LUCY CALKINS

A GUIDE TO THE WRITING WORKSHOP, GRADES 3-5

This book is dedicated to John Skorpen, my life partner, with love.

FirstHand
An imprint of Heinemann
A division of Reed Elsevier Inc.
361 Hanover Street
Portsmouth, NH 03801-3912
www.heinemann.com

Offices and agents throughout the world

Copyright © 2006 by Lucy Calkins

All rights reserved. No part of this book may be reproduced in any form or by any electronic or mechanical means, including information storage and retrieval systems, without permission in writing from the publisher, except by a reviewer, who may quote brief passages in a review.

Photography: Peter Cunningham

Library of Congress Cataloging-in-Publication Data

CIP data on file with the Library of Congress.
ISBN 0-325-00861-2

Printed in the United States of America on acid-free paper
10   09   08   07   06   ML   1   2   3   4   5

Acknowledgements

This series has the biggest undertaking of my life—other than the larger projects of leading the Teachers College Reading and Writing Project and of parenting Miles and Evan—and so it is fitting that I dedicate this project to John Skorpen, who has been my life partner through it all. There have been lots of books before now, but John is the sort of person to say, "Dedicate that one to your parents," or "Have you remembered…?" Just this once, I want to say to John and to the world that I am the luckiest person alive because I am married to someone who understands and cherishes me, who knows that my work gives me great joy, who cares for the family as much as I do, and who is always glad that we can come home to each other. John, thanks for your depth of understanding, your wise observations, your spirit of adventure, your sense of priorities, your forgiveness and your love.

When I write and when I teach, I reach through words to something that is deeper, older, purer than words…and I know that the source, way down deep inside of me, has everything to do with my mother and my father, and with the legacy of my family. I thank both Evan and Virginia Calkins for all that I am, for all that I believe in, and I thank each of my eight brothers and sisters—Sally, Steve, Joan, Ben, Hugh, Ellen, Geoff, and Tim— for understanding the preciousness of family.

Anyone who has ever read my writing or been part of my teaching knows that the sun rises and sets for me with Miles and Evan Skorpen, my two beloved sons who are now becoming young men. John and I could not be more proud of them.

I live and learn as part of the community of teacher-educators that comprises the Teachers College Reading and Writing Project, and there are a few people at the Project who have been especially important thought-companions. I especially thank Laurie Pessah, who has always helped me lead the organization, Kathleen Tolan and Mary Ehrenworth, Deputy Directors, Ruth Swinney, Director of English Language Learners, and Beth Neville, Associate Director. For the past year, this leadership team has been coached by a leader-of-leaders, Patsy Glazer, and we are all grateful to her. I am also grateful to Amanda Hartman who demonstrates what is possible in staff development, for Maggie Moon for assuming a leadership role at the Project, and for Brooke Keller who has helped me think more deeply.

The ideas about teaching writing that are essential in this book were introduced to me when I was a young teacher and I am eternally grateful to Don Graves and Don Murray for being my first mentors in the teaching of writing. Since then, I've learned from many others. Randy Bomer, author of *Time for Meaning* and former President of the National Council of Teachers of English, has been an especially important influence, and his insights and suggestions helped me create a form for and imagine these books. Many former Teachers College Reading and Writing Project colleagues—including Shelley Harwayne, Joanne Hindley, JoAnne Portalupi, Ralph Fletcher, Georgia Heard, Isoke Nia, Katherine Bomer, Katie Ray, Pam Allyn, and Carl Anderson— added layers of insight to my knowledge on teaching writing.

I am grateful to the co-authors who joined me in writing these books. Colleen Cruz has been a wonderful writing partner, and her ideas and experience at writing fiction made that book into what it is. Mary Chiarella not only contributed to the final book in the series, but has also been the teacher I rely upon most in all of these books. Her children's work stud the pages of every book, and I salute her for being Writing Teacher Extraordinaire. Kathy Collins, co-author of the CD-ROM, is a whiz at anything demanding creativity, energy, an intimate knowledge of the very real world of classroom teaching. I thank her for her gigantic contribution. I am also thankful to the contributing authors, each of whom pitched in on a particular book; I describe their contributions in those books.

Because of the scale of this writing effort, I recruited a few others to help me. Julia Mooney has brought her sparkling intelligence and her deep understanding of good writing to the pages of every book. She especially helped contributing and co-authors authors write their Tailoring your Teachings. Natalie Louis, Shannon Rigney Keane, Grace Enriquez and Kathy Doyle each helped as well. Katherine Bomer brought her special verve and her sense of intimacy with kids and texts to some of these books. Ruth Swinney provided invaluable assistance with the chapter on supporting English Language learners. Peter Cunningham, the photographer for these books and for every book I've ever written, graced this effort with magical talent.

The book stands on the shoulders of the Teachers Reading and Writing Project's alliance with the New York City schools, and that alliance relies upon a close relationship with Regional Superintendents and Deputy Superintendents. I especially thank Judy Chin and Brenda Steele from Region 3, Reyes Irizarry and Charles Amundsen from Region 4, Peter Heaney and Barbara Gambino from Region 9, and Marcia Lyles and Elaine Goldberg from Region 8. Their work relies upon leadership from Chancellor Joel Klein, Deputy Chancellor Carmen Farina and Director of Instruction, Laura Kotch.

Leigh Peake has led Heinemann's involvement with this effort, and I thank her both for channeling enormous support towards this project and for her responsiveness to me. With Leigh at the helm of Heinemann, the organization is able to maintain its very special identity as a think tank and a family as well as a service-provider. Jean Lawler has been the production mastermind at Heinemann. She has kept track of all the zillions of bits and pieces that create the mosaic of these books, and worked with terrific dedication and good will. Jean has been utterly and completely essential to the entire process. She's been lucky to have support from David Stirling. Charles McQuillen will take over once Jean has let go, and I thank him in advance for what he will do to usher the books into the hands of teachers.

Most of all, I am grateful to Kate Montgomery. Whereas John is my life-partner, Kate is my writing partner. I could not have written these books without her brilliant presence at my side. Kate cares as much as I do; her standards are sky-high, and she has the talent to see and to bring forth the lion that is hiding, still, deep in the marble. I've dedicated *Launching the Writing Workshop* to her— a small gesture when her name really deserves to be on the cover of each book!

A GUIDE TO THE WRITING WORKSHOP, GRADES 3-5

CHAPTER 1

ABOUT THE SERIES

This is the first in a series of books designed to help upper-elementary teachers teach a rigorous yearlong writing curriculum. The series stands on the shoulders of the Teachers College Reading and Writing Project community. The books have, in a sense, been coauthored by the entire staff of this professional development organization and by the teachers, principals, and superintendents who have become part of the community of practice, helping develop, pilot, and revise the ideas that fill the pages of these books.

Together, all of us have passed the baton to others, helping several hundred thousand teachers become skilled at teaching writing. Word has spread. Over the years, more and more teachers have heard that the writing workshop has given children unbelievable power as readers, thinkers, and composers of meaning—and that it has given *teachers* new energy and joy, reminding us why we chose careers in teaching in the first place. Demand for support in the teaching of writing has skyrocketed. This series is my effort to provide that support.

The increased focus on writing comes in part from the technological revolution that has transformed our lives. As the Internet and text messaging seep into every nook and cranny of our day, all of us are writing more than ever. In today's Information Age, it has become increasingly important that all children are given an education that enables them to synthesize, organize, reflect on, and respond to the data in their world. Indeed, three years ago, a National Writing Commission called for a Writing Revolution, suggesting that children need to double the amount of time they spend writing in their classrooms.

But above all, the escalating demand for professional development in the teaching of writing comes because when teachers receive the education we deserve in the teaching of writing and are therefore able to provide children with clear, sequenced, vibrant instruction in writing (along with opportunities to write daily for their own important purposes), we make a dramatic difference in children's abilities to write. The stories and essays that children produce as a result become far more substantial and significant, revealing the young authors in ways that are often poignant.

Strong writing instruction can also power dramatic increases in scores on standardized tests. Today, students need to write well to achieve on the SAT and on advanced placement exams. More and more states have either integrated writing into their standardized reading tests or added separate assessments of writing.

Educators who wonder whether adopting a reading and writing workshop will translate into increases in standardized tests will want to notice the impressive gains New York City has made since the Chancellor held a press conference at P.S. 172, a Teachers College Reading and Writing Project stronghold, in which he said that the approach in that school needed to be taken citywide. Since adopting balanced literacy, New York City's test scores have skyrocketed, with double-digit increases in state standardized tests in grades three, four and five. The most important gains in New York City have been on the NAEP, often referred to as the "nation's report card." This assessment is mandated by Congress and administered by the US Department of Education. Last December, recent NAEP scores were released showing that New York City's fourth grade school students outperformed their peers in other cities with populations over 250,000.

Sheila Ford, Vice Chair of the National Assessment Governing Board of the NAEP was quoted in a recent Education Week article saying, "New York City had the greatest gains of any urban city setting in the country in the area of reading." In a speech to the principals and superintendents from schools across the country which are affiliated with the Project, she elaborated saying, "The important thing to realize is that over thirty years, the NAEP scores nationally have been essentially flat. Since New York City adopted the balanced literacy approach citywide in 2002, New York City's scores have risen 7 points which is a statistically significant gain. New York City is also the largest school district in the nation with 1.1 million students, and 84 percent of its fourth graders are eligible for free or reduced lunch." New York is making progress bridging the achievement gap. New York City's Black and Hispanic low income fourth graders far outperformed similar students in large cities and in the nation as a whole on the percentage of students achieving at or above the basic level.

NAEP writing scores for major cities will be released in 2007 but even before the writing workshop was extended citywide, New York City children wrote better than children in any other major city except Charlotte. More generally, data from the NAEP assessment show clearly that children who are accustomed to writing more than one draft and who save their writing in folders—techniques that are hallmarks of a writing workshop—perform better as writers than do other students.

Although it is reassuring to realize that teaching children to write well can transfer into improved scores on standardized tests, those of us who put writing at the center of our professional lives do so for far more personal and compelling reasons. First of all, it is not only *children's* work that is transformed through professional development in the teaching of writing; *teachers'* work is also transformed. When a community of teachers embraces reform in the teaching of writing, teachers often become reinvigorated and renewed in the process. And individual teachers find that teaching writing taps new sources of energy within themselves. Over the years, teachers have continually told me that the teaching of writing has given them new energy, clarity, and compassion, reminding them why they went into teaching in the first place. I understand what these teachers mean, for writing has done all this—and more—for me.

Lifting the level of writing instruction matters because writing matters. I recently read an article that reminded me of the human need to tell and write the stories of our lives. The article was about Ivory, a man whose job had been to drive a garbage truck through New Orleans and who was, at the time of the article, living on a cot in the New Orleans Convention Center and had only a small cardboard box full of salvaged stuff left to show for his life. Sitting on that cot, bereft of all that he'd built for himself, Ivory asked to borrow a pencil and then began listing everything he'd lost in Hurricane Katrina: the framed photograph of his mother, the radio that had turned his little apartment into a pub, the table he'd found once beside the road . . . . I'm quite sure that as Ivory recorded each precious item on his page, it was as if those items were, in some way, still a part of him: "This is me," he seemed to be saying. Writing is a way for us to hold onto the moments and the selves that could otherwise slip through our fingers.

All of us rush through our lives: we wake up, we eat our breakfast, we hurry to school, into our classroom, we hang up our coat, we wave hello to this person and that, time passes and soon one day becomes the next. Behind us, we leave what John Updike calls "a litter of old selves." Ten-year-old Geirthruder wrote:

> I often think that my life is like a handful of sand, they fall, there's nothing you can do about it, it will keep falling until it's all gone, which is why I hate digital watches that count seconds.

Of course, no one is leaving behind old selves in faster, more dramatic ways than children. It is children who know the glee, and the sadness, too, of finding they can no longer squeeze through the gap in the backyard fence. It is children who find their voices changing, their legs getting longer. It is children who constantly outgrow trousers and roles. And children, like adults, need ways to set their lives onto the page, to hold on to their past and make meaning in their present.

It is not enough simply to go from here to there, from this moment to that one. We need our moments and our days to add up, to mean something, to cumulate. As Ernst Becker has said, "What human beings fear is not growing old, but growing old without things adding up." And so we write.

We write to hold on to the moments of our lives and to make them matter. Patricia MacLachlan, the Newbery Medal–winning author of *Journey*, writes, "Other animals have journeys far greater than ours. The arctic tern

crisscrosses the Atlantic Ocean many times. The monarch butterfly summers in the meadows of Maine and winters in the rain forests of Mexico." Then she adds, "But we are the creature that lives to tell the tale." During prehistoric times, human beings used whatever we could find—sticks, berries, pieces of rock—to record the stories of our hunts and journeys on stony cave walls. Then, standing in the company of one another, we reread, recalled, reconsidered the hunts and journeys that we'd been on and imagined the ones still before us. I am convinced this is how we human beings became human. We live through our days, and then we turn back and say, "This is my journey, and this is what I make of it." In the end, each and every one of us is the author of a life: *My Life*, we each write. *My Life*, by me.

We've written this series because writing matters. Demand for professional development in writing has far outstripped the Teachers College Reading and Writing Project's abilities to provide this support. These books reflect our effort to hand over what we know so that more children can be given opportunities to grow strong as writers and more teachers can experience the extraordinary benefits that come from participating in a community of practice that involves a shared inquiry into the teaching of writing.

The wonderful thing about learning to teach writing well is that there are just a few teaching methods that one needs to know and be able to use. In this series, I provide crystal-clear advice on how to lead efficient and effective minilessons, conferences, and small-group strategy sessions. I do so knowing that as you travel through the series, encountering scores of transcripts of minilessons, conferences, small-group sessions, and shares, you will learn not only from explicit instruction but also from immersion. This first book of the series explicitly describes the architecture of all our minilessons, conferences, and small-group strategy sessions and details the management techniques that make writing workshops possible. The subsequent books show these methods and principles effecting real life in classrooms. I know from helping thousands of teachers learn to teach writing that these units will scaffold and inform your own teaching, and you will develop finesse and flexibility with the methods and information conveyed in these books.

In an ideal world, every teacher deserves the chance to learn state-of-the-art methods for teaching writing not only by reading books but also by watching an exemplary teacher instruct her children day to day. Although we do not live in an ideal world, teachers who have relied on the *Units of Study for Primary Writing* (or on the binders containing very early and incomplete preliminary versions of the upper grade units) will assure you that these books can be a next-best substitute. They can give you the chance to listen in on and observe my teaching and, at times, the teaching of one of my colleagues. Each unit of study in this series contains the words of my teaching (and sometimes of a colleague's teaching) for between fifteen and twenty days, with suggested ways to extend each of those days if this seems merited. You will read the words I used to gather a class of students together on the rug for a minilesson, and then, once the children are gathered, you'll hear exactly what I said to them. You will hear me retell a harrowing moment with my dog, Tucker, and you'll see how I use that anecdote to illustrate a quality of good writing.

Ideally, you and every other teacher in the world should be able not only to observe exemplary teachers but also to do so with a coach nearby, highlighting the way the teaching illustrates a collection of guiding principles. Ideally, someone will be there at your side to point out the alternative decisions the teacher could and could not have made in any one moment. Therefore, as you witness this teaching, I will be an ever-present coach, highlighting aspects of the teaching that seem especially essential. My goal is to help you watch this teaching in ways that enable you to extrapolate guidelines and methods, so that on another day you'll invent your own teaching.

I already know, from talking with so many teachers who've used the *Units of Study for Primary Writing*, that sometimes you will take the words of my minilessons and bring them verbatim to your own children. I also know that more often you'll decide that the teaching I describe needs to be adapted or rewritten in order to fit you and your children. These books provide a detailed model; they are not meant as a script. Either way, the end goal is not the teaching that I've described here but the teaching that you, your colleagues, and your children invent together.

The most important thing for you to know is that the books are designed to put themselves out of a job. Once you have used this scaffold to support your teaching, you will find you no longer need it. You will see that your students need more help with one strategy or another, and you'll use the principles in these books to help you author minilessons, small-group work, and conferences tailored to the needs of your students. This series supports only six or seven months of teaching writing. In order to provide your children with a *yearlong* curriculum in writing, you will need to create your own units of study with your colleagues; these books will help you to do so.

The books are intended to be read and used in sequence, each book standing on the shoulders of the books that go before it. (The order of *Fiction* and *Literary Essays* could conceivably be flipped; other than that, they must proceed in order.) A few homemade units can be inserted between the fifth and the sixth book. I suggest one of these be a unit of study on poetry, and I will later direct you to sources of support for that unit and others. Together, these units (including the ones you author yourself) will combine to provide the curricular support necessary to take a class of upper elementary students on a learning journey. The series can also provide the backbone for a second or third year of study, as long as teachers in the succeeding years are increasingly willing to tailor their teaching to take into account what children already know and can do. That is, children profit from a spiral curriculum in writing: for example, in third grade they learn to write detailed, chronological personal narratives, but then in fourth grade, they have opportunities to deepen their knowledge of narrative writing. Because the teaching in these books is highly predictable, and because each bit of it draws on principles that are clearly articulated, you will find that these books will take not only your students but also you and your colleagues on a learning journey.

THE PARTS OF EACH SESSION

Here is what you can expect in each of the fifteen or so sessions in each unit book in this series.

GETTING READY

This list can help you be sure you have the materials you need for each minilesson. Further detail is included on the CD-ROM. The required materials are kept to a minimum!

Introduction

Just as minilessons begin with Lucy pulling children close to tell them what the upcoming lesson aims to teach, to explain how this lesson fits with previous ones and to convey why the teaching matters, so, too, each session begins with Lucy doing the same for you.

MINILESSON

Listen in while Lucy teaches. Hear the language she uses and hear, also, some of what children say in response. These won't provide scripts for your teaching because the lessons are tailored to a particular class of children, but you can learn from and adapt them. Each minilesson follows the same architecture:

CONNECTION: Children learn why today's instruction is important and how it relates to their prior work. They hear the teaching point that crystallizes the lesson.

TEACHING: The teacher shows children how writers go about doing whatever is being taught. Usually this involves a demonstration, which the teacher sets up and explains.

ACTIVE ENGAGEMENT: Children are given a chance to practice (for a minute) what has just been taught. The teacher scaffolds their work so they can be successful.

LINK: The teacher crystallizes what has been taught, adding it to children's growing repertoire. Children are reminded that today's lesson pertains not only to today, but to every day. The teacher often summarizes the conditions under which a child to reach for this new knowledge.

Italicized Commentary: As you read and picture the teaching, Lucy will coach you to realize why she's taught the way she has, to see other choices she could have made, to notice the aspects of today's teaching which are transferable to other days, to understand ways one day's teaching stands on the shoulders of previous days, and to consider ways the teaching could be adapted for children with different needs.

WRITING AND CONFERRING

Although children always catch us by surprise when we draw a chair alongside them to confer, the truth is our conferences are not as off-the-cuff as they may seem. Experienced teachers of writing can plan a minilesson and predict the coaching and instruction children will especially need. It is predictable, too, that some days children will need so much help that it will be important to devote the workshop to small group instruction. In some of these sessions, you will listen in on the conferences or small groups that Lucy led in the wake of that day's minilesson. Other times, this session will equip you to lead the conferences or small group work that are apt to be especially helpful that day.

MID-WORKSHOP
TEACHING POINT

It is inevitable that in the midst of a writing workshop, a teacher will want to interrupt the hum of the workshop to teach the entire class. Often this teaching builds upon the minilesson. Most mid-workshop teaching points are actually mini-minilessons!

SHARE

Every writing workshop ends with a share. This provides one more opportunity to sneak in some pointers. Usually during the share, Lucy will highlight one child's work in a way that create a trail that others could follow, and then she'll channel each child towards a productive conversation with his or her writing partner.

HOMEWORK AND LETTERS TO PARENTS

By the time children are in the upper elementary grades, they can do substantial work at home, and they will be more eager to do this work if we are careful to craft homework that helps children outgrow themselves. Each session, then, contains two or sometimes three different variations of homework assignments. These are written to be read by children. They

always include a pep-talk (a miniature minilesson) and sometimes include exemplar work. The homework section provides you with a way to communicate with parents about the important work children are doing in school. In addition, the CD also contains letters that can be sent home to parents describing each unit of study. You'll want to alter both the homework and the letters, and so they are packaged to make it easy for you to do so.

TAILORING YOUR TEACHING

With adaptations, the lessons that you read in these sessions can provide the backbone for your own units of study, but you will want to tailor your teaching based on what you see your children needing. After each session, then, there is a description of minilesson extensions. Here and on the CD, Lucy Calkins, Kathy Collins and the contributing authors and co-authors imagine ways in which your children may need further help. "If this is the second time your children are traveling through the unit…" we may write, and then suggest the kernel of a minilesson you might give to them. "If your children are struggling with…" we may say, and again suggest a minilesson. Each session provides a handful of extensions, some in the book and more on the CD.

ASSESSMENT/MECHANICS/COLLABORATING WITH COLLEAGUES

These three strands are woven through each of the units of study, with a 1-2 page discussion of one of these topics at the end of each session. The mechanics section suggests ways in which you can teach the conventions of writing both within and outside the writing workshop. Collaborating with Colleagues suggests ways that you and your colleagues can use study-group time productively in support of this unit. Assessment suggests lenses you might use as this particular time in your children's development, and helps you imagine ways to make sense of what you will probably see.

THE FOUNDATIONS OF A WRITING WORKSHOP

Whenever I work with educators in a school, a school district, or a city, I make a point of meeting with educational leaders to think together about the vision that guides that school system's course of study. Because I, too, am a leader of a large organization, I am aware that leadership involves gathering the community and, together, finding a North Star. Someone needs to say to the extended community, "This pathway is an important one for us to follow. Come, come...."

Teachers and school leaders together, need to think about the rights of learners: "What does the Bill of Rights in the teaching of writing consist of for the learners in our care? What conditions are so essential that every child deserves these conditions, these opportunities to learn?" A system must adopt common denominators that are within reach of the people in that system and that are aligned to the system's standards.

The educators that I work closely with tend to agree that the following are the necessary foundations for the writing workshop:

We need to teach every child to write. Almost every day, every K–5 child needs between fifty and sixty minutes for writing and writing instruction.

Although I strongly believe teachers should make decisions about their own teaching, none of us can decide not to teach math, nor can a teacher say, "I teach math across every subject area," and then merely sprinkle math here and there across the day, asking children to add up the number of pages they've read or to count the minutes until school is dismissed for the day and calling that a math curriculum. Yet in some districts it is acceptable for teachers to say, "I teach writing across the curriculum" and for those teachers to then not regard writing as a subject in the school day. I regard this as a problem. Children's success in many disciplines is utterly reliant on their abilities to write; children deserve writing to be a subject that is taught and studied just like reading or math. In school systems that are affiliated with the Teachers College Reading and Writing Project, it is nonnegotiable that every child spends time every day learning to write, that there is a planned curriculum for that time, and that during that time, the teacher is teaching writing.

It is also necessary that during that time, children actually write and do so for long stretches of time. Writing is a skill, like playing the trumpet or swimming or playing tennis or reading. There is very little a teacher can do from the front of the room that will help a learner become skilled at playing an instrument or swimming or playing tennis or reading—and writing is no different. Skills are learned through practice. As my sons' tennis teacher says, "Success in tennis has an awful lot to do with the number of balls hit." Similarly, success in reading directly correlates with the number of hours spent reading. John Guthrie's recent study illustrates that fourth graders who read at the second-grade level spend a half hour a day reading and fourth graders who read at the eighth-grade level spend four hours a day reading.[1] Similarly, success in writing directly relates to the amount of writing and rewriting a person does.

This means that day after day, children need to write. They need to write for long stretches of time—for something like forty minutes of each day's writing workshop—and they need to write for almost the same length of time at home most evenings.

Volume and stamina matter. It is almost impossible for a child to write well if that child doesn't write fluently, because writing well involves elaboration. (This is true enough that a recent study by an MIT professor found that a student's score on the writing component of the SAT correlated almost exactly with the length of the student's essay![2]) Because volume matters, many teachers help students set incremental goals for themselves. At first, the goal might be to write a half page within one writing workshop, but within a few months, the goal can be a page or a page and a half of in-school writing each day, and soon, a similar amount

of at-home writing. Students date each day's writing, and all writing stays in the students' notebooks and folders until the unit of study culminates in a publishing party. This means that teachers, literacy coaches, and principals can look through students' writing folders and notebooks and see the work that any student produced on Monday, Tuesday, Wednesday, and so forth. Of course, there may be a day when writers devote their writing time to a study of exemplar texts or to an especially long discussion about writing rough drafts. But those days are exceptions. Writers write, and a wonderful thing about writing is that it is immediately visible. This allows a school system to hold itself accountable for ensuring that every child has the opportunity and the responsibility to write every day.

We need to teach children to write texts like other writers write—memoirs, stories, editorials, essays, poems—for an audience of readers, not just for the teacher.

Donald Murray, the Pulitzer Prize–winning writer who is widely regarded as the father of writing process, recalls the piano lessons he was given as a child. The school system announced that anyone wanting to learn to play the piano should report to the cafeteria after school. Murray recalls his palpable excitement: at last, he was going to learn to make those beautiful melodies! In the cafeteria, children sat in rows, facing the front. Each child was given a cardboard keyboard and shown how to lay his or her hands on it so as to "play" notes. Children pressed their cardboard keyboards, but there was no music, no melody. Murray left and never returned.

Children deserve opportunities to write real writing; this means that instead of writing merely "compositions" and "reports," children need to

---

[1] "Engaging Young Readers: Promoting Achievement and Motivation." *Solving Problems in the Teaching of Literacy.* Guilford Publications, 2000.

[2] "SAT Essay Test Rewards Length and Ignores Errors" by Michael Winerip, *The New York Times,* May 4, 2005, article cites MIT Professor Les Perelman's research on SAT.

write in all the genres that exist in the world. A child should know that he or she is writing something—a poem, an essay, a book review, a lab report, a short story—that writers write and readers read.

Children not only deserve daily opportunities to write particular kinds of things—to write *something* that exists in the world—they also deserve opportunities to write for *someone*—for readers who will respond to what they have written. Children deserve to write knowing that their final pieces of writing—the ones writers produce after planning and drafting and revising—stand a good chance of being read by readers. Otherwise how will young writers learn that writing well involves aiming to create an effect? Craft and deliberate choice in writing are the result of thinking, as we write, "This will surprise them! They'll sit up and take notice right here," or "This will be a funny part," or "If I can pull this section off, I think it will give my readers goosebumps." In order to write with this sense of agency, students deserve opportunities to see readers' responses to their writing. They need these opportunities midway through their work with a text, and they also need their final pieces to reach responsive readers.

Giving children opportunities to write *something*—a memoir, a poem—for *someone*—a friend, a grandfather—makes it likely that writing will engage children and that they will feel as if the work they are doing is real, credible, and substantial. Children should not be asked to learn to play music on cardboard keyboards or to learn to write on ditto sheets.

Writers do not write with words and convention alone; writers write above all with meaning. Children will invest themselves more in their writing if they are allowed—indeed, if they are taught—to select their own topics and to write about subjects that are important to them.

Try this. Pick up a pen and write a few sentences about the sequence of actions you did just before picking up this book. Do it on paper or in your mind.

Now pause and try something different. Think about a moment in your life that for some reason really affected you. It might be the tiniest of moments, but it gave you a lump in your throat, it made your heart skip. The last time you saw someone. The time you realized you could actually do that thing you'd been longing to do. The encounter with that special person. Write (or mentally think through) the story of that indelible moment. On the page (or just in your mind's eye) try to capture the essence of that bit of life.

You will find that doing the one kind of writing—in which you throw out any old words —and doing the other kind of writing—in which you reach for the precise words that will capture something dear to you—are utterly different. In order for children to learn to write and to grow as writers, it is absolutely essential that they are invested in their writing and that they care about writing well. Children (indeed, all of us) are far more apt to be invested in writing if we are writing something real and meaningful and if we are writing for real, responsive readers.

It is hard to imagine an argument against letting children choose their own topics for most of the writing they do. Although the craft, strategies, and qualities of good writing and the processes of writing vary somewhat depending on whether someone is writing an essay or a poem (and therefore there are advantages to the teacher's suggesting that the whole community work for a time within a shared genre), good writing does not vary based on whether it's about the day Grandfather died or the first moments in a new school. Teachers can gather the entire class together and teach them anything—the importance of detail or strategies for making simple sentences more complex—knowing the instruction will be equally relevant to children who are engaged in writing about a wide array of different subjects.

The easiest way to help children love writing is to invite them to write about subjects they care about. When children have the opportunity and responsibility to choose their own subjects, they are not only much more apt to be invested in their writing, they are also much more apt to be knowledgeable about their topics. In addition, they can learn what it means to rediscover subjects through the process of writing about them.

Obviously, there may be some instances when you decide to ask the entire class to write on a shared topic; when there are compelling reasons to ask this of children, this other value will trump the value of topic choice.

Children deserve to be explicitly taught the skills and strategies of effective writing, and the qualities of good writing. This teaching will be dramatically more powerful if teachers are studying the teaching of writing and if they are responsive to what students are doing and trying to do as writers. Children also deserve a teacher who demonstrates a commitment to writing.

Although it is important for children to write every day, it is not enough for them simply to have the opportunity to write. Children also deserve instruction. They are extremely vulnerable to instruction. I can walk into a classroom, look over children's writing, and know immediately whether children are being taught to write well, because strong, clear instruction dramatically affects student writing.

It is not enough for we teachers to turn down the lights, turn on the music, and say, "Write." It is not enough for children to have time each day to crank out genre-less, audience-less, model-less, revision-less journal entries. Instead, we need to teach explicitly the qualities, habits, and strategies of effective writing; moreover, we need to assess the results of our teaching in order to ensure that every child has learned what we have taught. Most strategies and qualities of good writing are multileveled. Every child in every classroom can learn to write narratives that are chronologically ordered and detailed. Every child can learn to include direct quotations. Some children will spell better than others, some will use more complex sentence structures than others, but many of the skills and strategies of skilled writing are within reach of every writer.

Children not only deserve to be instructed in writing well, they also deserve to learn from a teacher who is well informed about the qualities, processes, and habits of skilled writing. This is most apt to happen if teachers participate in professional development on the teaching of writing and if teachers across grade levels plan teaching together, capitalizing on any teachers within the group who have invested time studying the teaching of writing and/or working on their own writing. Teachers' collaborative study in the teaching of writing will take on heart and soul, nuance and fire, when we ourselves try the techniques we ask children to try, writing our own personal narratives, essays, poems, and memoirs.

The quality of writing instruction will rise dramatically not only when we study the teaching of writing but also when we study our own children's intentions and progress as writers. Strong writing instruction is always tailored for and responsive to the writer. A writing teacher functions above all as a coach, watching from the sidelines as writers go through the process of writing, then intervening to help one individual after another see what she is doing that is or isn't working, ways in which she can work with more skill. The teaching of writing is always about helping individuals, small groups, and classes as a whole ratchet their work up a notch.

As important as it is for children to learn *how* to write well, it is equally important for them to learn to *care* about writing. It is enormously important that we, as teachers, demonstrate and expect a love of writing.

We need to provide children the opportunity and instruction necessary for them to cycle through the writing process regularly as they write, rehearse, draft, revise, edit, and publish their writing.

The scientific method is widely regarded as so fundamental to science that children use it whether they are studying sinking and floating in kindergarten or friction and inertia in high school. Likewise, the writing process is fundamental to all writing; therefore it is important that children of every age receive frequent opportunities to rehearse, draft, revise, and edit their writing. If a child is going to write an editorial, his first concern should probably not be, "How do I write the first sentence?" but rather, "What are the qualities of great editorials? What does the writing life look like for an editorial writer? What sorts of entries does an editorial writer collect in his or her notebook?"

Most of the time, children should be expected to proceed through the writing process. This means that, most of the time, they should anticipate and have opportunities to plan for and rehearse writing. They should usually write tentatively at first, producing at least a portion of a rough draft (or two). They should certainly have the opportunity to reread a rough draft, viewing it through a variety of lenses, including "What am I really trying to say here? How can I bring forth that meaning?" and "What sense will a reader make of this? How can I make my meaning clearer and more compelling for my reader?" A writer will always write with the conventions that are easily under his control, but once a text is almost ready for readers, the writer will want to edit it, taking extra care to make the text clear, forceful, and correct. Often the writer will use outside assistance—from dictionaries, peers, a teacher—in order to increase the level of clarity and correctness in a text.

Writers read. Writers read texts of all sorts, and we read as insiders, aiming to learn specific strategies for writing well.

Any effective writing curriculum acknowledges that it is important for writers to be immersed in wonderful literature. Children will not learn to write well if they are not immersed in and affected by texts that other authors have written. They need the sounds and power of good literature to be in their bones. They need a felt sense for how effective stories can go, for the way in which a poem can make a reader gasp and be still. They also need some opportunities to study closely a few texts that are similar to those they are trying to make.

Children especially need opportunities to read-as-writers. Imagine that you were asked to write a foreword for this book. My hunch is that you'd do exactly as I did when Georgia Heard asked me to write my first foreword ever. I pulled books from my shelf, and searched for forewords. I found half a dozen, and read them ravenously. "How does a foreword really go?" I asked. Children, too, deserve the chance to read like writers.

By studying the work of other authors, students not only develop a felt sense of what it is they are trying to make but they also learn the traditions of that particular kind of text. Poets leave white space, essayists advance ideas, storytellers convey the passage of time. All writers care that the sound of our words matches the tone of our meaning, all writers care that we choose precisely right words. By studying texts that resemble those they are trying to make, children learn the tools of their trade.

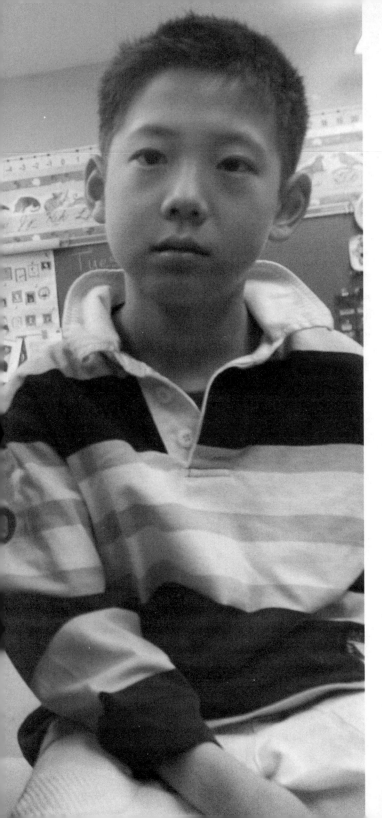

CHAPTER 3

THE WRITING PROCESS FOR UPPER-ELEMENTARY-GRADE WRITERS

When I was a fourth grader, my teacher taught writing by assigning us topics and page lengths. We wrote at home, bringing our completed stories, essays, poems, and reports to school a few days after they were assigned. After a bit, we'd receive the papers back, each with a grade for content, a grade for mechanics, and a few marginal comments. I expect many of us were "taught" writing that way. That was before the Writing Revolution.

Approximately two decades ago, a flurry of books and articles called for and created a Writing Revolution. Peter Elbow, Donald Murray, James Moffett, Ken Macrorie, and a series of edited volumes titled *Writers at Work* combined to popularize the message that when writers write, we do not sit down with a quill pen and immediately produce graceful, compelling prose. Instead writers work through a process of writing, a process that contains recursive "stages." Different people use different terms when describing those stages. For example, some use the term *prewriting* and some *rehearsal*, but either way, widespread agreement has emerged that writers spend time preparing for writing. This stage involves living "writerly lives," collecting material for writing, jotting alternative plans for how a piece of writing might go, talking about one's topic, and reading texts that resemble the text one hopes to write. Writers also *draft*. Early drafts are more like playing in clay than inscribing in marble; a writer might try alternative leads, explore different voices for a text, or free write, keeping her eyes glued on the subject and trying to capture the contours of it in tentative form. Writers shift back and forth between drafting and revising. *Revision* means, quite literally, to see again. During revision, a writer pulls back from a draft in order to reread and rethink, "What is it I really want to say?" Writers revise in order to discover and convey meaning. Revision may involve rewriting a lead, re-angling a story, elaborating on important sections, and deleting unimportant ones. It usually involves anticipating a reader's response: "What do I want my reader to feel? To know?" Revision may or may not involve a second or third draft. Finally, writers *edit*, which involves correcting, smoothing out, linking, clarifying. During editing, writers think about spelling, punctuation, and word choice, yes, but writers also think about language and clarity.

The news that professional writers go through a process of writing was accompanied by the equally important news that even young children can experience the writing process. More than two decades ago, a team of us from the University of New Hampshire—Donald Graves, Susan Sowers, and I, followed by many others—wrote articles and books showing that children, too, can rehearse, draft, revise, and edit their writing and suggesting that when we observe and coach young writers in their process of writing, their growth in writing can be spectacular. The research on young children and the writing process was the talk of the town in the eighties. Since then, the idea that educators need to teach the writing process has become so widely accepted that this is almost a mainstream premise. Many standardized tests even include planning pages and remind writers to leave time to revise and edit their essays. Most language arts textbooks have incorporated the terms (if not the real concepts) of the writing process into their curriculum. And in New York City, for example, every elementary school teacher is now expected to lead a writing workshop in which all students work their way through the writing process.

TEACHING EIGHT-, NINE- AND TEN-YEAR-OLDS THE WRITING PROCESS

Although the rhetoric behind the idea of teaching writing process involves talk like this—"Children should be invited to write like real writers"—the truth is that children can only approximate the processes that adult writers use. An eight-year-old will not write exactly like Robert Frost or Patricia Polacco, nor do adult writers all write exactly like one another! Even when a school system has adopted a writing process approach to teaching writing, teachers are still left with the job of thinking through the process that we plan to teach.

Some teachers decide to encourage each child to devise his or her own individual writing process. On any one day in these classrooms, one child will write leads to a story, another will begin and complete an all-about book, yet another will write several poems. Day after day, children in these classrooms cycle through the writing process in their own way and at their own pace. In a month, one child in a class may have written one very long rough draft, another will have worked two pieces through a series of revisions, still another will have produced a dozen lightly revised texts. Teachers in these classrooms also place a priority on each child choosing his or her genre and topic. The teachers, meanwhile, look for teachable moments in which they can extend what children do as writers.

Other teachers—and my colleagues and I fall into this category—imagine that at the start of a school year we will scaffold a class of children to progress through a version of the writing process in a roughly synchronized fashion, with some children moving more quickly and others more slowly along the same general path. Because children are traveling roughly in sync, the teacher can do a lot of explicit teaching. As the year unrolls (and as one year follows the next) the teacher provides scaffolds that support larger, more encompassing steps, giving children progressively more independence. For example, at the start of a school year, working with children who are new to the writing process, the teacher might teach one rehearsal strategy, asking all children to use that one strategy to generate ideas for that day's writing. A few days later, the same teacher might review three optional strategies for rehearsal, demonstrate a fourth, and suggest that each child select from this repertoire the one that works best for her that day. Two months later, this teacher might begin yet another narrative unit by saying, "You already know a lot of strategies for generating narrative writing, and I hope you'll again draw from that repertoire of strategies. But *this* time, I want to help you think about using those strategies to generate writing that feels more significant to you and to your readers."

Because my colleagues and I want to move upper-elementary-level children through a somewhat shared process of writing, we approach our teaching by asking, "Given that there is no *one* way to approach the challenge of writing a piece, what sequence of living, writing, and thinking feels close enough to what real writers do that we could imagine championing this approach within our writing workshops?" Of course, when we think about the process of writing that we will demonstrate for children, we also need to ask, "What will be doable (as well as worth doing) for all my children?" and "How will different children tailor this process differently in keeping with their specific hopes, passions, skills, and temperaments?"

Pacing and Materials

When trying to decide what is within children's reach, teachers need to invite not only upper-elementary students but also their younger brothers and sisters to approximate the writing process. In the schools I know best, children in the primary grades usually cycle fairly quickly through the entire writing process, producing several texts each week. Five-, six-, and seven-year-olds rehearse for writing simply by thinking of a topic, telling a partner what they will write, selecting paper with an eye toward how the text will go, drawing a sketch on each page, and saying or thinking the words that they will write on that page. Then children draft. They reread, fixing up obvious problems on their own. Otherwise, revision is usually prompted by conferences or minilessons which steer them towards particular alterations. At this age, it is easier for children to write many pieces of writing rather than linger on a single piece.

By third grade children can definitely work a bit longer and more deeply on a given piece of writing, but I do not think that in September most third graders yet have the skills or the temperament to invest a full month in working toward a single publishable piece of writing. At the start of the year, the third graders I know best cycle through the writing process at a good clip. Within a month they produce many narrative

notebook entries, develop and revise two of these, and select one of those narratives for further revision, editing, and publishing. As they become more experienced and develop a deeper knowledge of good writing and a bigger repertoire of strategies for rehearsing and revising writing, they cycle through the writing process more slowly. In this series, the first unit, *Launching the Writing Workshop*, supports children as they produce two pieces in a month, and the second unit, *Improving the Quality of Personal Narrative Writing*, supports children as they produce just one, more carefully written text in a month. However, you will adjust this rate of work to suit your own class, bearing in mind that as children become more experienced and skilled, they can work longer (not less long, as some might suppose) on any given writing project.

Third graders, like their younger counterparts, find it supportive to write on paper that physically embodies the expectations for a particular genre. In K–2 classrooms, children write narratives in small booklets, with each page carrying the story of the next thing that happened. Teachers in the primary grades make paper for children, leaving space on each page for a picture as well as for sentences. When the time comes for third graders to write a "stretched-out," detailed narrative about a small moment in their lives, many teachers suggest they do so in a grown-up version of the booklets one finds in primary classrooms. The third graders' booklets do not have spaces for drawing, but children are expected to put a dot from their timeline (and the sentence accompanying that dot) at the top of a page, and this functions much as the picture does for younger children. By third grade, teachers rarely make paper for these booklets, instead suggesting that children who are writing narratives draft on pieces of notebook paper, folded in half. If the school doesn't suffer a shortage of paper, it's ideal to put two such sheets of paper together to form a booklet, with children writing only on one side of each "page," leaving them flexibility to cut the pages apart in order to extend any one portion of a draft. Similarly, when third graders write essays, teachers suggest that children use a clean sheet of paper for each new paragraph of the essay, writing topic sentences at the tops of pages and then elaborating on them in the space below. By the time children are in fifth grade, it may be less important for the paper on which they write to physically support elaboration.

Rehearsal for Writing

The first stage of the writing process is often called "rehearsal," or "gathering entries." Children who have been in strong writing workshops during the primary grades will enter third or fourth grade able to gather and generate ideas for writing. Other children, however, are apt to sit over blank pages saying, "Nothing happens in my life," or "I don't have anything to say." In these instances, supporting rehearsal for writing means helping children learn strategies for generating whatever kind of writing they aim to write.

Although I did not always believe this, I'm now convinced that those strategies will be somewhat different depending on whether a child is writing a personal narrative, a literary essay, or a poem. For example, when teaching children to write personal narrative entries, I might suggest they take a minute to think of a person (or place or thing) that matters to them and then to list several times when they did something with that person (in that place, with that thing). Then I suggest they reread that little list, select one episode that they remember with crystal clarity, and begin to write the story of that one episode. When teaching children to write essays about literature, I might teach them to read with a set of questions in mind: "What is this text really about? What line or passage in this text captures what the author is really trying to convey?"

With a bit of instruction, children can quickly develop a small repertoire of strategies for generating writing in their genre of choice and learn to draw on their developing repertoire of strategies in order to generate writing within that genre. More than this, children learn that when they live their lives as writers, the details of their lives and of their thinking are worth writing about. They'll find themselves living with a writer's consciousness, thinking often, "I should write about this."

In upper-grade writing workshops, after teaching children a few strategies for generating writing, we encourage children to collect entries in their writer's notebooks. Ideally, we hope children will carry those notebooks (literally and figuratively) through their lives. Although it is fairly easy to teach children a few strategies for generating ideas for writing, it is less easy and more important to take the additional step and teach children to live with this perspective of being a writer, seeing potential stories, essays, and poems everywhere and thinking often, "I should jot this down. I may want to make something of it."

As soon as possible, we encourage children to carry notebooks between home and school, generating entries in both places. This doubles the volume of writing that children produce, and it also makes it much more likely that children will live their lives with the writerly consciousness of "I am one who writes," seeing their lives as full of raw material for writing. This is a very deep, important aspect of rehearsal for writing.

Teachers who are not able to rally children to write entries at home can still see growth in children's abilities to rehearse. In time, children come to the writing workshop already knowing what they want to write, which suggests that children are seeing their lives as full of stories to tell, ideas to share.

Rehearsal involves not only living like a writer and seeing potential stories and essays everywhere but also selecting from all these possibilities one seed idea that is worth developing and beginning to plan a first draft. As children become more experienced, they learn that writers select one seed idea over another because they have a sense that the chosen seed has more significance. Writers write, wanting to convey a meaning that matters. Writers think, talk, and write in order to come to an understanding of what it is we want to say.

As children become more experienced and skilled as writers, everything they learn through revision can move forward into the rehearsal stage of their writing. For example, some writers begin the year writing about gigantic topics—"my trip to my grandma's house." Only during revision do these children reread their writing and think, "Which *particular aspect* of my visit do I want to address?" With experience, however, these same children will soon learn to generate ideas for writing and to immediately screen those ideas, asking, "Will this story (essay) be focused enough?"

Similarly, the initial entries children write in their notebooks will not be detailed, written in paragraphs, and so forth. As children learn more and more, however, the work they do during rehearsal will incorporate features they earlier learned only through revision. These might include paragraphing, writing with details, showing rather than telling, developing the heart of the story, or a host of other skills. In other words, the more skilled and experienced a writer becomes, the more that writer can do during rehearsal.

A professional writer might delay drafting for six months or a year, using this time to write and critique a whole sequence of different plans for a text! Such a writer would prefer progressing through multiple *outlines* rather than multiple *drafts*. A nine-year-old child, of course, will not find it easy to scrawl a few words onto the page and then look at this outline or plan, imagining from the abbreviated notes the larger text and imagining also the problems such a text would encounter—let alone imagining another way in which that text could have been written.

Still, nine-year-olds can live like writers, seeing potential for stories and essays everywhere. They can use all they know about good writing (or good narratives, good essays, and so on) to lift the level of their entries, thus giving them taller shoulders to stand on when they select one entry to develop into a major piece of writing. These children can also learn to talk through the writing they plan to do, trying out one way and then another of approaching their subject, observing their audiences' responses to those "in-the-air" drafts and revising the drafts before they've even written a word.

Finally, upper-elementary students can learn to make simple outlines, revising these in preparation for writing. More specifically, children who are writing narratives use timelines or story mountains to plan and, more importantly, to revise the scope and sequence of an eventual draft. They can look at a timeline of a story and think, "I should start later in the progression, closer to the action," and they can look at a story mountain and think, "I need to really build up this part of my story, it is my rising action. I need to show how he tried, tried, tried." When children write expository texts, they can outline their main idea and their supporting ideas, adjusting these to be sure their supporting ideas are parallel to one another. They can conduct research as a way to gather information to support their ideas. They can gather a variety of supporting information and make sure that their supporting information is aligned with their ideas. All of this can be done in preparation for writing a draft.

Drafting

While rehearsal and revision both involve the deliberate use of one strategy or another, drafting is less strategic. After all the work of collecting and choosing among entries, planning how the piece will go, choosing paper and imagining the piece laid out on the page, telling the story or teaching the information to another person in order to develop a voice with which to convey the material, the writer takes pen in hand and writes.

I often teach children that narrative writers first try different leads, choosing between them. I expect that children who are writing narratives will try replaying a small action or recording a bit of dialogue. I expect that children will try starting the story at various places in the sequence of events, experimenting with a narrower and broader focus. As children try different leads, I give myself a bit of time to move among them, working toward what for me is a very important goal: when a child writes a narrative, I hope that the child will envision what happened in his or her mind's eye and write the story, fast and long.

Peter Elbow, the great writing teacher and author of *Writing with Power*, advises, "Don't *describe* the tree. *See* the tree!" Powerful writing does not come from thinking about penmanship, word choice, complex sentences, showing-not-telling as one writes. Powerful writing comes from being full of one's subject and keeping one's eye on that subject.

The felt sense of writing an essay is, I believe, very different from the felt sense of writing a narrative. Sometimes when we write essays, we are essentially teaching or persuading readers. The essayist assumes a teaching/explaining/persuading voice, feels full of his or her subject, and then puts pen to page, trying to write in ways that convey an idea to anticipated readers. The essayist sometimes literally copies material that she or he has gathered and sometimes leaves gaps in the draft that she or he will puzzle through later. For the essayist, as for the narrative writer, drafting is tentative, done in the spirit of exploration.

There is no question that as children grow older and more experienced, the drafts of any one piece of writing will stand on the shoulders of previous writing and especially of previous revisions. If Roy's first draft of a personal narrative in September conveyed what the characters said to each other but was only a sound track, without any mention of actions and settings to contextualize the dialogue, and if Roy worked arduously to revise that draft by adding a backdrop to the dialogue, then one would expect that in October, when he makes new narrative notebook entries and especially when he writes another first draft of a personal narrative, this time he will, from the start, intersperse dialogue with sentences conveying action and setting.

Revision

Revision means, quite literally, to *resee*. Writing is a powerful tool for thought precisely because when we write, we can put our first thoughts on the page and then take those thoughts and put them in our pocket or file and take those thoughts out another day. We can then reread and rethink our first thoughts.

As writers we learn, over time, a variety of lenses we can use to re-see and reconsider our first drafts. For starters, we shift to become readers of our own writing; we pretend we are strangers, encountering

the text for the first time. We read thinking, "What will a reader make of this?" We ask, "Are there sections that are unclear? That rely on more explicit information? That are misleading? Contradictory?" Then we revise our writing so that readers will be able to make sense of what we've said.

We can also reread in order to consider our own texts in the light of our aspirations, asking, "Can I see the quality of writing that I'm aiming to achieve in this text?" In other words, if a writer has studied effective essays and learned that essays often shift between precise examples and overarching ideas, the writer might look at her own essay asking, "Does my essay shift between the general and the specific?"

Writers can, more generally, reread our own writing asking, "What works here that I can build upon?" and "What doesn't work here that I can repair or eliminate?"

The most sophisticated and important sort of revision isn't fixing up one's text so that it works more effectively to convey one's meaning. Instead, the most sophisticated sorts of revisions involve the writer looking through his draft in order to come to a deeper, more nuanced, more thoughtful understanding of the writer's content. This sort of revision begins with the writer asking, "What am I trying to say?" and then revising to highlight that meaning. In time, this sort of revision becomes more exploratory. Writers venture into unexplored terrain and stumble upon new insights that illuminate a topic not only for the reader but also for the writer.

Writers sometimes write without knowing exactly what it is we want to say; then we turn around and read our writing to learn "What is it that I think?" and "What surprises me, astonishes me, makes me catch my breath?"

Between kindergarten and fifth grade, children's abilities to revise become more sophisticated. Kindergartners revise the first day of school, but those earliest revisions typically only involve adding more details onto their drawings. In time, kindergartners will add more pages to a story, more labels or sentences to a page. By first and second grade (although with some students this happens at the end of kindergarten) children will tape flaps onto edges of a draft and use those flaps to insert details and direct quotes and elaborating information. They will sometimes write new leads or endings, taping them on top of the earlier versions. They may re-sequence pages. They will certainly rewrite key pages in order to include more detail, show-not-tell their feelings, answer reader's questions, and so forth.

Revision for upper-elementary students begins much earlier in the writing process. By the time children are eight (especially if they have grown up participating in writing workshops), revision begins right when they select a topic from a list of possibilities. They'll draft a timeline if the writing will be a narrative or a very sketchy, informal outline (boxes and bullets) if the writing will be an essay and use these graphic organizers to help them anticipate difficulties and imagine other possibilities for how their planned entry might go. Once children are in third grade, they learn to begin revising very early in the process of writing, and they use revision as a way to bring their growing knowledge of good writing to bear on what they do.

Similarly, when upper-elementary students draft and revise leads, they are doing so not only with an eye toward a good lead but also because they recognize that each lead represents a different way the text could go: "If I start it this way, it'll take too long to get to the main part."

Revision happens earlier in grades three through five because whatever strategies children use as they write one text eventually move earlier in the writing process: postwriting revision eventually becomes part of their rehearsal. For example, at first children will write a narrative and then revise it by thinking, "What is the heart of this story?" and elaborating on that one section. In time, children will plan their narratives from the start with an eye toward concentrating on the heart of their story. As they draft, they'll be thinking, "I need to build up this part. I gotta make it more intense here."

Similarly, at first children will collect a great deal of supporting material for their essays, then they'll reread and reconsider it, eliminating the many passages that don't support their point. As they become more experienced, however, these same children pause as they're making their notes to ask, "How can I angle this material so that it makes my point?"

As children's revision work begins to occur earlier in the process and as children are able to do more and more during rehearsal, the amount of time that lapses between the day the child settles on a "seed idea" (the entry the child commits to turning into a final piece of writing) and the day the child begins to write his or her first draft will grow longer. This portion of a child's writing process also varies based on the kind of text the child is writing, with fiction and essays requiring more rehearsal. I find that at the start of third grade, when these youngsters are writing personal narratives, not much productive revision work happens in the abstract. I suggest these children try a few leads and that they draft and revise a timeline, but beyond that, they need to write a draft so they can then roll up their sleeves and begin a concrete form of revision. Once children are in fifth grade, if they are experienced with the writing process, they will be able to do much more productive work as they rehearse their narratives. For example, if they are writing personal narratives, fifth graders can ask themselves (and muse over in writing) questions such as: "What will this story *really* be about?" "What will I try to show about myself in this story?" "How will this story change the way readers feel?"

Editing

Professional writers tend to postpone editing until the text is ready to be published. Like adult writers, children learn the value of writing rough drafts quickly, without pausing to use *Roget's Thesaurus* or even a dictionary in the midst of drafting. And like adult writers, children do not pore over a draft, worrying that every convention is correct, until it is time for the writing to be published.

Once the main structure and content of a draft has been revised so that the text now feels stable, writers begin to reread, checking each sentence, word, and letter from a "when you falter, alter" perspective. In our writing workshops, we teach students to read each draft successive times, each time with a new lens. Among other things, the child will read for spelling. If the child senses that a word is misspelled, she circles that word and then tries it again in the margin. In order to do this, the child needs to look at the approximate spelling, asking, "Is this partly right?" and then copy that part of the word. The child also needs to ask, "What other words do I know that might be spelled like this one?" and to use the words the child can spell to help spell unknown words. Children are encouraged to use resources to help them, including a dictionary and each other.

Editing involves much more than correcting spelling, and children are taught to check that they've included end punctuation, that their verb tenses agree, that they use a variety of punctuation and sentence structure, that their words are precise, that their pronoun references are clear. "Does this sound right?" a writer asks. "Is this exactly true? Are the words precisely chosen? Will the punctuation give readers the road signs they need?"

Teachers teach editing within minilessons, and also within mid-workshop teaching points, share sessions, and homework assignments. Obviously, teachers will tailor their lessons so they are roughly aligned with what most of the class needs, using small group instruction to provide special support for children who need it. As the year unfolds, the classroom's editing checklist will grow, with children having access to a growing list of skills. That is, in September, teachers may expect children to edit their writing looking for high-frequency words which are on the class word wall, for end punctuation and for paragraphing. By May, children will check that their pronoun references are clear, and their sentences structures, varied.

Once children have been taught to edit with particular concerns in

mind, then those skills and strategies need to move forward in the writing process, becoming part of the writer's repertoire of skills that he draws upon while scrawling a rough draft. That is, although children are not expected to fret about writing perfectly correct drafts, it is also not helpful for them to postpone all thought of spelling and punctuation until the final throes of work on a manuscript. Over time, they need to write very fast rough drafts with roughly correct spelling and punctuation. It is also important that they learn to spell a growing bank of words (and syllables) automatically. And punctuation cannot be an afterthought, inserted into a manuscript just before it goes to press! So we, as teachers, help children take a few minutes as they write their rough drafts to make sure that the conventions they "almost know" are under control. Then, during editing, children can reexamine conventions that pose problems for them, relying on resources and one another to edit these problematic areas.

Once a child has edited her own writing, a teacher will need to confer with the child, teaching the writer another few strategies she can use to edit the text. Perhaps the child will have added quotation marks correctly, but will not yet have mastered the punctuation that is expected with quotations. In the editing conference, we would support the child's use of quotation marks, and show her the next step toward correct handling of quotations. We'd go over one quote with the child, and then ask her to read through the draft, fixing the others. Meanwhile, however, there will also be some incorrect spellings and some problems with verb tenses, and we might choose not to tackle those as well. That is, in editing conferences like in every other kind of conference, a teacher makes a choice, teaching the child one or two things which seem to be within the child's reach.

Meanwhile, before the child's work is published, many teachers go through the final draft as a copy editor would, correcting on it. The child then recopies the piece, correcting most (but rarely all) of the errors. This final step calls for a decision. If teachers correct the child's final work before children recopy it, then that text will be easier for others to read. On the other hand, if teachers do this, then the child's final work does not really show what the child can do with independence, and it will be harder for us to hold ourselves to being sure that children are growing in their abilities to correct their own writing. It is important, therefore, that the next-to-final draft is kept in the child's portfolio.

Cycling Through the Entire Process

Just as children need to have a felt sense of how a narrative or an essay tends to go, they need to have a felt sense of how the process of writing that kind of text is apt to go. For example, we don't want the stage of gathering entries to be so long that children can't feel that it is just a prelude to selecting one seed idea to develop. The gathering of entries can't feel like an end in itself—the stage of using those entries has to follow directly upon it, within a short enough time frame that kids recognize the reasons they collected those entries. I want children to plan and draft their writing anticipating the day they'll revise it and, better yet, anticipating the day they'll send the text out into the world. When I am creating a version of the writing process for a class, I look for indications that the version of the writing process that I imagine for them matches what they can do with only a little support. I want to see that children are productive, engaged, and purposeful throughout the entire process.

PLANNING A YEARLONG CURRICULUM

For more than two decades, writing workshops have been characterized by their structure. Workshops usually begin with explicit instruction delivered in a minilesson, followed by a long stretch of time in which students work with some independence on projects of great importance to them while the teacher circulates, conferring and sometimes leading small groups to lift the level of writing-in-progress and to teach students skills and strategies they can also bring to future pieces of writing. Workshops tend to end with some form of share, either among the whole group or between partners or members of response groups.

THE ARGUMENT FOR TEACHERS TO COLLABORATIVELY DESIGN SHARED CURRICULAR CALENDARS

One of the greatest contributions that the Teachers College Reading and Writing Project has made to this widely shared image of a writing workshop is the notion that workshops are characterized not only by these ongoing structures but also by changing units of study. Thirty years ago, when I wrote the first edition of *The Art of Teaching Writing*, I imagined that each class of children would probably progress through their own unique sequence of units of study. At that time, I imagined that some units might last three weeks, others six weeks, and that as one unit came to an end, the teacher and children would together envision a new unit of study, embarking on that upcoming inquiry when the time was right.

Since then, my ideas on a yearlong curriculum have become less informal and spontaneous and more planned and collaborative. Now, in most New York City elementary schools and in thousands of other schools, teachers across a grade level spend a full day or an afternoon in May or June thinking together about the units of study for their upcoming year's writing workshop. In general, teachers assume that all the classrooms at a particular grade level will move roughly in sync through a preplanned, collaboratively chosen sequence of month-long units of study. A letter containing an overview of the yearlong writing curriculum goes home to parents early in the school year.

There are, of course, lots of exceptions. For example, sometimes cohorts of teachers decide that the length of units will vary. One unit will be only three weeks long, another will take six weeks. Sometimes not all teachers and classrooms on a grade level join in on the shared curriculum—instead, a "friendship group" of several teachers across different grade levels embraces this chance to teach within a community of practice. Sometimes teachers agree to travel in sync for most of the year but also set aside a month or two to go their own ways.

But on the whole we find that when all the teachers across a grade level in a school agree to plan and teach in alignment with one another, this relatively simple decision can do more to improve the professional learning lives at the school than almost any other decision teachers and school leaders could possibly make. And few things matter more than the professional learning lives of the people who live and work together in a school.

Roland Barth, author of *Improving Schools from Within*, points out that all too often, relationships among teachers are like relationships among two-year-olds playing next to one another in a sandbox. When teachers engage in this "parallel play," we do not share our "toys"; one teacher has the teaching equivalent of a shovel, another, a pail. Not only that, we also do not talk to one another. We *do* talk, all the time,

but never to one another, and we would never think of combining efforts to make a shared "castle." Other times relationships among teachers can be hostile, as we battle for limited resources and limited recognition. And sometimes relationships are congenial, with teachers engaging in pleasant small talk together under the shared premise illustrated by a sign in one faculty room that said "No Children Allowed in This Room" before it was revised, by a handwritten addition, to read, "No *Talking About* Children Allowed in This Room." Finally, some faculty rooms are characterized by collegiality, and Barth argues that in these schools, teachers have the greatest system of professional development imaginable. In these schools, we plan teaching together, wish one another well as teachers, observe one another's teaching, and stand on one another's shoulders in order to make our teaching as strong as possible.

When teachers adopt a shared curricular calendar for writing and make the commitment to travel in sync with one another through a collaboratively designed curriculum, there are suddenly wonderful reasons to spend prep periods planning together. Teachers write together, sharing the stories of our own lives, and we gain insights from our own experiences as writers in a community of writers. We bring one another's drafts into classrooms, helping all the children in a school see all their teachers as richly literate people. Suddenly it becomes incredibly meaningful for us to convene around student writing, poring over the work that students in various classrooms are doing in order to think together about predictable problems students encounter and possible ways to support them. Teachers who are more experienced or more able to study the teaching of writing can lend a hand to those who need help writing minilessons, locating mentor texts, and evaluating student work.

When teachers across a grade level collaborate in this way on the teaching of writing, we provide one another with important support. Decades of work in the teaching of writing have convinced me that wise methods of teaching usually do not emerge *sui generis* from a single gifted and talented teacher. Wise methods of teaching do not come from our genes alone but from our communities of practice. How important it is for schools to devise schedules so that teachers across a grade level can meet together several times a week as a support and study group, collaborating around anticipated units of study. Within these groups, teachers write together, study children's literature together, assess student writing together, and draft, revise and share minilessons and small-group strategy lessons together.

This structure also allows professional development to be aligned with instruction. A staff developer, for example, can work for a month in four schools, one day a week in each, then move and spend one day a week in a second cluster of four schools, returning during the third month to the first set of schools. While the staff developer is working in a school, she can help several grade-specific groups of teachers plan and teach their units of study. Early on, the staff developer provides demonstration teaching and coaching to support that unit of study; over time, she provides coaching and guided practice as teachers assume more and more responsibility. In time, the teachers can be teaching one unit of study to kids—say, a unit on literary essays—and the staff developer can be teaching a different unit of study to teachers—a unit on supporting reading-writing connections, or on methods of teaching that support increasing independence, or on small group work in a writing workshop.

Let me explain the way in which staff developers might work in more detail. For example, an upper-grade staff developer might work Wednesdays in September at P.S. 260, starting each day with an 8:30–9:30 "lab site" class of third graders, with all the second- and third-grade teachers participating. Later in the day, the staff developer might work similarly with all the fourth-grade teachers and then with all the fifth-grade teachers. The staff developer then leads a study-group session for each of the

three groups of teachers, helping them learn from methods of teaching they saw demonstrated and also helping them plan their teaching for the upcoming week. As the unit of study comes to a close and the staff developer prepares to leave to spend the next month with different schools, she helps each of the study groups plan for and perhaps launch the upcoming unit of study, with these groups of teachers then teaching and developing curriculum on their own. A month later, when the staff developer returns, the teachers again, in collaboration, construct a third unit of study. When teachers across a grade level share curricular calendars, it is easier to ensure that professional development directly supports classroom teaching.

The Emphasis in This Writing Curriculum: Learning to Structure Text

All of this starts with a group of teachers asking, "How might a yearlong curriculum in the teaching of writing go?" In order to make headway with this question, it is helpful to ask a follow-up question: "What big ideas will underlie my idea—our idea—for how this curriculum will unfold?" For example, when teachers develop a social studies curriculum, we need to decide what aspects of history are so important that they deserve to be spotlighted. Perhaps the teachers will decide to highlight the relationship between geography and culture or to celebrate the variety of cultures that come together in America. Those choices angle the work of the year and the sequence of that work. Similarly, when teachers devise a curriculum for teaching writing, we first need to ask, "What ideas will take preeminence in this curriculum?" There is no right answer to that question, and over the

years I've found it exhilarating to explore several very different ways to imagine a yearlong curriculum.

This series of books grows out of the decision to highlight the importance of structure (as well as process) in the teaching of writing. I do not want to argue that there is something sacrosanct about this particular emphasis, only that it is one very worthwhile option. I came to believe that we'd do well to emphasize structure in writing after studying the written work that students were producing in writing workshops across the country. Many students were focused primarily on using writerly craft and reading–writing connections to "pretty up" their texts with fancy beginnings and endings, sound effects, sensory details, and metaphors and similes. But far too many of the pieces were structured in such hodge-podge fashion that it seemed as if the writers were worrying about door-knockers on homes that had no foundation or walls!

The written traces of kids' processes suggested the writers had written their first drafts by selecting a topic—summers at Grandma's house—and then piling on whatever loosely related material came to mind. Then it seemed the children had either asked the teacher, "Can I be done?" and been told no or had gotten a second wind; either way they'd again written whatever came to mind that was loosely related to the chosen topic, often repeating much of what they'd already said. Finally, the writers had set about revising these drafts by adding special effects—sound effects, a pretty metaphor, endings that referred to their beginnings. The resulting pieces might have some lovely sections, but the texts as wholes were often chaotic, hard to follow, and not representative of any particular genre. Studying them, I came to believe that young writers would profit from learning to approach a draft with a specific text structure in mind.

During this time, I had also been meeting periodically with literacy leaders from across the country who were hoping to revise the standards for literacy published by the National Center for Education and the Economy. My belief that structures—or kinds—of writing need to figure more preeminently in children's plans were echoed by other members of that committee, and together we posited that the texts fourth and fifth graders write can be divided into these main categories:

- Narrative texts: personal narratives, narrative memoir, short fiction, biography, narrative nonfiction

- Persuasive or expository essays

- Functional (also called procedural or how-to) texts

- Informational writing: reports, brochures, all-about books

- Poetry

In the primary grades (and especially in the series *Units of Study for Primary Writing*) children learn to do *all* these kinds of writing within the writing workshop, with the exception of the fairly advanced genre of persuasive or expository essays. By the time children are in upper-elementary grades, however, it seems to me that functional writing can take place mostly within math and science classrooms, informational writing in content area studies. (Both those claims, by the way, are debatable and could be rethought.) The writing workshop can then be dedicated to helping students write narratives texts, expository/persuasive essays, and poetry—and above all, helping them write these genres well and with enough enjoyment that children initiate this work within their own independent learning lives.

When thinking through a yearlong curriculum on writing, I generally begin with the idea that children will first write personal narratives, learning through this work about both the writing process and qualities of good narrative writing. After two months of narrative writing, it will probably be time for them to try their hand at expository writing, starting with the personal essay. After that I imagine children shuttling between narrative and expository writing. After writing essays, children benefit from returning to narrative writing, this time to write short fiction. This, in turn, nicely supports them to read short texts and write literary essays. Children also need the opportunity to write poetry.

In addition, teachers and children may plan a unit on revision or on author studies or on a particular quality of writing (such as show-don't-tell) or on another kind-of-writing (such as journalism or narrative non-fiction). If teachers want children to practice expository texts on-the-run, teachers may design a unit on Writing to Make a Difference, enabling children to write editorials and persuasive letters. Finally, before the year is over, students need to learn that writers do not always begin with a specific form in mind, pouring content into that form. Sometimes writers start with content and, as we write, consider a variety of forms (and create their own hybrid forms) for conveying their meaning. We encourage this very creative kind of writing in a unit on memoir.

There is no one "right way" for a yearlong curriculum to proceed. In this series, I lay out one curricular journey, one that is especially important to the community within which I teach. I deliberately do not include enough units to fill an entire year; later in this book, I suggest ways in which you and your colleagues can author additional units of study tailored to your children and to your own passions.

A Recommended Curricular Calendar

September

UNIT 1: LAUNCHING THE WRITING WORKSHOP

We start the year by teaching children some of the biggest lessons they'll ever learn. First and most important, we teach them that their lives and their thoughts are worth writing about. We help children realize that the small moments of their lives can be compelling stories, and we help them feel committed to capturing the truth of their experience in words.

The first lessons in this unit center on topic choice. We teach children a number of strategies they can draw on in order to generate their own ideas for writing, and we set them free from a dependency on the teacher. Children will benefit from knowing that writers think of a person, then brainstorm moments they've spent with that person, choose one moment, and write the story. Writers similarly think of places that matter to them, brainstorm moments that occurred in those places, choose one moment, and write the story. Writers know that objects and photographs from their lives hold stories and that by listening to the stories of others, we can recall our own stories. Naomi Nye's beautiful poem "Valentine for Ernest Mann" reminds writers that "poems hide . . . in the shadows of our room they are hiding." Stories hide too, and with just a few minilessons we can be sure that all our students know where important stories are likely to hide.

Many teachers find that in this first unit, it helps to celebrate the fact that stories of significance can be found in the smallest and most ordinary occasions. Perhaps after children throng back into the classroom after lunch, we will want to help them choose one small story from all the many that occurred while they were eating and tell that story as well as possible to their partners. In this fashion, we can teach students to reexamine the everyday routines of their lives in search of stories that have humor, beauty, and drama.

Meanwhile, during this unit children learn the essentials of narrative writing. They learn that narratives are just that—stories. In a personal narrative, one character (presumably the writer) experiences one thing, then the next, then the next. These texts are chronologically ordered. Children also learn that their narratives will be more effective if the writer has zoomed in on a small episode, written with detail, expanded the heart of the story, made their characters talk—and above all "made a movie in the mind" and then recorded that movie on the page. As children learn to write in ways that reflect all that they have already learned about focus, detail, strong leads, and so forth, their writing will improve in very noticeable ways. The improvements in children's writing should prove to them that learning to write well matters and thus launch them into the year.

One of the few nonnegotiable qualities of narrative writing is the hard-to-describe (and hard-to-achieve) quality that some teachers refer to as "writing in the moment" or "making a movie in your mind." If a child talks "all about" an event—summarizing it with sentences like "It was a good baseball game. We won 6 to 2. I got a lot of hits."—then the child is *commenting on* the game rather than telling the story of it. The child has not yet grasped the idea of writing in a storyteller's voice. If, on the other hand, his piece begins, "I grabbed a bat and walked up to the plate. I looked at the pitcher and nodded. 'I'm ready,' I said," then the child is writing a story. Most children need to be reminded to make movies in their mind and to write so readers can picture exactly what is happening.

During this unit, many children will profit from learning a very simple form of focus. For example, a child might initially plan to write a page-long piece depicting his whole day at the beach, but because of our teaching, he'll write instead about body surfing on one wave. Another child will decide that instead of retelling the entire trip to Grandma's house, she will focus on how she accidentally let the pigs loose. As children narrow the time span of their stories, it is crucial that they then elaborate on the portion of the event that remains in their spotlight. In other words, the main reason to "zoom in" or to "write about a little seed story, not about a big watermelon topic" is that this makes it more likely that the writer will relive an episode with enough detail that the reader, too, can experience the event.

As children learn about narrative writing, some of the lessons will be explicit, taught in minilessons and conferences. But some of the lessons will be implicit, gleaned as children are immersed in texts that sound like those we hope they will soon write. It is not always easy to find published personal narratives, so we also share realistic fiction, especially picture books and short stories that resemble the stories about small moments the children will write. Even just one dearly loved and closely studied text can infuse a writing workshop with new energy.

This unit of study is designed to launch a writing workshop that is well managed enough that children can proceed with some independence. Children learn the structures and rituals of a writing workshop. They learn to gather for a minilesson, to sit and listen throughout most of it, to "turn and talk" with a partner at the designated moment. They learn that they can get themselves started on writing, work past the hard parts, rely on one another as well as themselves, share their writing, and so forth. Soon children will be able to get themselves started writing new entries without needing any input from the teacher; this means that during one day's writing workshop they'll write one entry after another, working with independence.

During this launching unit, most children write two focused personal narrative stories and then select one for further revision, editing and publication.

October/November

UNIT 2: RAISING THE QUALITY OF PERSONAL NARRATIVE WRITING

Although this unit is titled *Raising the Quality of Personal Narrative Writing*, the real goal is to improve the quality of the writing—and of the writers—in general. We linger for another month of work in personal narrative writing, before shifting to a focus on expository writing, because we know that real progress comes not from constantly exposing children to yet another form of writing but from working long enough within one form to help children write longer, more significant, more conventional, and more graceful pieces in general.

We begin the unit by telling children they will be revisiting narrative writing and helping them understand this means they need to draw on all they already know. This is a perfect opportunity to teach children that writers carry with them and draw on a cumulative repertoire of strategies. For example, we can say, "You already have a whole repertoire of strategies for generating narrative writing," and briefly direct their attention to the charts listing strategies they learned during the earlier unit. When children begin to draft new personal narrative entries, we can ask them to look back at the piece they published (after revision and editing) at the end of the previous unit. Since they learned to write focused, sequential stories that included direct quotations, details, paragraphs, and end punctuation, we can suggest that their new entries should demonstrate all they have already learned as writers. This unit can definitely break children of the habit of regarding each day as nothing more than a time to practice that day's minilesson!

Once the unit has gotten underway with this emphasis on writers' drawing on all they already know, you will want to find important ways to lift the quality of students' work. Chances are good that the stories children wrote during the first unit of study were sequenced, detailed, and dull. One important way to lift the level of writing in this unit is to help children write stories that matter. There are many ways to help children bring out more significance in their writing. For starters, we may want to teach children strategies for generating narrative entries that stand a greater chance of having emotional weight and a story arc. In addition to drawing on the strategies they learned in the first unit, children also write narratives about the first (or last) time they did something, a time they learned something, and a time they felt a strong emotion—hope, worry, sadness. The resulting stories are often significant and shapely.

A second way to lift the level of student writing is to rally children to look really closely at the ways in which writers create texts that matter. We encourage children to read texts like those they will write, to let those texts affect them, and then to pause and ask, "What has this writer done that has affected me?"

Since we are guiding students to notice aspects of published texts that we believe will be especially important to them, this unit relies on assessment. Are children already writing focused, detailed, chronological pieces? If not, we'll want to teach the easiest way to focus personal narratives, which is to limit the time span of the story. Sometimes teachers refer to focused narratives as "small moment stories," although the technical word that writers use for this is *scenes* (as in scenes of a play, not scenery). But once children grasp what it means to write effectively about a brief episode, we can show them that narratives need not stay within the confines of a half-hour episode! Narratives actually comprise several scenes glued together with bits of exposition (or narration) between them.

In this unit we can suggest that a child look at any short story and notice that writers often put a few scenes (or small moments) one after another. This is what many people mean when they say that a story has a beginning, a middle, and an end. For example, the child who has written a small moment vignette about getting a bike for her birthday will construct a better story if she sets up the incident by first telling about an earlier time when she begged for the bike. Similarly, the child who writes about defending the goal in a hockey game will construct a more effective story if he first backs up to recreate the moment when he put on his goalie pads and worried they might not be thick enough.

Whether children are writing one episode or linking several together, we will definitely teach them that writers focus our pieces not only by narrowing the time frame in which we write but also by deciding on the angle from which to tell a story. We teach children to ask, "What am I trying to show about myself through this story? What do I want readers to know about me? How can I bring that meaning out in this episode?" We help children learn that the same story can be told differently, depending on the theme the writer wants to bring out. An episode about falling from the monkey bars could be written to show that the writer was afraid but conquered her fears or to show that peer pressure goaded the writer to take stupid risks.

In this unit, it is especially important to select a few touchstone texts for children to study. Ideally, they will be personal narratives—but sometimes teachers may choose instead a fictional story, explaining that although the text is really fiction, it is written as a narrative. I recommend the narrative about a red sweater embedded in "Eleven," by Sandra Cisneros. I also recommend selected pages from Jean Little's memoir *Little by Little*, Patricia MacLachlan's *Journey*, Gary Soto's *A Summer Life*, Amy Ehrlich's *When I Was Your Age: Original Stories About*

Growing Up, and *Chicken Soup for Kids*. Some picture books can be useful in this unit including Crews' *Shortcut*, Yolen's *Owl Moon*, Keats' *Peter's Chair* or *The Snowy Day* or Willems' *Knuffle Bunny*.

During this unit, we invite children to study narratives written by an author they admire, paying attention to what works in those texts. We help them read these texts as insiders, noticing sections that particularly affect them and then examining the text closely, thinking, "What has the author done to create this effect?" In the end, children also need to ask, "What effect do I want to create in my text and how could I create it?"

Once students have drafted, you'll teach them to revise, and this work will probably be informed by knowing how stories go. Stories have settings; have your students developed theirs? Children may also study effective leads and endings, the use of dialogue, and ways of showing the passage of time. Have they considered that stories usually contain a problem and a solution? If a child writes about the day he gets a bike, he may want to set up this vignette by telling how all his life he longed for a bike. Children can use their knowledge of good narratives to develop their writing; they also learn new strategies for generating story ideas that are apt to contain a story arc.

November/December

UNIT 3: BREATHING LIFE INTO ESSAYS

This unit of study is designed to help students with the difficult and exhilarating work of learning to write well within an expository structure. At the start of this unit, we point out that we could conceivably write about a topic—say a visit to Grandma's—as a narrative, retelling it chronologically, or as a non-narrative, or essay, advancing a certain idea (visits to Grandma's farm feel like time travel, for example). For some students, the fact that they can write about personal topics in a genre other than a personal narrative will be a new realization. The terms narrative and non-narrative or essay refer to structure and genre, not to

content. In this unit, each child will write a personal essay in which she advances a theme of personal significance, arguing, for example, that it's hard being an only child or claiming "my dog is my best friend."

A teacher could choose to hurry kids through this unit, showing them how to whip up modest yet well-structured and competent little essays. However, we argue that there are many reasons to take one's time, teaching students how to write these essays well and harvesting all the learning opportunities found along the way. If we help children write lots of rough drafts and do lots of revision with the goal of learning as much as possible about logical thought, this unit can have enormous payoffs. Then, after helping kids spend a month writing one essay, we can show students they also have the option of churning out a quick essay in a day—or even in fifteen minutes! This, of course, provides children with test preparation.

As with any unit of study in a writing workshop, we begin by helping children develop a repertoire of strategies for collecting entries— this time, entries that can grow into essays. It's important to teach students that their lives are provocative. Writers observe things in the world, recording what we see, and then we shift and write, "The thought I have about this is…" or "This makes me realize…." When teaching children to grow essays out of everyday observations, we are really teaching them to free write, the goal being to help them realize the value of keeping at it, writing without a preconceived content but trusting that ideas will surface as they go along. Children can observe and then write their ideas about anything that is before them in the writing workshop, but they can also learn the power of imagining themselves in a provocative place and generating ideas in response to what they "see."

During this early phase of the unit, we also teach children that they can reread entries they collected earlier in the year during narrative units of study and use those entries as starting points, perhaps again beginning, "The idea I have about this is…" or "The thing that surprises me about this is…." A child might jot down a topic, hobby, or issue that he or she cares about, then collect ideas about that big subject and write about one of them. Children should become accustomed to selecting the strategy that works best for them on any given occasion. That is, the strategy the teacher introduces in a minilesson on a particular day is not that day's assignment but joins a growing repertoire of strategies that writers draw on as needed.

Essayists need tools to push past their first thoughts, and many find it helps to use thought-prompts to prime the pump of their thoughts. "The surprising thing about this is . . ." an essayist might write in his or her notebook before spinning out a brand-new thought in letters that scrawl down the page. The important thing will be that once a child records an idea, the child has strategies to elaborate upon that idea. Using prompts such as "to add on . . .," "furthermore . . .," "this makes me realize . . .," "the surprising thing about this is . . .," "on the other hand . . .," "I think this is important because . . ." allows children to extend their first ideas and to use writing as a way of thinking. They find that new ideas come out of their pencils, ideas they never even knew they had.

After collecting possible seed ideas, young essayists select one and revise it until they've made a provocative, clear, compelling claim—or thesis statement. When it comes time for children to choose a seed idea, it helps to remind them that they already know how to reread their notebooks looking for seeds. In the earlier, narrative units of study, they selected a seed *story*; this time they will select a seed *idea* (a thesis).

Once students have selected and articulated an idea (it is hard to be an only child, for example), we teach them to elaborate on it by generating subordinate ideas (it's hard to be an only child because you get more attention than you want, it's hard to be an only child because you're often lonely, and so forth). The easiest way to support most claims is to provide a few parallel *reasons* for that claim; writers can restate the claim each time and add the transitional word *because* followed by a reason.

Usually children write support ideas through a series of parallel statements. One writer's thesis was, "It's hard being an only child," which she then elaborated on by saying, "Your parents shower you with

too much attention, your parents have too many of their hopes attached to you, and you can be very lonely."

During this planning stage, students can play around with their subordinate ideas and decide what they really want to say. In the end, we hope each child has a main idea (a claim or a thesis) and several parallel supporting ideas. We sometimes refer to the main idea and supporting statements as "boxes and bullets." We have found it helps if children take their thesis and record it on the outside of one folder, then make internal folders for each of their bullets (these become topic sentences for their body paragraphs).

When it is time for children to collect materials to support their topic sentences, we teach them that they can first collect stories that illustrate their ideas. It is also important to teach children to angle these stories so they support the idea the writer wants to advance.

Writers can also collect lists to support their topic sentences. We show children how statistics, observations, citations, quotations, and so forth can enrich their work. These bits are collected not in a writer's notebook but on separate bits of paper and filed in the appropriate topic-sentence folder.

It is important to help writers select *compelling* evidence from the material they collect in these folders, and to help them ensure that the evidence closely supports their claim. We teach them to look carefully from the claim to the evidence and back again, because often the two aren't as congruent as they appear at first glance. Eventually we teach writers to sort through the materials in each folder, writing well-structured paragraphs. Special lessons on transitions, introductions, and conclusions are important here.

Once writers have selected the most powerful and pertinent support material for each of their topic sentences, they staple or tape or recopy this information into a paragraph or two that supports each topic sentence, and in this manner construct the rough draft of an essay.

This unit ends with children learning that the long, involved process they've used to write personal essays can be abbreviated in order to write "instant essays." Writers learn not only *how* but also *when* to do this. This work is described in Chapter 11 of this book.

January

UNIT 4: WRITING FICTION: BIG DREAMS, TALL AMBITIONS

After students spend a month writing essays, they'll be eager to return to the land of narrative writing, especially if they are finally, at long last, able to write what students want to write most: short fiction. By this time, students will not be surprised that the unit begins with them learning ways to live like fiction writers, seeing ideas for stories everywhere. At the start of this unit, we let students know that fiction writers get ideas for their stories by paying attention to the moments and issues of our lives. We tell children, "When I was young, I thought fiction writers looked up into the clouds and imagined make-believe stories about castles and puppy dogs. But then I grew up and learned how real fiction writers get their ideas." We let them know that Robert McCloskey got the idea for *Make Way for Ducklings* when he was stopped in Boston traffic while a line of ducks waddled across the street in front of him.

Children collect story ideas in their writer's notebooks, learning to flesh the ideas out a bit so that they contain some of the elements of an effective story. Children learn to take the tiny details and big issues of their lives and speculate on how that could become stories. They might write entries in which they both recount a bit of their lives and then speculate (in writing) on how they could turn this into a story. A child who has recently moved could make up a story about a girl who moved, only this time she could give that girl a companion—a dog? a sister?—the writer wished she'd had. Children can reread their notebooks as well as live their lives collecting possible story ideas. In these entries, children will probably not actually write their stories; instead they will write plans for how their stories might go.

For a few days, children will collect entries in which they explore ideas that could possibly become fiction stories. As they do so, they will profit from trying story ideas out. A great way for them to do this is by "storytelling" those ideas to a partner. We teach children some storytelling techniques—for example, the beginning of their stories might sound like the beginning of a famous book or a fairy tale ("Once, not long ago, a little girl named Cissy…"). Elevating storytelling a bit helps each youngster bring a storyteller's voice—and an aura of literary language—to his or her own story plans.

Once children have each chosen a seed idea (which will now be called their story idea), it is important for children to develop those ideas. One way fiction writers do this is to develop their main characters, perhaps in notebook entries that never appear in the final story. A fiction writer once said, "Before you can begin writing your story, you need to know your characters so well that you know exactly how much change each one has in his or her pocket." When children are asked to develop ideas about their characters' traits, most children immediately list external traits (she has red hair, and so on). We encourage children to think also of a character's internal traits. What is she afraid of? What does she want? The trick is to help children create coherent characters with characteristics that fit together in a way that seems believable. When children use broad generalizations (for example, suggesting the character is a good friend), we ask them to open these terms up, to be much more specific (what are the unique ways in which this character is a good friend?). After writers gather entries developing their character, we may dramatize the character, having him or her perform action in a scene (a fiction writer's word for a small moment story).

Finally, it is important to be sure that young fiction writers think especially about a character's wants and needs. Usually a story line emerges out of the intersection of a character's motivations and the obstacles that get in her or his way.

Children use "story mountains" to plot the points of their stories and revise their story plans; these story mountains become the road maps for the stories. We help children see that these story mountains build to a high point and that their main characters make harder and harder climbs toward their goals. As they sequence their story, children learn that at the top of their mountain something happens that solves (or begins to solve) the character's problem and that when the character reaches the bottom, both the character and the reader should be satisfied with the journey.

Finally, children begin to draft their story, writing across the pages of a story booklet. Since the stories will be long, revision needs to begin early; it shouldn't wait until they've already written ten pages of text. We help students incorporate qualities of good writing as they revise the early sections of their stories. Children incorporate all they learned during the personal narrative units of study in their efforts to write short fiction. They use dialogue and small actions to draw their readers immediately into the story. They show rather than summarize character's feelings.

There are new lessons that children need to learn as they draft and revise fiction. For example, many children need to realize that a story can begin midpoint in a sequence of events, and that the opening scene can convey backstory. They need to learn to convey the passage of time, and to abut one focused scene against another. Above all, children are led to rethink the evolution of a story. Oftentimes, they approach a fiction story planning for the character to magically receive his or her fondest dream, often in the form of a solution that flies in out of nowhere like Superman. With help, we show children that in fiction as in life, the solutions we find are generally those that we make, and if there are magic answers to be found, they usually have been there before our eyes all along.

February

UNIT 5: LITERARY ESSAYS: WRITING ABOUT READING

In their personal essays, many children will have written about lessons they learned from people they know and interact with. But writing also helps us learn from the characters in the books we read. Just as writing allows us to pause in our hurried lives and really notice and experience and reflect on things that have happened to us, so, too, writing is a tool we can use to pause in our hurried reading and really pay attention to the characters in our books.

In order for children to write about reading in this way, they need to be reading! Children who are learning to write literary essays while they are still very young—in grades three, four and five—will profit from writing these essays about short texts they've read, reread, and discussed. In this unit, we invite children to read and study from small packets of short texts that merit close study. A teacher might thread one short story through many minilessons, showing children how she or he reads, thinks, and writes about that one story and then suggesting that children try similar techniques with a story from their packet. The stories in a child's packet need to be ones he or she can read. Therefore, children may not all have the same collection. We encourage teachers to provide stories that are rich, complex, and well crafted enough to reward close study.

On each of the first few days of the unit, we demonstrate a lens that readers can bring to a text, reminding children that all of these lenses accumulate so they have a repertoire of possibilities to choose from whenever they read. We teach children that just as essayists pay attention to our lives, expecting to grow ideas from this wide-awake attentiveness, so, too, literary essayists pay attention—but this time, the attention is directed to texts. Each child chooses a story that especially speaks to her or him and then collects entries about that story. The process of choosing a seed idea in this unit has two stages. First, a child chooses a story. Then, the child lives with that one story and gathers entries about it. Eventually, the child rereads those entries to choose a seed idea.

We remind children of their work in the personal essay unit, when they observed their lives and then pushed their thinking in their notebooks by writing, "The thought I have about this is . . ." or "This makes me realize that . . . ." In this unit, children can pause as they read to observe what is happening in the text and then develop an idea using the same conversational prompts. We teach children that their thoughts can be extended by using phrases such as "another example of this is," "furthermore," "this connects with," "on the other hand," "but you might ask," "this is true because," and "I am realizing." If we hope children will write literary essays in which they articulate the lessons they believe a character learns in a story or name the theme or idea a text teaches, then it is important to provide children with strategies for generating these sorts of ideas.

After children have collected reading responses in their writer's notebooks for at least a week, we remind them that they already know how to reread a notebook in order to find a seed idea. In the personal essay unit, students found seed ideas, and they'll need to do something similar now. We encourage students to search for a portion of an entry that tells the heart of the story in one or two sentences. We ask them to look for a seed idea that is central to the story and provocative.

We also help children generate possible seed ideas. I sometimes recommend that children try writing inside this general structure: This is a story about [identify the character] who [has this trait]/[wants/cares about such-and-so] but then [what happens to change things?] and s/he ends up [how?]. In other words, we may encourage students to try writing a sentence or two in which they lay out what the character was like at the start of the story, what happened to change things, and how this was resolved at the end: "*Because of Winn-Dixie* is the story of a lonely girl, Opal, who befriends a stray dog, Winn-Dixie. The dog helps Opal make friends with lots of people." "'Spaghetti' is the story of a lonely boy, Gabriel, who learns from a tiny stray kitten to open himself to love." I also encourage children to think of a story as containing an external as well as an internal story line, and to write an essay which highlights the internal (and therefore, sometimes the overlooked) story.

We help each child revise his or her seed idea so that it is a clear thesis, making sure it is a claim or an idea, not a fact or a question. We help children imagine how they can support the thesis in a few para-

graphs. Usually for children in grades three through five, the first support paragraph will show how the child's claim was true at the start of the story, and the next support paragraph(s) will show that it was true later in the story as well. It may be that the first support paragraph shows how the claim was true for one reason, the next, for a second reason.

Once children have planned their "boxes and bullets" for a literary essay, they will need to collect the information and insights they need to build a case. We encourage each child to make a file for each topic sentence and each support paragraph. For example, if the child's claim is "Cynthia Rylant's story 'Spaghetti' is the story of a lonely boy who learns from a tiny stray kitten to open himself to love," the child might title one file "Gabriel is a lonely boy" and another "Gabriel learns from a tiny stray kitten to open himself to love."

We also teach writers how to cite references from a text and how to "unpack" how these references address the relevant big idea. Before this unit is over, we teach children that writers of literary essays use the vocabulary of their trade, incorporating literary terms such as *narrator, point of view, scenes,* and the like. We may also want to teach students to write introductory paragraphs that include a tiny summary of the story and closing paragraphs that link back to the thesis and that link the story's message to the writer's own life, or to another story, or to literature as a whole.

March/April

A HOMEGROWN UNIT: POETRY

It would be incomprehensible to lead a yearlong writing workshop and not invite children to spend a month delving into a study of poetry. We didn't write this unit for several reasons.

First, it seems right that we provide fairly detailed support for half a dozen units of study and also leave space for you to author some of your own units of study. And what unit could be more satisfying to plan than a unit in poetry?

Then, too, we are confident that there are especially wonderful resources already available to help teach this unit of study. The unit on poetry that Stephanie Parsons and I wrote for *Units of Study for Primary Writing* could easily have been written for upper-elementary students; many teachers have that series in their schools. Our close friend and former Project staff member Georgia Heard has written two books (*For the Good of the Earth and Sun, Awakening the Heart*) that provide detailed help either in enriching that unit or in writing a new one. These books are available from Heinemann. In addition, draw on your own experiences writing poetry. You may find it helpful to read the summary below of one way in which this unit of study could unroll.

In a poetry study, children again practice all that they've learned thus far. Just as they have in all the previous units, youngsters will live like writers, finding significance in the ordinary details of their lives, gathering entries and images and lists that might be turned into publishable texts.

We may teach children to look carefully at everyday objects and pay close attention to their surprising beauty, to reconsider memories, to ponder conversations. They can also search for poems in past entries. A teacher may make this unit a time for close observation, teaching students to look for objects or scenes that capture their attention and intrigue them. (For examples of close observation poetry, see Valerie Worth's *All the Small Poems and Fourteen More*.)

All through the unit, children will read poems out loud so that they can learn how to savor the sounds of words. We can help them talk and think about the difference in sound and meaning between *fry* and *sizzle*, *shine* and *sparkle*, *cry* and *weep*. Ideally, they'll hear how the right choice of words can make a poem funny or wistful or sad. They'll learn how to create "mind pictures" by bumping an ordinary thing up next to something it's never been compared to before: "Today the sky looks soft and worn, like my old baby blanket." Children learn how to shape words on the page so that their texts not only sound but also *look* like poems. They learn that poets think about where to break a line so that the sound, rhythm, and look of each line achieve the overall tone and meaning that the poet wishes to convey. They learn how poets use the white space around the words to pause, take a breath, and make something stand out from all the other words. For many children, all of the year's lessons in word choice, writing with detail, and making mind pictures suddenly make sense in the context of a small, shapely poem.

The teachers I know emphasize free verse. Rhyming well is a precise skill that many adult poets find difficult to master! We teach children to aim first for meaning—to find a way to describe what matters with words that will make the reader see the world in a brand-new way.

Once students have many beginnings and first tries of poems in their notebooks, we teach them that as poets draft new poems and rework poems they have already written, they try out many different versions. Poets make changes to better express what they most want to convey to the reader. They sometimes find that the act of revision brings new and more powerful ideas: what they want to say may change as they play with the way they're saying it.

Above all, the secret of poetry is heart. Poets write from the heart. Poets teach all of us to look at the world differently. They help us celebrate small beauties. They inspire us to be outraged over injustices great and small. And so, in this unit, we focus on the work that poets do in the world, the way that poets love the world through words, the way poets sustain us in hard times, the way poets express outrage and grief and joy.

April/May

ANOTHER HOMEGROWN UNIT: TEACHERS' CHOICE

A yearlong curriculum in teaching writing wouldn't be complete unless a group of colleagues have the chance to author your own unit of study in which you take your passions and your students' passions and fashion them into your very own unit of study. For this reason, I've deliberately left this month absolutely open. Chapter 9 in this book helps you imagine possible units of study you could coauthor with your colleagues.

There are endless possibilities for this unit. In some schools, teachers devote this time to a unit on content-area writing, taking down the walls between social studies (or science) and writing and inviting children to write about a subject the class has studied. These teachers sometimes ask children to write essays linked to the content area. Sometimes, instead, they invite children to explore the wide variety of forms in which nonfiction texts can be written. Journalism is an especially popular unit of study. Some teachers embrace the idea of Writing to Make a Real World Difference: Editorials, Persuasive Letters, and Feature Articles as a way to teach children to create on-the spot expository pieces.

In other schools, teachers who are eager to venture away from specific genres decide to focus this unit on a part of the writing process rather than on a genre. For example, some teachers use this time to teach students to live writerly lives; they ask children to renew their attachment to the writer's notebook and their commitment to wide-awake living, this time emphasizing that in real life, writers often begin with something to say and select a form that reflects their content and their purpose. Some teachers decide to embrace a unit of study on revision, perhaps designing a unit not unlike the revision unit in *Units of Study for Primary Writing*.

Other teachers use this time to focus on an aspect of writing: writing with literary devises, writing with a variety of punctuation, (see Angelillo) showing rather than telling. Still others focus on an author study, inviting all children to participate in a shared apprenticeship to one author. That shared apprenticeship might also be the focus of whole-class minilessons while each child (or small group) chooses a separate author. Some teachers use M. Colleen Cruz' *Independent Writing* as a reference and teach a unit of study on writing with independence.

Whatever unit a group of colleagues decides to pursue, the process of designing that unit will probably follow a course similar to the one I outline in Chapter 9.

May/June

UNIT 6: MEMOIR: THE ART OF WRITING WELL

This final unit aims to teach children that they can compose not only pieces of writing but also a life in which writing matters. Children will write a memoir, and in order to do so, they will draw on everything they have learned all year, and they will also invent more strategies and imagine more possibilities. At the start of the unit, we invite children to search for Life Topics. We suggest that Life Topics can be found by rereading our notebooks, reconsidering our lives, and living, wide awake to the topics that feel intensely alive and close to the heart. But we also tell children, "This time, you need to compose a writing life for yourself. You can draw on any strategy you have learned this year, or invent another strategy. Your job is to compose a writing life for yourself, one which is exactly tailored to you as a writer."

This unit, then, recognizes that the scaffolds that we have provided for children all year long can also become boxes, and the unit encourages children to set aside scaffolds that limit, and to realize that writers not only create texts, we also create our own writing lives.

We help children learn that in order to put themselves on the page with honesty and intensity, they need to write within a community of trust. And so now, as children 'round the final bend of the year, we again teach them what it means to really listen to each other and to themselves.

When writers really listen to themselves and each other, an entry or a topic can grow in significance. We encourage writers to use writing as a way to develop their own ideas and associations around a Life Topic, writing-to-learn in their writers' notebooks. In some classes, children in this unit of study refer to their seed idea as a 'blob' idea, imagining a glowing, living, changing heartlike form. Children learn that the process of 'choosing' a seed idea is a more flexible one than they'd at first learned, for as they live with a Life Topic, their sense of what it is they really want to say changes.

In this unit, children search for and create the forms for their writing. That is, we do not say to them, "This is how your writing will be structured." Instead, we teach children that writers often begin with a topic, and then choose or create forms that allow us to say whatever we want to say. Some children will write their narratives as a story, some will write a collection of short texts, some will write essays that are more journeys-of-thought rather than traditional thesis-driven essays. Mostly, children learn that the structures they've learned to use throughout the year are not as inflexible as they once thought, and they create texts which are hybrids, containing perhaps one long narrative section set off against a thesis-driven expository paragraph rather than a thesis-driven essay. As children create structures that will support their content, they learn about revision in a whole new way. They come to understand that writing is a process of growing meaning, and that writers use strategies as needed, as we reach to create meanings which feel deeply significant and personal.

CHAPTER 5

PROVISIONING A WRITING WORKSHOP

In 1986, when I wrote the first edition of *The Art of Teaching Writing,* I emphasized the importance of simple and predictable workshops. Over all these years I have continued to believe that teachers and children both profit when our writing classrooms are structured in clear, predictable ways. Back then, I wrote:

> If the writing workshop is always changing, always haphazard, children remain pawns, waiting for their teacher's agenda. For this reason and others, I think it is important for each day's workshop to have a clear, simple structure. Children should know what to expect. This allows them to carry on; it frees the teacher from choreographing activities and allows time for listening. How we structure the workshop is less important than that we structure it. (25–26)

I also said:

> [T]he most creative environments in our society are not the kaleidoscopic environments in which everything is always changing and complex. They are, instead, the predictable and consistent ones: the scholar's library, the researcher's laboratory, the artist's studio. Each of these environments is deliberately kept predictable and simple because the work at hand and the changing interactions around that work are so unpredictable and complex. (12)

In this chapter, I describe, in-depth, a workshop environment.

THE CLASSROOM ENVIRONMENT

Teaching writing does not require elaborate methods or materials or special classroom arrangements. Teachers who teach in widely divergent spaces and ways can all lead writing workshops, and their workshops can be more or less formal and traditional. There are, however, a few ways of organizing materials and space that are so supportive that these room arrangements and routines have become widely associated with writing workshops.

One necessary structure underpinning the units is the creation of long-term writing partners. These liaisons last at least across a unit of study and sometimes across several; they are not ability-based, nor does one child function as the "teacher," the other, the "student." In many classrooms, one partner is Partner 1, the other, Partner 2. On any one day, only one of the partners is apt to share, while the other listens and supports. To be sure that the more garrulous child doesn't always step into the spotlight, teachers specify who will talk and who will listen. "Partner 2, read your lead to Partner One, 1 will you talk about . . . ." Usually teachers form these partnerships with an eye toward combining youngsters who'll do good work for and with each other. Partners do not write collaboratively, but they function as audiences for each other's writing-in-progress and frequently make suggestions to each other. In some classrooms, when work is published and celebrated at the end of the unit, the partner as well as the writer sits in the place of honor, and both writers are applauded for a job well done.

Room Arrangements

Many teachers arrange their classrooms to support a rhythm of children gathering for brief bouts of direct, explicit instruction, then dispersing for longer stretches of independent, partnered, and small-group work.

THE MEETING AREA Many teachers create a carpeted corner that serves at different times as a library, a meeting area, an arena for direct instruction, a place for reading aloud and giving and listening to book talks, and a quiet workspace. During minilessons, the teacher usually sits in a chair (kept nearby) and has both a chalk tray and a storage area of materials close at hand. Usually there is also an easel holding a giant pad of chart paper within reach. Some teachers also have an overhead projector at the ready, perhaps perched on top of a readily accessible bookcase, angled to project transparencies of student work or the teacher's writing onto the white board. An overhead projector, however, is totally expendable, and I urge teachers not to over-rely on it; too many projected images can make a minilesson feel more like a board meeting than a huddle among teammates.

When children gather for minilessons or share sessions, they usually sit in a clump or in rows on the carpet, drawn as closely as possible around the teacher. Most teachers assign children spots on the rug, moving the children who might otherwise sit on the fringes front and center. Each child sits beside his or her long-term partner.

Sometimes teachers tell us they do not have enough space for a carpeted meeting area. It is true that as our children grow older and our class rosters become longer, it can be more and more challenging to create a meeting space large enough to convene the class. On the other hand, as students get older, gathering and holding their attention becomes even more of a challenge, and a sense of community becomes all the more necessary. Because it is far easier to communicate with a whole class of students when they are pulled very close around us, teachers sometimes invent ways to make this possible. Many question whether they need a large teacher's desk at the front of the room and whether they need desks to be arranged so that all children can see the board (perhaps instead a system can be devised so that a few children know to move in a specified way when the teacher does frontal teaching with children at their workspaces). Tables and desks can be more easily consolidated into three quarters of the room if some space-hungry chairs are eliminated. By making some tables coffee-table height and positioning them along the edges of the meeting area, children at these tables can sit on the floor (perhaps on pillows) rather than on chairs—and the tables make perfect benches during meeting times. In other classrooms, children know the signal to convene means that half the class will squeeze onto a small patch of floor, another group will sit on turned-around chairs, and a third group will perch on the edges of a few well-placed tables. Whatever system the class agrees on, the important things are that the teacher can gather the children close and command their attention and the children can get themselves in and out of the configuration efficiently.

WORK AREAS Although the meeting space is important, the most important thing is the rhythm of children sometimes pulling close around the teacher for a short stretch of very clear, explicit instruction, then dispersing to their workplaces, the teacher now meeting with individuals and sometimes with small groups of children as they write. That is, the rhythm in a writing classroom should *not* be three minutes in which the teacher talks, elicits, and assigns, then three minutes in which the children work, then three more minutes in which the teacher again talks, elicits, or assigns, followed by another three minutes of "seat work," and so on. Instead, teachers teach explicitly for about ten minutes, then children disperse to work on their writing for forty minutes before the teacher either convenes the class for a concluding meeting or asks writers to work with their partner.

In many classrooms, children write at tables or at desks that have been clustered together to allow table-like seating. (It is important for teachers to check out the relative position of chairs and desks, making sure that no child is writing at armpit level! Try doing this yourself for five minutes, and you will quickly see this is not too fine a point.) During the writing workshop, children often sit beside their long-term writing partner. Many teachers ask children to use children "assigned writing spots" that are different from their permanent seat. If children "own" the inside wells of their desks, but the desktops are in the public domain, children can sit in different arrangements at different times of the day. Alternatively, children's permanent seat arrangements may

reflect their partnerships, with each child sitting throughout the day alongside his or her writing partner.

As I will describe in more detail later, a writing workshop is usually punctuated by a brief mid-workshop teaching point. At this time, teachers often ask children to join their writing partners to do a particular bit of work. For example, after twenty minutes of writing, a teacher might ask for every child's attention, make a brief speech about the importance of writing with punctuation, and then ask children to double-check that both members of each partnership are using end punctuation. It is important that partners are able to convene and disperse efficiently. If partners *aren't* sitting alongside each other, they usually have prearranged "meeting spaces"—a neutral patch of floor or one partner's permanent seat.

CONFERRING AND PEER CONFERRING AREAS While children are working, the teacher moves among the workspaces in order to confer with individuals and partnerships, carrying along a small chair or a stool in order to do this comfortably. In most classrooms, teachers work with small groups by gathering a cluster of children into little circles in the meeting area or in any spare section of floor space; some teachers do small-group work at a table designated for that purpose.

I discuss what happens during teacher-student conferences and small groups in another section of this book. Conferences, small-group strategy lessons and minilessons are absolutely crucial to a writing workshop.

THE WRITING CENTER Different teachers have different ideas of what a writing center is. For some, a writing center is a place for a small group of children to sit when they write, while other groups of children do other activities at other centers in the room. This idea of a writing center fits with the concept of language arts instruction in which the teacher works with one reading group after another while the rest of the children work independently on various other literacy activities. These teachers have decided to let writing take place without explicit instruction and without the benefits of the larger community.

For writing workshop teachers and other teachers who prioritize writing instruction, a writing center is something quite different: it is a writing supply area. The writing center is where supplies that are not site-specific are kept. For example, the three-hole punch might be here, along with the boxes containing cumulative folders, copies of touchstone texts, and paper of different shapes and sizes (this is more common in the primary grades). Books on writing well, grammar guides, dictionaries, and thesauruses might also be shelved in a writing center. But I'm spilling over into the topic of writing materials, which is dealt with immediately below.

MATERIALS

When writing is an important part of the literacy curriculum, it is crucial for the teacher to develop a system for managing children's actual papers. I suggest that each upper-elementary student needs to have a writer's notebook, a writing folder for writing-in-progress, and a cumulative writing folder or a portfolio for stored, completed writing.

Writer's Notebooks

Some schools order a writer's notebook for each child, but in most schools teachers show children a variety of optional notebooks and then ask them to purchase their own. The dimensions and binding matter: the notebooks should have room for a lot of writing. (The dainty four-inch-square diaries with a lock and key don't give children the space they need, and their bindings often keep the pages from lying open on the desk or table while the child writes.) Many teachers also steer children away from spiral notebooks, because they have a "required class work" feel—we're after a more magical aura. Ideally a writer's notebook gives the impression that it could have been the notebook of choice for one of the authors that a child loves most. This isn't always possible, however, so it is also fine to settle on the marbled-covered composition books that are readily available at stores everywhere—especially if children

personalize them, perhaps laminating a collage of pictures and words of wisdom onto the covers. Certainly children need to write, "If lost, return to So-and-So" inside the cover of the notebook. These are ways to help children bond with their notebooks, and this emotional attachment matters more than one could imagine.

Writing notebooks offer a subtle way to make assignments multi-level. Some teachers steer their struggling or younger writers toward slightly smaller and thinner notebooks. Some suggest that struggling writers skip lines while the rest of the children write on every line. If you ask every member of your class to write a page and a half entry for homework most evenings, you might nevertheless suggest to a particular child that it's easier to reread that child's writing if she skips lines. This is a way to make your assignments more multi-level. Obviously, if more inexperienced or challenged writers work in notebooks with a smaller page size, this, too, allows for assignments to be multi-level.

Children date each entry they write in their notebooks and generally proceed in order though the notebook. That way, teachers can readily see the amount of writing a child has done in a day or a week. (Teachers must also take into account the drafts written outside the notebooks.) Children in grades three through five will usually write at least a page a day in school (often more) and will often write approximately as much at home. It is common for children to fill two writer's notebooks in a year.

Writing-in-Progress Folders and Paper

In addition to a writer's notebook, each child will need a folder for drafts, rubrics, guide sheets, and mentor texts related to the current unit of study. Most of the teachers I know suggest using a two-pocket folder for storing these materials. Usually, during the first week or two of the unit children will do most of their writing in their writer's notebooks, and during the second half of the unit they will do most of their writing on draft paper that they keep in their folders. When children are writing in their notebooks rather than their folders, only the notebooks travel between school and home, with the folders for any one table of writers stored in a box or a tray and brought to the table for the writing workshop.

Children need loose sheets of lined paper on which to write their drafts. Teachers decide whether each child supplies her or his own or whether the paper is provided in a writing center stocked with writing tools and materials. In grades three through five, most children like to write drafts on white lined composition paper, unless they have access to computers. Often during the first unit or two, two pages of lined paper are each folded top to bottom and then combined to create little booklets, each containing four half-pages. Some teachers ask children write rough drafts on yellow paper, final drafts on white paper. I recommend using white paper for all writing because yellow paper is harder to read, especially if children are writing in pencil.

Cumulative Folders

When a unit of study ends with a publication party at the end of a month, children empty their writing-in-process folders. They staple or clip a sequence of rough drafts, mentor texts, and unit-specific rubrics together and file them in cumulative folders. Some teachers send a folder of work home after each publication party. Others keep all students' work in a cumulative file. Either way, children begin a new unit of study with freshly cleaned-out files. And either way, work is not sent home in dribs and drabs. Final drafts are published and eventually filed.

Writing Utensils

A wonderful thing about teaching writing is that it is easy to provision a writing classroom! Children need something to write on—and something to write with. Other than paper, the most important tools are writing utensils; although any writing utensil is acceptable, I recommend pens. Pencils smudge and break, require sharpening, are harder to read, and invite children to erase. We want to study our children's rough drafts

and revisions, so it is preferable for them to cross out rather than erase deleted sections of texts. Then, too, most of *us* prefer to write in pen rather than in pencil, so presumably children feel the same.

Teachers need to decide whether each child will purchase and keep track of her or his own writing utensils or whether there will be communal ownership. If children chip in to purchase a whole-class stash of pens or pencils, and if this stash is used to replenish cans kept in tool boxes, one for each writing table, this avoids the "He took my pen!" scraps. If children write with pencils instead of pens, it helps to keep a can of sharpened pencils at each table and to teach writers that if their pencil needs sharpening, they can simply put it in their "to be sharpened" can and take another sharp one. Otherwise it is not unusual to find the struggling writers spending lots of time at the pencil sharpener.

Some teachers like to have date-stamps on hand to make it more likely that students date their work. They aren't necessary, of course, but dating one's work makes it much easier to hold students accountable for being productive. We encourage revision when we supply writers with scissors and tape. We encourage stamina when we supply them with the staplers that turn loose sheets into booklets.

The particular system I describe here isn't essential. What is essential is that each child in the school needs to date each day's work; children's work needs to accumulate until the authors' celebration; after an authors' celebration, some work needs to accumulate as evidence of children's growth over time; and no work can be sent home until the first final draft has been published and until teachers have an opportunity to talk to parents about significant progress evident in children's spelling and writing. This usually means teachers keep work in school at least until Open School night, teacher-parent conferences, or grade-by-grade parent meetings. By then, explanations about the writing process will be accompanied by convincing evidence of growth. After that, student work does not go home in dribs and drabs but instead, after a celebration, certain work may go home in a folder bearing the name of the unit.

Chart Paper, Marker Pens, Easel

Teachers will need to have a supply of chart paper and magic markers for writing visibly on this paper, and the charts teachers make throughout a unit will need to be visible to writers. An easel is incredibly helpful in a writing workshop. Many teachers turn a magnetic white board into a large writing process chart, with a space down one side for each child's name. Children move their name-magnets from one column to another to signal their progress from one stage to another. This chart functions as a record of the whole class' progress through the writing process.

Exemplar Texts

Writers need to read widely, deeply, ravenously, and closely. A classroom full of wonderful writers is one in which teachers read aloud several times a day and the children, too, are passionate readers. Although children benefit from rich classroom and school libraries full of a great variety of texts, in order to learn to write well, children especially need to read texts that resemble those they are trying to write. And they need not only graze these texts but also study some of them incredibly closely, revisiting them time and again to learn yet more and more and more. The same text can be used to teach leads, semicolons, character development, showing-not-telling, lists, pronoun agreement, and a dozen other things. I've often led workshops for teachers in which I show how one single text can be the source for dozens of minilessons.

In addition to a wide, rich library, each teacher needs a short stack of dearly loved and closely studied short texts that he or she returns to over and over throughout the year. It is great if children have their own copies of these texts, and many teachers type up and duplicate exemplar texts (also called *touchstone texts*) so that each child can carry a copy of the text in her writing folder for reference. (This sometimes requires permission from the book's publisher.) It is important that the touchstone texts that weave through a year are not the same texts, year after year.

Word Walls, Dictionaries, and Thesauruses

Every writing teacher will want to find ways to encourage children to spell conventionally. Most teachers find it helpful to teach children the high-frequency words that constitute the majority of what they write. After teaching children to spell a specific high-frequency word, teachers often post that word on a large alphabetical "word wall," encouraging children to use this as a resource so that they always spell that word correctly, even in rough drafts. Often teachers add five new words to the word wall each week, deleting a few that no longer require attention. They may also send copies of the word wall home with children once a week so that children can study these words at home and refer to them in the writing they do at home. Word wall words are a perfect source for phonics lessons, because they contain chunks that can be applied to countless other words.

In addition to a word wall, a writing workshop needs dictionaries and thesauruses. Writers care about words and are willing to work hard to find just the right one. These tools help convey the message that words matter.

Writers don't need much: paper, a pen, a place to store yesterday's writing, a few wonderful published texts, a responsive reader of writing-in-process, crystal clear help in writing well, an anticipated audience—and time. Ideally, a writing classroom has a carpet on which to meet and an easel and a pad of chart paper around which to gather, but not much is called for! Because writers don't need much, it is entirely possible for a school system to provision writing workshops with all that is needed, and doing so is enormously important. I've watched writing workshops take hold within a year or two in every classroom up and down the corridors of a school, and when I try to discern the conditions that made it likely that teachers and children would embrace the writing workshop, one remarkably important feature was the fact that the provisions were available. Throughout the history of the human race, tools have made us smarter. The wheel, the stylus, the computer—these tools of the hand become habits of the mind, re-creating what it means to live and learn together. Teachers and school leaders, too, are wise to pay attention to the important work of provisioning writing workshops.

MANAGEMENT SYSTEMS

When teachers hesitate to teach writing using a writing workshop approach, it's usually for one of two reasons. The first is time, which is discussed in a different section of this book. The other is the fear that a writing workshop will pose insurmountable management challenges. Teachers who worry in advance about classroom management are wise to do so, because it is never a small achievement to establish the structures and expectations that ensure that children work with engagement and tenacity. How could it not be tricky to build an environment in which twenty or thirty youngsters each work and live within the confines of a small room for six hours a day, one hundred and eighty days a year? This challenge is inevitably more taxing when the goal is not only for children to live alongside one another but also for each child to maintain his or her own greatest possible intensity and receptivity for learning. In order for each child to learn well, he or she needs an individual mix of silence and collaboration, time and deadline, resources and support.

Why do so many people assume that it is only novice teachers who struggle with classroom management? Why is classroom management regarded as a low-level skill when corporate management is considered an executive skill? If the people working under our direction were grown-ups instead of children, the job of managing them would be regarded as highly demanding leadership. Executives take courses on designing accountability structures, structuring workspaces, and holding workers accountable. As classroom teachers, we need to give equal attention to these issues. Teachers should assume from the start that classroom management will inevitably be a challenge.

This does not mean, however, that classroom management is more difficult when leading a writing workshop than when teaching writing using other systems and methods. There are many ways in which the systems and structures of writing workshop make classroom management easier as well as more challenging. The important thing to recognize is that workshop teachers rely on different tools and techniques for managing children than do teachers who teach from the front of the room.

Long before the school year begins, then, we need to give careful thought to how we will institute the systems that will make it likely that our children will sustain rigorous work. When we plan our writing instruction, we must plan not only the words out of our mouths—the minilessons and the conferences that will convey content about good writing—but also the management structures and systems that make it possible for children to carry on as writers, working productively with independence and rigor. The good news is that none of us must invent management systems *ex nihilo*.

I recently visited the classroom of a first-year teacher. The writing workshop was about to begin. "Writers," Manuel said, "in a moment, I'd like you to bring your writer's notebook and your pen to the meeting area. Put everything else away and show me you are ready." As he counted ("Five, four, three, two, one.") children hurried to clear off their workspaces. "Table Two," Manuel signaled, "let's gather." Soon Manuel had signaled four other tables as well, and each time he gestured, his children stood, pushed in their chairs, walked swiftly and directly to the meeting area, and sat cross-legged, shoulder to shoulder with a long-term writing partner. Manuel had soon taken his place in the author's chair. "Writers," he said, touching his eyes to signal that he wanted children's eyes on him. Almost every child turned in his direction. Manuel then began a ten-minute minilesson in which he named a strategy that writers often use, demonstrated that strategy, gave the children a few minutes of guided practice with the strategy, and invited his writers to add that strategy to their repertoire. Soon the children had dispersed to their writing spots, each hard at work on his or her ongoing writing project. None of them waited for Manuel to offer a personalized jump-start.

As I watched all this, I marveled that Manuel, a novice teacher, was teaching in such efficient and effective ways. Had someone sprinkled Miracle-Gro on him? I remembered with a pang my first years as a teacher. "How did he get to be so good?" I wondered, but then I knew. Manuel is the teacher he is because although *he* is new to the profession, *his methods* are not new. His methods have gone through hundreds of drafts and have benefited from the legacy of scores of experienced teachers. This is how it should be!

In order to teach writing, we need to establish structures that will last throughout every day of our teaching. As I said earlier, the essential premise, one that undergirds any system of managing a writing workshop, is this: the writing workshop needs to be simple and predictable enough that children can learn to carry on within it independently. That is, children need to be taught how to self-manage.

Because the work of writing is complex and varied, because children need to be able to follow their texts toward meaning and because teachers need, above all, to be able to coach writers who are engaged in the ongoing work of writing, the writing workshop in most classrooms proceeds in a similar way through a similar schedule, using similar management structures. Managing a writing workshop becomes immeasurably easier if children are taught in similar ways through succeeding years, thus allowing them to grow accustomed to the systems and structures of workshop teaching. For this reason, it is easier to manage a writing workshop if children are also learning math, science, reading, and social studies within workshops!

MANAGEMENT THROUGHOUT THE MINILESSON

Most teachers find that it is helpful to circulate around the room five minutes before the writing workshop begins saying, "Five more minutes until writing," or something similar. This gives children time to finish up whatever they are doing prior to writing time. The workshop itself begins with the teacher using an attention-getting signal to secure writers' attention, and then asking them to convene. It is remarkably important for teachers to develop such a signal and to teach children that it is a meaningful one. The signal can be obvious. Most teachers simply stand in the midst of the hubbub and say, in a voice one notch louder than usual, "Writers . . . ." Some instead ask, "Can I have your eyes on me?" or the abbreviated version, "Eyes?" The important thing is that we use the signal we settle upon consistently and teach children to honor it. This requires that after we say, "Writers," we wait as long as necessary until every child has put his pencil or pen down, stopped talking, and looked at us. At the start of the year, we may need to wait as long as three minutes before further addressing the group.

Of course, waiting alone isn't enough: we also need to talk explicitly about our expectations. Some teachers are uncomfortable insisting on utter silence and therefore they speak over still-murmuring children. I'm convinced we do our children no favors when we collude with their tendencies to ignore our words. If our goal is to teach children that words matter, then our language, for a start, must mean something: when we ask for attention, we should expect that children will comprehend and honor our request. The same children who are "Teflon" listeners, regularly letting our instructions roll off without getting through, tend also to be "Teflon" readers, regularly moving their eyes but not their minds over the words on a page, then looking up to say, "I read it, honest; I just don't remember what I read." If we expect that we'll regularly need to repeat ourselves several times before children take in what we've said, we are enabling our students to live as if they have comprehension problems. The first step in remedying this is to develop a way to signal for children's attention.

Once we have our students' attention, we will probably want to ask them to take out materials they'll need for writing, and we'll no doubt want to convey that we hope they'll bring some of these materials to the meeting area. Many teachers have a ritual for mobilizing children for writing. "Please set yourself up for writing. Five (I love that you are getting your notebooks out of your knapsacks), four (thanks for remembering your folders as well as your notebooks), three, two (in a minute I'll be

calling you to the meeting area), one." If teachers want children to bring particular materials, they make a point of holding up those materials, creating a Technicolor illustration. Some teachers regularly list whatever they want children to bring to the meeting on a white board. This way, they need only say, "Let's gather," but children know this means they must check the white board and bring the listed items with them. In other classrooms, teachers expect each child to bring his or her writer's notebook, writing folder, and a pen or pencil to the meeting area, which of course means that children always have the basic supplies on hand.

If children do bring supplies to a meeting, the next question is: what happens to the supplies during the meeting? Do we want children to put their work on the floor in front or behind them? Literally sit on top their work? Any of these systems increases the chances that children won't be distracted by fingering through their materials. On the other hand, some teachers want writers to open their writer's notebooks before a minilesson starts and be ready to take notes.

In many classrooms, children gather on the carpet half a dozen times a day; it is obviously worthwhile to be explicit about how we hope they will do this. Experienced workshop teachers are apt to demonstrate—act out—showing children that they are expected to push in their chairs, make a beeline for their spot on the meeting area rug, sit (rather than hover), handle materials however they are expected to be handled, and begin rereading the charts containing teaching points from previous days. At the start of the year, after the teacher calls one table of writers to the meeting area, the teacher is apt to name (for the other writers) what children do well: "I love the way they pushed in their chairs, don't you? Look how quickly and quietly they're coming to the meeting area!" Of course, before long this behavior becomes automatic, and teachers merely need to say, "Table One, please join me," and children push in their chairs, come quickly and quietly, sit in their assigned spots, open writer's notebooks to the next available page, and begin rereading charts from previous minilessons. This is very efficient! In many classrooms, children are taught that when the teacher takes her place in the chair and says, "Writers," children should be sitting on their bottoms with their hands contained in their own space, looking at the teacher.

Some may question this detailed attention to how children move from one place to another, and there certainly will be teachers who prefer a more organic, easygoing approach. But for lots of teachers, especially those in crowded urban classrooms, transitions can be a source of delay and tension, and neither is advisable. A fiction writer once said, "The hardest part of writing fiction is getting characters from here to there," and this can be true for teaching as well.

I find it striking that in classrooms in which the transitions are long and mired in tension, teachers often assume this is par for the course. They shrug and say, "What are you going to do?" as if they assume this is how writing workshops proceed in most classrooms. I've come to realize that many aspects of classroom management are shaped more by our teaching and specifically our expectations, than by our children's developmental levels. When teachers make a point of teaching classroom management, thirty children can come and go quite seamlessly between the meeting area and their workspaces.

During minilessons, children usually sit alongside their partners. At the start of the minilesson, teachers typically talk about and then demonstrate a strategy; children are expected to listen, rarely to talk. Some children don't know that the start of a minilesson is a time for them to listen rather than talk. In those cases, the teacher might say, "You'll notice that at the start of a minilesson, I do the talking. This is my time to tell you something very important."

After talking and demonstrating, the teacher says, "Let's try it," or something of that nature, to signify that this is the Active Engagement section of the minilesson. Teachers set children up to be active during this time; usually this means either to "write in the air" or "turn and talk" with a partner. For example, if the minilesson taught that writers sometimes reread drafts, looking at action words and asking, "Is this the exactly true word?" the teacher would probably reread a draft of a few sentences in front of the class, pausing at each action word, musing

aloud whether it was the exactly true word. Then she'd say to the class, "So let's try it." She might set the class up to continue rereading the text, saying, "If you find a place where I used a generic word instead of a precise one, would you write in the air, showing your partner how you'd repair my draft," thereby channeling children to say aloud the word they recommend substituting. Alternatively, the teacher could ask children to notice and then discuss in pairs the steps she went through in order to replace a generic term with a precise one: "What steps did you see me taking when I replaced *went* with *crept*? Turn and talk with your partner."

Children need to know how to make a fast transition from facing forward and listening, to facing their partner and talking. Children can't spend five minutes getting themselves off the starting block for a turn-and-talk (or a stop-and-jot), because the entire interval usually lasts no more than three minutes! We need to teach children explicitly how to make the transition from listening to the teacher to interacting with a partner. I've watched teachers practice this with kids by saying, "What did you eat for breakfast this morning? Turn and talk," and then, after a minute, saying, "Back to me," and finally giving children feedback on their ability to shift between whole-class listening and turning and talking or jotting.

MANAGEMENT AT THE START OF WORK TIME

Once the minilesson is over, in a classroom in which some of the materials are centralized, table monitors distribute materials. That is, if folders are kept in boxes rather than in children's knapsacks, a table monitor will put a box of folders on each table. If tools are kept in a table-caddy, this will also be put on each table.

Just as we explicitly teach children how to gather for a minilesson, we also teach them how to disperse after the minilesson and get started on their work. The important thing is that children need to learn how to go from the minilesson to their workspaces, and then to open up their folders or notebooks, decide what they are going to do, *and get started doing it*. If we don't teach them otherwise, some children will sit idly by until we make our way to that table and give that child a personalized jump-start. Teachers have learned, therefore, that it is worthwhile to come right out and teach children how to get themselves started writing. Sometimes a teacher will disperse one cluster of writers at a time. While one cluster goes off to work, the teacher may say to those still sitting on the carpet, "Let's watch and see if they *zoom* to their writing spots and get started right away!" Sometimes the teacher will speak in a stage whisper ("Oh, look, Toni has her notebook open and is rereading the entry she wrote yesterday. That's so smart! I wonder if the others will do that? Oh, look. Jose is rereading too!"). This reminds both the dispersing and the observing youngsters what the teacher hopes they will do.

Sometimes teachers find it helpful to ask children first to envision what they will do that day. "Picture yourself leaving the meeting area. Where will you go, exactly? What will you do first? Thumbs up if you can picture yourself leaving and getting started," the teacher might say, signaling to the children who seem ready that they can go back to their writing spots.

Sometimes we disperse children by saying, "If you are going to be doing (one kind of work), get going. If you are going to be doing (another kind of work), get going. If you are not certain what to do today and need some help, stay here and I'll work with you." Soon we are leading a small group of children who've identified themselves as needing more direction.

Transitions are smoother if children always know where they'll sit during writing time. In most classes, children have assigned writing spots. But children also need help knowing what to do, especially in instances when the minilesson doesn't channel children in one specific direction. If children are in the earliest stages of work, they always know they can write a new entry, but once children have begun work on a piece, they are apt to be in the midst of revising. I usually tell children that if one is not sure what to do as a writer, the wisest thing is to reread recent writing, thinking, 'What does this piece need me to do next?' I

also suggest that if children are stymied, they can look at charts for strategies that writers often use and decide which of those strategies might work at that point for their particular piece. In some classrooms, children are expected to give themselves an assignment (also referred to as a planning box) each day. "Decide what you are going to do, record your plans in a self-assignment box, and get started! Walter Dean Myers doesn't wait for a teacher to appear at his elbow and to say, 'You can start now,' and you don't need to do this either."

In a classroom in which children tend to wait for individual jump-starts, I suggest teachers say to children, "At the start of each day's writing workshop, I won't be available for conferences. Instead, this is a time for me to admire and record the ways you get yourselves started in your writing."

MANAGEMENT DURING WORK TIME

What do I mean when I say that children give themselves an assignment? Isn't the teacher assigning the work through the minilesson?

In upper-grade writing workshops, children usually write one completed (final) piece each month. There are exceptions. During the *Launching* unit of study, I suggest that children (especially third graders) draft two personal narratives, choosing just one to revise and edit for publication. In a poetry unit of study, children will obviously write more than a single poem, and in a journalism unit, children will write many news articles. And when teaching a unit of study on revision, the teacher might ask children to look back over all the writing they've done all year and select, say, four pieces to put through further revisions. But on the whole, in a unit of study, upper-elementary students progress through the writing process and end up with one final piece. In a sense, the teacher "assigns" the writing of this one text.

In many units of study, the teacher has selected a genre of writing (or a structure of writing) for the entire class. That is, everyone may be writing a literary essay or a memoir or an editorial. There will sometimes be units of study which are open-genre (with each child deciding what form his content suggests), but it is more common for the class to investigate and write within a genre the teacher has selected. In a sense, the teacher "assigns" children to write within that genre.

Children are always expected to progress through a writing process that they learn about in the writing workshop. In the upper-grade classrooms I know well, each child is expected to live a writerly life, paying attention to what goes on around them day by day and collecting a variety of entries. Each child is expected to reread these entries and select one "seed idea" to develop in ways that match the genre (such as making a timeline if the genre is personal narrative), write a draft, then revise and edit that draft. In a sense, the teacher "assigns" children to work their way through this writing process.

But on most days, children still need to choose what it is they will do that day. Every child may know he or she needs to write a timeline for his or her story, consider whether the entire sequence represented in the timeline belongs in the story, choose some "dots" in the timeline on which to elaborate, try writing different lead sentences, study exemplar texts, and the like, but some children will spend more time in one portion of this work, some in another. And every writer is encouraged to use his or her judgment, making decisions about what the piece of writing needs and letting the piece of writing and the writer's own hopes come together in an individualized work plan.

The rule of thumb during a writing workshop is that during writing time, everyone writes. So there is no such thing as being "done." If a writer completes one thing, then he or she begins the next thing. On a given day, a writer might progress through a sequence of writing work. For example, a writer might study a few exemplar leads, try a few leads, select one, and start a draft.

As writers progress along through their sequence of work, many of them come to places where they feel stymied. "I'm stuck," they say. When a child feels stuck, the first instinct is usually to find the teacher and ask, "What should I do next?" These interactions between a writer and a teacher are referred to as conferences, and they may occur at the initiative of the writer or the teacher.

But in conferences (as well as in minilessons and small-group work), teachers explicitly teach children to be self-reliant writers and decision makers. In minilessons, teachers teach children what they can do when they feel stuck—or when they are done or when they don't know how to start writing or when they want to revise or when they encounter any of many other problems. Almost always, teachers teach children an array of expendable strategies that writers sometimes draw upon and then we expect children to draw on these strategies as needed to achieve goals which are not expendable. In conferences, teachers personalize this instruction, scaffolding children to become more self-reliant, strategic, and skillful writers.

Teach and Organize So That Children Rely on Each Other

If youngsters seem overly reliant on us for direction, we often teach them to help each other. "Writers, can I stop all of you? Would you look at all the people following me! I feel like a pied piper. Writers, today I want to teach you that there is not just one writing teacher in this classroom. Each one of you can be a writing teacher. And you need to become writing teachers for each other because this is how we learn to become writing teachers for ourselves—in the end, every writer needs to be his or her own writing teacher. So right now, let me teach you what writing teachers do for each other. Then those of you in this line behind me can help each other."

Teachers need to decide exactly what it is they think children in a particular class *can* do for each other. At a minimum, writers can listen to each other talk about their subjects. The first step in helping writers listen to each other is to teach children to ask open-ended questions. "Your job is to ask me questions that get me to talk at length about my subject. Ask questions that get me teaching you about the aspects of my subject that are important to me. Let's try it. I'll be a writer. 'I'm stuck. I don't have much to say. I wrote about my bike ride but nothing much happened. . . .' Remember, your job is to ask me questions to get me talking." One child asks, "How long did you ride for?" This is a closed question and we want children to ask open-ended questions. We answer curtly: "Two hours." "Was it fun?" Again, the question doesn't call for an expansive answer, so we don't give one: "Yes." Eventually a child will ask a more open-ended question: "What were the fun things about the bike ride?" "Oh! I'm glad you asked. I expected the bike ride to bring me into nature, but this particular bike trail was loaded with people, and it was almost as sociable as a neighborhood picnic." Children probably will have missed what we just tried to demonstrate so we come right out and name what we've done. "Do you see, writers, that Jeremy asked the kind of question that got me really talking? He didn't ask a yes-or-no question like, 'Do you like your bike?' Instead he asked, 'What were the fun things you did?' That's so helpful, because now I have ideas for what to write. And he could help me get even more ideas if he asked follow-up questions. Try it, Jeremy. Ask me to be more specific."

Children not only need to be taught to help each other in peer conferences, they also need a structure that allows them to do this. In some classrooms, children shift between writing and conferring as needed, and this can be workable. Sometimes, however, if children have standing permission to shift between writing and conferring, very little writing is accomplished, in which case teachers wisely insist that writers work silently, conferring only in specified areas of the classroom. For example, some teachers set two pairs-of-chairs up along the margins of the room; as long as two chairs in the "conference alley" are open, a writer and his or her partner can decide to meet for a five-minute conference (some teachers keep a timer in the conference areas to enforce this time constraint; others add the timer only if the length of conferences becomes a problem).

In addition to student-initiated conversations, teachers often ask the whole class to meet with their partners to discuss something specific.

Often these partner conversations follow a mid-workshop teaching point or come at the end of a writing workshop. That is, most writing workshops are punctuated by the teacher's standing up in the middle of the workshop hubbub, signaling for attention, and then giving a pointer. For example: "Most of you are having your character talk, including dialogue in your story, and that's great. But today I want to remind you that dialogue needs to sound right to the ear. It needs to sound like something a real human being would say. Get with your partner and read your quoted sections aloud to each other. Ask, 'Does this *sound like* a real human being?' If it doesn't, see whether you can alter the quoted section so that it does." A mid-workshop interruption like this sets partnerships up to talk with each other briefly about a topic the teacher specifies. Similarly, at the end of the writing workshop, teachers often ask partners to share with each other, "Find a place where your character's talk really rings true, and read that aloud to your partner. Then look together at what you've done and try to dissect why it worked." Of course, sometimes these interactions are more open-ended, "Writers, would you tell your partner what this mentor author has done that you'd like to emulate? Show your partner where in your draft you might use this technique."

Use Table Conferences and Strategy Lessons to Keep the Class as a Whole Productive

During a writing workshop, teachers spend most of their time moving among youngsters conducting brief conferences. I write about these conferences in a separate chapter, but for many teachers, the issue is not what to say in conferences. Instead, the problem is how conferences are possible in the first place; "What are the other children doing while I confer?"

True, teachers cannot devote themselves to one-to-one conferences until the whole class has learned to carry on as writers. On days when we know that lots of children are going to need our help, instead of conferring with individuals, we will probably decide to opt for the more efficient alternative of meeting with groups.

If, for example, we have just taught children that essayists elaborate on our thesis statements by making two or three parallel claims, each becoming the topic sentence in a support paragraph, we can anticipate that a third (or even half) of the class will need hands-on help translating our instructions into actions. With such a large-scale need for help, we will probably decide to blanket the room with "table conferences." Instead of gathering selected children together, we can go from one table to another, ask for every child's attention, then confer with one child who needs help while the others watch. Of course, the others will not want to watch unless we shift back and forth between demonstration and debriefing and do this work in a manner which helps not only the focal child but all the others who need similar help: "Do you see how Anthony just did such-and-so? Try doing the same thing right now." Then, as the children begin emulating Anthony's first step, I can help Anthony proceed to another step, one which the observing children see with only peripheral vision. Soon I'll point out to the table full of listeners that they, too, can do the work Anthony has just done.

I often blanket the room with table conferences during the first few days of the writing workshop and again at the start of each unit of study. At these times, there will be a reasonable chance that writers are all at the same place in their work, which is less apt to be true in the midst of a unit of study.

Another way to reach lots of writers efficiently is to sort them into need-based groups and gather each group for a brief strategy lesson. Again, I describe the methods and content of these lessons elsewhere; for now, the important thing to say is that we can easily lead four small-group strategy lessons in a single day. These are not formal events. Usually we convene the first group based on the student work examined the night before. Toward the

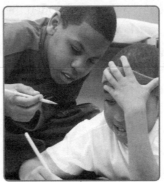

end of the minilesson, I am apt to call out a list of names and say, "Will these writers stay on the carpet after the minilesson?" Then I talk to this group: "I looked over your writing last night and I want to make a suggestion to all of you." I might show this group how they can get past their impasse and ask them to try what I suggested or demonstrated while they continue sitting together. As these children get started, I might move around the room, ascertaining what other children need. If I noticed, for example, one child who was writing without any punctuation, I might think to myself, "I wonder if there are others like this child?" Finding others with similar problems, I might gather this group. "I've been looking over your writing and I have one thing I want to teach you and to ask you to do." While this second group gets started, I might return to the first group. I might check in with each member of the group quickly, then say, "Can I stop you?" and make a point or two that pertains to them all. Alternatively, I might decide to confer with one child while the others watch, extrapolating larger points from this one situation.

In both of these instances, I set out to do small-group work. Sometimes, instead, we intend to conduct one-to-one conferences but find part-way through the workshop that we need to reach more children more efficiently and therefore shift into leading a small-group strategy lesson or two. We are wise to shift to small-group instruction when we find we are having what is essentially the same conference over and over. For example, if I have just helped one child who was writing about a giant topic—"My summer"—narrow it to something more focused and the very next child I approach needs the same kind of help, I am apt to say, "Will you wait for just one second?" while I peer over kids' shoulders to see which other children need the same help. Signaling, "Come with me," I soon have six children pulled into a tight circle on the carpet. Often I will then use the conference with the first child as a case in point.

Then, too, if I am trying to confer and can't because I am swamped with children who *all* need attention, I may triage these needy children and work with them in small groups. To one group, I'll say, "I called you together because it seems all of you are having a hard time getting much down on your page. We've been writing for twenty minutes today, and every one of you has less than a quarter of a page. So let me tell you ways that I get myself to write more, and then let's try those ways—because during writing time, writers need to write. One thing I do a lot when I'm having a hard time writing is thus-and-so." To another group, I might say, "I called you together because although you are writing up a storm and that's great, you are forgetting that writers try to use what we know about conventions as we zoom down the page. I don't want you to go to the opposite extreme and fuss over the shape of every letter and spend twenty minutes looking every word up in a dictionary, but I do want you to become accustomed to pausing for just a second as you write to ask, 'Did I spell that word right?' If you need to, you should be checking with the word wall as you write." I can also convene children who spend too long in their peer conferences, who never seem to light upon topics they care about, who forget their writer's notebook, who summarize rather than storytell in their narratives, who let dialogue swamp their stories, or who need to add transitions into their essays.

Support Students' Writing Stamina

What if children can't sustain work the whole time? Generally writing workshops involve ten minutes for a minilesson, forty minutes for writing and conferring (with a five-minute mid-workshop teaching point) and five or ten minutes for a culminating share session. At the start of the year, children who are new to a writing workshop may not be able to sustain writing for forty minutes. If children are not accustomed to writing for this length of time, after fifteen minutes the class will become restless.

If children have trouble with stamina, part of the problem will probably be that they are doing everything you suggest they do in such an underdeveloped fashion that the work is done within ten minutes. In that case we may decide to give them a series of additional directions (via

mid-workshop teaching points) that will sustain them for several more short intervals. Setting up these mid-workshop teaching points for children to talk with a partner will give them a break from the physical act of writing as well as a chance to rehearse whatever they will write next.

We may also decide that for a few weeks at the start of the year our writing workshops will be briefer than they'll be once children have developed more stamina. Just don't let abbreviated work periods become the norm. Children will never write well if they are accustomed to writing briefly. Elaboration is one of the very first and most foundational qualities of good writing.

If you see that even after your children have been in a writing workshop for several months, they are still not producing even a page a day during writing time (and more text at home), then you'll want to intervene to increase the volume of writing your students do. Start by talking up the fact that writers, like runners, set goals for ourselves, and ask children to push themselves to write more. Then during the workshop, go around cheerleading children to write more. Make stars or checks on their pages when they produce a certain amount of text. Watch for when a child is pausing too much and whisper, "Get going!" Mid-way through the workshop, intervene to ask children to show with a thumbs-up, thumbs-down whether they've produced whatever the aspired amount of text might be. Use share times as a time to count (and even to graph) how many lines of text each writer produced. Solicit children who have increased their volume to talk about what they did to reach this goal. Make charts of "Strategies for Writing More." Eventually, if some children aren't getting enough writing done during writing time, ask them to return to their writing at another time of the day—during recess, before or after school. Say, "You wouldn't want days to go by without getting a chance to write at least a page," or, "Writers do this. We set goals for ourselves. Sometimes it does take us a while to get the words on the page, but that's okay. We just rearrange our day so that somehow, we get the chance to write." You'll find that the amount of writing your children do can be transformed in short order if you go after this goal with tenacity—and the same is true for almost any goal you take on!

MANAGING ONE-TO-ONE CONFERENCES

Although there are times when so many children need us that it is much more efficient to work with small groups than with individuals, one-to-one conferences must remain the mainstay of an effective writing workshop. The writing process approach to teaching writing is also called the conference approach for a reason: teacher–student conferences play a critical role in the entire enterprise. In a later chapter I talk about the internal structure or pattern of conferences. Here I describe conference management practices that help lead children to independence.

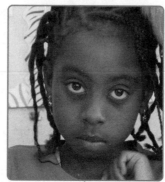

When we say that our children are not able to sustain work long enough to do much conferring, we need to look at ways in which we can scaffold children's independent work. Writing conferences, themselves, must be angled to teach children how to carry on with independence another time. Some conferences will begin with a writer coming to us and saying, "I'm stuck." Our first job is to learn what the writer has already done, has been trying to do, and has considered doing next. Then we need to help the writer extend his or her work in ways that make the writer more self-reliant in the future. "So you aren't sure what to do next. What I tend to do is reread my writing, starring the sections that I think really work and check-marking the sections that don't work so well. Then I decide which to work on first. Often I start with the sections that work well, and I think, 'How can I make these longer?' I ask, 'How can I make more of this good part?' Why don't you try that now? After this, when you aren't sure what to do, this is always something you can try."

Sometimes when we cannot carve enough time out of the workshop for one-to-one conferences with individuals, the underlying issue that keeps children from working independently involves not having the necessary materials readily available. If getting paper is a big problem in our class, our writers will be stymied and they'll all be at our elbow saying, "I need more paper." If we are the holder of the stapler, they'll line up behind us for staples.

Then, too, sometimes the issue is that children rely on us to help them come up with topics for writing. If we haven't taught children strategies for generating writing and for coming up with topics, then whenever a child is ready to embark on a new entry, that child will be at our elbow. If we haven't convinced children that we expect them to approximate spellings "as best they can" and keep going, then children will line up for help each time they come to a challenging word. Our goal is to enable writers to cycle through the entire process without needing help. Their independence gives us the time and freedom we need to be able to pull a chair alongside one writer and then the next, and to teach.

Choosing with Whom to Confer

Although the context for our conferences is created by the entire fabric of our teaching, conferring itself creates its own organizational challenges. For example, we will need to decide how we'll figure out which child to meet with next. Teachers develop their own idiosyncratic systems here. Some teachers enter a writing workshop with a little list in hand of writers they plan to see. The list may come from studying their records and noticing the children they haven't conferred with for a while and from thinking about previous conferences that need follow-up. Alternatively, the list may come from thinking about or reading through children's work and deciding on both children who need help and children who could, with help, do exemplary work that might fuel the next minilesson, mid-workshop teaching point, or share.

Personally, although I do enter a workshop with a list of the children with whom I hope to confer, I find it is important to be able to improvise based on the signals children give me. That is, if youngsters at one table seem unsettled, I'm apt to confer with a child at that table, knowing that my presence can channel the entire group to work rather than socialize. Then, too, if one child is especially persistent about needing help, I generally assume he needs to be a priority—unless he is always at my elbow, in which case I'll respond differently.

I tell children that if they need my help, they should get out of their seats and follow me as I confer. I find this keeps the child who feels stymied from derailing his or her companions as well; in addition, the children learn from eavesdropping on conferences. I also receive very tangible reminders of how many children feel confused or stuck at any moment, and this keeps me on my toes. If I have six children in tow, I'm not apt to overlook them for long.

Keeping Conference Records

We as teachers will definitely want to record our conferences, and it is important to develop a system for doing so that fits intimately into the rhythms of one's own teaching. The important thing is that the writing about teaching that we do must help us teach better and help our students learn better. This writing needs to be attuned to our teaching, reflecting, and planning. We will probably go through a sequence of systems before settling, temporarily, on one. Five or six systems are especially common among the teachers with whom I work.

Some teachers keep a page on a clipboard that looks like a month-at-a-glance calendar but is, instead, the class-at-a-glance. For the period of time this page represents (which tends to be two weeks) the teacher records the compliment and teaching point of any conference she holds. Sometimes the grid has light lines dividing each child's square into several parallel slots, with alternate slots labeled either *c* or *tp*.

Alternatively, teachers may carry a version of the record-keeping form included on the CD-ROM included with this series. Instead of recording what we say when we compliment and teach each new child, the teachers brainstorm what we are apt to compliment and teach (these will be the same things, just at different times) within a unit. We turn this into a prewritten list of possible compliments or teaching points, and use this list to jog our mind as to possible things we can teach. Teachers carry these prewritten lists of teaching points with us, checking off what the child is doing that merits a compliment, what we teach, and what we recognize we *could* but won't be teaching.

Some teachers have notebooks divided into sections, one for each child, and record our conferences with each child that way. Others do a variation of this, recording the conferences on large sticky notes and later moving the note to the appropriate section of their notebook. Some teachers do an enlarged version: they post their conference notes on a wall-sized grid, which reminds every child what he or she has agreed to do—and serves as a very visible record of which children have and have not received this form of intense instruction. I like to record conferences in the student's writer's notebook, the logic being that this way when I return for another conference, I can look at both the conference notes and the ensuing work. At the same time, the child has a very tangible record of the agreed-on work and the pointers I have made.

MANAGING THE SHARE TIME

You will want to have two or three alternate ways that share time generally goes in your classroom and to induct children into those traditions right from the start. You will certainly want the option of convening children in the meeting area. The logistics of this will match those you rely upon to convene children for the minilesson. A child might circle the room when there is just three minutes left before the share session—either you'll ask this child to do this, or, if the times for writing in your classroom truly ascribe to the daily schedule, then it could be a child's regular job to keep track of time and initiate these rounds. Alternatively, you could intervene to announce, "Three more minutes." In any case, children will need a bit of time to finish what they are writing. Then you'll bring children to the work area. You may simply say, "Writers" to get kids attention and then use hand signals, or you may convene children by table. Either way, you'll want children to bring their work with them and to sit in their rug spots beside their partner.

If you've convened children in the meeting area, you'll probably plan to talk with them for a bit, and you may plan to share one child's work. You may read the child's work aloud yourself, or ask the child to stand or sit beside you (or in your place) at the front of the meeting area, and to share his or her work. Then, typically, you'll invite children to talk with their partner. You may recap by repeating something you overheard, but more likely, time will be running short so you'll simply sum up the day's work and make a transition to whatever you'll teach next.

Just as often, however, you will decide to lead your share session without convening children. You'll want to stand in some prominent spot, to use your attention-getting signal to gather children's attention, and then to wait until you really do have full attention. You'll know you have children's full attention because they won't be writing any longer and they will be looking at you. This will provide you with a context in which you can teach using normal intonation and volume, and it is important to do so. If you have made the decision to not convene your children, chances are good that you'll curtail the length of your remarks, and devote most of the share session to a partner share. Partners either need to be sitting alongside each other, or they need a plan for meeting together which does not entail moving furniture or taking more than a minute of transition time.

Finally, you'll probably want another format for share sessions, and you can select the format which works the best for you. Some teachers like to use partnership shares when children are sharing work, and use table-shares when children are talking over their ways of solving a particular writing problem. That is, if your goal in the share is to encourage children to talk about how they are planning ways to end their stories, then you might suggest they have a table conversation about this. Some teachers use those table conversations as a prelude to a community meeting, which probably involves convening in the meeting area.

Alternatively, you may find that in your classroom, the ritual that I describe as a symphony works well. In this ritual, you ask children to search for an instance when they did something well. For example, you may have taught children that the way a character speaks, as well as the content of the character's language, needs to reveal the person. You may have asked children to find a place in their text where they use dialogue in ways that reveal the character. "When I tip my baton to you, would you read out one instance when you used dialogue to reveal character?" you could say, and then function like the conductor in a symphony, with one child after another reading a contribution.

Teachers that I know have devised a few other alternate rituals for share sessions, and you should certainly see this as one more place where you can draw on your own imagination of what's possible. Whatever you devise, however, I encourage you to be sure that you often use this same mechanism for sharing and getting responses to writing. If every day's writing workshop ended with a chance for writers to meet with a partner and to talk about whatever is on the writer's mind, those partnership meetings could still be endlessly interesting for children.

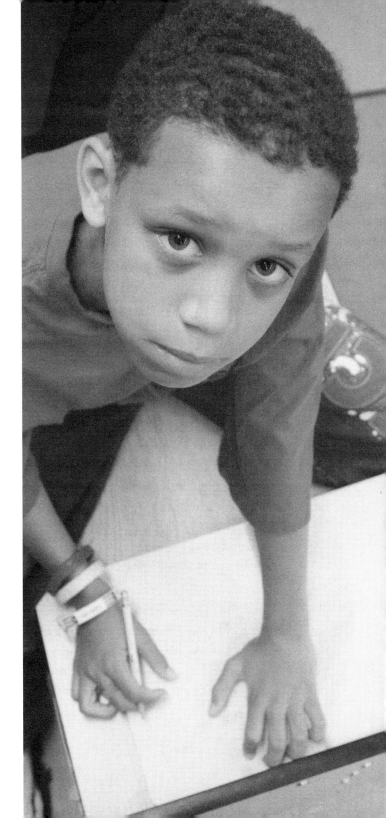

CHAPTER 7

THE PATTERNS OF MINILESSONS

Just as the art instructor pulls students together to learn a new glaze technique or a new way to mix paints, just as the football coach and his team huddle over a new play, so too the teacher of writing pulls children together for a minilesson which opens each day's writing workshop.

Minilessons power our curriculum. Once we learn how to lead strong, efficient minilessons, we find we have a power chip that never quits. It generates strong teaching each day, each year. The teachers I teach worry most over how they'll generate the *content* for their minilessons. I'm convinced, however, that it's equally important for teachers to learn the *methods* of leading efficient, effective minilessons.

Our most effective minilessons tend to follow a similar template. That is, while the content of the minilessons changes from day to day, the architecture of minilessons remains largely the same. The minilesson that follows illustrates the major components of most minilessons.

THE ARCHITECTURE OF A MINILESSON

Once the youngsters have settled onto their rug spots, I took my place and said, "Writers," and then waited until they turned their eyes and their attention toward me. "Yesterday you learned that writers write with details." To provide a small example, I added, "Remember how we admired the way that Josh rewrote his first draft, changing 'I gathered my school supplies' so that his next, more detailed version read, 'I zipped my four Bic pens and my puppy-eraser into the pencil case my mother had bought me.'"

Then I said, "Today I want to teach you that writers don't just write with any ol' details, we write with *surprising* details." This sentence, my *teaching point*, ended what I refer to as the Connection phase of the minilesson.

Moving on to what I refer to as the Teaching phase of the minilesson, I said, "Last night, writers, I decided to write a story about my day at the beach. So I wrote, 'We walked across the beach,' and then I thought, 'No, wait. I need to add a detail.' So this time I wrote, 'We walked across the *sandy* beach.' But then I remembered that writers don't just write with any ol' details, we try to write with *surprising* details. And I realized that *most* beaches tend to be sandy, so that's not really a surprising detail. Watch what I did to come up with a surprising detail."

Turning to the white board, I wrote:

We went to the

"Hmm. How shall I describe the beach so my readers can be there with me? Let me picture it in my mind (that's what I often do when I want to come up with a surprising detail). I'm picturing the waves, crashing in, and a stripe of seaweed running down the center of the beach . . . Oh! That's a surprising detail." I added that to my story:

We went to Seapoint Beach. There was a stripe of seaweed down the center of the beach. I stood and watched the waves crash onto the shore.

I ended this component of the minilesson with a little debriefing. "Did you notice that I *almost* wrote, 'I went to the *sandy* beach'? A famous writer, James Merrill, once pointed out that 'the words that come first are anybody's words. We need to make them our own.' Anybody's beach is a sandy one. Did you see that when I made a picture in my mind of exactly what I honestly saw, I came up with a surprising detail,

one that describes not *anybody's* beach but the *particular* beach I visited?"

Shifting into the Active Involvement component of this minilesson, I said, "So let's try writing with surprising details. Pretend you are writing a story about your hand. You write, 'I put my hand in front of me, and I looked at it.' You *could* say, 'I saw five fingers,' but hands *tend* to have five fingers. To write with surprising details, look closely at your hand." I do this. "What *exactly* do you notice? Be honest and precise." I let every one look at his or her hand, mentally reaching for surprising details. "Partner One, write in the air what you might say next in the story." I recited the start of the story: "I put my hand in front of me." Then I looked at my hand, cueing all the Partner Ones to do the same. Finally I mobilized the turn-and-talk: "I saw . . . ."

The room erupted with conversation. For a moment, I crouched among the children, listening to what they were saying. Then I reconvened the class for the final portion of the Active Involvement section of the minilesson. "I heard Sasha say, 'It's got wrinkles? Big ones and small ones? Like a tree.' That's a surprising detail, and it really helps us picture Sasha's hand."

To end the minilesson and Link it with students' ongoing independent work, I repeated the previous day's teaching point as well as that day's, and again mentioned a few of the tips I'd given in the minilesson. "So writers, yesterday you learned that we write with details, and today you learned that writers write not just with any ol' details but with *surprising* details. From this day forward, when you are writing, remember to take the time to picture your subject, and to reach for the surprising details and precise words that will help others picture your subject as well."

COMPONENTS OF A MINILESSON

Let me explain each of the components of the above minilesson in more depth.

Connection

The connection opens the minilesson. Though it is very brief, it is intended to catch children's attention, name the goal of the day, convey how this goal fits with previous work, and ideally, rally children to listen astutely and actively. Usually, it has two main sections. First, we situate today's lesson within the context of previous work, and second, we name the teaching point for the day.

In my example minilesson, the connection is plain, straightforward, and not very developed. I simply repeat the previous day's teaching point—saying something that is probably not new news to anyone: "Yesterday I taught you. . . ." This is a rather common way to start a minilesson, and it is especially appropriate in instances like this one in which the new minilesson extends the previous lesson. There are times when the link between the previous minilesson and the new one needn't be this tight; in those instances it is common for the connection to integrate many lessons that children have learned across a host of previous days or put a new spin on the old work.

One of the most powerful things we can do at the start of a minilesson is to consolidate earlier teaching in an effort to make that work more memorable and more readily useful for children. For example, this series of units begins with a minilesson suggesting that writers can generate ideas for writing by thinking about people who matter to us. The next day's minilesson suggests that writers can generate ideas for writing by thinking not only about *people* but also about *places* that matter to us. By the connection on the fourth day, I say, "So far you've learned that we can generate ideas for writing by thinking of people, places, and *things*

that are important to us." Because many of us are accustomed to the expression *people, places, and things*, this small collection of sources-for-writing-ideas has a catchy quality to it. If day after day I simply listed a hodge-podge of different sources for stories—favorite places, songs we remember, stories that are often retold within the family, memories that are attached to items—that collection of sources would be very hard to recall. It is much easier for children to remember and draw upon the knowledge that writers sometimes think of people, places, or things that matter to us, write one of those down, and then proceed.

Another move I often make during the opening seconds of a minilesson is to refer not to the previous day's minilesson but to work children have done at this same juncture in the writing process during an earlier cycle of writing. For example, when children choose their seed ideas during the essay writing unit, I'm apt to say, "Earlier this year, when you wrote narratives, you learned three strategies for choosing a seed idea. You learned . . . ." Then I go on to teach students ways in which choosing seed ideas for an essay unit is different and the same.

Sometimes during the connection I retell what children learned or did on an earlier day, highlighting a new nuance or aspect of that work. For example, I may have taught several minilessons focusing on strategies children can use to generate ideas for writing; in the connection I might simply mention those strategies and emphasize that as children learn strategies, they are also learning about characteristics of effective topics.

Often one of my goals during this early phase of a minilesson is to make children feel like authors. I may tell how I read their writing the previous night and phoned my sister so I could read her some of the choice parts. I might say that lately it feels as if the class is populated not only by all of them, but also by their wonderful, idiosyncratic characters.

When writing the Connection section of a minilesson, I often summarize previous teaching points. I've learned that it is very important to repeat the exact phrases I used in the previous lesson. If one day I taught the importance of "surprising details," I won't, a day or a month later, rename these as "unusual details," because I know many children will miss the fact that these are two different names for the same thing. If I name one strategy or skill or quality by ten different names, this can confuse children. They end up thinking each name refers to something different yet are unsure of the differences. On the other hand, there are times when I do call something by two interchangeable titles; then I try to use the two terms as synonyms in the same sentence: "When we write narratives, or stories, it is important to remember. . . ."

After the looking-back portion of the connection, I look forward by naming the teaching point for today's minilesson. That is, the teaching point is *not* contained within the Teaching section of the minilesson. After all, the entire minilesson is really an act of teaching.

THE TEACHING POINT After putting our teaching into context, we come straight out and tell children, as clearly as possible, exactly what we want to teach them today. Usually we do this in a sentence, although it may be several sentences. This is the teaching point. Listen to the language of some of my teaching points:

> Today I want to teach you that although there are oodles of things fiction writers can think about as we develop our characters, there are just one or two things that we *must* think about. Specifically, I want to teach you this: every fiction writer needs to know what his or her characters want, what they yearn for, and what gets in the way of their getting what they want.

> or

> Today I want to teach you that writers of nonfiction often live like magnets, collecting not only *our* stories but also the *stories of others* (as long as those stories illustrate our main ideas).

or

> Today I want to teach you that in order to learn to "show, not tell," writers often study instances when other authors have done this, and we notice particular strategies those writers have used and think, "I could try that too."

Trying to generalize these teaching points, one probably notices right away that all three begin with the phrase, "Today I want to teach you that . . . ." This exact wording is not crucial in and of itself—what *is* crucial is that the teacher does not say something like this: "Today I want you to make a chart. In the first column list the names of your characters. Beside each name, in the second column, record what that character wants or yearns for. In the third column, record what gets in the character's way of achieving that goal." I am not suggesting that it would necessarily be a bad thing for children to make such a chart—in fact, as I wrote this "bad example" I thought, "Such a chart could conceivably be a helpful one."' What I *am* saying is that minilessons are different from assigned whole-class activities. Minilessons aim to teach skills and strategies that writers use over and over for their own important purposes. Therefore, in a minilesson, instead of saying, "Today I want you to make four columns," we would say, "Today I want to teach you that writers sometimes invent little charts or grids that help us think through a story before we write it. Some writers, for example, find it helpful to make four-column charts."

My point is that in a minilesson, we are teaching a transferable skill that we want our students to draw on as needed from this day forward, throughout their lives. One way to do this is to couch the teaching point inside the phrase, "Today I want to teach you that writers often. . . ."

We must be very explicit in the teaching point. Each of the examples above could have been left vague. I could have said, "Today I want to teach you that although there are oodles of things fiction writers can think about as we develop our characters, there are just one or two things that we *must* think about." Perhaps I could have added, "Today I'll teach you those crucial elements of fiction." But after hearing my teaching point, learners would still not know what I'm trying to teach. My message would have been, "Wait and see." I think learners profit from the sense of control that comes from knowing what they are learning and why they are learning it. So I suggest that teachers come out with it—that we spill the beans—during our teaching point. This means either that we need to be as explicit as possible right off the bat or that it helps to add a second sentence in which we say something like, "More specifically, I want to teach you that . . . ." I tell teachers that the teaching point should be a line or two that a teacher might put onto a class chart and that writers will want to remember always. A teaching point that stops at, "Today I will teach you how to make your characters come to life," is hardly memorable. On the other hand, if that sentence is followed by another—"Specifically I will teach you that in order to bring your characters to life, you need to show them interrelating with each other"—then the teaching point has suddenly become valuable.

Some may ask, "Why is the wording of a teaching point worth fussing about? Is it really a problem if a teacher says, 'Today we will rewrite our leads,' instead of saying, 'Today I will teach you that in order to write an effective lead, it helps to put your character into action, to show what he or she is doing'? Why does the teacher need to frontload the minilesson so that everything is revealed within the teaching point?" And of course it's true that a teacher needn't use a set of specific words in order to teach an effective minilesson.

However, I have found that when we hold ourselves to a teaching point expressed as, "Today I want to teach you that (writers/fiction writers/essayists) often do such-and-such. Specifically, we do this by (a specific strategy)," it is vastly more likely that the minilesson will teach a skill or strategy that children draw on again and again in the future. Minilessons are not a forum for assigning work; they are part of a

workshop in which children make choices about the specific work they will be doing at any one moment. In this context, in which kids are engaged in their own ongoing work, teachers need to focus on giving writers a repertoire of skills and strategies they can draw on as needed. The wording in a teaching point matters because it reveals whether this is a bit of traditional instruction designed to channel students toward a curriculum requirement or it is a minilesson that orients and inspires a writing workshop.

I find that if we don't embed the specifics of what we will teach into the teaching point, we tend to use the Teaching components of our minilessons to tell students these specifics. If my teaching point in the minilesson at the start of this chapter had been, "Today I want to teach you how to select effective details," then later, during the Teaching component, I probably would have said, "Instead of selecting any ol' details, it helps to select surprising details." I might even have given an example of what I meant by a surprising detail. But *telling* is not *teaching*. I would have succeeded in telling children what to do, but I wouldn't have equipped them to do what I talked about.

In the actual minilesson, when it came time for me to teach, I had already told students that surprising details are more effective than any ol' details. Therefore I used the teaching component to demonstrate to students how I come up with those surprising details. I demonstrated the process I use to generate surprising details—a process that involves picturing the scene in my mind, asking, "What *exactly* do I see?" and reaching for the precise words to convey what I imagine.

Let's take an example. I might want to teach students to write more effective lead sentences for their personal narratives. The teacher could say, in the teaching point, "Today I will teach you how to write more effective leads." Such a teaching point would not have a lot of teaching value. Teachers could record it on a chart and repeat it over and over, and kids could learn it by heart, without any benefits at all ensuing! And if the teaching point is so very vague, then chances are good that during the teaching component, the teacher's time will be consumed with giving specifics. Perhaps the teacher would say something like, "To write more effective leads, it often helps to write what the character says or does."

A better option is for that teacher to spill the beans in the teaching point:

> Today I want to teach you that in order to write an effective lead for a narrative, writers often tell what the character says or does. That is, we can write strong leads by starting the story with a bit of dialogue or with a small action.

Then, during the ensuing Teaching component, the teacher will probably demonstrate the processes a writer goes through in order to come up with the dialogue or small action that the writer uses at the start of the story.

Teaching

The Teaching component of a minilesson requires several kinds of planning. We plan how we will teach, we plan the materials we will use, and we plan the content we will teach. Even though this component lasts only about five minutes, that's a lot of planning!

We can use one of several methods within the teaching component. We can demonstrate, we can explicitly tell and give an example, or we can provide scaffolded practice. It is also possible to use inquiry as a teaching method (although the minilessons in this series tend not to do so.) The vast majority of minilessons involve either demonstrating or explicitly telling and providing an example.

Imagine you wanted to teach someone to tie a special kind of knot. If you decided to teach through a demonstration, you'd start at the beginning and go through the process step by step, talking aloud about each step as you progressed. Alternatively, you might decide to explicitly tell how to tie the knot in a little illustrated talk. You'd try to make the talk memorable. You might consolidate all the steps into three main

steps, giving each one a name. Perhaps you'd use a metaphor, as I did when I taught my son to tie his shoes by referring to "bunny-ear loops." Finally, you might want to provide guided practice. "Take hold of the two ends of the ropes," you might say, waiting for your students to do that. "Now...," you'd continue, guiding the learner step by step.

Let's look at each of these methods in more detail.

DEMONSTRATION Using this method involves setting students up to learn from the demonstration; demonstrating step by step, highlighting what you want students to notice; and then debriefing, naming what you hope children learned from the demonstration that might be applicable to another day and another piece.

- Set students up to learn from the demonstration by telling them how you hope they'll watch the demonstration and by naming what you hope they will soon be able to do. You might say, "Pay attention to..." or "Afterward, I'm going to ask you to..." or "Notice how...."

- Demonstrate step by step what it is you hope the writers will soon be able to do. Highlight whatever it is you want writers to notice, sometimes by almost doing the wrong thing and then correcting yourself, sometimes by narrating a specific aspect of your process. Either think aloud or keep up a running commentary—whichever way you choose, reveal what you are doing in such a way that it is replicable.

- Debrief, usually by looking back on what you just did, naming the steps you took.

- Usually take children back to the beginning of the activity or suggest a situation in which they are apt to initiate the activity.

- Either help children practice the same strategy now, or help them recall what they have learned in a manner that sets them up to use this information later.

It is important to set up the demonstration so that students are aware of what you are doing and how they should be watching you. We usually preface our demonstrations by saying something like, "Let me show you how I . . . ." And we often are more specific, adding something like, "Watch and notice how I . . . ."

Here are some specific examples:

> Let me show you what I mean. I am going to reread my writer's notebook, looking for an entry that could grow into a whole story. Watch as I read; you'll notice I give each entry a little growing space, a little time to become an idea. I don't just race through entry after entry, saying, "Nope, nope, nope," as I flick past them.

or

> Listen while I tell the story "Three Billy Goats Gruff" in a summary way, like a stream of words rushing past me with no rocks to stand on . . . . Now listen as I write in the air a scene from that story. You should be able to hear the difference between a summary, when I am just telling, telling, telling what happened, and a scene, when my characters talk in their character voices and you see what is happening.

A demonstration is a form of procedural or how-to writing. Our purpose is to demonstrate the step-by-step process we used in order to do whatever it is we recommend students do.

In my minilesson about writing with surprising details, for example, I retold the step-by-step processes I had supposedly used the night before in order to write a detail about the beach. I started, as I am apt to do, by creating the context in which I would need to use the technique. I said, "Last night, writers, I decided to write a story about my day at the beach. So I wrote, 'We walked across the beach.'" Then I

demonstrated the step-by-step processes I might go through in order to generate a surprising detail, embedding a few practical how-to tips into this demonstration, ensuring that this portion of the minilesson was instructive. It needed to teach information that was not included in, but was subordinate to, the teaching point. Observe again how I tucked little tips into this small demonstration:

> "I thought, 'No, wait. I need to add a detail.' So this time I wrote, 'We walked across the *sandy* beach.' But then I remembered that writers don't just write with any ol' details, we try to write with *surprising* details. And I realized that *most* beaches tend to be sandy, so that's not really a surprising detail. Watch what I did to come up with a surprising detail."

Turning to the white board, I wrote:

> We went to the

> "Hmm. How shall I describe the beach so my readers can be there with me? Let me picture it in my mind (that's what I often do when I want to come up with a surprising detail). I'm picturing the wave s, crashing in, and a stripe of seaweed running down the center of the beach. . . . Oh! That's a surprising detail." I add that to my story:

> We went to Seapoint Beach. There was a stripe of seaweed down the center of the beach. I stood and watched the waves crash onto the shore.

Does this mean that whenever we choose the method of demonstration, we are going to do a bit of public writing in front of the class? No. There are three very common ways we can demonstrate and yet use someone else's writing.

First, we can act out what a famous author probably did. If my teaching point is that writers often start their stories using dialogue, I may use Ezra Jack Keats' book as an example. If I want to teach using demonstration rather than the more obvious choice of explicitly telling and showing an example, I need to fabricate Keats' actions. No problem! I'm apt to say something like this:

> Let me show you how Ezra Jack Keats went about writing the lead to his book, *A Letter to Amy.* I'm pretty sure that he picked up his pencil and thought, "Wait, let me make a movie in my mind of what actually happens." Then in his mind, he made a little scene—almost like a play up on the stage. He put Peter there, sitting at a table, probably, and he said to himself, "What exactly is Peter doing? What's happening?" Pretty soon the idea popped into his head that Peter is muttering to himself and his dog, Willie. Peter says, "I'm writing a letter to Amy." And Ezra wrote that sentence down—see, here it is at the start of his book.

In a similar way, we may demonstrate by reenacting what *a student* did, prefacing this by saying something like: "Watch what Caleb did when he went about writing his lead sentence. He first . . . ."

We may not only demonstrate what a writer did in order to produce a bit of text, we may also demonstrate what *we* do in order to learn from a text. Take the beginning of this day's teaching component:

> Listen to one of the most famous bits of non-narrative writing in the world. You've heard it before—it is Martin Luther King Jr.'s "I have a dream" speech. I think we can benefit from studying the way Martin Luther King Jr. uses lists to support his ideas. I want you to listen first to a bit of his speech and then watch how I, as a writer, go back and study what this author has done in order to borrow his techniques.

At the end of the demonstration, we often review the step-by-step processes we just walked though, extrapolating what we hope children

ascertained. Debriefing my minilesson on surprising details, I added in another bit of advice:

> "Did you notice that I *almost* wrote, 'I went to the sandy beach'? A famous writer, James Merrill, once pointed out that 'the words that come first are anybody's words. We need to make them our own.' Anybody's beach is a sandy one. Did you see that when I made a picture in my mind of exactly what I saw, I came up with a surprising detail, one that describes not *anybody's* beach but the *particular* beach I visited?"

More often, however, debriefing serves simply as a way to consolidate and crystallize whatever it is that we hope students take with them.

EXPLICITLY TELLING AND SHOWING AN EXAMPLE Using this method involves explicitly telling students a concept you hope can guide them today and in the future, then laying out an example that makes this as memorable or as helpful as possible.

- Perhaps begin by describing the context in which today's teaching point will be useful.

- Explicitly tell students a concept you hope can guide them today and in the future. Teach this in a way that makes it as memorable or as helpful as possible. Usually this means telling an anecdote or creating a metaphor or sharing a list—in some way trying to bring home your point—and often it means crystallizing your point in a catchy phrase.

- Show the example, highlighting the aspects that will enable children to produce something similar. One way to highlight what a writer did do is to remind people of the alternative choices a writer could have made. Tuck tips and pointers into this discussion in a manner that is informative for the learner.

- Reiterate what you have taught, often reminding learners of situations in which the concept will be useful.

Although there are advantages to *demonstration* as a method for teaching, sometimes when I want to convey a concept or an idea, I find myself wanting to give students a little talk rather than act something out. I am mindful that if I sit in the front of the class and blab on and on, the chances that my lesson will be memorable are especially weak. Therefore, I regard this method as especially challenging and I work especially hard to get it right.

I essentially use the same techniques to talk to kids that I use when I'm giving a keynote address to teachers. I often rely on a well-told, usually personal story. I may turn a story into a metaphor I hope will convey the concept I'm trying to teach. I often use parallel structure, with repeating phrases.

Some of my favorite minilessons rely on this teaching method. For example, in *Units of Study for Primary Writing*, I tell children that sometimes writers come up with great big watermelon ideas, thinking, "I'll write about my summer," or "I'll write about recess." Then I tell children that writers know that it helps to reach, instead, for a little seed story, writing about tubing down a creek or falling from the monkey bars. Many future minilessons reference this one; later when children write all-about books (or informational books), their job is to select a watermelon topic, and each seed becomes a separate chapter.

Another time, I tell children that revision means quite literally to "see again." Then I say that the one thing they need to revise is—here I reach for my prop—glasses. They are surprised, of course, and I laugh and say they don't really need glasses to revise but they do need

to put on a special lens and reread their writing with that lens. Then I tell them that writers can choose the lens we'll use, but that I especially recommend writers reread their essays with the lens of structure.

I also use the explain-and-give-an-example teaching method in a minilesson in which I invite children to build spaces in their lives that support them as writers. I can't very well create such a space before their eyes, so I rely on storytelling. Early in the minilesson, I say, "Today, I thought I'd tell you that when I begin a new writing project, I do one other very important thing: I clean my office. Many writers take the time to set up spaces in which we can do our best work." Then I tell the story of Annie Dillard, who turned a tool shed into a study, pushing a long desk against a blank wall so that she'd have nowhere to look but onto the page. Then I generalize from this example: "Do you see how Annie Dillard has built a place for her writing, a place that reminds her of what she wants to remember as she writes? She makes sure her place whispers a message to her." And then I name my teaching point: "Today I want to teach you that most writers set up spaces in which we can do our best work as writers, and we put into those spaces items and words that remind us of all we resolve to do and be as writers. Wouldn't it be great if instead of putting up portable classrooms outside this school, they instead put up tool sheds, one for each of us? It'd be great if we could each set up a writing shed for ourselves, but in this classroom we can only set up our writing spaces, our notebooks, our folders. Still, it is important to choose items that we can put near us as we write, items that carry with them bits of advice." Then I tell about how I put things near me as I write that remind me of lessons I've learned earlier and don't want to forget.

Each of these explain-and-give-an-example minilessons are deliberately written in such a way that the message is memorable. I think of these minilessons as little keynote speeches and try to inspire and entertain as well as inform.

GUIDED PRACTICE OR INQUIRY These two teaching methods are less common than explaining and giving an example. Both of them follow a similar sequence:

- Perhaps begin by describing the context in which today's teaching point will be useful.

- Explicitly and briefly tell students a skill or concept you hope to impart. Usually this skill or concept is one that writers use repeatedly in the midst of writing.

- Get them started doing the thing and interject lean prompts to scaffold the child's work. Your scaffolds may help the child progress through a sequence of activities, but they are more likely to ratchet up the level of the child's work.

- Debrief, naming what you have taught and reminding learners of situations in which the skill or concept will be useful.

This method is used fairly often in conferences, less often in minilessons. Rather than demonstrating or talking about what we hope students learn and then stepping back while children have a chance to try the thing we have taught, we sometimes teach by telling very briefly and then giving children scaffolded practice. For example, when I want to teach children to insert periods at the ends of their sentences, I tell them that writers think of a thought, say it in a sentence, write that whole sentence without pausing, and then, when we do pause, we insert a period. Then writers think of the next thought, say that next thought in a sentence, again write that whole sentence without pausing, then pause to think of what comes next, and again record a period. I show this very briefly by dictating a series of sentences to myself and punching the air each time I pause at the end of one. But within a minute or two, I've gestured for the class to join me, and now we are all punching the air whenever we reach the end of a sentence. Then I ask children to continue dictating their thoughts, this time to a partner. As they talk to each other,

I intercede with reminders: "Don't pause till you reach the end of that thought." "Don't forget the period (punch) when you pause."

In the above example, my interjections lift the level of the children's repeated actions. Sometimes, instead, I guide them, step-by-step, through a sequence of work. For example, when children are writing narratives and I want to help them avoid summarizing and instead *tell* the story, I'll walk them though a sequence of prompts. "Think of one particular time when you were doing something," I might say, giving children a moment to settle on one episode. "Now make a movie in your mind of the very start of this. Where were you, exactly? What were you doing, saying? Write this down. Now reread what you've written and in your mind, be there. Put yourselves in the shoes of your character. What happened next—exactly?"

When we use the guided practice method in conjunction with the inquiry method, we are essentially coaching children through the process of learning something about writing for themselves, usually through mentor texts. "Read lots and lots of examples of whatever it is you want to learn or learn from," we say. Then we coach children how to look for patterns in what they've studied, extrapolating rules or techniques to emulate. Then we coach them how to take what they've learned and apply it to their own writing to serve their own purposes.

The Teaching component of a minilesson usually follows the general design of an essay: explicitly and briefly we tell children what we hope they extrapolate from this minilesson, this text; then we show an example or give a demonstration; and finally we reiterate what it is we have told them.

Active Engagement

We learn more from our own actions than from words out of someone else's mouth. Therefore, after we have shown or told or demonstrated a strategy to youngsters, we try to engineer things so that children have a few minutes of scaffolded practice doing whatever they've just learned.

I usually use different texts in the Teaching and Active Engagement components of the minilesson. For example, in the surprising details minilesson, I demonstrated by talking about a story I'd worked on at home about the beach, but when it came time for children to be actively involved, trying the strategy, I didn't ask them to work on my beach story (they didn't have enough information about my day at the beach to do so!). Instead, I set children up by saying, "Pretend you are writing a story about looking at your hand," and got them started practicing the strategy in a miniature, short-term piece about that readily available and universal topic. Both my text about the beach and the text I asked children to use for practice were just "one-day texts." Neither the beach story nor the hand story threads its way through a series of minilessons. Their redeeming feature—and the reason they are used in this minilesson—is that they are instantly accessible. I could speak for just seconds about each story and the children could still grasp my meaning enough to focus on the particular point I was trying to make.

Often, in order to keep the Active Engagements as simple as possible, teachers will return to a text that the children worked with in previous minilessons. For example, throughout the personal essay unit of study, I demonstrate with references to an essay about my father, and children practice by working on a whole-class essay about their shared work with first-grade reading buddies.

Some teachers are surprised that we don't regularly ask children to pull out their own drafts and practice with them. For example, if I reference Keats' *A Letter from Amy* in the minilesson, showing how Keats probably went about imagining a bit of dialogue to use at the start of that story, people are sometimes puzzled that I'm not apt to then say, during the Active Engagement section of the minilesson, "So get out your most recent draft and reread your lead," and then help children get started transferring the lessons from Keats' book to their own writing.

First, asking children to look at their own drafts and either say aloud to a partner or begin incorporating what has just been taught into their own work is indeed an option and teachers may, in their own minilesson, make choices that differ from mine. If your children do not write anywhere near enough during the writing workshop and you want to give them a nudge to get more writing done, you might want them to use the Active Engagement component to get started on their own work. And if you are less concerned that children learn to use strategies with independence and more concerned that they are mobilized to do *something* productive, you might use this section of the minilesson as a time for them to rehearse aloud for the writing you desperately hope they will do that day.

My rationale for often using an "exercise text" rather than having children practice on their own writing is this: if every child essentially accomplishes whatever I have taught within the two-minute Active Engagement component of the minilesson, then when I say, "Off you go," and send children back to their seats, they will have mostly finished their work for the day. Then, too, I want children to become accustomed to initiating the strategies they learn in minilessons, reaching for these strategies only when the moment seems right for this within their own writing process. And although I may take just a few minutes to teach a strategy, I hope that when they incorporate this strategy into their own writing, the work becomes more complex and involved than anything that could fit into a few minutes of work in the midst of the minilesson. For these reasons, I often set children up to be able to work successfully with what is essentially a whole-class text. Because they are all working with the same text for a moment or two, they especially will be able to learn from each other's work.

For example, in my minilesson on writing with surprising details, I set children up to try what I'd taught this way:

> "Did you notice that I *almost* wrote, 'I went to the sandy beach'? A famous writer, James Merrill, once pointed out that 'the words that come first are anybody's words. We need to make them our own.' Anybody's beach is a sandy one. Did you see that when I made a picture in my mind of exactly what I saw, I came up with a surprising detail, one that describes not *anybody's* beach but the *particular* beach I visited?"

We went to Seapoint Beach. There was a stripe of seaweed down the center of the beach. I stood and watched the waves crash onto the shore.

"So let's try writing with surprising details. Pretend you are writing a story about your hand. You write, 'I put my hand in front of me, and I looked at it.' You *could* say, 'I saw five fingers,' but hands *tend* to have five fingers. To write with surprising details, look closely at your hand. What *exactly* do you notice?"

In this instance, as in many Active Engagements, because the children are all using a shared text, I am able to set them up and get them started doing what I want them to do, thereby orienting them to the work and building their momentum so there isn't a time lag at the beginning. In fact, I often get children started by joining them in doing the strategy in the way I suggest. That is, at the start of many Active Engagements, it almost looks as though this will be another demonstration—and then at the last moment, I pass the baton to the class. For example, in the minilesson about the importance of surprising details, I did not launch children in the Active Engagements component by assigning them to do some work. I did not say, "So would you examine your partner's hand and notice details, surprising details. Then tell your partner what it was you saw." Instead I joined the children in doing this, as if I was running along beside their bike, building up their momentum before pulling my hands away:

> "So let's try writing with surprising details. Pretend you are writing a story about your hand. You write, 'I put my hand in front of me, and I looked at it.'" I did this. "You *could* say, 'I saw five fingers,' but hands *tend* to have five fingers. To write with surprising details, look closely at your hand." I do this. "What *exactly* do you notice? Be honest and precise." I let everyone look at his or her hand, mentally reaching for surprising details. "Partner One, write in the air what you might say next in the story." I reread and

enact the start of the story: "I put my hand in front of me." Then I look at my hand, cueing all the Partner Ones to do the same. Finally I mobilize the turn-and-talk: 'I saw....'"

Usually the work that we set children up to do during this component is either "turning and talking" or "writing in the air." The difference is that the first prompt asks children to discuss, the second asks one child to dictate to the other what he or she could write. That is, if I said, "Turn and talk about surprising details you could mention if you were writing about your hand," I would expect children to say something like this: "Uh, I don't know. That it's got wrinkles? Big ones and small ones? Like a tree." Children would speak differently if instead I had said, "Partner One, write in the air what you might say next in your story. 'I looked at my hand. I saw....' Turn and write in the air." In that case the comment would probably be expressed like this: "Wrinkles, big and small ones, branching out like a tree."

Of course, there are lots of exceptions to what I've said about Active Engagement. One of the more common ones is that sometimes it is not easy to set children up to do what we've taught. In these instances, we sometimes ask children to function as researchers, telling each other what they saw us (or an author) do. We can also ask children to function as planners, telling each other what they plan to do. And certainly, there are times when we want them to get started doing some work on their own piece during this moment of scaffolded practice.

Usually the Active Engagement component of a minilesson leads up to some type of closure. If children have been working in pairs, we will have listened in on that work. The most common way to bring closure is to say, "I heard you (repeat the teaching point here). Listen to how (refer to one or two children who did the work well, providing yet more examples of good practice)." It is crucial, of course, that we don't refer to the same children over and over. Sometimes the child being spotlighted did especially strong work only because we were scaffolding his or her partnership conversation, but when we retell the child's achievements, we leave ourselves out, giving the child full credit for the effective work.

Link

During this final section of a minilesson, we restate our teaching point and either try to ensure that every child applies this new learning to their ongoing work today or encourage children to add today's teaching point to their repertoire of possible strategies or goals.

Pulitzer Prize–winning writer Donald Murray once told me that the single most important sentence in a paragraph is the last one. "This sentence needs to propel readers onward to the next paragraph. It needs to be not a closing, but a launch." I remember this advice when I reach the final bend in my minilessons. These last few sentences need to encapsulate the content of the minilesson in such a way that kids get their hands around it and carry it with them as they head off into the whole of their writing lives.

The challenge of teaching in a way that makes a real difference is not for the faint of heart. It's a tall order to believe that we can call children together into a huddle and take five minutes to teach a technique and they'll then add that technique to their repertoire, using it when the time is right.

And so we speak with great energy. "And so I'm hoping that today and every day," we say with great solemnity, knowing this repeating phrase may matter more than anything else in our teaching, "you'll take time to reread your work and ask, 'Does this make sense?' If it doesn't make sense, class, what do writers do?" "Fix it!" "That's so smart of you. Thumbs up if you are quite sure that from this day onward, you'll be the kind of writer who rereads your own work and asks, 'Does that make sense?' All of you?! Wow! That is so cool. The writers who are seated at the blue table can get started. At the green table . . . ."

I try to remember four things when I plan the Link between my minilesson and writing time:

- *Crystallize the lesson.* I consolidate the lesson into a clear, even catchy phrase that will be easy for children to hold on to and remember. I may repeat the key phrases several times during the last minute of the minilesson, and I know I'll weave these phrases into future conferences and minilessons. The key phrase in the minilesson might be, "Writers look with honest eyes," or "Remember, you are not just a writer, you are a writing teacher," or "Writers show, not tell," or "Take a small moment and make it big," or "Writers add, and writers subtract," or "Let Eve Bunting be your writing teacher." Whatever it is, I find ways to repeat those words so they become a song in children's minds.

- *Generalize the lesson.* As the day's minilesson ends, I want children to remember that it applies to every day's writing. Sometimes I'll make sure everyone uses the tool that very day, but just as often I'll want children to use the tool only when they need it. Either way, however, I need to remind children that the lesson is for "today, and every day" and that "from this day onward" they'll need to remember this tool. Sometimes it helps to put the lesson onto a chart where it accumulates alongside others and remains visible. Such charts might be titled How Writers Revise; Finding Topics for Writing; When Writers Are Done, They've Just Begun; What Good Writing Teachers Do; Qualities of Good Writing; Lessons Mem Fox Can Teach Us. It is also important that teachers move between specific examples and general principles. If the minilesson has been geared toward teaching one new trick for turning narratives into poems, I'll want to be sure to say, "So you can do any of these things when you want to turn a narrative into a poem," and then I'll reread the whole list, adding the new item.

- *Make the transitions smooth.* It's worth my time to think about how to move my twenty-five kids expediently from the carpet to their workspaces. It's worthwhile to develop and refine a system that will then remain in place almost every day. If the system is always changing, it becomes forefront in children's minds and in our own, and at this crucial juncture, our hope is that children's minds are on their writing topics and plans.

- *Boost the children's writing energy.* Don Murray once said, "Above all, in a writing conference, the writer's energy for writing needs to go up, not down." The same can be said about the Link. Above all, it needs to boost children's energy for writing, not sap it.

Studying the craft of effective minilessons can change our teaching not only in the writing workshop but also in other disciplines, and it can improve not only our whole-class but also our small-group instruction. The power of the template is that it is usable and strong for every kind of teaching, both throughout the school day and throughout our lives and interactions with other learners. Just as a powerful minilesson has a replicable, potent, portable lesson in it, the *template* for a minilesson has those same qualities. It is meant to be a framework that is useful to us forever, in many kinds of situations.

THE PATTERNS OF CONFERENCES

The writing workshop approach to teaching writing is also referred to as the conference approach, because one-to-one conferring is at the heart of this method of teaching. These conferences are essential: when a teacher talks with a child about the child's rough drafts, the child internalizes this conversation and, in the end, is able to talk with himself or herself in the midst of writing. The writing process, in a sense, is an internalized conversation that occurs *within* any skilled writer. The writer digs in to write, then pulls back to reread and rethink, shifting between being passion-hot, and critic-cold, between pouring words onto the page and pausing to ask, "What am I really, *really* trying to say? Does any of this draft capture what I want to say?"

Research on the teaching of writing has shown that if teachers habitually approach children in the midst of writing and ask, "What are you planning to do next with this draft?" or "What do you think is especially strong in this draft that you can build on?" or any similar query, children eventually internalize these questions. The child in the midst of writing, will pause and say, "Let's see, what do I plan to do next with this draft?"

It is tremendously important, then, that we confer regularly with children, and that we do so in ways that teach children to confer with themselves. We need to ask writers the questions that writers can profitably ask themselves. And we need, as much as possible, to hand over the conferences to the children, letting them become, with our support, both writer and reader, creator and critic.

It is no surprise that writing conferences (like minilessons) have a predictable architecture. After we listen in on this conference, I'll show how it typifies many conferences.

A Typical Conference

I watched Regio rereading his story about playing Frisbee® with his Labrador Retriever. At various points, he paused to insert a word or a phrase into his draft: the color of the dog's collar and the Frisbee®, a description of his lawn—lush and green. "Hi, Regio," I said. "What are you working on as a writer?"

"Frisbee® with my dog," he said.

"You are writing a story about playing Frisbee® with your dog, is that what you mean?" I said. "Huh! That sounds like fun." Then I added, "But Regio, my question is this—what are you working on, that is, what are you trying to do as you write?"

This time Regio responded, "I'm adding details."

"Can you show me?" I said. Soon I'd seen some of Regio's additions. I laughed appreciatively at a description of his dog biting on a Frisbee®, and for a few seconds we commiserated about owning retrievers who never want to stop retrieving. Then, wondering about Regio's rationale for adding the very small details he'd inserted into the draft, I asked, "What led you to add that the dog's collar was blue, and details like that? What specifically were you trying to do with that sort of detail?"

Regio explained that he wanted people to be able to picture it. Listening to him, I worried that he seemed to be reciting someone else's reasons for revising rather than really sharing any special commitment of his own, and I tucked this thought into a corner of my mind.

"What are you planning to do next?" I asked, wondering whether he had some other intentions up his sleeve. I learned that Regio thought he'd add a few similar details; then he figured he'd recopy the piece to make it look better, be able to pronounce it done, and publish it.

"Regio," I said, shifting now into the Compliment stage of this conference, "I'm totally impressed that you've chosen to write about this incident with your dog. You and I are kind of the same because we both have retrievers, and your story has reminded me that I could do the same. I could take just an everyday incident with Toby and try to write it really well—and it would almost be as if I were making a snapshot of Toby, only in words. I'm also impressed that without anyone suggesting it, you went back and reread your draft and added in more details to help readers really imagine your dog. I love that you're in charge of your own writing. You not only choose your own topics, you also go between drafting and revising all on your own. That's very writerly of you!"

"But can I teach you one thing?" I waited for a shrug or a nod. "When writers try to put details into our personal narratives, we add the true details that we really noticed when the event was happening. So if I were going to write about walking into the school's front foyer today, I wouldn't say, 'I walked into the front foyer of the school. I saw that the main office was beside the front foyer'—I've been coming here for years and I no longer notice it's there." But I *might* have said, 'I walked into the front foyer of the school. I noticed that the display case was filled with colorful flags. I looked closer and saw there was a flag from every state.' Do you see how as a writer of a personal narrative, I include the true details that I actually noticed when the event was happening? That allows a reader to read the draft and to picture the true details that stand out in the moment of the story."

"Why don't you try that? Reread your draft, and give each of the details you've included a test. Ask, 'Is it likely that I really noticed this detail at the time the event was occurring?' I'm pretty sure the answer will be no some of the time. You are the kind of writer who revises on your own, so it probably won't be hard for you to do what professional writers do—revise your revisions! Cross them out! Then you can go back and remember exactly what did happen when you and Banjo were playing on the lawn and this time try to add only the details that you would have noticed then." Turning the draft so that Regio could see it, I said, "Get started, reread a bit of your draft aloud while I'm here and give those details a test while I watch. Okay?"

Regio did that, crossing out a few of his details at the top of his page. "You are great at giving these details the Truth Test," I said. "Before you read on, will you try revising not only by subtracting, but also by adding?" I waited and saw him return to the passage he'd just read, rereading it. I murmured, "Smart decision to reread. Make sure you are picturing the True Thing that happened. What exactly did Banjo do?"

"He put the Frisbee between his paws and sorta said, 'You can't have it?'" Regio responded, his inflection rising as if he wasn't at all sure he was on track.

"Oh my gosh, that is *per*fect! Add that!"

THE ARCHITECTURE OF A CONFERENCE

My conference with Regio, like many of my writing conferences, follows a predictable structure. I begin by researching what he is in the midst of doing as a writer and what he intends to do next. I also try to glean what he feels about his draft and his work. I read sections of his draft that he has referenced, glancing over the whole piece. This phase takes a couple of minutes. Sometimes during this phase I look over a larger amount of the student's work.

Then I compliment Regio. I try to compliment something I believe either is a new accomplishment or at least is important to the writer. I try to name what the writer has done in ways that make that work transferable to another piece and another day. Sometimes I try to articulate the steps the writer probably went through to accomplish the thing I'm complimenting, making it likely that the writer will do similar work another time. Often I hope that my compliment will support a child's identity as a writer and/or the child's commitment to this writing project.

Then I name what I want to teach as explicitly as possible, again making sure that my teaching point will be transferable to another piece and another day, and teach it. Sometimes my teaching in a conference involves demonstrating; if so, I do this much as I might in a minilesson. Fairly often I ask a writer to get started doing the new work, as I did with

Regio, and I coach or otherwise support the writer's beginning efforts. Before my time with the writer is over (either that day or later) I try to extrapolate from this one episode some enduring lessons that I hope the writer has learned.

Let's look more closely at each of these components of an effective conference.

The Research Phase

In my conference with Regio, as in almost every conference, I begin with Research. Often my research starts with a bit of observation. From afar, I check out what various writers are doing, and muse over possible ways I might contribute. Often, it is only after I have a hunch about ways that I might help that I pull my chair close to a particular writer and begin to ask questions.

I ask Regio the one question I ask over and over during this phase of a conference: "What are you working on as a writer?" Because I ask this same question often, I make sure that children learn how to answer. I am not surprised when Regio responds by telling me his topic—this is what most writers do until we teach them otherwise. So when Regio says he is working on "Frisbee® with my dog," I let him know I've heard him—"You are writing a story about playing Frisbee® with your dog, is that what you mean?"—but then I clarify that my question has not actually been, "What are you *writing about*?" I say, "But Regio, my question is this—what are you working on, that is, what are you trying to do as you write?" This time Regio points out, "I'm adding details."

If Regio had struggled with that question, as children often do at first, I would have provided more support by turning it into multiple choice. Either using the chart of recent teaching points or glancing at his writing as a reference, I would have said, "Are you trying to make sure your characters come to life, or are you working on writing with details, or are you trying to make sure you write in paragraphs, or what?" giving Regio the idea for the sort of response I expect.

Because I don't want simply to draw children toward my own

assessments and plans for their writing, I think it is important to begin a conference by learning about the writer's intentions. For this reason, "What are you working on as a writer?" is an incredibly common question, although there are other ways to word essentially the same request for information. And because the question matters, we teach children how to respond to the question. That is, we teach them that we want to learn not just about their content ("playing Frisbee® with my dog") and not just about their genre ("a personal narrative about playing with my dog") but also about their goals and strategies ("I'm writing a personal narrative about playing Frisbee® with my dog and I am trying to write with a lot of details").

If a number of children in a particular class are struggling with the "What are you working on as a writer?" question, I am apt to stop the class and talk to all the children about the importance of having goals and strategies. I teach children the sort of goals and strategies I expect they might have, and ask them to assign themselves one at the start of their work by taking stock of where they are in the writing process and choosing their next step.

Once Regio tells me that he has been working on adding details, it is clear I need to study those efforts. "Can you show me?" I ask and soon see (and build some theories about) some of Regio's additions. I theorize that he doesn't feel especially committed to his revisions or to the writing itself, and I speculate that he is trying to add sensory details as a paper-and-pencil endeavor, simply inserting color words here and there without really envisioning his subject—his dog—at all. I want to check *his* rationale for adding these particular details, however, so I ask, "What led you to add that the dog's collar was blue, and details like that? What specifically were you trying to do with that sort of detail?" His answer confirms my hypothesis, as do his answers about his future plans for the piece.

The work I do during the Research component of this conference is fairly typical. The writer conveys the aspect of writing that has occupied

his or her attention, and the teacher tries to understand the writer's knowledge, intentions, assessments, and plans pertaining to that aspect of writing. This almost always involves probing to understand what the child means. Regio tells me that he has been trying to add details. Of course I know what it means to add details to a piece—but I don't know what this means for this nine-year-old! I could have asked any of these questions at this point: "What kind of details do you think are important?" "Do you just add details all over the draft or do you add them in particular places?" "Why did you choose these particular details to add?" The point of these questions is that we, as teachers, need to understand the writer's understanding. Often children will throw terms around, saying back whatever words we have said to them, and we need to get below the glib phrases and really understand the writer's concepts of revision and of good writing.

Especially when I don't feel that the area the child is focusing on merits more of the child's attention, I am apt to probe a bit to see whether the writer has any other plans up his or her sleeve. (Of course, I let the draft inform me as well.)

Usually when I try to help graduate students learn to confer well, I find that the source of most of their troubles lies in their research. They don't spend enough time trying to understand what the writer is doing and why. As a result, what they decide to teach is often an utterly generic point, perhaps just a recap of a minilesson. That is, when a conference doesn't begin with a teacher really taking into account what the child has done and is trying to do, then during the Teaching section of the conference, the teacher seems to be reciting canned material unaffected by this particular student and his or her work. Our conferences can be among the greatest sources of originality and new thinking in our teaching but only if they are truly responsive. The vitality and originality that characterize really powerful conferences require that we, as teachers, take in what the writer is doing, planning, working to achieve, understanding, and knowing. My first book was titled *Lessons from a Child*, and I continue to believe that conferences give us the chance to learn from the only people who can really teach us how to teach!

Sometimes I help teachers understand the importance of this Research phase by asking them to think about times when a principal has observed their teaching. How helpful it is if the person who coaches us first listens and observes to learn what we are already trying to do! One teacher I know always worries about the strugglers in her classroom. Realizing this, she set herself a correction course, deliberately focusing on her strongest students for a week or two. Her principal sat in on a few moments of her teaching and then told her that she mustn't focus so much on her strong students! If that administrator had prefaced the visit by asking, "What have you been working on? How's it been going?" the coaching interventions could have been far more helpful.

The Decision Phase

To an outside observer, a conference may seem fairly relaxed. But for me, as a teacher, conferences are anything but. As the young writer talks and as my eyes quickly take in the draft and any other available data, my mind is always in high gear. Malcolm Gladwell, the author of the bestselling book *Blink: The Power of Thinking Without Thinking*, suggests that he can observe a married couple for just half an hour and predict the chances that their marriage will be intact a decade hence. In a conference, I'm trying to do an equally astonishing feat of "thin-slicing." I take in all the data I can quickly assimilate, and as I do, I'm theorizing, predicting, connecting this writer to other writers I've known, determining priorities, imagining alternate ways to respond, and lesson planning! All this must happen while I smile genially and act captivated enough by what the child says to keep the data coming my way! This is no easy task, and teachers are wise to recognize that this invisible

aspect of teaching writing is the most challenging one of all.

In the Deciding phase of a conference (which in actuality happens simultaneously with the Research as well as in the handful of seconds between the Research and the Compliment), I quickly synthesize what I have learned and imagine possible paths to take that will best help the writer.

It is important to note that I deliberately delay acting on what I have learned until I have made a conscious decision. That is, I take in whatever I can and then say to myself, "Hmm," being very careful, at all costs, not to slip unconsciously between researching, complimenting, and teaching. Instead I hope that it will always be crystal clear to me, to the student, and to any observer when I move from researching to complimenting to teaching.

During the Decision phase, I am deciding at least two things: what to compliment and what to teach. In making this decision, I draw on these considerations.

- If possible, I equip writers to do what it is they intend to do. When I ask, "What are you working on as a writer?" and "What are you trying to do with this piece?" my purpose is to learn the writer's intentions so that I can support and extend what the writer is already trying to do (if that seems fruitful) and equip the writer with more (or better) strategies for achieving his or her intentions. That is, I do not want my interactions with children inadvertently to teach them they might as well not have any plans or intentions for their own writing, because when they bring their writing to me, I will always come up with a direction they could not possibly have imagined. Instead, I want children to feel as if they have some ownership over their writing, that their hands are on the steering wheel. Given that there are usually lots of ways children could improve their drafts, I will, whenever possible, align my teaching with their own plans and intentions.

- On the other hand, there are times when I think the writer's intentions are too constricted or are otherwise ill advised. When I don't want to get behind the child's existing intentions (or can't discern what they are), I first try to rally the child to take on a new intention. For example, if a child is writing in bare outlines but only wants help with spelling, one alternative is slyly to elicit details and get the child to record them. This would accomplish the goal of making the text more detailed, but it would not make a lasting impact on the writer. I am more apt, therefore, to talk to the writer about his or her goals, encourage him or her to see the importance of writing with detail or some other goal I've chosen based on my assessment, and then briefly talk up the overall direction and goals I'm advocating, before equipping the child to pursue those goals.

- I'm always teaching toward independence and growth. I try to decide on an intervention that will extend what children can already do but also to teach within their reach so that what they do with my support today, they can do independently tomorrow. This means that I sometimes act very excited about a goal that is not really an end goal but a halfway goal. I'll teach a child to add details and watch as the child rereads, using a carrot to add details that fit into a few phrases; while I well know that my real goal is for the child to write details that span paragraphs, I meanwhile act very pleased over what he or she has done.

- I am always informed by my goals. These goals come from an overall sense of what I value in young writers (the ability to write well-structured stories, a growing control of conventions, a readiness to emulate other authors, and so on) and what I value in learners (initiative, zeal, skills, a willingness to take risks and work hard, self-awareness, a commitment to social justice, and so on), as well as from the specific goals I have in mind for a particular unit of study and a particular child.

The Compliment Phase

When I listen to children talk and look over their writing, the first big question I ask and the first big decision I make revolves around the Compliment. That is, I am thinking first, "What has the child done—or gestured toward doing—that I could name and make a fuss over?" Either at the end of the Research/Decision phase or earlier, I spot something that the child has done (or has almost done) that has significance in the child's learning journey, and I name this in a way I hope makes it likely that the child will do this same wise work again in future pieces of writing.

The trick is I need to be able to extrapolate something transferable out of the details of the child's work. If the child added the sound her guinea pig makes when it squeaks into her draft, I don't say, "I love that you added the *ee, ee, ee* sound to your story. I hope you add that squeaking sound into your stories often!" Instead, I name what the child has done in a way that makes the action replicable: "I love the way you reread and added teeny details that could help readers create movies in their minds of exactly what happened. You made it so I can picture your guinea pig. Whenever you write, add details like these." Or, "I love the way you've brought out dialogue—even if it is guinea pig dialogue! You didn't just say, 'Freddy made noises to greet me,' you told us exactly what he said!"

After researching to learn what Regio is doing and trying to do and after deciding on my plan for the conference, I say, "Regio, I'm totally impressed that you've chosen to write about this incident with your dog. You and I are kind of the same because we both have retrievers, and your story has reminded me that I could do the same: I could take just an everyday incident with Toby and try to write it really well—and it would almost be as if I were making a snapshot of Toby, only in words. I'm also impressed that without anyone suggesting it, you went back and reread your draft and added in more details to help readers really imagine your dog. I love that you're in charge of your own writing. You not only choose your own topics, you also go between drafting and revising all on your own. That's very writerly of you!"

The truth is, of course, that Regio's revisions don't amount to much. It isn't especially valuable to insert the color of the dog's collar into the draft! And so it takes some discipline for me to see that there is something commendable about his teeny-tiny additions. But I'm glad that I force myself to get behind something Regio has done, because in fact it *is* impressive that he shifts from writing to rereading and revising and does this on his own. And I'm glad that my plan to begin a conference by making a fuss over something good that the writer has done channels my attention in such a way that I see that Regio's work merits support.

As I look for what I will compliment, I am usually thinking, "What has the child done—or gestured toward doing—that represents the outer edge of the child's development and therefore would be something wise for me to extol?" I always want to name what the child has done in such a way that this is exportable to other pieces and other days, and this means extrapolating something transferable out of the details of the child's work.

Often I am getting behind something that the child may have done almost accidentally, and so I try to reiterate the process the child may have taken in order to accomplish the commendable activity. "I can tell that you . . ." I say, naming the step-by-step strategies the child may or may not have taken. This way, I leave a pathway for the child to repeat his or her accomplishments another time.

The Teaching Phase

The Teaching phase of a conference is remarkably similar to a minilesson. I try to make it very clear that the conference has turned a corner and that I now want to explicitly teach the writer something that I hope will help him, not only today, with this piece, but also in the future. I'm apt to preface this component by saying something like, "But can I give you one tip, one very important tip, that I think will help you not only with this piece but also with future pieces?" Alternatively, I might say, "Can I teach you one thing that I think will really, really help you a lot?" Or, "One thing that I do when I want to (I repeat the writer's goal—convince my reader, write a really effective list, angle a story so that it makes my point) is that I. . . ." This prelude essentially sets me up to make a teaching point.

For example, in my conference with Regio, after complimenting him, I round the bend in the conference like this: "But can I teach you one thing? When writers try to put details into our personal narratives, we add the true details that we really noticed when the event was actually happening." I have carefully worded my teaching point so that I am giving Regio advice that will help not only today with this piece of writing but also other days, with other pieces of writing.

Yesterday, I conferred with half a dozen children who were in the midst of writing essays. These were two of my teaching points:

> "Daniel, what I do after I've written a story that I hope supports the point of my essay is this: I reread my story, chunk by chunk. And after I read each chunk of it, I say to myself, 'Does this part support my topic sentence, yes or no?' Then I go on to the end of the next chunk of text, and I ask that same question."

> "Cassie, after I've collected a few stories that I hope will support my topic sentences, I pause to reread what I've

gathered, and I sort of check over what I've done. I look to see if the stories I've collected really make the point I want to make."

Sometimes I am confident that after making my point, I can ask the writer to go off on his or her own and try the strategy I've just described. Sometimes I feel as if I need to give an example from my own work or even show the writer what this might mean if I were to start doing this sort of work with the writer's text. For example, after telling Regio, "When writers try to put details into our personal narratives, we add the true details that we really noticed when the event was actually happening," I am pretty sure I need to provide an example. So I say, "If I were going to write about walking into the school's front foyer today, I wouldn't say, 'I walked into the front foyer of the school. I saw that the main office was beside the front foyer.'" I explain why—I've been coming to the school for years and therefore I wouldn't be apt to notice the office. Wanting to contrast what I wouldn't do with a positive example of the sort of detail I hope Regio may learn to insert, I say, "I *might* have said, 'I walked into the front foyer of school. I noticed that the display case was filled with colorful flags. I looked closer and saw there was a flag from every state.'"

In Daniel's case, instead of bringing my own case in point to bear, I suggest we reread the first chunk of his story and work together to give it the test of, "Does this support your main idea?" The first chunk does, the second doesn't, and at that point I show Daniel how he can rewrite that episode so that it makes the point he wants to make.

I always begin the Teaching component by explicitly naming something I believe will help the writer not only with this piece but with many pieces. I usually word the teaching point in such a way that it can be generalized to other instances. For example, I might say, "When I am trying to (do what I see you trying to do), I find it is helpful to (progress step-by-step through a replicable strategy)." Of course, this can be worded differently to reference other writers rather than me: "Many writers find that in order to . . . . it helps to . . . . Specifically, they often . . . ."

After this, I decide whether or not the writer needs more detailed help. If yes, I might provide an example or do a demonstration by referring to my own writing or telling a story about another writer. Either way, I generally detail the step-by-step process that a writer goes through and then, often, summarize (still through a sequence of steps) the strategy.

Sometimes I decide to provide even more support by showing writers the sort of thing they might do with their own draft. For example, if the writer has summarized the events that occurred when he went to the airport to pick up his grandmother, saying, "We went and got her at the airport. It was great to see her. We were happy to see her. We took her to her room in my house," I might say, "This would be better if you tell it step-by-step. For example, I could imagine you might rewrite your story so that it went something like this: 'We walked in the big doors at the airport. The air was cold inside. We looked on the wall chart to see where her plane would arrive. "Gate 16," my Dad said. Then we turned to walk toward . . . .'" At this point, I'd say, "I probably didn't get it just right. Can you tell it the true way? Start 'we walked in the big doors . . . .'"

One way or another, I name a teaching point and provide as much support for that teaching point as I think is necessary. If I decide the writer needs more support, I might say, "So let's try this together" then read aloud the relevant portion of the writer's draft or otherwise set the writer up to get started doing the strategy. But, I might simply say, "So would you go off and try this? I think it will work for you this time. And any other time when you are (repeat the situation), remember this is a strategy that you can call on."

When I wanted Regio to reconsider the details he was inserting into his story of playing Frisbee® with his dog, I got him started by saying, "Why don't you try that?" Then I reiterated the sequence of activities. "Reread your draft, and give each of the details you've included a test. Ask, 'Is it likely that I really noticed this detail at the time the event was occurring?'" I anticipated his response and set him up to go farther on his own: "I'm pretty sure the answer will be no some of the time. You are the kind of writer who revises on your own, so it probably won't be hard for you to do what professional writers do—revise your revisions! Cross them out! Then you can go back and remember exactly what did happen when you and Banjo were playing on the lawn and this time try to only add the details that were true then." Turning the draft so that Regio could see it, I said, "Get started, reread a bit of your draft aloud while I'm here and give those details a test while I watch. Okay?"

As writers progress, I provide more or less supportive scaffolds. For example, if the writer is learning to tell a story through a sequence of small steps and needs very strong scaffolds, I can ask, "What did you do first? Exactly what did you say? And then what did you do?" After a few such questions, I can synthesize all that the child has said up to that point and then add one more extending question. But at some point, I need to withdraw some of these very heavy scaffolds so that the child moves toward independence. "Keep going," I soon say. Within another moment or two, my interventions may be just a supportive nod or hand gesture conveying, "Continue. Keep the story rolling."

After Regio crossed out a few of his details at the top of his page, I set him up for the next step by supporting what he'd done and naming what he needed to do:

> "You are great at giving these details the Truth Test," I said. "Before you read on, will you try revising not only by subtracting, but also by adding?" I waited and saw him return to the passage he'd just read, rereading it. I murmur, "Smart decision to reread. Make sure you are picturing the True Thing that happened. What *exactly* did Banjo do?"

> "He put the Frisbee® between his paws and sorta said, 'You can't have it?'" Regio responded, his inflection rising as if he wasn't at all sure he was on track.

> "Oh my gosh, that is perfect! Add that!"

Once the writer has done some work on her or his own (even if that work occurs in the conference, with the benefit of the teacher's scaffolding), it's important to step back and name what the writer has done that we hope the writer does again in another instance within this draft or when working on another piece of writing. In a sense, the conference ends with a second Compliment, one not unlike the first. This second compliment functions rather as the Link does in a minilesson. Usually I repeat the teaching point, this time not as a charge to the writer but as a record of what the writer has just done. These compliments are not unimportant. The single most important guideline to keep in mind in a conference is this: "The writer should leave wanting to write."

And so my conference with Regio ended, "What you are doing is brilliant, Regio. From now on, always remember that you are the kind of professional writer who not only writes but also rereads your writing. When you reread your writing, you pay attention to your details. You give them the Truth Test, don't you? You ask, 'Is this a true detail, one I would actually have noticed when the event was occurring?' And if the detail isn't true, you cross it out and add ones like you just did that are exactly true details."

When we follow the general pattern outlined above, conferences become more manageable. In a one-hour writing workshop, having half a dozen intense, meaningful teaching interactions, each one tailored to the individual needs of a child, is difficult enough. Reinventing the structure for each conference along the way would be virtually impossible. A general template allows us to channel our attention and our thoughts to the specific next steps each child can take in her growth as a writer, and to think "Out of all the options available to me, what can I teach that might make the biggest difference?"

CHAPTER 9

AUTHORING YOUR OWN UNITS OF STUDY

This series will have done its job well if it not only helps you to *teach the units* described to good effect, but if it also encourages you to work collaboratively with your colleagues to *author your own units of study*. My hope is that you and your colleagues will notice gaps in the yearlong curriculum that my colleagues and I have laid out, and that you will decide to work collaboratively to create units of study to fill those gaps. Better yet, I hope that teachers at one school (or one grade level) become especially knowledgeable about one facet of a writing curriculum, and teachers at another school (or grade level) become adept in a different area. Perhaps towards the spring of the year, before teachers across different grade levels meet to compose a curricular calendar for the upcoming year, there could be a gigantic conference with teachers sharing the units of study you've authored. Of course, the units will always need to be labeled "Under Construction."

In this chapter, I will turn the process of creating a unit of study inside-out, sharing the interior work.

DECIDE ON THE SUBJECT FOR YOUR UNIT OF STUDY

First, of course, you will need to decide on what it is you will teach. The units that I've detailed in this series may lead you to imagine that most units of study are genre-based. Certainly there are many genres that I have not tackled in this series and that merit study. For example, you may decide to teach a unit on news stories or feature articles, editorials or investigative reports. Alternatively, you may decide to develop a unit on narrative (or literary) nonfiction—children could study narrative nonfiction writing that chronicles a writer's process of investigating a subject. Then, too, once your children have written realistic fiction, you may decide to teach them historical fiction, science fiction or fantasy.

On the other hand, it is important for you to understand that units of study need not be based on a genre. You could instead teach a unit on aspects of the writing process—certainly many people teach units on revision, for example. You might begin such a unit by suggesting children identify three or four pieces they've written that they believe are "good enough" to merit revision, and then you could teach strategies of revision, supporting children in using those strategies on their portfolio of selected texts.

Alternatively, you could teach a unit focusing on a quality of good writing. For example, you could rally children to closely study places where authors "show-don't-tell." Children could find instances where writers show instead of telling within published texts, revise their existing texts so as to do this more, then draft new texts in which they use all they've learned from studying mentors and revising their own texts. There are other aspects of good writing I could imagine studying: characterization, for example, or the development of setting.

Then, too, you could study a social structure that supports writing. For example, you could design a unit of study called "Writing Friendships," in which you help children consider how to work well with a partner and perhaps with a writing club. How might a writing partnership best help us with rehearsal for writing? With drafting? With revision?

Revision of *teaching* is as essential as revision of *writing*, and front-end revision of teaching, like of writing, is especially efficient. Guard against seizing on the first topic of study that comes to mind and plunging forward. For example, if you and your colleagues see that there is no unit of study on poetry in this series, and decide to develop such a unit for your classroom, that could be a wise decision. But poetry is

surely something you will want children to study again and again across their school career. Perhaps you'd like each year's work with poetry to take on a different focus so that children perceive each year as new, and come to each study with fresh enthusiasm. If you and your colleagues decide to differentiate your poetry units so that you create a spiraling curriculum, you'll want to imagine and create a gradient of difficulty for studying poetry. What might be more accessible for younger writers? More demanding for older writers? Perhaps, for example, you will decide the third grade unit on poetry could highlight reading-writing connections and revision. Perhaps the fourth grade study could focus on language and imagery. Fifth graders, then, could study ways in which poems are metaphoric, noticing that even a poet's use of white space matters, for the poet lays words on a page in a manner that conveys the poet's meaning.

You may wonder whether some topics are more worthy of study than others, and whether there are predictable traps to avoid when selecting a topic for study. These are great questions to ask!

When you decide upon a unit of study, you are taking it upon yourself to channel the young people in your care to devote an entire month of their writing lives toward the subject you settle upon. It goes without saying, therefore, that you need to believe any unit of study you teach (any unit you impose upon your children) must be incredibly important. When a teacher suggests she may want to teach a unit on sea shanties, alphabet books or limericks, for example, I sometimes question whether those areas of study are the most important ways for children to invest their time. Sometimes the rationale for a writing unit is that the choice aligns to a reading or social studies unit. My response to that is that when we design units of study for a writing curriculum, I think we need to keep in mind that our choice should come from our sense of what children need *as writers*; I don't think the goal of aligning disparate subjects should take priority over other goals.

That is, the reason to select one unit of study over another may not be immediately obvious to an outsider. The guiding question for choosing a topic for a unit of study should, I believe, be this: "What writing work will be especially helpful for these kids?" That is, a unit of study contains a line of minilessons on a topic, yes, but it is far more important to realize that a unit of study comprises a month of writing work for the children in our care. Would it be especially beneficial for them to work on writing lots of short texts, whipping through a quick version of the writing process many times? If so, then a unit on poetry might be an option, or a unit on revision, or a unit on writing to make real world difference. Perhaps a teacher decides that she wants her children to become more skilled at writing proficient, first-draft writing on demand—for this reason, she may decide to turn the classroom into a newsroom and teach children to write news articles and editorials.

Here is a final word about one's choice of a unit: The other deciding factor is you. If you are learning to play the guitar and find yourself dying for the chance to dig into song-writing, then consider bringing that passion into the classroom. If you loved your fiction unit and yearn to do more, consider a unit on revision, or on character development (which could invite children to revise several earlier pieces so as to bring the characters to life more)or historic fiction. In the end, children can grow as writers within any unit of study. And whether you are teaching a unit on independence in the writing workshop or on writing to change the world, you need only remember that you are teaching children, and teaching writing. The rest is negotiable.

PLAN THE WORK CHILDREN WILL DO

It is tempting to start planning a unit of study by writing a minilesson for day one and then for day two. What I have found is that if I proceed in that manner, chances are great that those intricate, time-consuming plans will end up being jettisoned.

I'd recommend instead that you begin by thinking about the work that you envision your children will be doing in this unit. For example,

when I was working on the first unit of study in this series, before I could imagine the unit's flow, I needed to decide whether I would be channeling children toward writing one narrative during that month, or two, or several. Also, I needed to decide whether I imagined that the writers would proceed in synchronization with each other, or would some children write three stories and some one? Then, too, I needed to decide whether I imagined that children would progress quickly through rehearsal, spending more time on revision or vice versa?

Before you begin to think about the progression of your minilessons, then, you need to imagine different ways that the unit of study you've selected could proceed, and then weigh the pros and cons of those various alternatives. You won't, of course, be sure how long any stage will take, but you can and must approach a unit of study with some tentative plans.

If your children are fairly inexperienced as writers, then you will be more apt to keep them in synchronicity with each other and more apt to expect them to complete several pieces of writing. It is not an accident that the unit in this series that gives children the most latitude in pacing themselves and the most latitude in designing their own projects is the last unit.

As you plan the work that your children will do within the unit, keep in mind a few ways upper-grade writing units unfold. You might, of course, invent something altogether different, but these are a few common templates for a unit of study:

- Your children might generate lots of one kind of writing, perhaps taking each bit of writing through a somewhat limited amount of revision. Then your children could look back over all of it to choose one piece (presumably from the writing they've only lightly revised) to delve into with more depth, bringing it to completion.

- Your children may each work on one writing project that contains lots of parts or steps, with children working roughly in sync with each other, spending a set amount of time on each step (or aspect) of the piece.

Let's imagine that you decide to teach a unit on poetry. You'd probably find this fits best into the first template. Presumably, at the start of the unit, each child could write and lightly revise a bunch of poems. Then writers could commit themselves to taking one poem (or a collection of poems that address one topic) through more extensive revision and editing. A unit of study on news articles could fit into that same template. News stories are written quickly, so children could generate many of these at the start of the unit, bringing more and more knowledge to them as they learn more. Then you could explain that sometimes a writer decides to extend the news article into a more developed sort of writing, and you could teach children to rewrite one of their articles into an investigative report or an editorial (either project would require more research and revision).

On the other hand, you might decide that within one unit, children will work on a single, large writing project: say, a piece of literary non-fiction, perhaps one requiring research. Perhaps for this unit each child will investigate a different endangered species. You may decide that the first half of the unit will focus not on drafting informational writing but on note-taking. Then, during the second half of the unit, children could draft their literary nonfiction.

Before I write a single minilesson, I bring out a blank calendar for the unit to plan how the children's work is apt to unfold across the month. I imagine that for the first week or week-and-a-half in a unit, children will gather entries—so I mark those days onto the calendar. I do not yet know the specific minilessons I will teach, but I do know the broad picture of what children will be doing during those days. Proceeding in a similar fashion, I mark off the bends in the road of a unit. Even after this, however, I'm not ready to write minilessons.

GATHER AND STUDY TEXTS FOR CHILDREN TO EMULATE

You will need lots of examples of the sort of text you hope your children will write. That is, if you decide to teach a unit on writing descriptively and to emphasize the importance of developing the setting, you'll want to turn your classroom library upside-down looking for examples of the sort of thing you plan to teach. You'll become a magnet for this sort of writing and find examples of it throughout your life. You will very likely want to invite your children to join you in this, depending on where they are in their writing and reading lives at the time.

Soon you will have gathered a pile of writing, and you can begin to sift and sort through it, thinking:

- What are the different categories of texts here?

- What are the defining features of this sort of writing?

- Which of these texts could become exemplars for the unit of study?

In order to make these decisions, you'll need to think not only about the texts but also about your kids. You will want to aim toward goals which are achievable for them. You may well choose texts to serve as exemplars that are not the texts that you, personally, would choose to emulate if you were teaching this unit to a group of adults!

In order to decide upon the texts that you will use as exemplars for the unit, you'll need to take into consideration the particular focus you will bring to this unit. For example, when I taught children to write fiction, I knew that I wanted their stories to be simple, involving just two or three characters and just two or three small moments. I knew, also, that I wanted them to write realistic fiction. Fiction, meanwhile, comes in all shapes and sizes—so I needed to do some research before settling upon "Spaghetti" and *Stevie, Fireflies!* and *Peter's Chair.*

Often, you will decide to use your own writing as one touchstone text for the class, and you might also decide to use writing done by another child another year. These are perfectly reasonable choices. You probably won't rely exclusively on any one text, however. Each will have its benefits, and children will profit from studying a variety of texts. Usually in a unit of study, children will work collaboratively to write one shared class text. In the essay unit, for example, I began with an essay about my father, and meanwhile, during the Active Engagement section of many minilessons, children worked in pairs to write-in-the-air a class essay, "Working with Reading Buddies." Before you begin a unit of study, then, you may want to consider not only whether you want to thread an exemplar text through the unit, but also whether kids will work collaboratively on creating a class text.

or revise it in exactly the same ways that you suggest your kids try.

As you read and write, try to think about ways in which the current unit of study could build on previous learning. Not everything that you and your kids do in this unit can be brand new. What is it that kids already know that they can call upon within this unit? What will the new work be?

Think, also, about what is essential in the unit and what is detail. The answer to that question lies not only in the unit itself, but in your hopes for how this unit of study will help your kids develop as writers. If you are teaching poetry with a hope that this will lead children toward being able to engage in much more extensive revision, then this goal influences your decision about what is essential in the unit.

READ, WRITE, AND STUDY WHAT YOU WILL TEACH

I describe units as if they are courses of study for children, and of course the truth is they are courses also for us! In addition to collecting examples of the sort of writing you'll be asking kids to do, you will also want to scoop up all the professional books and articles you can find pertaining to your unit of study. You can learn a lot from books for adult writers, so don't limit yourself to books by and for teachers.

I cannot stress enough that you need to do the writing that you are asking your kids to do. You needn't devote a lot of time to this. The writing that you use as an exemplar text needs to be very brief anyhow, so even ten minutes of writing, four times a week, will give you tons of material to bring into your minilessons. The important thing is that during those ten minutes you work in very strategic ways. Usually you'll begin with a bare-bones, little text, and you'll develop

OUTLINE A SEQUENCE OF TEACHING POINTS

After all this preparation, it will finally be time to outline a sequence of teaching points. When I do this, I am usually not totally sure which teaching points will become minilessons and which will become mid-workshop teaching points or share sessions. Those decisions often come very late, as I revise my unit.

I make my plans within general time constraints. That is, I might say to myself, "I will use about three days for teaching kids to live like poets, generating entries which could become poems." I approach a set of days, then, feeling sure about the most important skills that I want to teach, and the most important content I want to convey. I might approach a poetry unit by saying to myself, "Everyone thinks of poetry in terms of pretty words. I want to emphasize, instead, that poets see the world with fresh eyes, reaching for honest and precise words." If this was my goal, I would try to be clear to myself what it is that I hope kids will know and be able to do after this work.

Before I can write minilessons, I need to set the goals that I will work toward in each part of a unit. I also need to name or invent some practical, expendable, how-to procedures that I believe these young writers can use to achieve the goals. For example, although I will be convinced that it is important for a writer to know how to show-not-tell, I will be less sure which step-by-step procedures, which strategies, will help each particular youngster do this. For this reason, I tend to teach by saying, "One strategy that some writers find helpful is…" or "One strategy that you might try is…." Those strategies are expendable.

Whenever we teach anything worth teaching, we need to anticipate that kids will encounter trouble. When I teach kids ways to use ministories in their essays, for example, I need to anticipate that this will pose difficulties for some kids. At least half our teaching does not involve laying out brand new challenges but instead involves coaching and supporting kids through predictable challenges.

When we plan a unit of study, it is important to anticipate the difficulties kids will encounter in the unit. We'll want to plan to provide them with the scaffolding necessary to have success with first a pared-down version of what we are teaching and, eventually, with higher level work. For example, I was pretty sure I would need to provide some scaffolding for kids when I taught them that they could reread an essay as from a plane, looking down at the structure, the overall chunks of text. When I told kids to look at the patterns of chunks and think, "What was the author doing in this chunk of text?" and "What about in this one?" I knew that some children would find this confusing. To scaffold children's efforts to do this, I boxed out the major sections of a text I found, explaining my thinking about the work each chunk was doing. Then I asked children to try this with another text, a text which I'd already boxed into sections.

Although we can anticipate lots of the difficulties that kids will encounter as we teach them, it is inevitable that new issues will emerge.

So, we keep our ears attuned, our eyes alert. We know from the start that as we teach a unit, we'll outgrow ourselves and our best teaching plans in leaps and bounds.

WRITE MINILESSONS

In writing workshops, kids generate ideas for writing, then they select one of those to develop. They make an overall plan on either a timeline, a story mountain or some boxes and bullets, and then they revise those plans. They try a few alternate leads—and then get started. They write with some tentativeness, expecting to revise what they write with input from others.

The process of authoring a unit of study is not so different. We generate ideas for a unit and then select one of these to develop. Then we make an overall plan for the unit and revise it. Eventually, we settle on a plan and get started. After all that planning and revising, we write the first word. Even then, we write knowing that our teaching plans will be what Gordon Wells refers to as "an improvable draft."

If teaching plans are only in our minds, or only coded into a few words in a tiny box of a lesson-plan book, then it's not easy to revise those plans. But ever since we human beings were cave dwellers, inscribing the stories of hunts on stony cave walls, we have learned that once we record our thoughts and plans, then the community can gather around those thoughts. Those thoughts can be questioned, altered, expanded. The ideas of one person can be added to the thoughts of another. In scores of schools where I work closely with teachers, we keep a binder for each unit of study. In that binder, we keep a collection of all the minilessons written that are related to each unit. Many of these are minilessons one teacher or another wrote, but others come from professional development teachers have attended or books they've read. In these binders, the teachers also deposit other supporting material.

Hints for Writing Minilessons:

1. **The Start of the Connection**

   Try to think of the first part of your Connection as a time to convey the reason for this minilesson. You are hoping to catch children's attention and to rally their investment. Fairly often, this is a time to step aside from writing for just a moment, telling a story or reliving a class event in a manner that will soon become a lead to (or metaphor for) whatever you will teach.

   If you have trouble writing the start of a minilesson, it is also possible to settle for simply saying, "Yesterday I taught you . . . ." and then referring to the exact words of yesterday's teaching point. These should usually be written on a chart, so gesture toward the chart as you talk. Ideally you can follow this with a memorable detail of someone who used yesterday's teaching point (a published author, you or a child). You can say something such as, "Remember that . . . ."

2. **The Teaching Point**

   This will only be a few sentences long but nevertheless it merits care and revision as it is the most important part of your minilesson. Plan to repeat the exact words of your teaching point at least twice in the minilesson. In order to learn to create teaching points, try temporarily staying within the template of these words or something very close to them. "Today, I will teach you that when writers . . . , we often find it helps to . . . We do this by . . . " The important thing to notice in this template is that we are not saying, "Today we will do this." A teaching point is not the assignment for the day! Instead, the teaching point is a strategy that writers use often in order to accomplish important writing goals. Then, too, notice that teaching points do not simply define the territory within which one will teach. That is, if a teaching point went like this: "Today I will teach you how to write good leads," then there would be nothing worth remembering in this teaching point!

3. **The Teaching**

   When planning how the teaching will go, begin by deciding what your method and materials will be. If you will be demonstrating using your own writing, go back and look at a few minilessons in which I used a similar method, and at first follow the template of these minilessons. You will probably see that I set children up to observe me by telling them what I hope they will notice and what they will do after I demonstrate. Then I tell the story of how I came to need the strategy. Then, I act out what one does first, next, and next in using this strategy. I often include in my demonstration an instance when I do something unhelpful, and then I correct myself, coming back on track. Throughout the demonstration, I tend to write only about four sentences; usually these are added to an ongoing piece that threads its way through much of the unit.

   I might demonstrate using a bit of a published author's text instead of my own writing, and again, if you decide to create a minilesson using that method, find instances when I did this and let them serve as an exemplar for you. You'll find that if I am demonstrating using a published author's text, I'll enact what the author probably did, prefacing my enactment with a phrase such as, "So and so probably did this. He probably . . . ."

   I might choose not to demonstrate. Instead, for example, I might talk about something and then show an example. These kinds of minilessons are more challenging to write, but again, I encourage you to find and follow a model as a way to induct yourself into this work.

4. **The Active Engagement**

   Almost always, this will be a time when children try the strategy that you have just taught, and they do so by writing-in-the-air (talking as if they are writing) to a partner. For example, if you have taught that toward the end of one's work on a text, a writer rereads her own writing to ask, "Does this make sense?" then you'll want to use the Active Engagement time as a chance to provide children with some scaffolded practice doing this. You have two common options. One option is for you to say, "So right now, while you sit in front of me, would you get out your own writing and read just the first paragraph as if you are a stranger, asking yourself, 'Does this make sense?' If you spot a place where it is confusing, put a question mark in the margin." The advantage of asking children to try the strategy this way is that you help children apply the minilesson to their own work and help them get started on their own work. The disadvantage is that sometimes kids can't use the teaching point of the day on just any paragraph (as they could in this example), and therefore it is not possible for them to find a place where the strategy applies and put the strategy into operation all within just a few short minutes. This portion of a minilesson shouldn't take more than four minutes! Then, too, you can't provide much scaffolding or do much teaching off this work because each child will be working with a different piece of writing.

You might, therefore, say, "Would you help me with my piece by becoming a reader of my next paragraph? Would Partner One read it quietly, aloud, and as you read, think, 'Does this make sense?' Partner Two, you listen and give your partner a thumbs up if yes, you think it is making sense." By using your writing for the Active Engagement, You'd have a common text to discuss if problems arise in applying the strategy. Also, when children have applied the strategy to your writing, they could also transfer the strategy to their own writing once the minilesson was over and they were on their own. Otherwise, the teaching of the minilesson won't carry into the workshop time, and may be less likely to carry into each child's writing life.

Sometimes the Active Engagement portion of the minilesson does not involve partner work; each child works individually, often guided by the teacher's nudges. Teachers listen in on what children do sometimes intervene to lift the level of a particular child's work. We often end the time by reporting back on the good work one child did.

5. **The Link**

During this portion of the minilesson, you will always repeat the teaching point verbatim, usually adding it to a chart as you do so. You won't have one amalgamated chart that lists every teaching point that has ever been taught! Each chart will feature a collection of strategies writers can use to accomplish a particular goal. That is, the title of the chart generally names the goal, and then below this there will be a growing list of strategies writers might draw upon to accomplish that goal. Charts lose their effectiveness if they are too long. Typically, charts do not contain more than five or six specific items.

Generally, the Link is a time for you to tell children when to use what you have taught them. You will be apt to say something like, "When you are (in this situation as a writer) and you want to (achieve this goal), then you might use any one of these strategies: (and you reread your charted list). Another option would be to use this strategy (and you add the new strategy to the list)." Usually, in the Link, you will say something like, "So today, you have lots of choices. You can do this, or that, or this, or that . . . ."

PLAN CONFERENCES, LETTERS TO PARENTS, RUBRICS, HOMEWORK . . . AND THE REST

Planning a unit can't be equated with just writing minilessons! First of all, once you have planned a sequence of minilessons, you can read through them imagining the challenges they will pose for your children. You'll be able to ascertain that for some minilessons, many of your children will need extra support, and those will be good places to plan small-group strategy lessons. You may decide that on some of those occasions, you will go from table to table, providing close-in demonstrations of whatever it is you hope children do first, then circling back for demonstrations of whatever you hope children do next. For these extra-challenging minilessons, you will probably want to plan follow-up minilessons, devising those after you study the particular ways in which your children are encountering difficulty.

Then, too, you'll want to plan how you will assess children's progress. You might think that the time to assess is at the end of a unit, but in fact, it is wise to mark mid-unit checkpoints. For example, in *Launching*, you can predict that after three or four days of collecting entries, you will want to check to see which of the children are writing about focused events, which are organizing their narratives chronologically, and which are storytelling rather than summarizing. In *Literary Essays*, you'll want to look over children's entries a few days into the study to see whether children have been gathering entries which contain possible thesis statements.

You can plan for any other aspect of your teaching as well. For example, you could plan how partnerships might be tweaked so that they support the goals of the unit. You might think about particular language lessons that English Language Learners may need in a unit. In *Personal Narrative*, for example, English Language Learners may need help writing in past tense and using temporal transition words. In *Breathing Life into Essays*, they may need support writing with logical transitions.

Because your units of study will be written down, you and your colleagues can put them on the table and think together about these plans. "What's good here that we can add onto?" you can ask. "What's not so good that we can fix?"

SUPPORTING ENGLISH LANGUAGE LEARNERS

These units of study have been taught in thousands of New York City classrooms. The writing workshop's success across New York City has been dramatic and that success is especially poignant in schools filled with English Language Learners. It was no surprise to us to learn that since the writing workshop has been brought to scale across the city, results from the National Assessment for Educational Progress (NAEP) show that our ELLs have made especially dramatic progress.

Because the Teachers College Reading and Writing Project works primarily in New York City schools, where classrooms brim with English Language Learners, we spend a lot of time thinking about ways in which the writing workshop can be adjusted so that it is especially supportive for our ELLs.

It is clear that the writing workshop, specifically, and more generally, the structures of New York City's version of balanced literacy, are tailored to support English Language Learners. Language development is embedded in the structures of this version of balanced literacy. These classrooms are organized in such clear, predictable, consistent ways that children quickly become comfortable participating in their ongoing structures. Very early in the school year, ELL children come to understand that writing workshops start with the teacher giving a minilesson, and that during the minilesson they learn strategies that they are then expected to apply to their independent work. Children know that after the minilesson, they will be expected to write independently, and that the teacher will circulate around the room, conferring with individuals and with small groups. Children also know that they will be expected at some point to share their work with a partner (more on this later). When their writing time is over, children know that they need to put their materials away and gather in the meeting area (or with a partner) for a share. When teachers follow these routines day after day, students can focus their energy on trying to figure out how to do their work rather than on worrying over what they will be expected to do. The predictability of the workshop provides tremendous reassurance to a child who is just learning English, and this is amplified if workshop structures repeat themselves across other subject matters.

In addition, writing workshops are characterized by a consistent instructional language. The consistency of this language scaffolds each child's classroom experience, making it easier for a child who is just learning English to grasp the unique content that is being taught that day. For example, it helps that every minilesson starts in a predictable manner, with teachers saying, "Writers," and then reviewing the content of yesterday's minilesson, referencing a bullet on a chart. It helps children that every day the teacher encapsulates the day's lesson in a sentence or two(the teaching point) that is repeated often and written on a chart.

Of course, the predictability of the workshop also means that teachers needn't invent a new way each day to support English Language Learners. Because the same classroom structures are in place every day, solutions that help on Tuesday will also help on Wednesday, Thursday and Friday.

Then, too, the work that children do in the writing workshop always, inevitably, provides wonderful learning opportunities for English Language Learners. Because the child always chooses what she will write about, chooses the words she will use, chooses the people and places and themes that will be brought forth in the texts, chooses meanings that are vibrantly important to her, chooses the level of vocabulary and of sentence and text structures, and so forth, the writing workshop is *by definition* always individualized. Yet—and here is the really powerful thing—the writing workshop is also, by definition, utterly interpersonal. You try it. Write about the things that are on your mind. Put your mom on the page, or your son; capture that memory that haunts you. Now bring this page to the table when you gather with the people who live and work alongside you. Share the text. Talk about it. You will find that by sharing your writing, something happens that makes you and the people with whom you shall see each other in a new way; sometimes it will almost seem as if you are seeing each other for the first time. You will see that if you share your writing with your colleagues, you will go through each school day with a different sense of yourself and of your workplace, and the same will be true for your ELLs. You'll understand that song, "No man is an island, no man stands alone. Each man's joy is joy to me, each man's grief is my own . . . ." For every one of us, the chance to work and learn in the presence of a community of others is invaluable. Could we possibly give anything more precious to our English Language Learners? To all our children?

But let us think now about specific ways in which each of the components of the writing workshop can be altered just a bit so that the workshop as a whole is especially supportive for ELLs. Of course, there is no such thing as "the" English Language Learner. Language learners, like all learners, differ one from the next in a host of ways. Two significant factors contributing to their unique needs will be the child's level of competence in his or her native language and the child's English proficiency.

TAILORING THE WRITING WORKSHOP TO SUPPORT CHILDREN IN ALL THE STAGES OF LEARNING ENGLISH

Support in the Preproduction and Early Production Stages of Learning English

It's critical that we, as teachers, think through how each of the components of a writing workshop can be altered to provide ELLs with the support they need. Second language learners go through predictable stages of language acquisition as they move to full fluency in English. When we plan the writing workshop, we need to think about how we are going to meet our children's needs as they develop English language skills and how we are going to adjust our expectations as children move toward full fluency.

Children who are in either the silent period (or preproduction stage) or in the early production stages of learning English will have few oral English skills but they will be listening carefully, trying to interpret what is going on around them. It is okay for children to be quiet at this stage, but we, as teachers, need to understand that they are taking in a lot of information. The English words, phrases and sentences which will make sense to them first will probably be the predictable sentences related to concrete classroom activities, such as, "Get your writing," and "Draw something on this paper," and "You can go to your seat now" or "Let's gather in the meeting area." Opportunities for listening, really listening, are important, and the expectation that these children will participate in the comings and goings of the class spotlights the importance of them learning the social language that is most within their grasp. It is definitely important that these children *are* being told, "Get out your pencil," and "Draw here," and "Let's gather in the meeting area," (with accompanying gestures) and that they are expected to do all these things along with the others.

The writing workshop is an especially rich context for language development because children are not only writing and listening; they are also talking—and much of that talk happens in the small, supportive structures of partnerships. Eventually, these partnerships will give children important opportunities to rehearse for writing, but when children are in the preproduction stage of learning English, a partnership with one other child could make the child at the early-production stage feel trapped, like a deer in the headlights, with nowhere to hide. Still, it is crucial that new arrivals are expected to join into the class as best they can from the start. There is never a time when new arrivals sit on the edge of the community, watching. Instead, the rug spot for the new arrival needs to be right in the center of the meeting area, and from the start, when children turn and

talk during the Active Engagement section of a minilesson, these children must know that they belong to a conversational group.

Children in the early stages of learning English benefit, however, from being in triads not partnerships; ideally one child in that triad will share the new arrival's native language but be more proficient in English, and the other will be a native speaker of English (and a language model).

Granted, children who are in the pre-production stage of learning English will mostly listen. Their more English-proficient partners can be shown how to speak with children who are at the beginning stages of learning English; like the teacher, more proficient partners can learn to use lots of gestures and to ask the child questions that can be answered with a yes or a no, a nod or a head shake.

I hope that I am making it clear that when a child in the first stages of acquiring English arrives in a classroom, the first goal is to make sure that child is immediately active and interactive. If this child is literate in his or her first language, than by all means, it is important for the child to write (and to read) in that language. If there are people in the classroom or the school who can speak the child's native language, we can rely on this buddy to convey to the child the kind of text that the class is writing, and some of the main ideas about that text. For example, this buddy might convey, "We are writing fiction stories, realistic ones with just a few characters in our stories and just a few different moments."

Whether or not the new arrival is literate in his first language, while that child writes as best he can in his first language, you will also want the child to begin doing some writing in English. Some teachers find that it helps for these children to have time-slots for first language and for English writing, with the child perhaps starting the writing workshop with fifteen minute to write in his language. (During this time, the child can write with volume that is comparable to other children and build his identity as a child who writes a lot.) But it is also important for this child to write in English.

Usually we start by asking the child who is at early stages of learning English to draw and label her drawing when writing in English. This, of course, is reminiscent of what we ask kindergarten and first-grade children to do. Of course, there is nothing "elementary" about learning a second language, and yet taking children new to English through the progression of work that younger children in a writing workshop experience has all sorts of advantages. After a child has drawn and labeled in English for a bit, we can ask the child to start writing in sentences. These children need the same range of paper choices that we normally offer to children in earlier grades. Examples can be printed from the CD-ROM available in the *Units of Study for Primary Writing* series. It is especially important that these children have access to paper that contains a large box on the top of a page, and several lines for writing under that box. The size of the box shrinks and number of lines increases as children develop proficiency in English. This progression of paper is an extremely powerful way to scaffold children's language development. Imagine that the child has written about a soccer game in her first language, and drawn a series of sketches showing what happened first, next, and last in the game. Then, with help from English-speaking children, the child labels each drawing with lots of English words, providing the child with a picture dictionary that is tailored to that child's exact story. It is not such a big step, then, to ask this child to use those words and write a sentence or two to accompany each of the child's drawings.

If a teacher has children who are in the early stages of English acquisition, it is especially important to provide them with extra help understanding the content of a minilesson. If there is an English as a Second Language teacher who is willing to provide support, this can also

be extremely beneficial. Some ESL teachers push in to classrooms, some ESL teachers pull out children for work in the ESL room. In either case, if classroom teachers and ESL teachers are provided with opportunities for planning together, the ESL teacher can support the children during writing workshop by preteaching the concepts and developing the vocabulary that will be necessary to understand what will be taught in the minilesson. For example, if the minilesson will teach children how to write with main ideas and support ideas, the ESL teacher might use a nonfiction content area book and lots of gestures to convey that the title of the book is the main idea or the big idea, and then to convey that some of the subtitles are support ideas (or smaller ideas). The teacher could reinforce the concept of ordination and subordination (without using those terms) by showing that the classroom represents a big topic, the library area could represent a subtopic.

There are ways to alter minilessons so as to support English language learners. First, we will want our minilessons to be as concise as possible. If you are working with such a population, you'll want to trim the minilessons in this series! Then, too, visuals can make a huge difference. It helps to draw and act as you talk. Sketch almost any story as you tell it. If you want to describe the way in which a writer can "stretch out" sections of a story, for example, it helps to tug on the ends of a rubber band whenever saying the term, "stretch out." We will also probably make a special point of using examples that children can relate to. It's helpful to repeat the teaching point more often with children who are just learning English.

Some teachers find that if we've used write-in-the-air to demonstrate something and want children to learn from our example, children profit from first retelling the teacher's version of the text before they then apply these principles to their own content. This leads some teachers to set up a double Active Engagement within many minilessons. Similarly, when we want children to turn and talk, it can help to set them up with cue cards. In *Breathing Life into Essays*, for example, we might give them cards that say "one example"..."another example...."

If the child has not received schooling in her first language or if that schooling has been especially interrupted, the child will face many more challenges. Expect this child to require extra support for a number of years. For children learning English, the writing workshop will provide a rich form of language education. Children will be learning to write, of course, but they will also learn to narrate, summarize, predict, describe, elaborate, question, to extend their vocabulary, and best of all, to use language to interact with each other and to set ideas and places, people and events onto the page.

Support in the Later Stages of Learning English

As children begin to acquire more fluency in English, they will be able to understand written and spoken English when they have concrete contexts (pictures, actions, sounds, and so on). As they develop these proficiencies, we often move them from triads to partnerships (or we nudge them to become one of the more vocal members of a triad, with a new preproduction ELL joining in as best he or she can). We know these learners will not always use correct syntax but we also know they can participate fully in partnership work.

As children become more proficient in English, their answers to questions will be more extended, but of course, their hold on English grammar and vocabulary will still be approximate. Again, partners (and teachers) can be coached to realize that this is not a time for correcting grammar. Instead, it is a time for extending what the child says. If the child points to a picture she has drawn as part of a story

she's written and says, "Mom," then we'll want to expand on this. "That's your mom?" [pause for nod] "You and your Mom" [pointing] "went in the car?" [pointing] "Where did you go?" [gesturing to illustrate that the question pertained to where the car drove]. If the child isn't sure how to answer, we can eventually supply options, "Did you go to the store? Or to the park?"

In order to help children bring a growing repertoire of language from the minilessons into their independent work, the teacher will often scaffold the writing that children do (and also the conversations that children have during work time with their partners) by providing them with conversational prompts. For example, in *Breathing Life into Essays*, the teacher might teach children to write or say, "I see...." and then to shift and write or say, "I think...." The thought can be elaborated on when the child learns to use transition phrases such as, "For example...." Children who are just learning English may rely heavily on these prompts, and teachers may even write cue cards for them.

It is important for teachers to celebrate the work that children at this stage of early emergent English are producing, focusing on the content and quality of the story not on the correctness of the syntax. These children are taking risks and teachers need to help them to feel successful.

But meanwhile, children also need instruction. For example, if children are writing personal narratives, a teacher might teach and then post transition words that show that a little time has passed such as, "Then...," "Later...," "After a while...," "Five minutes later...," or "Next...." The teacher might remind children that in their stories, as they move from one dot on a timeline to the next, they will often use a time word to show that time has passed. To practice this, the teacher might ask one partner to tell another what he or she did since walking in the classroom, remembering to insert words that show the passage of time. When partners meet, teachers can suggest that they talk through the sequence of events on each child's timeline, using time words as the storyteller progresses from one dot on the timeline to the next. Each child will also benefit from having a list of these transition words during work time, itself.

Support in Learning Academic English

As important as it is for us, as teachers, to tailor work time during the writing workshop so that children in the early stages of English acquisition receive the help they need, it is equally important for us to be cognizant that children who are in later stages of language acquisition also need special support. When children reach intermediate fluency, they demonstrate increased levels of accuracy and are able to express their thoughts and feelings in English. They often sound as if their English is stronger than it is—this is because although these children have developed conversational skills, often they still do not have academic English language skills. These children often seem to be very proficient in English. They have a strong command of social English, and can use English to chat with each other, to learn what the teacher expects them to do, to talk about the events of the day. They may sound "fluent" in social conversation where complex structures can be avoided, but it is often difficult to follow them when they describe events from another time and place.

The challenge for these children is that they need now to learn academic English; in order to learn this, they need input from people who can provide strong language models and from skilled teachers. At this stage it is very important for teachers to work on elaboration and specificity so as to help children use more descriptive and extended language. It is also important for these children to be partnered with children for whom English is their first language, children who can function as strong language models. The interesting thing is that often, when teachers have a handful of children who are in the earliest stages of language acquisition and a handful who are further along, teachers devote most of their special attention to the children who are the newest to English. However, the truth is that if we set new arrivals up with the proper invitations to work, support-structures from other children, and ways of being interactive, they can learn a huge amount from each other. Meanwhile, children who have a good command of social English but not of academic English need help which is less readily available from the peer group.

One way to determine whether a child needs help with academic English is to talk to the child about the story in a novel or about something that happened in another time and place. Invite the child to retell an episode from the book or from the child's experience; listen well. If the child's language is such that you have a hard time really piecing together what she is intending to communicate, chances are good this child needs support with "academic English." That is, the phrase 'academic' English does not refer only to the language that is used in discipline-based studies. The phrase refers to the language that a person must use in order to communicate about a time and place which are distant and unfamiliar, which must be created by the words.

Children who need help with academic English will profit from explicit instruction tailored to their needs. For example, these children benefit from instruction in connectives. They tend to write in simple sentences, linked together with the connector, *and*. It is important for children to study connectors because when English language learners learn to read as well as to write, these can become a source of confusion. Many readers assume that sentences are arranged in chronological order. However, in many sentences, that assumption is incorrect, for example, "I went to the office because the principal called for me over the PA system." In small-group instruction, then, teachers will want to provide English Language Learners with explicit instruction to help them understand connectors, tenses, pronoun references, and so forth.

Of course, English Language Learners also need support in developing a rich vocabulary, and again, children benefit from explicit instruction. If a child overuses a word such as *nice* or *beautiful*, a teacher will want to help children learn that there are many different, more precise words the child could use. Is the person lovely? Impressive? Unusual? Dignified? Cute? Some teachers help children to develop word files, with the overused word at the center of a card, and five variations of that word around the edges. Children keep these cards on hand throughout the day and look for opportunities to use specific words orally (some teachers ask children to place a check mark beside a word each time they use it orally).

This word bank would also be on hand when the child writes. If a child decides that her beloved mother is not dignified but cute, then the child's personal connection to the word will make it more memorable than had the child merely encountered it in a class on vocabulary.

Children learning English will need support as they come to understand and to use figurative language. Of course, literature is filled with metaphor and simile, as are the minilessons in these series. Children who are just on the brink of learning academic English will profit from some small-group instruction which gives them access to literary devices.

Similarly, if children are writing about a particular subject, the teacher or an English-speaking buddy may want to help the child build a domain-specific vocabulary to draw upon as he or she writes. If the child is writing about attending a carnival, the child would benefit from having a conversation about his experience at the carnival. This sort of rehearsal is important to every writer, but it can provide an extra language support to the English Language Learner who is ready to learn precise vocabulary.

OUR TEACHING IN EVERY UNIT CAN SUPPORT WRITING GOALS—AND LANGUAGE GOALS

When teachers approach a unit of study we need to think about the language needs of ELL children in the classroom: What are the language skills that our children need to have in order to understand the work that they are being asked to do? We need to think not only about the writing skills and strategies that will be developed in a unit, but also about the language language skills the unit will support. We need to think about the vocabulary, the idiomatic expressions, the connectives, the conjunctions, and about the grammar we want children to develop in a unit. There has to be a plan for content and a plan for language, side by side.

When approaching a unit in essay writing, for example, we can anticipate that we'll be teaching children to explain, describe, compare, categorize and question. We can anticipate that mostly we'll be helping children write in present tense, and that they'll benefit from learning connectives such as *if, when, because, for example, another example*, and so forth. We can plan that we might provide scaffolds such as a chart of phrases and we can know in advance that children may need help with instructional terms such as *fact, example, reason, thought*, and *idea*. We know we may teach the language of comparison, including, for example, the use of the '-er' and '-est' word endings, as in 'big, bigger, biggest.'

The power of written curriculum is that a group of teachers can hold our hopes for teaching in our hands, and talk and think together about how we can take our own best ideas and make them better. One of the most important ways to make our teaching stronger is to think, "How can we give all children access to this teaching?" The wonderful thing about a workshop is that it is incredibly supportive for English Language Learners—but if you bring your best idea to the table, you can make the writing workshop even more supportive.

CHAPTER II

PREPARING FOR STANDARDIZED WRITING TESTS

As I write this chapter, my son Evan is downstairs, working with a stopwatch at his side, practicing yet one more time for the writing component of his April SAT exam. He and I know that on that exam, he will have twenty-five minutes to read a prompt, then to plan, write, and edit a well-constructed essay. In the essay, he's been told to reference a classic novel and an episode from history. He also needs to write with an opening hook, an introductory anecdote, a thesis statement which lays out a framing idea, and two body paragraphs, each beginning with a transition and ending with references to his thesis statement and his framing idea. The essay will ideally end with yet another anecdote, with a nod to the thesis, and with a new twist on the original idea. And Evan needs to do all this in twenty-five minutes! Frankly, despite all the advantages that Evan has been given, he and I are both sweating over the demands of this high-stakes test.

Meanwhile, he will no sooner finish the SAT exam than it will be time for the ACT exam, followed by a whole series of AP exams. And of course, Evan is not alone. Children in all our schools are being subjected to high-stakes assessments as never before, and some of these assessments have life-changing consequences for children. There was a time when fourth and eighth grades were "the testing grades." Now tests tyrannize every grade, every year.

That tyranny is felt by teachers as well as by students. Our students' performances on standardized assessments have very real consequences on our right to teach according to our best beliefs. It is an understatement, then, to say that standardized tests have important implications for those of us who teach children. It is therefore important to take into account the demands of high-stakes writing assessments when we plan a yearlong curriculum in the teaching of writing.

KNOWLEDGE IS POWER

Knowledge of standardized tests can allow you to avoid being victimized by the testing and test-prep industry, and to teach test prep with the same clarity with which you teach anything else.

Several years ago, Kate Montgomery (the editor of this series), Donna Santman and I coauthored a book about standardized reading tests entitled, *A Teacher's Guide to Standardized Reading Tests: Knowledge Is Power*. When doing the research for that book, my colleagues and I came to realize that many of us were painfully uninformed about the reading assessments that hold such sway over us and our children. The fact that so many teachers are not knowledgeable about the tests is not surprising. Teachers often regard the tests with hostility—we don't want to give them any more attention than is absolutely required! But a lack of knowledge about the tests will backfire, making us easy victims. This remarkably unprincipled industry feeds on developing test-anxiety in teachers and school leaders and then providing test prep materials, at a price, to supposedly allay those anxieties. Our study further convinced us that much of what was being taught in the name of test prep added to students' confusion, consolidated their unhelpful test-taking habits, and in general, wreaked havoc. It was fascinating and frightening for us to find that teachers who would never dream of importing random bits of curriculum into their school day, who would never consider shoving any old materials that crossed their desks at their kids, were doing this with the test-prep materials. Meanwhile, those test-prep materials came at us from all sides, presumably from administrators whose anxieties translated into similar practices. It was as if everyone, at every level, was so anxious and out of his element that instead of constructing a crystal-clear approach to teaching test prep, we disregarded everything we knew about curriculum and teaching in the name of preparing kids for the craziness of standardized reading tests.

Thankfully, writing assessment has not yet escalated into quite the same frenzy. My clear suggestion is this: don't let a fear of writing assessment derail you from teaching writing well! Teach writing rigorously, following the pathways laid out in this series, and I promise you that the results will be dramatic, palpable, obvious, and lasting. I have received not dozens but hundreds—perhaps thousands—of responses to the primary series of books, with teachers saying, "I would never have believed that my kids could do so much." Those kids will be growing up and coming into your upper-elementary classrooms, so right there, you'll find that the tests are less daunting. And if you teach writing well and do so within a curriculum that emphasizes the structures of narrative and essay writing, your kids will be absolutely ready for you to show them how to take all they know and use it to shine on those assessments.

Writing assessments for children in the elementary grades differ, state by state. Some assessments require students to produce a narrative, others ask for one version or another of an essay (this is sometimes a literary essay, sometimes a personal/persuasive essay, and sometimes a persuasive letter shaped like an essay). Some writing assessments do not channel children toward one kind of writing or another, leaving this open. The units of study in these books will go a very long way toward preparing your students for any one of these assignments, but it will be important for you to analyze the demands put on your children so that you can tweak these units, if this seems called for, and provide the supplemental instruction your children need.

Of course, the first thing you will think about is that on their assessments, your children will need to read and analyze a prompt or an assignment so that they understand what they are being called to do and can go about planning a piece of writing which meets requirements set forth by someone else. As part of this, they need to be able to read their own writing with objective eyes, seeing ways in which it does and does not meet the criterion for success, and also seeing ways in which the paper could be altered so it would be judged more successful. These two skills are closely related, and together translate into the fact that students need to be able to read and analyze an assignment or prompt, to create a mental representation of what it is they are expected to do, and to proceed, letting their work fit the contours of what someone else expects them to do.

Then, too, in every state, children will be asked to write quickly, on demand, and in a relatively correct and well-organized fashion from the start; again, this will be addressed in some detail later in this chapter.

Although kids will not, in the writing workshop, be accustomed to writing under a stopwatch in response to a prompt or an assignment, the writing that they will be expected to produce on their assessments will be simpler versions of what they have been writing all along. That is, if a fourth grader is asked to write a narrative on a state test, the narrative the child produces will be vastly more impressive if she even gestures toward writing with detail, making characters talk, bringing out the internal as well as the external story, developing the heart of the story and so forth as she has learned to do in this yearlong curriculum. This curriculum expects much more of nine-, ten- and eleven-year-olds than any state test! Similarly, if children are asked to write an essay (or to persuade or argue), the child's writing will be vastly more impressive if the child remembers to develop a thesis with supportive claims, to embed stories which make the point, to return back to the thesis statement often. All of this WILL be asked of children when they are sixteen years old and hoping to ace the SAT exam, but there won't be any state which asks or expects nine-year-old children to do this.

On the other hand, there may be some small ways in which your state's assessments require something more than what children have learned through the units of study. For example, when children are asked to respond to quotations, they will need to reference texts and, in some instances, to ascertain and acknowledge the point of view (or bias) of a particular text. Similarly, by the time children are in middle school, some states expect that a persuasive (expository) essay will include a section in which the writer acknowledges and refutes opposing arguments. You will want to review your state assessments to determine

if there are any ways in which they ask children to do something a bit more than what they will learn through this yearlong curriculum.

And yes, there will be some things you need to teach under the auspices of test prep. When you do this teaching, remember that you will want to use the same methods to teach test prep that you use to teach anything else. Curriculum writers from the test prep company Stanley-Kaplan recently attended several Teachers College Reading and Writing Project institutes and then met with me to ask for my blessing in hiring a Project staff developer as a consultant to them as they wrote a series of test prep minilessons books. They did write those books—a whole series of them, each patterned after these *Units of Study* books, each containing minilessons which begin with a connection that includes a teaching point, and each of which follows this architecture of minilessons. My point is not to endorse those materials, my point is that if Kaplan, which has a tremendous knowledge of standardized tests and yet has hardly been a bastion of progressive teaching methods, has decided that writing workshop teachers could use workshop methods to teach a brief test-prep unit, then surely you and I should feel confident if we come to this same conclusion!

TESTS THAT CALL FOR PERSUASIVE OR EXPOSITORY WRITING

What do children need to know and be able to do in order to perform well on assessments that ask for persuasive or expository writing? How do these expectations align with and diverge from the writing skills developed in these *Units of Study*?

The first job is not for *students* to analyze prompts and internalize criterion, it is for *you and I* to do this. We need to do this while also keeping in mind what children will and will not have already learned to do. That way, we can plan ways to teach children how to apply what they know to the assessment and we can design teaching to help them learn what they may not yet know. Prompts which ask children to argue, persuade, or take a position and give reasons are common and I suspect these will become increasingly common as SAT-style tests trickle down into lower and lower grades.

Let's pause for just a moment to think about the SAT exams—that is, about the writing requirement that children will need to respond to six, seven or eight years *after* they are with us (and that is a long time).

On the SAT exam, students are given an assignment such as this: "Do you believe that that which doesn't kill you makes you stronger? Write an essay supporting your point of view. Use texts, experiences and observations to support your position."

The initial question can change: What is your opinion of the claim that honesty is not the best policy? What is your opinion of the claim that without knowledge of the past, we cannot truly understand the present? Of the claim that sometimes making a bad decision is better than making no decision at all? That disagreement leads to progress? That censorship is sometimes merited? In all of these instances, students are asked to write in a fashion that very closely resembles the essays they are taught to write in these *Units of Study*.

Granted, students who are writing their SAT exam essays are told to begin their essays with a hook, which might be a rhetorical question or a personal anecdote. For example, Evan began his essay on facing difficulties with a ministory about caving with his peers, crawling headfirst into a tunnel-like cave, then feeling a lump of fear and deciding to persevere, realizing that facing difficulties can make you stronger. In *Breathing Life into Essays* we downplayed the importance of a catchy lead. But teachers could make the decision to spotlight this facet of essay writing.

Then, in their SAT essays, students need to turn the question into a thesis, a claim. Evan's (very expensive) SAT

tutors have assured him that it is totally acceptable to write something strictly based on the prompt such as, "I believe that what doesn't kill us can make us stronger." Then writers must include what the makers of SAT exams refer to as a "framing idea." Your children will think of it as one, overarching reason for the thesis statement: "I believe that what doesn't kill us can make us stronger *because we learn to push past our limitations*." Then, on SAT essays, students are expected to write two body paragraphs and in each, they are expected to refer to and then talk about one example that supports this claim. Ideally, in one paragraph, the student will refer to an example from either literature or history; in the other paragraph, the writer could again do that or could draw on personal experience. Each body paragraph needs a topic sentence that begins with a transitional word or phrase and then also refers back to the thesis or framing idea. One body paragraph might begin, "Just as I faced fears when crawling into that cave, so, too, Hamlet, the protagonist of Shakespeare's tragedy, needed to face his limitations." The next body paragraph would also stack evidence, building on the previous example, with a topic sentence that might start, "The need to face difficulties is evident not only in literature but also in history." Finally, in the ending paragraph, the writer must restate the thesis statement, and refer back to the examples. The essay will have even more flair if the writer can add a little twist to the end. My son is practicing finding a way to bring the phrase, "in order to make a better world," into the last sentence of almost every trial-run essay he's written!

My point in detailing this is simply this: as you read this, those of you who have studied the *Units of Study* in personal and literary essay will see that the *Units of Study* teach third graders to do most of what eleventh graders are required to do! So, you can rest assured that yes, indeed, these *Units of Study* will provide your children with the preparation they need.

Remember, during this section I am specifically addressing the times when elementary students are asked to write persuasive or expository essays. These prompts are different than prompts that ask students simply to *address a topic*—to tell about an experience you remember—without specifying how students are to approach that topic. In those cases, the writer will need to define the kind of writing for himself. Prompts that call for expository or persuasive writing are also different from those that ask students to write narratives: "Write about one time in your life that you remember well."

For now, let me say that if our intermediate students are asked to write expository or persuasive pieces, these will be significantly lighter versions of the SAT prompts I've detailed. Students may be asked: "Do you think students should wear uniforms to school? Tell why or why not, and give reasons." This prompt could have a different spin, starting with the same question about school uniforms (or whether standardized tests are wise, or whether recess is important) but the invitation to argue for one's point of view is followed with an attempt to make the exam feel more "real-life." For example, students may be asked: "Write a letter to the school principal arguing your point of view. Be sure to give reasons to support your opinion." Sometimes the test asks elementary students to address claims such as these: "Decisions (mistakes, challenges, classes, people) can change lives. Tell about a decision (or a mistake, a challenge, a class, a person) that/who taught you an important lesson."

Sometimes students will be asked to write persuasive or expository pieces in response to a text they have read: "In such and such text, what does the main character learn about friendship? Support your answers with details from the text." Or "In such and such text, do you think so and so was a good friend? Explain why or why not. Use examples from the text."

Sometimes children are asked to argue a point, and to do so by providing reasons that will be available to them in the texts they are asked to read. For example, after reading two articles about the harm that pollution is causing birds, children may be asked to write in response to this question: "Do you think pollution is endangering birds? Give reasons to support your answer and use examples from both texts to support your argument."

It is important for us to read a prompt or an assignment and see the kind of text that students are being asked to write. When I analyze most of these assignments, it seems to me that the most demanding ones ask us to teach students to do these things:

- *Our students need to be able to write a crystal clear thesis in which they make a claim, rather than stating a fact or asking a question.* This claim is generally related to the prompt, but if the prompt asks "Do you think children should spend holidays with their family?" or "Do you think this character was a good friend?" the student needs to not only state his or her point of view on the question, but also provide a reason, probably using the connector *because*. For example, the student might write, "I think children should spend holidays with their families because it makes families closer," or "Charlotte, the main character in *Charlotte's Web*, is a good friend to Wilbur because she does everything she can to save him from being killed."

- *Our students need to provide more than one example to support the thesis and each must be linked to the thesis.* Children need to learn to preface examples with a transitional word, phrase, or sentence. This transition before each example might be a topic sentence that sets up the support paragraph, one topic sentence for each example and for each paragraph. In fact, however, it is very rare for children in third through fifth grade to be expected to support their thesis across several paragraphs. However, if children are doing this in school anyhow and if enough time is provided, you might suggest children do write two support paragraphs when writing their on-demand essay—paragraphing reminds a writer (and the assessor) to pay attention to structure. The bare-bones expectation for persuasive or expository writing, however, is simply that the child makes a claim—"I think children should spend time with their families because this makes families closer"—and then elaborates with an example or two, each prefaced with a transitional phrase. It might read, "One example is that last summer I went camping with my family...." And, later, "Another example occurred last week when..." Or, better yet, the transitions could be stacked, "I learned that spending vacations with my family made us closer *not only* when we went camping together, *but also* when we...."

- *Children ideally learn to unpack their examples after they've laid them out.* This tends to make essays very strong, though it is usually not required. Unpacking the example involves returning to the claim, and explicitly talking about how the example illustrates the claim. "This story about when I went camping with my family shows that families become closer when vacationing together. My family is usually too busy to spend time together but when we went camping, we became closer by...."

- *Our students need to learn to write a concluding sentence or two in which they restate their initial claim and refer to their examples.* Ideally the writer adds a little twist to this section of the essay, perhaps by referring to a greater good, or to a larger lesson, such as "When you sit down to think up all the fun things that you can do on your next vacation, be sure to consider spending time with your family."

I describe teaching to these ends in great depth during the units of study on personal and literary essays. Once a teacher has studied the

assessments, then, and related them to the *Units of Study*, it will be important to reassure students and their parents that when test day arrives, children will simply be asked to write a kind of thing they have been writing all along in the writing workshop. You will want to talk with students about how you will get them ready for the odd context that comes with testing situations—this writing is timed and written in response to a prompt.

It is important for us to look over the task and find a way to say to our students, "You definitely know how to do this already! This will be no big deal for you at all!" If that is not the case—if there ARE writing muscles students need to succeed on your district's assessment, then by all means weave these into your own version of the *Units of Study* in writing or into curriculum in other subjects. No matter what, you will need to approach test prep having already taught students the skills they will need to draw upon, so that test prep is simply a matter of showing children how easy it is to draw on the muscles they've developed elsewhere to produce something within the new (and yes, stressful) context.

TESTS THAT CALL FOR NARRATIVE WRITING

What do children need to know and be able to do in order to perform well on assessments that ask for narrative writing? How do these expectations align with and diverge from the writing skills developed in these *Units of Study*?

Some assessments will ask children to write narratives rather than to make and defend claims. The prompt might direct children to "Write a story about a time when you overcame a challenge (learned something new, made something special, met someone who changed you, were given a present, opened a door and found something surprising...). Include a beginning, a middle and an end, and write with details." Sometimes, instead, children will be asked to create short fiction. For example, they may be asked to write a story about a picture of a little girl and a dog standing under an umbrella, with rain pouring down around them. Perhaps there is something else in the scene—say, a kitten who is drenched, or a taxi cab approaching.

When children are asked to write a story, they will be expected to do exactly what they have learned in the *Units of Study*. That is, they will need to decide *who* is doing *what* in this story, and to imagine a timeline of events. If the writer writes all about the girl under the umbrella— "There is a girl under the umbrella. She is dry because of the umbrella. She is wearing a dress...."— then the writer would not fare well on this assessment. The task is to tell a story. The child would fare far better if he instead relied on what he'd learned in *Launching the Writing Workshop* and *Improving the Quality of Narrative Writing* and began the story with the main character doing or saying something, "'Move in close to me,' Hannah said to Rufus, her German shepard. 'This umbrella is big enough for both of us.' Just then, ..."

When children are asked to write narratives, the most important thing is that they do just that—write a Small Moment. Their stories will receive better ratings if they include:

- dialogue

- a character feeling something strong and therefore trying to do something

- details, especially descriptive details of the setting

- a resolution or a character learning a lesson

This last element of resolution can be created by the writer standing back from the story and writing a sentence or two of "reflection" on it: "That was the day when he learned ..." or, "Now, years later, she still remembers that time because...."

FROM WRITING WORKSHOP TO WRITING-TO-THE-PROMPT

It is late March as I write this chapter, and my son has agreed to spend half an hour on many days of his spring vacation, practicing writing-to-a-prompt, with a cell phone (masquerading as a stop watch) beside him. His SAT exam is two weeks away, and now is a good time for Evan to prep for that exam. When kids are subjected to high-stakes tests, there is no question that we need to set them up for success on those tests, and one part of this will entail teaching children how to read, analyze, and respond to prompts and other forms of writing assignments. But let me be clear: Evan is spending *two weeks* before the SAT exam practicing writing-to-the-prompts. This writing-to-the-prompt is a wonderful form of test prep, but it would be a lousy writing curriculum. He is able to rally what it takes to write-to-the-prompt because of the rich writing life which his teachers have given him all along.

I sometimes encounter schools where concern for test scores has led teachers to substitute a daily drill of test prep for writing instruction. Thankfully, I do not find it necessary to spend a great deal of time arguing that a steady diet of writing-to-the-prompt couldn't possibly take the place of a rigorous writing curriculum because the student work speaks for itself. I simply display our kids' work and say "Do your kids write like this? Like this?" Children's work speaks for itself, and it is inevitably the case that children who are taught to write well have vastly more resources to draw upon when they are asked to write under timed conditions in response to an assigned prompt.

But of course, it is still important to teach children to read and analyze the prompt. In the schools I know best, teachers ask children to read the prompts very carefully, and to look especially for the kind of writing they are asked to produce. Teachers sometimes ask children to circle the verb that tells what sort of writing they are to do. Does the prompt ask for them to argue? Convince? Tell a story? Explain? Those words will give writers a clue about what is expected, but they will also want to look for and underline words that name the genre they are writing. Are they being asked to write an essay? A story? A letter to convince?

The most important mental work that a child must do when analyzing a prompt is determining what the test calls for, and then fitting this call to action into his knowledge of how to write well. That is, if the child reads the prompt and learns that he is to write about a day when he felt scared, he needs to decide whether he will write this as a story, calling to mind all he knows about writing focused narratives, or as an essay, calling to mind all he knows about writing according to what he will think of as a "boxes-and-bullets" structure.

Of course, responding to prompts is immeasurably easier if children have writing experience to draw upon! Imagine what it must be like for a child who is asked to write a story about the picture of a girl, holding an umbrella, if that child does not know what writers do to go about writing a story. Imagine what it must be like for a child to be asked to argue that pollution is harming birds, drawing on information in two articles, if that child isn't accustomed to writing a concise, clear claim and supporting that claim with reasons and examples!

Test prep is no big deal, when writers enter into it having already developed the muscles they need to draw upon. But test prep alone can't possibly prepare our kids for the hurdles they will be expected to get over. For that, they need to be actively engaged in the writing process, thoroughly and often.

CHAPTER 12

ASSESSMENT

Our student writers put marks on the page and we, as teachers of writing, read the writing but also read the writer. We read as a reader, responding to the heartache and adventure, humor and information, that each child has encoded onto the page, laughing and gasping and inquiring in response to what we find there. We also read as a teacher of writing, noticing what the child has tried to do, has done, and can almost do.

Assessment occurs in little and big ways throughout every minute of the teaching my colleagues and I have described. As a school year unfurls, not only our curriculum but also our assessments change.

ASSESSMENT THAT INFORMS US AS WE DEVELOP A CURRICULAR CALENDAR

Toward the end of a school year or the start of the summer, when teachers across a grade level—or a lone teacher, if need be—devote a good deal of time to planning the upcoming year's curriculum, it is crucial to begin by assessing the year that is ending and the work our departing students have done during that year. We want to reflect on our teaching, on the work our students have done, and on the progress our students have (and have not) made. We do all this with an eye toward growing new curricular plans for the year ahead.

- What worked? Did my teaching feel especially vital and strong during particular units of study? What made it work then? How can I build on this so that more of my teaching feels this way in the year ahead?

- What didn't work? Where did my teaching seem to flounder? What lessons can be drawn from that? How can I make curricular (and other) plans for the year ahead so that my teaching gets stronger? Should I tackle different units of study? Secure more support for particular units of study? Develop my own muscles for teaching particular things? What game plan could I develop that might help me outgrow myself?

- What have students learned? In looking over my students' written products, what have almost all of my students learned to do as a result of my teaching? How can I be sure to provide next year's students with these same opportunities—and help next year's students go even farther?

- What do students need to learn? In what ways could my students' work be dramatically strengthened? Obviously, it will take more than curricular plans to strengthen student work, but how can I design units of study that will help take students on the journey I have in mind for them?

ASSESSMENT THAT INFORMS US AS WE PLAN FOR THE FIRST DAYS OF SCHOOL

Summer has a way of slipping away quickly, and all of a sudden a new academic year is upon us, with a host of new children. It is crucial for us to make real contact with each and every child as quickly as we possibly can. Children need to come into our classroom and feel seen and heard. They need this instantly—all of them. How helpful it is if we give ourselves a head start!

Toward the end of each academic year, many schools organize what some people call "up and down" visits. The fifth-grade teachers spend a week (or a day) teaching fourth grade, the fourth-grade teachers teach third grade, and the third-grade teachers, second grade. Ideally, these visits happen with the host teacher in the classroom, but usually isn't possible. The visiting teacher then follows the host teacher's plans (the host teacher may meanwhile be at his or her feeder-grade level). In either case the visiting teacher learns something about the nature and abilities of the children he or she will be teaching next year. The following September, the teachers can deliberately create consistency across the two years by reminding children what they were able to do at the end of the preceding year and telling them this will be the starting point for the new year. This makes a world of difference; too often teachers' expectations do not move children along a thoughtful gradient of difficulty from year to year. For example, children may be writing two six-page books a week at the end of second grade, then move on to third grade teachers who act pleased if they produce half a page in a day's writing workshop!

Some teachers find it helps to write children's parents a letter in the summer. "I know my teaching will be strongest if I connect with your child as quickly as I can. Could you take a few minutes to write and tell me about your daughter? Tell me about her passions and her worries; tell me about her friendships and her family. What does she like to do when she has a free day?" When we know our children as individuals, it is much easier to teach them.

Assessment must occur continually as we teach writing. The child does something—anything—and we, as teachers, think, "What is this child showing me? What might the child be trying to do? Able to do? What seems to be just beyond the child's independent grasp?" The child acts, and the teacher interprets those actions and thinks, "How can I best respond?"

The challenge in writing about assessment is that assessment happens in so many ways, for so many purposes, that it is hard to pin down. Assessment is the thinking teacher's mind work. It is the intelligence that guides our every moment as a teacher.

GUIDING PRINCIPLES FOR ASSESSMENT

When we, as teachers, assess a child as a writer, we try to discern what the child can do independently so that we can determine the next step this child should take. Just as readers benefit if teachers help them progress along a gradient of difficulty, help them read books that are just a tiny bit beyond their independent reach, so too writers need instruction that scaffolds them to extend what they can do one notch farther. The curriculum laid out in these *Units of Study* suggests one trail along which writers develop, but there are lots of lines of growth for writers, and a skilled teacher can note what a child is doing and where she could, with help, be able to go along any one of those lines of growth.

For example, the teacher can look at a child's ability to organize non-narrative writing. Can the child distinguish topic-based subcategories so that information on "feeding my dog" is in a different place that information on "training my dog"? If the child can do this, can she or he also organize the information within any subcategory according to some principle? Is there some logic—any logic—informing the sequence of information in the "feeding my dog" section?

Teachers of writing need to be able to look at a piece of writing with a particular growth line in mind, name what the child can do along that growth line, and imagine what a logical next step might be. This assessment is necessary in order to provide children with the scaffolds they need to develop as writers. What a child can do at one moment with support, he or she should be able to do at another moment with independence.

Our assessments will be more sound if, at any one time, we deliberately choose the lens through which we look. If we don't consciously make this choice, we probably apply different criteria to different children. That is, without even realizing we are doing so, we may end up looking at the strong writers' work with an eye toward organization and looking at less experienced writers' work only for spelling and penmanship. Of course, there are countless possible lenses through which teachers could view their students as writers. How are children doing at storytelling rather than summarizing a narrative? At elaborating in ways that build significance? At spelling sight words correctly? At writing story endings? At producing a lot of work? At getting started writing without needing a personal nudge? At rereading their own work? At writing with detail?

It is sometimes worthwhile to look over the entire class, thinking, "How are all my children doing in any one area?" For example, we could ask, "How are all my children doing at writing stories in which a character moves sequentially through time?" This will probably result in our gathering clusters of children together and providing each cluster with some small-group strategy lessons. We may, at times, decide to look across all our children in order to assess a particular aspect of their work. We could look at something as simple as the amount of text a child is producing in a given writing workshop. Which children wrote at least a page-and-a-half today? Which wrote approximately a page? Which wrote half a page or less? We could, on the other hand, look at something less obvious. For example, we could look at the conjunctions children use in their sentences, which will tend to reveal their sentence complexity. We could look at the scale of their revision work. How many add and delete pages? Paragraphs? Phrases only?

Of course, the reason to group children is so that we are ready to differentiate instruction in the area of consideration. The discovery that some children are revising by altering phrases only is not an assessment of them so much as of us—and it is a wake-up call as well. Obviously, there is nothing in the child's genetic makeup that means the child only revises minute portions of his or her text! How will we teach those children so that this changes?

If assessments are going to inform instruction, it is crucial that we understand that the questions are always "What can a child do now?" and "What can a child almost do now?" The question "What can't a child do?" doesn't tend to inform instruction, because there will always be vast terrain that is beyond any given learner. Just because a child can't synthesize information from six sources or write citations with correct footnotes does not mean this is what we should teach him to do these things! But if we notice that a child makes characters in her drawings speak in speech balloons but has never yet made characters in her written stories speak, then it is logical to think we could perhaps show her how to bring the contents of those speech balloons into the text of her story. The job of assessment, then, involves finding the growing tip of a child's writing development and nurturing it.

When we are learning a skill, it's great fun to see ourselves getting better. Whether we are learning to play softball or swim or roller-skate, it helps to have concrete goals and to be able to see and record our progress toward those goals. The fledgling swimmer works hard to swim from one side of the pool to the other. When he meets this goal, he is ready for the next one and will work hard to achieve it.

Writing development occurs on lots of fronts, and children can't consciously tackle all the goals we have in mind. They need to have a palpable, concrete sense of what good work entails and to be able to chart their progress toward at least some fairly obvious aspects of achieving it. Therefore, it is important to show children examples of good work that are within their reach and supply them with guidelines they can apply when assessing their own work.

It is also important that children join with us in noticing the pathway they've already traveled and in setting goals for the next phase of their development. People learn as much or more from attention to growth and celebrations of progress as from critique. Taking this into account, frank discussion should occur often in a conference. "I see you are able to do this now and that is great—what I think you need to reach toward now is this. Let me help you get started doing that, with me nearby to help. Okay, now see if you can keep going without me. Wow! You did it! From now on, do this whenever you write."

Whenever we assess what children know and can do as writers, it is important that we understand that the children are reflections of the effectiveness of our work with them. Whether we are classroom teachers, building principals, or involved staff developers, we need to understand that the information about what our children can and cannot do as writers is also information about what we have and have not done in our respective roles. What have we done well? What must we begin to do better? What could be the sources of trouble? How might we best respond? The most valuable assessment is always self-assessment.

OPPORTUNITIES FOR ASSESSMENT

Writers' Notebooks

The good news about teaching writing is that children regularly give us demonstrations of what they know and can do. The first step toward becoming a teacher who assesses children's writing is being sure that each child has a writer's notebook and a folder containing his or her current work. Each writer should also have a different portfolio containing samples of work accumulated throughout the year or throughout several years.

The most important work to save is that produced by the child's own hand. That is, there are lots of reasons to edit, word-process, and publish children's writing, but for the purpose of assessment, the writing that really needs to be dated, organized, saved, and studied are the rough drafts of what children themselves have written.

The first tool for assessment, then, is the writer's notebook. Page through any child's notebook and one is immediately given a window onto this child as a writer. What are the range of topics that the child tends to write about? Are there some topics that reoccur, and how does the child's writing on these topics evolve over time? What does the child tend to do most often when he or she sits down to write? What patterns can one detect in how a child goes about starting a narrative? An entry that aims to become an essay? How does the child seem to keep him or herself going? What principles of elaboration are evident in the child's writing? How much of the child's writing seems to be done in school? At home? What sorts of topics or genre or conditions seem to generate energy for the child?

One of the most important things to look for is this: to what extent do we see evidence that instruction is effecting what the child does? Obviously, children sometimes will be influenced by instruction without necessarily using the instruction toward fruitful ends. But it is still very important simply to look for evidence that instruction is having an effect on children's writing.

If in all of this assessment we see that synapses are broken between teaching and learning, or we see that some children are not making palpable progress, then it is important to ask "why?" Similarly, when we see that our teaching is absolutely making a difference in some children's writing, and if we let children know this (and let them know that we know), their growth takes off and along the way and we stand a chance of hitching some wagons to those stars!

Goals and Rubrics

It is also important that teachers and children work toward clearly-specified goals within a unit of study and throughout the year. Of course, end-of-year standards need to inform the day-to-day decisions we make as we teach. To that end, we have specified clear goals for each unit of study, goals that help us assess each child and our own teaching

within each unit. You'll find a rubric in each *Unit of Study*, and all of them are on the accompanying CD-ROM.

The rubrics provided with the units are intended to serve two purposes. First, they name the intentions we have for writers in our classrooms as we move through the various units. Second, they encourage us to step back and see the commonalities across units—the "big ideas" in writing that are embodied in the series as a whole.

We strongly encourage you to make these documents your own. Working with colleagues, adapt them to the goals you have for the children in your care and use this format as an opportunity to talk and write about what matters to you as a learning community.

Writing Conferences

Although assessment weaves through every moment of our teaching, we especially assess during one-to-one writing conferences. For many years, teachers in our community carried clipboards with them and scrawled anecdotal notes about the child's topic, genre, and process decisions. Recently, however, we studied those anecdotal notes and found that sometimes the expectation that we must keep records during our conferences distracts us from feeling duty-bound to teach the child something during these interactions. We can find ourselves dutifully recording whatever the child says in a conference and then moving on, oblivious to our not having taught the child anything. In order to make it more likely that our conferences actually provide teaching opportunities, we have recently begun speculating in advance on the sorts of things we will watch for in order to see what children do. We watch with a record sheet in hand, and if children do something we regard as significant to the unit, we make note of it. If we teach the child a particular skill or strategy, then we record a *T* (for teaching) and hope that in the days ahead we'll observe (and record) the child doing this independently. In this way, our record sheet of the conferences we hold with individuals also records what individual writers are able to do.

Assessment is not an end in itself. Assessment must be purposeful to be either effective or useful. If our notes and files stay in the drawer or on the shelf gathering dust, they have been for naught. They need to be brought into the public eye from time to time to show what children can learn to do when given the chance. They are the evidence that allows us to teach in the ways we know are best for children. Static assessment files have their purpose in allowing us to be held accountable to others and ourselves for our teaching. But changing, growing assessment notes are most useful to our teaching and learning. When we take what we learn about our students and use that information to teach them more, teach them differently, place them in helpful learning contexts, and show them how their hard work has made a difference in their ability to make sense of and participate in the world, then our assessment has truly been worthy of us and worthy of our students.

APPENDIX

Frequently Asked Questions About This Series...And Some Answers

Has this curriculum been piloted?

The units of study described in the two series of books—*Units of Study for Primary Writing*, and *Units of Study for Teaching Writing, Grades 3–5*—grew from the Teachers College Reading and Writing Project's deep, intensive and long-lasting affiliation with thousands of schools across the nation and the world. For almost three decades, my colleagues and I at the Project have collaboratively developed ideas on the teaching of writing, and then helped teachers and school leaders bring those ideas to classrooms and schools where, in turn, we learn from the young writers who help us outgrow our best-draft ideas about the teaching of writing. This cycle of curriculum development, teaching, action-research, assessment, and curricular revision has meant that for almost thirty years, those of us who are affiliated with the remarkable community that coalesces around the Teachers College Reading and Writing Project have been able to stand on the shoulders of work that has gone before us.

When the leadership of New York City decided several years ago to bring the writing workshop to every classroom throughout the city, I knew that teachers would need extra curricular support. At the Teachers College Reading and Writing Project, we wrote incomplete, fast-draft versions of these units of study and distributed them in loose-leaf binders. I gave schools throughout New York City approximately 30,000 binders, each containing several hundred pages. These were trucked to the elementary and middle schools which ascribe to our Project's work. For three years now, we have watched those materials be translated into teaching and learning, and have continuously revised our thinking based on what we have learned. So yes, the series has been piloted.

Is there scientifically-based data vouching for the effectiveness of these curricular materials?

The only assessment measure that has been used for many years (thirty) and has been used across every state is the NAEP (National Assessment of Educational Progress). The NAEP has often been referred to as "the nation's report card," and it has been used to compare and contrast different state exams. Several years ago the NAEP assessment found that New York City's children write as well or better than children in every other major city except Charlotte (New Yorkers jokingly question whether Charlotte qualifies as a *major* city!).

Across the nation, NAEP scores have been basically unchanging for thirty years. The current administration declared a triumph when this year's national average rose 1%. Meanwhile, scores in New York City rose a dramatic 7%, since the city's leadership brought balanced literacy and assessment-based reading interventions to scale. New York City's African-American students and English Language Learners improved in even more dramatic ways. According to the NAEP, New York City's lower income African-American and Latino children far outperformed similar studies in large cities in the nation as a whole.

From 2005 until now, NAEP has disaggregated data to show progress in ten large urban cities. From the first data point in 2002 until the most recent data in 2005, New York City has made a 10% gain. Sheila Ford, who announced the NAEP scores in a press conference in Boston, said, "This is a very significant gain." It is particularly important to bear in mind that meanwhile, New York City has 1.1 million children with 85% of them eligible for free and reduced lunch.

There is a great deal of data suggesting that improvements in writing will have a payoff across the curriculum.

If a school or district adopts the two series—*Units of Study for Primary Writing* and *Units of Study for Teaching Writing, Grades 3-5*—will the books within these series be enough to sustain children's growth and teachers' instruction across all the grades?

The answer to this is no. These series of books were never intended to replace all the professional reading and study that teachers have been doing for all these years! You and your colleagues will absolutely need to continue to read other professional books, and you will need to continue to author your own ideas as well.

But yes, the two series of books can provide the *backbone* to a K–5 approach to the teaching of writing, bringing coherence to your school-wide or district-wide writing curriculum.

These books absolutely support a spiral curriculum. For example, the books can help teachers of kindergartners to support children as they begin drawing, labeling, telling and writing simple Small Moment stories—and then over the years, the books will help teachers equip children to use more and more complex concepts, tools and strategies so that by fifth grade, children are not only writing sophisticated stories, they are also embedding those stories in memoir and personal essays, and using techniques developed in personal narrative to write short fiction. In a similar fashion, this spiraling curriculum supports teachers in scaffolding children's writing of expository and informational texts.

The truth is that at no point will the books suffice as a script for your teaching. They are a very detailed model. They convey the story of what I (and in some instances, what colleagues of mine) did in order to teach a unit of study to a particular group of children. The books are filled with examples of my writing, with anecdotes about my dog and my family, and they are filled also with examples that come from particular children. Teachers at every grade level in a school will need to revise these lessons so they reflect you and your particular children, and so they are tailored to what your children can almost do. This means that when third-grade teachers, fourth-grade teachers, then fifth-grade teachers all rely on the books, you will at every point need to bring yourself and your kids to this model.

But if you ask whether, in general, it is appropriate for third graders to proceed through these units and then for fourth graders to revisit these units, and for fifth graders to have yet another go at them, the answer is usually yes. It is like learning to play tennis. You work on serving the ball when you are starting to learn, and again when you have been playing tennis for a year, and you still continue to work on serving the ball when you are a member of a varsity tennis team. In a similar manner, those of us who write continue to work at the same challenges, year after year. I find that the lessons I teach to third graders are very much the same lessons, tweaked a bit, that I teach to graduate students, and then when I get a bit of time, alone at my desk, these are the lessons I teach myself.

If I teach children who have not grown up within a writing workshop, can I follow these units of study? Or do they require a foundation that I will need to provide children?

If your children did not participate in a writing workshop before this year, you will certainly want to start with *Launching the Writing Workshop* and proceed (for the most part) in sequence. The truth is that you will want to do this even if your children did have the benefits of a writing workshop throughout their primary grades! So the answer to your concerns is this: Don't worry. Carry on! These units were designed, knowing that this would be the case for many teachers and children.

How much time should I devote to a single unit of study? If my children do not write particularly well, or if I am new to the teaching of writing, should I extend the time frame?

These units are designed to support a month-long unit of study. If you or your children are new to writing workshop, then you should expect to progress more quickly, not more slowly, through a unit of study. That is, when your children are skilled and experienced writers, they'll be able to spend more time revising and improving their draft, but if they are less experienced (or if you are), they'll probably stay closer to the pathway I've laid out.

Which books and other materials do I need to purchase to support these units of study?

There is a chapter in this book which describes the pens, folders, paper and notebooks that your children will need. On the CD-ROM included with the series, you will find resources you'll use and suggestions for texts or additional materials organized on a session-by-session (day-by-day) basis. Of course, you'll want to be sure to have some children's literature. The texts that are referred to the most in this series include Sandra Cisneros' and *House on Mango Street*, Cynthia Rylant's *Every Living Thing*, an anthology of short stories, the picture books *Fireflies!* by Julie Brinkloe and *Peter's Chair* by Ezra Jack Keats.

LUCY CALKINS ✦ MARJORIE MARTINELLI

LAUNCHING THE WRITING WORKSHOP

This book is dedicated to Kate Montgomery.

FirstHand
An imprint of Heinemann
A division of Reed Elsevier Inc.
361 Hanover Street
Portsmouth, NH 03801-3912
www.heinemann.com

Offices and agents throughout the world

Copyright © 2006 by Lucy Calkins and Marjorie Martinelli

All rights reserved. No part of this book may be reproduced in any form or by any electronic or mechanical means, including information storage and retrieval systems, without permission in writing from the publisher, except by a reviewer, who may quote brief passages in a review.

Photography: Peter Cunningham

Library of Congress Cataloging-in-Publication Data

CIP data on file with the Library of Congress.
ISBN 0-325-00863-9

Printed in the United States of America on acid-free paper
10   09   08   07   06   ML   1   2   3   4   5

Excerpt from *Peter's Chair* by Ezra Jack Keats, copyright (c) 1967 by Ezra Jack Keats, renewed (c) 1995 by Martin Pope, Executor. Used by permission of Viking Penguin, A Division of Penguin Young Readers Group, A Member of Penguin Group (USA) Inc., 345 Hudson Street, New York, NY 10014. All rights reserved.

Excerpt from *Whistling* Text copyright © Elizabeth Partridge. Used by permission of HarperCollins Publishers.

Excerpt from *Fireflies!* Reprinted with the permission of Simon & Schuster Books for Young Readers, an imprint of Simon & Schuster Children's Publishing Division from *Fireflies!* by Julie Brinckloe. Copyright © 1985 Julie Brinckloe.

Excerpt from *The Witch of Blackbird Pond* by Elizabeth George Speare. Copyright © 1958, renewed 1986 by Elizabeth George Speare. Reprinted by permission of Houghton Mifflin Company. All rights reserved.

Excerpt from *Because of Winn-Dixie.* Copyright © 2000 Kate DiCamillo. Published by Candlewick Press Inc.

Excerpt from *Shortcut* Copyright © 1992 by Donald Crews. Used by permission of HarperCollins Publishers.

ACKNOWLEDGEMENTS

This book is dedicated to Kate Montgomery, who has edited all the books in both this series and in the series, Units of Study for Primary Writing. Kate has been my closest writing partner for the past decade. She's written sections of each of my books. More than this, she has trimmed and tailored every book, making each one more graceful as well as more explicit and more helpful. Kate has also managed the multifaceted organization that has formed around these books, keeping the contributing authors, co-authors, production crew, editors, teachers and publicists in close communication with each other. She has been my North Star and my compass, helping me steer a path.

I also want to thank Marjorie Martinelli, the contributing author of this book. Marjorie was a support in the Units of Study for Primary Writing as well as in this book. I thank her for her generous efforts throughout both these writing projects. She contributed to many of the extensions in this book and in the Launching section of the CD-ROM. Marjorie is a wizard with classroom management, and her years as a staff developer made her especially helpful at thinking through ways we could provide additional supports for teachers who will first encounter the writing workshop through this book. Marjorie helped locate specific samples of children's work, obtain permissions, and fill in gaps in the manuscript.

I want to thank all the children whose work has been featured in this book, and their wonderful, generous teachers. I specifically want to thank Teresa Caccavalle and Lis Shin from PS 116 in Manhattan, Mollie Cura from PS 28 in the Bronx, Larry Neal from PS 18 in the Bronx, Kathy Doyle from Smith School in Tenafly, and Mary Chiarella from PS 57 and, before that, from PS 199 in Manhattan.

Tasha Kalista took almost unreadable manuscripts of this book and all the others, and like the fairy godmother at work at her spinning wheel, transformed the flax into golden threads. Those of us who have had the chance to work with Tasha are convinced that she is magic. Her skill comes from understanding this work so much that she could co-author any one of the books.

The teaching that is described in this book and throughout the series is only possible because of the extraordinary leadership that New York City principals and superintendents have provided to their schools. I am especially grateful to a few of these New York City principals and superintendents who have especially supported the process of developing these units of study. These include Liz Phillips, Melanie Woods, Arlene Berg, Nora Polansky, Donald Conyers, Lillian Druck, Eileen Reiter, AnnaMarie Carillo, Daria Rigney, Leslie Zackman, Peggy Miller, Carol Wertheimer, Carol Stock, Anthony Inzerillo, Jack Spatola, Elsa Nunez, Maria Ciccone, Adele Schroeter, Cynthia Hunter, Joan Ratner, Jacqueline Jones, Peter MacFarlane and Janette Cuban.

LAUNCHING THE WRITING WORKSHOP

Welcome to Unit 1

WELCOME TO THE UNIT

LAUNCHING THE WRITING WORKSHOP

About the Unit

We start the year by teaching children some of the biggest lessons they'll ever learn. First and most important, we teach them that their lives and their thoughts are worth writing about. We help children realize that the small moments of their lives can be compelling stories, and we help them feel committed to capturing the truth of their experience in words.

The first lessons in this unit center on topic choice. We teach children a number of strategies they can draw on in order to generate their own ideas for writing, and we set them free from a dependency on the teacher. Children will benefit from knowing that writers think of a person, then brainstorm moments they've spent with that person, choose one moment, and write the story. Writers similarly think of places that matter to them, brainstorm moments that occurred in those places, choose one moment, and write the story. Writers know that objects and photographs from their lives hold stories and that by listening to the stories of others, they can recall their own stories. Naomi Nye's beautiful poem "Valentine for Ernest Mann" reminds writers that "poems hide . . . in the shadows of our room they are hiding." Stories hide too, and with just a few minilessons we can be sure that all our students know where important stories are likely to hide.

Many teachers find that in this first unit, it helps to celebrate the fact that stories of significance can be found in the smallest and most ordinary occasions. Perhaps after children throng back into the classroom after lunch, we will want to help them choose one small story from all the many that occurred while they were eating and tell that story as well as possible to their partners. In this fashion, we can teach students to reexamine the everyday routines of their lives in search of stories that have humor, beauty, and drama.

Meanwhile, during this unit children learn the essentials of narrative writing. They learn that narratives are just that—stories. In a personal narrative, one character (presumably the writer) experiences one thing, then the next, then the next. These texts are usually chronologically ordered. Children also learn that their narratives will be more effective if the writer has zoomed in on a small episode, written with detail, expanded the heart of the story, made their characters talk—and above all "made a movie in the mind" and then recorded that movie on the page. As children learn to write in ways that reflect all that they have already learned about focus, detail, strong leads, and so forth, their writing will improve in very noticeable ways. The improvements in children's writing should prove to them that learning to write well matters and thus launch them into the year.

One of the few nonnegotiable qualities of effective narrative writing is the hard-to-describe (and hard-to-achieve) quality that some teachers refer to as "writing in the moment" or "making a movie in your mind." If a child talks all about an event—summarizing it with sentences like "It was a good baseball game. We won 6 to 2. I got a lot of hits."—then the child is *commenting on* the game rather than *telling the story* of it. The child has not yet grasped the idea of writing in a storyteller's voice. If, on the other hand, his piece begins, "I grabbed a bat and walked up to the plate. I looked at the pitcher and nodded. 'I'm ready,' I said," then the child is writing a story. Most children need to be reminded to make movies in their mind and to write so readers can picture exactly what is happening. As the year unfolds, we will let children in on the fact that stories are not shaped like those we teach children to write in this unit, but for now, children find that they've got their hands full.

During this unit, many children will profit from learning a very simple form of focus. For example, a child might initially plan to write a page-long piece depicting his whole day at the beach, but because of our teaching, he'll write instead about body surfing on one wave. Another child will decide that instead of retelling the entire trip to Grandma's house, she will focus on how she accidentally let the pigs loose. As children narrow the time span of their stories, it is crucial that they then elaborate on the portion of the event that remains in their spotlight. In other words, the main reason to "zoom in" or to "write about a little seed story, not about a big watermelon topic" is that this makes it more likely that the writer will relive an episode with enough detail that the reader, too, can experience the event.

As children learn about narrative writing, some of the lessons will be explicit, taught in minilessons and conferences. But some of the lessons will be implicit, gleaned as children are immersed in texts that sound like those we hope they will soon write. It is not always easy to find published personal narratives, so we also share realistic fiction, especially picture books and short stories that resemble the stories about small moments the children will write. Even just one dearly loved and closely studied text can infuse a writing workshop with new energy.

This unit of study is designed to launch a writing workshop that is well-managed enough that children can proceed with some independence. Children learn the structures and rituals of a writing workshop. They learn to gather for a minilesson, to sit and listen throughout most of it, to "turn and talk" with a partner at the designated moment. They learn that they can get themselves started on writing, work past the hard parts, rely on one another as well as on themselves, share their writing, and so forth. Soon children will be able to get themselves started writing new entries without needing any input from

the teacher; this means that during one day's writing workshop, they'll write one entry after another, working with independence.

The Plan for the Unit

During this *Launching* unit, most children write two focused personal narrative stories and then select one for further revision, editing and publication. The major "bends in the road" of the unit are as follows:

- Children learn a variety of strategies for generating entries and begin to live like writers, collecting lots of entries in their writers' notebooks. We hope these entries are focused, detailed narratives (or "Small Moment" stories.)
- Children choose one of these entries to function as a "seed idea," and they write various lead sentences and storytell as ways to rehearse for rewriting this entry, this time as a rough draft, outside the notebook, in a story-booklet.
- Children collect more entries, drawing on strategies they learned earlier and on new strategies, and they again select a seed idea.
- This time, children rehearse for drafting by making and revising a timeline as well as by writing and selecting between leads and storytelling.
- Children write a draft of their second story. Hopefully each child makes a movie in his or her mind, envisioning the story as it unfolds, and each child writes in a step-by-step fashion.
- Children select the piece they like best and revise it. One way to revise it is to locate the heart of the story and to stretch that section of the text out, writing it in an even more step by step fashion. Another way to revise is to bring out the internal as well as the external aspect of the story.
- Children edit and recopy the draft they select as their best, checking especially their use of end punctuation, capitals, paragraphs and spellings of high-frequency words.

IN THIS SESSION, YOU'LL INVITE
CHILDREN TO BECOME WRITERS,
AND YOU'LL TEACH A STRATEGY
FOR GENERATING PERSONAL
NARRATIVE ENTRIES. YOU'LL
SUGGEST THAT WRITERS OFTEN
THINK OF A PERSON, BRAINSTORM
FOCUSED STORIES OF TIMES WITH
THAT PERSON, THEN SKETCH AND
WRITE ONE OF THOSE STORIES.

GETTING READY

- Your own filled writer's notebook
- Daily schedule with plans for a distasteful subject, which you'll replace with a writing workshop
- Memories of people who matter to you, for use in demonstrating strategy
- Chart paper and markers
- Notebook and pencil for each child
- Sheets of paper, each with the names of two children numbered 1 and 2, to place on the floor to indicate partners' spots
- See CD-ROM for resources

STARTING THE WRITING WORKSHOP

Years ago, the poet Lucille Clifton gave me some advice that I've cherished ever since. "Nurture your sense of what's possible," she said. "We cannot create what we cannot imagine."

This advice has changed how I work in many ways. As a staff developer I now realize that before I help teachers with the brass tacks of implementing a writing workshop, I need to show them what a whole writing workshop sounds and feels like. I encourage teachers to visit effective workshops, immersing themselves in the workshop environment.

Children, too, need to imagine what's possible in a writing workshop before they begin writing. Today you'll nurture children's sense of what's possible. You'll describe the writing workshop to them, helping them imagine what this time in their day could be like and helping them anticipate its rhythms.

Children need not only to imagine the workshop, but also to imagine themselves as writers, and so in this session you'll show them they have important stories to tell. You'll teach children to take small, true stories of their lives and tell those stories in ways that strike a chord in their readers. During the first week of this unit, you'll help them collect a dozen focused, detailed personal narrative entries. Children will write these in their writer's notebooks. Then they'll select one and eventually a second of these entries to develop, then draft, and then revise. Finally, they'll choose their favorite to further revise and edit, publishing it. Today, you'll teach writers to recall an episode, quickly sketch a sequence of events within that one episode, and then write the story as an entry in their notebooks.

You will find that your work flows beyond writing time. Throughout the day, you'll want to listen with rapt attention to children's stories. Say often, "You'll definitely need to write about that!" You'll also want to immerse children in the sort of literature you hope they will write. Read books and poems about writing, and read books and stories that resemble the first-person narratives your children will write. Say, "This story by Eloise Greenfield reminds me of the stories you wrote earlier today!" Draw from our list of recommendations on the accompanying CD-ROM or from any texts you love. Read to them, read to them, read to them.

MINILESSON

Starting the Writing Workshop

CONNECTION

Build your children's identities as writers by exclaiming over the stories they've told.

"Class, can I have your eyes and your attention? I want to tell you something very important. I have been listening to the stories of your summer—to stories of helping your grandma shuck the corn and stories of building model trucks and stories of learning to whistle—and these stories are so extraordinary that we can't let them float away. We have been together for only one day, one hour, and twenty minutes, but I'm already awed by all of you. You have amazing stories from your lives!"

Build your children's enthusiasm for writing and explain writing workshop.

"You have such extraordinary stories to tell that I'm thinking that this year, I should teach you how to write like professional writers! We need to save these stories forever! We need to hold on to them so that as we learn how to be better and better writers, we can make our stories better and better too! To be writers, you need the tools that real writers use, and the most important tool is this: a writer's notebook. I've been learning to become a writer, too, and so I keep my own writer's notebook." I held up my own well-decorated and much-used notebook and turned through a few pages so the children could see my pages filled with writing, sometimes also containing a sketch or a photograph.

"We will also need to spend time writing every day, just like professional writers do. Our writing workshop will be at the heart of our whole year. Starting right away, I am going to change our daily schedule so that every day we give a big chunk of time to writing." On the daily schedule, I erased "ditto sheets" and wrote "writing workshop."

COACHING

If you pattern a minilesson after this one, you'll want to name the true stories your own children have brought to school. As you read all these minilessons, remember that they are not meant to be a script for your teaching, but rather, they are meant to convey the story of my teaching, providing one example of how your teaching could go.

Often, children enter the classroom in September not believing they have anything to say. "Nothing happens in my life," they'll say. Our first job is to help children see that they do, indeed, have stories to tell. We want each child to think that, as Faulkner puts it, "my own little postage stamp of native soil [is] worth writing about and that I [will] never live long enough to exhaust it" (Cowley 1958, p. 141).

In this minilesson, I act as though it is because the kids' stories have given me goose bumps that I want them to have writer's notebooks and an hour-long writing workshop every day. The truth is that I approach the start of a new school year planning to be astounded and amazed by the great things that kids do. I try to approach each year with that mind-set, expecting to be touched and awed by my children and their stories. I know that it is all too easy to spend the first weeks of school mourning the loss of last year's kids. I know, too, that my responsiveness to these kids is vastly more important than any lesson I could teach.

"Our workshop will be like all sorts of other workshops. Usually workshops begin with the artists—they might be writers, they might be painters—convening to learn a new strategy. The teacher says, 'Let me show you a strategy, a technique that has been important to my work,' and then she models it. After about ten minutes together, everyone goes to work on his or her own project, and the teacher becomes a coach."

Name the teaching point. In this case, tell children that you will teach them a strategy for generating personal narratives.

"For now, let's write true stories, personal narratives. Today I want to teach you a strategy I use to help me decide which story to write (because writers aren't usually given topics; we decide which stories we will tell). If I can't figure out what to write, one strategy I use is this: I think of a person who matters to me and then I list small moments I've had with that person. I list moments that, for some reason, I remember with crystal-clear clarity. Then I sketch the memory and write the story of that one time." I turned to the chart paper and wrote:

Strategies for Generating Personal Narrative Writing

- Think of a person who matters to you, then list clear, small moments you remember with him or her. Choose one to sketch and then write the accompanying story.

TEACHING

First, teach your children the contexts in which a writer might use the strategy you are about to teach. Then, teach the strategy: one way to generate personal narrative writing.

"So let's say it's writing time, and I've got my writer's notebook in front of me, open to the first blank page. I *might* pick up my pen and think, 'I already know what I want to write,' in which case I'd just get started writing an entry."

"But, on the other hand, I *might* pick up my pen and think, 'Hmm . . . What am I going to write about?' When I don't know what to write, I think, 'What *strategies* do I know for generating narrative writing?' and I use a strategy to help me generate an idea for a story."

You'll notice that I explicitly teach children how the writing workshop generally goes. During the next few days, I plan to teach children specifics. If I see a child waiting for a personalized nudge to get started, for example, I'll say, "In a workshop, whether it's a painting workshop or a writing workshop, after the short lesson, the people go back to their workplaces and figure out what their painting needs next or their writing needs next, and they just get started on their own."

Notice that every minilesson begins with a section titled Connection that is patterned like this first one. Every Connection ends with the teacher naming precisely what it is he or she aims to teach. We call this the teaching point. Some people refer to this instead as the goal. Usually the teacher embeds this teaching point in a sentence that literally says, "Today I will teach you that . . . ." You will notice that the teaching point is reiterated often throughout a minilesson.

Intonation is important. I use my voice to suggest that if I think, "I already know what I want to write about," then today's strategy wouldn't be relevant or necessary. On the other hand, if I'm stuck over what to write, then today's strategy will be useful indeed. A strategy is only a strategy if it helps you past a challenge, if it is a tool you select to achieve a goal. When something that could have been a strategy is assigned, and done for no purpose except because it is assigned, then it is no longer a strategy, but merely an activity. You'll notice that often, before I demonstrate how I use a strategy, I set up the context in which the strategy will be useful.

Demonstrate the step-by-step process of using the strategy. In this case, think of a person, list focused memories related to the person, choose one of these stories, then sketch and storytell it.

I gestured to the chart that now contained one strategy. "Using our strategy, I'll think of a person who matters to me and list small moments connected to that person, moments I remember with crystal-clear clarity. So watch me while I use that strategy."

You'll notice that when we want to teach children how to use a strategy, we often teach by demonstrating. We role-play that we are a writer, and then we use the strategy in front of children. Your role-play is meant to function as a how-to or procedural guide, so act out the sequence of steps you hope children will undertake. You are showing them how to proceed when using the strategy. In your role-play, show children the replicable steps to take whenever using the strategy.

Picking up my marker and turning toward the chart paper, I said, "The person I write down should be someone who really matters a lot to me, because if I just put down any ol' person, like, 'the man at the checkout counter at the deli,' I'm not going to want to write about my list! So let me think . . . hmm, I'll write, 'Dad.' It's a good choice because my dad matters a whole, whole lot to me, and also because I have a zillion tiny stories I remember with crystal-clear clarity that I could tell about him."

Here I am teaching kids a strategy for coming up with a topic in a way that directs them toward writing personal narratives. The strategy will yield personal narratives only if each item in the list represents a small moment or an episode the writer experienced with the special person. If I had abbreviated my description of the strategy so that children simply wrote about a special person, they'd be apt to produce informational not narrative texts.

"I'm thinking of my dad. The first thing that comes to my mind is that last Saturday I woke up, and he said, 'I'm going to make breakfast for you,' and so I sat and read my book while he went into the kitchen. I heard him get out the bowl, and pretty soon I started to smell bacon." I wrote on the blank chart paper:

I could have pretended that I almost dismissed this story as too insignificant. That would have helped me make the point that writers tend to shove memories aside as unimportant, but that they should try not to do this. You'll decide how many minor tips you can tuck into your lesson.

Dad

When Dad made me Saturday breakfast

"What else . . . oh, I know! A moment I remember is the first time I saw him cry. It was kind of shocking and scary to see him cry, but I learned that he has deep feelings inside him, just like I do." I added to the chart:

Dad

When Dad made me Saturday breakfast
First time I saw my dad cry

Notice both entries represent stories of common, small episodes that could easily be written chronologically. Both entries have personal meaning to me, the writer. They are the sort of stories that children could conceivably write about—I try to steer clear of ideas that will resonate only with adults. I'm aware that the stories I tell provide models for children, and therefore I try to tell stories that will set children up for success.

"And I remember a basketball game I went to when I was your age, when my dad embarrassed me by walking right into the gym and sitting with me." I added to the chart:

Dad

When Dad made me Saturday breakfast

First time I saw my dad cry

When my dad walked into the basketball game

"I've got a lot more moments to add to my list, and I can add them anytime! But for now, I'm going to choose one moment from my list—I'm going to write about the basketball game because I really remember it! In all our lives, there are some moments that imprint themselves onto our memories, and they are ones worth writing about because they often have special, sometimes hidden, meaning for us."

"Watch how I go about picturing the memory in my mind, and then start telling the story of what happened in a step-by-step way."

Tuck bits of advice into your demonstration. In this case, tuck in pointers about envisioning your story and sketching quickly.

Switching into the role of writer, and speaking in a musing sort of way, I said, "So which part of that basketball game do I especially remember? (I need to zoom in on the part I remember most.) Well, what I really remember is that I arrived just before halftime and I didn't know where to sit. I'm going to make a movie in my mind of exactly what happened, in a step-by-step way, and sketch what I picture in my mind. I walked along the basketball court, looking up at the bleachers full of kids. I worried because all the kids were already sitting with other friends and there weren't any open spots for me. Then Sarah signaled for me to join her group. I was relieved!"

"I'll sketch this so I remember it: Here I am, walking alongside the court, looking up at the bleachers." I made a rapid sketch. "Here is Sarah, in the crowd, signaling to me." I drew a box in the top half of my page and sketched inside it.

Then, as I talked, I moved to the lower half of the page and made a second sketch to show what happened next. "So I clambered up the bleachers and sat with that group. Everything was fine until my father came to pick me up. He didn't wait in the car like all the other parents—instead he came marching right into the gym." Turning towards the chart

Three examples are plenty. Notice they are varied; they are meant to illustrate a range of possibilities so that students will realize a wide range is open to them as well. It is important to teach children that listing topics involves a few minutes, not a few days, and to show them how to shift from gathering to selecting and writing.

This first unit of study could have encouraged children to write in their choice of genre rather than channeling them toward personal narratives. In fact, my book The Art of Teaching Writing *describes a curriculum that welcomes a huge variety of writing at the start of the year. You, as a teacher, have choices to make! I have come to believe the lessons writers can learn through shared work around personal narrative writing are so foundational that it's valuable to channel children toward personal narrative writing right from the start. But some of my colleagues still prefer to begin the year by inviting children to write in a wide variety of genres. There are compelling reasons for starting the year either way.*

Notice that for now I demonstrate (but do not discuss or draw attention to) a few qualities of good personal narrative writing. I've "zoomed in" on, or focused, the narrative. I "make a movie in my mind" and retell what happened in a step-by-step way to help me recall and record tiny details. Before long, I'll devote whole minilessons to these qualities of good writing.

I deliberately decided to write about an episode from my own childhood, one in which I worried about fitting in and being judged. I want to create a community of trust, one in which we can leave behind our armor. I know that by telling stories of my own troubles, I can make the classroom into a safer place for others to share their vulnerabilities.

paper, I said, "I'm going to sketch that. (Here I am sitting with Sarah. Notice I'm sketching really quickly.) Then I saw my father come walking into the room. (Here he is, with his silly red hunting cap that he always wears!) I remember that he walked in front of the bleachers, scanning the crowd of kids. Then he saw me and called, 'Lukers!' and started climbing up toward us. I wanted the floor to open up and swallow me."

"The memory is really clear, so now I am ready to write. I need to go back and remember what happened first." I looked at my first sketch, then dictated to myself: "When I arrived at my first basketball game . . ." Returning to the chart paper on which I'd made my sketches, I fast-wrote, repeating my text as I scrawled down the page."

> When I arrived at my first basketball game, all the other kids had already found seats. I walked in front of the bleachers hoping to find an empty seat but everyone seemed ensconced with a group. Then I saw a hand wave. Yeah! I thought, as I climbed up the bleachers, flattered that popular Sarah had signaled for me to join her. When the game was almost over, I glanced toward the doorway and saw my father striding across the gym floor toward me, his red plaid hunting cap perched on his head.

"And I'll keep writing . . ."

Debrief. Help children recall the situation in which writers would use this strategy and the sequence of actions the strategy requires.

"So writers, I want you to know there are lots of ways to come up with stories to write. One strategy I use often is I think of a person who matters to me and write that on my paper. Then I list Small Moment stories connected to that person. I take one of these, one I remember with crystal-clear clarity, and zoom in on the part I remember most. Then I sketch and write what happened first and later."

When you are coming up with your own story to sketch, keep in mind that the simplest way to help children improve their stories is to teach them to focus. One way to focus a narrative is by writing a story that occurs within a tight time frame— retelling an episode that occurred in an hour or less. Writing about small episodes encourages writers to enrich the moment by writing with details.

Be sure to retell the first thing (and then the second thing) that happened in the story so that the children will feel the chronological structure of this genre.

This may be the longest story I'll ever write in front of the class. Minilessons need to be brief so that children have lots of time for their own writing. The last thing kids need to do is to watch us write on and on. Still, I think this one bit of public writing can give children an image of the way we hope they shift from drawing to writing and a sense for the genre. Notice I've zoomed in on one episode and written it almost as if this was a bit of fiction. You'll want to substitute your own story.

You will notice that I tell my story in more detail than is necessary for the teaching point I am trying to make. I do that because on this, the first day of the workshop, I am trying to build a relationship of trust with the class, and also because I know the power of shared stories.

ACTIVE ENGAGEMENT
Set children up to try the strategy. First, help them imagine themselves in the situation that calls for the strategy. Then, lead them through the steps you've demonstrated.

"Class, let's practice this strategy. Pretend it's writing time and you open *your* notebook," I opened an imaginary notebook, "and you pick up *your* pen to write and think, 'Hmm, what should I write?'"

"If you aren't sure what to write, try the strategy we've been learning." I pointed to the chart I'd begun."

> ### Strategies for Generating Personal Narrative Writing
> - Think of a person who matters to you, then list clear, small moments you remember with him or her. Choose one to sketch and then write the accompanying story.

"Right now, sitting here, think, 'Who is someone that matters to me?' Now, try listing across your fingers two or three little moments you and that person had together, moments you especially remember." I gave them a minute to do this. "Now choose *one* moment, one time. Give me a thumbs up when you've done this."

"Think back to the event. Which part do you want to tell? Zoom in on the most important part." I bring my hands together to contain a smaller area. "Remember that I didn't tell *everything* about the basketball game—getting ready, getting there, the start of it. I just zoomed in on the middle of the basketball game, when Sarah signaled me to join her group, and the end, when my father embarrassed me by climbing up the bleachers to join us!" I gave children silence in which to think. "Thumbs up if you have thought of how your zoomed-in story begins."

"Make a quick thumbnail sketch of whatever you did first." I watched just a minute while children sketched their opening action. "Now make a second quick sketch to show what you did next." I whispered with a few children to learn what they were sketching.

"Now tell the person beside you the story, starting with what you did first. Tell it with tiny details."

Notice the rhythm of a minilesson. First I tell children what I'll teach, then I teach it, and then I give children the chance to practice the strategy with my support. You'll see this in all of our minilessons.

Before I set children up to use this strategy, I establish the conditions in which the strategy would be useful. First a writer sits in front of the blank page, unsure what to write. Then (and only then) the writer reaches for a strategy that can help her generate a story. I am not only trying to teach kids a strategy— I am also trying to show them when, in their lives, they can use the strategy.

Notice that when I give directions, I word them in a very sequenced, step-by-step way.

The most important part of this may be the moments of silence. Don't skip past this! Give children a chance to think . . . watch their brains work.

This Active Engagement portion of the minilesson provides children with scaffolding as they try a new strategy. You'll notice that I don't just assign the work; instead I guide kids step-by-step through the process of using this strategy. In a few minutes, they will try the strategy again in their writing places, this time without scaffolding.

I am channelling children towards stories in which the first-person narrator is the active agent, not the passive recipient of events. "Sketch what you did first . . . next . . . ."

Debrief. Share the good work one child has done in a way that provides yet another model.

The room erupted into talk, and I circulated among the children, listening to their stories. After two or three minutes, I said, "Writers, can I have your eyes and your attention please?" I waited an extra long time until there was absolute silence. "Thanks. Next time, could you give me your attention a bit more quickly so we don't waste one precious minute of writing time?"

"I heard amazing stories, just as I knew I would with this class. Jessica told about riding her bike through her neighborhood one evening. First one kid joined her, then a bunch of little kids from across the street joined, and the group kept growing until there were ten of them riding bikes together! These are the stories of your lives, the stories writers put onto the page."

LINK

State your teaching point. Remind children that whenever they want help thinking of a true story, they now have a strategy they can use.

"So writers (with stories like these, I need to call you *writers*), without wasting another second, let's start putting these amazing stories onto the pages of your writer's notebooks."

"As you work today, and every day for the rest of your lives, remember that as writers we *choose* the stories we write. If we aren't sure what story to tell, we sometimes use a strategy to get us started. One strategy is to jot down a person and list small moments connected to that person. Then we take one Small Moment story that we remember with crystal-clear clarity. It often helps to ask, 'What was the most important part?' so we can zoom in on that part of the story and sketch or remember it with a lot of details. After we make thumbnail sketches of what happened, we write the story!"

Send children off to write, reminding them of your expectations for their independent work.

"As you work, I'll come around to admire your amazing stories, and later we'll share them with a friend or two."

"When you write today, the room will be totally quiet because writers need silence to be able to think and remember and sketch and write. The only sound will be pencils or pens on paper. When I call your name, you can come to me, get your writer's notebook, and go quickly to your seats. Antonio. Samantha." I gave each a notebook. "Don't you love how they are going quickly to their seats! Let's watch them while they get started. Look how well these writers get down to business."

Notice the example I highlight is a sequential story of a single brief episode—one that retells a rather ordinary, everyday occurrence. The writing that I make a fuss about will tend to be the sort of writing I hope kids will produce at this point in the year. For now, I am steering kids toward sequential, detailed personal narratives.

During the link, I articulate again what I have taught, reminding children that this is a strategy they can use for the rest of their lives. You will see my closing words "As you work today, and every day for the rest of your lives," end many minilessons.

Over the next few days, you will want to develop and practice a system for getting students from the meeting area to their workplaces smoothly. You might say, "Table monitors, will you please get the tools your table needs for writing?" Or "Supplies managers, please check that every table has supplies for writing." Each table will need a toolbox containing writing utensils and, soon, a box containing the writing folders for that table. Usually children carry writer's notebooks home each night and therefore have their notebooks in their backpacks at the start of each day, but you won't institute that ritual for a few weeks.

During this first week of writing workshop, you'll want to establish a serious working tone by pointing out behaviors you want to reinforce: "Let's admire how quickly that group got to their seats to write!" or "I love the way you have gotten straight to work. It feels like your minds are on fire!"

WRITING AND CONFERRING

Using Table Conferences to Reinforce the Minilesson

Listen to your children so you learn what they know. Donald Murray, the Pulitzer Prize–winning author widely regarded as the father of the writing process, describes teaching writers this way:

> I am tired but it is a good tired, for my students have generated energy as well as absorbed it. I've learned something of what it is to be a childhood diabetic, to raise oxen, to work across from your father at 115 degrees in a steel drum factory, to be a welfare mother with three children, to build a bluebird trail . . . to bring your father home to die of cancer. I have been instructed in other lives, heard the voices of my students they had not heard before, shared their satisfaction in solving the problems of writing with clarity and grace.

> I feel guilty when I do nothing but listen. I confess my fear that I'm too easy, that I have too low standards, to a colleague, Don Graves. He assures me I am a demanding teacher, for I see more in my students than they do—to their surprise, not mine.

> I hear voices from my students they have never heard from themselves. I find they are authorities on subjects they think ordinary. . . . Teaching writing is a matter of faith, faith that my students have something to say and a language in which to say it. (1982, pp. 157–160)

I was one of Murray's students, and I can still recall the great hope that welled up in me when he leaned toward me, listening with spellbound attention to my stories of growing up on a farm, struggling to find my place among the brood of nine Calkins children. If you can give your children just one thing right now, it must be this: your unconditional faith that each one has a story to tell, and your rapt attention to these stories.

Once the writing workshop is well under way, your conferences won't always reinforce your minilesson; but for now, you need to make sure your minilesson affects kids' actions. So go to a table full of writers, crouch low, and say something like, "I am just watching to see if you are looking at your sketches, and remembering your stories, and then writing these stories down, like your minds are on fire. Oh, look, Christina's looking back at her sketch and getting the whole story down!" When you go from one table to

---

MID-WORKSHOP TEACHING POINT   ***Writing More*** After ten or fifteen minutes of the workshop, you may feel that your students' attention is waning. This is a good time to intervene. You will probably stand in the middle of the room gathering students' attention. It could simply be that you say, "Writers . . ." and wait until they freeze, eyes on you. Then you can proceed to talk. You can use this mid-workshop time whenever necessary to teach additional, smallish points. Today, you might want to teach your students ways to write more.

"Writers, can I have your eyes and your attention? (When I say this, that means stop what you are doing, pens down, and all eyes on me, please.)"

continued on next page

another like this during a writing workshop, we call these interactions "table conferences." In a table conference, you don't select kids who need specific help and gather them as you'll do for strategy lessons. Instead you blanket the whole table and often the whole room with support. For now, your job is simply to rally the group to do what you just taught.

Shifting from extolling what one child is doing to rallying them all to follow suit, you might say, "Don't stop working because I'm here. I am just researching to see if any of you are finished writing about your first sketch and are about to make a second one to show what happened next. Oh my goodness! Look at what Antonio is doing! This is so spectacular!"

Once a child has sketched or written a bit of a story, it can be helpful to set the child up in such a way that he tells his story to you, starting at the beginning and proceeding in a step-by-step, sequential fashion. Show your interest in the story. "Oh my goodness! Did you really go to the SPCA and choose your own puppy? How did the story start—with you opening the door? With your mom saying, 'Let's go?' Or what?" Don't hear the entire tale. You need to move to other children, but also, once the child has told the entire story, he or she will often lose interest in writing it. So help the child tell the start of the story well, then say, "Before you do anything else, you need to get that down!" Wait while the child gets started and then slip away.

continued from previous page

"I want to teach you one more thing. Some of you are telling me that you are done. Writers have a saying, 'When you're done, you've just begun.' That means that when you think you are done, there is a lot more to do. One thing we writers do when we're done is think, 'What's another Small Moment story that I've experienced—maybe about the same person, maybe about someone else?' Then we leave a little space on our page (or move to another page) and we think, 'How did it start? What happened first?' and we sketch and then write another story. Or we simply think, "What's another true story I could tell, another memory that for some reason lingers for me?' How many of you think you are done with your first story, your first entry? Thumbs up. Okay. Well, for the rest of writing time I am going to admire what you do now that you know the saying, 'When you're done, you've just begun.' Return to your work."

For now, I also want to teach students that during the writing workshop, there is no such thing as finishing early and then doing something else—drawing, reading, or just waiting. When a writer finishes one entry or one draft, he or she starts the next. You may wonder why I don't encourage revision. In the end, I will expect many kids to sustain work on a particular entry for much longer than ten minutes. But at this point, I anticipate that children won't find it easy to sustain work on a single text. It is easier to write several underdeveloped stories than to write one good one—and for now, my first goal is simply to have children work productively, putting the stories of their lives onto paper.

Alejandra
• sleding in central park and racing against balin and losing
• saying good-bye Alejandra moved
• the sleepover with Kacey and Alejandra eating pizza
• when I first got to her birthday party
• When I find out Alejandra not in my class for 3rd grade

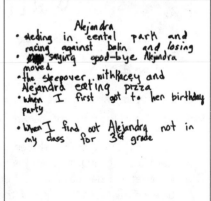

Fig. I-1 Notice that she names a person and then lists several small moments they shared.

SPECIAL Person
Laura
• I remember the time when Laura got me a Scrabble game for my birthday.
• I remember the day my aunt, Laura, and Boo came to my house and I had chickenpox

As I was preparing to leave my aunts house, she handed me a long flat rectangular box wrapped in birthday paper. "Mommy look! Can I open it now?" I asked "OK but you have to carry it home" she said. While my heart pounded, I opened the box. It was a scrabble game! I had never seen a scrabble game before then. All the way home I hugged my new game. I wondered

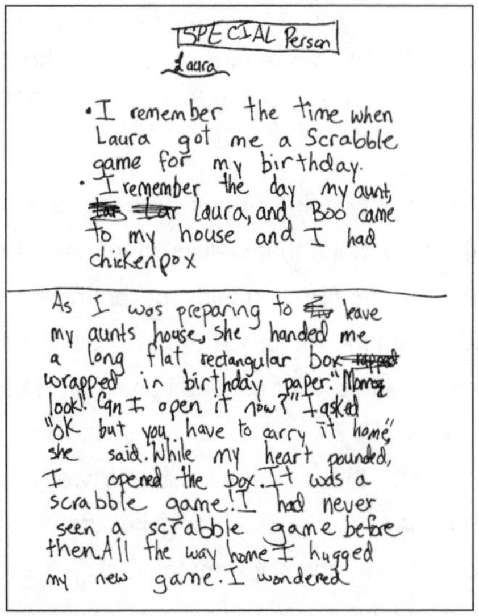

Fig. I-2 Notice how quickly the writer shifts from listing to writing.

SHARE

Establishing Writing Partnerships

Convene children in the meeting area. Establish the seating arrangements and systems that underlie partnership conversations.

"Writers, can I have your eyes and your attention? (I love the way most of you stopped what you were doing as soon as you heard me say that! Thank you.) Let's gather in the meeting area because I need to talk with you today (as I will at the end of nearly all of our writing workshop times)."

"When you go to the meeting area, you'll see a paper that has two names on it—your name and another child's name—and a number, 1 or 2, next to each name. Sit where I've put the paper containing your name and your number. You and your partner will sit facing each other, knee to knee, and each hold two corners of the paper."

"Writers, these papers are really important because they signify that the two people whose names are listed will work together as writing partners for our first unit of study in our new writing workshop. You won't write the same stories, but you'll sit alongside each other in your designated place every time we gather and you'll help each other write really great stories. The numbers 1 and 2 are just a management system to help us know who will talk first or share first. If you are partner 1, give me a thumbs up. If you are partner 2, give me a thumbs up. Terrific."

Set children up so they name some qualities of effective writing partners, then plan with their partner how they can assume this role for each other.

"As partners, you'll help each other write well. In my life, I've had a few people who have helped me as a writer tremendously. Would you each think of a person who has helped you in your writing life. Partner 2, will you tell partner 1 what that person did that helped you?"

After the children talked for a while, I added, "Now would you and your partner make some plans for how you can be effective writing partners for each other? (Some of you were

Share sessions often involve children convening in the meeting area, but when you want to expedite things, you can simply stand in the middle of the room and call for children's attention. For now, however, your children's stamina for writing probably isn't especially strong, and you will want to create a sense of solidarity among writers. So for the next few days, you'll probably convene children in the meeting area for all your share sessions.

You'll see that I institute partnerships. You could, of course, simply have children talk with whomever sits beside them in ever-shifting talk arrangements, waiting a few days before you establish firmer partnerships. I establish partnerships right away because I know that before the next unit of study, I'll have a chance to tweak these arrangements.

Notice that we generally ask for a thumbs up instead of asking children to raise their hands. This is less obtrusive, a signal rather than a call for attention or a claim on the teacher. You'll need to demonstrate. When you do so, keep your hand low, at knee level so that thumbs up is not a way to raise one's thumb (instead of one's hand.)

Notice that only one partner spoke and the other listened. This wasn't a typo! Children benefit from both roles, and another day I'll reverse the parts.

talking partners and some listeners today, and we didn't reverse roles. That'll be the case often in our workshop.) Again, will you talk together about how you two can be really helpful to each other?" The partners talked together for a few more minutes, making plans.

Bring closure to today's workshop: Recall and share one thing that was learned.

"Can I have your eyes and your attention? I wonder if writers like Walter Dean Myers and Cynthia Rylant and Patricia MacLachlan can remember back to the day they began keeping *their* writer's notebooks or the day they first had a person who really helped them as writers."

"We are lucky because all year, we will remember today, the day when we launched our writing workshop. Right now, will you each think of one thing that you did today or that a friend did or that you learned—one thing that you are going to remember—and tell it to your writing partner."

The children spoke in pairs, and I listened in. After a moment, I convened the group. "I heard you say so many smart things! Tiffany said, 'I learned I can write any story from my life that I remember.' And Abraham said, 'Sketching helps me picture my story like a movie video.' And Christina said she learned that writers can ask, 'What's *another* story I can write?' so that when we're done, we've just begun."

Notice that we try to teach children how the workshop tends to go. Transparency is a good thing in classrooms, just as in government. Today I have two conflicting goals. I want to bring children smoothly into a writing workshop, conveying to them that this will be easy and rewarding. On the other hand, I want to help children understand that the writing workshop in general and the work they began today is a very big deal. I want to rally their energy by saying, "This will be hard work, but it's worth it!" I do this in part by likening children's work to the work done by beloved authors.

⊙ HOMEWORK *Decorating Notebooks and Collecting Ideas for Tomorrow's Writing*
Tonight, at home, would you decorate the cover of your writer's notebook? You'll see I laminated pictures that I love onto my cover, and Marjorie did the same thing, only she used dried flowers and blades of grass. If you decide to paste a collage of pictures onto the cover like I did and want to borrow our rubber cement and contact paper, bring the pictures in tomorrow and I'll have the materials ready for you. One way or another, you will need to personalize your notebook, to make it special, because it will hold your writing, it will hold your stories—which means it will hold your life.

And as you decorate your notebook at home, keep in mind that tomorrow you will have another chance to write in it. So tonight, when you are home with your family, be on the

You may wonder why I suggest that you and your students take time at the start of the year to decorate your notebooks. This may seem excessive or extraneous, but I don't believe it is. If you think about it, we outfit our children for the roles they play as soccer players, Scout members, and cheerleaders. We do this, I think, because we know that something as simple as a new T-shirt can help a child assume the identity of being a soccer player, an athlete, and a team member. Isn't it just as important to help each child assume the identity of a writer?

lookout for stories. Listen for stories. When things happen at home, let them jog your mind so memories surface. When you feed your cat, maybe you'll remember the day you picked her out from a litter of kittens. When you take out the garbage, maybe you'll remember the time you saw a big raccoon on top of the garbage can. Tomorrow, come to the writing workshop already remembering some stories you could write.

⊙ TAILORING YOUR TEACHING   We call each component of this book a *session*, not a day, because we know that you may want to devote several days to one session. We also know that it is likely that this book will support teachers across two or three years, and that in each grade, teachers will teach variations of the same minilessons as well as invent new ones. There are many ways you and your colleagues can teach the concepts in this session. The following are a few suggestions. More ideas are included on the CD-ROM.

If your students are having difficulty thinking of stories from their lives . . . you may decide to weave storytelling into your days so that each child is simply bursting with stories before you hand out writer's notebooks. Perhaps you'll want to begin or end each school day (at least for a while) by suggesting children storytell to a partner. You'll find that if you create conditions that welcome stories, one child's story will remind every other child of a story she too has to tell. You might start storytelling time by simply letting the children know that you are dying to hear their stories. "Let's tell stories from times in our lives that for some reason are very clear in our memories," you could say, and then choose your own story to tell. I recommend telling a story from your own childhood, ideally a story of a small moment in which you were vulnerable; this helps bring you and your class together quickly. I might tell the story of when I was given the role of Abraham Lincoln's mother Sarah in a school play. "I'll need an old-fashioned dress," I said. The teacher looked me up and down and said, "You can wear the one you have on!" I can still feel my cheeks burning in shame over my hand-me-down clothes.

If your students need help listening well and responding respectfully to each other's stories . . . you can teach students to wait until they have the listeners' full attention before they continue to tell their stories. You can teach listening also by modeling this. When a child tells a story, listen in deep, responsive, respectful ways and rally the rest of the class to do the same. Be vigilant, too, for even the tiniest shows of disrespect, and be ready to shift from teacher to preacher when needed, espousing your absolute commitment to helping everyone listen to the stories told in the room.

ASSESSMENT

I remember taking my sons, Miles and Evan, to our local public pool in summers past. I was struck time and again by the cheerful, energetic scene at the pool—the packs of children in their bright swimsuits like the colorful plumage of birds, and the packs of moms and sometimes dads lounging on the grassy sides of the pool, reading books and magazines. Those parents always maintained peripheral vision. As they read, they were picking out their own precious children from among the dozens of others, surveying the situation, ready to rise at any instant should there be a safety problem. I noticed two important truths about how kids and parents act at swimming pools and I wondered if one begets the other: The children never tired of trying new stunts in the water, getting braver and braver by the day, and every time, they begged Mom or Dad, "Watch me!" For their part, parents consistently shouted back, "That's great!" And some even commented on some aspect of the dive or swim stroke that was improving.

Why does it seem that in schools, children seem to slouch, sigh, and give up trying to improve things like writing? I think it's the way that schools assess children. When a person is trying to learn how to do something, nothing squelches courage and enthusiasm more quickly than criticism.

I believe that writing assessment can be just as loving, constructive, and vigilant as the assessments at the pool in which parents watch their children and admire their energetic efforts. And it begins the same way, with kid-watching. In the classroom, we watch how kids get started with their writing and how they procrastinate. If our children self-select spots to write in, we watch where they sit, and with whom they sit. We notice when they use tools to write, such as the word wall and our instructional charts. We see them rereading and making changes to their texts. And we watch for signs of risk-taking and growth, making note of them so we can give feedback to individual children. Pretty soon, children learn to trust that we are watching with loving, interested eyes, and they begin to perform for us, almost shouting, "Watch me!"

Since we are not parents watching only one or two children, but teachers who are responsible for twenty to thirty children, it becomes necessary to track in writing what we see and hear kids doing. Methods of record keeping range from checklists to rubrics to anecdotal note taking, and the best system is the system that works for you. I scrawl notes as fast as kids talk, so there will be times in the year when I write down everything they say to me in conferences. But I also devise checklists based on what my hopes and expectations are for a unit of study and these checklists help me keep an eye on goals that are important to me. For example, during this unit of study, it is very important to me that children learn their lives are worth writing about, and that in time they find it easy to generate ideas for writing. It is important to me that children learn one very simple and concrete way of focusing a narrative—that is, that they zoom in on a relatively small period of time. Therefore, as I confer with writers in this unit, I'm apt to carry with me a checklist which reminds me of these and other goals. If a child is generating focused narratives, the checklist will remind me to compliment the child on this and to record the child's success. If the child needs help focusing his or her narrative, the checklist can remind me that this might be something to teach, in which case I'll want to record that I did this teaching so that in a later conference, I can reinforce the teaching point. No matter what kind of records you keep, the key is to be sure that your record keeping improves your teaching. You will find your system changes as your goals change.

GENERATING MORE WRITING

Today you will teach children a second strategy for generating their own topics for personal narrative writing, and you'll encourage them to write with stamina, self-assessing their volume and devising strategies to keep themselves productive. These will be the explicit lessons you spotlight.

Meanwhile, however, you will implicitly teach children the norms of a writing workshop and continue to help them develop identities as writers and cohesiveness as a writing community. Throughout today's session, you'll tuck in comments that socialize children into the culture of your workshop: "Remember to check the board, because every day it will tell you what to bring—that way, we won't need to waste one precious minute of writing time." Because you want to teach children that what they learn in one day's workshop applies to other days, you will repeat any ritual you established on day one. For example, you'll use the same attention-getting phrase today that you used in the previous session, and the same means of sending children off to work on their own writing. You'll also rely again on the partnerships you instituted in Session I.

You'll want to convey high standards around each of the rituals you've established. For example, wait the necessary time for quiet so children learn that when you ask for their attention, you expect nothing less. Expect children to gather for the meeting quickly; you may need to help them practice this so they "don't waste even a second of writing time."

You'll notice that my minilesson reminds children that they are developing a repertoire of strategies from which to draw for the rest of their lives. My message today is, "When you are stuck on what to write about (and are hoping to write a true story), draw on yesterday's or today's strategies."

As I teach particular strategies for finding a topic, I am also conveying some very basic expectations for narrative writing, showing children their stories will probably involve a character who progresses through a plot line. I choose stories that celebrate everyday life moments. Continue to read to the children; marinating them in writing that resembles what they'll write. Don't hesitate to reread texts, and to show children that you savor them. Gasp over writers who put the truth of their lives onto the page. Say things like, "She writes with exact, honest words, just like so many of you did today!"

IN THIS SESSION, YOU'LL TEACH CHILDREN THAT WRITERS SOMETIMES THINK OF A MEANINGFUL PLACE, LIST SMALL MOMENTS RELATED TO IT, THEN SELECT ONE AND WRITE ABOUT IT.

GETTING READY

- Instructions on chalkboard telling children to bring their writer's notebooks (pens tucked inside) and sit with their partners in the meeting area
- Donald Crew's *Shortcut* and *Bigmama's* or other texts children know well
- Strategies for Generating Personal Narrative Writing chart from previous session
- Chart paper and markers
- Storage baskets or boxes for children's notebooks on each table
- Tool containers on each table with sharpened pencils
- See CD-ROM for resources

MINILESSON

Generating More Writing

CONNECTION

Establish the systems you will use every day to convene the writing workshop.

Before the children convened, I said, "Please remember to check the section of the board that says 'Writing Workshop,' because every day it will tell you what you need to bring to the meeting area. That way we won't waste one precious minute on logistics. Today it tells you to sit beside your writing partner on the rug spot I gave you yesterday, and to bring your notebook with a pen tucked inside."

Build your children's identities as writers by celebrating that they live like writers, paying attention to the stories around them.

"Writers, can I have your eyes and your attention?" I waited for them. "I had a chance to peek at many of your writer's notebooks as you were coming in this morning, and you did a beautiful job making them your own by inscribing and decorating them. And many of you told me stories of what happened last night! I could tell you lived like writers—you paid attention to the stories that were around you. Some of you even went ahead and wrote them in your notebooks! Donald Murray, a Pulitzer Prize–winning writer, once said, 'Writers see more, hear more, think more because we are writing,' (1968) and I could tell that was true for you. Evan took one tiny moment and wrote this entry." [Fig. II-1]

> It's 8:30 and Dad's not home. I walk upstairs, me and my book. I lay in bed listening but Dad doesn't come home. "Turn off the lights," Mom calls. I switch the switch. I drift away. The garage door opens. Dad opens the door, walks upstairs to kiss me good night.

"Isn't that an amazing moment Evan caught?!"

COACHING

I introduced these rug spots and partnerships during Session I. Therefore, I must refer to them again today. I need to teach children that lessons they learn on any one day make a lasting impact. It is important to set up and maintain everyday procedures so these become automatic and free us to focus on other teaching. For now, don't hesitate to devote teaching time to management issues.

Minilessons generally begin by contextualizing the lesson by referring to the previous day's lesson, to children's related work, or to the prior instruction upon which the minilesson builds.

> It 8:30 and Dads not home
> I walk up stairs
> Me and my book
> I lay in bed listening
> but Dad donst come home
> "tarn off the light s mom
> calls I switch the
> switch. I drift away
> the garbe door opens
> Dad opens the door
> Walkr upstairs to kiss me good night

Fig. II-1 Evan

Remind children that writers draw on a repertoire of strategies for generating writing.

"Although we did great work in writing yesterday, it was also hard work. At the start of writing time, some of you sat with the blank page in front of you and thought, 'Nothing happens to me. I don't have anything to write.'"

"This happens to *every writer*. So today I want to teach you that writers do not have just *one* strategy for coming up with ideas. We need a whole repertoire of strategies for generating writing." I gestured toward the chart I had started the preceding day. "Yesterday we learned a strategy writers use to generate ideas for narrative writing."

> Strategies for Generating Personal Narrative Writing
>
> • Think of a person who matters to you, then list clear, small moments you remember with him or her. Choose one to sketch and then write the accompanying story.

Name the teaching point. In this case, tell children you'll teach them a second writing strategy—think of a place and list small, memorable moments linked to it.

"Today I want to teach you that writers sometimes think not of a person but of a *place* that matters; then we list small moments that occurred in that place, moments we remember with crystal-clear clarity. Then, just like we did when we thought of the person, we choose just one Small Moment story from our list. Sometimes we take a second to sketch what happened first; sometimes we just go straight to writing."

TEACHING
Name the context that might lead a writer to use today's strategy. Give an example of a writer using the strategy.

"Donald Crews may have used this strategy when he came up with the idea for his Small Moment story, *Shortcut*," I said, holding up the familiar book. "I think that for a moment, he wasn't sure what to write. Then, probably, he decided to use the strategy of thinking of a place."

It is important to teach the kids that first a person has a need for a strategy, then that person reaches for the strategy. Writers who approach the desk already knowing what they want to write about don't need to rely upon a repertoire of strategies for generating topics. So I first help kids recall times when they have been stuck, unsure of what to write about, and then I introduce the idea that writers profit from having a repertoire of strategies. This is important because throughout the reading and the writing workshop, we will often use minilessons as a time to demonstrate new strategies or more effective ways to use strategies. In these early minilessons, we need to teach kids the whole concept of having a repertoire of strategies that one draws upon when the situation demands.

At the start of a minilesson teachers are apt to say something like: "Today I will teach you another strategy for generating narrative writing." I urge you to include a follow-up sentence in your teaching point as well, so that you name exactly what that strategy will be. This means that by the end of the connection, kids have a good grasp of what they will be learning. When we have already named the strategy before we even enter the teaching component of a minilesson, we are less apt to confuse naming the strategy with teaching it.

Whereas in my first minilesson I used demonstration as the method in the teaching component, here I use the teaching method I refer to as explain and give an example. This is not a demonstration because I do not reenact a sequence of actions; instead, I simply talk about an example—I talk about how Crews probably used the strategy.

"Crews decided to write about his grandma's place—Bigmama's place—down south, because he spent every summer visiting there." I held up the book *Bigmama's*. "I bet he probably thought to himself, 'What Small Moment stories do I remember that happened to me at Bigmama's place?' He probably remembered lots of different times and then decided to choose just one story to tell. Crews did what writers often do. Instead of writing about 'my summer vacations at Grandma's,' he wrote about when he and his friends were walking on the train track, and a train came bearing down on them. He thought of a place that matters (his grandmother's place down south) and then of episodes that have happened in that place. Then he chose just one episode to write."

ACTIVE ENGAGEMENT
Set children up to try the strategy you've just taught. Scaffold children through the first step by brainstorming together a place they care about and a small moment related to that place.

"So let's try this together. Pretend you were stuck and not sure what to write about. You might look up at our list of strategies," I gestured toward the chart, "and decide to think of a place and then list episodes we recall that happened there. So let's think of a place that matters to us." I paused to let them begin thinking on their own of a place. "Hmm, how 'bout . . . the playground? Thumbs up if the playground is a place that matters to you."

"So now let's make a list of small moments that happened on the playground. Think for a moment about a small moment that has happened to you on the playground, a memory from the playground. Give me a thumbs up when you have remembered one thing that happened on the playground. Okay, now turn to your partner and share the story that came to your mind." As students talked to each other, I leaned in to listen to one pair and then another, each for only thirty seconds, so that I had some stories to bring back to the whole class.

I actually do not know how Crews came up with his topic. This is why I tuck the words "I bet he probably thought . . ." and "He probably remembered . . ." into my speech about Crews. You'll see that when I ask kids to learn from an author, I often speculate on how that author probably went about doing the writing. I do this because I don't think it's enough to show an example of good work and urge children to do likewise. We need also to show them or tell them how to proceed.

In the Active Engagement, I could have suggested each member of the class think of a place that matters to him or her and jot that down. Then I could have prompted each child to list a couple of small moments connected to that topic. I could even have asked children to star the one Small Moment story that they particularly care about and tell this story to a classmate. That active engagement would have started each child on that day's writing. Try this if many children are staring at blank pages during writing time, or if you are teaching a class full of struggling and reluctant writers.

There are advantages (described above) and also disadvantages to having kids work on their own pieces while in the meeting area. One disadvantage is that once kids go back to their seats, they have already used the strategy you've taught—they miss the opportunity to try the newly learned strategy on their own while it's fresh in their minds. Therefore, I often use what I call an exercise text in the minilesson—a group piece of writing. For example, here I help the kids try out the strategy of thinking of a place and then recalling moments that occurred in that place by doing it together on a place I select. I definitely do not expect children to write about this exercise topic—it exists just as place to practice and I intend for children to transfer the strategy (not the topic) in their independent writing. I know in advance some children will need reminders about this.

"Writers, can I have your eyes and your attention?"

I waited for silence. "I loved hearing your tiny moments from the playground! Like hearing about yesterday when Christina, Yazmin, Abraham—oh, a lot of you—crowded up under that one puny tree in the schoolyard to get out of the sun! Or the time last year when Gabriella finally got a group of girls to agree to play soccer with the boys." As I spoke, I made a list:

The Playground

- When we crowded under one puny tree
- When the girls joined the boys' soccer game

Notice the predictability of workshop instruction. Day after day, we use the same attention-getting device to ask for children's attention.

Two examples are plenty. More than two makes the minilesson unnecessarily long and less focused. I could have called on children to say their ideas, but it's faster if I name who I overheard. I also make a point of wording the children's ideas so they sound like focused vignettes. Notice that I use quite a few words to represent each moment. Sometimes when children list small moments, they try to use a single word to represent an episode, writing "soccer" instead of a longer phrase. The longer the "title," the more apt it is to be focused.

Debrief. Remind children that when stuck for a writing idea, they can use the strategy of thinking of a place and listing and selecting moments in that place.

"Now that we have this list of moments that all fit under the bigger topic of the place we've chosen (the playground), you could go back and write the story of one of these times. Of course, the strategy that you have learned today is not, 'Write about small moments that happen *on the playground.*' We just *practiced* this strategy using the playground—but Donald Crews used his grandma's place down south, didn't he? The strategy is, 'Take *any* place—a big chair in your bedroom, the school bus, your grandma's apartment—and then list moments that happen there, like we did with the playground. You will choose your own places, and make your own lists of small stories."

You'll notice that when I say, "It could be any place," I follow this with specifics—"a big chair in your bedroom, the school bus, your grandma's apartment." The reason for doing this is that qualities of good writing are also qualities of good teaching. Writers know that often the best way to convey a big idea is through details. I use this principle also when I teach. Chances are good that more students will grasp what I am trying to say if I use emblematic details. I often use two or three details so as to open up a range of options in students' minds.

LINK

State today's teaching point and set it alongside the previous session's. Remind children that whenever they want help thinking of a true story, they can draw from their growing repertoire of strategies. Send them off to write.

"So writers, from this day forward and for the rest of your lives, remember that whenever you are sitting in front of an empty page feeling stuck over what to write about, you can take a place, and then list Small Moment stories that happened in that place, like Donald Crews did when he wrote *Shortcut* and like we did today, when we thought of stories we could write that occurred on the playground. You could also think of a person," I said, gesturing to the item from the previous minilesson. "Either way, you might jot a list of Small Moment stories you could write and then choose one that you remember really well."

You will notice that whenever we talk about a strategy, we first create the situation in which a writer might reach out to use one of those strategies. In this instance, I remind children that these strategies will be useful if they are sitting in front of a blank page and thinking, "I don't know what to write about." I am also careful to remind writers of yesterday's as well as today's strategy.

"Today, you'll go to your writing spot, and you'll open your notebook and pick up your pen, and then you will decide what to do." I had already added the new strategy to the chart.

Strategies for Generating Personal Narrative Writing

- Think of a person who matters to you, then list clear, small moments you remember with him or her. Choose one to sketch and then write the accompanying story.
- Think of a place that matters to you, then list clear, small moments you remember there. Choose one to sketch and then write the accompanying story.

"I'm going to circle among you, noticing and recording what I see you've chosen to do."

"Let's watch how quickly and quietly the writers in the back row get started writing. Oh, look, Joe is rereading what he wrote yesterday to decide what he wants to do today. That's smart. Writers in the front row, you can disperse and the rest of us will watch to see how quickly you get started." I stage-whispered to the remaining kids, "Do you see how everyone is walking so quietly and quickly to their tables! That's great. Let's watch the rest of you get started just as beautifully."

A fiction writer once said, "The hardest thing about writing fiction is getting a character from here to there." The same could be said for teaching. It is very important that, at the start of the year, we purposefully teach kids how to use every minute of the writing workshop productively. This send-off is one way to do so. Even with very young children, transitions do not need to be full of dilly-dallying!

WRITING AND CONFERRING

Using Table Compliments and Small-Group Strategy Lessons to Address Predictable Problems

Eventually, while children work, you will pull close to one child and then another, conferring with writers individually. But for now, one-to-one conferences probably don't suffice because too many children still need you in order to work productively. If this is the case, you will probably want to divide your time between table conferences and small-group strategy lessons. For now, your table *conferences* may actually be table *compliments*.

The concept of table compliments originated from the recognition that it is sometimes best to use fragments of conferences rather than entire conferences when we interact with kids. If you study some of the transcripts of our conferences in our book *One to One,* or our CD-ROM *Conferring with Primary Writers,* you will see that conferences typically begin with time for research. This is our time to figure out what it is that a writer is trying to do, to think about what is already working for that writer and what the writer might benefit from doing differently. Then we usually give the writer a compliment, using this as a time to make a fuss over something the writer is doing well that he would benefit from doing other days on other pieces. For example, suppose in one conference we encounter a child who began by writing about his trip to the Dominican Republic, then realized the topic was too large and shifted to writing about when he first saw his dad. We might say, "I love the way you realized your topic was so, so huge, and you zoomed in on a more focused one. It is brave of you to not feel as if you need to tell everything, and to realize that if you zoom in on a smaller topic, you'll actually see more treasures! For the rest of your life, whenever you write narratives or stories, always remember that writers are like photographers. We zoom in on the specific story we really want to tell."

MID-WORKSHOP TEACHING POINT   ***Generating More Personal Narrative Writing*** "Writers, can I have your eyes and your attention? We already learned that, as writers, we can take a person or a place that matters to us, then list small stories connected to that and write one of those. But I want to also teach you that we can look at the stuff of our lives and let the *things* around us remind us of memories. Sometimes writers look at the things near us, and let those *objects* jog memories."

"For example, right now I am noticing my shoes. I'm going to let my shoes jog a memory. Hmm ... Now that I'm thinking about it, they remind me of one time I've never forgotten when I saw a homeless man walking onto the subway on a cold day with no shoes on at all. His feet were very dirty and callused. I've always wished I'd given him some money to get some shoes, but for some reason, I just looked at his feet, and then he got off the subway before I could react."

"Can you all try the strategy of taking an object and letting that object remind you of a Small Moment story? Just for a sec, look at something in the room or something you're wearing or something in your desk. Let what you see remind you of a story." I gave the children time to think. "Tell that story in your own mind." I again paused. "Thumbs up if this strategy worked for you. Did you find that not only a person or a place but also an object could remind you of a story?"After the children nodded I said, "The good news is

continued on next page

In a usual conference, after we give writers a compliment, we decide upon a teaching point and then teach it, rather like we would teach a minilesson. Although ideal conferences contain all these components, early in the year, when we wish we had roller skates to get to every writer ASAP, we often forgo the research and the teaching parts of conferences and just use compliments to rally writers' enthusiasm and channel their energies toward habits we know will serve them well.

You will probably go from table to table, watching what writers are doing. At one table, then another, you'll watch for a moment and then convene that small group's attention. "Writers, can I have your eyes and your attention please?" Then you'll name what one child has done (or what the group seems to be doing) that is exactly right. For example, you might say, "I love the way the group of you has gotten started. You didn't wait for me to come around and help each one of you, one by one. No! Instead you've done exactly what real writers do. You've picked up your pens and gotten started. I can tell, some of you came to the table already knowing your topic and you just started zooming down the page. Others of you used a strategy to help you generate a story to tell. That is so, so smart. You are doing what writers do. Get back to work, and I am just going to admire what you do for a minute."

In a similar fashion, you could extol the way some writers have remembered to record what they did first in the small moment, reliving an episode starting at the beginning. You could make a fuss over the fact that some writers didn't tell *everything* about their trip or their day, but instead zoomed in on just one small moment. Or that writers selected small ordinary events, or invented their spellings as best they could and kept going, or filled one page and then moved on to the next, or ended one entry and began another.

The very things that you could compliment are also things you could teach in small-group strategy lessons. If you see a handful of kids having problems with something, beckon for them to pull close in a circle around you, and teach them what they need to know. Be direct: "I pulled you over here because it seems like you are having trouble with . . . . Sometimes I have the same trouble. One thing that helps me is . . . . So let's together help Sasha do this, and then all of you can try it."

---

continued from previous page

that now you have another story you can write. More important, you have another strategy for generating personal narratives."

"Let's add this strategy to our chart, because now we know that writers can look at (or think about) *objects*, and then let an object (as well as a person or a place) spark memories." I added this strategy to the chart:

- Notice an object, and let that object spark a memory. Write the story of that one time.

"Remember that when you finish one entry, you can use any of these strategies—or make up a new strategy that works for you—just so you are able to get yourselves started on some good writing. Now you can return to your work." I watched as Alexa looked over her jacket, noticing her badges and buttons. She took one from a gymnastic meet and put it in front of her, then wrote an entry about a memory that object sparked. *[Fig. II-2]*

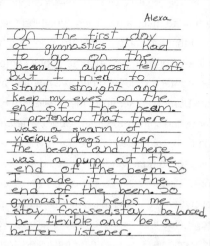

Alexa

On the first day of gymnastics I had to go on the beam. I almost fell off. But I tried to stand straight and keep my eyes on the end of the beam. I pretended that there was a swarm of viscious dogs under the beem and there was a puppy at the end of the beem. So I made it to the end of the beem. So gymnastics helps me stay focused,stay balanced, be flexible and be a better listener.

Figure II-2 Alexa

SHARE

Building Stamina for Writing

Convene children. Rally your children's enthusiasm for writing more and for a longer time. Set children up to self-assess and to set goals with partners.

"Writers, can I have your eyes and your attention? Nice work today. You really seemed to push yourselves to get a lot of writing done, and that is important. I think it is hard to write well unless a person writes quickly and can sustain writing for a long time."

"I have been thinking that we, as writers, can take some lessons from runners. I have been trying to jog every day. I have strategies that I use to get myself to run farther and faster. I keep records of how long I run and compare what I do one day with what I do the next day. Sometimes I set goals for myself. I say to myself, 'Yesterday, I ran for a mile, today I am going to try to run a mile and a half.' I not only set goals for myself, I also have strategies for meeting those goals. If I get tired, I have ways to keep myself going. Sometimes I give myself a break halfway through the run so that I have a second burst of energy. Have any of you ever pushed yourself to run farther, or to do more in gymnastics or swimming or some sport? What did you do to keep yourself going? Would partner 2 tell partner 1?" They talked.

"What I am wondering is this: If we have all these ways to push ourselves as runners and soccer players and gymnasts, might we use similar techniques to push ourselves to write longer and more? For starters, could you look back on the writing you've done since the beginning of our writing workshop and ask yourself, 'Did I write more today than on the first day?'"

"Then look at how much you usually write, and ask yourself this question: 'What could I do to push myself as a writer, like some people push themselves as runners?' I'm going to give you some time to just think about this." I paused.

Ask writers to talk with partners, listen in, then reconvene the group and list what you overheard.

"So, please talk with your writing partners. Show each other how much writing you've done today and the day before, and talk about plans you have for how to push yourselves to

At the start of the year, you need to induct children into the norms and mores of a writing community. Unless your children are accustomed to a writing workshop, you'll find they are probably accustomed to doing a bit of writing, then stopping for the day. You need to explicitly teach them to keep going. It is crucial for them to learn that when they finish one entry, they start the next one, which removes any incentive to finish entries quickly by writing in a cursory fashion. When you push for volume, you push for making the workshop a place for productive work, and this helps with classroom management.

Be sure that children date each day's writing, and that one entry follows the next, gradually filling the notebook. If they jump hither and yon, you'll have a hard time keeping track of their progress and their volume. (Perhaps they are onto this and this explains their propensity to jump around!)

write more." They talked. "Writers, here are some of the thoughts I heard from you":

- When I finish one entry, I should start the other one because some of mine are little.
- I think I worry about making it really good even if it is an entry and that slows me down.
- One day I wrote a lot and a different day I did not. I think I gotta talk less.

"Writers, these goals (and others that you haven't had a chance to say aloud) are really, really important. Starting tomorrow, we are going to work harder to make sure everyone gets a lot of writing done every day. For today, leave your notebooks in the box or basket on your table, because I'm dying to read them tonight."

You'll see that I haven't collected these comments in a chart. My decision was that they're worth saying, but not worth taking the time to record. I am conscious, however, that sometimes I am orally constructing a list. I usually lift one finger, then another, to give children a visual scaffold that helps them to recognize that I'm listing.

HOMEWORK ***Noticing Stories Like Writers Do*** Writers, the poet Naomi Nye once said: "Poems hide. In the bottoms of our shoes, they are sleeping. They are the shadows drifting across our ceilings the moment before we wake up. What we have to do is live in a way that lets us find them" (1990, p. 144). I think that stories, like poems, hide. Tonight when you are at home, writers, will you pay attention to the stories that hide in places of your life? Think about the places in your life that hold stories, and come to school ready to talk about lots and lots of ideas you have for Small Moment stories you can write during writing workshop. You should find yourself living differently because you write. Be like a magnet, pulling story ideas in to you.

TAILORING YOUR TEACHING The minilessons in this book were tailored for a class of children that's different from your own class. Borrow whichever parts of this model work for you, but substitute your own life stories and your children's own drafts. You may decide to slow down the teaching we describe, spending two days on concepts you think merit more time. And next year's teachers may return to these sessions, bringing a new twist to them. These ideas and the others that you will find on the CD-ROM can help you develop extension minilessons as well as small-group strategy lessons, mid-workshop teaching points, and share times.

You'll need to decide when to institute the ritual of the children taking their writer's notebooks home. Eventually, it will be crucial for your children to write at home, as this will double the amount of time they have to write each day, and it will allow parents to see and celebrate children's progress. If your children already carry reading books between home and school, you may decide they are able to carry writer's notebooks as well. If you worry terribly that the notebooks won't return to school, you might make little portable notepads so your writers can become accustomed to carrying those between home and school without the risk, yet, that the notebooks will be left at home. If your children record in notepads, at the end of a week they can tape pages from the notepad into the writer's notebook. You may, however, postpone writing homework that includes actual writing for now. If you institute homework, you need to provide a great deal of follow-up. If you assign homework and aren't prepared to address the fact that some children don't do it or don't bring it to school, you are allowing children to develop problematic habits. You'd be better off to postpone assigning it until you are ready to be vigilant.

If it seems that most of your students are struggling to stay focused throughout writing time and if you are overwhelmed with management concerns . . . it is important to remember that a host of challenges are to be expected at the beginning of the school year, especially if you or your students are new to writing workshop.

In general, if your kids are having difficulty, it helps to first specifically name the difficulty. Try not to say, "Writing workshop doesn't work," or "My kids have no stories to tell." Instead, ask yourself, "What exactly is the problem? When does it occur? Who is having this problem?"

For instance, if your room is too noisy during writing workshop, you need to ask why. Instead of just saying, "My room is too noisy during writing workshop," and spending time reminding kids to whisper or banning talk altogether, you'll want to get at the root of the problem. Perhaps the noise is a symptom of another issue. Maybe your students need more strategies for generating notebook entries. Maybe they need a specific time to talk with a partner to help them plan what they are about to do.

Another question to ask about any problem is, "When does it mostly occur?" Maybe it seems like it's noisy throughout writing workshop, but it is more likely that the noise happens in patterns. Perhaps your children are only noisy when they are trying something new or only when they are revising. Maybe your students need a shorter writing workshop for a couple of weeks because it's chaos in the last ten minutes. Perhaps you'll want to build the length of writing workshop gradually rather than beginning with a too-ambitious expectation.

You'll also need to figure out exactly who in the class is having the difficulty. It usually isn't every student, although at first glance it can very often feel as if everyone is struggling. Watch for a day or two to see exactly who is having the problem so you can get to the bottom of the problem while also addressing her needs as a writer. Notice children who are not having the particular problem. If we notice a table of students who work quietly during a writing workshop, we can find out how they do this and then teach the rest of the class the strategies they use.

You could also choose to let the whole class in on the problem and brainstorm with them a strategy to help the problem go away.

ASSESSMENT

A great treat lies waiting for you—you can spend some time poring over your students' work. Gather up their notebooks and give yourself a block of time so that you can really take in what these children are telling you about their lives and their literacy.

When you first read their entries, try to use them as a way to know your children. The author Avi was wise when he said, "If you can convince a child you love him (or her), you can teach that child anything" (1987). Of course, falling in love with children is tough in September, when you're still mourning the loss of last year's group. Remember, you'll be a much more powerful teacher for your kids if you find ways to fall in love—fast!

Try to see past your children's errors and past their writing skills to their content—to what is important to them, and to what they are trying to say and do. If you are able to do this, you will go a long way toward understanding and supporting the children as writers and toward creating a community conducive to writing. Your children's errors and skills matter— but now is not the time to focus on either. Jane Yolen, author of *Owl Moon, (1973)* once told a story about a child who came to her and said, "I love *Owl Moon*. I like your metaphors." Jane was pleased, of course, that the child responded to her book but sorry that it had been the *metaphors* that the child loved most. "I want children to open my books and fall through the rabbit hole of the story," she said, referring to Alice's adventures in Wonderland. Children, too, want and deserve to have readers who listen *through* their attempts at descriptive language and high-frequency words, to hear and care about their content. If we can give children readers who really listen to the content of their stories, we enable children to feel how powerful it can be to write the stories of their lives.

So begin the year by trying to use your children's writing as a way to become an expert on the little ones you teach. Learn what each one knows and cares about, and then make specific, individual plans to let children know that their writing has gotten through to you. Prepare to tell them, "I had no idea you have a beagle! I've always loved those dogs," or "Someday you need to bring in pictures of your town in the Dominican Republic."

Meanwhile, however, you may also want to make some mental groupings of your children according to the support you want to give them right away. You may, for example, plan to convene the children who have not done much writing of any kind for a strategy lesson in which you help them get more down on the page. You may make another mental group of children who are writing all about a topic rather than telling a story in narrative form (this will probably be a huge group). You may also notice a few children who are writing focused narratives that could be exemplars for other children.

Hopefully, some of your more struggling writers will be among those who have zoomed in and told a focused story—this is something even kindergartners can do, so prepare yourself to find focused stories hiding behind problematic spelling and penmanship. A writer need not have fancy spelling or a sophisticated control of syntax in order to zoom in and tell a story in a chronological, step-by-step way. If you can find some exemplar texts among the writing your strugglers have done, and make a big fuss over the smart decisions those children have made, other strugglers will see children like themselves meeting with your approval, and their expectations for themselves will skyrocket.

IN THIS SESSION, YOU'LL TEACH CHILDREN THAT WRITERS FOCUS THEIR STORIES, AND THAT THEY TELL STORIES IN SCENES RATHER THAN SUMMARIES.

GETTING READY

- Instruction on chalkboard telling children to bring their writer's notebooks (pens tucked inside) and sit with their partners in the meeting area
- Chart Qualities of Good Personal Narrative Writing
- List of story topics, some watermelon-sized and some seed-sized
- See CD-ROM for resources

QUALITIES OF GOOD WRITING:
FOCUS, DETAIL, AND STRUCTURE

You are still at the very start of the school year, and you and your students have months still stretching ahead of you. You could argue that it's not urgent to lift the level of student writing right now, that instead what's needed is to teach students to proceed independently through the writing process. I argue, however, that it actually is important to teach children what they need to know so their writing becomes dramatically more effective, quickly. Ultimately, children will invest themselves in learning to write if they see their writing becoming stronger— and you will invest yourself in teaching writing if your hard work pays off!

In this session, you'll explicitly teach some qualities of good writing. First, you'll teach some ways writers focus. Children are much more apt to write organized, detailed pieces if they closely focus their writing. The easiest kind of focus is temporal focus— writing about a short span of time. For now, help your children to do this. Eventually, you'll acknowledge that good stories need not fit into twenty minutes, but for now, encourage children to "zoom in" and to write with detail about brief episodes.

In this session, I point out that writers often think first of watermelon topics and then focus on a story the size of one tiny watermelon seed. The metaphor of a watermelon topic is one I will revisit later, pointing out, for example, that there are lots of seed-sized stories in a single watermelon topic. After teaching about focus, I remind children that writers use specific details. It is impossible to overemphasize the value of detail.

There is another quality of good writing that I do not overtly address in this session but that matters tremendously: significance. When we write well, we convey that we are invested in our own stories. It is important to write in such a way that readers do not read our stories and shrug, thinking, "So what?" Steer children toward writing stories that matter to them. As Robert Frost said, "No tears in the writer, no tears in the reader." (1963, p. 32) Whereas E. B. White can take a subject like warts and write well about it, most of us will have an easier time writing well about moments that bristle with significance. You'll notice, then, that the stories I spotlight in this session are ones in which everyday events (a goodbye kiss before the school bus arrives, decorating a classroom for the first day of school) carry emotional resonance.

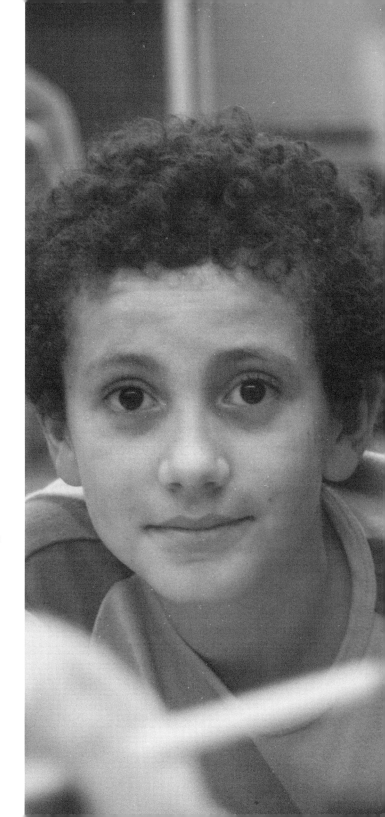

MINILESSON

Qualities of Good Writing: Focus, Detail, and Structure

CONNECTION

Celebrate that your children are using the strategies you've taught in order to write stories that matter. Do this in such a manner that you help writers recall these strategies.

"Writers, can I have your eyes and your attention? You have been coming up with people, places, and objects that matter to you, and I am so glad you realize your lives are worth writing about!"

"When you think of a topic and then list specific instances, sometimes those specific instances are still too big. After you jot down a place that matters—say the beach—your list may contain items like 'my summer at the beach.' You won't yet have come upon a small moment. So, here's some advice I can give you that will help your writing get better."

Name the teaching point. In this case, tell children that writers focus.

"Today I want to teach you that in addition to strategies for generating writing, writers keep in mind qualities of good writing that help us shape our ideas. Specifically, writers know that to write a story that draws readers close to listen, it helps to write about a small episode, something that happened in twenty minutes, or even in just three minutes! It is important to zoom in on one small story and to tell the parts of the story that matter, leaving out sections that don't matter. Writers retell the sequence of events in our stories, writing with details, telling the story in a step-by-step way."

"I wrote these qualities of good writing on a chart to help you remember that as writers, we think about not only *what* we're going to write about but also *how* we'll write our stories so they really affect our readers. The chart will be called Qualities of Good Personal Narrative Writing and we will continue to add to it as we learn other qualities of good writing that writers use when they write."

COACHING

Notice that I've not only reminded writers of the previous teaching points, I've also tried to consolidate the strategies I've taught to make them easier to remember. We hope our teaching gives students ready access to a handful of tools.

It is typical that a unit of study will begin with the teacher equipping children with a small repertoire of strategies for generating that particular kind of writing. The strategies will be a bit different depending on the genre or structure of writing under consideration, and embedded in the strategies will be some information about the genre or structure. I think it is important to limit the number of days you spend introducing strategies so that by the third or fourth day of a unit, you encourage children to draw from their repertoire of strategies, self-selecting one, while you shine a spotlight on qualities of writing that also merit attention.

> Qualities of Good Personal Narrative Writing
>
> • Write a little seed story; don't write all about a giant watermelon topic
> • Zoom in so you tell the most important parts of the story

TEACHING
Highlight what you hope children will do. Contrast a less-than-ideal topic with a better writing choice.

"Let's examine the first quality of good writing on the chart: 'Write a little seed story; don't write all about a giant watermelon topic.' Usually, after we think of a place, for example, what comes to mind first are great big *watermelon* topics like 'My summer at the beach' or even 'My day at the beach.' But to get a really good story, it helps to select a particular, smaller subject, to tell not a watermelon story but a little seed story, like the story of one time at the beach when I made a sailboat out of some driftwood and a shirt."

"The other day, I was going to write about playing with my cousin," I said, spreading my arms wide. "But then I realized, 'Wait, that is a great big watermelon topic,' so I decided instead to write about how my cousin and I made a fort out of blankets." I held my thumb and forefinger a tiny bit apart. We draped the blankets between the sofa and the chairs."

ACTIVE ENGAGEMENT
Set children up to practice distinguishing between big topics and focused stories.

"Just before you write a personal narrative, a true story, pause to ask yourself, 'Is this a big watermelon idea, or is it a little seed story?'"

"Let's practice asking that question and discerning the difference between big watermelon ideas and little seed stories. Signal with your hand to show me whether I'm about to write a big watermelon topic or a little seed story." First I held my arms apart then I held my finger and thumb near one another.

"Let's see, I *could* write about the time when I was your age and I snuck away from the playground during recess to buy candy. I was waiting in line at the store, my hands loaded with candy, when my mother walked in and saw me there. Is that a big watermelon topic or a little seed story?" The children signaled by holding their fingers together, as if to hold a tiny seed, that this was a seed story. "What if I planned to write about my trip to Disney

---

In the series Units of Study for Primary Writing, *I used the metaphor of "big watermelon topics" and "little seed stories" to distinguish unfocused stories from focused stories. Writers of every age need reminders to focus. In life, of course, there must be a place for stories that encompass more than twenty minutes of time. But one of the fastest ways to improve the quality of your children's writing is to help them focus, and the easiest way to focus a narrative is to write about a smaller chunk of time. Eventually, we will help children write with a thematic focus where they will create effective stories that span larger chunks of time. In the examples I provide here, notice that the unfocused and focused versions of a story match in every aspect but focus. Whenever I contrast two examples, I try to be sure that the only difference between them is the quality I'm highlighting.*

In minilessons specifically and the writing workshop in general, we are teaching children to use knowledge on the run about writing. This means that when we teach children qualities of good writing, we attach these qualities to strategies and procedures. I don't want to tell children about a quality of good writing without showing them how they can put their knowledge into action. In the Active Engagement section, I essentially set children up to join me in reading over a list of topics. I know that in life, writers aren't given generic lists of topics and told to decide whether or not those topics are focused. So I try to engineer this active engagement in such a way that I show how and when I, as a writer, actually might pause for a second and think, "Wait, would that be a focused topic?"

World? I could tell all the stuff I did." The children used outstretched arms to try to encircle this gigantic watermelon topic.

"Now, what if I planned to tell the story of how I stood next to the sign that tells if you're tall enough to go on the roller coaster, and this year I was tall enough?" They signaled that this was a seed idea. "How about these?"

- "Fun times I have with my dog?" [watermelon]
- "When I first saw my dog in the cage at the SPCA and knew he was the one for me?" [seed]
- "When the person who is now my best friend first arrived in our classroom and we met each other?" [seed]
- "My best friend?" [watermelon]
- "The year I was on the soccer team and we won six games and lost two?" [watermelon]
- "I broke my leg and went to the hospital and had to use crutches for a month?" [watermelon]
- "The time I was playing with Susan Downer at recess and she and I found a quarter frozen in the ice so we chipped it out of the ice?" [seed]

"Would you and your partner look over the entries in your notebooks, the stories that you've written. At the start of each story, write 'watermelon story' or 'seed story.'" The room filled with chatter, and I listened to conversations.

Share the good work of one partnership in a way that allows you to explain that watermelon topics have many seed story ideas in them.

"Writers, I was listening in on Paul and Abraham, and they realized that Paul had written a great big watermelon story about his old school. But then Paul realized that *inside* that one watermelon, there are a lot of seed stories! He doesn't have to throw the watermelon topic out—instead, he can reread his entry and at the bottom of the page, make a list of all the little seed stories he could get from that one topic. The rest of you may want to try the same smart work."

LINK
Remind children that whenever they use qualities of good writing to think of a true story, they can pause to consider whether their story idea is focused.

"So writers, whenever you start writing a personal narrative story, pause for a second to ask yourself, 'Is this a little seed story?'"

This can progress really quickly, and needs to do so. Of course the list will work best if it's created out of your life together.

You can't make writers perfect overnight. Allow some kids to get by with drafts that are not totally focused and with narratives that sound rather like summaries. Remember, your primary goal for this first unit is not phenomenal writing. Instead, your goal is for kids to be engaged with writing for an increasing length of time, for them to begin to grasp some concepts of good writing and of the writing process, and for kids to work with some independence. If a child initially writes all about a vacation and then checks herself, zooming in to write all about one brimful day, note to yourself that the child will need further coaching. But for now, celebrate that the child independently drew on a concept she'd learned. Each month you will have more time to strengthen the lessons on good writing you have taught in your minilessons.

WRITING AND CONFERRING

Teaching Writers to Draw on All the Strategies They've Learned

I have sometimes compared a writing workshop teacher to the acrobat in the circus who gets plates spinning on the ends of sticks. The acrobat gets four plates spinning, then six. The first plate begins to wobble and with a touch, he helps that plate regain momentum. From across the room, he sees another plate wobble dangerously and rushes over to prevent its fall. You probably resemble this circus performer as you rush about, trying to keep your writers writing!

As you confer with one child and then another, remember that your conferences, table compliments, and small-group strategy lessons should reflect the cumulative content of your teaching. So today, for example, guard against the temptation to go from table to table, child to child, working only to help kids zoom in on smaller topics. Instead, you will help some kids generate ideas for personal narratives, you'll help others set volume goals for themselves and write toward those goals, and you'll remind some children that when writers are done, they've just begun. Of course, you will also see that some children have great big watermelon topics, and you'll help them focus on little seed stories, reminding them if their initial entry was all about a topic, they'll need to begin an entirely new and focused story.

Keep your priorities clear. You want every child to believe that he or she is able to generate topics, writing chronological and true entries; you want every child to work through a process that involves choosing a topic and perhaps rehearsing for the story by sketching or saying it. But you need to expect that some of your instruction will fall on rocky soil and that, until you intervene, some kids will continue to write unfocused and chaotically organized entries. It is more important for you to keep your plates spinning (and your writers engaged) than to fuss over whether each child is doing exactly what you had in mind.

Today you will especially want to confer with kids who haven't yet written any entries that seem to be in

---

MID-WORKSHOP TEACHING POINT *Telling a Story Instead of Writing All About a Topic* "Writers, can I have your eyes and your attention?" I paused until the room grew absolutely silent. "I want to teach you a smart thing Brooke did. She began writing an entry that went like this." *[Fig. III-1]*

> My family and friend
> Jamie is one of my Best friends! I knew her for almost all my life.
> My mom is thirty years old, and has brownish gold hair. And works.

"Then she paused and said to herself, 'Wait a minute! I'm writing all about two people (my mom and my friend). If I want to write a story, I gotta choose one. I'm going to try to list stuff my mom and I have done together.' So she stopped right smack in the middle of writing her entry and wrote a list about her mom that went like this."

> Kissing me good bye before school
> Putting green ribbons in my hair

continued on next page

> My Family and frend
> Jamie is one of my Bestl frends. I new her for almost all my live.
> My mom is thirty years old, and has brownish gold hair. and works

Fig. III-1 Brooke's initial unfocused entry

the ballpark. Within a few days, you'll be asking students to reread all their entries and to select one to work on for the next week, and it'd be great if every student could go into that endeavor with some strong entries from which to choose. To help your students write strong entries, help them select focused topics in which they tell a story they care about, and help them to tell the story in a sequential and detailed fashion. If you've heard some children telling lively stories to their friends during snack time, by all means help them put those same stories onto the page.

Pay attention to the volume of writing your children do. If they're not producing much text, you'll probably want to lead a second mid-workshop teaching point, this one reminding them that writers are like runners: we push ourselves toward goals that we set. You may resort to making smiley faces in the margins of writer's notebooks as a way to signify, "I love to see you are writing more!"

continued from previous page

"Brooke picked the goodbye moment. She tried to remember it—not the whole before-school time, but just the things that happened right before and after her mom kissed her goodbye. This time, Brooke made a movie in her mind of exactly what happened and wrote what she remembered. Listen." *[Fig. III-2]*

Mom's kiss goodbye

One lovely day, on the first day of school, I told my mom to hurry up and get my back-pack full of things like my lunch, my snack, my special pencils and pen, my very special, powerful writing notebook and my glue stick. And so I zipped my back-pack and I walked outside, and the bus was already there and mom gave me a kiss, and ever since that day, I can still feel that exact same wonderful lovely kiss!

"Can you hear what a good start Brooke got when she zoomed in? So remember, if your writing feels like it's about a lot of things, you can stop, make a list like Brooke did, and zoom in! Okay, back to writing!"

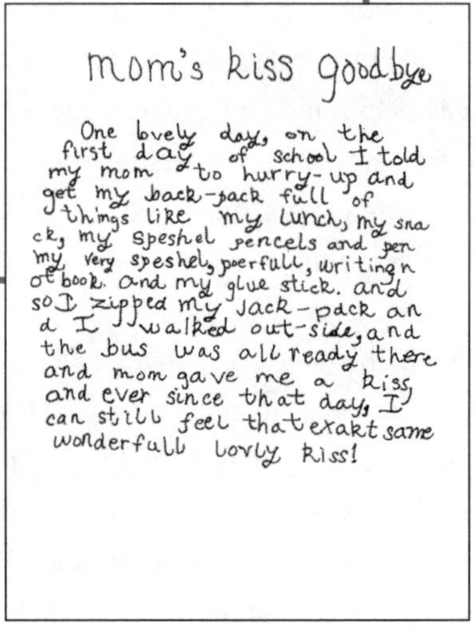
mom's kiss goodbye

One lovely day, on the first day of school I told my mom to hurry-up and get my back-pack full of things like my lunch, my snack, my speshel pencels and pen my, very speshel, poerfull, writing notbook. and my glue stick. and so I zipped my back-pack and I walked out-side, and the bus was all ready there and mom gave me a kiss, and ever since that day, I can still feel that exakt same wonderfull lovly kiss!

Fig. III-2 Brooke's later, more focused entry

SHARE

Writing with Specific Details

Convene children. Find an example of a child who has used a strategy you want more children to try. Tell what one child did in such a way that others could follow a similar procedure in their own writing.

"Writers, can I have your eyes and your attention, please? When I gesture toward your table, come find your spot on the rug."

"Your writing is giving me goose bumps. You are getting so good at writing Small Moment entries! I want to show you something Lizzie did that you can try also, a strategy that will make your writing even better. Lizzie did a *smart* thing in her writing. She didn't just write 'I got in the car'—a short, general sentence—and then stop. Instead, she added on, writing with specifics. Listen." *[Fig. III-3]*

> I got into the car with my feet scrunched up so I wouldn't smash the plants.
>
> My mom and I were decorating her classroom for the new school year. There were calendars, posters, plants and supplies. We carried them in, up the stairs and into room 205. I set up a magnetic calendar, did a puzzle of the USA, stuck short biographies on the walls and hung my Mom's tacks up high so she could hang up high things . . .

"Lizzie didn't just say, 'I got in the car' and then stop her sentence, did she? Instead she said more. She said, 'I got in the car *with my feet scrunched up so I wouldn't smash the plants.*' She didn't just say, 'I set up the classroom' and then stop, did she? Instead she kept going, telling how she set up the classroom."

You may wonder when to call an end to workshop time. Frankly, at the beginning of the year, one important factor to consider is the children's ability to keep working. Although eventually you'll want the actual workshop section of your workshop to last at least forty minutes, at the beginning of the year children's stamina for writing may not be strong enough for them to perservere this long. When the students get restless, end the writing portion of your workshop by asking them to put their work in its storage place. (You'll probably have a box to hold notebooks for each table.) Then convene writers for a longer than usual share session.

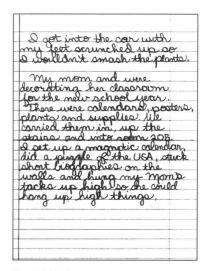

Fig. III-3 Lizzie

In this Share, I act as if I want to celebrate Lizzie's success. But actually, I chose Lizzie not only because she merits praise but also because lots and lots of kids were writing short sentences lacking detail, and I wanted them to recognize this and be able to self-correct. I use the positive example of Lizzie to get the point across. If the class had had different needs—say, a bunch of children staring at blank pages—then I would have had a different share.

"Another thing I love—Lizzie told us *exact* details. She could have written, 'I helped my mother unpack *a lot of things.*' If she'd said that, we wouldn't really be able to picture precisely what Lizzie did. Because she instead wrote, 'I set up *a magnetic calendar, did a puzzle of the USA, stuck short biographies on the walls . . . ,*' we can picture how she helped her mother unpack. I'm hoping some of you can learn from Lizzie's smart decision to write with precise details, even if it took extending her sentences."

Ask children to work with their partners to check for places in their own writing where they could apply this technique.

"Now let's help each other find places where each one of us could try saying more and writing with exact details. Will partner 1 from each partnership raise a thumb so we know who you are? Partner 1, will you read one of your entries? Then partner 2 (show me which of you is partner 2), see if there is a place for saying more and saying exact details. Your job is to listen and then point out specific places in the text where the writer could try this."

"If there are short sentences like 'I got in the car,' you and your partner may want to add to them, saying more. 'I got into my car with my feet scrunched up so I wouldn't smash the plants.' You can use a caret," I wrote one on the board, "and then add the details above your writing, or you can use the caret to point to a star and then, at another place on your page, write another star and write out the specifics you'd like to insert into your entry." I gave them time to do this.

Remind writers that they can use this technique in their own writing every day from now on.

"From this day forward, try to remember that specifics like 'I set up a magnetic calendar and did a puzzle of the USA' are more powerful than generalizations like 'I unpacked a lot of things.' To help you remember these qualities of strong narratives, you can refer to our chart." I pointed to the chart onto which I'd added a line about details.

Qualities of Good Personal Narrative Writing

- Write a little seed story; don't write all about a giant watermelon topic
- Zoom in so you tell the most important parts of the story
- Include true, exact details from the movie you have in your mind

Here I do something we often do in share sessions: I took one student's work and thought, "What actions has this writer taken that others could emulate?"

I don't really know how Lizzie went about writing, but I notice that, whereas many children write in simple sentences (the subject did [the verb] to an object), Lizzie extended her sentences by providing more details. She made a similar gesture to tell more when she told an action and then added a few sentences that elaborated on it with more details.

I always try to teach both a quality of good writing (writing with details) and also a procedure for achieving this quality in writing. That way, I hope, the writer can achieve this quality later, in her own writing. I teach the goal and the step-by-step procedure for achieving the goal.

HOMEWORK *Living Like Writers, Noticing Details* Today we talked about the importance of *writing* with details, but I want to remind you that we can't record details unless we first see details! Tonight, instead of writing with details, *live* with details. Watch your dog slide between you and the newspaper you're trying to read, as if she's saying, "Read me!" Notice that the tower of books beside your bed shows how your reading tastes have changed over the last few weeks. Pay attention to the fact that in your household, there is only one person who can find the heads to Lego-people. Does your little sister have a stash of heads hidden away so that she can save the day? Most people wouldn't wonder about this. Most people walk right past details. But writers are people who pause and say, "Hmm . . . this is interesting!" The poet Naomi Nye says it this way: "Truly, I feel irresponsible when I don't notice things well enough, when I slide or slip through a day. . . . I want to hear the cat down the street turning the block."

TAILORING YOUR TEACHING

If your students need more support with zooming in on small moments in their stories . . . you might design a minilesson like this: "Writers, we're going to write in our notebooks today, choosing our own topics from our lives. Before you get started, I want to share with you something that I learned from my husband, who's a photographer. When he takes pictures, he doesn't swing the camera like this," I indicate a 180° panorama, "but instead he zooms in by focusing the camera on one small frame at a time. He usually doesn't take a picture of a whole meadow, but of three daisies. He usually doesn't take a picture of the whole city, but of a pigeon roosting on the arm of a statue in the park. Writers are like photographers. We focus when we write personal narratives; we focus on tiny incidents from our lives. Today I'm going to teach you how to focus, or how to zoom in on small moments from your lives."

Then, for the teaching component of the minilesson, you might demonstrate, focusing. You could say, "Sometimes when I sit down to write, what comes to my mind first are the things I've been doing. The events of my life. But here's a secret. When one of these events comes to mind, I don't start writing. Instead I say to myself, 'Wait, I need to zoom in on a small portion of this event.'" Please turn to the CD-ROM for suggestions for how the rest of the minilesson might go.

Notice that these early homeworks don't spell out how much actual writing you expect. In fact, they ask writers to live writerly lives but don't ask them to produce entries. This will change soon, but for now I'm aware that it may still be too early in the year to pull off assigning a significant amount of writing at home. These assignments, then, channel children to live as writers, coming to school prepared to write. You could tweak them and specify writing in either a portable take-home notepad or a writer's notebook, if you can shepherd children to do the writing you assign.

If you step back and look over this entire series of books, you'll see that there is never a time when I shift away from a focus on detail. Youngsters so often think that they write with words, and especially as they become more facile with language, they throw a lot of words around fast and loose. We write with information, with specifics, with facts. Our readers want information. They want specifics.

So begin now to encourage children to collect exactly, precisely true information. If they mention that their refrigerator door is covered with papers fastened with magnets, encourage them to describe the magnets. Are they china pigs and cows? Advertisements from local shops masquerading as magnets? Of course, once you encourage writers to write with detail, you'll need to go a step further and celebrate emblematic or revealing details.

COLLABORATING WITH COLLEAGUES

In the schools in which my colleagues and I work closely, the decision to support children's growth as writers is a whole-school decision, and every teacher devotes time each day to a writing workshop. Those writing workshops are structured similarly, so that children grow up expecting that they'll be explicitly taught skills and strategies of effective writing, and so they know that every day they'll have time to draw on all they've learned as they pursue their own important projects.

In these schools, teachers find it incredibly helpful to follow a shared curricular calendar so that at any one time, children across a grade level are delving into a shared unit of study. This means that teachers needn't invent our teaching alone, in isolation, but can instead teach alongside each other.

If you or your colleagues have decided to support each other through shared units of study, I can't emphasize strongly enough the enormous benefits you receive from using some of your grade-level meetings as opportunities to write alongside each other. If you live through a unit of study first as writers and only then as teachers, you'll be able to bring your own drafts and those of your colleagues into your

minilessons, and there is nothing that could make a bigger difference than this! Of course, the fact that you've tried the strategies I suggest will also give you an insider's appreciation for the challenges they pose, the detours to avoid, the tips that can make a big difference.

Joyce Chapnick is in a writing group, and I'm sharing the narrative she wrote and shared with her students so as to give you a glimpse into what you might decide to do as a writer. Remember, however, that Joyce's narrative evolved slowly, across a month of work.

Narrative: First Day of Third Grade with Reflection

It was September 1983, my family moved to a new house within the same town, but I had to start at a new school. I hated new. As a child I loved structure and routine.

My mom pulled through the circular driveway of my new school. The car halted. She said, "Good-bye, have a great first day," and she waited for me to get out. I couldn't move. It wasn't like I was trying to move. I didn't want to move. No part of me wanted to leave the safety and comfort of my Chevy station wagon.

I looked up at my mom and did everything in my power not to cry. I tried to talk, but nothing. Finally, I heard myself say with a quiver in my voice, "Aren't you going to take me in?" She knew that if she didn't act fast the tears would flow.

As I walked into Fox Meadow Elementary School gripping my mom's hand all of the children looked like they belonged; some were carrying backpacks, chatting with friends; one was me, frightened and nervous, the new girl at school.

I held my mom's hand tightly as we moved down the hallway from left to right dodging and avoiding all of the children and backpacks. Every time we had to wait for someone to move I breathed a sigh of relief because it delayed the inevitable for at least one more minute. The door to my new classroom became visible. I grabbed my mom's hand tighter hoping that the sweat would bond us like glue. My knees felt weak and my heart beat quickened.

My mom looked down at me with her warm eyes, "Joyce, you will be fine." Why couldn't she just stop, turn us around, and take me home? The classroom door was open. I saw so many children, talking and laughing. They all knew each other, and I knew no one. With that first glance, I felt it, first in my toes, then in my knees, then in my stomach. I was totally overwhelmed. Oh no," I thought,

"Please don't cry." But it was too late the tears were on in full force. It was like someone unscrewed the cap on a fire hydrant.

Just as the geyser blew I felt a hand on my shoulder. I looked up and through the glaze of my tears I saw a woman. She had curly dark hair and was wearing a blouse and long skirt. "You must be Joyce," I heard her say; "we have been expecting you." How did she know my name? "I am Miss Vopicelli." She reached down and took my hand. I looked up at my mom pleadingly. She smiled and whispered in my ear, "You are in good hands. Have a great day. I love you." And with those words she was gone. I had no choice but to follow the woman with the pretty voice who knew my name.

I learned that day that my mom couldn't always hold my hand and that change is not easy; especially change you don't choose. Right after I entered the classroom with Miss Vopicelli she introduced me to another little girl. At recess the girls asked me to play with them. I don't remember most of the details of the rest of that day, but I will always remember Miss Vopicell. Ten years after that frightful September day in 1983 I reentered Miss Vopicelli's (changed to Mrs. Banks) classroom…this time by choice. Today, I teach third grade and every September I am reminded of her when I welcome my new students. As each child enters the classroom, somewhere in the back of my head I hear her saying, "we have been expecting you."

Fig. III-4 Joyce

IN THIS SESSION, YOU'LL INTRODUCE CHILDREN TO THE STRUCTURE OF A WRITING CONFERENCE AND TEACH THEM WAYS WRITERS TALK ABOUT THEIR WRITING.

GETTING READY

- Instructions on chalkboard telling children to bring their writer's notebooks (pens tucked inside) and sit with their partners in the meeting area
- List of questions asked during a conference (see a sample in the Connection section)
- Short transcript of two conferences (effective/ineffective)
- Strategies for Generating Personal Narrative Writing chart
- Qualities of Good Personal Narrative Writing chart
- See CD-ROM for resources

THE WRITER'S JOB IN A CONFERENCE

The writing process approach to teaching writing is sometimes referred to as the conference approach. This title is an apt one because writing conferences are not only occasions for teaching children, they are also occasions for us to be taught. In a conference, a young writer teaches us how we can teach. The writer teaches us what she has been trying to do, has already done, hopes to do next. Children as well as teachers need to be let in on the plan for writing conferences. If children aren't told otherwise, they sometimes see the initial phase of a conference as merely a time for pleasantries, before the teacher lays out the directives.

In this session, then, you will teach children that in a conference, they become the teacher. Specifically, you help children know that when you ask, "What are you working on as a writer?" you do not want to learn simply the topic ("I'm writing about my dog running away") or even just the topic and the genre ("I'm writing a personal narrative about the time my dog ran away"). You also need to know what it is the child is trying to do as a writer ("I'm trying to show, not tell, that I was worried"). After you ask, "What are you working on as a writer?" you will have to show some children the sort of answer you have in mind. Look over the child's entry and then answer the question yourself, saying, for example, "It looks like you have been experimenting with different leads—some include dialogue, and some include setting. Is that right?"

Once you and the child have established whatever it is that the child has been trying to do, you might say, "Can you show me where you tried that?" Then compliment. Try to compliment something that you hope writers will do another day in another piece. "I love the way you told where you were when you were bowling," I said to one writer. "Always remember that it can be smart to bring out the setting." Then you can teach them a strategy to help them reach their writing goal today and forever more.

MINILESSON

The Writer's Job in a Conference

CONNECTION

Tell children that, just as they can expect a daily minilesson, they can count on frequent writing conferences.

"Writers, we've been working together in a writing workshop for almost a week, and I think you've come to understand that you can count on every writing workshop beginning with a minilesson where I teach you a strategy that writers use. You can count on having lots of time to write and a chance to write on topics that are important to you using all the strategies you've learned. You can also count on the fact that often, I'll pull up a chair alongside you to confer with you about your writing. Many people believe that writing conferences are at the heart of a strong writing workshop."

Name the teaching point. In this case, tell children that writing conferences have a reliable structure. The child's job in the conference is to talk to us about their thinking.

"Today I want to teach you that you can also count on how a writing conference will tend to go. This can help you do your part of the writing conference well."

"When a writing teacher confers with you, the teacher will want to know what you are trying to do as a writer, what you've done so far, and what you are planning to do next. So the writing teacher will start by interviewing you, asking questions about your writing (not your topic). The writing teacher will tend to ask questions like these:"

- What are you working on as a writer?
- What kind of writing are you making?
- What are you doing to make this piece of writing work?
- What do you think of what you've done so far?
- What will you do next?
- How will you go about doing that?

"A teacher's job at the start of the conference is to study the writer in order to figure out how to help—and a writer's job is to teach the teacher. You are teaching us not about your subject, but about the ways you've figured out to write. That way, we can be helpful."

COACHING

It's a good sign when your children have enough momentum and direction as writers that they don't rely on the daily minilesson as their source of direction. If children know how to carry on as writers and have a small repertoire of strategies to draw from, then our teaching can focus on the finer points of their work, as this minilesson does. Minilessons aren't designed to set children up for what they'll do on any one day; instead, they are always designed to lift the level of what children are doing in general.

It's not important that children learn the exact questions writing teachers tend to open conferences with—this is not a chart. This list is intended to help children understand the kinds of topics writing teachers want to learn more about from them. Meanwhile, however, you will definitely want to take note of these questions!

TEACHING

Contrast a writing conference in which a child talks about his thinking with one in which he talks about his topic.

"Listen to this conference with a child who hadn't yet learned how to do his job well, and then listen how it changed after he learned to do his job well." I signaled to my young volunteer, who held a copy of the transcript and played the part of the student before and after. "In this first conference, you'll see that the writer doesn't yet know his job in a conference."

Teacher: What are you working on as a writer?

Child A: Writing about the baseball game.

Teacher: What are you trying to do as a writer?

Child A: Writing about winning the game.

Teacher: What will you do today in your writing?

Child A: Write about how I hit the ball.

"Now compare that exchange with this one. You'll see that by now, the writer has learned his job in a conference, and does it well."

Teacher: What are you working on as a writer?

Child B: I'm writing a personal narrative about baseball and I've zoomed in on the last time I was up at bat.

Teacher: What are you trying to do as a writer?

Child B: I want to really write with details, but I'm not sure I remember them.

Teacher: What will you do today in your writing?

Child B: I was going to sketch the scene to see if that gets me remembering details I've left out.

Debrief. Point out that in a good conference, the writer articulates what she is trying to do.

"Did you see the difference? During this early part of both conferences, the teacher asked the same questions: What are you working on as a writer? What are you trying to do as a writer? What will you do today in your writing? The difference was that in the second conference, the writer knew that he needed to teach the teacher the specific goals that were important to him and the strategies he used to reach those goals." I gestured to the Qualities of Good Personal Narrative Writing and the Strategies for Generating Personal Narrative Writing charts.

In this teaching component, I set up two contrasting examples: the first is a don't-do-this example, the next is a do-this example. To highlight what I hope writers will do, I often contrast my hopes with what I don't want to see. The trick is that in order to highlight one feature, the two versions need to be identical in all ways but the one feature I'm trying to showcase.

Notice that in the first conference, the child talks about his topic only. In the second conference, the child talks about his writing goals, strategies, and challenges.

If we want children to rely upon the charts of our teaching points, then it is important for us to demonstrate times when a writer might reference a chart. This is one such time.

ACTIVE ENGAGEMENT
Set children up to practice their role in a writing conference. Specifically, ask the questions you are apt to ask during a conference, and give them time to prepare responses.

"So I'd like you to practice the part of a conference that is your job. Right now, I'm going to ask you the same questions I asked our writer. Think about your answer, and if you aren't sure what to say, try looking at one of our charts. For now, no one will talk—just think—and when you have an answer in mind, give me a thumbs up."

"First, what are you working on today as a writer?" I gave them thirty seconds of silence in which to silently answer this question and then I said, "Remember, you can say your topic, but a good answer reveals more specifics about your writing goals than that. The chart might help. Here's a further question: What are you trying to do as a writer?" I waited, and when most children gave a thumbs up, I signaled, "Tell your partner what you are thinking."

The room broke into a hubbub of talk. "Here is one last question for you to answer first, silently, in your mind: What will you do today in your writing?" Again, I paused until most gave a thumbs-up signal. "Remember our example. The writer didn't just say, 'Write about my dog' or 'Write.' He said, 'I'm going to sketch to see if sketching it will get me remembering details I've left out.' Try to be as purposeful and planful as a writer. The answer to this question is what you need to do now, so go ahead and start writing."

LINK
Reiterate the active role children will be expected to play in writing conferences.

"So writers, from this day forward when I confer with you, remember that you have a job to do in conferences. I'll be coaching you not only on your writing but also on your conferring!"

Don't underestimate the importance of silence. When I ask the question, "What are you working on today as a writer?" it is critical that I actually sit there and wait for a length of time that communicates to the children that it's their job to fill the silence with real thinking. Only then, after time for thinking, do I say, "Tell your partner . . . ."

If your children don't seem to know yet how to answer these kinds of questions, you might try modeling a writing conference with one child in front of the whole group. Figure out as a class ways the writer might respond to each question, or process together the answers she gives. If this too seems a stretch, you could ask another adult to role-play being a student writer and hold your conference with this colleague in front of your students. This modeling offers the students language to use in describing their own situations.

WRITING AND CONFERRING

Teaching Children the Basics of Conferring

Let's work on the basics of your conferring. First, make your body language convey that a conference is a respectful conversation, not a lecture or an assignment. Sit alongside the writer, and let the writer literally maintain control of the paper by being the one to hold the text. Then say something like, "Hi, Amanda, what are you working on as a writer today?" Today your children will be ready for that question, but even so the child is apt to answer by telling you her topic, not telling about what she is working on as a writer. If the child says, "I'm writing about playing Capture the Flag," you want to convey interest in the topic, but don't linger in a conversation about it. Say, "Oh! Great! I love that game." Then restate your question about the child's intentions. "And what, exactly, are you working on, are you trying to do, as a writer?" The child may look at you blankly, because she is still not sure the sort of answer you expect, or she might shrug and say, "I'm just writing." Ask to see her paper. Look to see if you can glean from the text itself some sense for what she has been trying to do as a writer. Could she have been trying to do one of the things you have taught the class? Name what you see or almost see. "Oh! I see. So you've written an entry about a time you remember. It looks to me like you tried to make your characters talk, you've recorded their exact words. Is that one thing you were working on?" The writer will probably nod. "Am I right that you were rereading it just now? Were you thinking about whether you'd zoomed in enough?"

The writer will probably go along with whatever you see in the entry. If she nods to indicate that yes, she had just been about to reread the entry and to think whether it was a focused story, you can say, "So why don't you do that while I watch."

> **MID-WORKSHOP TEACHING POINT**
>
> ***Writing Stories Step-by-Step*** "Writers, can I have your eyes and your attention? I want to show you the smart work that Amanda just did. I came over to her and asked (as I often ask), 'What are you working on as a writer?' She answered that she was rereading her entry, trying to decide if she'd talked all about an event or told it like a story. Listen to her entry and ask yourself the same question. Is this a summary or is it a story?" I read it.
>
> > I was 4 and my brother wanted to play capture the flag with me. It took about 20 minutes to finally understand how. He got frustrated from all my questions and threw a snowball at my face.
>
> "Amanda decided she'd written a summary," I said, tweaking the truth a bit so as to make Amanda look like she'd been in the driver's seat more than was accurate. "So Amanda made a movie in her mind of exactly what happened on one day and then asked herself, 'What happened first? Where was I?' This is her next draft.
>
> *continued on next page*

In this instance, Amanda's entry went like this:

> I was 4 and my brother wanted to play capture the
> flag with me. It took me about 20 minutes to finally
> understand how. He got frustrated from all my
> questions and threw a snowball at my face.

Before you proceed to teach, find something to compliment as well as something to teach. "You didn't just *tell* the reader that your brother was frustrated. You thought about what he did to show his frustration, and you added a tiny detail. That detail brings your brother to life on the page."

Then I said, "Can I teach you one thing?" and proceeded to tell her that she'd actually written a summary, not a story, of the event. So I helped her to tell this episode as a story. To do so, I gave her prompts that I use countless times over the first few weeks of a narrative unit of study. "Amanda, can you remember exactly how this started? Where were you at the beginning? Then what happened? Exactly what did he say? Can you say what he did, exactly? What did you do then?"

Once Amanda began telling this like a story, I repeated back what she said. Then I got Amanda to write the words.

continued from previous page

Listen and give me a thumbs up if you think this version sounds like the start of a story."

> I was at the kitchen eating macaroni. My big brother, Chris,
> came in and said, "You gotta play Capture the Flag with me
> and Nate. You are on my team." I followed him out to the
> front lawn...."

The children signaled that this was indeed a story. "You are right! What a difference. Listen again." I reread the two versions again, emphasizing the differences with my voice— reading the summary in a monotone and the story with a "once-upon-a-time" lilt.

"So writers, right now would you get with your partner and read one of your entries aloud, and decide together whether you have written a story, telling it step-by-step, or a summary. If your entry is not yet a story, try to start it over, telling exactly what happened first and then next."

SHARE

Naming Exactly What Works Well in Writing

Convene writers. Ask them to study their partner's writing and name what is working well in it.

"Writers, can I have your eyes and your attention, please? Now let's share with our partners a little bit of what we've written. Partner 1, will you read what you wrote today to your partner? Then partner 2, please talk about your classmate's writing. Instead of just saying, 'It's nice,' name some specific technique the writer used that really worked. If the writer helped you get a movie in your mind, point to the part of the writer's story you can really envision. If the writer wisely zoomed in and told a whole lot about one tiny time, tell that to the writer. Perhaps the writer wrote what happened first, then next, in a step-by-step way. Or perhaps the writer included true, exact details of what happened. Your job is to listen and then to name exactly what the writer did that worked well. Then point out specific places in the text where the writer did this."

Remind writers to use the Qualities of Good Personal Narrative Writing chart as they write.

"The chart we created earlier can help you remember qualities of good writing that are worth celebrating. When you look at your partner's writing, I'm sure you'll find examples of those qualities."

You should be finding that the format and methods of minilessons are beginning to feel familiar to you. Usually in a share, we celebrate what a few children have done in a manner that allows us to reiterate what we hope all children are doing. The teacher needs to name what one child has done in such a way that the one instance of good work is transferable to other days and other children. Then, children often get an opportunity to work in pairs, seeing if they've already done similar work or planning how they, too, could do that work.

You may decide to make copies of this chart so that each child can hold onto his or her own copy. See the CD-ROM for a master copy. You may go a step further and turn this chart into a self-assessment checklist.

Qualities of Good Personal Narrative Writing

- Write a little seed story; don't write all about a giant watermelon topic
- Zoom in so you tell the most important parts of the story
- Include true, exact details from the movie you have in your mind

I listened while Raymond read his entry to Christina: [*Fig. IV-1*]

> When I was in the train to Canal Street I was fooling around with my sister. I keep on tickling my baby sister and my baby sister was tickling me. Then we stop and I was bothering her and when she looks at me, I say, "I did not do nothing." And my baby sister did the same thing I did. We both laughed and so did my Mom and we did not notice that everybody was staring at us. I laughed a little.

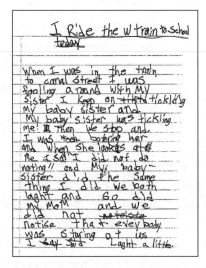

Fig. IV-1 Raymond

Christina said, "You told about one time on the train."

I added, "That was smart of you to notice that he zoomed in on one time. Let's listen again and Christina, can you try to give more specific compliments? Try to name exactly what Raymond did that works."

Raymond again read the entry. This time, Christina said, "I could picture that 'cause the same thing happens with my brother!"

"Can you point to where Raymond wrote that one part you especially liked?" I asked, and Christina did.

Addressing the whole class, I said, "Writers, I've heard some *amazing* conversations just now. Many of you referenced the chart, which was a brilliant thing to do. Remember that when you write, you can look up at our charts to remind yourself of goals that can lead you to write really well."

● HOMEWORK **The Writer's Job in a Conference** Today you learned about your job in a writing conference. For homework, you'll rehearse for that job. Tonight imagine that a teacher pulls up a chair next to you. Think about your writing so you'll be ready to talk about it with the teacher. Remember, teachers tend to ask questions like the ones below in conferences, so be ready to answer them:

- What are you working on as a writer?
- What are you trying to do as a writer?
- What will you do today in your writing?

I'll be looking forward to talking with you and teaching you based on what you say!

TAILORING YOUR TEACHING During the first few weeks of this unit, you will need to teach children self-management skills. For example, you will need to teach children what writers can do when they are stuck, or how they can get help if the teacher is busy, or how to talk more quietly.

If your students need strategies for working independently through difficulties . . . you might teach a minilesson that begins like this: "Writers, something happened to me last night when I was writing, and I know that the same thing happens to you. Last night, right before bed, I was trying to write about this memory I had of chipping a precious dish when I was little, and I got stuck. I know that sometimes happens to you, too. You get stuck. Well, in my case, I forgot exactly what my mom had said when she found out I broke the dish. I could have called my mom to ask her to help, but it was too late at night. I didn't have anyone around to help me, so I had to help myself. Let me tell you how I helped myself— because you may want to try the same technique. I thought about what she probably would have said if I'd gone to her for help. I helped myself without asking anyone else! That way, I kept on writing without needing to wait for help. So one way we can help ourselves as writers," you might say, "is to ask ourselves the question instead of taking it to someone else. Usually we can answer our own questions, usually we don't have to wait for help!"

If your students wait for help with the same predictable questions . . . you might show a list on chart paper of some questions students have asked you over the past week. "Let's take a look at this first question that was asked of me this week. When you think you have an answer, thumbs up." Give them a moment to think. "Wow, a lot of you answered that question quickly. Let's try the next question on the list." After one or two more, underscore how quickly and easily they were able to answer these questions when they took the time to ask themselves. "From now on, whenever you have a question, remember, the first person to ask is yourself. If necessary, you can also ask one of your fellow writers. Maybe they have had this problem before and you two can work it out together."

ASSESSMENT

If several people read and comment on the same piece of children's writing, the variety of their responses will be startling. The reason for this diversity is that what we see in our students' writing comes as much from us as it does from the children. The good news is that we can look at our students' work through lenses we've deliberately chosen, and not be limited by our instincts and habits. At this point in the year, I strongly urge you to look at your children's writing to see if and how your instruction has influenced it. As you do this, you are, of course, learning as much about your own teaching as you are learning about your children's work.

Ask yourself:

- "How many of my children have learned to write about small moments, about events that begin and end within a short span of time?" Jot lists of the children who have and who haven't yet learned this.

- Or ask, "How many of my children write a sequence of events, telling one after another?"

Don't ask yourself whether your children do any of this well yet—only ask if they've written a sequence of events.

I encourage you to make a pile of notebooks that don't contain much evidence that your instruction has made a dent. The authors of those notebooks need more of your attention. Assume for now that you, not the child, have some catching up to do and set out with great resolve, planning to do more to connect with the child who doesn't seem to be grasping what you are trying to teach. These children need to become your teachers, teaching you how to make a more significant difference in their lives. Study their written work and observe them during class time in order to untangle the puzzle. Give each of these children your best attention and gather data

that can inform you. Realize you may need to recruit a colleague to join you in puzzling through the mysteries of these children.

As you study these strugglers, consider whether your teaching perhaps asked them to take a step that was too giant, all at once. For example, you've asked these children to write about *small* stories that are nevertheless significant to them. The paradox involved in that charge may have been confusing, and perhaps for now you'll decide to forgo the emphasis on writing about significant stories, and to focus only on writing about tightly focused events. Although you may not have emphasized writing conventionally correct entries, some of these children may be obsessed with a concern for correctness and may, therefore, have little brain space to devote to envisioning precise details. If these children seem to you to be struggling because you or they have taken on a challenge which is too demanding for them at this time, then be sure to talk with the child about the goals that really matter right now, and those that can wait for a later time. Then be vigilant in watching for signs of progress toward the newly clarified goals. Keep in mind that a child may still be doing lots of things that are less than ideal . . . Yet if you see palpable progress toward a goal, this merits a celebration.

Meanwhile, think also about the whole class again. Look at their written texts as windows onto their growth processes. You've taught stamina; look to see if their notebooks suggest they've developed more stamina. Which children show that they can finish one entry and begin the next without needing your help?

If your instruction is making an impact, you'll want to celebrate this even if the resulting pieces are still laden with other problems, problems you have yet to address. As you look at what children *are* doing, you'll see next steps.

BUILDING STORIES STEP-BY-STEP

Since the start of this unit, *your children have spent their writing time collecting one entry after another. In the next session, they will select one of these entries to develop, revise, craft, and edit toward publication.*

The writing process is cyclical. This means that the phase you and your children have just experienced is not over. Each time your children write, they'll always begin their work by watching the world, living like writers and then collecting entries that could eventually grow into the kind of texts they're aiming to write.

You will want to be keenly aware of what you and your children have and haven't accomplished thus far. Look back at your goals for this unit and notice which you've met. Hopefully by now, most of your children have come to realize that their lives are full of stories to tell, topics to write. Hopefully most children live with a writer's consciousness, noticing funny predicaments or poignant moments and saying, "That'd make a great story!" Hopefully they've grasped the concept that during this writing workshop, they can draw on strategies they learned before. If any of these lessons have been learned, this is cause for great celebration.

Today's session is crucial. We need to move heaven and earth to be sure children have made the gigantic leap from summarizing to storytelling. When children summarize, they will probably be the first to feel that their writing is not very effective. That feeling will quickly lower their enthusiasm and lessen their investment in writing. Just as troubling, when children summarize instead of storytelling, it probably means that they have not yet realized that writing is a process of making choices about what to say and how to say it. Once children begin telling their story moment by moment, however, a world of writing choices opens up for them. Writers begin to sense all the possible ways to tell a story when they realize there are endless possibilities even for leads. "It was a damp day and my shirt was sticking to me" or "My little brother looked up at me and asked, 'Are you happy?'" Storylike openings imply choices and reasons not implied in summaries.

In this session you'll help children see their own writing as a crafted story, not just a recounting of thoughts as they occurred to the writer. In this session you'll help children feel their power as creators.

IN THIS SESSION, YOU'LL TEACH STUDENTS THAT WRITERS UNFOLD STORIES BIT BY BIT, RATHER THAN SUMMARIZING THEM.

GETTING READY

- Instructions on chalkboard telling children to bring their writer's notebooks (pens tucked inside) and sit with their partners in the meeting area
- Two versions of a story to tell: one a summary, one a sequential unfolding narrative
- Chart paper and markers
- Idea for a shared class event the children can retell orally, step-by-step
- See CD-ROM for resources

MINILESSON

Building Stories Step-by-Step

CONNECTION

Celebrate that your students are writing with some focus.

"Writers, I took your stories home last night and, reading them over, it was clear to me that most of you remembered to write not about a big watermelon idea but about a tiny, tiny seed story. Instead of writing about your visit to your grandmother's and telling the whole day, you zoomed in and wrote focused stories—writing, for example, a story about planting hyacinth bulbs with your grandma. That is so smart."

"But there is one thing I noticed in your writing that I want to talk about with you. Sometimes, after you get a small story in mind, like the story of planting bulbs with your grandmother, you aren't writing the story in a step-by-step way, telling *a story* of what happened. Instead you are making comments about the gardening (or whatever the episode is that you are capturing). For example, instead of writing what you did first and then next like this:"

> I knelt down under the tree with my grandma. "Is this a good place for one of the flowers?" I asked.

"you instead *talk about* (or comment on) the gardening."

> I did some gardening with my grandma. It was fun. We planted about five bulbs. She showed me how to plant bulbs so a deer can't dig them up.

Name the teaching point. In this case, tell children you want to teach them that personal narratives are often organized chronologically, told as a sequence of events.

"Now, writers *do* sometimes write all about a topic. But for now, in this class, we are writing true stories, or personal narratives. And today what I want to teach you is that stories, or narratives, are almost always organized to tell what happened first and then next and then next. One writer's strategy we can use to help us write true stories is to start by thinking back to the very start of the memory; then we make a movie in our mind of what happened first, then next, and next."

COACHING

You'll notice this minilesson opens the way so many of our writing conferences with children open: with a compliment. In every case, we strive to make the compliment focus on something that a writer has done that is worth emulating often. The trick is that we can't say to children, "From this day on, write about planting hyacinth bulbs with your grandma." We need to determine what it is that the child has done that is replicable, and name the action in ways that can guide not only today but also tomorrow.

This is a great time for hand gestures. You'll find that often this year, you'll need to highlight the difference between commenting on a subject (imagine a gesture that suggests the writer swipes this way and that over the subject) and writing a sequentially structured narrative (imagine a gesture that suggests a horizontal timeline).

It is important to me to give kids precise, clear instructions, which means that sometimes I oversimplify things to make a point. But I try to maintain intellectual honesty. So in an instance like this, instead of saying, "Writers do not talk about an event; we instead retell the story of the event," I acknowledge that writers do sometimes write all about a topic, but then I go on to explain that in this class right now, we are writing narratives. It is important to me that I acknowledge that it is entirely possible to write an effective all-about piece; on the other hand, I want to make it clear that for now, I am asking the class to generate narratives. All-about (informational or expository) writing involves quite a different skill set, and I'll help children do that kind of writing during other units of study.

TEACHING

Demonstrate that you resist talking all about an event and instead storytell the event.

"Let me show you what I mean. I'm going to write about the first time I saw Dad cry (remember that was one story I thought of when I used the strategy of thinking of a person and then listing small moments the person and I shared). I could just talk about that time, commenting on it."

> I remember when my dad's brother died and my dad cried. I never saw my dad cry before and I didn't know what to do. I was worried. My dad isn't the sort who cries often.

"But I'm trying to write a story, and to do so, I want to tell what happened first and then next and then next. So watch and notice how I go to the start of the memory, then make a movie in my mind of what happened first, then next, and next."

"Before I get started, I need to remember to ask myself, 'What am I trying to show in this story?' In this story, I want to show that it was really surprising to me when my big, tough dad cried."

"Now I'll remember that episode, getting the memory in my head. Then I think, 'What happened first? What did I do or see or hear first?'"

"So let's see. I'm remembering Dad crying. What did I do, see, or hear first? Oh yes. I heard dad talking on the phone." I touched my thumb as I recalled this, wordlessly demonstrating how I use one finger and then the next to scaffold the chronological progression. "He said, 'Oh no,' and 'How bad is it?' and 'He's gone?' I didn't know what he was talking about. Then he hung up the phone," I touched a second finger, in a way that suggested this was the second event in the story, "and he sat down on the chair like this." I reenacted my dad plopping himself down and sitting heavily, like the weight of the world was upon him. "He looked awful, and I knew something bad had happened. 'Grove died,' he told me. I sat beside my dad." I touched a third finger. "I looked at Dad and said, 'He was your big brother.' Dad nodded. I saw tears filling in his eyes, real tears. They started to stream down his face. I didn't know what to do or to say." I touched a fourth finger. "Then I hugged him." I touched the final finger.

Often when I am trying to teach children how to do something, I first dramatize the option I don't want them to do. By showing that I could have written all about the time my dad cried but rejected this in favor of writing a sequential story, I hope to draw attention to the point I am trying to make. I don't think my teaching would be explicit enough if I simply wrote a story about one time my dad cried, and assumed kids would attend to the chronological structure of the text.

In the teaching component of most minilessons we are giving writers a set of how-to directions. Part of the challenge in designing minilessons is that often we are teaching a strategy that is second nature to us. In order to make it accessible to kids for whom it is not second nature, we need to become conscious of the work that we do instantly and effortlessly, so that we can teach this to kids. The trick is to be explicit and clear. In an effort to teach the separate steps of a strategy, we can inadvertently describe the strategy in a way that doesn't ring true, and that is something to check for and avoid.

In the series for K–2 writers, teachers and children "told stories across their fingers," but did so with one sentence for each finger. As children get older, one important development will be that they write not in sentences-of-thought but in paragraphs-of-thought. It was intentional that each new finger (or dot) in my story sequence represents several sentences.

Debrief. Emphasize that instead of discussing the event, you retold it as a story.

"Writers, do you see how I didn't just talk about when Dad cried?" Sweeping my hand to illustrate that I could have commented this way and that way about the subject, I said, "I also didn't just say, 'I remember when Dad cried. It was really sad. He cried because his brother died.' Instead I thought about that time as a movie, almost, and thought, 'What happened first? If this was a movie, what would I see first?' I made the movie in my mind and told it, scene by scene."

"Now I'm ready to start writing." Touching my first finger, I repeated the start of the story: "I heard Dad talking on the phone. He said, 'Oh no....'" I pointed to the piece of chart paper, to signal that I'd write those words.

ACTIVE ENGAGEMENT
Set children up to practice what you've demonstrated, using a whole-class topic.

"So let's try it together. Remember yesterday when we had a fire drill? We could talk all about the fire drill, saying, 'We had a hard time at the fire drill because the first graders slowed us down and because it rained and we had to stand far from the building.' But today, we are writing stories. To tell the story of the fire drill, we need to recall what happened first. Scroll back in your minds and think, 'What happened first?' I'll start you off and then you can try telling the story to a neighbor. 'Our teacher told us to copy the math problems and so I got out some paper and started copying numbers from the board. (Do you have the movie in your mind?) Just then I heard . . . . ' Keep going. Tell your neighbor what happened, step by step, bit by bit. If you want, tell it across your fingers."

Debrief. Highlight what students just did that you hope they use another time, with another text.

"Writers, can I have your eyes and your attention? I loved hearing how you retold the story of the fire drill. I was really able to make a movie in my mind as I listened to you tell this story across your fingers. You didn't just say, 'Tuesday we had a fire drill. The bell rang while we were copying a math problem and we all had to go outside and we got in trouble because we followed the first graders down the stairs and they were so slow they made us late.' No."

Don't write the story! It is tempting to progress from one part of the writing process to another and another in the teaching component of a minilesson. Such a demonstration would no longer illustrate the targeted teaching point! Become accustomed to fragmenting your writing process so that you show kids only what they need in order to see that day's teaching point put into action. In this instance, the point was that writers need to guard against writing all about an episode and instead tell the episode as a story. You can demonstrate this without doing any writing at all. If you want to write something, write only the first sentence or two. In general, it is wise to constrain yourself so that you write three to five lines at the most during a minilesson.

In this Active Engagement section of the minilesson, I made the choice to have all writers practice the strategy while working with what I call an exercise text. I deliberately rallied the group around the story of the fire drill because it is certainly a sequential narrative with an obvious beginning (the blast of the fire drill), middle, and end. Then, too, I knew this particular class was in an uproar already over what they regarded as unfair treatment during the fire drill, so I knew they'd have a great time reliving the event. I was trying to recruit their enthusiasm for writing and, more specifically, for storytelling. However, if I was teaching a class of struggling and reluctant writers, I might have asked each child to think about what he or she would write that day, then to storytell it and even write the first sentence while the children sat together in the meeting area.

In the series Units of Study in Primary Writing, *we also used a fire drill story to introduce kindergartners and first graders to the idea of writing focused chronological stories (the introduction of Small Moment stories). There is nothing magical about fire drills, of course, but it might be interesting for you to look at the instruction involving the fire drill story in* Small Moments *and to notice ways in which instruction in writing is similar and different depending on children's grade levels.*

"Listen to Takeshi's retelling of the fire drill and notice how he tells it, like this is an amazing story that could be in our libraries. While you listen, see if you can get the movie in your mind of what happened, because great authors write so that readers can feel like they are there, in the story."

> Just then I heard the fire alarm. Everyone stopped writing and looked around. I counted each dong: one, two, three. After a pause, the alarm began again. I jumped up and headed toward the door because I was the line leader. I walked quickly to the stairs. We hurried down the stairs. We got to the second floor at the same time as the first graders. We had to let them go first. Man, were they slow."

"Did you see how Takeshi took a tiny event that happened to him (to all of us) and he thought about that time as a movie? He thought, 'What happened first?' He made the movie in his mind and told the story, step by step. We could really picture the whole story, couldn't we!"

LINK
Tell the children that you expect all of them to write their stories in a sequential, blow-by-blow fashion from now on.

"From now on, whenever you are writing a story, don't just talk all about what happened; instead say exactly what happened first, then next, and next. Retell the story just like Takeshi did in a step-by-step fashion. This strategy will help you anytime you want to write stories. Let's start today by rereading our stories from yesterday and making sure we have told them as stories."

You'll notice that usually after children turn and talk in their Active Engagement section, I only cite one child's work as a model. I'm always aware that other children did good work too, but I'd rather develop the one example in some detail than rush to convey several good examples. Always, my decisions are influenced by a sense that time is limited. Above all, children need to be writing.

Remember to use the gesture for swiping this way and that way past a subject, juxtaposing that gesture with the one you use to represent the process of writing a sequentially organized narrative.

WRITING AND CONFERRING

Addressing a Host of Writing Situations

Sometimes, we need to stop teaching, step back, and take a bit of time to watch children as they work, trying to ascertain patterns that merit attention.

You may see that a bunch of children leave the minilesson and then simply sit until you arrive to give them a personalized jump-start. If you've got this group, resist the temptation to deliver each child his own personalized pep talk. Instead, gather these kids together, tell them what you've noticed, and help them think of a strategy or two for getting started on their own. Then watch them use one of these strategies to do just that.

You might find that another cluster of children write incredibly slowly, producing only half a page or so in a day. Gather these youngsters together and tell them that you're going to help them double the amount of writing they can do in a day. First, these writers need to be clear what they intend to write. So set them up, making sure each child has a story to tell and is proceeding chronologically through that story. Don't worry about the quality of writing just now—to focus on fluency and speed, these children need permission to lower their standards (temporarily). Now help children to dictate a full sentence to themselves and write that whole sentence without pausing. These children are apt to pause at the ends of words or phrases—that won't do! Then help children dictate the next sentence to themselves and write it quickly, too, without rereading in the midst of writing.

In general, cluster children into smaller groups based on your diagnosis of what they need. Every child's writing will have a host of issues. Try to prioritize. You can't repair everything at once, so ask yourself, "What are the really fundamental issues?"

> **MID-WORKSHOP TEACHING POINT** *Spelling High-Frequency Words with Automaticity* "Writers, can I have your eyes and your attention? You are remembering to do so many things. Instead of writing about big huge watermelon ideas, you are writing tiny seed stories. Instead of telling all about an event, you are reliving the event in a step-by-step fashion. You are using strategies that grown-up professional writers use. What I want to remind you now is that when you are writing for readers, it is important to spell common words as correctly as you can. That way, everyone can understand you easily."
>
> "So when you are writing, take a second to spell the words on our word wall (and other words you know) correctly. Right now, would you reread what you've written so far, and if you find a word wall word that is misspelled, would you fix it? If you aren't sure how to spell it, look at the word wall. But instead of copying the word letter for
>
> *continued on next page*

You will eventually find that a small group of children need more help shifting from summarizing and commenting on one episode toward storytelling that episode. That is, some children will write like this: "My sister and I played at the beach. We made castles and buried ourselves in the sand. It was fun but it was hot. I had a good time with my sister. She is nice." In an instance like this, recognize that the writer summarized the story, commenting on several main things that she did. She probably then realized her story was too short, leading her to add some sweeping comments to the end. This is a very common thing for writers to do. We can give a child a predictable sequence of prompts to help that youngster loosen her hold on summarizing and begin to storytell. Try something like this:

"You've written about lots of moments! Do you want to tell about the time when you [possible topic for this child]? Or maybe the time when you [alternative topic]?"

"Oh! Great choice! I'm dying to picture how that really happened. So how did it start? What exactly did you do first? What did you say?"

Then you could retell what the child says in story form, and press for more story from the child. "So one morning you [did a specific action] and then you thought [a specific thought]. Then what did you do?"

"What a story!" Then, you would retell it. "Write this down." Finally, dictate the start of the story as the child records his or her own words.

continued from previous page

letter, when you look at the word wall, go through all the steps we go through when we are learning new words. Look at the word. Think about what you notice about it. Now try to imprint the word on your mind. Close your eyes and try to see the letters in your imagination. Say the letters aloud. Now open your eyes and check to see if you were right. When you have the correct spelling fixed in your brain, write it. Check that you were right."

"And after this, for the rest of this year and for the whole of your life, remember that it's important to get into the habit of correctly spelling the words you use a lot. If you are writing a word and you think, 'This is on our word wall' and you aren't quite sure how to spell it, take an extra fifteen seconds to try to spell (and write) like a pro!"

SHARE

Appreciating Children's Writing

Convene writers. Use one child's story to demonstrate how a good story allows readers to live alongside the narrator.

"Writers, when I read the stories you are writing, it is almost like I am with you at your kitchen table, on the subway, in the park. Listen to Song Moo's story of an adventure he had in the park last Saturday, and see if you don't agree that a good story allows readers to live in it. Listen." [Fig. V-1 and V-2]

On Tuesday I wanted to go to the park, so I asked my father to go to park with me. At the park, I saw Ttomy waving at me and saying "Hi Song Moo!" Then I say back to Ttomy, "Hi Ttomy!"

While we were walking, Ttomy saw a worm wiggling in the dirt so Ttomy said to me, "Look, there is a worm." And then he pointed at it and then I said, "Oh, it's a worm." And then Ttomy said, "So let's cut the worm. It will be fun!"

Next to the worm we saw a piece of glass so Ttomy picked up the piece of glass and he cut the worm into $1/2$ but the worm didn't died so Ttomy cut the worm into $1/4$ but the worm didn't died so I said, "This is interesting" and Ttomy said, "Yes, this is interesting." but we had a trouble to know which side was head and which side was tail so we decide to cut both sides but the worm was still wiggling in 6 little pieces so I said, "Let's just wait until the worm died because it will not died even if we cut the worm into $1/10$." So we wait and wait and finally the two pieces of worm died but the other pieces of worm didn't died so we wait another while. After a while the wiggly worm died so I said, "Finally the wiggly worm died."

When you select writing to read aloud, be sure that you don't find yourself drawing on the same six or eight children day after day. A child once showed me that in the back of his writer's notebook he'd collected a list of every child that his teacher mentioned by name in minilessons and shares. Looking at that list, I was reminded of the agony I felt in gym class when team captains took turns choosing children to be on their teams. As teachers, we have more power than we realize. With a single gesture or word, we can raise or dash a child's hopes.

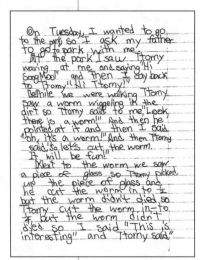

Fig. V-1 Song Moo

Fig. V-2 Song Moo

Ask children to share their story with a new partner.

"I can't wait to read all of your stories! Right now, would you get with someone who has not yet heard your story, and read what you've written aloud to that person? When you finish reading, storytell the part you haven't written. Remember to storytell it in a way that gives your listener goose bumps."

It's not likely, of course, that you'll actually read Song Moo's story aloud. Instead, you choose an entry that one of your children has written. When you read the text aloud, read it as well as you can. Focus through the words to whatever the writer is saying. When I read the section where Song Moo wrote, "and then he pointed to the worm," I see that worm, squiggling in the ground. When I read how he and Ttomy studied the worm, trying to decide which end was the head, I picture the two friends squatting close to the writhing worm. This matters. If we read aloud well, seeing not just the words on the page but the life drama, then listeners, too, can see through the words to the drama.

HOMEWORK *Practicing Spelling* There are many things you may know by heart: addition facts, your phone number, the lineup and batting averages for the New York Yankees, the order of the planets, your best friend's e-mail address, and so on. Of course, there are lots of words we can spell by heart, too. The great thing is that this list of words we can spell by heart just keeps growing!

Even so, brave writers still use words in their writing that they may not be quite sure how to spell. We give these words our best try, but then we move on in our piece, even if we aren't quite sure of the spelling. Fortunately, writers reread their work often, and when we reread, one of the things we can do is take another try at spelling these tricky or unfamiliar words.

Your job tonight as a writer is to go back at least three entries and circle words that you think you have misspelled. Ask yourself, "What seems right here? What seems wrong here?" Next, you'll find space in the margins of the page to give the spelling a couple more tries. You can then pick the try that seems to be most correct and change the spelling in your piece.

Here are some things to remember to do:

- Reread a piece and when you get to a word that you think is spelled incorrectly, circle it.
- Think about what is right with the word and what is wrong with the word you spelled.
- Try to spell it a few different ways by asking yourself, "Are there other words I know that can help me with this word?"
- After you've spelled it a few different ways, decide which try looks the best. Change the word in your piece to match your best try.
- Do this spelling check in your last three entries. You can do it in more entries if you want!

Here's an example of what you'll be doing, right on your notebook pages:

Example sentence: I got chills when I heard the aplaws. (Note: aplaws needs a circle around it)

Then try using what you already know about other words. For example:

applaws (change the beginning to look like *apply* or *appear,* but the *w* looks strange)

applaus (change *aw* like *law* to *au* like *auto,* but it still looks weird)

applause (change the end of the word to look like *cause*)

TAILORING YOUR TEACHING

If you have students who struggle with oral storytelling or with sequencing events . . . you could offer them the option of creating a storyboard to help them move through their narrative bit by bit. Create a storyboard template with squares for quick sketches and lines beneath them for jotting quick notes, four per page, like this:

It's important to consider which students will benefit from working from a storyboard. For some students, doing so will only delay their drafts; for others, the necessity of doing so will support their drafts.

If you notice students getting into a writing rut, always writing one page a day or always starting a new entry each day . . . break the rut. You may decide to change the structure of your writing workshop, for example, by having writers start each day with some time devoted to rereading what they worked on the day (or night) before. Writers often begin any writing session looking for places to add on to, places to fix, places to elaborate upon, etc. They may also reread to make sure their pieces sound the way they want them to, so they might decide to make different word choices, to restructure sentences, to fix parts that don't make sense.

If you notice your students growing careless with their writer's notebooks . . . you might spend a minilesson or a share session teaching your students how you expect them to take care of their writer's notebooks. "Writers, yesterday at lunch time I was reading through your writer's notebooks. I can't think of a better way to spend my lunch hour than reading your stories. I loved them! But you know what? I want to talk about something that seems to be a growing problem. As I looked through your notebooks, I saw that many of them are beginning to look messy. There were pages with missing dates, some pages were skipped, some notebooks even had pages that were ripped out or crumpled up! I was so surprised, because a writing notebook is a very important tool for writers and it's so important to take care of the tools that help you do your work."

"So today, I want to spend a bit of time talking about how to take care of your notebook. We treat it like a book from the library as we handle it and turn the pages. Then when we write in it, we should respect it, because it's holding the stories of our lives. We can show respect by writing as neatly as we can, by going page by page, and by not using it for scratch paper. Watch me as I pretend I'm a student during writing time. Notice whether or not I'm taking care of my notebook, and then think of suggestions that would help me become more careful with it."

If you notice lots of abandoned entries in the notebooks or lots of similar entries about recurrent subjects, such as particular birthday parties or first days of school, for example . . . you may decide you need to help children get more invested in their writing. Over and over again, writing workshop teachers see that if writers do not take seriously the job of choosing a subject, then they will not be emotionally invested enough in their story to continue writing it until it is finished. You may want to teach a minilesson where you model the thought process behind topic choice. Teach your writers that if a story is important, you should be able to talk for a few minutes about it—even on a first telling. Demonstrate picking one story that is a thirty-second tell and another story that is only a two-minute tell.

MECHANICS

It is important for you and your grade-level colleagues to spend some time reflecting on what you notice about your children's control of written conventions and devising a plan for how you will support this aspect of their writing development. You'll probably find that it is challenging to decide on strategies for spelling and punctuating that will be applicable to all children. That is, whether a child is spelling with just initial and final consonants or spelling perfectly, that child can still benefit from learning to tighten her narrative to tell a focused story with detail. But a child who is spelling with just initial and final consonants won't benefit from studying why writers do or do not double a final consonant before adding an ending. Instruction in conventions must be tailored to the individual child more than other kinds of instruction. Use your judgment before transferring what I teach about the conventions of written language into your classroom!

When you and your colleagues think together about written conventions, you will probably choose to talk about spelling because it will be the elephant in the room. I suggest you devise an approach to spelling that you can discuss with parents, and that you do so right away. Send a letter home to parents in which you let them know that, across the year, you will definitely be helping children become more conventional as spellers. You'll want to write your own letter but this one may give you some ideas.

In general, there are principles that can guide you as you and your colleagues devise an approach to spelling. First, you need to convey to the parents of your children that you recognize that spelling matters. This is important for your students, but it is especially important right now for the parents of your students. Research has shown that when parents are becoming acquainted with you as a teacher, one of their biggest concerns is your approach to spelling. If you show parents that you value their child's progress in spelling, they will be more apt to trust you. Since you certainly do care about the children's progress in spelling, among other areas of writing, your letter to parents should convey this.

Second, it should be a priority to help children spell high-frequency words with ease and automaticity. Fifty percent of the words children write come from a list of thirty-six most common words, so helping children master those words has great payoff.

Finally, it is important to teach children strategies for tackling tough words so they aren't hesitant or ill-equipped to do so. That is, the job is not only to teach lists of words; the job is also to teach tools and strategies for spelling. One strategy that you'll teach is that you'll help children know they can approximate a spelling and return to it later to problem-solve. If a child believes she has misspelled a word, suggest she look at what she's written and think, "What part of this seems right? What part seems wrong?" This is helpful because it gives the child a sense of control. The child who is writing "international" may believe she's spelled "inter" and "na" correctly. So now she's working only on one or two problematic syllables. Next, suggest that writers think: "What other words do I know how to spell that can help me spell the hard parts of this word?"

Dear Parents,

As we start this year together, I want to take a moment to convey to you some of my plans for helping your children grow in their abilities to spell conventionally. I have been assessing your children's spelling during these first few days of school, and I've come to believe that some children in the class are choosing only "easy" words to write because they are worried over whether they can spell the more precise words correctly. My first goal, then, will be to make sure that every child is a fearless and inventive writer, and that every child is willing to write "enormous" rather than sticking with "big" even if that child cannot spell "enormous" conventionally. You will see that I do not expect perfect spelling in children's first-draft writing.

The second thing I have noticed is that many children in this class haven't yet learned to spell some of the most important high-frequency words—words like *because, said, although*—correctly. So, each week, I will directly and explicitly teach children a list of high-frequency words. Children will bring that list home on Mondays, they will be quizzed on those words on Fridays, and more important, they will be expected to incorporate those spellings into their writing whenever they write. I'll help them do this!

Meanwhile, there are a few children who will need extra help with spelling. We all know that many great writers and thinkers struggle with spelling. I'll be meeting with a few children to let them know that they will need to put extra time and receive extra help in spelling, and that together, we can make huge progress. Meanwhile, these children need to be reminded that although their progress in spelling matters and merits attention, they meanwhile need to also work towards other goals as well. Like all children, I'll encourage these youngsters to write a lot, and to write with voice and detail. I look forward to supporting and studying your children's progress towards writing more correct and more effective pieces of writing.

IN THIS SESSION, YOU'LL TEACH CHILDREN THAT WRITERS REREAD THEIR NOTEBOOKS, SELECTING AND COMMITTING THEMSELVES TO AN IDEA THEY'LL DEVELOP INTO A FINISHED PIECE OF WRITING.

GETTING READY

- Instructions on chalkboard telling children to bring their writer's notebooks (pens tucked inside) and sit with their partners in the meeting area
- Your own filled writer's notebook
- Selected books with great leads (*Salt Hands, The Paper Boy, Shortcut* to read aloud; varied collection of books for a reading table)
- Paper clips
- Blank booklets with four or five pages, one for each child
- Writing folders, one for each child, to hold the booklets and future loose-leaf work
- See CD-ROM for resources

CHOOSING A SEED IDEA

Jerome Bruner, the great American cognitive psychologist, once said that the ideas that are essential to any discipline "are as simple as they are powerful." Children at any age level can experience the essentials of a discipline, "learning to use them in progressively more complex forms" (1960, 1977, pp. 12–13). This understanding of discipline-based knowledge underlies a writing process approach to composition. The approach is based on the belief that even very young children can experience a version of the professional writer's process.

In this curriculum, we invite children to experience the writing process. So far, we've helped children live like writers, seeing the fine fiber of their ordinary lives as worth recording. Today, we show children that writers return to their writer's notebooks, rereading them and asking, "Of all that's here, is there one story that says the most about me or my life, or one story that I especially want to share with readers? Which one story will I choose to develop and publish?"

Today, then, you are inviting children into revision, which means quite literally re-vision, to see again. You will help children discover that because they've put their life stories onto the page, they can now hold their lives in their hands, rereading those lives. And in doing so, they can take the rush of life, and slow it down in order to re-experience it, this time seeing the colors, feeling the wind, hearing the words all the more intensely. They can take one of the ever-so-fleeting episodes of their lives and pause long enough to see it, to frame it, to share it.

When we write the stories of our lives, we reread them and select one to linger with and to develop. It is as if we press the pause button of time. Pause. Rewind. Replay. This is what you will teach your children to do today. It's exquisitely important work.

MINILESSON

Choosing a Seed Idea

CONNECTION

Solidify what children already know by summarizing the early parts of the writing process they've learned so far.

"Writers, so far in this class, you've lived like real writers, learning that you can think of people, places, and things, and these can jog your minds to recall particular small moments, and you can write those into detailed entries. You've also learned some essential qualities of good writing, and these help you shape your entries into ones readers will draw close to hear."

Name the teaching point. In this case, tell children you'll teach them to choose one entry to develop into a publishable piece.

"Today I want to teach you that writers don't just write one entry and then write another and another as we have been doing. As writers, after we collect entries and ideas for a while, we reread and we find one story, one entry, that especially matters to us, and we make a commitment to that one entry. We decide to work on it so that it becomes our very best writing ever."

TEACHING

Show children that writing allows us to slow down and find treasure among the everyday events of our lives.

"I love the picture book *Roxaboxen,* by Alice McLerran. In it, some children are playing on a desert hill. There's not much there: just sand, some cacti, a broken crate. But then Marian finds a rusty tin box, and the children circle around her, declaring it to be treasure. And it is. Inside the box are smooth black stones. The children lay them out on the sand to make roads, and soon they've created a pretend kingdom of Roxaboxen. And it all started with Marian finding a rusty tin box and declaring it to be treasure."

COACHING

If you scan all the opening passages across a sequence of minilessons, you'll see that I almost always compliment children on what they've been doing in a way that also summarizes what I've taught, and you'll see that each time I accumulate more specifics. That is, in Session II, I said, "You are coming up with people who matter to you," and this time I say that they've learned to "think of people, places, and things . . . to recall small moments and write those into detailed entries." By consolidating what I've taught thus far, I hope to keep previous lessons accessible and alive for youngsters so they carry this content in their mental backpacks, drawing on concepts and tools as needed.

Notice that in some teaching sections, I rely on my writing. In some, I rely on a child's writing. In this minilesson, I refer to a published picture book. Variety adds interest.

"I write because writing allows me to take the stuff that is all around me in my life—the little stories, the everyday events—and hold one small piece of life in my hands, declaring it to be a treasure, declaring it something worth thinking about. Our new white sneakers get grass stains during recess. Our hamster circles round and round before curling up into a golden pom-pom. A best friend shares a secret at lunch. Writing gives me a way to declare one of these events to be a treasure. It gives me a way to pause."

"When I write, I reread my notebook (and rewind my life). I find one entry that for some reason sort of matters, and I say, 'This is the one that I'm going to linger with, and make into a publishable book.'"

Ask children to notice exactly what you do as you demonstrate choosing an idea from your notebook to develop into a finished piece.

"Watch me while I reread my notebook, thinking about whether one of my entries might be worth developing into a story that I'd like to publish. Later I'm going to ask you to tell each other what exactly I did, as a writer, in order to choose one story, one entry, to turn into my best writing."

"Hmm . . . I'm reading this entry about seeing a homeless man without shoes. That doesn't really say that much about me. Here is an entry about how I longed for a crow as a pet, and had a crow cage ready in case I caught one. I'll star that as a possibility because I bet I could explore that one and find some interesting stuff there. Here is that list of small moments about my father. I like that one about the first time I saw him cry . . . . Now I'm reading the entry about the first time I saw my dad cry. That's a possibility because it really mattered to me, and I have a lot more I could say about it. I will star that one and keep on reading. After I read all these entries, I'll decide between the entries I've starred."

During these early days of getting the writing workshop up and going, I have choices to make and priorities to set that will ultimately affect the tone and the energy that will drive the workshop forward throughout the year. If children think their stories are irrelevant or insignificant, they will not be able to sustain the energy necessary to be writers. I want each child to declare his story to be a treasure.

Notice that before I slip into the role of writer and demonstrate, I usually frame the demonstration with remarks meant to orient children so they know what they are watching, and what they're expected to do with what they see.

When you demonstrate, as in this instance, be sure your intonation and gestures suggest you are mulling over, thinking aloud. You aren't talking to the children. Your eyes aren't on them. Instead you are poring over your notebook, thinking aloud as you do, letting children eavesdrop on your thinking. But don't look at the children or direct these remarks to them.

You may notice that after the demonstration, I didn't debrief as usual. That's because I'm going to incorporate debriefing into today's active engagement.

ACTIVE ENGAGEMENT
Give children a chance to think through the process you've demonstrated.

"Writers, you've probably already noticed lots of strategies that I used in order to choose an entry that matters to me. Would you turn and tell your partner three specific things you saw me doing that you could try?" The children talked, and I listened to several pairs.

Your intonation will change at this point, and now instead of thinking aloud, you are talking directly to children.

This is not a usual Active Engagement. When possible, we try to give children a chance to actually do what it is we have talked about and demonstrated. In this Active Engagement, children instead talk about what they have heard and seen; they do not actually use the strategy themselves. I think their talk gains energy when I give the specific instruction to list three things I did.

Voice the observations children make in a way that allows you to review the process you demonstrated.

"I heard some of you say that I carefully reread my entries. You noticed that I didn't just flip, flip, flip through the pages of my notebook when it was time for me to choose an entry. I took my time and reread thoughtfully."

I know to tell children that I don't just flip, flip, flip through my notebook only because I've taught this minilesson before and been dismayed to see kids choose seed ideas by racing through their notebooks saying, "Nope, nope, nope!" Every time you give a minilesson and children's work doesn't proceed the way you hoped, take note and amend your minilesson for the next time!

"And you realized that when I reread, I thought about whether the episode matters to me, and whether it says something true about me. I thought about whether I had more to say on the entry. Some of you noticed that I starred some entries as possibilities and kept on reading, planning to come back when I'd read through them all so I could choose one. You can do all these things as well when you reread your writing today, deciding which entries you'll star, which entry you'll declare to be treasure."

Years ago, I suggested kids "nurture" their seed ideas in their notebooks for several weeks before beginning a draft. I have come to believe, however, that until youngsters have had a lot of experience with the writing process, they can be swamped if they collect too much loosely related material. I don't want children to lose hold of their organizational structure or their focused message. So during the first units of study, I keep this "nurturing one's seed idea" phase streamlined. It will become longer and more elaborate in later units in this series.

LINK
Remind children that after they start collecting entries like writers do, they'll want to choose an idea to develop into a publishable piece.

"Today, and whenever it is time for you to stop collecting entries and begin working on one writing project, remember that you—like writers everywhere—can reread your entries and think, 'Which of these especially matters?' Look for entries that draw you in, that seem to be saying, 'Pick me!' Off you go."

WRITING AND CONFERRING

Learning to Be Best Listeners

In any unit of study, my favorite day for conferring is always this one: the day when children reread all their entries in order to select just one to nurture, revise, and develop. Usually I find children are tentative about their choices. "This one?" they say, looking for confirmation.

"It's a hugely important one, isn't it?" I respond, and I say this acting on faith, whether or not the evidence is there yet on the page. After all, out of all the child's life, he has already made the decision to record this story in an entry, and now, out of all the entries, the child has chosen this one. The significance is not always apparent to me, but I find that if I confirm the entry's importance and then lean in to listen, saying, "Tell me all about it. How, exactly, did it start?" I can help children tell the story with engagement.

The challenge of this day is that every child will want this intense attention, and we can't listen respectfully and offer generous amounts of time and focus to every single child! On this day, especially, I try to make appointments to confer at lunch or recess, but I also set children up to listen well to each other. "Now that you have your seed idea chosen," I'll say to one writer, "will you listen to Robbie like I listened to you? Get him to tell you the whole story and to tell it with detail. Help him tell it in a way that gives you goose bumps."

For some children, today's work will require all of thirty seconds. Some children will know exactly which entry they want to develop, and you may find yourself in an awkward situation because you won't yet have had a chance to teach the class ways to develop their seed ideas. My suggestion, in this instance, is to either confer with those children, or interrupt the class to offer a mid-workshop teaching point to solve this problem.

MID-WORKSHOP TEACHING POINT *Rehearsing for Writing by Storytelling* "Writers, can I have your eyes and your attention? Thumbs up if you've chosen one entry that matters to you, an entry that you think you could work on more. Great. I'm going to pass out paper clips. Mark your entry with a paper clip—we'll call it your 'seed idea' because we are going to grow the entry, like one grows a seed, into something wonderful! Before you write the story of that entry, please turn to the person next to you, and partner 2, *tell the story* of your seed idea. Tell it long. Tell it in ways that gives your listener goose bumps."

After just a couple of minutes, I intervened. "Writers, let me stop you. I'm not surprised you selected these particular stories from your notebooks. They are incredible! I loved hearing that the stories grew as you told them; you seemed to remember more things right in the middle of the stories! That's exactly why we often storytell before we write. But let me tell you something else. Writers don't just tell our stories once before we write them—we tell and retell them. Robert Munsch, author of *Thomas' Snowsuit*, says that he never writes a story until he has told it at least a hundred times!

"When you go back to your writing, would you tell your story again to yourself, not to your partner. I'm going to give you blank booklets and I'd like you to *storytell to yourself* across the pages." I showed children what I meant by this. Holding a blank book, I storytold the first bit of my father-crying story, then turned the next page and storytold the next bit. Then I sent children off to storytell . . . and to write.

SHARE

Immersing Ourselves in the Kinds of Texts We Plan to Write

Convene children. Suggest they immerse themselves in the kind of text they plan to write. Read some texts aloud.

"Writers, can I have your eyes and your attention? You are on the brink of beginning your first draft. Now that you've found your seed idea, try doing what writers the world over do: read. Read books and stories that remind you of what you want to write. I've put a collection of books and short texts out on this table—ones that remind me of what we are writing. Most of them you know, which is the way it should be."

"With your seed idea in mind, take some time to read one of those books. Read it and reread it til you get the sound in your bones. A man named Hirsch wrote, 'I feel words creating a rhythm, a music, a spell, a mood, a shape, a form.' You'll want to feel that. So that you can create it with the entry you've chosen."

"To get you started, I want to read aloud the beginnings of some published stories so that you get the music and rhythm and lilt of a storyteller's voice into you. After I read, I'm going to ask partner 2 to tell your stories again, this time as if your stories are books on library shelves." I read aloud the lead to Jane Chelsea Aragon's *Salt Hands*, Dav Pilkney's *The Paper Boy*, and Donald Crews' *Shortcut*. After both members of each pair told their stories, I asked for everyone's attention again.

Suggest children ask themselves, "What do I want my listeners to feel?"

"Writers, your stories are sounding like literature. What a difference this makes! I want to suggest one more thing that'll make a world of difference. Before you continue your story, ask yourself this: 'What am I trying to make my listeners *feel*?' It might be that you are trying to convey one feeling at the start of the story and another feeling later, in the middle of the story. Tell the story so that your listeners *feel* what you want them to feel. Embellish it a bit, build up certain parts, get through to your listeners."

Hand out folders where kids can store their booklets and other related papers to keep with their notebooks.

"Now that you are about to write drafts, you need a new kind of paper and a place to store it, so it's always easy for you to find. Here are some folders you can keep with your notebooks to hold your drafting booklets and eventually all your final pieces."

As writers progress from writing entries toward writing a publishable piece, it is especially important that their writing takes on the cadence of literate language. The music and voice of stories are important. Mem Fox has said that for her, the ability to write well "came from the constant good fortune of hearing great literature beautifully delivered into my ear, and from there into my heart, and from my heart into my bones." The "rhythms," she said, "remain in the marrow of my memory" (1993, pp. 113, 116). In this share, I'm trying to get the lilt of story into the marrow of children's memory. I'm urging children to say their stories aloud, and to tell their stories in ways that give listeners goose bumps in hopes that "I went rollerblading in the park" shifts to "One morning last summer, before anyone was up, I put on my skates and headed to the park."

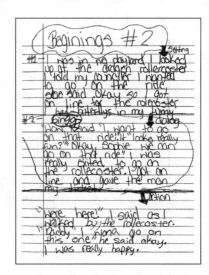

Fig. VI-1 Sophie experiments with leads

HOMEWORK *Storytelling, Over and Over* This afternoon on your way home from school or at home, retell your story again to yourself. Tell it to your mom or to your friend. And think about your story too. Stories get much better if we play them over in our minds, trying to tell them in ways that really affect listeners and readers. Do you want to make people shiver with worry, laugh aloud, gasp, wince? Try telling your story so that you make listeners feel whatever it is you want them to feel.

TAILORING YOUR TEACHING You may not want to devote more than one minilesson to helping your children choose a seed idea. There is plenty to teach at this juncture, but your children probably can't keep themselves productively busy for days of work on this. If your children are revisiting this minilesson in their second year in writing workshop, you'll want to remind them of what they already know and teach something new such as the following:

If your students are skilled at thoughtfully choosing a seed idea . . . they may need help in reflecting on the significance of their chosen seed idea. You may decide to use your own writing. "Watch how I think and write about why I have chosen this entry about seeing my dad cry for the first time." Then I thought aloud about the hidden meaning in the entry, writing as I did so, "Hmm, I picked this entry because I had never seen my dad cry before. But why is that such a big deal? What does this say about me?" I tucked in a comment to the children, "Do you see how I am asking myself questions? Then I write a bit: 'Seeing my dad cry still surprises me to this day. I felt so surprised and worried at this one moment and all I wanted to do was help my dad feel better.'" I paused, and then I asked the children to turn to their seed idea. "Writers, always reread seed ideas, thinking about why it matters. Writers ask, 'What does it say about me?' Writers, whenever you are choosing a seed idea from your notebook, it is important to ask yourself questions about it to make sure it will be an idea worth developing."

ASSESSMENT

Because this lesson marks the end of collecting entries and the start of developing one entry, today marks a bend in the road. You'll probably want to look over your children's writing and notice ways in which they've changed as writers. What seems to be getting better? What hasn't changed?

Try reading this small collection of one child's work. Simeon goes to school at a public school in Harlem and the work you see comes from his first year—in fact, his first few weeks—in a writing workshop. Try reading this work looking for his strengths, assessing his growth, and thinking about future instruction for him. *[Figs. VI-2, VI-3, VI-4, and VI-5]*

The first thing I notice is this boy has the soul of a writer. He's a dreamer; I love the image of this child, living among the huge buildings in Harlem, thinking about how he'd climb to the rooftop in Trinidad, lie in a hammock under the stars, looking up into the sky and thinking about a lot of stuff. My heart went out to him when I read in the fourth entry about him wearing a pink tuxedo because he was to be the ring bearer in his cousin's wedding, then falling in the mud and feeling so messed up that, as he put it, "I felt to hit somebody."

Next I notice the dazzling, dramatic growth toward understanding the genre of narrative writing. In the fourth entry, Simeon is writing with setting and dialogue. His story focuses on a dramatic event and is even structured like a traditional story with a problem, rising action, and solution.

1. This is my house when I was in Trinidad. It has a lot of memories the motorcycle that I use to ride and I was good at riding it. I also had a nice ladder I use to climb on the roof. I had hammock and up into the sky and think about a lot of stuff up there and I like to in Trinidad because it had a pool in the back yard and I all ways went swimming.

2. My dog Brownie
   It saved me
   The day my dog died
   First day with my dog

   One day when I was in Trinidad for summer vacation I was sleep and I heard somebody footsteps my dog Brownie was there with me and the bandit walked to the living room. I was scared so I got up to see who it was I went to get my dad but he was in the bathroom. When I caught my step mother I said look somebody is in our house.

Fig. VI-2 Simeon

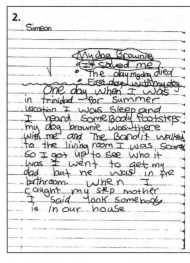

Fig. VI-3 Simeon

3. My dad came over and said "What happen with Brownie" I said "I don't know." So we took it to the veterinarian And he said the dog is getting old When we got home it was useless and I went to sleep and when I got up and looked outside it was dead and I cried a lot so we buried it.

4. One day it was a rainy day and I had on a pink tuxedo and it was my cousins wedding so I was so excited I ran to her. I was like "Are you excited" I said. "Yeah" she said. So I ran to my dad and then I fell in the mud and I was messed up so I got so mad that I felt to hit somebody.

Simeon's syntax suggests he hasn't done a lot of writing. His sentences are composed of a long chain of very simple, short independent clauses (they could be short sentences) chained together with either *and* or *so*.

> So we took it to the veterinarian
> And he said the dog is getting old
> When we got home it was useless and
> I went to sleep and when I got up
> and looked outside it was dead and I
> cried a lot so we buried it.

Simeon would profit from being encouraged to write with end punctuation, trusting that readers will read on to the next sentence without the overuse of connectors. His teacher may want to say "Think one thought, write that thought and then put a period. Think your next thought, write it out and then put the next period." Once he is writing sentences which do not run-on, he could be taught how to include subordinate clauses. Another possibility is to teach him to use alternative connector words so that instead of relying exclusively on *and* or *so* he begins to also use connectors such as *because* or *while*.

Simeon could also be explicitly taught to be more specific in his use of references. When looking at his second entry, for example, I might ask who or what he meant by the word *it*. Simeon would probably answer, "That's my dog, Brownie. He died and we had to bury him." It would help Simeon if his teacher encouraged him to reread, checking to be sure that readers would always know who or what he referred to in his sentences.

By explicitly teaching Simeon something about referents and alternative connectors, his writing can become more cohesive and elaborate. But meanwhile, if Simeon continues to write and read a lot, if he is encouraged to use end punctuation, to convey feelings, and to include dialogue, all of this work will lead him toward more mature syntax.

3.

My dad came over and said "What happen with Brownie" I said I don't Know" So we took it to the veterenarian, And he said the dog is getting old when we got home it was useless and I went to sleep and when I got up, and looke outside it was dead and I cryed alot sowe berried it.

Fig. VI-4 Simeon

4. Simeon

One day it was a rainy day and I had on a pink tuxedo and it was my cousins wedding So I was So exited I ran to her I was like are you exited I said yeah she said SoI ran to mydad and then I fell in the mudd and I was messed up so I got so mad that I felt to hit some body when I went in every body looked and laued at me I was so scared that she might not want me to carry the rings

Fig. VI-5 Simeon

IN THIS SESSION, YOU'LL TEACH STUDENTS THAT WRITERS CRAFT THEIR LEADS. YOU'LL SHOW CHILDREN HOW WRITERS CAN LEARN TECHNIQUES TO TRY IN THEIR OWN WORK BY STUDYING PUBLISHED WRITING.

GETTING READY

- Instructions on chalkboard telling children to bring their folders holding their notebooks and drafting booklets and sit with their partners in the meeting area
- Examples of children's leads that show improvement
- *Peter's Chair* (Ezra Jack Keats), *Whistling* (Elizabeth Partridge), *Fireflies* (Julie Brinckloe), *The Witch of Blackbird Pond* (Elizabeth Speare), *Because of Winn-Dixie* (Kate DiCamillo), or any familiar books with great leads
- Example leads on chart paper
- Chart paper and markers
- Two different leads in mind for your story from previous session
- Qualities of Good Personal Narrative Writing chart
- Plan for how you will tell your story using the pages of a drafting booklet
- ⊙ See CD-ROM for resources

REVISING LEADS:
LEARNING FROM PUBLISHED WRITING

In some ways, the word lead *to describe that first sentence or first paragraph of a piece of writing is so misleading! A better word might be grab, pull, or yank. Writers of every genre know that the first bit of text on a page must cajole, beg, or even jerk the reader into the text so that she will invest the time and attention it takes to finish, to appreciate, the story.*

Inexperienced writers often become paralyzed when writing the first words or sentences of a story because the words represent a huge mental decision: Out of all the information that I have swimming about in my head, where do I start? I tell students that it's like standing on a high diving board, looking down that scary distance to the water. It seems impossible to step off, yet once we do it, we realize it's not that hard; in fact it's a blast, and we can't wait to climb up the ladder to dive again!

In this session, I help students gather their courage and take the plunge; I try to make it less frightening to get started on a draft by encouraging children to expect revision. They don't pick up the pen and write the lead. Instead, they write several possible leads, then choose one.

By looking closely at several leads in published texts, I help students notice and name some techniques authors use to craft some good leads. I then teach students how to apply one or two of those techniques immediately to improve their own leads. Children's lead sentences are utterly and easily revisable, and when we help them start a story with specific action, dialogue, setting, and so forth, we lead children to write stories that sound like literature. At the same time, we can tuck into this lesson a reminder that writing is pliable, claylike.

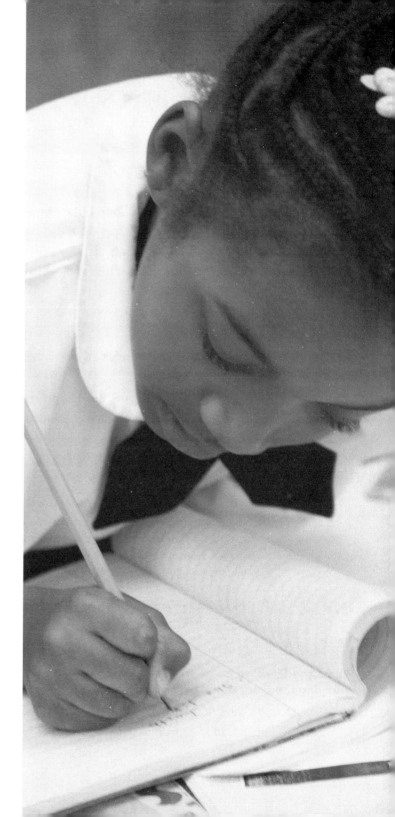

MINILESSON

Revising Leads: Learning from Published Writing

CONNECTION

Celebrate that your children's stories sound like literature.

"Writers, something magical happened in this classroom yesterday. You told your stories, and then I read aloud the leads that Mem Fox and Dav Pilkney and Donald Crews wrote to their picture books. And you told your stories again—only this time, the stories sounded like literature!"

"Lizzie's first version of her story about reading with her reading buddy began like this." *[Fig. VII-1]*

> My buddy is absent. She's sick so Mrs. B found another k student for me.

"Listen to the miraculous changes that happened after Lizzie heard other authors! She wrote several new drafts of leads, and each one sounds like it could be the start to a picture book on our library shelves! Listen." *[Fig. VII-2]*

> On a warm September afternoon, we strolled outside to find our buddies.
>
> I scan the playground, in search of my kindergarten buddy. "Why don't I look from someplace high I think like the slides! I sprint across the playground and using my legs and arms, I climb up the tan colored slide. This I think should give me a good view! I check again. She's nowhere in sight. Puzzled, I go down the spiral slide, without a clue about my buddy. Wth my head down, I begin walking slowly toward the steps, where the kindergarteners poured onto the jungle gym.

Name the teaching point. In this case, tell children that writers improve leads by studying the work of authors and then applying their techniques.

"Today I want to teach you that the lead in a story matters. It matters tremendously because a great lead sets us up to write a great story."

COACHING

Learning to read as a writer is not a small undertaking. Not so long ago, we were coaxing these same children to learn to see right through the words on the page, into the story. Now, in this session, we are asking them to do the opposite, to step back from the story and to think about the words themselves and how they are put together to make the story. It is easier for children to do this when the examples we use are ones they've already read. They have already thought about the story, and now they can think about how the story is told.

"More specifically, I want to teach you that we don't just improve our leads by trying and trying to make them better on our own, or by simply reading beautiful leads written by other authors. We improve our leads by closely examining work we admire, asking, 'What exactly has this author done that I could try?'"

TEACHING
Demonstrate how to study the work of mentor authors. Show children that setting, tone, and action in leads can create mood.

"Watch how I study the lead of Ezra Jack Keats' story *Peter's Chair*." I turned to chart paper on which I'd written the lead and reread it aloud to myself. I read it once, then reread it. "Do you see that I read and then reread it, and I read it quietly but aloud to myself? I'm trying to get the feeling for the lead."

> Peter stretched as high as he could.
> There! His tall building was finished. CRASH!
> Down it came.
> "Shhhh," called his mother. "You'll have
> to play more quietly. Remember we have a
> new baby in the house."

Again I read the text. "I'm thinking, 'What has Ezra Jack Keats done that I could do?'" I muttered to myself.

"The first thing I'm noticing is that Ezra Jack Keats has Peter doing a small action in the very first line—if this were a play, as soon as the curtain opened, the main character would be up on stage doing something. He is putting the last brick on the top of his building. In a second, the building will collapse and we'll imagine Peter's feeling of disappointment. I also notice dialogue—Peter's mother's words are here." I reread the starting lines again and said, "Right from the start, Keats has the main character doing something very specific, very particular. If this were a movie, I know what I'd see on the screen—and it'd be the main character doing a small action. I'd know he would first do something and then he would think something. Then his mother would speak. In this lead, the author includes these elements:"

- the main character doing a specific action
- the main character saying or thinking something
- another character doing an action

It's not necessary for you to use these exact pieces of literature. Refer to children's books you and your class love. You may need to practice putting into words what you see the lead achieving and how it achieves it. It's not easy to explain the work a given sentence does in a way that helps young writers try the same thing!

Notice that this story begins with an action, then there's dialogue. Eventually I'll teach children that stories are often built from a tapestry of actions, dialogue, and thoughts.

You may find that at first, some children interpret "the main character doing a specific action" very generally, and in that form, it won't help their writing much. They might start their writing with a line like, "We drove to the airport to pick up my mother." It is important for you to notice that the child who starts a narrative in such a way is attempting to start the story with the character doing something. The action is still general and therefore it won't be an especially effective lead. Still, celebrate the child's approximation, and help her understand that starting with a small action might, instead, mean starting, "I walked through the big doors and into the airport."

You could easily pull different replicable qualities from Keats' lead. Perhaps your list would include:
- *one character acting and another responding*
- *actions that reveal a character's wants and struggles*
Guard against telling children too many characteristics of a strong lead all at once—the real work of the session is to write differently, not just to talk differently about writing!

Demonstrate taking what we've learned from the published writing and using it to improve our own writing.

"So let me think how I can use those same techniques in my story about my dad crying. I want to try a lead which starts with me doing an action, or maybe with me talking. Um . . . I don't *really* remember exactly what I did, but I'll write what I probably did."

> I held the phone receiver against my chest.
> "Dad, it's for you," I said. "I think it's your sister."

"Did you see how I tried to follow part of the pattern that Ezra Jack Keats set? That's one way the lead to my story could go." Then I said, "Let's look at the lead another author has written. Let's look at Elizabeth Partridge's *Whistling*."

> "Jake," Daddy whispers. "It's almost time." I poke my head out of
> my warm sleeping bag. The air is tingly and cold.

"Partridge also uses action and this time, the lead also establishes the setting," I said. "And again she incorporates the character's exact words. I will try the same thing in another draft of a lead."

> I held the phone receiver against my chest.
> "Dad, it's for you," I said. "I think it's your sister."
> "At this hour?" Dad said, his face clouded with worry as
> he took the phone from me.

"See how I put in the time to add some more setting? I chose to put in that part about it being very early so my reader might know why my dad and I were already worried the instant the phone rang."

ACTIVE ENGAGEMENT

Share a lead written by one student. Ask children to revise the lead out loud with their partners by using an action or a setting.

"Writers, listen to the work Milan has done. He's writing about a Tae Kwon Do meet. In his first lead, he begins with dialogue—the words the announcer says. That's one way the authors we studied started their stories. Listen." *[Fig. VII-1]*

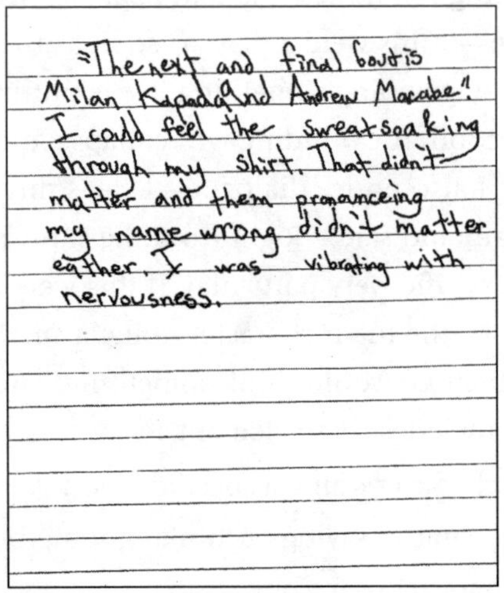

> "The next and final bout is Milan Kapada and Andrew
> Macabe." I could feel the sweat soaking through my shirt.
> That didn't matter and them pronouncing my name wrong
> didn't matter either. I was vibrating with nervousness.

If the goal of the session is to teach children that writers draft and revise lead sentences, and to show children some of the qualities of an effective lead, then it is much more helpful to examine the leads to several texts rather than to read one lead . . . and then continue reading that entire text. When we incorporate texts that we and the children already know well into our minilessons, it is reasonable to examine just one aspect of one text, then of another text.

Fig. VII-1 Milan

"Did you hear the exact words of the announcer start us off? Now, let's pretend to be Milan for a minute and see what other leads we can try for this story. He might end up sticking with this one, but let's just experiment for a moment. With your partner, try writing another lead for this same story, this time starting not with dialogue but with an action or with the setting. You won't know the real story since you aren't Milan, but that's okay, just imagine what it might have been like." I paused while partners worked together to draft a lead for Milan's story.

"Those are some great leads you are making! Before Milan rewrote his lead, he studied *Fireflies!* by Julie Brinckloe."

> On a summer evening
> I looked up from dinner,
> through the open window to the backyard.
> It was growing dark.
> My treehouse was a black shape in the tree
> and I wouldn't go up there now.
> But something flickered there, a moment.
> I looked, and it was gone.

"He noticed that she began by showing the setting in a way that created a mood, so he made a lead patterned after hers." *[Fig. VII-2]*

> The stadium dark with one single light.
> The spotlight shining on my face, the stadium quiet as the forest in winter.
> I could feel the sweat soak through my shirt, I was vibrating with nervousness all around me. I see the referee standing there in the light waiting for me.

"Wow, that's quite a lead, right? Do you see how he added to the setting in a way that created a mood just like Brinckloe did?"

As you listen to the children tell their revised leads to their partners, you will soon see how well your minilesson is taking hold. If it doesn't seem that the kids yet understand how to examine a lead, see what it does, and try doing the same thing, you could extend this minilesson by repeating the process again for them with another mentor text's lead.

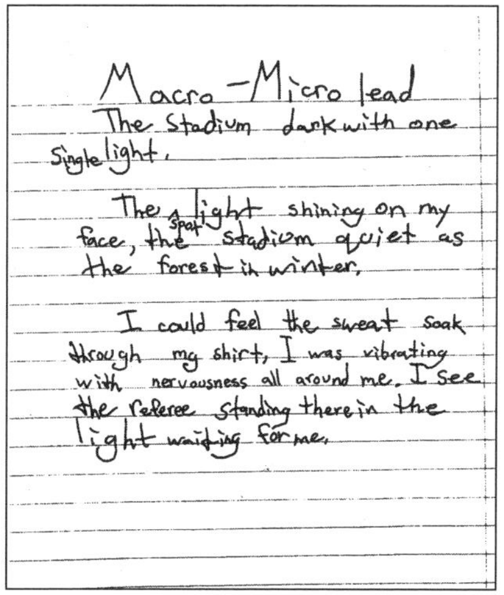
Macro-Micro lead
The Stadium dark with one Single light.
The spotlight shining on my face, the stadium quiet as the forest in winter.
I could feel the sweat soak through my shirt, I was vibrating with nervousness all around me. I see the referee standing there in the light waiting for me.

Fig. VII-2 Milan

Restate your teaching point. Send children off to write new leads, using the techniques they've learned from mentor authors.

"If we want our stories to continue sounding like literature, we need to closely examine the work of other authors, asking, 'What has this author done that I could do?' Today we did that with leads. You noticed that some authors begin their stories by telling us actions, and some start with dialogue, or with setting. I'm going to add that to our Qualities of Good Personal Narrative Writing chart."

I believe that children are well served by working on their leads early in their writing process. The leads can bring life and possibility to their writing—they can lift the level of the whole piece of writing to follow. Leads can also point out new directions stories can take, and it's much easier to explore those directions before the whole draft is written than it is afterwards.

Qualities of Good Personal Narrative Writing

- Write a little seed story; don't write all about a giant watermelon topic
- Zoom in so you tell the most important parts of the story
- Include true, exact details from the movie you have in your mind
- Begin with a strong lead—maybe action, setting, dialogue, or a combination which creates a mood

"When you go back to your tables to write, think about what you have learned about writing leads and then try out three or four different leads in your notebook. Try starting with the setting, or actions, or dialogue, or a combination of these. If you'd like, study the leads other authors have written, to expand your repertoire of options. And from this day on, for the rest of your life, always remember that your lead matters—it merits attention."

Writing and Conferring

Teaching Writers to Talk Well about Their Writing

I often remind children that on any given day, their work during the writing workshop should draw not just upon that day's minilesson, but on all the strategies they've learned. Similarly, your teaching needs to draw upon all the strategies you've taught. Today, however, is a bit of an exception because everyone will be doing the same work—studying and drafting leads. The one prior lesson you can draw upon, though, is the one helping children consider their role in a conference.

Children will be able to assume their roles only if you set them up to do so. Try starting your conferences by asking children to teach you what they've been working on as writers. "How's it going?" you might ask. "What are you trying to do with the lead you are writing?"

If a child doesn't respond to your questions by teaching you what he or she is trying to do, give the writer some feedback. "When I ask, 'What are you trying to do as a writer?' I'm expecting you to tell me not so much what your story is about, but the decisions you are making over how to write the story well. What did you notice another author doing that you are trying to do? How's it going?" In this instance, it should be relatively easy for a child to tell you, "I'm trying to begin with an action." Prepare to extend that. "How'd you decide on this particular action? What other ones did you consider?" You may end up teaching some children that it helps to start with actions that are close to the main event of the story, or that it helps to select actions that reveal what the character cares about and that set us up to understand the character's main struggles. Of course, *Peter's Chair* can help you make that point!

You can enter today anticipating that some children will pop out a lead and want to call it a day. Be ready to help those children embrace revision, perhaps by shuttling between reading and writing leads. If your own memories of revising writing are such that you cringe at the prospect of revision, try to put your

> **MID-WORKSHOP TEACHING POINT** *Using Quotation Marks* "Writers, can I have your eyes and your attention? I love that you are trying out different leads for your story. That's amazing. Now I want to teach you a rule for using quotation marks, because many of you are trying leads that begin with people talking. You need quotation marks; otherwise the sections where you have people talking will be confusing."
>
> "Quotation marks signal the exact words a person has said. They let the reader know that someone is talking. Let's look at the lead from Elizabeth Partridge's *Whistling*, (2003) looking closely at where she places her quotation marks."
>
> > "Jake," Daddy whispers. "It's almost time." I poke my head out of my warm sleeping bag. The air is tingly and cold.
>
> "Notice that she surrounds the daddy's exact words in quotation marks. The quoted section begins with a capital and ends with punctuation. It's usually a comma or a period. And the quotation marks have surrounded it all."
>
> *continued on next page*

distaste for revision out of your mind and role-play the part of being a writer who loves revision. Like most other writers, I love tinkering with sentences until they are just right. I listen to the sounds of the words, fiddling with the punctuation, syntax, and word choice until the sentence sounds pleasing. I say my sentences aloud, testing them for sound just like I say proposed names for a newborn baby aloud. I mimic the sentences of writers I admire. Act as if you can't possibly imagine how it could be that a child doesn't love this work as you do.

continued from previous page

"Let's try this together right now. I am going to talk. As I begin, capture the beginning of my talk by hooking your two fingers on your left hand. When I finish talking, catch my last words with two fingers on your right hand." I did this, and they made quotation marks in the air. "You can do the same thing in writing by using quotation marks. Look over your story right now and check to see if you have included talk. If you have, make sure your quotation marks surround the exact words being said, and that what is said includes its punctuation."

I moved among the class, coaching children to help each other punctuate the dialogue they'd already written. This seemingly straightforwad lesson was not at all straightforward when children tried to apply it to their drafts. Some, like Takeshi [*Fig. VII-3*], had sections of text in which one character and then another talked back and forth, interjecting brief comments. When the text didn't name the speaker or include any actions, it was often difficult to discern when one voice ended and another began. Then, too, some writers summarized conversations rather than quoting verbatim.

One day I was playing on the playground at school then Takuma came and said, what do you want to play. I said I don't know so he said "play by yourself because I'll play kickball." "Okay." "Sure," I said, but in my mind I said to myself I can't believe that he just said that.

Fig. VII-3 Takeshi's first entry with beginning attempts to mark the dialogue using quotation marks.

SHARE

Listening to Leads

Convene children on the rug. Ask writers to share their best work of the day—in this case, a favorite lead.

"Milan's whole story will be different because he's taken the time to try different leads, and modeled his leads after those he admires in books. I know many of you did similar work. Would you share your leads with your partner? Talk over the techniques you tried to use."

I listened as Rebecca read her favorite lead to Sofiya, and Sofiya in turn shared her choices. *[Figs. VII-4 and VII-5]*

Rebecca Leads:

I peered into my bag. Nothing. No gym tights, no leotard. I felt tears welling up in my eyes. I thought back: yes, no, yes. I hadn't putten my leotard back in the bag. I jerked down my head and pulled my tea shirt over my school tights.

Sofiya Leads:

"I like snakes, don't you, Sofiya?"
She's got to be joking.
"No I don't!"
I don't know since when, but I dont like snakes.

I was sitting in the circle waiting. What kind of animal was the lady about to bring out? A bird, a parrot, a spider or two, maybe a fish in a bowl of water? A snake!

I listen in as children share with one another to show my interest in hearing what they have to say. Listening also gives me important insights into the children's understandings and interpretations of what I have asked them to do.

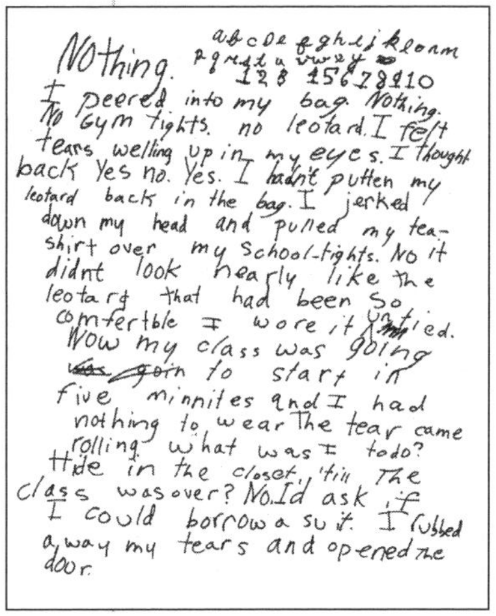

Nothing. abcdefghijklonm
nprqstuvwxyz
123 1567 8910
I peered into my bag Nothing. No Gym tights. no leotard. I felt tears welling up in my eyes. I thought back Yes no. Yes. I hadnt putten my leotard back in the bag. I jerked down my head and pulled my tea-shirt over my school-tights. No it didnt look nearly like the leotard that had been so comfertble I wore it Untied. Wow my class was going was gorn to start in five minnites and I had nothing to wear The tear came rolling what was I todo? Hide in the closet, till The class was over? No. Id ask if I could borrow a suit. I rubbed away my tears and opened the door.

Fig. VII-4 Rebecca

" I like snakes, don't you, Sofiya?" She's got to be joking. "No I don't." I don't know since when, but I don't like snakes.

I was sitting in the circle waiting. What kind of animal was the lady about to bring out? A bird, parrot, a spider or two, maybe a fish in a bowl of water? A snake!!!!!!!!

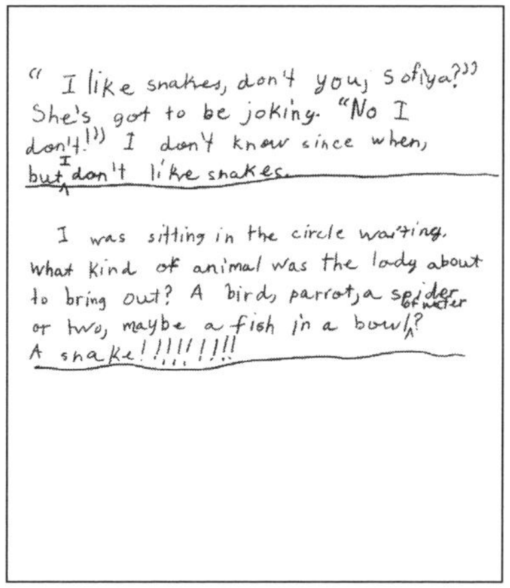

Fig. VII-5 Sofiya

Show children the next steps. Introduce drafting booklets.

"I want to show you what I mean about how your story will flow from your lead. Right now, take out the blank booklets you were storytelling into yesterday. Those booklets are what writers call *drafting booklets*. This is where you'll write your rough draft story. Right now, copy the version of your lead which you've selected onto the first page of this booklet, and then try telling your story across the pages of the booklet. Watch how I repeat the lead I chose and then storytell, touching each page as I say the next bit of my story."

> "Dad," I said. "The phone's for you." Dad arched his eyebrows as if to say, "For me? So early?" All of us kids looked up from our sections of <u>The Sunday Times</u>. We listened while Dad said into the phone, "Hello?" The silence was deadening as we waited.

I turned the page.

> "Oh no," we heard Dad say. "When did it happen?" My mind raced through catastrophes. Who'd died? Who was hurt?

Again I turned the page. "Do you see how I turn the page when I shift to the next part?" Then said, as if dictating:

> A few minutes later . . .

Pausing, I said, "Try telling your story across the pages of your booklet!"

In this share session, my reference to drafting booklets sets children up for the next day's lesson. By having each child copy his lead onto his first page, a lot of the preparation work for tomorrow's workshop is done ahead of time. This will allow me to get right to the point of what I want to teach in the next session—how to write a draft.

I find that if I want children to tell or to write a story with a clear plot, with one event leading to the next, it helps for them to write across a sequence of pages. If your classroom has a shortage of paper, a single piece of notebook paper can be folded in half to create a booklet with four pages.

HOMEWORK *Studying Leads* When a chef goes out to dinner, he pays attention to the sauces and the spices he admires, thinking, "How was this made?" Similarly, you will want to find sections of the books you've read that you admire and pause, asking, "How was this made?"

Cynthia Rylant once said, "I learned how to write from writers. I didn't know any personally. But I read." She is not alone. The writers we love will all agree that they learned to write from authors. So tonight, would each of you spend some time reading like a writer, noticing not only what authors say, but also how they say it. Bookmark places in beloved books where an author has used a technique you'd like to try.

Especially notice leads. Come to school ready to talk about what you learned by studying the work of a pro. For example, last night I noticed that books often begin with a paragraph that establishes a big context, then zooms in to a small action. Sometimes these leads seem shaped like a funnel. For example, *The Witch of Blackbird Pond* begins:

> On a morning in mid-April, 1687, the brigantine Dolphin left the open sea, sailed briskly across the Sound to the wide mouth of the Connecticut River and into Saybrook harbor. Kit Tyler had been on the forecastle deck since daybreak, standing close to the rail, staring hungrily at the first sight of land for five weeks. "There's Connecticut Colony," a voice spoke in her ear. (Speare, 1958, p. 1)

Because of Winn-Dixie also begins by establishing context, but when I compared this lead with the lead to *Witch of Blackbird Pond*, it seems to me that in *Because of Winn-Dixie* it is the narrator and main character, Opal, who creates the context:

> My name is India Opal Buloni, and last summer my daddy, the preacher, sent me to the store for a box of macaroni-and-cheese, some white rice, and two tomatoes and I came back with a dog. This is what happened: I walked into the produce section of the Winn-Dixie grocery store to pick out my two tomatoes. (DiCamillo, 2000, p. 7)

So tonight do similar research. Come to your own conclusions about techniques authors use that you could emulate.

◉ TAILORING YOUR TEACHING

If your students each write only one kind of lead over and over again . . . you might introduce them to a variety of leads, each other's leads, as inspiration. One way to do that is to ask every student to star a lead he's written in his writer's notebook and then leave the notebook open at his writing spot in the room. Then, ask everyone to walk around the room, reading and researching the types of leads on display. Then, gather writers together, and ask them to discuss their findings. After you have charted the types of leads they've discovered, suggest they try making their own leads in these new ways—first aloud with their partners and later independently in their writer's notebooks.

If many children in the room have all written the same kind of lead, this sort of museum walk won't be inspirational to writers. In that case, you will want to find leads from published writing and make those leads available to students to study and discuss and imitate.

Another way to approach this problem, as any problem, is to simply point out to the students the patterns you notice in their work, why the pattern isn't one to settle into. Then ask children to brainstorm with you possible solutions to the problem. Then, you can chart these suggestions and send children off to try them, taking note of which invented strategies help and which ones don't, revising them along the way.

If your students don't seem excited by spending time revising leads . . . bring excitement to the topic by making a big deal out of leads you notice throughout the day. Show children your collection of "favorite leads" that you've accumulated over the years (or maybe over the last few days) and ask their opinions of them. Make a fuss when chapters start with great leads in your read-aloud book. Bring in leads you find in magazine articles that are either horrid or wonderful, and ask children to join you in thinking about them and collecting others. Start a bulletin board of great leads from the students' notebooks; ask students to keep an eye out for leads in their own and others' notebooks to join the display. Reiterate overheard comments that could make great leads, "Did you all hear what Paul said just now when he was talking about how things used to be arranged on that back shelf? He said 'Back when the daisies were alive . . .'. That could make a great lead to a narrative if you were looking for that particular ominous tone, don't you think?"

COLLABORATING WITH COLLEAGUES

It may appear as if your instruction in this session has put a spotlight on the characteristics of an effective lead, but really your teaching in this session, as is usual within this unit, has focused above all on ways children can improve the quality of their personal narrative writing.

If your education in the qualities of good writing was anything like mine, you'll probably find that you are learning about narrative writing right alongside your children. Know, first of all, that you are not alone.

When I was in school, I was taught to write with my five senses, to use adjectives and adverbs, and to include similes and alliteration. But I was not taught anything else about narrative writing until I was out of graduate school and teaching third graders. I wanted to write an article about my students and therefore got hold of Donald Murray's *A Writer Teaches Writing*, and the rest is history.

I strongly advise you to read some books on good writing as you teach this unit and the one that follows it. I also suggest you talk with colleagues about this professional reading, working together to use what you learn in your own writing and teaching. Start with chapters 4 and 5 of Katherine Bomer's *Writing a Life*. Then try Ralph Fletcher's *What a Writer Needs* or the

book that started me on my journey, Murray's *A Writer Teaches Writing*. Or William Zinsser's *On Writing Well* if you want to teach toward clear, simple prose. Or Barry Lane's *After THE END*.

But you needn't learn qualities of good writing only by reading professional books. Good writing itself will teach you. Open any great narrative text and put to words what the author has done. Try examining the first chapter of Kate DiCamillo's *Because of Winn-Dixie* (mentioned in the Homework section). Try any page of Patricia MacLachlan's *Journey*. Find "Mr. Entwhistle" in Jean Little's *Hey World, Here I Am*. It's two pages long and my colleagues and I spent hours poring over it. If you hear yourself describing these texts by relying on clichés, saying, "The author paints a picture," force yourself to go past those words to be more precise, exact, replicable. What exactly has the author done that you could try?

Once you name the technique, what's there to stop you from trying it yourself? Pull out the entry you began earlier and see how your sentences turn out, rewritten under the influence of Julie Brinckloe, Jane Yolen, or Alma Flor Ada.

GETTING READY

- Instructions on chalkboard telling children to bring their folders with drafting booklets to the meeting area
- Piece of writing, preferably a child's discovery draft, copied onto a transparency
- Overhead projector
- Chart paper and markers
- See CD-ROM for resources

WRITING DISCOVERY DRAFTS

The world is bursting with options, but a writer and a teacher both must reach into the hurly-burly of life and select just one word, then the next—just one teaching point, then the next.

I've helped thousands of teachers launch writing workshops, and there is a dazzling array of options for how one might proceed into drafting. Do we begin by teaching children to make a timeline of the event, then tell the story following that timeline? Do we begin by studying a touchstone text closely, then encouraging children to write in the same fashion or with the same structure? Do we start the year with an emphasis on content only? "Teach your readers what you know," we could say, postponing discussion about structure until later.

Out of all the options, I've chosen to channel children toward writing well-structured, chronological, focused narratives because I've come to believe that structure is absolutely fundamental to good writing, and that children—and teachers, too—care more about writing when it turns out well.

I've decided to put forth the concept of a discovery draft because I want children to understand that drafting is an exploratory process that resembles shaping in clay more than inscribing in marble. I want children to write fast and long so they feel that a first draft is tentative and improvable. Then, too, I've chosen to emphasize writing discovery drafts because I find that sometimes when children are fast-writing, those who have regarded themselves as struggling writers find an internal source of power and surprise themselves (and us too) by writing with a passion and freshness that takes our breath away.

MINILESSON

Writing Discovery Drafts

CONNECTION

Remind children of the work they've done so far in the process of drafting, and tell them they are ready to go one step farther.

"So far, you've rehearsed for your writing by storytelling and by thinking of leads. Now is the time to write a draft!"

"There is no one right way to go about writing a draft. This year, I'll teach you a variety of strategies that writers use to draft, and I'll ask you to try them on for size. You know how we try shirts on for size, saying, 'This one is too bulky for me,' or 'This one's arms are too short for me,' and 'This one is just right.' In a similar fashion, writers try writing processes on for size. Some writers find one method of proceeding fits best, others prefer another. But no matter which strategy, all writers rehearse for writing, and all writers write a rough draft. And when we are done with our rough drafts, all writers reread and revise what we've written, just like we will do."

Name the teaching point. In this case, teach children that some writers fast-write discovery drafts to get their story out on paper.

"Today I'm going to suggest you all try writing a discovery draft. Writers sometimes decide that after carefully crafting each word of a lead, it's a good next step to do the opposite kind of thing and just fix our eyes on our subject, writing our story fast and long, without stopping."

TEACHING

Use a metaphor to tell children that writers sometimes fast-write a discovery draft. Tell how this is done and show an example.

"A friend of mine is studying to be an artist, and in her class on painting portraits, her professor has taught her that one way to get unbelievable power into her drawing is to look at her subject, to gaze deeply and totally at the person she is portraying, and to sketch what she sees without even looking down at her paper. She keeps her eyes on the person, and sketches with the goal of putting down the truth of what she sees—all of it—onto the page."

COACHING

Notice that whenever I summarize the work children have done to date, I try to name parts of the writing process I hope they will cycle through again and again. I know that when children first progress through the writing process, they sometimes proceed with tunnel vision, seeing only the next step. In the movie Platoon, *a character says that war means putting one foot in front of the other, trying to see three inches in front of us. I know that by retelling the broad vista of the writing process, I help children gain a greater sense of control.*

Once a thoughtful lead has pointed a way through the story, the draft can follow more easily.

The friend I am referring to here is the writer Georgia Heard. She writes about this technique in her book Writing Toward Home *(1995, p.121)*

"Writers do something similar. We fill ourselves with the true thing that happened to us. We remember the very start of the episode and storytell what happened first (only we scrawl the story onto the paper rather than tell it) and then, without worrying much about perfect spelling or word choice or anything, we keep our minds fixed on everything that happened and write fast and long without stopping."

"Let me show you Felix's discovery draft. I'm going to show it using the overhead projector so you can see that it doesn't need to be well spelled—listen to the power of this fast-write." [Fig. VIII-1]

> "Felix, wake up, we have to go to the church." We went to the church. I started seeing all my family members. I did not know what was happening. Then I saw a big box coming out of the church. My grandma laied her head against the big brown box and stared crying. I tugged on her shirt, "Grandma grandma what's in there?"
>
> "Just look."
>
> I stared through the screen. It was my grandfather. He was as pale as glue. "Grandfather get out of there, come and help me make the paper airplanes you make! Don't go. Don't! I am sorry about what I said to you." I knocked on the screen. It did not help. He would not wake up. "I want to see my grandfather now." I knew now what was going on. My grandfather had just died. I did not know what to say to myself. I felt scared. What was I going to do without my grandpa?
>
> No no no. There's no paper airplanes that he's going to make me. Who is going to say the funny stories everyday? Whose going to put a smile on me everyday? I stop. A tear runs through my face. I stomp over to my grandfather but my uncle holds me back. I see his white face. His hard boney hands on his sides.
>
> "Grandpa, let's go to the window and throw the paper airplanes." I see him coming, his pale white face grinning at me. He slowly starts walking with a long brown stick, his weak hands holding on the stick.

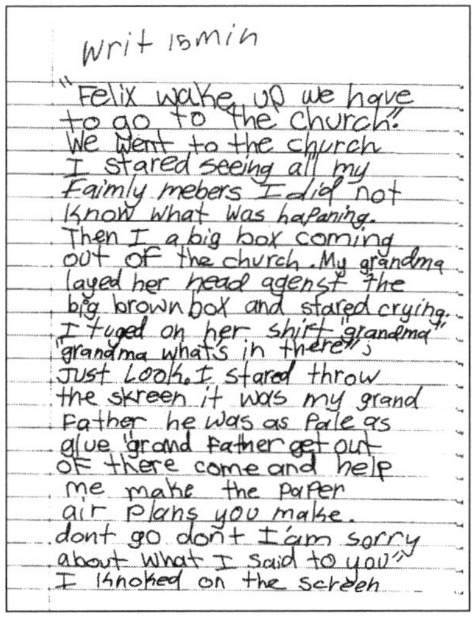

Fig. VIII-1 The first page of Felix's draft.

Felix has gone through school with the reputation of being a struggling writer. Like some other children with this reputation, Felix is in fact a very powerful writer—but one who struggles with the conventions of written language. He needs explicit instruction in these conventions, but more important, he needs a teacher who can see the power of his work. This piece reveals his difficulties with the surface mechanics of language, yet it also reveals his willingness to write honestly, with deep emotion, and his enviable gift for metaphor: "pale as glue." I want children to see Felix's handwriting and spelling errors because I want every child in the classroom to realize that powerful, honest writing is within grasp. Spelling well does not necessarily correlate with writing well. Both are important. Children who care about writing and believe they have something to say will be much more willing to do the work of becoming more effective spellers.

ACTIVE ENGAGEMENT

Recruit children to be willing to write discovery drafts and channel them towards being ready to start this work.

"A famous writer named Faulkner once said, 'There are some kinds of writing that you have to do very fast, like riding a bicycle on a tightrope' (Murray 1990, p. 143). To stay up on bikes, we need to pedal fast and go full speed ahead! Many writers find that in order to make listeners feel what they want them to feel, it helps to write fast and long. Today we'll do that, writing the same stories (only better) that we told each other yesterday."

"To get started, reread the lead you already copied onto page one of your drafting booklet, and then just touch each page of the booklet and say the story you'll write on that page. Do this for the whole story, spreading it out across pages, and then go back to page one. Reread your lead and remember the beginning of the event. Pretend you are storytelling the story to listeners. Make them feel whatever you want them to feel. Start writing and write fast, keeping your eyes on the true story. Then I said to children, "Get started while you are here on the carpet, and once you feel like you are ready to keep going, go to your seat."

If this is the first time you have asked your students to write while sitting together in a clump of bodies in the meeting area, you may run into predictable problems with kids finding it difficult to sit still, to concentrate, and to get words flowing onto the paper. Don't despair! Every aspect of writing workshop requires practicing over and over until it becomes routine. Throughout the units in this curriculum, there will be opportunities for children to practice and get better at both "writing in the air" and literally writing while sitting in the meeting area. Also, as your students become more independent and begin to draw from your instruction to help themselves get better at writing, they will welcome any and all variations on the usual procedures as a new way to stretch themselves!

LINK

Remind writers of what you've taught today, and tell them they can use this new strategy for the rest of their lives.

"So writers, you know that we sometimes storytell a story to ourselves or aloud before we write it, as a way to take a story idea and stretch it into a wonderful, long story, the kind of story that can give people goose bumps. Today, you learned that writers often write discovery drafts, writing fast and long in order to get your story down on the page. Try on this way of drafting just like you might try on a shirt. See if it fits!"

The poet and novelist Naomi Shihab Nye says it this way: "Write luxuriously, abundantly, fill whole pages, making little notes to yourself in the margins. Don't worry about saying it perfectly." (Flynn and McPhillips 2000, p. 46)

WRITING AND CONFERRING

Supporting Writing Fluency

When the children in your room are writing discovery drafts, trying to write quickly and for a long time, your conferring will probably be a little different than usual. Most of the time when you confer, you won't hesitate to interrupt children at work since you know that your interruption—your conference—will provide a strategy to help them strengthen their work. The nature of conferring is that you engage with children in the midst of writing, teaching them about their work as they are doing it. If the conference is not an interruption, it's probably not your strongest conference.

Today's situation is a bit different, however. Today, many of the children are pushing themselves specifically to write without interruption—to write fast and long. Interrupting them to determine if there is a way to help them write without interruption might seem like a contradiction. On the other hand, if you can tell without much research that some children could be writing faster and longer and stronger, you should go ahead and interrupt them to confer.

> **MID-WORKSHOP TEACHING POINT**   **_Rereading to Build Writing Stamina_**   "Writers, can I have your eyes and your attention? When I feel myself lagging in energy, I reread my writing. But I reread in a special way. I reread it to myself as if the story is an utter masterpiece."
>
> "I don't fuss over the details; if a word is awry I mentally fix it, and keep going because I want to read with a rapt focus on my content, filling myself with the story so it wells up in me. When I come to the last word I've written, I just pick up my pen and write for dear life, scrawling down the page."
>
> "So writers, if you are lagging in energy and want to give yourself a second wind, pause and reread. Reread your own writing as if it is a masterpiece, and let your rereading give you a boost for more writing."

- If a child is tapping the page and staring into space instead of writing, you might teach the child that he can get a running start into writing by going to the first page of the booklet and storytelling the parts that belong on each page.

- If a child is using the word wall to help her spell a word exactly right and that process is more than a slight diversion from getting the story down, you might teach the child that she can write the word as best she can, circle it so as to keep writing and then come back to it later to rethink the troublesome spelling.

- If a child is stopping to erase, you might teach the child to put a light line through the part of the writing that is leading him astray and simply keep writing.

- If a child is thinking and rethinking how any given part of the draft goes, teach that child to make marginal notes about alternatives to how she's written the draft and just keep going.

- If a child is judging every sentence, encourage the child to think, "Oh well, I'll just do the best I can and keep going."

SHARE

Savoring Favorite Parts

Remind writers of the strategies they already know for giving themselves more writing stamina. Lay out a new one.

"Writers, in our share session today, I want to teach you another strategy that writers use to give themselves that 'second wind'—one in addition to rereading our writing like it is a masterpiece. Sometimes we take time to reread parts of our writing that we know just sing, parts that we are proud of because we have found the right words to express what we want to say. When I do this in my writing room at home, I pretend I'm on a stage, reading that particular part of my writing out loud to an audience. I use my best reading voice; I even give the characters different voices. I slow way down when I come to the dramatic parts, I speed my voice up when I come to exciting parts. Sometimes I ask people in my family to listen to the small part of my writing that I think I've written well."

Ask students to try this strategy by reading favorite parts to the whole class.

"So take a moment to reread what you wrote today. Choose a phrase or sentence you particularly love, either because of the way it sounds or because you think it is exactly true. When you have found a section you like, show me with a thumbs up." I waited until most thumbs went up. "Let's read these parts to everyone, into the circle. Read your line whenever you are ready, whenever there is a space for you to speak. Let's begin now."

I gestured towards Ahra. She read, "The trees were swaying back and forth like they were dancing." My eyes caught Tasnim's. She whispered, "My bravery was blowing away with the wind." I smiled and nodded towards Genesis. She read, "The cake was mush as if I was holding oatmeal." Joseph followed with, "The icicles pointed north." Soon the room was filled with powerful phrases and favorite lines.

Voice your appreciation for the writing the children have read aloud. Remind children to use this strategy when they need writing energy.

"Wow, what exquisitely chosen words you've read! Can you feel all the writing energy in the room right now? I bet you can hardly wait for the next opportunity to write! Remember, you can always do something like this when you need writing energy!"

Notice that this is a new way of conducting the share session for this unit, but it's one that you will see my colleagues and I use often, with variations, throughout the school year. We love this one because it reminds us to celebrate the power and beauty of writing. We forget sometimes, in keeping our noses to the grindstone, to appreciate where we are and how far we have come.

Even though there might not be a formal teaching point in this type of share, the lessons learned carry more weight than you might imagine. Children learn, for instance, that their words have the power to move others to laugh, to frown, or simply to think about something. They learn that everyone in the community has written something beautiful or amazing, and not just the "good writers." This share also spurs revision because sometimes after a writer reads out loud, he hears parts that need to be changed.

Some people refer to the previous share as a "Quaker Share" because children can just begin to read when they feel ready, rather than going around the circle round-robin style. Keep in mind that the first few times you try a Quaker Share, the silences between each reading might feel awkward. Children are accustomed to being called on when it is their turn to speak, so asking them to "speak when the spirit moves you" might cause some fidgeting. With repetition, however, students learn how to enter their voices into the stream of sound, and the results are always beautiful! Use this format to share small bits of writing, such as leads, titles, and favorite lines, perhaps once each week. This offers the opportunity for everyone's words to be heard and celebrated in a quick and joyful manner.

HOMEWORK *Finding a Favorite Writing Place* Writers, we will begin writing at home pretty soon, in addition to the writing we do in school. And writers need a place to write, a place they can call their own. So tonight, look around your home for a place you might be able to make into a writing place. It doesn't have to be big or even your own space. It can be a corner of a room or a table that travels. Find a spot where you can think and write without being easily distracted. Try out a few different spots, then pick the one you like the best and think of ways you might make it your own. One way writers try to create a special writing place is by surrounding ourselves with objects that mean something special to us. Writers often gather our favorite books, photographs, objects, inspirational quotes, poems, artwork, music; anything that makes us feel comfortable. You will also need to gather the tools you will need to write. Ralph Fletcher in his book *How Writers Work* (2000) recommends this:

> Make sure you have what you need to start writing. These may seem
> like small details, but I have found they matter a great deal. Just as a
> carpenter has tools particular to his or her trade, so does a writer—
> pens, a notebook, paper. If you have these tools in your writing
> place, you won't have to go rummaging around when it's time to
> write. Everything you need will be right where you want it. (p.10)

Draw a picture of your special writing place. Label the picture showing the things that will make it a good place to write. Remember, it may be the kitchen table or a favorite chair or your bed. Your objects and tools may be on a shelf or in a basket or a bag. There is no one kind of place writers find to write. The important thing is that it is a place you can go to anytime you want or need to write.

You will continue to find ways to help students develop identities as writers. Writers love to gather objects and tools that might stimulate writing. Carving out a place at home will also encourage both the children and their caregivers to provide a time and a place and the tools required for homework.

TAILORING YOUR TEACHING

If you notice that students' writing fluency is hampered by their worries about accurate spelling . . . you may want to show them a strategy for getting their words down the best they can so they can keep going. From spelling expert Sandra Wilde, I learned that it can be helpful to teach children the concept of placeholder spelling. In order to do this, I said, "Writers, yesterday I taught you one method for drafting: writing long and fast. Some of you were slowed down by trying to spell hard words exactly right. Today I am going to teach you a strategy for getting words down the best you can by using placeholder spelling."

"Watch how I use placeholder spelling to help me get my tricky words down quickly enough that I can focus on what I want to say." Using chart paper, I wrote, "I stood by the lake watching the sun . . ." I paused, and then said the next word to myself several times. ". . . shimmering, shimmering, shim-mer-ing." Turning away from the chart paper, I explained, "I am saying the word a few times, then once slowly, so I can hear all the sounds. Then I will write the word the best I can, underline it so I know to check it later with a dictionary or a friend, and keep writing. This is a great strategy for when you need to write a word you are not sure how to spell, because it doesn't slow you down."

I then set the class up for guided practice by preparing a practice sentence that contained a couple of words that I knew would stump the class. I reminded children, "When you get to a hard word, say the word out loud, out loud again, then slowly, listening for all the sounds. Okay, get the word down the best you can, underline it, and let's keep going."

If you notice that your students simply copy their writer's notebook entry into their drafting booklet . . . explicitly teach them that when writers turn a notebook entry into a draft, we usually enlarge and elaborate on the entry. You may want to use an entry from your writer's notebook that is familiar to your students. "Writers, when I move this entry to my drafting notebook, I'm not going to just copy it in word for word. Instead, I'm going to use the entry and build on it. The entry is almost like an architect's blueprint for a house. The blueprint gives an idea of what the building will be like, where the rooms are, how long the hallways are, but when it's actually being built, you can begin to see all the details, like the color of the paint, the view from the windows, the noise the floor makes when it's stepped on. That's what happens when you move from your entry to your drafting booklet. You add more and sort of build upon the entry. Watch me as I do this." Think aloud as you write in your drafting booklet, showing students how writers might add details that are not in the entry, elaborating on certain parts of the entry.

MECHANICS

Earlier, I suggested that you and your colleagues gather your children's writing and look at their control of conventions in order to devise a plan for supporting this aspect of their writing development. Some of the overarching questions to ask yourself are these: Are my children generally on track in their spelling development? In their control of punctuation? In their use of standard English syntax and grammar? In their sentence complexity? In their vocabulary development?

To answer that, you need general guidelines. Here are some of my recommendations for finding or setting them:

- Pat Cunningham has provided a recommended list of high-frequency words that she suggests teaching at each elementary grade level. For example, the second-grade list contains words such as *about, before, didn't, into, many, other, then, were*. The fourth-grade list, on the other hand, contains words such as *because, become, guide, journey, laugh, straight, through, question*. It's worth obtaining her list of high-frequency words that she believes are appropriate for each grade level, and determining which grade-level list is aligned to most of your children. Ask yourself, "Do 80% of my fourth graders spell the second-grade words correctly when they write?" If the answer is no, then it is fair to say that your kids are definitely not on course as spellers! Ask yourself whether the majority of your fourth graders are able to spell the words on her fourth-grade suggested list. This will give you one indication of how you can assess your children's spelling . . . and will meanwhile suggest starting points for their continued growth.

- Then, too, by the time children are in third grade, they should be able to tackle a word they do not know how to spell—say, *subordination*—and their spellings should reflect that they have broken the word into syllables and used a knowledge of how those syllables are usually spelled in order to produce an approximation that is at least as informed as these: *subordenasion, subordanation,* or perhaps *subordenaysen.*

- Sandra Wilde, author of many books on spelling, once gave me this as a rule of thumb. She said, "By the time children are in fifth grade, 90% of the words on their rough drafts should be spelled correctly, and children should also have the skills necessary to find correct spellings for many of the misspelled words."

If your kids need some extra help with their control of conventions, then chances are great that your children also need extra help with their writing. Please don't let a focus on mechanics overrun your writing workshop. Instead, provide a separate time in your day for mechanics, spelling, and vocabulary, while still weaving this work into the writing workshop. During the writing workshop, you can show children how to incorporate what they've learned during mechanics time into their ongoing writing.

REVISING ENDINGS:
LEARNING FROM PUBLISHED WRITING

Narrative stories have a plot and also a resolution. *A good story needs a good ending. Many writers I know say that the endings of their stories and poems and essays are their favorite parts. Some even say that they know their endings before they know anything else about their piece! The writer Katherine Anne Porter claimed, "I always write my last line, my last paragraph, my last page, first." Our students may not feel that their endings are their favorite parts, but endings are crucial. For if leads have to do the work of inviting, even begging readers to spend time with the story that follows, the endings are what stay in readers' minds the longest. Endings can cause readers to sob, to applaud, even to get up and vow to change themselves or the world. Writers know this, so we spend extra time on the last paragraphs and last sentences of our stories. Long before you teach this lesson, you can convey the power of a good ending to your children during your read-aloud time. Let the pace and intonation of your voice showcase each story's final passages.*

As Frank Smith says in his groundbreaking book Joining the Literacy Club, *"Children must read like a writer in order to learn how to write like a writer. There is no other way in which the intricate complexity of a writer's knowledge can be acquired" (1988, p. 23).*

While teaching children to draft and revise endings, then, you'll also be teaching children that writers read the works of other authors as insiders, noticing not only the content but also the craftsmanship. You'll teach, also, that writers pull in to write, then pull back to look at what we've written thinking, "What's good about this?" "What could be better?"

In Session VII, we learned how to craft powerful leads by studying the opening paragraphs of several mentor texts. In this session, we will do the same work with endings. After this session, we'll support those children who are ready to leave this first piece of writing and begin another.

IN THIS SESSION, YOU WILL TEACH CHILDREN THAT WRITERS DELIBERATELY CRAFT THE ENDINGS OF THEIR STORIES. YOU'LL SHOW CHILDREN HOW TO LEARN TECHNIQUES FOR IMPROVING THEIR OWN WORK BY STUDYING PUBLISHED WRITING.

GETTING READY

- Instructions on chalkboard telling children to bring their writer's notebooks (pens tucked inside) and sit with their partners in the meeting area
- Ending of *Fireflies!* by Julie Brinckloe, or another strong ending that kids know well, written onto a transparency
- Mental notes about what makes that ending strong that kids can try
- Overhead projector and marker
- Qualities of Good Personal Narrative Writing chart
- See CD-ROM for resources

MINILESSON

Revising Endings: Learning from Published Writing

CONNECTION

Remind children of the writing work they have been doing and prepare them for learning something new.

"I love the way you have been writing fast and long on your discovery drafts. I have something incredibly important to tell you today, now that you've done that! It's a kind of a secret that good writers know, but many beginning writers don't know. You will need to listen carefully."

"Remember when we worked really hard to get leads that would capture and hold the attention of a reader? Adam took his lead *[Fig. IX-1]*: 'Last night my dad, Harrison and I were in the car going to a restaurant.' and turned it into 'One warm evening last Spring, Harrison, my dad, and I climbed into our car and zoomed off toward the highway.' What a big difference just putting in a few words about the weather and using strong verbs like *climbed* and *zoomed* made! Adam's little changes set a mood for the story. I get a picture in my mind of a warm night, when you drive in your car with the windows rolled down, the wind blowing in your face—when you feel excited, like anything can happen."

Name the teaching point. In this case, teach children that authors craft not only beginnings, but also endings that have an effect on the reader.

"You've all discovered how we writers lead into stories, luring the readers to follow us with a special lead. But the secret that many beginning writers don't know is that writers work just as hard—well, maybe even *harder*—on our endings. Today I want to teach you some ways to do that using the ending of one of our mentor texts, *Fireflies!* by Julie Brinckloe."

TEACHING

Demonstrate using a mentor text to learn ways to make writing more powerful. Read the text aloud and explain your thinking.

"We have to be sure that we make something at the end that fits with the idea we're writing about, something that will stay with the reader. Let's look at the ending of *Fireflies!* I've projected it using the overhead projector so we can study Brinckloe's writing and learn ways to make our endings powerful. Watch while I reread and think about what Julie

COACHING

At the start of the minilesson, your tone and words need to convey the message, "Listen up. I've been thinking about you all and I have just one crucial tip to share." You may want to scan through lots of minilessons, collecting various ways in which I try to rally children's attention. This Connection (and specifically the invitation to hear a secret) is one of my favorites.

Notice that over and over, I point out good work and then name what is good about the work in a way that is generalizable to another day and another piece. You and your colleagues may want to practice doing just this because if you are skilled at this, you'll find it also comes in handy during connections, mid-workshop teaching points, the compliment section of conferences, and share sessions.

NHL Game 7,

Last night my dad, Harrison and I were in the car going to a restaurant or where me and Harrison thought we were going Then we got to the continental Airlines Arena we still thought we were going to a, restaurant. Third we went in the Stadium and I got a little suspicous. After that we went to our seats. Finally we relized we were all going to a restaurant we were at the 12th game 7 in all of hockey history and the Devils won.

Fig. IX-1 Adam's first draft

Brinckloe did here to make her ending powerful." I read the following section aloud, marking the things I noticed on the transparency.

> I flung off the covers.
> I went to the window,
> opened the jar,
> and aimed at the stars.
> *"Fly!"*
> Then the jar began to glow,
> green,
> then gold,
> then white as the moon.
> And the fireflies poured out into the night.
> *Fireflies!*
> Blinking on, blinking off,
> dipping low, soaring high above my head,
> making circles around the moon
> like stars dancing.
> I held the jar, dark and empty,
> in my hands.
> The moonlight and the fireflies
> swam in my tears,
> but I could feel myself smiling.

"This is such an ending, isn't it?! Let's read it again, and this time, I'll think out loud while we read it. Look, the first thing in this ending is the boy flinging off his covers. Julie made it so the boy is doing something, right? But not just doing any old thing, he's not scratching his nose, he's flinging off his covers. I bet the author chose that action for him to do because it's just like he's flinging off the comforting idea that he can keep those fireflies forever in the jar. I think she put that action in the ending because it can give us more thoughts about the important parts of the story. I'm going to write 'important action' right here to remind me of something I can try in my endings." On the transparency, I wrote a marginal note and continued reading the ending. "Yes, these are all important actions, right? I'm really getting the idea I can put important actions in my ending."

"Now here it has exactly what the character says—one carefully chosen word! It says: *'Fly!'* That makes me realize I could try putting important dialogue, the exact important words people say, into my endings. I'll write that." I wrote "important dialogue" in the margin and read on.

As always, you needn't use the exact text I've chosen to demonstrate using a mentor text to learn about writing. As long as you choose a narrative text with which children are already familiar, one with an ending that is succinct and memorable and has moves in it children can see, then this minilesson will be strong.

Notice that when I read aloud the book's ending, I am not reading only the last sentence. Usually an author regards both the lead and the ending of a story as longer than a line or two.

Two decades ago Mem Fox, author of Koala Lou, led a workshop on children's literature at the Teachers College Reading and Writing Project. I was a member of her class. She taught us many things that I'll never forget and one was this: When you read aloud and come to the end of a text, slow . . . your voice . . . down . . . to . . . a . . . stop.

Notice the assumption that writers have characters doing actions for a reason. Brinckloe didn't need to tell that the boy flung off his covers, and does so for reasons that are not accidental.

"So much of the rest of this ending is helping us understand what the moment looked like, isn't it? All those colors and comparisons help us picture how it went. Julie uses a lot of images. I could try that too." I wrote "images" in the margin and read the last sentences.

"This very last part—'I held the jar, dark and empty, in my hands. The moonlight and the fireflies swam in my tears, but I could feel myself smiling'—brings our attention back to the boy. It helps us see him, sad and happy at the same time. That sort of makes us remember the whole story—how he saw the fireflies and then, all excited, he caught them in the jar and loved them there and then he decided to set them free. Julie reminds us of all the things that happened and all the feelings the boy had in just one short bit of writing." I wrote "reminds us of whole story" in the margin.

"Maybe later you can find some other things that Julie did as a writer that make this a powerful ending for you. The things I notice she put in were important actions, important dialogue, images, and a short reminder of the whole story. We can try doing those things ourselves with our endings!"

Debrief. Name what you hope children learned from the demonstration. Add this lesson to the ongoing chart.

"Did you notice how I didn't just read the ending? I read it several times and studied it closely to see what the author did to make her ending powerful! Let's add what I noticed to our Qualities of Good Personal Narrative Writing chart." I wrote:

Qualities of Good Personal Narrative Writing

- Write a little seed story; don't write all about a giant watermelon topic.
- Zoom in so you tell the most important parts of the story.
- Include true, exact details from the movie you have in your mind.
- Begin with a strong lead—maybe use setting, action, dialogue to create mood.
- Make a strong ending—maybe use important actions, dialogue, images, and whole-story reminders that make a lasting impression.

You always need to decide whether your teaching aims to nudge children one small step along in their development, or whether it aims to immerse them in a world of literary language. So far, this unit has leaned towards giving simple, do-able guidance. Here—just for a patch of time—I break loose and immerse children in the heady world of literary language. There's no question that I'm teaching over their heads here— what else is a sky for?

Of course, you could decide to make a short-term chart titled, "Good Endings." The chart could list important actions, important dialogue, images, and reminders of the whole story.

Some teachers highlight that writers often try to make the reader feel like the character feels. Others highlight the technique of making an ending reminiscent of the story's beginning. Some teachers help children focus on choosing the emotion they want to convey at the end of their story. Choose only a few techniques to try—ones that are well illustrated in the mentor text, and that your children can have success with.

ACTIVE ENGAGEMENT

Remind children that writers work hard on endings. Writers study mentor endings, make plans for their endings, then write rough draft endings.

"Before today, you might have thought that writers write endings in a snap! I used to think that when it came time to end a story, I could just slap, 'And they lived happily ever after' onto my last line. But I think now you understand why some writers say that when we come to the last page of a story, we're halfway home!"

"While we're here in the meeting area, we can't each write an ending for our stories. That would take too much time. But we can begin to plan—to rehearse—for an ending. One way to do this is to reread our drafts, asking, 'What is the important message I've conveyed?' Would you reread your draft and mark the places in the text which seem to you to be especially important—your ending will want to somehow relate to these places."

After a few moments of silence, I said, "Will you reread your draft again and this time mark any important actions, words, images that could maybe be woven into your final scene, your final image?" Again I let children work quietly.

LINK

Rename your teaching point.

"Writers, today I'm not going to ask you to tell your partner your thoughts. I don't want to break the spell! Just slip back to your writing space, and start drafting an ending. Remember that now, if you've reached the final page, you're halfway home!"

If you and your class have also been working on a shared text, you could instead ask students in the Active Engagement to turn to their partners and talk about strong actions, images or important ideas that could come into the story's ending of that text. Another option is to reread the final page of a beloved novel—say, Where the Red Fern Grows—and to invite children to talk with a partner about ways in which that ending illustrates the characteristics listed on the chart.

WRITING AND CONFERRING

Grouping Writers for Conferences

You'll probably wish you could clone yourself so that you can be at every child's side today. You'll want to get this child back on track, and that one, and this one—so breathe. Realize that the agendas you've laid out for children represent the writing work of the year (or really, of a lifetime), not the work of a week. It's okay that the children who are trying to write focused narratives are still swamped with other problems (perhaps they are including mind-numbing detail, or perhaps they are writing with run-on sentences). It's okay if a large group of children still struggle to fully understand what it means to write a narrative. When we're teaching writing, we're teaching people entirely new habits, a whole new way of living and thinking. That cannot be easy!

But, having said that, yes indeed, you need to work hard at your conferring today. You will need to group children who currently need the same kind of support. Perhaps five children really need you to remind them about end punctuation. Another four need a push into focusing their narratives. These two write and write and write, but their stories are hard to follow. These three write with detail, and now need to learn to be selective in which details they include.

After you've figured out a group of students to confer with, you can just stand up and announce, "Can I meet with . . . " and read your list. Once you've convened the group into a huddle, tell them, "I called you over because I've noticed you are ready to learn . . . " Then tell them, "What I do in this situation is I . . . " and show them how you punctuate as you write, or how you narrow your topic. You need to have examples at their writing level and you need to highlight the one thing you intend for them to learn how to do. Then say, "So work on that right here, right now." Be specific. Do you want them to reread and correct, to list, to start a new piece or page? Should they work alone or with a partner? Tell them you need to meet with another group but you'll be back in five minutes to see what they've done. Then call the next group. Don't limit yourself to working with only one group just because you perhaps haven't had a chance to plan a careful lesson for more than that one group. Wing it! These children need face-to-face talk, and they need to be noticed more than they need your teaching to be perfect.

MID-WORKSHOP TEACHING POINT *Checking for Sense* "Writers, can I have your eyes and your attention? I've noticed a bunch of you are having a problem that I have too, when I'm writing. When I write a true story, I already know how the story goes because I'm the one it happened to! Sometimes I forget that my readers weren't there. I'll say, 'Michelle got lost,' and my reader doesn't know if Michelle is a cat or a child! When I leave out important details, my story doesn't make sense!"

"This is what I do to fix that problem: Now and then, I read my draft to a person who doesn't know the story. I ask 'Can I read this to you? Will you stop me if it's confusing?' Sometimes instead of reading to another person, I pretend to be a stranger and I read my draft through the stranger's eyes. As I read, I find places where it's confusing and then I fix those places."

"Could everyone take a moment right now and read your draft through a stranger's eyes? If you find confusing places stop and revise. You'll need to do this from time to time from now on."

SHARE

Appreciating Endings

Convene children. Share the work of one child who wrote several possible endings, trying to be sure they referred to important actions, dialogue, images from the story.

"Writers, can I have your eyes and your attention? I want to remind you that writers know our endings will be the last thing readers encounter, and so we usually write several drafts of them. Jill did some smart work today. She reread her narrative about waterskiing, deciding she wanted her ending to emphasize the pride she felt in herself afterwards because she'd circled half the lake. So she wrote three drafts of endings. She's planning to combine them into one best ending." *[Fig. IX-2]*

> "Wow" I thought. That was me. I went around half of the lake. I couldn't wait to rest my legs. I was ready to do it again.
>
> I walked off the boat with a smile on my face and excitement flowing through me. I couldn't wait to talk to my parents and tell them I got half way around the lake.
>
> "Bye" I said, "Thanks." I was so happy that I wanted to jump right back into the lake and do it again! I walked onto the dock and was ready to do it 50 more times.

Jill read aloud the entry she planned to stitch together:

> "Wow," I thought. "That was me. I skied half of the lake." I walked off the boat with a smile on my face and excitement flowing through me. I walked onto the dock and was ready to do it again.

Extract lessons from the one child's work.

"Writers, did you notice that Jill reread her whole narrative, paying attention to what it was she really wants to say in her ending? Then she drafted three versions of an ending. Next she plans to take the best of all three—but she could have selected one. At the end of today, she'll have produced four lines of text—but that'll be a good day's work."

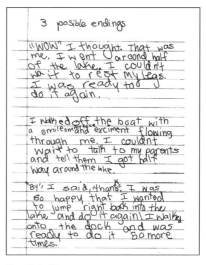

Fig. IX-2 Jill

HOMEWORK *Studying Endings* Today, writers, we studied the endings in one or two picture books, noticing that the author wove together important actions, important dialogue, images, and short reminders of the whole story. Tonight, would you be investigators? Return to books you've loved, and especially to those whose endings have worked for you. Would you copy down two endings that you think merit more study. Choose endings in which the author does something you imagine that you, too, could do, and choose two endings that represent different kinds-of-endings. Tomorrow, we'll see if we can lay out some of the options, mapping the field of possibility. When you arrive in school tomorrow, let's use our empty bulletin board as a place to sort kinds of endings. Tomorrow, when you come to school, post the ending you've brought in alongside others that are somehow similar, and write labels or diagrams to show how these endings are similar. Maybe in the end, we'll put endings you write on the bulletin board, in the same categories we design for Kevin Henkes' endings and Lucille Clifton's endings!

TAILORING YOUR TEACHING

If students tend to write flat endings such as, "After that we went home." Or "Then I had to go finish my homework." . . . you could teach your students that if the ending tells an action, that action needs to be closely related to the main event of the story.

You can share examples from the work of published authors, and highlight the choices the authors made by reminding children they could have chosen otherwise. For example, Jane Chelsea Aragon could have ended *Salt Hands* with, "Then I went back to bed." Instead she ended with a small action, one related to the heart of the story. The story is about a nighttime visit from a deer. It starts with the deer's arrival, and ends with his departure. Describing the giant deer, Aragon ends the story like this: "When he was finished, he raised his head and turned away slowly and walked off into the night." You could, in a similar fashion, help children notice Polacco's craftsmanship. What if she had ended *Thunder Cake*, her story of getting over her fear, "After we made the Thunder Cake, I had to wash all the dishes." Instead, Polacco's ending revisits the heart of her story. She writes, "We just smiled and ate our Thunder Cake. From that time on, I never feared the voice of thunder again." You could teach children that some writers do decide to write endings which involve an event that isn't closely related to the main event, but usually these contain reflections rather than actions. In *Bigmama's*, Donald Crews ends by saying: "Some nights even now, I think that I might wake up in the morning and be at Bigmama's with the whole summer ahead of me."

MECHANICS

As you read your students' writing, guard against the temptation to conclude that no one has ever taught them about periods, capitals, and other forms of punctuation. Chances are good that your students have heard lessons about punctuation marks since first grade!

But, as you may be seeing in their writing, it is not enough for us to simply teach rules for using conventional punctuation marks—we also have to help children apply this knowledge as they write. Do your children the favor of reminding them that writers always put end punctuation at the end of a sentence, and capitalize the start of the next sentence. Sometimes children believe because it isn't crucial that their rough drafts and their entries are totally correct, this means they are free to write for days on end without any end punctuation. They sometimes think that just prior to publication, they need to reread their drafts and insert periods and capitals.

Of course, there is a grain of truth to these perceptions. It is true that writers focus more on content and craft during early drafts, and don't obsess about every last mechanical detail until it's time to publish. But this certainly does not mean that children should postpone writing with end punctuation until just prior to publication!

Instead, they need to develop ease and automaticity with end punctuation. Therefore, children need to write with punctuation even when they are only writing entries in their notebooks. You may need to find times throughout the workshop to insert punctuation prompts. "Writers," you might say, "I'm finding that a few of you are so focused on what you are saying that you are forgetting to write with punctuation. Forgetting punctuation reminds me of a time when I drove to work and realized as I pulled into the parking garage in the middle of Manhattan that I'd forgotten my shoes! I had to walk in stocking feet on the sidewalk to my office, and I had to spend the whole day without shoes. I bet that anyone I spoke to that

day had a hard time listening to me because they probably kept thinking, 'How weird! She's in her stocking-feet!' Forgetting your punctuation is like forgetting your shoes. It's just not done! Go back over your writing in your notebook and make sure it's punctuated. Remember to punctuate as you go so that readers can listen to your message!"

If children use what they know about punctuation to punctuate, then you can see their developing understandings. If writing with punctuation (and I'm not saying with complex punctuation or even with correct punctuation, but with *some* punctuation) is a challenge for your children, you'll need to carve out a separate time in each day to teach mechanics. You might, for example, teach them to correctly punctuate quotations and ask them to reread their notebook looking for instances in which they could improve their punctuation of dialogue.

Errors in punctuation, for example, often begin to show when children attempt to write more complex sentences than they have in the past. Their mistakes may be signs that the children are pushing themselves beyond the syntactical structures they already know; they may be signs of learning and growth, not simply signs of ignorance about the rules governing comma or period use.

You might also remind them that a writer usually tries to write in a consistent tense. If we tell a story of an event that occurred in the past, we usually would use past tense. Some writers choose, however, to use present tense as a way to help readers feel in-the-moment. I find, however, that writing stories about past events and doing so in present tense, often leads writers to either teeter between time frames, or to be locked into a sportscaster–like, "I am running down the field. I am catching the ball. I am throwing the ball . . . " Again, writers can reread entries in their notebook, noticing their tenses and perhaps making New Year's resolutions.

IN THIS SESSION, YOU'LL
EMPHASIZE THAT WRITERS MAKE
DECISIONS ABOUT THEIR OWN
WORK, INCLUDING WHEN TO FINISH
PIECES AND TO START NEW ONES.

GETTING READY

- Directions on chalkboard telling children to bring their folders and sit with their partners in the meeting area
- Strategies for Generating Personal Narrative Writing chart
- Monitoring My Writing Process checklist on chart paper
- Monitoring My Writing Process checklist in each child's folder
- Qualities of Good Personal Narrative Writing chart
- Writer's notepad for each child to take home
- See CD-ROM for resources

TAKING CHARGE OF OUR WRITING WORK:
STARTING A SECOND PIECE

When I help teachers design their own units of study, I tell them that although it's tempting to focus on the content of our minilessons, the truth is that the words that come out of our mouths are not as important as the work that our children do. When planning a unit, we're wise to think first about the nature of our children's work. Will children write one piece or two? Will all children progress in sync with each other? Will they write in booklets, stretching their stories across a sequence of pages, or on single sheets?

I decided in this unit of study that I would give children extensive opportunities to rehearse for writing, expect minimal revision for now, and support them in writing two narratives rather than just one. In this session, you'll see that after children write one narrative, instead of revising it immediately, I ask them to write a second piece, only then selecting just one of their two stories to revise and edit.

You could decide on a different course. There is not one answer to the question of how many stories you should expect children to write within a month–long unit. When deciding, keep in mind this general principle: The more skilled a writer is, the longer that writer can profitably sustain work on a single piece of writing. At the start of kindergarten, children are apt to write fifteen stories in a single month. Meanwhile, a professional writer will often work many years on a single story! Your third, fourth, or fifth graders will be somewhere in between.

The words of this minilesson emphasize independence, but in truth, it is a limited sort of independence. We're really saying, "Some of you will start your second story today; some need more time and will start the second one tomorrow." Your implicit message is that everyone will progress through the same sequence of writing work. You will support more diversity in writing work as the year progresses because in the end, our goal is to help children author rich writing lives for themselves.

MINILESSON

Taking Charge of Our Writing Work: Starting a Second Piece

CONNECTION

Celebrate your children's rough drafts.

"Writers, I have been reading your stories every chance I get. When you were at music earlier this morning, I didn't go to the faculty room. I just sat here with your stories. I read about how violins sound when you first try to play them, I laughed about the pigeon with the wink that Carl saw on the sidewalk, I tried to guess the ending of the mysterious disappearance in Christina's story . . . Then I looked up and saw I was out of time! I was so disappointed! When I had to stop reading, I felt like someone was taking a prize right out of my hands. You all are turning into such strong writers—congratulations!"

Name the teaching point. In this case, tell children that writers need to take charge of their writing, assigning themselves jobs.

"Some of you have reached the end of your drafts; others still have lots to write. Either way, what I want to teach you today is that you don't need to line up alongside me and ask, 'What should I do in writing time today?' You are in charge of your writing—writers make their own writing decisions."

TEACHING

Tell children the work you expect them to do next, explaining the options: continue drafting or begin a second story.

"A girl I knew once wrote, 'I am the mother of my story. No one else can tell me, "Do this with your story" or "Do that" because I am the mother of my story.' And it is true that you are the parent or the boss or the job captain of your own writing."

"You do not need to come to me and ask, 'Is my story done?' You can decide if you have reached the end. You do not need to come to me and ask, 'What should I do now?' You can decide whether you have more to write in your story, whether you want to revise your first story right now or whether you are ready to move to your second story. In the next week, all of us will write a second story; some will start it today, some will start it tonight, some will start it tomorrow or the next day. After we have written two stories, we will look back on them both and choose the one we like best to revise again, edit, and publish."

COACHING

Time and again you will notice that I try to convey general messages through details. Madeleine L'Engle, the great fiction writer, once told me "If you say, 'I once saw some flying elephants,' that isn't particularly believable. But it feels more believable if you say, 'Last Tuesday, when I walked from the school to my car, I saw something flying over the far parking lot. At first I thought it was a blimp but then I looked again and it was two pinkish purple elephants, with a baby elephant trailing behind them.' Because I want children to believe me when I say that I have really, truly enjoyed reading their writing, I don't rely on generalizations, saying only, "I have enjoyed reading your writing. The stories are really great." Instead I try to use details that will make my words more convincing.

The truth is that your children have probably not yet internalized the writing process enough to take over the task of being job captain. You are only making a first move toward handing over this responsibility. Although you tell them they're in charge, for now they are mostly in charge of the timing for when they progress to the next bit of work rather than the decision as to what that work will be.

"Of course, if you are going to start writing another story, you know what to do—start gathering some new entries in your notebook. You already know strategies you can use to generate personal narrative writing," I reminded them, gesturing toward the chart listing those strategies. "On the other hand, you may not need to gather entries—you may simply reread your notebook and say, 'Wait, I already have another seed story that I want to develop!' Either way, once you've chosen a seed idea, you already know that you can tell the story to yourself or write leads as ways to develop that seed idea. The important thing is that you can be your own job captain and tell yourself, 'The next thing I should do is to collect some new entries' or 'I think now I should write a few different leads.'"

Explain how you use a chart to keep tabs on your progress through the writing process, and give children a similar chart.

"When I'm organizing my writing life, I keep tabs on my progress. I know my writing process usually involves certain steps, so I have a list of them near me and a system for checking off when I have completed each step. That helps me know what to try next."

So often in schools, we try to act as if everything children do is always new, new, new! Let me caution against this. Recall how important it is to you when the principal, at the start of the year, says, "This year we'll continue working with last year's initiative." We breathe a sigh of relief because this means we'll have a chance to revisit what we tried once, to gain some sense of mastery. Children, too, long to hear that they'll have a chance to return to work they've done before. Now is their chance!

It is very important to teach children the way in which a writing curriculum cumulates, leaving the writer with a repertoire of skills and strategies. Today gives you a chance to convey the cumulative nature of your teaching.

Make sure the language you use on your Monitoring My Writing Process chart matches the language you've used to explain each step in the unit so far. Repeating the same words is yet another way to help children recall the previous teaching and learn that each new lesson will be referred to again and again in future lessons, just as these past lessons are referred to here.

Monitoring My Writing Process	First Piece	Next Piece
Gather entries		
Select and develop one seed idea		
Storytell to rehearse for writing		
Read published writing that resembles what I want to write		
Draft leads—try action, dialogue, setting		
Choose paper, plan story across pages, copy lead		
Write draft with each part on a separate page		
Reread and revise for clarity		
Draft endings—try using important actions, dialogue, images, or reminders of the whole story		
Revise and edit more now or decide to wait until later, or not to revise		

ACTIVE ENGAGEMENT
Set children up to use charts to track and plan their progress through the writing process.

"I think it will be helpful for you to have these steps laid out so that when you act as job captain for yourself, you can keep tabs on your progress and remember what you usually do next. Therefore I've put a checklist like this inside each of your writing folders."

"Right now, before we head off to work, will you think about your writing process? Look over the chart in your folder and ask yourself, 'Which of these steps have I already done for my first piece of writing?' Then think, 'What will I do today?' Ask yourself also, 'Does this chart contain all of the steps I've been taking as a writer lately?' As the year progresses, we will definitely learn other things writers do, and we'll add those to this checklist. For now, though, tell your partner which of these things you have done, and which of these represent work you will do today."

LINK
Remind children that they need to decide whether to continue working on their existing drafts or to shift to new stories. Tell them writers are always job captains for themselves.

"For now and for the rest of your life, keep in mind that we writers are job captains for our own writing. It is important to always keep one eye on our subject and another eye on our progress along a sequence of work. You can keep tabs on your progress by charting what you have already done as a writer."

"When you go off to work today, reread your draft and decide upon a plan of action. Since you are your own job captain, decide whether to add to or revise your existing draft, or whether you will start collecting new entries in your notebook and finding a new seed idea for a second story. You can use the chart to help you remember your options."

Some teachers keep a whole-class, wall-sized version of the chart, with each child moving his or her magnetic plaque along on a white-board chart. You'll need to decide whether this chart is an individual one kept in writing folders or a whole-class one, displayed on a wall, or both. If your school leader wants you to use charts and rubrics, then by all means turn this into a whole-class, white-board chart. It has more potential to function as a living representation, one that actually helps children, than do most charts and rubrics.

Later you'll find that I teach children they can write a planning box or a self-assignment box for themselves at the start of a day's work. If you prefer to teach that now, you could do so.

WRITING AND CONFERRING

Encouraging Independent Problem Solving

In your conferring today, try to teach independence. Invite children to identify and solve their own writing problems. As teachers, especially, we love to feel useful, and we love to feel as if we are teaching something, so we often rush to suggest solutions to every problem. It's wise to remember, however, that our job is to put ourselves out of a job. I sometimes enter a workshop planning to turn issues back to the child. So if a child says that he feels "done," I do not generate a list of five things the writer could do next. Instead, I say, "I know that feeling of being finished with something. But since I know (and you do too!) that when I'm done, I've just begun, I look back to find what else I can work on. You try that now. Figure out what else you can work on. I'll check with you at the end of writing time to see what you came up with!" When I expect the child to find his way out of a predicament, I find the child rises to the occasion.

So guard against being the problem solver. For today, anyhow, if the writer expresses a problem, try mulling the problem over aloud, as if you are thinking of a solution: "Hmm . . . I'm trying to think of what writers do when we encounter this problem. Hmm . . . ." The writer will probably supply a possible course of action. Go with it! "So are you suggesting . . . ?" you can say, and as you retell what the child has suggested, sneak in a few little tips of your own.

Keep a copy of the Monitoring My Writing Process checklist in hand as you confer. If a child isn't certain what he or she might do next, help the child use the checklist to find what she has done and might do next: "Where are you in the process and what on this list might you plan to do next?" Turn the question or problem back to the children, and soon enough, children will find their ways to independent solutions.

MID-WORKSHOP TEACHING POINT **Solving Our Own Problems** "Writers, can I have your eyes and your attention? Look what I have following me!" I gestured to the line of children trailing me. "Writers, listen while I talk with each of the writers who are in line for help. Listen closely, because this could be you, lined up for help."

Then I said to the first child, "What is it you are wanting?" The child explained that he was done and wasn't sure what to do next. I kindly but firmly asked if he thought he could figure that out, and he admitted that he probably could. "Okay, off you go then," I said.

The next child wanted to know if I liked his lead. "Hmm, is it vitally important to know whether *I* like your lead? Do *you* like it?" The writer confessed that he really wasn't that fond of it. "So I bet you can figure out what to do next, can't you?" and he, too, went on his way. After one more child went back to handle his own problem, I turned to the class. "Writers, do you get my point? You need to become your own job captains and make your own decisions. I can't be the person who decides what every one of you should be doing. From this day on, when you feel like coming to me for help, take a

SHARE

Remembering Qualities of Good Writing

Convene children. Ask writers to examine their work for examples of some qualities of good writing from the class chart.

"Writers, I was really blown away today to see that so many of you could figure out what you needed to do and pleased that you were able to resume gathering narrative entries in your notebooks. You also wrote those entries much more quickly than you wrote them earlier this year. But what especially impressed me was that you kept in mind the qualities of good writing that we talked about earlier this month."

"I'm going to read a quality of good writing from our chart, and then I'd like you to look at what you've written so far in this unit and see if your writing illustrates that quality. If it does, give me a thumbs up."

Qualities of Good Personal Narrative Writing
- Write a little seed story; don't write all about a giant watermelon topic
- Zoom in so you tell the most important parts of the story
- Include true, exact details from the movie you have in your mind
- Begin with a strong lead—maybe setting, action, dialogue, or a combination to create mood
- Make a strong ending—maybe use important actions, dialogue, images, and whole-story reminders that make a lasting impression

"So first of all, did you remember that when you are writing personal narratives, it's easier to write well if you don't write all about a giant watermelon topic, but instead tell a small seed story? Thumbs up if your writing today included a focused story."

"And would you look at the writing you did and think whether instead of writing all over the place, making comments about and chatting about your focused story, you instead told the story in a bit-by-bit fashion. Thumbs up if you focused and then let the story unfold bit by bit," I said. Then I added, "Writers, let's listen to Jake's story and see if we agree that he did these things." *[Figs. X-1 and X-2]*

> I sat behind the bleachers, waiting for my race to be called. "Second- and third-graders, please line up by the entrance," the announcer said.
>
> Just like last time, I thought. We always go there.
>
> Quickly, I jogged to the asphalt by the start point.
>
> When it was my turn, I leaned forward. I was ready for the gunshot.
>
> BANG! The gun went off, and I did too.
>
> For the first half second, I stayed in position by Daniel Fabrezio. This time I'm going to win, I know I will.
>
> Then, I started to fall back. But, I didn't notice until I saw three or four kids in front of me, some even on their third turn!
>
> Then, I decided to give up, and I realized I ought to give up. But I knew I would regret it later.

Then, pointing to another item on the chart, I asked the writers, "Did you write with true, exact details? Right now, find a particularly nice detail in the writing you did today, and share it with your partner." After a minute of talk, I said, "Isaiah found a lot of details in his writing. Let's listen to it and see if we agree that he has written with true, exact details." *[Fig. X-3]*

> I looked inside the tank. There he was, Hissy, my beloved pet snake. I looked at my mom eagerly. The moment I had been waiting for was almost here. The time to take Hissy out of his tank. I watched excitedly as my mom took Hissy out. I held out my hands. They were a little shaky but I was still excited. Mom gave Hissy to me.

"Isaiah, you have definitely zoomed in on one moment, and you stretched the moment out so much that I feel as if I am right there with you, leaning over the tank." Then

Then, I decided to give up, but realized I ought to give up. But I knew I would regret it later.

The 400 Meter
Jake

I sat behind the bleachers, waiting for my race to be called. "2nd and 3rd graders, please line up by the entrance," the announcer said. Just like last time I thought. We always go there. Quickly, I jogged to the asphalt by the start point. When it was my turn, I leaned foward. I was ready for the gunshot.

BANG! the gun went off, and I did too.

For the first ½ second, I stayed in position by Daniel Fabrezio. This time I'm going to win I know I will.

Then, I started to fall back. But I didn't notice until I saw 3 or 4 kids in front of me, some even on their 3rd turn!

Figs. X-1 and X-2 Jake

beginning I looked inside the tank. There he was, Hissy my beloved pet snake. I looked at my mom eagerly. The moment I had been waiting for was almost here. The time to take Hissy out of his tank. I watched excitedley as my mom took Hissy out. I held out my hands. They were a little shaky but I was still excited. Mom gave Hissy to me. I could kind of tell we shared the same feeling. I just wanted to be with Hissy. We belonged with each other. We were really best friends. I sat down on the floor, still holding Hissy.

Fig. X-3 Isaiah

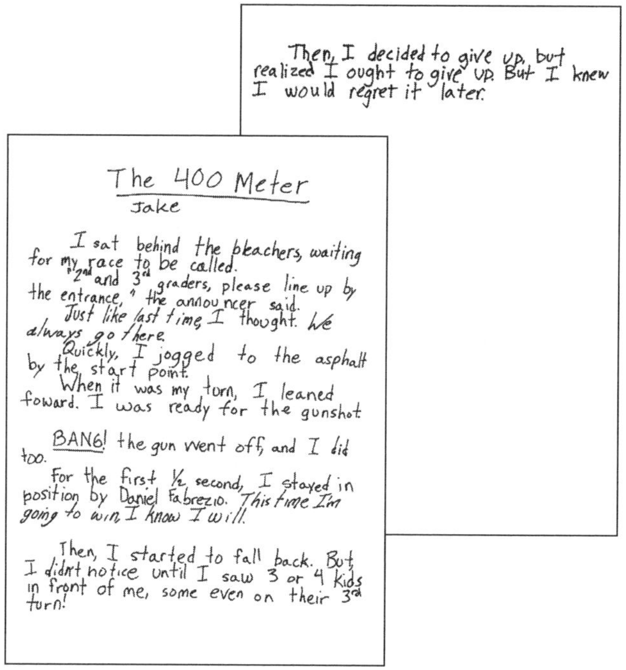

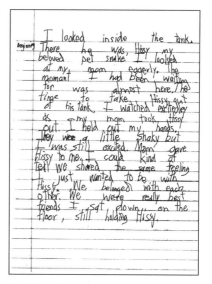

I asked the class, "Do you think Isaiah wrote with true and exact details?" When children confirmed that he'd done this, I said, "As you continue working tomorrow and for the rest of your life, remember to keep these qualities of good writing, as well as this sequence of writing work from your checklist, in mind."

HOMEWORK *Writing Every Night* You've graduated. We've only been together for two weeks but you've already been through one whole writing cycle, and you're already acting as job captains for yourselves, deciding what writing work it is that you need to be doing. The time has come, I think, for you to have your own time, away from the classroom, when you can decide what you need to do as a writer and then do it.

So I've made a writer's notepad for each of you, and every day after school you'll have a chance to gather an entry or two in your writer's notepad. Bring those entries to school because when it comes to choosing a seed idea, you may decide to select an entry that you wrote when you were in your own home space, giving yourself a job to do.

All the writers I know have little spirals tucked in their pockets or purses, and they're always ready to write. I once sat in a school with a gigantic hospital across the way. As I watched, I saw a window on the fourth floor open, and suddenly a telephone was flung out the window! I had my notepad there and recorded the whole episode.

It'll definitely be important to carry your notepad with you—and definitely have it in school every day.

TAILORING YOUR TEACHING

If your students could be more productive and focused during writing workshop . . .
you could show the children how to use the Monitoring My Writing Process checklist as a guide for making plans. Remind them of the chart and show an example of how one child filled it out. Then the class can work on helping that classmate come up with plans for what she might work on today. And if you want this to become one of your rituals, you could end the lesson by saying, "So remember that before a writer starts writing, the writer often takes stock of where he or she is in the process of writing. The writer often gives himself or herself a little self-assignment. So every day for the next few days, anyhow, before you start writing

Eventually, you'll want to instruct students to tape or paste the pages from this portable notebook into their more permanent writer's notebook so that all their writing will be available to reread and glean from.

would you take a look at your progress through the writing process, as recorded on your chart. Let that help you make plans for your work."

If your students need help to make plans that are more closely related to their needs as writers . . . one way you might build upon this lesson is to have children assess themselves as writers, making goals and giving themselves assignments. "Today I want to teach you that another way in which you can become more independent is by looking over your writing and thinking, 'What am I doing that is working well?' and 'What do I need to work on more as a writer?'" You might then demonstrate how you look over your writing with those questions in mind. You will want to mimic the types of things you would like your students to notice as they self-assess. For example, "I have used two of these strategies on the chart for coming up with ideas. I've written about a special person, my sister, and I've written about a special place, Aunt Rose's house. And I've written them as stories. But one thing I am noticing is that sometimes I forget to use punctuation. Also, none of my stories seem to be very long." Show children how this self-assessment leads you to decide on the work you need to do next, recording it in an assignment box you made in your notebook.

ASSESSMENT

When you collect your children's finished first-draft stories, remember that you can choose the lens through which you want to look at that writing. You *can*, if you want, search your children's writing for flaws. You can point out errors, bemoan misspellings, list areas of weakness. But if your role is to help your children grow as writers, you would be wise to consciously and deliberately put those lenses aside and look, instead, with an eye toward celebrating growth.

Look for ways in which your instruction seems to have made a difference—even if the result isn't perfect yet. Has the writer begun the story with dialogue? Started close to the action in a zoomed-in, focused way? Retold the event step-by-step instead of summarizing it?

Look for approximations of higher-level work, and for evidence of risk taking. Cultivate the habit of celebrating the shaky steps writers take en route to new prowess. Pay attention to evidence that children have taken your instruction to heart and tried to use your guidelines as they write. The resulting texts won't be perfect—but even at this early point in the year, they should provide evidence that your writers are growing and your teaching is making a difference.

You will also want to pay attention to the children who seem to be made of Teflon™—all of us have those children, especially at the start of the year. When you find a writer of any ability level to whom your teaching never sticks, you have a choice. You could push the writer out of your mind. But the wiser decision is to let that writer become your teacher.

Speculate over what could be going on for the writer, and try to discover why your teaching has not taken hold for this individual.

Your children's work can give you feedback on your teaching— imagine getting feedback without an administrator or staff developer even coming into the room, without a letter in your file! What a gift! But for this to happen, you need to get out of the mind-set of blaming the child. If you see that your teaching hasn't made a dent for a particular child, you need to resist the impulse to regard this as the child's problem. Instead, see the evidence as providing a window on *your teaching*, not on the child's capacities. And do this without putting yourself through a guilt trip— which should be easy since it is still the start of the year!

Try to remember right now that your job is to be an avid learner of teaching. So yes, look for affirmation that you have made a difference, but expect and search for evidence that all is not perfect, too. Your teaching can't possibly be perfect—you don't yet know your children—and in the end, your real challenge will be to teach in ways that enable all your children to learn. I am reminded of a comic strip I saw once in which a little boy confides to a friend that he taught his dog to whistle. The friend is impressed and astonished, but then the little boy reminds him, "I said I taught him to whistle—I didn't say he learned to whistle!"

Learning to write, like learning to teach, doesn't happen overnight. Let yourself become a student of your students.

TIMELINES AS TOOLS FOR PLANNING STORIES

GETTING READY

- Instructions on chalkboard telling children to bring their writing folders (containing writer's notebook and notepad) and sit with their partners in the meeting area
- Monitoring My Writing Process checklist on chart paper
- Story from your own childhood (plan parts for timeline)
- Idea for shared class story (event class experienced together)
- Two leads for your story (one using dialogue, one with an action)
- See CD-ROM for resources

You may find it surprising that the children are suddenly done with one piece of writing and back at the rehearsal stage. It's true that we've skipped revision altogether, and begun a second piece. I chose to do this because I think that at this stage, children need more practice planning and drafting narratives than they do revising them. I think the opportunity to cycle through the process again right away, this time accumulating new strategies and knowledge for each phase, is an important one. Before long children will have written two narratives, and then I'll ask them to select their best, and revise and edit it.

So this session returns to rehearsal, reminding children of what they already know about collecting and selecting entries, then adding a new technique that can accompany or replace storytelling as a way for children to plan the whole flow of the story. Specifically, in this session children learn to draft timelines as a form of planning their pieces, revising those timelines by thinking about where, in the sequence of events, their story really begins and ends, and thinking also about other options for where it could begin and end.

This session helps writers learn they have choices not only about what they will write, but also about how they will write. Many children assume that writing true stories means the writer acts as a stenographer, recording what actually happened. In this session, children learn that writers need (at the very least) to decide where in the sequence of events they will begin their story. By showing children that writers experiment with different entry points into the sequence of events, you give children a concrete tool for planning and revision. You can also teach them to look at what they've written and ask, "Are all the dots on my timeline crucial to the main story?"

Children learn that they can weigh different ways a story can start; they can tell the story aloud one way—and soon they're ready to scrawl a draft, writing fast and long.

MINILESSON

Timelines as Tools for Planning Stories

CONNECTION

Summarize the work children did yesterday in the previous session to provide context for today's lesson.

"In the previous session, you all acted as job captains, deciding what it is you, as writers, need to do. Some of you are still finishing your first story, but most of you gathered entries for a new story yesterday, and chose a second seed idea. Some of you storytold that new idea or tried writing different leads for it. Please keep track of what you've done on your writing process checklist." I pointed to the one on chart paper to remind them.

Monitoring My Writing Process	First Piece	Next Piece
Gather entries		
Select and develop one seed idea		
Storytell to rehearse for writing		
Read published writing that resembles what I want to write		
Draft leads—try action, dialogue, setting		
Choose paper, plan story across pages, copy lead		
Write draft with each part on a separate page		
Reread and revise for clarity		
Draft endings—try using important actions, dialogue, images, or reminders of the whole story		
Revise and edit more now or decide to wait until later, or not to revise		

COACHING

This could easily have been preceded by a minilesson that reminded children of all they have already learned to do. Such a minilesson would have entailed re-visiting charts and reminding children that when they want to begin a new piece, they use their repertoire of strategies to gather entries, then reread those entries looking for a seed idea. The minilesson could have allowed time for children to storytell their stories. They'd then be even more ready for this new session.

By citing the variety of choices children have made, you accentuate the options open to them.

Tell children you will teach them another strategy for developing a story idea: making timelines.

"Today I want to teach you another technique narrative writers sometimes use to imagine how a story might go and to get ready to write a draft. We sometimes make timelines of the story we want to write. This helps us organize our writing because the timelines can help us remember what happened first, then next, until the end of the story."

TEACHING
Demonstrate the strategy of developing an idea by making a timeline with your own writing idea.

"Have you ever followed a diagram to build a model? As writers, we sometimes make ourselves a pattern, a plan, before we write and then use that plan to help us know how to write our drafts. When we are writing a narrative, one way to make a plan is to write a timeline."

"Yesterday, when we were collecting entries for our second story, I wrote one about walking home in a rainstorm and another about a bumblebee I rescured from a rain puddle. I think I'll try developing the latter entry into a story—it's a small story, but I think I can make it big."

"I don't know how to start though, so making a timeline could help me plan. Watch how I make a timeline for the story I've chosen so you can do this too, when you need to." I drew a horizontal line on the chalkboard.

"Let me see, what happened first? I had lunch." I wrote "Lunch" near a dot at the beginning of my timeline. "Then I grabbed a frisbee and went out to toss it around." I added "Brought frisbee to yard" near a second dot. "I threw the frisbee." I wrote "threw frisbee" by a third dot, placed a bit farther along the line. "It landed in a mud puddle." I wrote "Mud puddle" and explained, "You'll notice I write just a few words on each dot of my timeline, and that each dot represents a new action. I noticed bees swarming around the frisbee and one bee buzzing and swimming across the puddle. It looked like it was frantic, like it was drowning." I labeled another dot "Bee drowning," and then I described bringing a stick near the bee, letting it climb up the stick to my hand—only to sting me. Before I was done, I'd added "Rescued bee," "Bee stung me," "Stepped on it," "Ran away," and "Got frisbee" onto my timeline.

You'll see that I use this story for a few days of this unit. When planning a minilesson, you will want to ask yourself, "Which piece of writing will I use for the Teaching section of my minilesson?" and "Which piece of writing will I use for the Active Engagement section?" Frequently, as in this session, we will thread two or three pieces of writing throughout a unit of study. Kids benefit from using the same text over and over because it is familiar. If the whole text is new to kids, they appropriately focus on the content and other aspects of the story—their attention is diffused.

Notice that the writing I have done is as brief as possible. I try to be a minimalist for several reasons: I don't want to suck the energy out of the room by going on and on about my own stories. As often as possible, I want the children's stories to fill the air in the classroom. Also, children can become overwhelmed when the teacher writes on a much more sophisticated level than they can. And finally, the bare-bones quality of this writing allows me to return to it later to demonstrate revision by stretching out the details, reworking the plot line, and adding what I was thinking and feeling.

By this time, my timeline looked like this:

```
↑  Lunch
•  Brought frisbee to yard
•  Threw frisbee
•  Mud puddle
•  Bee drowning
•  Rescued bee
•  Bee stung me
•  Stepped on it
•  Ran away
•  Got frisbee
↓
```

"Do you see how making a timeline helps me set the parts of my story in order? When I write, I can use my timeline to remind me to tell what happened first, second, next, and after that."

ACTIVE ENGAGEMENT

Set children up to try the strategy you've taught. Recall an event the class experienced together; help children make their own timelines of that event.

"Let's try making a timeline together. I'm thinking we could practice by making a timeline of when that dragonfly flew into our room—remember him?"

"With your partner, say how a timeline could go of the other day when the dragonfly flew in while we were reading. Tell what happened first, then second, then third, and so forth. For now, use your fingers as dots on a timeline." The children talked to their partners. I listened, jotting notes.

Convene the class. Share what you overheard individuals doing in a way that allows you to reiterate the steps you hope all children will follow when making timelines.

After a minute, I asked for the children's attention. "I heard some ideas for our timeline dots. Carl, you said the first dot would be, 'We were doing math.' So I'll make 'Math' our first dot." I wrote "Math" on a new timeline on the board.

"Olivia, you said, 'We were listening to a story when Jonathan saw the dragonfly.' I'm going to make that into two dots because first we were listening to a story, *then* Jonathan saw the dragonfly and called out, didn't he?" I started to write "We were listening to a story." Then I pointed out I could abbreviate that phrase as "Story" and wrote just that instead.

You'll notice that I use just a word or two for each dot of the timeline. Each dot on the timeline represents the next action. For now, the personal narrative I am writing and expecting kids to write consists primarily of a character progressing through a series of actions (a plot). If your kids are writing at a more advanced level, you might include dots that represent smaller actions. By leaving these out, however, I have set myself up to add them later. Notice that I begin the timeline before the story really starts, with lunch, and end it with other bits that could be extraneous. I am deliberately messing up, setting myself up to demonstrate how writers revise timelines in order to focus their stories.

Your teaching will have more meaning for you if you use a story from your own life, though we've deliberately chosen a story that could be yours in case you don't think of one.

You will create a wonderful sense of community as you mine the true dramas of your class, using events you experience together as the raw material for minilessons such as this. If your ceiling falls in or a mouse runs across the floor during reading time, take secret pleasure in these mini-disasters because each will make a great story!

I deliberately started this second timeline with a dot (and an event) that are irrelevant to the main story. This will again set the stage for a subsequent mid-workshop teaching point.

It is not an accident that I almost wrote this bullet to represent two linked events. We try to embed little tips into our demonstrations, and one way to do this is by deliberately making the mistakes that kids are apt to make and then self-correcting them, saying aloud why the correction is preferable.

"What should the next dots be, Sam?"

"Add the part about Jonathan seeing the dragonfly. And then tell that it landed on the rug and we were totally silent."

"And then?"

"You started to read *The Lion, the Witch and the Wardrobe*."

"And then?"

"And it listened to Chapter six before it flew out the window!" As the children recalled the episode, I added to the timeline until the completed version looked like this:

Math

Story

J. saw dragonfly

Landed on rug/silent

Read Chapter 6

Flew out

"Did you see how we took a tiny event that happened to us and we remembered the story, then made a timeline that helped us retell what happened first, next, and then next? The timeline can help us organize our writing because we will tell the story of what happened first, then second, then next."

Link
Compile the new list of strategies students have learned for developing their seed idea before drafting.

"Let's go back and add, 'Make a timeline' to our Monitoring My Writing Process checklist. And after you have found your seed idea for your second story, try planning it by making a timeline. In the end, this might be something that really works for you—in which case you will do it often—or it might not work for you. But for this cycle through the writing process, give it a try. Making a timeline shouldn't take more than a few minutes. When you've finished making it, you know other ways in which writers get ready to write. You can try writing different leads, or you can storytell your draft to yourself over and over, thinking, 'How can I tell this story really well, even better than last time?'"

It is great to weave a love of literacy into as many stories as possible. I'm always trying to send subliminal messages to kids.

Some writers will make timelines that are overly full because they write every last bit of the story on it. These writers write a full sentence beside each dot. Teach these children that when writers make timelines, we just jot a quick word beside a dot, using that word later to spark a detailed memory.

Because the concept of a timeline is a rich one, you may want to support this across your day. For example, children may also learn that readers notice the major events (the important dots) in the timeline of a story, and can retell a story by recalling those events in sequence. Of course, if you have a flow of the day chart or a daily agenda, these are timelines of a sort and you'll want to point this out to children.

WRITING AND CONFERRING

Writing Timelines: Predictable Problems

During writing time today, you'll want to convene small groups based on the assessments you made when you studied children's notebooks and specifically their timelines. You will probably have some children who do not really understand the nature of timelines. They may not grasp that the line represents the passage of time, that the dots signal events or actions, or that their job is to write only a word or phrase alongside each dot, something that is a reminder of the much more detailed story they will eventually write. You can probably gather all the children who are confused about timelines and show them that your flow-of-the day chart in which you overview the day's agenda is already a timeline of their day. They could work with you to make another timeline – perhaps of that day's start of school. They could also make a timeline of a well-known story such as *Owl Moon*. As you work on one of these shared timelines, you can tuck in little pointers and show the group that timelines are tools for telling or retelling stories. You will want to take the time to teach this organizational tool because children will need it throughout the year.

Your children's timelines will also sometimes reveal problems with their personal narratives. Some children will still not have zoomed in in a manner that allows them to retell an event with detail. You may decide to let this go, for now, especially if these are writers who struggle. Many children find it easier to write about an adventure-filled day than to write about a single episode. On the other hand, you may want to help your writers focus—and it's vastly easier to help them now, before they begin their drafts, rather than later. These writers are sometimes reluctant to focus for fear their narratives will end up being too short, so you may need to help writers understand that once they've narrowed themselves to a small number of dots, they can expand their timelines and eventual drafts. Prompts that help

> **MID-WORKSHOP TEACHING POINT**
>
> *Resetting the Tone* "Writers, can I have your eyes and your attention?" I said, waiting an extra long time and sweeping the room with my eyes to convene children. "Writers, I need us to gather now in the meeting area because we need to have a serious conversation." Once children had gathered, I said, "Lately you've been restless and distracted. When I look around the room, instead of seeing you pulled intently towards your paper, I see many of you leaning back in your chairs as if you're just slopping some dots onto the page. You are missing the entire point of timelines, because timelines are meant to be tools of thought."
>
> "Let me explain. Pretend you have a very generous grandmother and she asked you to mail her your birthday list. I know for sure you wouldn't just slap any ol' word onto a page and mail it to her. You'd do a ton of thinking in order to produce even one word on that list, and equal thinking for the next item on the list. Making timelines requires the same sort of dedication, the same level of attentiveness, because each dot represents a whole scene in the story you'll eventually write, and it represents a writer's choice."
>
> "So our classroom needs to become a place where writers can focus. We're going to institute a system of silent work places. If any one of you needs help from a partner, the two of you can go to one of the two conferring stations I've set up on the margins of the room. There are only two of these, however, because I'm going to be admiring the ways in which you're able to help yourselves.

writers do this include, "Can you think of exactly what you did (or said, thought, felt) at that moment?" Or, "Show me, act it out." "Say out loud the exact words you said." This type of guided practice usually helps the child to "write in the air," so you will want to follow up by prompting the child to start putting the new timeline on paper.

Some children may write feelings and thoughts on dots in the timeline, not understanding that each dot represents a new event or a new moment in time. You might see one dot labeled, "I peeled all the bark off the tree" and the next dot, "It was a long piece" and next, "It was fun." You could help such a writer by teaching her to make a movie in her mind of the event, starting at the very beginning and slowly moving through it, writing down dots and labels for every key scene in the movie. What would the scene be for "It was fun"? Was it a big smile on your face? Was it a look of concentration? The action of smiling or looking serious is what should be written on the timeline's dot, if there is going to be a dot for that part.

If any of these issues are troubling a sizable portion of the class, you will want to address them in a mid-workshop teaching point, or even during the next minilesson.

You can anticipate that many children will finish work on their timeline fairly quickly (this doesn't mean the timeline will necessarily be an effective one), so you may move quickly toward your mid-workshop teaching point. In it, you lay out further work that your children could do once they feel as if they've finished with their first timeline. However another alternative is to not rush towards this particular Mid-Workshop Teaching Point, and to instead convene the class and remind writers that whenever they're 'done' they need to function as their own job captains.

In a conference you can use the work of one child to show other children examples of the way work can progress quickly from a list of story ideas [Fig. XI-1] to timelines [Fig. XI-2] and then on to a draft [Fig. XI-3].

Fig. XI-1 Sophie lists possible stories she could write about her grandmother.

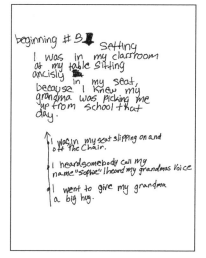

Fig. XI-2 Sophie makes a timeline for the story she's decided to tell.

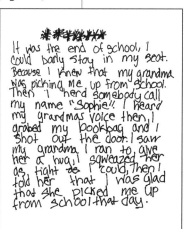

Fig. XI-3 Sophie's first draft

SHARE

Revising Timelines

Convene writers. Celebrate that they are imagining various starting points for their narratives.

"Writers, earlier this year you planned stories across your fingers and across the pages of booklets. Today you learned that you can also plan stories as we plan our school day — by recording a timeline. The important thing to realize is that timelines are meant as quick ways to jot some notes—and they are meant as tools for revision."

Explain that timelines can be used to help writers focus and revise our writing before it is even written. Give an example.

"Timelines give us a way to revise our stories before we've even written them. Let me show you what I mean," I said, turning to my timeline. "After I have made a timeline, I reread it and think, 'Are all the dots on this timeline important to the real story I want to tell?' Sometimes I cross out parts of a timeline that aren't that important. Watch me as I reread my Bee timeline and reconsider which parts are important to the story I want to tell."

- Lunch
- Brought frisbee to yard
- Threw frisbee
- Mud puddle
- Bee drowning
- Rescued bee
- Bee stung me
- Stepped on it
- Ran away
- Got frisbee

"I'm realizing that if I want to zoom in on the most important part of my story, I can cross out the part about lunch. It doesn't really matter to the story." I crossed out that event on my timeline. Then I held my pen poised over the final dots on my timeline. "I'm not

Timelines are amazing tools for teaching children that they can take control of their writing. It's easy to feel that the way writing is on the page is the only way it could be—after all, there it is. The choices writers make are easier to see when children learn to manipulate timelines.

sure how to end the story. Running away and getting the frisbee doesn't really relate to the bee part. I might want to end the story with me stepping on the bee. But that is an angry ending. Is that what I want? I'll have to think about that some more and try to remember more about what happened. I want to think more about what the important thing is in my story."

Ask children to consider revising the timeline of the class' story.

"Right now, would each of you think about our class dragonfly story? Look at the timeline—are there any events on this timeline that are *not* important to the heart of the story?" I waited half a minute, giving children time to do this. "Give me a thumbs up if you see some dots we could take out of our timeline."

↑
● Math
● Story
● J. saw dragonfly
● All saw
● Landed on rug/silent
● Chapter 6
● Flew out
↓

Naomi suggested, "We don't have to keep the part about doing math because it doesn't have anything to do with the dragonfly."

"That's smart! So let's cross off the first event—Math—and we could just keep going, asking, 'Is there anything else on our timeline that isn't part of the real story?' And then we'd cross it out if it's not."

Remind children they can use this strategy on their own.

"So, writers, whenever you are working with timelines, look back and think, 'Is every dot on my timeline important for the main story I want to tell?' Your story will get better if you cross out unnecessary dots. Often, the first few dots on your timeline, and sometimes the last ones as well, aren't essential to the story. A writer I know said, 'If you are writing about a waterfall, start when you can just hear the falls ahead of you.' So if you are writing about rescuing a drowning bee, start just a bit before you extend a helping hand."

I added very obvious bits into my timeline which aren't integral to the story I'm writing. I did this deliberately, in order to make the point. Because the example is an obvious one, it's all the more likely that children will grasp the lesson. I generally find that I make my point best in minilessons when I'm not subtle in the least.

Later in this series, we'll teach writers that story mountains are a more sophisticated way to plan the plotline of a narrative. The big difference between a story mountain and a timeline is that in the former, the writer makes a decision over what to highlight.

Whatever children suggest in terms of revising timelines can work, of course, since the point is that timelines CAN be revised. Whether the decision of what to revise is the best or not matters little.

HOMEWORK *Storytelling from Timelines* Tonight, at home, use your timeline to jog memories of the sequence of your story. Storytell this new piece of writing in preparation for drafting it tomorrow.

Remember, the story about a drowning bee will not sound like this: 'Lunch, brought frisbee to yard, threw frisbee to puddle . . .'

When you storytell or write a draft from your timeline, don't just read the labels off the dots! Instead, look at a dot, and then tell a whole story that goes with that one dot. For example, the first dots of the bee timeline says, 'lunch' and 'brought frisbee to yard.' The story that goes with those dots may start like this:

> After lunch I grabbed my new frisbee and went to the yard. The sun
> was shining bright. "See you later, Mom," I said, and ran through
> the back door, letting it bang shut.

The dot says, 'frisbee' but the story will contain not only this, but other details I recall:

> I threw the red frisbee up into the sky. It flew up, up, up, rebounded
> off the garage door and then . . . it landed with a plop in a mud
> puddle right next to the sticker rosebush. Surrounding the muddy
> frisbee was a swarm of buzzing bees.

Remember Robert Munsch's advice and storytell your story several times, to yourself and to others. Use the dots as a guide, but say a whole lot for each dot. Add to the story in ways that aren't on the timeline. Make your stories sound like the stories we read in books—and tomorrow, you'll have a chance to write them on the page.

Notice that I am tucking a cautionary note into my teaching. This cautionary note comes from prior experiences doing this work with children. I'm presenting an extreme version of what not to do.

If you want to raise the stakes of children's storytelling, ask them to try to tell their story in such a way that the story commands attention. It's likely that your child will need to recruit an audience. While she washes the dishes, a student might say to her father. "Can I tell you the story of a memory I have?' The father will agree and as the story starts, he may listen politely. But if the storyteller succeeds, she will draw the father in to really, really listen. Ruth Sawyer, author of The Storyteller, *writes: "I have never told a story that I have not wondered if this were not after all the supreme test of the art: To command attention, not trade on mere willingness of others to listen. To take the center of the market-place, or a table at the inn, and, whether by the sharing of great adventure or taking the gentle road of fancy, be able to lift the soul with exaltation or move it with amazement. To hold 'children from play, and old men from the chimney corner'—nothing short of this, I take it, can be called storytelling" (1942, p. 71).*

If your students are new to timelines and tend to include too many items or too many details . . . you could make and talk through a timeline of a class event like a birthday celebration or trip. You can highlight the brevity of each label on the timeline and highlight also that each dot represents a step forward in the sequence of events.

If your students have experience with timelines . . . you could show them how to angle the timelines in ways that help to get to the heart of their story. Writers can make different timelines of the same event, depending on what they decide they want to show. For example, if you wanted to show that a class visitor was greatly anticipated, your timeline might start before the visit and convey the class' excitement—one dot might represent the narrator peeking into the hall to see if the visitor was approaching yet. On the other hand, if you wanted to show that the visitor brought odd animals with him, the timeline might start as the visitor entered the room carrying a wriggling bundle.

If your students could use more support in using timelines effectively . . . you might create a minilesson in which you ask children to join you in studying timelines that other children have made, noticing their different choices and the effects these choices might have on the stories. They might notice the following:

- Some label each dot with a word, some with a sentence
- Some are interesting just by themselves, some seem flat already
- Some start with a small event, some start broad
- Some have a lot of cross-outs, some are untouched

If your children already know how to make timelines and want other tools for planning their narratives . . . you could teach them that writers keep in mind the kind-of-text-we'll-be-writing, and use our knowledge of the genre in which we're writing to help us prepare for drafting. This means that when children know they're writing narratives (or stories), it's helpful for them to think in advance about their setting, their characters, and their plot. Children can be reminded to use all they know as readers of stories to guide them as they plan the stories they will soon write.

COLLABORATING WITH COLLEAGUES

Sometimes people ask me for advice on using these units of study. They want to know whether it's important for a group of teachers to read through an entire book or series of books before launching the work in classrooms. They have questions about whether it's best for a teacher to hold the book in his or her lap while teaching a minilesson, or to let the particular words slip away in favor of teaching the big ideas of a minilesson.

I believe there are many right answers to these questions. As the song goes: "Different strokes for different folks."

But there is one right answer that I believe pertains to all of us, and this is it: Our teaching will be immeasurably deeper and richer if we do the work ourselves in the minilessons we plan to give to children, and then refer to our own writing and learning from those minilessons as we teach them to our students.

In many schools, one teacher agrees to read ahead in a unit of study, and during grade–level meetings, this teacher gives a very abbreviated version of an upcoming minilesson to the group of teachers. Then for a few minutes – even just five minutes works – the room is quiet as everyone does a tiny bit of fast writing. The pieces we produce are written on topics we're willing to share with our children, and they are abbreviated – which works perfectly for minilessons.

When teachers write together, we experience firsthand what it is we are asking children to do. When we're asked to make a timeline of a small moment in our lives, we'll find ourselves confronting all the questions that children will confront. Do I label each dot with a word? A phrase? How small are the steps I take through an event?

The fact that we write ourselves will have giant payoffs, but the conversations we have with our colleagues as a result of the writing will be even more powerful.

Finally, let me emphasize that the children need to know that you and the other teachers are learning this work alongside them. Roland Barth, the author of *Improving Schools from Within*, recently reminded Teachers College Reading and Writing Project principals that schools need to be places where everyone's learning curve is off the charts. "Write down the areas in which you find you are learning, learning, learning," he said to principals. After giving people a moment to record, he pressed further. "Here is the question: Who knows about this learning you are doing?" Barth's point was that in schools, those of us who are called upon to mentor children need to be very public about our learning. So strut your stuff!

IN THIS SESSION, YOU WILL SHOW
CHILDREN THAT WRITERS CAN
DEVELOP SEED IDEAS BY CHOOSING
ONE DOT FROM A TIMELINE AND
EXPANDING THAT EVENT INTO A
NEW TIMELINE.

GETTING READY

- Instructions on chalkboard telling children to bring their writer's notebooks and sit with their partners in the meeting area
- Sample second timeline made from one dot of first timeline, written on chart paper
- See CD-ROM for resources

TIMELINES AS TOOLS FOR DEVELOPING STORIES

Writing is a powerful tool for thought *because it allows us to put our words, our thoughts, onto paper. Then we can hold our thoughts in our hands, and we can think about our thinking. In this minilesson, you'll teach children that once they've jotted a timeline of their story onto the page, that graphic organizer can become a tool for thought. They can look at what they've written and ask, as they did in the previous session, "Are all the dots key to the story I want to tell?" They can also think, "Which dots are so important that I should expand them?"*

Eventually, children will learn that in order to decide where and how they will start and develop a story, they first need to decide what their story aims to show. For now, however, it is enough for children to realize that writers have choices. Whereas many children have assumed that writing true stories means telling what happened, children will go away from these two sessions aware that writers can select just one part of their story, just one dot of a timeline, and expand that single dot into a timeline, a story, of its own.

By showing children that writers not only eliminate unnecessary dots or actions, but also add actions that are important, you will give children a practical introduction to revision. For now, you spare them the work of writing a sequence of long drafts, and yet you still give them an experience in thinking, "How else could I have written this?"

Your children will think through different ways their story could star. They will tell the story aloud one way and then another. Soon they'll choose one and scrawl out a draft, writing fast and long.

MINILESSON

Timelines as Tools for Developing Stories

CONNECTION

Remind writers that making timelines can help them plan and draft stories.

"Yesterday we learned that writers can get ready to draft stories by making timelines to lay out what happened first, next, and next. In the process of trying to remember everything that happened, some of you came up with so many dots! Jonathan had eleven! Remember that we also learned we can look back at our timelines to cross out parts that are not important."

"We also learned that writers sometimes try starting the story at one dot on the timeline, then we try starting at another dot. Writers ask ourselves, 'Where, in a sequence of events, is the best place for me to start my story?'"

Name the teaching point. Specifically, tell writers that they can zoom in on just one dot of a timeline, expanding that single dot into a timeline of its own.

"Today I want to teach you that as writers, we revise not only by eliminating dots that seem unnecessary to the timeline, but also by adding dots, expanding the most important events."

TEACHING

Show children an example of a timeline that has been made from a small part of another timeline.

"I noticed that Sasha found that by zooming in on the important part of her story, she ended up with just one dot on her timeline! Sasha started out with a timeline with seven events on it. She ended up deciding none of them were important except one: 'We twisted and spun on swings.' Then Sasha did something that all writers sometimes do—she made a second timeline out of that one dot since it was the most important part, the part she wanted to focus on! To do this, a writer makes a movie in our minds of what happened inside that one dot. Here's the new timeline Sasha made out of 'We twisted and spun on swings.'"

COACHING

It would be very easy for me to describe yesterday's work by saying, "Yesterday you all made timelines of your seed ideas." But by saying instead, "Yesterday we learned that writers can get ready to draft stories by making timelines," I aim to help children grasp the larger purpose of what they did yesterday and what they will learn today.

Notice that I tell the class that Sasha shows us how writers sometimes make a second timeline. Over and over, you will see that we try to attribute insights we aim to teach to particular kids. To do this truthfully, we must have an eagle eye for the great strategies kids invent and the insights they voice so we find opportunities for children to teach the whole class. We do this because we want kids to be famous to each other. We want them to regard themselves as people who grow important ideas about writing. We want to create a community in which we learn from each other.

Notice that I tuck in a passing reminder that when writing timelines—as when writing narratives—a writer makes movies-in-the-mind of what happened.

- Got on swing
- Tried to touch leaves
- A girl beside me tried to do it too
- Bumped each other
- Her name was Lizzie
- We laughed

"Can you see how Sasha took that one event and really thought about exactly how it went, and made a new, more focused timeline out of it? That is the strategy you can try when you need to get to the heart of your story before you draft."

ACTIVE ENGAGEMENT
Ask children to try this new strategy for developing a seed idea.

"Open up your notebooks to the timeline you made in the last lesson. Find one important dot on your timeline, just like Sasha did. See if you can zoom in on that one dot and make a movie in your mind of what happened inside that single moment. Try to remember the tiny little actions in it." I gave the children a few minutes to read over their timelines and to choose an important dot to expand upon.

"Partner 1s, please tell partner 2 the story of just one dot on your timeline. Tell the story so your partner can make a movie in his or her mind of your tiny actions." The children did this.

"I heard many of you remembering more small events by zooming in on one dot on your timeline and replaying that one small moment of your story like a movie in your mind. Yazmin, will you please share what you discovered when you tried to do this?" [Fig. XII-1]

"I remembered lots more about my reading buddy being restless." Yazmin pointed to his next finger. "He started fidgeting and pulling up grass." Yazmin pointed to a new finger. "Then he rolled back and forth. He even tried to run off." Pointing to yet another finger, Yazmin said, "I had to jump up and bring him back to our reading spot."

"Wow, Yazmin, it sounds like you could turn that one dot into four more dots on your timeline. Now that you know you can do this with this one dot, you'll realize you could do the same thing with other dots. So you'll need to look back at your original draft of a timeline and think again about the story you want to write. What's not important in that story and can be deleted? What is important and can be expanded? Writers fiddle with our timelines as a way to weigh possibilities for our drafts."

Be sure that children don't get the idea that the timelines are important as products. They are only important as tools for revision, as a shortcut method to weigh alternatives.

I usually don't have children practice on their current writing work in this way because this often doesn't leave any work for them to do when they go off to their seats to write. But today I thought that by having the children try to zoom in on one existing dot during the Active Engagement, they would be more likely to go back and make revisions they might not otherwise make on their timelines. Notice that I ask partner 1 to do this work, and partner 2 to listen. Another day, these roles will flip. Both benefit from this tiny interlude of closer practice—and from the brevity of the minilesson.

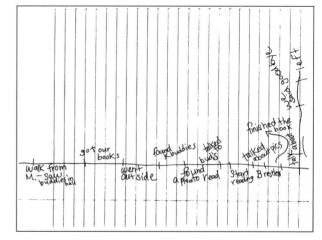

Fig. XII-1 Yazmin's timeline

LINK

Remind children that after they select a seed idea, they have a repertoire of ways to begin developing that idea.

"Writers, you have learned that after a writer decides on a seed idea, there are some things the writer can do to get ready to draft. Today you can choose from all those things. You may decide to make and rethink your timeline, eliminating dots that don't really go with the story and expanding dots that are especially important. You may decide to storytell your stories and to use storytelling as a way to get a new trajectory on your story. You can experiment with different leads, trying out a lead which begins with a small action, then trying one which begins with dialogue or with the setting. Of course, you can also try leads which start at different places in the timeline. I can't wait to see the choices you make during today's writing workshop!"

Ideally, when we send kids off to do their work, we want to remind them that they can draw on what they learned earlier in the year as well as on what they learned today. This is a nice link because it reminds writers that they have choices to make and lots of work to do. As often as possible, I try to use the link as a time to reference and revitalize classroom charts which spell out strategies I've taught earlier in the unit and in the year.

WRITING AND CONFERRING

Getting a Good Start

You may question whether timelines really merit two full days of minilessons and mid-workshop teaching points, and my answer is a resounding yes.

One reason timelines matter is that your children are probably still more willing to do initial revisions, revising leads and timelines, rather than final revisions, producing a sequence of full drafts. Because they are still fairly inexperienced writers, your students probably can't yet entertain and discard a whole sequence of ideas simply by mulling over their plans. Timelines, like leads, allow children to make their abstract plans into a concrete object—manipulating that concrete timeline makes it easier for them to rethink those abstract plans.

But the other reason to work on timelines for several days is so you can keep children working productively while at the same time stalling them from drafting until you can confer with each of them! That way, you can help them get this next piece of writing off to the best possible start. Just because children are working on timelines does not mean you need to focus on timelines as you confer. Instead, I suggest you study the child's writing, look over and listen to the child's plans, and decide how you can help the child have as successful an experience as possible writing the upcoming piece.

If the child is not yet writing about a tightly focused event, you will have time to intervene. Rely on the standard questions: "Of all the things that you did while at your grandma's what's the one particular event that you most remember?" "How did that start?" "What exactly were you doing at the start?"

If the child you are conferring with did, in her last piece, focus on a specific event, and if she did seem to make a movie in her mind and retell the story as she recalled it, you will very likely find that the previous draft is detailed and lively but that the story is swamped by dialogue. Danielle's draft is typical of the personal narratives I saw in those New York City schools where writing workshop has only recently been instituted.

MID-WORKSHOP TEACHING POINT *Choosing a Starting Moment* "Writers, can I have your eyes and your attention? Let me stop you for a minute. Wow! It's so quiet in here, another dragonfly might come for a visit!"

"I want to show you one more way in which I use timelines to help me get ready to draft. Remember how, during our first piece of writing, we spent time trying out different leads? Well, writers not only weigh different ways to word their leads, we also consider different times in the sequence of events to start with. Watch how I try this out, asking myself, 'When, in a sequence of events, do I want to start my story?'" I pointed to my bee timeline, at the dot labeled "Mud puddle," and said, "I could start then." I voiced that lead:

> I stood beside the mud puddle, staring at my brand new frisbee that lay in the center. "I'll get you," I said to the frisbee, but then I saw a buzzing swarm of bees circling it.

Then I pointed to a later dot, and said, "Or I could start it when I got a stick to rescue the bee."

> I nudged the bee gently with my stick. It climbed onto the stick unsteadily, clinging to the bark. Then it inched up and up, away from the muddy water, higher and higher, toward my finger.

"I bet I could even start my story with this dot—'Rescued bee'."

> "I can't believe it!" I thought to myself. The wet bee was inching up my finger.

"Do you see how I looked at my timeline and experimented by beginning my story at different times in the sequence of events?

continued on next page

Danielle is in fourth grade, but she is an inexperienced writer. Still, this first story of hers shows evidence of instruction: it is focused, chronological, detailed, and includes direct dialogue. In fact, the draft reads like a soundtrack of a film, without any actions!

When I conferred with Danielle, I celebrated the fact that she clearly has made a movie in her mind and recorded that movie *[Fig. XII-2]*:

> I was in the pool. Me and my sister was playing water fight so I was scared because I thought that I was going to drown so my sister said, "You are not going to drown. I got you. Don't' worry I have you." So I said "Okay." She said, "Go on your back." I was telling my sister "Please don't drop me, please don't drop me," and she said "I'm not going to drop you. If you keep saying that I will drop you!". . . .

I pointed out, however, that because she knows the people, the place, and the actions, she only paid attention to the sound track in her movie. For the sake of her reader, she needs, in the next piece, to play that mental movie to record not only the dialogue, but also to tell who spoke, to tell how she spoke, and to tell what she did along with the dialogue, so that the next draft reads more like this:

> She said, "Go on your back," and she rolled my body over in the water. I held my sister's arm and yelled, "Please don't drop me!" with panic in my voice. . .

I could, of course, have suggested Danielle revise this piece so as to add the speaker, the speaker's intonations and actions . . . but it was just as effective for me to use knowledge gleaned from her last piece to set Danielle up for her next piece. And in this way, I gave her more confidence and energy for the writing ahead of her.

continued from previous page

> Let's try that with our class story. Look over our timeline, think in your mind about one dot you could use as a starting time for a story, and say that lead in your head." I waited a half-minute.
> "Now try a second starting time, and a second lead."

Tashim said, "We could start it when we were reading and Jonathan saw a dragonfly."

Picking up a sheet of paper, I said, "So your story would go like this: 'When we were reading?'"

Giggling, Tashim said, "No. I'd write, 'We were so quiet, we could probably have heard ants crawling along the floor. Then our teacher stopped reading, and we were just about to say, 'Don't stop! It's the most exciting part!' But she was looking at Jonathan because he was looking up at the top of the bookshelf where a dragonfly had landed. 'He wants to listen to the story,' he said'."

"That is so beautiful! There are also many other places in the timeline we could begin the story about the dragonfly. Writers, do you see that all of your stories can begin in different places? You can return to your own writing now."

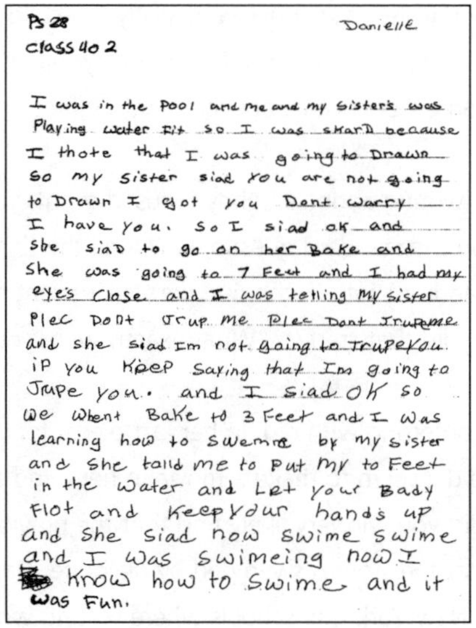
Ps 28
class 402
Danielle

I was in the Pool and me and my sister's was Playing water Fit so I was skarD because I thote that I was going to Drawn so my sister siad You are not going to Drawn I got you Dont warry I have you. so I siad ok and she siaD to go on her Bake and She was going to 7 Feet and I had my eye's Close and I was telling My sister Plec Dont Jrup me Plec Dont Jrupme and she siad Im not going to TrupeYou. iP you Keep Saying that Im going to Jrupe you. and I siad OK so We Whent Bake to 3 Feet and I Was learning how to swemme by my sister and She talld me to Put my to Feet in the Water and Let your Bady Flot and Keep your hands up and She Siad now swime swime and I Was swimeing now I Know how to Swime and it was Fun.

Fig. XII-2 Danielle

SHARE

Planning and Goal-Setting

Explain to children that writers can keep themselves on course by making and sticking to plans and goals. Ask them to make some goals and plans with their partners.

"Writers, most of you have shifted from drafting to revising timelines and leads to beginning your draft, and that's great. When you write, you'll keep you timeline near you and it can act as a silent teacher, a quiet coach, reminding you of your hopes for this new piece of writing. Some people tie yarn around a finger to remind themselves of how they want to act. Writers have our own ways to keep ourselves on course, and one way we do that is to use plans. Timelines are a form of a plan."

"But you may want to give yourself other reminders as well, and you need to decide on the particular reminders you need. I told you earlier that you need to be job captains for yourselves, deciding when it is time for you to start this second piece of writing. Well, you also need to decide on a goal and reminders that will help you do your best work."

Explain that writers can make goals for themselves by looking at their past writing and deciding what to aim for in future writing. Share the story of one child who did that.

"You can glean those reminders from looking back on your first completed piece and thinking, 'What did I do in this piece of writing that I want to always do as a writer?' Then jot yourself a reminder on a sticky note, and put it beside you as you write. Perhaps you remembered to write with periods and capitals—well, you definitely don't want to go back to the old days before you did that! So write a reminder."

"Natalie realized by looking at her first piece that she wrote what one person said and the next person, but her writing was like a sound track. It told what people said, but didn't tell the actions, their intonations, so she's written herself a note which says, 'Not just a sound track!'"

In other places in this series, you will have the chance to teach children that they can also form goals for themselves by aiming to work on certain qualities of good narrative writing, either qualities they name for themselves or qualities they pick from the class chart. Any of the class charts can become the spark for writerly aspiration, and future sessions in this series will offer you a place to explore this use of the charts more with children.

Ask children to get started on this work now, with partners.

"Right now, get with your partner. Look over each other's first pieces, and create together some goals for your future writing, starting with this next piece."

HOMEWORK *Collecting Words* This year we are going to travel on a journey through language, and our souvenirs will be words. We are going to collect words like a tourist collects postcards in order to remember all our new experiences with language.

After you leave school today, listen for words that catch your attention. You may overhear a conversation where someone uses a phrase that strikes you as special. Jot it down in your notepad. As you are reading, pay attention to any words that you can practically taste. Write them down in your notepad. Pay attention to words, savor them, then use them.

From this day forward, gather words that seem to be just right for saying hard-to-say things, words that are somehow remarkable, jot them down, and then we will try to use these words when we talk and when we write. We will begin to collect these words in our very own album.

TAILORING YOUR TEACHING

If your children are skilled at drafting and revising timelines for their stories . . . you may want to remind them that writers can plan other elements of a story in addition to the plot. For example, teach children that before they begin a draft, some writers take a few minutes to envision the place in which the story is set. Teach children that it helps to go back to the beginning of the story and to think, "Where was I exactly?" If the writer's first thought is a general one such as "I was in the park," teach the child that it is important to press on for more specifics, for example, "I was sitting on the bench under the giant willow tree in Central Park." Then you can teach children that writers sometimes take a second to sketch the place, and do so thinking, "What can I put in my story that will help readers see the scene clearly?" Of course, the challenge will be to paint the picture using not a drawing but words.

Words hold power, and the language we use and the way we use it often impacts our success and status in this world. Whether the language is academic or poetic, our students need constant exposure and encouragement in its usage. You can encourage this language study during your daily read alouds and throughout the day. Math, science, and social studies vocabulary sets also offer numerous opportunities to explore and celebrate words!

COLLABORATING WITH COLLEAGUES

In the New York City school district, leaders sometimes conducted school "walk-throughs." Often a team consisting of the superintendent, the principal, and assorted other people in power would walk in and out of every classroom in a school, sampling bits of data. In one room they might ask to see the teacher's records of reading assessments, in another they might look closely through a randomly selected child's work. In some rooms, they might stay five minutes and in other rooms, much longer.

Sometimes, in the wake of these walk-throughs, harsh mandates and memos would go out. Sometimes the walk-throughs added to a climate of mistrust between schools and their leadership.

New York City's current deputy chancellor, Carmen Farina, has instituted a different kind of school visit. She calls these *Glory Walks*. "Show me what's working, or almost working, in this school," she says, and uses her visits as a time to celebrate, to study characteristics of successful practice and to spread success stories.

After Carmen visits a school, she invariably talks about that visit with everyone she meets with over the next few days, always sending others to see and emulate what she most admires. Schools that have never been regarded as exemplary are suddenly hosting visitors, displaying what it is they do well.

Word had spread through New York City. This is a place where good work is often recognized and celebrated. Walk-throughs are often now *Glory Walks*. Morale is rising, efforts are redoubled, and schools are improving.

Keep this message in your mind as you study your children's work. Look at the children who've never been regarded as mentors and models. What can you see in their work that you can glory in? Can you find ways for unlikely children to be touted as teachers and asked to help others?

Try learning from Carmen Farina's model. People work harder and grow faster when we are seen and our work is recognized.

IN THIS SESSION, YOU WILL TEACH CHILDREN THAT WRITERS REPLAY LIFE EVENTS TO HELP OURSELVES WRITE IN WAYS THAT LET READERS FEEL THE EXPERIENCE.

GETTING READY

- Instructions on chalkboard telling children to bring their writer's notebooks and sit with their partners in the meeting area
- Examples of memories that have been seared into your mind—big and small
- Chart paper and markers
- Qualities of Good Personal Narrative Writing chart
- Example of paragraph formatting on chart paper
- Two drafts of a child's writing, one without paragraphs, one with, copied onto transparency or chart paper
- Overhead projector and marker
- Copies of a child's writing with paragraphs indicated by boxes (one copy per partnership)
- Copies of a story retyped with no paragraph formatting at all (one copy per child)
- Tool containers on each table with sharpened pencils (for use during share)
- See CD-ROM for resources

WRITING FROM INSIDE A MEMORY

Yesterday your children tried one timeline and another, and you helped them to feel the elasticity of their plans for their narratives. Today you'll teach towards an almost opposite goal. Today's session aims to help children understand that in order to write an effective narrative, after weighing possible plans, a writer commits himself or herself to one trajectory and then relives that story, holding onto the unfolding storyline with the same rapt attention that a reader might give when lost in a book.

The fiction writer, John Gardner, has pointed out that when reading, we first see letters on the page. But soon we are seeing not ink marks on a page but a train rushing through a Russian countryside or rain, pelting down on a ramshackled house. "We read on, we dream on," he says.

But here is the secret. Readers can read words and see a train hurtling through the Russian countryside or rain pelting down on a ramshackled house if first, we as writers have seen those scenes. We must first write, seeing not words on the page but the events of our lives. We see these events, relive these events, so that readers can, in turn, do the same.

If you don't actually do this work on the page, do it in your conversations with friends, and notice yourself doing it. The other day my husband brought me to the window to look out at what had been a small garden and was now a patch of scorched earth. "You know what happened?" John said, and launched into this story. "Matt told me that every spring, he burns his dead plants, and new growth shoots up," he said. "So I brought out the garden hose and left the water running into the lawn, just to be safe. Then I took a match and set fire to the dried grasses we used to have in the center of the garden. It smoldered. I wondered if it would catch fire. I blew on the sparks. Then I glanced away. Out of the corner of my eye, I saw an explosion of fire. The whole garden was wreathed in flames. I grabbed for the hose, but the little stream of water seemed like nothing! I thought the house was going to burn down!" As John retold the escapade, he relived it in Technicolor and I, in turn, felt as if I had been right there with him. For both of us, the story made our hearts leap. I didn't tell him the whole event was great for my book!

MINILESSON

Writing from Inside a Memory

CONNECTION

Put today's work into the context of the writing process as a whole so that children can see the writing cycle of rehearsing, drafting, revising, and editing.

"We've talked earlier this year about the fact that writers don't just sit down in front of a blank sheet of paper, pick up a pen, and write. Instead, as writers, we live in a way that gets us ready to write. We first see possible stories everywhere and gather entries, then we select an entry that we believe particularly matters, storytell the story to our friends and ourselves, and draft and revise timelines of the story sequence. We often explore different leads and plan how our story will lay out across pages in a booklet or down the page in paragraphs."

"And then the day comes when we write a whole draft. As you know from earlier in this unit, we usually write fast and long. While we write, we try to keep our minds on our subject."

Name your teaching point. Specifically, tell children that writing involves reenacting their own experiences.

"Today I want to teach you that writing personal narratives well involves reliving episodes from our own lives."

TEACHING

Point out to children that we all have memories that are seared into our minds forever. Give examples.

"Writers, I'm sure that for every one of us, there are moments in our lives that are seared into our memories forever. For me, one of those is the time I heard that a second plane had just flown into the World Trade Center towers, and all of a sudden the awareness flooded into me that this was not an accident. I can close my eyes and relive where I was in that moment, what I heard on the radio, what I thought, what I looked at, what I said, what I did. I can, and I do, go back to my experience of that event and replay it."

"As a writer, I have come to realize that I can go back and relive not only the traumatic, life-changing events, but also little moments that for some reason have mattered to me. I do not know why I remember the story of saving that drowning bee. Maybe I feel like my

COACHING

So far this year, children have inched along through the writing process. In this connection, I'm helping them to look back over the terrain they've traveled as if they're finally standing on a hilltop, surveying the route they've traveled. By helping them trace the path they've taken, I'm teaching towards independence. I want them to understand that whenever they write, they'll make a similar journey. It is important, then, that they see all the steps of the process as a single trail of work.

In order to teach children ideas that are deeper than the usual ones, you'll want to revisit content you have talked about earlier, layering the content with new insights and interpretations. Ideas grow like onions, in successive rings of thought.

We teach not only explicitly but also implicitly. By treating a little story about a bumblebee with such respect, I hope to convey to children that gigantic life issues can be contained in the seemingly mundane details of life.

whole life has been about trying to give folks who are drowning a stick to hang onto—I don't know. But I do know that when I wrote that story, I could feel again the wash of pride when that little bee climbed higher and higher up my stick, safe at last. And I know when I wrote that story, I can feel again the sudden throb in my finger as that bee turned on the very hand that had rescued it."

"Whenever I write a personal narrative, I relive my own experiences. Remember my story about Dad coming in to that basketball game? That was almost forty years ago but right now, I can still hear Dad's booming call, 'Lukers!' and the blood rushes to my face all over again. The truth is, I am not totally sure Dad really called out 'Lukers' that night. He called me that a lot, but did he holler that across the gym? I don't really know. When I write, I bring all the memories to my pen, and I imagine what probably happened. When I write, I remember an afternoon from years and years ago, and I reenact it in my mind."

"And the experiences that we remember and relive become all the more intense and searing and beautiful because we are living through them a second time, a third time."

Demonstrate to show that you write by reliving.

"Let me show you how I go about doing this kind of writing, and then we'll try it together. I'll never forget the day when Jeremy came running into the class with a cricket— that's the topic I've chosen to write about for now."

"I'm going to close my eyes and really put myself back into that memory. I remember exactly where I was, over here. And I remember it was hot out and I was feeling sticky. Now I'm going to look through the same eyes I had then and see what I see and hear what I heard then and write it! If I can't remember something, I'll picture how it might have gone and write that."

> I stood at the easel, copying something out of a book.

Then I paused, reread, and crossed that out. "I want to be more detailed about what was going on before Jeremy interrupted me."

> I stood at the easel, trying to hold <u>Peter's Chair</u> open with one hand while I copied the lead with the other.

The juxtaposition of these distinct stories is no accident. By showing children that there are many episodes in our lives that for some reason are seared into our memories, I emphasize the power writing has to imbue small moments with meaning. It is through writing that we discover the particularities of how and why moments matter.

Notice that when I write in front of children, I generally work on just a tiny excerpt of text. I think aloud, letting children in on the thoughts as I weigh them. I deliberately show myself struggling in ways which resemble the struggles children also encounter.

"I could include the lead I was copying but that's not the main story. Instead, I want to get to the main event."

> I stood at the easel, trying to hold <u>Peter's Chair</u> open with one hand while I copied the lead with the other.
>
> Suddenly I heard a commotion behind me and turned to see Jeremy, who was holding a cricket.

I paused, and reread, testing what I'd written against my true recollection of the scene. "No, I didn't know at the time that he was holding a cricket. Let me stay true to what I knew at that moment."

> I stood at the easel, trying to hold <u>Peter's Chair</u> open with one hand while I copied the lead with the other.
>
> Suddenly I heard a commotion behind me and turned to see Jeremy, who had his hands clasped as if in prayer. A circle of kids gathered around and Jeremy opened his hands so a few kids could peek in. "What is it?" I asked.

"Did you see how I recreated the event in my mind, then wrote it, trying to stay specific, detailed, and true to the unfolding story?"

ACTIVE ENGAGEMENT
Ask kids to try the strategy you've introduced. In this case, have them relive an important moment from the day before and write it down as they lived it. Then share one child's writing as an example.

"To practice, think of something important that happened to you yesterday. For now, maybe you want to recall a time when you entered or left a place as the sequence of events should be clear. For example, recall how you entered the lunchroom and found a seat, or how you left school at the end of the day and boarded the bus. Some small episode. Now remember how it started. Where were you? What did you do? What did you say? Thumbs up if you can recall what you did and said."

I've chosen to write this sequence of tiny drafts because I want to highlight that it is very important for the narrator in a personal narrative to stay inside a specific perspective. If I'm standing at the easel, copying from a picture book and a child approaches me, I'm not apt to discern instantly that the child is holding a cricket!

I tuck a lot of teaching into this demonstration. I model envisioning, adding specific details, getting to the main event, replaying the episode, and slowing down the key part. I also demonstrate how I work through these predictable problems. I think, I write, I cross out, and I try again. This is what I want students to do as they write.

Watch the way I move kids quickly past topic indecision, shepherding them along so they have a moment in mind and can proceed to learn from my pointers on how to write about that moment.

When most thumbs were up, I said, "So quickly, scrawl that small moment down in your notebook, just as I wrote mine on the easel. Imagine yourself right inside the story. Stay detailed, specific, and true to the story. This is just an exercise; you won't actually regard this entry as a draft to develop."

After a few minutes I asked children to share what they wrote with partners and I listened in.

"Listen for the details in Ellie's try-it." *[Fig. XIII-1]*

> "Oh man! I am late to lunch," I said as I glanced at my watch. I rushed through the quiet hall, clutching my lunch bag in my right hand. I wove through the Kindergarteners with my arm stretched like a football player ready to push the wood door open. My other hand gripped my paper bag lunch.

"Do you hear how Ellie got right inside the moment and wrote thoughts from her head at that moment and wrote the things she saw at that moment? She was really reliving it as she wrote, wasn't she?"

LINK
Remind writers of all you've taught so far about the qualities of good personal narrative writing, adding this new one aloud.

"Before you get started, writers, will you think for a moment about the work you will do today? There are probably some of you who began your draft yesterday and have decided you're going to start over, revising like writers revise, so that you really live inside your story. Some of you haven't yet begun your draft. Remember you are job captains for your own writing lives. I can't wait to see what you decide to do today."

As the year unfurls, there will be more and more times when you ask children to stop and jot in lieu of turning and talking with partners. This is the first such time, and you may need to take special care to help children realize that they're simply creating a tiny exercise-text. You aren't looking for a class full of lunchtime or bus line publications!

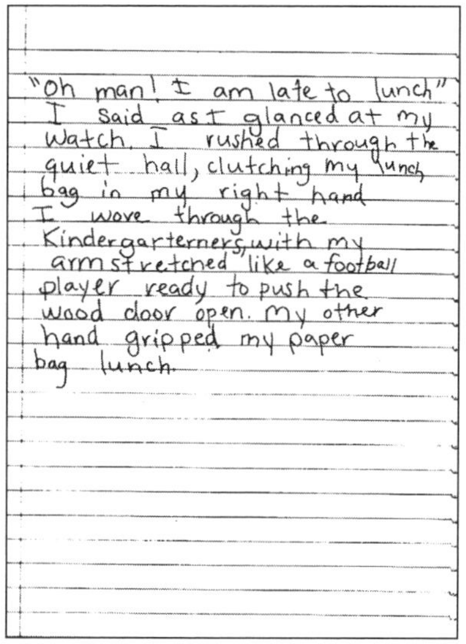

Fig. XIII-1 Ellie

Qualities of Good Personal Narrative Writing

- Write a little seed story; don't write all about a giant watermelon topic.
- Zoom in so you tell the most important parts of the story.
- Include true, exact details from the movie you have in your mind.
- Begin with a strong lead—maybe use setting, action, dialogue, or a combination to create mood.
- Make a strong ending—maybe use action, dialogue, images, and whole-story reminders to make a lasting impression.
- Relive the episode as you write it.

Keeping these charts alive in our classrooms is extremely important. It is not enough to simply hang charts on our walls and expect kids to look at them, let alone use them. The more a chart is referred to, the more likely it will be used by your students.

"And remember to relive the episode as you write it. This is how we make our writing intense and real."

Writing and Conferring

Conferring Effectively

By now, your kids are probably engaged enough in their writing that you can think less about simply getting them going and more about conferring well. As I have mentioned earlier, I recommend that teachers generally begin a writing conference by learning what it is the child has been trying to do as a writer. If we know the writer's intention, we can support that intention by equipping the writer to do what he wants to do, or we can explain why we think he should be aiming toward a different goal.

I recommend opening most writing conferences by asking, "What are you working on as a writer?" At first, children will answer by telling you about the topic. If the child does that, ask a follow-up question: "And what exactly are you trying to do as a writer? What strategies have you been using?" Sometimes you will need to show the child the sort of answer you have in mind. You can do this by looking over the child's draft and then answering your question yourself, saying, for example, "It looks like you have been experimenting with different leads, and some include dialogue, some include the setting. Is that right?"

Once you and the child have established whatever it is that the child has been trying to do, I recommend saying to the child, "Can you show me where you have done that?" Then I look at what the child has already done and as I look, I am trying to think of what I can compliment. I try to compliment something that I hope writers will do another day in another piece, which means I need to find something transferable. "I love the way you told where you were when you were bowling," I said to one writer. "Always remember that it is smart to bring out the setting for your story like you did just now." In a writing conference, after I've complimented the child, I tell the child that there is one thing I'd like to teach. Then I name the teaching point and teach it, just as if this were a brief minilesson.

Before any one day's writing workshop, it helps to anticipate the sort of things you might find yourself

> **MID-WORKSHOP TEACHING POINT** *Paragraphing* "Writers, can I have your eyes and your attention? Today I want to remind you that writers are always working on more than one thing. While you are reliving your life, reexperiencing an episode, you also need to keep an awareness in your mind that paragraphing matters, just like punctuation matters. Words can be like books—I bet you agree with me that when every inch of a bookshelf space is crammed with books and you can't see how they are organized, it's hard to appreciate any of them. We pass them by."
>
> "On the other hand, if a bookstore has its books nicely grouped—a round table featuring a selection of mysteries, a special shelf of biographies, and a display of store favorites—and if each of these groups is set out carefully with space around it, then it's easier to take the books in, to decide which ones to read."
>
> *continued on next page*

teaching. Your list of possibilities will be cumulative, and will pertain to many days. For now, your list of possible teaching points for a conference might look like this:

- Writers focus on small incidents.
- Writers envision, then storytell, rather than summarize, starting by telling a small action that we did at the start of the envisioned story.
- Writers write with specifics; so that instead of saying "I played a game," the writer names the game.
- Writers include exact speech.
- Writers spell word wall words correctly.
- Writers punctuate as we write.
- Writers write with paragraphs.
- Writers sometimes pretend to be strangers, rereading a draft for the first time and thinking, "Can I follow this? Does it all make sense?"
- Writers sometimes recruit readers who can tell us places where our draft is confusing.
- Writers try to solve our own problems, inventing solutions rather than simply lining up behind the teacher.
- Writers begin their stories with a small action, with dialogue, or with the setting.
- Writers stretch out the important sections of a story.

continued from previous page

"Writers, we need to make sure people's eyes don't fly right past our words and our ideas like they fly past books when they are crammed too close together with no organization! Group your thoughts and your writing. The micro-event that happens first in your story and that is represented by the first dot on your timeline is probably one grouping, one patch of words. After you write about that first micro-event, indent the next line, moving those words far in from the edge of the page to signal readers that this is a new group of thoughts—a new paragraph. You've seen how this looks in books, and you may have been doing it already yourself. Here's what a new paragraph looks like in handwriting—see mine here on the chart paper? From now on, as you write, chunk your story into paragraphs. And for now, mark a box around the sentences that you think go in a chunk. When you make the next draft, you can put in the paragraphs. We'll talk more about this at the share. Okay, writers, back to work!"

SHARE

Paragraphing

Convene writers. Tell the story of one child's writing in a way that demonstrates how that writer decided to use paragraphs.

"Writers, you all are doing smart, intense work reliving parts of your lives and writing it down from your insider's perspective. And I am really pleased that you are keeping one eye on your content, and one eye on your paragraphs. Earlier, Abraham reread his story about his cat, Ginger, and realized that his story had different sections in it, almost like different chapters. I'll show you how he added a code that signified a new paragraph. This is what he'd written," I said, reading from my chart paper copy of his story:

> Ginger stretched out on the carpet and yawned. I scratched behind her ears and she leaned her head into my hand. She purred. My mom was in the kitchen baking cookies. She was singing a Spanish song. She always sings when she's in the kitchen.

I selected an example that isn't subtle, and abbreviated it for this purpose. Minilessons aren't times to be subtle—the message goes by children too quickly.

"Abraham realized that his piece really had two parts: one about his cat and one about his mom," I said, and added the paragraph sign at the appropriate place. "Abraham was really smart because when he saw he had two topics, he paused and thought, 'If I have two topics, does this mean I have two stories? Or do they really fit together into one small moment, just not in one paragraph?' In this instance, he decided they belong in the same story because they are both parts of a longer story about Ginger eating one of his mom's chocolate chip cookies and getting sick. On Abraham's second draft, he'll leave a bit of white space between the first message and the next bit. That will give us, as readers, a chance to get ready for content that is a little bit new."

> Ginger stretched out on the carpet and yawned. I scratched behind her ears and she leaned her head into my hand. She purred.
>
> My mom was in the kitchen baking cookies. She was singing a Spanish song. She always sings when she's in the kitchen.

Paragraphs are more important than many people realize. When children learn to paragraph as they write, they are on their way towards internalizing the importance of structure in writing. If a child who is writing a narrative knows that each new step forward in time probably merits a new paragraph, this internalized feel for how writing goes will nudge the child to expand on rather than simply mention each incident. The child will know that writing in one–sentence paragraphs is not a reasonable option.

"In Abraham's story, the need for a new paragraph came from a new subtopic, but sometimes the need for a new paragraph comes because time has moved forward, and sometimes it comes because a new person is speaking."

Set children up to practice what you've taught. In this case, help them practice thinking about how to group sentences to alleviate dense, unbroken text.

"Right now, I'm going to give each set of partners a copy of Michela's draft. You will see that she is working on paragraphs, so she has boxed her story in ways that reflect the paragraph divisions she thinks will work. Each time she makes a new paragraph, would you and your partner think, 'Why does she think this is a new paragraph? Is it that time has moved forward? Is there a new subtopic? Is someone new talking? Has the story turned a corner?' Work with your partner to decide and jot the reason for the new paragraph beside the paragraph box that she made. There may be places where you disagree with her judgments. If so, write, 'We disagree because . . .' alongside the box and mark the text the way you would paragraph it." [Fig. XIII-2]

Getting ready to go to California

"Beep, Beep, Beep" the alarm clock went off. It was 4:00 in the morning.

"Go, Go, Go!" I screamed.

We peeled off our pajamas and jumped into our clothes as fast as we could.

"Get the toothbrushes, get the suitcases!" yelled my mom.

"Get the entertainment, get the extra pillows!" bellowed my dad.

"Where's my cell phone?" screamed my sister.

"Get everything!" I yelled.

"Honk, Honk!"

"The car service is here," I said, hitting my head with my palm.

We bolted out the door and slammed it behind us.

The car door opened with a creak and we hopped inside.

As the children read and marked the paragraphs in Michela's draft, I listened in. "Writers, I heard you doing some smart work as you read Michela's draft. You noticed lots of reasons for using paragraphs. Some of you noticed reasons for paragraphing we haven't even mentioned yet! Remember from now on as you write, to use these reasons to group your thoughts in paragraphs."

I'm mentioning things in passing that could easily be developed more fully!

Alternatively, I could have shown children a teacher-written draft and said, "Would you and you partner help this author paragraph this piece? Tell each other your reasons for recommending she make paragraphs where you think they belong."

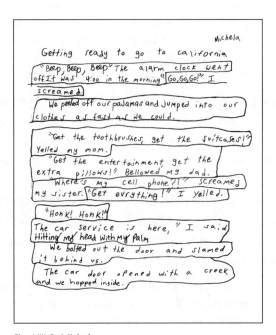

Fig. XIII-2 Michela

HOMEWORK *Paragraphing Text* Writers, I've typed up a short picture book for you with no paragraphs in it at all—I took them out! I did that so we can all experiment together with ways to make paragraphs. Tonight, read the entire excerpt first to get a sense of the story. Then, think about how paragraphs could best help this story make sense and have an effect on readers. When you decide the places you think make the most sense to paragraph, will you jot a note alongside it explaining the reason you paragraphed there? Tomorrow when you come to school, you and your partner can compare what you did with each other and then we can look at the actual book and discuss what the author chose to do. Then you'll have more thinking to draw from as you paragraph your own writing.

TAILORING YOUR TEACHING

If some of your students try to make a movie in their mind of the memory they want to storytell, but when they close their eyes, they say they don't see anything . . . you might want to try leading those students on some guided imagery practice. Begin by asking the group of children (or the child) to get comfortable and close their eyes. Then, ask the children to imagine they are somewhere you know they can picture like a park or a beach. At first, be very specific with the words you use to describe the place. You might say, "You are heading toward the ocean, but first you have to walk through the beach grass and climb up a giant beach dune. Your feet feel heavy and for every step you take, you slide back a step or two. At the top of the hill, you are surprised to see another dune." In later days when you practice guided imagery with the students, you can be less exact, removing a bit of the scaffolding. You might say, "You are heading to the ocean. Notice what is under your feet. How do you feel?" Your specific language in the beginning days of guided imagery practice will not only help children grow an image in their minds, it will also help them see ways to put together words to make images. After several sessions of guided imagery, some students may be ready to lead the guided imagery sessions themselves. Of course, getting images in their minds is only the first step to writing from within images, and in a fully constructed conference or minilesson you'll need to help children transfer what they've learned under your guidance to their own writing. "Remember how you closed your eyes and pictured yourself walking on the beach when we practiced guided imagery?" you might ask. Then, "Try that same process now. Where were you when this memory begins? Put yourself there and take a few steps, just like we did at the beach. Tell me what is happening. . . ."

You can use any short picture book for this exercise. We've sometimes used an excerpt from Bill Cosby's The Meanest Thing to Say.

One day, a new boy, Michael Reilly, came into our class. It didn't take long for him to start trouble— just until recess.

I walked to the basketball court with my friends— Andrew, José, and Kiku. My cousin, Fuchsia, was waiting for us. She's in a different class.

José was dribbling when Michael showed up.

"I know a better game," Michael said. "It's called Playing the Dozens. You get twelve chances to say something mean to a person."

ASSESSMENT

Earlier I emphasized the importance of trying your hand at the work you are asking children to do. Frankly, I want you not only to experience what it's like to write, I also want you to experience the rush that comes when you see your own writing improving. There are a few minilessons in this series that have special power to lift the level not only of the children's writing, but also of your own – so let me channel you towards them.

First of all, you do need to keep in mind that adults, like children, usually reach first towards big watermelon topics and our writing will be light years better if we instead write about a tiny seed story.

The paradox, however, is that it is much easier to write well if we select a story that matters to us. So you will find it helps to use a strategy like recalling a person you care about (I'll take my son Miles, for example), and then listing tiny 30-60 minute vignettes that you recall involving that person. I'd steer you to select a small moment that has seared itself into your memory. For example, I won't forget being at the beauty parlor, seeing my cell phone vibrate on the hair dresser's counter and thinking, "Who would call me now?" I picked up the phone, and it was a policeman saying, "Your son has been in a bad accident."

You'll have your own small moment; it needn't be a traumatic one but you will write the narrative more easily if the moment is one that you recall with crystal clarity. Those moments are, I believe, already congealed into coherent stories in our memory banks, and so when we write the story,

relive the story, those moments are easy to capture on paper.

Finally, I'd give yourself today's minilesson. It is very likely that when you first write the story you've selected, you stand outside the story, discussing it, rather than reliving it. A teacher I know wrote her first draft like this:

> After I got home, I went into the house and I could tell something was wrong. I realized the painters had painted the wrong wall!

After taking in the minilesson, she rewrote her draft doing her best to stay inside the story as she wrote it:

> I drove up the driveway, then stopped the car. Putting my keys into my bag, I thought, "I'm going straight to bed." But when I entered the kitchen, something seemed wrong. I stood in the doorway, letting my eyes scan the room. The oven was fine (no fire). The counters. Then my gaze fell on the wall, and for a moment I just stared. "What the..." I thought.

After going through the process of writing and then revising based on the minilesson she was about to teach, she felt much more equipped to help children do the same writing work.

WRITING IN PASSAGES OF THOUGHT:

PARAGRAPHING TO SUPPORT ELABORATION

IN THIS SESSION, YOU'LL SHOW CHILDREN HOW WRITERS CAN BRING OUT MORE OF THEIR STORIES BY WRITING WHOLE PARAGRAPHS FROM SINGLE KEY SENTENCES.

GETTING READY

- Instructions on chalkboard telling children to bring their writer's notebooks and sit with their partners in the meeting area
- Sample of a first draft, a child's or your own, with numbers inserted to indicate where the writer decided to elaborate (on chart paper or overhead transparency)
- Second page on which the numbered inserts are written (on chart paper or transparency)
- Sample of another child's writing that needs elaboration, for use as a class text (one copy per partnership)
- Example of another child's writing that illustrates elaboration
- Tool container on each table with sharpened pencils
- See CD-ROM for resources

One of the first essential skills to teach writers is the skill of elaboration. Inexperienced writers tend to write in what Mina Shaughnessy (1977) calls "sentences of thought" instead of "passages of thought." They write one sentence when a more skilled writer would write three sentences, or ten.

When a child writes, "I sat on the bench at the ball game. Then the game started. The first player made it to first base," we need to teach the child that the draft would be much stronger, the reader could more easily put herself in the narrator's place, if the child wrote two sentences for every one. "I sat on the bench at the ball game. It was still damp and the water soaked through my pants. Then the game started. People stopped talking and started watching. . . ." As humans, we need help empathizing with others—generally, the more we know about others, the more easily we can see ourselves in them and can put ourselves in their shoes. We need to teach our writers how to say enough to help the reader feel the person in the story.

Elaborating is important for more pedestrian reasons as well. The New York Times recently showcased research that showed that by considering length alone, one can accurately predict the score a student will receive on the new writing component of the SAT exam. The longer the answer, the higher the score. The Educational Testing Service, the designer of the test, has hastened to challenge that claim, but the research stands. On standardized tests, length matters. Elaboration matters.

I believe that one way to help children develop the habit of elaborating is to encourage them to think and write in paragraphs rather than sentences. If children begin to group their thinking in clusters of sentences, whole passages of thought, rather than in smaller clusters of words, they will draw more language, more thoughts, out of themselves and onto the page. Used in this way, paragraphing is not an afterthought or a postwriting organizational structure.

MINILESSON

Writing in Passages of Thought: Paragraphing to Support Elaboration

CONNECTION

Celebrate that your children are writing from inside their stories and not summarizing them from a distance.

"Writers, I love the way you are reliving parts of your life and writing down what it was like as though you are right in it all over again! Carl knew he wanted to write about his first checker game, so he made a tiny thumbnail sketch on his paper to remind himself of the topic for that page. He *could* have written, 'My opponent and I sat down and began to play.' Instead, what Carl did was he sat back and closed his eyes and really transported himself back to that moment. Then he played a movie in his mind of what happened at the very start of the checkers game, and then he told the story as though he were right there doing it all over again. Listen": [Fig. XIV-1]

> At my first game of checkers I sat down on my chair. I was getting ready for my match. I took a deep breath. I rubbed my hands together. Then I had my eyes glued to my opponent like I was going to murder him. He sat down with me. We started to shake hands to one another. I said may the best man win. My opponent had a strange little smile on his face.

"Many of you, like Carl, are taking the time to relive the moments you are writing about, and that's great for your writing!"

Create the context for today's lesson. Point out to children that many of their paragraphs are tiny, a signal that their texts are underdeveloped.

"Yesterday, you were not only reliving your stories, you were also starting to chunk your stories into parts that go together and parts that need a little space between them—you were making your writing into different paragraphs. What I learned yesterday as I watched you work is that right now, the way you are writing, a lot of you have zillions of tiny paragraphs! Now, on the one hand, that's wonderful, because that means you have zillions of small, step-by-step actions, and narrative writers all wish to spell out the small steps in a progression! But on the other hand, it's almost always true that your paragraphs deserve more than just one quick, thin sentence in them. Probably, each new micro-moment in your story needs more words and sentences."

COACHING

I am always pleased when minilessons dovetail together as this one does with others around it. This minilesson extends the teaching share from last session and leans towards the minilesson in the next session.

It makes sense that children will need additional scaffolding to have success with what we teach. So in this instance, you'll tell children that when their writing involves lots of tiny paragraphs, this is a signal that they need to elaborate more. Teach them that at the very least, elaborating means writing two sentences instead of one.

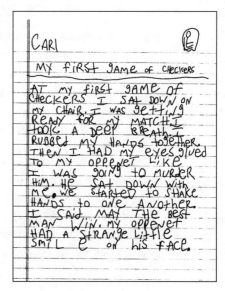

Fig. XIV-1 Carl

Name your teaching point. Tell children that tiny paragraphs signal a need for elaboration.

"Today I want to teach you that when your piece has lots of tiny paragraphs, this is a sign that you need to elaborate more. It means you need to say more about a topic, a moment, a scene before you move to the next paragraph. It's great to elaborate in your first drafts as you write, but you can also go back to a complete draft and realize there are places where you need to say more."

TEACHING

Spotlight one child's revisions in a way that illustrates elaboration.

"Let's look today at Michela's writing and let her teach us. Yesterday, we looked at how she boxed her writing into paragraphs. Remember how she found she had lots of one- and two-sentence paragraphs in her story? After Michela realized this, she inserted little numbers in her draft where she thought she could say more, and then on another sheet of paper, she wrote those numbers and additional sentences that could elaborate on her initial writing. Michela realized that in her first draft, she tended to write conversations but not actions or descriptions. In her revised version, she wrote not only what people say but also what they do, and she described the scene. This is her first draft with numbers inserted wherever she added more text:" [Fig. XIV-2]

Getting ready to go to California

"Beep, Beep, Beep" the alarm clock went off. It was 4:00 in the morning. *1 "Go, Go, Go!" I screamed. *2

We peeled off our pajamas and jumped into our clothes as fast as we could.

"Get the toothbrushes, get the suitcases!" yelled my mom. *3

"Get the entertainment, get the extra pillows!" bellowed my dad.

"Where's my cell phone?" screamed my sister. "Get everything!" I yelled. *4

"Honk, Honk!" *5

"The car service is here" I said, hitting my head with my palm.

We bolted out the door and slammed it behind us. *6

The car door opened with a creak and we hopped inside.

We can learn some qualities of good writing from the expert authors who write books on the topic – but some of the lessons that will matter for children will come simply from looking at children's work and thinking, "What next step might I suggest for this writer?"

I like using Michela as an example because her original draft isn't especially developed or strong, and yet she does an extraordinary amount of work on it. The model, then, conveys to all children that this work is doable.

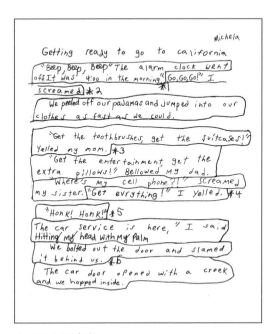

Fig. XIV-2 Michela

"Her next page (on which she'd written the inserts) looked like this." *[Fig. XIV-3]*

1. You'd think we would be exhausted but . . . we ran around in circles, trying to figure what to do.

2. Our birds whistled to cheer us on, saying "Run, run, run."

3. I was shoved into the small wooden bookcase as my sister ran to get the toothbrushes and suitcases.

4. It was a mad, mad house. Every which way people bumped into each other struggling to get ready. When we were finally ready we all plopped onto the couch. I let out a loud sigh and closed my eyes for a quick rest.

5. Suddenly the house was in motion again.

6. We ran down the dark, deserted street toward the blinking taillights.

Debrief. Extrapolate principles that can be deduced from the one example. Explain that writers can often see how to elaborate by looking for what they have left out of stories.

"In her next draft, Michela will intertwine the original draft and her inserts. Some of you may decide you need to do similar work to expand your paragraphs and to be sure readers really can picture the events in your narrative. If you aren't sure what to add to your paragraphs, it can help to think, 'What have I put into my story? What have I left out?' Good stories usually have actions, dialogue, descriptions, and thoughts. When you reread your drafts, think about which element of successful narratives you have already incorporated into your draft, and which you might still want to add."

ACTIVE ENGAGEMENT
Set children up to practice the strategy on a class text with partners.

"Remember Jake's story? Let's practice elaborating by pretending Jake's story is our story, and thinking, 'How could the paragraphs be a little longer?' Let's just look at the start to his story." *[Fig. XIV-4]*

I sat behind the bleachers waiting for my race to be called.

"Second and Third graders, please line up by the entrance," the announcer said.

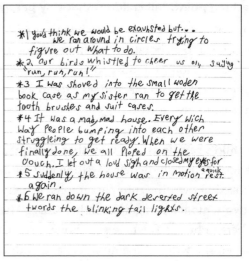

Fig. XIV-3 Michela

Your revisions will be more effective if they are informed by self-awareness. It is extremely telling to look at your own writing asking, "Do I include actions? Dialogue? Thoughts?" Most of us have ways we tend to write and we use those tried and true ways often.

Fig. XIV-4 Children practiced elaborating by trying to do so with Jake's lead.

"Would you and your partner read over this draft and think, 'What element of effective narrative does Jake tend to exclude in his story? Does he include dialogue? Small actions? Thoughts? The setting?' If you can figure out what is usually not there in his draft, then you know one way to elaborate on the draft. Please tell your partner what the writer could add."

After the children worked in partners for a bit, I reconvened the group. "Christina thought that Jake didn't include a lot of setting, so she and her partner invented ways he could add it. Christina especially added the setting in places where the paragraphs were a bit too short to be very meaningful."

> I sat behind the bleachers, waiting for my race to be called. All around me, kids stood about wearing the colors of their school. The sun was hot.

> "Second and Third graders, please line up by the entrance," the announcer said. From all parts of the crowd, kids separated from their friends and started to go toward the gate.

Joseph waved his hand. "We thought he could include what he was thinking, like wondering if he would win or not."

> I sat behind the bleachers, waiting for my race to be called. I wondered if all my practice would pay off. I wanted to win.

LINK
Restate today's lesson in a way that helps children see how to use it today and every day. Here, remind children that when they need to elaborate, they can think of what types of information are missing and add them.

"When you go off to write today and every day, remember you can elaborate on your sentences and paragraphs by adding actions, dialogue, descriptions, and thoughts, just like we did here together with Michela's and Jake's drafts. If you have zillions of tiny paragraphs and realize you need to elaborate, start today by rereading your draft and asking yourself, 'What have I put into my story? What have I left out?' Then you can mark where you want to add parts and write them into the next draft."

Someday, you'll want to help children cull through all the details they could add to choose the most meaningful ones – leaving the others behind. Someday, you'll explain to children that authors include (and exclude) different kinds of information for different reasons – dialogue has its place and time, as does description. For now, we want to banish kids' censors and loosen their inhibitions about writing. To write well, kids first need to write voluminously, not worrying whether the writing is marvelous or not.

WRITING AND CONFERRING

Focusing on English Language Learners

As these first few weeks of school fly by, you are quickly coming to know each one of the children who comprise your diverse classroom community. One of the things I love most about the writing workshop is the time I have to confer with each of these unique individuals. Conferring gives me the time to teach in a highly customized manner. One group of children who require this customized teaching are those whose first language is not English. In New York City these children are called English Language Learners (ELLs).

A single description cannot adequately represent this diverse group of learners. Each English Language Learner is different and will need a different kind of attention. We must take care not to assume that because these children share a designation, they also share strengths and weaknesses. Thank goodness for the writing workshop—a time in the day when the bulk of instruction is responsive and based on assessments.

When studying ELLs, it is helpful to understand that many grammatical errors are due to assumptions the children make about English based on their native language. English doesn't work in the same manner as many other languages and this causes children confusion. In Spanish, for example, the adjective follows the noun, so the child says "la casa blanca," not "the white house." If a child whose first language is Spanish writes "the flower blue," we can acknowledge that if the child were writing in Spanish, this would be perfect, but in English, the words are sequenced differently.

MID-WORKSHOP TEACHING POINT **_Answering Readers' Questions_** "Writers, can I have your eyes and your attention? I was just conferring with Simeon, whose writing the teachers and I examined earlier this month (see Session VI). Simeon discovered a way to elaborate by thinking about questions the reader might have and adding the word _because_ to expand and clarify what he was saying. First he wrote this sentence." [Fig. XIV-5]

> When I went in everybody looked and laughed at me.

"Then he thought about the reader. Would the reader understand why everyone was laughing at him? So he went back and added the word _because_ and that pushed him to say more."

> When I went in everybody looked and laughed at me because I was covered with mud.

"Sometimes, when you are reading your writing, think about your readers' possible questions, like Simeon did, and try to answer them. One way to do this is by adding _because_. We make things clearer by answering questions like why, what, who, or when."

Simeon

One day it was a rainy day and I had on a pink tuxedo and it was my cousins wedding so I was so exited I ran to her I was like "are you exited I said "yeah" she said so I ran to my dad and then I fell in the mudd and I was messed up so I got so mad that I felt to hit some body when I went in every body looked and laued at me I was so scared that she might not want me to carry the rings

Fig. XIV-5 Simeon

Another area that will improve a child's writing as well as their comprehension is language and vocabulary development. Expanding a child's vocabulary will help the child elaborate, make a text cohesive, and communicate complex ideas. For example, when Ahra first wrote about a thunderstorm, she wrote with the basic facts only. [Fig. XIV-6]

> One night when I went to sleep, I heard a thunderstorm. I saw a lot of rain. I thought it was a hurricane. When the storm came I hide under my blanket all over again. Finally, the storm has cleared.

When I conferred with Ahra, we brainstormed words and phrases that come to mind when we think of a thunderstorm: loud, boom, pow, like fireworks, hard rain, dark, wind blowing, hot, humid, lightning bright as day, trees swaying back and forth. She then sketched a quick picture of the scene, labeling the picture with the English words that I helped her access. The labeled sketch, then, functioned as a personal word-bank when she shifted from sketching to writing. Ahra's text was vastly richer as a result, but more importantly she devised a strategy she can use again when she writes. She learned she can brainstorm or research words she may need before she starts writing [Fig. XIV-7].

> It was a hot and humid night. I went to bed around 7:30 pm. It was dark in my room. My grandma was sleeping in the bed next to me. The wind started to blow as hard as a hurricane.
> I got out of my bed and looked out my window. I saw the trees swaying back and forth like they were dancing. Then the lightning started. The lightning made the sky look like it was daytime. Then came the thunder, BOOM! POW! which sounded like fireworks. Then it started to rain, which sounded like a waterfall. I started to get scared.
> I hid under my blanket. I was so scared. I started to shiver and I screamed. My grandma said, Don't worry. It's okay."

Once I help equip a child with some tools of language that enable her to tell a story more fully, I can move to support the child with some of the smaller words and sentence level details. By focusing on one or two things at a time, I can push a child toward becoming a more successful writer.

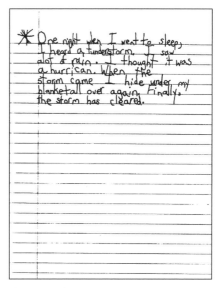

Fig. XIV-6 Ahra

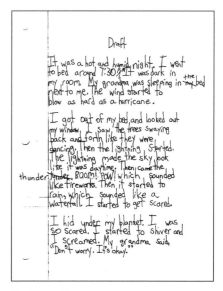

Fig. XIV-7 Ahra

SHARE

Listening to Elaboration

Remind children of the day's teaching. Invite them to share their work with a partner. Share one example of elaboration. Remind children to try this whenever the context calls for it.

"Writers, can I have your eyes and your attention? Many of you tried to elaborate on your sentences and paragraphs today by adding actions, dialogue, descriptions, and thoughts. Your writing seems to be growing before my very eyes. Nice work."

"Take a moment and show your partner a place where you elaborated on a sentence or a paragraph." They did. "Writers, let me share with you what Cameron did to expand upon his story about the tennis match. When Cameron reread his story, he decided to revise it. He added numbers into his draft as we saw Michela doing earlier, and then on another page wrote text he'd like to insert. *(Fig. XIV-8)* For example, he wrote a #1 beside:"

> I looked towards Cafelnnacaulf from the front row. He tossed the ball into the sky and I kept my eyes focused on the ball, as the racket smashed the ball I thought it must have been going 100 mph, because it landed in the box.

Revision *(Fig. XIV-9)*:

> It hit the cushioned wall. It came hurling toward me and the speed decreased slowly but surely by about 60 mph.

"Writers reread their writing thinking about the reader. Then they add to places where they want the reader to see and feel exactly what they did, just like many of you are trying to do. Remember to elaborate on your tiny paragraphs in any of the ways we learned today whenever you need the reader to really be there!"

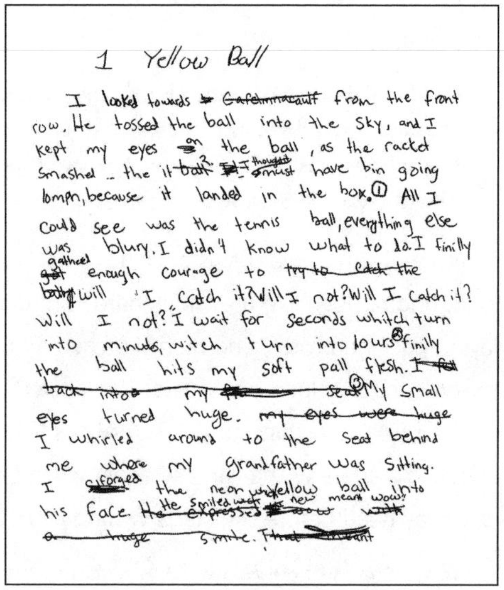

Fig. XIV-8 Cameron's first draft

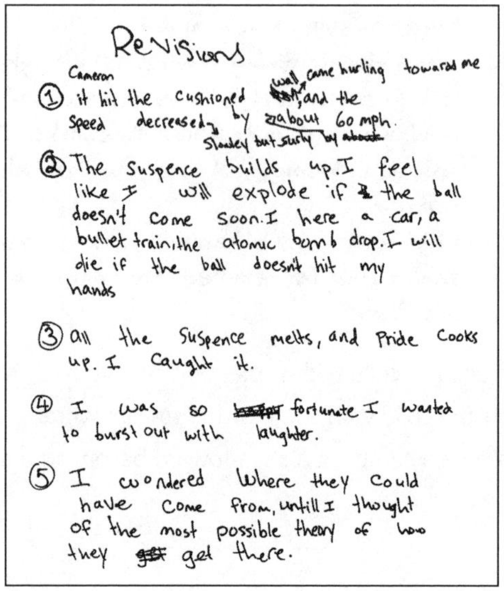

Fig. XIV-9 Cameron's revision

HOMEWORK *Building Paragraphs, Elaborating on Each Sentence* I was in the convenience store last night and the store was offering several "2 for 1" specials. "Buy two bags of chips for the price of one." "Buy two deodorants for the price of one." I liked this idea. It made me think of our writing. What would happen if every sentence offered the same "2 for 1" deal as my local convenience store? How would that work?

If we start with one sentence from our fire drill story, "We got to the second floor at the same time as the first graders," can we get two sentences out of that one image? "Some of them looked nervous and they were very quiet!" You might elaborate on that sentence in a different way. Think about our talk, what we saw and heard, and what we felt and thought, because this is one way to elaborate on stories.

For homework, return to some of your one-sentence notepad entries and try to elaborate on them using the strategies you have learned so far. We have learned that writers can elaborate on a sentence by adding specific actions, dialogue, descriptions, and thoughts. This evening try elaborating on your single entries using the same strategies.

TAILORING YOUR TEACHING This session is an important one to revisit throughout the year, no matter what genre is being studied. After you have read through your students' drafts, you will have a better sense of their understanding, not only of paragraphs, but their methods of elaboration. Most children tend to find and use one favorite way to elaborate, like adding dialogue.

If your children tend to overuse dialogue as a method of elaboration . . . you will want to follow up this session with a lesson on how to balance the actual talk included with actions and internal thinking. You can point out what you have learned about what they have tended to put in and what they have tended to leave out.

"Writers, yesterday as I was conferring with all of you, I noticed that many of you have tried to elaborate by adding dialogue. And that is definitely one way to elaborate. But we also want to make sure we keep a balance and use dialogue where it will have the biggest impact and support your meaning. Today I am going to teach you that you can also elaborate by adding actions." Then you can use a text like Julie Brinckloe's *Fireflies!* to show how she surrounds her dialogue with lots of actions that show the reason for the dialogue. Ask children to practice by finding places in the class story where they can add more actions that will help create a clearer picture in the reader's mind. Suggest that this is something they can do anytime they want to elaborate on one of their sentences or paragraphs.

You need to remember the importance of helping children speak in paragraphs, rather than in short phrases or single sentences. We often settle for the first words a child expresses. Just think how much more we might hear by simply asking each child to say more. Of course we will want to teach some explicit strategies for elaboration, such as remembering exact actions, dialogue, descriptions and thoughts. But, by helping children speak in paragraphs rather than short expressions or individual words, we help increase not only their fluency, but their confidence as well.

MECHANICS

During the time in your day set aside for mechanics, you will want to show children how they can use their writer's notebook as a place to practice and get control over whatever you've been teaching them. So if you have taught them ten high-frequency words, you can ask children to reread the entries they've written since the beginning of the year, double-checking that they have spelled those word wall words correctly.

You will have a handful of children for whom the word wall words are No Big Deal. You'll want to gather these strong spellers and tell them that you know that often the work you teach the rest of the class during mechanics time will be easy for them. Ask whether they are game to do some advanced work, working together in a small group. They will probably be thrilled at the suggestion.

If you are working with the rest of the class on spelling, you may suggest your strong spellers reread their own writing to check for spellings they think may not be right (they need to learn to ascertain this for themselves) and then bring their writing to someone. While most of the class is looking at *because* and discussing what they notice about how it is spelled, these strong spellers can do similar work with their words. While most of the class takes a spelling quiz on Fridays, the strong spellers can figure out how to quiz each other.

Meanwhile, you will have some children who do not even find it easy to spell the word wall words correctly as they write. Teach these children that when they come to a stopping place in their writing, it is helpful to

reread it, and to choose the lens they will use to guide their rereading. (Sometimes they need to reread simply to regain momentum and remind themselves of what they have written so they can add on. If that is their goal, it is fine for them to overlook misspellings as they reread.) Sometimes they will want to reread to check their spellings. Teach children to mark—to underline or circle or leave a marginal dot—words they believe may be misspelled.

A child may think that twenty of his words are misspelled, and it is not reasonable for that child to look up twenty words per page in the dictionary! So don't suggest that once a child has marked a word as "probably wrong" she necessarily needs to fix it. It is very important for children to get better at simply sensing when a word isn't right. This, in and of itself, is a very helpful skill because that child can then work on that spelling if the writing will be public and accuracy therefore matters. But I do suggest asking children to repair the spellings on any word wall words that they've misspelled. Make sure that even your most struggling writer knows how to use the word wall as a sort of enlarged dictionary.

You do not need to wait until the child is officially editing a piece for publication before asking the child to repair his or her misspellings of word wall words. Your goal is to have children spell those words accurately and automatically whenever they write them, so at any point in the writing process you can remind children to double-check that they have done this.

GETTING READY

- Instructions on chalkboard telling children to bring their writer's notebooks to the meeting area
- Sample draft of a child's piece of writing that needs revision, written on chart paper
- Guest speaker—the child whose piece needs to be revised (prepare the child ahead of time so the child knows what to expect)
- Child's version of the class story you used in the timeline session, written on chart paper
- *Shortcut* (Donald Crews)
- Scissors and tape
- Chart paper and markers
- See CD-ROM for resources

DEVELOPING THE HEART OF A STORY:
REVISION

The day the very first copies of my book The Art of Teaching Reading arrived, a few teachers were beside me watching while I, with trembling hands, opened the box and brought out one copy of the book. My hand ran over the glossy cover with delight. I clasped the book against me, loving its heft. "I can't imagine you wrote all those words!" one of the teachers said. I remember thinking, "If she only knew." The words that I held with such pride were just the tip of the iceberg. In making that one book, I had written hundreds of thousands of words that no one would ever see. When people build houses, they fill a truck-sized trailer with the rejected materials. When I write, I need one of those trailers parked next to my desk.

In life, I go through my days knowing that the work I do will go into the world, good or bad, as it is. In life, I can't take back my words. As I move through my days, if I am clumsy or hurtful or obscure, I can't rewind and make myself into a more agile or lucid or savvy person. I can't call back a speech I have given, a workshop I have led, a meeting I have facilitated, a conversation I have participated in. But I can call back my writing, and I can take whatever I've done and make it much, much better. Revising my writing (and in doing so, revising myself) is a great and powerful opportunity. Revision is my favorite part of the writing process. It is pure pleasure to be able to stand back, scan what I've written, and think, "How can I make my best work better?"

Children, however, often come into our classrooms dreading revision. We cannot tarry a moment, then, before inviting children to see revision in a whole new light. In this session you let children know that revision begins with selection. Writers reread and say, "This is my best work." We revise because the work merits the compliment of revision. And then revision itself is all about giving a piece of writing the respect, the listening attention that will allow that piece to become even stronger. The most important thing I do when I revise is to find the life in my piece, and create space for it. I say, "This is beautiful." When children see their own work become dramatically stronger through revision, sermons on the importance of revision are not necessary. That is our work in today's session.

MINILESSON

Developing the Heart of a Story: Revision

CONNECTION

Remind writers of the work they've been doing; rally their energies toward revision.

"Writers, you have been using timelines to develop your ideas, you have been paragraphing and elaborating on each paragraph, you've been experiencing the writing process that writers go through with every piece. Now many of you are about to finish drafting your second story. When writers have a collection of drafts, writers often look over the drafts of several stories (you have two) and select the best piece to really delve into and revise."

"I talked to a few of you earlier today about revision and I learned something surprising. I learned some of you don't like to revise! Some of you actually think of revision as something you have to do when you aren't writing well enough! So today I want to set you straight. When your writing is lousy, you throw it out. When your writing is alive and beautiful and full of potential, you revise it. Revision is a compliment to good writing!"

Name the teaching point. In this case, tell writers that revision is not about fixing errors; it is about finding and developing potentially great writing, sometimes by adding more to the heart of the story.

"More specifically, I want to teach you today that revision is about finding and developing the potential in your piece. This means, first of all, that when we revise, we return to drafts that seem promising to us. So today you'll reread both the stories you've written and decide which one has special promise; that will be the piece you revise and publish."

"And then, once it is time to settle into serious revision, you again need to reread, asking, 'Which section of this do I think works especially well?' That is, after looking for the piece that is good enough to revise, you look for the *section* that is the heart of it!"

"Usually in any story, there will be a part where the readers should pull in to listen—the part that really matters, the heart of a story. And one important thing we can do when we revise is find the heart of a story and develop it further."

"So revision is not about cleaning up messes; it is about finding and developing powerful writing, and one way we develop writing is by adding more to the important parts of the story."

COACHING

Stories often begin by setting a character into a setting and in a sense, this minilesson (like so many others) establishes the setting, the content, for today's teaching. If your students seem to have no resistance around revision, you will not want to begin the minilesson this way. If they have no reason to have reservations about revision, why offer them any? On the other hand, if you know there is resistance to revision in the air, acknowledging it may be the best way to begin.

In the K-2 Units of Study, *the fourth unit is* Revision *and the unit starts with me asking children if they are very proud of the piece they just published. After children respond with the resounding 'yes.' I tell them, "Because when writers really like a piece of writing, we revise it." In that unit, children not only revise their recently published piece, they also go back and scour their folders for other pieces "that are good enough to be revisited."*

TEACHING
Spotlight what one child did in a way that illustrates the teaching point. Retell the story of the process.

"Yesterday, Gregory did some powerful revision work. I want to tell you the story of his revision because some of you may want to follow his example. When I pulled my chair alongside Gregory, he'd already written a quick draft about the day he learned that his fish, Al, had died. I told him that what I usually do after I've finished a draft is reread it, thinking, 'What's the most important part of this story? What's the heart of this story?' So Gregory reread his draft. I copied it onto chart paper so you can see it." [Fig. XV-1]

> **Al is Dead**
>
> Dead. Ever since I had fish, I had Al: the best algae-eater in the world. Once I heard he was dead, I did not cry. I just was still. Then I asked, "Where is he?" My Dad said, "In the trash." I asked to see him. I saw it was true. My Dad put him back. For a second, I thought, then I said, "We can give him a funeral." My Dad looked doubtful for a minute but I picked him up and said, "He was special." Then I cried. Al was gone.

"Gregory reread his story, looking for what he thought was the heart of the story; then he motioned to a line in the middle of the draft: 'I asked to see him. I saw it was true.' Gregory said, 'That's the most important part. That was the saddest part.'"

"Gregory," I said. "After I find the most important section in a story, I cut my page apart like this." At this point I started cutting the chart-paper version of his story into two at the place he'd identified. "Then I tape a lot more paper into that important section of the draft." I taped a half page of chart paper into his story. "Then I reread up to those blank lines, and try to make a movie in my mind of exactly what happened. And I write the story of that moment, trying to tell it with more details." To get Gregory started, I read his draft aloud to him, stopping at the section he'd identified.

Then I imagined aloud what Gregory might say for just another sentence or two, trying to give him an idea for what I meant by stretching out the important part. "I walked over to the trash can and looked in. I saw . . ." Then I said, "Take it, Gregory."

" . . . lots of trash . . ."

"Be exact. What exactly did you see? If you can't remember, make it up," I said, and repeated what I'd already said to give him a new jump start.

By now you have seen that there are several common methods you can use in the teaching component of a minilesson. You can write publicly or bring in writing you have done at home. You can tell children about a published author's process or show the author's work. You can reenact a conference you had with a child, or you can retell the story of a child's process. Another option is to invite the child to be a guest speaker, telling the class what he did to make his writing better. Knowing this list of options should enable you to invent minilessons more easily, and to realize that you could teach the same content about writing in any one of many different ways. In this Teaching component, I retell the story of one child's process of revision.

Notice that I copied this story onto chart paper for the purposes of this minilesson.

This draft is a great favorite of mine. Read it aloud well. Your children should get goose bumps!

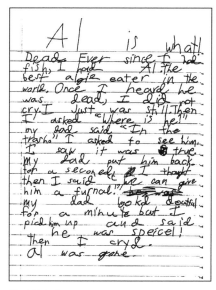

Fig. XV-1 Gregory

Gregory reiterated the last line of the story and then added on to it.

"I walked over to the trash can and I opened it. I looked in and saw . . . wet paper towels, orange peels, and a pile of coffee grounds."

"Keep going. What exactly did you do?" I said.

"I picked up Al."

"Be exact. What *exactly* did you do? What did you say?"

"I flicked off the coffee grounds, and said, 'Al, I'm gonna miss you.'"

Debrief. Point out what the one child did to find and develop the heart of his story.

"Class, do you see what Gregory did? He reread his story, determined that this part about looking in the trash can and seeing his beloved fish was the heart of the story, and then he added a chunk of paper right at that section of the story. He went back, recalled exactly what happened, and wrote that section with much more detail:"

First draft

> Dead. Ever since I had fish, I had Al: the best algae-eater in the world. Once I heard he was dead, I did not cry. I was just still. Then I asked, "Where is he?" My Dad said, "In the trash."

Insert added to the second draft

> I asked to see him. I walked over to the trash can and I opened it. I looked in and saw wet paper towels, orange peels and a pile of coffee grounds. I picked up Al. I flicked the coffee grounds, and said, "Al, my friend. I'm gonna miss you." My dad put him back. For a second, I thought, then I said, "We can give him a funeral." My dad looked doubtful for a minute but I picked him up and said, "He was special." Then I cried. Al was gone.

"Today you'll want to look at the two stories you have now written in rough draft form. Decide which you like best—which is worthy of revision. Try this revision strategy once you have selected the story you want to revise. Reread your story, find the heart of it, and then develop that section of your text."

Details are magic. These details transform this story. Notice that my interjections are lean. I do not want to overwhelm his story. But my prompts are calculated. I shift Gregory from generalizations to specifics of what he saw, what he did, what he said.

When I debrief, I try to describe the actions a writer has taken that are transferable to another day, another piece. I describe what the writer has done in a step-by-step manner, because this is meant to serve as a how-to text for the class.

Be explaining that every child in the room can follow in Gregory's path, finding the heart of a story and expanding on it as Gregory has done, I show children that Gregory's work is replicable and worth replicating — and it is! This revision strategy has proven to be accessible and powerful.

ACTIVE ENGAGEMENT
Set children up to do similar work on the class story.

"Let's practice it. Let's revisit our class story about the dragonfly and develop the heart of it. I've written a version of that dragonfly story on this chart paper. Would you each pretend it is your personal story and reread it, trying to find the heart of it? Then think how you could tell that one part with more detail. Let me read it aloud."

> We were so quiet, we could probably have heard ants crawling along the floor. We were barely breathing. Then our teacher stopped reading, just for a minute, and we were just about to say, 'NO! Don't stop! It's the most exciting part!' But she was looking at Jonathan because he was looking up at the top of the bookshelf where a dragonfly had landed. 'He wants to listen to the story,' we said.

"Tell your partners where the heart of this story might be for you. Make a movie in your mind of what happened at that part and tell your partner how you'd stretch that part out. Write it in the air with details. " I gave them a few minutes to do this.

"Okay, writers, can I have your eyes and your attention? Most of you felt that the heart of this story was right at the end, when the whole class saw the dragonfly. If we hadn't spotted our unexpected visitor, the day would have been like any other. I heard lots of you adding details to embellish (that's a word for 'add on to') that part," I said, and began to write what I'd heard them say. "Milan, you said this:"

> The dragonfly was perched on the highest shelf.

"Jonathan, you added this next bit."

> It was purple and green.

"What else could we add?"
Ahra dictated, "It twinkled like tinfoil."
I nodded and transcribed as directed. Then I said, "I think we should tell what we did. Did we say something or do something?"
"The dragonfly was so beautiful that we all gasped," Sam said. I added this and then read the entire story aloud again, starting from the very beginning:

Of course, there is no one right answer to the question "What is the heart of this story?" If children choose a part and have reasons for their choice, they could certainly take the story in that direction. Theoretically, it could be valuable to let children discuss their decisions about which part is the heart of the story. But for now, you will probably decide to keep the minilesson as lean as possible.

I love this revision strategy because essentially we are asking children to do what they've worked hard to learn to do—make a movie in their mind, telling the story in a step-by-step way. But now they're doing this to expand a moment within the moment. They should have a lot of success with this.

When I say, "Write in the air" I am asking children to dictate to a partner the exact words they would write if they were writing instead of talking. I take some time to explicitly teach children what this injunction means.

We were so quiet, we could probably have heard ants crawling along the floor. Then our teacher stopped reading and we were just about to say, "Don't stop! It's the most exciting part!"

But she was looking at Jonathan because he was looking up at the top of the bookshelf. We all followed her gaze and there, perched on the highest shelf, was a green and purple dragonfly that twinkled like tinfoil. It was so beautiful that we all gasped. "He wants to listen to the story," we said.

LINK

Summarize the lesson in a way that directs children through the steps of using this strategy.

"Writers, you really revised this story! You reread it, found the heart of it, and added more to the part where readers should really sit up and take note. That's what writers do all the time when we revise! You can do that every time you have a really deserving draft in front of you. I can't wait to see how you stretch out the heart of the story you pick to revise—if you decide you need to do that!"

Remind children to be job captains for themselves.

"Once you decide on your best story, remember that you need to be job captain for yourself, and figure out what jobs you need to do to make your story the best in the world. You may decide to divide it into paragraphs if you haven't done that already and to use codes—perhaps numbers inserted into the text—to help you elaborate by writing two sentences instead of one. You may decide to find the heart of your story, and then make a movie of it in your mind, adding details to stretch it out. You may have other ideas for how to make this story so, so much better. We'll be revising for a few days and editing. Then we will have a gigantic author celebration in which we publish the best of our two stories. Okay, writers, get going."

We are not obligated to include every child's suggestion every time. If we elaborate on the heart of this class story with empty words and cumbersome phrases, the whole lesson falls flat. If children can feel the story improve, if they can feel that this kind of revision helps, then they will be drawn to the strategy. If you worry that the suggestions for revision of the class story that kids make won't be strong, ask them to turn and talk with their partners about what they'd add. Walk among them, listening in for suggestions to take. If there are none, let that inform your teaching for tomorrow! In the meantime, make up great suggestions yourself!

Notice that in this minilesson, as in most minilessons, I leave children aware of their options for the day ahead. Just because I've taught something in a minilesson doesn't mean everyone must spend the workshop doing the content of that day's minilesson.

WRITING AND CONFERRING

Getting Children Off to a Strong Start

In today's minilesson you sang praises to revision, but the real sales job will need to occur now, during the work session. Today your children will reread their two stories and choose the one they like best. Once they've made a choice, affirm their decision. "I can tell this story is really important to you, isn't it?" you can ask. You may not be able to discern this from what's on the page, but clearly the writer has weighed in on this story. Then help each writer decide what he or she wants to do to revise. Many children will decide to locate the heart of their story, and to use all they know about writing strong narratives to stretch out this section. When you talk with children, you can make this revision much more powerful if your conferring is informed by two principles.

The first is this: If the writer can determine what it is she really wants to say in a piece, then this decision needs to steer her efforts to elaborate. This means that it helps if you ask, "Why do you think this is the story you decided to write? What do you really want to say to the world through this story?" You can help a writer realize that her story about bees descending on a class picnic is really a story about a week when everything seemed to be a disappointment. Alternatively, the same sequence of events could really be a story about how three best friends make even a class picnic into an adventure. In a conference, you can show a child that the same story can be told in different ways. Once a writer has decided what he or she really wants to say, this decision can inform the writer's choice of where and how to elaborate.

A second principle is this: everything you know about effective stories can inform your conferring. For example, you know that stories have settings. If a child seems at a loss for how he could improve a draft, you could always point out that he is writing a story, and like the stories read during reading workshop, his story needs to have a setting. Similarly, the child might consider the characters in his story. Has he made them seem real?

The results of this revision work are often amazing, and children feel this when you read what they've written. The author thinks, "Wow! I wrote that! It's really good!"

> **MID-WORKSHOP TEACHING POINT**   *Inserting Paper to Help Revision*   "Writers, can I have your eyes and your attention? As I watch you work today, cutting your draft apart and adding more space into it, I am reminded that writing is more like playing in clay than inscribing in marble. You are all realizing that drafts can be cut and spliced. Ellie did something smart. She realized that she didn't like her lead sentence, so she wrote a new lead and taped it on top of the old one! And Isaiah realized that he needed to expand not just one section of his draft (the heart of it) but also another section where things weren't that clear. So he sliced open his draft in two different places, inserting some extra paper into both spaces."
>
> "I want to remind you of another system for making drafts malleable. Remember how Michela put little numbers into her draft and then, on another sheet of paper, wrote what she wanted to add next to that number? You can do something similar, if you want."
>
> "Okay, writers, you can return to your work now."

SHARE

Expand Key Sections By Bringing Out the Internal Story

Highlight a child who took the minilesson to heart. Tell the story of that child's work in a way others can learn from.

"Writers, today many of you tried to find and develop the heart of your story. Let me show you how Michela stretched out the important part of her story. First she wrote her story step-by-step. Listen to this first version." *[Fig. XV-2]*

First Version

> It was the night before Halloween, my Mom comes in the door. "Mommy, Mommy, Mommy," I shout. I run to her giving her a hug and a kiss. Then I notice she's carrying a little tiny brown box. "Pitter pat, pitter pat." Something's moving around inside of the box! I squeeze her arm. "What is it Mommy, what is it?"* My mom slowly opens the box as if she was afraid something would pop out. I peer into the box. An animal with black beady little eyes, a small orange beak and a pair of wings looks up at me with its head cocked to one side. "It's a bird!" I shout. "A bird?" My sister Alex comes running. She peers into the box. "He's sooo cute," says Alex. "What should we name him?" I ask. "I've got the perfect name, we'll name him Twinkle." Twinkle whistles. "Then Twinkle it is!" says Alex. Then we hurry off to bed and go to sleep dreaming of our new pet.

"Then Michela realized she'd rushed past an important part—the suspense of opening the box. So she rewrote that section of the story, using a star as a code to show where she'd add the new section. What I want you to notice is that Michela stretched out the important section of her story by telling not only what she and her mother did, but also what she thought. This is an important strategy writers use often. We don't only tell the external story,

> When I got my bird
>
> It was the night before Halloween, my Mom comes in the door. "Mommy, Mommy, Mommy!" I shout. I run to her giving her a hug and a kiss. Then I notice she's carrying a little tiny brown box. "Pitter Pat, Pitter Pat" something's moving around inside of the box! I squeeze her arm. "What is it Mommy, What is it?* My Mom slowly opens the box as if she was afraid something would pop out. I peer into the box. A animal with black beady little eyes, a small orange beak and a pair of wings looks up at me with it's head cocked to one side. "It's a bird!" I shout. "A bird?" My sister Alex, comes running. she peers into the box. "He is soooo cute" says Alex. "What should we name him? I ask. "I've got the perfect name, we'll name him twinkle!" Twinkle wistle's. "Then twinkle it is!" say's Alex. Then we Hurry of to bed and go to sleep, dreaming of our new pet.

Fig. XV-2 Michela

the sequence of actions that can be plotted on a timeline. We also tell the internal story, as Michela does in this instance. Listen for how she shows what she thought as she stared at the box in her mother's hands:" *[Fig. XV-3]*

> What could be in that box? I wondered.
>
> "Pitter pat, pitter pat!" a noise came from the box.
>
> "Pitter pat, pitter pat!" There it was again for a second time. Something was moving inside that box." Maybe there's a monster in there!" I thought. "A mini one!" I started backing away slowly.
>
> "What's in the box, Mommy?" I asked. "A monster?"
>
> "No, no," said my mom.

"This is such important work that, writers, I'm going to ask you to take out a sheet of paper and write just the heart of your story on that paper, telling what you did in small steps, and telling also the internal story, as Michela taught us to do. And for the rest of your life, always remember that writers write not only the external but also the internal story."

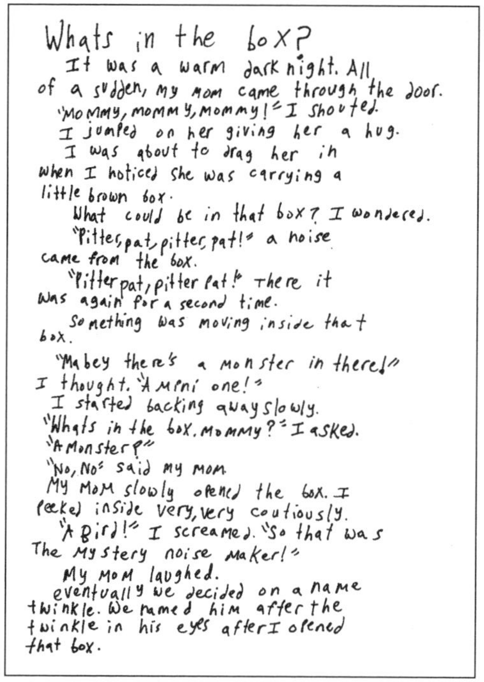

> Whats in the box?
> It was a warm dark night. All of a sudden, my mom came through the door. "Mommy, mommy, mommy!" I shouted. I jumped on her giving her a hug. I was about to drag her in when I noticed she was carrying a little brown box.
> What could be in that box? I wondered.
> "Pitter pat, pitter pat!" a noise came from the box.
> "Pitter pat, pitter pat!" There it was again for a second time.
> Something was moving inside that box.
> "Mabey there's a monster in there!" I thought. "A mini one!"
> I started backing away slowly.
> "Whats in the box, Mommy?" I asked. "A Monster?"
> "No, No" said my mom.
> My mom slowly opened the box. I peeked inside very, very coutiously.
> "A Bird!" I screamed. "So that was The mystery noise maker!"
> My mom laughed.
> eventually we decided on a name twinkle. We named him after the twinkle in his eyes after I opened that box.

Fig. XV-3 Michela's Insert

⊙ HOMEWORK ***Bringing Out the Internal Story*** Writers, in another few days we will hold our first Author Celebration of the year. You could say that we are approaching our first deadline, then. For me, however, the word *deadline* is all wrong. When I know I need to hurry and make my writing ready for publication, I feel as if I've been given not a *deadline*, but a *lifeline*. Tonight is one of your last chances to add more to the heart of your story, so spring to life! In your writer's notepad, take time to try one final, best-in-the-world draft of just the heart of your story.

Take a key moment in the story. Begin by timelining that episode on the page or across your fingers or in your mind. The manner in which you do this doesn't matter but it does matter that you recall the step by step, moment by moment sequence of events. Now recall how the story started. Where, exactly, were you and what, exactly, were you doing? Make a movie in your mind and record the start—write what you said, what you did. Then continue writing the movie as it spins out in your mind, but this time remember to use words that access the internal as well as the external story. Write, I thought . . . I noticed . . . I remembered . . . I wanted to say . . .

Bring this to school, of course, and you'll have a chance to insert it into your draft.

TAILORING YOUR TEACHING As publication day comes closer, you'll find yourself wanting to shoehorn in all the lessons you haven't yet had a chance to teach. It's probably wiser to remember that you have an entire year ahead of you, and many of those lessons are probably best reserved for a later unit of study. For now, you may want to shift towards teaching children that the rhythm of writing changes when we can see a publication date around the next bend. For one thing, writers become readers, rereading our own work and asking, "How will someone else read this?"

If you decide to teach children to anticipate their readers responses and to revise accordingly . . . you may want to tell children that as publication date nears, writers need one thing more than anything else. We need the gift of an honest, attentive reader, one who will truly listen to what we have written and who will help us understand places in our text which are confusing, places where the reader goes, "Huh?" These very special readers need to be honest, but also supportive. Don Murray, my writing teacher, once summed up the role of a writing partner this way: "Above all, the writer needs to leave, wanting to write." So listen and ask questions, yes; listen and convey when you are a bit confused, yes; but communicate also that you are dying to understand this writer's very important content.

MECHANICS

At this early stage in the school year, we need to determine our priorities regarding the conventions of written language that we will teach our children. High on my list would be conveying that conventions matter enough that children should take the extra ten seconds to stick a period at the end of what they believe to be a sentence, and should recall, for just a second, that *said* and *say* are the same words, really, and that the spelling of *say* is a good reminder that *said* contains the vowel *a*.

But while I'm playing Tough Guy Enforcer with bottom-line mechanics and spelling expectations, I also want to demonstrate that as a writer, I'm ravenously hungry to learn interesting and wonderful ways in which other writers use the conventions of written language. I want to model that sometimes I read a sentence that an author has written, and I just gape over the sounds of it, and the punctuation that created those sounds.

Crews' story *Shortcut,* which opens with some inventive and effective punctuation is a perfect place to begin. Ellipses aren't threatening to anyone. Children haven't usually been subjected to years of drills on ellipses, or seen their papers scrawled with red because they've gotten ellipses wrong. So marvel at the ellipses at the start of Crews' story:

> We looked . . .
> We listened . . .
> We decided to take
> the shortcut home.

Invite kids to join you in speculating over why Crews decided to use ellipses. How would the story have been different had he written it like this: "We looked. We listened. We decided to take the shortcut home"?

I'm not sure there is a right answer to that question. I suspect that in

this instance, the ellipses represent time going by, and they convey that the children stood still on the train tracks, looking and listening, for a long time. They deliberated. Had the text not had those ellipses, I think I'd imagine the children took a quick, fleeting look up and down the tracks and, after seeing and hearing nothing, made their decision.

Then, too, I love thinking about why some of Crews' paragraphs are longer and some are incredibly short. While the children did lots of things, simultaneously, as they walked down the tracks, Crews' writing looks like this:

> We laughed. We shouted. We sang.
> We tussled. We threw stones.

When the sound of the approaching train makes time freeze and hearts stop, Crews' paragraphs (and pages) are incredibly abrupt:

> "I HEAR A TRAIN!"
> Everybody stopped.
> Everybody listened.

If you invite children to speculate with you why Crews varied his paragraph length or used ellipses, children will have their own theories. That's great. There is nothing magical about my theory. But I suspect there will be something magical about asking children to study the ways in which an author has used punctuation and paragraphs artfully. Your real goal is to change children's concepts of themselves and of the conventions of written language so that they are thinking, "I'm the kind of person who needs to understand how writers use punctuation to create effects in their stories." My hope is that this change in perception can matter more than you might dream possible.

GETTING READY

- Instructions on chalkboard telling children to bring their writer's notebooks and sit with their partners in the meeting area
- Editing checklist for each child
- Chart-sized editing checklist
- Example of writing that needs editing to make more sense (written on chart paper)
- Qualities of Good Personal Narrative Writing chart
- Tool containers on each table containing colored pens or pencils
- See CD-ROM for resources

USING EDITING CHECKLISTS

When I was in school, *if there was any instruction about editing at all, it had the tone and purpose of correcting faults. I knew that at some point I'd let go of my writing and it'd come before the teacher who would scrutinize it, line by line, red-marking each flaw and error. Frankly, I always felt as if it was me, not my writing, that my teacher would scrutinize.*

This part of writing made me feel naked and exposed, judged and humiliated. I wasn't alone in these feelings. Mina Shaughnessey, author of Errors and Expectations, *writes that for many people, "Writing is but a line which creeps across the page, exposing all that the writer does not know. Writing puts us on the line and we don't want to be there."*

In this session and in this series, we approach teaching children to write conventionally and to edit their writing in the same way in which we teach children to do anything as writers do. We rally children to care about this important aspect of writing, we induct them into the role of being writers who do this sort of work, and we demonstrate strategies that are do-able and worth doing.

Just as children in this unit learned a rudimentary sense for the essentials of narrative writing and were empowered to use that introductory knowledge with independence and confidence, so, too, in this session, you'll hand over to children a very rudimentary understanding of how writers edit our rough drafts. Watch to be sure that your instruction gives children roots—and wings.

MINILESSON

Using Editing Checklists

CONNECTION

Create a context for today's lesson by talking about self-help books that fill bookstores and top best–seller lists.

"Writers, I thought about you last night when I stopped at the bookstore (I only have one book left in the pile beside my bed so I needed to replenish the pile). At the bookstore, I noticed a rack of best-seller books and it was full of what I call self-help books: *How to Become a Millionaire, How to Win Friends and Influence People, How to Start Your Own Company.* I started to realize that it's human nature to want texts in our lives that can act as personalized coaches, whispering bits of advice to us. And I realized that you and I as writers have our own miniature library of self-help texts, and those are our charts."

"Today, I want to give you one more self-help book. It's time for one of my favorite parts of the writing process: editing. And you all deserve to have a self-help text that can act as a personalized coach, whispering bits of advice to you."

Name your teaching point. Specifically, tell children that writers use editing checklists to remind us of strategies we can use to edit our writing.

"Specifically, I want to teach you that most writers rely on an editing checklist—either a concrete physical list or a mental one—and each item on the checklist reminds us of a lens we can use to reread and to refine our writing. If we have six items on our checklist, we're apt to reread our draft at least six times, once with each item as our lens."

TEACHING

Tell children they each have a personalized editing checklist. Demonstrate how to read through a draft, using an item on the checklist as a lens.

"You'll see later that I've put an editing checklist inside each of your writing folders, and you'll see that the lists are somewhat personalized so they can each function as a personal coach. But every editing checklist will contain some shared items, so let's look at one of those shared items. I want to show you how writers use an item or an editing checklist as a lens, rereading the draft through that lens."

"Every writer's editing checklist always says something to the effect of 'Read your writing to be sure it makes sense to strangers.' I'm a lot older than you, and yet, in all these years, that first

COACHING

Did you notice that in this connection, I bypassed the usual process of contextualizing today's session by recalling previous learning? If you did notice this, it suggests you are internalizing the architecture of minilessons. But of course you'll also want to remember that our teaching needs to be shaped to our specific purposes. And today, it didn't seem necessary to go backward before going forward.

Name_____ Date_____		
Title:_____ Unit of Study:_____		

Reread your writing carefully. Put a check √ in each box under "Author" as you complete each editing item. Once all the boxes are checked, give this editing checklist to the teacher for the final edit.

Editing Checklist	Author	Teacher
1. Clarity - Read, asking, "Will this make sense to a stranger?" Find confusing spots and rewrite to make them more clear. Note places where you stumble as you reread and revise to make them easier to read.		
2. Punctuation - Read, paying attention to the actual road signs you've given readers. If you followed the punctuation as you've written it, will the piece sound the way you want it to sound? Have you guarded against sentences that run on and on? Have you punctuated dialogue?		
3. Spelling - Do your words look correctly spelled to you? Circle ones that feel as if they could be wrong, try them again, get help with them. Check that the words on the word wall are correctly spelled.		
4. Paragraphs - Narrative writers use a new paragraph or a new page for each new episode in the sequence of events. Do you paragraph to show the passage of time? Do you also paragraph to show changes in who is speaking?		
Optional Items: Punctuation *For strugglers...*Have I written with periods and capital letters? Do I avoid using 'and' or 'so' to scotch tape lots of short sentences together into one run-on sentence? *For more experienced writers...*Have I used complex punctuation and varied sentences to help readers read my story with expressiveness and in a way that creates the mood I want to create? Have I used a mentor author to give me ideas for new ways to use punctuation to create a powerful effect in part of my story?		
Spelling When tackling long and challenging words, have I tried to record every sound I hear in the word? Have I used what I know about how other words are spelled to help me spell parts of the challenging word? Have I reread my spelling and circled the parts of a words which I think could be wrong? Have I used spellings I know (and especially those on the word wall) to help me tackle words of which I'm unsure?		

Fig. XVI-1 Editing Checklist (see CD-ROM Resource List)

item has never left my checklist." Referring to a chart-sized editing checklist which contained only two items, I read the first item: "Read, asking, 'Will this make sense to a stranger?'"

"To check for sense, I pretend I know nothing about the topic or the writer. I pick up the paper and start reading, and as I read, I watch for places where I go, 'Huh?' I mark the places that cause some confusion. Later, I go back and rewrite those places so they're clearer. I also mark places that are for some reason hard to read correctly. Writers have a saying, 'When you falter—alter!' If I stumble as I read something or, need to reread to figure out what a part is saying, then I figure the section needs more work."

"Let me show you what I mean by showing you a draft that one of my students from last year wrote." I revealed a chart-paper copy of a child's story. "Follow along while I read just the start of Esther's story. We'll pretend we're Esther, and we're using the first item on our checklist to prompt us to reread the draft, checking for sense. See if you find yourself going, 'Huh?' We'll want to come back and clarify those confusing places." [Fig. XVI-2]

> "Ring, ring!" I ran out of Polish school.
>
> I saw my friend Paulina. "Hi Paulina," I said. "Hi." I ran to her dad's car. I jumped inside.

"Hmm . . . I'm a little confused. I understand the words, the vocabulary, in this story, but if I try to make a picture in my mind of what's really happening, I can't do it. Why is she jumping inside her friend's car?"

> "Where is your sister?" I asked her. "I don't know." My friend's dad looked sad. He was not talking. We were in the car driving. His daughter's name was Paulina. We were friends.

"Now I'm even more confused . . . and if I was Esther, I'd want to clarify so no stranger would read this and go, 'Huh?'" Then I said, "Writers, in Esther's case, she'd been trying to do exactly what we taught her, writing her story step-by-step—but she'd written her piece in such a step-by-step manner that we couldn't understand the big things that were happening. So she went back and clarified:"

> "Ring, ring!" The bell rang, telling us we could leave the Saturday Polish school. So I ran out to the street to find Paulina's Dad because he drives me home. I got in the car and noticed Paulina's sister wasn't there. She was always there. . . .

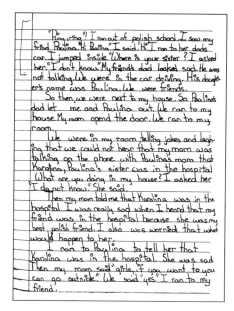

Fig. XVI-2 Esther

Your intonation should suggest this is already confusing.

It was as if, instead of saying, "I picked the flower," Esther had written, "I leaned down. I put my fingers near the flower's stem. I squeezed them. I pulled up . . ." but she hadn't made it clear that she was describing picking the flower! In instances such as this, if you can figure out the intelligence behind students' errors, you can help them enormously. Esther was following my instructions to a T—and going overboard doing so. This happens with nearly every lesson we teach—children often overuse the teaching of the minilesson when they try it for the first few times. Embrace their enthusiasm even as you help them see the teaching in its proper perspective.

"Writers, did you see that I took the first item on the checklist and acted as if it was a personalized assignment? I read, using that item as a lens, and then I did the work that item led me to do. Then I move on to the next item on the checklist. On all our lists, this item says, 'Check the punctuation,'" I said, gesturing towards the second item on an enlarged list on chart paper. "So I reread a whole other time, and this time I pay special attention to the road signs that tell us how to read. Sometimes I see that I've left out periods, and my sentence goes on so long I forget what the beginning was. So I repair that. If I have dialogue, I check to make sure I have the punctuation that shows the reader that people are talking and these are their exact words."

"The third item that I put on everyone's checklist is spelling," I said, gesturing to this item on the enlarged chart. "To check my writing for misspellings, I read it very slowly, looking at each word. Does each word look right? If I get to any that I think might be wrong, I circle that word and then go back and check. To check words, I ask someone, look at our word wall, or find them in a dictionary or other book."

ACTIVE ENGAGEMENT

Ask children to read through their draft with their partner, focusing on one item on the editing checklist.

"Writers, right now, with your partner, let's work with the next item on that checklist." I gestured to the chart and read aloud, "Make sure your paragraphs work the way you want them to in your story. Partner 2, will you spread out your draft and will the two of you read it, checking paragraphs together? If you both find a way the paragraphs could be better for the story, make sure you mark that spot, and maybe make a note in the margin about what needs fixing. Okay, go ahead." The children worked for a bit on that item from their checklist before I interrupted.

Using a different color pen or pencil, or one with a special flair to it, can be a tool that inspires editing: A fancy editing tool can spark kids to make changes just for the thrill of using it—especially when it comes to adjusting spelling and punctuation.

At some point, the children will need to assess their writing and decide which editing tasks in particular they need to add to their own editing checklists. The checklist is also a place you can add items you and the child discuss in conferences and strategy lessons. This is another way to help hold the child accountable for all the teaching to date.

LINK

Remind children that they can use this strategy forever when they write.

"Writers, I hope you've learned that editing checklists, like self-help books, can function as personalized coaches, giving us a to-do list. Today, find the editing checklist in your writing folders and use each item as a lens. Reread with that lens, and do the refinements that work prompts you to do. Later today and tomorrow, you can start your final draft and from this day on, always remember that whenever you are going to put your writing into the world, you need to edit it very carefully so that the people reading it will see exactly what you intend for them to see. So when you get started on this important editing work—your last chance to make the writing as perfect as you can get it—you can always use a checklist to help you remember the areas to consider carefully. Someday, you will have used a checklist so often that you won't need it on paper; you can use it right out of your mind!"

WRITING AND CONFERRING

Focusing on Tenses and Pronouns

Two areas where children can easily help themselves in the editing stage are tenses and pronouns.

As you confer with children, pay attention to the tenses they've used in their drafts. Sometimes children misunderstand what we mean by making movies in one's head and recording what we recall, and they write personal narratives exclusively in the present tense, almost as if the story is a caption to a movie. In the following draft, for example, John has tried to write in the present tense.

Lost Dog

My family, my cousin and I are driving home happily from lunch. As we get out of the car we notice the driveway gate is wide open. I find myself yelling, "Pepper, Pepper!" I'm looking everywhere in my green yard. I can't find my dog. My happiness turns into sorrow. Then my sorrow turns into cold tears that are dripping down my face.

In general, past tense is the usual tense used for storytelling. There are reasons why a writer might deliberately break-stride and write about a past event in present tense, but that'd be an unusual choice. In the story cited above, the writer simply misunderstood the instructions and thought that when he was told to 'make a movie in his mind and record what happened,' this required present tense. His piece worked more easily when he was given permission to rewrite it in past tense:

My family, cousin and I drove home from lunch. As we got out of the car, we noticed the driveway gate was wide open. "Pepper, Pepper," I yelled. I looked everywhere in my green yard. I couldn't find my dog.

If you see a child trying to maintain present tense, you may want to help the child start the draft over again, this time writing in past tense.

Pay attention also to pronouns. You'll see that children often overuse he or she, and the reader can't keep track of the characters. Tell children that writers are careful to match pronoun references with proper nouns since the pronoun always refers to the person mentioned just before it. You could tell them that one way, then, to edit for clarity is to read while asking: "Is it clear who the character is in every part of my story?"

MID-WORKSHOP TEACHING POINT — *Reading with Writing Partners* "Writers, may I stop you for a moment? You're doing a great job finding places in your own writing that you can make better by editing.

"Right now, I want to teach you that after you have looked over your own writing carefully and edited it, you can also ask a writing buddy to look it over to see if they find other areas where editing would make the piece stronger. All writers have a friend who helps us edit, or we rely a lot on our editors who help us publish our poems and stories and articles. No one on this whole planet can see every opportunity to make something a little better by herself; we need another pair of eyes!"

"Please exchange papers right now and be another pair of eyes for your partners. When more than one person edits a piece of writing, it helps keep all the changes straight if you use different colored pens. So partners, choose a different color from what the writer used, and put on your best 'editing glasses!'"

SHARE

Preparing for a Celebration

Ask children to show each other what they've done, what they've learned, and what they've resolved to do next.

"Writers, would you gather in the meeting area?" Once the class convened, I said, "Writers, don't you love the days just before a holiday, when everything takes a special significance and special urgency? I love the prelude to Valentine's Day as much as I love the day itself. It's fun to make lists of what I need to do, to busy myself with preparations, to anticipate the actual day. I'm telling you this beause today is the prelude to another sort of holiday—our first author's celebration—and I love the quickening in the air as we ready ourselves."

"Tonight, I'm going to look over the drafts that you've edited today. I'll function as your copy editor. Every author sends his or her books to a copy editor who reads the manuscript over and makes added corrections."

"Tomorrow won't be a usual writing workshop because every minute of the day will be reserved for making final copies of our pieces."

"Before you leave your draft with me, take a few minutes to savor this special time. Meet with your partner and tell your partner what you did to make your story even better today, and what you learned as a writer that you'll carry with you always."

You will probably be uneasy about the idea that publication day is just around the bend. "Shouldn't I send the drafts off to parents who'll type them?" you may ask yourself. It is true that the day is apt to arrive with some children who haven't finished their final draft. I strongly urge you to go forward anyhow. Children need to finish a unit and to celebrate the work they've done right then and there . . . not two weeks later when every loose end is tied up. You can celebrate the end of the unit – whether or not every detail is completely finished. Your real purpose in this celebration is closure on one unit, and a drum roll to the next. Your hope, too, is to make writing authentic for children by ensuring that they are writing for readers.

My mission today is to create a sense of occassion around the upcoming author celebration, and to be sure that editing takes on special importance because it is a way of preparing one's work to go out in the world.

I'll probably have a chance to look over and correct some children's drafts during today's workshop or during other portions of the day. If I've made corrections on some drafts, I'll certainly send those children home with encouragement to begin making their final copies at home.

⊙ HOMEWORK **Preparing for the Celebration**   Writers, our first Author Celebration is just around the bend. Tonight I hope you will help with preparations for that event. You might think this means that I'm hoping you'll bake brownies or mix Kool-aid, and it's true that I want you to think about ways to make the occasion a special one. But the truth is that when a person writes, when we send our words out into the world, what we long to receive is not a brownie . . . but a response. One writer said that sometimes, authorship feels like tossing rose petals into a well and waiting, hoping to hear a splash.

Let's be sure that every writer in our community knows that someone has truly heard that writer's work, and truly recognized the time and care invested in that story. And who is in a better place to take notice of what a writer has accomplished than the writer's partner?

At our celebration, it will be your job to introduce your partner to his or her audience. You'll say to the second graders, "I want to introduce you to . . . " and then you'll say, "This writer is especially famous for her ability to . . . Notice the way she (or he) . . . " You will need to think tonight about your partner's writing, and try to use precise details to exactly name what your writer has done that is especially noteworthy. Keep what you write to yourself, just as you keep Valentines to yourself, until the 'Big Day' comes.

TAILORING YOUR TEACHING   One of the goals of this session is to encourage students to regard themselves as people who have important reasons not only to write well, but also to spell and punctuate well—they are writing for an audience who wants to know exactly what they are trying to get across! The editing work you focus on during this first unit of study will depend on the grade and the experience of the children you teach and on you, the teacher. You will want to consider how much time you want to spend on editing and how specific you want to be. You also want to remember to celebrate all that your children do know about language, conventions, and writing.

If your children need extra help to edit for spelling accuracy . . . you might begin a lesson in which you equate editing to getting dressed for a special occasion or celebration. You might say, "One way writers edit is that we check the spelling of each word. Writers ask, 'Does this word look right?' Then we either fix the word in a snap or we try out a few different spellings and choose one that looks right." Demonstrate how you read closely for spelling by pointing under each word, asking questions, and stopping when a word doesn't look right.

If your students need extra practice editing for spelling mistakes . . . you could use a child's piece of writing as a class text to work on editing together. In the minilesson you might say, "Let's practice together what it's like to edit for spelling. A little girl, Jenna, who lives next door to me asked if I could help edit her writing, so I figured we could all help her." Pass out a copy to each partnership along with editing pencils. "Working with your partner, read this excerpt of Jenna's writing very slowly and carefully, touching each word with your pencil. Ask yourself, 'Does this look right?' If you find a misspelled word you know in a snap, cross it out and write the correctly spelled word above it. Underline any words that don't look right, but you're not sure how to spell. Try writing those three different ways at the bottom of the paper and choose the one that looks right to you."

> I was running fast then I triped over something. I fell in the air. Ahh! I scramed. I was falling off the edge of the street. I was almost going to hit myself on the floor. I put my hands doun so I would not hit myself on the hed so hard.

You could harvest insights by saying, for instance, "Who found some words that were misspelled that you knew in a snap?" Or, "Who found a word that didn't look right, but was not sure exactly how the word was spelled?" Point out what they did. "You did a really good job editing this writer's story for spelling. Because you read slowly and carefully, touching each word with your editing pencil, you were able to catch and fix some of the misspelled words." Bring the lesson to a close by saying, "So writers, whenever you want to get your writing ready for readers, for an audience, you need to become an editor by checking your spelling and fixing anything that does not look right or sound right, just like we did here together. This will help your readers be able to read and enjoy your stories easily. And your stories will be ready for our publishing celebration."

ASSESSMENT

One day on my way home from work, I was listening to a radio interview with a famous visual artist. The interviewer was asking him how he kept himself on track through his starving artist days—the days when he was working well under the radar of gallery owners, art collectors, and paparazzi; the period when he was a bricklayer by day and a painter at night. "Did you ever consider just giving up?" she asked.

I remember the artist taking a few seconds to answer. He began by saying that although he often longed for an income that wasn't fraught with gaps and surprises, he always had energy and hope for his art. He said he had a variety of tricks to help him stay motivated and focused, even when an eviction notice had been slipped under the door. One of the most important things he did that helped him to keep moving forward as an artist was looking backward and taking time to reflect on how his art had changed. He said that looking back regularly through his body of work helped him to notice ways he'd grown, how he'd changed, and what he still needed to work on as an artist. For this painter, the act of reflecting was incredibly motivating.

Taking time to step back and reflect is incredibly important as we try to grow, no matter whether we're trying to become better painters, golfers, spouses, parents, cooks, teachers of writing . . . or writers. All of this suggests to me that it would be time well spent to tuck in opportunities for our students to step back and reflect on their work as writers.

It's important to consider, however, that reflecting on one's writing work isn't just about rereading old entries and drafts. The more important and challenging work of self-reflection requires naming what you see and considering its significance.

This first unit then provides a perfect opportunity to give students time to self-assess, to reflect on their work so far, and to answer questions such as:

- What do I notice about myself as a writer as I read through my work?"
- How have I changed as a writer so far?
- What are three things I do well as a writer?
- What are some things I want to get stronger at as a writer?
- What is my favorite piece, and what are the things I love about it?

In some classrooms, teachers have students do this work during homework for a couple of days at the end of the unit. Then, in class, the students talk in small groups about their self-reflections as the teacher listens in on their conversations. If students write self-reflections, they will be powerful artifacts to accumulate over the course of the year and analyze at the year's end.

Although this self-reflection may benefit the student primarily, certainly we, as teachers, can use the responses to help us plan instruction. When we see that we have several children who feel strong at writing authentic, accurately punctuated dialogue, we can suggest those children become mentors to other children who may have a more difficult time with this. If we find that we have several students who say they still struggle with coming up with ideas for writing, we can pull these together for some small group instruction. Assessment is one way to channel growth.

GETTING READY

- Empty bulletin board prepared to receive each child's writing
- Tacks
- Assorted stickers
- Juice and cups
- See CD-ROM for resources

PUBLISHING:
A WRITING COMMUNITY CELEBRATES

This first celebration of the year is a momentous occasion for both you and your students! Your students have learned to work productively and independently, to use a repertoire of strategies to generate and develop ideas, and to be able to capture moments on the page, minding the conventions of standard English. This day is a celebration of a great accomplishment; your children are writers!

Today your young writers will feel how their work can affect others; they will share compliments and celebrate each other's work. Some children will be astounded that they've made their classmates laugh; some will be shocked by the attention their words get from the others in the class. Most will be thrilled, as we all are, to feel that they have made something, an artifact that can stay in the world forever. Writing celebrations help our young students regard themselves as authors in a working, thriving community of other authors. In Ralph Peterson's brilliant book, Life in a Crowded Place, he explains that celebrations contribute to our sense of belonging by helping us learn to focus on others and their achievements rather than just on our own (1992, p. 39). The gallery wall of writing you create today is an announcement to the world: "Look! Here we are all authors."

Celebrations need to build in grandeur from the beginning of the year until the end. This first celebration needs to make your writers feel proud and strengthen their motivation for writing while still leaving room for fancier celebrations to come. As children's writing strengthens and deepens, so must the celebrations that honor that work. For now, plan to celebrate children's change into writers rather than celebrating exquisite writing. The truth is, the pieces of writing may yet be far from exquisite— after all, for many writers this may be their first time working through the entire writing process! Don't succumb to the temptation to postpone the celebration until the writing is fantastic, or until you've had time to work individually with each child until they've written something impressive. Let the children's finished work stand as examples of their best work to date. This way, the children, and all the grown-ups watching their development, can see their growth throughout the year more clearly— something they couldn't see if these first pieces are "propped up." This particular celebration is truly a lovely way to appreciate where children are and encourage their growth as writers from this day forth.

CELEBRATION

Start the school day by building up excitement toward the approaching celebration.

When children lined up on the playground in the morning, ready to come into the classroom for the day, I heightened their excitement. "You all seem bursting with energy this morning," I said. "No wonder—it's our author celebration!" When children convened in the meeting area to review the schedule for the day, I said "I know for certain what your first question will be: 'When will we have our celebration?!'"

For the celebration, bring the guests into the classroom. As a welcome, describe a reading that you attended at the local bookstore. Explain the structure for today's celebration.

"This is a very special moment," I said once the little children, the class' younger reading buddies, had settled in the meeting area alongside my class. "Today we are gathering to celebrate that Room 203's children are truly becoming writers. Last Saturday, I went to a reading at our local bookstore. Lots and lots of people gathered in a corner of the bookstore, just like we've gathered in a corner of our classroom, and the author's writing partner, a person known as her editor, spoke first. She said, 'I want to introduce you to someone whose writing I know very well.' Then the editor went on to tell us what this writer did so remarkably."

"Afterwards, the author read her writing aloud, and we got a chance to ask her questions about her writing life, questions like, 'Where did you get the idea for your story?' or 'Who especially helped you to write this story?' or 'What did you learn from writing this?'"

"I'm telling you this because today we will celebrate your writing just as we celebrated that famous author's writing. In a few minutes, we will gather in one of our four corners (remember we gathered in a corner of the bookstore!) and then, in each corner, an author will take her place in the author's chair (you'll see I have one set up in each corner). The author's writing partner will sit beside her, and our reading will begin. First, the writing partner will introduce the author. You will read the introductions you wrote at home last night!"

COACHING

I know that it is not truly the case that every child in the class is beside herself with excitement over the fact that today is our author celebration day, but I'm going to act as though, of course, children feel thrilled at the prospect of sharing their writing. At the start of the year, especially, we are building a culture in our classrooms, and the values of that culture make a very big difference. So I will do everything possible to be sure that this community is one that honors the written word, one that regards author celebrations as one of our most important occasions.

Younger children, not parents, are the audience for this celebration. At the start of the year, your emphasis will have been on helping children cycle through the writing process with independence. In order to be sure that your workshop is a productive one, one where children are able to carry on with independence, you will not have been able to coach and guide every writer about his final piece of writing. Chances are very good that some children will be publishing stories that are laden with problems. At this early stage, it is crucial that you accept that children's best work is worthy of celebration. You will have lots of time to raise the level of that work—for now, some children will publish stories that are still unfocused, underdeveloped, and so forth. For this reason, I suggest you postpone the celebration with the high-stakes audience until a bit later in the year. Meanwhile, this is a wonderful way to induct younger children into the writing culture of your school.

"Then, Authors, read your stories. When you have finished, please leave a little bit of time for silence. Let there be just a moment when no one speaks and everyone lets the story sink in. Then one of you can ask the writer a writing question—just one, for now."

When each member of each group has shared her piece and answered one question, ask everyone to gather in the hallway beside a shrouded bulletin board.

"Writers, the work that you shared deserves to be sent out into the world. At the bookstore, after the reading, the bookstore created a gigantic display of the author's work, and that made me realize we, too, needed a way to display your work. So you'll see," I dramatically pulled the shroud off a beautifully matted bulletin board, "I've created a special display case for your masterpieces!" I paused for the oohing and awwwing. "Now, when I gesture to you, please say the name of your writing partner and that writer please come to me for some stickers to decorate your piece. Then you will hang your writing in our display case!"

In this fashion, one child after another was named, then approached me for a few stickers and then hung her writing on the bulletin board.

Here is Terrance's final draft: *[Fig. XVII-1]*

"Matches!" I thought. I picked them up. I flipped them open and took out a match. "This is not right," I thought. "I'm going to do it anyway," I said. I rushed to my room to set a string on fire. I crawled under my bed. "No one can see me now," I thought. I set the string on fire. WOOOF!—the sheets burst into flames. "What's that smell?" Mom yelled! "Nothing," I said. That's when I heard running footsteps. The last step she took was to my room.

She saw the flaming sheets. She ran to my room. She flipped the bed over. The flames burst into her face, almost leaving her hair like rice crispies. She backed away from the fire. I crawled out from under my bed! My Mom ran to the bathroom. She got two big buckets of water. She threw the water on the bed to make the fire stop. But the fire was too strong to put out, so my Mom called the fire department. They brought fire hoses and other materials. They put out the fire. Then I got on punishment for 4 months.

If possible, it would be great to station an adult in each of the four corners, though, of course, the grown-ups can also keep an eye on two corners at once. Your hope is that the author takes his place of honor, the partner sits beside the author. The partner uses the class' attention-getting signal to ask for everyone's attention and waits (help them do this) until the group is focused and ready to listen. Then one partner begins, saying, "I'm proud to introduce you to my writing partner. I think Terrance has a special talent for conveying excitement . . ." Then the author reads aloud, and when the listening children hear evidence of what the partner described, the listeners signal with a quiet thumbs-up.

You may wonder what, exactly, the work looks like that children are pinning onto the bulletin board. Your first and biggest question is probably this: is the work totally correct? Although children will have devoted earnest effort to making their writing their best, and you will have had three or four editing conferences in which you teach three or four editing tips in relation to this one piece, there is no way every child in your room (or even most children in your room) will have been able to fully correct their own writing.

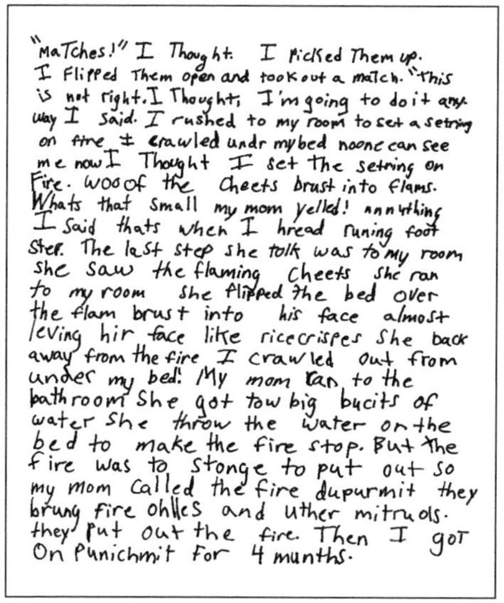
"MaTches!" I Thought. I Picked Them up. I Flipped Them open and tookout a match. "This is not right. I Thought, I'm going to do it any way I said. I rushed to my room to set a setring on fire I crawled undr mybed noone can see me now I Thought I set the setring on Fire. woooF the Cheets brust into flams. Whats that small my mom yelled! annything I Said thats when I hread runing foot Step. The last step she tolk was to my room she saw the flaming Cheets she ran to my room she flipped the bed over the flam brust into his face almost leving hir face like ricecrispes She back away from the fire I crawled out from under my bed! My mom ran to the bathroom She got tow big bucits of water She throw the water on the bed to make the fire stop. But the fire was to stonge to put out so my mom Called the fire dupurmit they brung fire ohlles and uther mitruols. they put out the fire. Then I got On Punichmit for 4 munths.

Fig. XVII-1 Terrance's final draft

Bask in the glory of progress as writers. Remind writers that a whole year for writing stretches ahead of them. Create time for children to compliment each other's writing.

"Writers, I need to tell you that frankly, I am incredibly excited because I listen to this writing and I think, "And this is still Unit One!" I know it will be an amazing thing to see how your writing gets even better. Maybe our last celebration better be at that bookstore . . . because look out world, here these writers come!"

"Before we end our celebration, could we hear from our young guests? Second-graders, what did you notice about these bigger-kids' writing? Will you guys turn and talk, and let's hear from our visitors, and learn from their observations." We heard from several.

"Writers and guests, before we go back to our other work, would everyone get yourself something to eat and drink, and let's have a party!"

Here is Olivia's final draft: [Fig. XVII-2]

The Place: the Finish Line

I held my sled in my hand tight. My heart pumped as me and Alejandra walked over to Balin. The words, "Balin, do you want to race?" wouldn't come out. Finally, they did. "Hey, Balin, do you want to race?" I said. "Sure, why not? On the count of three," was his response.

"I must have sweated buckets as we got our sleds in place. "1," said Balin. My heart pumped. "2," said Balin. I sweated ten buckets. "3," said Balin. I nearly wet my pants.

After three, we were off. It was going very smoothly and we were tied for the lead. Then suddenly me and Alejandra hit a big root and went in the air and landed with a plop, and slowed down. I wondered what we hit but reminded each other we had a race to finish.

So we dug our hands in the cold snow and pushed ourselves forwards. We tried and tried to win. But as we trailed behind Balin we heard him cheering, "I win! I win!" I reminded myself everybody's a winner.

You may wonder what, exactly, the work looks like that children are pinning onto the bulletin board. Your first and biggest question is probably this: is the work corrected, and if so, how did it get that way? If you are thinking that, for your children, the only way for the work to be absolutely correct is for you to correct it, and even retype it, and then you need to know that you are in good company. All of us teach children with needs like that, and frankly, even grown adults rely on copyeditors. It goes without saying that although children devote earnest effort to making their writing their best, their texts will not be perfect.

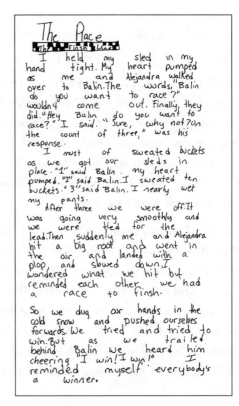

Fig. XVII-2 Olivia's final draft

Here is Felix's final draft: *[Fig. XVII-3]*

It was a warm, sunny day. It was also the day before Easter, around the time for me to have lunch. Just me and my Mom all alone in the car. She was driving somewhere, and I had no idea where.

"Hmmm, I wonder where we're going," I said in my head. I tried to think of something that I told her I wanted really bad, but I couldn't think of anything. So I just asked her.

"Where are you going?" I asked her.
"You'll see," she answered.
"Can you just tell me?" I begged.
"Nope," she said.
"Please," I said.
"No!" she said so loud she almost screamed.
"Fine," I said in an angry voice.

She drove up to some animal shelter.

"Yay! So what kind of animal can I get?" I said.
"A cat," she said.
"Yay! A cat. I love cats," I said happily.

So anyway we got out of the car and went into the animal shelter. I started walking down the aisles, and this one cat started staring at me and I started staring back. We were staring at each other for about 2 minutes. They my Mom saw me.

"Mom, watch this," I said. So my Mom came over to see.
"Why don't you get that cat?" she said.
"Okay," I said.

So the person who worked took him out of his cage. The shelter worker gave us a box so I could carry him home on my lap. "Hmmm, now what should I name him?" I said in my head.

You will certainly want to have had editing conferences with children to improve their use of conventions in their writing. But, even if you have taught three or four editing tips in relation to this one piece, there is no way every child in your room (or even most children in your room) will be able to fully correct their own writing.

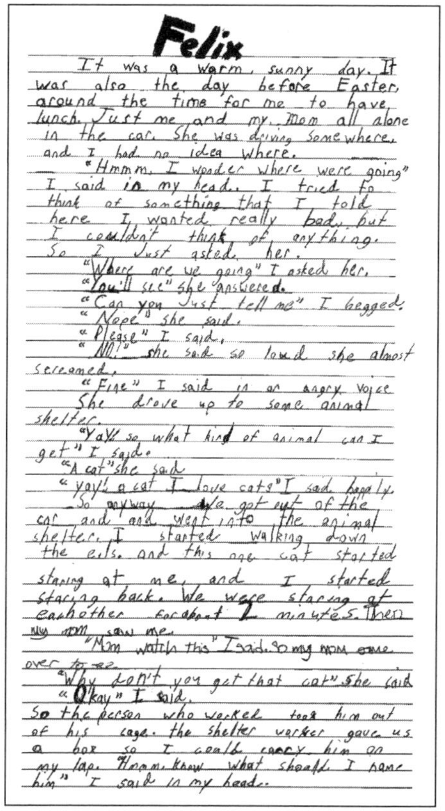
Felix
It was a warm, sunny day. It was also the day before Easter, around the time for me to have lunch. Just me and my Mom all alone in the car. She was driving somewhere, and I had no idea where.
"Hmmm. I wonder where were going" I said in my head. I tried to think of something that I told here I wanted really bad, but I couldn't think of anything. So I just asted her.
"Where are we going" I asked her.
"You'll see" she answered.
"Can you Just tell me" I begged.
"Nope" she said.
"Please" I said.
"No!" she said so loud she almost screamed.
"Fine" I said in an angry voice
She drove up to some animal shelter.
"Yay! so what kind of animal can I get" I said.
"A cat" she said
"yay! a cat I love cats" I said happly.
So anyway we got out of the car and and went into the animal shelter. I started walking down the eils. and this one cat started staring at me, and I started staring back. We were staring at eachother for about 2 minutes. Then my mom saw me.
"Mom watch this" I said. So my mom came over to see.
"Why don't you get that cat". She said
"Okay" I said.
So the person who worked took him out of his cage. the shelter worker gave us a box so I could carry him on my lap. "Hmm. know what should I name him" I said in my head.

Fig. XVII-3 Felix's final draft

Here is Gregory's final draft: *[Fig. XVII-4]*

Al is Dead

Dead. Ever since I had fish, I had Al: the best algae-eater in the world. Once I heard he was dead, I did not cry. I just was still. Then I asked, "Where is he?" My Dad said, "In the trash." I asked to see him.

I walked over to the trash can and I opened it. I looked in and saw wet paper towels, orange peels and a pile of coffee grounds. I picked up AL. I flicked off the coffee grounds and said "Al, my friend. I'm gonna miss you."

My dad put him back. For a second, I thought, then I said, "We can give him a funeral." My dad looked doubtful for a minute but I picked him up and said, "He was special." Then I cried. Al was gone.

Here is Michela's final draft: *[Fig. XVII-5]*

GETTING READY TO GO TO CALIFORNIA

By: Michela

"Beep, beep, beep" the alarm went off. It was 4:00 in the morning. You'd think we would be tired but . . .

"Go, go, go!" I screamed.

We peeled off our pajamas and jumped into our clothes as fast as we could.

"Get the tooth brushes, get the suitcases!" yelled my mom.

I was shoved into the small, wooden bookcase as my sister ran to get the suitcases and toothbrushes.

"Get the entertainment, get the extra pillows!" bellowed my dad. I was yanked to the side to make room for my mom while she ran to get the entertainment and extra pillows.

"Where's my cell phone?" screamed my sister. I was pushed into the stereo as my sister grabbed her cell phone from the top of the CD rack.

"Get everything!" I yelled still rubbing my head from my past incidents.

It was a mad, mad house. We ran around in circles trying to figure out what to do, when finally we realized we were done packing. We all plopped on the couch. I let out a loud sigh and closed my eyes for a quick rest.

"Honk, Honk!" the car service is here.

We bolted out the door and slammed it behind us. We ran down the dark deserted street toward the blinking taillights.

The car door slowly opened with a creek and we hopped inside. We were on our way to the airport.

Fig. XVII-5 Michela's final draft

You will decide, based on the expectations of your community, whether you need to go through and correct each piece, asking each child to recopy your corrections, or whether you can publish children's best work at this point in the year. I hope you can do the latter. If we are always propping children's work up so that it looks perfect, then how can we keep track of their development over time? How can we hold ourselves responsible for them learning to do significantly more on their own? If your school community has trouble with displays of imperfect work (they no doubt accept this for clay sculpture and portraits, but if they do not regard approximation in writing with equal trust,) then I recommend moving the display case inside the classroom and perhaps titling it, "See Our Work In-Progress" or "Celebrate Rough Drafts and Revisions!"

Al is what!
Dead. Ever since I had fish, I had Al the best algie eater in the world. Once I heard he was dead, I did not cry. I just was still. Then I asked "Where is he!" my dad said "In the trash." I asked to see him.
I walked over to the trash can and I opened it. I looked in and saw wet paper towels, orange peels and a pile of coffee grownds. I pick up al. I flicked off the coffee grounds, and said "al, my friend. I'm gonna miss you."
my dad put him back for a seconed I thought then I said "we can give him a furnal" ~~he was~~ my dad lookd doutful for a minute but I pick him up and said he was speicel! Then I cryd. al was gone.

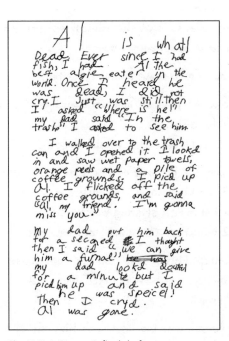

Fig. XVII-4 Gregory's final draft

LUCY CALKINS ✦ TED KESLER

RAISING THE QUALITY OF NARRATIVE WRITING

This book is dedicated to Laurie Pessah.

FirstHand
An imprint of Heinemann
A division of Reed Elsevier Inc.
361 Hanover Street
Portsmouth, NH 03801-3912
www.heinemann.com

Offices and agents throughout the world

Copyright © 2006 by Lucy Calkins and Ted Kesler

All rights reserved. No part of this book may be reproduced in any form or by any electronic or mechanical means, including information storage and retrieval systems, without permission in writing ʾom the publisher, except by a reviewer, who may quote brief passages in a review.

ʾraphy: Peter Cunningham

ʿongress Cataloging-in-Publication Data

ʾ with the Library of Congress.

ʾ7

States of America on acid-free paper
ʾ   ML   1   2   3   4   5

Excerpt from "Eleven" from *Woman Hollering Creek*. Copyright © 1991 by Sandra Cisneros. Published by Vintage Books, a division of Random House, Inc., and originally in hardcover by Random House, Inc. Reprinted by permission of Susan Bergholz Literary Services, New York. All rights reserved.

Excerpt from *Little by Little* by Jean Little. Copyright © Jean Little, 1987. Reprinted by permission of Penguin Group (Canada), a division of Pearson Canada Inc."

Excerpt from *Owl Moon* by Jane Yolen, copyright (c) 1987 by Jane Yolen, text. Used by permission of Philomel Books, a division of Penguin Young Readers Group, a member of Penguin Group (USA) Inc., 345 Hudson Street, New York, NY 10014. All rights reserved.

Excerpt from *Smokey Night*, text copyright © 1994 by Eve Bunting, reprinted by permission of Harcourt, Inc.

Excerpt from *My Pig Amarillo* by Satomi Ichikawa, copyright © 2003 by Satomi Ichikawa. Used by permission of Philomel Books, a division of Penguin Young Readers Group, a member of Penguin Group (USA) Inc., 345 Hudson Street, New York, NY 10014. All rights reserved.

Excerpt from *Salt Hands* by Jane Chelsea Aragon, copyright (c) 1989 by Jane Chelsea Aragon. Used by permission of Dutton Children's Books, a division of Penguin Young Readers Group, a member of Penguin Group (USA) Inc., 345 Hudson Street, New York, NY 10014. All rights reserved.

Excerpt from *The Leaving Morning* by Angela Johnson, illustrated by David Soman. Published by Orchard Books, an imprint of Scholastic Inc. Text Copyright © 1992 by Angela Johnson. Illustration Copyright © 1992 by David Soman. Reprinted by Permission.

Excerpt from *Peter's Chair* by Ezra Jack Keats, copyright © 1967 by Ezra Jack Keats, renewed (c) 1995 by Martin Pope, Executor. Used by permission of Viking Penguin, a division of Penguin Young Readers Group, a member of Penguin Group (USA) Inc., 345 Hudson Street, New York, NY 10014. All rights reserved.

Excerpt from *Homesick: My Own Story* by Jean Fritz, copyright (c) 1982 by Jean Fritz. Used by permission of G.P. Putnam's Sons, a division of Penguin Young Readers Group, a member of Penguin Group (USA) Inc., 345 Hudson Street, New York, NY 10014. All rights reserved.

Excerpt from *Fireflies!* by Julie Brinckloe, copyright © 1985 by Julie Brinckloe. Reprinted with the permission of Simon & Schuster Books for Young Readers, an imprint of Simon & Schuster Children's Publishing Division.

Excerpt from "Papa Who Wakes Up Tired in the Dark" from *The House on Mango Street*. Copyright © 1984 by Sandra Cisneros. Published by Vintage Books, a division of Random House, Inc., and in hardcover by Alfred A. Knopf in 1994. Reprinted by permission of Susan Bergholz Literary Services, New York. All rights reserved.

Excerpt from *Fly Away Home* by Eve Bunting. Text copyright © 1991 by Eve Bunting. Reprinted by permission of Clarions Books/Houghton Mifflin Company. All rights reserved.

ACKNOWLEDGEMENTS

This book is dedicated to Laurie Pessah who has, for several decades, joined me at the helm of the Teachers College Reading and Writing Project. Laurie is the organizational and interpersonal heart of the Project. She brings all the people, places, and projects together, matching eighty-five staff developers to hundreds and hundreds of schools across the nation. Laurie's unerringly astute instincts inform these decisions, and then she also keeps track of all the work and all the players. All of us at the Project regard Laurie as utterly indispensable to all that we do and all that we are.

I am grateful also to Ted Kesler, who has been a contributing author to this book. Ted contributed to some of the extensions in the book and especially, on the CD, and he read through the manuscript half-a-dozen times, filling in gaps, working on the charts, tracking down the drafts of children's work, and supplying model texts. His input was enriched by his knowledge of children's literature and of qualities of good writing. I thank him for his help.

The book stands on many shoulders, but there are a few classroom teachers have made especially strong contributions to it. The brilliant teaching of Mary Chiarella, Lis Shin and Kathy Doyle helped this book immeasurably. Their children's work fills the pages of this book, and for years, I have learned about teaching writing by teaching in their company. Mary Chiarella joined me in a think tank during the final months when I was revising this book, and her ideas about the relationship between elements of story and narrative craft made a difference. Natalie Louis, a spunky, creative, child-centered co-author from the primary series, helped me break new trails for this unit.

Katherine Bomer, author of *Writing a Life* and a close friend of the Project, added her ebullient love of writing and her insights; I am grateful to her for her help on this manuscript and for her support in professional development. My ideas on narrative writing have been enriched by the wisdom of Ralph Fletcher, Barry Lane, and especially Mary Ehrenworth; Mary, along with Janet Angililo, also helped me think about teaching grammar and punctuation. If it takes a village to raise a child, it takes close to that many people to plan a unit of study! I am grateful to all these brilliant educators.

I want to especially acknowledge Katie Ray, whose brilliant work on reading-writing connections informs all I do. Katie was a staff developer at the Project years ago and continues to enrich our thinking, especially on the topic of reading-like-a-writer.

The photography in this book and in all of my books is the work of Peter Cunningham, an extraordinary artist. It has been a great joy to see the beauty in New York City schools through his eyes. I thank Peter MacFarlane and the teachers and children at P.S. 180 in Harlem, Carol Stock and the teachers and children at P.S. 199 in Manhattan, and Melanie Woods and the teachers at P.S. 29 for welcoming Peter and his camera into their midst.

Finally, the book grew out of a close partnership with my editor, Kate Montgomery. This book required extra-care because when I finished work on it, the manuscript was like the Secret Garden, overgrown with flowers, vines, fruit trees of all sorts, all needing to be trimmed and brought under control. I have written about Kate's contribution in detail elsewhere, but this book, like every book in the series, bears the special imprint of her brilliance.

RAISING THE QUALITY OF NARRATIVE WRITING

Welcome to Unit 2

WELCOME TO THE UNIT

RAISING THE QUALITY OF NARRATIVE WRITING

Although this unit is titled *Raising the Quality of Narrative Writing*, the real goal is to improve the quality of *writing*—and of the *writers*—in general. We invest another month of work in personal narrative writing (before shifting to a focus on expository writing) because we know that real progress comes not from constantly exposing children to yet another form of writing but from working long enough within one form to help children write longer, more significant, more conventional, and more graceful pieces in general.

We begin the unit by telling children they will be revisiting narrative writing and helping them understand this means they will need to draw on all they already know. This is a perfect opportunity to teach children that writers carry with them and draw on a cumulative repertoire of strategies. For example, we say, "You already have a whole repertoire of strategies for generating narrative writing," and briefly direct children's attention to the charts listing strategies they learned during the earlier unit. When children begin to draft new personal narrative entries, we can ask them to look back at the piece they published (after revision and editing) at the end of the previous unit. Since they learned to write focused, sequential stories that included direct quotations, details, paragraphs, and end punctuation, we suggest that their new entries should demonstrate all they have already learned as writers. This unit, then, emphasizes that learning to write is cumulative, and that any new work that writers do will always stand on the shoulders of previous work. Among other things, this unit, then, can definitely teach children that each day of writing is much more than a time to practice that day's minilesson!

Once the unit has gotten underway with this emphasis on writers' drawing on all they already know as they begin a new cycle of writing work, it will be important to find ways to lift the quality of students' work. Chances are good that the stories children wrote during the first unit of study were sequenced, detailed, and, sadly, a bit dull.

One important way to lift the level of writing in this unit is to help children bring forth more significance in their writing. For starters, we teach children strategies for generating narrative entries that stand a greater chance of having emotional weight and of following a story arc. Specifically, we teach children a few new strategies for generating narrative writing that, over time, have proved to evoke especially powerful, shapely stories. For example, we teach students that when a writer wants to write a powerful personal narrative, we sometimes write about the first (or last) time we did something, or about a time we learned something, or a time we felt a strong emotion—hope, worry, sadness. The resulting stories are often significant and shapely.

A second way to lift the level of student writing is to rally children to look really closely at the ways in which writers create texts that matter. We encourage children to read texts like those they will write, to let those texts affect them, and then to pause and ask, "What has this writer done that has affected me?" That is, this unit places a new importance of reading-writing connections.

Since we are guiding students to notice aspects of published texts that we believe will be especially important to them, this unit relies on assessment. Are children already writing focused, detailed, chronological pieces? If not, we'll want to teach the easiest way to focus personal narratives, which is to limit the time span of the story. Sometimes teachers refer to focused narratives as "small moment stories," although the technical word that writers use for this is scenes (as in scenes of a play, not scenery).

But once children grasp what it means to write effectively about a brief episode, we can show them that narratives need not stay within the confines of a half-hour episode! Narratives actually comprise several scenes glued together with bits of exposition (or narration) between them. For children who are ready to learn this, then, we can point out that in any short story, writers often put a few scenes (or small moments) one after another. This is what many people mean when they say that a story has a beginning, a middle, and an end. For example, the child who has written a Small Moment vignette about getting a bike for her birthday will construct a better story if she sets up the incident by first telling about an earlier time when she begged for the bike. Similarly, the child who writes about defending the goal in a soccer game will construct a more effective story if he first backs up to re-create the moment when he put on his goalie pads and worried they might not be thick enough.

Whether children are writing one episode or linking several together, we will definitely teach them that writers focus their pieces not only by narrowing the time-frame in which they write but also by deciding on the angle from which to tell a story. We teach children to ask, "What am I trying to show about myself through this story? What do I want readers to know about me? How can I bring that meaning out in this episode?" As part of this, we help children learn that the same story can be told differently, depending on the theme the writer wants to bring out. An episode about falling from the monkey bars could be written to show that the writer was afraid but conquered her fears or to show that peer pressure goaded the writer to take reckless risks.

In this unit, it is especially important to select a few touchstone texts for children to study. Ideally, they will be personal narratives—but sometimes teachers may choose instead a fictional story, explaining that although the text is really fiction, it is written as a narrative and can therefore demonstrate narrative craft. I recommend the narrative about a red sweater embedded in "Eleven," by Sandra Cisneros. I also recommend selected pages from Jean Little's memoir *Little by Little*,

Patricia MacLachlan's *Journey*, Gary Soto's *A Summer Life*, Amy Ehrlich's *When I Was Your Age: Original Stories About Growing Up*, and the anthology, *Chicken Soup for Kids*. Some picture books can be useful in this unit including Crews' *Shortcut*, Yolen's *Owl Moon*, Keats' *Peter's Chair* or Willems' *Knuffle Bunny*.

Once students have drafted, it is important to teach them to revise. Of course, we'll encourage children to draw on all they already know about revision, and the lessons from the first unit are not inconsequential ones! In addition, in this unit we teach children that a writer's revisions are always informed by our sense of how stories tend to go. This, then, becomes our entrée into teaching students that stories are not, in fact, chains of equally-developed mini-stories (as illustrated by a timeline), but that instead, stories include problems and solutions, and are characterized by rising action, increasing tension. Of course, when children develop the heart of a story as they did in the previous unit, what they are really doing is turning a timeline into a story mountain . . . and this is the graphic organizer that we spotlight as a tool for revision in this unit. Once we've helped children realize that it can help to think of one's personal narrative as a story, then it is not hard to teach children that the beginnings and endings of their stories need to relate to their story mountains. That is, if a child writes about the day he gets a bike, he may want to set up this vignette by showing first that all his life he longed for a bike. Children learn, then, significant ways to craft effective stories, and all of this knowledge will be important as they continue to grow as writers.

The Plan for the Unit

The bends in the road for this unit are as follows:

- Children first look at texts that resemble the sort of thing they hope to write, raising their expectations for what it can mean to write powerful personal narratives.
- Children draw on all the strategies they already know for generating personal narratives and also learn new strategies including the idea that writers sometimes write about first

times, last times, turning points in our lives, or about times we felt strongly. Children gather entries in their writers' notebooks, and we aim for those entries to be focused narratives. Children are encouraged to remember all they learned during the preceding unit and to think, "Am I drawing on all that I know in order to write these entries?" That is, what children learned once through revision now, hopefully, becomes part of drafting.

- Children select a seed idea and rehearse for the draft they will soon write. They recall strategies they learned earlier in the year for developing a seed idea, and they learn to ask, "What is it I *really* want to show in my story?" and to realize that a narrative can be told differently depending on the meaning the writer wants to bring forth. Children study leads of published books and draft and revise their own leads.

- Children draft, writing fast and strong and trying to maintain a point of view.
- Children draw on a growing repertoire of strategies for revising writing, including bringing out the internal story, moving forwards and backwards in time, weaving actions, dialogue and thoughts together, and so forth.
- Children reconsider and revise their draft in the light of a story mountain, asking, 'How might my beginning and my end link to the main thing that I want to show in this story?"
- Children edit drafts, drawing on all they've learned.

READING WITH A WRITER'S EYE

When I first began teaching, I was overwhelmed and disheartened. I even wondered if this profession was for me. I met with Don Graves, who has been a mentor of mine since I was an adolescent. "I'm not sure I'm cut out to be a teacher," I told him. "I can't seem to make it work for me."

Don gave me the best advice of my life. "Lucy," he said, "you need to surround yourself with examples of good teaching, to spend time with teachers who are the kinds of teachers you want to become."

I was at that time reading Charles Silverman's Crisis in the Classroom, a book that extolled the British Primary Schools. And so, even though I'd been teaching (or trying to teach) high school, I flew to England to spend a year apprenticing at the best school I could find, Bicester Primary School. That one year gave me an image of what schools can be like, and for the rest of my career, I've revised, adapted, and built upon that image. Now when I work with teachers across New York City and in other parts of the country, the first thing I suggest is this: Visit a school where the writing workshop is thriving. This will give you an image of what a writing workshop can be.

Children, too, need images of what good work looks like, so when we teach writing, we need to immerse them in the sorts of texts we hope they will write. We launch this unit by inviting children to read several mentor texts, noticing not only the content but also the craft of those texts, learning from what the authors have done. Today's session aims to convey that writers study texts they admire and ask, "What did this author do that I could try?"

In this unit, we ask kids to do something unusual: to repeat what they just did (write a narrative), only this time, to do it better. The school curriculum often has kids traveling through a sequence of one-shot studies. In the writing workshop, we instead ask kids to cycle through the same writing process over and over, each time with greater independence and skill.

In this session, I try to rally students for the important work ahead, to inspire them, and to give them a taste for what is possible in personal narrative writing. I hope that by examining their own lives, they will begin to live with new alertness, seeing more, hearing more, noticing more, and caring more.

IN THIS SESSION, YOU'LL TEACH STUDENTS THAT ONE WAY WRITERS MAKE WRITING POWERFUL IS BY EMULATING NARRATIVE WRITING WE ADMIRE.

GETTING READY

- Copy of Cisneros' "Eleven" for each student
- Excerpt of red-sweater scene from "Eleven," on chart paper or overhead
- Lessons from Mentor Personal Narratives chart
- Copies of other published focused personal narratives (refer to Bibliography for choices), in folder on each table
- See CD-ROM for resources

MINILESSON

Reading with a Writer's Eye

CONNECTION

Support your children's identities as writers by telling them anecdotes to show that their published writing affected their readers. Rally their enthusiasm for writing other stories that matter to readers.

"Writers, at our celebration yesterday, each of you became a published author. As you came in this morning, did you see your work displayed on the bulletin board? Did you pause to appreciate it again, or reread parts one of your classmates wrote?"

"This morning, I saw Ms. Manning come into school with her arms laden with books and boxes. She paused, her arms full, to glance at one of your pieces on the bulletin board; she planned to keep on walking so she glanced like this." I gave a fleeting glance. "Then watch what she did. After glancing at one person's story (I think it was yours, Joey, but I couldn't tell for sure), she stopped glancing and began reading (like this). Then she set her books and boxes down on the floor (like this), and read and read and read through the bulletin board. I watched her say, 'Ahhh . . .' at some parts, and laugh aloud at other parts. Watching her, I thought, 'This is so huge!' Writers dream of writing in a way that makes people stop in their tracks and go, 'Ahhh . . .'. And you've done that!"

"So from this day on, remember that you are writing for readers. Rise to the occasion by making your writing as true and as important as it can be, so your words make readers stop in their tracks and go, 'Ahhh.'"

COACHING

Your children will have just published their first pieces. It is important to use that experience to help them see themselves differently—to develop their identities as writers. I remember when I first studied writing with Pulitzer Prize–winning writer Don Murray. "Writers like you realize . . ." he said. I don't remember what he said after that because I was so blown away by the phrase, "Writers like you." Then a week later he wrote me a letter and addressed the envelope to "Writer Lucy Calkins." I found a discarded door in my cellar, set it between two file cabinets to make myself a desk, and began an intense regimen of writing that has continued ever since. Now I try to always remember that for me, being regarded as a writer allowed me to grow into that role.

If you wish to revise any partnerships or shuffle children's seating arrangements so that certain children are more accessible, the start of a new unit is a natural juncture for doing this.

At the start of a unit, the connection needs to set children up not only for that day's minilesson but also for the month's unit of study. It is always important to me at the start of a unit to promote the unit goals because I want them to be in the kids' hands as well as in my own. I have tried, therefore, to introduce the big concepts of this unit. I tell children that in this unit, we will return to personal narrative writing, but this time, our goal will be to improve the quality of writing. We will aim especially to write in ways that affect readers. To do this, we will learn from mentor authors.

Name the teaching point. In this case, tell children that to improve their writing, they can emulate published authors.

"Today, what I want to teach you is this: When we want to make powerful writing, one strategy we can use is to study the writing of authors we admire. We can read their writing and ask, 'What did this author do that I could do also in order to make my own writing more powerful?'"

TEACHING

Show children that to emulate a piece of writing, we first search for an appropriate mentor text, then we read and experience the text we select. Then, we reread as writers to derive techniques worth emulating.

"In a few weeks, my friend is getting married, and she asked me to make a toast. I will need to stand up at the wedding reception, clink on a glass, and then, when everyone is quiet and looking at me, I'll give a toast to my friend and her husband. But what kind of thing should I say? Should I aim my words *to* her or should I address the crowd and talk about her? I need to know how toasts at weddings usually go, so I'm doing what writers the world over do: I am researching. I am asking people, 'When you've been to wedding receptions and someone gives a toast, what do they usually say?'"

"Today, we're going to begin a new unit of study on personal narrative writing, and this time, we're aiming to write even more powerful stories, stories that will make our readers gasp or nod or wince or laugh aloud or change themselves or even try to change the world. Before getting started, writers often read writing that resembles what we hope to do. We need to not only read that kind of writing, but to reread it, and reread it again. We are going to try that today."

"Earlier this year, we read Sandra Cisneros' story 'Eleven.' A section of the text resembles what we will write in this unit of study, so that's why I'm choosing it as our mentor text. Watch me as I reread the red-sweater excerpt. Notice, especially, that this time I'm going to study the excerpt like I'm studying wedding toasts. I'm going to ask, 'How does this kind of writing mainly go? What has the author done here that I could try?'"

I read the excerpt aloud, as if I were reading to myself, trying to demonstrate experiencing the story as I read it. To show this, I acted out little bits of the text subtly; I became Mrs. Price, holding the sweater gingerly, and with disdain, between two fingers.

On the next page, I include the text of "Eleven." This text will weave through this year long curriculum. Children will revisit it often and you'll find you know it by heart! Of course you may select another text as a touchstone. I refer to "Eleven" as a touchstone becaue it beomes a mentor text for the entire class.

In this session, I will help students learn from a mentor text. As part of this, I want to teach children the process of reaching for such a source of help and of deriving their own lessons from a text. The truth is that whenever I am asked to undertake a new kind of writing, I search for examples that can help me envision the tone, structure, and voice that I want to assume. When I study a mentor text at this very early stage in the process, I'm not apt to notice the decorative details in that text; instead, I hope to gain an overall impression.

In this minilesson I mention that I'm investigating how wedding toasts tend to go so as to write one myself. On other days, I've talked about similar investigations of birthday cards—and of book dedications. I tend to choose tiny texts, and to refer to texts that kids interact with and may not even regard as texts worthy of study.

The decision to use "Eleven" as the mentor text was a tricky one. If the text is a personal narrative at all, it is a disguised one. (The narrator's name, Rachel, is not the author's name.) The truth is, usually before authors publish their personal narratives, they turn them into another genre. They may attribute their personal narrative to another character, embed the personal narrative into an essay, or recast it as fiction. I decided to use this excerpt from "Eleven" despite that ambiguity because it is written in ways that make it a perfect exemplar for kids. You might choose a different mentor text to use in this session. The text you select will travel through the entire unit so choose it with care and read it really well.

ELEVEN

By Sandra Cisneros

What they don't understand about birthdays and what they never tell you is that when you're eleven, you're also ten, and nine, and eight, and seven, and six, and five, and four, and three, and two, and one. And when you wake up on your eleventh birthday you expect to feel eleven, but you don't. You open your eyes and everything's just like yesterday, only it's today. And you don't feel eleven at all. You feel like you're still ten. And you are— underneath the year that makes you eleven.

Like some days you might say something stupid, and that's the part of you that's still ten. Or maybe some days you might need to sit on your mama's lap because you're scared, and that's the part of you that's five. And maybe one day when you're all grown up maybe you will need to cry like if you're three, and that's okay. That's what I tell Mama when she's sad and needs to cry. Maybe she's feeling three.

Because the way you grow old is kind of like an onion or like the rings inside a tree trunk or like my little wooden dolls that fit one inside the other, each year inside the next one. That's how being eleven years old is.

You don't feel eleven. Not right away. It takes a few days, weeks even, sometimes even months before you say Eleven when they ask you. And you don't feel smart eleven, not until you're almost twelve. That's the way it is.

Only today I wish I didn't have only eleven years rattling inside me like pennies in a tin Band-Aid box. Today I wish I was one hundred and two instead of eleven because if I was one hundred and two I'd have known what to say when Mrs. Price put the red sweater on my desk. I would've known how to tell her it wasn't mine instead of just sitting there with that look on my face and nothing coming out of my mouth.

"Whose is this?" Mrs. Price says, and she holds the red sweater up in the air for all the class to see. "Whose? It's been sitting in the coatroom for a month."

"Not mine," says everybody. "Not me."

"It has to belong to somebody," Mrs. Price keeps saying, but nobody can remember. It's an ugly sweater with red plastic buttons and a collar and sleeves all stretched out like you could use it for a jump rope. It's maybe a thousand years old and even if it belonged to me I wouldn't say so.

Maybe because I'm skinny, maybe because she doesn't like me, that stupid Sylvia Saldivar says, "I think it belongs to Rachel." An ugly sweater like that, all raggedy and old, but Mrs. Price believes her. Mrs. Price takes the sweater and puts it right on my desk, but when I open my mouth nothing comes out.

"That's not, I don't, you're not . . . Not mine," I finally say in a little voice that was maybe me when I was four.

"Of course it's yours," Mrs. Price says, "I remember you wearing it once." Because she's older and the teacher, she's right and I'm not.

Not mine, not mine, not mine, but Mrs. Price is already turning to page thirty-two, and math problem number four. I don't know why but all of a sudden I'm feeling sick inside, like the part of me that's three wants to come out of my eyes, only I squeeze them shut tight and bite down on my teeth real hard and try to remember today I am eleven, eleven. Mama is making a cake for me for tonight, and when Papa comes home everybody will sing Happy birthday, happy birthday to you.

But when the sick feeling goes away and I open my eyes, the red sweater's still sitting there like a big red mountain. I move the red sweater to the corner of my desk with my ruler. I move my pencil and books and eraser as far from it as possible. I even move my chair a little to the right. Not mine, not mine, not mine.

In my head I'm thinking how long till lunchtime, how long till I can take the red sweater and throw it over the schoolyard fence, or leave it hanging on a parking meter, or bunch it up into a little ball and toss it in the alley. Except when math period ends Mrs. Price says loud and in front of everybody, "Now, Rachel, that's enough," because she sees I've shoved the red sweater to the tippy-tip corner of my desk and it's hanging all over the edge like a waterfall, but I don't care.

"Rachel," Mrs. Price says. She says it like she's getting mad. "You put that sweater on right now and no more nonsense."

"But it's not—"

"Now!" Mrs. Price says.

This is when I wish I wasn't eleven, because all the years inside of me—ten, nine, eight, seven, six, five, four, three, two, and one—are pushing at the back of my eyes when I put one arm through one sleeve of the sweater that smells like cottage cheese, and then the other arm through the other and stand there with my arms apart like if the sweater hurts me and it does, all itchy and full of germs that aren't mine.

That's when everything I've been holding in since this morning, since when Mrs. Price put the sweater on my desk, finally lets go, and all of a sudden I'm crying in front of everybody. I wish I was invisible but I'm not. I'm eleven and it's my birthday today and I'm crying like I'm three in front of everybody. I put my head down on the desk and bury my face in my stupid clown-sweater arms. My face all hot and spit coming out of my mouth because I can't stop the little animal noises from coming out of me, until there aren't any more tears left in my eyes, and it's just my body shaking like when you have the hiccups, and my whole head hurts like when you drink milk too fast.

But the worst part is right before the bell rings for lunch. That stupid Phyllis Lopez, who is even dumber than Sylvia Saldivar, says she remembers the red sweater is hers! I take it off right away and give it to her, only Mrs. Price pretends like everything's okay.

Today I'm eleven. There's a cake Mama's making for tonight, and when Papa comes home from work we'll eat it. There'll be candles and presents and everybody will sing Happy birthday, happy birthday to you, Rachel, only it's too late.

I'm eleven today. I'm eleven, ten, nine, eight, seven, six, five, four, three, two, and one, but I wish I was one hundred and two. I wish I was anything but eleven, because I want today to be far away already, far away like a runaway balloon, like a tiny o in the sky, so tiny-tiny you have to close your eyes to see it.

From *Woman Hollering Creek* Copyright © 1991 by Sandra Cisneros

"Whose is this?" Mrs. Price says, and she holds the red sweater up in the air for all the class to see. "Whose? It's been sitting in the coatroom for a month."

"Not mine," says everybody. "Not me."

"It has to belong to somebody," Mrs. Price keeps saying, but nobody can remember. (Cisneros, p. 7)

"Do you notice how I try to take in what's happening? I try to read in a way that lets me experience the moment of the story." I continued reading with total absorption:

> I move the red sweater to the corner of my desk with my ruler.
> I move my pencil and books and eraser as far from it as possible.
> I even move my chair a little to the right. Not mine, not mine,
> not mine. (p. 8)

Putting the story down, I leaned in to talk directly to the class. "I can picture the story exactly. As I was reading, I practically felt like I *was* Rachel, moving the sweater to the corner of my desk with my ruler (so I don't have to touch the nasty thing)."

Demonstrate that you shift from reading and experiencing . . . to reading and extrapolating pointers about good writing.

"Now I'm going to pause, shift, and think, 'What do I notice about this story? What are the main things that Sandra Cisneros has done that I need to keep in mind if I'm going to write like this?'"

My eyes scanned the text. Touching one finger to show I'm making a list and that I'm about to name the first item on it, I said, "She's written about an episode in her life that other people might not realize was a big deal, but that really did matter to her." I turned to the chart paper I had entitled Lessons from Mentor Personal Narratives and wrote:

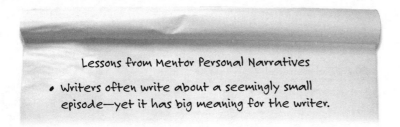

Lessons from Mentor Personal Narratives
• Writers often write about a seemingly small episode—yet it has big meaning for the writer.

In this session, I read aloud a fairly long mentor text. Usually minilessons contain only tiny excerpts for reading aloud. I'm diverging from the norm here because at the start of any new unit, it is important to try to motivate children for the big work ahead. Reading aloud a text that illustrates what we hope children will write is one powerful way to do this. For now, I won't dissect the text. I am helping them be absorbed by the story, and then I will help children step back to examine the text like writers.

I want to show that there are different ways to respond to a story: as a reader, one who gets lost in the text, and as a writer, one who turns the text inside out, asking, "How did she do that?" My body language and tone will accentuate that I shift between two different ways of relating to the text, and between reading aloud and talking to the class. When doing the latter, I put the text down and lean as close to the class as possible.

Little actions such as touching one finger and then another when we progress through a list can make it much easier for children to follow what we say in minilessons.

Again I scanned the story. "She writes it from start to finish with so much detail that I practically feel as if I am reliving the episode." Then I added, "One way she does this is by recording the exact words Mrs. Price said, which was probably how the episode started."

Lessons from Mentor Personal Narratives

- Writers often write about a seemingly small episode— yet it has big meaning for the writer.
- Writers often tell the story in such a way that the reader can almost experience it from start to finish. It helps to record the exact words a character uses.

Debrief. Name what you have demonstrated in a way that is transferable to other texts and other days.

"Do you see how I reread 'Eleven' as thoughtfully as I could, and then, after a bit, I asked, 'What are the main things this author has done that I need to keep in mind if I'm going to write like this?' I'm not focused just yet on the little tiny details—on the repetition of 'not mine, not mine,' for example. Instead I'm trying to understand how her text mainly goes."

ACTIVE ENGAGEMENT

Suggest children read first like readers (envisioning and experiencing the text) and then like writers (analyzing what the author has done). Ask them to list the main things the author has done and then share their lists.

"So let's try it. I'll continue to read, starting after the section in which Rachel pushes the red sweater to the corner of her desk. As I read, try first to simply experience this text, making a movie in your mind. Then I'll reread it, and this time, think about the story as a writer, trying to notice the ways the author has written that allow you to experience her story. Think, 'What are the main things she's done with her writing that I could do?' You'll have a chance to jot these in your notebook."

I resumed reading aloud, starting with this section:

> In my head I'm thinking how long till lunchtime, how long till I can take the red sweater and throw it over the yard fence, or leave it hanging on a parking meter, or bunch it up into a little ball and toss it in the alley. Except when math period ends Mrs. Price says loud and in front of everybody, "Now, Rachel, that's enough . . . ."

You'll notice that the techniques I extrapolate come not only from what I notice in the text but also from what I know children will need to do as they embark on writing another personal narrative. I won't, for example, point out the way an author has ended his or her narrative if I'm guiding children toward how to start their narratives! When I'm studying an exemplar text as a way to start writing that kind of text, I point out the overarching and essential characteristics of the text, and those that might influence how apprentice authors get started on their work.

The Active Engagement section of minilessons begins with the teacher saying, "Let's try it." One trick is to name what students will be trying in a way that is transferable to other texts. So I didn't say, "Let's read 'Eleven,' picturing Rachel's experience with that red sweater." Instead I worded this differently so that what we are practicing is something that I hope writers do over and over, with lots of texts. "As I read," I said, "try to experience this text, making a movie in your mind." The truth is that children will be apt to do that if I make my own mental movie as I read aloud.

I read about Mrs. Price telling Rachel to put the red sweater on, and then I read this:

> I put one arm through one sleeve of the sweater that smells like
> cottage cheese, and then the other arm through the other and stand
> there with my arms apart like if the sweater hurts me and it does, all
> itchy and full of germs that aren't mine. (p. 8)

I gestured toward the text on chart paper, reminding children that the text was available for them to reread. Then I said, "Stop and jot. What did Cisneros do in her text that you could emulate?" After giving children long enough to generate a few items, I said, "Tell your partner what you noticed." As children talked, I listened for an observation that I wanted to highlight.

Ask children to report on their findings, and then add their observations to the class chart.

After a minute, I nodded at one child to repeat what I'd just overheard her saying. Jocelyn said, "She has a lot of feelings."

After I nodded to signal that another child could add on, Rafael added, "And she doesn't just tell that the sweater was disgusting and all, she showed it by describing it carefully."

I added their observations to the list, and now the chart looked like this:

Lessons from Mentor Personal Narratives

- Writers often write about a seemingly small episode—yet it has big meaning for the writer.
- Writers often tell the story in such a way that the reader can almost experience it from start to finish. It helps to record the exact words a character uses.
- Writers often convey strong feelings, and they often show rather than tell about those feelings.

Practice reading aloud. Mem Fox once taught a group of us to read (and storytell) well. She cautioned us that instead of aiming to read expressively, we'd be better off to aim toward truly experiencing the text as we read it. When I read that it's an "ugly" sweater, if I am seeing the ugly thing, then my voice will reflect the ugliness of it. When I read about putting one arm in one sleeve, I need to mentally slide one arm into that sleeve so that as I speak, my voice allows listeners to also feel as if they are sliding their arms into that sweater, full of germs that aren't even theirs.

You may, of course, select a different text to thread through this unit, and I'd certainly advise this for your children's second cycle, in a subsequent year. The reason I like "Eleven" is its clarity. The decision relates to your image of good writing. Some teachers of writing (and I am one of these) lean toward an image of good writing that highlights clarity, detail, order, simplicity, and others prefer writing that is lush, poetic, descriptive, and decorative. Select a mentor text that matches your goals for your children, and hope that children study in progressive years under the tutelage of teachers with different preferences.

Notice throughout all of this that I use silent gestures often to cue children. I gestured to the chart paper to remind children to read it. I nodded (instead of calling out) to draw more voices into the conversation. When we use gestures instead of our voices to manage children's behavior, we are using less visible and concrete scaffolds, thus helping children transition toward proceeding with independence.

There is no question but that you could elicit lots more observations from the class community and you could spend half an hour making a gigantic list of all that children notice in the text. I wouldn't do so because the goal here is to demonstrate the strategy of studying a mentor text and noticing features worth emulating; the goal is not to produce a gigantic list. In fact, the great reading researcher, Marie Clay, once visited our classrooms and confided that she wonders if any list of more than five items is worth much—an intriguing thought! In any case, I'd keep the list brief now so that you can soon send children off to do this sort of work on their own.

LINK
Reiterate the teaching point and send children off to study mentor texts.

"So writers, today we launch a new unit—our goal will be to write personal narratives that make even more readers, like Ms. Manning, stop in their tracks! We learned today that writers read first as readers, trying to experience the story. Then writers read as writers. Just as chefs taste a great apple tart and then think, 'What was the recipe?' and seamstresses turn a particularly interesting dress inside out to study the seams and hems, thinking, 'What pattern did she follow to make this?' so, too, writers read the work of other authors, asking, 'How did she write this? What did this author do that I could try?'"

"Today and for the rest of your life, whenever you want to gear yourself up for an important writing project, I hope you remember to study texts that are like those you want to write. I've put a small folder of personal narratives on the middle of your tables. Instead of writing, today, let's read. Read these first to experience them, then read them again to study the main things the author has done. List what you see the author has done that you can try in your writer's notebooks, and get ready to talk together about your lists. We'll work silently for about fifteen minutes, and then we'll talk."

Don't hesitate to put texts that children already know into the folders on their desks. For example, they studied Shortcut *in the first unit of study—include it! You may want to retype* Shortcut *(and any other picture book you hope children will study) onto a single sheet of paper so that children have a copy of the text that they can mark up as they study it. Be sure to include "Your Name in Gold" if you plan to discuss it later (as I do). You'll find it listed (along with many other possible mentor texts) in the Bibliography.*

Writing and Conferring

Studying Mentor Texts

Today, prepare to gasp at the texts your children are reading and do so in a way that draws children into the reading. If a child points in a half-hearted way to a section of a text as you circulate, pretend the child has just jumped up and down with excitement over the words and that you are joining in. "Oh my gosh!" you'll say. "You are right. This is so powerful, isn't it?" Then read that section aloud. Read it like it's worth a million dollars. Don't question the child's judgment, and for now, don't interrogate the child to get him or her to produce a defense for the selection. At least at first, don't even analyze the text to unpack the writing techniques that it illustrates. Instead, begin by reading the texts deeply and well. This will help children to also read in such a way that the texts can make a difference to them. Read the selection aloud so that the hairs on the back of your neck prickle. Read it slowly. Gasp at it. Read it again.

> **MID-WORKSHOP TEACHING POINT** *Rereading Texts* "Writers," I said, standing among the children as they worked. I waited for all eyes to be on me. "When someone asked the great poet Robert Frost, 'How do I learn to write?' Frost said, 'Read *Anna Karenina*, read *Anna Karenina*, read *Anna Karenina*.' He could have said, 'Read "Eleven," read "Eleven," read "Eleven,"' or 'Read *Shortcut*, read *Shortcut*, read *Shortcut*.' The point is that to learn from a text, we need to not only read it, but to reread, and reread, and reread it."
>
> "Would you reread a section of a personal narrative text that you've already admired, and this time try to see more? Read the words aloud in your mind and listen to them. Think, 'What has this writer done that I can emulate in my writing?' In a bit, you'll have a chance to talk with your partner about what you noticed and admired."

Then after you have joined the child in reading at least a section of the text, model how a reader sometimes turns back to name the effect the passage created. Speak in true words, naming what the passage did for you and avoiding hackneyed phrases like "made a picture in my mind." Instead say something like, "When I read this, I realized I have done the exact same thing. And when I read these words, I was doing it in my mind." Or you might say, "This part gave me a hollow feeling. The words are so stark. 'Not mine. Not mine. Not mine.' It sounds like *amen* or *goodbye*."

Encourage the child to say what he was thinking or feeling or noticing. Help draw words out of the child through gestures and body language; listen, nod, respond in ways that say, "Yes, yes, I know what you mean, say more . . . ." Don't worry today about whether your conferences follow the usual architecture of conferences or whether you are explicitly teaching anything. You will teach *implicitly* today. You'll help children immerse themselves in the sort of text you hope they will soon write—and meanwhile, you will create a drumroll for a unit of study that essentially asks kids to go back and do what they did before, only better.

SHARE

Discussing the Genre of Personal Narrative

Set children up to talk about their general sense of the genre, deduced from looking at many personal narrative texts.

"Writers," I said, and paused until all their eyes were on me. "Let's gather in the meeting area to talk about the incredible observations you are making. Bring your folders of mentor texts and your writer's notebooks, and sit with your partners." Once children had gathered, I said, "We're going to talk with our partners, but first let me help you prepare for those conversations. Our goal now is to think and talk about these texts in ways that help us write our own true stories even more powerfully than we ever have before. So I think it is important to look, think, and talk about the overall design of the writing we've just read. Here's my question: What were all these writers doing? Another way to put it is this: What is the shared form that you saw in this writing?"

"Would you reread and jot notes to get ready for partnership conversations on this topic: What is it that all of the narratives have in common?" I allowed time for children to quickly scan the stories they'd just read. After a few minutes, I asked them to discuss this topic with their partners.

Reconvene the class. Solicit and chart the shared characteristics they saw in personal narratives.

"So writers, during our minilesson today we began a list, Lessons from Mentor Personal Narratives. What observations have you made that we could add to our list?"

Caleb said, "Well, 'Your Name in Gold' really is two small moments. It first tells about when the girls read the cereal box and saw you could send away for your name in gold. Then it jumped and told about when the package arrived in the mail. So it was two small moments, stuck together."

Ori agreed: "And *Shortcut* told about when the kids walked on the train tracks before the train came, then when the train came, and when it rattled off."

You may wonder why I'm asking children to study personal narrative writing as if it's a new genre, when in fact they just finished a unit in which they wrote this way. I think that often in life, we do something and then later we reflect on that familiar action. I taught minilessons for several decades before undertaking a study of effective minilessons, which led me to design what I now refer to as the architecture of minilessons.

The endeavor I ask children to undertake here is not easy. It isn't clear to me that most eight and nine year olds can extract the common features across an assortment of short texts. However, the fact that I've invited children to try something which may prove difficult for them is okay with me, as long as they'll still benefit from the effort.

There is nothing magical about these particular texts I reference. I like "Name in Gold" because it is simple and straightforward—and shows that focused personal narratives can contain a few closely related moments. The sisters read the cereal box advertisement for a name-necklace, one makes off with the coupon to the other's disgust. In the end, it turns out the one sibling sent for her sister's name in gold.

I nodded. "This is a huge discovery! These authors zoomed in. But they didn't just write about one moment—the name plaque arriving in the mail. Author A. F. Bauman set that moment up by first writing about an earlier moment, when the girls read the cereal box's offer to send one name in gold. And you are right, Crews also didn't write just about the one moment when the train came, did he? He first told about walking, carefree, on the tracks with his friends, didn't he? It is as if his picture book included a Before Moment, then a Super Important Moment."

"Writers, I'm thinking we should definitely add your insight to our chart."

If students haven't noticed this particular aspect of personal narrative, the last item on the list, you will need to point it out as your own observation, after you have added their observations to the chart. One of the strongest ways to help children write more sophisticated narratives in this unit is this time you'll encourage them to build personal narratives which follow a story arc—with moments leading up to (and perhaps following) the main small moment of their story. You will build on this item in later lessons, so you need to be sure it's mentioned here.

Lessons from Mentor Personal Narratives

- Writers often write about a seemingly small episode— yet it has big meaning for the writer.
- Writers often tell the story in such a way that the reader can actually experience it from start to finish. It helps to record exact words a character uses.
- Writers often convey strong feelings, and they often show rather than tell about those feelings.
- Writers often include two and sometimes three small moments so that there is a sense that the stories have a beginning, a middle, and an end.

Notice that in Unit 1 I taught children to zoom in on a single moment, and in this upcoming unit, I teach children to outgrow that somewhat rudimentary notion of focus. I believe that our teaching will often progress in such a fashion. After all, we teach beginning readers to point under words as they read . . . and then we teach them to stop pointing under words as they read. This doesn't mean that it wasn't helpful that children did, for a passing interval, point as they read. Similarly, expect in other ways that I'll teach in overly simplified ways that are later made more complex.

Remind children of the strategy that can help them today and every day: Writers can learn writing techniques from great literature.

"Now we have made a list that you can look at when you are thinking about how your own personal narrative will go. More than this, I hope you have learned that always, you can do what writers do—look at literature similar to that which you want to write and let it help you figure out what to do!"

The Lessons from Mentor Personal Narratives chart is likely to have similar, if not nearly identical, items to the Qualities of Good Personal Narrative Writing chart from the previous unit. This is intentional. Children are likely to need various ways to think about these qualities of good personal narratives. This session offers children a new approach to the same topic. Children can learn from this session that they can always turn to writing they admire to find ways to emulate good writing.

HOMEWORK *Studying Mentor Texts* Painters visit art museums, and stand before the giant canvasses, studying the techniques of the masters. Scientists apprentice with researchers, working alongside them in laboratories. Writers, too, learn from studying mentors. We find texts that resemble the text we want to write, and we study those mentor texts.

It takes imagination to learn from a text that another author has made because we need to look at the text and think, "What kind of life did this writer lead which allowed her to write like this?" We wonder what sort of entries she may have collected in her writer's notebook. We speculate over whether she wrote a timeline first, or tried several lead sentences. We won't, of course, know the answers to those questions, but it is important to look at writing we admire and to think about the processes the writer probably used in order to write like this.

Tonight, would you read another narrative by Sandra Cisneros, this one called "Papa Who Wakes Up Tired in the Dark." Think about the sorts of entries Cisneros probably collected in her notebook. Why do you think she decided to write about this moment? Do you think she made a movie in her mind in order to write this?

Because you'll read "Papa Who Wakes Up Tired in the Dark" as a fellow writer, you'll no doubt want to star parts that are especially beautiful and to think, "How did she write this part?" Write all over the copy of this text that I'm giving you. Tomorrow you'll have a chance to write your own entries! Be thinking about moments that you, like Sandra Cisneros, can capture on the page.

TAILORING YOUR TEACHING

If you think your class needs some inspiration and motivation as they approach another unit of personal narrative writing . . . you could also seize this opportunity to teach children how to turn "Eleven" or the touchstone text you select into a symphony share. After giving children a few minutes to find and reread favorite parts, say to them, "I'm going to be the conductor of an orchestra. When I point my baton at you, would you read aloud a tiny excerpt, an excerpt you especially like? Read the excerpt in such a way that it gets through to us. Look up to show me you've found your excerpt and then I'll start conducting. Your excerpt can be just a sentence or a phrase." When I did this recently, I began the recitation by saying aloud, "Powerful Writing, by Sandra Cisneros," as if this were the title of the improvisation. The title adds a touch of extra dignity to the event. Then I pointed to one child and another. I didn't respond verbally to what a child read—instead, I moved to the

If you suspect that children will have a hard time making generalizations about the content and structure of the genre, it might help to set examples of personal narrative writing against examples of another genre of writing. Comparing personal narratives to short stories or short essays or short newspaper articles will make features of narrative writing pop out to young readers. Of course, if the genres being compared are similar, more emphasis will fall on the details of what makes personal narrative writing unique. When the two kinds of writing being compared are vastly different, the biggest differences will be the most pronounced. When choosing texts to contrast with personal narrative writing, keep in mind that generally the shorter the texts, the more easily readers can grasp a sense of the form of the whole.

This is from Cisneros' The House on Mango Street, *which is a book that you'll return to often for examples of powerful narrative writing. "Papa Who Wakes Up Tired in the Dark" could be your touchstone text for the entire unit—it is beautiful!*

next and then the next so their voices cascaded together. If a child chatted about his or her response, I intervened and asked the child not to do this; then we redid that one section. Soon the room filled with voices:

"with sleeves all stretched out like you could use it for a jump rope."

"I said in a little voice that was maybe me when I was four."

"'Not mine,' I finally say."

I find that the work required to pull this off is worthwhile because this symphony share is a ritual you can return to often over the year. While in this instance, children read lines they love from a published text, another time, you may instead ask them to select and read details from their own writing or instances of alliteration or strong action words. Just be sure to allow children to prepare before they perform by finding instances of whatever is being celebrated within their own or a published text.

If you decide to extend this work . . . you may invite children to join you in a search for either well-written personal narratives, or for texts that illustrate narrative craft so well that they can be instructive in this unit. Just as the red-sweater excerpt from "Eleven" functions well as an example of the narrative craft, children may also decide to study chapters in *Because of Winn-Dixie*, by Kate DiCamillo, for example. You may share a few examples and then ask children to help you search for others, compiling a basket of texts that resemble those they aspire to write. The day wouldn't follow a traditional workshop structure—and the children would benefit from the break.

ASSESSMENT

It has been said that we see and hear not with our eyes and ears but with our beliefs. The list of things that a child sees in a mentor text will reveal more about the child than about the text. Study your children's observations of published mentor texts. Ask children to study also a text written by another child, making observations about what the child has done (see CD for suggested texts). Your children's observations will reveal what they know about good writing. Of course, these observations will also reflect previous instruction. If many of your children report seeing similar things in mentor texts, these may be qualities of good writing that previous teachers have valued or that your students have come to believe you value. You may need to allow children more time to see past their first observations.

Very often I find, for example, that teachers have emphasized writing descriptively, and children are quick to admire any instances in which an author has used his or her senses or written with figurative language. But often children are *not* taught to read with an eye toward other qualities of good writing that have particular power to lift the level of their own work. You'll want to observe whether your children are carrying the work from the previous unit with them. For example, do they notice focus, commenting on whether the author has written a focused Small Moment story rather than writing all about a topic? Do they notice how the author has included true and exact details from within a scene? Do they see that the story develops in a step-by-step sequential fashion on the page?

Save your children's notes about the stories they read and, toward the end of the unit, ask children to reread the narratives they read today, again jotting down what they notice about the authors' craftsmanship. They should be able to see many techniques they didn't observe at the start of the unit, and this should provide you with a great sense of satisfaction. In a sense, this simple activity will convey to you whether your instruction is lifting children's

sense of standards, giving them more informed ideas about effective narrative writing. Even if some of your children end this unit still unable to turn their images of good writing into realities, simply developing a richer image of what they are working toward when writing a story is a huge accomplishment. *[Fig. I-1]*

Meanwhile, of course, it is important for us, as teachers, to become much more skilled at reading writing. When you gather with your colleagues, try doing what you ask your children to do. Read a story and talk together about the characteristics of the writing that make the story an effective one. Put two narratives alongside each other, and try to find words for ways in which both texts incorporate a similar form. Resist the tendency to use prepackaged language. For example, it would have been helpful if I asked myself, "What exactly do I mean when I say, 'This story has a beginning, a middle, and an end'?" If I can expand on that cliché, I can make it more personal and meaningful for me and for my students.

Ingredients for a Small moment		
1. one focus/small amt of time (stretched out)		
2. action		
3. sensory details /images		
4. 8x in the moment (present tense)		
5.*what is the big thing? so what?		
6. some dialogue (not much)		
7.		

Fig. I-1 Ilana reminds herself of the ingredients for a Small Moment narrative

IN THIS SESSION, YOU'LL REMIND STUDENTS TO USE STRATEGIES THEY ALREADY KNOW FOR GENERATING NARRATIVE WRITING. YOU WILL ALSO TEACH THEM THAT WRITERS THINK OF FIRST TIMES, LAST TIMES, OR TIMES OF IMPORTANT REALIZATIONS TO GENERATE WRITING.

GETTING READY

- Strategies for Generating Personal Narrative Writing chart from first session
- See CD-ROM for resources

STARTING WITH TURNING POINTS

Although the preceding session was the start of this unit, because children spent that day reading rather than writing, today's minilesson actually launches the writing work in this second unit of study. Approach this session knowing that your minilesson will need to set children up for the earliest stages of their writing process. As you plan today's minilesson (and the initial lessons of all units), you will need to help children consolidate, carry forward, and draw upon the lessons they have already learned. This will be especially important in this unit because children will be writing personal narratives again. Teach children that the strategies they learn during previous writing workshops will be useful throughout their lives. Of course, as children develop facility with these strategies, the strategies themselves will no longer be the focus of their attention. Instead, writers will be able to use them almost automatically, concentrating on new writing goals.

When I introduce a strategy, I make a big deal of it: I lay out every part of it, turning it into a mechanical, step-by-step operation. This may feel odd at first, a bit unbalanced, but I believe that when we teach any complex activity, we need to explicitly lay out each step with exaggerated attention, keeping in mind that soon, the learner will master the procedure, repeating it as one flowing, almost automatic activity. For example, the tennis coach will show the novice how to grasp the tennis racket, then how to turn the racket so that it fits properly in the hand. But before long, the learner just grabs for the racket, swiftly taking—but no longer fussing over—the same steps.

In Launching the Writing Workshop, *we helped children develop a set of strategies for personal narrative writing and we asked them to carry these in their mental backpacks. In this unit, you'll help children use those strategies to more powerful effect. You'll teach a few new strategies, but this time, you'll focus less on the strategies and more on writing narratives like those the class is studying, narratives that contain more than a single small moment—narratives that have a story arc. The early lessons in this unit will help children generate not only topics for writing but also fleshed-out story ideas—topics with a ready-made plot line. This will help children write stories that revolve around (but are more than) accounts of single, small moments. That is, the narratives that children begin generating today should begin to feel like real stories—stories that resemble those your children have been studying.*

MINILESSON

Starting with Turning Points

CONNECTION

Tell children that in this unit, they will be writing even more powerful Small Moment stories—and one way to do this is to start with turning points.

"Writers, yesterday we pored over stories that resemble those we hope to write and we asked, 'What did this author do that I could try?' We especially looked at the way in which all the stories have a shared form. They all contain more than just a small moment, they have writing leading up to the main small moment in the middle, and then they sometimes have more moments to make an end. For example, in "Your Name in Gold," you noticed that the story starts with a scene at the breakfast table when Annie and her big sister both read the cereal box and both yearn to be the one to send the coupon off for a golden name plaque, and the story ends with a second small moment, a second scene (as writers call it) in which the big sister gives Annie her name in gold. We also read other stories—like *Shortcut* and 'Papa Who Wakes Up Tired in the Dark'—and afterwards, we realized that stories often have a shared form."

"In the stories we read, there is a beginning—and then something happens to change things, and then there is an end. The moments that change things are all different, but all are important: In one, the big sister does a surprising act of generosity; in another, the girl realizes that it could have been her own papa who died; in another, the train almost flattens a group of kids. In all of these moments, the character feels or learns something important. The stories we studied (and the stories we will be writing) are Small Moment stories, and if you study them even harder, you will see that they all include some kind of turning point."

COACHING

It is all too easy to begin our minilessons with an empty introduction: "Yesterday, we began our unit on writing powerful personal narratives," or "Yesterday we read and talked about mentor personal narratives." There is nothing terribly wrong about starting a minilesson like this, but if leads are important in children's writing, they are also important in our minilessons. And those ho-hum introductions may send this message to kids: The beginning of a minilesson is old hat, so you can tune out till later. Why would we want to convey such a message? Don't we risk having kids tune out for the whole minilesson? Instead think, "What can I say at the start of a minilesson that recaptures some of yesterday's learning but also consolidates and packages that learning so that it's ready for the road, or adds new nuance and energy to that learning?" In this instance, I try for the latter. I am also angling my account of the previous session so that I highlight one of the more complex and rich lessons, a lesson that I definitely want in the forefront of children's minds as we go forward.

Remind children that they already have a repertoire of strategies for generating narrative writing, represented in charts that can become vitally important tools for them.

"Today, as we begin to work on new pieces of writing, I want to remind you that *you already know* strategies for coming up with stories that make readers sigh and laugh and pull in to read more. Last month, you wrote two personal narratives and this month we'll work on the same kind of writing again! As writers, we each carry with us an invisible backpack full of all the strategies we've ever learned, and we pull them out as needed. It's not an accident that the charts from our first unit are still in the room. You'll look at those charts often throughout the whole year to remind you of strategies you've already learned. Later today, when it is time to generate narrative entries, I bet you'll use this chart to remind you of the strategies you might use."

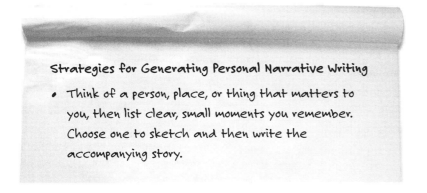

Strategies for Generating Personal Narrative Writing
• Think of a person, place, or thing that matters to you, then list clear, small moments you remember. Choose one to sketch and then write the accompanying story.

Name the teaching point. In this case, teach children that when writers want to generate ideas for personal narratives, they often think of turning point moments.

"Today, before you start generating personal narrative entries, I want to teach you one more strategy that I often use when I want to write personal narratives. This is a strategy that especially helps me write entries that can become powerful stories. Specifically, I find it helps to list moments in my life that have been turning points for me. These are often first times, last times, or times when I realized something important."

Sometimes I see teachers disguising the fact that children will recycle, in this unit, through the same process they experienced earlier, once again writing personal narratives. Don't downplay this! Instead, seize on the important opportunity you have to teach children to draw on yesterday's and last month's teaching as they continue their work. Until children learn to do this, they can't be independent writers. The image of an invisible backpack is one I use again and again. Substitute your own metaphor, if you prefer, but find a way to help children learn to draw on all they know, not just the most recent lessons.

Note that the first bullet in this chart now consolidates three strategies introduced individually in the first unit: focusing on a person, place, or object. For conciseness, you too may want to group these items as I've done before adding to the list.

Notice that I do not phrase the teaching point like this: "Today we will think of turning point stories." That wording would have simply assigned children a task. That is not my goal! A minilesson is not a forum for telling children what we want them all to do in the upcoming workshop. Instead, it is a place for explicitly teaching children the skills and strategies of good writing—skills and strategies we want them to call upon as needed not only today, but always. In today's minilesson, I am hoping to teach children one more technique that they can carry with them in their invisible backpacks of strategies.

TEACHING
Demonstrate the step-by-step sequence of using the strategy. In this case generate ideas for personal narratives by listing first times, last times, or times when you realized something important.

"Let me show you how I use the strategies of thinking of first times I did something, thinking of last times I did something, and thinking of when I realized something important, because these are all ways for me to think of turning point stories."

"In order to come up with a first or last time, I take something—anything I do all the time. So I pick ice skating. Then I think, 'When is the *first time* I ice skated?' And suddenly, I remember a time (it might not have been the very first time, but it was an early time) when I skated out to an island, pushing a little red chair in front of me so I wouldn't fall. I write that time on my list, knowing I might come back and tell the story of it later." I jotted a phrase representing the episode on chart paper. "In order to come up with a last time I did something, I go through the same steps . . . and this time, I end up remembering the last time I saw my grandfather, on a visit to the nursing home."

"I can also think, 'What moment can I recall when suddenly I realized something important?' That's harder! But I think about 'Your Name in Gold,' and I think Anne wrote about that moment—her name in gold—because that's when she suddenly realized her sister really cared for her. And in 'Papa Who Wakes Up Tired in the Dark,' Sandra described the moment when she hugged and hugged and hugged her father because in that moment, she suddenly realized it could have been *her* dad who died!"

Debrief. Remind children of the purpose for the strategy. In this case, remind them that thinking of turning points can help them generate ideas for personal narratives.

"When I want to pick a topic for a personal narrative that will make a really good story, one that will have the shape of a story—a beginning, a middle, and an end—and one that matters, it often helps to think about turning point moments. And now you've seen that to do this, I sometimes brainstorm first times, last times, and times when I realized something important. My brainstorming leads to a list, and then I choose one moment from the list that I believe is the most significant to write about in detail."

Don't bypass this lesson! It works like a charm to ask children to think about first times, last times, and times when they realized something important. When children think about these turning points, they automatically generate story ideas that have a before and an after, or a beginning, middle, and end. In other words, finding topics in this way helps children build a story arc because the arc is inherent in the story. This is most obvious in the "times when I realized something" stories. For example, a child might tell about how he'd always taken his dad for granted. Then a turning point happened, and he appreciated him. Another child may have thought a particular teacher would be terrifying, but then a turning point happened and the child realized his fears were unfounded. Last- and first-time stories also often have a before and an after, or a beginning, middle, and end. For example, first-time stories often begin with a prelude: "I always wanted to do such and such," and then the stories progress until the crucial moment happens. This way of finding topics puts a tension into the personal narrative—an element so many good stories contain—even though the writer may not yet be completely conscious of crafting to create the tension.

While you teach children qualities of good writing, keep in mind that those same qualities can meanwhile transform our own minilessons. One quality of good writing that we have not yet highlighted for the kids is cohesiveness. By the end of this year, you'll see that I teach children how they can create a more cohesive text by repeating an important phrase at the beginning, middle, and end of a narrative, or by having images or symbolic objects recur. Cohesion is also important in our minilessons. You'll notice that I repeat the teaching point several times in a minilesson, and also that I carry phrases, images, and titles from one day's minilesson into the next.

ACTIVE ENGAGEMENT
Ask your children to think of turning point stories they could write and to jot those ideas in their writer's notebooks so they have a list of story ideas for later.

"Let's try it. I'm going to suggest some general topics, and you try to think of a turning point story you could write. If you think of one, jot it down in your writer's notebook so that later, you'll have a list of ideas you can come back to." I posed one idea, then another, leaving time after each item for children to scrawl their thoughts into their notebooks.

"Think about the first time you did something that felt, at the time, like it was hard for you, like swimming across the pool, or climbing to the very top of a mountain, or taking the subway by yourself."

"Think about the first time you did something that now you do every day, like seeing your younger brother, or coming into this classroom, or walking to school from your apartment, or playing a sport, or reading a book."

"Think about the last time you saw a person (or a pet) who died, or the last time you saw someone who left you."

"Think about the time you realized something about yourself, or about a person you know well."

"Think about a time you realized something almost happened to you—something that would have changed your life."

"Thumbs up if you found it helpful to think about first times, last times, and times when you realized something," I said, revealing the more specific Questions to Ask to Find Turning Points chart I had written.

Keep your suggestions simple, common, and general. Your goal is for children to be able to prompt themselves the way you are now prompting them. For a strategy to be useful, the writer has to be able to use it independently, without a teacher, later. Therefore make sure your prompts are the sort that kids can internalize and use for themselves.

Don't underestimate the importance of leaving little pools of silence after each injunction. Give children time to think and to jot. The best way to do this is to have your notebook on hand, and to take a second after each injunction to do your own very quick thinking and jotting.

In this minilesson, you may wish to highlight the fact that the process of brainstorming possible story ideas involves five minutes, not a full workshop! Explain that writers shift between brainstorming, selecting, and writing.

Questions to Ask to Find Turning Points
- first/last time you did something hard to do
- first/last time you did something you now do every day
- first/last time with a person, an animal, a place, an activity
- a time you realized something important about yourself or someone else
- a time you realized a huge change in your life almost happened

LINK

Remind children that writers draw from their growing repertoire of strategies. Add the turning point strategy to the Strategies for Generating Personal Narrative Writing chart, and therefore to your children's repertoire.

"So writers, I hope you remember that you carry with you an invisible backpack full of strategies, including all the strategies you learned earlier this year for generating personal narratives. And today you learned one more strategy to add to your backpack. You learned that if you want to turn a small moment in your life into a really good story, it can help to start by thinking of turning point moments, and more specifically, to think of first-time or last-time moments, or times when you realized something important. I'll add that to our chart over here."

> **Strategies for Generating Personal Narrative Writing**
>
> • Think of a person, place, or thing that matters to you, then list clear, small moments you remember. Choose one to sketch and then write the accompanying story.
>
> • Think of first times, last times, or times when you realized something important. Write about one of these moments.

"As you gather entries today, draw on any strategy from this chart. Remember that it should take you just a few minutes to jot a few quick lists of ideas for entries, and then you'll need to select an idea from your list and write it. You may have time to write two entries (as well as some lists) today."

"Give me a thumbs up if you think you'll choose to write about a first time, last time, or a time when you realized something important. Give me a thumbs up if you think you'll start with a person, a place, or an object, and then list and choose between small moments connected to that." Children so indicated and I sent them off to work.

Although these strategy "backpacks" are invisible, your charts are very visible. Be sure to add each strategy to your chart of Strategies for Generating Personal Narrative Writing.

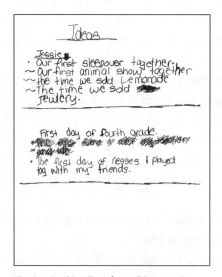

Fig. II-1 Sophie's list of possible narratives

Fig. II-2 Sophie lists more possibilities

WRITING AND CONFERRING

Generating Energy and Writing

When you launch a new unit, you'll want to rally the children to do the new work, creating a burst of energy around it. You hope that by the end of the day, lots of children have used the new strategies you've taught and that their energy for the new unit is high. Because I always want to be sure the first minilessons in a new unit empower children, I scanned this session's teaching plans in advance, asking, "What problems can I anticipate the children might encounter today?" I don't want any problems to interfere with children's sense that the upcoming work will be do-able and exciting. I did not expect that children would have trouble with today's work because it is not very different from the work they did during Unit 1. However, some children may simply list turning points, not shifting from listing to writing, so I entered this work time ready to make a quick whole-class interruption, if necessary, to clarify that once a child had listed some moments, the challenge is to take one and write it as a story in his notebook—a story that resembles those he's been studying.

As children generate ideas for their writing, you'll remind them to draw on what they have already learned. Recalling the strategies for generating narratives shouldn't be too difficult. A bigger challenge will be to make sure children recall the qualities of writing they learned in the previous unit. For example, if Jacob worked hard during Unit 1 to focus his story on a smaller moment, you will want to act totally astounded if he forgets all that he learned in the first unit now and returns to writing about a huge, broad topic. If Maria learned during the last unit to write with detail, you'll want to act as if you can't comprehend why someone with her talent for detail would now be writing with generalizations. In your conferences, convey your expectation that children will use their accumulated knowledge every time they write.

If you know certain students are struggling, immediately give them the help they'll need to get off to a great start in this unit. Convene a group of your least experienced writers and read with them the chart of strategies for generating personal narrative writing. Help them select one strategy, then say, "Let me show you how that strategy works." With your help, the kids could (for example) each think of the first time they did something. Prompt each child to orally list and choose between a few story ideas;

MID-WORKSHOP TEACHING POINT — *Making Planning Boxes* "Earlier today you learned a few new strategies for generating true stories, and I've loved seeing your stories about first times, last times, or times when you realized something important. But I want to remind you that you needn't draw only on this list of new strategies. Remember how Cisneros' character points out that when she is ten, she is also nine and eight and seven? And that is true for us as writers as well. When we are in our *second* unit of study, we are also in our *first* unit of study, because as writers, we grow in layers like onions, or like trees in rings, with one unit of study inside the next."

"You'll want to draw on your full repertoire of strategies, and to do this, you'll want to use stuff—old charts, old entries and rough drafts, finished writing—to get you thinking about strategies that worked for you that you'll want to carry with you into this new unit."

"When I want to remember strategies that I've used before, I don't just sit at my

continued on next page

> Pay attention at lunch time so I can write a small moment from lunch or recess today.

> Write a scene use all you know about slowing down! Internal + External

> pick another entry from my notebook Visualize and write the new entry in tiny little steps

Figs. II-3, II-4, and II-5 Examples of Planning boxes

listen for and steer children toward story ideas that sound like they will pay off. Don't take too long helping children to generate story ideas because you'll also need to help them get those stories started.

Once every child in the group has a story idea, help them frame their writing as stories, not summaries. Try working with one child while the other children watch. Ask, "What were you doing at the very start of this event?" Once the child specifically describes her opening action, help her say more: "Then what?" Be prepared for the child to speak in generalizations, and help her speak in details. "What exactly were you playing?" The child's story should not have sweeping statements such as "I was playing and he yelled at me," but should instead be specific: "I was playing Frisbee with my dog, Banjo. Banjo grabbed the Frisbee. Then my Dad yelled, 'Cut it out!'"

The child will probably articulate her story one sentence at a time; once you have lured the start of the story out of the child, say her story back coherently, synthesizing the fragments into a flowing lead. If the lead you articulate is what the child wants to say, repeat it but this time say a phrase and wait while she writes it. Say the next phrase, and wait. After a bit, have the child reread what he or she has written. Then say, "Keep going." Once the child has said what comes next, signal for her to add that to the page. That child should be off to a great start.

Meanwhile, the other children in the small group will be ready for you to nudge them to use these same questions and prompts to help them with their writing. In this manner, you can get your strugglers off to a strong start. Plan to use their work soon as examples for other kids to emulate. You will totally alter their experience of the entire unit of study if you give these children an early boost toward success.

---

continued from previous page

desk and stare into space. Instead, I look back on my experiences as a writer and remember strategies that have helped me improve my writing. For sure, I reread old charts." I referred to the Strategies for Generating Personal Narrative Writing chart.

"As I look over old charts and the writing I've already done, I get ideas for the strategy I want to try next. I give myself an assignment for what to do next, and I record the strategy I will use in a planning box in my notebook." I showed children how most of the pages in my notebook begin with a little planning box. Leaning close to the children, I said, "Here's the important thing. Writers do not just plan *what* we are going to write about. We also plan *how* we're going to go about writing. Right now, would you reread what you've written, look over your charts, and think, 'How will I go about writing my next entry?' If you haven't already reused a strategy from our first unit of study, pick one to reuse today. And before you write (today and from this day on), make and fill in a planning box for yourself in your notebook. Then get going, following your plan."

What I did not say, but thought, was this: The fact that a child must take a moment to record his or her plan before proceeding makes it much more likely that children do make plans as writers. They are less apt to simply proceed as if on autopilot.

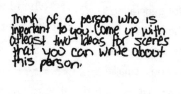

Fig. II-6 Sophie's planning box

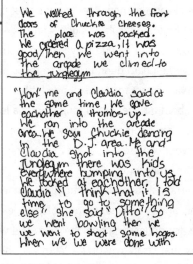

Fig. II-7 Sophie's writing based on her plan

SHARE

Noticing Features of Personal Narratives

Ask partners to share and discuss their own writing just as they did the day before with texts written by published authors.

"Writers, yesterday we read folders full of mentor texts written by famous authors, and we talked about all those texts, noticing what most of those authors tended to do. Today we have new texts that we can look at—texts you all have written. Would you and your partner get together, and partner 2 (thumbs up so I can see that you know who you are), please share the entry or the entries you wrote today with partner 1, and then talk together about that writing. What is it that you've done? What were you trying to do? How is the form of your writing similar to (and different from) the form you noticed in the folder of mentor texts? Talk deeply and read closely, and in a few minutes, I'll bring us back to talk as a group."

Ask one partner to share an entry, and the other to share observations of it. Then debrief in a way that reminds writers of the lessons they can hold on to.

After a few minutes, I convened the class. Joey read his entry: *[Fig. II-8]*

> Jumping in the pond really late at night
>
> Me and John were going to jump in the pond really late at night. John kept on telling me, "Come on! Jump!" I just could not. John kept on encouraging me to do it. He said, "You can do it, come on. Nothing is going to happen."
>
> I had to do it. I jumped. I closed my eyes and tried to think of good things. Splash. "I did it!" I yelled.
>
> John ran up to me and said, "Great job. You did it! You're the best."

Joey's partner Felix said, "He told about one moment, and he had the beginning before the jump and all."

Joey added, "And I showed I was nervous, I didn't just tell it."

I nodded. "Yes, you noticed that like the other personal narratives we read, your story has more than just plop, there's the moment, right? Although the climax of the story is the moment when you jumped into the pond, you led up to it, didn't you? Just like a diver

If students are skilled at discussing their writing, you may choose to ask them to look at the writing they did in the previous unit as well as the writing they've done today. If children can assimilate the information about personal narrative writing offered by a whole folder of their own writing rather than just one piece, their conclusions will be deeper and more advanced.

Fig. II-8 Joey

often has a three-step approach before diving in! And Joey, you also spiced up the way that you told the story, adding dialogue and showing your feelings. Doing these things will serve you well for a long time, Joey." Turning to the entire class, I said, "All of you can do these things that Joey has done. You can consider having a beginning as well as a middle to your story, keeping in mind Joey's prelude and a diver's three-step approach to the dive. You, like Joey, can spice up the way you tell your stories, too. And do whatever else you learn from studying great personal narratives! So writers, give yourselves a thumbs up for all the hard work you did today. I can tell this is going to be an amazing unit of study."

● [HOMEWORK]   *Emulating Writers' Lives*   We can learn from authors' *texts*, like we did yesterday, and we can also learn from studying authors' *lives*. We can research how an author did whatever we are trying to do. For example, if we are trying to come up with story ideas, we can find out how certain authors came up with their own story ideas. Since you all are working on getting story ideas, I want to tell you about how two authors we know got their story ideas. Then, you'll have a chance to write a planning box for the writing work you plan to do this evening.

When Cynthia Rylant was asked about how she gets her ideas, she said, "We are talking about art, thinking about art, and creating art every single day of one's life. This is about going fishing as an artist, having relatives over for supper as an artist, and walking the aisles of Woolworth's as an artist." (1994) I think Rylant keeps a writer's notebook, and often, as she lives her life, she opens the notebook and writes the story of catching a fish, shopping for slippers, or of other tiny little events that make up her life. It sounds like she collects ideas all the time; even when she is also doing other things, part of her mind is on writing.

Robert McCloskey, the author of *Make Way for Ducklings*, was in Boston in his car one time and the traffic stopped. "What's going on?" he thought, wondering if there had been an accident or something. So he got out of his car to look, and walked ahead a few cars—and saw a long line of ducks crossing the highway. The traffic on all sides had stopped while each little duckling waddled along. McCloskey said to himself, "I could write a story about this! I could tell about the day I was driving in the traffic, then everything stopped, and I could tell about how I got out of my car and watched . . ." That story became *Make Way for Ducklings*.

The concept that personal narratives generally have a moment leading up to the Big Moment (and another time I'll emphasize that stories also have a moment leading away) is a concept we will keep coming back to in this unit. Eventually, we will talk with students about story arcs, and help them find the story arc in their own personal narratives, probably by adding a moment before the Big Moment (the rising action) and a moment after the Big Moment (the resolution or falling action). For this share, if you know there is a student who has been noticing features of personal narrative related to these concepts, it will be helpful for you to choose her to share her thinking and work.

If these stories of Rylant's and McCloskey's lives have given any of you an idea for how you could live your life as a writer, please jot these ideas in your notebook.

I anticipate that some of you will write that, like Cynthia Rylant and Robert McCloskey, you could carry your writer's notebooks with you, recording little things that happen in your life. I think you are ready to do just that. Many of you will probably notice that writers pause and pay attention to details that others might just walk past. We see ducks crossing the road and instead of just thinking, "Come on, come on! I'm in a hurry!" we get out of our cars and watch the line of ducks quacking across the street. In school tomorrow, we can perhaps add this idea to our Strategies for Generating Personal Narrative Writing chart: Carry your writers' notebook with you, paying attention to details and thinking, "I could write a true story about this."

You have lots of options, then, for ways to come up with personal narrative entries tonight and evermore. When you decide which of these strategies you want to use (and you can invent a new strategy instead of using one of these) record it in a planning box on the next blank page of your notebook and get started!

TAILORING YOUR TEACHING

If your students would benefit from spending a bit more time reviewing the strategies for generating personal narratives from the first unit of study . . . you could reteach each of these strategies. Be sure to reference the earlier instruction rather than acting as if these are new strategies. For example, you could say, "Earlier this year we learned that one strategy writers use to generate ideas for writing is that we think of places in our lives that matter to us, then brainstorm small moments that we experienced in these places." Then you could proceed to retell how one child in the class did this effectively, weaving little pointers into your description of what the child did. Alternatively, you could demonstrate (role-play) the writer who begins by thinking of a place, a person, or an object, or you could cite the example of a child or a published author who used a strategy well. You won't know, for a fact, how an author went about generating the idea for a story, but you could say, "I'm pretty sure Ezra Jack Keats got the idea for this story by . . ." For example, you could suggest that *The Snowy Day* probably came from thinking first of a place—his neighborhood. The idea for *Peter's Chair*, on the other hand, could have come from noticing an object: a small child's chair.

If your students are skilled at using the strategies for generating personal narrative that you've already taught . . . you may also decide to teach children that *they* can create their own strategies for generating writing. Children are inventive, and sometimes you need only share what one child comes up with. Other times, you might guide a child in applying a strategy for generating writing. Once a child has used the strategy successfully, that child can teach the rest of the class how the strategy works. Remember to go to unlikely children who aren't usually in the academic spotlight; consider, also, going to a child who has some social power in the classroom—other children may be more apt to learn from her. You might start your minilesson like this: "Writers, I want to tell you about something smart Felix has done. He has come up with a new strategy for getting writing ideas—we will need to add it to our list. The strategy is this," and I wrote: "Listen to other people's stories and let them remind you of your own" on the Strategies for Generating Personal Narrative Writing chart. You could easily demonstrate the strategy. "I'm like Felix," you might say. "Oftentimes, when I listen to someone else's story, I think, 'That reminds me of something that happened to me,'" and show how one writer's idea acts a springboard for your own. Then you could suggest, "Right now, while we're here on the rug, let's all try Felix's strategy. Let's all let one person's ideas nudge us to think of new ideas. Will partner 1 share a story—choose one—and partner 2, will you listen really well? Then partner 2, say, 'That reminds me of a time when . . .' and tell *your own* story, a story that comes to mind just now as you listen." This minilesson could also be condensed into a mid-workshop teaching point.

COLLABORATING WITH COLLEAGUES

I know that during the first unit, I encouraged you to spend time writing together with your colleagues. If you resisted taking that plunge then, you have a new chance to do so now. My hope is that all of the talking you've been doing with your children about writing will lure you toward the idea of your own writing. I promise you, you won't regret it if you and your colleagues devote a grade-level meeting or two to your own writing workshop. My mother recently had seven hours of back surgery, and I returned to the old family manse to help her in the week after her surgery. I won't forget that first moment, after we'd carefully maneuvered things to get her into the kitchen, walker and all. She shifted onto the edge of the kitchen chair, pulled herself up by leaning on her walker, and said, "So now I'll try going to the bathroom," and she started shuffling off toward the john. As I watched my tough, all-powerful mother inch from the kitchen toward the bathroom, I thought, "Is she going to need my help?" And I thought also about how I'm not ready for a change of roles, and how odd it felt to have this woman who is the strongest force in my whole life in a vulnerable position.

Later, at my desk, I began to write the story of just that one small moment. All the techniques that we talk about become so dear and so huge when we use them to bring our moms to life on our pages, and to wrestle with what it means for us to grow old, to need each other, to face those huge life issues.

If you and your colleagues are reluctant to actually write entries alongside each other, at least use the strategies I've suggested to generate ideas you *could* write, and storytell one or two of these to a partner. That, alone, will give you a feel for this work's vibrancy and significance when our own life stories are at stake.

If you storytell together, I know that after leaving your meeting, in the privacy of your own home or your classroom, many of you will write.

So write. Write alone, without your colleagues, or write with each other. And write about your mother, your son. Write about your last times, your first times, and about the turning points that have given shape to your life. Your teaching will be utterly and totally different if you take the plunge and try all that you are asking your children to do. As you write, don't aim to write *well* so much as to write *true*. Don't aim for colorful or fancy words. Aim to put the truth of your story on the page, using the words that come first and most easily to you. You'll find that without trying to write well, you'll end up doing just that.

If you share your writing with your children, something magical will happen between you and them. I promise. Don't wait—that magic will mean more than any minilesson!

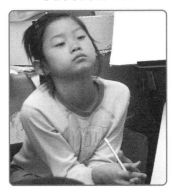

STARTING WITH STRONG FEELINGS

IN THIS SESSION, YOU WILL TEACH CHILDREN THAT WRITERS CAN GENERATE PERSONAL NARRATIVE WRITING BY CHOOSING A STRONG FEELING AND WRITING THE STORY OF ONE *PARTICULAR* TIME FEELING THAT FEELING.

GETTING READY

- Chart paper listing a strong emotion and several instances when you experienced it; second example ready to share
- Your own Small Moment story, based on a strong emotion, ready to "compose" on chart paper
- Strategies for Generating Personal Narrative Writing chart
- When to Use Paragraphs in Narrative Writing chart
- See CD-ROM for resources

When children grow as writers, this growth is not represented simply by greater and greater mastery of the conventions of English. Growth as a writer has many facets. One is that as children work within any genre, they progress from writing in simple versions of it toward writing in more complex versions of that genre.

When children first learn to write narratives, they usually aren't writing narratives at all. That is, as they strive for narrative writing, they usually first produce all-about or attribute entries in which they list their thoughts and ideas and feelings about a personal topic. With some instruction, young writers can shift toward writing a simple narrative, one in which the writer (the central character) does one thing after another after another. These narratives are chains of actions that often are connected only sequentially with each other. That is, there may be no cause-and-effect relationship between the events. The connection is mostly a temporal one; the main character does one thing and then the next thing: "I went to the beach, then I went to McDonald's."

As writers develop a more complex understanding of story, their writing revolves around not only a central event but also around a person who has feelings and motivations. In a personal narrative, that person is almost always the writer, presented as someone who has wants or hopes or ambitions or worries that lead the character into a sequence of actions. Because of something inside a character, one action leads to another; something happens and sets in motion a reaction.

The previous minilesson and this one both appear to provide children with strategies for generating personal narratives, but in fact, these minilessons also represent efforts to scaffold children toward telling and writing stories that are more shapely and more complex than those that involve a simple chain of events. For example, today's strategy for generating story ideas leads children to begin thinking about true stories by focusing on a time when a character (the writer) had motivations (which we refer to as strong feelings). The specific feelings I suggest—worry, hope, embarrassment, sadness—are all ones that likely mean the character will encounter trouble (as characters tend to do in stories). I haven't highlighted the role of trouble or the traditional structure of stories yet because I'm trying to scaffold children so that they suddenly find themselves telling well-structured little stories before I tell them that this is what they are doing!

MINILESSON

Starting with Strong Feelings

CONNECTION

Celebrate the way children share their entries with each other, and celebrate that the children are living like writers.

"Writers, I love the way those of you who arrived first in the meeting area opened up your notebooks and showed each other what you wrote last night. I listened in as you shared some of those entries, and I am totally impressed with the way you lived like writers last night. I remember at the start of this year, I read Naomi Nye's poem to you. She wrote, 'Maybe if we re-invent whatever our lives give us, we find poems,' (1990) and she challenged you to live in a way that lets you find poems and stories, too. But back then, some of you came in the next day saying, 'Nothing happened that I could write about last night.' Ipolito, do you remember saying to me, 'All I do is watch TV. Watch TV, feed the pigeons, watch TV; that's it.' But you ended up taking your writer's notebook up on the roof while you fed the pigeons, and you realized significant stories were hiding there, didn't you?"

"I walked down the street the other day with a photographer friend of mine, and every few steps, he'd point to something that could make a great picture. Because he is a photographer, even if he doesn't have his camera with him, he's always seeing possible photographs. And in the same way, you all live your lives seeing possible stories everywhere. Thucydides, a historian in ancient Greece, once said, 'Stories happen to those who tell them.' Because you all are writers, stories happen to you!"

Name your teaching point. In this instance, tell children that you will teach them another strategy writers use to generate powerful personal narratives.

"Today I am going to teach you one more strategy that writers use to generate personal narratives. This one is especially good for generating entries that can be turned into really powerful true stories. We know it is easier to write well if we are writing about small moments that are, for some reason, important ones. So usually, we'll want to recall times when we wanted something badly or felt something strongly. It sometimes works to think first of a strong feeling—worry or hopefulness, embarrassment or sadness. We can write a feeling on the top of a page, and then ask ourselves, 'Can I remember one *particular* time when I felt that feeling?' Then we write the story of that time."

COACHING

Even if you aren't 100% supportive of everything that your children are doing as writers, it is important, as Dr. Benjamin Spock often advised, to "catch them in the act of doing something good" and praise whatever they've done that merits support. Writing is a risky enterprise, and all of us who do it feel vulnerable. A little positive support goes a very long way toward increasing our energy for writing. So if a few children read aloud the entries they wrote at home last night, make a big fuss over how the class as a whole is changing. Do this even if it is only partly true.

It helps to liken writers to painters, photographers, runners, teachers . . . because this is a way of helping more children see this as a just-right role!

Earlier, you and the children read published personal narratives and realized that usually these are stories of small moments that convey really big feelings. Often we suggest children start with small moments that they somehow, for some reason, recall. Today's strategy suggests that writers can generate story ideas by thinking first not of the small moment but of the big feeling, going from that feeling to a tiny time when the writer remembers feeling that way. Whether you start big and go small, or start small and go big, the resulting topic will be both detailed and enormous.

TEACHING

Tell children about a time when you needed help generating ideas and reached for this strategy. Share what you did, then demonstrate to show the step-by-step sequence.

"Before you came in this morning, I was thinking I should get going on my own entries, but I wasn't sure what to write about. So I decided to use a strategy that writers use often, especially when we want our stories to have significance right from the beginning. Specifically, I wrote down a feeling I have sometimes—I just picked any feeling—and then I tried to list small moments I could remember when I had that strong feeling." I showed children that I had written the word *worry* on chart paper, and listed several times when I felt that:

Worry

The time I knew my mom had gone to see the doctor. The phone rang and I answered it, worried over what the news would be.

The time I came home, collected the mail, and saw that one envelope held a report card. "Oh no," I thought.

"So watch me while I use this strategy again—I will take another feeling, write it down, and think of small moments when I felt it." This time, I wrote *embarrassment* and started brainstorming in front of the children, recording vignettes.

Embarrassment

The time when my dress ripped and I had to go to the party with scotch tape holding my clothes together

The time when the kids told me the dress I was wearing looked old-fashioned enough to serve as a costume in the Civil War play

"After I take a minute to gather a few ideas, I select one that seems the most significant to me. I'll take this second one because I think it says something about who I am even now, and that's a sign that it is significant! First I'll make a movie in my mind of what happened, and think, 'Who said something or did something that could get this started, that would make a good lead?'"

I captured the small moment linked to worry in a few sentences that show the specific step-by-step sequence of the phone ringing and me answering it which conveys to children that the lists I'm advocating are still of small moment stories. I'm not planning to write an entry in which I summarize all that I feel when I am worried! Instead, I will recount one small episode. It's the marriage of a strong feeling and an episode (one which evolves through a sequence of actions) that will lead to a powerful narrative.

When possible, I try to use stories that are either from my childhood (because I know these are evocative for kids) or that could happen in a child's life. My mother, in fact, just went to the doctor, in my adult life, but this could easily be a child's topic as well. I deliberately try to share stories in which I admit my vulnerabilities because I know that writing is a risky, revealing thing to do; I try to create a place of safety and compassion in the room by being willing to share hard, though appropriate, parts of my own life.

Soon I was writing on a pad of chart paper, voicing each word as I scrawled it down. I wrote the text in one solid paragraph so that I could go back later to teach about paragraphing:

> "Those of you with parts in the play, stay after class to talk about your costumes," Miss Armstrong said just before the bell rang. I smiled as I packed up my books. Eliza, Becky, Richard, and I were to be the stars. We'd probably need to stay late often. We'd probably go to each other's houses on Saturdays to study our lines. I knew Eliza's house because, many times, the school bus had drawn to a stop in front of it and she and a whole group of girls had thronged off the bus. I always wondered what they did at Eliza's and now I'd find out. I pulled my chair over to where the others had already gathered. Eliza ripped a page from her spiral, and said, "It's from the 1860's, so we'll need antique costumes . . . oh!" She giggled and pointed at me. "You won't need a costume. You can just wear the dress you have on!"

The text I wrote is really too long for any minilesson and especially for this one, which is not really about writing entries but specifically about generating topics. Sometimes I know my minilesson is problematic in one way or another and I let it be anyway, as we all will at times. Nonetheless, you should know that I try to refrain from writing long entries in front of the class because the long bits of writing usually distract from the main teaching point of the minilesson.

I paused at this place in the story (not before it) because I wanted to return to the plot line before I stopped, lest my story contain too much internal thought and not enough plot. In general, I hope children write a sequence of occurrences. One advantage to the length of this particular bit of writing is that I can now use this same piece of writing to teach paragraphing. For these reasons, I rationalize the fact that I let the writing go on a bit long. But the real reason I did this is that the piece, to this day, makes my heart ache. And I'm a better teacher if I can share my heartaches with young writers.

Debrief by reiterating the sequence of actions involved in using this strategy to generate personal narrative stories.

I paused. "Do you see how I first wrote a feeling, and then listed small moments when I felt that feeling? Then I took another feeling. Soon I decided I had one that was significant and would make a good story—and I began writing the story-idea out as a real story, just like the stories we've read. I didn't worry about doing my best writing yet. Instead I kept my mind on my subject and got down to writing. (I think I'm already getting somewhere, because now I see it's really about two big feelings—hope and embarrassment.)"

I added this new strategy to our class chart.

Although I do not dwell on the fact that my story actually contains two feelings—hope and embarrassment—I believe this is worth exploring. In a story, the main character changes, so it makes sense that the character will experience more than one feeling. In our final unit of the year, you'll see that I revisit this concept. For now, I just mention it. Because I am an adult and also am someone who has been writing for decades, there will be lots of things I know and think about effective writing that I decide to not mention or mention only lightly. If I think most of the class is not ready for a concept, I don't talk much about it because then children will learn to tune me—and the concept—out.

ACTIVE ENGAGEMENT
Set children up to try the strategy, reiterating the moves students will have to make by sharing one child's work.

"So let's try it. Open your notebooks to a blank page. Let's take . . . um . . . let's take hope. Write that down. Now, think back over your life to very particular times when you were hoping for something," I said, and let there be silence while children recorded the feeling in their notebooks and started brainstorming times they felt this. "You may have been hoping for a present. For recognition. For someone to come, to call, to say yes. If you write something general like, 'hoping for a bike,' think also of a very specific time when you had that feeling. Then record the actions you did: 'Looking through the Sears catalog, I stared at the bike I wanted, then tore that page out and put it on our refrigerator door.' Once you list one time, go back into your memory files and come up with another very specific time you felt that feeling."

After two minutes, I intervened. "Writers, listen to Leath's list," I said, and read her list aloud. *[Fig. III-1]*

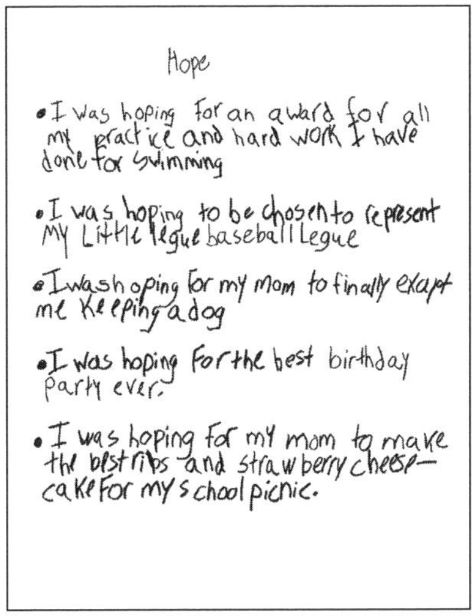

Hope

I was hoping for an award for all my practice and hard work I have done for swimming.

I was hoping to be chosen to represent my little league baseball team.

I was hoping for my mom to finally accept me keeping a dog.

I was hoping for the best birthday party ever.

I was hoping for my mom to make the best ribs and strawberry cheesecake for my school picnic.

Fig. III-1 Leath's list of topics are in sentences

"Do you see how Leath used the big emotion to help her remember specific times in her life when she's felt that feeling?"

Strategies for Generating Personal Narrative Writing

- Think of a subject (or a person, place or thing) that matters to you, then list small moments you remember. Choose one to sketch and then write the accompanying story.
- Think of first times, last times, or times when you realized something important. Write about one of these moments.
- Carry your writer's notebook with you, paying attention to details and thinking, "I could write a true story about this."
- Think of a strong feeling, then list small moment stories pertaining to that feeling. Choose one to sketch and then write about.

Notice that when I'm asking children to try a strategy during this component of the minilesson, I deliberately do part of the work for them, leaving for them the work that I think they especially need to practice. Because I bypassed topic choice and gave them an "exercise topic"—hope—I know they'll spend less time hemming and hawing before they get started.

Restate today's teaching point in the context of the children's writing strategy repertoire in particular and writing life in general.

"So today, we'll continue writing entries that could grow into stories like those we read. Remember to record the strategy you will use to generate writing in your planning box before you write. I've put some examples of planning boxes on the bulletin board, if you want to see them. You already know lots of strategies for collecting Small Moment stories and *any* of these can help you today if you need help getting started." I pointed to the Strategies for Generating Personal Narrative Writing chart. "If you are having trouble getting started, I especially encourage you to try the strategy of writing an emotion on a page of your notebook, then listing moments when you felt that emotion. Then take a very significant one of those moments, and write it as a story. Today, let's write for half an hour in absolute silence, so we can do the important work of putting our true stories on the page. Then we will read our stories to our partners, and after that, we'll have a chance to write even more."

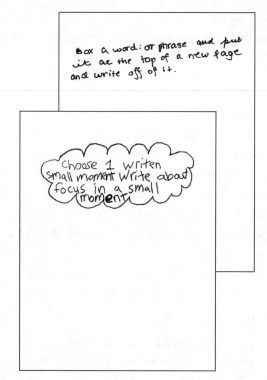

Figs. III-2 and III-3 Planning boxes

WRITING AND CONFERRING

Letting Observations Inform Your Teaching

Until now, I've talked about assessment as if it is something you do at home when sitting with a stack of your children's writing. It's crucial to pay attention to these drafts, but you can also assess during the workshop itself. You can especially assess on days like this one, when your children should have a large enough repertoire of strategies to be able to carry on with some independence. By now, most of your children should be able to choose topics for their entries, compose entries, and finish one entry and begin the next. This should enable you to take some time off from conferring and leading small groups and instead assess by observing.

When you survey the room during work time, notice, first, your students' levels of engagement. This is not a minor detail! If some children seem disengaged, resolve to study the situation so that you can address the underlying issue rather than simply nipping at their feet. Watch, also, to see what seems to derail or distract your writers. Does the layout of your classroom mean that children need to walk across the room to get another sheet of paper, and does that walk leave disengaged writers in its wake? Notice what your children do when they look up from the page. Hopefully, they spend a fair amount of time rereading. If they don't, make note of this.

It's all too easy for us to spend all our time *fixing* problems. As teachers, we very much need to study, as well as to fix, problems, and then to step back and think about solutions that are deeper and more long term than those we can imagine and execute amid the hurry of our teaching.

For example, you may find that some children always seem to be without a writing tool. Chances are good that these writers prefer to spend their time sharpening pencils or searching for pens rather than writing. One response is to provide a can full of sharpened pencils at each table, but another response is to study these writers' engagement during writing time to see what *does* draw them in. Does the threat of needing to stay in for recess if they

---

MID-WORKSHOP TEACHING POINT — *Remembering to Paragraph* "Writers, the stories you are writing today are really powerful ones. What you're doing, which is what I did with my Miss Armstrong story as well, is you are letting your words flow quickly on the page. You are fired up over your stories, and you are writing fast and long. That is great."

"But just like we talked about in the last unit, since you and I want readers to really take in our writing, we need to chunk our writing into paragraphs. Paragraphs give readers pauses in which to envision what we've said, allowing them to take in one thing we've said before the next thing happens. In general, we use new paragraphs when—" and I pointed to a new chart I had prepared, and read from it.

When to Use Paragraphs in Narrative Writing

- new character comes along
- new event happens; new idea is introduced
- new setting
- new person speaking
- time moves forward (or backward) a lot

"But those guidelines don't tell us exactly what to do—we need to make artful decisions. Watch while I reread my Miss Armstrong story, dividing it into paragraphs, and then you'll be able to do the same with your entry."

continued on next page

"haven't had a chance to write a page" seem to spur the child on? Does the child profit from continuing to make a timeline and to rely on it as a scaffold? Would the child accomplish more on the word processor? My suggestion is to ask the writer. Say, "What could I do, or could *we* do, that would make writing time go better for you?" Ask, "What makes writing hard for you?" And when a child names a problem, try to first *understand* the problem rather than simply rushing for a short-term remedy. "Can you tell me more about that?" you might ask.

A second suggestions is this: You may have some children in your class who write at the level of many first graders. So visit a first grade and notice all the ways in which paper choice and writing tasks are designed to scaffold such a writer. Could you provide some of that support to your struggler?

When you observe your writers, expect that these observations will inform your mid-workshop teaching points. The ones I give are embedded in classrooms other than your own. You'll find that your own class is like an orchard of fruit trees, waiting to be harvested.

---

continued from previous page

As I reread, I said aloud my reasons for paragraphing where I did.

> "Those of you with parts in the play, stay after class to talk about your costumes," Miss Armstrong said just before the bell rang.
>
> I smiled as I packed up my books. Eliza, Becky, Richard, and I were to be the stars. We'd probably need to stay late often. We'd probably go to each other's houses on Saturdays to study our lines. I knew Eliza's house because, many times, the school bus had drawn to a stop in front of it and she and a whole group of girls had thronged off the bus. I always wondered what they did at Eliza's and now I'd find out.
>
> I pulled my chair over to where the others had already gathered. Eliza ripped a page from her spiral, and said, "It's from the 1860's, so we'll need antique costumes . . . oh!" She giggled and pointed at me. "You won't need a costume. You can just wear the dress you have on!"

"There isn't a rule that will tell me where to make that second paragraph. When Miss Armstrong talks at the start of the story, I'm already there in the room (even though the story doesn't say so), which means that when I pack up my books, I don't qualify as a new character entering the scene. I made a paragraph there because the spotlight now shifts onto me, but also because I know my story won't have lots of actions and I'm trying to get readers to realize that the little movements I make will comprise the action in this story."

"So each of you please reread what you've written, and be sure you are making artful decisions about where to paragraph!"

SHARE

Retelling Family Stories

Congratulate writers for writing personal narratives of significance. Tell children that another strategy for generating personal narrative stories of significance is to retell our family stories.

"Writers, can you gather?" I said. "You all are writing up a storm, and the stories you are telling are poignant ones. I think during our first unit of study, some of you took the phrase *small moments* literally and wrote about moments that were so tiny that they didn't really matter. You'd want to write about playing dress-up with the seaweed at the beach but to write a small moment, you'd tell just about getting a drink of water: 'I opened my mouth. I drew my mouth near the water fountain, I pushed the button, and the water spurted up.' The problem was this: You weren't necessarily telling important stories. But today, in this room, I saw many of you writing really important stories. They are still focused, but you've come to realize that when we writers say we are writing about small *moments*, we really mean small *episodes*. Small episodes that carry big meanings."

"Watching you work, I remembered another strategy that helps me when I want to generate entries for true stories. I think about the stories that I enjoy telling. In my family, we have stories that we tell and retell and retell. When relatives gather, we bring out the muffins, and we bring out the stories. Usually we tell trouble stories."

Demonstrate telling a family story that could become a personal narrative entry.

"For example, the other day my brother, Hugh (who is a single father) told one of his many trouble stories about how he messes up, trying to be the perfect parent. Last week, the parents at his daughter's school were supposed to bring cookies to the class celebration. Hugh isn't the best cook, but the night before, he bought sugar dough, sliced it up, made cookies, and covered them with a loose piece of plastic. The next day he went to work but left early, hurried home, grabbed the little plate of cookies, and raced into the classroom in time to join all the mothers at the celebration. Just as the last child was performing, Hugh looked over to the counter where his cookies sat. He noticed the chocolate chips on his cookies . . . and then thought to himself, "Wait. I didn't make chocolate chip cookies! I made sugar cookies!" The performance was just

Use the fact that this unit is similar in structure to the last unit to continually point out to children the lessons they've learned and the growth they've achieved. They are the kinds of writers who get better and better—they are going places!

When you choose a family story to tell, try to choose one that will remind listeners of their own family stories. Choose something memorable and vibrant—let it put zest and humanity into the classroom as well as the yearning to tell stories.

Notice that I tell this story in a step-by-step fashion, using all that I know about personal narrative writing. I could have summarized instead of storytold. I could have written, "Last week Hugh made cookies for Eliza's school event, but he realize after he'd brought them into the class they were covered with ants." Instead, I storytold, hoping that by doing so I could let children experience the event . . . and learn from the model.

ending. As the children thronged toward the food, Hugh reached his arm to the buffet table, pulled out his plate of cookies, and looked down to see that his contribution was teeming with ants. He whisked the plate away, breathing a sigh of relief to have somehow avoided yet another crisis in his life as a single father."

Set children up to share their own family stories. Add this strategy to the chart.

"I bet some of you have stories that are told and retold in *your* families, and I bet that your stories, like mine, might be trouble stories about times when you narrowly escaped mess-ups. If you are thinking of a story that is told a lot in your family, give me a thumbs up," I said. Since five children had stories, I created informal storytelling groups and set these children up to captivate their audiences. After a few minutes, I interceded. "Writers, the stories you are telling now, and any of the family stories that you tell and retell, can be ones you record in your notebooks. (When you do record them, remember to give readers space to think by writing in paragraphs.) Let's add this to our chart," I said.

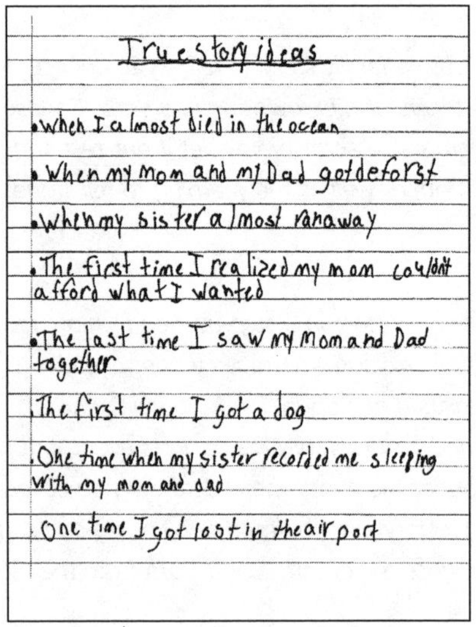

In my family, we do actually refer to these as trouble stories. I write about the importance of sharing our trouble stories in my book for parents, Raising Lifelong Learners: A Parent's Guide.

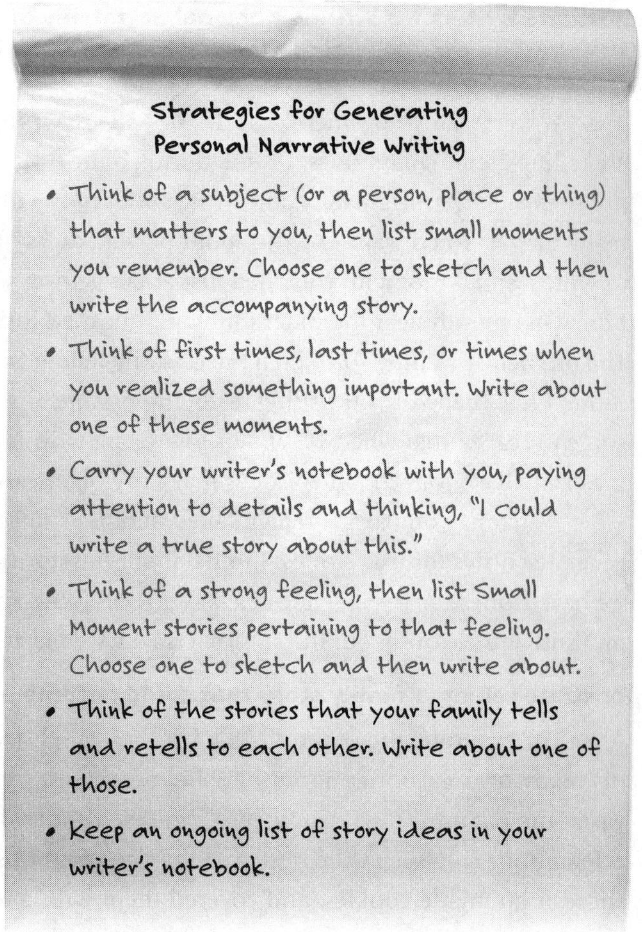

Strategies for Generating Personal Narrative Writing

• Think of a subject (or a person, place or thing) that matters to you, then list small moments you remember. Choose one to sketch and then write the accompanying story.

• Think of first times, last times, or times when you realized something important. Write about one of these moments.

• Carry your writer's notebook with you, paying attention to details and thinking, "I could write a true story about this."

• Think of a strong feeling, then list small Moment stories pertaining to that feeling. Choose one to sketch and then write about.

• Think of the stories that your family tells and retells to each other. Write about one of those.

• keep an ongoing list of story ideas in your writer's notebook.

True story ideas

• when I almost died in the ocean
• When my mom and my Dad got deforst
• when my sister almost ranaway
• The first time I realized my mom couldn't afford what I wanted
• The last time I saw my mom and Dad together
• The first time I got a dog
• One time when my sister recorded me sleeping with my mom and dad
• One time I got lost in the airport

Fig. III-4 Rafael's list of topics

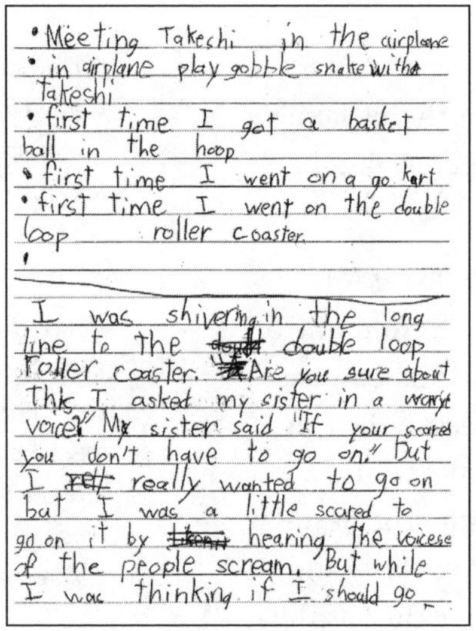

• Meeting Takeshi in the airplane
• in airplane play gobble snake with Takeshi
• first time I got a basketball in the hoop
• first time I went on a go kart
• first time I went on the double loop roller coaster

I was shivering in the long line to the double loop roller coaster. "Are you sure about this I asked my sister in a worryd voice." My sister said "If your scared you don't have to go on." But I really wanted to go on but I was a little scared to go on it by hearing the voices of the people scream. But while I was thinking if I should go

Fig. III-5 Takuma shifts from listing to composing

⦿ HOMEWORK   *Making and Using Topic Lists*   Writers, I love the feeling that your minds are bursting with stories, because this means that during writing time, you aren't just *thinking up* stories, you are *selecting* the stories that you feel will especially work. Just to make sure you are brimming with possible stories, would you take some time tonight to gather a list of possible stories on a special page of your writer's notebook? That way, if you ever finish an entry and, for a moment, can't think of something to write about, you can always also draw from your very own well. Here are some more ideas that can help you find your own stories.

- Take a topic from your life: your hair, your glasses, your hobby, a pet, a relative, one part of school, your home. Make a timeline of things that have happened connected to that one topic. Choose one dot from one timeline, and write that story.
- Start free-writing a list, using a recurring phrase. It could be *I remember,* but be sure to remember very specific, sensory moments: "I remember the sound of the last bit of milk being sucked from my school milk cartoon." "I remember standing at the edge of the mountain stream up to my ankles in freezing water." "I remember putting my head inside my sleeping bag and trying to warm myself up with my breath."
- Alternatively, you could start with a more specific phrase such as "At my cousins, I . . . " or "Sleep-overs mean . . . " and then list different ways to complete it. After creating a list, reread what you have written, circle one item, and then begin to write this as a story.

"Writers, collect your lists in your writers' notebooks, and from this day forward, you will always have more possible ideas than you need." I added this to our chart.

⦿ TAILORING YOUR TEACHING

If you notice that many of your students' notebook entries seem uninspired, lacking significance or power . . . you might want to teach them to follow the strategy that poet Georgia Heard once heard when she was learning to draw. Her instructor suggested that she fix her eyes on a subject—say, a tree—and draw fast and furiously, never once glancing away from the subject. The drawings that result often contain a life force that is remarkable. You can teach the students to apply the same kind of focus to the stories they are working on. You'll suggest that a life force, or power, can emerge in our writing when we keep our eyes (and minds) intently on the mental movie of our memories as we write them.

ASSESSMENT

For now, look over your students' writing with an eye toward the essentials of effective personal narratives. Above all, make sure that they are letting their stories develop on paper in a step-by-step fashion. You don't want to see them summarizing or swiping at or commenting on events. Instead, you want to sense that each writer is reliving an event as he or she writes. Instead of writing, "I went to the ball game and it was fun," you hope the child writes, "I paid for my ticket and walked into the stadium. I found my seat and sat down."

Then, too, check to make sure the kids are writing about fairly focused events. If they are writing about a whole day or the whole afternoon, the writing will sometimes feel like a list of generalizations: "I went on the swings, then I went on the slide. Then I went for lunch." Of course, the child who zooms in to tell the story of hurting herself on the monkey bars will still need a set up (presumably approaching the monkey bars) and a resolution (perhaps talking or thinking about the monkey bars after the incident is over). That is, out of a commitment to focus, see that children don't take the expression "small moments" too literally!

Look, also, at the volume of your students' writing and at the typical length of their entries. For grades three through five, you should expect that most kids will write entries that are about a page long, and soon most of them should be able to write at least a page a day in school (and eventually, more than that) and an equal amount at home. If your kids' entries tend to be only half a page long, it will be hard for them to write well because good writing requires detail, dialogue, development—and all of these require some breathing space on the page. So if their entries are brief, teach toward the goal of faster writing and more stamina. And be sure you are giving enough time for actual writing during writing workshop!

When I study Marco's writing, *[Fig. III-6]* it seems to me that he's written two drafts here about lunch in the park, and has tried to write the second version of the story in a more step-by-step, stretched-out manner. The resulting story is not yet an especially effective one, but I still do notice that instruction has influenced Marco. Whereas his first draft began with the crucial moment—the picnic lunch where there is no food for him—in the next draft, Marco attempts to stretch out the moment. He continues his narrative writing in a step-by-step fashion. He even includes direct dialogue—another example that instruction has affected him. Although the "story" is really a chain of events, without the elements that make for a story, it is organized sequentially in a step-by-step fashion and some details are included.

> When I went to central park with my cousin and we played baseball fist we all ate but me because by mistake I told my mom that I washt hungry so she didnt bring me eneything Then I got really really hungry but when I started to play baseball I didnt care about my hungernis.
>
> I steped in my godmothers car with my sister and my cousin. Then we went to pick up my mom so we can go to central park. After we picked up my mom we drove off to central park. But then we hade to wait outside because my godmother went to podke her car. So then we waited and waited and waited until finally my mom said "lets go setting up the chairs wail we wait for her." then afterthat my godmother finally came so then we all started to eat but me. Because when we were picking up my mom from her house by mistake I told my mom I washt hungry so she didnt bring me eneything. But then when I started playing baseball with my cousin I didnt really care about my hungernis.

Fig. III-6 Marco's entry

Next, I study Adam's writing. *[Fig. III-7]* Like Marco, Adam has written an entry which shows that he understands that narratives are organized chronologically by time, with one event leading to the next and the next. Neither writer is simply compiling all that he knows that pertains to the topic on hand. Instead, both children have tried to narrow in on an event, and to recreate that event sequentially on the page. Early stories are often written as chains of events rather than as an integrated, cohesive story, and both of these boys have written narratives that are chains of events. One thing happens, then the next, then the next.

In time, Adam will learn to think, "Who is the main character here? What is he—(in this case, what am I)—really wanting? What gets in the way? What's the main event of the story? How is that one event developed?"

Pay attention to Adam's entry. His notebook in the autumn of the year was filled with entries like this one. At the end of the final book in this series, you'll follow Adam's process as he writes a heartbreaking and poignant story about his brother's departure for college. It will be important for you to remember, when you read his final piece, what his writing was like at the start of the year.

When my son Miles was three, he planted popcorn in his sandbox. A month later, tiny lime-green tufts of grass poked through the sand in his sandbox. Then we moved. As Miles and I walked through the old house one last time, he stood beside his sandbox, tears welling. "But I'll never see it grow into a cornfield," he cried. Teaching is like that. We plant seeds, we see the lime-green tufts poke through the soil . . . and we rarely have the chance to see our plans grow into a cornfield. When teaching writing, however, the growth is palpable and dramatic.

First we all climbing into the car to go to Degentrro's a Pizza Parlor. When we got there we went into the bathroom to wash our hands. When we finished washing our hands we all picked out a bottle of soda. Then we sat down at a table and talked. It was my friend who used to live in tenafly's birthday so he had alot of us over to his house. When we got the pizza pie we were all hungry we each ate about two pieces of pizza. All of us left then we filed back into the cars and we drove to an ice cream parlor called Coldstone. We got to pick an ice cream and a couple of toppins to mix in. It was really good.

Fig. III-7 Adam's entry

YESTERDAY'S REVISIONS BECOME TODAY'S STANDARD PRACTICE

IN THIS SESSION, YOU WILL GUIDE STUDENTS TO SET GOALS FOR LIFTING THE QUALITY OF THEIR NARRATIVE ENTRIES BY USING ALL THAT THEY'VE LEARNED SO FAR ABOUT WRITING WELL.

GETTING READY

- Qualities of Good Personal Narrative Writing chart from first unit
- Student example demonstrating an item from that chart
- When to Use Paragraphs in Narrative Writing chart from previous session
- Student example that demonstrates focusing on the subject and writing fast and long, using true, exact details
- Student example that demonstrates paying attention to the details of life
- Overhead projector and markers
- See CD-ROM for resources

Those of us who teach writing often say that we are helping children cycle through the writing process. And it is true that throughout a year and across children's school years, we give them the time and support to cycle again and again through the process of rehearsal, drafting, revising, and editing.

But when we teach writing, our aim is actually not just for children to cycle through the writing process; our aim is for children to spiral through that process. With each new cycle, we hope that the level of work our children do increases. And this happens not just because they accumulate knowledge and experience. Children's work becomes progressively more sophisticated in part because we explicitly teach them to incorporate yesterday's lessons into today's work.

By this time in the year, you'll be very aware that our teaching accumulates, with one day's minilesson often building on previous minilessons, and with one unit of study building on previous units. The cumulative nature of this curriculum will be very clear to you—but it is probably less clear to your children.

Today, your goal will be to remind children that as they draft entries in this new unit of study, they need to draw upon all they've learned in the previous unit. If a child's final draft from the last unit was written in paragraphs, then you'll wonder why her early drafts in this unit are not written similarly. If she stretched out the heart of her story during revision in the first unit, you'll suggest that this time, she can do that work as she drafts.

In this way, you'll give children a spiraling process for ratcheting up the level of their writing work.

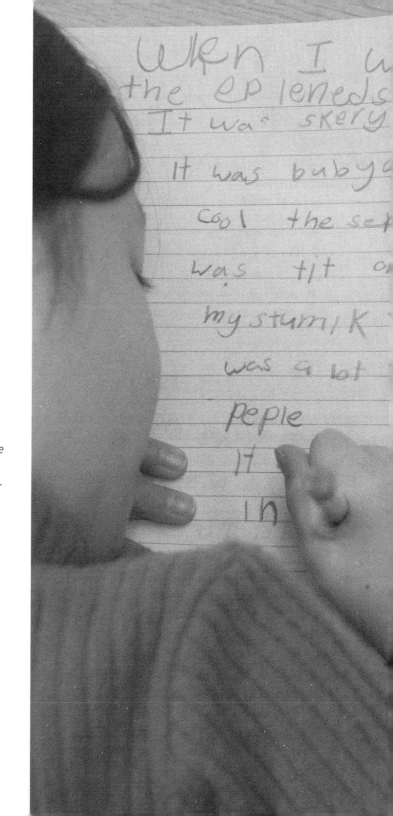

MINILESSON

Yesterday's Revisions Become Today's Standard Practice

CONNECTION

Point out that children now have a repertoire of strategies for generating writing ideas, but that many of them aren't needing these strategies as they now come to school brimming with ideas.

"Over the past few days, you've learned lots of strategies for generating ideas for true stories. I know you can continue to use those strategies—and others that you learned earlier this year—whenever you are unsure of a topic for writing. I also know that more and more of you are coming into the writing workshop already brimming with ideas for your writing—and that often you don't need a strategy to jump-start your writing. Your life itself sparks your writing . . . and that's true for lots of writers."

Name your teaching point. Specifically, tell children that what they once did through revision and editing can now become part of planning and drafting.

"Today, instead of helping you think about *what* to write, I want to help you think about *how* to write. And specifically, I want to teach you this. Everything that you did to revise and edit your last piece of writing can now move forward in your writing process, becoming part of what you do naturally as you write an entry or a first draft. What was at one time a revision and editing strategy ends up becoming part of planning and drafting."

COACHING

It is important for you and your children to keep in mind that the strategies they've learned for generating writing are all tools a writer can call upon when needed. But the truth is that for many, many writers, the challenge is never to come up with ideas for writing . . . the challenge is only to choose between all the possibilities. So expect to only devote a couple of days in any unit to teaching strategies for generating writing, and be ready to shift towards teaching strategies for writing more effectively.

Over and over you will notice that I use parallel construction. "Today, instead of helping you think about what to write, I want to help you think about how to write." I do this because minilessons are an oral genre. Effective speakers often use repetition and parallel construction. Think of Martin Luther King's "I have a dream" speech or John F. Kennedy's famous words from his inaugural address: "Ask not what your country can do for you; ask what you can do for your country." This parallel construction makes what we say easier to remember and therefore easier to take to heart.

TEACHING

Show children how one child studied the first paragraphs of her first publication, gleaning from it lessons she could incorporate into upcoming drafts.

"Remember that earlier we talked about the importance of studying authors and the texts they write? Well yesterday, Sophie studied a really important author. She studied herself."

"She went in the hall to the bulletin board and took off the tacks holding her published story on the wall. And she read her story over, reminding herself of all that she already learned as a writer."

"Let me show you how she did this," I said. "Sophie got some paper, and as she read her last publication, she paused whenever she reached something which she'd done on purpose, and she jotted down the strategy she'd used, the goal she'd reached towards."

"So she read this." I showed her text using the overhead projector: [Fig. IV-1]

> Tic- toc, tick toc. I was sitting anxiously in my seat. I was wondering when Mrs. C was going to line us up to go home? I was looking at the clock every 5 seconds to see if it was 3:00 yet. I knew that my grandma was picking me up from school that day. I hoped that when my grandma picked me up, we could get ice cream together. I couldn't wait for her to come to get me.

"After reading her first paragraphs, Sophie made this list." I revealed a copy of it on chart paper:

- Indent! Write in paragraphs
- Zoom in on a small moment
- Start at the beginning
- Start with dialogue or small action
- Follow the timeline step by step
- Tell what I was thinking

Research has shown that we need to explicitly teach toward transference. That is, we can teach all the strategies and qualities of good writing that we can imagine, but none of this amounts to a hill of beans unless we also teach children to draw on what we have taught when they are actually writing on their own.

The idea that children are expected to make a planning box before they begin an entry, and to record in that box whatever they intend to do, might seem an unnecessary step, but it is more significant than many people realize. If children learn to pause before writing, reflect on their options, review what they have been taught, and make a conscious decision about how they'll proceed, it is much more likely that they will access what they've been taught long enough for these strategies and qualities to become habitual.

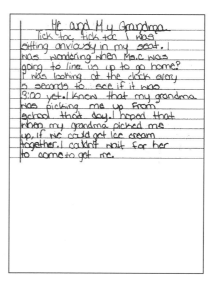

Fig. IV-1 Sophie's entry

ACTIVE ENGAGEMENT

Recruit children to help the child study the next sections of her publication, gleaning more lessons. Then ask them to help the child apply these to her new entries.

"Then she read on. As I read aloud the next two paragraphs in Sophie's story, be thinking about other things that she's learned to do, things that she also added to her list":

> I looked at the clock it was 5 to 3:00. I heard somebody call my name "Sophie!" Joy ran through my body. I heard my grandmas voice a smile shot on my face. I got my bookbag and walked out the door. She looked so beautiful. When I looked into her eyes I remembered all the good times we have together and I knew that we were going to have a great time together today.
>
> I went to give her a hug and when I got there I wrapped my arms around her. I felt so happy to be with her. When I hugged her I squeezed her as tight as I could. She squeezed me back. When I hugged her I had a feeling it felt like I was just safe with her. "Mimi, thank you for picking me up from school today." "No problem Sophie."

"Tell each other things that Sophie has learned to do, as evidenced in her first publication," I said, and the room erupted into partner conversations. After a minute, I elicited a few suggestions from children and added to the list:

- Indent! Write in paragraphs
- Zoom in on a small moment
- Start at the beginning
- Start with dialogue or small action
- Follow the timeline step by step
- Tell what I was thinking
- Show not tell feelings
- Write with precise details

I looked at the clock it
was 5 to 3:00. I heard somebody
call my name "Sophie!" Joy ran
through my body. I heard my
grandmas voice a smile shot
on my face. I got my bookbag
and walked out the door.
She looked so beautiful.
When I looked into her eyes

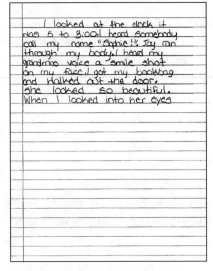

Fig. IV-2 Children studied the first page of Sophie's story booklet in order to practice deducing what she's learned to do.

I went to give her a hug
and when I got there I wrapped
my arms around her. I felt so
happy to be with her. When I hugged
her I squeezed her as tight as
I could. She squeezed me back.
When I hugged her I had a
feeling it felt like I was just safe
with her. "Mimi, Thank you for
picking me up from school
today." "No problem Sophie."

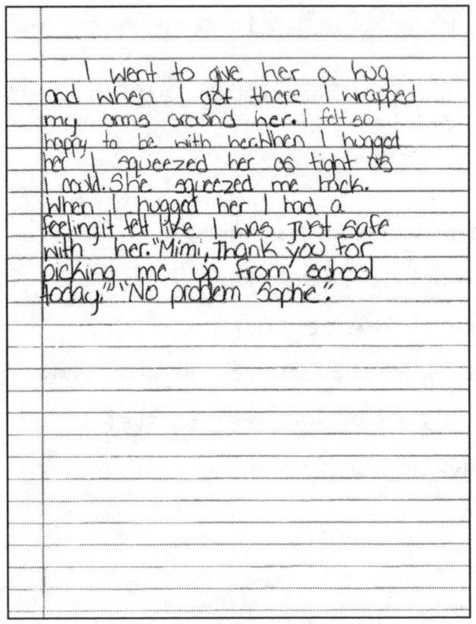

Fig. IV-3 Children also studied the next page of Sophie's narrative from the first unit.

"Writers, eyes on me. I need to tell you what Sophie did next because it is hugely important. She opened up her writer's notebook to an entry she'd just recently written and she did this—watch!" *[Fig. IV-4]* (I looked back and forth, slowly, between the publication and the entry, the publication and the entry.) Then I added, "After a few minutes, she said, 'I can do better,' and she began a new draft of her Chuck E. Cheese entry. Let me show you the start of it—that's as far as she's gotten—and will you check and see whether Sophie is incorporating many of the things she learned in our first unit of study into this entry? *[Fig. IV-5]* Is she writing in paragraphs? Does she seem to zoom in on a small moment or two? Start with action or dialogue? What else do you notice?"

LINK
Rename your teaching point: Writers can draw from all we've learned from past writing experiences and apply those lessons early in the process of writing future texts.

"Writers," I said, waiting for the children's attention. "I often end my minilessons saying, 'From this day forward, for the rest of your life, remember that writers . . .' and you know this is an important task—to remember the lessons you've learned so that you can grow stronger and more skilled as writers. But I want to tell you that becoming stronger and more skilled as a writer takes more than just remembering—it takes action. You have to take what you've learned and do it, use it, again and again until it's easy enough for you that you can learn something even newer and even more challenging. So go ahead, make some plans and take some action!"

In this session, you'll notice that during the active engagement children practice what I've taught using what I call "an exercise text." That is, I set them up so they can try what I'm suggesting writers do, trying this on a text other than their own. Later they will transfer and apply this with some independence to their own text during the writing workshop. When I teach classes full of reluctant and struggling writers, I alter these minilessons so that children do the work on their own texts instead of on exercise texts, as this makes it easier (and more likely) that they'll do the work at all.

Fig. IV-4 Sophie contrasted her first publication with this entry and resolved to improve her entries

Fig. IV-5 Sophie lifted the level of her entry, incorporating lessons from Unit One.

WRITING AND CONFERRING

Participating in a Writing Conference

Your minilesson today set children up so they should be able to talk to you in conferences about what they are trying to do as writers. After you ask, "What are you working on as a writer?" and follow up with, "Can you show me where you've done that?" you'll want to consider how effectively you think the child has done the work he or she set out to do. You'll want to know the child's assessment as well. "How are you feeling about what you've done?" you can ask. Plan in advance to ask the child to elaborate on any generalizations. "What do you mean when you say you feel okay about it?" you might ask. "What do you like that you've done? What don't you like?"

When children have trouble with your questions, try to ascertain if the trouble is the way you have worded the question or if the child has simply learned that whenever he or she resists, you'll go away. Don't let a child shrug off your questions; instead, try rephrasing the question. Say, "The question I am asking you is really important. What's making it hard for you to answer?" You may need to give the child a few minutes to reread and to think about what you've just asked, then come back to the child to learn his or her thoughts.

You may need to help children understand the sort of answers you imagine them providing. For example, when you ask a child, "What are you working on as a writer?" if the child doesn't seem to have a clue, follow up by asking, "What did you notice that you learned in our first unit of study? What did you see yourself doing in that publication?" If the child doesn't seem to have an answer, you could ask more supportive questions. "Did you, like Sophie, learn to start a piece with small actions or dialogue? Did you do that in your entries?" Alternatively, you could ask, "Which of the

> **MID-WORKSHOP TEACHING POINT** *Paragraphing* "Class, I want to share with you what Jake learned when he looked back at his last publication. He realized he'd learned to write in paragraphs and decided that now as he writes his entries, he wants to keep in mind that paragraphing matters," I said and gestured to the When to Use Paragraphs in Narrative Writing chart from the previous session. "It's not the paragraphs alone that Jake cares about—he knows he tends to write one sentence describing the first thing that happened in his narrative sequence, and then one sentence describing the next thing, so he's written in his planning box that he's trying to write a whole paragraph (even if it's just a little one) about each new event in his story, so that he really gets out more of what happened. This kind of elaboration is something Jake did late in the game for his last piece, so he's planning to try it sooner in this piece. One of these days, his writing is going to come right out of his brain in full paragraphs!"
>
> *continued on next page*

qualities on our list [point to it] are you thinking you want to work towards in your next entry?" If the child isn't sure, use the child's work to clue you in, and take a guess.

Children will probably name goals but be unclear about the strategies they could use to achieve those goals. If a child says he's working on writing it so that readers can picture the story, support this intention. "That is such a huge goal!" you could say. If the child is less clear how he is achieving that goal, you could show him how you go back and make a movie in your mind of what happened, drawing on telling details from that movie. "If I was to write about this writing class," you might begin, and then proceed to show how you'd go about starting your entry.

"So why don't you try this when you write your new entry," you could say, and coach the child to recall some part of the episode and to articulate a detail. "You can add that to your entry, just like I added details to my story about how Eliza teased me about my out-of-fashion dress," you might say.

If in another conference, a child tells you she is trying to paragraph, ask if Cisneros has helped her. Show her that once you decided to work on paragraphing your story, you first reread a mentor text, attending only to the paragraphing. Don't go into all the reasons you found—one is enough for a start, but slyly choose one that you know will pay off for the child's own writing. Remember, if every gesture to paragraph the child makes is not necessarily well informed, it still is important if the child is now thinking in paragraphs.

Make sure that you not only support the child in attaining her writing goal, but also support her in drawing on all she knows to reach her goal.

continued from previous page

Then I said, "To figure out where his paragraphs should go, Jake did something I'd like to teach you to do."

"Choose any page of a book and sort of squint your eyes so you can't exactly see the print. Instead of the print you might see gray blocks that get longer and longer as they move down the page—or shorter and shorter. It's kind of like standing on a rooftop and looking down at the streets and blocks below. They look all organized. You can't see any little details like curtains on the windows, or the bike on the fire escape, but you might notice a kind of pattern in the sizes of the paragraphs. Sometimes just the look of the paragraphs—the bunches of words on the page, the white spaces in between them—helps to shape the story the way the author wants it. *Everything* counts in writing! Now read the page for real and notice how the paragraphs organize and separate the parts of the story the way the streets organize and separate the houses and buildings and city blocks. You can try with your own entries, too."

SHARE

Using Precise, Engaging Details

Demonstrate for children studying a mentor author's work to learn ways to achieve a writing goal.

"Writers, I love the plans that you gave yourselves today. I have one hint that can help you do whatever you aspire to do. This is the hint: Whatever writing goal you take on for yourself, a mentor text can usually give you examples of ways to get there! Marco's goal is to keep his eyes glued onto what really happened, mentally acting it out, writing with exact, true details that reveal what the scene was really all about."

I pointed to the copy of "Eleven" written on chart paper. "Marco can look at 'Eleven' and see the ways Sandra Cisneros goes about writing with true, exact details. Cisneros' mind was probably fixed on Rachel sitting next to that sweater. In Cisneros' mind, she could see Rachel sitting herself in that hard little school chair. Cisneros probably envisioned exactly how the scene went. She probably thought about what Rachel noticed when she looked at that red mound on the corner of her desk. Cisneros' mind was fixed on Rachel and how she would act, and Cisneros aimed to write details that would tell the truth."

> I open my eyes, the red sweater's still sitting there like a big red
> mountain. I move the red sweater to the corner of my desk with my
> ruler. I move my pencil and books and eraser as far from it as
> possible. I even move my chair a little to the right. Not mine, not
> mine, not mine. (Cisneros 1991, p. 8)

"Studying 'Eleven' can give Marco inspiration about how he, too, can write with true, exact details."

"Marco already knew that in his next entry, he would be writing about a *first time*, and specifically about the first time he took his puppy to obedience class and put him in a 'sit-stay' line with all the other dogs. But after he looked back at this chart, Marco decided that when he wrote his entry, he was going to work especially hard to keep his eyes on the sit-stay event and to include true, exact details, trying to see and hear and recreate what happened. He said, 'When I tried that before, it felt as if I was *acting the story out* in my head as I wrote and that really worked for me.' Marco wrote those plans in his planning box. This strategy started out as a class lesson, but it is becoming a part of who Marco chooses to be as a writer!"

Writers, teachers often describe the writing process by saying writers first rehearse for writing (making leads and timelines and plans), then draft, then revise, and then edit and publish their writing.

But when *writers* describe their writing process, we don't always start by talking about desk work—about entries, leads, or timelines. Instead, writers start with life work. Remember how Cynthia Rylant talked about going fishing as an artist, walking the aisles of Woolworth's as an artist, and having relatives over for supper as an artist?

She *could* have said, "Writing is playing dodge ball as a writer, watching a rainstorm blow in as a writer, going to Starbucks as a writer." Zora did just that. She went to Starbucks *as a writer*, and she saw more, heard more, felt more because of that. You might think, "What's there to see, to notice, at Starbucks?" But listen to this entry Zora wrote last night and continued today: [Figs. IV-6 and IV-7]

Trips to Starbucks

Whenever my family goes to Starbucks I sit in the same chair. It's a ragged old chair in the corner where the men play chess. Its arms are shagged with gold cloth and patches of red and silver. Its legs are chipped and have the smell, old, stained in. There is dust on top of the chair and if you sit in it and pull this long pole back, you fly back also. When you sit in that chair you feel as if you are gliding on air. Like your worries about the big multiplication test that you know you are having on Monday because your teacher forgot to give it to you on Friday vanishes in thin air. That smell of coffee beans grinding is just what you need on that Saturday when you're sitting in that same old ragged chair with gold cloth and patches of red and silver, with chipped legs, and the smell of old stained in.

When your mom gets that Double café mocha or whatever. With the hazelnut and orange extract. And the half low fat soymilk with the whip cream that has no flavor, cappuccino (she's on a diet, you know) with a couple of sweet and low sugars it will make it taste just like a milkshake with coffee ice cream. You ask your

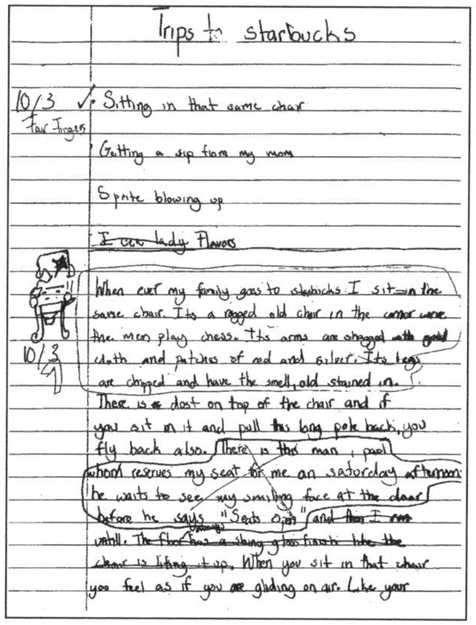

Fig. IV-6 Zora

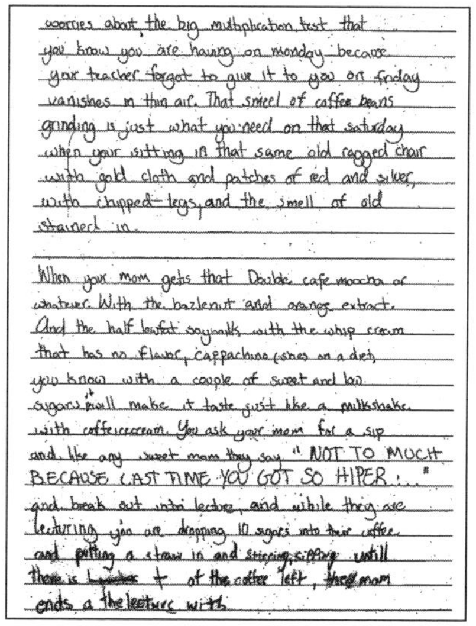

Fig. IV-7 Zora

mom for a sip and like any sweet mom they say "NOT
TOO MUCH BECAUSE LAST TIME YOU GOT SO HYPER..."
and break out into lecture, and while they are lecturing
you are dropping 10 sugars into their coffee and putting
a straw in and sipping, sipping until there is 1/4 of the
coffee left, then mom ends the lecture with ...

Do you see that Zora is applying what she has learned about being a writer to the earliest, earliest, earliest parts of writing, even before it gets near a notebook? Zora is doing the part of writing that comes before writing—noticing the world! And she's noticing in true, exact details, just like you were writing your first drafts using true, exact details. She has taken this goal back even farther into herself. It's like she put a planning box in the corner of her mind, not just on her page! She has details here that she could only remember if she tried to catch them, tried as a writer to catch them for writing down later. And that's what she did! Try that—put a goal, maybe the same writing goal as Zora, in a planning box in your mind and live your life with that writing goal.

TAILORING YOUR TEACHING

If your students need support to try the new strategies they're learning...you can suggest they use the class charts almost like checklists as they reread their entries. As they reread, they can check off the strategies on the charts that they use often, so that it's easy to see which strategies they don't use as much. After rereading a few entries, they can make a plan to use some of the newer strategies either as they revise an older entry or begin a new one. You'll want to emphasize the importance of trying new strategies by saying something like, "I also look at charts and think about strategies that I never got a chance to try, that I might try now." You could look back at the chart and say, for example, "I never reread old entries and let them remind me of new stories. I have a feeling that would work for me. So I am going to plan on rereading all the entries I have collected so far, letting them jog other memories. I'll write 'reread old entries' in a planning box on the next page." You might add, in an aside, "This is sort of cool because I really am acting like I'm my own job captain, giving myself jobs to do!"

Strategies for Learning from Previous Writing

- Reread old charts and think about strategies that have already worked for us.
- Reread old charts and think about strategies we have yet to try that might work.
- Give ourselves self-assignments, writing things we plan to do in our notebooks.
- Look back over old writing, noticing what we did in revision that we might want to do earlier.
- Look back over old writing, noticing what made our writing strong that we want to remember to do, and noticing what got us into trouble that we want to avoid.

MECHANICS

In the previous unit, I suggested you write a letter to parents letting them know that you care about their children's control of the conventions of written language. Before long, it will be time for parent-teacher conferences, and you can be sure that some parents will bring up this topic. The fact that those conferences are coming soon should nudge you, then, to do some work you need to do in any case.

So do this: In your mind, sort your children into clusters based only on their issues around the conventions of written language. Perhaps you'll group children like this:

1. Children in the first group are so swamped with problems that you hardly know where to begin. They have problems with spelling, handwriting, punctuation, stamina, syntax, making sense, length—the works.

2. Children in the next group write quickly and generally write with 90% accuracy (although at first you thought they were worse because their errors stand out). These children make all the common mistakes that many kids do: mixing up *to*, *too*, and *two*, forgetting to double consonants when they add endings, and so forth.

3. These children are English language learners who are literate in Spanish and use their knowledge of Spanish to help them write in English. While this has helped them in some ways, it also creates its own set of problems. For example, a fair percentage of the errors these children make in English result from relying on their knowledge of Spanish in ways that don't work for English. These children sometimes put an adjective after the noun it modifies, mix up their gender-related pronouns, struggle with tenses other than the present, and spell phonetically (which works in Spanish but not in English).

4. Children in this group write with fairly correct conventions. They concern you not because they make errors but because they are not using complex sentences or vocabulary. You worry that their zeal to be correct and in control has led them to cling to safe terrain. As a result, much of their writing reads as if it is a list. They don't seem at home with literary syntax, and they don't use a diversity of connectors, relying almost entirely on *and, so,* and *then*.

5. These children have an easy command of the conventions of written language. Some seem to be trying new things and pushing themselves to experiment, to create effects on the page, to use mentor texts as models; others do not, but all of these children seem to have this aspect of writing well under control and avoid making errors.

You may have clusters of children who fit into other groupings. I'd sort children according to whatever groups you see emerging, and then look closely at the work of at least one representative child from each group. Consider whether that one child's progress (or lack thereof) is representative of the others from that group as well. Ask yourself, "What progress am I expecting from this group of children?" Based on your answer, you should be able to think about how your teaching thus far has or has not been appropriate for each group, and you'll begin to become accustomed to gauging whether a child is or is not making dramatic progress in the control of written conventions.

Chances are good that you will need to begin working regularly, for five or ten minutes a day, with some of these groups of children. You might think that, right off, you'll want to zero in on the children who are so swamped with problems that you hardly know where to begin. If you do decide to work with these children, you may work first on their use of end punctuation. The first step is not for them to reread their entries, inserting punctuation, but instead for them to get some sense for the rhythm of writing with punctuation. Help these children think in sentence-long bites instead of word-long bites. "Say your thought," you nudge. "Now write that fast, without stopping, and then put a period." They do this. "Now say your next thought." They do that. "Now write that fast without stopping and put a period." Meanwhile, asking these children to rehearse for writing by saying the story across their fingers, or across several pages, can help them focus on large chunks of the story instead of on small bits. This can help them avoid losing the thread of their story amid the complexities of the individual words they are trying to write. Composing the stories aloud first can also help; students find ends to their sentences. This can keep them from writing idea after idea, connected simply by the word *and*.

But you may find that children who struggle the most with mechanics are getting better in leaps and bounds, leading you to suspect that above all they needed chances to write and to be respected as writers. You might, for example, help children in the fourth category (above) make the transitions from run-on to simple sentences—a transition that can set them up so they are ready to next learn to write with subordinate clauses.

If children write in a structure of subject, predicate, conjunction, subject, predicate, conjunction, on and on, in one run-on sentence after another, then it is hard to help them introduce commas and clauses into that writing. And if kids aren't composing their writing with commas, they probably aren't composing their thoughts with subtle relationships between them, with one slightly less important thought, another slightly parenthetical, another deserving of a full breath. Those different levels of importance and relevance are there, of course, and may even be intended, but many children aren't yet crafting their writing to reveal them. Adding commas hither and yon to make the writing correct after the fact does not help children learn to tease out these relationships.

The first step, then, is to help children see that strings of simple sentences linked with the words *and* or *so* don't work. Then once these children have begun to write in simple sentences, it is powerful to show them that authors use clauses and more complex transition words to convey their ideas. We need to help children understand that relationships exist between parts of sentences as well as parts of stories. We can help them to

learn that writing with commas and subordinate phrases can help them to convey what really matters. But these are tall orders!

You might, for example, gather some children in category four together and tell them that you often admire the way a certain author writes his or her sentences and sometimes try to revise your own writing under the influence of that author.

You might study Cisneros' artful use of sentences in "Eleven." She could have written:

> I don't know why I'm feeling sick inside. The part of me that's three wants to come out of my eyes. I squeeze them shut tight. I bite down on my teeth real hard. I try to remember today I am eleven, eleven.

Instead, Cisneros uses some connectors, such as *but, like, only,* and *and,* to make one fluid sentence.

> I don't know why *but all of a sudden* I'm feeling sick inside, *like* the part of me that's three wants to come out of my eyes, *only* I squeeze them shut tight *and* bite down on my teeth real hard *and* try to remember today I am eleven, eleven. (Cisneros 1991, p. 8)

Encourage children to learn from this aspect of Cisneros' craftsmanship as well as from her other qualities of good writing.

All of this work will help you to show the parents of your children that you are tailoring instruction based on what you see their child needing.

LISTENING FOR SIGNIFICANCE IN SEED IDEAS

IN THIS SESSION, YOU WILL TEACH CHILDREN TO BE STRONG LISTENERS, LEARNING TO DRAW OUT THE POSSIBILITIES IN THEIR OWN AND EACH OTHER'S SEED ENTRIES.

GETTING READY

- Monitoring My Writing Process checklist from first unit (with blank spaces for adding new strategies)
- Student copies of the Monitoring My Writing Process checklist (also with blank spaces for adding new strategies)
- Student seed idea that shows qualities of strong personal narrative that the class has studied so far
- Lined paper
- Set up place where two students can confer
- See CD-ROM for resources

I hope that by now, you and your children have become accustomed to the rhythms of the writing process. I'm hoping that even before today, your children have been rereading their entries and thinking, "Which of these will I choose to develop into a publishable piece?" This process of collecting, selecting, and then developing is an important one for teachers, for writers, for human beings. It is tempting in life to try to do all things. We rush about as teachers, as writers, as people, trying to do and be everything. But in life, one thing we know for sure is that there will never be enough time. And so we, as human beings, are called upon to make choices. "Out of all that I could say and do and be," we think, "what matters most to me?"

When choosing a seed idea, it's helpful for children (and for us) to be able to look at a quickly written, abbreviated, less-than-artsy entry and see potential. Some people can look at a room and imagine it redecorated, or look at a piece of raw marble and imagine a finished sculpture. Writers need to eye entries, seeing potential. This is a talent that teachers as well as children need to develop. What an art it is to be able to look at a fragment of an entry, the skeleton of a story, and imagine the tale it might become!

You'll want to remind children that they've traveled this road before, and that they already have strategies for developing a seed idea and for planning the draft they will soon write. Just as earlier you asked children to recall their strategies for gathering personal narrative entries, now you will ask them to recall their strategies for developing those entries in their notebooks prior to writing their stories. You will remind children that they can draft and revise timelines and leads, especially.

In Writing and Conferring, I emphasize the spirit that needs to be woven throughout this session.

MINILESSON

Listening for Significance in Seed Ideas

CONNECTION

Remind children that they are job captains for their writing and that they can use the writing process charts to guide them as they progress along a predictable course. Invite them to choose seed Ideas when they feel ready.

"Many of us have organizers and calendars to make sure that we use our time productively, and earlier this year, we learned that writers often keep tabs on our writing process by charting our progress. Because we know that our writing process will generally proceed along a fairly predictable sequence of work, we keep a chart of the writing process near us as we work, and check off when we have completed each step in that process. (Of course, we'll need to revise this chart as we go to reflect all that we're now learning about the writing process.)"

COACHING

This chart scaffolded children's work in the Launching unit of study, and will grow alongside them in this unit as well. Charts support students' independence as long as we reference them consistently and as long as they contain clear, concise language that becomes part of the class lexicon. We also emphasize "less is more." In other words, we use only a few charts, but use them often, with the expectation that students will do the same. This chart is the most important chart in many teachers' writing workshops.

Monitoring My Writing Process	First Piece	Next Piece
Gather entries		
Select and develop one seed idea		
Storytell to rehearse for writing		
Read published writing that resembles what I want to write		
Draft leads—try action, dialogue, setting		
Make a timeline		
Choose paper, plan story on pages, copy lead		
Write draft with each part on a separate page		
Reread and revise for clarity		
Draft endings—try writing with important ideas and images from the story, and with details that are reminders of the whole		
Revise and edit more now or decide to wait until later, or not to revise		

"I want to remind you that you can decide when you are ready to move along in your process. When you are ready to choose a seed idea, you'll want to make a check in the first column on your chart to indicate that you have collected entries, and then you'll want to reread all your entries carefully, giving every one a chance, perhaps marking several possibilities, and finally selecting one entry as your seed."

You'll notice that although I talk up the idea of moving from gathering to selecting entries, I do not suggest that all the children choose their seed ideas today. First, I want to give children a sense that they are in control of their own writing process. Then, too, it would be hard for me to get around to every child in one day, so if half the writers continue to gather entries for another day or two, that will only make life easier. I have no hesitation saying at some point, "If you haven't chosen your seed idea, do so now."

Confide that for you, it's comforting to share writing decisions with a partner.

"For me, it is always a little scary to make a choice, to say, 'This will be the entry that I develop into a publishable piece.' Sometimes when I reread my notebook looking for an entry that's worth developing, I fret. 'I wonder if this is good enough,' I say to myself. When that happens, what I really need is a listener. I need someone who'll say, 'Tell me your story . . .' and who listens with such rapt attention that I find myself saying more than I thought there was to say and getting to the heart of my writing."

The fact that the writing process is cyclical means that we, as teachers, are freed from always needing to teach children what their next step should be as writers. We need only to reference that next step, and meanwhile we can teach them how to do that step especially well, or we can address the predictable problems they'll encounter. In both your conferences and your minilessons, be sure you don't let yourself get into the trap of reteaching steps and strategies that you know your children already know. Allow yourself to spotlight something new.

Name the teaching point. In this case, tell writers that in order to write a great story, writers need to become writing teachers for ourselves, listening raptly to our own stories.

"Today I want to teach you to become good teachers for yourselves and for each other, because each of you needs someone who can listen so deeply and so intently that you find yourself saying more than you thought you had to say. Good writing teachers listen, and allow writers—the writer in each of us—to uncover layers of an idea. Good writing teachers help us know we've chosen a good seed idea, and help us get started finding the words to write about that seed idea."

TEACHING

Tell the story of one time when you listened so intently to a writer that you helped the writer find significance in a seemingly small moment.

"Has a friend ever gotten you talking—a friend who listens so intently that all of a sudden it's as if a dam broke inside you and suddenly you are telling the whole story, feeling words pour out as you talk? Writers need listeners like that. I want to tell you about one time when I was a good writing teacher because I listened, and then I'm going to help each of you become a good writing teacher for yourselves and each other. I remember one time when I pulled my chair alongside a fifth grader, Kenny. Most of Kenny's classmates had produced long narratives, but Kenny's writing amounted only to these lines."

> My Life Story
>
> I saw my father. We had coke, and then we had a hot dog.
>
> The end.

"Looking at his entry, I was tempted to say, 'Kenny, you need to produce more!' But I reminded myself that writers need listeners who are affected by our stories. So I told myself to really listen. I read what Kenny had written again and really tried to listen to it: 'My Life Story. I saw my father. We had coke, and then we had a hot dog. The end.'"

"This was, indeed, huge. And tragic. 'Kenny,' I said. 'This is huge. This is so important.'"

"Kenny looked at me, his eyes widening.' Yeah?' he said, tentatively."

"I asked Kenny to tell me all about his visit with his father. At first he just repeated what he'd already written—they had Coke and a hot dog—and instead of being impatient, I tried to really picture the moment. 'Kenny,' I said, 'I can picture it. You and your dad having Coke and a hot dog.'"

"Kenny nodded. And I waited. After a long silence, Kenny added, 'My dad showed me buildings.' Again Kenny paused, and again I waited. Kenny added, 'I still have the soda can.'"

"It was three years since Kenny met with his dad and ate a hot dog and soda. But all these years later, he is still holding the soda can and the memory of that afternoon."

"When I trusted that Kenny's entry was important, *Kenny* finally realized his story is important, and he began using words and details that showed what made that story so important. The reason I care about writing true stories is that for all of us, life amounts to just, 'We had Coke, and then we had a hot dog.' But when we write and think and talk about those moments, we find that a little story about having a soda with one's dad—or about a red sweater—is not so little after all."

You'll want to begin collecting your own stories and your colleagues' stories of young writers. We all have countless times, like this one, when a child struggles and then makes a breakthrough. As these teaching moments happen, you need to become accustomed to thinking, "I could write about this." You are lucky to be in the classroom every day because stories like this are all around you! Harvest them. Cherish them. Use them in your teaching.

When you turn these teaching moments into entries, keep in mind that you are essentially writing a narrative. Mine begins with a small action. I pulled a chair alongside Kenny. Soon the problem presented itself: Kenny's draft, unlike the drafts of his classmates, was tiny. In my story of this teaching moment, I include the internal story: Looking at Kenny's draft, I wanted to say, "Is this all?" This episode is shaped like a story. A teacher encounters a problem, tries for a solution, and finds a breakthrough—one that has universal ramifications.

Notice that I tell this story like a small moment, then I step back and reflect on what the story shows. This is one model for what you may want your children to do.

ACTIVE ENGAGEMENT

Set one child up to share her seed idea, and use this as an opportunity to coach children in listening responsively to each other's writing.

"Writers, we not only need strategies for developing our seed ideas, we also need to respect our own words. We cannot write a good story if we don't respect the story we are trying to tell. The best way I know to respect our own words is to have a listener who really listens and who says, 'Whew! This is going to be huge!'"

"Let's practice being that kind of listener. Cindy is going to read an entry that she thinks might be her seed idea, and will you tell each other what you might say to her to show her that you are listening to her, just as I listened to Kenny." Cindy read her entry aloud. [*Figs. V-1 and V-2*]

> I was standing in the middle of the kitchen arguing with my Aunt Blanca about some party she wanted to go to and to take me to.
>
> "I'm going to call your Father and you're going to get into big trouble, you brat," Blanca said as she pushed my dad's phone number.
>
> "Can I speak to Ramon Benitez?"
>
> "Hello?" my dad said. Blanca threw her hands out at me and I snatched the phone.
>
> "Dad, I don't want to go to the party!" I screamed.
>
> "What?" my dad said, expecting something bad for Blanca to say.
>
> "I don't know the people. I'm going to be so bored!"
>
> "Sweetie, you have to—"
>
> "No, I hate you! I hate everybody! Why? Because no one loves me or cares about me and no one listens to me." There was silence on the phone and in the house.
>
> "Oh, my God! Cindy, I can't believe you!" Blanca said shaking her head.
>
> "Shut up! Please shut up!" I couldn't believe my words! They had come out one by one. BANG! I dropped the phone. I closed my eyes. I swung my hands. My aunt was standing right next to the stove with the vegetables right on top. At that moment, I wished I could go back in time and change what I said and done.

When you teach children about the importance of listening, you may want to read aloud Byrd Baylor's I'm in Charge of Celebrations. *One could look at Baylor's subjects and shrug them off. She's writing about seeing a green cloud in the sky, that's all, and some dust blowing around in a spiral. But Baylor knows that we human beings have choices to make. We can pass by the details of our lives, hardly noticing them, or we can let a green cloud stop us in our tracks. "We're in charge of celebrations," Baylor says, and her advice is gigantically important.*

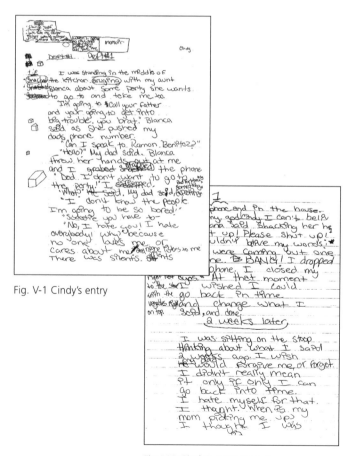

Fig. V-1 Cindy's entry

Fig. V-2 Cindy's entry page 2

"What could you say to help Cindy feel heard?" I asked. The room erupted into talk

After a moment, I called on one child to talk to Cindy, cautioning, "Remember, your job is not to ask questions. Your job is to let Cindy know you listened."

"I know how you felt because I once did that to my mom. It's like you love them, but you just get so angry sometimes that you end up saying mean things."

Mellora interjected, "Yeah. It's like you don't mean it, it just comes out, and then you regret it."

Cindy said, "Yeah. That's *exactly* how I felt. It was bad news, like I'd *never* live it down." She looked down at her feet as she spoke. "I hated what I'd done."

"Cindy, I hope what these listeners are saying is making you realize that you had feelings that day that are really an important part of what you want to say. You might reread your draft and figure out how you can expand the part about your sense of regret, if that's the main message." Then I turned to the whole class and said, "When a writer has someone who really listens to us, we often end up realizing the aspect of our story that moves us, that fills us with feelings. When we have a listener, and we take in our own story, realizing what it is that matters most to us."

LINK
Remind children that when they are choosing their seed ideas they can be listeners for each other and themselves, using this as a way to find significance.

"At your desks, you will each find a copy of our Monitoring My Writing Process checklist," I said, holding up a copy to signify that children needed to record their progress on their own charts. "Writers, remember that as writers, you need to be job captains for yourselves. Some of you will collect entries for another day or two, and some of you will decide you are ready to choose your seed idea now. If you do choose a seed idea, and you think it'll help, say to your partner, 'Can we confer about this?' You'll probably want to leave your workspace and sit together in the meeting area, or in one of the conference areas I've set up in the margins of our classroom. Partners, be listeners who help writers want to write."

"Once you've chosen your seed idea and talked about it, you may want to draft a timeline, you may want to try some leads, you may want to start a draft. If you are starting a draft, do so outside your writer's notebook, on lined paper."

It is important to keep concepts we teach earlier alive. Even by making just a passing reference to job captains, planning boxes, or charts, we remind children of these concepts.

WRITING AND CONFERRING

Listening to Teach Listening

If I had a writing teacher's magic wand, I'd use it to make sure that every single writer had a private teacher on the day that he chose a seed idea. I'd tell all the private teachers to listen to the entries that kids have chosen and say, "Wow. This story is going to be huge," or "Whew. You've chosen an important story, haven't you?"

But because you and I do not have magic wands, the wisest thing we can do is to teach children to become listeners for each other. Teach children that in a good writing conference, the writer leaves wanting to write. The writer's energy for writing should go up. That is the single most important hallmark of an effective conference.

You'll want to move among children who have decided on their seed idea, and help them tell their stories so well that they give their partners (and you) goose bumps. Say to the child, "This is going to be an amazing story." Help the child believe that he or she is poised at the brink of a remarkable writing venture.

If you aren't sure how to get writers to tell the story well to you, remember what therapists know. They listen and then say back what they've heard. "It sounds like you are really mad at your mother," the therapist says, using the technique they refer to as active listening. You will see that the technique elicits more than a battery of small questions could possibly elicit. The important thing is not the fact that you say back what the writer has said. Instead, what matters is the listening. Listen with rapt attention to just a chunk of the story, then respond by reiterating or exclaiming over what you've heard and *then by not talking.* "You were really worried as you stood there, ready to jump into that pond, weren't you? And John kept saying, 'You can do it'?" Then wait. Be quiet. Let the writer talk. If you do want to prompt for more information, instead of asking specific questions, say things like, "I'm not sure I can picture it. Exactly how did it go? What did he say? What did he do? Oh! So he said . . . Then what?" Once a child has told the start of a story with voice and passion and detail, scrawl it down if necessary to hold on to it. Then say the start of the story back to the writer while he or she records it, and say, "You're off to a good start. Keep going."

Sometimes I make an even more pointed effort to rally a child's energy for the work ahead. "Takuma," I might say. "I have a feeling that this is going to be the most important story you've ever written. Do you feel that too? You're onto something here." Or I might say, "Sophie, I'm not sure you realize that the detail with which you're talking about your writing plans is very special. You are talking like you are a real published writer. I hope you take this talent of yours seriously."

> MID-WORKSHOP TEACHING POINT **Drawing on Strategies** "Writers, I want to remind you that you have a backpack full of strategies for developing your seed ideas. Right now, before I go any further, would you list across your fingers three things writers do to choose and develop their seed ideas?" I watched as children whispered to themselves, moving along their fingers as they did so.
>
> "You already know that to choose a few possible seed ideas, we reread every entry in our notebooks thoughtfully. We don't just flip past them; we give each entry a chance."
>
> "Thumbs up if any of you remembered that now is also a good time for storytelling your seed ideas . . . great!"

SHARE

Reading Aloud Powerful Writing

Plan a way for every writer to read a bit of his writing aloud to the group as a means to celebrate children's stronger and stronger writing.

"Our goal this month is to write in ways that make readers stop in their tracks like Mrs. Manning did. I thought we would spend the next few *weeks* trying to put some powerful writing on the page, but you've *already* written entries that are powerful! Some of you selected entries which will become your seed ideas today, and you made wise choices! Remember earlier this year, I acted as the conductor of your orchestra? When I pointed my baton at you, you read aloud a tiny excerpt from your writing. We're going to do the same thing today; when I point to you, read aloud a tiny excerpt of the entry that you've chosen as your seed idea. You may read your lead, or you may choose the heart of your entry to read aloud. I'll give you a few minutes to look through what you've written and choose what you'll read. Practice reading your words in your head like they're precious jewels, so that you can do justice to them."

Soon I gestured with my "baton" and one child after another read aloud.

Khalid: *[Fig. V-3]*

> I balanced on the bike with my feet. I looked down the long hill. Gulp! I swallowed hard. Camillo pushed me. The wind was blowing hard. I kept going into the dark night. Would I crash? I was kind of scared.

After a few others, Sabrina read: *[Figs. V-4 and V-5]*

> I spent about three seconds in the air partly tripping and partly jumping. As I was in the air, I thought, please let me land on my feet. I don't want to fall with Mya in my hands. Mya is just a baby, what if she gets hurt? It will be all my fault if Mya gets hurt. I really don't want Mya to get hurt!

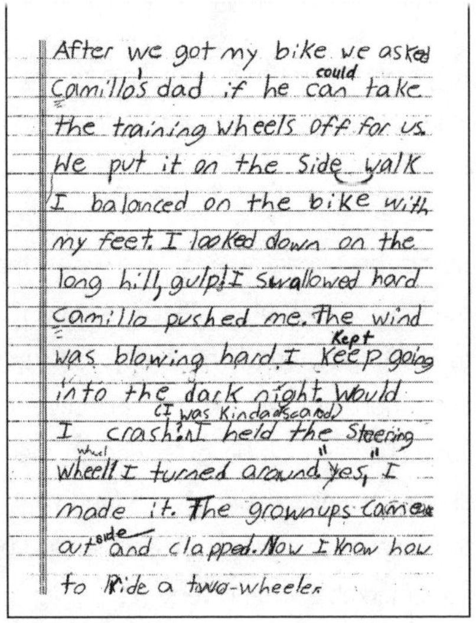

Fig. V-3 Khalid

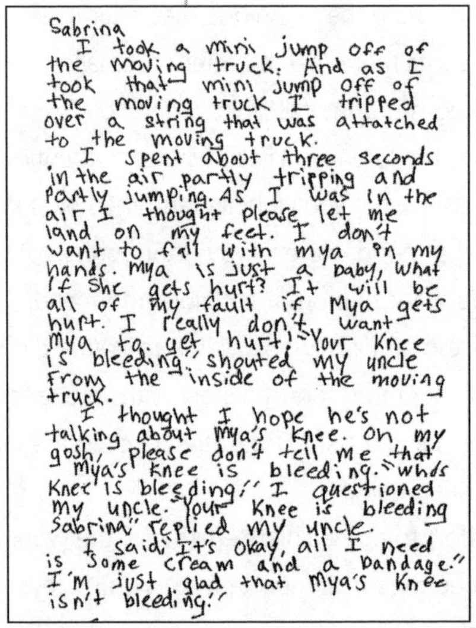

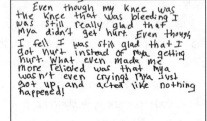

Fig. V-4 Sabrina

Fig. V-5 Sabrina

After hearing five or six other snippets as well, I said, "Writers, this writing definitely gives me goose bumps. It gives us all goose bumps. Listening today, I realized that one thing you each did in these entries which makes your writing really strong is that you shifted between telling an external action, telling what you said, and telling an internal thought. Listen to Juliana's excerpt from her entry retelling the story of how she met her father for the first time and notice how she shifts between action, thought, and dialogue": [Fig. VI-6]

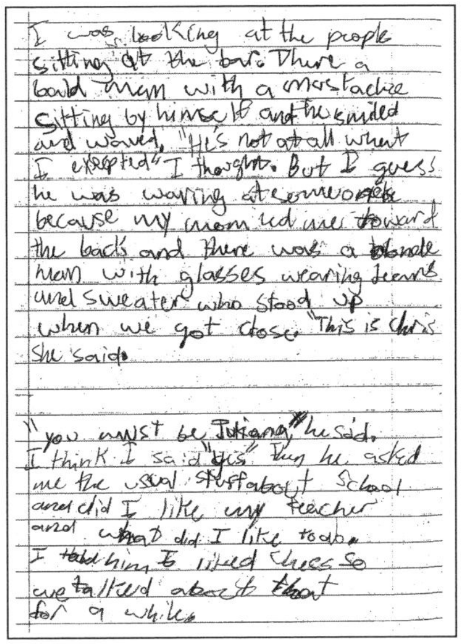

> I was looking at the people sitting at the bar. (action) There was a bald man with a mustache sitting by himself, and he smiled and waved. "He's not what I expected," I thought. (thought) But I guess he was waving at someone else because my mom led me towards the back and there was a blond man with glasses wearing jeans and a sweater who stood up when we got close. (action) "This is Chris," she said.
>
> "You must be Juliana," he said. (dialogue)

"When you go from writing an entry to writing a draft, remember that this is one more strategy that you already know how to do as writers."

"Congratulations!"

Fig. V-6 Juliana

⬤ HOMEWORK *Collecting Details Related to the Seed Idea* Once we have decided on a seed idea, we need to be like magnets, attracting details that pertain to our story. So tonight try to collect details that will help you write your personal narratives especially well. If I've decided to work on a story about when I got my new fish, I can't go back to that day—it is done—but I might spend time trying to describe this fish, putting words to the fact that it comes to me when I tap on the glass. I'll notice that the fish looks silvery sometimes, and orange at other times. I'll watch him closely. I can also go back and remember the time when I got him. Why did I pick him from all the other fish in the pet shop? How did he behave when I put him in with the other fish in my tank? How did my mother word that advice she gave me? Writers reach for the specific details that will help them develop their stories. Tonight, when you are home, collect those details.

If you notice that students need extra help with stretching out key moments in their writing to reveal their importance . . . you might share examples by students who have done this successfully because students often attain concepts best through peer examples. For example, you might say, "Francesca selected her seed idea and made a timeline of it. The actual actions are simple ones. Her timeline goes like this:

↑
• Phone rang
• Can I hamster watch?
• She's given the cage and hamster

"That's it! But pay attention to the way Francesca helps us appreciate that this moment is monumental to her. Watch the way she stretches this moment out, telling not just the external story but also telling the internal story of what she is remembering and wondering and noticing." [Figs. V-7 and V-8]

Hamster for a Day

I am picking up my black cold phone. I almost drop the phone at what I'm hearing. I am going to hamster sit Homer Rezler for 27 days. I feel half excited, half scared. I thought about my 13 pet worms that I got from Seattle, 3 months later they died. I don't know why. Maybe it was because they did not have the same soil? What if the same thing happens to Homer? I think. I know how hard it is to lose a pet. So I will try to be as careful as I can with him.

With a nervous look she handed me the cage and him. I felt brave that she chose me over anyone else to watch Homer. As I saw the half sad, half relieved look on her face I slowly picked up the cage. Homer was one of the cutest things I had ever seen in my life! With his little wet pink nose and orange soft fur. It was like watching a little tiny baby.

You could show students the internal events Francesca included at the start of her draft and ask them to locate and discuss with partners those she included in the second half of her draft. By naming Francesca's craft, they will be more able to apply it themselves.

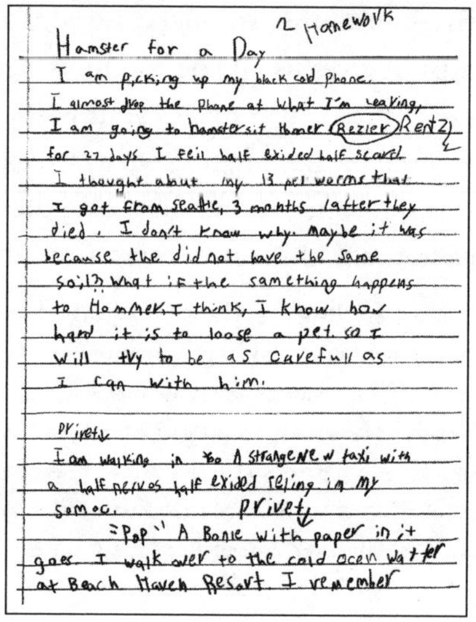

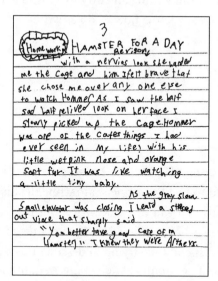

Fig. V-7 Francesca

Fig. V-8 Francesca

ASSESSMENT

You will want to spend some time assessing your children's writing at this point so you can tailor the minilessons and strategy lessons you teach over the next few days to lift the level of their stories. The minilessons I suggest assume that children have graduated past the phase of writing all about their subjects. But I know from experience that some of the children will still be listing all their thoughts and feelings and memories related to a personal topic, a topic such as "The Soccer Game" or "Bowling at My Birthday Party." And their writing will look something like this:

> I love soccer. I'm good at it. I am good at making goals
> because I am sly. Once I went behind the other kids and got
> a goal in. They didn't see me. But one time I twisted my
> ankle. "Ow, did that hurt!"

You need to watch for children who still believe that texts like these are narratives. At the very least, a narrative—and this includes a personal narrative—involves a central character progressing through a sequence of events. If your children are instead gathering a pile of the thoughts and ideas and memories associated to a personal topic, then they are on the verge of writing an all-about or informational piece, not a narrative. They either need to go that way with the piece—chunking their information so one paragraph (or chapter) tells why the child is good at soccer, one paragraph tells about injuries the child has incurred during soccer—or they need to stop and ask a question such as, "What is one particular small event that I experienced during soccer that might make a good story?"

There are other essential lessons that I do not teach in this unit of study, but which you may decide to revisit. Perhaps your children are trying

to write about the whole mountain climb, the whole day at the park, the whole soccer game, and they need to realize that any one of those topics contains dozens of focused stories. You may protest, saying, "Doesn't there need to be a place in life for a narrative that depicts the whole mountain climb?" and of course you are right. But to be effective, those narratives probably will comprise several vignettes (or scenes or small moments—those are all words for the same thing) linked together with tiny bits of exposition (as students noticed in "Your Name in Gold," back in Session I). Perhaps the whole-day-of-mountain-climbing story begins with a vignette about starting up the hill, then jumps ahead to depict the last strenuous moments of climbing, then leaps forward to retell the triumphant moment when you crest the top of the mountain and see the world spread below. For now, you may teach children who are still struggling with narrative form to write just one of those vignettes.

Be willing to look at your children's writing with honest eyes. Look through their command of spelling, through their use of adjectives, and try to see what they are doing as writers of narratives. Be sure they have learned to write focused narratives, and to storytell rather than summarize. If they're doing these things, the minilessons that follow will be helpful. If they are not doing these things, go back and find the minilessons from *Launching the Writing Workshop* that were designed to help with these skills. Draw on our list of mentor texts so that you bring fresh examples into minilessons, and try to understand what the challenges are that are derailing your children. Drawing on these resources, you'll be able to revise and reteach minilessons.

IN THIS SESSION, YOU'LL TEACH
STUDENTS THAT WRITERS ALWAYS
CONSIDER WHAT THEIR STORIES ARE
REALLY ABOUT SINCE THIS DECISION
GUIDES ALL CHOICES IN CRAFTING
AND REVISING NARRATIVES.

GETTING READY

- Excerpt of red-sweater scene from Sandra Cisneros' "Eleven," written on chart paper
- Whole-class common experience that can be told from various angles
- Monitoring My Writing Process chart
- Example of student writing before and after revising to reveal a particular meaning
- *Little by Little,* by Jean Little
- See CD-ROM for resources

WRITERS ASK, "WHAT AM I *REALLY* TRYING TO SAY?"

Once again, you will help students shift between collecting entries and writing a draft. This is a good time to mentally back up for an aerial view of the curriculum, seeing how you are helping children spiral through the writing process over and over, each time drawing on a bigger repertoire of possible strategies and each time carrying a more complex knowledge of the qualities of effective writing.

Knowing that your students—and your teaching—will continue to cycle through the writing process should help you realize that it is okay if your children do not grasp all the nuances of your teaching. At any one point, some children will be mastering a concept while others are still acquiring it. Those in the latter group will know the concept is important, but they will not yet be able to use it without your support. This shouldn't surprise you. Whenever we are learning to do something, we often understand the teacher's words long before we can master the trick of making our actions fit those words. I recall my mother teaching me tennis. Over and over she'd tell me, "Keep your eye on the ball!" and over and over I would want to say to her, "What do you think I'm doing? Watching birds?" But then one day I actually watched the ball spin toward me, and I saw it hover for a minute at the top of its arc. I saw my racket make contact with the ball—and I realized that until that moment, I had never before followed my mother's advice.

Today, your lesson is as essential as my mother's advice to me. It is, in a sense, the same message. You will be saying to children, "Keep your eye on your subject," and they will think, "What do you think I am doing? Counting elephants?"

Some children will grasp the power of this teaching today; others will not yet fully take in your words. Still, teach them with the full knowledge that this is enormously important and complex work. Because actually, everything else that a writer might do—drafting and revising a timeline, exploring different leads, considering which section of a story to tell in detail and which to summarize in passing—is contingent upon the writer first asking, "What am I really trying to say?" and then keeping his or her eye on that meaning.

MINILESSON

Writers Ask, "What Am I *Really* Trying to Say?"

CONNECTION

Celebrate the stories you heard yesterday.

"Writers, yesterday many of you chose your seed idea, and you told your stories to each other in ways that made people gasp or laugh or want to hear more. The stories that I heard yesterday are incredibly significant ones. You all are doing hard and important writing work, aren't you! Because of the amazing, *big* stories I heard you tell yesterday, I believe you are ready for this: today I want to teach you one of the most important lessons I will ever teach you about writing."

Name your teaching point. Specifically, tell children that writers need to ask, "What am I really trying to say in this story?" and then let that question guide us as we develop seed ideas into drafts.

"Before you can decide which lead will work best for your story, or whether you want to stretch out one section or another, you need to decide what you really want to say in your story. You need to ask, "What is my story *really* about?" and to realize that the same story could be written to show very different things. You could write about going on a Ferris wheel, and your story could show that you conquered your fear of heights. Or you could write about the same ride on the Ferris wheel and show that when you are in a crowd of people, you always find ways to be alone. As a writer, once you have chosen the entry that will be your seed idea, you need to pause and think, 'What am I *really* trying to say in this story?' and then let your answer to that question guide your work as a writer."

TEACHING

Tell children that their mentor author probably asked, "What am I really trying to say in this story?" Show that she could have angled her story differently.

"When Sandra Cisneros wrote 'Eleven,' I am pretty sure she remembered that story of the red sweater and thought, 'What is it I really want to say about that incident?' She could have written the story in a way that highlighted that the kids kept losing stuff that ended up in their coat closet, in which case she would have had Mrs. Price come out of that coat closet carrying a big pile—not just the red sweater, but also a whiffle bat and ball, some old coats, and maybe some left-behind lunch bags. Cisneros could have told the story to

COACHING

You may want to glance back across a whole series of minilessons, noticing the variety of ways in which I ask for children's attention. In the booming, crazy chaos of a classroom, commanding attention is no small feat. I do this by saying the opening word, "Writers," quietly, leaning toward the class, and by waiting until I see that I have their eyes before continuing. But I also try to find words that say, "What I'm about to say is really important." Today's lesson has a bigger than usual drumroll preceding it, and so I want to lean forward to you as well as to the children, to say, "Teachers," and I want to help you step aside from the chaos and take in the significance of today's lesson.

The qualities of good writing pertain to minilessons. I could have simply stated the generalization: Cisneros could have angled her story of the red-sweater incident to highlight any one of a range of meanings. Instead of simply telling kids this, I try to show it with examples that detail how Cisneros might have told the story differently.

emphasize that Mrs. Price was mean to Rachel; in that case Cisneros might have shown the teacher raging more, and made a bigger point of how Mrs. Price saw Rachel cry and instead of offering comfort, Mrs. Price turned her back on Rachel."

"Instead, I think Cisneros decided she wanted to highlight the idea that people have all different levels of maturity in themselves and different ones show up according to different situations. Even though Rachel is old enough to stand up for herself, when Mrs. Price says, 'Of course it is your sweater. I remember you wearing it once,' and puts the sweater on Rachel's desk, Rachel can't get words out of her mouth to protest. Because this part of the story matters a lot, this section is described carefully, with lots of words, in detail, and with paragraphs all to itself." I point to and read aloud the excerpt from "Eleven."

> Mrs. Price takes the sweater and puts it right on my desk, but when I open my mouth nothing comes out.
>
> "That's not, I don't, you're not . . . Not mine," I finally say in a little voice that was maybe me when I was four . . . Not mine, not mine, not mine, but Mrs. Price is already turning to page thirty two, and math problem number four. (pp. 7–8)

"When we write, we always need to ask ourselves, 'Which part of this story will I tell with lots of details, and which parts will I write only a little about?' One way to emphasize a part of the story that really says what the story is about is to take tiny steps through that bit, writing down every little part. Sandra Cisneros could have decided to pass quickly by the part of her story that involved putting on the red sweater. She could have written only a little about it, like this."

> "You put that sweater on right now," Mrs. Price said. I put it on.

"But instead, she decided that this section of the story could help convey what she really wanted to say about Rachel not having the courage to say, 'It's not mine.' So she took tiny steps through this partial episode and wrote every bit down as she went."

> I put one arm though one sleeve of the sweater that smells like cottage cheese, and then the other arm through the other and stand there with my arms apart like if the sweater hurts me and it does, all itchy and full of germs that aren't even mine. (p. 8)

It is a great treat to be able to rely on published authors as co-teachers, helping us demonstrate the skills and strategies of good writing. Cisneros writes so beautifully that when we borrow her text, inserting it into our minilesson, some of her magic rubs off on our teaching. But the challenge when using published texts is that we only have the finished product, and it's not enough to say to children, "Go and write like this." So we often need to imagine what a writer's process might have been, as I do in this instance.

As I teach this minilesson, I know that writing with great detail and in small steps is not always better than writing that traverses the terrain in big strides. But I also know that children come to us, writing in giant steps, and that it is definitely a good thing for a writer to vary the amount of detail according to the content of the story and its relative importance. The fact that I oversimplify the goal is acceptable to me. Later in the year, you'll see children learn a more nuanced sense of good writing.

During the teaching component of minilessons, you may use your writing or a child's writing or a published author's writing. Usually it helps to revisit the same piece of writing often because you can zoom in on specific sections, knowing that children can recall the entire text enough to contextualize the point you make.

You'll notice that to highlight the choices an author has or has not made in ways that guide children's choices, I often say, "This author could have . . . but instead she . . . "

ACTIVE ENGAGEMENT
Invite children to retell a familiar event twice, angling the story differently each time to bring two different meanings to the event.

"What I hope you are learning is that, as a writer, once you have decided on a story you want to tell, you need to pause and think, 'What am I really trying to say?' Once you have decided on the meaning you want to convey, all other decisions will be affected by that decision."

"Let's try it. Remember yesterday when our window was stuck and we couldn't open it? Let's pretend we want to write that stuck window–story and we want to angle the story to show that it is really hard for us to get through even one read-aloud without interruptions because so many things in our room don't work. I'll start the story, and then partner 2s, you continue it. Everything you say doesn't need to be exactly true; you can take some poetic license."

> Yesterday, our teacher read aloud. It was so hot that
> sweat was rolling down our faces, so our teacher stopped
> and went over to open the window. She pushed. Nothing
> happened. Flakes of paint rained down. So she . . . (Did
> what? Partner 2s, continue the story.)

Intervening after a few minutes, I called for children's attention to revert to me. "Let's say that instead, we want to tell about that same episode but this time, we want to show how we all work together as a community, solving our problems by helping each other. How could we tell the same story? I'll start it, and partner 1s, add on."

> Yesterday our teacher read aloud. She looked out and
> saw that we had sweat rolling down our cheeks. So she
> knew she had to help us. She went over and tried to open
> the window. It was stuck. Soon Ori had jumped up . . .
> (partner 1s, continue the story.)

I listened in as children carried on, telling their partners about how first one, then another and finally four children gathered around the window, pushing with all their might until, with a groan, the window creaked open.

Notice that the for portion of the minilesson in which I debrief, my teaching can fall either at the end of the Teaching component or at the start of the Active Engagement component, or in both places.

I know that what I am asking children to do is not easy. This is why I get them started, telling a good deal of the story. I try to provide enough scaffolding that it's feasible for them to carry on where I've left off, and I know that even if they can't, they will probably learn from these added illustrations of my point.

I could have chosen a more accessible example. I could, for example, have asked children to describe entering the classroom that morning, putting their things away and convening in the meeting area. They could tell this as if they came to school in high spirits, looking forward to the day—or as if they came to school in a depressed mood, dreading even the writing workshop.

"You told the same event really differently, didn't you?" I said. "You told the story of that event once to show that nothing works very well in the school, adding details about the paint flakes raining down on us and the hissing radiator that won't stop whining and groaning. Then you told the story of the same event a second time, this time showing how we jumped up to help each other, and how, when we all worked together, we could get that window to creak open. You brought out different details in each story because you were aiming to show something different in each version."

LINK
Reiterate that writers need to pause and ask, "What am I really trying to say?" and then revise and craft the stories to convey that chosen meaning.

"So, from this day forward and for the rest of your life, when you decide to work on a story, remember that one of the first and most important things you can do is to pause and ask yourself, 'What am I *really* trying to say in this story?' Let's add that to our Monitoring My Writing Process checklist as one important way to develop our seed ideas." I took a moment to add "Write an entry about what I am *really* trying to say in this story" to our class chart.

Monitoring My Writing Process	First Piece	Next Piece
Gather entries		
Select and develop one seed idea		
Write an entry about what you are really trying to say		
Storytell to rehearse for writing		
Read published writing that resembles what I want to write		
Draft leads—try action, dialogue, setting		
Make a timeline		
Choose paper, plan story on pages, copy lead		
Write draft with each part on a separate page		
Reread and revise for clarity		
Draft endings—try writing with important ideas and images from the story, and with details that are reminders of the whole		
Revise and edit more now or decide to wait until later, or not to revise		

This is a writing lesson, but of course it is also a life lesson. The truth is that as teachers, too, we need to remember that we are the authors of our lives. It will always, for each of us, be My Life, by me.

I'm convinced that until a child has decided what she wants to highlight in a story, it's fairly likely that her revisions won't actually improve the text. The single move to decide on one's meaning makes enormous contributions. As I've said before, this lesson is only the beginning of teaching children how to write and revise their stories based on what those texts are "really" about. At first, children may not have the experience to know how to answer that question—thinking about it is a start, however, and we will teach them more about this in later units.

"After you have chosen your seed idea, you will want to do that—write an entry about what you are really trying to say, and that will help you determine what goes on your timelines and what details to include in your story." Then I said, "If you want to see an example, I have an entry one of my students from last year wrote *[Fig. VI-1]* and I'll leave copies at our writing center."

What's the big thing/really important?

I want the reader to know that my father and I are so intensely into the game that we're nervous and biting our lips. I want the reader to know that I am hoping with all my heart that Soriano gets a hit, or even a homerun. I think the big thing of the story is leading up to the hit and how everyone's very tense.

How am I going to show this?

I'm going to show more of my surroundings, and what the people around me are doing. Also, show mine and everyone's actions more thoroughly, so the reader gets a sense of all the tension even more, so the reader is tense or excited.

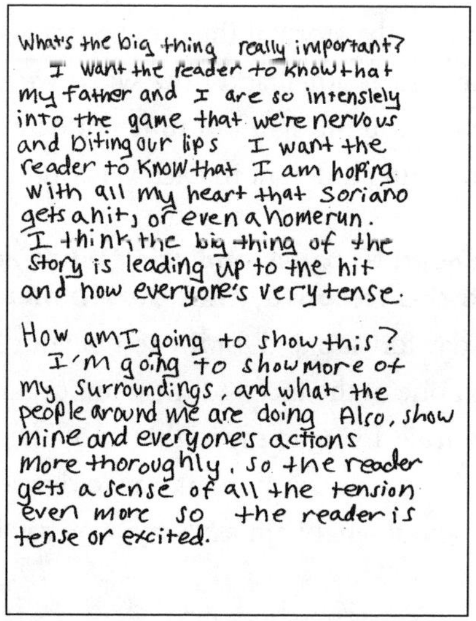

What's the big thing really important?
I want the reader to know that my father and I are so intensley into the game that we're nervous and biting our lips I want the reader to know that I am hoping with all my heart that Soriano gets a hit, or even a homerun. I think the big thing of the story is leading up to the hit and how everyone's very tense.

How am I going to show this?
I'm going to show more of my surroundings, and what the people around me are doing Also, show mine and everyone's actions more thoroughly, so the reader gets a sense of all the tension even more so the reader is tense or excited.

Fig. VI-1 Notice how this writer reflects on what it is he really wants to convey in his piece.

WRITING AND CONFERRING

Teaching Children to Confer with Each Other

I pulled my chair alongside Sophie. "How's it going?" I asked her.

"Good," she said, her intonation suggesting that in fact she was in a quandary.

A rule of thumb that guides me when I do research in a conference is the advice that journalism students are often given: to get information, you need to give information. If I detect something in a writer's demeanor or her drafts and can name what I see, letting my further questions stand on the shoulders of that knowledge, that will usually yield more insight. So this time I said to Sophie, "You say you are doing well, but your voice isn't convincing. Are you in a quandary, in a puzzling situation?"

"I can't decide what my entry is really about," she answered, "'cause it's just about going to Chuck E. Cheese's with Claudia and I told what we did,' cause we had pizza and we got tokens and we did this squirt gun game and all."

"What a time you guys had!" I answered. "And you are so wise, trying to decide what the main thing is that you really want to show in your story. Writers do exactly what you are doing – and it's a hard question for all of us. What have you done so far to figure it out?"

"I was rereading it and voting – you know, one check for the pizza, two for the games, like that."

"Let me see if I understand," I said. "You've been rereading your draft and you have a coding system to decide which episode, which moment, from the dinner was the most important one. Is that right?"

Sophie nodded.

"I love that you aren't just sitting here holding your paper expecting that the answer about what really matters to come out of thin air!" I said. "It is smart that when you found yourself in a quandary, in a puzzle, you thought, 'So how could I go about solving this?' and then you came up with a plan for proceeding. That is so like you, Sophie, to be such an active problem solver!"

MID-WORKSHOP TEACHING POINT *Angling Writing* "Ori's seed idea tells the story of a Saturday morning when he got up early and brought his little brother downstairs, fixing him breakfast. Ori's first version of his story went like this." [*Fig. VI-2*]

> This Saturday I woke up at 7:17 am. I rolled out of my bunk bed and crouch to the hall when I see that my little brother, Alon, was lying in my mom's extremely large, brownish bed with my dad. Mom must be in the bathroom, I think to myself. I crawl into bed when my mom comes out of the bathroom.
>
> "Good morning Ori," she says. She goes in the bed on the left side next to Alon. "Alon, do you want to go downstairs?" I ask.

"So today, before working on leads and starting his draft, Ori took the time to write an entry in which he asked, 'What am I trying to say in my story?' He realized that he wanted to show that on this particular morning, he decided to let his parents sleep in. So even though he was very sleepy and didn't feel like getting out of bed, he did so, and soon had invited his brother,

continued on next page

Fig. VI-2 Ori's first version of his story

Then I added, "But can I give you one tip?" Waiting for her assent, I said, "The really important part of a story is not always one moment of the story, one small chunk of the story. Sometimes, the really important thing is a relationship or a feeling, not a single episode or event. For example, maybe you want to tell about the evening at Chuck E. Cheese's because you want to show that this was a time when you and your dad felt really close. Or maybe there is a different relationship or a different feeling that you want to spotlight."

"It's Claudia!" Sophie said. "'Cause we gave each other our prizes and that's when we decided to be best friends."

"That was the very night?" I exclaimed. "How did it happen?" I tried to mask my smile, to not show that I found it entertaining to notice how closely this conversation resembled ones I have had with colleagues who've recently announced their engagement. "Who asked whom?" I queried—but didn't linger long before telling Sophie that she definitely knew the big thing in her story!

Sophie decided to write an entry in which she recorded what it was she really wanted to say in her story, and then she set out to make a new timeline, this time being sure to put the events on it that pertained to her friendship with Claudia.

> Why is this idea important to me?
> The idea is important to me because it makes me realize that me and Claudia are very good friends and we can trust each other and count on each other to be there for each of us like if I fall back she will always be there to catch me and so will I.

continued from previous page

Alon, downstairs. Listen to Ori's lead, and see if you think he angles his story to show how tired he was." [Fig. VI-3]

> Last Saturday, I woke up at 7:17 am. "I'm s-s-s-so tired," I whisper. I snuggle in my warm bed and let my body sink into it. It's 7:20 am. Wow it's early I think to myself as I look sideways to the clock on the wall. 1,2,3! I roll out of bed and land in a big "boom!" "Ouch, that hurts" I say.
>
> I crouch into the hall and stand up when I get there. I decided to check if my brother is awake yet. I walk slowly and open my brother door. No one there. I walk even slower to my mom and dad's room...

"A famous poet, Emily Dickinson, once said, 'Tell all the truth but tell it slant.' You will need to decide what truth your story will contain, and you will also need to decide how to slant your story so your truth shines through. Ori did something really smart when he paused to ask, 'What's the big thing I'm trying to show?'"

"Now Ori is going to try starting his Saturday morning story at a different place in his sequence. If any of you want Ori's help thinking about what you want to show in your story, he's agreed to help anyone who needs it."

> last saterday I wake up at 7:17 AM "Im s-s-so t-t-tired." I whisper. I snuggle in my warm bed and let my body sink into it. It's 7:20 AM, wow Its early I think to myself as I look sideways to the Clock on the wall. 1,2,3! I roll out of bed and land in a big "boom!" "ouch, that hurts" I say. I crouch into the hallway and stand up when I get there. I dicided To check if my brother is awake yet. I walk slowly and open my brothers door ho one I walkeven slower to my mom and dad's room. It was half way opened so I peeped inside to see if my brother is there I see that

Fig. VI-3 Ori has tried to angle his new lead to highlight his tiredness.

SHARE

Storytelling with an Angle

Convene the class and remind children of strategies writers use to bring out their meaning. Ask one partner to storytell his or her story in ways that highlight the meaning.

"Writers, please bring your writing notebooks with you to the meeting area. Let's gather." When the class was settled, I said, "Last month we learned to expand the heart of our stories by slowing the action, by giving details, by adding thoughts, and by adding dialogue. These are great strategies not only to expand the important parts of a story but also to bring out what we want to say. Let's practice these strategies right now."

"Right now, take a second to look over your seed idea and also look over the entry you wrote exploring why you want to write this story. Then close your notebooks, and practice telling at least the beginnings of your story to your partner. After you've told the start of your story, see if your partner can guess what it was you were trying to show, bringing out your angle by using actions, details, thoughts, and dialogue, like Ori did earlier." I listened and coached individuals as they practiced.

You'll decide whether storytelling is an important way for your writers to rehearse, and whether your children benefit from the props you provided in the last unit when they storytold using fingers and booklet pages and dots on a timeline to remind them of the march of time. If possible, I'd let those props fall away for most of your children as they can limit as well as support.

HOMEWORK **Angling Your Writing as You Draft** Writers, in her memoir *Little by Little*, Jean Little wrote one scene about her first day in a new school. It happened in April, when all the children already knew each other. Jean was struggling because of her poor vision, which made her different from the other children. At the end of the scene she tells us what she wanted to show most of all. She wrote: "I was gradually learning that if you were different, nothing good about you mattered. And I had not really understood, until now, that I *was* different" (p. 36).

Read the first part of this scene, and notice and mark up ways Jean angled her writing. In fact, every part of the scene brings out her stated intention. Listen.

"This is Jean Little," my new teacher told the class. She led me to a desk.

"This is Pamela, Jean," she said, smiling at the girl in the desk next to mine. I smiled at her, too.

Pamela's cheeks got pink. She looked away. I thought I knew what was wrong. She was shy. I sat down and waited for lessons to start. I was glad that reading was first.

When it was my turn to read out loud, I held the book up to my nose as usual. The other children giggled. The teacher hushed them. Then she turned to me.

"Are those your reading glasses?" she asked.

I was not sure. I snatched the glasses off and switched. But I still had to hold my book so close that my nose brushed against the page. Everybody stared. Nobody noticed my good reading.

That afternoon when the teacher left the room, Monica pointed at me.

"Look!" she crowed. "She's got black all over her nose!"

I clapped my hand to my face. The class burst into peals of laughter. They only broke off when the child nearest the door hissed, "Shh! She's coming."

After you have learned from Jean Little's craftsmanship, take time to think again about what it is that you most want to show in your story. If you haven't made a timeline of your story, do so now and if you've made one already, try another draft. Be sure your timeline brings out what the story is mainly about. If you are writing about an early morning fishing trip, and you want to show your closeness with your dad, your timeline will feature the things you and your dad did and said and felt. If you really want to show the impatience you felt, just waiting and waiting and waiting for a nibble on the end of your line, then your timeline of events will reflect this."

In this example from Rie, notice how she identifies what it is that makes this small episode matter to her. *[Figs. VI-4 and VI-5]*

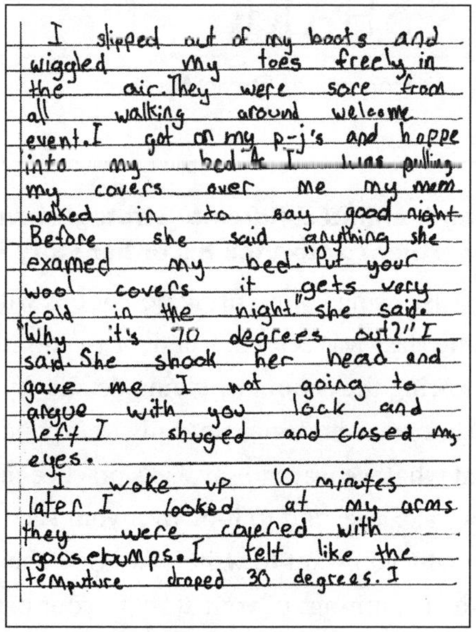

I slipped out of my boots and wiggled my toes freely in the air. They were sore from all walking around welcome event. I got on my p-j's and hoppe into my bed. As I was pulling my covers over me my mom walked in to say good night. Before she said anything she examed my bed. "Put your wool covers it gets very cold in the night" she said. "Why it's 70 degrees out?" I said. She shook her head and gave me I not going to argue with you look and left. I shuged and closed my eyes.
I woke up 10 minutes later. I looked at my arms they were covered with goosebumps. I felt like the temputure droped 30 degrees. I

Figs. VI-4 Rie's entry

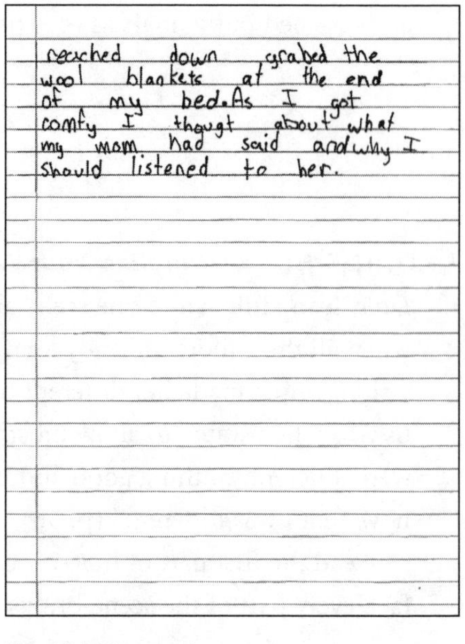

reached down grabed the wool blankets at the end of my bed. As I got comfy I thougt about what my mom had said and why I should listened to her.

Figs. VI-5 Rie page 2

TAILORING YOUR TEACHING One of the most important qualities of good writing is something which people refer to as "voice." Don Murray suggests that voice involves the imprint of the author, the sense that a real person is behind the words. Children are more likely to write with this magical quality if they've first storytold or otherwise voiced their draft.

> Writing and speaking are different but writing, without an understanding of its roots in speech, is nothing. The human voice underlies the entire writing process, and shows itself throughout the life of the writer. It is no accident that children enjoy reading their selections aloud, that professional writers have public readings of their work, or that writing compels us to speak to others, or to voice to ourselves. (Graves 1988, p. 162)

If your students could benefit from oral storytelling in ways which strengthen particular aspects of their writing as they move from seed ideas to drafts . . . you may find it worth the time to provide more storytelling sessions, each time teaching children that writers sometimes keep in mind specific goals. One time, you might teach students that writers sometimes make a point to incorporate dialogue in our storytelling. "Make your characters talk. Say their actual words." Another time, you might teach children that writers sometimes keep in mind what we want listeners to feel. "If you want us to know you were devastated, then tell the story so we know just how devastated you were!"

If your students need more opportunities to rehearse their drafts by storytelling them . . . you might teach children that writers sometimes rehearse for drafting by telling our stories to one person then another. You might begin by saying, "Writers, I know most of you have chosen a seed idea (and some of you have a few possible seed ideas in mind). You've been spending time getting ready to write. Remember that you're going to be writing these stories in ways that will—you hope—get through to your readers, that will make your readers gasp and wince and laugh. So right now, why don't you do what writers do and try telling your stories to people who've never heard them. Aim to make your listeners gasp or laugh or wince." Then pair children with new temporary partners. These temporary partners can provide a fresh audience for each student's seed idea.

COLLABORATING WITH COLLEAGUES

The lesson today is one that will require conferring support. If your primary-level colleagues have been using the *Units of Study for Primary Writing* and if they have our DVD called *Big Lessons from Small Writers*, I encourage you to borrow it and watch my conference with Lisa. She is a first grader, writing a story about a sleepover at her friend's house. You'll see that I asked her, "What is this story really about?" and there was a very long pause while she mulled that question over before finally admitting, "I'm not sure." So then I suggested two options, based on what she had already told me about the story. Might she be writing about the fun times that she and her friend had together? Or perhaps she could be wanting to show that sometimes, when you are over at a friend's house, you get a little homesick? Lisa knew right away that she wanted the latter option. So I asked, "Where does that lonesome part start?" I added, "When you got to Romi's house—at the start of the story—page 1—that wasn't really the lonesome part, was it?"

If you study that segment, you will see moves that I make repeatedly as I help children decide what the story really is that they want to tell. You'll see how I help children use their answers to this question to help them rethink their drafts. You'll also see that conferring with a six year old is not all that different from conferring with a ten year old.

After watching the segment, I suggest you try out this conference with your colleagues, helping each other to look again at your own writing and ask, "What am I really trying to say?" I want to tell you a secret that I don't

bring out until later with the kids. Usually, there is a timeline to what you are trying to show, just as there is a timeline to the events in the story. That is, usually what a writer wants to show changes across the draft. For example, in my Miss Armstrong story, at the start of the story, I want to show how hopeful I am that I will finally be included in Eliza's group of friends, and then later in that story, I want to show my bitter disappointment when it becomes clear that having a role in the play doesn't give me a role in the popular group of kids. You may realize, too, that there is one thing you want to show at the start of the story you are writing, and another thing at the end of that story.

Try to utterly rewrite your story, bringing out what you want to show. This means that if some detail actually happened in real life, but that detail doesn't convey your point or add to what you are trying to show, you will probably not mention it. You'll also need to take some liberties to angle your story to convey the meaning you select.

This work is not easy, but it is extraordinarily powerful. If you want an added challenge, look at children's literature thinking, "How does this author use every means possible to convey his or her meaning?" Study, for example, Ezra Jack Keats' *Peter's Chair*, and notice how everything in that story works together to support the message that Peter first feels his world is threatened because of the arrival of a little sister.

STUDYING AND CREATING LEADS

In this minilesson, I invite children to study leads in touchstone texts, learning from the work that other authors have done. The lead to Owl Moon can teach us that authors begin a draft thinking, "How can my lead link to the heart of my story?" From the start, readers need to sense what the story is really about.

Then, too, a close look at Owl Moon and other published texts can help you and your children pay attention to the grammar and syntax of leads.

When demonstrating how to study the craft behind Yolen's lead, you can help children notice what adults refer to as a subordinate clause, one that modifies the independent clause that is the heart of the sentence. Although you probably won't try to teach the complex grammar of this structure just yet, children benefit from knowing that when writing narratives, we often begin our sentences with a clause that sets the scene, establishes the time or location, or describes the action. Children tend at first to write simple subject-verb-object sentences: "I rode the merry-go-round." As their skills and experience increase, they learn to begin sentences with subordinate clauses.

- One sunny morning, I rode the merry-go-round. (States the time)
- Inching forward, the merry-go-round started. (Describes the action)
- At the top, I looked out. (States the location)

You'll help writers push beyond the simple subject-verb-object sentences that fill so many of their drafts.

You may wonder why the lead (which is also the topic of Session VII in Unit 1) is worthy of such attention. First, I think that in writing (as in teaching), beginnings are important because they channel what follows. Of course, revising the lead can channel what follows only if children revise their lead prior to writing the narrative; it's less powerful if they return to a completed story and plop an improved lead in place of a preexisting one. I also think it is worthwhile to teach children to revise their leads because working with leads gives us a microcosm in which to teach children the process and payoffs of revision. When suggesting a child write one lead, then another and another, we aren't putting especially high demands on them. Meanwhile, children can get a taste for revision.

GETTING READY

IN THIS SESSION, YOU'LL HELP STUDENTS LEARN THAT MENTOR TEXTS CAN GUIDE THEM AS THEY DRAFT AND REVISE LEADS.

- Lead of Yolen's *Owl Moon,* written on chart paper
- Lead for a Small Moment story the whole class experienced, written on chart paper
- Collection of well-crafted narrative picture books very familiar to your students [see CD]
- Copies of chart with three columns: Author's Lead; What the Author Has Done; Our Lead Using the Same Technique
- Monitoring My Writing Process checklist
- Student examples of leads that support intentions of their narratives
- See CD-ROM for resources

MINILESSON

Studying and Creating Leads

CONNECTION
Remind children of the techniques they learned when studying leads in Unit 1.

"Writers, remember that we talked about leads in our last unit? By looking at the work of published authors, you learned some techniques to try. You learned, for example, that it often works to start a narrative by telling a small action, by establishing the setting, or by having a character say something. This time, because we are more experienced as writers, we'll notice even more. Today we're going to look again at the way mentor authors write texts we love."

Name the teaching point. In this case, remind children that by studying the leads in mentor texts, they can learn new techniques.

"Have any of you tried to do a skateboarding trick? Or a skiing trick? Or a new dance step? If so, I bet you've watched someone who can do these things—maybe in real life, maybe on TV—and then you've tried to follow that person's prowess. I'm bringing this up because today I want to remind you that in the same way, writers study other writers whom we admire. This is how we learn moves that we want to use in our writing. Today I want to teach you to expand your options for writing leads by looking closely at how writers whom we admire begin their stories."

TEACHING
Demonstrate a process children can go through as they study the craftsmanship in another author's lead. Highlight the author's technique by contrasting it with what the author could have done.

"When I reach out for an author to study, I reach for one whose writing reminds me of what I'm trying to do, and I reach for an author who has written a text I admire. I've always admired Jane Yolen's lead to *Owl Moon*." I had copied her lead onto chart paper, and now I read it aloud.

COACHING

One of the challenges in this unit is to find ways to raise children's expectations so they tackle narrative writing with a new ambitiousness. By roping in authors as coteachers, I borrow their power and put it behind my teaching.

You may wish to peek ahead to Session XI. In that session, I teach children that narrative writers often plan our stories by thinking of them as story mountains. We sketch a story mountain, and keep in mind that the lead of a story needs to relate to the story's apex. If I was teaching skilled and experienced writers, I might move that session to this place in the unit because in fact, the decision over how to start a story relates to our sense of the story as a whole. I worried, however, that for many children this would be too complex. It is usually preferable to introduce a new and complex idea as a tool for revision, moving it forward in the process during a later cycle of work.

I would normally have returned to the one text that I hope will thread its way through much of this unit. The problem is that the children and I have been studying an excerpt from "Eleven" The start of the excerpt is not actually Cisneros' lead to the essay. In the final unit of this year, children revisit "Eleven," this time noticing the exposition at the start of that text. For now, I chose to study Owl Moon because it allows me to make the points I want to make and because children know it well.

It was late one winter night,
long past my bedtime,
when Pa and I went owling.

There was no wind.

The trees stood still
as giant statues.

And the moon was so bright
the sky seemed to shine.

Somewhere behind us
a train whistle blew,
long and low,
like a sad, sad song. (p. 3)

"When I study this lead, the first thing I notice is that even in her first sentence, Yolen has highlighted the narrator's relationship with her father—and the silence of the night, too. I'm pretty sure that for Jane Yolen, this story is really about a silent, wordless closeness she and her dad shared when they went owling. Those elements are present even in her opening lines."

"When I study this lead, I also notice that Jane Yolen isn't hesitant to give us all the vital facts we need to know to understand what's going on in her story. I'm mentioning that Yolen gives us all the vital facts because some people start their stories in ways that are confusing. For example, some authors might start a story like this.":

"Son," my dad said.

"Yes," I answered.

"Come here," my dad said. I walked over to where he lay face down on the grass.

"You read the lead and you think, 'What's happening here?' Granted, creating a puzzle in the first line of a text can sometimes be effective, but I personally prefer leads that answer the reader's questions. In *Owl Moon*, Jane Yolen puts all the vital facts into the start of her story. She tells us *who* is doing *what*, *where*. She even does this in one single sentence, answering *where* and *when* ('Late one winter night, long past my bedtime'), then *who* ('Pa and I') and *what* ('went owling'). But she doesn't answer these in a boring way. Instead, her chock-full-of-information lead has a 'pull in and listen' tone. You can feel that she's going to tell a story."

There is no one way to describe all the techniques Yolen has used that are worth emulating. I think many people would use more flowery language to name what she has done: She paints a scene, she creates a mood. Those things are true. But I want to highlight a few aspects of her craft that children may not notice but which will make a big difference to their writing. For this reason, I point out that her lead links to her message; this was, after all, the subject of the previous session. I could have proceeded to say that Yolen first paints the background, the big picture, and then zooms in to details, the footsteps on the snow. I decide instead to point out that she starts her story with information because in this class, I found many of the children's stories were confusing and disorienting. In any case, simply saying, "She paints a picture" wouldn't seem helpful enough to me.

You'll notice in all these units of study that the examples we present closely match what the students themselves might produce.

When I weigh the success of a minilesson, I tend to focus on whether it is memorable and replicable. I find that little things can make minilessons more replicable—like the fact that I refer to the well-known terms: who, what, when, where and why.

Debrief by naming the author's craft moves and showing how you could use similar moves in a lead about a class event.

"What I've learned, writers, is that if I want to write like an author, it helps to really study what the author did *exactly*. Let me look more closely at Jane Yolen's sentences. I'm going to try to think, 'How is this different from what I usually do?' When I'm talking or writing in a regular way, I think I tend to say *what I did* first (or what another person did), and only then tell *when* or *where* I—or we—did that thing. I think if *I* had been the one to go owling, I'd say (or write) this. 'I went owling late last night.'"

"Jane Yolen brings a story feeling to her writing partly because she changes the usual order of the sentence. She puts when and where first, then adds a comma and then tells the action. 'It was late one winter night, long past my bedtime, when Pa and I went owling.'"

"If I want to write a lead following Jane Yolen's template (only mine will be about *my* story, not hers), I could try to write a sentence that answers the *who, what, where,* and *when* questions, and one that sequences these in the way that she did."

"So if my story is about how Hermie tried escaping from his cage during today's read-aloud time, I could write the lead this way."

> It was early one Friday morning, just at the start of read-aloud time, when Hermie tried escaping from his cage.

"Of course, tiny specific actions sometimes help, so I could also start the story like this."

> It was early one Friday morning, just as we were settling in for read-aloud, when Katie noticed the empty cage.

"Later today, or whenever you write, some of you may want to emulate Jane Yolen's *Owl Moon* lead."

ACTIVE ENGAGEMENT
Rally children to study the lead in another published text and to name what that author has done.

"But my bigger point is that, as we learned in our first unit, we can study any author's lead really closely, asking, 'What has this author done that I could try?' I'm going to pass out some other books that all of us know really well. When you get a text, will you and your partner find the lead. Read it once, twice. Read it aloud and then talk together about what your author has done. Has your author written a lead which is similar to the lead of *Owl Moon*? Has your author done something different—and if so, what has the author done? Dissect the sentence like I did when I said Yolen wrote *where* and *when*, and *who* did *what*.

You may be surprised to see this detailed attention to syntax when students are just on the brink of beginning a first draft. It is true that I believe syntax is more a matter of rehearsal and drafting than of editing. I believe we can launch children in writing with more literary syntax, and that doing this can evoke a quality of writing that can never be achieved through red pen corrections. Then, too, I want children to know that writers love the sounds and textures of language, and pay attention not only to what we say but also to how to convey our content.

When you pass out books for children to study, I recommend you fill the collection with books which have opening sentences which resemble that which you studied as well as with books which demonstrate another option or two. Classics such as Mike Mulligan and His Steam Shovel, ("Mike Mulligan has a steam shovel, a beautiful red steam shovel.") or McCloskey's One Morning in Maine, or MacLachlan's Sarah Plain and Tall follow the same pattern as Owl Moon.

You needn't use these words —*where, when, who, what*—invent your own words for describing exactly what the author has done. If you can, try saying a lead to the Hermie story that would follow the same pattern as the lead you study."

One partnership pored over *My Pig, Amarillo* by Satomi Ichikawa. The lead begins:

> One summer day, my grandpa arrives home with a tiny pig on a leash.
> "Pablito, it's for you," he says. I am so excited. I do not know what to say.

The children decided the story began like *Owl Moon*. The author told when the action happened, then added a comma, then included a simple sentence, telling "who did what." They tried inventing a similar lead to the Hermie story:

> One fall afternoon, my teacher read aloud in the meeting area. "What's that noise?" I whispered. It sounded like Hermie. I was nervous.

Similarly, the children who studied *Smoky Nights* by Eve Bunting saw that the opening sentence told "who did what" and then added a comma, then explained how the action was done:

> Mama and I stand well back from our window, looking down. I'm hiding Jasmine my cat.

The children need not report on their conversation to you. They gain from having the chance to talk about something whether or not you hear and record what they say! If you decide to extend the minilesson by soliciting the class' help in filling out a chart see the CD for advice.

Author's Lead	What the Author Has Done	Our Lead, Using the Same Technique
Mama and I stand well back from our window, looking down. I'm hiding Jasmine, my cat. We don't have lights on though it's almost dark. People are rioting in the street below. Mama explains about rioting. "It can happen when people get angry . . ." (Smoky Night, by Eve Bunting, p.5)	The first sentence tells who is doing what, and then there is a comma, followed by a tiny explanation of their main action. Then the story names the circumstance—the rioting —that happens around the characters.	My classmates and I listened to the story, picturing the scenes in the book. Hermie's cage was empty. Robert pointed out that he'd left a trail of shavings. "We can follow them."
One summer day, my grandpa arrives home with a tiny pig on a leash. "Pablito, it's for you," he says. I am so excited. I do not know what to say. (My Pig, Amarillo, by Satomi Ichikawa, p.5)	The story begins by telling when, then with a main character doing an action in a place, followed by dialogue. Then the narrator expresses her feelings.	One fall afternoon, my teacher read aloud in the meeting area. "What's that noise?" I whispered. It sounded like Hermie. I was nervous. I did not know what to say.

LINK

Rename the teaching point, reminding children that today, and whenever they write, they can let authors become their teachers. Before sending children off, remind them of the strategies on the writing process chart.

"So writers, remember that if you want to do a trick on your skateboard, you watch someone who can do it. You watch really closely, noticing their technique. Perhaps the skateboarder shifts his weight, or leans to one side, or puts his hands out for balance. Whatever he does, you try the same thing."

"Similarly, you learned today that if you want to write a really powerful lead, it helps to carefully study the leads of writers we admire, just like we did for *Owl Moon*. Writers and skateboarders aren't that different from each other! Let's change the wording on our Monitoring My Writing Process chart to match what we now know about leads." On the chart, I quickly wrote "Study published leads."

"So during writing time today and often, you may want to look closely at what an author you admire has done. Let that author become your teacher by paying close attention, studying the craft the author has used."

"If you are admiring a lead, ask, 'Why did it work?' If you are studying anything—the setting, the character development, the question, 'What's this story really about?'—you can pay attention to what the author did pertaining to whatever it is you are studying. Of course, you will want to refer to our Monitoring My Writing Process chart, making sure that you are progressing along in the process of writing your own story." I pointed again to the Monitoring My Writing Process chart as a reminder of all their options. "Let's get started."

We hope that children's learning is cumulative. Because we want children to hold on to what they learned from previous minilessons as they progress, you'll see that we often weave language from early minilessons into our teaching.

You may want to literally count up how many times our link reminds children of the array of optional activities they could pursue during the day, versus how many times the link channels children to do a particular activity right away. I'm quite sure that most of the time, before sending children off, we remind them of their options.

Monitoring My Writing Process	First Piece	Next Piece
Gather entries		
Select and develop one seed idea		
Write an entry about what you are really trying to say.		
Storytell to rehearse for writing		
Read published writing that resembles what you want to write		
Study published leads. Pay attention to what the author did and how the author did it. Let this influence your own writing.		
Draft leads—try action, dialogue, setting		
Make a timeline		
Choose paper, plan story on pages, copy lead		
Write draft with each part on a separate page		
Reread and revise for clarity		
Draft endings—try writing with important ideas and images from the story, and with details that are reminders of the whole		
Revise and edit more now or decide to wait until later, or not to revise		

WRITING AND CONFERRING

Getting Ready for Drafting

Today might be a day to help kids confer with each other. I sometimes emphasize this on a day when a particularly long line of kids seems to be following me, looking for assistance, in which case I am apt to ask for all children's attention and tell them there are twenty-nine writing teachers in the classroom, not just one. But I might also choose to teach this lesson now because at this particular juncture in the writing process, it is very important for writers to have listeners.

Most of your children will still be rehearsing for their first drafts. They'll probably be writing in their notebooks, making and revising timelines, trying alternate leads, telling their stories to listeners. As children do this, it's a great thing for them to say aloud the story they plan to write, and to cumulate goals for the draft they'll soon produce.

If you do decide to help children confer with each other, before you can teach them to do this, you need to decide the kind of help you can imagine kids giving each other. The easiest thing for kids to do is to help each other talk a lot about their subjects. That is, if a child has written about her guinea pig, another child can listen with interest and say, "I didn't even know you had a guinea pig. Tell me more about it."

With coaching, some children can learn to steer the writer, asking, "What's the most important thing you want to say?" or "Can you tell the whole story, and tell it in a way that makes that important?"

In general, I hope that as the year moves along, you'll be able to spend less and less time listening to writers talk about their guinea pig and their sister and their basketball game, and that you'll be able to spend much more time listening to writers talk about their writing strategies and goals and assessments. That is, as you confer, if a child answers your inquiry about what she has been working on as a writer by simply telling you her subject—"I've been writing about my guinea pig"—I hope you'll respond only briefly

---

MID-WORKSHOP TEACHING POINT **Elaborating on the Important Parts** "Writers, earlier you learned that a writer needs to decide whether to write in big steps or in tiny steps. Rena just realized that usually we'll slow down and use tiny steps to tell the *important parts* of our stories. Rena began writing about a bike ride. She started inching her way through the story starting with getting a drink on the way to her bike."

> I slowly raise the glass to my lips and settle my mouth on the rim. I tip the cup so that the lemonade pours down my throat. I shiver. I put too much ice in it, and it's over-refreshing. One cube slips down with my last sip.
>
> I feel much cooler now. I know I won't be cool for much longer, though. I am going on a bike ride.

"But then Rena realized the drink didn't matter to her bike trip story! She said to me, 'I stretched out the story of how I gulped down some lemonade, but now I realize I stretched out something that doesn't really matter.'" [Fig. VII-1]

continued on next page

> I slowly raise the glass to my lips and settle my mouth on the rim. I tip the cup so that the lemonade pours down my throat. I shiver. I put too much ice in it, and it's over-refreshing. One cube slips down with the last of my sip.
>
> I feel much cooler now. I know I won't be cool for much longer though. I am going on a bike ride.
>
> We go downstairs, to the basement where our bikes are locked up. My mom takes out the keys and fiddles with her U-lock while I fasten on my bike helmet. I need to adjust the straps on it. It feels too tight. My head must have grown. My mom is ready to go, but she doesn't have to adjust her helmet because her head stopped growing a long time ago.

Fig. VII-1 Rena

to the subject and will, above all, channel the writer to talk about what he or she has been trying to do on the page and the strategies he or she has used to accomplish these goals. So it's a great thing to invite children to take over some of the role of being listeners as writers talk about their subjects.

As you move away from conferences that focus exclusively on content, help children assume the role of being good listeners for each other. Recall that in Session V, I emphasized the experience of talking to someone who listens with such rapt attention that we end up saying and recalling more than we dreamed of saying. This is what children can do in peer conferences.

The jury is out over how to teach children to help each other. Some people start right in with fairly explicit instructions: Look at the writer while he or she reads, tell the writer what the draft made you think and feel, ask the writer open-ended prompts like, "Can you tell me more about this?" or "How did you feel?" or "Can you help me picture it?" or "Start at the beginning, and tell it bit by bit." Other teachers try to instill in children an appreciation for good listeners, and then send kids off to be good writing partners for each other, relying on authentic relationships more than scripts to lift the level of peer conferences.

---

continued from previous page

"Looking back on the draft, Rena crossed out most of what she'd written, which was so smart of her!" Then I said, "Writers, the most important thing to realize is this: sometimes when we learn something new, we over learn it! When I teach first graders exclamation marks, they add them in all over a draft! And some of you have over-learned what I said about writing in tiny steps, stretching out your story. As Rena said, now she realizes that the main thing in her story was bike riding but she got stuck in the kitchen having a drink of lemonade!"

"You will need to keep in mind that some parts of your story will need to be written quickly, in big steps, and some parts of your story need to be written slowly, in tiny steps. You will know what to skip past and what to stretch out when you know what your story is really about."

"Would each of you look at your writing right now, and put a mark in the margin indicating the really important parts of your story?" After a moment, I said, "These are the parts you'll probably want to write in tiny steps."

SHARE

Learning from Techniques Classmates Have Used

Share the process by which a student has crafted a stronger lead than the one she had.

"Writers, I want to share with you the work that some of you did on leads today. Emily remembered she could start her lead at more than one place in her timeline. Here are two leads that she tried for her story about losing her math homework at a Chinese restaurant." I read aloud the following entries. *[Fig. VII-2]*

> Lead #1: "Do I really have to do my homework now?" I asked.
>
> "Yes" answered my mom. Then I started to think of an excuse. "But then how are we going to do it without scissors?"
>
> "I can rip out the cards, now just stop asking." My mom replied. She started to rip out the cards. "It is sooo dim in here!" I said.
>
> Lead #2: The lights were dim as I walked in. I could already smell a whiff of Chinese food. The people were as quiet as ever. I thought, they must like there food.

"Did you notice how one lead starts at the point on the timeline when Emily and her mom were already sitting at the table, and the other starts at the point when they first entered the restaurant? I also want you to notice that Emily created a sense of the setting. She got the idea for doing this from both *Owl Moon* and also from Eve Bunting's *Smokey Nights*. I love the way she came up with her own goals, wrote them in her planning box, and then pursued those goals."

Fig. VII-2 Emily

Share the process of another student who had success using a mentor author's techniques to revise her lead.

"Sophie, you remember, had initially begun her draft this way."

> We walked through the front door of Chuck E. Cheese.
> The place was packed. We ordered a pizza. It was good.

"But the other day, she realized that her narrative is really a story about she and Claudia, so she tried a new lead. She labeled it 'Beginning Action' but really, she's beginning with action *and* with Claudia. I'm going to read this now and will you list four smart things that Sophie's done. Tell these across your fingers and then get ready to share them." *[Fig. VII-3]*

> We walked into the Chuck E. Cheese. I held Claudia's
> hand tight, my palm was sweating. I was feeling really
> happy to be with Claudia. "Hey, Claudia! What game do
> you want to play?"

"What did you list? Turn and share." After a few minutes, I said, "What smart things have you done? Share your leads and point out each other's smart decisions."

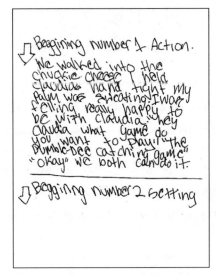

Fig. VII-3 Sophie

⊙ HOMEWORK   *Studying and Writing Leads* Today we studied some leads in stories we know well in order to name the things the author did that made these leads really work well. Tonight your job is to do the same things. Reread the lead in the book you're reading right now and then reread the leads in some books you love. They could be chapter books, short stories, or picture books.

When you reread these leads, do the same work we did in school today. Notice what the author does in the lead and name it on a sticky note. Now, take a look at the leads you've written and revise them using one or some of the things you noticed in published leads. Bring these revised leads to school tomorrow because you'll have a chance to talk to your writing partner about what you did in your lead revisions.

If your students could benefit from studying different kinds of leads to expand their repertoire of possibilities for their own writing . . . you might spend a writing session studying powerful, well-loved leads together with your students and categorizing them. In *Live Writing*, Ralph Fletcher suggests categorizing powerful leads from well-loved books. One category of powerful leads he describes is the Grabber Lead, in which the writer begins deliberately with an element of surprise. Fletcher also discusses Introducing the Narrator leads; the Moody Lead, in which the writer sets the mood or tone of the story; Beginning at the End, in which the writer reveals the ending at the start before unfolding the story; and the Misleading Lead, in which the writer deliberately sets you up for something other than what unfolds. In some strong writing classrooms, teachers and students chart different types of leads with examples from both professional and student writers. After your students know a variety of categories of leads, you can guide them to try out different leads before choosing the one that best fits the overall intentions they have for their stories.

If your students seem so intent on writing titillating or exciting leads that they forget that a lead needs to orient the reader . . . teach them how authors describe actions in ways that answer readers' questions and provide orienting information. You may want to cite the famous lead to *Charlotte's Web*, and you'll also find Takeshi's skilled efforts can be a resource for you in your minilesson. *[Fig. VII-4]*

> I got off the taxi cab with my mom, my brother and me to go drop Faiki off to his piano lesson. When we got off the taxi and the taxi went away, right in front of me was the old deli I used to go to.
>
> "I'm going in the deli, okay?" I asked my mom.. I walked up to the cashier and said. "Hi, do you remember me?" The cashier turned his head and said. "Oh, I remember you," he said.

Takeshi finally decided to start his story like this.

> "I'm going in the deli, okay?" I asked my mom as I ran up to the deli. "Okay," she said. I was already walking up to the cashier. "Do you remember me?" I said as I stood up to the cashier. He turned his head to look at me. "Oh, hi." he said and I was relieved that he remembered me.

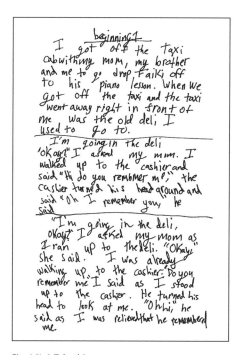

Fig. VII-4 Takeshi

COLLABORATING WITH COLLEAGUES

One of our goals in this unit of study is to teach students to make strong reading/writing connections. We want them to realize that mentor texts can teach them everything they need to know about any kind of writing they want to compose. Webster's dictionary defines a mentor as "a close, trusted, and experienced counselor or guide," which perfectly describes the relationships we want our students to have with mentor texts.

You may find yourself tempted to bring great armloads of wonderful literature into your grade-level faculty meetings or study groups. I caution against this, and urge you instead to devote long chunks of time to study a single mentor text closely (and then, perhaps, another one).

For example, you could decide to study Ezra Jack Keats' *Peter's Chair* together. On first glance, this book might appear easy to dismiss. It's written for young children, and can seem to be no big deal. Look again. Members of the Teachers College Reading and Writing Project staff spent perhaps six hours studying just that one book and we were amazed by the craftsmanship. In Session XI, you will help children discover its perfect arc of story structure. But also notice how every part demonstrates Peter's emotional journey. For example, consider the beginning:

> Peter stretched as high as he could.
> There! His tall building was finished.
> CRASH! Down it came. "Shhhh!" called
> his mother. "You'll have to play more
> quietly. Remember, we have a new baby
> in the house." (pp. 7–9)

Peter's world literally crashes down around him.

Notice how Keats provides three examples to show Peter's world collapsing: his cradle, his high chair, his crib. These collapses trigger Peter's decision to run away. Likewise, Keats lists three items that Peter packs when he runs away: his blue chair, his toy crocodile, his baby picture. Keats trusts that these few details are enough for the reader to understand the larger picture. Similarly, Keats suggests Peter's emotional change through a series of actions: sitting in his baby chair that is now too small; playing a trick on his mom that she plays along with; eating lunch with his family; and offering to help paint his chair pink. Keats has crafted a story whose seemingly simple elements take the main character—and the reader—on a meaningful emotional journey.

If you know a book really well, you can carry that book with you as you confer, referring to it often. If you want to teach a youngster the importance of precise action words, you can find them in this book. If you want to teach that characters have motivations and they encounter struggle, you can also show this using *Peter's Chair*. If you want to highlight the use of metaphor, you'll find this one book is laden with them. If you want to teach point of view, show-don't-tell, alliteration, answering reader's questions, or a host of other things, you can do so with this one book. When you encounter students who include details that don't support their intentions, you could look together at the details that Keats included (or may have excluded). When a student writes, "We got ready to go," you could teach her to list at least three specific details such as Keats does. And the secret is: you can probably teach qualities of good writing using *any* well-written narrative!

GETTING READY

- Your own writer's notebook
- Your own story draft, showing a point of view that needs work
- Qualities of Good Personal Narrative Writing chart
- *Homesick*, by Jean Fritz
- Student samples of personal narrative writing showing work of the minilesson, one from a previous year to use before the Share
- See CD-ROM for resources

TELLING THE STORY FROM INSIDE IT

When I read Ori's writing aloud *during the session on the importance of asking, "What am I really trying to say?" I was drawn to a puzzling detail in his story. He described looking into his parents' room and seeing his mom's "extremely large brownish bed." Later, he also said that he walked down the "brownish stairs." I noticed these details because it was absolutely clear to me that I would never, in a million years, describe my bed or stairs that way. So why had Ori done that? This was the question that led to this minilesson and to the one in Session VII (Revising Leads) in Unit One.*

This minilesson reminds children to write their story through their narrator's eyes. As we taught students in Launching the Writing Workshop, there are details a person in a particular situation would be apt to notice—and details a person in that position would be unlikely to note. If I've just opened my door and sleepily entered the long hallway, I might notice the morning light on the hallway mirror, but I wouldn't attend to the details of the floral pattern on the rug at the end of the hall. I also wouldn't notice mundane details—why would I remark that the floor was brown if it was brown every day? Thinking through the story from inside it, as though it's happening, is what helps us choose which details to include and which to exclude.

Earlier in this series, we encouraged students to write with their full attention on their story, acting out the story in their heads, getting the whole true story down, without concern for whether they were writing well or badly. Now it seems as if we are emphasizing the opposite: asking students to be critical readers of their own writing. The truth is, this is a dichotomy that writers live with. Writers always switch back and forth between writing passionately about a subject, then rereading critically. This unit reflects these two roles that writers must assume; the next few sessions, in particular, emphasize this critical reader role.

Try letting this minilesson lift the level of your writing as well. As you try to make sense of what I say, and apply it to your own writing, make note of your thoughts. You could turn this lesson into a two-day sequence, and on the second day, tell your children how the minilesson affected you and your own writing.

I'm pretty sure your children will come away saying the minilesson you wrote, the one sharing your process, was their favorite!

MINILESSON

Telling the Story from Inside It

CONNECTION

Help children see where they've been and where they're going in their writing process.

"Writers, many of you have written several leads and you've also written entries *about* your seed idea, exploring what it is you want your story to show. Many of you have used Robert Munsch's idea and storytold your story as preparation for writing it."

"If you haven't started your first draft, do that today. Drafting, for a writer, is a lot like sketching is for an artist. Drafts and sketches are fast and tentative and imperfect—but both drafts and sketches can capture the tone and feeling of a subject. Once you get started on your first draft, you'll be lost in your writing like most of us get lost in a good book. Your mind will be on what happened in your story, seeing and hearing and feeling the episode all over again, and you'll try to get it down as fast as you can."

Name your teaching point. In this case, tell children that when writing a personal story, they need to step into the point of view of their narrator.

"As you work on your drafts, I have one bit of advice that I think can set you up to write an especially true story. This is it. You need to put yourself inside the skin of the main character. (The character is you, of course, just you in a different time and place.) Your job as a writer is to tell the story as you see it unfolding, looking through the narrator's eyes."

TEACHING

Tell the story of one time when you wrote a story, staying inside the constraints of your particular perspective.

"I first learned about writing inside a point of view when I was in the middle of washing dishes (in a story) and the phone rang. My arms were deep in the soap suds, so I couldn't answer it. My sister picked up the receiver and I heard her say, 'Hello?' into the phone."

"And then what happened next was that I learned a big lesson. (Remember my advice. I need to put myself, as the storyteller, inside the skin of one person. When I tell this story that means I'm standing at the sink with my arms deep in the dishwater.) I'm still at the sink when my sister picks up the phone. I want to write about the phone call. But my arms are still in the dishwater so the story can't go like this.

COACHING

The truth is that some people write messy, tentative, rapid drafts and some inch along, refining each line as they go. Both ways can work. I tend to talk up the value of fast, tentative drafts because I want children to be game to revise, and I know if they worry about writing a draft perfectly, they sometimes become wed to it.

I believe that when writing, as when reading, we actually can become lost in a story and that doing this yields amazing writing.

When I use the phrase "narrator's point of view" throughout this session and this series, I don't mean it as a way to distinguish the first-person (meaning "I") or third-person (meaning "he" or "she") points of view. Instead, I mean the words more literally: what exactly is in the mind's eye of the narrator at any given time? I use the phrase "narrator's point of view" to help writers understand that if details of the scene aren't in that narrator's perception at that moment, perhaps they don't belong in the writing either!

My sister picked up the phone. It was my mom telling her that she had been to the doctor.

"I'm at the sink. How would I know whose voice was inside that phone? The story has to unfold as it occurred to me. I'm standing at the sink, my hands in the suds, looking at my sister as she talks on the phone. So the story as I experienced it must sound like this.

My sister picked up the phone. I heard her say, "What'd he say?" and "Did he give you anything for it?" After she hung up she said, "That was Mom. She's been to the doctor."

ACTIVE ENGAGEMENT
Set children up to practice telling a story from within the narrator's perspective. Ask them to reread a pretend draft where the point of view needs to be remedied.

"Once you get used to staying inside your own perspective, it's not that hard to watch for instances where, oops, you slip out of it."

"To practice noticing when a story suddenly loses its grounding, listen to my story and decide, 'Is the point of view working?' in which case make a thumbs-up gesture, or 'Did I just lose it?' (show thumbs down)." I pretended to write on my spiral pad, zooming quickly along, and meanwhile voiced this story aloud.

I stood alongside my bike at the top of the hill. My brother, Alex, and his friend, Brian, waited as I made up my mind. In front of me the road lay like a ribbon. "I'm ready," I thought. I swung my leg up, climbed onto the seat, and pushed on the pedal. [Thumbs up.] Soon I was gently slipping down the road, faster and faster. The world zoomed past me: trees, boulders, woods . . . browns, grays, greens—a blur of color. [Thumbs up.] Then I saw something dart out in front of me. Was it a squirrel? A chipmunk? I swerved to avoid it, lost my balance, and headed into the wild brush on the side of the road. [Thumbs up.] My bike flipped and I went flying. Suddenly I saw nothing. [Thumbs up.] My brother raced down the hill and then they went inside. Brian looked at Alex and wondered if I was alive. [Thumbs down.]

I like the visual effect of this minilesson. I can imagine telling this portion of it and I know that within the minilesson, I'll act out how my arms are elbow-deep in sudsy water, and while I still stand there with arms immersed, my sister picks up the phone. And then I can imagine that just by my intonation the children will discern that something has been knocked asunder by the sentence, 'It was my mom telling her that she had been to the doctor.' My intonation and my gestures can make it easy for children to grasp why this story defies reality.

It's always challenging to think, "How can I set things up so children can have a few minutes to practice and apply the concept I've taught?" Part of the challenge is that we want to act as training wheels, enabling children to have success with the concept. In my examples, I deliberately try to use words which make it clear when I'm writing within the first-person point of view, and when I slip out of it. But intonation helps as well.

Ask children to continue saying the story aloud, maintaining the point of view.

"Pretend you are the author. Continue the story from where I leave off. Make it up, based on what you think could have happened, but stay in the point of view of me lying on the ground after the accident."

To get children started, I went back and reread the story before I lost the point of view. "'My bike flipped and I went flying. My arm crashed on a rock with a thump. Suddenly I saw nothing . . .' Okay, take over. Partner 1, begin."

LINK
Rename your teaching point. Send children off to copy their leads and to climb into the skin of their narrator.

"So writers, if you haven't done so already, find your favorite lead. Copy it onto lined paper outside the notebook (or write a new lead on draft paper). You can write on single sheets or fold paper in half to make story booklets, in which case please think about which dot on your timeline will go on each page. Then remember, before you can write, you need to recall the story. And you need to put yourself inside the skin of the person in the story. Are you at the top of the hill, your bike beside you? Or are you at the kitchen sink, up to your elbows in suds? Are you in bed on a cold autumn morning? Wherever you are in the lead of your story, go there mentally before you write. See what's around you, taste it, live it, and as you write, write the step–by–step of what you experience." Then I added this item to our Qualities of Good Personal Narrative Writing chart.

Qualities of Good Personal Narrative Writing

- Write a little seed story; don't write all about a giant watermelon topic
- Zoom in so you tell the most important parts of the story
- Include true, exact details from the movie you have in your mind
- Stay inside your own point of view. This will help you to write with true and exact details.

You'll notice that this is a double-decker Active Engagement and you may decide to delete this final portion. I included it because my goal is to set children up to actually do (not to talk about) whatever I've taught.

Let's talk about paper. First of all, paper matters. The kind of paper that children use is not inconsequential. You'll notice that most of the writing that I include in this book has been written on single sheets of notebook paper. Some are pages from within writer's notebooks and others (the rough drafts and final drafts) are loose pages which writers store in their folders. I don't have many examples of children writing in booklets, and yet I continually mention them.

This is why. In just the past few months, my colleagues and I have come to believe that many writers, and especially those who struggle, benefit from writing narratives across pages in little booklets. The booklets only work, however, if the writer first allocates one step of the story to page one (one dot of the timeline), one step to page two, and so forth. This means that the pages are not apt to be full, leaving space for revision.

WRITING AND CONFERRING

Reenacting Events

As you confer with children, you'll find that by studying their work and trying to understand their understandings of writing, you become much smarter as a teacher. I suggest you pay special attention to children's use of details and try to articulate what you ascertain. My observations tell me that when teachers encourage children to add descriptions, especially to write with sensory details, the resulting text often doesn't ring true unless the details are those that the narrator would notice from his or her vantage point. So I sometimes think that even if the goal is for writers to write with detail, the one strategy that can best produce those details is for writers to make movies in their minds, reenacting the events as they write about them.

But it is important for children to remember that, as James Merrill said, "The words that come first are anybody's words. You need to make them your own." If a child wrote, "I walked up the walk and inside the front door. I had a snack. Then I went to my bedroom." you might say, "Your story could tell about walking inside *anybody's* front door. Listen to how Jean Fritz, in her memoir *Homesick*, describes walking inside *her* house."

> I flung open the iron gate and threw myself through the front door.
>
> "I'm home!" I yelled.
>
> Then I remembered that it was Tuesday, the day my mother taught English at the Y.M.C.A. where my father was the director.
>
> I stood in the hall, trying to catch my breath, and as always I began to feel small. It was a huge hall with ceilings so high it was as if they would have nothing to do with people. Certainly not with a mere child, not with me—the only child in the house. Once I asked my best friend, Andrea, if the hall made her feel little too. She said no. She was going to be a dancer and she loved space. She did a high kick to show how grand it was to have room. (p. 13)

MID-WORKSHOP TEACHING POINT *Noticing if the Details Ring True* "Writers, when you are writing from inside the skin of a character (you), remember that the details you see and include in your draft will be the details that the character notices *in the moment of the story*. Do your details ring true? For example, last year, one of my students, a boy named Andy, wrote about sitting down at the lunch table. Think about the real, true details you focus on when you sit at the lunch table and then think about Andy's piece. Does it seem to you these are the details he truly noticed when he sat at that table?" *[Fig. VIII-1]*

> I carried my tray full of food from the lunch line. I went over and put my tray on the yellow metal table. I pulled the red metal chair in as I sat beside the table.

"I don't think that during his lunch, Andy really paid attention to the metal or to the color of tables and chairs in his cafeteria, do you? I think he was trying to add sensory details because he knows writers do that, but he'd forgotten that the sensory details need to be *true ones* that he noticed from the narrator's point of view. Talk with your partner about your own writing so far today."

> I carried my tray full of food from the lunch line. I went over and put my tray on the yellow metal table. I pulled the red metal chair in as I sat beside the table. Everyone was sharing snack. William had cupcakes and I wanted some. Thomas shared some popcorn with me. He put it on my tray. "Thanks, Thomas," I said.

Fig. VIII-1 Andy

I might show this excerpt to a child in a conference, saying, "Do you see how Jean Fritz describes that hallway in a way that reveals not only the hallway, but also reveals her as a person? If your first draft said, 'I walked up the walk and inside the front door. I had a snack. Then I went to my bedroom' and you wanted to revise this to show yourself—your point of view, your kitchen—what might you write? Would you say, 'I walked into our kitchen and opened the refrigerator to see if Mom had made the casserole for tonight's dinner'? Would you say, 'I sifted though a pile of mail but it was all bills to my mom, and this time they had threatening labels: "Third bill,"' and so on. What might you say to show yourself entering your kitchen?"

Then I'd look for a few places in the child's draft where he or she could apply this same concept and help the child get started.

"Francesca's draft describes the day her cat died. I might cite this in a conference, instead of referencing a text by a published author. The power of this writing comes, I think, because Francesca put herself back into the story moment, losing herself in that moment as she wrote. I might say to a child, "Try, as you listen, to be there: to stand in Francesca's shoes, to see through her eyes, to feel right along with her. I think you'll see that her details about her cat ring true because she wrote this draft, keeping her attention focused on the true story of what really happened "

It was a Sunday, a strange Sunday. I knew that something was going to happen. Sam was walking weakly, as usual, but worse than other days. I went to play with my friend Lucy. When I came home, Sam was barely walking but still alive.

Camilla (my little sister) picked Sam up and put her on a soft white chair. Everyone was looking at her, even Lucy. I knew she was probably going to die so I cried. My Dad started making tea to calm us down but it did not help. What would it be like without Sam? "It will be really quiet," I started thinking. I looked at Sam, with her little white paws and her cute tail. She was almost dead. She took three breaths of air. On the last one, I was looking at a dead cat. The room was silent. Too silent. I could feel Sam's spirit floating up to heaven. I don't know why but I had a big feeling that today was her 19th birthday. I looked at the candles. They were still burning like Sam's spirit was still alive and here. It was a good feeling.

SHARE

Using Details from the Moment

Share an example of a child's writing that includes details from inside the story.

"Writers, I want you to think about how you might describe a brand-new house that you just moved into. You *could* write something like this: 'There are three bedrooms along the hall. Each is about the same size. There is also a dining room.' But *anyone* could see those things. A stranger to the house or a real estate agent might describe it that way. In a really good story, characters (and you are the main character in your story) let the reader see the world as the character saw the world in the moment of the story."

"I think Kim Yung does this really well. The way she writes about the new house—the one she's just moved into—lets me feel as if I am seeing that new house through her eyes. It's almost like she's got a video camera, and as she goes from room to room, we go from room to room with her. Remember what rooms look like when there is no furniture in them yet—when they contain just carpet and sun? Listen to how Kim Yung writes about her new house." [Fig. VIII-2]

> After looking through this never-ending house, I went to my room that I chose and sat down on the furry carpet. The sun shined through all the windows until it reached the soft carpet. It was nice and warm when you stepped on it. It made you want to stay in that spot. I was going to like this house. It had everything. I would rise up every morning with a happy and bright smile. I would like that feeling. I would go downstairs and eat a healthy breakfast. Life would be the greatest in this house.

"Sensory details work in a story when they are the details that the character (that's you) really, truly notices in the moment of the story. Kim Yung's details about her new house ring true. Remember Felix's story about his grandfather's funeral? In the story he wrote about when he realized it was his grandfather in the coffin. He wrote, 'I grabbed my grandma's hand tight. I felt her bones.' He wrote that as he tried to reconcile himself to the fact that his grandfather had died, he looked down and found that he was staring at the new shoes on his feet that his grandfather had bought for him. These details let us, his readers, see through Felix's eyes."

After looking through this never ending house I went in my room I chose and sat down on the furry carpet.
The sun shined through all the windows until it reached the soft carpet. It was nice and warm once when it was stepped on. It felt nice. It made you want to stay in that spot. It felt like it was made to be a bed.
I was going to love this house. It had everything. I would rise up every morning with a happy and bright smile. I would like that feeling. I would go downstairs and eat a nice healthy breakfast. Life would be the greatest in this house. I would take nice walks along the gray streets. I

Fig. VIII-2 Kim Yung

If your students could use another example of writing from inside the story, inside the moment, inside the narrator's mind, bring them back to Francesca's piece about the death of her cat. Francesca writes second by second about the last bits of life of her cat, never once pulling away or offering descriptions outside of that intense focus on her beloved pet.

Children could also take out Felix's piece and study this same aspect of writing in-depth, to emulate. [Launching the Writing Workshop, Fig. VIII-1]

Ask children to reread their drafts and note, and perhaps revise, their use of details.

"Right now, would you reread your own writing and look at your details. Which ring true, as if you have lived through this event? Which don't seem like they are really true to what you saw, felt, or noticed that day? Talk with your partner; see if you can revise more details to make them ring true."

● HOMEWORK   *Rereading While Visualizing the Story*   Remember in reading today, we tried to make pictures in our minds as we read. Remember how I read about the girl who walked step-by-step up to the school, then pulled open the big front door? Remember how I stopped at that point, and asked you to tell your partner exactly what you were picturing? You all pictured the girl pulling back the handle and drawing the door open. The details the author gave us about the steps up to the door, and the heaviness of the door really drew us to make those pictures. Some of you hadn't pictured the school itself. You said, 'It doesn't say what the school looks like,' and I told you that readers nevertheless draw on all the schools we've ever been to, using all we know to mentally paint pictures in our minds. Today you have learned that both readers *and* writers need to make movies in our minds. As you reread your drafts, are you able to mentally paint pictures in your mind of your story world? Where are those pictures strong in your draft? Where do they need work? Use that lens to guide your important revision work.

● TAILORING YOUR TEACHING

If your students are able to write, staying in the moment . . . they may be ready to try writing from slightly more difficult-to-enter moments. When we write a personal narrative, often we tell a story of a childhood experience. It's helpful, in writing these experiences, to try to time-travel back to the age we are in the story. As an adult, Sandra Cisneros may not compare that old red sweater, with its sleeves all stretched out, to a jump rope—but that's the way Rachel, the eleven-year-old narrator of "Eleven," sees that sweater. And chances are that as an adult, Sandra can think of many smells that are far worse than cottage cheese, but that's the smell that Rachel experiences, since she is eleven.

It is not always true that when the narrator of a text is five or eight or ten, he or she uses the language and the metaphors that are suitable for his or her age, but it's helpful, in writing these experiences, to try to time-travel back to the age we are in the story.

If your students are able to write in a way that maintains the narrator's point of view consistently . . . you might want to stretch them to include the narrator's state of mind. Suggest that what writers see in an event can reveal their state of mind or emotions at that time and that a writer's state of mind or emotions can become part of the narrative.

For example, I could look at my dog, snoozing in the corner, and see the burls and snarls in her fur. Alternatively, I can look at the same snoozing dog and see the gentle rhythmic rise and fall of her ribs, and I could notice her eyes, flickering underneath her eyelids as she dreams. These two different views of the dog reveal a difference in the writer, not in the dog, who sleeps through it all! A writing teacher once said, "We do not see with our eyes or hear with our ears but with our beliefs."

Another way to approach this is to use a whole-class shared experience. Again, you could use the story of the bus that broke down on a field trip: the narrator's state of mind could be relief that she's off the bus because she feels nauseous or dread because she has to use the bathroom and just wants to get back to school.

This idea of using a narrator's state of mind will most likely be a challenging nuance to teach young writers, but it can work if we mine our class for an example of student work in which a clear state of mind is revealed.

You could turn to a student's piece and ask him what his state of mind or emotions were in the moment the writing is about. Put the piece on an overhead and then ask students to turn and talk about how a different state of mind would change the piece.

For active engagement, ask the students to think about their state of mind in their story and to find places where they show it. If they can't find any places where they reveal their state of mind, they may decide to revise the piece to better reflect it.

Remember, this is a high-level strategy and may not be an appropriate lesson for the whole class. You could gather small groups of writers who are ready for it.

ASSESSMENT

While your children are working within a narrative frame, you'll want to give special attention to their abilities to handle the elements of narrative writing. Look, for example, at their abilities to handle the passage of time. You may notice that at first, some children are so worried about conveying a sequence of events that they rely exclusively on the transition words *first*, *second*, *third* or *first*, *then*, *next*. The resulting writing is odd, but you'll want to keep in mind that this writer is merely trying to do as you've taught and to show a sequence of events.

Invite children to study how Sandra Cisneros shows the passage of time. Cisneros often shows that as one action is ending, a second one has started, usually with the one causing the other. In this paragraph, for example, three events fit together like tongue-and-groove joints in woodworking.

> Maybe because I'm skinny, maybe because she doesn't like me, that stupid Sylvia Saldívar says, "I think it belongs to Rachel." An ugly sweater like that, all raggedy and old, but Mrs. Price believes her. Mrs. Price takes the sweater and puts it right on my desk, but when I open my mouth nothing comes out. (Cisneros 1991, p. 7)

Cisneros doesn't say, "After that Mrs. Price puts the sweater on my desk. Next I open my mouth." The passage of time is implied; in this instance one event causes the next. Between these sentences, Cisneros could have written the connective *and* but readers supply that transition for her. Children can study this paragraph and try to emulate this way to sequence events in their own writing.

Sometimes Cisneros wants to shift between telling what happens externally and telling what Rachel is thinking and feeling. She has cues

that she uses to switch between describing an action and revealing a thought or feeling.

> I don't know why but all of a sudden I'm feeling . . . and I try to remember . . . In my head I'm thinking . . . This is when I wish . . . That's when everything I've been holding in . . . I wish . . . but I wish . . . I wish . . . because today I want . . .

Children can take this set of phrases and tuck it in the back of their notebooks to help them manage these transitions. Again, like tongue-and-groove joints, Cisneros blends dialogue with description, action, and Rachel's thoughts, often within the same paragraph. You could consider again, with your children, the Sylvia Saldívar paragraph above using subtle cues to help the reader follow along. Also, like many writers, Cisneros doesn't always say outright who's speaking. The speaker is implied based on the flow of dialogue. Children can try this too.

> "Rachel," Mrs. Price says. She says it like she's getting mad. "You put that sweater on right now and no more nonsense."
>
> "But it's not—"
>
> "Now!" Mrs. Price says. (p. 8)

You may want to sort your children's writing into piles based on their use of conventions related to narrative writing. It's likely you'll see a group that could use some support in each of these areas where the writer needs to cue the reader to a shift of some sort, be it a shift in sequence, a shift between external and internal events or a shift in speaker. Assessing your children's understanding and control of various transitions in writing will help you plan some quick, helpful teaching to various small groups.

BRINGING FORTH THE INTERNAL STORY

IN THIS SESSION, YOU WILL TEACH STUDENTS THAT WRITERS CAN STRENGTHEN OUR PERSONAL NARRATIVES BY BRINGING FORTH THE DEEP CONNECTION BETWEEN EXTERNAL ACTIONS AND INTERNAL RESPONSES.

GETTING READY

- Student anecdote that can be used to introduce importance of internal events
- Red-sweater scene from Sandra Cisneros' "Eleven," written on chart paper
- Passage from Chapter 11 of *Olive's Ocean*, by Kevin Henkes, one copy for each partnership
- Qualities of Good Personal Narrative chart
- Student examples of revising to bring out the internal story based on overall intentions
- See CD-ROM for resources

I recently observed a teacher lead a very nice minilesson. She said to her class, "Yesterday you learned that you can improve your stories by making your characters speak," and she reminded the students how they'd added a line of dialogue into a little class story about flying a kite. "Today," the teacher said, "I want to teach you that you can also improve your story by writing not just the external story, but also the internal story." And she showed the class that she could add a line in which she looks up at the kite and thinks that she loves to fly kites.

> I loosened the string on my kite. "Fly, fly," I whispered. I thought about how much I liked flying kites.

That line was added to the story, and all the children dispersed to insert lines of thought into their own narratives.

That teacher was right to teach children that writers shift between recording an action, transcribing a bit of dialogue, and conveying a thought. But as I reflected on this lesson, I realized that in the teaching of writing, most lessons can be taught either as little tricks that writers can do easily, or as gigantic truths that underpin our entire understanding of life. I ended up writing a keynote speech about that minilesson, and in my speech I argued that sometimes, in our efforts to lure children to try a technique, we convey, "This is easy. It's no big deal!" And that is both true and not true—because bringing out the internal story can be a very big deal indeed.

When we teach children to record not only the event but also their thoughts during the event, we are teaching them that in the end, their lives are not just what happens to them, but also their responses to what happens. Another child could fly that same kite, loosen that same string, whisper those same words of encouragement, and have entirely different thoughts.

For this reason, each one of us is ultimately the author of our own lives. We do not always control what happens to us, but we control our response to what happens.

In this session, I try to help children understand that it is not a small thing to develop the internal story. I try to give them a few specific tools for doing this well.

MINILESSON

Bringing Forth the Internal Story

CONNECTION

Tell a student anecdote to illustrate the writing challenge many children may be facing by this time in the unit.

"I've been talking with many of you about the importance of focusing your stories. But some of you worry that if you focus your story too much, it'll be too short. Caleb, for example, wanted to tell about going to a sports store with his dad to buy a baseball mitt and then riding his bike to his friend's house and playing a game with the mitt. I said, 'Caleb, it seems to me that you have two or three different small moments, different scenes in this story. Is there one that is particularly important?'"

"Caleb answered that above all, he wanted to write about going into the store to pick out his mitt, but he worried about narrowing the story down to just that. 'Won't it be awfully short?' he asked."

Name your teaching point. In this case, tell writers that our lives are not just what happens to us. They are our response to what happens to us.

"What I said to Caleb and what I want to teach all of you is this. Our stories are not just what happens; they are also our response to what happens. I used to worry that real writers had richer lives than me, and a great writer named Roethke said to me (actually he wrote this, but I put his quote on my bulletin board and I pretend he said it just to me), 'Lucy,' he said. 'It is an illusion that writers live more significant lives than non-writers. Writers are just more in the habit of finding the significance that is there in their lives.'"

"These are hugely important words for me. It means that I can write about any moment in my life—a ride on the Ferris wheel, a time when my dad picked me up from the basketball game, a few minutes after school with some classmates when they told me my dress looked antique enough to be a costume in the Civil War play—and I can make that moment carry the biggest truths of my life. You can do the same."

"Specifically, I want to teach you that if I'm going to write not only what happens but also my response to what happens, then much of the story will be the internal story, and not just the external one."

"In a story, I can run, spin, climb, clamor, dig, holler—but I can also yearn, fantasize,

COACHING

You'll notice that today's minilesson picks up a point which was taught in yesterday's mid-workshop teaching point, and will be woven into our instruction across the year. Qualities of good writing are easy to name but challenging to pull off!

The picturebook, Roxaboxen by Alice McLerran has always seemed to me to be a metaphor for writing. A few children play on a desert hill. There is not much there—just some broken crates, cacti, sand. But then one girl, Marion, finds a rusty tin box and declares it to be treasure. And it is. Inside the box there are smooth black stones. The girls use them to frame roads, and soon they have build themselves a kingdom of Roxaboxen. This is why I write. To take the rusty tin boxes of my life, to declare them to be treasures, and to make something of them—and of myself.

I've learned that three examples—from Keats and Rylant, or any number of master writers—are enough to illustrate a point. Notice that I reference stories both from previous units and our present unit that are now part of the lexicon of the class community.

remember, regret, worry, imagine. Often a character's internal life is as rich and as poignant as her external life. If you think about it, in the entry that I wrote a couple of weeks ago, nothing much happens: 'The teacher says some of us are to stay after school, I gather my books and sit with the kids, one girl makes a list of costumes people will need, and she records that I already have my costume.' Though nothing much happened *externally* in that story, *internally* I've traveled a roller coaster of hope and heartbreak."

TEACHING
Return to the class mentor text (in this case, "Eleven") to study the balance of external and internal story.

"When I pause in the middle of a draft to reread my writing, I sometimes say to myself, 'Let me reread and pay attention to whether I've told the internal as well as the external story.' And when I make a planning box for the writing work I'm going to be doing in the day ahead, I sometimes say to myself, 'Today, I want to be sure to tell the internal story.'"

"And I sometimes study mentor texts, thinking, 'How has this author written the story of what she was thinking and feeling?' I ask, 'What has she done that I could do also?'"

I pointed to our chart-paper copy of the red-sweater scene in "Eleven." Then I said, "Watch me as I study what Cisneros has done, and try to extrapolate lessons that can help me. Hmm. One thing I notice is that she seems to seesaw back and forth between writing what happens and writing what she's thinking. For example, the phrase "Not mine, not mine, not mine" conveys an internal thought, but this passage, " but Mrs. Price has already turned to page thirty-two, and math problem number four (p. 8)" is external—it's what happens."

> I move the red sweater to the corner of my desk with my ruler. I move my pencil and books and eraser as far away from it as possible. I even move my chair a little to the right. [external gesture]
>
> Not mine, not mine, not mine. [internal gesture]
>
> In my head I'm thinking how long till lunchtime, how long till I can take the red sweater and throw it over the schoolyard fence, or leave it hanging on a parking meter, or bunch it up into a little ball and toss it in the alley. [internal gesture]
>
> Except when math period ends Mrs. Price says loud and in front of everybody, "Now, Rachel . . . " [external gesture]

I will want to help children know that they can convey the internal story not only with the words 'I thought,' but also with 'I pretended,' 'I worried,' 'I remembered,' 'I wanted to say,' 'I noticed,' and a dozen other such phrases.

I liken the emotional journey of my story to a roller coaster ride. Metaphors are one way to pack a punch.

The minilesson is predominantly an oral form. As my colleagues and I work across the New York City public schools, we often need to provide modifications and supports for our English Language Learners and for other students who need more than just the oral mode of learning. Throughout these units, notice the supports we provide, such as charts, student copies of texts, clear and consistent language that we chart and reference, use of gestures, use of demonstration texts. Here I return to our class copy of "Eleven" (Cisneros 1991, p. 8) and provide support for key concepts through the use of gestures.

As I read each of these passages aloud, I tapped the side of my head as a gesture to emphasize internal section of the text and showed open hands as a gesture for external sections.

"My writing teacher, Don Murray, once told me that if you want to have a character in the kitchen, thinking about something and getting more and more angry and worried, you might as well have that character chopping carrots. Then your writing could go like this."

> "Where is he?" I thought, looking out the door to see if my son's car was in the driveway yet. Nothing. "Dang it all," I thought, getting the giant cleaver and the cutting board out. I lay a carrot on the board. "Why's he late?" Chop, chop, chop, the little slices piled up. "I said to come straight home," I remembered, lining another carrot up under the giant blade. Chop, chop. I went to the door again, but still no car. "This is the last time," I thought reaching for a head of lettuce. Slamming it onto the counter, I turned to see if I'd broken the stem, the heart, I always called it. Then I glanced at the clock.

I try to teach writers that usually the internal story needs to be carried by an external story. If the writer wants to sit on a stool in the kitchen and experience a whole sequence of thoughts and feelings, in between each new thought or feeling, the character will need to slice a carrot or turn down the teakettle, even if the actions exist only to support the internal story.

ACTIVE ENGAGEMENT
Provide a brief scene from another mentor text and ask students to study the balance of external and internal stories.

"You'll see examples when you read. I recently read a chapter book called *Olive's Ocean*, by Kevin Henkes. One small chapter in this book tells how the main character, Martha, was standing outside the airport (she was going to her grandma's at the beach), with her mom, dad, and brother, Vince, waiting for the shuttle bus to take them to the car rental place, and then she was jostled while boarding the bus. That's all that happened *on the outside* in this chapter. But meanwhile, things were happening *inside* of Olive. Listen to part of this chapter. She begins by describing the glittery feeling she has when she is en route to summer vacation at the beach with her grandmother, whom she calls Godbee. Partners, look at the copy I gave you now. Later, I'm going to ask you to tell your partner the external and then the internal events of this story."

Olive's Ocean is a beautiful novel but the content of some chapters makes it a better choice for middle school children. The chapter I share is fine for elementary school children!

> They were outside, at the airport, waiting for the shuttle bus to take them to the car-rental lot. Martha thought she smelled the ocean already and was immediately excited. She breathed deeply, letting the feeling sink in. They would be at Godbee's shortly, right on the water, and every molecule, every atom, knew it.
>
> She called the feeling the glittery feeling, and she always experienced it when they were this close, when they were at this part of their trip to Godbee's.
>
> The glittery feeling. She'd named it because it felt to her as if her skin and everything beneath it briefly became shiny and jumpy and

This choice of texts to illustrate the teaching point is time-consuming, but crucial. Several factors make this scene from Olive's Ocean a strong choice. First, notice its brevity. In a minilesson, unless it's a familiar text like "Eleven," you don't have time to both introduce and teach from a new, longer text. Second, notice the balance between external and internal, and how most of the scene occurs internally, which reinforces the focus of this minilesson. Third, notice how the main character, Martha, like Rachel in "Eleven," connects with a group of fourth-graders. I try to choose texts with a keen awareness of my audience.

bubbly, as if glitter materialized inside her, then rose quickly through the layers of tissue that comprised her, momentarily sparkling all over the surface of her skin before dissipating into the air.

Martha closed her eyes and let her arms drift slightly upward. She couldn't help herself. A small joyful squeak escaped from her throat.

"What do you think you are? A bird?" It was Vince.

Her arms fell.

"The bus is here," said her father. "Grab everything and hurry."

Her mother accidentally bumped her with a suitcase as they jockeyed for a place on the curb among the crowd. "Move, honey," she said.

The glittery feeling was gone.

"Writers, will you tell your partner the sequence of external events that happened in this story." I listened while children talked. "Many of you said, 'Not much happened. A girl is jostled while getting on the bus. That's it!' But now, follow along in your copy while I read the story again, and this time tell your partner the *internal* events or feelings, or thoughts that occur in this story." I reread the text, and again children talked.

"So you see that the only external thing that happens in this episode is a girl is jostled while getting on the bus. But meanwhile, she has gone through a whole sequence of internal changes. You can learn from what Kevin Henkes has done!"

LINK
Remind students to reread and revise their drafts, bringing out the internal story, and to rely on mentor texts for support.

"Writers sometimes talk about rereading drafts with particular lenses to make the drafts stronger, and there are many lenses that writers use. For example, we could reread our drafts noticing word choice, or clarity, or our use of dialogue. We could reread noticing especially our use of punctuation."

"Writers, as you go off to work today, you may decide to reread your drafts, and to do so in a manner which allows you to notice the internal story. You may ask yourselves, "Did I provide a balance of internal and external? Did I seesaw back and forth between writing what happens, and writing what I'm thinking? Alternatively, you can draw on anything you've learned in order to write or revise your draft, making it the best it can be.""

As students went off to work, I added this revision strategy to our Qualities of Good Personal Narrative Writing chart.

Again, notice the supports I try to provide to meet the needs of all students in the class. It helps that, during this active engagement, I have students work with their partners and provide them with copies of this text. This facilitates their ability to both read and analyze it. But also notice that I read aloud the text, twice. I want to provide a fluent rendition of this text so the children can hear its tone, its coherence, and can better attend to the challenging textual analysis that is the aim of this activity.

Just as we see the world differently when we view it through different colored lenses, we can look at a draft and attend to different aspects of it. The metaphor stays consistent with the word revision itself, which literally means "to look again." It's a metaphor that I return to often.

Qualities of Good Personal Narrative Writing

- Write a little seed story; don't write all about a giant watermelon topic
- Zoom in so you tell the most important parts of the story
- Include true, exact details from the movie you have in your mind
- Stay inside your own point of view. This will help you to write with true and exact details.
- Make sure stories tell not just what happens, but also the response to what happens.

WRITING AND CONFERRING

Uncovering Internal Details by Reenacting the Story

I pulled my chair up next to Becca. She'd written an entry about cotton candy, then moved on to an entry about beach combing. "What are you working on as a writer?" I asked.

"Well, I figured out what I really wanted to show. I found a really nice piece of sea glass. And I wrote a little about it—details about it being lime green, and how I held it up to my eye. But it is still pretty short," she said. "So I was gonna think, 'What else do I want to show?' and tell about the cool rides." I looked over her piece: *[Fig. IX-1]*

> Combing the beach, sifting the sand. We are looking and digging carefully for seaglass and shells. I am a scientist digging up the past at an archeological site. I am a pirate searching for buried treasure. But so far, all I've found is smashed Corona bottles, and crushed beer cans, while Mabel kept running over to me, beautiful pieces of broken china and big, pretty shells. All of a sudden, something incredible happened—I found a nice piece of seaglass, for a change!!! It was bright, bright, lime green and when I held it up to my eye it was a grass-green world that looked back at me. Happily I sipped water from my bottle.

"Becca," I said, "I love the way your entry shows that you have already done so much work with it. Even before I pulled up my chair, you had already switched from being a writer to being a reader, and you reread your own draft and thought, 'Have I done the things I wanted to do?' I love that on our own, you boxed in a place which you thought was especially important, your focus. And I also love that you thought through the writing challenge that you face. Lots of kids just say, 'I don't know what to do next,' but you figured out that the hard part is writing extensively about a topic as small as a piece of sea glass. It's not doing anything much, so it isn't easy to describe it in detail, is it?"

> **MID-WORKSHOP TEACHING POINT** *Working with Partners on the Internal Story* "Writers, give me your eyes and your attention." I waited for complete attention, as students finished their sentences. "Juliet is writing about a toy sculpture that she admired in a store window near her apartment. Not much action happens, sort of like the glittery feeling scene in *Olive's Ocean*. But Juliet has worked hard on bringing out the internal story. Listen to how she seesaws between writing what happens and what that makes her think and feel, like Cisneros does in 'Eleven'."
>
> *continued on next page*

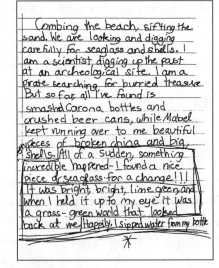

Fig. IX-1 Becca

"I love the way you are taking charge of your own writing. It really feels like you are your own job captain. Congratulations." Becca beamed, pleased that I had noticed.

Then I said, "You are right to think, 'My story is a bit short,' because it is, but the answer doesn't need to be to move on and tell about the rides. Because if you did that, then when you asked yourself, 'What am I really trying to say in my story?' you'd have to answer, 'Well, I say this one thing and then I say this other thing—and your message would get all blurry. So instead, you can either make this sea glass story bigger, or move on and find something else that you'd like to highlight. I'll help you do either one of those. Which makes more sense to you?"

She answered, "The sea glass?" with intonation that suggested she wasn't too sure.

So I said to her, "Let's pretend it is right here on the floor. You see it. You reach down and pick it up." Then I gestured, "Do that now." I picked up a similar piece of imaginary sea glass. "Hold it. Turn it over in your hand. What are you thinking?"

Becca said, "I feel lucky. I can't believe I just found pretty sea glass for a change."

"What does it remind you of?" I watched as she began writing a new passage with plans to insert it in her original piece. [Figs. IX-3 and IX-4]

I am slowly walking along the beach, looking for a beautiful shell or rare piece of sea glass. But so far, I haven't had much luck; and all I've found is crushed soda cans and broken Corona bottles. Then, I step on something cool among the sticky, hot sand. I walk past it; then realize that it might have been seaglass. I walk back to where I thought it was. I feel around with my foot. I hit it again. I look down at the piece of something that I have just stepped on. I pick it up. I can't believe that I have just found a pretty piece of sea glass for a change. I decide to examine it, just in case it's a phoney piece of plastic.

continued from previous page

Juliet read aloud: [Fig. IX-2]

One afternoon, I stepped off the bus, like usual. I said hello to my mom, like usual. I looked at the store window to see the sculpture, like usual. But . . . where was the sculpture? OH NO!!

Maybe I had seen it wrong, I thought. I decided to look one more time.

OH NO!! Where was my favorite sculpture from the store window? Where was it? There was an empty space in the store window, where the sculpture used to be. Like a building getting knocked down, and becoming a vacant lot.

"Did you notice how Juliet showed her thinking by asking questions in her head? She also repeated "like usual" to show the routine of these actions. We could feel Juliet's disappointment in not seeing that sculpture anymore."

"Right now, get together with your writing partner. Share a section of your draft where you worked on bringing out the internal story, as Sandra Cisneros or Kevin Henkes did, as Juliet did. Ask your partner if the feelings you tried conveying in that part come through. Then return to your work plans. Okay, get started."

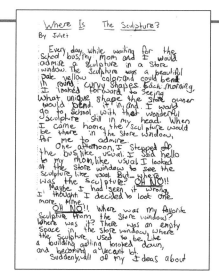

Fig. IX-2 Juliet

I run my fingers over the cool, smooth surface like a pond in January. I enclose it in my sweaty palm. It feels like I am holding a flat sheet of ice. I hold it up to my eye, to make sure that it is transparent like sea glass is, and a limey sort of fluorescent green world is looking back at me.

Definitely sea glass, I decide. I hold the grassy, neon green triangle up to my chest, and call, "Mabel, look what I found!!!!!" I can't believe that I finally found a nice piece of sea glass. So what if Mabel has found 2 pieces of china along the shoreline?

"Becca," I said. "After this, when you want to write the internal story, remember it helps to reenact whatever it is you are describing, because sometimes when you act things out, you think up more to say."

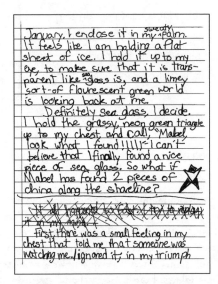

Fig. IX-3 Page 1 of Becca's revised story

Fig. IX-4 Page 2 of Becca's revised story

SHARE

Listening to the Internal Story

Ask children to meet with partners and to share their writing before they added the internal story, and after they added it.

I listened in as Joey and Felix shared their writing with each other. I'd heard Joey's original entry earlier in the unit: [Fig. IX-5]

> Jumping in the pond really late at night
>
> Me and John were going to jump in the pond really late at night. I just could not. John kept on encouraging me to do it. He said, "You can do it, come on. Nothing is going to happen."
> I had to do it. I jumped. I closed my eyes and tried to think of good things. Splash. "I did it!" I yelled.
> John ran up to me and said, "Great job. You did it! You're the best."

"Joey," I said, "It is clear you brought out the internal angle so much more by showing more actions and details, by including more dialogue. But I also love the way you paid special attention to the external story—the actions—as well!" [Figs. IX-6, IX-7, and IX-8]

> I was terrified. I never was going to do it. I just could not. I was totally scared. I was thinking in my head about jumping in the pond and feeling the water touching me. The ice cold water. It was not pretty. I was trying to think of good things like beautiful skys and seawaters. But it did not work. John went over to me and said to me that its ok, really, knothing is going to happen to you. Then he said "Here, why don't I show you? Then you can do it." I saw John walk up to the dock with full confidence in his eyes. He lifted his feet and flew in the air. I saw a big smile across his face and his mouth wide open screaming his guts out. Then his foot went under. It only made a tiny splash but then his knee started to go under and I was really amazed because he still had that wide open smile all the way across his face. He was great. Then the splash was greater each

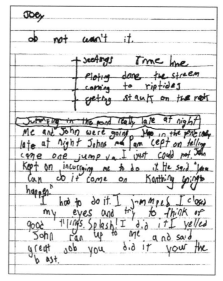

Fig. IX-5 Joey's original entry

Fig. IX-6 Joey, page 1

time his body went down more into the pond. Then his whole body was down under the water. It kind of reminded me of the time me and John went canoeing, white water class 2. The riptides turned white because of the strong current. When John jumped in the water/pond the water turned white. Then he spurted out of the water like a cork. He swam over. He climbed up the ladder and stood on the dock. He said "Its your turn." Then I walked to the end of the dock bent my knees and I jumped in the air. I opened my eyes and actually felt kind of fun. Then I screamed. My feet went in, then my knees and my waist. I was almost in shock because I thought it would be the worst moment of my life. I guess I was wrong. My head went under. I smiled under water and then flew out of the water. I saw John. Then he started clapping his hands. I really felt good because John really comforted me and also he thought I did good and I really liked that.

"It's clear that Joey was reliving that moment as he wrote this draft—seeing it, feeling it, hearing it—which helped him not only to include actions, details, and dialogue that rang true, but also to weave in his thoughts and feelings that bring out his angle."

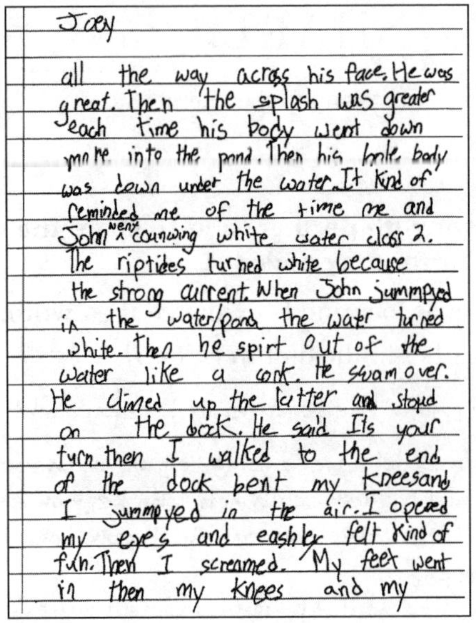
Joey

all the way across his face. He was great. Then the splash was greater each time his body went down more into the pond. Then his hole body was down under the water. It kind of reminded me of the time me and John went canuwing white water class 2. The riptides turned white because the strong current. When John jummpyed in the water/pond the watr turned white. Then he spirt Out of the water like a cork. He swam over. He climed up the latter and stoud on the dock. He said Its your turn. then I walked to the end of the dock bent my kneesand I jummpyed in the air. I opened my eyes and eashler felt kind of fun. Then I screamed. My feet went in then my knees and my

Fig. IX-7 Joey, page 2

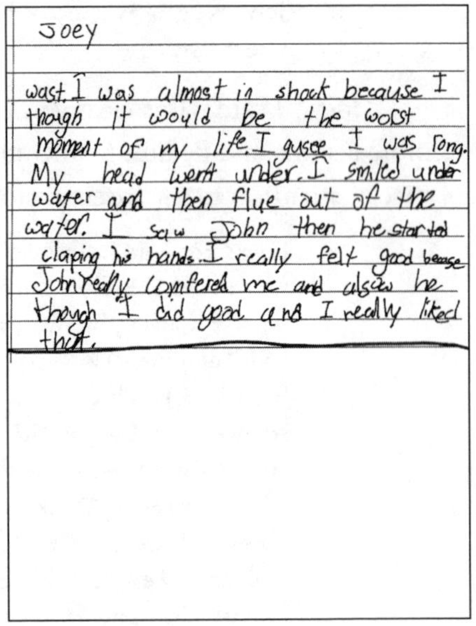
Joey

wast. I was almost in shock because I though it would be the worst moment of my life. I gusee I was rong. My head went under. I smiled under water and then flue out of the water. I saw John then he startid claping his hands. I really felt good beause John really compfered me and alsow he though I did good and I really liked that.

Fig. IX-8 Joey, page 3

HOMEWORK ***Writing the Internal Story*** Today at the start of our lesson I suggested that our lives are made up of not only what happens to us but also our responses to what happens to us.

As writers, this means that we pause in our actions and ask, "What was I thinking?" We offer our readers clues to reveal our thoughts and feelings. This is especially true in the heart of our stories.

Tonight for homework, your job is to reread your draft and find the heart of your story. Reread that part as if you're using a stop-action camera. For each chunk of action, ask, "What was I thinking/feeling?" Check that you give clues that reveal your thoughts and feelings. If you haven't included clues that reveal your thoughts and feelings in the heart of your story, you will want to add some tonight.

If your students have difficulty finding places in their pieces to include the internal story . . .
you might tell them that writers add the internal story into the most important parts of our pieces. This will be more manageable than sweeping through their whole piece to find places to include internal thoughts. Remind them of the storytelling work they did when they were developing their story ideas. Remind them how they tried to make their readers (or listeners) have strong reactions, how they made them gasp and laugh and cry. Now, ask your writers to storytell the important parts again, this time interspersing phrases that begin "I thought," "I noticed," "I remembered," "I pretended," "I wanted," and so on. They can do this oral storytelling work with their partners and then go back to their pieces to include the internal story. Make sure to remind them they can always storytell the important bits of their story with the internal story added to try to strengthen their writing.

If your students are writing stories with tiny actions that move through time, but still need help showing how each action reveals the internal story . . . teach them that each action is attached to a feeling and that writers choose action words that fit the feelings they want to convey. Each action can be a tiny window into the character's feelings. Often, students add in internal thought. Of course, this works in many cases. But it can often be more powerful to show students how the actions that they choose for their characters to make can reveal a great depth of feeling.

You might show them an excerpt from your writing that first states what the character is thinking. You might say, "Writers, you know that one way to show what's going on inside a character is to add the words that the character is thinking in his head. Here's a part of an entry from my notebook where I am on the boardwalk at Coney Island and I am really frightened to go on the Cyclone. I'm telling the reader how I'm feeling through my thoughts."

> I walked along the boardwalk. I don't want to go on the Cyclone, I thought. Why do I need to go?

But I can make my feelings much more powerful by showing them through the actions I take and don't take. For example:

> I stood frozen on the boardwalk, my feet refusing to take one more step toward the Cyclone. I squeezed my sister's hand tightly, tugged on her arm and turned to walk back to the car. But I was unable to escape as my sister dragged me in the direction of the screaming people.

MECHANICS

As I've pointed out earlier in this series, a very common issue to see in children's writing is that it is swamped with dialogue and there's little else there. This may seem at first to be a problem children are having with the mechanics of integrating dialogue into their pieces, but the problem is often a bit more intricate than that. Oftentimes, it helps children to learn that writers aim to create a working balance of strong pictures and strong sounds in their writing.

When conferring, I often carry the familiar children's book *Yo! Yes?* by Chris Raschka. I use the book to point out to children that there are two elements that make up this story. There is dialogue, and there are pictures. On every two-page spread, there are a few words—these are the exact words the characters are saying. That dialogue is crucial to the story. However, every two-page spread also holds illustrations, and those illustrations add equally crucial information to the reader's understanding of what is happening. As writers, there is a lot we can learn from this book.

When we include direct dialogue in a story, this adds tremendously to the story. But Raschka's book wouldn't make sense if it was only dialogue: "Yo! Yes? Hey! Who?"—the book's first four pages—make no sense without the pictures which convey who is talking, how that person acts, the intonation in the voice . . . .

When I confer with a child who has written chunks of text which read as a sound track only, I point out that the child's draft resembles Raschka's book without the pictures—and as such, it does not yet make sense. Raschka filled in the missing information with pictures, but the writers with whom I confer need to do this with words. Every chunk of dialogue needs a written image, created by words which reveal who is talking, what action that person makes or what intonation the person uses.

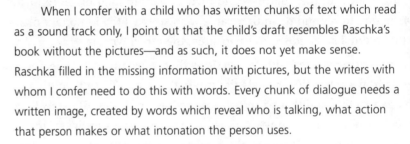

GETTING READY

- Passage from "Papa Who Wakes Up Tired in the Dark," by Sandra Cisneros, written on chart paper
- Timeline of "Papa Who Wakes Up Tired in the Dark," written on chart paper
- Student examples of narratives that show moving back and forth in time
- Whole-class Small Moment story written on chart paper (you might reuse the class story from Session VII)
- See CD-ROM for resources

ADDING SCENES FROM THE PAST AND FUTURE

When we write, we take the booming rich, nuanced, chaos of life itself and we simplify and channel and shoehorn all that into a single line of print that unrolls across the page. When we write curriculum, we work in similar ways. We take the vastness, richness and complexity of all our dreams and worries, all our disciplinary knowledge and practical know-how and somehow we cut and craft, select and simplify, until our plans and hopes are set onto the page in what is temporarily, at least, a best-going-draft.

In order to write a line or to create a curriculum, we make choices along the way that temporarily compromise the multi-layered, multi-faceted nature of what we want to say as teachers and as writers. And so early in the year, when we sense that many children are accustomed to writing in such an unrestrained, unstructured manner that they record anything tangentially related to the last word they've written into their pages, this series of books suggested teaching children that stories proceed chronologically, with a character doing one thing and then the next in a step–by–step fashion. But of course, that was over-simplifying, and today we open the door, wander outside, and let children peer at the sky. Today we teach children that in the midst of their tightly controlled sequential narratives, they—the main character—can blast through barriers of time and space by the simple miraculous act of remembering, or of fantasizing.

MINILESSON

Adding Scenes from the Past and Future

CONNECTION

Invite children to recall a fantasy story in which the character suddenly steps into another world. Explain that time travel can happen similarly in personal narratives when the narrator remembers the past or envisions tomorrow.

"Most of you have read or seen the film version of *The Lion, the Witch and the Wardrobe*. You'll remember that in the midst of a hide–and–seek game, Lucy hears her brother's footsteps coming and slips into a wardrobe, a closet. It's full of coats. She pushes towards the back of the closet, rustling in through the soft coats, and suddenly something cold brushes against her arm—a tree bough, covered with snow. Lucy looks down and she sees she is standing in snow. Ahead, a lamp gleams golden and from afar she hears the sound of approaching sleigh bells. She's in another world."

"When you and I write, we put one foot in front of the next. We are playing hide–and–go–seek. We hear someone approaching, worry that we'll be found, and slip into the closet. One thing—the sound of footsteps—leads to another."

"And sometimes in the sequence of these actions and reactions, we take a step that transports us to another world. In the stories we are writing this month, we aren't transported to a magical kingdom—but in just as magical a fashion, we may well burrow into a coat closet and find ourselves startled by the brush of a tree bough, by something from another time or place, something that signifies that suddenly we are in another space in the world of yesterday, or of tomorrow."

Name the teaching point. Specifically, tell children that in a personal narrative, characters can time travel—by remembering or by envisioning tomorrow.

"Today I want to teach you that characters in personal narratives sometimes travel through time and place. We do this by remembering and by fantasizing."

TEACHING

Share examples by both professional and student writers that show writing about both imagined future events and remembered past events.

"Let me show you an example of a writer who wrote a story of something that actually involved just about five minutes of real time. In this story, the narrator thinks *ahead*,

COACHING

This is, of course, an elaborate way to teach children that they can break out of the confines of sequential time when they write narratives. My detour will be suitable for some classes of children but it could confuse others. Use your professional judgement, then, to revise this session (and every one) so that it will work well for your children. As you weigh your choices, it may help you to know that the reason I rope The Lion, the Witch and the Wardrobe, *into this lesson is that I want children to realize that there can be a very concrete, physical, embodied quality to the memories and fantasies which we tuck into a personal narrative.*

imagining what will happen in the future. (In others stories, the narrator may think *backward*, recalling what happened years ago.) You'll see in this story we're going to study, that the narrator still moves step–by–step through time—but her mind jumps into the future, and for a little bit of the story she imagines a scenario that has not yet actually happened. Then she returns (like children in Narnia return) to the very real sequence of events."

"This example, written by Sandra Cisneros, is a text you have already studied: 'Papa Who Wakes Up Tired in the Dark.' Listen," I said and I pointed to the chart paper as I read aloud.

> Your abuelito is dead, Papa says early one morning in my room. *Está muerto*, and then as if he just heard the news himself, crumples like a coat and cries, my brave Papa cries. I have never seen my Papa cry and don't know what to do.
>
> I knew he will have to go away, that he will take a plane to Mexico, all the uncles and aunts will be there, and they will have a black and white photo taken in front of the tomb with flowers shaped like spears in a white vase because this is how they send the dead away in that country.
>
> Because I am the oldest, my father has told me first, and now it is my turn to tell the others. I will have to explain why we can't play. I will have to tell them to be quiet today.
>
> My Papa, his thick hands and thick shoes, who wakes up tired in the dark, who combs his hair with water, drinks his coffee, and is gone before we wake, today is sitting on my bed.
>
> And I think if my own Papa died what would I do. I hold my Papa in my arms. I hold and hold and hold him. (Cisneros 1989, p. 56)

"When I want to study a text so as to learn from what the author has done I don't just read it once or twice. I reread, reread, reread. I turn it inside out and study how it was made. So watch me do that," I said.

"I'm going to reread it with special glasses," I said, "with special lenses. I could notice Cisneros' word choice because it is beautiful, or the way she uses tiny details to make the character of Papa come to life. But I'm going to give myself the job of rereading this and paying attention to the timeline of events, watching for when Cisneros moves from telling about the sequence of events in her bedroom that morning to telling about another time and place."

The text I show as a model only gestures towards what I've described. You and your colleagues will surely be able to find texts which are more clear examples. Look through any Calvin and Hobbes *books and you'll see countless examples of how, in the midst of an all-too-real sequence of events, Calvin is suddenly transported into his own little Narnia, returning to the reality of his life in time for the next event. In truth, this is exactly what happens in Sendak's beautiful story* Where the Wild Things Are. *I didn't reference that text because I don't want to fan the flames of fantasy writing—not just yet, anyhow—although of course fantasizing is very much a part of all our comings and goings.*

I've studied this beautiful text for years, admiring so many aspects of Cisneros' craft that I won't mention in this particular minilesson. I won't mention the way her text begins with dialogue, and the dialogue—written in Spanish—reveals the character of Papa. I won't admire the way this narrative begins not with the narrator doing an action, but with the abrupt intrusion of her Papa's words, and the narrator's dawning realization of what happens. There's more, too; the alliteration of harsh sounds as Papa crumples like a coat and cries, the repetition of 'cries' as the narrator takes in the fact that here, before her very eyes, her brave Papa is crying (she's never seen him cry before). I say none of this for now, but my respect for the craftsmanship shines through my reading of this text, and for sure I carry it with me so the text can help me launch a thousand ships as I confer.

I reread, and at the start of the second paragraph I said, "Here, I can tell she's traveling in her mind, thinking of what will happen later today, tomorrow. It's as if she has a second timeline inserted into the first." I showed them the following timeline.

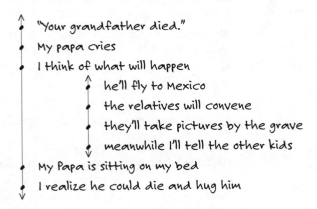

"Your grandfather died."
My papa cries
I think of what will happen
    he'll fly to Mexico
    the relatives will convene
    they'll take pictures by the grave
    meanwhile I'll tell the other kids
My Papa is sitting on my bed
I realize he could die and hug him

Then, looking back on the timeline of actual events, I said, "Do you see that the actual events only involve a few minutes?"

"But meanwhile, in the second paragraph, the narrator pictures what will happen soon, that her father will go to the funeral in Mexico, and she imagines sharing the news with her siblings. These events happen only in the narrator's mind."

ACTIVE ENGAGEMENT
With a whole-class exercise text, practice jumping forward or backward in time.

"So writers, I'm hoping you realize that you can decide, in the sequence of your narrative, that you want to leave the physical sequence of events on a timeline and tell the story of another time and place—one you imagine, that might happen in the future, or one you recall, that happened in the past. When you do this, as when C.S. Lewis wrote *The Lion, the Witch and the Wardrobe*, something very concrete and specific will happen and suddenly you'll be transported to another time and place."

"Let's try it. Remember Gregory's story, "Al is Dead" which we studied earlier this year? As you'll recall, Gregory had written a story about the day his dad told him that his fish Al was dead. I'm going to read you Gregory's revised story about when he saw his fish lying in the trash. Partner 2, pretend you wrote the story, that Al was your fish, you got him and six others at a pet store, with a bag of turquoise sand and all . . . I'm going to set you up to time travel. Write in the air how you might add on to Gregory's story." Then I read and dictated the following story:

Dead. Ever since I had fish, I had Al: the best algae-eater in the world. Once I heard he was dead, I did not cry. I just was still. Then I asked, "Where is he?" My dad said, "In the trash." I asked to see him.

I walked over to the trash can, stepped on the pedal and the lid opened. I looked in and saw wet paper towels, orange peels, and a pile of coffee grounds. Lying on top of the coffee grounds was my golden fish Al. I picked him up and flicked off the coffee grounds that had stuck to him. "Al," I said, "What happened?"

I remembered back to the day I'd gotten him. My dad and I pushed open the door to Carver's Pet Store. I walked over to the fish tanks, and started eyeing them . . . (take it from there, Partner Two).

For a minute, only, partner 2 wrote in the air the words he or she might say. Then, before the child could get lost in the pet store, I spoke up, and pointing to Gregory's draft, I read the remaining section of it:

I looked at Al, lying dead in my hands. For a second I thought, then I said, "We can give him a funeral." My dad looked doubtful for a minute but I picked him up and said, "He was special." Then I cried. Al was gone.

LINK
Remind children that as writers, they need to draw on their entire repertoire of strategies to accomplish whatever it is they want to do.

"Writers, whenever you are writing a narrative, remember that you have the option of having your narrator or main character either imagine a future event or recall a past event. Today, you have lots of options. You could check for true and honest details in your writing, study mentor texts for powerful leads, or bring out the internal as well as the external story. You could make sure that you angled your writing to show your intentions or that you wrote the heart of your story in a step-by-step way." As I spoke, I pointed to our class charts, including the Qualities of Good Personal Narrative Writing chart, as references. "Most of all, you want readers to dream the dream of your story. So as you reread, stop and ask, 'Is this what I really wanted to show? Is this what's most true and honest about my story?' Let the lens of truth be your guide for revision. Let's get started."

Often in a unit of study, the minilessons you teach early on introduce children to some goals and strategies that are essential to the work of the unit, and the teaching you do later in the unit is more of an option children may or may not draw upon. That is surely the case in this instance.

WRITING AND CONFERRING

Revising with Scenes from the Past

I pulled my chair alongside Joey, who was working with an enormous sense of industry. "What are you working on?" I asked.

"I'm doing time travel," he answered, his face flushed with excitement. "'Cause when John dove in the water and it was all wave-y, I had already put that thought about when we were canoeing in Class II rapids. So now I wrote about what we did when we were canoeing and I'm gonna make myself think of that," he said, showing me that he'd inserted a code into the swimming story: *[Fig. X-1]*

> Then the splash was greater each time his body went down more into the pond. Then his whole body was down under the water. It kind of reminded me of the time me and John went canoeing white water class 2.*

This was the section Joey planned to insert into the swimming story: *[Fig. X-2]*

> We got pulled in by a riptide. We paddled as hard as we could. It was getting us even closer and closer to the big rock. We tried the draw, that didn't work. We tried the back paddle, that didn't work. We tried the J-stroke, that didn't work. Suddenly we hit the rock.

MID-WORKSHOP TEACHING POINT **Using Flashback to Convey the Main Feeling**   "Writers, what I'm noticing as I confer with you is that many of you are finding that when you want to build up the feeling that you had in a story, to really make readers feel what you were feeling, it helps to tuck just a tiny bit of time travel into your draft. For example, Becca has been writing about when she stayed for a week at her friend Clarissa's house, and suddenly experienced a pang of homesickness and worry. In her first version of her narrative, she just *told* about that. She wrote:

> "I do this every year," and I smiled to myself, thinking it would be a wonderful time. I looked down the hill at the rest of the Catskills and thought, "This is a beautiful house." But then in the night I felt a rush of pain in my stomach. Tears built up in my eyes, until they paused at the brim of my lower eyelids, then the tears suddenly flowed down my cheeks like small rivers. "I don't know what to do . . . I miss my family . . . I need them!" I sobbed. Then I imagined them in a car accident and cried even more.

continued on next page

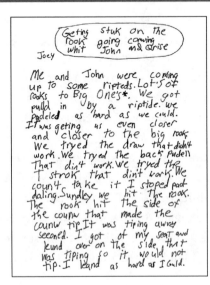

Fig. X-1 Joey's entry shows a code

Fig. X-2 Joey's insertion text

I looked over what Joey had done and thought, "Now what?" He'd done exactly what I'd taught, and done it with great excitement—yet his revisions were in all likelihood going to detract from the story, distracting the reader away from the main idea which was Joey's appreciation for his friend's mentorship. I scrolled through my options. Clearly what I'd like best to do is to teach Joey that when a writer moves from one sequential story to a secondary one, that secondary story needs to enhance the story's main message. Joey could have written the paddling story so that it illustrated that yet again, while paddling together, John had been willing to go first and had paved the way for Joey. But it wasn't clear to me that any such thing had happened during the paddling story. And more to the point, Joey had just a very short while to bring his story to completion. It was far and away his longest story ever and his proudest accomplishment.

"Joey," I said. "Can I shake your hand? Congratulations. You've just done exactly what authors do. You told the story of one moment, and it sparked the memory of a second, related story. I love that you didn't summarize this secondary story, the one you'll insert, but that you instead told it step by step. Congratulations!" I moved on, noticing that another day I had a pointer that I'd want to share with the class—and with Joey.

continued from previous page

"Becca decided she could actually go into her mind and tell about what she imagined could happen to her parents, so she wrote this."

> A terrible feeling came over me and took control of my mind. Words appeared in my mind and turned into worries. I saw my dad driving the car and my mom beside him. I saw a deer jump in the road. I saw the car bang into the rail and flip over. "What If My Parents Get Into a Car Accident!" I thought.

"Then Becca returned to the sequence of her story events, writing this."

> I was shaking. And my insides didn't know what to do. I called my mom and she told me that it's okay, that I should calm down . . .

"She's finishing the story now. I think Becca can teach all of us that one way to build up the main feeling that we want to convey in a story is to consider detailing what exactly we remember, or worry will happen, or hope for . . . "

SHARE

Showing Significance through Adding Scenes from the Past or Future

Share an example of a student's writing that shows moving to a new scene at a new time, making sure that it strengthens the writer's overall intent.

"Writers, many of you are moving backward and forward in time, and your pieces are becoming richer as a result. Caleb's first draft went like this." *[Fig. X-3]*

> I looked up. Shelves upon shelves of mitts stared back down at me. The air conditioner made me feel like a snowstorm was forming in my intestine. I had tried on more than ten mitts and was about to give up. Finally I found one. It was perfect.

"But then Caleb thought, 'What am I trying to show in my story?' and he wrote a note to himself, 'I want the reader to know that my mitt is special to me.' He again wrote about shopping at Sports Authority, but this time he shifted between telling about shopping and telling about what he imagines himself doing with the glove in the future. He moves forward in time. Listen." As I read aloud, I emphasized the parts that revealed Caleb's intentions by shifting to an imagined future. *[Fig. X-4]*

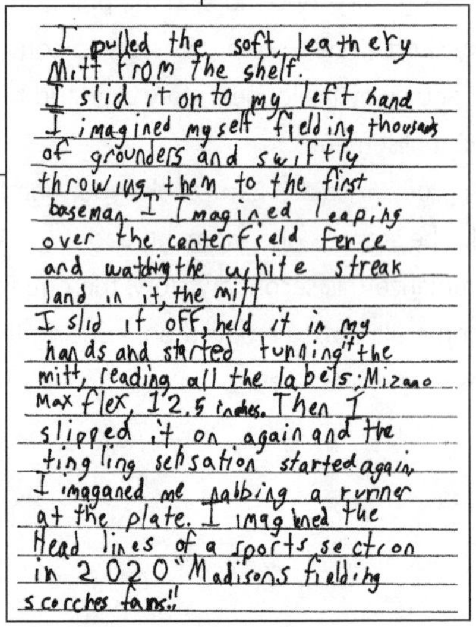

> I pulled the soft, leathery mitt from the shelf. I slid it onto my left hand. I imagined myself fielding thousands of grounders and swiftly throwing them to the first baseman. I imagined myself leaping over the centerfield fence and watching the white streak land in it, the mitt. I slid if off, held it in my hands and started turning the mitt around, reading all the labels: "Mizono, max flex, 12.5 inches." Then I slipped it on again and the tingling sensation started again. I imagined me, tagging a runner at the plate. I imagined the headlines of a sports section in 2020, "Madison's fielding scorches fans."

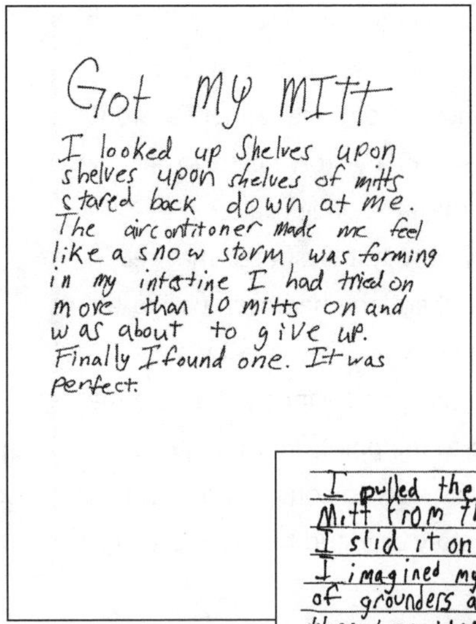

Fig. X-3 The start of Caleb's draft

Fig. X-4 Caleb rewrote the middle of his draft so now he leaps forward in time.

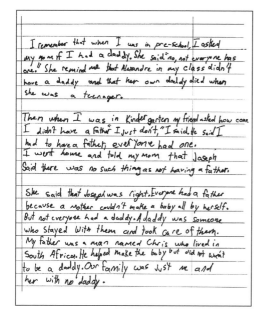
Fig. X-5 Juliana

HOMEWORK *Using Past Memories to Emphasize Meaning* Tonight, please work some more on adding a scene from the past or future to emphasize the significant part of your writing. Here's an example from Juliana to again show you what I mean.

Juliana is writing about meeting her dad, Chris, for the first time at a restaurant. But, she interrupts the story with this memory to emphasize how much this meeting matters to her. *[Fig. X-5]*

> I remember that when I was in pre-school, I asked my mom if I had a daddy. She said "No, not everyone has one." She reminded me that Alexandre in my class didn't have a daddy and that her own daddy died when she was a teenager.
>
> Then when I was in kindergarten my friend asked how come I didn't have a father. "I just don't," I said. He said I had to have a father, everyone had one. I went home and told my mom that Joseph said there was no such thing as not having a father. She said that Joseph was right. Everyone had a father because a mother couldn't make a baby all by herself. But not everyone had a daddy. A daddy was someone who stayed with them and took care of them. My father was a man named Chris who lived in South Africa. He helped make the baby but did not want to be a daddy. Our family was just me and her with no daddy.

Juliana uses *I remember* as a starting point for her flashback, and this flashback leads up to and gives importance to the story that she is writing. Try that tonight.

TAILORING YOUR TEACHING

If your students would benefit from studying the words and phrases a mentor author uses to move back and forward through time . . . select some text passages to analyze, and then have students select one (or more) of these passages to use as mentor texts as they add scenes from the past and the future into their own pieces.

For example, in *Stevie*, by John Steptoe, once Stevie leaves to live with his mother and father again, Robert starts to remember all the fun they used to have together. The text includes passages like these:

I remember the time I ate the last piece of cake in the breadbox and
blamed it on him.

We used to play Cowboys and Indians on the stoop.

I remember when I was doin' my homework I used to teach him
what I had learned. He could write his name pretty good for his age.

I remember the time we played boogie man and we hid under the
covers with Daddy's flashlight.

And that time we was playin' in the dark under the bushes and we
found these two dead rats and one was brown and one was black.

And him and me and my friends used to cook mickies or
marshmallows in the park.

We used to have good times together.

Ask your students to study the words and phrases John Steptoe uses to insert these
memories into his story. Your students will surely notice how Steptoe uses phrases like, "I
remember," "We used to," "That time we," and so on. Developing a list of these words and
phrases that authors use to move back in time will help your students figure out how to
insert their own memories into their pieces.

**If your students seem to plop scenes from the past or future into their narratives, and if
this movement through time tends to distract from the big idea of their stories rather
than reinforce it** . . . you could use the same passages from Stevie listed above; however, this
time your lens is how they each show the big idea of Robert's regret that *Stevie* left. Begin by
suggesting that when writers add backward and forward movement to their stories, they do
it for a purpose. Authors try to heighten the big idea of their story, and often it helps to add
some scenes from the past or future to make the big idea clearer to the reader. In other
words, they ask themselves, "What am I really trying to say here?" and add past and future
scenes in order to strengthen the overall meaning of their pieces.

For Active Engagement, return to a piece of writing that is familiar to the class but that
doesn't have any future or past scenes included. (It could be one of your entries, a whole-
class text, or a student piece.) Have your students consider where and how to add past or
future scenes to make the overall meaning of the piece shine through.

If your children studied this unit in a previous year . . . you'll want to cite a different
mentor text and to create a new sort of active engagement. You might return to the example
of a class event, such as when the class hamster got loose. You might say something like,

"Let's write a story about the other day when Hermie escaped from his cage during our read–aloud. Here is a draft of the start of that story." You could point to the story on chart paper. "Let's pretend we wanted to show that Hermie has escaped before, and that we get worried whenever this happens. Where could we think backwards, recalling what happened before, or think ahead, imagining what might happen in the future? Let's try to embed these jumps in time right into the middle of the narrative." Then you could take a moment to read the draft aloud.

> One fall afternoon, my teacher read aloud in the meeting area. "What's that noise?" I whispered to my partner. It sounded like Hermie. I looked over at his cage. Hermie was standing on top of his exercise wheel, pushing open the corner of the lid to his cage with his nose. Then I saw the brick. Someone forgot to put it back on top of the lid. I was nervous. I did not know what to say.
>
> When I looked again, Hermie was gone. I noticed the lid was pushed open, and I knew that Hermie escaped again.
>
> A moment later, I heard scraping sounds under the radiator. I saw Hermie poke his head out. He was in the same hiding spot as last time. Should I raise my hand and tell the teacher? Interrupt the read-aloud or wait until we finished? How were we going to catch him this time?

"Work with your partner on this. Get started."

COLLABORATING WITH COLLEAGUES

As your children near the editing phase of the writing process, their attention will need to turn to the smaller and smaller details of their writing. To prepare yourself for this, you too may want to study the smaller choices writers make.

Writers learn to value the true word, the word that actively leaps to mind in the moment. You can teach children that writers reach not for the ornate or the impressive word, but for the true word, the precise word. It is unlikely that we'd see our canine ambulating with its nostrils declined toward the earth. We might, on the other hand, see our beagle running, its nose to the ground, chasing a scent. Point out to children that the sections of stories that seem beautiful often are not fancy ones. For example, I love Rylant's description of sleeping in a house full of relatives in *The Relatives Came*. She writes, "It was hard going to sleep with all that new breathing in the house." There's not a fancy word or a bit of figurative language in the sentence, but it's one of my favorite examples of descriptive writing. Part of its power is Rylant's choice to use that one word, *breathing*, usually a verb, as a noun.

With colleagues, study the careful word choices, the true words that authors use in mentor texts, particularly nouns and verbs. Strunk and White, in *The Elements of Style*, state: "It is nouns and verbs, not their assistants, that give to good writing its toughness and color" (p. 72). Carefully chosen nouns allow writers to be specific. So, instead of, "I grabbed a bag for the trip," it's more accurate to say, "I grabbed a *suitcase* for the trip." Instead of, "I packed my things," it's more accurate to list, "I packed my *shorts, T-shirts, and tennis racket*." If I want to show that I packed for a big trip, and the suitcase was heavy, instead of, "I took the suitcase off the bed and put it on the floor," it's more revealing to write, "I *wrestled* the suitcase to the floor."

For example, notice the beautiful choice of words in *Salt Hands*, by Jane Chelsea Aragon. Consider the following excerpt:

I went to the door. It was dark. It was still. The night air was warm.

I didn't want to frighten the deer, so quietly I went in and sprinkled some salt into my hands.

I tiptoed outside and stepped toward him silently. He looked at me. His eyes were big and brown. He watched me for a long time.

I knelt on the grass. The deer flicked his white tail back and forth. I sang a song to him softly, while he nibbled on fallen pears.

He shook his head and twitched his ears. He was listening to my song.

He moved closer to me cautiously. I whispered my song. Then slowly, I held out my hands.

Notice the careful choice of verbs: *tiptoed, stepped, knelt, flicked, sang, nibbled, twitched, whispered*. Notice the simple and true choice of nouns: *salt, eyes, grass, tail, pears, head, ears, song, hands*. Or the sparse, careful use of adverbs and adjectives that convey the author's intentions of silent communion: *quietly I went in . . . stepped toward him silently . . . his white tail . . . sang a song to him softly . . . fallen pears . . . moved closer to me cautiously . . . Then slowly, I held out my hands.*

Then bring this awareness to your students. For a Mid-Workshop Teaching Point, or other teaching opportunity in the writing workshop, you might try angling some common situations by working the nouns and verbs. For example, you could start with the common sentence, "I walked into the room." Show how you might change *walked* to *snuck* if you wanted to show that you were there without permission. Then you might change *room* to the *kitchen* to make that more accurate. Students could try changing *walked* and *room* for other specific scenarios as practice for careful word choice, especially for nouns and verbs.

BRINGING FORTH THE STORY ARC

In Session XI of Unit 1, we introduced timelines as a construct to support students' planning and revision. In this session, we introduce students to a similar but more complex structure: a story arc.

IN THIS SESSION, YOU WILL TEACH STUDENTS THAT ONE POWERFUL WAY TO REVISE THEIR NARRATIVES IS TO BRING OUT THE STORY STRUCTURE.

GETTING READY

- *Peter's Chair*, by Ezra Jack Keats, and *Shortcut*, by Donald Crews; be sure students are familiar with both
- How Stories Tend to Go, drawn on chart paper
- Your own example of using story structure to tell a common, everyday event
- Story mountain for *Peter's Chair*, sketched on chart paper
- See CD-ROM for resources

As teachers of reading and writing, we are keenly aware of the underlying structures in the genres we encounter. It is for this reason that my colleagues and I emphasize the format, the architecture, of a minilesson. We know that by uncovering the form of minilessons, "the way minilessons tend to go," we let you in on the genre's secrets. An awareness of a genre's form allows writers to compose in that form. This is true for any human endeavor. Music has its minuets, waltzes, and sonatas; law has its hearings, plea bargains, and trials. Mastery requires an awareness and application of forms.

In this lesson we introduce students to story arcs as a way of describing the pattern stories usually follow. In a very rough sense, narratives usually have some description of the situation, then something happens, and then there are some results. Another way of describing "the way stories tend to go" is to say that stories revolve around a character who yearns for or reaches towards something, who encounters trouble, and who as a result, finds new resources within himself or herself or the world . . . and changes in the process.

In this minilesson, we analyze very simple texts. But don't be fooled by these texts' simplicity. Some people maintain that it's the mark of genius to make the complex seem simple. This is true for these stories. My colleagues and I have used Peter's Chair for countless craft lessons. Look at this text closely, and you will notice that Keats has no wasted words; every word forwards Peter's emotional journey through the story. After guiding students to perceive story structure, we show them how this newfound awareness gives them power to revise their narrative drafts.

This session, then, invites substantive revisions, suggesting that just as the sculptor finds a lion emerging out of his block of marble and works the material to bring forth his vision, so, too, writers can sometimes see a story arc hidden within the details of a rough draft, and work with his or her material to bring forth that design. It's a wonderfully complex, rich way to revise—one which has everything to do with vision as well as re-vision.

MINILESSON

Bringing Forth the Story Arc

CONNECTION

Let your students know that revision begins with seeing possibilities in drafts that at first we think are finished.

"Some of you have been coming to me saying, 'I'm done.' That's a great feeling, isn't it? To reach the end of a draft! When I get to the end of a draft, I sit back and enjoy being done. I take time to clean up my writing folder. I get a drink of water . . . and then I get back to work!"

"As I told you earlier this year, writers have a saying: 'When you're done, you've just begun.' Once we've reached the end of a draft, we're in a very special place because now we can make our best work even better. I know you are thinking that your drafts are already pretty good—as good as your final pieces from Unit 1, that's for sure—and you are right. And over the next few days, you'll have a chance to take the best that you can do so far . . . and make your best, better. That's how learning goes."

"The word *revision* comes from the word *vision*. It literally means to look again. Today I want to teach you one way to revise (to resee) your writing."

Name your teaching point. Specifically, tell children that they can revise their drafts by bringing out the story structure.

"Today I want to teach you that, just as our writing workshops usually follow one general plan or format, so, too, stories usually follow one plan or format; they both have a 'way they usually go.' Writers know how stories usually go, and when we write stories, our stories tend to follow the same general plan. One way to revise our writing is to bring out the story structure that is probably hiding underneath our personal narratives."

TEACHING

Analyze aloud the story structure of a well-known story, such as Ezra Jack Keats' *Peter's Chair.*

"Writers, by now you have come to realize that our writing workshops usually begin with a minilesson, then there is work time, then we meet to share. You can count on that.

COACHING

I want children to embrace the concept of revision and to anticipate major, significant changes. The message is that revision is not a time to tweak and polish. It instead offers a chance to reinvent, to reimagine. I want children to approach their revision work with zeal and resourcefulness.

This session will work best if your students already know the text you'll refer to later in the session. I refer to Keats' Peter's Chair but any simple story with a traditional story arc will suffice. Williams' Knufflebunny is perfect. The red sweater excerpt from "Eleven" in Cisneros' Woman Hollering Creek and Other Stories is not suitable.

Pause for just a second to realize how many words related to the teaching of writing are linked to sight: point of view, focus, zooming in, vision, lenses, perspective . . . but the greatest of these is re-vision.

When planning this unit, I went back and forth over the question of whether to teach this lesson on story structure as part of planning, just before children begin their drafts, or as part of revision. For me, a sense of structure is one of several magnetic poles exerting a force on my content from the very start. For this reason, I was tempted to make this Session VI. But, on the other hand, I worried that children might let their sense of story and their attentiveness to form overpower everything else so that writing a narrative became filling in a format rather than dreaming the dream of an event. So this session is here, at this late point in the sequence of the unit, and probably it will be most influential for your stronger students, allowing others to gain time for continuing with trajectories you set earlier.

You know how writing workshops usually go. In a similar way, stories, like writing workshops, have a pattern, a way that they usually go. Most stories begin by introducing the *main character* and usually that main character has hopes or desires. Then, the main character's hopes or desires usually lead to that main character getting into some sort of a *problem* or *trouble* or *tension*. Finally, *things happen* related to that problem, and the story ends in a re*solution*."

Notice my emphasis on the predictable nature of the writing workshop. Here I build on students' growing awareness of the structures of both their daily life and of stories they read.

How Stories Tend to Go

- main character (wants, hopes, desires)
- problem (trouble) (probably an emotional response)
- things happen related to the problem
  (the problem gets bigger? there is another problem?)
- a resolution

We will, of course, revisit this content in the unit on writing short fiction. But it is fascinating to realize that our personal narratives work best if they are not just true chronicles of a life experience, but if they are also shaped like a story. Consider the implication of this in relation to the narratives you've been writing.

"So let me show you what I mean by showing you the *story arc* as I see it in Ezra Jack Keats' *Peter's Chair*." I read the story as if to myself, almost murmuring, skipping irrelevant passages to keep the rendition quick.

> Peter stretched as high as he could . . .

"Yup, there is the character and he's physically reaching for something—he already wants something. I guess he's wanting to make a tall tower. He may have deeper wants, too."

> "Shhh. Remember we have a new baby."

"Yup, there is the problem! His tower falls down and all that his parents worry about is waking the baby." Then I added, in an aside, "Do you notice that the story never really comes right out and says that Peter has a problem? It just shows it: Peter has to tiptoe around because of his sister. His parents aren't paying attention to him, they are paying attention to his sister's needs."

> "That's my cradle. They painted it pink!"

"More stuff is happening about the problem—and again, the story doesn't really come right out and *say* it is a problem for Peter that his parents are taking his stuff and painting it

Of course, not all stories go like this. Starting with this common, simple structure, however, can help children craft their narratives into pieces of writing that feel like stories, pieces that have a touch of suspense, or that have, at the very least, an unfolding of interrelated events.

Donald Murray has suggested that the secret of all dramatic writing (as he calls this sort of narrative) is the quality that can be summed up in the adage "show don't tell." This is simple to say and enormously complex to put in action.

pink for his little sister, but we can figure that out. So let me keep reading and you see if the ending of this story follows the plan for most stories."

> Peter picked up the chair and ran to his room . . . "Let's run away, Willie," he said.

"The story is winding up, isn't it? Peter is upset enough that he's taking action. He took that chair and ran away because he didn't want his chair painted pink too! I think he's trying to get his parents' attention in a drastic way! I think this is the heart of the story, the problem Peter is facing has gotten so bad that Peter wants to run away with Willie. Let's read on":

> But he couldn't fit in the chair. He was too big!

"You know what? I'm sensing a turning point to the problem, a resolution, which is how stories go. I bet that Peter is starting to realize that he's too big for his baby things." Skipping past other details which add to the sense of resolution, I read from the ending:

> Then Peter says, "Daddy, let's paint the little chair pink for Susie."

"That definitely shows resolution: Not only does Peter rejoin the family, but it seems that he's learning to accept Susie. He is offering to paint his little chair pink! Ezra Jack Keats doesn't come out and say that the problem is resolved, but we're able to figure it out."

"Writers," I said, taking hold of a marker pen and drawing a mountainlike arc across chart paper, "here's an easy way to see the story structure in *Peter's Chair*. We'll call it a *story mountain* because of its shape. The main character, Peter, *wants* his family to be the way it was: just him and his mom and dad." I locate this in a dot at the base of the story mountain, and continue making dots, as on a timeline. "*But then* there's a new baby, Susie, in the house. Things happen to Peter that make the problem get worse." As I spoke, I moved up the incline of the story mountain, marking key moments. "*And so finally*, he and Willie run away: Peter can't take it anymore." Then I pointed to the top of the story mountain. "Then comes the resolution, starting with Peter finding he no longer fits in his old chair and including Peter's mom inviting him in for lunch. In the end [and I pointed to the last portion of the story mountain], Peter helps his dad to paint his blue chair pink for Susie."

ACTIVE ENGAGEMENT
Retell *Shortcut*, using voice intonation to help children perceive the story's structure.

"Let me retell the story of *Shortcut* to you. Please listen and in a minute I'm going to ask you to talk with your partner about whether this book has the same structure as *Peter's Chair*."

Sometimes I help children realize that writers don't show-not-tell all parts of our stories, but we do use this adage to develop the heart of a story.

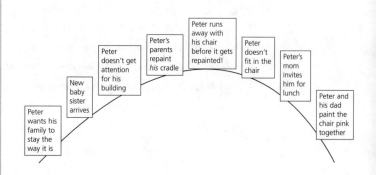

The big difference between a timeline and a story mountain is that in the latter, one section of the story is given prominence. We can refer to that one section as "the heart of a story" or as the rising action and climax or as the peak of the story—and the way this teaching is evolving, we'll end up using all of these terms despite the fact that this means we're using mixed metaphor. If children are confused, the confluence of different terminology probably won't be the main cause for that confusion. Instead, the hard part will be applying what they learn about Peter's Chair *to their own drafts.*

Remember how stories tend to go," and I pointed again to the story arc. "So in *Shortcut*, the children take the shortcut home and a train comes clackity clacking down the track, bearing down upon them. They holler, they run, they leap out of the way. Then they hear the train, clickety clacking away from them. Walking home, they resolve not to tell anyone . . . and never to take the shortcut again. Turn and talk to your partner. See if you can plot *Shortcut* on the same structure as *Peter's Chair*. Be sure to explain your thinking. Ready? Begin."

LINK
Remind children that stories, like the writing workshop, follow a form. Help writers realize that a knowledge of story structure can help them re-vision their work and decide upon their next steps.

"So writers, always remember that stories, like the writing workshop itself, have a way-they-usually-go. Knowing the way-things-usually-go helps a person to be more planful. Because I know that I'll only have thirty or forty minutes to confer during writing time, I can look over my plans for a day and realize I'll never get around to all the one-to-one conferences I hope to hold, and so I can revise my plans with the constraints of the workshop in mind. I can, for example, decide to hold a small group strategy lesson rather than to try conferring with eight of you individually."

"In the same way, writers, because you know how stories usually go, you can look over what you've written so far and revise what you've done and what you plan to do next, keeping in mind that your personal narrative will probably be stronger if you bring out the elements of story that are buried in it."

"You will need to look at whether your story is still more like a timeline, with one event leading to the next, each of equal size and importance. If that's the case, you'll want to be sure to figure out what your story is really about and what you can do to show that. Turning a timeline into a story mountain is the same process as building up the heart of your story. Remember how Peter's feeling builds as one thing after another happens, and he feels worse and worse? If you haven't built up the incline in your story, take the key section and stretch it out. If knowing how stories go gives you other ideas for revision . . . do those now! This is your chance. Off you go."

If you feel that the students need another example, you could add: "Writers, do you see that all these stories have a structure that is the same as the one in The Little Engine That Could*? Remember from when you were little, that story of a train that makes it over the mountain, carrying toys and treats to all the good little girls and boys? It starts up the mountain, but the load is heavy, the train is small, so it chugs along, going, 'I think I can, I think I can, I think I can,' until finally—Hurray! Toot toot! It's on its way to all the good little boys and girls."*

WRITING AND CONFERRING

Developing Elements of Story

I pulled my chair alongside Sirah. I knew, even before I began the conference, that Sirah was well on her way to writing an effective piece of writing, and looked forward to helping her make a good story into a great one.

"Sirah," I said, "I'm wondering how you decided which parts of this event to include in your writing?"

Sirah answered, "Well, I was telling the story the way it happened. I went to the hotel to go swimming and I was playing in the pool when a hurricane hit. Then, we thought the hurricane was gone, so we all went in the pool, but then it came back so we all went home."

"So, you remembered the way the story happened from the beginning to the end and that's the way you wrote it?"

Sirah nodded. "Yep. The whole story was not even one hour so it's focused."

"That's smart of you, Sirah. I'm glad you are thinking about keeping it focused and you are right that one way writers focus is by limiting the amount of time that passes."

Then I said, "But Sirah, I'm going to give you another very important tip that will help you to focus your writing. Another way we check that our story is focused is we check to make sure that all parts of the story relate to the story mountain. And for you, the peak of your mountain is . . ."

Sirah interjected, "When the hurricane hit."

I nodded. "So, that's at the peak of your mountain. If you want to be sure your writing is focused, you need to think how all the other parts of your story relate to this part," I said, sketching her story mountain. "So, for example, you started your story when you arrived at the hotel for your swimming lesson. Could you think of a point in time that is more closely related to when the hurricane hit? You can still be enjoying yourself and having fun. But you want your starting place to begin to lead the reader to the most important part of your story."

Sirah replied, "Well, my cousin and I were on the beach collecting shells. We had a whole bucket. This is where I first had a feeling that the hurricane was coming."

> **MID-WORKSHOP TEACHING POINT** *Developing Story Mountains* "Writers, many of you are struggling a bit with your story mountains and that's as it should be. You're wise to go through several drafts of a story mountain—it is lots more efficient than writing several drafts of a story! Let me remind you of a few pointers."
>
> "Remember that your story will probably contain only two or three small moments, two or three vignettes that perhaps each occupy about twenty minutes. To pull this off, remember that you don't need to start the story at the start of the action. If you are writing about a ski trip, you needn't start it with the drive! You could start it with the moment when you slide off the ski lift at the crest of the mountain. Usually, it helps to start the story close to the trouble, to the rising action, when you can see the story's mountain peak rising ahead of you."
>
> *continued on next page*

"Okay, so you might start it when you were on the beach and you had a feeling that a hurricane was coming?" As I spoke, I graphed what Sirah said on a story mountain. Then I said, "Sirah, do you see that one way, then, to be sure your story is focused is to check that your beginning and your ending relates to the main part (the peak) of your story? You've done that for your lead; try it now with your ending. You have everybody leaving and going home at the end. But, just like your beginning, you want your ending to be related to the most important part of your story. Don't leave and go home! Think of other possible endings that stay close to the heart of the story."

---

continued from previous page

"Be sure that you ask, 'What's my story really about?' and be sure that your answer to that question translates into your story mountain. If Rie's story is really about how her father helps her feel safe when they're surfing in big waves, she's not going to want to start her story with a description of eating lunch at the beach sitting under a colorful umbrella, even if that is what she did before she went surfing in the waves. If her story will end up being that she was very scared and her father made her feel safe, her lead needs to at least hint at those scared feelings. So she can only have herself eating lunch at the start of the story if her father disrupts the lunch to cajole her into the waves."

"That leads to my third point. You may need to invent some actions to show what you are feeling. If you want to show that you are afraid to go out in the thundering surf, then you can make your father plead with you to go out. You can have him grab your hand and say, 'Come on, scaredy-cat!' Every single bit of the story need not be exactly true."

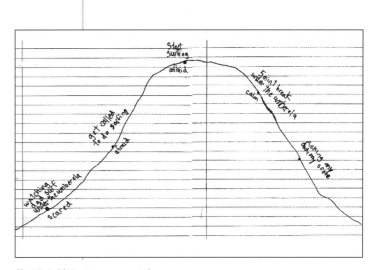

Fig XI-1 Rie's story mountain

SHARE

Mapping Internal and External Story Arcs

Show children a story arc drawn in "mountain" form. Show another story arc for the same story, this time for the character's internal changes.

"Oh my gosh writers, I've got to stop all of you because the work I am seeing right now is so drop-dead amazing I can't stand it! Holy-moly. I go from desk to desk, from writer to writer and I feel like I'm on some sort of magic carpet because one moment, I'm walking with Takeshi into a delicatessen, seeing the very same man behind the counter who was there five years ago, and the next minute I'm with Sirah, living through a hurricane. You are building up the important parts of your stories in such powerful ways that I feel as if I need to hold my hat or I'll be swept away by your words!"

"Listen to Sirah as she reads to you just the story mountain where trouble grows. Remember her story starts with her gathering shells when she was on the beach near her home in Senegal. She'd been taking swimming lessons at the hotel, when she saw a dark cloud coming. She worried it was a hurricane but no one believed her. Then—listen. See if you think she has what writers call rising action! *[Figs. XI-3, XI-4, and XI-5]*

Sirah's story is a spectacular illustration of rising action, but my worry is that children will feel as if they need high winds to flatten buildings and raise roofs in order to create the increasing tension, the drama, of an effective story. I might, therefore, decide to instead share a story such as the one Sophie wrote. She brought out story tension by showing that she had butterflies in her stomach as she rehearsed for the moment when she'd ask Claudia to be her best friend.

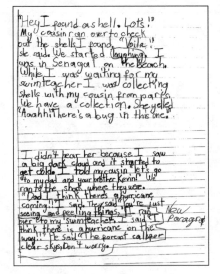

Fig. XI-3 Sirah, page 1

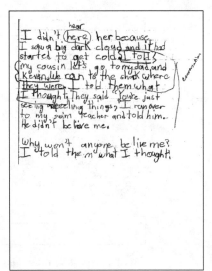

Fig. XI-4 Sirah, page 2

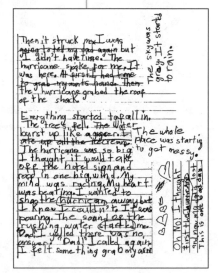

Fig. XI-5 Sirah, page 3

HOMEWORK *Planning Revision with Story Arcs*   Earlier today, when we looked at the story mountain of *Peter's Chair*, I noticed that Keats built gradually toward the heart of the story. He showed a few events that made the trouble seem worse, before it resolved, and that helps build Peter's feelings of jealousy, exclusion, and anger.

Right now, think back on the story mountain that you imagined for your own narratives, and compare it to the story mountain for *Peter's Chair*. What's missing from yours? What final revision could you do that would bolster the structure of your own narratives? Your time for making changes is almost up, so work fast and furiously.

TAILORING YOUR TEACHING

If your students are hesitant to revise, perhaps because they are not sure what parts of their stories could benefit from revision . . . you may want to teach them that a big part of revising is having a strong sense of audience as you reread your writing. Show your students how writers actually envision particular readers as they revise. Teach them to reread with this strong sense of audience in mind by asking questions like these:

- What parts will the reader enjoy? Where does the writing sound good and give a clear picture of what was happening?

- Are there any places where the reader might get confused? Where do I lose focus?

- Have I left out actions, details, and dialogue the reader needs in order to follow my story?

- Where might I include more thoughts and feelings to make my intentions clear to the reader?

Using your own narrative draft, demonstrate how you jot notes in the margins or underline or circle parts that help you revise for your audience. For active engagement, students could practice this careful reading and rereading with their own drafts, or with a whole-class narrative draft on chart paper (or projected on overhead transparency).

ASSESSMENT

You are nearing the conclusion of your second unit of study, and of this round of work with narrative writing. Soon you and your children will move to the brave new world of essay writing. Before you do that, take a bit of time to review the journey that you and your children have traveled thus far, and to reflect on their growth.

When you think about your children's growth, remember that the word *evaluation* includes in it the word *value*. Reflect for a moment on what you are really after as a teacher, on what the values are that led you into this profession in the first place. Then look at your children's growth (and your own) towards those things you choose to value.

Consider, for example, the progress your children as a group and individuals in specific have made toward composing writerly lives for themselves. It wasn't long ago when you were preoccupied with teaching your children strategies for generating ideas for writing, and with helping children realize their lives are worth writing about. Has your class as a whole come to understand that topics for writing are everywhere? Which children continue to need help generating topics for writing? Which choose small topics but struggle to bring out the significance in those topics? Which

choose gigantic topics and have trouble trusting that "the smaller you write, the bigger you write?"

In thinking about your children's writing lives, consider their initiative as writers, and their investment in their own writing. Which of your children seem to have caught the writing bug, coming to you with stories of writing while at home, on the playground, at a sleepover?

In a similar fashion, you will want to consider children's progress towards your other values. For example, I care very much that children develop increasing independence as the year progresses. I'll want to consider children as a group and as individuals, weighing the extent to which they've developed independence. How likely is it that I'll teach a minilesson on one strategy, and a writer decides to work, instead, towards a whole different goal? How often does a particular child initiate revision? Reach to make a reading-writing connection on his or her own? Then, too, which children can sustain work for long periods of time without needing me to carry them along?

Today's a good day for assessment—and not just the sort of assessment that comes from looking at written products.

IN THIS SESSION, YOU WILL TEACH CHILDREN THAT WRITERS DON'T JUST END STORIES, WE RESOLVE PROBLEMS, LEARN LESSONS, AND MAKE CHANGES TO END THEM EFFECTIVELY.

GETTING READY

- Your ongoing writing with several possible endings
- See CD-ROM for resources

ENDING STORIES

One of the extraordinary things about the teaching of writing is this: almost any lesson we could possibly teach is equally applicable to a six-year-old and a sixty-year-old. The challenges of writing well are enduring ones.

Whether writers are six or sixty, the challenge to end a story well is an important one. Abby Oxenhorn, a kindergarten teacher who co-authored the Small Moments *book in* Units of Study Primary Writing: A Yearlong Curriculum, *found she finally resorted to laying down the law for her youngsters. "You are not allowed to end your story 'and then we went to bed!'" she said. Five-year-old Emma responded by ending her story about a ride on the ferris wheel by saying, "and we lived happily ever after." Soon that ending, too, was on the off-limits list. Of course, Abby and I were secretly thrilled that even these littlest writers knew that stories need something special at the end.*

In this session, you'll help children consider ways to end their stories. You may not need to lay down the law as Abby did, saying, "No fair ending your story with 'then we went to bed' or 'we lived happily ever after'" . . . but you will need to decide how to nudge children to take on the challenge to write a good ending as an invitation to fashion a new insight, develop a new thought, resolve an issue, or learn a lesson. Because although you may not have a chance just now to teach this to your children, the truth is that when we consider ways to end our stories, we are also inventing ways to resolve our problems. This is life work, at its richest!

MINILESSON

Ending Stories

CONNECTION

Remind children that they've learned to consider personal narratives as stories.

"Writers, yesterday we thought about *Peter's Chair* and about our own stories, too, as stories which are structured like story mountains. Whenever you write a personal narrative, remember that you can get a lot of power by using story structure—the structure we saw in *Peter's Chair* and in *Shortcut*, too. A friend of mine describes the structure that one finds in most stories this way: 'Somebody wanted . . . but then . . . and so, finally . . .' This structure makes people read stories on the edge of our seats, wondering how the problem will turn out!"

Name your teaching point. Specifically, tell children you'll teach them how to write the resolution to their stories.

"Today, I want to help you wrestle with just one part of your story arc, and that's the part represented by the words 'and so, finally . . .'. Today, I want to remind you that writers don't just *end* our stories, we resolve our problems, we change our feelings, we learn our lesson."

TEACHING

Tell children that writers draft possible endings, and do so by asking ourselves a series of questions meant to elicit the story's real meaning.

"What I want to tell you today is that just as writers often take time to draft and revise different leads for our stories, so, too, we need to draft and revise alternate endings. But when we think about how we'll end our stories, we don't think so much about whether we'll end our stories with dialogue or with a small action or with a thought. Instead, we think this: What is my story really, really about? What was I wanting or struggling to achieve or reaching towards in my story? How does that story end? And what is it I want to say to my readers about this struggle, this journey?"

"For example, let me pull out the story I began writing earlier in this unit. I'm going to read it over now and see if I can ask myself those questions and begin considering possible endings. It will be harder to figure out an ending to my story about Eliza insulting me, because there wasn't a happy ending or a resolution in my life . . . not that I can remember,

COACHING

Crafting resolutions, whether in writing or in life, is no small task. Learning a lesson, realizing the nature of life, making a change, or finding meaning in the events around us is tough! To write well about it, we need to have experienced it with awareness. Celebrate your students doing the best they can at this!

In this minilesson, I am going to use my own writing to demonstrate how I go about considering and drafting alternate endings. I could instead have decided to use a mentor text. "Papa Who Wakes Up Tired in the Dark" would have been a good choice. If I wanted to use this text, I'd need to imagine what Sandra Cisneros probably did in order to arrive at her ending. I might, for example, tell children that she may have considered ending her story, "I ran off to tell my sister that our abuelito had died." Then I could say, "But she probably thought, 'Wait, this isn't really a story about the narrator and her sister,'" leading her back towards the ending she arrives at.

anyhow. I do have a somebody, namely me, who wants to be liked by the popular kids in my class. But then, things get in the way, there is trouble. They make fun of my clothes. They still don't accept me. And so, finally . . . Huh, you know what I am noticing? There isn't any resolution in my story. The story essentially goes like this."

> Lucy got a part in the play. She hoped that would help her gain acceptance by the in-group. It didn't help.

"And the story is left hanging, isn't it? To make the story better, I need to figure out how to bring the story to some resolution. But I need to remember what my story is really about—which is my longing to be popular—and I need to think, 'What action could I put at the end of my story that goes with the real message of my story?'"

Picking up a marker pen, I wrote on chart paper:

> That incident happened more than forty years ago, but I still remember it. And now I try to help children grow up understanding that popularity isn't the only thing that matters.

Rereading that ending, I said, "Sometimes I do that. I stand way back from the actual event and look at it from a distance." Then I picked up my marker pen and tried another ending:

> "I think your dress is fine. It's not antique at all," Emma said, shooting an angry look at Eliza.

> Then I said to Emma, "Do you want to meet after school and figure out our costumes?" Eliza made a big huffy noise and turned away.

"In a similar way, I hope that thinking of story structure might help you form a vision for how you can revise your endings."

ACTIVE ENGAGEMENT
Ask children to think of making the same sort of "mountains" for their own narratives.

"So, let's try it. Take out your drafts, and imagine the story mountain structure for your own narratives. Use that story mountain to help you revise your endings. Ask yourself, 'What is my story really, really about? What was I wanting or struggling to achieve or reaching towards in my story? How does that story end? And what is it I want to say to my readers about this struggle, this journey?' Now look through your draft for the journey. What are the emotions that you, the main character, are feeling in the beginning? Do they

If you wonder whether this might be too sophisticated for your children to really grasp, you are probably right . . . but children learn by the seriousness with which we address them, by the earnesty in our voices. They certainly will not master the content of today's teaching . . . but it's okay that some days suggest a horizon.

It may be that your students would benefit from another example. You can add other examples from your own writing to this minilesson or you could use an example of a student's writing.

build toward the heart of your story? Do your emotions start to change at the turning point? Do you reach a different emotional state by the end?"

"Okay. Turn and talk to your partner about how you can imagine revising your ending to show the heart of your story—to reinforce what your story is really, really about."

LINK

Assure writers that you understand the tendancy to slap any ol' ending onto a completed story, but rally children to invest themselves in drafting endings that convey what they want to say.

"Writers, if you are like me, then you probably are accustomed to ending your stories any ol' way. I know that I'm usually tired by the time I reach my ending, and so I just slap something down on the page. But when I revise, I look closely at my ending, because I know that it is what readers will read last. It's what they'll carry with them. Today, I hope you learned that our endings need to link back to the top of our story mountain. Our endings, like our beginnings, need to help convey what it is we most want to say. Today is your last day to work . . . so let's not waste a minute!"

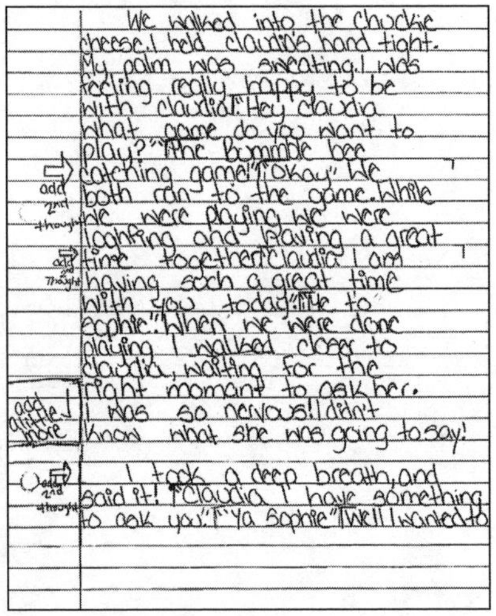

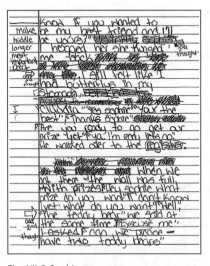

Fig. XII-1 Sophie

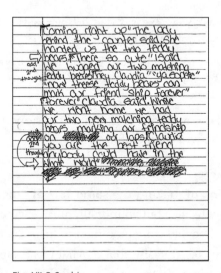

Fig. XII-2 Sophie

Fig. XII-3 Sophie

WRITING AND CONFERRING

Using Story Mountains to Improve Our Narratives

I watched Sophie make the finishing touches on her story mountain. She looked up and said, "I can't decide whether to start with driving to Chuck E. Cheese, or with when we're there, 'cause I want to have a beginning part before we, you know, say we'll be best friends."

"That's a wise question. I love that you aren't just thinking about what would make a catchy beginning—you are thinking about how the beginning will set readers up for the middle," I said.

"But Sophie, my hunch is that your story could work starting either place in the sequence of actions, but that the really crucial question to ask yourself is this: what is the internal story you want to tell at the beginning? You've graphed the events, the external story, but not the internal storyline. You've written the external events on your story mountain. Can you think (at least for the start of it) what your internal feelings are and graph those?"

Sophie pulled close to her draft and added the words, "feeling happy to be with Claudia," and "feeling even more happy" onto her story mountain.

"I love your sense that the feelings grow, that they become more intense! That's just what happens when a story picks up its pace," I said." But I'm wondering how the story will work if it goes like this: 'I was happy to be with Claudia. I was even happier, I was the happiest. Then we said yes, we were happy.' When we read novels during the reading workshop and we talk about characters, we often talk about characters struggling and overcoming struggles. Or at least we talk about a character going through some kind of change." Then I said, "Can I leave you for a bit to think more about your story? My question for you as a writer is this: Was it all just happy, happier, happiest? And even if it was all just one growing feeling of happy, could you maybe tweak the truth so there was some change of feelings, some development? Could you make a story mountain so it showed changing feelings, paralleling the changing sequence of events?"

Later that morning, Sophie told me she decided to start by telling that at first she'd been scared Claudia wouldn't want to commit to the friendship, and that just before she popped the question, Sophie's happiness had been tinged with anxiety. With all this in mind, she set out to begin another draft. [Fig. XII-4]

MID-WORKSHOP
TEACHING POINT

Focusing Story Endings   "Writers, can I have your eyes? Rie is stuck on an ending. Can you see if you could help her? Remember Rie's story? She's writing about how she let her dad convince her to go surfing this summer even though she didn't want to and she was so happy that she did, because she realized afterwards that she could do anything. The most important point in her story is when she's actually up on her board—surfin'."

"Let's say that Rie is going to end her story where she walks out of the water with her dad to have some lunch. In her first draft, the story ends with her thinking about the mac n' cheese that she's going to eat soon . . . but Rie realizes that feels like a whole new story. She knows it will throw her writing out of focus."

"Who can help Rie write an ending? So far she's written: 'My dad and I walked out of the water. "I've got mac 'n' cheese, guys!" my mom yelled from under the umbrella.' Can anyone help?" Soon Rie had a plethora of suggestions, and I sent all the children back to help themselves, as they helped Rie.

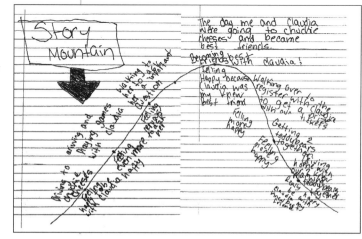

Fig XII-4 Sophie's story mountain

SHARE

Partners as Editors

Ask children to share drafts with their partners, who will function as editors.

"Writers, tomorrow we'll work on editing your drafts, and in the blink of an eye, your parents will be here and we'll read these stories out into the world. So during today's share, it's really important that you swap papers with each other, and spend some time functioning as editors."

"Exchange your writing with your partner. Readers, please read the draft as if you are a stranger to it. You won't be double checking for perfect spelling because this is still a rough draft. But double-check for sense, for clarity. If there are places where you are confused, leave a sticky note, explain the confusion, and perhaps suggest a way to clarify the draft. If you see small sections that could easily be spruced up, tell that to the writer too. Now is not the time to suggest a whole new draft . . . but it is the time to lend a hand."

HOMEWORK *Reading Aloud for Clarity* Writers, tomorrow we'll begin editing your pieces and recopying them into final drafts. Tonight, read what you've written for clarity, for sense. If your partner found places that were confusing, you'll want to clarify them.

Then read your draft again, this time reading it aloud. Pretend that you have a circle of people listening. Hear places where you stumble, where you can't read the draft really well. Those are probably places that merit revision and editing. So revise tonight to make sure the draft sings.

TAILORING YOUR TEACHING

If your children are revisiting this unit for a second time and you want to vary the minilesson . . . you might approach this work with endings as a lesson on focus. You could say, for example, "Writers, we've spent a good bit of time thinking about how and where to begin our stories so that we can keep them focused. We've thought a lot about what's important in our stories and we've angled our beginnings so that they are focused towards this point."

Then you could elaborate, "The way we choose to end our stories is equally important. We need to end on a point that will keep stories in focus. The end is the last point that our readers will remember. We want them to remember what's most important to us!" Shifting, you could say, "Today I'm going to teach you that writers decide where to end their stories by asking themselves: 'How does this ending connect back to what's most important in my story?' We think about the final action that will happen in our stories as well as the final thoughts that our characters have and we look to see if these fit with the most important point of our story. This helps to keep our stories focused!"

In the teaching component, you'd want to use your own story as an exemplar. Mary Chiarella said to her class, "I'm going to show you what I mean by using my story. You remember, it's the one that I'm not at all proud of. The one about 'the time I told Maria Guadagno that she couldn't hang out with my group of friends anymore.'" Then Mary reviewed the main points of her story:

- I'm sitting with my new friends happy to be part of a crowd
- Ann Margaret tells me that I need to go and tell Maria that she can't be part of our crowd anymore and I'm feeling bad about it, but relieved that I'm not the one being kicked out
- Then, I walk across the field with my new friends feeling fierce and powerful to be part of the group
- I tell Maria that she can't be part of our group anymore and I'm feeling powerful because I have all my friends around me—this is the most important scene, because it shows how I would have done anything, even something completely dreadful, to be popular!
- Then we walk away and I turn back and see Maria crying. For a moment, I'm feeling sad for her.
- But then my friends call me over to play dodge ball and I run away feeling happy that they want me to be part of their game.

Mary said, "The last action in my story is when I go off to play with my new friends. But, I need to make that fit with the most important part of my story—the part where I treat Maria horribly." Thinking aloud, she said, "So, let's see. I need to end with actions that somehow connect back to the most important part. I also need to ask myself: What's the last thought that my character, that's me, will have? It needs to have something to do with Maria. I'm going to hold the most important part in my mind while I envision this last point in my story. Maybe it can go something like . . . " and she tried one ending:

> "Hey Mare, come on and play kickball with us!" I
> continued to follow my friends to the playground. But
> something didn't feel right. What had I done? How could
> I treat someone so badly? I should go to her, tell her how
> sorry I am, ask her to come play with us.
>
> "Hey Mare, we can't start without you!" my new friends
> called again.

Pausing, Mary said to the kids, "Now I'm also trying to show that I would do anything to be popular, even treat another person badly." Looking back at the chart paper, she said, "I think I'll end with—'I'd been waiting to hear that for so long. When will I get this chance again? I wondered. I turned on my heels and ran to the playground.'"

Debriefing, Mary said, "Writers, did you see how I decided where to end by thinking about the most important point in my story and how the last actions and thoughts fit with what's most important? If I had ended by just running off and playing with my new friends thinking about how much I love dodge ball, it would feel like the ending belonged to another story! It would bring my writing out of focus!" You could, in a similar way, use your story to teach children that when we work on endings, we bring out our focus.

ASSESSMENT

You and your students are approaching the end of the second unit of study and your students' work with personal narrative writing. In this unit of study, your students learned more about working through the stages of the writing process, about crafting writing that engages and affects readers, and about using the conventions of written language with higher levels of accuracy and fluency than ever before. Although you and your students will soon move on to another genre, essay writing, the lessons learned in the personal narrative unit are foundational to all the writing work that follows—across the year and throughout your students' lives.

Because this second unit of study provides opportunities for students to deepen their understanding of personal narrative writing, one way you might assess your students' writing is by comparing the drafts of students' published personal narratives from the first unit of study with their drafts from this unit of study. As you compare the two pieces of writing, you'll be able to note changes in their understandings of the genre and of the writing process.

In this unit, your students have also learned two extremely important skills that will serve them well in writing workshop and beyond. First, you taught your students how to be resourceful learners who bring all they've learned before and apply it to new and more challenging situations. They know how to use class charts, and they understand that the strategy they learned during last Tuesday's minilesson might be applicable in their work tomorrow. Another important thing your students know is that they can use their favorite authors as mentors to guide them as writers. They've learned

how to read like writers, noticing the things authors do that make a piece of writing compelling. These two grand ideas, bringing everything you know to the table and mentoring yourself to an expert in order to become stronger at something, are life skills that your students will be able to apply to their writing, their art, their relationships, their athletics . . . and so on.

Another kind of assessment you might consider takes these two grand ideas into consideration. You could give your students copies of their published pieces from the launching unit and ask them to revise these pieces. You might think about setting up their work by saying something like, "Writers, you've had another few weeks to learn more and more about writing strong personal narratives, so I'm going to give you a chance to show what you know. I'm going to give each of you a copy of the personal narrative you published in the first unit of study. I want you to reread it with this question in mind, "Knowing what I know now about writing, how would I change this piece to make it stronger?" The students would write their revisions right on the copy of the piece of writing. This will give you invaluable insight into what your students have brought away after two units of study on personal narrative. If you have a student who only edits for punctuation, you may consider spending more time working on revision strategies with that child down the road. If you have a student who revises to elaborate more on the heart of the story, you know he's grown an understanding about the structure of personal narratives.

EDITING:

THE POWER OF COMMAS

We all resist doing what we're told. Even if the truth is sound advice, good counsel, and the right thing to do, it's still irksome. Following rules too often and too carefully chafes.

It's simply not enough, then, for our students to see editing as simply a matter of following the rules of English grammar at every turn. In this session, we aim to present editing as an adventure, potentially full of exploration, discovery, and invention.

As I discussed in A Guide to the Writing Workshop, *the book that opens this series of units, there are four methods for conveying a teaching point that we use over and over again in our minilessons: demonstration, telling and offering an example, guided practice, and inquiry. Of course, we also use combinations of these methods. The majority of minilessons we've laid out in this series so far have used the first three methods. In this session, we use the inquiry method of exploring a teaching point.*

To use the inquiry method, we set up a situation in which children can explore a problem. In this case, we'll set the stage for kids to ask and try to answer the question, "How can commas help us in our writing?" Of course, this same basic minilesson can be used to help children start exploring any punctuation mark or any grammatical structure or any aspect of language. Just as children studied powerful published texts to think about techniques for writing leads, so too can they study mentor texts to think about techniques for using commas—or any other meaning-making mark. Then, once they've determined some uses and effects of the comma, they can try doing the same thing in their own writing.

Two wonderful books that you can turn to for more about teaching conventional English grammar, including punctuation, are A Fresh Approach to Teaching Punctuation, *by Janet Angelillo, and* The Power of Grammar, *by Mary Ehrenworth and Vicki Vinton.*

IN THIS SESSION, YOU WILL SET STUDENTS UP TO LEARN ABOUT PUNCTUATION, COMMAS IN PARTICULAR, FROM WRITING THEY ADMIRE. THEN YOU WILL ASK STUDENTS TO TRY USING COMMAS IN THE WAY THEY'VE SEEN THEM USED, IN ORDER TO MAKE THEIR WRITING MORE EXACT.

GETTING READY

- Copies of three familiar texts containing commas (one set per partnership)
- A chart on the blackboard or chart paper with three columns, labeled "Examples of Commas in Mentor Text, What Does the Comma Do?, and Using the Comma in My Own Writing"
- Prepare for Share by reading celebration in the next session
- See CD-ROM for resources

MINILESSON

Editing: The Power of Commas

CONNECTION

Remind children they will be cycling through the writing process again and again, each time learning new strategies for creating better writing.

"So writers, many of you are now satisfied with the big shape of your stories. You've made sure the important parts are developed, you've crafted your stories so that they contain a story arc—a story mountain—and now you are ready to turn your attention to the detailed changes you could make, the final editing you could do to polish your story. Every time you go through the writing process, every time you make a piece of writing, you'll go through these steps, and you'll have an opportunity to learn new ways to make your writing stronger."

Name the teaching point. In this case, tell children that one way to learn how to use punctuation marks is to study their use in published works.

"What writers know is that every single punctuation mark that exists in the world— now what are some punctuation marks? Right, periods, commas, quotation marks, dashes— every single punctuation mark has hidden power. As a writer, you are allowed to use any punctuation mark you want, but if you want it to bring its hidden power to your own writing, and not just sit there doing nothing on the page, then you have to know that punctuation mark's secrets. And they all have secrets!"

"Whenever you want to learn a punctuation mark's secret, when you are ready to add its power to your writing, what you have to do is study that mark. You have to scrutinize it, examine it, study it with both your eyes and your whole mind to figure out what it does. Today, what I want to teach you is this: You can figure out any punctuation mark's secrets by studying it in great writing."

TEACHING

Explain that just as children learned to write strong leads from studying mentor texts, so too can they learn to use commas powerfully.

"A little while ago, you studied leads in published writing to see what the author did and then you tried those same things in your own leads, remember? Well, I told you then and I'll tell you now that you can use that same technique for learning just about anything about writing. We can do the same with punctuation marks! First, we'll study the

COACHING

One way you can tailor the level of difficulty of this minilesson is by compiling sets of examples of comma usage of varying levels of complexity. You might, for example, select examples of commas separating items in list. On the other hand, you might select a set of unconventional comma uses, or omissions, as in the opening passages of Toni Morrison's The Bluest Eye.

punctuation mark. What would the writing be like without it? What message does the mark send to readers about the words? Does the mark change the sound or speed of the words?"

"Then, after we've figured out some of the secrets of commas, some of what their power is to change and frame words, we'll put commas into our own writing, both things we've already written and things we've yet to write, and we'll try to bring that same power to our own writing."

When you use the inquiry method to teach, you'll find that you always have the option to angle your teaching toward improving children's methods of inquiry or toward ensuring that children understand and can use the information they've derived. In this minilesson, I try to do both, but I emphasize the process of learning from mentor authors over the content of how to use commas. You may tip the balance in the other direction for your students.

ACTIVE ENGAGEMENT
Set children up to explore the punctuation mark with their partners.

"Okay, to study a punctuation mark, you'll need to read aloud parts of a text with the mark in them, and think about it and talk about it. Remember, some of the questions you and your partner can think about are: What would the writing be like without it? What message does the mark send to readers about the words? Does the mark change the sound or speed of the words? Here are three books you all know well for you to examine. Now take some time to copy this chart into your notebook and then with your partner fill in the first two columns, which are similar to the ones we used when we studied leads. Leave the last column blank for now:"

Examples of Commas	What Does the Comma Do?	Using the Comma in My Writing

As children studied the texts, I listened in and began compiling a list on chart paper of comma uses that children had discovered. After a bit, I stopped them.

"So children, let me stop you now, even though I know you haven't finished. The comma has many different powers, doesn't it? You are finding some of them; I heard you.

Now take some time to use a comma in your own writing (you can look back for a place in your notebook)." I gave them a few moments and then gathered their eyes. "This is some of what you said, and how you filled in your chart."

Examples of Commas	What Does the Comma Do?	Using the Comma in My Writing
"For one minute, three minutes,maybe even a hundred minutes, we stared at one another" (Owl Moon)	"Commas make you think about what goes in between other things happening."	(James) I saw three, seven, a million mitts piled on the shelves.
"If you go owling, you have to be quiet, that's what Pa always says." (Owl Moon)	"Commas mean 'stop' but not all the way."	(Olivia) I hated her, but she was still my sister.
"A farm dog answered the train, and then a second dog joined in." (Owl Moon)	"Commas mean that's one part of it, but there's another part coming up."	(Hanna) There was pink frosting, rainbow candles, and a plastic ballerina with a silver skirt.

"Will you turn to your partner again and talk about how these discoveries about commas are the same or different from what the two of you discovered about commas?"

LINK
Remind children of what they learned, both specifically and generally.

After a short time to talk, I signaled for children to turn back to me. "Is there anything absolutely pressing that you mentioned with your partners? No? Okay, then, today in your writing work, and from now on when you are writing, do two things: You need to try to make commas use their full power, not just sit there; you also need to keep noticing commas in the writing all around you—in your own writing, in your friend's writing, in your favorite books, on your milk carton at lunch, everywhere! Keep learning about the power of commas so that you can put it all in your own writing when the time comes for you to edit. So remember, we learned today that you can always, as a writer, study the work of an author you admire, and learn ways to make your own writing better! Go ahead and get started."

When you teach children by giving them materials to explore and learn from instead of simply waiting for them to find what you've told them to find, you won't know exactly what they are going to come up with. This means that you have to trust their intelligence and powers of observation to lead them to conclusions about what they are studying. You will have to decide for yourself how far to let children lead the study. If they come up with a hypothesis about the functions of commas that you know from experience will prove to be false or undependable, you have a choice to make. Will you ask them to test their hypothesis until they discover for themselves that it won't hold? Will you point to an example that will show them that it won't hold so that they can test it quickly? Will you take the rule and treat it as correct until the class discovers the error? Each teaching path has its purposes, and you will have to choose the one you believe will be best for your class.

In this Active Engagement, I have highlighted discoveries from three sets of partners that will serve the class well although the "rules" are not yet honed to perfection. That will come. The other discoveries by other partnerships are still in the air, but by highlighting these three and offering children a chance to talk about how their observations relate to these, I hope our class knowledge will be consolidated. If any invented rules conflict with these statements, they are likely to come to light here, and we can decide as a class which to follow.

WRITING AND CONFERRING

Studying Commas by Studying Mentor Authors

Today's session has been about commas, but in the larger sense, it has been about teaching children that they can learn from authors if they study the writing they admire with a writing question in mind. If you decide to confer to support today's minilesson, you can either support children in learning from mentor texts, or you can help them use commas with greater skill. Of course, one path does not necessarily exclude the other, but it may help you confer with greater clarity if you decide which is your primary goal in each conference. Which lesson will give the child a leg up at this moment in his writing development?

You may want to confer with several examples of comma uses from mentor texts at your fingertips. You could lay out a sentence and together puzzle over the comma use it demonstrates. Working through the process of discovery with the child and then helping him apply that discovery to his own writing is the same as giving the child another active engagement part of the minilesson.

If the child has shown you that he knows how to learn from mentor texts and is now trying to apply that learning, to be more correct and pointed in his use of commas, then you will want to research his understanding of comma use by asking him questions and studying that use in his own writing. Alongside the child, you could ask two questions of his writing. (Limiting yourself to two questions makes it more likely the child will internalize and ask himself the same questions.)

- Is there a place (or another place) in this sentence where a comma's power would help?
- How is this comma affecting this sentence?

If a child seems able to put commas into her writing after it is written, the next step can be to help her compose her drafts with commas, inserting them as she goes. If she already does that, the next step can be to help her write her notebook entries with commas. The more automatic comma use is for the writer, in other words, the earlier in the writing process she is able to use commas, and the more fully she can utilize their power. This concept of helping children use language and grammar automatically, earlier and earlier in the writing process, so that they can reap its full power, is true for all conventions of our language— grammar, punctuation, vocabulary—all of our syntactic structures. We can create only what we can imagine, and learning the relationships and possibilities offered by grammar educates our imaginations.

> MID-WORKSHOP TEACHING POINT **_Discovering Uses for Commas_** "Can you all stop for a minute? I want to tell you what Raji learned just now. He was studying the commas around him and he noticed another power they have. He said, 'They go around words, to say "I'm gonna say more about it."' Do you know what he means? Here's the example he gave from his book."
>
> To make words seem off to the side
>
> Example: It was cherry-flavored, my favorite
>
> "That's another power for commas that you can use if you need to in your own writing. Remember, if you want to know ways to get power out of every mark on your page, you can study great writing. I'll add this observation to our list for powers of the comma! Okay, you may get back to your writing."

SHARE

Celebrating Comma Use

Ask children to share with their partners their most successful implementation of a comma from today's minilesson.

"Writers, please read though the writing work you did today, and show your partner the place where you think you used a comma very, very well. Talk with your partner about why you think that comma belongs there, and how it's using its full power! If you didn't use a comma today, you can talk with your partner about where you might be able to use one, or how you could rewrite so that you'd use one correctly. Partner 2s, you start, please."

Ask children to work with their partners to prepare for the upcoming celebration. Ask them to practice reading their writing until they are ready for the celebration. Rehearse as necessary.

"Now I know that tonight you are going to read over your pieces and make every last tiny little change you need to make them perfect. And tomorrow, we will have our celebration! Some very special people are going to be here tomorrow listening to your pieces. We need to practice a bit to make sure we read exactly the right parts aloud, and read them just the way we want to read them, with the voices and tones we want to use. So we're going to practice. Practice reading your writing aloud with your partner until you are ready. Then, we will rehearse the whole celebration, right here in our meeting area!"

This is a share that you can use after any minilesson: Simply ask those children who applied the strategy of the minilesson to their writing to share with their partner. Those who didn't have the writing context to try the strategy at this time can talk about their plans to try it.

Before you get to this portion of the share, you will need to read ahead to the next session's celebration. Once you can imagine your class having the celebration I describe in that next session, you'll be able to foresee exactly those moves your children need to rehearse. Of course, you might vary the celebration to suit your children's needs.

[HOMEWORK] *Preparing for the Celebration* Writers, can you believe our writing celebration is tomorrow? The first day we share our finished writing with the world is finally here! I'm so excited! I know exactly what you'll be doing tonight with your writing—you'll practice a bit more of the reading aloud that we practiced in our Share today, won't you? To make sure you can read that portion of your writing that you've chosen just how you want to read it, you'll need to read it aloud a few more times, making sure everything is perfect. You might want to call someone to read it to her, or you might want to read aloud in front of a mirror, so you can practice having an audience too. What a day tomorrow will be!

If you think your students would benefit from more instruction and inquiry about using commas in their writing . . . you could try the same work that this minilesson presents using a passage from one of the mentor texts.

Consider, for example, this passage from *Fly Away Home*, by Eve Bunting.

> Once a little brown bird got into the main terminal and couldn't get out. It fluttered in the high, hollow spaces. It threw itself at the glass, fell panting on the floor, flew to a tall, metal girder, and perched there, exhausted.
>
> "Don't stop trying," I told it silently. "Don't! You can get out!"
>
> For days the bird flew around, dragging one wing. And then it found the instant when a sliding door was open and slipped through. I watched it rise. Its wings seemed OK.
>
> "Fly, bird," I whispered. "Fly away home!"
>
> Though I couldn't hear it, I knew it was singing. Nothing made me as happy as that bird.

You might first consider some of the word choices that Eve Bunting used, such as fluttered, the high, hollow spaces, glass, fell panting on the floor, tall, metal girder, perched, exhausted. Then analyze her phrasing and punctuation, even for the first paragraph. What are some ways you and your students might punctuate it to change its meaning and its sound? Which way best matches the intention of this scene?

If you notice that most of your children are writing without much variation in sentence structure . . . use your own or a mentor author's narrative to study sentence length and the use of connectives and conjunctions. For example, in *Salt Hands*, Jane Chelsea Aragon intersperses short sentences alongside longer ones, like this:

> My heart beat quickly as I sat as still as the grass, as still as the night. I didn't want him to run away.
>
> There was not a sound as he came near me. He came very close.
>
> As I looked up at him, I could see into his eyes. They were gentle, and I knew he was not afraid.

Ask your students to focus on the use of the connectives *as* and *and*, the effects these words have on the sound of the story. Then have students go back to their own writing to see if they have varied sentence lengths and to find places where they could use a connective to combine two small sentences.

MECHANICS

In this session, you've invited children to study mentor texts to discern the special powers that commas have to change meaning in various, subtle ways. You might take this minilesson's structure and use it to guide you in creating more minilessons about grammatical structures.

1. Assess children's writing and goals as writers.

To do this, you will want to first study children's writing to determine which kinds of mechanics instruction would be most likely to improve the quality of their writing. Are they writing with sentences of various lengths and structures? Are they comfortable using colons, semi-colons, parentheses and ellipses? Are they marking dialogue? As you ask yourself each of these questions, you might also ask yourself if students are using these structures and marks for a purpose that matches with their writing intentions. If you see an enthusiasm for colons for example, but you don't see students using them effectively, or if you see no colons in students' writing at all, colon use might well be a prime candidate for a minilesson's teaching point.

2. Choose the teaching method, in this case, inquiry.

Once you have chosen the teaching point, as always, you have several methods of teaching from which to choose: demonstration, explain and give an example, guided practice, and inquiry. (Of course, a combination of these is also possible.) You may well select the inquiry method in the manner of this session's minilesson about studying commas.

3. Assemble the texts containing the grammatical structure or punctuation mark.

Your next step is to assemble the material your students will study; in this case, you'd find a bunch of passages or short texts that hold colons. You could also leave the search for the materials, the search for texts that demonstrate colon use to the students. This would take a bit longer than assembling them alone, but it would help children form a wide-awakeness to the texts in their lives. For now, they'd be looking everywhere for colons, then they'd be looking everywhere for semi-colons until eventually they would acquire the habit of noting punctuation use in texts!

You'll want to make sure that the text to study are passages that contain the punctuation mark, in this case the colon, and are long enough to allow readers to feel the impact of the colon on the whole text, not just the isolated sentence. Punctuation marks' powers come not only from their specific effect on the sentences in which they are found, but also from the contrasts they present with other sentences and punctuation marks.

4. Research examples to hypothesize about the particular effect on meaning the punctuation mark or grammatical structure has.

Once the excerpts and short texts are assembled, whether that phase takes two minutes or two days, the next step is to study the examples of colon use and to make some generalizations about them. We generally do this in groups or partnerships and then compare notes, trying to make a coherent, comprehensive class chart of our findings. We'd then post that in a public place in the classroom as a reference.

5. Take the newfound knowledge to writing and reading.

Oftentimes, the charts start as long lists of very specific uses of the punctuation mark. Over time, we will edit the list down as a class, deleting incorrect assumptions, combining the observations that overlap, and making new rules that seem to apply nearly all the time. In the end, the class might hone a chart about colon use to two simple facts: colons are used to introduce and colons are found after independent clauses. At that point, the guidelines belong on an editing checklist.

To keep the study of colon use alive and well, you will want to celebrate and make public and open for discussion students' uses of colons in their writing. At first, that colon use is bound to be a bit incorrect and a bit overdone—that's to be expected! With practice and feedback, though, children's use of the newfound structure or newfound mark will settle into its proper place among the other language skills and bits of information they are learning. As that knowledge settles, you will want to hold students accountable to using colons earlier and earlier in their writing process, eflecting that they've integrated knowledge of that mark's use.

READING ALOUD OUR WRITING:
A CEREMONY OF CELEBRATION

In this session, children will read their writing to an audience of parents and each other. People will write letters in response to the writing.

IN THIS SESSION, STUDENTS WILL HAVE AN OPPORTUNITY TO SHARE THEIR WRITING WITH AN AUDIENCE AS WRITERS STRIVE TO DO. CHILDREN WILL READ ALOUD THEIR PIECES, ADDING A CHORUS TO GIVE THE OCCASION APPROPRIATE CEREMONY.

GETTING READY

- Prepare four children to read their writing or an excerpt from their writing to the whole group
- Preassign each child to one of four groups
- Prepare rest of children to read their writing or an excerpt from their writing to their small group
- Set up room to allow for all present to hear first four children and then divide into four groups
- Children need to have memorized a few lines of a poem, one they've written or found, to chant as a chorus; write this on a chart
- Invite guests—parents, another class, teachers—as appropriate
- Prepare refreshments
- Baskets of note cards, enough for 3-4 per child, set up in prominent places around the room
- See CD-ROM for resources

I want to encourage you to take Author Celebrations very seriously. Just as authors create alternate worlds through stories, so we, too, create alternative worlds through our teaching. When we teach, we create a counter-culture within our classrooms. If we've done our job well, just as surely as Lucy and Edmund and Peter and Susan in The Lion, the Witch and the Wardrobe *knew they were in another world, so, too, the children who enter our rooms can sense that we have created a Different Kind of Place. We teach by helping children know they are indispensable to a community of writers. We teach by helping children live in a place where words are cherished, where people lean in to listen deeply to each other's words, and read words as if they have magical powers. We teach helping our children to regard each other as authors, and by relishing the different tones and textures, passions and purposes in their stories.*

Of course, an Author Celebration is an extraordinary form of parent education too. These celebrations teach parents about what's happening at school and about qualities of good writing. Author Celebrations also give parents another chance to learn about their own sons and daughter. I will not forget last June, at the final Author Celebration of the year, when a young boy who'd come into the year writing only the shallowest of sports stories read a piece aloud in which he'd written with a wide-open heart and with exquisite sensitivity and talent. His father came up to me and to his teacher afterwards, with eyes brimming, and said quietly, "I never thought he had it in him."

It is incredibly important to create a sense of occasion around these celebrations, and to give children the extraordinary gift of knowing that their stories are reaching readers.

CELEBRATION

Welcome children and their family members. Explain that when we read stories, authors bring us into other worlds. And today, the writers in the class will read aloud, bringing all of us into other worlds.

"Writers, many of us have read or watched C.S.Lewis' *The Lion, the Witch and the Wardrobe*. We've seen Lucy enter that wardrobe, pushing past the coats, and then suddenly something cold brushes against her arm. It is a tree branch, covered with snow. She looks down and sees she is standing in snow, and looks up and sees a lamppost, burning bright among the trees. From far away, she hears the distant jingle of sleigh bells, and soon the evil Snow Queen has approached.....and hold your hat! The plot thickens!"

"In that story, as in every story that has ever been told, listeners are invited into a world. It is not just Lucy, but all of us who push past the furry coats into the back of the wardrobe, and all of us feel something cold, and find we are standing in snow. That is the magic of story. C. S. Lewis' story takes us into a land of Narnia, where four children are called upon to save the world."

"In this classroom, stories can also take us to other worlds: to the terrifying world in Terrance's apartment that day when someone smelled smoke, to the day in this class, when Sofiya conquered her fears and actually touched the skin of a snake. Stories can take us to stand with Joey, on the edge of the dock, looking into the murky water of the pond."

Explain the plan for today's Author Celebration. In this case, explain that after a few children read to the group, everyone will disperse to a corner to share writing in small groups.

"Today, we'll hear a few stories together as a community. And then we'll disperse to our story corners (the young writers know their corners and grown-ups, you can tag along). It is here where we can have a more intimate audience."

Tell writers that after each reading, listeners will respond not by clapping but by reading a poem chorally.

"All weekend, I thought and thought, trying to decide how we could best respond to each other's writing. And I came to the decision that this Author's Celebration needs to be

You will notice that this celebration is a bit grander than the previous one; as you continue through the units, this trend continues. But your October celebration will only be a step or two fancier than the preceding one—if an Author Celebration is too splashy too soon, you'll find you are soon in over your head!

If we say to a child, "Your writing reminds me so much of Naomi Nye's writing," a decade later, that child will still remember those words, and for all these years, those words will have sustained her.

treated like the big occasions in our lives: like a graduation, a wedding, an anniversary. When we people gather for those big celebrations, we often share poetry. The poet, Erica Jong, once said, 'People think they can do without poetry. And they can. At least until they fall in love, lose a child or a parent or lose their way in the dark woods of life.'" (*In Their Own Voices: A Century of Recorded Poetry*)

"So, after a writer reads, let's join in a choral reading of a poem. We've chosen a favorite that we can all read together.

"To start us off, will our four readers come and sit in the chairs here at the front of the room. I will read the poem, and then one reader will read. The room will be absolutely silent after Claudia reads (no clapping please), and then Claudia's mother, would you start us in the poem and we'll all join in. Then Zora? And Zora's mom or dad . . . ? Let's get started."

"Let's disperse into our corners. Writers you lead the way, parents follow. Begin right away with one child reading and remember to honor that reading with the choral reading."

Disperse the readers, providing everyone with snacks. Ask parents and children to circulate, writing notes to the readers. They can respond to writing they already heard and also read more children's writing during this interlude.

When everyone had read, I brought out the snacks and said, "For the next little while, every child will keep his or her narrative on hand. Could you get some food, and then would all of you—parents and children— circulate among each other, reading each other's stories. You'll see that I've left little note-cards in baskets around the room. Please take the time to write responses to the writing you heard earlier today, or to what you read now. Write responses that let writers know the parts that resonated for you, the way the writing made you feel. I've got a mail box up here, and as you write a response, could you bring it up here and I'll distribute them later."

As parents circulated among the kids, I kept an eye on the responses, and from time to time made a point of steering a particular parent towards a child whose work wasn't being read. In this fashion (and by adding my own notes), I checked that every child was receiving several writing 'valentines.'

If you are looking for a poem to use, I especially recommend "Things," by Eloise Greenfield, which is cited in a minilesson in Literary Essays. "Things" ends with a child who "went to the kitchen/made me a poem." When using this as the refrain in a celebration of stories, we alter the word accordingly.

This ritual may seem unnecessary, but on the last day of Teachers College's summer institute, people read their writing aloud to each other and oftentimes, listeners write notes in response. For decades now, I have seen teachers gather up those notes as if they were the love letters we'd desperately wanted. People have told me that, years later, they still keep those notes. I know what they mean because sometimes I, too, receive a note from a reader. After putting oneself on the line, as writers always do, it is a rather extraordinary thing for someone to write back and say, 'Your words mattered.'

Compliment the class as a whole, but also use this as an occasion to seek individual children out, to look the child in the eyes, and to tell the child what you have noticed that he or she can do uniquely well. Does one child have the knack for writing with rhythm, for prose that makes the reader read aloud so, so well? Tell the child that you see this. Does one child know how to speak the truth in words that are straight and true, words that go directly from the child's heart to the reader's heart? Tell the child this. I will never forget the Author Celebration when my son's teacher introduced Miles by saying, "Our next writer, Miles Skorpen, has a gift for seeing the world. He lives and writes with his eyes wide, taking in the details that others might never see. He loves telescopes, microscopes, magnifying lenses…and he uses language as all these." Now, fifteen years later, Miles' hobby is photography—and writing. And I wonder whether that teacher, long, long ago, created a pathway for him by seeing more in my son than he saw in himself.

Here is Takeshi's final personal narrative: *[Figs. XIV-1 and XIV-2]*

Alert Alert Typhoon Alert!
By Takeshi

I sat down on the seat. I was shivering, and getting sick from all the shaking because of the typhoon. I tried to sit down and relax. I took the remote and started to watch TV, but it felt more and more worse every second.

The airplane was still shaking. Would the plane crash right before I ever even get to be at Japan? It felt that we were inside the typhoon, twirling over and over again. Would we make it through? I wondered over and over again. I checked how close we were to reach Japan. It was just about 300 meters to reach Japan, but my mom couldn't hold it anymore. She asked to person who helps the pilot "Could I lay on the floor?" They said "Yes." I noticed that me and my brother were alone. "What should we do?" I asked my brother. My brother said, "Sleep and forget that this ever happened." I tried to sleep, but it felt like every time I was about to sleep the airplane started to shake. Did someone put a curse on me, I wondered as I looked around to see if anybody was there. 300 meters passed. I was relieved.

I was waiting for them to land, but it didn't land. After a while I heard the pilot say "Sorry, we are going to land to a different airport." My brother and I both said at the same time, "WHAT!" What did I do to deserve this, I thought.

Landing to the other airport took about an extra three hours. When we landed we waited an extra two more hours for our mom to come. I told my brother, "That took at least eighteen hours." He said, "You're right." When our mom finally came we got on a bus to go to our grandma and grandpa's house. After we got off the bus I told my mom "We finally made it." My mom said, "Yeah, you're right." We finally made it I thought again as I started to walk down the street to our grandma and grandpa's house.

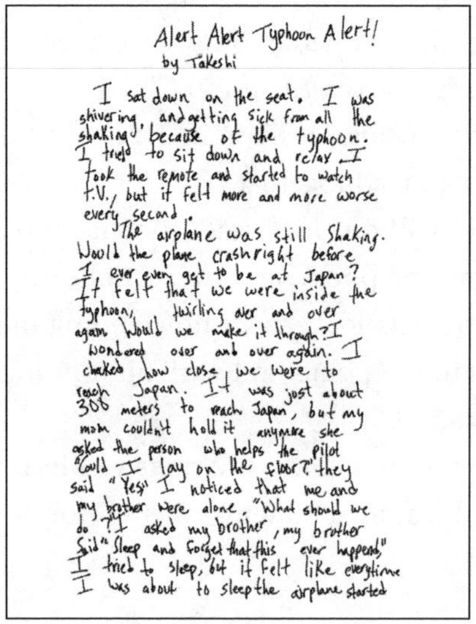
Alert Alert Typhoon Alert!
by Takeshi
I sat down on the seat. I was shivering, and getting sick from all the shaking because of the typhoon. I tried to sit down and relax. I took the remote and started to watch t.V., but it felt more and more worse every second.
The airplane was still Shaking. Would the plane crashright before I ever even get to be at Japan? It felt that we were inside the typhoon, twirling over and over again Would we make it through? I wondered over and over again. I checked how close we were to reach Japan. It was just about 300 meters to reach Japan, but my mom couldn't hold it anymore she asked the person who helps the pilot "Could I lay on the floor?" they said "Yes" I noticed that me and my brother were alone. "What should we do?" I asked my brother, my brother Said "Sleep and forget that this ever happend," I tried to sleep, but it felt like everytime I was about to sleep the airplane started

Fig. XIV-1 Takeshi's final draft

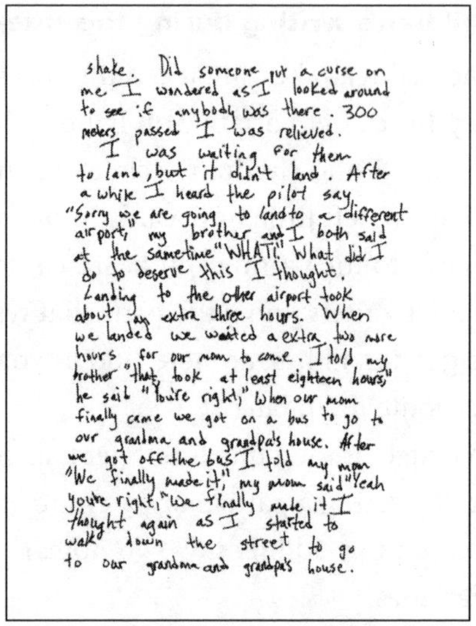
shake. Did someone put a curse on me I wondered as I looked around to see if anybody was there. 300 meters passed I was relieved.
I was waiting for them to land, but it didn't land. After a while I heard the pilot say "Sorry we are going to land to a different airport," my brother and I both said at the sametime "WHAT!" What did I do to deserve this I thought.
Landing to the other airport took about an extra three hours. When we landed we waited a extra two more hours for our mom to come. I told my brother "that took at least eighteen hours," he said "You're right," When our mom finally came we got on a bus to go to our grandma and grandpa's house. After we got off the bus I told my mom "We finally made it," my mom said "Yeah you're right," We finally made it I thought again as I started to walk down the street to go to our grandma and grandpa's house.

Fig. XIV-2 Takeshi's draft page 2

This is Sophie's final draft: [Fig. XIV-3]

Excitement in My Heart
By Sophie

We walked in the Chuck E. Cheese. I held Claudia's hand tight. My palm was sweating. I was feeling really happy to be with Claudia.

"Hey, Claudia! What game do you want to play"?

"The bumble bee catching game."

That's my favorite. How did she know? I thought to myself. We were made to be friends!

"Okay." We both ran to the game. While we were playing, we were laughing and having a great time together. I don't want anything at all to ruin this day for me, I thought to myself.

"Claudia, I am having such a great time with you today!"

"Me too, Sophie!"

When we were done playing, I walked close to Claudia, waiting for the right moment to ask her. I was so nervous! I didn't know what she was going to say!

Okay. Sophie. Time to ask, I said to myself. I took a deep breath and said it!

"Claudia, I have something to ask you,"

"Yah, Sophie?"

"Well I wanted to know if you wanted to be my best friend and I'll be yours."

"Um, well..." Oh, no, is this a no? I thought to myself.

"Of course, Sophie!" I was so relieved I hugged her. She hugged me back. I still felt like I had butterflies in my stomach. I didn't understand why she stumbled on her answer but I was still happy.

"Claudia."

"Yes, Sophie?"

"You're the best!"

"Thanks, Sophie."

"Are you ready to go get our prize yet?"

"Ya, I'm ready. Let's go, Sophie!" We walked over to the register. When we got there, the wall was full of prizes.

"Hey, Sophie. What prize do you want?"

"I don't know yet. What do you want?"

"Well... the teddy bear," we said at the same time.

"Excuse me. Can we please have two teddy bears?" I asked.

'Coming right up," the lady behind the counter said. She handed us the two teddy bears.

"They've so cute," I said. We hugged our two matching teddy bears.

"Hey, Claudia."

"Ya, Sophie?"

"Now the teddy bears can mark our friendship forever."

"Forever," Claudia said.

When we went home we had our two new matching teddy bears marking our friendship on our laps.

"Claudia, you are the best friend anybody could have in the whole world."

Right then and there I knew we were going to be best friends forever.

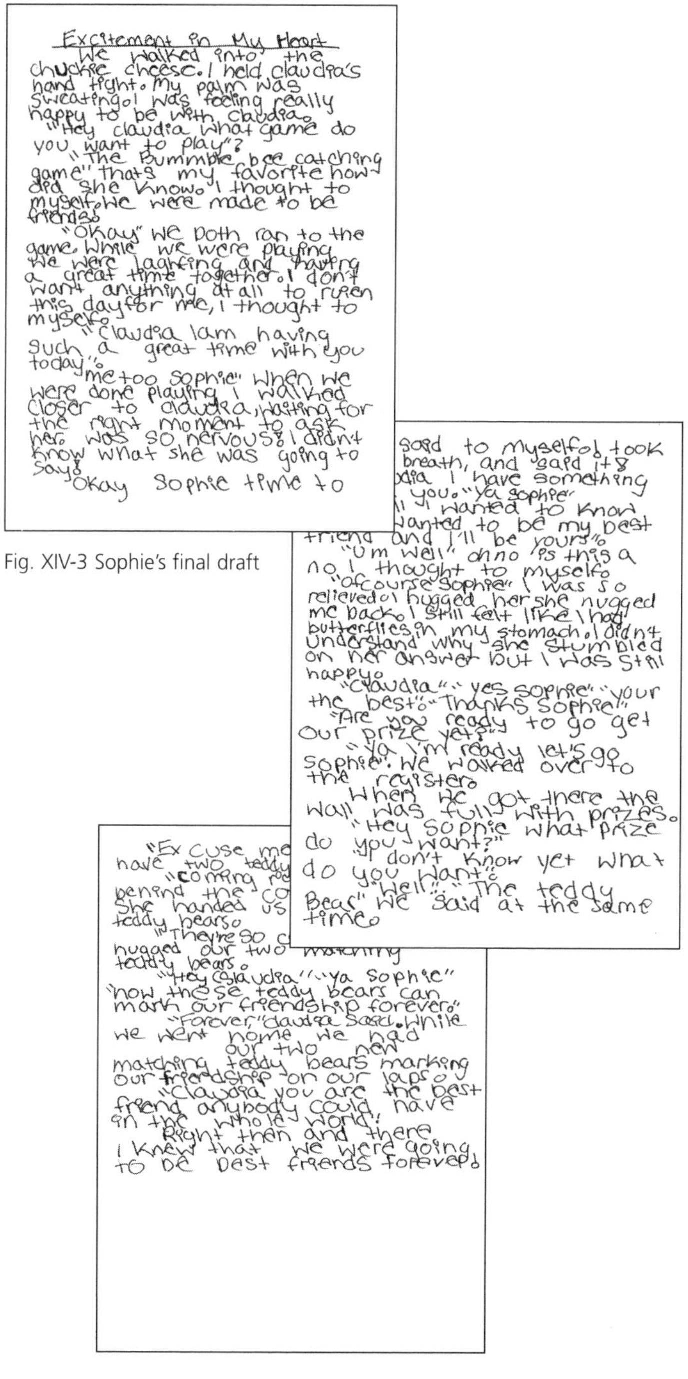

Fig. XIV-3 Sophie's final draft

Here is Miles's final draft: *[Fig. XIV-4]*

Gifts That Count
By Miles

On Father's Day morning, I woke up in an Adirondacks campsite. I watched the beautiful red morning sun and thought about what I had planned for my Father's Day present: a piece of land that had been snatched from my heart.

I tip-toed over to my dad's tent and unzipped it, waking Dad. I said, "Dad, let me show you your Father's Day present."

"OK," he answered.

I shepherded hi between the two rows of trees, out into the sunlight, onto my point. The point was covered with soft meadow grass, sprinkled with tiny wild flowers. I watched Dad take in this precious bit of the world and knew I had given him the right gift. Then from its hiding place I drew forth a fishing rod and laid it triumphantly in Dad's hands. His eyes sparkled and I said, "You deserve the honor of being first."

Dad nodded and cast. The line sailed through the air.

We watched in silence. We all waited: Dad, Evan, and I. Dad held his breath, his fingers tense.

Suddenly the line jerked. A huge dark shape struggled under the water. Dad slowly brought it to the surface. We gasped. A huge bass . . . Suddenly, Snap! The string broke under tension and the monster fled to the bottom of the lake. So we christened the point, "Bass Point". On that day, Evan and I gave the love of fishing to Dad.

Fig. XIV-3 Miles' final draft

Here is Jasmine's final draft: *[Fig. XIV-5]*

Practicing for My First Communion
By Jasmine

I sat in a church pew, with all of the kids who will make their communion with me. Talibia my teacher walked down to us and pointed to me and five other kids. Talibia said, "You six kids are going to be reading from the gospel."

Right then I thought I was going to make a mistake when I was going to read. Me and the five other readers went up to the altar in a line and started to read.

After we finished we went home. When I got upstairs my mom was mopping the floor. I said, "Mom guess what?" "What?" my mom said. "I'm going to read something in the gospel."

My mom was so happy she had a smile on her face. She went to the phone and she called the whole family. My aunt drove to our house. My grandma took the bus, My uncle walked there. My cousin took the train.

Soon the whole family was in the kitchen working together making me a cake. I felt like it was my birthday.

For two months we rehearsed. I had a hard time reading two paragraphs from the gospel. There were words I didn't even know. My mom said, "every day we will practice at home." We pretended the table in the living room was the altar and the living room was the church. My mom said to me, "Practice makes perfect."

On the day of my communion I was so nervous. The whole family came to watch me. When I went up to read I thought I was going to make a mistake. But I looked at the paper and read the words one by one. When I was finished reading I was proud of myself.

Me and my mom were so tired that night we fell asleep on the couch together hugging each other.

Fig. XIV-4 Jasmine's final draft

LUCY CALKINS ✦ CORY GILLETTE

BREATHING LIFE INTO ESSAYS

This book is dedicated to Kathleen Tolan.

FirstHand
An imprint of Heinemann
A division of Reed Elsevier Inc.
361 Hanover Street
Portsmouth, NH 03801-3912
www.heinemann.com

Offices and agents throughout the world

Copyright © 2006 by Lucy Calkins and Cory Gillette

All rights reserved. No part of this book may be reproduced in any form or by any electronic or mechanical means, including information storage and retrieval systems, without permission in writing from the publisher, except by a reviewer, who may quote brief passages in a review.

Photography: Peter Cunningham

Library of Congress Cataloging-in-Publication Data

CIP data on file with the Library of Congress.
ISBN 0-325-00866-3

Printed in the United States of America on acid-free paper
10   09   08   07   06   ML   1   2   3   4   5

Excerpt from *Envisioning Literature*. Copyright © 1995 Judith Langar. Published by Teachers College Press.

Excerpt from "I have got these" published in *Soda Jerk* by Cynthia Rylant. Published by Orchard Books/Scholastic Inc. Copyright © 1990 by Cynthia Rylant. Reprinted by permission.

Excerpt from *The Lightwell*. Copyright © 1992 Laurence Yep. Published by HarperCollins.

Excerpt from *Writing Down the Bones* by Natalie Goldberg; © 1986. Reprinted by arrangement with Shambhala Publications, Inc., www.shambhala.com.

Excerpt from *A Writer's Guide to Nonfiction*. © 2003 by Elizabeth Lyon. Used by permission of Perigee Books, an imprint of Penguin Group (USA) Inc.

Excerpt from *Destinations: An Integrated Approach to Writing Paragraphs and Essays*. © 2005 by Richard Bailey and Linda Denstaedts. Reprinted with permission of The McGraw-Hill Companies.

Excerpt from "I Have a Dream" reprinted by arrangement with the estate of Martin Luther King, Jr., c/o Writers House as agent for the proprieter, New York, NY. © 1963 Martin Luther King, Jr., copyright renewed © 1991 Coretta Scott King.

Excerpt from *Write to Learn* 7th edition by Donald M. Murray. © 2002. Reprinted with permission of Heinle, a division of Thomson Learning: www.thomsonrights.com. Fax 800-730-2215.

Excerpt from *A Writer Teaches Writing* Revised 2nd edition by Donald M. Murray. © 2004. Reprinted with permission of Heinle, a division of Thomson Learning: www.thomsonrights.com. Fax 800 730-2215.

ACKNOWLEDGEMENTS

This book is dedicated to Kathleen Tolan, the Deputy Director for Reading at the Teachers College Reading and Writing Project. Kathleen functions as the Project's master teacher. She adopts schools in deep need of support, and develops close partnerships with the leaders and teachers at those schools, helping these people to transform their schools into lab sites that demonstrate the best of what's possible in urban literacy education. In the process of doing this, Kathleen challenges, deepens and models the Project's best thinking about methods of staff development and methods of teaching of reading and writing. She especially helps the organization adjust our methods to provide the special support that children and teachers in high-need schools deserve. It was Kathleen's close work with the teachers at PS 28 in upper Manhattan and PS 18 in the Bronx, which allowed me to develop, pilot, revise, re-think the ideas in this book. I am grateful to Kathleen for her spectacular teaching, her generosity with her ideas, her extraordinary work ethic, and for her unremitting belief in all children as readers and writers.

I am grateful also to Cory Gillette for her input as contributing author of this book. As a Project staff developer, Cory helped me bring these ideas to the schools throughout New York City. Once we had developed the beginning plan for this unit and piloted it at PS 18, Cory brought it to a study group of teachers, and joined them in learning from their children's efforts to write essays. Cory channeled ideas to me and contributed to Tailoring your Teaching's, as well as to some other sections of the book. Readers will appreciate Cory's commitment to straight-talk and her grounding in the very real world of classroom teaching. I know I do.

This book has relied tremendously on input from Julia Mooney, a writer-in-residence at the Project. Julia helped me fill in gaps in the book—an italics here, some bolds there, a missing mid-workshop teaching point, a tailoring your teaching . . . She is an astute student of literature and of writing, and helped me also to see where my prose bogged down, where my meanings became obscure. Julia Mooney wrote many of the 'Tailoring Your Teachings' for this book, as did Grace Enriquez, a doctoral student at Teachers College and a staff developer and Kathy Collins, co-author of the CD.

This book has benefited also from input from a few teachers in particular. As I mentioned earlier, I developed many of the ideas for the book while learning from the teachers at PS 18 in the Bronx, especially Sue Ottomanelli, and I thank them for opening their classes to me. As I rewrote the book one final time, Mary Chiarella and I were in a study group together; Mary piloted the book's final iteration with her fourth graders, and I thank her for this. Medea McEvoy brought these ideas to life in her fifth grade classroom, and her children's work is important in this book. Laura Schiller and Linda Demstadt added their knowledge on this topic, and I thank them.

It is impossible to end one of these acknowledgements without giving an extra nod to the contribution made by Kate Montgomery, my editor. Kate is a passionate advocate for the richest possible literacy education, and the fact that she believed this book, on this subject, could be written without compromising all that she and I believe, gave me the courage to try.

BREATHING LIFE INTO ESSAYS

Welcome to Unit 3

WELCOME TO THE UNIT

BREATHING LIFE INTO ESSAYS

About the Unit

This unit of study is designed to help students with the difficult and exhilarating work of learning to write well within an expository structure. At the start of this unit, we point out to writers that they could conceivably write about a topic—say a visit to Grandma's—as a narrative, retelling it chronologically, or as a non-narrative, or essay, in which case they'd need to advance a certain idea ("Visits to Grandma's farm feel like time travel," for example). For some students, the fact that they can write about personal topics in a genre other than a personal narrative will be a new realization. The terms *narrative* and *non-narrative* or *essay* refer to structure and genre, not to content. In this unit, each child will write a personal essay in which she advances a theme of personal significance, arguing, for example, "It's hard being an only child," or claiming, "My dog is my best friend."

A Rationale for Teaching Traditional Essay Structure

Before describing the sequence of this unit, I want to share my rationale for teaching students to write fairly traditional thesis-driven essays. I know that some of the nation's writing process advocates will feel as if this unit of study doesn't follow the tenets of that school of thought. I can hear these critics say, "Why would we ask students to write thesis-driven essays when essayists approach essays as journeys of thought, as wandering ruminations? Why would we teach kids to do a kind of writing that *we* don't do and that writers in the world don't do?" I've posed similar challenges in my day, and so I respect these questions.

These are my reasons for teaching children to write traditional thesis-driven essays. First, although I *do* want children to write like writers all over the world write, this does not mean that everything I ask a child to try will be something that Wadsworth or E.B White or Thoreau would have done. If we simply show children rich, complex finished

publications and say, "Have at it! Write like this!" I agree that some children will progress with remarkable success through a series of approximations. But because I try to truly hold myself accountable to being sure that *all* children truly do make palpable, dramatic progress in their abilities to write well, I think it is important to admit that some children profit from more scaffolding and support. I believe that it is the teacher's job to reduce some of the complexity of finished essays, to highlight the most essential moves an essayist must make, and to show all children that these moves are within their reach. We ask beginning readers to point underneath words as they read, and we later tell them that actually, pointing under the words is not necessary or even forever helpful. In the same way, I think we can teach children to write explicit thesis statements and topic sentences and later tell them that actually, essayists often write towards main ideas that are implied but not explicitly stated, and that actually, essayists often advance one idea for a time, then turn a corner and advance a second idea, creating a text that takes readers on a journey of thought. Although this book teaches children to write within a traditional thesis-driven essay structure, the final book in the series shows children that actually, the structure they learn in this unit is not the only way to structure an essay and that they can in the end, use this structure in flexible ways.

Another reason for teaching children to write traditional thesis-driven essays is that in fact, I do think this is a structure that real-world writers rely upon often. Most of the chapters in my professional books pose an idea, and then elaborate upon that idea in parallel categories, each introduced by a sub-head. Many of my speeches, grant applications, persuasive letters and editorials all rely upon this fundamental structure. Then, too, I teach this to children because I think the unit can help teachers as well. Classroom charts and staff development workshops, too, often rely upon structure. Some educators have never been explicitly taught that in a strong presentation, information is organized within parallel categories—a classroom chart entitled, say, Revision Strategies should not include materials or qualities of good writing. Then, too, I think that when children learn that they can, if they so choose, think and write according to what I refer to as a "boxes and bullets" format, this helps them construct a mental model comprised of main ideas and support information as they read expository texts and as they take notes on books and class lectures. Finally, I know that in middle school and high school and on standardized tests, this is the form of writing that children will rely upon most. They will need to write in this form with speed and finesse while also carrying a heavy cargo of disciplinary ideas and information. In most secondary schools, students receive very little introduction in this challenging kind of writing before they are assigned to write an expository essay on books they can barely read. Secondary school teachers, often responsible for well over a hundred students, assign and grade this work but rarely teach it.

Lastly, the reason that I include a unit on the thesis-driven essay (and a subsequent one on writing literary essays) is that I believe children benefit from teachers working together to create a shared curriculum that spirals through the grades, and I am convinced that the only way to take staff development to scale is to adopt a curriculum that incorporates aspects of teaching writing that are priorities to a variety of educators who approach the teaching of writing from a variety of perspectives.

An Overview of the Unit

A teacher could choose to hurry kids through this unit, showing them how to whip up modest yet well-structured and competent little essays. However, I argue that there are many reasons to take one's time instead, harvesting all the learning opportunities found along the way. If we help children write rough drafts and do lots of revision with the goal of learning as much as possible about logical thought, this unit can have enormous payoffs. Then, after helping kids spend a month writing one essay, we can show students they also have the option of churning out a quick essay in a day—or even in fifteen minutes! This, of course, becomes a form of test-preparation.

As with any unit of study in a writing workshop, it is important to begin by helping children develop a repertoire of strategies for collecting entries—this time, entries that can grow into essays. It's important to teach students that their lives are provocative. Writers observe things in the world, recording what we see, and then we shift and write, "The thought I have about this is . . ." or "This makes me realize . . . ." When teaching children to grow essays out of everyday observations, we are really teaching them to free write, and the goal is to help them realize the value of writing

at length without a preconceived content, trusting that ideas will surface as they go along. Children also learn the power of imagining themselves in an evocative place and generating ideas in response to what they "see."

During this early phase of the unit, I also teach children that they can reread entries they collected earlier in the year during narrative units of study and use those entries as starting points, perhaps again beginning, "The idea I have about this is . . . " or "The thing that surprises me about this is . . . ." A child might jot down a topic, hobby, or issue that he cares about, then collect ideas about that big subject and write at length about one of those ideas. Children should become accustomed to selecting the strategy that works best for them on any given occasion. That is, the strategy the teacher introduces in a minilesson on a particular day is not that day's assignment but is one of many in a growing repertoire of strategies that writers draw on as needed.

Essayists need tools to push past their first thoughts, and many find it helps to use thought-prompts to prime the pump of their thoughts. "The surprising thing about this is . . . " an essayist might write in her notebook before spinning out a brand new thought in letters that scrawl down the page. That is, once a child records an idea, the child will benefit from having strategies to elaborate upon that idea. Using prompts such as, "to add on . . . ," "furthermore . . . ," "this makes me realize . . . ," "the surprising things about this is . . . ," "on the other hand . . . " allows children to extend their first ideas and to use writing as a way of thinking. They find that new ideas come out of their pencils, ideas they never even knew they had.

After collecting possible seed ideas, drawing on what they already know about rereading notebooks looking for seeds, young essayists select one idea. In the earlier, narrative units of study, they selected a seed *story*; this time they will select a seed *idea*. Writers then revise that idea until they've made a provocative, clear, compelling claim—or thesis statement.

Once students have selected and articulated an idea ("The Dominican Republic feels like home to me," for example), we teach them to elaborate on that idea by generating subordinate ideas ("The Dominican Republic feels like home because my childhood memories are there," and "The Dominican Republic feels like home because my extended family is there," and so forth). The easiest way to support most claims is to provide a few parallel *reasons* for that claim; writers can restate the claim each time and add the transitional word *because* followed by a reason. There are other ways to support a claim (or thesis), and a teacher may or may not teach those alternatives.

Usually children write support ideas through a series of parallel statements. The child elaborated on the thesis, "It's hard being an only child," by saying, "Your parents shower you with too much attention; your parents have too many of their hopes attached to you; and you can be very lonely."

During this planning stage, students can explore their subordinate ideas and decide what they really want to say. In the end, we hope each child has a main idea (a claim or a thesis) and several parallel supporting ideas. I sometimes refer to the main idea and supporting statements as "boxes and bullets." I have found it helps if children take their thesis and record it on the outside of one folder, then make internal folders for each of their bullets (these become topic sentences for their body paragraphs).

When it is time for children to collect materials to support their topic sentences, we teach them that they can first collect stories that illustrate their ideas. It is also important to teach children to angle these stories so they support the idea the writer wants to advance, and for them to learn to "unpack" those stories, just as a teacher debriefs after a demonstration in a minilesson.

Writers can also collect lists to support their topic sentences. We show children how statistics, observations, citations, quotations, and so forth can enrich their work. These bits are collected not in a writer's notebook but on separate bits of paper and filed in the appropriate topic-sentence folder.

It is important to help writers select *compelling* evidence from the material they collect in these folders, and to help them ensure that the evidence closely supports their claim. We teach them to look carefully from the claim to the evidence and back again because often the two aren't as congruent as they appear at first glance. Eventually we teach writers to sort through the materials in each folder, writing well-structured paragraphs.

Once writers have selected the most powerful and pertinent support material for each of their topic sentences, they staple or tape or recopy this information into a paragraph or two that supports each topic sentence, and in this manner construct the rough draft of an essay. Special lessons on transitions, introductions, and conclusions are important here.

The Plan for the Unit

The major "bends in the road" for this unit are as follows:

- Children learn a variety of strategies for living like essayists. They learn to observe the grit of their lives, pushing themselves to develop thoughts in response to what they see. They learn to travel in their minds' eyes to provocative spots, again shifting between describing and ruminating.

- Children learn to generate lists of people, places, issues or passions and then select any one item and generate ideas about it, selecting one idea to develop in a notebook entry. Similarly, children can reread old entries and grow thoughts in response to them.

- Children learn that one way to elaborate on their ideas is to use the conversational prompts they have used to grow ideas in book talks, phrases such as *in addition . . . another example is . . .* and *the important thing is . . .* to think and write more about their first ideas.

- Children reread their entries and select a seed idea. They tighten and revise this until it is a clear, straightforward thesis statement such as, "It is hard being an only child." Children freewrite to consider if this is really what they want to say.

- Children generate a plan for an essay by considering ways to elaborate on their thesis. Most children add the transitional phrase *because* to their thesis statement: "It is hard being an only child *because . . . ,*" and then generate several reasons. These support ideas (or topic sentences) are each written on the outside of a folder, and children begin collecting material within each folder. We teach them that writers collect stories angled to support the idea and also lists, observations, interviews and so forth, filing everything in the appropriate topic sentence folder. Children revise some of this material as it is collected.

- Children construct one portion of the essay at a time. For each topic sentence, children lay out all the possible support material, select the most convincing material, and design a sequence for it. Then they staple component sections together, rewriting this later to strengthen it with transitional phrases and key words from the thesis.

- Children learn to write introductory and concluding paragraphs.

COLLECTING IDEAS AS ESSAYISTS

When you launch children into a new kind of writing, *it is important to teach them the strategies writers use to generate this new kind of writing. In order to teach this first session, you need to think, "Where do ideas for essays come from?" "What is the life work of being an essayist?"*

This question is dear to my heart because the keynote speeches and book chapters I write are essays of a sort. So for me, the question is a very personal one. How do I grow the ideas that eventually become themes in my own nonfiction writing?

For me, the challenge is to develop ideas that feel new and significant. I find that the ideas that matter to my listeners, that take them on significant journeys of thought, are those that dawn on me as I pursue the process of writing. The best way I know to grow new ideas (rather than simply restating old, clichéd ideas) is to start with data. I start by putting myself into the hubbub of real life—for me, into classrooms—and I try to observe keenly. I record, and then I push myself to have a thought about what I observe.

My research on writing tells me this is how many writers grow ideas. Malcolm Cowley edited a series, Writers at Work, in which he interviewed dozens of our most famous writers. At the end of that experience, he was asked what he learned about the processes writers use. He answered that above all, he learned that every writer is idiosyncratic, that there is no one shared process all writers experience. But then he added that most writers begin with a precious particle—an observation, an image, a phrase, a bit of data—and grow their writing from that particle.

When I teach children to write essays, I first teach them to pay attention. I teach them to collect bits of life—and then I teach them to take a leap of faith, declaring those bits to be precious, and then surrounding them with the thoughts and responses that make them significant.

IN THIS SESSION, YOU WILL TEACH CHILDREN HOW TO COLLECT WRITING THAT CAN BE DEVELOPED INTO ESSAYS AND INVITE THEM TO BECOME ESSAY WRITERS. YOU'LL SHOW THEM THAT WRITERS OBSERVE THE WORLD WITH EXTRA CARE AND ALERTNESS AND THEN THINK HARD ABOUT THEIR OBSERVATIONS, RECORDING THEM IN WRITING.

GETTING READY

- Non-narrative notebook entries from students that demonstrate observations, questions, musings, ideas
- Sample essay entries from students, past and current, or from you and your colleagues
- Strategies for Generating Personal Narrative Writing chart (from Units 1 and 2)
- See CD-ROM for resources

MINILESSON

Collecting Ideas as Essayists

CONNECTION

Support your children's identities as writers by exclaiming over their stories and rallying them to write essays.

"Writers, when I heard your personal narratives yesterday, I felt as if I was right there with you, experiencing the small moments of your lives! Congratulations. I think you are ready to graduate."

"The entries you've collected and the stories you've developed are wonderful—but writers don't just write Small Moment stories. We write lots of things—songs and speeches and picture books and essays—and we write in lots of ways. Today we are going to begin writing in a radically different way. Instead of writing *stories*, we will write *essays*. Instead of writing about *small moments*, we will write about *big ideas*."

Name the teaching point. In this case, tell children that essayists observe and then grow ideas about those observations.

"Today, what I want to teach you is this: When writers want to grow ideas, we don't just gaze up in the sky and wait for thoughts to descend. Instead, as writers, we live especially wide-awake lives, giving thoughtful attention to the stuff, the grit, that others might walk past. We listen to the purr of our cat, we notice how each person in our family reads the newspaper differently, we study the stuff that accumulates in desk drawers, we overhear arguments—and we let all this sink into our minds and our notebooks. Then we write, 'This makes me think . . .' or 'I'm realizing that . . .'."

TEACHING

Tell children the story of a writer who first observed, then pushed herself to develop insights, and then recorded those insights.

"Let me tell you about two writers who've grown ideas by paying attention to the stuff, the grit, of their lives. You'll notice that they first notice, observe, and then they push themselves to think of a new idea, right there on the page."

"You all know Katherine Paterson, author of *Bridge to Terabithia*? Well, when she was asked, 'What is essential to writing?' she told of standing with her son, watching a cicada bug shed its skin. Katherine wrote about how she and David first saw a tiny slit in the bug's back. It grew larger, as if the bug had a waist-length zipper, and then they saw a hint of color as the

COACHING

You'll find your own ways to talk about the work your children did in the preceding unit and the effect their published writing had on you and others. Recall times in your own life when your hard work was recognized, and remember the way in which this recognition spurred you to work harder. Your children will work harder for you if you can help them feel that their efforts are recognized.

I like beginning a unit by conveying a sense that we're entering a new chapter in children's writing lives. And I do believe that essays are fundamentally different from stories.

Although essays are fundamentally different from narratives, the process of writing is remarkably similar. Whether we are writing stories or essays, we begin by living writerly lives, collecting bits that we grow into developed texts. The bits we collect are structured differently depending on whether we're planning a narrative or an expository text, but the topics can be the same. Keep in mind that people can follow an expository structure while writing about very personal topics— and that's the plan for this unit.

One of the challenges in this unit of study is that I don't have published examples of essays that resemble those I'll ask children to write. The essays by authors like E. B. White and John McPhee are far more complex than those that children can write, and children's bookshelves don't contain anthologies of essays written specifically for youngsters.

wings emerged, first crumpled ribbons and then stretched out. As they stood there, the cicada bug swung like an acrobat onto the twig and flew away, 'oblivious,' Katherine said,' to the wake of wonder that it left behind.'"

"I hope you realize that Katherine *could* have just let the cicada bug's wake of wonder wash over her; but because she was gathering entries for a speech, an essay, she not only put her observations onto the page, she also went one step further. She pushed herself to have a thought about watching that cicada bug with her son. She wrote this passage."

> As I let that wake of wonder wash over me, I realized this was the real gift I want to give my children because what good are straight teeth and trumpet lessons to a child who cannot see the grandeur that the world is charged with. (1981, p. 20)

"And that is a big idea! That cicada bug helped Katherine Paterson realize that it is more important to watch a bug shed its skin with your child than it is to rush your child to trumpet lessons and orthodontist appointments."

"Today I want to teach you that, like Katherine Paterson, you can notice the cicada bugs—the small stuff of your lives—and you can record what you see and hear. Then you can push yourself by saying, as Katherine did, 'This makes me think . . .' or 'I'm realizing that . . . .'"

"Writers do not usually sit and gaze at the sky to grow big ideas. Instead, we live wide-awake lives, noticing the small stuff and letting it provoke big thoughts."

Tell children another example of a writer who first observed, then pushed herself to develop insights, and then recorded those insights.

"Francesca also grew big ideas and did so by first paying close attention to the stuff of her life. Here's what she wrote." *[Fig. I-1]*

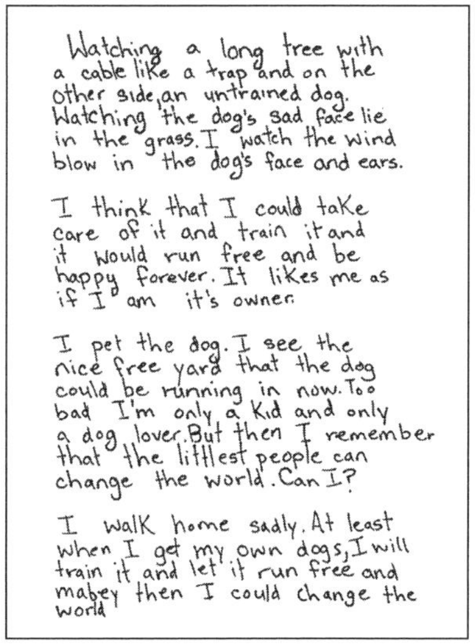

> Watching a long tree with a cable like a trap and on the other side, an untrained dog. Watching the dog's sad face lie in the grass. I watch the poor dog lie there. I watch the wind blow in the dog's face and ears.
>
> I think that I could take good care of it and train it and it would run free and be happy forever. It likes me as if I am its owner.
>
> I pet the dog. I see the nice free yard that the dog could be running in now. Too bad I'm only a kid and only a dog lover. But then I remember that the littlest people can change the world. Can I?

On the other hand, there are lots of places where authors use the muscles that we are asking children to use. I use some of those instances as illustrations.

The teaching component of this minilesson is structured in a manner that should be familiar to you. I name what I plan to teach, then teach by showing an example, and soon you'll see that I debrief. In this instance, I'm not teaching by demonstration but instead by referencing a finished product. Because the children need to know how to do likewise, I imagine and describe the process that the author probably used to create the product. It is this process that I am inviting children to adopt.

Of course, writers needn't literally say, "This makes me think . . . " but I find that when I give children the language to get themselves started, I'm giving them a powerful temporary scaffold.

Notice that I shift from describing a published writer to describing a child's writing. I'm hoping to show respect for all children by elevating one child in this way. In this instance, I'm not teaching by demonstration but instead by referencing a finished product.

Watching a long tree with a cable like a trap and on the other side, an untrained dog. Watching the dog's sad face lie in the grass. I watch the wind blow in the dog's face and ears.

I think that I could take care of it and train it and it would run free and be happy forever. It likes me as if I am it's owner.

I pet the dog. I see the nice free yard that the dog could be running in now. Too bad I'm only a Kid and only a dog lover. But then I remember that the littlest people can change the world. Can I?

I walk home sadly. At least when I get my own dogs, I will train it and let it run free and mabey then I could change the world

Figure I-1 Francesca's notebook entry

I walk home sadly. At least when I get my own dog, I will
train it and let it run free and maybe then I can
change the world.

"Francesca's entry begins with an observation of a dog, tied to a cable, and ends with
her yearning to make a difference in the world. She began by living a wide-awake life, letting
what she sees nudge her into big thoughts."

ACTIVE ENGAGEMENT
Ask children to try observing and making a thought about what they observe.

"Let's practice living like essay writers. Look around our classroom or look at
something you are wearing, or at some part of you—perhaps at the skin on the inside of
your elbow. Partner 1, write in the air (remember, this means to say the exact words you
could write) something you observe, and then say, 'This makes me realize . . .' or 'The
idea this gives me is . . .' And then push yourself to make a thought." The room erupted
into conversation.

**Debrief. In this case, describe what you heard partners say that could be models for the
observation-then-reflection entries you hope children will write.**

"I heard Jack noticing that our big clock has the numbers 1 through 12, and then Jack
said to Tyrone, 'I'm realizing that my watch doesn't have any numbers, only lines, and my
watch looks like a wheel with spokes.' Jack, you remind me of Katherine Paterson—the way
she looked at the bug's wings and saw they were like crumpled ribbons—you looked at a
watch and it reminded you of a wheel!"

"And Alexis said, 'I notice our library corner is surrounded by books and plants. It's the
heart of our classroom.' That could definitely become an essay or an editorial in our local or
school newspaper."

"Writers, your observations and ideas could make great essay entries, and today you'll
be able to start collecting entries in your writer's notebooks."

*Notice that the structure of this teaching component is actually
similar to the structure we're trying to hand over to children in
this unit of study! I name the idea I will advance, then
elaborate on the idea by discussing an example, and finally I
summarize the discussion, putting the content into a larger
context. That's the structure of a traditional school essay.*

*When I ask writers to say to a partner the exact words they might
write, I call this writing in the air. You'll ask your students to do
this often, so it's worth checking to be sure children actually do
say the words they could write instead of simply talking about
their ideas. If their conversations do not sound to you as if they
are dictating the words they could write, stop and clarify the
directions. Then hold children to following those directions even if
this requires you to stop them midstream yet again.*

*Obviously you will want to celebrate your own children. In this
instance, notice that I select tiny specifics that children said,
ones that seem original and provocative, and I help children
imagine how these could be developed. You may notice that I
rarely come straight out and compliment children's work,
preferring to treat the work with such respect that the child
feels complimented and yet does not become reliant on an
external judge's praise.*

LINK
Rename the teaching point. Send children off to begin work in ways they can use now and every day from now on.

"Writers, today we learned that when we want to write essays or other kinds of non-narrative writing (I'll talk later about what I mean by non-narratives), we live like writers—with extra alertness, paying attention to everything we can see, hear, read, notice—and then we can push ourselves to have ideas about what we see. We learned that entries in our writer's notebooks change based on the kind of thing we are writing. Today, you'll start a new section in your writer's notebook, and you'll begin collecting entries that might grow to become essays. You may want to begin your entries with phrases such as *I notice* and then, after you write your observations for a bit, skip a line and switch to phrases such as *I am starting to think that* or *I realize that.*"

I have lots of background information on essays (and non-narrative writing in general) that I could have included in this minilesson, but I decided to save some of this for later so that today I can immediately help children begin to live like essayists. I tend to avoid dumping a lot of information about a genre on kids in minilessons, because I want to teach "how to" do things, not "all about" things.

If you feel as if the content of any one minilesson is repetitive, you are right. During the final moments of a minilesson, I reiterate what I've taught, and I usually show that this new information can be integrated with students' prior knowledge. I also try to send children off with both clear directions (for those who are ready to try the strategy) and an awareness of their choices (for students who are not yet at this stage of the writing process).

Writing and Conferring

Guiding Small Groups

Although most of your students will by now be very capable of sustaining their work when they write personal narratives, you may find that many of them want encouragement and direction now that they are working in a radically new genre. If lots of kids need you at once, the easiest way to support them all is to go from table to table, providing children with table compliments. That is, draw a chair alongside one table full of kids. Watch what they are doing (or are almost doing) that matches your hopes for today. Then ask for the attention of everyone at the table. "Writers, can I have your attention for a moment?" Wait until you have their full attention. "I need you to know that . . . " You'll need to decide if you want to compliment all of them at once or to spotlight one child. If you decide on the latter, you could say something like, "Nadine is doing something really brilliant. She realized that the things right on her desk are interesting and started to write about her pencil, of all things! She wrote what she sees, using exact words. Listen." After sharing what a child has already done, you could decide what you hope the one child will do next and say something like, "I bet soon Nadine will write about what she thinks. She will probably write something like, 'Looking at this pencil, I realize . . . ' or 'Looking at this pencil makes me wonder . . . ' This is really smart work. She first took something she saw and *described* it, and in a moment I bet she will write what this gets her to think. I bet some of the rest of you will also do this sort of smart work."

Of course, there are lots of things you could notice and compliment. You could notice a child who finished writing one entry and then went on to the next one. The entries will

---

MID-WORKSHOP TEACHING POINT *Gathering Essay Entries* "Writers, can I have your eyes and your attention please?" I paused. "When we studied personal narrative writing, we had a chart of strategies for gathering entries that might become true stories, and with the help of those strategies we kept our notebooks brimming with true stories. What I hope you are realizing is that when we write essays (instead of stories), we tailor the strategies we use so that now we come up with material that will lead us toward this new kind of writing."

"Listen to what one of your classmates wrote when she observed the small stuff in her life and then let her observation get her thinking about big ideas. Chloe wrote:

> Sometimes when my three-year-old cousin is watching Tellytubbies or Barney, she dances or sways to the music. It's like she is hypnotized! If Barney jumps, so does she. If the Tellytubbies are dancing, she does it. It's fun to watch the things kids do when they're comfortable around you because they do silly things.

"Of course, essayists use lots of strategies to collect entries. You have all been observing, you've been paying attention to the small stuff of your lives—but as essayists, you can also gather entries by writing about big issues that matter to you, issues you think about all the time. Essayists sometimes put an issue on the page and then list a few ideas we have about the issue, taking one of those ideas to write about at length. Adam tried this strategy. He decided to write an entry about his illness, and the bigger issue of how children treat people who are different from themselves. He first wrote an entry about how he feels when people stare at his bald head. He circled that idea for a while.

continued on next page

---

probably be short, so writing several entries in a day will be essential. You could notice that a child wrote not just about his or her own life, but also about things that happen in the larger world.

You can predict ways in which your children will need direction. For example, you can be sure that some will continue to write narrative accounts. Plan to tell those children what you see and encourage them to shift from retelling to asking, "What did that make me think?" or "What new idea does this provoke?" This way you'll help children move between recording events and reflecting on ideas. When children write entries in which they first observe and then shift to think about what they've observed, some of them will jot *phrases* instead of writing *sentences*. If a child, for example, wrote just the word *Mom*, nudge that child to add whatever his thought might be: "My mom is one of my best friends." Then, too, some children will write lots and lots of questions. Help these children to entertain those questions.

Above all, your challenge will be to help children see more, think more, feel more. They're apt to want to write one sentence about what they see and one sentence about what they think! Teach them to really look, to take in the world, to be moved by what they see. And then help them understand that they can grow ideas as they write. You'll return to the work of helping writers develop ideas in a later session.

continued from previous page

Then he started a second entry, which I want to read to you. You'll notice that this time he stands back a bit from his own disease and addresses his entry to children who ignore those who are different. Adam generated this entry by recording an issue, then listing the detailed ideas he has about it." *[Fig. I-2]*

> People shouldn't judge people by what they look like. When kids are discriminated by what they look like they are treated very cruelly. It is really mean to do this because you don't really know this person. For example, let's say someone wears a shirt with a stain on it and everybody doesn't want to be your friend because they think your dirty. The person who did not want to talk to you could have been your future best friend. When I was in kindergarten in this school a lot of people avoided me because I am bald. It took me a long time to make friends. It is harder to go into a new school if you have something different like I do. Before people judge people by what they look like they need to tell themselves, "What would I feel like if I was that kid? With everybody staring at me and nobody talking to you." Then you look at you and your friends, with everybody admiring you and including you. Then you go over there to the "different kid" and include him and talk to him.

"So remember, you can use the strategies you already know for generating writing—you can start with the small observations and let them lead you to big ideas *or* you can start with big ideas and let them lead you to the details. Okay, go ahead and get back to writing."

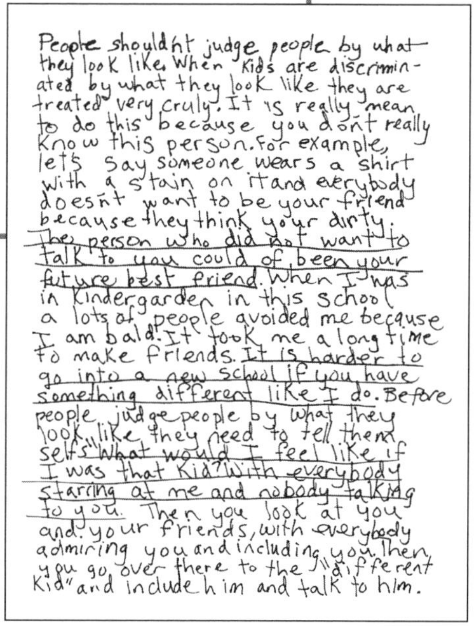
People shouldn't judge people by what they look like. When kids are discriminated by what they look like they are treated very cruly. It is really mean to do this because you don't really know this person. For example, let's say someone wears a shirt with a stain on it and everybody doesn't want to be your friend because they think your dirty. The person who did not want to talk to you could of been your future best friend. When I was in kindergarden in this school a lots of people avoided me because I am bald. It took me a long time to make friends. It is harder to go into a new school if you have something different like I do. Before people judge people by what they look like they need to tell themselfs "What would I feel like if I was that kid? With everybody starring at me and nobody talking to you. Then you look at you and your friends, with everybody admiring you and including you. Then you go over there to the "different kid" and include him and talk to him.

Fig. I-2 Adam's notebook entry

SHARE

Collecting Essay Entries

Rally children to reread and reflect on their essay entries, talking with partners about how these differ from narrative entries.

"The *strategies* for generating entries will be a bit different when we write essays, and the *entries* themselves will also be a bit different. Would you and your partner look back at the entries you collected during our first two units, and then look at the entries you collected today? How are your entries changing?" The children talked with their partners for a few minutes, and I listened in with my clipboard in hand, writing snippets of overheard conversation.

Convene the class, share a few observations.

"Writers, can I have your eyes? I am blown away by your insights. Let me talk about what you said."

"It's true that essay writers are a bit less apt to gather *stories* in our notebooks, and more apt to write observations and ideas."

"It's also true that essay writers sometimes collect tiny entries; some of these entries may not even fill half a page."

"And it's true that essay writers often write with information and facts, as well as with ideas and wonderings. And it is true that essay writers address big topics that exist in the world. The fact is that essayists write with information, with facts, and they also grow ideas about big topics!"

"Today we talked about the differences between personal narrative and essay entries. Another day, we could think and talk about ways in which good writing is the same whether we are writing essays or writing narratives—because the truth is, it's both different and the same."

Because this is the first session in a unit, you should anticipate that it will resemble (and refer back to) Sessions I and II of the previous two units. In this session, as in the first sessions of every other unit, you will again need to teach writers strategies for generating entries. It's important that your students realize this new teaching stands on the shoulders of (and contrasts with) earlier work on generating narrative entries. It is also important for you to see that one unit of study expands upon another.

When we ask children to talk in pairs, then listen in on their conversations and report back some of what we hear, we can word our reports in ways that provide the class with clear guidelines. To report back on a conversation overheard during the turn-and-talk, the teacher is essentially using the same muscles we use when we notice what a child has done and turn that observation into a mid-workshop teaching point.

Those of you who worried that the first two units produced overly constrained and channeled writing and put undue emphasis on focused, chronological entries will perhaps feel more comfortable now as this unit reclaims the value of entries in which the writer observes, questions, wanders, meanders, backtracks, sidetracks.

HOMEWORK ***Collecting and Thinking About Small Surprises*** Writers, a while ago I spent time with Karla Kuskin, the author of *The Philharmonic Gets Dressed*. I asked her, "What do you do when you sit down to write a picture book?" and she answered, "I don't *sit down* to write." She went on to say, "My writing starts with catching glimpses or snatches." To demonstrate, she told me that on her way to our meeting, she'd seen a big, beautiful truck bearing the name Manhasset Imperial Sewage—and she thought, "I could make something out of that." For her, writing often begins with catching a glimpse of something which lends an idea to dawn on her. She went on to explain that her book about the philharmonic orchestra getting dressed actually began when she was at a child's birthday party. The child was given a doll and the first thing she did was lift up the doll's skirt to check out the underpants. That one observation sparked the idea for a whole book about the layers of clothing the orchestra members don each day.

Tonight, would you try to live an especially wide-awake life? Pay attention to anything surprising. Record what strikes you: a phrase, an observation, a little kid checking out her doll's underpants. You won't write long entries, but I am hoping you will, as Don Murray says, see more, hear more, think more, notice more because you are writing. Describing his notebook as "a great garage sale of life," Don Murray says, "I compost my life, piling up . . . lines overheard in restaurants, scenes caught in the corner of my eyes, pages not yet understood." Do that sort of collecting, that sort of paying attention, tonight. Your writing should fill up at least a page, which may mean you collect several entries. Be sure you observe—*and* have a thought about what you see. Notice that Takuma takes the time to really see the fake butterflies, before letting them spark memories and ideas.

I'm enclosing Takuma's writing to give you an idea for the sort of writing—and living—you might do tonight. *[Figs. I-3 and I-4]*

I could my see the fake
butterflies hanging down
the string. The butterflie
shines when a light
comes to it as if
it was a mirror
Slowly shaking by the
wind. Almost as if
They were real live
butterflies. They are all
lined up on one string,
all wobbling almost
falling. Purple, orange, green, light
blue, dark blue, all
lined up on one
single string. It reminds
me of my family
because there lined up
in one house. One wing
reminds me of my dad
all fall. The others wing
would remind me about
my mom. And the body
would remind me of
my sister. flap flap flap

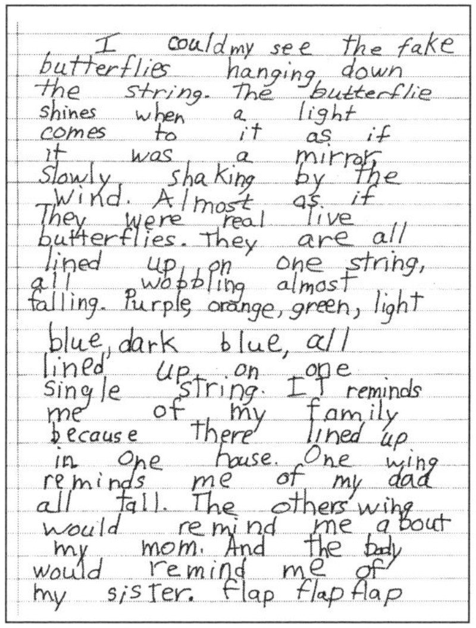

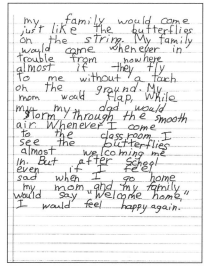

Fig. I-3 Takuma observes and has a thought

my family would come
just like the butterflies
on the string. My family
would come whenever in
trouble from nowhere
almost if they fly
to me without a tuch
on the ground. My
mom would flap, while
my my dad would
storm through the smooth
air. Whenever I come
to the class room I
see the butterflies
almost welcoming me
in. But after school
even if I feel
sad when I go home
my mom and my family
would say "Welcome home,"
I would feel happy again.

Fig. I-4 Takuma's notebook entry page 2

If your children don't seem to have grasped the concepts of this minilesson ... don't be surprised. They have just spent two units writing texts that follow an entirely different structure. You have now asked them to shift gears and start moving toward a new way to look at the world as writers. You might decide to move forward even if many of your children are still writing narratives because Session II will provide more strategies for generating non-narrative entries.

If your children have worked through this unit in previous years, and you'd like to vary the minilesson ... keep in mind that in *Living Between the Lines*, my theme is that writing well is not only desk work but also life work. You'll find the book brims with examples of children who've collected entries that reflect this wide-awakeness and examples, too, of writers who celebrate the importance of wide-awake attentiveness. You can take any of these bits and develop minilessons around them. Take Faulkner's quote, for example, "I have finally found that my little postage stamp of native soil is worth writing about, that I will never live long enough to exhaust it." (Cowley 1958, p.141) Or take this observation referenced in *Living Between the Lines* but made by journalist Roy Peter Clark:

> The ordinary person walks down the street and sees a bar, a wig shop, a grocery store, a pharmacy and a shoe store. The journalist sees dozens of story ideas behind the facades of those businesses. He sees people and issues and asks himself, "Who drinks in that bar at 9:00 in the morning?" "What kind of market is there for those huge rainbow-colored wigs in the shop window?"(Calkins 1991, p.226)

If you set a quote such as one of these alongside an excerpt from a familiar read-aloud book (an excerpt in which the author relays a bit of life and then reflects on it), and then add a bit of practical how-to advice for how writers can gather and combine and record in similar ways, you'll soon have a brand new minilesson.

If your students' observations tend to be characterized by statements of the obvious or by generalities rather than specifics ... you may want to do a lesson where you help your students slow down and observe not only the object or subject of observation, but also the world around it. For example, you might begin a lesson by saying something like, "Over the weekend my friend Diane visited me. She's a painter, and she designs textiles, you know, the designs on wallpaper, sheets, and dishes, and I noticed that she makes observations like an artist. For example, we went out for a walk after the rain, and she told me she loves the shades of green that come alive after the rain. I had never noticed that before, but once she said that, I couldn't help but see all the different greens around us. That got me thinking about observations, how people observe differently. Like my neighbor, who is nurse. She notices the littlest things about how people look. She once mentioned someone's fingernails! She said that this guy must smoke a lot because his fingernails have the 'smoker's curve' to them. Who knew! I never noticed fingernails before. Anyway, today I want to teach you one thing I think I know about how writers observe . . . when we observe, we try to take in all that we see and then have some sort of thought about it. I tried it. For example, last night, I looked at my bed before I got into it. I jotted down my observations and I wrote this: "My pillow, full and fluffy at the head of my bed, seems to be luring me there. It's as if it is smiling its warmest smile at me, inviting me to lie down." You see, I didn't just describe my pillow—'My pillow is fluffy and it's got a yellow pillow case on it. It's at the head of my bed.' No, I added some thought to the observation."

For the active engagement, you could say, "So right now, let's try it. Let's take our notebooks over to the window. Look outside at something that catches your eye. Then as you're writing, have a thought about what you're observing. We'll share with our partners in three minutes."

COLLABORATING WITH COLLEAGUES

When you and your colleagues meet to learn together about this new work, it is important to begin with the understanding that this unit will be very different from the previous two. In fact, many linguists, philosophers, and literacy scholars have suggested that there are two fundamentally different ways of thinking and of organizing discourse. People use different terms to distinguish between the two different modes: literary and nonliterary (Langar), aesthetic or efferent (Rosenblatt), narrative or paradigmatic (Bruner), spectator or participant (Britton), subjective or objective experience (Langar), and narrative or expository (secondary school teachers).

The important thing to realize is that people can choose how we will relate to, learn from, and think, talk, or write about an experience. Judith Langar, in *Envisioning Literature,* writes about this:

> Say, for example, you are taking piano lessons and want to play well. You might study sight reading and musical theory . . . tape record your own playing in order to critique it. (1995, New York: Teachers College Press, p. 6)

That is, you could study music in a nonliterary, objective fashion in which you strive to gain control of the topics and subtopics, applying ideas to the material. But, Langar points out, there is another option. You could learn about music in a more literary (subjective, participant) way, immersing yourself in a few musicians and their playing:

> You could let their music invade your senses and seduce you by their sounds, as their best playing can do. By internalizing their music, you respond ... you put yourself in their places, you can even begin to sense the feel of their (your) fingers on the keys and the sounds in their (your) ears—the same, but different, heard through the filter of your own experience. (p. 6)

To explore the fundamental differences between narrative and expository ways of thinking, you and your colleagues may want to select a shared experience—say, a recent faculty meeting—and try thinking about it in a narrative and then in an expository way, noticing and discussing how those two views feel fundamentally different. You will find you use different language in general, and in particular for transitions (when you are in the narrative mode, you'll rely on chronology to tell the story, whereas in the expository mode, when you analyze what happened, you'll rely on categorization and comparison). You may also notice that the point from which you, as narrator, experience the event seems different. When I'm in a narrative mode I find myself starting at the beginning and walking chronologically through time. When I'm in the expository mode, on the other hand, I feel as if I'm flying overhead, looking at the event from a more removed perspective.

It is crucial for you to become comfortable with the subject you are teaching. In this instance, you and your colleagues may want to recall and discuss television shows that are organized in an expository way versus those that are narrative. News reporters on one channel, for example, may teach the main ideas about say, a big weather-related event, whereas on another channel, the same content will be conveyed through a first-hand narrative, as when one person relives his or her experience of the event. The two "texts" will use different organizational frames, different voices, different perspectives, different vocabulary, and different transitional phrases.

GROWING ESSAY IDEAS IN NOTEBOOKS

I once asked a group of teachers to tell me the one time when professional development most mattered to them. I wondered if they'd choose summer institutes, or cite a particularly brimful course of study. To my surprise, each teacher selected a moment when a literacy staff developer or an administrator came into that teacher's classroom, observed the teaching, and then met with the teacher to say, "This is what I notice about your teaching." For us, as practitioners, few things are more precious than the gift of recognition. By recognition, I do not mean prizes and awards. I mean that it is enormously helpful if someone we respect watches us as we work and then demonstrates that she understands our struggles and notices our successes.

Children, too, want the gift of recognition. If we can, in a minilesson, let children know that we understand the predicaments they encounter and the struggles they face, then they'll trust our teaching. If children first feel seen and heard, they'll draw close when we say, "I have one tip I want to share."

You'll find that although my purpose in this session is to address a predicament I see many students facing (their entries are short), I use the session to repeat everything I said in the first session. I cycle right back to the idea that writers who want to compose personal essays live wide-awake lives, but this time, I address problems I notice many children have encountered with that charge. One problem is that their entries are short. A related problem is that many children seem to suffer a crisis of confidence. They write about the loose buttons in their pocket or the homeless man who sells poems in the park, but then they look at these entries with wavering doubt, thinking, "So what?" I help children realize it is okay to have those doubts, and encourage them to take the risk of investing themselves in their little observations, using those observations to prompt big thinking about the details of their lives. If my theories about these children apply to your children as well, borrow them. If not, try to put into words whatever it is you see your children doing.

Later I teach children another strategy for generating essay entries. Under the auspices of teaching this second strategy, I share writing that resembles the writing I hope children will do.

IN THIS SESSION, YOU WILL AGAIN TEACH CHILDREN WAYS WRITERS COLLECT WRITING FOR ESSAYS. YOU'LL TEACH THEM ESPECIALLY TO BE MORE THOUGHTFUL ABOUT WHAT THEY SEE, WRITING AT GREATER LENGTH.

GETTING READY

- Non-narrative notebook entries from students that demonstrate observations, questions, musings, ideas
- T-chart written on chart paper, headed "What I Notice" on one side and "What It Makes Me Think" on the other, filled in with an example
- Strategies for Generating Essay Entries chart
- Writing samples by published authors (e.g. *The Lightwell*, by Laurence Yep; *Alone*, by Jean Little), you, or students that demonstrate observation and reflection
- Writing sample with a subject (a person, place, or object), ideas related to that subject, and one developed idea
- See CD-ROM for resources

MINILESSON

Growing Essay Ideas in Notebooks

CONNECTION

Support your children's identities as essay writers by exclaiming over the entries they collected at home. Then name the problem your teaching point will address. In this case, children seem to feel their entries are insignificant.

"So, many of you have been living like writers collecting bits and pieces of your lives. Listen to a portion of John's writing:" *[Fig. II-1]*

> Imagine you have been looking at the floor and it just comes into your mind tan, red, tan, red. Then all of a sudden it goes red, red, tan. Sometimes I feel like ripping out the tiles and replacing them. When I look at the tiles I start to wonder why is this tile here? Or is this a mistake. HOW CAN THE SMALLEST THING STAND OUT SO MUCH?
>
> "Why does it really matter?" my mom said.
>
> "It just caught my eye," I said. "It's that, why are the tiles different? Instead of tan red tan red it went tan, tan, tan. Will it leave my mind? Why do I care?"
>
> "I think that titles shouldn't matter", my dad said.
>
> As the thought stayed in my mind, I started to change my mind, but something wouldn't let it go away.
>
> The titles—red tan tan red—it doesn't sound like a pattern!

"When I see what you all collected last night, I am reminded of Donald Hall, who says that as a writer, he goes through life collecting 'string too short to be saved.' And I'm reminded of Malcolm Cowley, who says that every writer always begins writing with 'a precious particle.' You all have lots of little strings, lots of precious particles, in your notebooks. You are becoming essay writers!"

"But some of you told me this morning that you aren't sure whether your entries are precious. You told me, 'I just wrote down what I saw.' You aren't sure whether your particles are significant."

COACHING

It is incredibly important to teach children to value the details of their lives. So many children come to school saying, "I don't have anything to write about" and "My life is boring." Just as photographers go through life seeing potential pictures (whether or not they have a camera with them), writers go through life seeing significance in the ordinary fabric of our lives. I can think of few goals more important than that of helping kindle children's interest in the stuff of their lives. Although this is a unit on personal essay writing, some of the instruction addresses goals that don't fit into the confines of a single unit.

> I can hear my mind saying don't
> look at them DON'T!
> I feel like taking a bat and instead
> of hitting balls I would smash
> the tiles.
> surprising
> imagine you have been looking at the floor
> and it just comes into your mind tan,
> red, tan, red Then all of a sudden it
> goes red, red, tan.
> Sometimes I feel like ripping out the
> tiles and replacing them.
> When I look at the tiles I start to
> wonder why is this tile here? or is
> is a mistake
> HOW CAN THE SMALLEST THING
> STAND OUT SO MUCH?
>
> Why does it really matter My mom
> said I just caught
> my eye I said It's that why are the
> tiles diffrent? Instead
> of tan red, tan red it went tan tan Will it
> leave my mind? Why do I care?
>
> I think that tiles shouldn't matter
> My Dad said.
> As the thought stayed in my mind
> I started to change my opinion but something
> wouldn't let it go. with
> the tiles go tan tan red it
> doesn't sound like a pattern!

Fig. II-1 John's notebook entry

Name the teaching point. In this case, tell children that essay writers develop systems that help us not only to observe but also to grow ideas.

"Today I want to teach you that when we collect the stuff of our lives in our notebooks, that stuff doesn't come with ideas attached. We just have a bunch of buttons from our inside-out pockets, or the image of a child checking out her doll's underpants, or a yellow truck with the name Manhasset Imperial Sewage. In a way, we don't start with much."

"But if we are going to make something out of the stuff of our lives, we need not only to collect it, we also need to grow ideas around it. To be sure that our entries begin with our observations and end with our thoughts, we can do one of two things: We can push ourselves to shift between observing and saying, 'and the thought I have about this is . . . ' Or, we can write in two columns, one for what we see, hear, and notice and the other for what we think."

TEACHING
Name and then demonstrate a system you use to push yourself to develop thoughts from your observations.

"Writers, I am like many of you. I often begin my entries by writing what I see or hear in the world around me. But I know that to get a good seed idea for an essay, it is important for me to shift from seeing (or hearing or noticing or remembering) to thinking. I have two ways to push myself to go from noticing to thinking."

"One thing I do a lot is this, after I put the stuff of my life onto the page, I turn a corner in my writing. I do this by almost forcing myself to write, 'and the idea I have about that is . . . ' I don't always use those exact words. I might instead write, 'This makes me realize . . . ' or 'This reminds me of . . . ' Either way, though, I give myself an assignment to switch gears so that I stop recording what is actually there in life and begin instead to record my thoughts about what I noticed."

"I'm going to try this right now. I'll begin and describe something I notice. After I describe for a few sentences, Emily, will you coach me by saying, 'And the idea I have about this is . . . ' Then I'll try to have an idea (at that very second, right in front of you)."

Shifting into the role of writer, I said, "I'll start," and I took a big breath. "I'm looking at our fish tank. I see that there is some fine, hairy green stuff growing on the pebbles on the tank floor. It's practically invisible, but it waves a bit as fish swim by, and when it does that, you can see it."

When I got married, the writing researcher Don Graves (who'd been my minister when I was a child) conducted the service. He began by describing John and me to the congregation, and said of me, "Lucy, who knows how to live off the land. Who turns sticks and stones into toys for little children." At the time I was taken aback by the description, but over the years I have come to think Graves was paying a beautiful compliment. As a writer, teacher, thinker, person, I so hope that I live off the land. I want to be the kind of person who takes the everyday stuff of life and declares it to be significant. And I believe that significance is made, not found.

The teaching component of our minilessons is designed to teach youngsters 'how to' do something. For this reason, this section of most minilessons will be structured chronologically. We retell the step-by-step procedures we follow to solve a problem or to use a strategy. We do so in a sequenced, chronological way. We sometimes come out and literally say, "First I . . . then I . . . finally I . . ." The Teaching component of a minilesson is usually a procedural (or how-to) text.

Notice that I observe for a while, lingering to see specifics. When children are asked to take over my role and continue observing, on the other hand, they tend to observe one thing, then move to another, then to something else.

It's not an accident that I observe something that all of us have passed by. I'm hoping to show that our everyday world is waiting to be rediscovered. I am writing in the air, not writing on chart paper. I do this to save time.

When I nodded to remind her to do so, Emily interrupted me and said, "And the idea I have about this is . . . "

"Thank you, Emily. And the idea I have about this is . . . I'm wondering if this green stuff is good for the fish. I know we sprinkle fish food into the tank, but I wonder if fish also eat the stuff that grows in their tanks. How do they know what to eat and what not to eat? It's interesting how animals have ways to take care of themselves."

Debrief, naming what you did in such a way that it is transferable to another day and another topic. Spotlight a child who already used the strategy you just demonstrated in his writing.

Stepping out of the role of writer and back into my role as a teacher, I said, "Did you see how I first observed and then used the phrase, 'And the idea I have about this is . . . ' to help me switch gears and have a brand new thought, sparked by what I'd just observed?"

"Sophie started her entry by recording what she noticed. If she had just stopped there, her entry wouldn't be much. But the great thing is that she pushed her writing to take a turn, and asked herself, 'What does this make me think? What does this remind me of?'"[Figs. II-2 and II-3]

> When I look at the wind chime, I think about my great-grandmother Evelyne. And how my wind chime has an angel on it, and angels are in heaven. My great grandmother is in heaven. I think about how strong she was, before she passed away. I think about how she held my hand and she kissed it, and how I thought that she would be alright. When I look at my wind chime, I think about how much time we spent together. I realize how hard it must have been to be her and how she went through all that pain. When I empathize with my great grandmother, I think about how she laid in bed, and how she could not get up, it'll be to painful. When I empathize with my great grandmother, I think about how nervous she must have been for her to be passing away. I think about how she might want to live longer. That is how I empathize with my great grandmother. When I really think about it, I think about all the time we could of spent together, but instead I was doing something else. It's like I didn't even care. When I really think about this deeply, I think we had the time but I wasted it, but then I just close my eyes, and talk. We still have the time. All the time we want together, me and her.

I try to coach Emily to say this with rising intonation so that her phrase serves to prime my pump, to help me generate ideas. If you think the partner's intervention puts words into writer's mouths, you are right. But I find it also puts words into their minds, and the words become tools for thought.

Notice that in both Sessions I and II, I incorporate two examples into the teaching component of the minilesson—one adult example and one child example. You may decide your children need briefer minilessons, in which case you will use only one example. Of course, it is best if you use examples from your own writing and your own students, but if need be, borrow these examples.

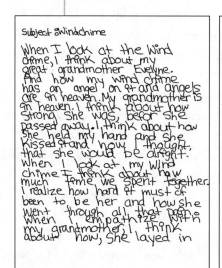

Fig. II-2 Sophie's notebook entry   Fig. II-3 Sophie's entry page 2

"Do you see how Sophie uses what she sees to spark a thought, and then she keeps herself going? She looks at the chime, then writes what it makes her think, and then looks back at the chime, and thinks more on the same topic. When her new thought subsides, she pushes herself to keep going, 'When I empathize . . .' she writes. 'When I really think about it . . .' and 'When I really think about this deeply.' Study the ways Sophie pushes herself to think more and more deeply. This entry ends up as the source for an essay on her great grandmother."

Name and then demonstrate a second strategy you use to nudge yourself to shift from observing to growing ideas.

"Another system I sometimes use is that I gather observations and information on the left-hand side of my notebook and then use the right side as a place to think about what I've written. The chart could look something like this."

What I Notice	What It Makes Me Think
Two girls sit together, showing off their lunches to each other.	I used to show off my lunch. Why are kids so competitive? It is not fair to kids whose parents have less money. Or to kids with moms who won't buy sugary foods.

"Now you have two ways to push yourself."

Debrief, reminding writers that they can use either of these systems.

"So writers, yesterday you were collectors, gathering bits and pieces in your writer's notebooks. Today I showed you two ways in which we can give those bits the attention they deserve. It is important not only to collect entries in our notebooks, but also to collect and to think. Writers have strategies for doing both. Sometimes after we put the stuff of our lives onto the page, we then write a phrase like, 'The idea I have about this is . . .' to spark a thought. And sometimes, we use the white space on the left-hand side of our notebooks as an invitation to mull, to grow ideas."

It is very important to notice that minilessons are not a vehicle for doling out a daily assignment. Instead of saying, "Today, I'd like you to each make a two column chart. On the top of the left column, write . . . ," I say, "Another system I sometimes use is . . ." The goal of a minilesson is to add to students' repertoire of skills and strategies, not to dole out that day's assignment.

You may, of course decide to teach this second strategy for generating entries in a separate minilesson, or you may not teach it at all. One thing to notice is that this strategy involves filling in a chart rather than writing full pages. Decide if you want to encourage listing and charting as ways to generate ideas in a notebook, or if you prefer that children write more expansively, as we saw Sophie doing on the preceding page.

It's probably accurate to say that essayists are collectors. We collect, sort, categorize. Children, of course, are collectors as well. They may collect stickers, sea glass, Barbie dolls, comic books, or bean bag animals, but collecting almost seems to be part of childhood. So build on this! This is an idea that could be made into a Big Idea. It could be the subject of a chapter, a minilesson, a keynote speech. You'll want to become accustomed to noticing big ideas—and mentally starring them. That is, as someone who is teaching essayists, cultivate in yourself the ability to recognize passing comments that could be developed into big theories, because this is part of the mind-set that essayists and nonfiction writers bring to our lives.

ACTIVE ENGAGEMENT
Set children up to try thinking within a mental structure in which they shift between observing for a while, then reflecting for a while.

"So let's try this together. Partner 1, look around the room (or open your desk, your backpack, and look in it). Let your eye fall on something, anything, that you can describe. Thumbs up if you have something. Okay, now you are going to write in the air, saying aloud the exact words you'd write if you had a pen and were writing one paragraph of observations. Partner 1, describe what you see to your partner. Start by saying, 'I see . . .' and keep observing that one thing until I guide you to do something different."

After a minute, I interjected, saying loudly, with rising intonation, "and the thought I have about this is . . ." I tucked in the quick instructions: "Repeat what I just said and keep going." I said this in such a way that the children shifted gears, incorporated the phrase 'and the thought I have about this is . . .', and continued talking.

Again set children up to observe and then to articulate a thought about that observation, but this time teach them to observe a distant place that they must conjure up in their minds' eyes.

"Let's try it again. Partner 2, this time you are going to see something in your memory. Pretend you are at home. Put yourself in your kitchen, your living room, on the front stoop, or the branch of your climbing tree. Watch something—your cat as she purrs on the couch, the pile of books beside your bed. Thumbs up when you've got something in mind that you are observing. Okay, you'll start by just describing exactly what you see in your mind's eye. Say, 'I see . . .' (and keep going)."

After a minute, I again interjected, saying loudly and in a way that channeled the speakers' remarks "and (repeat after me) the idea I have about this is . . .". The children carried on, talking now about the ideas they generated from their observations.

"Writers, you've come up with great ideas!"

You'll recall that yesterday you also asked children to write essay entries in the air. You'll probably find that it is much easier for children to write narratives in the air (to storytell) than to write essays or expository texts in the air. You may want to encourage children to watch television shows that are designed to teach, like the shows about exotic animals or news features, and listen to the language on these shows. It's important that they become comfortable talking in this genre. Terms such as, 'on the other hand,' 'consequently,' 'three factors account for,' or 'notice that' all need to become part of your children's speaking, reading, and eventually writing repertoire. To encourage children to listen to teaching shows on television and acquire some of the lingo, you could videotape such a show and view a bit of it together. If you can, go a step further and encourage children to role-play being professors or news reporters, teaching each other about any subject at all. You could even take the time that once was set aside for children to storytell and now designate it as a time for informal speeches designed to teach or to persuade.

Notice that the strategies I teach become progressively more sophisticated. First children observed what was before their eyes, then they traveled in their minds to another place, and observed what they conjured up. When I design units of study, I plan to move children up a gradient of difficulty as we proceed. It is always important to teach so that children can be successful, but we want them to be successful at progressively more demanding work.

The idea of observing in one's mind is an empowering and important twist to this minilesson. If your children can't take it in today, save it for another day, but don't miss the chance to teach children that we can sit at our desks and mentally conjure up distant places and events, writing what we see and what we think about what we see. This technique opens worlds.

Link

Remind children that today and always, when they want to collect entries that can become essays, they can draw on their growing tool chest of strategies.

"I hope that from this day on and for the rest of your lives, you always remember that we not only collect the stuff of our lives, but we also grow ideas about what we collect. In your notebook, you can use any of these strategies to generate more entries. I put them together in a chart—draw on them as needed."

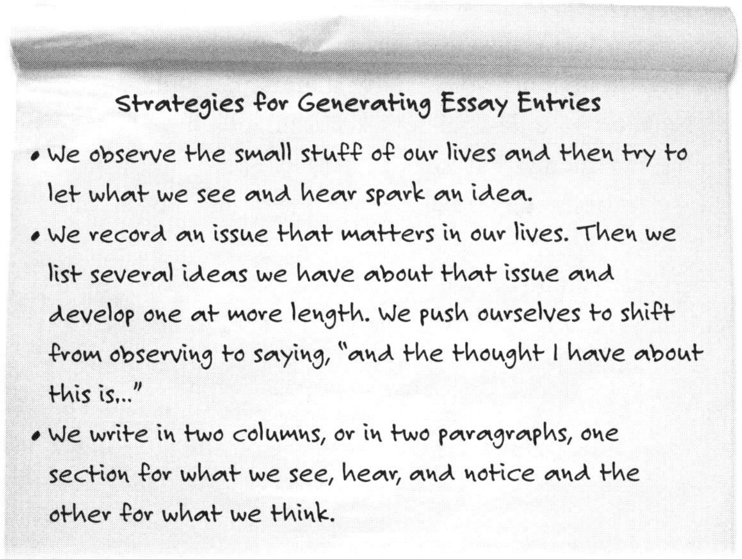

Strategies for Generating Essay Entries

- We observe the small stuff of our lives and then try to let what we see and hear spark an idea.
- We record an issue that matters in our lives. Then we list several ideas we have about that issue and develop one at more length. We push ourselves to shift from observing to saying, "and the thought I have about this is..."
- We write in two columns, or in two paragraphs, one section for what we see, hear, and notice and the other for what we think.

I notice that some kids are not dressed nice on picture day. Why do kids not dress nice on picture day? Do they even care how they look for their pictures? If they don't I certainly do! I think that their parents should make their kids wear nice clothes for picture day don't you? The Kids responsibility is to make shure they look nice because they are going to have that picture forever and it is not faira for the kids who look nice. The kids who look nice really care that their picture looks good. I am one of those kids who wants to look nice.

Fig. II-4 Alejandro's notebook entry asking questions as a strategy for developing ideas

The white tall blank coffe cup stood tall on my teachers desk. The way it sat tall on the desk it reminded me of the chysler building. That also, reminded me about my dad because he used to work there. This is important to me because on half days my mom would pick us up from school bring us there. We would ride the elavator to his floor. The elavator was quick even though his office was up high. When stepped off the elavator my dad would greet us at the door and lead us down a narrow hallway. The he would open the door to his office. Me, my brother and sister would in. My brother went in the wind up train and my

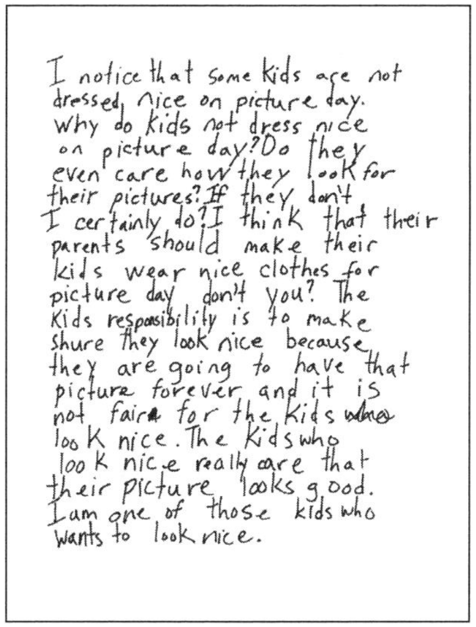

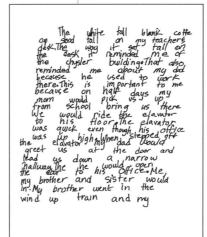

Fig. II-5 Olivia's notebook entry with brief observations then a well-structured entry

sister would go putting hole. I headed towards the Nova Nordis puzzle. I would take it apart then put it together again and again. My fingers would fumble each time holding the blue, white and light blue pieces until my dad would call lunchtime.

HW Prewrite an old entry to make an idea.

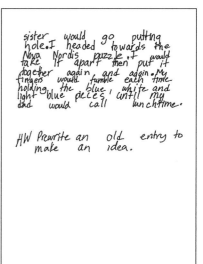

Fig. II-6 Olivia's entry page 2

WRITING AND CONFERRING

Providing Guided Practice

If you notice that several students are having difficulty making the transition from writing stories to writing about ideas, you may want to do a shared writing activity to support these children. Gather them and grab chart paper and a marker. Tell them that as a group, they're all going to write one shared entry and that doing this will help them feel the difference between writing a story—a personal narrative—and writing about an idea— an essay. Point out that one possible first step is to make an observation.

When I did this recently, Sydni offered her observation: "All the kids are running around like crazy at recess."

Then I said, "So if we want to write an entry starting with Sydni's observation, we need to say thoughts about it."

Aidan said, "Recess is when we get to be free."

I guided, "Say more about that—tell a reason or give an example or compare recess to something else." Then I showed children that to get themselves started thinking more, they could reread the one idea Aidan had already shared, letting the thought hang in the air.

Roy did this and then piped in, "There aren't any assignments."

I wrote this and again we reread what we'd written so far and waited. Then I quietly muttered, "We've got to say more," and eyed those who hadn't spoken. "What is your idea about recess and how there aren't any assignments?" I asked Chris, adding, "Remember, we try to think of more to say about the main thought." I reread it again.

Chris dictated, "Kids should have more recess!" and I recorded this at the growing edge of the paragraph.

MID-WORKSHOP TEACHING POINT   *Generating More Essay Entries* "Writers, your entries are briefer than they were when you were collecting true stories. So you'll need to write more entries in a day. Let me teach you another strategy that writers use to gather essay entries. You won't be surprised to learn that I often think of a subject (perhaps a person, place, or thing) that matters to me, and then I list specific ideas (this time, not stories but ideas) that I have about that subject. I take one of those ideas, and think more about it in an entry."

"Remember when I wrote personal narratives, I wrote, 'My Dad.' Then I asked myself, 'What small moments do I remember about my dad?' When gathering essay entries, I again jot down a subject that is important to me—I can again write 'My Dad,' but this time, because I am writing essays, not stories, I am going to list ideas about my dad. I'll list them on my fingers."

My Dad

- one of my most important teachers
- always been a colorful character
- helped me care about writing

Debriefing, I said, "Did you notice that when generating ideas for essay entries, I again started with a subject—a person, place, or thing—that matters to me, but this time I didn't list small moments; rather, I listed ideas related to the subject? Now I will take one of those ideas (the second one) and begin to write about it."

continued on next page

In this manner we continued to write an entry together about recess. The entry consisted of a list of related ideas, each written in a sentence. This wasn't perfect writing, but my goal wasn't perfection! After a few minutes of work, I reviewed what we had done together, asking the children to talk about how it felt to write about ideas instead of writing stories. Then I told them to take that "idea–writing feeling" back to their seats and try writing another idea in their own notebooks—this time on their own topics. "I'll come soon and see how you're doing," I said.

You might find it helpful to notice and name what children are doing when they observe and then write their ideas about observations so that this concept becomes familiar to them. So if one child writes, "I see the green plant. It has one long stem which only has two tiny leaves," I'm apt to say, "I love the way you first named the big picture of what you see—the whole plant—and then instead of moving on to observe something else, you zoomed in and noticed details. You described those details about the plants' leaves with lots of words." I'm apt to end my comment by saying, "Writers do this. We see the big picture of whatever we are observing, but then we don't just move on to look at something else. Instead we linger, we see closely, we elaborate, and we say more."

As you make teaching moves such as this one, notice that you are essentially doing what essayists do all the time. Like writers, you will also shift between a particular example and an overarching generalization. You will make mountains out of molehills! What I can describe now – the teaching move that involves naming what you see a child or an author doing and then making a fuss about what you see—is an essential move that teachers and writers, both, make all the time. Learning to do this well will lift the level of your teaching from this day forward, for always.

continued from previous page

My dad has always been a colorful character. On Christmas Day, he went to move a log in the fireplace and gouged his head on one of the nails from which the Christmas stockings hung. To stop the ferocious bleeding, he held a bag of frozen peas on the top of his bald head. Guests arrived for our Christmas party and he greeted them with the peas draped over his forehead. The guests weren't surprised to see Dad's odd ice-pack because he's always done what he pleases without much concern for fitting into social norms. It isn't important to him to dress "right." He wears his red plaid hunting cap everywhere. When I was a teenager and he wore that hunting cap to my school events, I was embarrassed by him. But now I'm proud of his values and hope my life demonstrates similar values.

"You may think, 'Isn't that a personal narrative?' and it's true that essayists often illustrate our ideas with stories. The entry does contain a story, but it also contains a discussion of how that story relates to my main idea. You'll notice that the entry definitely advances the idea that my dad is a colorful character."

continued on next page

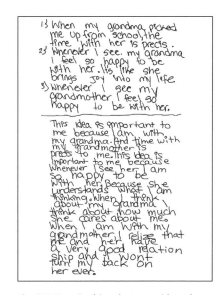

1) When my grandma picked me up from school, the time with her is precis.
2) Whenever I see. my grandma I feel so happy to be with her. It's like she brings joy into my life.
3) Whenever I see my grandmother I feel so happy to be with her.

This idea is important to me because I am with my grandma. And time with my grandmother is precis to me. This idea is important to me because Whenever I see her I am so happy to be with her. Because she understands what I am thinking. When I think about my grandma I think about how much she cares about me. When I am with my grandmother I relize that she and her have a very good relation ship and it wont turn my back on her ever.

Fig. II-7 Here Sophie selects one idea—her first—and writes about it.

Remember that your Mid-Workshop Teaching Point provides you with an opportunity to respond to the specific challenges you see in your classroom. So if it seems that an inordinate number of children are lining up behind you, then you have a forum for reminding them that they can be teachers for each other. If they've forgotten to punctuate now that they are in this new unit, remind them that forgetting to punctuate is as odd as forgetting one's shoes.

I like to tuck management pointers into discussions of what writers often do. You could, for example, say, "I notice that you are talking among yourselves a lot during this unit, more than when you were writing narratives, and my hunch is this is because your entries are getting you excited about ideas. This happens a lot for writers. What I want to suggest, however, is that writers try to write instead of talk; we want to channel our thoughts onto the page rather than into the air."

continued from previous page

"Writers, did you notice how I first took a subject that matters to me, then listed ideas I have about that subject, and then selected one of those ideas to write about? Let's pretend you were gathering entries for this unit and you started by saying, 'What is a subject that matters to me?' Let's say you thought not of a person but of a place, and you wrote, 'Our Meeting Area,' on your paper. Then you'd need to ask yourself, 'What ideas do I have about our meeting area?' Right now, list several ideas about our meeting area across your fingers. Then take one idea and 'talk long' about it." The children talked to their partners for a moment.

"So writers, remember that writers have a saying, 'When you are done, you've just begun.' After you write one entry, leave a space and write another. To do that, you can use any of these strategies for generating essay entries from our chart," and I added the new strategy to the chart.

Strategies for Generating Essay Entries

- We observe the small stuff of our lives and then try to let what we see and hear spark an idea.
- We record an issue that matters in our lives. Then we list several ideas we have about that issue and develop one at more length. We push ourselves to shift from observing to saying, "and the thought I have about this is..."
- We write in two columns, or in two paragraphs, one section for what we see, hear, and notice and the other for what we think.
- We pick a subject that matters to us, then list ideas about that subject, then select one of those ideas to write about.

SHARE

Generating Even More Essay Entries

Offer students an example of how living like a writer can help generate entries. Let children share their entries with their partners.

"Writers, you've learned a handful of strategies for generating essay entries, and gotten good at shifting between observing and thinking. I know these strategies have helped you collect some interesting material in your notebook. I also hope the writing you've been doing has helped you see that writing can change your life. A writer I know once said, 'Writers notice the things that others pass right by.' I think many of us, in our lives, are so busy running here and there that we don't see what's in front of our noses. Have you ever found yourself at school, hardly able to remember how you got there? Well, writing is one way people stay alert to our own lives. And when someone writes, suddenly, parts of life that once seemed mundane become interesting."

"In this entry, notice that Emily is riding the school bus home as a writer, seeing things that she—and many people—never noticed before. Then she pushes herself to name her idea about what she sees."

> When I ride the bus home after school, I notice that things change in different neighborhoods. Like where the school is, the houses look so bad. They are kind of beat up, like crumpled up paper. And then when the bus goes a few blocks away, the houses have lots of pretty colors, flowers everywhere, and nice yards. Also, by the school, there is a lot of trash in the gutters, but in that other neighborhood, it looks like somebody sweeps the whole street every day!
>
> Everybody should have nice houses, not just some people. My bus ride home shows me that the world is not very fair.

"The extraordinary thing about Emily is that she not only sees—she also lets what she sees get through to her. Would you give me a thumbs up if you, like Emily, wrote what you saw, and then let what you saw affect you, and wrote your response to what you saw?"

I think of the first sessions in all of these units as a course in living writerly lives and keeping writer's notebooks. As you'll recall, at the start of the year, I didn't yet expect children to carry notebooks between home and school. By now, expectations for children to live writerly lives have grown. Later sessions across all the units will combine to form a course on drafting; still later sessions across all the units combine to offer a course on revision and editing.

When I ask children if they've ever found themselves at school, hardly able to remember how they got there I'm referring to an anecdote Don Graves once shared. He talked once about how many of us sometimes drive to school as if on autopilot. We pull into the parking lot and think, with a start, "How did I get here? Am I dressed?" In my minilesson, I left out the latter question—and didn't feel the need to tell children the source of the anecdote. You can, in a similar way, borrow from every source possible when you teach.

HOMEWORK ***Finding Significance in Ordinary Moments*** In school, you learned how writers gave our attention to a time in the day that most people don't regard as especially provocative—the bus ride home, for example. Tonight, would you take a time in your day that you usually don't think much about, and play the believing game. Say to yourself, "I know for sure that a lot of really interesting ideas occur to me at this time." 'Say that to yourself even if, frankly, you are not convinced.' You might choose to pay attention to moments just after the final bell at the end of school when you go to your locker. You might choose the instant when you walk into your house, into your kitchen perhaps—what happens? What do you think? Notice? What observations can you collect if you pay close attention to that time? What ideas can you gather?

The other evening, a teacher I know shared his writing with me and he'd done just what writers do. He paid attention on his walk home from school, and he recorded what he saw. Then he pushed himself to have a big idea about all that he'd seen. Listen, *[Figs. II-8 and II-9]*

Observations

Trees with lime green leaves

Trees with lemon yellow leaves

Trees with fire red leaves

People walking to and from

Boys behind the school partaking in drink

Children talking in their native West Indies accents

People getting hair cuts.

> The South Bronx is my Home Sweet Home! I love all that it is, and all that it is not. I love the Projects. Yes, I know people talk down the Projects. The Projects for me are opening presents on Christmas morning. They are washing dishes with Grandma when everyone goes home after Thanksgiving dinner. In the Projects, I learned how to ride my first bike. In the Projects, I cried when my training wheels were taken off. In the Projects, this is where I saw all four seasons—winter, spring, summer and fall. It's where I learned the importance of street smarts, but it's also where I learned the importance of a good education.

You all can learn from this how to shift between observing—and having a thought.

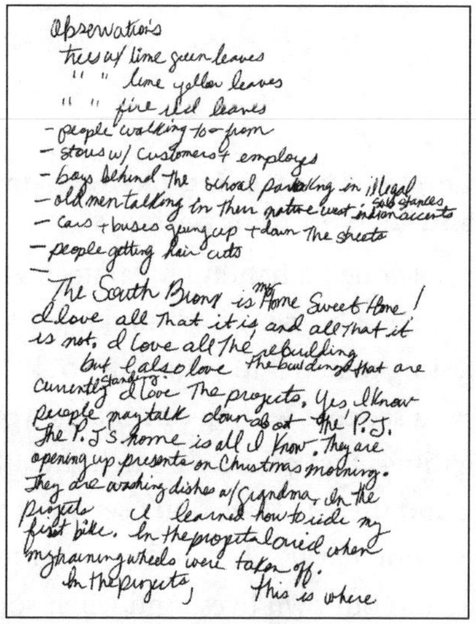

Obsewation's
trees w/ lime green leaves
" " lime yellow leaves
" " fire red leaves
- people walking to-from
- stores w/ customers + employes
- boys behind the school partaking in illegal substances
- old men talking in their native west indian accents
- cars + buses going up + down the streets
- people getting hair cuts
-
The South Bronx is my Home Sweet Home! I love all that it is and all that it is not. I love all the rebuilding but I also love the buildings that are currently standing. I love the projects. Yes, I know people may talk down about the P.J. The P.J.S home is all I know. They are opening up presents on Christmas morning. They are washing dishes w/ grandma. In the projects I learned how to ride my first bike. In the projects I cried when my training wheels were taken off. In the projects, this is where

Fig. II-8 Dyon's notebook entry

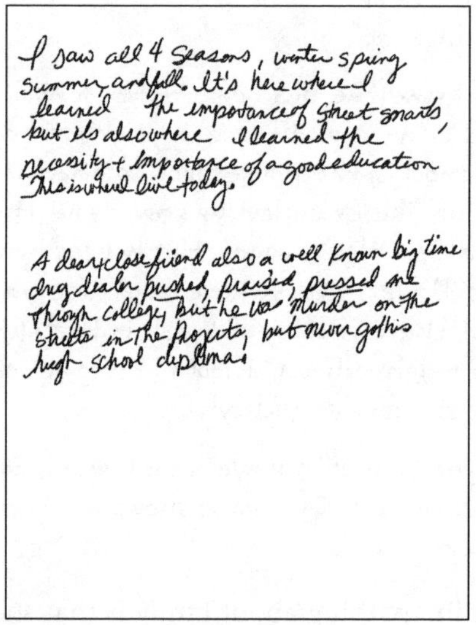

I saw all 4 seasons, winter spring summer and fall. It's here where I learned the importance of street smarts, but its also where I learned the necessity + importance of a good education. This is where I live today.

A dear close friend also a well known big time drug dealer pushed, praised, pressed me through college, but he was murder on the streets in the projects, but never got his high school diploma!

Fig. II-9 Dyon's entry page 2

If your children are looking for unusual things to observe and therefore struggling . . . you might teach them that anything can prompt reflection—even a piece of blank paper, as in this entry, *[Fig. II-10]*

> A paper is a mysterious object. It's blank, white coat makes it seem to be daring you to write on it. It can contain a poem, a story, a document, or a project. It can be any one of these, and can't be predicted. A paper can be cut, ripped or crumpled. It can be written on by pen, marker, crayon, paint, or a pencil. It can be a magical object that can destroy one's hope, or rise one's. A paper can be all of those things and more.

If you notice that your students' observation entries tend to be rushed or bland . . . it may be helpful to teach them strategies for slowing down an observation so that it is fresh and detailed. Often, you may find that students name just what they see in this way: "I see my friend waiting for me. She's standing in front of her door looking at the street." In essence, they are observing only the "outline" of the scene. You'll want to teach them how to take the scene in and slow down so they can really capture the details and write the true words that fit what they see. When a writer does this, an entry can turn into something like:

> "I see my friend waiting for me, her face turned toward the street. I don't mean to be late again, so I begin to run. She's wearing her light blue down jacket and her white hat is pulled down low. Her arms are crossed in front of her chest and her book bag is on the ground, which probably means she's cold and has been waiting for a little too long . . . "

For the demonstration part of the lesson, you might decide to show two entries that contrast, such as the observations above. You'll want to read the first one, the surface-level observation, and respond in a "hmm, so what . . . " sort of way. Then read the second one aloud followed by a quick accounting of the differences. "Writers," you might say, "did you notice how in the first entry, the writer just told the very basic stuff? It's like we got a sketch in our minds. In the second entry, the writer shared more details, so it's like we got a painting (or a movie) in our minds." You'll want to tell them that in order to write observations well, writers train themselves to push for the precisely honest words that fit what they see. For the active engagement portion of the lesson, you might cite examples of

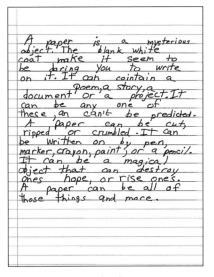

Fig. II-10 Sadie's notebook entry

powerful observations from literature. For example, you could reference *The Lightwell*, by Lawrence Yep. He writes, " the lightwell seems to stretch endlessly upward and downward among the many buildings. At its brightest, it is filled with a kind of tired twilight." After you share the example, you may ask your students to turn to a partner and talk about what the author did to write the observation well. As you listen in to the partner talk, you can gather items for a chart that may be entitled Tricks to Writing Observations.

Collaborating with Colleagues

The work that you'll ask your children to do in this unit is much more challenging and intriguing than it appears to be on the surface. The best way to appreciate its hidden complexities is to try your hand at it. In even just twenty minutes of writing time, you could use a few of the strategies for generating essay entries that you've invited your students to use. Try it! The added bonus is that you'll have your own entry to use in place of the one about my dad. That entry about my father threads its way through this unit, so I strongly recommend you come up with your own replacement. If this feels a bit scary, stay close to my model at first. Try choosing a person who matters to you and then list some of the ideas you have about that person. Be precisely honest, and you'll find your writing flows from a power source within you. If it's hard for you to generate ideas, try thinking of the person as a character and ask yourself, "So what are his/her character traits?" Be sure you state your idea with crystal clarity—don't equivocate or say too much. Then write an entry in which you elaborate on your claim about this person. You might want to borrow my structure and write a short, angled anecdote that illustrates your point, and then talk briefly about one or two other ways in which the person demonstrates whatever you are trying to say.

Try, also, the strategy of observing a place that matters to you, then writing specifics about it. Write about your mother's kitchen, your front yard, wherever—and as you write, try to capture the details that keep your yard from being just anyone's yard, your mom's kitchen from being anyone's kitchen. Then push yourself to skip a line and start with the phrase, 'The thought I have about this is . . .'

You'll definitely want to use your own writing in an upcoming lesson. To create the text you need for Session IV, put an entry that you wrote in a previous session in front of you. If you haven't yet written one, then select a person or place that matters to you and write one thought about that person or place, extending it with a second or third sentence. Or observe something for even just a few sentences. In any case, put an entry in front of you.

Now ask a colleague or a child to dictate a series of prompts to you, one prompt every three minutes. When that person says the prompt, write down the exact words of that prompt, and quickly continue from where the prompt leaves off, writing whatever comes to mind. Try these prompts (or others):

- To add on . . .
- An example of this is . . .
- I'm realizing . . .
- The surprising thing is . . .
- This is important because . . .
- On the other hand . . .

Try, as you do this work, to experience the way in which you can let brand-new thoughts come out of the tip of your pen.

CONTRASTING NARRATIVE AND NON-NARRATIVE STRUCTURES

IN THIS SESSION, YOU WILL ORIENT CHILDREN TO THE GENRE OF ESSAYS BY CONTRASTING ESSAY STRUCTURE WITH THAT OF NARRATIVES. YOU WILL TEACH CHILDREN THAT WRITERS NEED A SENSE OF WHAT THEY ARE AIMING FOR IN ORDER TO COLLECT, ELABORATE ON, AND STRUCTURE THEIR WRITING.

GETTING READY

- List of features of non-narrative writing, written on chart paper
- Your own writing sample that tells the story of a subject and a non-narrative version that discusses ideas about the same subject
- Photocopies of narrative and non-narrative writing examples, one set placed on each desk
- See CD-ROM for resources

Children have a way of cutting to the chase, of pointing out the elephant in the room that no one wants to admit is there! So when Sophie told me she didn't really 'get' what essays are, I had to face the question. The question is challenging because if you look at the variety of essays published in books, journals, and magazines, you'll see essays come in many types.

Technically, the term 'essay' comes from a Latin root word that means "to wander." Great essayists such as Lewis Thomas, John McPhee, and E. B. White don't write with a single controlling idea and with paragraphs that are tightly linked to that thesis! Yet on College Entrance exams, Advanced Placement exams, and in their coursework, secondary school students are expected to write a school version of the essay and those school essays do require a thesis, elucidated by a series of supporting paragraphs, each beginning with a clear topic sentence related to the thesis.

You will need to come to terms with what you want your children to learn. You may resist teaching the genre of school essays, arguing that it is not an authentic form of writing—a reasonable concern. As the mother of two teenage sons, I feel that as long as secondary schools and standardized assessments require thesis-driven five-paragraph essays, I will argue that upper-elementary-grade children need to be explicitly taught the skills required to write them. It's not fair to withhold teaching when the stakes are high.

Then, too, the writing muscles children develop as they learn to craft thesis-driven essays are valuable. Although I do not write five-paragraph essays, most of the nonfiction texts I do write (speeches, grants, chapters) are structured similarly: I propose an idea; then I develop different parts of the idea.

These, then, are my reasons for teaching Sophie and her classmates to write in a genre that is rarely found in libraries. The next challenge is to explain the genre, and to do so without the benefit of published examples. You'll see, in this session, how I attempt to do this.

MINILESSON

Contrasting Narrative and Non-Narrative Structures

CONNECTION

Establish the reason for today's teaching point: writers need to imagine the kind of text they're writing.

"Writers, yesterday Sophie asked me a really smart question. We were waiting for the buses together, talking about our new unit of study, and she said, 'I'm not totally sure what I am trying to make.' She went on to say, '*Before*, I knew we were writing stories, true stories. But what is an essay?'"

"I wish there was a simple description that I could give to Sophie and to all of you, but the truth is that different people mean different things when they talk about writing essays. And across this year, you will learn about several different ways to write essays. Sophie is so smart to think, 'What kind of thing are we writing?' Writers do need to know what a genre is like in order to write well in that genre."

Contrast the features of narrative and non-narrative writing.

"One thing you need to know for starters is this: Essays are a kind of *non-narrative* writing. You already know a lot about writing *narratives*, or stories. In this unit, we are going to write *non*-narratives. So what does that mean? Well, *non* means 'not.' Nonreturnable purchases mean that you can*not* return the purchases to the store. Nonfat milk means there is *not* fat in the milk. So when I say we will be working on *non*-narrative writing, this means that the writing we do will *not* be the same as the narratives we've been working on."

"Here are some ways to distinguish *non*-narratives from narratives."

- Stories tell what happened first, next, and next. Non-narrative essays don't.

- Stories show a character—in our personal narratives, we are the main character—going through a sequence of events. Non-narratives don't.

- Stories lead the reader through the sequence of events. Non-narratives don't.

COACHING

When I first work with teachers to help them learn to give effective minilessons, I emphasize the architecture of a minilesson, showing the contribution that each component makes to the whole. But after a short while, I think the spotlight needs to shift. Next, I encourage teachers to notice that minilessons are meant to be replicable and memorable. In this minilesson, I open with a tiny, tiny anecdote. I'm trying to win children's attentive interest.

It always helps learners to know the big picture of what we're trying to do before focusing on fitting the small pieces together. It's easier to fit together the pieces of a jigsaw puzzle if we've seen the picture on the box! So it is best to give children a big picture of what they will (and will not) be writing during this unit. This is challenging, however, because the sort of essay I will help them write is a school genre, one that secondary school students write all the time in literature and history classes, but not a genre that fills the bookshelves of our libraries.

When I list items orally, I try to help listeners grasp that my text is a list. It's also an option to make a quick chart. When listing, I often use the same opening word or phrase for each new item in the list. Especially if the class contains many English language learners I'm apt to touch first one and then the next finger while naming items in the list.

I pointed to the first characteristic on the chart and said, "Instead of being organized by time (this happened, then this happened, then finally this happened), non-narratives are organized by ideas. They might go, "I think this one thing, I also think this other thing, and furthermore, I think this third thing." Or, they might go, "This is true because of A, because of B, and most of all, because of C."

I pointed to the second characteristic on the chart and said, "Instead of being held together by a character who travels through the whole story, non-narratives are held together by an idea that is developed (or an argument that is advanced) across the whole text."

I pointed to the third characteristic on the chart and said, "Instead of being written so the reader can participate in the event, non-narratives are written so the reader can think about the topic."

"What do non-narratives, essays, contain?" I asked. Then I revealed a chart.

Characteristics of Non-Narratives (and of Essays)

- Non-narratives are organized by ideas. (They might go, "I think this one thing, I also think this other thing, and furthermore, I think this third thing.")
- Non-narratives are held together by an idea that is developed (or an argument that is advanced) across the whole text.
- Non-narratives are written so the reader can think about the topic.

Name the teaching point. In this case, tell children that writers can usually choose whether to structure a text as a narrative (a story) or a non-narrative (an essay).

"Today and throughout this unit, I will teach you that, as a writer, you can often choose to write in either genre. Whenever you are writing, it is helpful to have a little voice in the back of your head that asks, 'Wait, am I writing a narrative (which means a story) or am I writing a non-narrative (an essay)?' This is an important question to ask because these two major kinds of writing are usually organized and written in different ways. They are also judged by different criteria."

There are many visual clues I can give to help children grasp what I'm saying. For example, when I talk about the sequence of a narrative, my hands progress along a horizontal line. When I talk about the logical hierarchy in an expository text, my hands create an outline in the air.

Notice that I first listed three characteristics of narratives, and then said non-narratives do not have those three characteristics. Then I returned to the list and said non-narratives do have three alternative characteristics. The two lists follow the same sequence. That is, the first item in both lists addresses contrasting ways to structure texts, the next item in the lists deals with contrasting ways to unify the text. It is worth noticing that the patterned way in which this minilesson is written illustrates a feature of non-narrative texts! Writers of expository texts often think about the design, shape, and balance of a discussion.

Life is not really this definitive. Many texts have sections that are narratives and sections that are organized in a more expository fashion. Eventually we'll show children that within a single piece they can shift between these two ways to organize texts. The last unit of the year invites children to draw from and integrate both narrative and expository structures. And even this unit will show children that narratives are often embedded into essays.

TEACHING

Demonstrate how you might write about one topic in either a narrative or a non-narrative fashion.

"So watch me as I decide whether I am writing a narrative or a non-narrative piece. Let's see . . . I think I want to write about my visit to the park."

"Hmm . . . is this going to be a narrative or a non-narrative?" I asked, pausing for an extra long time as if mulling over the right answer to the question. Then, leaning in to the group as if to tell them a secret, I said, "Writers, you need to realize that I could write about this topic (or almost any topic) and make my writing be either a narrative or a non-narrative! For example, I could write about my trip to the park yesterday and tell the story of what happened first, next, and next. Or I could write about the same visit as a non-narrative and teach people my ideas about the park."

"Watch how I write in the air about this topic first as a *narrative*. I want to remember what happened and make a movie in my mind." I said, as if writing:

> It was windy yesterday when I got off the subway. First I
> headed to the park. I held my coat around me and still
> the wind was cold. When I got to the park, I passed people
> walking quickly with their coats drawn around them.
> Soon after that, I got to the dog park. Only one guy was
> there with his dog. I just stayed a little bit and then I
> hurried to the pond. No one was there so I left.

"Now watch while I write about this in a *non*-narrative way, and see if you can list across your fingers ways that this writing is different."

"Okay, let me look over the notes I took about how to get an essay started, and think, 'What idea do I have about this?' Oh! I know," I said, as if just realizing how to go about it. I began voicing:

> When I visited the park yesterday, I saw signs of winter
> everywhere:

To show I was about to articulate my first subordinate thought, I touched one finger.

> People walked differently from how they walked just a
> few weeks ago. We pulled our coats around us closely,
> leaned into the wind, and walked with our heads down.

I use the teaching method of demonstration to act out the process and the mind work I go through to write as a narrative; then I provide a contrasting demonstration showing the process and mind work involved in writing an essay. Notice that I'm not displaying two finished texts. I'm instead composing in front of the children. My tone reveals that I'm mulling things over. My tone would be very different if I were simply holding up examples to illustrate that I wrote about one subject in two different ways.

You can decide whether to actually write the entry with a marker on chart paper, or to scrawl it on your clipboard, voicing aloud as you proceed. The latter allows you to move much faster because you can write in shorthand, or not write at all. If you decide on the chart paper alternative, abbreviate the text! Another choice is to write in the air, dictating what you "write" as you move your hand across the chart paper, leaving no visual trace.

When I ask children to list something across their fingers, I'm giving them a graphic organizer and practice at doing something that is fundamental to essay writing: organizing information.

Notice that the text I create begins by advancing a main idea, and then this idea is developed in two parallel sections. Each of those two sections begins with a big idea and then that idea is supported. Obviously essays often are not this symmetrical, but for now I'm putting forth a very clear model. I don't, however, point these features out to children just yet. I'm trying to give them the felt-sense for how narratives and essays contrast with each other.

I raised a second finger to address a second subordinate thought.

> Places that used to be full were empty now. There was only one man and his dog at the dog park. Just two weeks ago, dozens of dogs scampered there. And there were no longer kids, lining the edge of the pond.

Debrief. Remind children that writers can decide on the structure with which they will write.

"So you see, as writers you need to decide whether you are going to end up writing a story (a narrative) or an essay (a non-narrative). And if you are writing a non-narrative, your piece will be organized not by a chronological sequence but instead by different reasons or different examples or different categories."

ACTIVE ENGAGEMENT
Set children up to write in the air about a class event, first as a narrative, then as a non-narrative.

"You should realize by now that you could write about one topic—maybe about arriving at school this morning—in a *narrative way*. You could retell what happened with phrases like *First we . . . , and then we . . .* Try telling a quick narrative to your partner about this morning." The room erupted into talk.

"Can I stop you? Now, what I want you to realize is that you could also write about arriving this morning in a *non-narrative* way. To do this, you need to have an idea you want to convey. So before you can write a non-narrative, an essay, in the air, you need to ask yourself, 'What's my idea about this morning?' Squeeze your mind and see if you can come up with an idea, an opinion, about this morning." I gave children a minute to do so, and then said, "If any of you are having a hard time coming up with something, try thinking to yourself, 'What did I notice or observe this morning?'" I left a little space for silence. "Then, in your mind, say something like, 'The idea I have about this is . . .'."

"Give me a thumbs up if you have an idea about this morning," I said. "Good. If you don't have an idea yet, try this one: 'Mornings in school are chaotic.'"

"Okay, now, because you are writing a non-narrative (or an essay) piece, you will need to teach us about your main idea, and then you'll need to share reasons for it, or make points about it. In your mind, repeat your idea about this morning, and then list across

Because I'm trying to highlight the impact of the decision to write this as a narrative or a non-narrative piece, the only thing that distinguishes the two versions is that one conveys the information through a narrative, the other, through an essay. I try to keep the other variables constant, so the two pieces are otherwise the same.

I ask children to try what I've just demonstrated, using a topic I give them because I hope this will serve as a quick practice exercise. Later, once they disperse, they'll apply what they've learned to their own topics.

Notice that although there is one main teaching point in a minilesson, this doesn't stop us from tucking lots of subordinate tips into our teaching. Not every student will catch and hold every teaching point, but those who are ready will. This is one way to differentiate our instruction, providing more instruction for students who are ready for it.

I want everyone to have a chance to get aboard this work, so I'll resort to giving a thesis if necessary. Of course, in a few minutes children will disperse to work on their own writing, and they'll find their own topics and ideas about those topics.

your fingers a few points you could make about your main idea. You might come up with your points by using the word because." They did this quietly in their minds. "Now partner 1, teach partner 2 your main idea about this morning, making specific points."

Earlier children told stories across their fingers; now they do corresponding work with essays. They again list (and elaborate upon) points by talking across their fingers. The hand is a perfect graphic organizer! Some children will not totally and immediately grasp what you want them to do, but others will, and soon they'll learn from each other.

LINK
Rename the teaching point. Set children up to spend some time reading exemplar texts, dividing them into narratives and non-narratives. Then ask children to study the exemplar non-narrative texts.

"So today, you are going to continue to use all those strategies that we've imagined for growing ideas. And when you pick up your pen to write about a topic—like 'My cousin came over last weekend'—remember, you already know that you can write about that topic as a narrative, telling what happened first and then next. Now you also know you can try writing about it instead as a non-narrative, in ways that state (or claim) an idea and then support that idea."

"Before you get started writing today, I've left a very small stack of narratives and non-narratives in a basket on each of your desks. Would you take some time to read through these, making two piles so that you separate the narratives and non-narratives, the stories and the essays? Then, with your partner, find an essay you like. Talk about what the writer has done that you admire."

You'll want to share a variety of texts with your children, choosing texts which are somewhat within your children's reach. If you'd like a published text, I recommend Judy Blume's The Pain and the Great One, which rather closely resembles an essay. Depending on your children's writing abilities and interests, you might include a sample essay from the ACT writing test (www.act.org). Remember to include narratives as well as essays so children have a chance to differentiate.

WRITING AND CONFERRING

Supporting the Minilesson

You will probably want to use some of your conferring time to bring children together in informal small groups to talk about what they notice in the essays you've given them to read. Help children distinguish narratives from non-narratives, and help them see the overall structure in the essays they're studying. You will have chosen essays that follow a very obvious, heavy-handed organizational pattern, so children should be able to spot the fact that near the start of each piece, the writer states his or her big idea (the thesis). Then in subsequent paragraphs, the writer develops this thesis with examples and discussion. Point out that each paragraph addresses one subtopic, starting with an overarching sentence that lays out a main idea.

It is not crucial that children notice all the fine features of the essay genre. They will have plenty of time later in this unit to notice transitional phrases words, to study the job that the final paragraph does in the essay, or to see the variety of evidence that authors use to support their claims. For now, you are simply trying to give kids a general sense of what it is they will be making, while at the same time reminding them that writers take the time to read the sort of thing they aim to write.

Meanwhile, you'll also want to remind writers that they have many choices for how they'll spend their writing time today. Soon you will herd all children through a very set sequence of work, so for now, it is important to emphasize that writers have options. In conferences, encourage children to realize that they are expected to make wise choices. Do they want to write entries in which they observe and then push themselves to think? And if so, do they want to try a double entry format or to write in paragraphs, shifting at some point between observing and reflecting? On the other hand, perhaps a child wants to take a subject and list ideas related to that subject, then develop one of those ideas. Many writers will spend most of today reading and talking about the sample essays you've distributed, and that, too, is an option.

MID-WORKSHOP TEACHING POINT **Studying Essay Structures** "Writers, you all are making incredible discoveries about the essays you are reading. Some of you noticed that essays have sections or parts. Give me a thumbs up if you noticed that essays are often organized into categories, or sections, of information. You should be able to box out the sections, the categories in a text, and write a subheading for each section or each category. Later today, see if you can do that. You can write on the texts I've given you."

"Others of you noticed that often there is a sentence or two toward the start of an essay that lays out the main premise, the main idea, of the essay. There are also main-idea sentences (some people call them topic sentences) at the beginning of many paragraphs. See if you can find the sentences that lay out big ideas in your paragraphs and underline those sentences."

continued on next page

Teach your writers to think, "What can I do with my time that will help me to write thoughtful, original, significant entries?" Help each child feel that he or she is "the boss" of his or her own writing. Remind children that once they decide on a strategy, they need to make themselves a planning box, as they did in the previous unit, (Raising the Quality of Narrative Writing) in which they recorded the strategy they planned to use.

When a child decides to follow a particular strategy—say, observing and then having a thought—be sure the writer knows that the strategy is not a goal. It's only a means to a goal—and the goal is to write in ways which are provocative, insightful, original, and significant.

continued from previous page

"Let's look together at this one brief essay," [Figs. III-1, III-2, and III-3] I said, and used an overhead to enlarge one of the essays. "I'm going to read it aloud; will you and your partner see if you can help me figure out how to box and label the main chunks, the main categories, of this essay? How could we name each major chunk?" They did this, and two children offered suggestions. "Now will you and your partner see if there is a big-idea sentence that sets up the entire essay and others that set up each separate paragraph?" They did this.

"So writers, I'm hoping that you are beginning to sense the sort of thing that we are making, and that having a sense for this will help you. I know when I put together a jig saw puzzle, it helps me if I've seen the picture on the cover—and always, when you write in a form or genre that's new to you, it's helpful to spend a bit of time reading pieces that resemble what you want to write."

EFFECTS OF PARENTS FIGHTING
Parents fighting effects kids very much. Two people a kid loves yelling at each other really penetrates a kids mind. It makes kids yell for things, it makes them choose sides between their parents, the most terrible thing abut parents fighting is that it makes the kid start not trusting people.

Parents fighting makes kids yell for things instead of asking nicely. One time my parents fought and I watched. So when I went to school I wanted the glue so I yelled for it because that's how my parents get things from each other. Another time my parents had a fight and I watched and then I went to my cousins house and yelled at them for the controller because it was my turn to play Nintendo. Another time my parents had a fight and I watched and then I was hungry and I yelled at Mom to make

dinner faster. All this was encouraged by my parents fighting.

Parents fighting also makes kids choose sides between their parents. One time my parents were fighting and my Mom said something totally inappropriate and snap I'm on my Dads side. Another time my Dad said something totally inappropriate and snap I'm on my Moms side.

Another time my parents were fighting and my Dad said something totally inappropriate and snap I'm on my Moms side, but then my Mom said something just as bad back so snap . . . I couldn't decide both sides were pushing me and I felt like I was falling apart and that was what it was like during a lot of their fights.

The worst part about parents fighting is that it makes kids not trust people. One time my Mom couldn't trust Dad to get a

carton of milk so when I went to school I couldn't trust my friend to watch my lunch. Another time my Dad couldn't trust my Mom to give him his mail so when I went to my friends house I couldn't trust my friend to look at my cards because I thought he'd steal one. Another time my parents couldn't trust each other to watch me and my sisters so I couldn't trust Dad to stay with me at the Yankee game.

Parents fighting is an ugly thing. It really does penetrate a kid. I know what it's like to choose sides and yell for things and not trust people. It doesn't exactly feel good. Imagine having a war going on insides your head. Well that's what it's like when parents fight.

Fig. III-1 Andy's essay, page 1

Fig. III-2 Andy's essay, page 2

Fig. III-3 Andy's essay, page 3

SHARE

Clarifying "Writing About Ideas"

Share a conversation you had with a student that could be helpful to the whole class. In this case, clarify the meaning of "writing about ideas."

"Writers, I want to tell you about a conversation I had today with Neha. I complimented her on the ideas that she had come up with and asked if she could tell me more about her ideas. She looked at me with an odd expression and said, 'I am confused. I don't understand what you mean when you say you want to hear more about my *ideas*. What *are* my ideas about drama?' Neha and I realized that she wasn't sure which part of what she wrote constituted an idea, and we thought some of you might be unsure, too."

"You have ideas every day. You have ideas about people, school, your family, the texts you read. You have ideas about what your mom said last night, about school lunches, about our president. An idea has two things: a subject and something you think about the subject; a subject and a point you want to make about it."

"But an idea is not quite the same as a fact. It's not usually something you just plain know, like 'My idea is that our benches are made of wood,' because it would be hard to keep thinking about that fact and talking about it in interesting ways. I suppose you could, but it would be difficult. On the other hand, your *thoughts* about our benches are your ideas. If you said that benches help us keep things fair in our discussions, that is an idea that you could say lots and lots about."

"If you said, 'Benches are good things to have,' that would be an idea, but it would not be a focused or specific idea. If, on the other hand, you said, 'Sitting on benches (that'd be your subject) helps kids listen to each other (that would be your point),' then you'd be voicing a specific idea—and we'd all want to hear your reasons for believing this!"

"So listen to just the start of Neha's writing, and I'm sure you'll agree with me that she has lots of ideas."

> Taking drama is hard work.

"That's an idea."

> We usually have little contests in which we have to say certain expressions while the rest of the class can laugh at you. Doing drama is worth it because it is fun to pretend you are someone else.

"That's an idea, and a specific one. I'm dying to hear her reasons, aren't you?"

Every discipline has its own lingo, and this is as true for those of us who teach writing as it is for a blacksmith, a botanist, a sculptor. If children are going to become active agents of their own writing development, we need to be able to discern their sources of confusion and to teach as explicitly as possible. When Neha suggested she wasn't clear what I meant when I asked her to write her ideas, I realized she was not alone. Therefore, I used a share session as a teaching opportunity.

Clearly, you will choose a different teaching point if your students are having no problem generating ideas. You could use this time instead to share some of the ideas children have written in their notebooks. This will prime the pump for more ideas to pour forth, just as sharing stories inevitably leads to more stories. Alternatively, you could use any of the extensions as a way to angle this share session.

Ask partners to talk with each other about their writing so far, pointing out each other's ideas, or noting starting points for ideas.

"Let's read each other's entries and search first of all, for ideas. Then secondly, let's search for ideas that leap off the page, ideas that seem insightful and note worthy. Put a little check in the margin beside any passage which contains ideas that make you, as the reader, go 'Wow,' or 'Hmm!' and mark places where there is an idea that you could turn into an essay. You can also mark places that are just crying out loud to become longer pieces—bits of writing where you are curious about where the thinking might lead. Okay, go ahead."

I listened as Olivia shared this entry with Rebecca, who wanted to give a stream of check marks alongside the margin of the entire entry. *[Fig. III-4]*

When I am cranky sometimes I act up and say words I don't mean to say. For example, I started getting cranky one night in Montana to wear a certain pjs and gave my mom a hard time with out even caring.

That made me realize to not give my mom a hard time because she works hard to make me happy and I didn't care about that. So that shows me it's not okay to only think about yourself.

This event also reminds me mom's give good advice and I rejected that and only cared for myself. I really just forgot about my mom as a piece of dust and went on with my life. Then later on I feel like wow, I just rejected one of the most important people in my life.

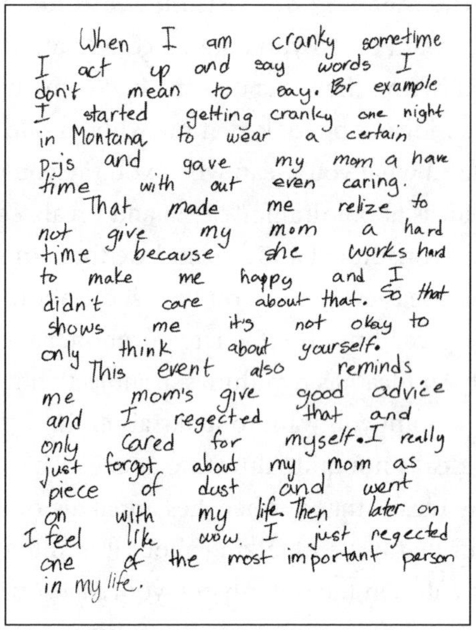
When I am cranky sometime I act up and say words I don't mean to say. For example I started getting cranky one night in Montana to wear a certain p.js and gave my mom a hare time with out even caring. That made me relize to not give my mom a hard time because she works hard to make me happy and I didn't care about that. So that shows me it's not okay to only think about yourself. This event also reminds me mom's give good advice and I regected that and only cared for myself. I really just forgot about my mom as piece of dust and went on with my life. Then later on I feel like wow. I just regected one of the most important person in my life.

Fig. III-4 Olivia's entry

HOMEWORK ***Collecting Essay Talk from Life*** Recently, I spoke on the phone with my dad and he told me how much he likes having grown-up children. His reasons were that we can take care of ourselves, we become more like friends, and as we get older he sees more and more of himself in us. As I listened, it seemed like he was writing an essay over the phone, and I could almost picture how his essay could go. I wrote down his idea and his reasons.

I like having grown-up children.

- because they can take care of themselves
- because they become more like friends
- because I see myself in them as they grow into themselves

You will find that once you get into this unit, you see the world through the lens of essays, finding examples everywhere. Make sure you collect at least some of these examples to share with your students!

Writers, the reason that I shared this story with you this story is that tonight I want you to record a few conversations you overhear in your family into your notebook. Record a conversation in which one person claims a big idea and then supports that idea with reasons. If no one talks like this naturally, then you'll need to prompt people to talk in this way. If you know your father worries about the president's decision, ask him what his reasons are. Have your pen ready! If your friend is angry that her visiting grandmother is sleeping in your friend's bedroom, ask her why this is so inconvenient. Catch what she says in the pages of your notebook. Collect several overheard essays—and be sure that in one of those entries, you are transcribing your own talking!

TAILORING YOUR TEACHING

If you'd like to help children glean a big picture of how essays tend to go . . . you may decide to box out sections of one essay, labeling each box and then asking children to do similar work with an unmarked essay. You could, in the first essay, identify these component parts :

- a catchy lead
- a thesis statement that overviews the main idea of the essay
- the first of several body paragraphs
- the topic sentence of this paragraph.
- supporting information—a story angled to support the topic sentence
- a discussion of the story that is cited for evidence
- other evidence supporting the topic sentence
- a second body paragraph
- a second topic sentence
- evidence supporting the second topic sentence
- a conclusion that repeats the thesis and adds a new spin

If children would benefit from seeing more examples of essays and parts of essays . . . you may want to tell children that this form is also very prevalent in their content area textbooks and in some nonfiction books. You might, as an example, show them an excerpt such as this one from Vogel and Goldman's *The Great Yellowstone Fire* (1990).

Yellowstone's patchwork of habitats provides homes for many
kinds of animals. Near steaming geysers, and hot springs, bison
graze in upper meadows. Moose and deer browse on tender
shoots of cottonwood and willow. On steep mountainsides,
golden eagles build nests on rocky ledges, and bighorn sheep
traverse the jagged rocks. The rivers and lakes of the park provide
food and resting sites for trumpeter swans, white pelicans, and
other water birds. (p. 6)

You could steer the children to their social studies or science textbooks to see if they
can spot examples of texts which are constructed similarly. Chances are not good that you'll
see the entire structure of an academic essay in these texts, but you'll see paragraphs such as
the one I cited.

If children could benefit from further orientation to the genre . . . you could teach them
how to assess essays.

Anne Ruggles Gene and Kelly Sassi's book, *Writing on Demand* is designed for older
students—it's touted as helpful for SAT, ACT, AP, and State Assessment Exams—but the
rubric they suggest using for evaluating essays is certainly within reach for fifth graders.
You may show children how you to use a rubric to assess an essay, using one of the essays
we provided.

**If you notice that in their attempts to clearly express ideas, your students tend to write in a
repetitive, circuitous manner . . .** you will need to remind your students in a minilesson, mid-
workshop teaching point, or a share session that writers reread their writing for lots of reasons.
One of the reasons is that they want to make sure it's crystal clear. You might say something
like, "Writers, you know what I've noticed? So many of you have really compelling ideas you're
trying to share in your writing, which is great! Sometimes, though, as you try to really help the
reader understand the point you're trying to make, you repeat things often. People think that
when you repeat things, you make your point stronger. But think about it. If your babysitter
tells you fifty times to clean your room before your parents come home, does that make you
do it faster? No, I bet it kind of drives you a little crazy and you begin to tune it out. Well the
same thing can happen to readers. If a writer repeats something over and over and over, the
writer might tune it out or else go crazy!"

"One of the things I've learned from essayists is that they make their points as clearly and as briefly as possible. In other words, they try not to repeat things. When you reread your piece, look for places where you're saying the same thing over and over again, and cross out the repetitive parts. You don't need to say the same thing over and over again!"

If you'd like to use a sample text to illustrate this point but don't want to use a student's writing as a troubled example, you can create your own repetitive text. Here's an example of one.

> Last night when we watched the news the weatherman warned that there would be a huge snowstorm coming over the weekend. Everyone in my family started to complain about it except for the kids. I don't understand why grown-ups complain about it. They didn't have any good to say, just complaining and whining. They complained but the kids were like, "Yeah! Snow!" My grandma was crabby when she heard about the snowstorm and my dad was swearing about it and my mom was annoyed and like, "They better not call off school!" I couldn't believe that they were complaining so much. I said, "I think it's good news!" I think grown ups should just relax a little and not complain about snowstorms because snowstorms can be good for us.

For an active engagement portion of a minilesson, you could ask children to work with their partners to revise this example.

ASSESSMENT

It is always a special treat to collect children's work after the first few days of a new unit of study. When you look over what children have done, you may see that a few of them haven't yet ventured out from the haven of narrative writing. It probably took your kids a while to grasp what it meant to write narratives, so it's not surprising that some will now be reluctant to loosen their hold on that structure! Alternatively, you will find some children who've put aside the confines and structures of narrative writing, but who now seem to be writing in an utterly unstructured fashion. Their writing may seem to have gone haywire. Their entries may be stream-of-consciousness, repetitive, general, chaotic, or all of these! For example, look at what Rie wrote. [Figs. III-5, III-6, and III-7]

Practice finding something to celebrate, even in the writing that doesn't at first impress you. When children are new at something, it may not be immediately obvious what you want to celebrate, so look closely. In conferences, mid-workshop teaching points, and shares, you need to be able to name what one child has done that you hope they repeat and others emulate. I notice that Rie writes with honesty. She risks putting herself on the page. She also cuts to the quick. Her entries are brief, but each one says something important. And although Rie may not realize it, there is a message that unites her entries. In a sense, this is already shaped as an essay, with one idea being advanced across the pages, and with a collage of support materials assembled!

Practice, also, reading your children's writing as if you are seeing it from an airplane, looking down at the whole text. Notice how the text is structured in the same way you might study a landscape from the air—you can see its divisions into fields, roads, and cemeteries. What main parts does a child's entry contain? How long are those main parts? How does the child seem to connect one part with another?

Very often, when I look at children's entries, it will seem as if a sentence about an overarching topic contains a single word that then triggers a discussion of that word. The writer may, for example, begin by writing about basketball, which leads him to mention his sneakers, and soon he has followed that trajectory and written about shoe stores (something utterly unrelated to the initial topic of basketball). I notice that children often use this train-of-thought system when they first write non-narratives. They don't have an overarching idea that acts as a big tent over the whole text, pulling everything together. Instead, they have one idea at the start of the entry and another idea (often only tangentially related to the first) later.

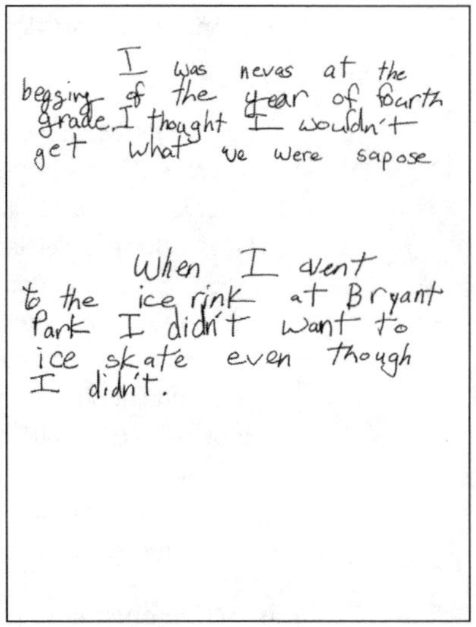

I was never at the begging of the year of fourth grade. I thought I wouldn't get what we were sapose

When I went to the ice rink at Bryant Park I didn't want to ice skate even though I didn't.

Fig. III-5 Rie

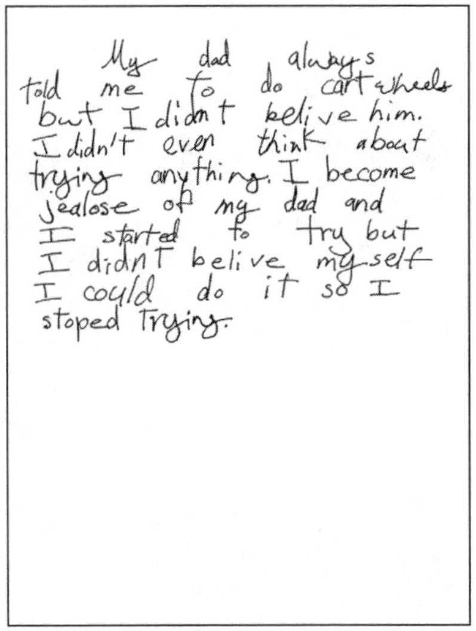

My dad always told me to do cart wheels but I didn't belive him. I didn't even think about trying anything. I become jealose of my dad and I started to try but I didn't belive myself I could do it so I stoped Trying.

Fig. III-6 Rie's second entry

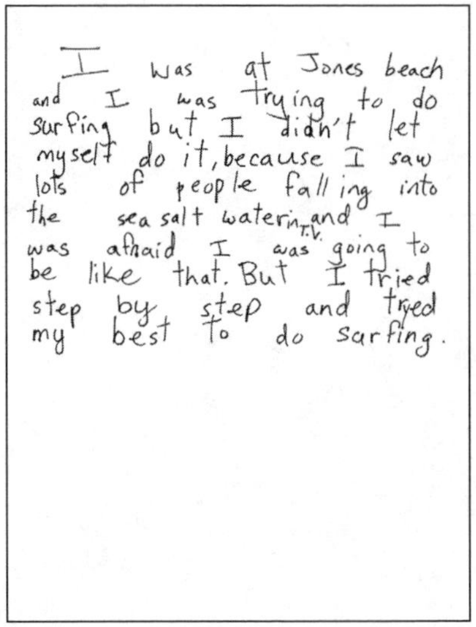

I was at Jones beach and I was trying to do surfing but I didn't let myself do it, because I saw lots of people falling into the sea salt watering and I was afraid I was going to be like that. But I tried step by step and tried my best to do sarfing.

Fig. III-7 Rie's third entry

Sometimes a single paragraph, as in Figure III-8, can contain many different, only loosely related ideas.

> This photo reminds me of how my mom would carry a camera everywhere we went and would at anytime save that moment forever. But now I hate having pictures taken because I always have to look nice and pose. I think, 'My mom is going to frame it and I want to remember a perfect moment.' But I love to see my face on a photo and many years later wonder about that moment when you posed, smiled, and said cheese. I think a picture tells a lot about someone. But it doesn't show the "truth" about yourself.

> This photo reminds me of how my mom Would carry a camera everywhere we went and would at anytime save that moment forever. But now I hate having pictures taken because I always have to look nice and pose. I think my mom, going to frame it and I want to remember a perfect moment. But I love to see my face on a photo and many years later wonder about that moment when you posed, smiled, and said cheese. I think that a picture tells a lot about someone.

Fig. III-8 This single paragraph contains many ideas

At first glance, I noticed that this one entry contained lots of loosely related ideas. But when I took a wider view and looked down on the terrain of this piece, I could see how it could turn into an essay. I could map it like this:

> The photo shows my mom carried camera everywhere to capture moments (no example)

> I both like and don't like my mom's inclination to take photos

Pros	Cons
• You can keep photo forever	• I worry about posing to make a perfect moment
• I love to see myself in an	
• old photo and ask questions	• It doesn't show the truth about yourself
• I think photos tell about someone	

I think it is very helpful if we, as teachers, can look at some of the entries children write and see nascent expository structure hiding within their texts. How helpful it is when we can see what students are almost doing, instead of seeing only what they can't yet do.

USING CONVERSATIONAL PROMPTS TO SPUR ELABORATION

IN THIS SESSION, YOU'LL TEACH CHILDREN THAT THEY NEED TO STAY WITH THEIR ESSAY TOPICS FOR LONGER STRETCHES OF TIME BY TALKING ABOUT THEIR IDEAS.

GETTING READY

- Transcript of an earlier book talk in which students used prompts to push their thinking, on chart paper
- Idea to build on using prompts
- Pushing Our Thinking list of prompts, written on chart paper
- Idea the class can build on using prompts
- Examples of student entries where thinking is extended, either with prompts or another way
- See CD-ROM for resources

When you invite children to write essays, you are inviting them to have, develop, and share their own ideas. You'll find that many students begin by writing (and perhaps thinking) in what the great writing researcher, Mina Shaughnessey, referred to as "sentences of thought." Your goal will be to push children to write, instead, in passages of thought.

It's easiest to teach children to elaborate on their ideas in writing if they've already done this in conversations. This session depends on your first helping children not only to have ideas about books, but also to grow those ideas through talking about them. If you haven't done so already, read aloud a text and when you pause, ask children to turn and share their ideas about the text with a partner. After a few minutes, ask, "Could someone get us started in a conversation about what we just read?"

Once one child has said something provocative and central to the text, repeat that idea as if it is fascinating to you; let the class see you mulling over the idea. Then say to the group, "Let's all talk and think more about Raffi's idea." You might say, "Would you look back at the text and talk with your partner about ways you agree with what Raffi said and want to add to it, or ways you disagree with his idea and want to talk back to it?" Then convene the class and help them work together for ten minutes to add on and talk back to that one idea. At first, you'll need to provide the conversational prompts. "Raffi said . . . who'd like to add on to that idea? Do the rest of you agree or disagree? Tell Raffi. Tell him why you agree. Give him examples."

"So Marco agrees because . . . Let's look at that part of the text, and think whether the rest of you want to add on, or whether we see another example of this, or whether you see this differently." Children can very quickly learn that once an idea is "on the floor," they need to elaborate upon it and talk back to it. And once children can do this sort of accountable talk in their whole-class conversations, they'll be ready for this session.

MINILESSON

Using Conversational Prompts to Spur Elaboration

CONNECTION

Celebrate that children are writing provocative ideas and point out that they could be saying even more.

"Writers, I brought your notebooks home last night. I made myself a cup of tea, wrapped myself in a blanket, and put the pile of notebooks beside me. You know what happened? I would read a few sentences in one of your notebooks, and then your writing would get me thinking. I'd look further on the page to learn what *you* thought next about the topic, and then I'd find that you had jumped onto a whole new topic! That happened over and over with so many notebooks. I wanted to phone you guys. I wanted to say, 'If this is true, then...?' or 'What's an example of this?'"

Name the teaching point. In this case, tell children that essayists talk back to our own ideas.

"I think we've turned a corner in this unit of study. You have gotten really great at coming up with entries that spark all kinds of thoughts. Today I want to teach you that *you need to hold on to those thoughts for longer stretches of time*—right on the page. Specifically, I want to teach you that after you've written a provocative idea, stay with it. Our ideas can get bigger when we talk back to them, just like I talked back to your ideas when I read them at home last night. When we write, we have a discussion with ourselves about our own ideas."

TEACHING

Tell children that the phrases they use to grow ideas during whole-class book talks can also be used to grow ideas in their entries. Use a transcript of a book talk as evidence.

"You already know how to grow ideas by talking back to them, because you've been doing this a lot during our book talks. This is a transcript of a book talk you had earlier this year about *Because of Winn-Dixie*." I projected a typed transcript onto the wall using an overhead projector. "Notice how you used a bunch of phrases to talk back to—to grow—Rashid's idea, his claim."

COACHING

When children are learning to write expository texts, they need to learn elaboration. This was an important quality of good expository writing even before The New York Times reported that Les Perelman, director of writing at MIT, found a stunning correlation between longer SAT essays and higher scores. "I have never found a quantifiable predictor in twenty-five years of grading that was anywhere near as strong as this one," he said (The New York Times 2005).

I'm hoping children will understand the need for elaboration if I situate this within the context of an interested reader who's dying to get into a grand conversation over their ideas.

When I say, "I think we've turned a corner in this unit," I mean that quite literally. When I plan units of study, I think of bends in the road. Usually children will work at one kind of thing for a few sessions; then I'll try to raise the level of their work or redirect the course of their journey—hence the image of turning a corner.

It is crucial to teach children to talk back to each other's ideas. The single most common limitation in children's writing is that ideas are underdeveloped. By teaching children to talk back to each other's ideas, you also teach them to talk back to (and extend) their own ideas.

As I read each line of the transcript aloud, I underlined the phrases that children had used that could help them in writing essays.

Rashid: I think Opal is lonely <u>because</u> she's new in the town, so she hasn't yet made many friends. That's why she wants Winn–Dixie, the dog.

Jason: <u>To add on</u> I think she is lonely also <u>because</u> her father never talks to her. He is too busy being a preacher.

Joline: <u>For example,</u> the book says he is too busy with suffering souls to go to the grocery store, so she goes alone. <u>This is important because</u> she doesn't have a mother either, so she feels like an orphan.

Rashid: <u>This gives me the idea</u> that the reason Opal talks so much to the dog is that she doesn't have friends and she can't talk with her father. <u>This connects with</u> how I sometimes tell my cat things I don't tell anyone else.

Leo: <u>The thing that surprises me</u> is that this stray dog has the power to change Opal.

Roy: <u>I am getting an idea that</u> the book might be all about how a dog changes a person and that is why it is called *Because of Winn-Dixie*.

"Did you notice the phrases we used in this book talk helped us say more and grow our ideas?"

Demonstrate that conversational prompts help a person grow ideas.

"Writers, you and I can use these same phrases to push ourselves to say more when we write essays. I'll read you a very short entry that I wrote."

> Lots of teachers ask kids to line up in two lines, one for boys and one
> for girls.

"Rebecca, would you choose from the list of prompts," I said, signaling to a list I had prepared on chart paper. "Coach me by saying a prompt you want me to use, and I'll use that prompt to think more about my claim. I won't actually write my further thoughts; instead I'll say them aloud." I began by repeating the entry.

Rebecca interjected, "In addition . . ." I repeated my claim and the prompt, paused in thought, and then completed that sentence.

> Lots of teachers ask kids to line up in two lines, one for boys and one
> for girls. In addition, boys and girls sometimes only play with each
> other on the playground.

Remember that our goals always extend beyond the reading and writing workshop. It is important to teach writing in part because writing is a powerful tool for thought. This session goes a long way towards helping children use writing as a tool for growing ideas on the page. We're explicitly teaching children to say more and think more, to extend their first thoughts, and to know what it is to see new ideas emerge from the tips of their pens. This is important!

When children begin to bring these phrases into their writing, you'll notice a child may write a phrase such as "This makes me realize . . ." without being aware of the meaning in that phrase. If you see a writer write that phrase, point to the words and say, "Oh! This tells me you are having a brand new idea right now. I can't wait to see it!" If the writer writes, "This is important because . . ." exclaim, "I can't wait to see what you figure the real significance of this is! I can't wait to see your decision." In this fashion, you can induct children into a culture that values words, and you can teach children what these hard-to-pin-down words mean.

As I said earlier, this minilesson presumes that you've taught your children to build on and develop each other's ideas within book talks. I describe this instruction in The Art of Teaching Reading.

You'll recall that earlier I taught children to use prompts to turn the corner from simply observing to having a thought about what they observed: "The idea I have about this is . . .". In this minilesson, you use a wider array of prompts to promote thoughtfulness.

Then Rebecca said, "For example . . ." Reiterating her prompt, I smiled in thanks and said:

> For example, yesterday, I saw a large group of boys playing kickball outside during recess, and a large group of girls playing on the swings.

Rebecca inserted, "This is important because . . ." I again repeated her prompt and said:

> This is important because I know both boys and girls like to play kickball and play on the swings, so I don't understand why they wouldn't be playing together most of the time.

In a similar fashion I proceeded to add:

> "The thing that surprises me is that boys and girls play together so much in this classroom, and then interactions change when kids leave the classroom. I now realize that the forces that make boys and girls divide are stronger than anything I've so far built in this classroom, and I need to try harder."

ACTIVE ENGAGEMENT
Set children up to practice using conversational prompts to extend an idea you give them.

"Now it's your turn to try this, and this time, let's try it through writing, not talking. Let's all start with a shared, whole-class idea, just as a place to practice. I'm going to show you how to use the prompts to push yourselves. Let's start with this idea."

> I learn new things during lunch time.

"Write that down and listen for a prompt that I'll say. When I say the prompt, even if you aren't finished with what you are writing, write the prompt and use it to push yourself to say more." Pausing to make certain every child had his or her pen poised, I said, "Okay, I'll first reread our claim. Then I'll add a prompt." I did so, saying first, "I learn new things during lunch time. For example, today . . ." I left time for children to record the prompt and then use it to generate more. When it seemed that they'd finished writing a sentence or two, I inserted a second prompt "Another example is . . ." Before long, I said, "To add on . . ." I prefaced my next prompt with a parenthetical aside, "Here's a hard one," and then dictated, "This makes me realize . . ." Again I said in an aside, "One last hard one," and then I said, "This is important because . . ."

As I do this, I try to demonstrate that a writer can use one of these prompts even without having a clue what she'll say next. We write (or say) a thought and then write (or say) one of these conversational prompts, such as "This is important because . . ." As we articulate those words, our mind leaps ahead, thinking, "Why is it important?" In this fashion, then, I'm hoping to demonstrate that writing can be a tool to grow brand-new thoughts. Children already know that we write to record well-fashioned ideas that we've decided to present to the world; now I'm helping them learn that we also write to muse, speculate, meander—to go out on a limb and risk having new insights.

You'll notice that I'm upping the ante. I demonstrated by talking (or by writing in the air), and now I'm suggesting that children can do similar work on paper.

This may seem a bit crazy to you but it is astonishingly successful. Just don't let kids slow you down. Teach them to write whatever they can and to keep going.

Ask children to reflect on what it feels like to use conversational prompts to extend thoughts.

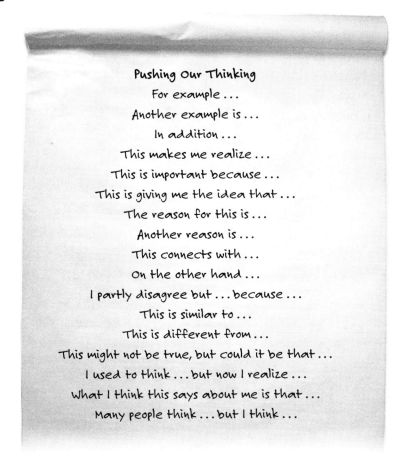

Pushing Our Thinking

For example . . .

Another example is . . .

In addition . . .

This makes me realize . . .

This is important because . . .

This is giving me the idea that . . .

The reason for this is . . .

Another reason is . . .

This connects with . . .

On the other hand . . .

I partly disagree but . . . because . . .

This is similar to . . .

This is different from . . .

This might not be true, but could it be that . . .

I used to think . . . but now I realize . . .

What I think this says about me is that . . .

Many people think . . . but I think . . .

"Okay writers, let's stop. How was that?"

Jonathan said, "My hand and my brain are tired."

"Your brain should be tired, because you were really focused! Now take a minute to read over what you have written." After a minute, I said, "Would you read what you've written to your partner and talk about how it felt using these conversational prompts to get yourself writing new ideas?"

Try this work yourself. It's almost magically powerful. The children become tickled by seeing their ideas emerge on the paper, and you will as well.

One interesting thing to realize is that different prompts channel children toward different kinds and even different levels of thinking. A prompt such as "For example . . . " or "Another example is . . . " or "To add on . . . " can lead children to provide examples and then to add on, to think associatively. My hunch is that prompts such as "This makes me realize . . . " or "This is giving me the idea that . . . " can lead them to progress from one thought to another thought, probably in a free-association fashion. "On the other hand . . . " and "But" and "I partly disagree because . . . " can lead a child to question. The prompts "This is similar to . . . " and "This is different from . . . " can lead to comparison.

> My mommy
>
> My mommy is very special to me because she takes care of me. One reason is that she cooks my favorite meals. To support that she cooks collard greens. They are sweet and out of this world. Another reason my mom is very special to me is because she understands me. To add on to that I can tell her anything and she won't criticize me. To support that she does not criticize me one time I was in a fight with my best friend. I told my mother what happened in the fight and she gave me advice. I told her "I won't do that!" But she understood. For example she gives me advice. One reason is she told me "don't be her friend any more." That really helped me

Fig. IV-1 LaKeya has used conversational prompts to extend her first thought.

LINK
Rename the teaching point. Rally writers to use prompts as scaffolds to help them extend their own ideas as they write.

"What I am suggesting, writers, is that our writing needs to get us thinking. When we hope to develop essays, our writing needs to get us into a conversation with ourselves that will yield wonderful ideas, like our book talks do. Only when we write, we are having a conversation on the paper, and we carry it on with ourselves." I pointed to the chart. "The conversational prompts that helped us talk back to each other in our book talks can now be prompts that help us talk back to (and think with) our own ideas, as we meet them on our pages in our writing. Of course, we can use all the prompts in the world and go nowhere in our thinking, so keep in mind as we use these prompts, the whole idea is to push ourselves to grow insightful, surprising, provocative ideas."

Notice the journey of thought I try to scaffold in this little speech. I make a point, and then push off from that point to a higher-level point. This journey-of-thought work is at the heart of what, in the end, we need to teach essayists to do. If you practice this yourself, you may more readily see it in your children's papers.

WRITING AND CONFERRING

Noting Qualities of Good Essay Writing in Children's Work

When you confer with children, try to let their entries teach you (and your students) ways to talk and think about essay writing. Notice entries that children have written that for some reason work especially well, and then join children in trying to put into words why those particular entries work. Be very specific and ask children to be specific, too. For example, ask "What do you mean when you say, 'It's detailed?' Point to the details you used."

Notice problems that you see in children's essays as well, and again, join children in trying to put those problems into words. We all need to develop a vocabulary for talking about our goals as we teach writing.

I suspect you'll notice that we always have the option of writing about an idea at a greater or lesser level of abstraction. For example, earlier I jotted ideas I had about my dad. One idea was that he has been one of my most important teachers. That is a fairly general idea, high on a ladder of abstraction. Think of it as roman numeral I in an outline. I could move down a notch in level of generalization and write, "My dad has taught me to fail with grace." Think of that as the A in the outline. Or I could move toward an even more specific/less abstract idea (the number 1 in the outline) and say, "When my dad was fired, he taught my brothers and sisters and me the truth of the saying, 'When one door closes, another opens.'" My feeling is that essay writing works best when there is only a little bit of writing at the highest level of abstraction, and much more writing at the lowest level. But all of the writing at the lower levels of abstraction needs to fit under the reach of the writing at the higher levels of abstraction. It is important for children to learn to shift between greater and lower levels of abstraction, and for our teaching to support that flexibility.

MID-WORKSHOP TEACHING POINT *Sharing an Example* "Writers, I want to compliment you. You are making important choices and gathering intriguing entries. I want to share with you another example of an entry that is poised to be an essay, so that you get more and more of a sense of how this kind of writing can start." *[Figs. IV-2 and IV-3]*

> I've been thinking about civilization. Civilization is a big word. When I hear it I conjure up images of the beginning of nations and empires. I think of Rome with its seven hills and I think of its future of beauty. It makes me think.
>
> What does Civ really mean? I think it describes the essence of our race, it is our culture, our technology, and our cities all combined. It is the computer program Civilization II that made me really think. Evan and I always call it . . .

continued on next page

Fig. IV-2 Miles' civilization notebook entry   Fig. IV-3 Miles' notebook entry page 2

You'll probably also notice that some of your children's entries feel fresh and others feel clichéd. Try to discern what makes some writing feel brand new, alive, unique, and why other writing feels prepackaged. I suspect you will find that when writing feels fresh, it is characterized by honesty. The writer may not use fancy words, but he or she reaches to put into words something that defies language, and the effort to pin down the truth gives those words power.

Look, for example, at Emily's entry about how she once referred to one color of crayon as dinosaur skin. *[Fig. IV-4]*

> When I was little I called crayons—
> dinosaur skin. Nobody knows for sure
> what color dinosaurs really were.
> For years I looked at pictures of
> them, trusting that whomever was
> in charge of coloring them was
> doing it based on a scientific fact,
> but the truth is they were guessing.
>
> If it was up to me to put a wrapper
> around a crayon and name its
> color, I would call it dinosaur skin. I
> used to think I knew what color
> that was, I believed when I was
> little that dinosaurs are neon pink.

I think you will find that texts also work when they are cohesive, and one important way to make a text cohesive is through the use of repetition and parallelism. You may notice that in some essay entries, a key phrase or word (perhaps from the opening line) recurs, almost like a refrain. As the text unfolds, bits of the text harken back to earlier passages. This creates resonance, and it is often what takes my breath away in an essay. When children do this it is usually a lucky accident. Find these accidents and let the young author (and his or her classmates) know the effect on you!

continued from previous page

> . . . Civ II. I wondered why. I now think it is because Civilization is such a massive word to describe this game, Civilization II is a big and complex . . . but it might not be big enough. I think that to make an ultimate civilization, the closest to true civilization, you would need to be able to make a theater and be able to walk in and watch a play that would be affected by your culture so it tells you something about your nation. You would need to be able to say a speech and have it affect your population.
>
> On <u>that</u> game's box, the creators could say that the game was worthy of the title 'civilization.'
>
> Maybe Civ II might be worthy, but I have not felt perfection yet. I might never.

"I know many of you have entries that muse like this, and it's a great way to begin the process of writing an essay. You can carry the flavor of this thinking with you as you go back to your own writing."

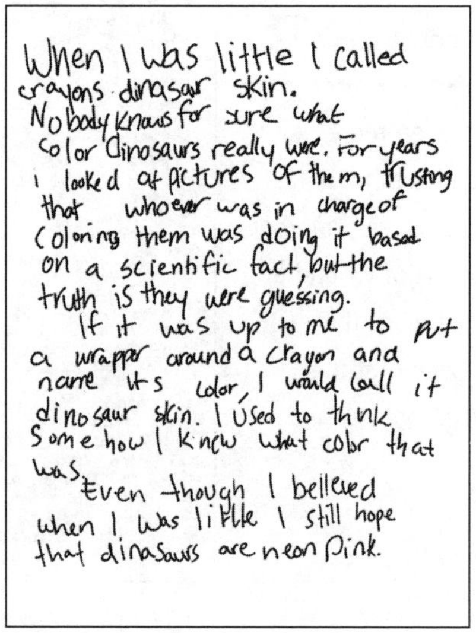
When I was little I called crayons dinasaur skin.
Nobody knows for sure what color dinosaurs really were. For years I looked at pictures of them, trusting that whoever was in charge of coloring them was doing it based on a scientific fact, but the truth is they were guessing.
If it was up to me to put a wrapper around a crayon and name its color, I would call it dinosaur skin. I used to think somehow I knew what color that was.
Even though I believed when I was little I still hope that dinasaurs are neon pink.

Fig. IV-4 Emily's notebook entry

SHARE

Celebrating Extended Thinking

Ask partners to talk over the development of the thinking in their notebooks—with or without prompts.

"Would you get with your partner and share an entry in which you really pushed yourself to talk back to your ideas, or to follow a journey of ideas? After you've read the entry, talk together, sharing your observations about whether the writer used any of the prompts on our class list, or tried another way to grow ideas."

Share examples by students who used prompts to extend their thinking.

"Listen to these examples from your classmates! See how their thinking grows and grows?" You'll notice that Ellie definitely uses thought prompts, and she uses more and more sophisticated ones as her entry progresses along. First she uses 'for example' but soon she's nudging her thinking with, 'I realize …' and 'What surprises me is …'."

> I hate it when I am doing something important and then I get interrupted.
>
> For example, when I'm reading a book and my mom calls, "Ellie, it's time to go to sleep" but I really want to finish the book because that's what I am into. I realize that this happens a lot to me, like when I'm watching TV or having fun with my friends. What surprises me is I always have a lot of time and no one interrupts me when I am doing things I don't like, like homework or practicing my oboe or other things.

"Listen to Max's writing. You'll see he also goes on a journey of thought, only he does not use thought prompts. Listen for the way Max grows an umbrella idea towards the end of his entry. Later you'll have a chance to tell your partner about a strategy Max has used that you think you could use as well."[*Figs. IV-5 and IV-6*]

> We got a dog when Mom came from Africa because she said we could when she left. We all thought she would not keep her word, but I should have known better because she did, the weekend she came back.

> We got a dog when mom came from Africa because she said we could when she left. we all thought she would not keep her word, but I should have known better because she did, the weekend she came back. Mom was also the first person who the dog, Monty, really loved. Both monty and I really have a lot of emotion for mommy. mom takes care of me, cooks for me, and makes me feel happy.
>
> I love her so much. I also love my dad so much because he is the nicest guy I know, he works five days a week – just so he can support my family and me. sometimes he even goes to work on the days you usually have off. And he does our house, our food, our clothes. And I am gald to have a father like that. But sometimes I don't think I

Fig. IV-5 Max's entry represents a journey of thought

Mom was also the first person who the dog, Monty, really loved. Both Monty and I really have a lot of emotion for Mommy. Mom takes care of me, cooks for me, and makes me feel happy. I love her so much.

I also love my dad so much because he is the nicest guy I know, he works five days a week—just so he can support my family and me. Sometimes he even goes to work on the weekends! You have to really have a good reason to work on the days you usually have off. And he does. Our house, our food, our clothes. And I am glad to have a father like that.

But sometimes I don't think I appreciate him enough, even though I should.

There are a lot of people/things that I think we should appreciate more. There should be a holiday called 'National Appreciation Day' when we take time to appreciate the things that we usually forget to. There are many people in the past that invented things for us, our troops who give their lives for us, teachers.

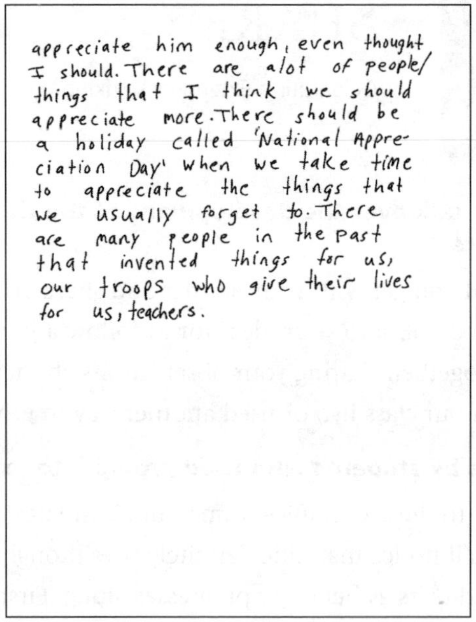

"Turn to your partner and talk about what these two writers have done that you'd like to try."

appreciate him enough, even thought I should. There are alot of people/things that I think we should appreciate more. There should be a holiday called 'National Appreciation Day' when we take time to appreciate the things that we usually forget to. There are many people in the past that invented things for us, our troops who give their lives for us, teachers.

Fig. IV-6 Max's notebook entry page 2

I'm enthralled by Max's writing and his mind, and haven't yet figured out just what it is he is able to do. You'll come to know him well in the last two books of the series.

🔘 HOMEWORK   ***Elaborating on First Thoughts***   Tonight, practice using some of the thought prompts at home. Have a little conversation with yourself while you are walking down the street, or brushing your teeth, or looking out the window. For example, you can walk down the street and pick a prompt out of the air. Say to yourself "I'm learning that . . . " Fill in the sentence in a way that surprises you. Then add on. Say another prompt "For example . . . " Or try more complicated prompts (they're the later ones on your list), like "I used to think that . . . but now I think that . . . "; "What surprises me about this is . . . "; or "Many people think . . . but I think . . . "

When you do this work, try to make sure that you don't only say these phrases but that you use them. Use the phrases to make your initial idea become richer, more complex, and more original. Suppose I say, "I like dogs" and add, "This is important because . . . " but then I simply say, "it just is" and add, "Furthermore, I like cats too." I wouldn't be using these terms as tools for thought. What a difference there would be if instead, my thought train went like this:

> I like dogs. This is important to me because my mother's dogs sometimes seem to matter as much to her as we, her children, do. I find myself growing up to be like her. Furthermore, now that my oldest son is going off to college, I've been thinking of getting myself a new puppy.

Most of your homework tonight won't be written, it will instead be thought, said, or lived. But also, in your writer's notebook, recreate and extend one train of thought, one that leads you into especially provocative areas.

TAILORING YOUR TEACHING

If your students are skilled at using conversational prompts for extending their thinking . . . you may want to try a more sophisticated variation on this lesson where you teach students that these prompts can be categorized and used for particular kinds of elaboration. You can show them that by selecting particular prompts, they can channel themselves into a kind of elaboration. For example, if a writer wants to think of more examples of something, he could use transitional words such as: for instance; for example; most importantly; in addition; and so on.

If a writer is trying to provide examples, you could suggest that instead of piling them up, one after the other, careful essayists think about a hierarchy of importance when offering examples. Some transitional words they might use are: of course; more importantly; equally important is; most importantly; and so on. Another way a writer might sort examples is temporally by using phrases like: in the beginning; later; next; in the end; finally, etc. If a writer is trying to think of reasons behind the points she is trying to make, she could use other transitions such as: because; this is caused by, one reason for this is; another reason is; and so on. If the writer wanted to imagine counter arguments (which by the way, is a lesson worth saving for another day), he might use phrases such as: on the other hand; however; yet; still; but; another way to look at this is; etc.

ASSESSMENT

One of the most important things to keep an eye on as you work with kids is their level of energy. Ask yourself, "Is this unit tapping into my children's motivations to write?" Take some time to watch during the writing workshop and also to read through the entries your students have written. Look at their products as windows onto student engagement, because few things matter more. If your students are invested in this work, anything's possible. But if they are proceeding in a perfunctory, passive fashion, it'll be hard to achieve any successes until you rally their enthusiasm. If your children haven't yet become invested in essay writing, it will be important to address this.

Guard against trying to hook kids into their writing by throwing compliments around fast and loose. You can inadvertently create compliment addicts. Then, too, if you offer too many compliments, the positive things you say will no longer carry real weight. Try instead to build student energy by showing respectful attention to kids' writing and to their subjects. This works!

One sure way to generate energy is to allow the children's work to bowl you over. You may not love their writing (often, in fact, it'll seem like their writing is dramatically worse once kids leave the safe haven of narrative). But if you look more closely and with forgiving eyes, you'll probably see that amid all the bad writing, some kids have recorded quirky, funny, provocative, or fresh ideas. Pay attention to those ideas, and let the less-than-great stuff float away. Repeat the powerful fresh bits to yourself as

if you were letting the idea the child has articulated dawn on you for the first time. Take the idea in. Let it matter. Be intrigued or surprised by bits of your children's thinking. Then, tomorrow, be ready to convene your class and share with all your children some of the ideas that their classmates have written. If your children see that their words matter to *you*, this will help them listen to their own and each other's words with new attentiveness.

I recently visited a class of special needs students. My intention had been to just stick my head into their classroom and say a few words to their teacher. But then I saw that their classroom was a converted bathroom. The room was so despicable that I couldn't leave without somehow trying to bring sunlight to the children. So I simply asked if I could read their writing. As all the children listened, I turned through the stack of work, reading aloud the start of one story and then another, and another. I read as if the stories radiated beauty. I did nothing but read parts of each text aloud—but the children's mouths were open in astonishment at what they'd written. To tell you the truth, a fair portion of this was due not to what they had written, but to the way I read their words. Try it. You can read "I once had a dog" like those are Shakespeare's words. If you read your students' essay entries as if they sizzle with insight, your children's deep freeze will thaw and they'll begin to care about this new unit of study.

Be sure to channel students' energy toward more writing. Say to one, "You've *got* to add on to this!" Whisper to the next child, "I can't wait to read what you write next!"

GENERATING ESSAY WRITING FROM NARRATIVE WRITING

Katherine Paterson, author of Bridge to Terabithia, *says, "Writing is something like a seed that grows in the dark . . . or a grain of sand that keeps rubbing at your vitals until you find you are building a coating around it. The growth of a book takes time . . . I talk, I look, I listen, I hate, I fear, I love, I weep, and somehow all of my life gets wrapped around the grain." (Paterson 1981).*

This quote exactly matches my understanding of how writers build depth and intensity in a piece of writing. For example, I might jot down an anecdote. When I reread it, something stirs inside me. I find myself layering the anecdote with an insight. I drive in my car, thinking of my writing, and pass something by the side of the road that somehow fits with the original anecdote and its accompanying insight. By now my mental seed idea takes on extra skins, like one of those surprise balls given as favors at a child's birthday party, the kind with layers of crepe paper hiding all sorts of embedded treasures. I write, I reread, I remember, I listen, and all of this gets wrapped around the initial idea.

One way to teach children to layer their ideas and memories is to teach them to reread entries—especially narrative entries—and to catch the thoughts they have as they do this rereading. For example, I might reread my story about my father with his improvised ice pack, and suddenly I'm thinking of how there are never enough classroom supplies, so teachers, too, are always jury-rigging things together to make do. I've sometimes defined creativity as a willingness to live off the land, to improvise in a resourceful fashion. Now, I think, "This is no longer about my dad, this is a bigger idea, an idea about creativity— what it is and where it comes from. Where do I want to go with this trail of thought?"

In this session, we teach children to reread, rethink, and to layer their experiences with insights. We teach them to reread entries and ask themselves questions: "Why did I write this? What surprises me here?"

This session is about finding meaning and messages in the stories and lessons of our lives, and I hope it can bring you and your children to the heart of writing.

IN THIS SESSION, YOU'LL TEACH CHILDREN TO REVISIT NARRATIVE ENTRIES COLLECTED EARLIER IN THE YEAR, THIS TIME LAYERING THEM WITH INSIGHTS AND EMBEDDING THEM INTO IDEAS.

GETTING READY

- Student entry showing how writing extended the level of thinking
- One of your personal narrative entries from last unit of study to revisit
- Questions Writers Ask of Earlier Entries, listed on chart paper
- Strategies for Generating Essay Entries chart
- Student entry where a previous entry inspired ideas
- See CD-ROM for resources

MINILESSON

Generating Essay Writing from Narrative Writing

CONNECTION

Celebrate that your children are extending their initial ideas.

"Writers, yesterday I watched many of you slow yourselves down so that instead of writing one new idea after another and another, you wrote an idea and then extended that one idea using a prompt that got you to think more."

"This is really smart work because you are writing an idea and then having more thoughts about it. A lot of people believe that the most important reason to write is that when we write, we fasten our first thoughts onto the page so we can think about our thinking."

"When you write something like 'It is important to have a best friend' and then reread what you have written and push yourself to write and think more, this is powerful work! Your ideas become more complex. Listen to what Tyrone wrote."

> It is important to have one best friend. This is important because having one best friend is like having a home in the world. Some people think that it's best to have lots of friends and to think of them all as equal, but I find it comforting to know that Amy will always be there for me no matter what.

"Do you see how this writer started with a rather simple, straightforward thought— 'It is important to have a best friend'—and he actually used writing to ratchet up the level of his thinking?"

Name your teaching point. In this case, explain that writers can become inspired by rereading and reflecting on their own previous entries.

"Today I am going to teach you that as writers we push ourselves to write not only from what we've just written but also from ideas and moments we recorded days, weeks, and months earlier. I often reread my old writing, find an entry I care about, and write *another* entry in which I reflect on and think about the first one. This is a way for writing to grow like the rings of a tree, with layers of insight and thoughtfulness."

COACHING

You'll recall that at the start of this unit of study, I told children that when writers want to write about big ideas, most of us don't sit in an armchair and squeeze our brains, hoping to produce an insight. Instead, we head into the fray of life, and do so with an extra effectiveness. That session nudged children to observe and to grow ideas from those observations. But it could have instead nudged children to reread their notebooks, attending to the particles of life collected in those pages, trusting that those bits of life could evoke big ideas. Don't miss teaching this lesson. It's one that has unbelievable potential!

You plan for your students to write in paragraphs of thought, not sentences of thought. Over time, watch whether their initial ideas always fit into the confines of one sentence. As writers become more sophisticated, they'll use the whole paragraphs not so much to elaborate upon a one-sentence idea, but to lay out the idea in the first place. If you wanted to do so, you could explicitly teach this.

Notice the reference to ideas growing like rings of a tree. You'll recall that Sandra Cisneros used this metaphor in "Eleven." It's great when your teaching can contain echoes from another day's teaching. This gives a new layer of meaning to your earlier instruction, just as you are asking children to give new layers of meaning to their earlier words.

TEACHING
Demonstrate returning to a personal narrative entry and using it to inspire a new entry.

Earlier this year I wrote a narrative entry about my father picking me up at a basketball game. I want you to watch how I now reread part of that entry and reflect on what I had written. First let me reread the end of the entry to get myself started."

> When the [basketball] game was almost over, I glanced toward the doorway and saw my father striding across the gym floor toward me, his red plaid hunting cap perched on his head, his rubber galoshes flapping. Why couldn't he wait in the car like all the other dads, I thought. Then, in a voice that boomed through the room, my dad called, "Lukers!" and began to climb the bleachers toward me and the other kids. I wanted the floor to open up and swallow me.

"I've read this over, and now I'm going to try asking myself some questions." (Pay attention to the questions I ask myself because they might work for you as well.) I read from the list I had prepared on chart paper.

Questions Writers Ask of Earlier Entries

- Why is this important to me?
- What is the important thing about this?
- Why am I remembering this? How does it connect to who I am or to important issues in my life?
- What other entries does this connect with?
- What does this show about me? About life? What does this make me realize?
- Why did I write this?
- What do I want readers to know about this?
- What surprises me about this?

One important reason to keep a writer's notebook is that this allows us to revisit earlier writing. There are many reasons to invite children to reread their notebooks. During word study, you may want them to practice their new high-frequency words by rereading early entries, correcting any instances where they've misspelled them. If you have taught children to think about structures in their writing, you can ask them to reread old entries and categorize them according to the structure in which they are written. Today, you are showing children how they can take inspiration from these early pieces. Once you have a narrative and some big ideas about that narrative, you have the ingredients for a strong essay.

You may decide to share only one or two of these questions. I'm quite sure I don't gain much by listing all of them. You'll want to pick the one or two that work for your children, however, so I'll leave that up to you. There are, of course, other ways to phrase these questions, and other questions you could ask instead. "What emotional truth do I want to share with my reader?" Or simply, "So what?"

"I'll try the first question. I'm not sure of the answer, but I'll try to let some ideas come out of my pen."

> Why is this story about the basketball game important to me? I think I wrote about being embarrassed by my father because when I was young, it bothered me that my dad didn't act like other fathers.

"I could leave it at that, but I'll try to push myself to say more. Let's see . . . I'll reread and then just tell myself, 'Keep going.'"

> Why is this story about the basketball game important to me? I think when I was young, it bothered me that my father didn't act like other fathers.
>
> For example, he didn't wait in the car like other fathers, but instead, tromped right into our basketball games. He didn't know parents were expected to stay in the background. He'd go up to my friends, introduce himself, and soon he'd be deep in conversations with them. My cheeks would burn because he didn't stay inside the traditional father role.
>
> That was long ago, however, and I've since come to see the beauty in my father's arrival at that basketball game . . .

Debrief, naming what you've done in a way that is transferable to other days and other topics.

"Did you see how I reread an entry I had already written, and then asked myself just one or two questions? In that way I explored the meaning of the first entry. Writers do this often."

Whenever I model, I try to make my processes transferable. Notice that these questions could be asked of any personal essay entry. I want to teach kids to ask (as well as to answer) questions such as these.

My writing has a quality that suggests I'm hemming and hawing a bit. I do this because I'm trying to support the concept of writing as a tool for thinking and not just as a vehicle for conveying thoughts.

Notice that I'm asking children to think deeply about the significance of and larger ideas behind an entry they've gathered—even though that entry may not be a critically important one. It may surprise you that I'd suggest they probe behind a randomly selected entry, but the important thing is this: whatever skill I want writers to learn needs to be recycled through the unit and taught in a variety of ways. Today's strategy will of course be all the more important once writers have selected a thesis and are committed to a plan.

ACTIVE ENGAGEMENT
Set up partners to practice what you demonstrate.

"Right now, partner 1, please open your notebook and turn to a narrative entry from our first or second unit. Read the entry you select aloud to partner 2, and then try to have some thoughts about what you have written. Partner 2, you may want to ask one of the questions from our chart," I said, gesturing to the Questions Writers Ask of Earlier Entries chart.

"After you have said a thought and talked about it until you feel talked out, partner 2 can interject prompts from our list," I gestured to the Pushing Our Thinking list, "one that might work to keep you thinking more. For example, partner 2 might insert, 'This is important because . . .', 'To add on . . .', or 'This connects with . . .' The goal is for partner 1 to write in the air what he or she could conceivably write in an entry."

Notice that these minilessons contain echoes of each other. In prior lessons children have already written in the air, inserted prompts to nudge each other's thinking, and used language to elicit new ideas. Therefore, this should all be accessible for them. This teaching wouldn't have made a lot of sense, however, had prior sessions not taught these strategies.

LINK
Ask children to list and share ways they can live like essayists during today's workshop and their lives.

"Writers, today you have forty-five minutes of writing time left. You should have lots of options in mind for productive ways in which you could spend your time today. Would you look over our charts, think over your writing, and work with your partner to come up with four possible things that writers in this room could be doing today?" Each child turned knee to knee with his or her partner and the room buzzed with talk.

You'll see that this link has a different spin to it than most. I ask children to list four options, instead of doing so myself. If you feel your kids need to be more active in more sections of your minilessons, you could do this sort of thing often.

"I heard you say that you could use our Strategies for Generating Essay Entries chart, which now has a new item on it."

Strategies for Generating Essay Entries

- We observe the small stuff of our lives and then try to let what we see and hear spark an insight or an idea.
- We record an issue that matters in our lives. Then we list several ideas we have about that issue and choose one of those ideas to develop at more length. We push ourselves to shift from observing to saying, "and the thought I have about this is . . ."
- We write in two columns, or in two sections, one section for what we see, hear, and notice and the other for what we think.
- We take a subject (a person, place, or object) that matters to us, and list ideas related to that subject. Then we take one of those ideas and write about it.
- We reread our earlier writing, and we have new thoughts about it. We sometimes ask questions of those earlier entries.

"I also heard you say that you could try to have discussions on paper in which you grow your first ideas, using the same thought prompts that we use in book talks. Some of you will try free writing. And some of you didn't get a chance to look at the non-narrative examples we brought in, so you'll be doing that today. I can't wait to admire the work you do!"

WRITING AND CONFERRING

Encouraging Children to Make Choices

The good thing is that this unit of study allows you to teach your students many things that will be new for them. The bad thing is that this unit is more directive than the others and does less to strengthen children's ability to make choices and work independently. That is, because this unit brings children to a new and challenging kind of writing, you'll often need to ask them to spend the workshop doing whatever you taught that day, instead of adding the day's strategy to a repertoire to be called on at will.

You have a little window of time now before the complexity heightens in which you can encourage children to make choices, so I suggest you make a special point of doing this. Begin your conferences by researching what it is they've chosen to do. Ask, "What are you working on as a writer?" and expect from their response not only a topic but also a strategy—one they've chosen for particular reasons to meet particular goals. Be aware that children will quickly learn the words to use to impress you; nudge and probe to be sure they mean what they say. Ask, "Where exactly did you do that?"

Once you know what a writer is trying to do and the strategies he or she has used, you'll want to learn more. Ask that writer how the strategy is working and if he needs any help with it. Wait for the child to articulate an answer, so that the child feels responsibility for what to write and for how his choices are working. Try to help the child judge whether a strategy is working well by encouraging him to notice whether he is learning during writing. Ask, "What did you learn by writing this entry?" and "What new idea did you form as you wrote?" Your questions show that writers can expect to learn new things as they write, and can choose ways to make sure that happens.

> **MID-WORKSHOP TEACHING POINT**   *Generating Essay Writing from Literature*   "I want to congratulate you on the decisions you are making about how to use your time. And I want to point out that you can not only choose from all the strategies on our chart—you can also invent your own strategies for generating essay entries. You already have! Marcus just told me that instead of writing from his earlier entries, he has been writing off of *Because of Winn-Dixie,* our read-aloud book. He went back to reread parts and now he has an entry about fathers and kids, and one about how dogs can be company—and both entries were sparked by that one book! Listen to what Marcus wrote about fathers and kids."
>
> > When I reread the part in the beginning of Winn Dixie where Opal was trying to get her dad's attention, it made me think about my relationship with my dad. My dad works at home and it seems like he is always working. I try to talk to him, but he says, "Can't you see that I'm in the middle of something?" Opal's dad was like that too. He was always working on his sermons so he didn't spend time with her or tell her about her mom. That's what she wanted to know. I just want to spend time with him. I wish he was like other dads.
>
> "Some of you may want to borrow Marcus' strategy (I'll add it to our list) and some of you may want to invent other strategies that you'll teach to the rest of us."
>
> *continued on next page*

Remember that after learning what a child is already doing, you'll want to find something to compliment. Then tell the writer that you could, if she is game, offer a tip, a pointer. Say, "Can I teach you one thing that'll make what you are doing even more effective?" After this, your conference will resemble a mini-minilesson.

If you feel unsure of what to teach during the teaching component of the conference, keep in mind that the class charts can be a resource for you as well as for young writers. If the child is unsure of what to write and a chart is posted titled, Strategies for Generating Essay Entries, then you'll want to remind the writer that when he is stuck, he can reach for a strategy from his mental tool box. Another resource which you and the child can draw on are the final drafts of previous year's student essays that children brought home to study earlier. For example, if a child says that her problem is she doesn't know what to write after she's recorded a big idea (or if she hasn't paused for a moment, instead blithely moving from one idea to a totally disconnected idea) then you can say, "Well, let's look at what some of our mentor authors have done that you could try – that's what I often do when I'm stuck." Then, a glance at the mentor text might suggest that one way a writer can say more is to shift from the level of generality to that of specificity, using a phrase such as, "For example, one day . . . " to help.

Remember as you confer with children that they are still writing entries, and are not writing formal essays. The authors haven't intended to write these entries in an essay shape, with a topic sentence and then support, and there is no reason that their entries need to follow this pattern. The goal has been thoughtfulness and insight.

Strategies for Generating Essay Entries

- We observe the small stuff of our lives and then try to let what we see and hear spark an insight or an idea.
- We record an issue that matters in our lives. Then we list several ideas we have about that issue and choose one of those ideas to develop at more length. We push ourselves to shift from observing to saying, "and the thought I have about this is . . . "
- We write in two columns, or in two sections, one section for what we see, hear, and notice and the other for what we think.
- We take a subject (a person, place, or object) that matters to us, and list ideas related to that subject. Then we take one of those ideas and write about it.
- We reread our earlier writing, and we have new thoughts about it. We sometimes ask questions of those earlier entries.
- We write off of the books we read.

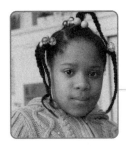

SHARE

Hearing Essays Based on Narratives

Share an example of idea-based writing generated by narrative writing.

"Writers, I want to share with you what Francesca did. She went back to a personal narrative story she wrote earlier this year about how, when she was sledding, she accidentally bumped into a child and the father yelled at her so harshly that she felt like a little kid again. And Francesca wrote a couple of pages of thoughts about that one entry! Listen." *[Figs. V-1, V-2,* and *V-3* on next page*]*

People can bring change in other people. I felt a little scared and guilty. As I sat down near Logan, guilt filled my head. I could feel heat building up in my head as I lay in the snow.

I feel like a little little kid that was about three years old. I was not that excited big kid, I felt like I was going backwards in life, like I was going from nine to three.

I am the kind of person who gives up easily when something like a mistake happens. I try to never mess up or do something wrong so I'm too hard on myself. Unlike Camilla, my little sister, or Logan, my younger friend. Why am I the only one who feels like it's all my fault? I always seem to take the fall for everything. Why do I care so much, I'm just a kid?

Growing up can have a rough color. Kids think that growing up is so great and so simple but they have no idea what they're in for. Growing up can feel really good but it does not happen fast and its not as easy as it looks. It's like a train where at every stop you get a little farther in life. I still remember when I thought growing up was so easy and so fast and I accidentally bumped into a man and his kid. After that I felt scared and little and did not sled again. So growing up can be great but it isn't as easy and smooth as it really looks.

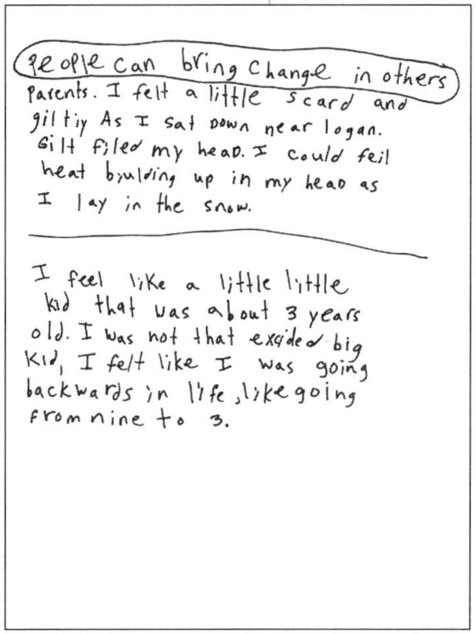
People can bring Change in others Parents. I felt a little scard and giltiy As I sat down near logan. Gilt filed my head. I could feil heat buulding up in my head as I lay in the snow.

I feel like a little little kid that was about 3 years old. I was not that exsided big Kid, I felt like I was going backwards in life, like going from nine to 3.

Fig. V-1 Francesca's notebook entry

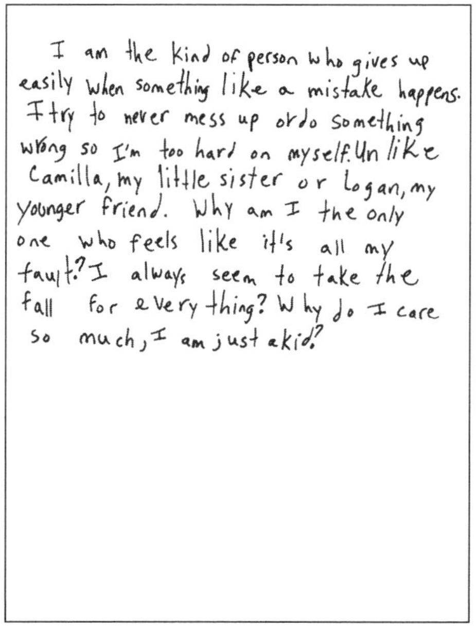
I am the kind of person who gives up easily when something like a mistake happens. I try to never mess up or do something wrong so I'm too hard on myself. Unlike Camilla, my little sister or Logan, my younger friend. Why am I the only one who feels like it's all my fault? I always seem to take the fall for every thing? Why do I care so much, I am just a kid?

Fig. V-2 Francesca's notebook entry

Ask students to share their own essay-like writing, born of narrative entries.

"Francesca's ideas are taking on new growth-rings of meaning, growing like a tree grows. She began with an experience on the sledding hill, and she's used that experience to think about how quickly her big-kid strength can vanish. She's pondered why she beats herself up, and she thinks grown ideas not only about herself but about growing up in general. Her writing has shifted from a detail about sledding to broad insights about life. This is what essayists do."

"Would each of you share with your partner an entry that you wrote based on one of your personal narratives? If you haven't yet done this, would you do it now, out loud, writing in the air so you get a chance to feel what this work entails?"

Growing up Can Have A Ruff color. Kids think that Growing up is so great and so simple but they have no Idea What there in For. Growing up can feel really good but it does not happen fast and It's not as easy as it looks. It's like a train where at every stop you get a little farther in life. I still remember when I thought Growing up was so easy and so fast and I accidentally Bumped into a man and his kid. After that I felt scared and lyttle and did not sled again. So Growing up can Be great but It isn't as easy and smooth as it really looks.

Fig. V-3 Francesca's notebook entry

HOMEWORK *Writing from Earlier Entries* Writers, remember Naomi Shihab Nye's poem "A Valentine for Ernest Mann," where she writes that poems hide in everyday places like sock drawers, and unlikely places like in the eyes of a skunk?

Today I want to remind you that it's not only *poems* that hide. *Issues* hide as well. They hide in the seemingly small events that haunt us, that resurface over and over in our minds.

Tonight, write an entry in which you step back from the hurly-burly of life and say, "There's a bigger issue here." That's important not only for life, but also for writing. I recall a fifth grader named Daniel who longed for a cat. Finally, after lots of preparation, he brought his case for a cat to his mother and she snapped back at him, 'Daniel, I don't have time for a cat.' Later, Daniel wrote about that moment in his notebook. He recreated the moment with his mother, recording her retort.

"Daniel, I don't have time for a cat."

But this time, Daniel added on. Here's what he wrote.

In my mind, I thought, "That's why I need one." I need a cat because I want someone who has time for me, who's there for me.

Daniel's next entry was about how, ever since his family moved from a little apartment in the city to a big suburban home, the rope that held his family together has been strained to the breaking point. His father leaves the house early, returns late. He and his brother no longer share a bedroom. His mother is busy all the time with the community. *All* of that was lurking behind Daniel's initial entry about wanting a cat! This is what I mean when I say, 'Issues hide.' The writer who questions, probes, connects can find the real issues that lurk behind minor heartaches, behind an argument over whose turn it is to take out the trash. Do that work in your writer's notebook tonight unless you, as a writer, have plans that take priority over this, in which case, follow your own plans.

TAILORING YOUR TEACHING

If your children need support before they can benefit from this minilesson . . . by all means revisit it. There are few minilessons in the series which matter more. Give your children an extra day or two in which to reread their prior writing and to write entries about that writing. The minilesson that might mean the most to your children is one in which you say to them, "Last night at home, I decided to try my hand at the work you all did here in school yesterday. So I remembered that writers can reread a story we wrote earlier, and then ask questions of that story." Here you can recall the specific questions. Then tell the children that you tried this and show them your text and teach them whatever insight about the initial event you gleaned from doing this work. If an insight doesn't leap to mind, show them how you can look for insight by asking yourself, "Why is this event in my life important to me?" Then talk and write about ways in which the event matters.

If your students are having trouble making decisions about which piece to choose or about what matters most in a particular piece . . . they may be paralyzed by the options, especially if they are fluent and prolific writers. If this is the case, you may want to narrow their task a bit by structuring their work more. You might begin this lesson by saying, "Writers, last night I decided to do the same work I asked you to do. I went back through my notebook and reread my entries. I was trying to catch the thoughts I was having so that I could start a new piece. But it was hard to do! I ended up reading through old entries. It reminded me of when I had to clean out my huge box of photographs. I wanted to throw some away, give some away, and put some in albums. But, I spent hours just looking through the photos and remembering the moments and the people in them. I never got my work done. That's what happened when I was rereading through my notebook. I'd read an entry and then I'd stop and begin to remember times in my life, and the next thing I knew it was midnight!!! Time to go to sleep! This morning, on my way to work, I thought about what could help us with this situation and I tried it again before you guys arrived. Here's what I learned. First, we just need to pick an entry. So, if you have several entries that really matter to you, just pick one of them! No big deal. You can flip a coin if necessary! Then reread that piece, and list out the thoughts you're having. I put a stcky note on the bottom of the page and as I reread, I jotted quick notes to myself. Then, once again, I had to make a quick choice. I think I came up with five ideas from rereading my piece about when my dad came to the basketball game and yelled "Lukers!" So again, I just had to pick one to write an entry about. It was hard, and I was having trouble deciding, but then I just made a decision. You know what helped? I realized that I have my whole life to write, and so I can write about those other entries, and those other ideas I have in the future. For now, it was important for me as a writer to just pick something!!"

For the Active Engagement part of this lesson, you could give students a timed minute or two to choose the entry they want to work off of and have them put a sticky note on the bottom of the page. Next, ask them to reread it and jot the thoughts they are having. Finally, tell them to make a quick pick of the idea they want to work on. You can ask them to tell their partner which idea they've chosen and to say a thing or two they plan on writing about it.

If your students struggle with the multi-layered task of rereading entries, picking one to probe, and then generating an essay narrative from it . . . you might want to make the task a bit smaller by adapting an idea from *Writing Down the Bones*, by Natalie Goldberg. In her book, Goldberg suggests taking a poetry book and opening up to any page. She tells writers to grab a line, write it down, and keep writing off of the line. For the purposes of the essay unit, you might suggest to students that they pick an old narrative entry and find a line to copy on the next blank page in their notebook. "Writers, pick a line that is sort of meaty, a line that seems to be telling you, "Say more here. Then write, write, and write some more off of that one line." Chances are your students will pick a line that matters to them, and the writing that they do off of the line might help them generate a piece that has significance.

MECHANICS

Although much of our teaching at the start of this new unit will support children as they work with expository writing, we will also want to continue to support children's ongoing development as writers and spellers. Developmental instruction needs to be tailored to support specific groups of children. It's important to ensure that children don't interpret the shift to a new genre as an invitation to stop using the conventions of grammar or the spelling rules they've learned!

To help plan your teaching of spelling, take an inventory of your class. Look at whether your students have mastered these challenges:

- Do they represent all the sounds they hear in a word?

- Do they spell most high-frequency words correctly?

- Are their short vowels correct most of the time?

- Do they use generalizations in ways that lead to correct (and sometimes to incorrect) spelling? For example, do they add final "E"s when they should, by logic, be necessary?

- Do they understand generalizations pertaining to word endings, such as doubling a final consonant before adding the ending?

If you sit with a stack of children's work and a set of questions such as this, you'll soon form a list of names of children who need help representing all the sounds in a word and spelling most high–frequency words correctly. Those children will no doubt also need help determining whether to double

the final consonant in a word before adding an ending, but such help might overwhelm them at this point. Once you have formed small groups and have an agenda for each group, then you simply need to be sure of how and when to teach whatever you wish to teach. You'll want to rely on a good book to help you plan your spelling instruction. I suggest Snowball and Bolton's *Teaching Spelling K–8*, Marten's *Word Crafting,* or Wilde's *You Kan Red This!*

In addition to keeping records of each child's knowledge of conventions, you will also want to know at which stage of the writing process the child uses that knowledge. For example, does this one child insert commas correctly in her final drafts, but not yet use them correctly in her very rough notebook entries? If so, this suggests that commas are still challenging enough and new enough for her that using them requires conscious, deliberate, focused attention. Encourage this writer to begin to draft-with-commas, even if she doesn't use them absolutely correctly. You want her to learn that what she at first does towards the end of the writing process then moves forward in the process, becoming an acquired habit that is incorporated into drafting. It is important that children begin to use conventions with automaticity in early drafts. So guide children to apply their knowledge in a stage of the writing process which is one step earlier than whatever you see. Coach them into the new groove by helping them get the feel for using that knowledge more quickly as they write. If you are seeing the same level of control of conventions in all stages of a child's writing process, that could be a sign that the child is ready for more teaching—she may be able to push herself further at the end of the process.

IN THIS SESSION, YOU WILL TEACH CHILDREN THAT WRITERS REREAD THEIR WRITING TO FIND OR INVENT A SEED IDEA—A THESIS.

FINDING AND CRAFTING THESIS STATEMENTS

Prepare yourself. Over the next three days, *your children will spend all their time drafting and revising what will amount to a frame—an outline—for their essays. Today you'll teach them to draft and revise a strong, clear thesis. In the next session, they'll plan topic sentences and paragraphs to support their thesis. And then, in the following session, one which is especially optional, they'll talk and free write about their plan and then reconsider it in light of what they discover they really want to say.*

You'll definitely want to do this writing work along with your students. There won't be a great volume of writing in the next few days, but you and your children can learn far-reaching lessons about logical thinking if you do this work alongside each other. By trying the same things that you ask your students to do, you'll get an insider's feel for why this work is harder than it looks, and for how you can help children do it more effectively.

Before you proceed, I suggest you read aloud some of the essays provided on the CD-ROM, paying attention to the thesis statement and the topic sentences for each one. These essays may seem simple and repetitive, even dull. I promise that although the products may not seem as luscious as other writing you've seen across this series, the lessons in logic and language that you and your children can learn through this work are crucial and long-lasting.

The work you launch today may not occupy children for a full-length workshop. Very skilled and experienced writers could invest weeks in today's work, but many children will find themselves done in short order. Because the next session's workload is gigantic, you can't collapse the two days into one. Instead, rely on conferring and small group work to support revision, and be prepared to end today's workshop a bit earlier if children seem to be finished.

GETTING READY

- Your own or a colleague's non-narrative notebook entry to demonstrate finding a thesis
- Student entry to illustrate the process of drafting a thesis
- List of questions for assessing a thesis, written on chart paper
- Student entry to illustrate the process of reviewing and revising a thesis
- See CD-ROM for resources

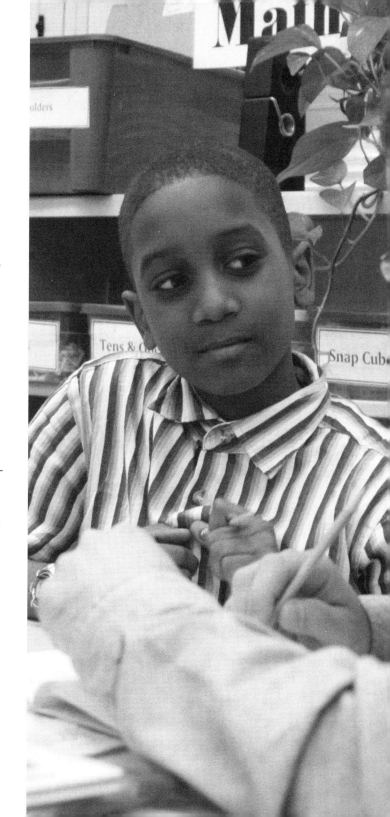

MINILESSON

Finding and Crafting Thesis Statements

CONNECTION

Connect the work of today to work writers did in previous units.

"Writers, earlier this year when we wrote our personal narratives, we collected entries in our notebooks for a week or two, and then looked back at everything we had collected and chose a seed idea that we developed into a major piece of writing. Our notebooks are again brimming with possible seed ideas that could be developed, and now we want to select one that could become an essay."

Name your teaching point. Specifically, teach children that writers reread to find a seed idea, in this instance called a thesis.

"Today I want to teach you that when I reread my notebook to select a seed idea for an essay, what I'm looking for quite literally is a seed *idea*. When we wrote personal narratives, we used whole entries as our seed ideas—they were really seed *stories* rather than seed *ideas*. But when we write *essays*, it helps if the writer has an idea—or a claim—that the writer wants to advance, that the writer wants to explore or defend."

"Sometimes we find our seed ideas in the pages of our notebooks, but sometimes the idea we want to address isn't yet crystallized on the page. That's why we reread our notebooks and ask, 'What is the big thing I *really, really* want to say?' Then we write our claim, or our thesis (that's the term essay writers give to this claim), in a sentence or two."

"So, writers, today I hope you learn that each writer needs to reread his or her entries to find (or invent) a seed idea, which is also called a *claim* or a *thesis*. We write that seed idea in a sentence or two. Before we begin to develop our seed idea, our thesis, we try it on for size, asking, "'Could I imagine writing an essay about this? Is this what I want to say?'"

TEACHING

Demonstrate the way essayists try a few seed ideas on for size.

"I know you can imagine how writers go about rereading their entries, looking for seed ideas, because you've done similar work earlier this year. The only difference is that now we look for or write just *a sentence or two* that states the idea we want to develop. You can probably figure out how to reread looking for a seed idea; I'd like instead to show you how my friend Cory tried a few seed ideas on for size."

COACHING

The Connection usually begins by consolidating what we've already taught as a way both to review and to ready children to integrate a new bit of knowledge into their prior learning. Usually this means that the Connection summarizes the preceding minilessons. Sometimes, however, as in this instance, the Connection section of a minilesson refers back to (and prepares writers to build upon) the lessons they learned during parallel minilessons in earlier units.

Every new study carries with it new terminology, new vocabulary. In these sessions, I tend to tuck synonyms alongside the new terminology. Some of your children (including your English Language Learners) may need more explicit instruction in the vocabulary of the unit. For this unit, the terms include claim, thesis, evidence, idea, argue, persuasive, statistics, citations, parallel, support, counterarguments, outline, transitions, *and* bullets. *All of these terms will resurface in the later unit on* Literary Essays.

If we want children to really attend to our minilessons, our teaching needs to be deserving of their attention. We can't say, "All eyes and ears up here, please" and then proceed to fill ten minutes with an elaborate demonstration of something the kids already know how to do! On the other hand, we do sometimes need to nudge kids to do some work they've learned previously. This minilesson, then, can provide a template for one way to handle this situation.

"After Cory read all the entries she'd written, asking herself, 'Which of these might make a good essay?' she found an entry she'd written about her friend Jen. It was a long entry; she reread it and underlined the two or three sentences that really captured her main idea about her friend. She underlined: <u>My friend Jen and I are so much alike.</u> She also underlined <u>Jen and I are close because we've been friends for years. We've been friends through the best and worst times.</u> She figured maybe one of these sentences could become her seed idea."

"Cory thought about building an essay around the first idea—that Jen and she are so much alike. She tried to picture what she might say in that essay. She said to me, 'It's true that we are alike, but when I think about writing an essay on that, I'm not sure that idea captures what I really want to say.' So Cory did what essayists do. She tried out the other idea, that she and Jen are close because they have been friends for years. She found that was better. But she still wasn't sure that was exactly what she wanted to say. I nudged her to ask herself, 'What exactly do I want to say about my topic?' That question led her to say, 'I want to tell about how good it is to have a best friend.' So she tried to write that in a sentence or two. She wrote, 'Best friends are like comfortable jeans.' She liked that but she still tried writing her main idea another way. This time she wrote, 'The world is a softer place when you have a best friend.' She liked that best of all."

Debrief. In this case, point out that the seed idea is smaller here than in narrative, and it takes revision and projection into the future to settle on one.

"Writers, I hope you noticed that Cory first reread all her entries, then she found one she liked and underlined a few key ideas about it. When we are writing essays, our seed idea is not usually a whole entry, a whole story. We cull out a single sentence or two (or write a sentence or two) that really says what we want to say. I also hope that you noticed that Cory didn't just settle on her first version of a seed idea. She wrote a few drafts and asked herself, 'What exactly do I want to say?' and finally, after she imagined how several would go, she had a thesis she really liked and knew she had things to say about."

ACTIVE ENGAGEMENT
Ask writers to join you in helping one member of the class go through the process of crafting a thesis.

"Writers, let's practice this by seeing if we can help Joe settle on his seed idea. He's already reread his entries and he underlined this idea: '<u>Kids should be able to get exercise more often.</u>' I'm going to ask Joe to tell us what he *really* wants to say in his essay. Often our

Notice that each of these statements contains a subject and a point.

You'll also find times to bring a colleague into your minilessons. You can literally have someone co-teach a minilesson, or simply tell the story of their work as I do here with Cory Gillette's work. Cory is doing some very complicated and important work here, drafting and revising her thesis. If you tell the story of another teacher's work, you can process what the writer is doing so the class can learn from both your colleague's mental moves and from your analysis. You can, of course, play both the role of the writer and of the teacher yourself, but be sure if you do this that you signal with your body language when you are being the writer and when you become the teacher.

As Cory revised her initial thesis statement, her thinking became more complex.

You can't expect children to see that the two different thesis statements each require different forms of elaboration, but you'll come to understand that the goal when writing a thesis is not one great sentence—it is, instead, a workable essay.

You'll be surprised to see that it is complicated to write a good clear thesis statement.

first effort at a thesis is vaguer and broader than the thesis we finally settle upon. Then would you work with your partner to see if the two of you can help Joe word his thesis in a way that really captures what he wants to say?"

Joe said, "See, I think it's not right that kids just eat junk food and watch TV and play video games. And I think kids need to exercise more. Schools should have gym more."

"So writers, the challenge will be to figure out how to consolidate Joe's main idea into a single sentence or two." I reiterated what he'd said. "Work with your partner, and then let's list some suggested thesis statements for Joe."

After a few minutes the class had compiled this list.

- Kids should be able to exercise more often.
- Schools should have gym more often.
- Instead of plopping on the couch, eating junk food, watching television, and playing video games, kids should get up off the couch and go exercise.

Reread each of the class' suggestions, projecting how an essay might go based on that particular thesis.

"These at first seem so similar, right? But if you project into the future and imagine how these theses might become essays, I think they'd be very different."

"'Kids should be able to exercise more often'—an essay from that thesis might name the reasons why kids should exercise more often. Maybe kids should do this because exercise is good for their hearts, their muscles—and maybe for their morale? Or there could be a different set of reasons why this matters."

"The next thesis, 'Schools should have gym more often,' is a little different, isn't it? That essay will need to defend why schools need to have gym—so maybe one reason is because exercise is important (that one part could tell about how exercise is important for kids' hearts, muscles, and morale, couldn't it?). Maybe another reason might be that kids are no longer playing out of doors during their free time, instead they are couch potatoes. Do you see how each thesis statement sets up a different plan for an essay?"

Joe will probably draft other versions of a thesis statement and that's the process all of you will need to go through today and every time you want to draft a thesis."

As you work with children, keep in mind that more general thesis statements are easier to develop but often lead to less stellar work. Nudge your more experienced writers, those who are game for a challenge, towards more specific thesis statements.

During the Active Engagement, it's often a reasonable option to ask children to work in partners, thinking through a way to help one child do whatever has been taught.

Elizabeth Lyon, author of A Writer's Guide to Nonfiction, suggests (claims!) that there are three kinds of claims: of fact, of value, and of policy. She writes, "Claims of fact offer objectively verifiable data. Claims of value express approval or disapproval of taste or morality. They evaluate desirability. Movie reviews are a good example. Claims of policy suggest institutionalizing change as a solution to problems, such as 'There ought to be a law.'" (Lyon 2003, p.119).

You'll probably find that your children aren't exact, precise readers; to many children all these sentences say the same thing. Help children to really read what's written on their own pages.

You will want to use a child in your own class, and the suggested thesis statements will then be very different. You'll find that often children suggest statements that have two or three branches in them—"kids need exercise and there should be more gym." Help children to prune these so the seed idea makes one big claim. This, in and of itself, will still be challenging to defend! You'll want to describe briefly the fact that each thesis leads to a different essay, although children will not tend to grasp this yet.

LINK

Repeat the teaching point. In this case, explain how to choose and make a thesis.

"So, writers, from this day forward, remember that after collecting ideas for a bit, the time will come to make a decision. Specifically, if you are writing an essay, after developing a bunch of entries and ideas, you'll want to reread and select what is, quite literally, a seed idea. To do this, reread your entries, and find or write sentences that get to the heart of your intentions. We usually write our seed idea, our claim, in at least six or seven different ways until we have the words and the meaning right. Today, each of you will want to begin rereading your entries, selecting a seed idea, and then you can draft and revise a thesis statement." [*Figs. VI-1 and VI-2*]

You'll notice that on this particular day, the minilesson is designed to channel every child to do the same work. This is unusual.

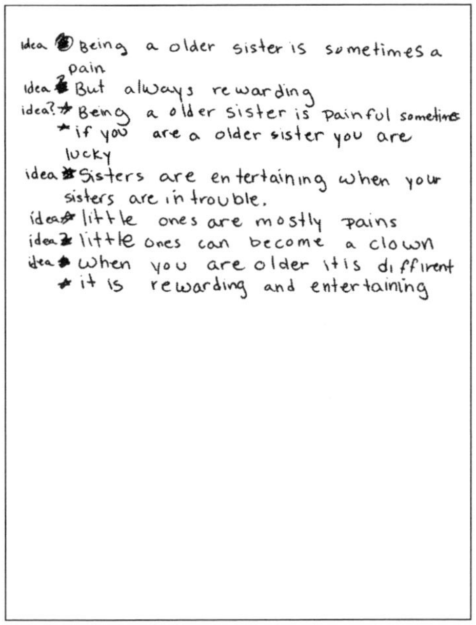

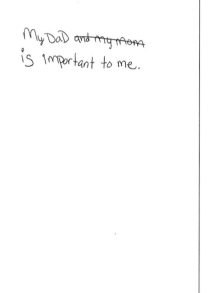

idea ❶ Being a older sister is sometimes a pain
idea ❷ But always rewarding
idea❸↗ Being a older sister is painful sometimes
★ if you are a older sister you are lucky
idea ★ Sisters are entertaining when your sisters are in trouble.
idea↗ little ones are mostly pains
idea↗ little ones can become a clown
idea ★ when you are older it is diffirent
★ it is rewarding and entertaining

Fig. VI-1 Various seed ideas

My Dad ~~and my mom~~
is important to me.

Fig. VI-2 Randolio's thesis

WRITING AND CONFERRING

Crafting Thesis Statements

Your minilesson probably did not feel particularly confusing to you, but the work you've set out for kids today and especially over the next few days will pose lots of challenges for them. These challenges are best addressed through one-to-one conferences and small-group strategy lessons. I recommend you look ahead to tomorrow's minilesson and the write-up on conferring in that session, and today as you work with children, set some of them up to have success tomorrow. I'd especially do this with some of your strugglers.

In terms of today's work with developing a thesis statement, you can anticipate that some kids will write and select questions rather than statements. Teach them that instead of writing, "Why do I love my dad so much?" they need to make a stand, to claim a position: "I love my father because he makes me improve myself." Some children will resist making clear, concise statements and instead hedge their claims: "One of the reasons why I love my dad is that some of the time he doesn't let me be anything less than my best." Help writers who hedge to create a lean, clear thesis that doesn't waffle.

MID-WORKSHOP TEACHING POINT *Checking Thesis Statements* "Writers, can I stop you? I hope you understand that your entire job for today's workshop is to write one sentence. You might think 'Whoopee! Not much work today!' But what I want to teach you is that it is crucial that today be your most intense, hard-working day of the unit. Your job is to work hard at writing and revising your thesis. To do that, you need to be willing to say, 'No, that's not quite it,' or 'Let me try writing another just to be sure.' So let me teach you two ways to go about revising your thesis statements."

"First, I mentioned to you earlier that after Cory and other writers have written a few possible thesis statements, they ask themselves questions and use those questions to help them revise those all-important sentences. These questions should nudge you, as well, to revise."

"Then, too, sometimes when you reread your entries, looking for a sentence which could become your thesis, you find that no one sentence really captures the complexity of what you want to say. Alejandro, for example reread his notebook and found an entry he'd written about his friendship with Mike. He figured this might be a topic he'd like for an

continued on next page

Questions Writers Ask of Theses

- Is this topic something I know and care about? Can I imagine writing about this general topic for the next few weeks?
- Is my thesis an idea or an opinion—not a fact and not a question?
- Is my thesis exactly what I want to address? Is it as specific as possible?
- Is my thesis a strong, clear claim?
- Is there only one claim I'll need to support in this thesis?

Steer children away from a thesis that has two branches, as in "My mother and my father are important to me." That essayist would have to prove that both his mother and his father are important. It is simpler to start with one single claim. Then, too, sometimes a thesis is really making two points, as in this example: "Because children care a lot about their parents, sometimes they are embarrassed by them." There is nothing wrong with this thesis, but defending it poses an extra layer of writing challenge, because now the child needs to show not only that kids can be embarrassed by their parents, but also that this feeling is motivated by care. Later, writers can always address counterarguments or further claims, but for now, help children write straightforward, clean, crisp thesis statements.

Some kids will write a fact in lieu of a thesis. The child who writes, "My father picks me up after school," has written a fact, not an idea. I prompt children to go past the fact to an idea by asking "What are your ideas or your feelings about this?" Soon the child will have a thesis: "I love it when my father picks me up after school."

continued from previous page

essay, so he reread his entry, looking for a single sentence that summed up the entry and his feelings for Mike. *[Fig VI-3]* Listen."

> I have been thinking about my friendship with Mike. I thought that it is sometimes hard to be friends with Mike because he is interested in things that I am not interested in. For example he is interested in movie making and I am not, he likes to make up comic book characters, he likes to play video games and I don't, he likes to watch the Simpsons and I don't. I sometimes have fights with him. For example, we play card games that he made up and he sometimes changes the rules in the middle of the game. On the other hand Mike is a good friend because the games that he makes up are fun.

"Alejandro realized that he didn't have one line that captured what he thought, because he had both good and bad feelings about Mike. So he thought, 'Maybe the one thing I am saying is that my friendship with Mike is complicated.' He wrote that down."

> My friendship with Mike is complicated.

"Then he tried to revise that idea by saying his feelings more precisely. He tried to compare the friendship to something everyone knows. Here's what he wrote next."

> My friendship with Mike is like a seesaw. Sometimes it is up and sometimes it is down.

"Then he tried to write this in a stronger fashion, adding in his emotions."

> It is hard to be friends with someone who is so different from me.

"You may need to do this kind of work to find or craft your thesis too."

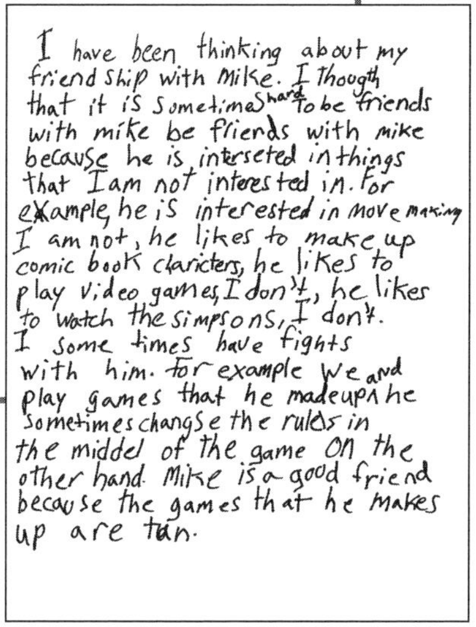
I have been thinking about my friend Ship with Mike. I Thougth that it is Sometimes hard to be friends with mike be friends with mike because he is intrseted in things that I am not interested in. For example, he is interested in move making I am not, he likes to make up comic book claricters, he likes to play video games, I don't, he likes to watch the simpsons, I don't. I some times have fights with him. for example we and play games that he madeup he Sometimes changSe the ruls in the middel of the game On the other hand. Mike is a good friend because the games that he makes up are fun.

Fig. VI-3 Alejandro's notebook entry

SHARE

Let Small Stories Evoke Big Ideas

Ask writers to postpone closure on their theses, and to imagine another possibility. Teach them that writers sometimes begin with a powerful story, using it to generate an umbrella idea.

"Your thesis statement will frame all the work you do for the rest of this unit, so I want to suggest you devote this share session to imagining that your thesis statement could be altogether different than the one you've temporarily settled upon. So for today, you arrived at your thesis by rereading your notebook and searching for a sentence or two that named a big idea that matters to you. Later, as you write, you'll generate details that support this big idea."

"You could, on the other hand, arrive at a thesis by progressing in the opposite direction. Many writers find it helpful to begin with detail, a specific, and then write their way toward the big idea. Writers talk about the importance of "revealing detail" and I recently realized, with a start, that details can be revealing for the writer, not just for the reader. A revealing detail can help a writer realize a big idea. In this way, a revealing detail can shine a light on a larger concept for the writer."

Get children started rereading their notebooks, identifying a precious particle, and developing an idea.

"Right now, would you sit quietly and just reread your notebook? Look for the anecdote or small story that catches your heartstrings or that makes your mind feel as if it's on fire. When you find this, reread that entry, and consider that you may want to put this entry at the heart of an essay. To do this, you'll need to discover a big idea that comes from your small story. Try writing as a way to mull over the meaning of your anecdote. Ask, 'What does this little story really show about me? About life? About a particular topic?' Try asking, 'What surprises me about this?' Try writing about this one bit of writing, prefacing your words with a phrase such as: 'The real thing I want to say is . . .' Write several different entries in which you explore the big ideas that might be hiding within this bit of powerful writing."

"If doing this brings you towards writing that feels more alive and provocative than the work you already did, try to produce a seed idea, a thesis statement, that crystallizes your new thinking. You can use this as your thesis and after this, you can use this pathway (going from small to big) to generate big ideas for yourself."[*Figs. VI-4, VI-5, VI-6, and VI-7*]

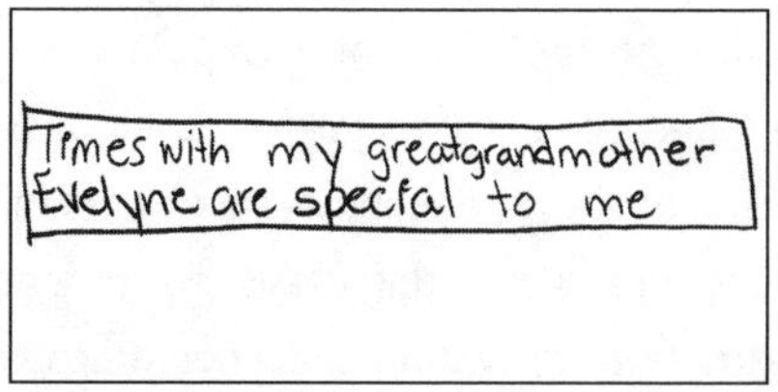

Times with my greatgrandmother Evelyne are special to me

Fig. VI-4 Sophie

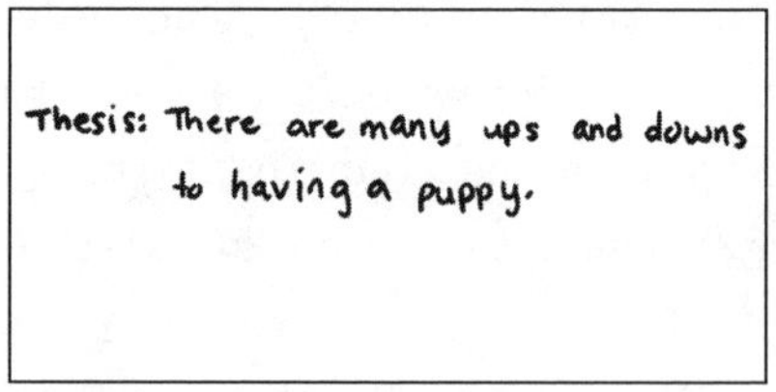

Thesis: There are many ups and downs to having a puppy.

Fig. VI-5 Elsie

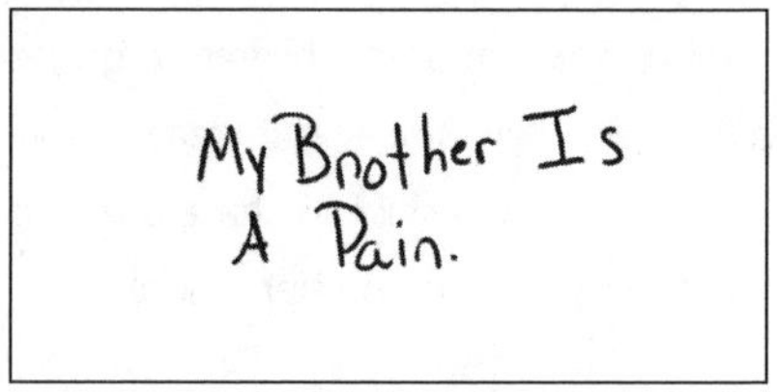

My Brother Is A Pain.

Fig. VI-6 Tray Sean

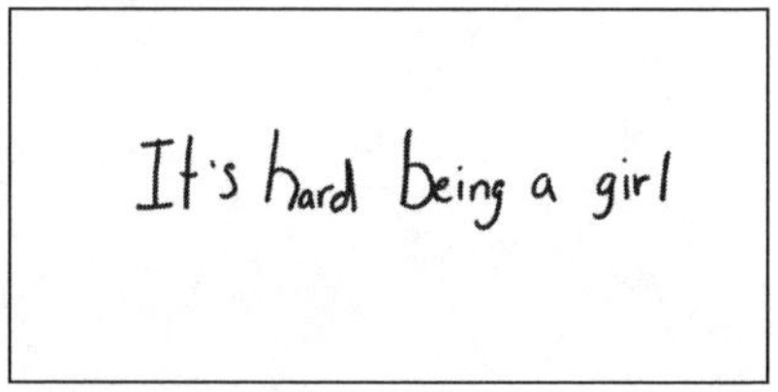

It's hard being a girl

Fig. VI-7 LaKeya

You can of course turn back to any of the minilessons in other units about finding and developing seed ideas since the process of finding and developing thesis ideas can be similar.

HOMEWORK | ***Comparing Narrative and Expository Writing Processes*** Writers, we haven't been talking a lot about the *writing process*, but I hope you realize that we're progressing through the stages of the writing process just as we did when we wrote personal narratives. Tonight, would you look back at our Monitoring My Writing Process checklist from our last unit of study, and think, "How is our process for writing essays the same as, and different from, the process we cycled through when we wrote personal narratives?" I'll send a blank chart home with you. Will you fill it out so that it accounts for the process you've experienced so far in this unit?

I'm also sending home our chart of the Qualities of Good Personal Narrative Writing. Would you think about this question: "Which qualities of good writing are shared in both genres? What qualities of good writing should we emphasize on a chart of Qualities of Good Expository Writing?" I'm sending home a blank Qualities of Good Expository Writing chart—please fill it out as well as you can.

The charts and lists that we make are ways to organize, consolidate, and make available all that children are learning so that they can draw on these strategies in the midst of writing time. If we want children to refer to charts, we need to do so in our minilessons, conferences, and small-group instruction. You may want to eventually turn some of these charts into checklists or rubrics, giving them to children to keep on hand as guides while they work.

Monitoring My Writing Process	First Piece	Next Piece
Gather entries		
Select and develop one seed idea		
Write an entry about what you are really trying to say		
Storytell to rehearse for writing		
Read published writing that resembles what I want to write		
Study published leads. Pay attention to what the author did and how the author did it. Let this influence your own writing		
Draft leads—try action, dialogue, setting		
Make a timeline		
Choose paper, plan story on pages, copy lead		
Write draft with each part on a separate page		
Reread and revise for clarity		
Draft endings—try writing with important ideas and images from the story, and with details that are reminders of the whole		
Revise and edit more now, or decide to wait until later, or not to revise		

To help you, I've also given each of you an essay that is worth studying.

Parent Pressure

By Harriet

Lately, I've been feeling like I have a huge weight on my back. I worry about every decision I make and every test I take. I feel like I always have to give 110 percent. I realize that I feel this way because I am under a lot of pressure from my parents. They put a lot of pressure on me in academics, sports, and even my social life.

My parents put tons of pressure on me when it comes to grades and tests. The subject doesn't matter. It could be math, reading, writing, gym or drama! Any time I do anything at school I have to get a good grade. One time I studied really hard for a social studies test on the American Revolution and got three wrong. For two days my mom kept insisting that I didn't study. So on my next social studies test my mom timed me. I had to study one hour each night for four days. I was so nervous to take that test. My stomach felt like a million bees were buzzing inside of it! I didn't want to let my parents down.

Also my parents pressure me about my career. I had to get into a good elementary school. Now that I am there they say I have to go to a great high school, get a thousand scholarships, then go to a top college. It doesn't end there. I have to get another thousand scholarships to go to medical school. Then I have to study hard to become an incredible doctor. It feels like this pressure will never end. I am only nine years old!

My parents also pressure me athletically. My parents want me to be the absolute best in sports. In soccer they want me to kick the most goals, be the star. In swimming they want me to win every heat. They also want me to play a variety of sports like tennis, basketball, bowling and golf. One time when I was playing soccer the star on the team, Cate, passed me the ball right in front of the net. I realized that if I made the goal my team would win. There was only a little time left. I could hear my dad cheering from the sides, "Go go go!" he shouted. "Kick it in!" I felt like time was slowing down. I was so afraid to mess up that I couldn't move. Suddenly a player from the other team kicked the ball from out between my feet. I never made a goal that game and I could tell that my dad was disappointed in me. There was too much pressure.

Finally, my parents pressure me socially. When I was little they wanted me to make the "right choice" when choosing friends. To be my friend kids had to be smart and never get in trouble. My parents really cared about the influence I got from other people. This was also true for my friend Angeli. Her parents only let her hang out with kids that got hundreds on tests. Angeli told me that she felt very limited with her friendships. She said there were a lot of kids that she wanted to have play dates with, but she wasn't allowed. She didn't want those kids to know that her parents wouldn't let her play with them. She didn't want to be mean. The pressure did not make her happy.

My parents put a lot of pressure on me and I hate it, but I realize that they probably don't realize how they make me feel. Adults can be oblivious to kid's feelings, but I also have never told them how I feel. Maybe if we talked about it they would understand that they don't have to worry about me. I always try my hardest.

Qualities of Good Personal Narrative Writing

- Write a little seed story; don't write all about a giant watermelon topic.
- Zoom in so you tell the most important parts of the story.
- Include true, exact details from the movie you have in your mind.
- Stay inside your own point of view. This will help you to write with true and exact details.
- Make sure stories tell not just what happens, but also the response to what happens.

If your students have difficulty understanding what a thesis statement is and if they have trouble finding one in their entries . . . you might teach your students that we make thesis statements all the time in life. You can suggest to them that when they are trying to convince their parents about something, they often begin the discussion by making a thesis statement and then offer evidence to support it. "Dad, I need pierced ears. Here's why . . . " or "I have too many chores! I have no time for fooling around anymore."

Another real-life example you might share is that people make thesis statements when they argue. In arguments, people often talk in thesis statements and provide evidence to further the points they are trying to make. You could say, "Imagine you and your friend disagree about which sport is the best, and you tell your friend something like, 'Soccer is a better game than basketball.' That's a thesis statement that you'll have to prove by offering evidence that supports your claim. Right now, think about some arguments you've had or think about some things you've been trying to persuade your parents to let you do. Turn and tell your partner about the example you've come up with, but try to tell it by starting with the thesis statement."

Another way to approach this is to ask your students to consider a concern they have about school. You might say something like this, "Writers, you guys always come back from recess complaining that it's too short. Let's pretend we're going to write an essay about it to give to the principal. What is your thesis statement or claim?" You might have the students turn and talk while you listen in. "Writers, I heard lots of different thesis statements. Some of you said things like, 'Fourth graders need longer recess time after lunch.' I also heard some of you say, "It's not fair that fourth graders have the same amount of recess time as third graders." Hmm. A few of you said, "More recess time will help fourth graders behave better in class." Wow, what thesis statements. Each of those claims would be great beginnings for an essay—as long as you can supply evidence!"

From these examples, you might ask your students to go back into their notebook and find a thesis statement that could turn into an essay.

COLLABORATING WITH COLLEAGUES

As you will have noticed, writing thesis statements is not easy for children. To better understand the challenges involved in creating a thesis statement, you might read this notebook entry with your colleagues, then together write several potential theses based on its contents. After a few minutes, come back together and compare what you have written.

> Our dad is quiet. My brother wishes he weren't. My brother's father-in-law is not quiet, and my brother spends almost all of his visiting time with his father-in-law and not with our dad. Our dad does not make a lot of phone calls to check in on us, his children. My brother's father-in-law comes over to his house most days. I see how well he knows my brother's house—he knows how to move the door to the baby's room just to keep it from creaking. Our dad gets lost on the way to my brother's house because he has been there so few times. My brother wishes our dad was different in so many ways. My brother forgets what our father did with him when he was little. Every Saturday, our dad would take my brother and me to the park to pitch to us until he was sore. Later that night, my mom would rub Tiger Balm into my dad's stiff arm. My brother's basketball team just won the championship. Dad heard about it from an acquaintance. My brother knows his wife's family so well, and he knows us less and less. I miss my brother.

When we tried this exercise, we came up with these possible thesis statements.

- Having a quiet father is hard.
- Quiet people have a difficult time maintaining relationships.
- Kids often wish their parents were different.
- Adult children don't value what was done for them as a child.

- Getting married doesn't expand your family, it shrinks it.
- People don't change just because you wish they would.
- People can really only have one father, not two.
- Adult children need to find ways to stay connected to their parents.
- My brother's hobby, basketball coaching, could repair the relationship between him and my dad.

As you look at this list or the one you and your colleagues generated, think about where a thesis statement comes from in relation to exactly what's written on the page as a notebook entry—then you can more easily help your children craft them. Sometimes we can form a thesis by taking a statement and attaching a judgment to it: "My dad is quiet" becomes "Having a quiet father is hard." Some thesis statements are a generalization based on the specifics in the writing. For example, "Quiet people have a difficult time maintaining relationships," generalizes the situation between this particular father and this son. Some thesis statements seem to come as potential solutions to problems: "My brother's hobby, basketball coaching, could repair the relationship between him and my dad." With your colleagues, you can find words to describe the ways in which different theses statements are created. However, this process of studying writing with colleagues and describing together what the writer has done can help your teaching of any stage of the writing process.

BOXES AND BULLETS: FRAMING ESSAYS

IN THIS SESSION, YOU WILL TEACH CHILDREN THAT ESSAYISTS FRAME THEIR WRITING BEFORE THEY DRAFT. YOU WILL DEMONSTRATE SOME STRATEGIES FOR DOING SO.

GETTING READY

- Simple example thesis that is easy to support with reasons, parts, or examples
- Class thesis statement
- Copies of two student essays from a past year, one set per child
- See CD-ROM for resources

Before you embark on today's session, you will definitely want to have a thesis in mind so that you can write your own essay along with your students. Unless you try your hand at this work, you won't grasp why and how it is challenging. To an outsider, the process described in this book may look simple, but it's vastly more complicated and more interesting than it appears from a distance.

Your goal today will be to help your children imagine several alternative plans or outlines for an essay. You will teach children that essayists sometimes support their thesis by providing reasons for a claim, sometimes by offering examples, sometimes by explaining how the parts of a subject support the author's point. Students will begin with their thesis statement(s) and then mull over the smaller points they want to make. Will they support the thesis by providing reasons? Examples? Kinds? By elucidating how the parts of the subject relate to the whole premise?

If you look closely at what your children do in response to today's teaching, you'll find this work is vastly more complicated than you ever imagined—and hence, it will present you with lots of teaching and learning opportunities.

This session will not follow the usual pattern of a writing workshop. Instead of a ten-minute Minilesson followed by a forty-minute Writing and Conferring, this minilesson will be a double-decker, with time for work interspersed throughout the extended minilesson. Let children know this plan at the start of the minilesson. As children sit around you in the meeting area, confer with individuals and small groups. Most of the lessons over the next few days will come from the ways you help writers confront and overcome difficulties. You'll definitely want to move quickly from child to child, helping them explore and learn from the writing that emerges on their pages. Perhaps you can have a small group of children gather around you during lunch or a prep period to give yourself extra time to read and think about their work.

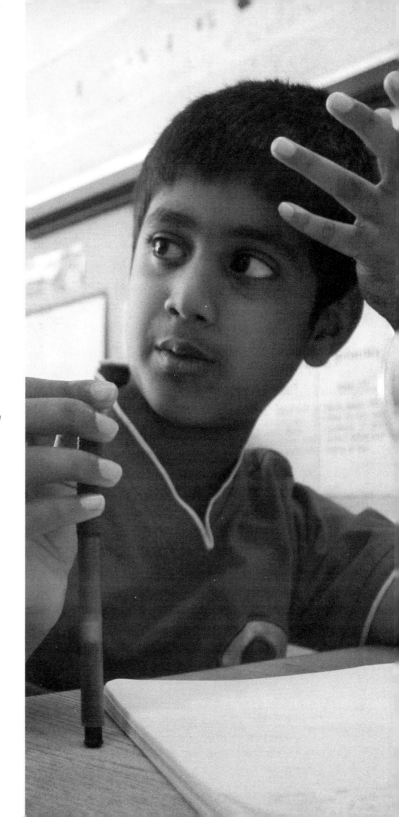

MINILESSON

Boxes and Bullets: Framing Essays

CONNECTION

Summarize the writing process your essayists have experienced thus far, referring to their homework.

"Writers, today marks a big day in our unit. Before we go forward, let's pat ourselves on the back for the work we've done so far. For homework, you thought about the writing process for us as essayists. We've been gathering entries by paying attention to things in our lives and thinking hard about them. Then we reread asking ourselves, 'So what do I *really* want to say?' Then, we each wrote our seed idea as a thesis statement."

"I hope that right now, each of you has a thesis that you feel fired up about, one that you can hold in your two hands like this." I showed the children how I held a construction paper plaque containing my thesis between my two hands. "Right now, would you each write your thesis statement in a big box at the top of a clean notebook page?"

COACHING

During a unit of study, we walk children through the writing process slowly, step-by-step, so that we can be present at crucial moments to lift the level of what children do. But eventually, we hope children will be able to cycle through the stages of the writing process with independence, at whatever speed matches their methods and constraints. It's important, for now, to help children get an aerial view of the process, so they grasp the main contours of it, and will be more ready to propel themselves through the process another time.

Name the teaching point. In this case, tell children that essay writers frame the main sections of essays before researching and drafting them.

"Today I am going to teach you that essay writers, unlike narrative writers do not make a timeline or a story mountain and then progress straight into drafting. Instead we often pause at this point to plan (or frame) the main sections of our essay. We plan the sections of our essays by deciding how we will elaborate on our main idea."

I have taught this session using fairly physical props, such as a construction paper "plaque" on which each child writes his or her thesis. When I do that, I'm trying to convey subtle messages through the use of materials. The plaque helps children to let go of their previous writing and give attention to their thesis. It helps them to feel as if they've made a commitment to a single thesis. The entire rehearsal and entry-gathering phase culminates in the commitment to this one- or two-sentence claim. I didn't do that today because for this class, I felt having their boxed thesis and list of bulleted sections all on one page would be more helpful for them in conceiving the essay as a whole.

TEACHING

Show children that writers often elaborate upon a thesis by discussing the reasons for their claim.

"Let me show you how I consider different ways to elaborate on my thesis. For now, I will use a really simple (and not all that interesting) example. Pretend that my thesis is this: 'Bikes are fun.' My job is to think about what I really want to say about my thesis, and then to design categories or sections for my essay that match what I want to say. I'll first think of what I have to say." I role-played the part of the writer who does this thinking silently.

"Now let me think of how I could categorize what I have to say."

After just a bit, pause to debrief, pointing out the replicable steps you followed. Then continue to role-play the next steps in the process.

"Notice that I physically (or at least mentally) take hold of my thesis." I grasped my plaque labeled "Bikes are fun" with both hands. "Then I think of all I've written and thought about that topic and ask myself, 'What do I really want to say about bikes?' I'm considering whether I want to tell the different *reasons* they are fun, and I'm asking whether the ideas I have are *reasons*." Then I said, "Often I'm not totally sure, so I give it a try. Watch."

I shifted from the role of teacher to the role of writer. "Okay. My main idea is 'Bikes are fun.' I'm going to think about different reasons and see if those categories contain what I really want to say." I wrote my reasons in a bulleted list:

Bikes are fun

- Bikes are fun because you can do tricks on them.
- Bikes are fun because you can go places on them.
- Bikes are fun because you can fix them when they break.

Debrief by articulating what you did that you hope children will also do.

"I call this work 'planning out possible boxes and bullets.' As you can see, after I choose my seed idea and write it as a thesis, I always spend a while—sometimes an hour or so, sometimes less—imagining different possible sections I could include in my essay. I do this by trying out different 'boxes and bullets.' Each time I think, 'Is *this* what I really want to say?' So far today you learned that one way to develop a thesis, a claim, is by writing the different *reasons* for an idea, like I just did."

Notice that I settle for the most bare-bones thesis imaginable. You may be uncomfortable with this, in which case I encourage you to choose a more insightful thesis. The thesis I use here has advantages because it is so bland and uninteresting that my listeners' eyes and ears are drawn to the specific ways I elaborate on it, and thus to the focus of this minilesson.

I think silently because I don't want to add unnecessary detail and risk cluttering what will already be complex instruction. Never underestimate the dramatic effect you create by simply thinking silently for several seconds at the front of the meeting area.

There is nothing fancy about this example, but it is so simple and concrete that I think it works well. The more complex and specific a thesis is, the harder it is to think through these support categories.

It is challenging to defend a claim by discussing several reasons, but most claims can be supported in this way. Your children may not even need to consider other ways to elaborate. If you decide to teach only this one way to elaborate on an idea, you can tell children that once writers have made a claim, they need to provide evidence (give reasons) why their idea/claim/opinion is true. You can, if you choose, ask your children to use the transitional word because.

ACTIVE ENGAGEMENT
Set children up to practice using reasons as a way to elaborate on a whole-class thesis.

"Why don't you try this? Just for now, pretend each one of you is in the midst of writing and your thesis is 'Working with first-grade reading buddies is fun.' Think for a minute about what you have to say on this topic." I wrote the topic on a construction paper plaque while the children thought silently. "Try asking yourself the same questions I asked: 'What if I thought of different *reasons* for this? Will that give me the categories that can contain my thoughts?'"

"To get yourselves started, I suggest you always repeat the stem of your thesis. So reiterate the stem (Working with first-grade reading buddies is fun), then add *because* and name one reason. 'Working with first-grade reading buddies is fun because . . . (this reason).' Then say, 'Working with first-grade reading buddies is *also* fun because . . . (that reason).'"

"Partner 1, write in the air to convey what you'd say are the main reasons why working with first-grade reading buddies is fun. Help each other if you get stuck." The room erupted into talk.

Listen in. Interject lean prompts that lift the level of what individuals do.

I pulled in to listen to children talking in partnerships. Leo said to his partner, "'Cause we teach 'em?"

I interjected, "Leo, the tone of your voice is important. Try saying your bullets as if each one is a claim, a pronouncement. I know you are just trying these out to see if they sound right and make sense, but use the voice of a teacher or a lecturer. And remember to repeat the whole sentence. Start 'Working with reading buddies is fun because . . .'"

" . . . we teach them to read."

I nodded and continued, repeating the thesis stem again and leaving a space for him to add a second reason. "'Working with reading buddies is also fun because . . .'"

" . . . we get to read cool books."

I nodded, gesturing for him to continue.

"And they look up to us."

I chose this whole class "exercise thesis" because it was a topic these kids knew about and one that would work for all the kinds of elaboration I want children to practice. You'll select a thesis that will work for your specific children—choose it with some care and plan on returning to the thesis often. Some teachers have found that "Fifth (or fourth) grade is challenging" works.

Instead of using a whole-class exercise text, you could ask children to try this work on their own theses. We rarely ask children to use their own work in the Active Engagement sections of the minilessons because that leaves them unable to initiate the work of the minilesson when they go back to their seats—they would have already gotten started on the work. When I teach classrooms full of struggling writers, however, I am apt to use the Active Engagement time as a chance to get everyone to initiate the work of the day.

"Great, but repeat the stem. 'Working with reading buddies is *also* fun because they look up to us,' I said, and Leo dutifully repeated the sentence after me. "Now put it all together—say the whole thing to your partner," I said, and listened while he got started. "Working with reading buddies is fun because we teach kids to read. Working with reading buddies is also fun because we get to read cool books. And working with reading buddies is fun because the little kids look up to us."

You may find that you resist having your children repeat the stem of their thesis over and over. It runs against all our training for children to be so repetitive! If you decide to encourage children to word the stem differently each time, you'll be in good company. We tried this too. But we have come to believe that if children don't repeat their stem (at least during their first experiences with this unit of study), they end up with categories (bullets) that aren't cohesive. This disjunction becomes increasingly problematic when the main idea is elaborated upon in an entire paragraph that also doesn't align. I strongly recommend that you stop worrying that the topic sentences will be dull if children repeat the stem.

Spotlight what the child has done in a manner that demonstrates what you hope all children have learned to do.

I jotted down what Leo said onto chart paper. Then I said over the buzz of conversation, "Writers." I waited for silence. "At first when Leo tried to cite reasons for our idea, he said, 'Working with reading buddies is fun because we teach 'em?' but I told him he needed to use a teacher's tone, a lecturer's tone. He is making a claim. And he remembered to repeat the whole sentence for each point. Listen to what he says now." I read from where I'd copied his ideas onto chart paper.

In this unit, the work you do in response to kids' efforts will be especially important because the intellectual work of the unit has everything to do with muddling through the hard parts. So insert yourself into partner conversations and listen for what you can support and teach. You may find that you need to convene the whole class' attention several times, intervening to lift the level of children's work during the prolonged Active Engagement. For example, often a close look will reveal that two of the reasons a child has produced are the same, just worded differently—you could mention that now or save it for a later time. Perhaps the child's points don't sound aligned—you could adjust them subtly by repeating them, with small tweaks that make the child's language fall into parallel structure.

> Working with our first-grade reading buddies is fun.
>
> - Working with our first-grade reading buddies is fun because we get to teach them to read.
> - Working with our first-grade reading buddies is fun because we get to read really cool books.
> - Working with our first-grade reading buddies is also fun because they look up to us.

"Try your claims again and make sure you speak in a teaching voice, and that you repeat your stems. You can also trim them a bit so they go like this if you want," I said, and revised Leo's boxes and bullets so they looked (and sounded) like this:

Leo's actual words used the second-person "you." "Working with reading buddies is fun because you get to teach them to read." I've switched his pronouns to one I prefer: "we." It's not unusual for me to make tiny refinements before I spotlight a child's work.

> Working with our first-grade reading buddies is fun.

- One reason that working with reading buddies is fun is that we get to teach our buddies to read.
- Another reason that working with reading buddies is fun is that we get to read really cool books.
- And finally, working with reading buddies is fun because they look up to us.

This final revision is optional, of course. Eventually you'll want to teach children to use transition words such as these, but it needn't be now. Leave the child's work that you have spotlighted on display as a mentor text.

Try not to use too many words, to be too chatty, when your intent is to scaffold children toward independence.

LINK

Instead of sending children off to work at their desks, ask them to apply what you've taught to their own writing while they work in the meeting area.

"I would usually send you off to work now, reminding you that whenever you have a thesis and want to plan the categories in your essay, you can always consider whether the ideas you want to convey would fit into paragraphs in which you write, 'I think this because . . .' and then, 'Another reason I believe this is . . .'."

You'll find that sometimes, for some thesis statements, elaborating by discussing kinds or examples will work better than reasons. So if several children don't find their content falls into the categories they establish by elaborating upon their reasons, then you'll definitely want to show these children that they can instead elaborate on their claims in ways I describe later in this mega-minilesson. And if your writers are experienced enough that you'd like to show more possibilities, then you'll also want to show other ways to elaborate.

WRITING AND CONFERRING

Framing Essays

The minilesson was over, but I didn't send children off to their work spots. "Instead of sending you off to try this with your own thesis statements, for today, let's have a tiny workshop right here on the rug. Each of you has your thesis. Take a minute and ask, 'Can I think of different reasons—will reasons give me categories in which to write?' Write boxes (your thesis) and bullets (your reasons), as Leo did, in your writer's notebook." As I spoke, I pointed to Leo's thesis and bullets about first grade reading buddies. "Remember to repeat the stem of your thesis over and over as Leo did," I said as I pointed to the repetition of "Working with first-grade reading buddies is fun because . . . " I told children to show their tentative plan to a partner. "Help each other. Talk about whether you actually want to write within the frame you've proposed. You need to be sure the categories hold what you want to say." As children worked, I moved among them.

I helped one child after another set up possible frameworks for an essay, and I encouraged nearby children to listen in as I worked with their classmates. I especially helped kids "try on" a variety of optional ways their essays could go. My conversations sounded like this:

"So what is your thesis, Diana?"

"My mom is important to me."

"That's such a huge, important idea. 'My mom is important to me!' What reasons will you provide?"

"I don't know. 'Cause she's nice?"

"Smart work. That definitely could be a reason why she is important to you. Can you say it in a whole sentence—and then keep going, listing another reason?" To show Diana, I said, "'My mom is important to me because she is nice. She is also important to me because . . . ' What else?"

MID-WORKSHOP TEACHING POINT *Finding Alternative Ways to Support a Thesis* "Writers, let's try *another* way to develop your thesis. Earlier I suggested telling my *reasons* behind the thesis. I could also consider whether the ideas I want to convey would fit into paragraphs in which I tell about different *kinds*. So watch me think about kinds of things to back up my thesis." Gripping the page on which I'd written my thesis, I said, "Okay. I'll go back to my main idea, 'Bikes are fun.' I'm going to think of all I've written and all I've thought about that topic and then ask myself, 'Do I want to tell how different *kinds of bikes* are fun?'"

"I could write a paragraph about how *two-wheeler* bikes are fun, another one about how *tricycles* are fun, another one about how *bicycles built for two* are fun, and one paragraph about how *dirt bikes* are fun,'" I said, writing these in boxes and bullets format on chart paper.

> Bikes are fun.
>
> - Two-wheeler bikes are fun.
> - Tricycles are fun.
> - Bicycles built for two are fun.
> - And most of all, dirt bikes are fun.

continued on next page

"She takes me places?"

"Okay, but say it in a whole sentence," I said.

I'm not worried right now about whether Diana's claims are especially original or specific. Although ordinarily, I wouldn't accept something as vague as "My mom is important to me because she is nice," in this instance I keep in mind that I have asked kids to write *big ideas*. I have asked for generalizations. Although it is true that even big ideas often become more compelling when they are more specific, it can then be harder to elaborate on them when they are more specific. (For example, recently a child tried to work with, "Being a kid and not being able to drive till you are eighteen is hard.") So for now, I don't necessarily push for more specificity than "My mom is nice." My goal is to help kids grasp the concept of an umbrella idea that is supported by several distinct and parallel subordinate categories.

As I worked with one child and then another, I often intervened when kids' categories didn't "go together." If a child said, "My mom is important to me because she is nice, my mom is important to me because she is patient, my mom is important to me because she got me a DVD for my birthday," I tended to help the child feel in his or her bones that those didn't match. The first two categories describe character traits, and they are fundamentally different from the last category. This gets more complicated when children's ideas are more complicated. Tyrone, for example, had written: "I don't want to let my grandmother down" as his thesis, and his bullets were "by not taking care of the baby; she'd be all alone with no one to help her; so she isn't sad." To help this struggling writer understand why those three bullets didn't go together, I told Tyrone that if my thesis was "I like oranges" and my supports were "because they are juicy, because they are tasty, and [I said the next phrase in a way that accentuated that it didn't fit] one day I saw an orange plant in a rainforest," people would say my categories didn't go together. To help a child recognize when things aren't parallel, I often point out, "This should sound like a song. Listen." For example, I read the claim "I like oranges because they are juicy/I like

continued from previous page

"Why don't you try elaborating on our class topic by discussing different *kinds*?" I read aloud, "Working with our first-grade reading buddies is fun," and said, "Ask yourself, 'What if I think about different *kinds* of things, will that give me categories that fit with what I want to say?' Let's try thinking, specifically, about all the different kinds of work that you do with those guys. Talk with your partner and think through the different kinds of work that you and your reading buddies do that is fun." Soon I convened the group and shared Sophie's suggestions.

> **Working with our first-grade reading buddies is fun.**
>
> - Telling our reading buddies to stop fooling around and to stay with us is fun.
> - Teaching our reading buddies to read the words is fun.
> - Reading great stories aloud to our reading buddies is fun.

continued on next page

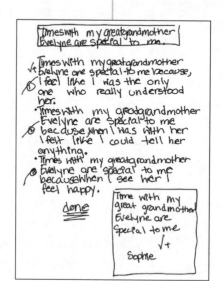

Figure VII-1 Sophie's first draft of her boxes and bullets

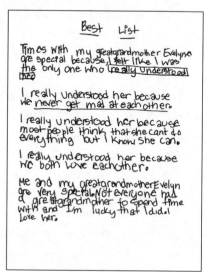

Figure VII-2 Sophie's second draft is more specific than her first draft.

oranges because they are tasty" with rhythm and intonation that accentuated the fact that the first two bullets matched. Then I read the third bullet ("I like oranges because one day I saw an orange plant in a rainforest") in a way that caused dissonance. To help the child construct a revised bullet, I almost always go back and reread the first two bullets in a song–like way and then get the child to construct a third statement that fits rhythmically alongside the other two. As I do this work, I also show children that in the end, we can collapse topic sentences so that, for example, my thesis about liking oranges, can, in the end, look like this: "I like oranges because they are juicy, tasty, and healthy."

Children seem to grasp the point when I use a very obvious example. Tyronne, for example, could see that my original sentences about oranges weren't aligned so he rewrote them to say, "I like oranges because they are juicy, because they are tasty, and because they are beautiful on the tree." With some help, Tyrone went back and revised his claims about his grandmother: "I don't want to let my grandmother down or else she'll be all alone, she'll have no one to help with the baby, and she'll be sad."

continued from previous page

"In a minute you'll have a chance to see if it works for you to think about different *kinds* of things related to your claim. But first I want to teach you another way to plan categories. As you've already learned, writers sometimes write *reasons*, we sometimes write *kinds* —but we also sometimes write *parts*." I demonstrated, saying, "Watch me recall my thesis (Bikes are fun) and ask "What if I think of different *parts*?" Soon I'd mentioned that the wheels of bikes are fun, the handlebars of bikes are fun, and so forth. Then I pointed out that sometimes writers write about different times, or instances their claim has been true to support it.

"So writers, let's go back to our desks where we can really concentrate. You'll be writing lots of different possible boxes and bullets in your notebooks so that you can figure out which way best matches what you really want to say," I said, gesturing to Leo's example, which showed the layout for this strategy. "Some of you will elaborate on your idea by discussing *kinds*, some will discuss different *reasons*, some different *parts* or *times*. Writers always try several ways to support a thesis, and we try wording whatever we come up with in lots of different ways until we feel we've hit the nail on the head. The important thing is to try several variations and after each one consider, 'Is this what I want to say?'"

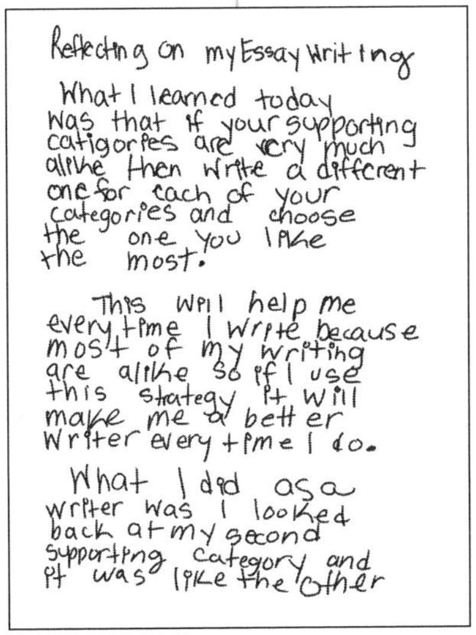

Reflecting on my Essay Writing

What I learned today was that if your supporting catigories are very much alike then write a different one for each of your categories and choose the one you like the most.

This will help me every time I write because most of my writing are alike so if I use this strategy it will make me a better writer every time I do.

What I did as a writer was I looked back at my second supporting category and it was like the other

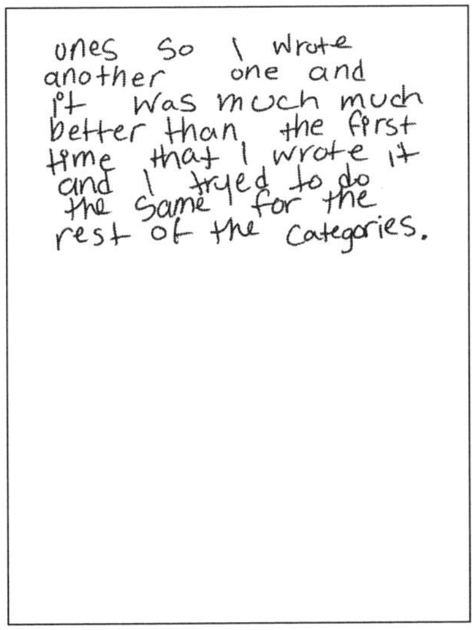

ones so I wrote another one and it was much much better than the first time that I wrote it and I tryed to do the same for the rest of the categories.

Figure VII-3 Sophie explains, in this entry, what she learned from a conference that led to her next draft of boxes and bullets.

Figure VII-4 Sophie's entry page 2

SHARE

Revising Thesis Statements

Teach students that revising their thesis statement is an option when they have difficulty supporting it.

"Today you have been figuring out how your essays will go by deciding how you will support your thesis statements. I saw all of you trying this out. You decided whether you wanted to talk about the *reasons, kinds,* or *parts* and you made sure that you had enough to say about the categories you selected. I noticed that some of you were really struggling to find bullets that support your thesis. When a writer has trouble supporting a thesis, one option is to revise the thesis statement."

"I want to share what Vianca did while she was trying to plan her essay. Her original thesis was 'Playing sports is fun,' and she planned to discuss how sports are fun for kids and grown-ups. When she thought about finding the evidence for this essay, however, she realized that she didn't want to write about *grown-ups* playing sports! So she decided to revise her thesis. Her new thesis is 'Playing sports is fun for kids.' She took one of her topic sentences and made it into her new thesis. In Vianca's case, this made her thesis more specific."

Have students go back to their plans to see if this strategy might be helpful to them.

"Can you share your current plans for your essay with your partner? Make sure to discuss the choices that you have made. Also, check your thesis. Will you have a lot of evidence to go with your topic sentences? Does your thesis match what you plan to say about it?"

If you believe that children have already revised their thesis statements well enough, you may want to use this share time to again emphasize the importance of building essays with parallel supporting paragraphs. You could list thesis statements and then supporting paragraph ideas, each with one that is off-kilter, so that children can learn to spy the ones that need revision.

> Sometimes I hurt peoples feelings
> • Sometimes I hurt peoples feelings to get back at them.
> • Sometimes I hurt peoples feelings to fit in.
> • Sometimes I hurt peoples feelings because I am man.
> • Sometimes I hurt peoples feelings when I am cranky.
> • Sometimes I hurt peoples feelings when I am having a hard time.

Fig VII-5 Olivia's thesis statement and possible support ideas.

Checking Thesis and Support Alignment For homework tonight, practice being a reader of essay drafts. I've made copies of the work two students wrote in my class last year. Pretend these are your essays, and ask, "Is the support material really aligned to the claim?" If it isn't, think about what you'd suggest the writer do.

For example, you'll see that Shanice claims, "I'm proud of my cat." One of her reasons is "I'm proud of my cat because she just had kittens." Think about the topic and think about the point that Shanice's support material needs to advance. Now read this entry and think, "Does this support Shanice's claim?"

> For example one morning I woke up to a screaming noise.
> It was the sound of a baby kitten. I looked under my
> bed. My cat was giving birth. Later on I found out there
> was 4 baby kittens and we were giving them away. We
> were only keeping the mother and a brown kitten.

You'll probably agree that although yes, much of this *is* about the fact that the cat had kittens, it does not support the fact that Shanice is proud of her cat. Think, then, about how Shanice could have revised her writing to solve this. One of her friends suggested she revise her writing like this:

> For example one morning I woke up to a screaming noise.
> It was the sound of a baby kitten. My cat was lying
> peacefully and being a perfect mother. I didn't even
> know she was old enough to be a mother. She is young to
> have babies and I'm proud of her.

Tonight, read the essays I'm sending home with you in just this manner, and carefully consider whether the support material is really aligned to the points.

If your students are struggling to support their thesis statements . . . you could teach them that writers can revise their thesis statements by either making their subject more specific or making it more general. Recall the share when Vianca made her subject more specific by revising from "Sports are fun" to "Sports are fun for kids." "Sports" is a very big topic so she narrowed it a bit by making it more specific to sports for kids. When the thesis statement is very broad, it can be paralyzing for young writers to decide which approach to take in order to support it. For example, in Vianca's case, she could have talked about playing different kinds of sports, reasons that playing sports are fun, being a spectator at sporting events, and so on. If the thesis is this broad and if there are so many evidence options, it's easy for the young writer to develop supporting evidence that doesn't quite fit together. Consequently, the essay may veer wildly from point to point.

Conversely, writers who are having trouble supporting their thesis statements may want to make their subject more general by opening it up. For example, Alexa was trying to find support for her thesis statement, "Violent television is bad for kids." She couldn't find enough reasons that supported this statement, so she made her subject more general. She changed "violent television" to "television." Her new thesis reads, "Television is bad for kids" and she easily came up with evidence to support her idea.

In a minilesson, you might model a struggle to support one of your thesis statements, and then demonstrate how making it broader or narrower can help a writer develop evidence that supports it. For the active engagement, you might use a student's thesis statement that needs some revision and ask the students to consider how they'd tweak the statement to more easily support it.

ASSESSMENT

You will definitely want to spend time this evening poring over the work your children have done. You'll probably want to categorize children so that tomorrow you can gather those who need a particular kind of help and give them that support right away.

Some children will profit from help developing *parallel* bullets. For example, John's plan was as follows:

> I'm proud of myself because I'm a good baseball player.
>
> • I got good sportsmanship.
> • I know the game well.
> • Characteristics of a good baseball player.

Once he'd lopped off the final bullet and revised the third bullet to "I got good skills," he was stuck because he couldn't imagine anything more to say! He was dead set against settling for only two categories, and ended up realizing he could divide his second category (I got good skills) into more specific points:

> I'm proud of myself because I'm a good baseball player.
>
> • I'm good at bat.
> • I'm good in the field.
> • I'm good as a team member.

Similarly, Estefan realized these categories weren't parallel:

> My dad is important to me because . . .
>
> • I have fun when we play baseball.
> • He makes sure I get a good amount of sleep so I am ready for the next day.
> • He shows me math.

He worked on making them match, and ended up writing:

> My dad helps me . . .
>
> • with baseball
> • with math
> • with daily life

Other children need to consider what they've said very carefully, checking to be sure their words are precise. Sarah wrote:

> My dog is like my best friend.
>
> • He keeps me company.
> • He understands how I'm feeling.
> • He licks me all over.

She realized that her best friend doesn't lick her at all.

The most common problem, however, was that bullets often reiterated the same point, as in Takuma's example:

> Without my grandparents, I would have felt lonely.
>
> • It's hard to play alone.
> • It's difficult and lonely not to be able to talk to others.
> • It's hard to be walking all alone.

LEARNING TO OUTGROW A FIRST THESIS

An essay represents a mind at work. *Effective essays not only contain strong writing, they also contain strong thinking. From the start, then, we need to nudge children to think deeply as they write. It's easy to say that we will teach children to think deeply—but what might such instruction entail? We can't very well say, "Writers, watch me as I think deeply. Now I want all of you to think deeply."*

Typically, in our minilessons, we advocate a goal—a skill—and help children reach that goal by providing them with a small repertoire of optional strategies, each of which is, in effect, one set of step-by-step instructions a person might follow to reach that goal.

Today's minilesson aims to equip children with a set of strategies that may help them write more perceptive essays. A word of caution: Developing writers sometimes need to choose between writing thoughtful essays and writing tidy essays. If you are teaching inexperienced writers, and this is their first experience with this essay unit, you may decide to detour around this minilesson, saving it for next year. Alternatively, you may use this as a strategy lesson for only your more agile writers. On the other hand, if your children are very experienced writers, you may teach this lesson and repeat another version of it later in the unit.

The lesson itself is not especially challenging, but it will nudge children to forgo generic (and easy-to-develop) thesis statements for more original, specific, and hard-to-develop claims. For many children, it is challenging enough to write an essay from a thesis at this level: "I'm good at baseball. I'm good when I'm in the field and I'm good when I'm up at bat." Proceed with this session if you hope your children will replace such a generic thesis statement with a more specific claim, such as, "Playing baseball well requires intelligence. When I'm at bat, I try to outwit the pitcher. When I'm in the field, I try to predict how other players will act." The latter essay is likely to be more perceptive, but it will also be more challenging to research and to structure.

IN THIS SESSION, YOU WILL TEACH CHILDREN THAT WRITERS FREE WRITE AND ASK QUESTIONS IN AN EFFORT TO OUTGROW EARLY DRAFTS OF A THESIS STATEMENT.

GETTING READY

- Story you can tell about a writer who discovered the value of postponing closure
- Notebook entries showing how children tried to push their thinking about their thesis statements
- Thesis you can use to demonstrate telling an essay aloud
- See CD-ROM for resources

MINILESSON

Learning to Outgrow a First Thesis

CONNECTION

Explain that writers postpone closure so as to *write* and also to *think* well.

"Writers, most of you drafted a thesis statement and plans for several support paragraphs in the two previous sessions. If you wanted to, you could probably write your whole essay in the next day or two. Especially once you are familiar with the expectations of this genre, you'll always have the option to either delve deep enough to write a provocative, ground-breaking essay, or to whip up a quick, adequate essay. But for now, our job isn't to rush along as fast as possible. Instead our job is to take the time needed to learn along the way. And today I want to remind you that our goal when writing essays is not only to *write* well, but also to *think* well.

Name the teaching point. In this case, tell children that essayists revise early, using free writing to deepen thinking and outgrow their earliest claims.

"Specifically, I want to teach you that essayists don't wait until an essay is done before revising. Instead, we revise all along the way to make our words and our ideas as true, as significant, and as provocative as possible. Many writers use free writing as a strategy to help us do this."

TEACHING

Tell a story about someone who finished writing an essay, sensed there was more to say, and took the risk of revising the completed text.

"I want to tell you a story, a story that will end up being a lesson about writing. A few years ago, my father flew to a nearby airport to visit me. As we drove home from the airport, he told me, 'I finished writing my essay about my childhood.' I knew the text—it was a reflection on his childhood, written in part to pay homage to his parents for all they had given my dad and his siblings. As we drove, Dad explained that he had made copies of the essay for each of us nine kids and bound each copy professionally. He'd boxed up each copy to mail to us, too. Then, as Dad and I continued driving home, he said, 'But as I put the last manuscript into the last box, I realized *I left out a story*.' As he spoke, Dad punctuated each

COACHING

At the end of the unit, I will teach children to use all they've learned about essay writing so as to write quick, well-structured essays on demand, when called to do so. They'll need to do this on standardized tests.

In New York City classrooms, where these units of study have been piloted, some teachers take a shortcut through this unit, arguing that in the end children need to write only the most bare-bones sort of an essay, and they need to write these very quickly. I question such a decision, believing it circumvents many teaching and learning opportunities, but it's a choice you can make.

Many writers and teachers argue vehemently against the restrictive, constrained form of a five-paragraph essay. They protest the notion that a writer decides early on what he will say and isn't allowed the journey of thought that is essential in creating thoughtful texts. This session's emphasis on writing to learn and on revising one's thesis is one of several ways in which I help children experience some of the musing, reflective, tentative, self-critical thinking that is at the heart of thoughtful writing.

Notice that this minilesson breaks stride. Instead of demonstrating or talking about a step-by-step strategy, this lesson advocates the importance of postponing closure in writing. I know that if I simply launched into this long story about my father without orienting the children, they might have sat there thinking, "Why is she telling us this?" I try to ease their minds by saying, at the start, "Sit back and listen. This will be circuitous, but in the end you'll see how it fits together."

word by banging on the dashboard of the car. '*I didn't just leave it out*,' he said. '*I boxed it out. Do you know why? Because it was just so sad. That's why.*'"

"My dad proceeded to tell me the story that he'd boxed out of his essay—a story of how, after he and his father won a sailing race together, the town circled him, celebrating by throwing him into the water, and how my dad resisted with feeble protests about having athlete's feet. Now, sitting beside me in the car, my dad continued, 'As we walked home, the water squeaking in my sneakers, my father didn't say a word to me. Not a word about the sailing race. Not a word about them heaving me into the sea.' Dad went on to say, 'The truth is, he didn't say a word about the athlete's feet or anything else. I'd failed him by not being the kind of boy who is thrown into the water with grace. And in our family, that wasn't okay. Failure wasn't okay. And talk—real talk—was rare. My father didn't say a word about the whole episode that day because, frankly, we couldn't talk about much of anything.'"

I shifted from storytelling that episode with my father to summarizing the events that ensued. I said to the children, "The visit with my dad ended, he flew home, and I waited to get the manuscript that he'd already boxed up to mail to me. Weeks went by and it didn't come. When I traveled home for Christmas, I asked my dad about it. His eyes twinkled. 'Look under the Christmas tree,' he said. There I found the long-awaited box, containing the manuscript. After I pulled it from the box, Dad directed me to a particular section. Reading it, I saw he had recounted the sailing race after all and the silence between him and his father, even though on the day of his visit to me, Dad had told me that the manuscript (without this story) had been professionally bound and boxed to mail. After retelling the sailing story, Dad had written this:"

> The story, as I wrote it, fills me with intense sadness. The most important part of the story may not be the episode itself but the fact that I rejected it from the initial log. I didn't include it because it was just so sad . . . for all I was given in my childhood, one thing was missing—a father who understood and cared for me, not just in a collective sense as one of his brood, but for me as a person.

Explicitly name the message you hope the story conveys. In this case, the message is that when a writer has the courage to resist premature closure and to revise, the writing becomes stronger.

"My father's final essay is more powerful because he had the courage to open the box and to mess up his original neatly packed manuscript," I said.

Notice that I refer to my dad's text as an essay. Really, it was a book-length memoir. I stretch the truth a bit to make my point to kids.

Readers who know my writing well may recall reading other versions of this story. I've told it often, each time angling it to make a different point. When I told the story in The Art of Teaching Writing, *my emphasis was that it's powerful to bring literacy home. When I told it in* The Art of Teaching Reading, *my emphasis was that we, as teachers, need the courage to outgrow our initial teaching ideas. This third version is a plea for writers to postpone closure of their writing.*

You may notice that I use all the narrative writing skills I teach children in order to write the little stories that are embedded in this minilesson. In the blink of an eye, I'll teach children that the first step to writing an effective essay is to collect miniature stories that illustrate the idea we hope to advance. As you read along through this story, take note.

"Writers know that courage matters. Writers resist the instinct for closure. We're willing to say, 'Wait. Is this *really* what I want to say?' We're willing to reopen our nicely completed thesis statements to try to be more precisely honest."

"And we try to be honest from the very start so that we don't end up, like my dad, reading the completed essay and feeling, in our bones, that we didn't really convey the true message we wanted to tell."

ACTIVE ENGAGEMENT
Tell children that you'll show a second instance in which a writer—this time, a child—revised. Set children up to research and then to name the replicable strategy the writer uses.

"I want to show you one child's work and to ask you to join me in researching the specific strategies she used to outgrow her first thesis statement. We'll look again at Francesca's entry (and more specifically at her work from a previous minilesson). I'll describe a bit of what she did, then ask you to tell your partner what you notice that she's done that you could conceivably do as well."

"First, let me tell you a bit about the overall writing situation. Francesca found a personal narrative story she'd written about a time when she was sledding and accidentally crashed into a little child. When I approached her, she had already done the work many of you did last night, growing a big idea, a generalization. She'd settled upon this thesis."

Grown-ups can really hurt a kid's self esteem.

"She'd put her thesis through the battery of questions and decided it was clear, strong, and clean. But she felt uneasy about her thesis, partly because it seemed to blame grown-ups, and she wasn't sure she wanted to write an anti-grown-ups piece. So Francesca got out a sheet of paper and began to restate what she really wanted to say."

Pause early on. Ask children to list two things the writer whose story you're telling has done that they, too, could do.

Although my recount of Francesca's writing process had just begun, I nevertheless paused and said, "Turn and talk with your partner. List two things Francesca has done that you could also do as a writer. Talk about each thing and be specific. Make sure you are giving yourself advice on how to write more honest, true essays."

This minilesson tells the story of my father revising a completed text, and you may therefore wonder why I tell it now when each writer has merely written a thesis sentence. Why am I pushing revision when children have just begun to draft? The reason is that it's most likely that they'll revise in substantial ways if revision begins early. Then, too, the thesis and the plan for the essay control all that follows. They are crucial. Aristotle was right when he said, "Well begun is half done."

I like speaking of the qualities of good writing using terms such as courage and honesty. I do believe that there is a thin line between writing well and living well.

The Active Engagement section in this minilesson has an extra job to do. So far in this minilesson, children have only fleetingly heard about one specific strategy (free writing) they can use to accomplish the goal (early revision) I've advocated. The minilesson has been high on inspiration and low on instruction. Children will need me to offer more how-to help in this section.

By now, you should realize that asking children to research what a writer has done and to name what they see is one of the common choices for this section of any minilesson. It's never an ideal active engagement because the children aren't actually getting a chance to do the work—they are instead talking about it—but sometimes this seems to be the best course.

You may be surprised that I no sooner began telling Francesca's story than I was saying, "Turn and talk. What do you notice?" This is deliberate and common. I want children to listen with alertness, expecting that they'll be called upon to make meaning. I don't want them to sit back in their seats and wait for meaning, significance, to jump up and bop them over the head.

The children talked, I eavesdropped, and then I asked for their attention. "I heard you say several things that Francesca did."

- She really looked closely at what she'd written.
- She gave her own words the truth test.
- She listened to her uneasy feeling.
- She was willing to mess up a perfectly okay, tidy thesis.
- Finally, Francesca tried to restate what she wanted to say.

"I especially want to emphasize that smart, thoughtful writers don't just settle for words that are in the ballpark. We are willing to feel uneasy; we have the keen eyesight required to see little untruths and contradictions and problems hiding in the shadows and cracks of our own sentences, and we're willing to flush them out."

"Let me continue with my story of Francesca. She tried to write more, to say more, and to talk not only about sledding—the particular story—but also about her biggest topic, self-esteem. She wrote this entry."

> Your self esteem pretty much stays the same in your life unless you really change who you are. The way you interact with the world controls how you feel. Say you were riding your bike all summer and you are about to show everyone, then you fall off. It may not change how you look at yourself if you have really good self esteem. Self esteem is very important to everyone on this earth. It is important to like yourself all throughout your life. Your self esteem needs to be treated right. If people abuse you and make you feel really bad your self esteem can change. If you are not around people who care about you, your self esteem (can) really change. You need to always want to grow up but you need to know that it isn't really smooth.

Pause and ask children again to list two things the writer has done that they, too, could do. Generate a list of advice gleaned from eavesdropping.

"Turn and talk with your partner. Again, list two things Francesca has done as a writer that you could also do. Talk about each thing and be specific. Make sure you are gleaning advice that you can use as you think about free writing today."

It is unlikely that I actually heard children saying these points, and certainly not in this chronological order. You may decide to reiterate what your children do in fact say, or you may use this as a chance to restate what you hope children have deduced.

The children talked, I eavesdropped, and then I reconvened the class. "I heard you say a lot of smart things."

- Francesca wrote really long about her original thesis. She wrote a full page.
- She really looked closely at what she'd written.
- She journeyed from one idea to another and related ideas as she wrote, hoping (probably) to move toward saying more true, more significant ideas.
- She became more and more willing to face the hard, and in her case, the sort of sad truths about life. She started out saying, "Self-esteem is important" and ended up writing, "Growing up isn't smooth."

"Those are all things you too can do in your own writing, aren't they?"

LINK
Restate the teaching point and describe upcoming work.

"Today, then, and whenever you write an essay, remember that many writers deliberately try to take a journey from one thesis to another. We do this to make our thinking more powerful. I'd love to have you put the exact wording of your thesis aside as Francesca did with her early statement, 'Grown-ups can really hurt a kid's self-esteem,' and free write so you can rethink what it is you want to say about your topic. After you've written long, you'll reread what you've written, then again lift out your seed idea, and write it as another draft of your thesis."

I will often say, "I heard you say . . . " and I do incorporate what I heard into my report. But I'm apt to have thoughts about what I want to cumulate for kids, and if I didn't hear a child make a point that I want emphasized, I nevertheless add it to the list.

I am pushing the students to write quickly here. I don't want them to think through every word before they put it on the page. I want them to write and write and then go back and mine their writing for emerging ideas.

WRITING AND CONFERRING

Aiming Toward Your Precise Meaning

If you see (or anticipate) that several children will need your help, cluster them together and teach a strategy lesson that gives them extra practice and support. Perhaps you'll see that one child in the group has already settled on a thesis. For example, I saw that Chris' thesis was "My dog is important to me." I convened a small group of kids who I knew all needed a bit more practice pushing themselves past their first ideas. I suggested that together they help Chris rethink his thesis. "This doesn't mean it's not a good thesis—it is! But writers shouldn't be afraid to make our best ideas even better." Then, to bring the whole group in on the work, I said, "Remember, Chris will be trying to say the same general idea, but he'll aim to be more exact and more honest. Pretend you are Chris. You want to say that your dog is important to you but you want to be more exact. Tell each other, in twos, what you might say. Keep talking and thinking (pretending you are Chris and that your dog is important to you) until you have something more true, more specific to say."

I listened as they said, "My dog is my friend," "I'd die if I had to lose my dog," and "My dog is like a brother to me."

Intervening, I said, "What I do, as a writer, is I write my thoughts down, and then I reread them, looking for the one that seems more precisely true." I asked Chris which of the statements rang especially true. He said, "My dog is like a brother to me," and wrote it. Then, I told all the children, "Now you need to explore *that idea* like you might explore a patch of forest. Instead of turning logs over to see the bugs underneath them, turn words over. Ask, 'What exactly do I mean by . . .' and choose a word, any key word. Open it up. Try more precise words. Then do that again with other words you are using." Soon the children had said, and Chris had written:

> My dog tags along behind me like a little brother. He's like Velcro. He's like a tag along little brother because whenever I go anywhere, he seems to say, 'Take me.' He's like a tag along little brother also because he's never the one to go first.

MID-WORKSHOP TEACHING POINT   *Writing with Insight and Honesty*   "Writers, today I find myself admiring your *thinking*. Many of you are asking tough questions of your own first ideas. You are saying to yourself, 'Is this *exactly* what I mean?' and trying to be more precise. Listen, for example, to the way Rebecca pushed herself to be more truthful. She began with this thesis."

> My grandfather and I have a good relationship.

"This is what she wrote next."

> My grandfather and I have a good relationship. But I don't think it is good enough because he hates noise and he hates my brother and me fighting. I know my grandfather well, but I don't like him much. I like him, but I think he yells because his back is hurting. My grandfather can always find something to tell me to stop doing.

continued on next page

"Wow, you are getting more and more precise!" I said. "Keep it up!" Then, turning to all the children, I reiterated the steps we'd just taken and launched each one into similar work.

If I spend some of my time working with small groups of children, this then can free me to spend the rest of my time in one-to-one conferences. When I asked Rie how she was doing with her boxes and bullets, she looked at me a bit nervously and muttered something about wanting to do this right. Glancing at her papers, it was clear she'd been revising—or struggling. Every page contained lots and lots of crossed out lines. Meanwhile, her thesis was, "Making a mistake in front of a crowd frustrates me." Just before I'd approached her, Rie had crossed out the line, "Not only people laugh at me I also laugh at myself." Rie overviewed for me her various attempts to create support categories for her essay, and each attempt struck me as a reasonable one (although sometimes the different categories overlapped). My real concern, however, was over whether it would be productive for Rie to spend weeks during the upcoming unit of study perseverating over why it is so utterly humiliating for her to make even a minor error in front of an audience. My concern was not that this would produce a flawed essay—but that I'd like to see Rie use writing as a way to name her nemesis, and to look it in the eye. So I celebrated her willingness to revise and to write the truth, both, and then asked if I could teach her one thing.

"Rie," I said, "In class over the past few days I've taught you all one way that an essay could go. But the truth is—there are other ways that writers sometimes structure our essays. Could I teach you a different template, a different pattern, for an essay because I have a hunch it would work for you." Soon I'd explained that some essays make a claim—say, "It can be boring to be home alone"—which we support for a bit. But then we make a second claim, one that pushes off from the first. "Because it's boring being home alone, I've become an avid reader." Often these essays first highlight a problem, then propose a solution, as occurred in that example. Before long, Rie had new plans for her essay, which started this way: [Fig. VIII-1]

> I hate to make mistakes in front of a crowd
> because I always want to do my best.

> continued from previous page

> I know I can count on my Mom for things but this is hard for me to tell her about. I know I'll never be stuck with him, but I still can't stand him sometimes. It's hard to believe he's my Mom's dad.

"Rebecca started off writing in what could be called a cliché: 'My grandfather and I have a good relationship.' She's now writing with honesty that takes our breath away. 'I can't stand him sometimes . . . I can't tell my Mom about this.' My hunch is that writing the hard parts will help Rebecca *live with* those hard parts. Okay, back to your own honest writing."

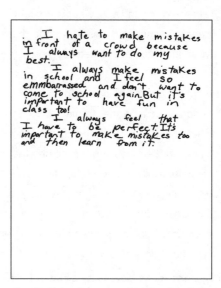

Fig. VIII-1 Rie trying to outgrow her first thesis.

SHARE

Teaching as a Form of Rehearsing for Writing

Tell students you are about to ask them to say their essay aloud. Show them how to use their fingers to organize their thoughts before they begin.

"Writers, earlier this year you wrote stories, and to get ready for writing those stories, you storytold them to each other. Soon you'll be writing essays, and it's also helpful to try talking about your essays to each other. I know you haven't yet figured out exactly what you'll write in your essays, but let's move forward anyhow. Right now, would you get ready to teach a course, to give a lecture, on the topic of your newest and truest thesis? To get ready, say your thesis aloud in your mind until you can imagine delivering it in a definitive voice to a whole roomful of students. Then plan across your fingers some of the points you could make to support your thesis, to teach your 'students.'"

Demonstrate by saying your thesis, and listing your supportive ideas across your fingers. Elaborate on each.

"My thesis is 'My father has been my most important teacher.' One point will be, 'My father's been my most important teacher because he taught me to adore my work.'" As I mentioned that point, I gestured to my first finger. Moving to the next, I said, "Another point will be, 'My father taught me that it's okay to fail.'" Then I told children, "I could, in a minute, give a little speech in which I announce my big claim, give my first reason [I gestured to one finger] and then talk a lot about it. Then I'd go to my second reason and talk a lot about it."

Ask students to plan and then tell their essay aloud.

"Would you right now take a minute to prepare a speech on your thesis?" I gave the children a few minutes. "Partner 1, will you pretend your partner is a roomful of listeners and give your speech?" I listened in as the children spoke with each other. Then I asked Partner 2 to take a turn.

This step has proven transformational. When I worked once with fifty teacher-researchers, just after they'd drafted tentative rough outlines for an article they wanted to write and before they set to work on their lead paragraph, I gave them fifteen minutes to plan how they might lead a staff development workshop on the topic and set them up to give these instant workshops to each other. What a difference! I'm convinced that when we write as a form of teaching others, it's transformational to do some actual teaching in lieu of an early draft of writing.

This will be a great opportunity to see how well children understand what you have tried to teach them. Make sure to listen. If it seems that most are making points and organizing their information under these big ideas, you can listen for the finer points of their structure—are the reasons parallel in construction and importance? Are the reasons illustrated with precise and interesting details and stories? What you see your kids do will help you tailor your next day's teaching.

HOMEWORK *Supporting Theses in Various Ways* For homework tonight, try this exercise. Practice using different kinds of sets of evidence to support one thesis statement.- Read each thesis statement below and try supporting it using: kinds, parts, reasons, ways and finally, times when. Try to come up with three statements that support the claim for each of those kinds of support. If another way of supporting the thesis makes sense to you, of course try that way too!

Here's an example of a thesis followed by ways to set up evidence that could support it:

Essay Possibility #1 (Kinds)

Fifth graders work hard; we study, babysit our siblings, and help our parents.

Essay Possibility #2 (Parts)

Fifth graders work with three parts of themselves. They work with their bodies, emotions, and intelligence.

Essay Possibility #3 (Reasons)

Fifth graders work hard because we want to do well at school, because we want to please our parents, and because we want to develop skills.

Essay Possibility #4 (Places/Ways)

Fifth graders work hard. We work hard in school, at home, and during sports.

Essay Possibility #5 (Times)

There are three times when fifth graders' lives are filled with work. Fifth graders work before school, during school, and after school.

You may wonder what the impetus was for me to teach children that a writer can elaborate on his or her thesis by writing about reasons, parts, kinds, and so on. This is my attempt to take the lessons my son struggled to learn in high school and scale them down so they're accessible for children.

You may protest, claiming, "Why simplify high school-level-work and teach it to nine-year-olds?" But of course, in the writing workshop as a whole, we are constantly taking the strategies, habits, and goals of adult writers and finding ways to invite even five- and six-year-olds to "have a go" with those aspects of writing.

● TAILORING YOUR TEACHING

If your students need more practice using writing to grow ideas . . . you could decide to teach another minilesson on this strategy. It might begin like this, "Writers, I had a conversation with a friend last night that reminded me of the work we did in class yesterday where we free wrote to outgrow and revise our thesis statements. I had just gotten back from my swim class. I told my friend that swimming was frustrating. 'What do you mean?' she asked. 'Well, every time I feel like I am getting better, there is something new to learn.' 'What do you mean?' she asked. 'It feels like it is impossible to become a good swimmer.' I said. 'What do you mean?' she asked again. Getting a little annoyed I answered, 'I guess that getting better at swimming is like getting better at anything in life. The more you know, the more you realize what you don't know.'"

"Later that evening I realized that as much as I was annoyed with her for repeating 'What do you mean?' over and over again, her question helped me figure out what I was trying to say. My first claim, 'Swimming is frustrating,' didn't fully represent what I was feeling."

"This strategy of asking repeating questions might be something that you can try with yourself on paper. Just write your idea, then ask yourself, 'What do I mean?' and try to restate it in a clearer, stronger way. Or do this with a partner if you are having trouble getting your words to match what you really want to say. And from now on, anytime that you feel like your ideas do not match what you mean to say, try asking yourself clarifying questions until you feel like your writing matches with what you really think."

If you feel that in order to revise their thesis statements, your children would benefit from a clearer understanding of the qualities of an effective essay . . . you might tell them what you admire in the work of one essayist, and ask them to note what they admire in the work of another. For your part, you might say something like, "Writers, last night I was reading a book of essays by one of my favorite authors, Barbara Kingsolver. She usually writes novels, so I was very interested in reading her essays. I was thinking about you guys the whole time I was reading! I noticed that the essays in Barbara Kingsolver's book had a couple of characteristics that made them so interesting to read. First, it felt like she knew what she was talking about. She chose to write essays on topics that she knew quite well. Her essays sounded smart! Then the other thing I noticed was they had a kind of passion. I could tell that she really cared about the topics in her essays. It's like her essays had brains and heart—knowledge and passion." Then, of course, you'd want to give children a similar opportunity to name what they admire in the work of an essay they've previously studied. You could then say something like, "Today, I want us to think about the thesis statements we've come up with to see if, like Barbara Kingsolver, we have chosen to write about topics we know and care a lot about."

COLLABORATING WITH COLLEAGUES

For homework the other day, you asked your children to consider which qualities of good writing pertain to both narrative and expository writing. You also asked them to think about the qualities of good writing that are especially important for essayists. These questions merit your attention as well.

Earlier in this series, I quoted Lucille Clifton, the great American poet, who said, "We cannot create what we cannot imagine." When helping children write well, it is terribly important that we and our students are guided by a clear vision of what we are trying to create. During our earlier work with personal narrative writing, we helped children write with focus and detail, and we encouraged them to "show, not tell." Do those same qualities pertain to expository writing?

If you or your colleagues pore over op-ed editorials, feature articles, essays, and persuasive letters, trying to ascertain what makes some of this writing especially strong, I suspect you'll find that specificity is crucial when the aim is to be convincing. You know this already. If you phone a friend, and the person who answers says something vague like, "She's not here. I don't know where she is. Why don't you call back?" you may well suspect your friend is avoiding you. But if that person responds, "She's driving Jimmy to his Boy Scout meeting. It starts at 7:00 p.m. so she should be back by 7:20 p.m.," then you don't doubt the veracity of this response. Specificity elicits trust.

In narrative writing, details can stand on their own. In expository writing, details are provided and then "unpacked," or discussed. That is, in expository writing, one expects that examples will be linked in an explicit way to ideas. In fact, details and anecdotes and examples usually abut generalizations or citations.

Cohesion is another important quality of good expository writing. Of course, cohesion is also important in stories. In a good story, the beginning, the middle, and the end all relate to each other. Characters don't come and

go from nowhere. Cohesion is equally important in a good essay—any one part of the essay needs to relate to the whole of the essay—but the techniques for creating cohesion are different in expository than in narrative texts. I often tell children that the need for cohesion translates into the fact that it's important for them to write sentences throughout their essay that refer back to the thesis. But it is also true that expository writers create a sense of cohesion by repeating a word or a phrase from the thesis often. Certainly at the end of any chunk of text, readers expect to be told how this new information advances the essay's premise.

I've found it very helpful to read books written for high school and college students on the essay and on nonfiction writing. For example, I love poring over Richard Bailey and Linda Denstaedt's *Destinations: An Integrated Approach to Writing Paragraphs and Essays*. It's a textbook for college freshmen and clearly light years beyond reach for elementary students, but I'm interested, for example, in their description of cause-and-effect, comparison, and definition essays. Linda and her colleague, Laura Shilling, have helped me think about expository writing.

They suggest that to write a cause-and-effect essay, for example, a student might generate ideas by asking questions that elicit causes: Does this thing have one or more causes? Does it have one or more effects or consequences? Does it help to think in terms of reasons for this thing? On the other hand, to help write a definition essay, a student might ask questions such as: Does this thing have components or parts? What are its origins? How does it change over time? (Bailey and Denstaedt 2005, p. 300).

Find books like this one and share them with your colleagues. You'll find your minds and conversations soon buzz with possibilities.

COMPOSING AND SORTING MINI-STORIES

IN THIS SESSION, YOU'LL TEACH CHILDREN TO WRITE, ANGLE, AND UNPACK MINI-STORIES THAT SUPPORT THE IDEAS THEY WANT TO ADVANCE.

GETTING READY

- Colored file folder for each student
- Several manila folders for each student (one per supporting topic sentence)
- Your own thesis, topic sentences, and supporting list of true stories
- One story you've developed to support a topic sentence
- Colored file and manila folders labeled for your own essay
- Class thesis and supporting topic sentences from the preceding minilesson, written on chart paper
- Guidelines for Writing Essays chart
- See CD-ROM for resources

I remember the first research report I ever wrote. My older brother and sister had each written reports, so I knew in advance that I'd need to buy index cards, a file box, and pens of different colors. I traveled by bus to the big library in the center of Buffalo, spending several Saturdays surrounded by books, proudly accumulating index cards full of information.

Now when I write nonfiction books, I no longer record information on index cards. But I do still collect bits and pieces of related information: quotes, stories, examples of student writing, data, and ideas. Later, when I prepare to write, I lay the bits alongside each other, noticing that two citations say almost the same thing, that this one text illustrates that citation, that some of my sources contradict each other. I realize some people do most of this work on the computer, but I still rely on the old-fashioned system of collecting, sorting, making headings, and so forth.

In order to bring children into the realm of writing that is organized logically instead of chronologically, it is crucial that they have opportunities to manipulate their information in physical and concrete ways. When teaching children to add and divide numbers, we initially ask them to combine and share buttons or blocks. In similar ways, children benefit from physically manipulating bits of information and ideas. In this way, they can grasp that two chunks of data are similar, that one story literally fits under a main idea, that a large pile can be divided into two smaller piles.

In this session, you'll teach children a system for collecting information and ideas, and then you'll help them start collecting and filing the materials they'll need to support their theses. For now, you'll teach them to collect stories that illustrate their ideas, knowing that this is a task they should be able to do with confidence and skill.

Your teaching needs to rally children to rely upon what they already know about writing stories, and to help them with the new challenge of angling (and unpacking) their stories to support their main ideas.

MINILESSON

Composing and Sorting Mini-Stories

CONNECTION

Tell children that the boxes and bullets they wrote in the previous session will provide the frame for their essays.

"Have you seen the huge building they are constructing down the block? I walked by it this morning and saw iron beams; they formed the shape of the building. In the last session, all of us worked on creating the iron structure for our essays. Most of you have chosen the boxes and bullets that will be your iron beams. From looking at the structure you've made, you can imagine your essay. Others of you are still working on this."

"The builders will soon truck in materials and begin to fill in the parts of the building outlined by the iron beams. They have pictured in their minds what the building will look like when the walls are in place, and they will bring in materials that will fit around the structure they have erected."

"Once you have the iron structure for your essay, once you have at least a tentative plan for your boxes and bullets, it is time for you (like the builders down the block) to cart in the materials you will need to build your essay. Before builders or writers can truck in a lot of building materials, they need to decide where to store those materials so the stuff that belongs in one part will be separate from the stuff that will make a second part."

Explain that writers use files to store the materials that will fill in the frame of an essay. Provide an example.

"Builders create piles; writers make files. I've put a stack of colored file folders and a much larger stack of manila folders at the center of each table. I suggest that you write or tape your thesis across the top of a colored outer folder. Don't make your letters too large or bold because you may alter your thesis as you proceed, so save space for future revisions. Then, in the same way, write one of the support sentences you've chosen—writers call these topic sentences—along the top of each manila folder. Then set each of these topic-sentence folders inside your thesis folder."

COACHING

There are lots of advantages to using a metaphor in a minilesson. We're trying to teach abstract and complicated ideas. Sometimes a metaphor can make our ideas more concrete and memorable. It is important, however, to avoid using multiple metaphors. We can't one day liken the frame of an essay to the frame of a building and then the next day suggest that an essay is shaped like a butterfly with separate but similar wings or like a three-leaf clover or a tree with branches. You'll see that I return often to this session's metaphor, that an essay is like a building, and that I generally return later to any metaphor that I use in a minilesson. Before you choose a metaphor, then, be sure it can be sustained across more than just one minilesson.

Sometimes it is tempting to use the minilesson as a time to tell your students what you'd like them all to do. It would have been easy to state as my teaching point, "Writers, today I want to show you how I'd like you to organize and collect writing. You're each going to make three files . . . " But I guard against letting minilessons become occasions to simply assign work to children, and I carefully watch my wording so that I am teaching children strategies that writers use often rather than nudging them to jump through a particular set of hoops on a particular day. Watch how I circumvent a teaching point that merely assigns today's work so as to hold to the principle that minilessons are occasions for teaching a strategy or an idea children can use often.

"You'll remember Andy's essay in which he claimed that parents' fighting affects kids very much (see CD-ROM for complete essay.) His skeletal plans had looked like this:"

> Parents' fighting affects kids very much.
>
> - Parents' fighting makes kids yell for things.
> - Parents' fighting makes kids choose sides between their parents.
> - Parents' fighting makes kids start not trusting people.

"He wrote his thesis," I pointed to it, "on a blue folder." Then, showing that his blue outer folder contained three inner manila folders, each labeled with one of Andy's bulleted sentences, I said, "Look how Andy created three different folders so he had separate places in which to collect and store the materials he planned to use when he was ready to build each of his three body paragraphs."

"Whenever you write a non-narrative piece, one that will require a lot of materials, a lot of information, it helps to set up a system for gathering and collecting the materials you'll end up assembling."

Name your teaching point. In this case, tell children that writers collect (among other things) mini-stories that illustrate our ideas.

"But today what I want to teach you is this. The most important materials writers collect when writing essays are—stories!"

TEACHING
Demonstrate that writers bring knowledge of personal narratives to this new task, only this time, we collect and write mini-stories that are angled to illustrate the bulleted, topic sentence. First we generate stories to support our claim.

"The good news is this: You can use all that you already know about writing good stories to help you collect powerful materials in your folders. Watch how I go about collecting stories in my folders, stories that could fit into the plan I've made for my essay. Here is my plan for my essay."

> My father has been my most important teacher.
>
> - My father taught me what it means to regard a job as a hobby.
> - My father taught me to love writing.
> - My father taught me to believe that one person can make a difference.

Some teachers use pocket folders instead of file folders, with the inside-the-cover pocket set aside to hold drafts of the title and introductory paragraph, and with one half of a pocket folder (yes, each child needs a folder with one half of another folder set inside it!) providing a place for materials that will end up becoming the first and second body paragraphs. Then the final pocket can be for either just the third body paragraph or for that and also, eventually, the concluding paragraph.

I could have made this sentence the teaching point. If your students risk being on instructional overload, you may decide to do so. It is reasonable to devote a minilesson to teaching children that writers need to set up systems for assembling their materials. The problem with this teaching point is that the work involved won't keep kids busy for the whole workshop. Therefore, I move on to introduce what is essentially a second teaching point—the notion that stories are some of the most important materials that writers collect.

"To get myself writing a story that relates to my thesis, I take one of my topic sentences, one bullet—I'll take 'My father taught me what it means to regard a job as a hobby'—and I ask myself, 'What true story can I think of related to this?' Let me list several." I then began jotting quickly on my clipboard and saying aloud what I wrote.

- On the last day of summer, Dad and I sailed together. He confided that he couldn't wait for vacation to be over so he could return to work.

- On Christmas mornings, my father always goes to the hospital carrying a waffle iron, ready to make waffles for the doctors and patients. I asked why he didn't send someone else. Dad admitted that he liked going to work. "It's my hobby."

- When Dad was a kid, he heard a book about Louis Pasteur read aloud. Dad said, "Listening to that read-aloud, I realized that the research which Pasteur loved so much was his job." Until then, Dad had always thought a person's job was a chore. Dad vowed that he'd grow up to love his job.

Select one story, recall the process of writing stories well, and draft.

"Next, I will choose one of the stories. Before writing it, I need to remember what I know about writing focused stories. I'll make a movie in my mind of how the story unfolded, starting at the beginning. When I write the story, I'll also keep in mind that it needs to highlight one particular idea—in this instance, that Dad taught me what it means to regard a job as a hobby. I know from the start that I'll play up the parts that make this be a story about Dad loving his job. I also know this needs to be a tiny story." I picked up my clipboard and began writing (and voicing).

My dad regards his work as his hobby. For example, on Christmas mornings, right after the presents have been opened, my dad always goes into the kitchen and begins the one bit of cooking that he does all year. He stirs Bisquick and eggs in a huge bowl and sets off for the hospital, leaving us to finish Christmas without him. For Dad, Christmas mornings are not just a time to be with family, they are also a time to serve hot waffles to the medical students and patients. When I asked him once why he didn't send someone else with the waffles, he told me he loves being at the hospital on Christmas mornings. "It's my hobby," he said.

I could have made my point in a briefer fashion, but when I write about topics that really matter to me I find it hard to be brief. I think children can tell when we are authentically engaged in our own writing, and they respond in kind. So I decided to forgive myself for offering examples that are longer than is ideal. You'll notice that I jotted this writing on my clipboard, not on chart paper—the advantage of the clipboard is that I can scrawl and abbreviate (and if necessary, prepare a cheat-sheet ahead of time to remind me of what I want to say).

It is very powerful to write detailed stories that carry gigantic ideas. The writer Richard Price once said, "The bigger the issue, the smaller you write."

I worked on this story before I met with the kids, trying to keep it brief, to make sure it was a step-by-step story, and to highlight the sections that illustrated my main idea. I tried to be explicit about the connection between this example and the overarching idea. I deliberately used the phrase, 'For example, . . . ' You will, of course, want to write your own story. Bring your dad into your teaching! Look ahead to Session XIV, when you'll want to use the draft you write today again.

Debrief, highlighting the process and pointing out that you told the story step-by-step rather than summarizing it.

Then pausing in the midst of the story, I shifted away from the role of writer and into the role of teacher. "Writers, I hope you saw that I collected this mini-story outside my notebook on loose-leaf paper. I did that because now I'm going to put the mini-story in the folder titled, 'My father taught me what it means to regard a job as a hobby.'" I did this.

"I hope you also noticed that to get myself started telling a story, I rewrote my claim and then wrote '*For example* . . .' Writers don't always use those exact words, but for today, use the phrase '*For example* . . .' or '*One time I* . . .' Finally, writers, I hope you noticed that when writing a story, I asked myself, 'How did it start?' I made a movie in my mind of what happened and wrote the story in a step-by-step way."

ACTIVE ENGAGEMENT
Set children up to try this while writing in the air. Ask them to write a story that can be embedded into the whole-class essay.

"So let's practice doing this; it's a lot to remember. Pretend it is writing time and I've said, 'Okay writers, time to work. Off you go.' Pretend Leo's bullets for 'Working with our first-grade reading buddies is fun' are your bullets. Remember Leo suggested," I turned back to the boxes and bullets from the preceding day's minilesson, "that the essay could be framed liked this:"

Working with our first-grade reading buddies is fun.

- One reason that working with reading buddies is fun is that you get to teach them to read.

- Another reason that working with reading buddies is fun is that you get to read really cool books.

- And finally, working with reading buddies is fun because they look up to us.

It's important to notice that although there is one teaching point in a minilesson, we often tuck instructive comments throughout the minilesson. My goal is to pack any minilesson with enough good stuff that an alert student can learn, learn, learn. How else can I justify taking up students' writing time?

I am scaffolding kids so the writing they produce will end up clicking into a nicely structured written essay. Asking kids to use specific transitional phrases such as for example *and* one day *may make you uneasy—it made me uneasy at first. But I've seen that once children have successful experiences writing essays, they use the forms we teach with increasing flexibility. Of course, you must discard any parts of these lessons that make you uneasy, finding your own ways to teach whatever you decide your children need to learn.*

Notice that this piece about reading buddies threads its way throughout much of this session, and this unit. If you teach a classroom full of struggling writers and if you are always working to just get your kids producing more volume of writing, you may want to revise many of my minilessons so that this component of the minilesson becomes a time for kids to work with their own texts. You could, for example, ask each child to take his or her first topic sentence, and to think of a story illustrating it, signaling with a thumbs up when they have that in mind. Then coach Partner 1s to say their bullet point again, to add for example, *and to tell the beginning of the story starting with what exactly they did first.*

"Assume these are your bullets. Now, you're at your workspace, ready to start. You have your boxes and bullets. What do you do next to get yourself organized? Tell your partner." They talked for just ten seconds. "Writers, I heard most of you remembering that when any of us plan to work on an essay, it helps to set up a system for sorting the materials. Specifically, you talked about getting folders ready before you start assembling the materials, the data."

"Stay with me, because now this gets harder. Let's say that you have labeled your folders. Now you want to begin collecting some entries, some materials that you'll put in those folders. Let's say you decide to start by collecting stories for the folder labeled, 'One reason that working with reading buddies is fun is that you get to teach them to read.' You'll get a piece of paper. You'll copy the bullet and then write 'For example . . .' and you'll probably add a time phrase. So you might write, 'One reason that working with reading buddies is fun is that you get to teach them to read. For example, one morning . . .' and then keep going, telling a mini-story. In this instance, your story needs to illustrate that it's fun working with reading buddies because you get to teach them to read. So think of one time when it was fun teaching your buddy to read. Partner 1, write in the air to your partner."

As you recall, the early section of this minilesson mentioned the importance of setting up a system for gathering materials, and only later did it highlight the fact that writers can collect stories that elaborate on their topic sentences. I need to be sure the children keep the first point (the need for systems) in mind, so I tucked in this reminder.

Some teachers describe the materials that get collected in this phase as mini-stories, suggesting that they can often be just three to four sentences long. Mini-stories need a sentence to begin the story, one or two sentences to tell what happened, and an ending sentence to wrap up the story and relate it to the main idea of the essay. You'll see that I decided not to highlight brevity just yet, but that was an option I considered.

Listen in on your children's work with partners. Intervene to lift the level of what individuals are doing. Then debrief.

As the partners turned to talk, I listened in. After a moment, I heard Diego say, "I taught my buddy the /sh/ sound 'cause she was going /s/."

"Class. All of you, I need your attention. Diego just said, 'I taught my buddy the /sh/ sound.'" Then I said, "The reminder I'm going to give Diego is one that probably pertains to many of you. So listen closely." Looking at Diego, I said, "Diego, while I don't question that you *did* teach Sari the /sh/ sound, you have not told this as a story yet! For now, we're writing stories to illustrate our points—another day we'll quickly list examples. To write a story, remember that you need to go back to that day in your mind (and if you don't remember it exactly, make it up). How did the moment when you taught Sari the /sh/ sound start? Use the words I gave you—'For example one morning . . .' to get yourself started."

It's very likely that your children, too, will shrink their stories, bypassing the beginning to get to the middle. There's logic in this—the one sentence Diego has told spotlights the time in the episode that fits with his point. For Diego to tell this as a story, however, he needs to provide the windup that precedes the climax. Of course, sometimes people end up providing too much windup! I believe that is a small price to pay for the vitality and honesty that real stories add to writing.

Diego started again, while the class listened. "For example, one time, Sari was reading a book about a sheep's car getting stuck in the mud. She read the words, *sheep shove* so it sounded like *sheep sove*, and she was stuck. I said, 'Sound it out,' but she didn't have the right sounds."

"Now you are telling this as a story, Diego!" Turning to the class, I said, "Try again; this time ask yourselves that question, 'How did it start?' and tell your example like a story. Use the phrase *for example, one time* or *for example, one sunny day* to get yourself started telling this as a story."

LINK
Restate the teaching point and remind students of the metaphor you established earlier describing their upcoming work.

"Writers, the builders have built their iron beams, and most of you have built yours as well. Once builders and writers have constructed a frame, it's time to gather the materials needed to fill in around the girders. Builders will truck in boards and cinder blocks; as writers, we build with words. Today (and whenever you have built an iron structure for an essay) begin to cart in materials—stories—to build your essay. When you write stories that will be tucked into essays, remember to use everything you already know about writing powerful stories."

You'll find that when the challenge is to tell a story in such a way that it illustrates a point, writers often delete the beginning of the story (which therefore means the story is not a story after all). For example, if my topic sentence is, "It is dangerous to drive to work," I could "tell the story" of yesterday's near accident by cutting to the chase in a way which relates to the topic sentence, saying, "Yesterday, I was almost in an accident." But that is not a story. To tell this as a story, I need to tell the start of the story, angling it towards the point I wanted to make: "Yesterday, I drove to work as usual, drinking coffee, talking on the cell phone, and steering around potholes. Suddenly . . . " That's an angled story!

WRITING AND CONFERRING

Supporting Thesis Statements

You will have your hands full today. First, you'll need to help any child who hasn't yet arrived at a workable thesis buttressed by several support statements, to finalize that work. If a child is still struggling, help out. For example, I am apt to say, "What do you want to say about losing your grandfather? Tell me what this meant to you."

Then the child will talk: "Well, I felt hollow. Because he was sort of, not really a grandfather; it was as if he was my age. Plus he was like a father."

I'll nudge the child on, murmuring, "Say more."

The child says, "I didn't have any tears in me. I didn't want to talk about it."

Listening, I will try to grasp the main categories the child seems to want to address, and then I will say these back to the child. "So do you want to write, 'When I lost my grandfather, I felt sad,' and then write about the *kinds* of sadness? You could write, 'I felt hollow, I felt silent, I felt...' Or, on the other hand, do you want to write, 'When I lost my grandfather, I lost a friend, I lost a father ...' (and write the different kinds of roles he played in your life?) Or do you want to write, 'When I lost my grandfather, this was a huge blow to me. For example, I . . . ; for example, I . . . ' It's up to you because you are the author, you are in charge."

You may ask, "Aren't you doing the child's work for him?" and the answer is partly yes. The child, however, is probably oblivious to the fact that I am giving him a piggyback ride across the high water. The child will probably think he has done the work independently, and meanwhile I will have helped him begin to be comfortable with the new text structure. There will be lots of other occasions for the child to do this work alone without scaffolds. For me, the question is not whether or not I helped the child; the question is whether my help lifts and supports the writer beyond today, and I think that setting up writers who struggle a bit for future success qualifies.

> **MID-WORKSHOP TEACHING POINT**   ***Angling Stories to Support Theses*** "Writers, can I have your attention? Eddy and I just discovered something important that I suspect pertains to many of you. Eddy's thesis is that he loves to spend time with his parents. In one of his folders, he's collecting material to support the idea, 'I love to spend time with my parents when we go on vacation together.' He collected a story about staying overnight in a hotel with his parents. I want you to listen to the story he collected, and see if you can discern the problem that Eddy faces (and I suspect many of you face as well). Listen."
>
> > I love to spend time with my parents when we are on vacation together. For example, one time we went to a hotel in New Jersey. First we went to the zoo in the hotel. It had really cute baby animals. Then I went swimming. Then I watched three TV shows.
>
> "Eddy, tell the kids what you discovered," I said.
> "I realized I left my parents out!"
>
> *continued on next page*

Today you'll also want to confer and lead small groups to help children gather stories that illustrate their ideas. You'll find that when children reach for stories that illustrate an idea, usually the idea comes at the end—the climax—of the story. Children, therefore, often bypass the setup and windup sections of their stories. When Jay Jay wanted to tell a story to illustrate that he loves being with his father because his father teaches him roller skating moves, he wrote:

> One day my father taught me a skating trick and I like him cause he did that.

I helped Jay Jay see that he needed to back up and tell how the story started (though now the problem became the other extreme—too much windup!). Soon Jay Jay's story went like this:

> One sunny Sunday, my dad came and picked me up to go to his job at the Skate Key. On the way I asked him how to do a 360°. When we got there, he said, "Jay Jay put your skates on." He putted his skates on. He did it first then I did it next but I fell on the floor. My head was . . .

Often children will tell a story without developing the part that illustrates the bullet point, the topic sentence. When I see this, I often say to the child, as I said to this child, "Would you box the part of this story that goes with your bullet point?" Then I state the child's bullet point, the statement labeled on the folder. In the example above, Jay Jay decided that only one line of his story, "He did it first then I did it next," advanced his idea which was, "I love being with my father because he teaches me skating moves."

continued from previous page

Nodding, I added, "Eddy made a really important discovery. If his story is going to illustrate that he loves vacationing with his parents, then he needs to angle his story about staying at the hotel so that the story shows that he likes to stay there because he gets to be with his parents! Listen to Eddy's next version of this story." [Fig. IX-1]

> I love to spend time with my parents when we vacation together. For example, one time we went to a hotel in New Jersey. First we visited a zoo that was in the hotel. It had really cute baby animals. My Mom loved the baby sheep so much that she pretended she was going to sneak it up the elevator to our room. My Dad and I had to drag her away. We were just joking. Then we watched three TV shows; one that was my choice, one that was Mom's, one that was Dad's. We usually don't watch each others' shows.

"Right now, before you do anything else, would each of you reread one of the stories you have collected and talk with your partner about how you could rewrite that story so that it really highlights whatever it is you need to show? Then rewrite that one entry, that one story. I'll be admiring the revisions you make."

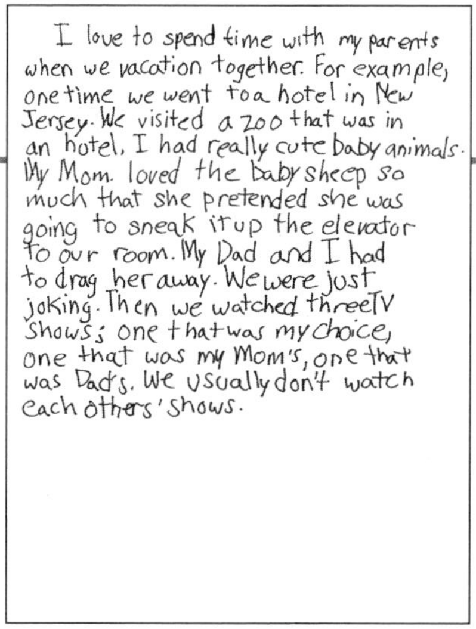

> I love to spend time with my parents when we vacation together. For example, one time we went to a hotel in New Jersey. We visited a zoo that was in an hotel. I had really cute baby animals. My Mom. loved the baby sheep so much that she pretended she was going to sneak it up the elevator to our room. My Dad and I had to drag her away. We were just joking. Then we watched three TV shows; one that was my choice, one that was my Mom's, one that was Dad's. We usually don't watch each others' shows.

Fig. IX-1 Eddy's revised story

I typically then ask children to take the underlined/boxed section and write a long paragraph just about that. Jay Jay wrote this to insert into his original paragraph: [Fig. IX-2]

> My dad whirled so fast—fast like a roadrunner. I couldn't see him. He jumped in the air. I thought he was going to fall back. Bang with his strong skates. I thought his wheels popped off. My eyes was spinning fast like I got dizzy. I thought that he fell head first into the floor. I thought he broke his leg when he came down.

The story tells more about Jay Jay's father as a skater than about the fact that Jay Jay loves his father because he taught him the 360° and other moves, but I let this go and moved on to teach one other tip. Once children have written a story, I often teach them to add a sentence at the end of the story that refers back to their bulleted reason. For example, Jay Jay's story at first had ended this way:

> I fell on the floor. My head was bloody.

I taught Jay Jay that essayists try to add a sentence at the end of a story that links back to the topic sentence (I love being with my father because he teaches me skating moves). Jay Jay added:

> I came to in the locker room still thinking how I love my Dad for teaching me skating moves.

The ending makes all the difference! Now he'd accumulated material in his folder which read like this:

> I love being with my father because he teaches me skating moves. One sunny Sunday, my dad came and picked me up to go to his job at the Skate Key. On the way I asked him how to do a 360°. When we got there, he said, "Jay Jay put your skates on." He putted his skates on. He did it first. My dad whirled so fast-fast like a road runner. I couldn't see him. Bang with his strong skates. I thought his wheels popped off. My eyes were spinning fast like I got dizzy. I thought that he fell head first into the floor. I thought he broke his leg when he came down. He did it first but next I did it. I fell on the floor. My head was bloody. I came to in the locker room still thinking how I love my Dad for teaching me skating moves.

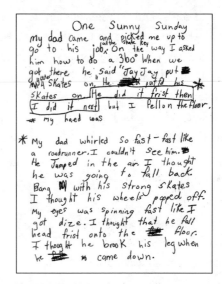

Fig. IX-2 Jay Jay's revised story about his father

SHARE

Honing Supporting Stories

Share your realizations about the process of essay writing to practice evaluating a piece of writing for what qualities are there and what qualities are missing.

"Writers, you've each collected a story that supports one of your topic sentences."

"As I've worked with you today, I've realized that together we have figured out a bunch of guidelines to follow as we write our essays. I've written them out for you here, so you can refer to them whenever you want."

Guidelines for Writing Essays

- Essayists frame the main sections of their essays.
- Essayists revise early, using free writing to deepen thinking and outgrow their earliest claims.
- Essayists set up a system so we can sort and compose material to support our ideas.
- Essayists collect and write mini-stories that are angled to illustrate our topic sentence.

"Now you've collected mini-stories to illustrate the ideas you want to advance in your writing. And what stories these are! We've learned guidelines for writing stories to support our ideas, too."

Never underestimate the power of story as the conveyer of ideas. The Bible is written in stories—parables, often—and these stories convey ideas. How lucky we are that Melville didn't write a book about whaling in general, but instead wrote about one man and one whale. And how lucky that Jane Austen didn't write about pride and prejudice, but instead wrote about one man and one woman struggling with and against their pride and their prejudice (Zinsser 2004, p. 107).

Guidelines for Writing Supporting Stories for Essays

- Usually writers include a transition into the story.
- The story needs to have a beginning, middle, and end.
- The story needs to be told to especially reveal the part of it that illustrates the thesis and bullet points.
- At the end of the story, it is usually wise to include a sentence that refers back to or repeats the main idea of that paragraph.

"Writers, let's listen to Tony's story and notice which of these guidelines he's followed and which he can still follow." *[Fig. IX-3]*

> Drawing is really fun. I can express myself in drawing. One time I was mad at a kid for bothering me. Instead of settling it in a violent way, I controlled myself, for a minute I thought about all I knew about drawing. Then I took out a paper and a pencil. I drew him running around, screaming with snake hair, a rat's head, and a slow turtle body. Drawing helps me express myself.

"Let's look next at Olivia's story," I said. "She's written two different stories, and although it's possible she could bring both these stories into her essay, she will probably need to decide which one better illustrates her topic sentence, which is, 'Sometimes I hurt people's feelings to fit in.' Let's listen to one of her stories, and think—as we did with Tony's entry—whether her story matches our guidelines for writing stories to express our ideas." I read one of her stories aloud. *[Fig. IX-4]*

> Sometimes I hurt people's feelings to fit in.
>
> An example was at lunch one day. I was sitting with a cool group of kids trying to get with the conversation. I put down my sandwich. I looked at everybody around me. I was sitting with them ready to make my move to be their friend. They talked about people who were geeks.

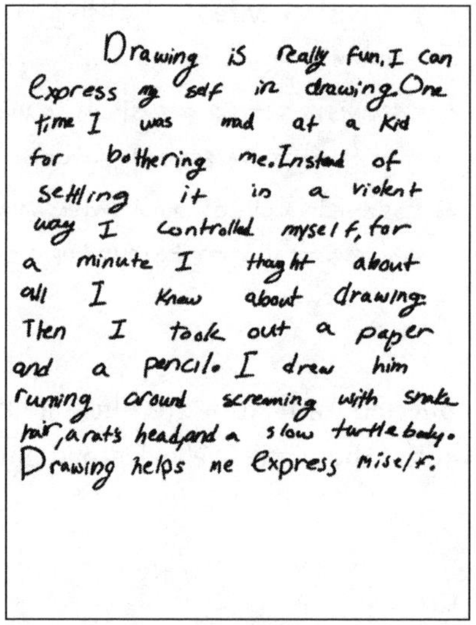

Drawing is really fun. I can express my self in drawing. One time I was mad at a kid for bothering me. Insted of settling it in a violent way I controlled myself, for a minute I thaght about all I know about drawing. Then I took out a paper and a pencil. I drew him running around screaming with snake hair, a rats head and a slow turtle body. Drawing helps me express miself.

Fig. IX-3 Tony struggles with spelling but he successfully uses a story to illustrate his idea

"I know somebody who plays with polly pockets," I said. They looked at me and said, "Really? Who?"

"Alejandra," I said. They looked at me and said, "Come and play with us."

"Ok," I said feeling so happy inside that I was going to play with them.

I got up to go line up with them but I ended up face to face with Alejandra. I could see tears in her eyes. She turned around and left. I knew I had hurt her feelings. I felt bad inside like someone punched me in the stomach.

"Come on Olivia," I started walking to them. But instead of feeling really happy, I felt really sad because I had just left my best friend out.

"Olivia!" I started running towards them.

Sometimes you can be so eager to fit in you hurt people.

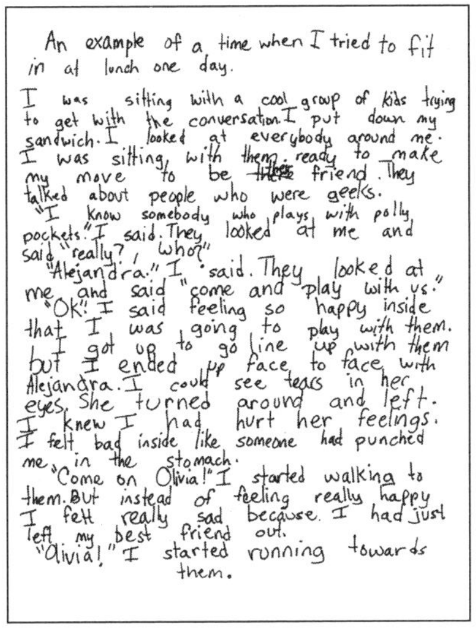

Fig.IX-4 Olivia's story is angled to support her idea

Ask students to assess their writing using the Guidelines for Supporting Stories chart to see what work to do next.

"Writers, can you take a minute and look through your own writing? Talk with your partners, referring to the chart. How do your stories fit our guidelines and how might you revise them?"

HOMEWORK *Angling Oral Stories* Writers, remember how much better our stories became after we rehearsed them, telling them before writing them down? Tonight please practice angling another story to support one of your points. Tell it to someone before you write it down. Try telling the same story a second time, even if you need to recruit your dog as your listener! Once you are happy with how the story sounds, write it down. I'm enclosing copies of our guidelines for telling stories to support ideas. Use those guidelines to help you revise your story. Bring it tomorrow and file it in the appropriate file.

If your students need a push into revision . . . you might tell them a story like this: "Writers, yesterday at lunch I was talking to my colleagues about writing. As we ate our sandwiches we shared our experiences with revision. After a lot of discussion we realized that writers need courage to be good revisers. When we figured that out, it was like a light bulb went off in my head! I realized that this is what had made revision so difficult for me for so long. I would go to revise and find myself physically tightening up because I was so afraid to lose what had taken me so long to write. I would make teeny tiny changes to my old ideas and then I would reread what I'd written and wonder why it had not gotten any better. Writers, all that time I didn't realize that what I really needed was courage. I needed the courage to erase and make big changes. I needed courage to trust that I could write better. I needed courage to believe that my first work was not my best work. Finding that courage has changed my writing so today I want to tell you: be brave writers!"

If your students are writing supporting ideas that are too long, too detailed, or too much like personal narratives . . . you'll probably need to revisit the difference between telling a story as a personal narrative and using a story as a way to support a claim. One of the ways you can demonstrate this is to show the difference between the two in your own writing. It helps to have a focused personal narrative entry that you've adapted so that it can work as a story within an essay paragraph. You may decide to show the two pieces of writing side-by-side so students can see and name the differences themselves. Inevitably, you'll notice that the thesis-supporting text is shorter, leaner, and to the point, whereas the personal narrative entry offers the reader the whole story.

For active engagement, during the lesson, you might decide to have your students go though their notebooks and find an entry that could, if it were leaner and more to the point, support one of their claims. Each writer could tell their partner about plans for revising that entry.

ASSESSMENT

When you look at your students' work, pay attention to goals that span all units. For example, you will want to carefully watch your children's fluency as writers. As the year progresses, you should see that your kids now write much, much more than they wrote at the start of the year. Watch them closely and you will notice that some children get the idea for a paragraph in their heads, and then tuck their heads down and write, write, write until that unit of thought has been written. Others think of a sentence and then write until that thought is on the page. Yet others think of a word, write it, reread, and only then think of the next word! You might be tempted to excuse these differences as being simply a matter of speed, but actually it is crucial to help children think and write in longer units of thought. If children are not writing quickly and with fluency, they are not apt to elaborate, to spin out believable stories, to write with details, or to develop convincing ideas. This means that you need to actually push kids to write faster and for longer stretches. Ask all your students to record where in their notebooks they start and stop writing each day in school and at home. Help them to join you in looking for trends related to their volume of writing.

If children's writing stamina (and the resulting volume) is a priority for you, you'll want to look across all the notebooks from a class, dividing them into two piles: strong stamina and weaker stamina. There might be a third pile for intermittently strong stamina. I suggest you record the names of kids in each group; then during writing time, convene the group that most needs your help and teach them a strategy which you hope can help them write with more stamina. You'll also want to set up a structure to check on their progress. If the problem persists, you may need to work with some children outside of class time to address the issue (and to signal to the writer that progress on this front is nonnegotiable).

When you study student work, you may notice predictable problems that crop up in children's writing and group those children who could profit from a specific kind of help. For example, I find that when children write about ideas, their writing often becomes repetitive because they circle back to say something again and again, hoping perhaps to clarify. Teach these children to reread their writing immediately after they've written it, deleting cumbersome iterations of an idea and leaving only the clearest version in place. Allow them to feel great about brief, clear writing.

You may find some children have regarded this unit of study as an invitation to write in bland, obvious generalizations. Encourage them to write more specifically and to say more in a sentence—usually when they write an idea using more words, they write with more specificity. Help them reach for more precise language. Coach them to push past words like good and fun toward words that name their feelings more exactly.

Notice whether the child uses any of the transition terms one would expect in non-narrative writing. Does the child use phrases such as *one reason, for example, I also think, it is important that, also, because, on the other hand?* If the child is not using any of these transition words, determine whether the child is instead using words such as *next, after this, and then*— transition terms one expects to see in narrative writing. If children aren't using transition words at all, this may or may not be a sign that they are not elaborating on or developing their ideas. Remember, using transition words is not our goal! Thinking of whole ideas in varying relationships to one another is our goal, and using certain transition words is one indicator that children are doing that. Children can use transition words without understanding or intentionally creating relationships between ideas, and they can leave out transition words while still creating these relationships.

SEEKING OUTSIDE SOURCES

When I studied writing with Donald Murray, *he told me that I needed to learn that I could put other people's voices and stories into my writing. For several years, all of my articles had been about my own teaching, and Murray was determined for me to expand my repertoire. "Think of a story you'd like to tell," he said to me, "that is not your own story. Then phone people and say, 'I want to write your story. Can I come visit you? Can I talk with you?'"*

Three days later, I set off on a four-day trip to visit teachers across the state of Vermont who'd studied in the National Writing Project's summer program at the University of Vermont. Looking back now, I laugh to realize that my first steps into the world of investigative journalism had been cautious ones, for I hadn't exactly explored a topic too far afield from my area of expertise! Still, I learned a lot from traversing the state, gathering the stories of people I did not know, as told in their own voices.

Now it is important to me that we nudge youngsters, too, to include stories and quotes from people they have interviewed, as well as the voices of people they meet in the pages of books. William Zinsser said, "Whatever form of nonfiction you write, it will come alive in proportion to the number of quotes you can weave into it as you go along" (Zinsser 2001).

How important it is for writers to learn to listen. Byrd Baylor, the author of the children's book The Other Way to Listen, *tells the story of an old man who teaches a young child how to listen. "Do this: go get to know one thing as well as you can," he advises. "Don't be ashamed to learn from bugs or sand or anything" (Baylor 1997). The old man's advice can aid your students as they begin the journey to support their thesis statement. Invite them to look around, to listen hard, and to be collectors of stories.*

IN THIS SESSION, YOU WILL TEACH CHILDREN THAT WRITERS SEEK OUTSIDE SOURCES, SOLICITING OTHER PEOPLE'S STORIES, TO SUPPORT THEIR IDEAS IN ESSAY WRITING.

GETTING READY

- One incident from which you have written two stories: one that illustrates your topic sentence, one that illustrates a different point
- A few sentences from an interview that support a bullet point from the class story, written on chart paper
- Example of a child's story and topic sentence requiring revision to support the main idea
- See CD-ROM for resources

MINILESSON

Seeking Outside Sources

CONNECTION

Remind children that authors collect and angle stories to highlight the idea we want to convey. Show that a familiar shared story could have been angled differently, conveying a different idea.

"Writers, in the previous session you learned that as writers we collect stories, we write those stories in such a way that we highlight the idea we really want to convey. For example, I wrote a story about how on Christmas mornings, my father used to leave us for the hospital, where he cooked waffles for the doctors and patients. I angled the story to show my dad's dedication to his work, but I *could* instead have written about the fact that on Christmas mornings, I have often felt swamped with cleanup chores, partially due to Dad's trips to the hospital. I *could* have written this:"

> When the living room was a sea of torn wrapping paper
> and empty boxes, my father would head out of the
> house, leaving us to clean up. He was adamant that he
> needed to cook waffles for the people at the hospital.
> So my brothers and I were left to lug load after load of
> trash to the garage.

"However, if I'd written about my Christmas morning job overload, this would not have advanced my thesis about my dad loving his job. The details about our living room being a sea of torn wrapping paper and the loads of trash would not have been aligned with my point; they would not have provided supportive evidence for the idea that Dad taught me what it means to regard a job as a hobby! I hope you have learned that when we write stories—stories we hope will become part of our essays—we need to keep in mind the messages we want to convey, and we need to tell the stories in ways that make readers *feel* our messages."

COACHING

You will notice that today's Connection is much more extensive than usual. I practically reteach the preceding minilesson. I do this from time to time when I think the preceding lesson was particularly new or complicated. Another option could have been to spend a day revisiting the previous session's instruction, and only then move on to the new teaching.

Notice that I revisit earlier stories, using a familiar story in a new way to make a new point. Again and again, you'll see a particular story thread through four or five minilessons. I do this so that children can focus on what is new about my story, and about today's teaching point, instead of focusing on the story's content. For the same reason, when I use children's literature to illustrate a teaching point, I try to choose stories with which students are already familiar.

Notice, too, that I once again highlight the feature I want children to notice in writing by juxtaposing a "do this" example with a "don't do this" example. I present contrasting examples as a way to bring a particular feature into focus.

"When I wrote the Christmas morning story, I kept in mind that it was supposed to provide evidence that Dad loved his job; now I'll underline sections of my story that I hope bring out that idea."

> I remember on Christmas mornings after the presents had been opened, my dad always went into the kitchen and began <u>doing the one bit of cooking that he did all year.</u> He stirred Bisquick and eggs in a huge bowl and set off for the hospital, leaving us to finish Christmas celebrations without him. <u>For dad, Christmas mornings were not just a time to be with family, they were also a time to serve hot waffles to the medical residents and patients.</u> When I asked him once why he didn't send someone else with the waffles, <u>he told me he loved being at the hospital on Christmas mornings.</u> "It's my hobby," he said.

"In a similar fashion, yesterday you all angled your stories to convey certain ideas. When Jay Jay looked back at a story he wrote to illustrate that he loves spending time with his father, Jay Jay realized that he hadn't yet made the point, so he rewrote the story. Listen to his first draft and then to the revised version of it."

> *1st Draft*
> One sunny Sunday my dad came and picked me up to go to his job at the Skate Key. On the way I asked him how to do a 360°. When we got there he putted his skates on. He did it first then I did it next but I fell on the ice.

> *Revision*
> I love being with my father because he teaches me skating moves. One sunny Sunday, my dad came and picked me up to go to his job at the Skate Key. On the way I asked him how to do a 360°. When we got there, he said, "Jay Jay put your skates on." He putted his skates on. He did it first. My dad whirled so fast~~fast~~ like a road runner. I couldn't see him. Bang with his strong skates. I thought his wheels popped off. My eyes were spinning fast like I got dizzy. I thought that he fell head first into the floor. I thought he broke his leg when he came down. He did it first but next I did it. I fell on the floor. My head was bloody. I came to in the locker room still thinking how I love my Dad for teaching me skating moves.

A third move I make in this minilesson, one I make in many minilessons, is that after I state a general rule, or an overarching idea, I follow it up with a very specific example. Notice that this shift from big idea to specific example is a mainstay of any essay—and it is a mainstay also of any course of study! If you feel as if this genre is not home terrain for you, think again because much of your teaching follows the structures of an essay.

This is Jay Jay's first year in a writing workshop. He has lots of trouble spelling conventionally, but he has already learned a gigantic amount about the craft of effective writing. One of the interesting things that you will no doubt see with your kids is this: It is not that hard to teach a struggling writer the craft of effective writing. Strugglers like Jay Jay can learn to angle their stories and to recap a main idea after they've told a story that they hope illustrates that main idea. But it is less easy to teach strugglers to write with strong spelling and complex sentence structures. Their learning on this front will be incremental, not exponential.

Notice that I used a student sample as well as my own sample in the Connection. This is more examples than usual, and more teaching in the Connection than usual.

"All of you, like Jay Jay, are learning to reread your stories, checking that you highlighted whatever matched your main idea."

Name your teaching point. In this case, tell children that essay writers often collect stories from outside sources.

"Today I want to teach you that writers of essays are collectors, collecting not only *our* stories but also stories of others, as long as these stories illustrate our main ideas."

TEACHING

Teach children that writers can rely on outside sources, on other people's stories, to support their ideas. Present an example.

"For example, Caleb's been working on collecting stories that illustrate his thesis that when learning sports, practice makes perfect. Caleb has lots of stories from his own life—we all know Caleb spends lots of time practicing sports—but he decided to search for stories from other people's lives as well, and to put those in his folders. I want you to notice, in this story about Michael Jordan, specific things Caleb does to highlight his point that, in sports, practice makes perfect. Listen and notice that Caleb's stories are shaped like stories. He tells about Michael Jordan encountering a problem, then struggling, then resolving the problem. Even though he writes mini-stories, his stories follow the same story arc that Keats' uses to write *Peter's Chair*. Listen." *[Figs. X-1 and X-2]*

> As a kid, famed basketball player Michael Jordan was heartbroken when he heard that he had not made his high school basketball team. He was so heartbroken that that summer he spent most of his free time on the basketball court, practicing. And guess what? The next time he tried out for that team, because of all that practice, he made the team, and was one of the best players.
>
> Michael and most other athletes will tell you that the key to their success is mostly practice. When you're practicing, someone else isn't, and when you two meet up, who's going to be better? You: the person who was practicing.

It is easier to recall bits of information when those bits are nested in familiar concepts or otherwise related to what a person already knows. I try to make my new point easy to remember by showing how this new lesson relates to and extends the previous lesson. I do this sort of thing often.

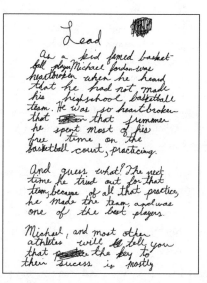

Fig. X-1 Caleb collects anecdotes to support his thesis

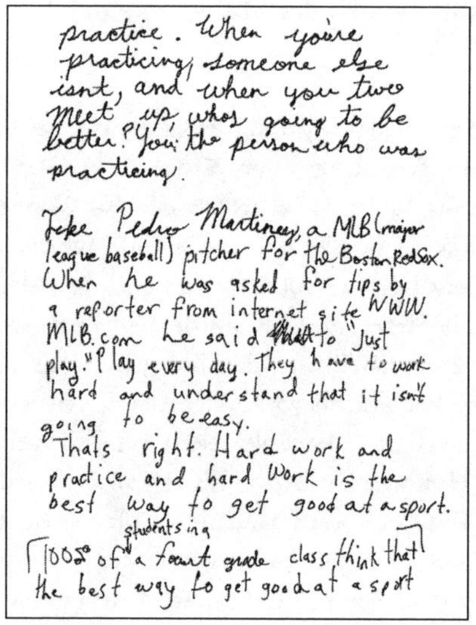

Fig. X-2 Caleb's anecdotes illustrate his thesis

"Did you notice that Caleb's story started like stories often do, with Caleb telling the problem Michael Jordan had, and then Caleb shows how Michael Jordan tried—and eventually resolved—his problem. But the other important thing I hope you noticed is that after telling the story, Caleb did just what Jay Jay did when he wrote about his father teaching him to roller-skate. Caleb came back and talked about how the story goes with his main idea. Listen again." I reread it, stressing the last paragraph.

"Sometimes when we go to collect stories from others, we end up collecting quotes more than stories, as in this next example. But again notice how, at the end, Caleb talks about how this bit of information connects with his idea, which is that practice, in sports, is important."

> Take Pedro Martinez, a MLB (major league baseball) pitcher for the Boston Red Sox. When he was asked for tips by a reporter from internet site www.mlb.com he said to just play. "Play everyday. They have to work hard and understand that it isn't going to be easy."
>
> That's right. Hard work and practice and hard work is the best way to get good at a sport.

"Did you notice that Caleb connected this story to his claim at the end as well, almost as if he were saying, 'Notice this story really builds my case!' It's like the story is evidence in a trial, and Caleb is the lawyer, showing people that the evidence proves the case."

ACTIVE ENGAGEMENT
Ask students to use the class piece to practice seeking outside sources and writing them into an essay.

"So let's try it on our class essay about first-grade reading buddies. Imagine you are writing a page to go into your folder labeled 'Another reason that working with reading buddies is fun is that you get to read really cool books,'" I said, holding up the folder with that label. You need some stories to support that bullet point, don't you! Now pretend you interviewed Randolio to learn whether he thought the first-grade books were cool. I did that, and I wrote down what he said right here." I pointed at the chart paper on which I had transcribed Randolio's comments about books.

Notice how I am really slowing down this instruction. This work is not easy, and I am teaching it by sharing an example rather than by demonstrating. I want to make sure that my students are seeing and hearing what I want them to notice. For this reason, I make a great point to share the example in a way that highlights the aspects I want highlighted. In this minilesson I am doing what I taught kids to do in the preceding lesson: I am telling a small story and angling it so that it illustrates my point.

In high school English classes, students learn that you can't make a claim, cite a passage from a text to illustrate that claim, and call it a day. Instead, it's important to write another sentence or two that digs into the passage, discussing specifically how this citation relates to the claim. Elementary school students can do a junior version of this if they learn to write about how their story illustrates their thesis.

Over and over you'll notice that to set children up to efficiently practice what I've taught, I do 80 percent of the necessary work, leaving just a bit for them to do. The part of the endeavor I leave for the children exactly matches what I've just taught them to do. I usually get them started doing this, almost as I might help a child get started riding a two-wheeler.

A lot of books have parts that pop up and squeak and quack and all. I love the ones that have sound effects. Once my buddy had a pile of books. He opened the first one and it mooed and neighed. It was so funny. The second book played, "Old Susannah." The third one didn't make sounds. He also had a book with a wheel that spun around.

"What part of Randolio's comments would you quote to support that bullet point? Partner 2, write in the air, saying aloud to your partner exactly what you'd write if you were quoting the section of Randolio's comments that make your case. What part of his comments prove that working with reading buddies allows you to read really cool books?"

The children did this, and I listened in. "I love the way you let some parts of what Randolio said drop away," I said, "but most of you aren't quite finished. You forgot to talk at the end about how Randolio's comments fit with the claim that working with reading buddies is fun. Pretend you ended by saying, 'Randolio's buddy, for example, had a pile of books. One mooed, another played "Old Susannah."' How could you explicitly connect this [I pointed to the line about first-grade books being cool because they have sound effects] to your topic sentence? Turn and talk. Write that final sentence in the air to your partner and then go off to your own writing, keeping this in mind."

Notice how I don't let children leave the meeting area until they connected their comments with their claim. I am tucking this in here because I know this is an area where many students struggle. I want it to become habit for them.

WRITING AND CONFERRING

Checking That Stories Match Topic Sentences

Whether your writers are collecting their own stories or retelling the anecdotes of others, there are a few predictable lessons you'll teach them as you confer and work with small groups. You'll need to teach children to angle their stories to make their point, and I've discussed this already. You'll also need to teach children to reread whatever they collect in their files, asking, "Does this really support my topic sentence?" Often, the evidence will be only tangentially related to the topic sentence.

For example, I pulled in and listened to Emily, whose thesis was "December is fun." One of her topic sentences said, "December is fun because of Christmas parties." I taught her to underline the two or three key words in her topic sentence, and she underlined *December, Christmas parties,* and *fun.* Then I told her that what I do to check that my material matches the point, the meaning, is that I reread my material and ask whether the information is related to each of the key words. So Emily read one of the stories she'd collected aloud, checking to see whether it supported the three things she'd decided were key (*December, Christmas parties*, and *fun*). *[Fig. X-3]*

> One time that <u>December</u> was fun at a X-mas party. Me, my cousins and my sister were eating <u>Christmas dinner</u> in my room and when we finished we decided to play this game on my bed. We put pillows under my bed and against the wall then we would all sit in the crack and the bed would move forward fast and we would drop down fast and land on our pillows.

"It goes with my point?" she said, her intonation suggesting she wasn't sure.

"Let's check. For this to 'go,' it needs to be about December. Is it? Yes. It needs to be about a Christmas party—is it? Yes. It needs to be about the party being fun—is it?"

"Yes?" Emily asked, but on closer inspection she realized that although she'd described a game that she does indeed find to be fun, she hadn't made clear to readers that the game was a lot of fun (and in fact, because the game involved crashing from the bed onto the floor on one's butt, she could not assume readers would just 'know' that this was sheer joy).

<u>MID-WORKSHOP</u>
TEACHING POINT

Showing* and *Telling "Writers, can I have your eyes and your attention? I have a quick but very important tip for you. As you are rereading your essays to make sure your stories prove your claims, you can also reread checking for something else. Remember how we've talked about how writers show, not tell? The truth is, essay writers nearly always both show *and* tell! As you reread what you've written, check to see that every story you've collected has times in it where you tell—outright explain what's important—and also times when you show—describe how something goes. You already know how to show—by making a movie in your mind and describing what you see and hear and sense. Emily is going to tell that her Christmas party was fun by saying that's where she and her cousin invented some of her favorite games. She's going to show it was fun by describing how they were laughing while they were playing them. You can show *and* tell in every essay you ever write, and that will make your essays all the more powerful."

> one time that December was fun at a X-mas party. Me, my cousins and my sister were eating christmas dinner in my room and when we finished we disided to play this game on my bed. We put pillows under my bed and agaist the wall then we would all sit in the crack and the bed would move forward <u>fast</u> and we we would drop down <u>fast</u> and land on our pillows.

Fig. X-3 Emily's notebook entry

I complimented Emily on the way she angled her story even though she hadn't done it perfectly. In my compliment, I walked her through the steps of angling, naming each turn she took or should have taken. "I love the way you didn't just tell your story any ol' way. Instead you said, 'I better make it clear this was a Christmas party,' so you put that fact up front in the story. And later you reread to check that key words—or key ideas— were in your example." This made my compliment reteach the process. Then I reminded her she always needs to reread the stories she collects to be sure they illustrate every important part of a topic sentence—she still needed to make clear that the party was fun. I suggested she could come right out and say something like, "Many of my favorite games are those that my cousins and I invented during those Christmas parties."

As you confer with individuals and teach small groups today, keep in mind that not only will you want to teach children to show and tell, but you'll also want to draw on all that your children have learned during the launching and personal narrative units of study. Be sure the old charts of Qualities of Good Narrative Writing are displayed in a prominent place, and be sure to remind children that they can draw on those early lessons, that they were indeed lessons that were meant to last a lifetime.

When I drew my chair alongside Rie, she told me she'd already written a story to support each of her topic sentences. Her stories were each brief—no more than half a page. "I'm impressed that even your tiny stories actually feel like stories," I said to her. Then I pointed out, "One thing I try to do is vary the length of my stories." I suggested she look them over and decide on a few stories to tell with more detail. Rie decided to stretch out this story which she hoped illustrated the idea that she hates to make mistakes in front of a crowd. She'd written: *[Fig. X-4]*

> I was in Japan in school waiting for my test score. My teacher was really shocked. "Rie!" he called, "You got sixty!" I was shocked about what I heard. I usually got ninety or hundred or ninety-five. Kids started to laugh at me. I felt my face grow red. I heard kids whispering and I heard an insult name.

This is her new version of it: *[Fig. X-5]*

> I wasn't happy doing a test because the teachers in Japan says the test score out. "Rie," called out a voice. It was my teacher's voice. I knew that I wouldn't get a hundred percent. I went up front. He said my score out to the class. "Rie you got sixty." My jaw dropped open. I couldn't believe my ears. I usually got ninety-five or ninety. I saw everyone giggling in front of me. I wanted to cry. But I was in school. Everyone would laugh at me even more. I wished if only I had magic powers and I disappeared.

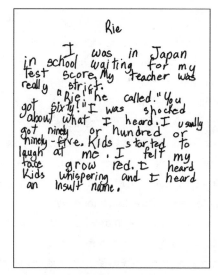

Fig. X-4 Rie's notebook entry (first draft)

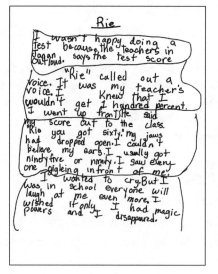

Fig. X-5 Rie's revised entry

SHARE

Checking That Stories Support Topic Sentences

Remind writers that they need to angle stories to support their topic sentences. Present an example of a student's story and a topic sentence, and describe how the writer checked his alignment and then revised his story to support his claim.

"Writers, I want to remind you that we need to check to be sure that our stories address our main ideas. Alejandro realized today that this is hard to do. At first, he thought, 'My story definitely supports my idea.' His topic sentence is 'Mr. Lee is a great teacher because he taught me how to do art.' His story is all about learning to do art. Listen, and see if you think Alejandro's example illustrates his point that Mr. Lee is a great teacher because he taught Alejandro to do art."

> We made self-portraits. We used tissue paper to make the color of our skin. We glued the tissue paper on to the picture of our head. It looked like skin. We made eyes using wax . . .

"At first Alejandro said, 'My story matches my main idea because it *is* all about doing art.' But then he said, 'Wait a minute!' and he reread. 'Now I get it,' he said. 'My thesis is "Mr. Lee was a great teacher (for all these reasons)," but in my self-portrait story, Mr. Lee is missing!' So Alejandro rewrote the story this way."

> Mr. Lee taught us new art techniques. For example he taught us that when we want to show skin, we can use tissue paper. Mr. Lee knows a lot of tricks like that. He taught us that to make eyes . . .

Ask partners to reread their own and their partner's stories, checking to see if their stories support their topic sentences.

"Writers, would you each reread your thesis statement with your partner and underline the two or three key words, the parts that need to be supported by your story. Alejandro will need to underline *Mr. Lee* (the subject), *taught* (what he did), and *taught us new art techniques* (the specific point). Then look together at your stories and see if they illustrate all these parts of your topic sentence. If they don't, help each other revise the story so that it does the job you need it to do."

It is very easy to give data just a cursory glance and to say, "Of course that supports the claim." But often, when one really looks, there are problems that need to be addressed.

The truth is that I had conferred with Alejandro and helped him realize that no, his example did not exactly support his claim. When I tell the story to the class, though, I leave myself out of it. I act as if Alejandro first thought his story matched his claim, and then on his own came to the realization that he'd left Mr. Lee out of the story. I do this because the contrast between his first, problematic version and the revised one brings home the point I am trying to make. Because I erase my role from this and act as if Alejandro, on his own, thought, "Wait a minute!" and revised his initial idea, I'm able to tell the "before" version without it seeming like a public insult. This is a very common way for me to show an example of a child traveling on a path that I hope other children will travel. I use the story not just to praise but also to teach others what they can do.

HOMEWORK   *Waiting for More Stories to Illustrate your Ideas*   I know at home tonight, stories related to your topic sentences will come to the surface of your thinking. That happens to every writer. We live with a topic, waiting on it. Eudora Welty once said that we sit, waiting for stories like we wait for a mouse to emerge from a hole in the wall. Don Murray says that all writers need to wait. "Waiting takes time, time for staring out windows, time for thinking, time for dreaming, time for doodling, time for rehearsing, planning, drafting, restarting . . . for moving closer, backing off, coming at it from a different angle, circling again, trying a new approach (Murray 1989, pp. 22–23). And Kafka had, over his writing desk, just one word: wait.

So as you travel home, wait for related story ideas to emerge. As you walk into your home, wait for a related story idea. When you tell folks at home what you are writing (and do that—talking helps ideas come out), wait. The stories will come, just as the mouse comes out of the hole. Plan to write two or three stories, each on separate sheets of paper because you'll file these in your folders, each telling a different story related to a different topic sentence. Combined, do a total of a page and a half or two pages of writing—which means you'll need your stories to be efficient ones!

TAILORING YOUR TEACHING

If your writers are having some trouble angling their narratives to support an idea . . .
you can demonstrate that sometimes it helps to write the story, keeping in mind the main idea, almost as one would hold onto a mantra. You could say, "I want to show you how I create my narrative, repeating phrases to remind myself the meaning I want to highlight in my story, almost as if it is a mantra. First, I create my mantra. If my thesis is 'Friendships are complicated' and the topic sentence is 'Friendships are complicated at school,' the mantra might go, 'friendships . . . complicated . . . school,' 'friendships . . . complicated . . . school'. Okay, now I have it. Now I am ready to write my story about the time I saw my friend Emily cheating on a test." Then I'd write, stopping every once in a while to say the mantra out loud. "Did you see how I took the subject of the thesis, 'friendship', and the main idea about friendship, 'complicated at school', and recited this over and over as I wrote out a narrative?"

MECHANICS

When you read over the writing your children do under the auspices of this unit, you will probably notice that at least a few children are trying to make their essay-entries sound more objective, formal and academic than their narratives. Chances are good that this well-intentioned effort will create lots of new issues involving mechanics and grammar.

First, you may see children writing unnecessarily in the passive voice and using abstract rather than concrete and specific words. A college student who is trying to be impressive might get caught in convoluted sentences such as: "The influence exerted by leaders upon the citizens extends to voting and . . . " Children can create their own versions of this: "A true friendship contains being helpful, showing that you understand and care, not being made fun of, and laughter. The obstacles in a friendship can be hurtful, but they also teach you a lesson about yourself and about your friends, and how to handle a situation like this later . . . "

If your children are trying to write like this—stop them! Teach them first of all to trust simple sentences in which a doer does something. The power in a sentence comes from the active agent, the subject, and from the actor's action, the verb. Sentences will always work best if they contain a clear, forceful, imaginable subject. "My best friend, Kara . . . " will work better than "Friendships contain . . . ".

In Session I, for example, you read Adam's entry in which he mulled over classmates' reactions to a disease. Notice Adam's struggles with pronoun agreement:

People shouldn't judge people by what they look like. When kids are discriminated by what they look like they are treated very cruelly. It is really mean to do this because you don't really know this person. For example, let's say someone wears a shirt with a stain on it and everybody doesn't want to be your friend because they think your dirty. The person who did not want to talk to you could have been your future best friend. When I was in kindergarten in this school a lot of people avoided me because I am bald. It took me a long time to make friends. It is harder to go into a new school if you have something different like I do. Before people judge people by what they look like they need to tell themselves, "What would I feel like if I was that kid? With everybody staring at me and nobody talking to you." Then you look at you and your friends, with everybody admiring you and including you. Then you go over there to the "different kid" and include him and talk to him.

Notice, too, that some of your children will probably struggle with *anaphora*—the use of a pronoun to reference an earlier noun. Take this passage:

Leo made errors, including telling the joke to his brother. He was embarrassed. Now that he'd told one, he needed to tell another.

Is "he" intended to be Leo or his brother? Is "one" intended to be "one person" or "one joke"? Is "another" a person or a joke?

The author of an expository text must use pronouns to represent not only nouns—people and objects—but also *concepts*. For example, I might write a whole paragraph describing the architecture of a minilesson. Later in my discussion, all of that information would be contained in the simple phrase *the architecture of a minilesson;* moreover, the information might later still be referenced in the tiny pronoun *it.* This means that pronouns carry a heavy cargo!

Many times, however, the writer needs to use synonyms or repeat the noun (rather than use a pronoun) to avoid an unclear referent. Watch Ali, a proficient fifth grader, struggle with the new demands of expository writing. I put her intended meaning in parentheses:

> My brother is his own person. Sometimes it is kind of hard *to tell a thing like that* (to discern that he has this character trait) when *they (people)* are little. But he is almost nothing like me, my mom or dad. *That* (my brother's uniqueness) is something I love about him. In some aspects of his personality he is very much the same (as others in the family).

It's important that we, as teachers, are able to look at our students' writing and recognize and categorize their miscues. Then we need to prioritize our instructional plans for responding to these miscues. If a child hasn't yet studied the concept of pronoun reference, it's probably not reasonable to try to devise lessons on anaphora. But it may make sense to ask these children, when they *read* expository texts, to notice that over and over again, an entire paragraph or page ends up crystallized into a single term that is then referenced later by just a pronoun. When reading these lines:

> The network of canals forms an irrigation system. Irrigation systems are vital to the success of a farm. These systems . . .

the reader needs to draw mental arrows backwards in the text.

From Irrigation to network of canals. From these to Irrigation.

Some readers do this without requiring direct instruction, but others need us to explicitly teach these reading and writing moves.

GETTING READY

- Example of published writing where author used lists ("I have a dream" speech by Martin Luther King Jr. used in this session) on chart paper
- Your own topic sentences and supporting lists to illustrate use of repeated phrases and parallel wording
- See CD-ROM for resources

CREATING PARALLELISM IN LISTS

I love to make lists. I list my priorities for a day, a week, a vacation, a year. I list the names of flowers I've planted in my garden. I list names for the dog I'll someday get. I list books I've read and books I want to read. I list places I'd like to visit someday. I list the days when my son will be away, and the days when he'll be home again.

Lists reflect the human instinct to collect, sort, order, and select. When we cannot physically gather all the flowers we've planted in our arms and line them up on the counter, we list their names, and those names make the flowers present. Simply by naming them, we conjure them up: dahlia, daisy, lily—yes, I've got them all in my garden.

During today's session, you'll help children make lists that may help their essays. There are lots of possible ways to teach this concept. You could share your own propensity to list and to collect, and share also what you know of your children's similar tendencies. One child collects baseball cards, another barrettes. Both children spend time sorting these into categories. Writers do similar work.

Specifically, today you'll teach children to write what I refer to as "tight lists," or lists of items linked by a repeating phrase. The lesson, then, will be not only about lists but also about parallelism.

For writers, the challenge of this lesson will be to attend to both content and form. It would be easy to write tight lists of anything in the world—but remember, Rebecca's tight lists need to advance her claims about her fury with her grandfather, and Caleb's tight lists need to show that practice is essential to success in a sport. Trying to convey a meaning while writing within a tight list structure is like trying to tap your head and rub your belly at the same time—it is not easy. Try it and you'll see!

MINILESSON

Creating Parallelism in Lists

CONNECTION

Remind your students that writers collect material, especially stories, to use in their essays. Spotlight the work of one child in a way that serves as a model for all children.

"Writers, over the past few days you learned that while builders build with plasterboard and lumber, writers build with words. Before we can draft our essays, we need to collect the materials we might use to build our boxes and bullets. You have already collected stories, and some of you used phrases such as *for example* to get yourselves started writing step-by-step stories. Diego did this when he wrote about Sari getting stuck trying to read the phrase *sheep shove*, and Caleb did this when he collected stories about Michael Jordan and Pedro Martinez."

"Emily, for example, collected a story to support her idea 'Having a dog is a big responsibility.' She wrote the story in a step-by-step way with a lot of detail, and those details make the story enthralling. Listen to it."

> Having a dog is a big responsibility because when they are adults they are playful. For example one day when I was sleeping my dog woke me up in the middle of the night to play. She was bouncing all over the place. She barked then jumped on my bed and started wiggling all over. I pushed her off and she jumped back on. I got up, walked her to her dog bed and put her to sleep. It took a long time, but it paid off.

"Do you see how Emily highlighted the parts of the story that show that dogs are a big responsibility because they are playful? And she continued, writing one more tiny story that also illustrates her main idea."

> This also reminds me of when I was in the park. I saw a boy walking his dog. It looked like the dog was walking him. He was yelling at the dog then he took out a ball. The dog started jumping all over the place. He threw the ball, the dog got it, he threw it again, the dog got it. He put the ball away and the dog walked him home.

COACHING

I know this unit can be complicated. One day children learn to write personal stories; another day, to collect less-personal anecdotes; and on another day they learn to write lists. I try to consolidate all they've learned so that it feels simple and portable. I do that here when I say builders build with plasterboard and lumber, writers with words.

I've tried to immerse children in examples of the sort of thing I hope they write. But meanwhile, I've slowed down my minilesson by including a fairly long example in the Connection phase. You may decide to streamline this lesson if you don't believe your children need the immersion.

"I know you have more stories in mind and you'll continue collecting them in your files. Once you get started writing stories, more and more examples will float to the surface of your mind."

Name your teaching point. In this case, tell children that sometimes writers collect lists of examples.

"Today I want to teach you that when writing essays, writers sometimes collect examples that we do not stretch out and tell as stories, but that we instead list."

TEACHING
Illustrate the importance of lists by referencing the parallel construction in a well-known speech.

"Listen to one of the most famous pieces of non-narrative writing in the world. I have a copy up here on the overhead so you can read along."

"You will surely have heard this text before—it is Martin Luther King Jr.'s 'I have a dream' speech. The whole speech is not structured exactly like the essays we are writing, but we can learn from studying the way Martin Luther King Jr uses *lists* to support his idea. I want you to listen first to a bit of his speech, and then watch how I (as a writer) go back and study what this author has done in order to borrow his techniques. Then we'll move to a second bit of King's speech and you'll have a chance to name the techniques you see him using that you can emulate."

> We have come to this hallowed spot to remind America of the fierce urgency of now . . . Now is the time to make real the promises of democracy; now is the time to rise from the dark and desolate valley of segregation to the sunlit porch of racial justice; now is the time to lift our nation from the quicksands of racial injustice to the solid rock of brotherhood; now is the time to make justice a reality for all of God's children.

"Listen to how King has one main idea here—that it is urgent to work toward civil rights *now*. Then he gives example after example of that main idea, telling what we need to do now. His examples echo each other. The key words are repeated so they sound like a

This is an odd Connection. I elaborate about the stories that writers sometimes tell but then instead of incorporating this somehow in my point for the day, I just end that topic and shift to another. I simply say, "Writers also do something else," pushing off from the first kind of writing to a second kind. The minilesson might have been better had I brought some of the content from this session's introduction into it, or pointed out the significance of lists within the classroom. By this time in the year, you will have lists of strategies, lists of qualities, lists of tools. You may decide to point out these lists, and then suggest that essayists are teachers of a sort and like all teachers, we rely on lists to consolidate a lot of information.

Note the way I try to orient listeners at the start of the Teaching component of a minilesson. I want children to know what I'll be doing and why, and I also want them to know what they'll be expected to learn and to do. I began deliberately adding bits of orientation after visiting hundreds of classrooms where I sit among the children in the meeting area listening to a minilesson, and finding myself often disoriented as the teacher launched into a story or an example. Readers can skim the page and see from sub-headings and other text features where the text is going, but listeners have none of those supports. It's helpful, therefore, if speakers give us a bit of orientation.

Notice that I sometimes use exemplar texts that are not exactly essays, and in those instances I use the larger umbrella term of non-narrative to describe those texts.

song." I reread several of them, accentuating the repeated phrase. "They all start with the same phrase—*Now is the time to …!*"

Ask children to watch as you use the techniques the author used to write a tight list pertinent to your topic.

"So let me try to borrow some of these techniques and use them for this idea: 'My father taught me that one person can make a difference.' So let me see . . . " I reread my sentence.

> *My father taught me to believe that one person can make a difference.*

"I'm going to take the stem of this claim. Maybe if I repeat it, I can jog my mind to come up with a list of examples."

> *My father taught me to believe that . . .*

"I need to come up with things that fit under the idea that one person can make a difference. And I need to remember to write with details."

> *My father taught me to believe that . . . that . . . one person could start a hospital clinic . . . that one person could rally all the members of a family to write their memoir, that one person could turn a rainy drab day into an adventure, that one person could change the spirit at a hospital . . .*

"Do you see how I took a key phrase and repeated it? Some of the lines I've come up with aren't all that great and some sort of repeat each other, but I think I've got some good stuff here." I put the entry in the appropriate file folder.

ACTIVE ENGAGEMENT
Remind children that to learn techniques for their own writing, they can study the writing of a published author. In this case, they can study parallelism.

"I hope you noticed the way I took just a bit of what Martin Luther King Jr. had written and I read it again. Then I asked myself, 'So what has Martin Luther King Jr. done that I can do too?' Whether you are writing a story or an essay, it always helps to study the work of the pros. Let's each try to do that with the copies of King's speech that I've given you. Would

Above all, I want children to sense the rhythm of King's language. You may decide that King's writing is too complex to serve as a mentor text for your children. You could use "Hairs," a passage from Sandra Cisneros' wonderful anthology The House on Mango Street, *as a more accessible example, or "Alone," a chapter from Jacqueline Woodson's* From the Notebooks of Melanin Sun. *Alternatively, you could choose any great picture book or poem that relies on repetitive lists. Search for titles by Charlotte Zolotow if you are looking for a picture book that's written as a list—she's written dozens of wonderful ones!*

Say this with intonation that signals children to fill in what could go next.

It is important to notice that I don't start with a neat mental list and then record it. I write what I refer to as a stem of a sentence, and in this instance, it is the stem of my topic sentence. Only then do I generate and record one idea for how to complete the sentence. After I've written one idea, I push toward a second idea. I find that simply repeating the pattern generated by the first line makes it easier to produce a list than trying to pull a full-blown list out of the air. Simultaneously conceiving of both the pattern and of the elements that will fill the pattern is quite difficult. "When you catch someone a fish, they eat for a day. When you teach them to fish, they eat for a lifetime." I'm trying—lightly—to demonstrate the process of learning from a mentor text while also showcasing the way this writer used lists.

you and your partner take the next paragraph, read it aloud, then try to name specifically what King has done that you can do too?"

> With this faith we will be able to work together, to pray together, to struggle together, to go to jail together, to stand up for freedom together, knowing that we will be free one day. And this will be the day.
>
> So let freedom ring from the prodigious hilltops of New Hampshire; let freedom ring from the mighty mountains of New York; let freedom ring from the snow-capped Rockies of Colorado; let freedom ring from the curvaceous slopes of California . . . And when this happens, and when we allow freedom to ring, when we let it ring from every village and every hamlet, from every state and every city, we will be able to speed up the day when all of God's children, black men and white men, Jews and Gentiles, Protestants and Catholics, will be able to join hands and sing in the words of the old Negro spiritual, "Free at last. Free at last."

"Once you and your partner have got an idea for something that Martin Luther King Jr. has done that you could try, would you use the technique you admire and work together, planning a list that you could insert into our class essay."

Reiterate your writing process, highlighting the steps you hope writers will take as they write lists for their essays.

"Remember that whenever you decide to write a list, you also need to figure out what the stem of your list will be because this is what you'll repeat and this is the part all the items in your list have to match with." I held up the folders, each displaying a topic sentence. "You could, for example, take this folder—'Working with our first-grade reading buddies is fun because you get to read really cool books'—and you could decide to list particular books. You could say, 'You get to read *Where the Wild Things Are*' and then say a phrase about that book; 'You get to read *Toot and Puddles*' and say a phrase about that one. *Or* you could choose a different stem and write, 'The books are cool because they have magic.' 'The books are cool because they have great pictures!'"

Alternatively, you could work with a different folder, a different topic sentence, and write, 'My reading buddy taught me this. My reading buddy taught me that.'"

If children need more support, I'll either read the paragraph aloud to them and ask them to talk in pairs about it, or I'll read it first, and then ask one of the partners to reread it aloud.

This is a long excerpt. You may want to read it aloud to help your children read it and hear its rhythms. You may also select just a part of it as your example. Alternatively, you may select a text that will be easier for your children to read. Picture books are full of examples!

Sometimes it can be a little jarring to take great works of literature and give their structure more attention than their content. Then, too, it can feel jarring to study magnificent writing and then apply a facet of it to everyday writing. However, I feel it is appropriate to do this in the classroom at times, for several reasons. First, nearly every text we study is one whose content is already familiar. We are not honoring form over content; we are simply continuing our study of the text by also studying its structure.

Second, we need to bring great literature and literature about great topics into the classroom at every opportunity. Even if the focus of our study is not the content of a piece of literature, some children will learn things from the content. Why not have the literature in the classroom be the most important literature we can possibly study? Last, as we've heard, imitation can be the sincerest form of flattery. Even the most awkward and ordinary bit of prose written to emulate a great work can be seen as a tribute to that great work. Our children and their work deserve the best writing we can bring them. Perhaps then, someday, they can create work that teachers across the country bring into classrooms as classic and heroic writing.

LINK
Restate the teaching point. Remind writers that today and always, essayists collect not only stories but also lists that illustrate their ideas.

"So writers, builders use cinder blocks and lumber. Writers use materials too, and so far you have learned that writers use stories. Today you learned that writers like Martin Luther King Jr. also use lists."

"The final point I want to make is that often we can choose to put the same content into *either* a list or into a story. When you think of an example today, think, 'Should I stretch this out as a story? Or should I combine it with other examples and write it as a list?' Both have their challenges, and today you'll probably write both lists and stories. But I would not write the same content over and over, in different forms. Make choices."

"Stories take a while to write because they are long, but lists also take a while to write because you need to work on many drafts so that you word them in ways that are parallel, concise, and make sense. I can't wait to admire and help you as you do this new work! Off you go."

Toward the end of a minilesson, I often try to put the day's teaching point alongside earlier teaching points, and if possible, show how they are related. In this instance, I refer back to the metaphor of writers as builders because this conveys the main concept of this minilesson. I also remind children that writers make choices, and that they can draw on previous teaching points as well as today's point.

It's not wise for a child to write the exact same content in a list and then again in a story. If a child is writing that his mother cares for him and he wants to say that she gives him Tylenol, penicillin, and cough medicine, the child needs to decide whether to write that in a list or in a story—but not to put the same specifics into both forms. The child may try it both ways and choose the way that seems to work best, but in the end, an essay can't contain the same content, written twice, each time in a different format.

WRITING AND CONFERRING

Making List Items Parallel

Any time we read students' writing or have a conference with one child, we need to ask ourselves, "Is this a lesson to teach one child—or should I pull in another writer or two?" As we read over our children's work, then, we create groups of kids. We think to ourselves, "Emily and Chris are both having trouble with . . . " and then later we pull them together and teach them a strategy we suspect will help them both. The following is an example of a strategy lesson I often teach in the wake of this minilesson.

"I gathered you together because I want to show you a trick I discovered when I was trying to make the items in my list parallel to each other. It's not easy to make them parallel, is it? I've noticed you guys are struggling with that, and you're not alone! So let me tell you what I learned from working on a list to go with my claim, 'My father taught me what it means to regard a job as a hobby.'"

"I had already written, 'My father doesn't just *like* his job, he *loves* his job.' When I read that line over, I knew it had a certain snap. I liked it. I didn't intend for the line to come out that way—I just wrote what I thought, and then I reread it and liked it. So I looked closely at the sentence to see if I could write more sentences in the same pattern. I noticed it has two parts, and they echo each other."

My father doesn't just like his job, he loves his job.

"So I built the next item on my list in the same way. I knew it had to go something like this: 'My father doesn't just *bing*, he *super-bings*. My father doesn't just like (something), he super-likes (something).' You see how it had to go? So I this is what I wrote:"

My father doesn't just care about his patients, he identifies with his patients.

MID-WORKSHOP TEACHING POINT — *Revising Lists* "Some of you are having some trouble getting started on a list. You aren't sure what to use as the repeating stem of the list. One thing to do is to think of a story, tell it to yourself in your mind, and then ask, 'How can I write this information—or the important parts of it—as a *list* and not as a story?' So listen to a story Eddy could have written to go with his general idea, ' I love spending time with my parents,' and with the specific idea (and folder), 'when we vacation together.' Remember his story? You've heard it before, but this time, listen so you can tell your partner what Eddy could *list* instead of *storytell*." [Fig. XI-1]

> I love to spend time with my parents when we vacation together. For example, one time we went to a hotel in New Jersey. We visited a zoo that was in the hotel. It had really cute baby animals. My Mom loved the baby sheep so much that she pretended she was going to sneak it up the elevator to our room. My Dad and I had to drag her away. We were just joking. Then we watched three TV shows; one that was my choice, one that was Mom's, one that was Dad's. We usually don't watch each others' shows.

continued on next page

> I love to spend time with my parents when we vacation together. For example, one time we went to a hotel in New Jersey. We visited a zoo that was in an hotel. I had really cute baby animals. My Mom. loved the baby sheep so much that she pretended she was going to sneak it up the elevator to our room. My Dad and I had to drag her away. We were just joking. Then we watched three TV shows; one that was my choice, one that was my Mom's, one that was Dad's. We usually don't watch each others' shows.

Fig. XI-1 Eddy's story

"Do you see how I followed the pattern of the first sentence I wrote? I started with the same phrase, '*My father doesn't just . . .*' and then I put in '*care about his patients.*' I knew the next part had to be something that tells he does more than just care about them, he 'super-cares' about them. And the phrase I chose was *identifies with his patients,* because that is so much more than caring."

"LaKeya did this too. Would you read this aloud and listen for the pattern, the song in her words and then look closely and point out to each other what she did that you could do as well."[Fig. XI-2]

> Being a girl is hard because we
> go through a lot of changes, and
> have mixed/sensitive feelings. I
> can be happy but in a moment I
> can be mad. I can not care how I
> look and then in a moment I can
> look in the mirror every minute. I
> can feel thin and then all of a
> sudden my rear end is getting
> bigger. I can smell good one
> moment and then the next
> moment my armpits stink.

"Now, each of you, try making a list or revising the one you've started to put into your own essay. Remember that first you reread what you've written or find a line you like, then you study what you did in that line to see if you can make another like it. I'll be right here helping you while you get started."

continued from previous page

The partners talked, and then I intervened. "I heard you finding lots of ways to do this, and of course there is no one right way. Theo first tried this."

> At the hotel, my family went to the zoo. At the hotel, my family
> watched TV. At the hotel, my family rode the elevator.

"But then he realized he'd left out the part about the family doing this *together* (which is, of course, the main idea!). He also left out all the interesting details. So he tried it again and this is what he came up with."

> I loved spending time with my parents when we stayed at
> a hotel. Together, we watched three TV shows (one that
> each of us had chosen). Together, we visited the hotel's
> zoo (where my Mom tried to sneak a baby lamb onto the
> elevator.) And together we ...

"Do you see that Theo has come up with a way for Eddy to repeat the important parts—that he, his mom, and his dad did these things *together*—and he has also included the details that bring his story to life? Coming up with this list isn't easy; Theo tried the list first one way, then another, then another. If you are working on lists that you can include in your folders, I should see draft 1, draft 2, draft 3 as you try your lists one way, then another, then another."

> Being a girl is hard because we go
> through a lot of changes, and have mixed/sensit
> ive feelings. I can be happy but in a moment
> I can be mad. I can not care how I look
> and then in a moment I can look in the
> mirror every minute. I can feel thin and then
> all of a sudden my rear end is getting bigger. I
> can smell good one moment and the next mom
> ent my armpits stink.

Fig. XI-2 LaKeya's lists

SHARE

Balancing Details and Parallelism

Name the problem that you have noticed. In this instance, children are so focused on parallelism that they forget the importance of honesty and detail.

"You are writing your lists in patterns and that is great, but you know how sometimes when we try to write poems that rhyme, we get into trouble—our poems end up having almost nothing *but* rhyme? Well, some of you are writing *lists* where one sentence matches with the next, but it's as if you are so worried about matching your words that you forget all you know about good writing! When you are writing a list (as when you are writing anything!), it is important to try to write well."

Showcase sections of an exemplar text that can teach the importance of using active verbs and precise details.

"There are a few qualities of good writing that you especially need to remember as you work on gathering lists. First, your word choice matters. If possible, write with precise, active verbs (or action words) and very specific nouns (or name words). King could have written, 'Let freedom *sound*,' but instead he wrote, 'Let freedom *ring*.' He could have said, 'From *north* to *south*,' but instead he wrote, 'From the *snow-capped Rockies of Colorado* . . . from the *curvaceous slopes of California*.'"

"The other thing that matters a lot when you write lists is using *specific* details. When Eddy wanted to write a list about staying in the hotel with his parents, this meant that he'd need to squeeze his whole long story into items in a list. He was probably tempted to leave out the details about watching one television show that he chose, one show that his mother chose, and one that his father chose. He was probably tempted to leave out the detail about his mother wanting to adopt a baby lamb, but Eddy wisely knew those details were the strongest part of his writing, so he kept them."

"Sometimes when writing a list, the details can't fit into sentences that sound just right—in that case, sometimes writers decide to keep the details and let go of the parallelism. That's the decision Jamile made when he listed examples to show how his pets are good entertainers, and I think his decision was really wise. Listen." *[Fig. XI-3]*

> I think pets are good entertainers. My little sister has tea parties with my dog; he has carrots and she has bread. I read with my dog and he shares his thinking with me. Most of his thoughts have to do with snuffle, snuffle, snuffle.

This share deals with an issue that we see in writing workshop all the time. We teach a strategy, students approximate it, and then they over-use it, to the exclusion of everything else. This is part of the learning process. Rejoice that your students are approximating because then you can teach them how to make choices as a writer, pulling from a variety of strategies.

I decided to refer back to the text I used in the minilesson because I wanted to be able to make a quick reference. You can choose any piece. Also notice that my second example is a child's. I like to put a professional writer's text alongside a child's text, as a way to elevate the work all children are doing.

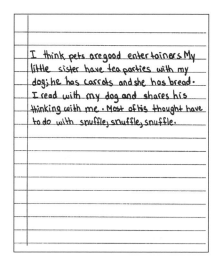

Fig. XI-3 Jamile's list does not have parallelism; he opted instead for details.

"The items in Jamile's list don't perfectly match each other. He decided that content mattered more than sound, and he was probably wise to make that choice. I call this an elaborated—not a tight—list."

Debrief by naming what you did that is transferable to another day on another topic.

"So when you work on your lists, try to remember that strong action words and specific, precise nouns matter (it is better to say 'from the snow-capped mountains of Colorado' than 'from the north'). And try to remember that even when you are squeezing a whole story into a sentence or two, you need to leave in the details like the dog eating carrots at the tea party and Mum wanting to sneak a baby lamb up the elevator to her hotel room!"

"Right now, would you and your partner look over your lists, and think and talk about whether your effort to give your list a musical sound, with one line matching the next, may have dominated too much. Ask whether you have written the truth and used exact details. If you've sacrificed truth or detail, try rewriting your lists."

HOMEWORK *Finding the Specifics That Bring Pieces to Life* Writers, you are learning that writers don't just write with words, they write with information. Don Murray, the Pulitzer Prize–winning writer, once said, "Beginning writers often misunderstand this. Young writers often become drunk on their way to becoming good writers. They dance to the sound of their own voices. They try to substitute style for subject matter, tricks for content, ruffles and flourishes for information. It doesn't work."

"The writer who has a warehouse of specific, detailed, relevant information has the advantage over any other writer," Murray continues. And writers, you are collecting files full of information. So tonight, would you collect specific information related to your topic? Live like magnets. Last night Philip did this, collecting information about how cats can be a lot of trouble, and he recorded this detail on his clipboard: "My cat trampled over me when she was catching a fly." What a detail—and he has it in his files because even when he was at home, he lived like a magnet, letting things related to his topic stick to him. Would you all do what Philip has done? Carry a clipboard with you, and let things that relate to your topic stick with you.

Specificity always helps.

When teaching children to write lists, after they do so in a way that repeats the stem over and over, you may want to show them that writers can collapse our lists. Instead of writing, "My grandfather is precious to me because he teaches me card tricks. My grandfather is precious to me because he let's me stay up late," you can tell a child to consolidate and write, "My grandfather is precious to me because he teaches me card tricks, let's me stay up late, and (whatever else the child wants to say).

If your students are skilled at creating parallelism . . . you might want to offer them yet another example of it that is more complex for them to emulate. Martin Luther King Jr. uses parallel sets of opposites to make his point in the following excerpt:

> Now is the time to rise from the dark and desolate valley [dark, lifeless place] of segregation to the sunlit porch [light, social place] of racial justice;

> Now is the time to lift our nation from the quicksands [unstable, dangerous place] of racial injustice to the solid rock [stable, safe place] of brotherhood.

In a mid-workshop teaching point, you might show students this example and say something like: "Look how King starts with a phrase—Now is the time—and then he makes a word pattern. The pattern is something like this: Now is the time to go up from the bad something to the good something. Can you fill in the pattern to make a new sentence that could have gone next? Tell your partner your sentence."

ASSESSMENT

When I was young, my older brother (whom I idolized) had a quote on his bulletin board that said, "I can live three months on a good compliment." I've sometimes thought that I've managed to live thirty years on good compliments! Sometimes I give workshops to teachers called *The Art of Complimenting Learners*. You'll recall that in every writing conference, after the teacher researches to understand what the writer is trying to do and has done, the teacher then compliments the child.

When I compliment a writer, I try to name what the writer has done that seems to be at the top of her game—what she's done that would serve her well if she does it (or tries to do it) forever. I'm particularly attentive to what the writer has been *trying* to do (even if she is only halfway there). Take this entry, for example, and think about how to compliment this writer.

> Worms are not just small creatures on the earth, or garden lepers. They can be your friend. Even though they can't interact with you or play with you, you can observe them for hours and write about them. They are very interesting pets to have and watch. Worms look small but they're pretty strong. When they dig into the dirt.

So when I look at Lydia's entry about worms, I'm not going to say, "I love that you spelled *worms* correctly." This seems like no big deal for her. And it is not particularly helpful for me to encourage her to spell *worms* correctly for the rest of her life. But it could be helpful, it could be a powerful compliment, to make a statement like one of these:

- I'm really impressed that you can take something seemingly ordinary like worms and make it significant by writing about it.
- I'm really impressed at how much you've found to say about a worm. Lots of people would just say a line or two and then would shrug and think, "So what else can you say about a worm!" But you've really pushed yourself to think, then to think again, then to think some more.

- I'm really impressed that you looked hard at worms and tried to find true things and true words to say about them. Most people don't look at worms and think "strong," but you really cleared a space to think your own thoughts about your topic, didn't you? That is am amazing thinking quality you have shown here—finding your own associations and words for things!

I know that I'm often complimenting something that a writer tried but didn't completely do. I might also compliment something that a writer did accidentally to help encourage the writer to do it intentionally the next time. I name the replicable process I suspect the writer went through en route to the results I see. For example,

- "I can tell you lived a writerly life, paying attention to details other writers would walk by—even to a worm! And it seems like you almost pretend to argue in defense of worms as you are writing. So you say, "People think that worms are just these slimy gross creatures but they're not!" Then you give one reason (you can observe them) and another (you can keep them as pets). Later you come back to these arguments and say even more ("You can observe them for hours and write about them. They are interesting to watch . . . "). You even provided evidence by referring to how your friends learned by observing them."

Finally, I'd make sure to help the writer take this compliment personally. The adage goes, "Don't criticize me, criticize my actions." But when complimenting, by all means, compliment me as a person! Then, too, I want to remind this writer and others who may hear the compliment that what she has done is transferable: "This is brilliant work! For the rest of your life, remember that you have a talent for finding meaning and majesty in small stuff that others would overlook, and specifically, that you are great at rallying to someone's (or something's) defense."

Learning to compliment children in powerful, lasting ways is a skill that is worth mastering. Your colleagues, friends, and family will certainly appreciate any practicing you might care to do!

GETTING READY

- Example of writing (your own or another writer's) that needs to be revised for honesty
- Passages from class essay that can be revised for honesty, written on chart paper
- See CD-ROM for resources

REVISING TOWARD HONESTY

You'll probably find that once your children grasp what is entailed in writing these very structured essays, it's as if the green light goes on and they are raring to go. And you may be tempted to bring this unit to an expeditious close. You may tell yourself that after all, in real life, children need to churn out thesis-driven essays within forty-five minutes.

I want to caution you against encouraging your students to whip up quick essays and call it a day. This unit is a journey, and at every bend in the road you have extraordinary lessons to teach. The most important learning and teaching will happen as you and your students grapple with the complexities and challenges of thinking and writing logically. And the complexities are legion!

In this session, you'll alter your focus to teach a quality of good thinking. Specifically, you will emphasize that good writing and good thinking are honest. You'll highlight precise, clear, accountable, honest thinking. This is a complicated idea because it is also true that writers take poetic license (and therefore are not always exactly honest)! Writers strive to tell an honest experience that does not always match the exact events. We may combine two events that actually took place at different times or places, we may allow a character to speak in direct quotes when we can't really recall the exact words used—but we do this in an attempt to convey a truth. And, it is crucial for writers to yearn to represent truth on the page. The writer's intent to convey a meaning that is exactly true gives the resulting text a ring of reality, an authenticity and power that listeners feel.

It's important for a writer not only to strive to tell the truth, but also to be able to discern when writing isn't true. Ernest Hemingway once said, "Every writer needs a 100 percent foolproof crap-detector." And William Zinsser suggested that often writers need to cross out their opening and closing paragraphs because that's where we tend to do the most lying. As writers, we need to develop a critical eye to turn on ourselves. We need to read over our words with skepticism and doubt. "Is this exactly what I want to say?"

MINILESSON

Revising Toward Honesty

CONNECTION

Remind writers that they've been working on improving the quality of their essay writing and then name the teaching point. In this case, tell children that writers also try to improve the quality of their thinking by aiming for honesty.

"Writers, yesterday we worked a bit on improving the quality of our writing, but today I want to remind you that when writing essays, it is even more important to improve the quality of our *thinking*. But it's not that easy to sit down, pen in hand, and *think* really well. What does it mean to *think well?*"

"To me, it means telling the truth, and that's the most important thing I do as a writer."

TEACHING

Tell a story of one time when you (or another writer) wrote first in easy glib words, then rewrote for honesty.

"Telling the truth is harder than you think. When I write, my words tend to fall into easy grooves. It's easy to write in words we've heard before, or to describe the way we assume things to be. When describing the snow, it is easy to write, 'I looked at the white snow.' It takes a mental effort to be sure I'm really saying the truth: 'I looked at the snow, speckled with ash.'"

"When I finished writing my first big book, *The Art of Teaching Writing*, I wrote my Acknowledgments. After I'd thanked all the people who helped with the book, I got to the final paragraph, to the place where writers traditionally thank their family members. I picked up my pen and wrote the words that came to mind."

> I want to thank my husband, John Skorpen, for not minding the long hours of desk work.

"Then I pulled back, read what I'd written about my husband not minding my work, and thought, 'This is a pile of baloney. John is *always* complaining that I work too much.'"

COACHING

In this session, I support honest and precise thinking. I'm convinced that when authors reach for the language to articulate something true, the intention to be honest brings power to a text.

This story is in The Art of Teaching Writing. *Many such books are filled with anecdotes and quotes that you can mine as you develop minilessons. The stories in your minilessons needn't all be ones that have happened to you. You can always say to children, "A writer I know told me that . . . " and retell stories you've heard or read.*

"So then I decided to try and write the truth (knowing I could always publish the sweet platitudes if I couldn't come up with anything better to say). I picked up my pen, held it near the page, and thought, 'So what *do* I want to thank John for?'"

"This time, I aimed to write the exact truth. Here's what I wrote."

> Although it is traditional to end one's Acknowledgments by thanking one's spouse for not minding the long hours of desk work, I want instead to thank my husband, John Skorpen, for calling me away from the desk. I want to thank John for the days of hiking in the Wind River Range and for the quiet adventures with our cat, dog, home, and family.

Debrief. Point out what you hope students learned from the story.

"The new version is a much better Acknowledgments because I have written with exactly true words. It takes mental energy to write the truth, and it takes courage, too. I always tell myself, 'I'll *try* to put the exact truth on the page—if I don't like what stares back at me, I can change it.'"

ACTIVE ENGAGEMENT
Set children up to practice rewriting with more honesty. Give them a few tiny excerpts that they could have written and invite them to revise them for honesty.

"Let's practice this. You all have been writing a lot about working with reading buddies. I've put a few passages that some of you have written on chart paper. Would you pretend that you, personally, wrote these? Reread them, giving them the truth test. Ask yourself, 'Does this say the exact and precise truth of what I want to say about working with reading buddies?' If it doesn't, spend a minute working in your notebook to rewrite one passage until it is truthful. Here are the passages."

> Another reason that working with reading buddies is fun is you get to read cool books. I really love books like The <u>Cat in the Hat</u> and <u>Mrs. Wishy Washy.</u>

> Another reason that working with reading buddies is fun is that they look up to us. They think we are smart and important. They make me feel special.

Notice that I rely again and again on the very same form that we teach our students. I could have made sweeping comments all-about my experience writing the Acknowledgments section of The Art of Teaching Writing. *I would then have summarized that process. Instead I retell the event in a step-by-step fashion, making characters speak, highlighting the problem and the solution. Try to do likewise with small writing moments you've experienced, and embed those narratives in your essays . . . and your teaching.*

This Teaching section does not contain a demonstration, as so many do, but instead relies upon a story. Still, I set up the story and afterwards, debrief it.

As I mentioned earlier, Hemingway once suggested that to write well, we need a 100 percent foolproof crap-detector. I've always loved the image of a writer rereading his or her text, moving his or her crap-detector over the words like a divining rod, waiting for it to start crackling. I'm apt to tuck quotes like this into my teaching when the spirit moves me. Draw on all you know when you teach.

Convene the class. Point out that the new more honest versions of their writing tend to be more specific and precise.

After children worked in their notebooks for a few minutes, I said, "Would you give me a thumbs up if you were able to rewrite one of these passages so that you were more honest? I'm wondering—how many of you found that you also became more specific? And how many of you ended up using more precise words, perhaps substituting a more exact term for *fun* or *cool*? I'm so interested to see that writing with honesty seems to have a lot to do with writing with specific and precise words. Would you turn and show your partner how you rewrote and rethought the writing so as to be more honest?"

LINK

Rename the teaching point. Remind children that they can draw on all they've learned as they continue to collect entries in their folders.

"So writers, I know that today you'll draw on all that you know as you collect entries for your files. You'll collect stories (using what you know about effective stories), and you'll collect lists. As you write—today and always—try to hold yourself to the goal of telling the truth."

Notice that at this juncture in a minilesson the teacher usually debriefs, but here, children assume that responsibility. In this instance, I think that giving children the opportunity to reflect on what they've just done will cement their learning. You may decide to adopt this as a regular ritual in your minilessons. Just guard against minilessons becoming maxi-lessons.

Notice the cumulative quality of this section of a minilesson. I'm hoping to keep alive the fact that during any one day's workshop, writers will be drawing on all they've learned thus far.

WRITING AND CONFERRING

Reading Writing Closely

Over and over when teaching this unit, I have found that skills and strategies that sound simple when I talk about them in minilessons prove to be vastly more complicated than I'd ever dreamed possible when a child actually tries to do the work. Every minute of the writing workshop, then, is an intensely packed learning adventure. How important it is for you to draw your chair alongside children, welcoming the chance to see and to understand the difficulties the child is experiencing! Develop an attitude of welcoming signs of trouble. These indications of trouble are requests for help. They'll make you feel needed!

To spot signs of trouble, you need to scrutinize your students' work. Don't just scan a child's words. Take them in. Think, "What is this child trying to say and do?" Ask, "Is this writing basically working? What has the child done that I can name in a fashion that will transfer to other pieces? What isn't working? How can I equip the writer to handle this area of difficulty in this piece and in future pieces?" Consider Estefan's entry with these questions in mind.

> My dad is important to me because I have fun when he teaches me baseball. One time my dad woke me up to tell me if I want to go play baseball. I said, "Ok I'll get ready." When I washed up and got ready we went to the baseball field. There we got out the baseball bats and balls. At the baseball field, my dad was throwing fast balls so I telled him to slow down. My dad said, "Alright but you got to get used to fast balls." I said, "Ok, I will."

MID-WORKSHOP TEACHING POINT

Celebrating Writers Who Are Telling the Truth   "Writers, can I stop you? Many of you are finding out that your writing becomes more powerful when you bear down and tell the truth. The great nonfiction writer, Milton Meltzer, says it this way: "The best writers of nonfiction put their hearts and minds into their work. In the writer who cares, there is a pressure of feeling which emerges in the rhythm of sentences, the choice of details, in the color of language." (1976, p. 21)

"Listen to these places where you all are bearing down, trying to write the precise truth. This is what some of you have said."

- I find that when I am sad, my dog is too. He makes me think feelings are contagious. (Jamile)

- If you made your team lose, you feel responsible for your actions but you feel like you have no power so you blame everything on yourself. (Felix)

continued on next page

There are many things Estefan has done well:

- Estefan has adroitly shifted from stating a big idea (My dad is important to me) to telling a specific story, and he's done so using the transitional phrase "one time."

- Estefan has transferred what he knows about writing stories to this new work with essays. His story is told in a step-by-step, chronological way and as a reader, I can re-experience it. He includes dialogue and details.

- Estefan's story is generally about the idea he wants to convey. The part of the story that he has elaborated upon (his father's efforts to instruct Estefan) is the part that matches his idea.

In a conference with Estefan I'd probably choose just one or two of these points to compliment. In this case, because of what I know I will soon teach, I created a compliment by combining the second two points. "Estefan," I said, "I absolutely love the fact that you brought all you know about stories to bear on the miniature story you tell inside this essay! And, more than that, you knew to elaborate with precise details."

There are a number of qualities and strategies I could teach Estefan. Most important, I'd want him to realize that although it's great that he used all he knows about stories to write this one, we place special demands on the stories that we embed into essays. These stories need to efficiently and directly address the main idea of the essay. I'd teach Estefan that I reread the stories I write within nonfiction texts, pausing after almost every line of the story to ask, "Does this go with my main idea?"

When Estefan read his first sentence, asking, "Does this go with my main idea?" the answer was yes. It is really smart of Estefan to not just say that his dad woke him but to say that his dad asked about baseball. I didn't point out to Estefan that he could have done even more to highlight the role baseball played in waking up. For example, he could have written, "I lay in bed and thought about how much fun it is to play baseball with my father. Even though it was early, I raced out of bed. I didn't want to miss this chance." I didn't bring out this point because I felt it wasn't something that Estefan could learn to do on his own just yet—and because I had less subtle instruction in mind. Estefan and I noted that yes, his first sentence pertained to his main idea. But as Estefan read on, pausing after each sentence to ask, "Does this further my

continued from previous page

- Imagine having a war going on inside your head. Well, that's what it's like when parents fight. (Andy)

- Teddy bears are good friends. You can tell them secrets and they stay quiet. I told my bear that I was wearing my sister's clothes. I told my bear that I was wearing my sister's makeup. I told my bear that I like 2 boys at the same time. (Camille)

"Right now, would you reread your writing and find a place where you told the truth. Search, especially, for a place where your writing is so truthful that it makes you realize something you didn't even know you knew. If you don't find a place where you wrote the truth in such a way that your writing comes to life, find a place where you used hackneyed, trite words and rewrite that section, this time telling the truth."

main idea?" he realized that none of the next details—that he got ready, woke up, and traveled to the field—advanced his main idea. I taught him that he had choices. He could include the fact that he washed up *if* (and only if) he could find a way to integrate his father teaching him baseball into washing up. (This might seem like a ridiculous suggestion, but of course, all Estefan would need to do is to scrub his face, thinking as he did so about the upcoming game.) Alternatively, Estefan could fast-forward his story, skipping past events that didn't relate to his main idea, which is what he in fact decided to do.

My larger point is that we need to read our children's entries with care, expecting that they'll struggle with aspects of this work. Be prepared to compliment them on what works, to teach skills they need to know—and to learn volumes in the process.

SHARE

Revising Claims to Fit Stories

Tell students that writers have to guard against using stories that don't support their claims.

"Writers, I've watched you holding yourselves accountable to writing the precise truth; by trying to be precisely honest, some of you have actually had brand-new ideas come out of the tips of your pens! This is incredibly important."

"Now I want to show you another powerful way to discipline your mind as you write. Just as it is easy to be a careless thinker and to write 'snow is white' rather than telling the precise truth, it is also easy to be a careless thinker and say that story supports your claim, even though it doesn't. That means that we have to check to make sure every story in each folder supports the claim on that folder."

Tell the story of a child who checked to see if her story supported her claim and found that it didn't.

"For example, Camille has a folder with the claim on it, 'Teddy Bears are like friends that stay quiet but deep down you hear them talking to you.' Camille started to add this entry to the file, but first she asked herself, 'Does this support my claim?' See what you think." [Fig. XII-1]

> Teddy Bears are like friends that stay quiet but deep down you hear them talking to you.
>
> Teddy bears are good friends because when you are sad teddy bears cheer up. They cheer you up because one time I came from school and a boy said a nasty thing to me so I went home and I talked to my teddy bear. She made me feel good.

"Camille realized that her information didn't show anything about teddy bears 'talking' deep down. Instead, her information was all about how she—Camille—talks freely to her bear, sharing secrets."

"Things became even more complicated because Camille had another file titled 'Teddy bears are good friends because you can share your secrets with them,' and that file was bulging!"

Ideally when children write essays, they develop their ideas through the process of writing. The work described in this Share suggests one way in which children use writing an essay as an appointment to think in disciplined, logical ways, and to grow new ideas through the process.

> ### Teddy Bears
>
> Teddy Bears are good friends. I feel this way because when you're sad teddy bears cheer you up. I also feel this way because they are like friends that stay quiet but deep down you hear them talking to you. My third feeling is that you tell your teddy bears all your secrets and you know they won't tell know one.
> Teddy bears are good friends because when you are sad teddy bears cheer up. They cheer you up because one time I came from school and a boy said a nasty thing to me so I went home and I talk to my teddy bear, she made me feel good. Teddy bears are also good friends because when my friend fell down she was crying and everyone was laghing at her so she talk to her teddy bear and he cheared her up. Teddy bears are good friends because when I fell down my cut really hurt badly so I went to my teddy bear and she cheered me up.

Fig. XII-1 Camille realized her examples didn't support her claim.

Point out through the example that writers can revise their claims to match their stories, just as they can revise their stories to match their claims.

"So Camille did something really important. She emptied all her files and then read through all her information. As she did, she asked, 'What are the big ideas here?' And, listen to this, she found the big ideas and then she renamed her files! All of us need to have Camille's courage. Reread the stuff you've collected, and have the strength to see when some of it doesn't go in the file in which you placed it. Let this lead you to revisions! You already know that writers revise stories to support claims, and now you know that writers also revise their claims to fit their stories!"

Expect that this lesson will pertain to half your writers. It's an incredibly important lesson, too, because it teaches people to read with great attentiveness. This is clearly a point that merits emphasis. You may want to give it more attention by writing a minilesson that celebrates the work specific children have done.

⊙ HOMEWORK *Balancing Writing Volume* Writers, before long we'll turn a corner in this unit of study. Instead of continuing to collect materials in folders, we'll begin to combine these into paragraphs. Before you can do that, you need to be certain that you have three or four solid and pertinent entries in each of your folders. Think about your folders and recall which ones need the most attention.

Tonight, your homework assignment is to collect two or three entries, amounting to at least a page of writing but written on separate sheets, that you can add to whichever folder is most empty.

If you feel that this will be hard, then chances are you need to rethink the claim on that folder. Consider developing a different bullet and renaming the folder; then gather information for that folder about your new topic sentence, your new claim.

⊙ TAILORING YOUR TEACHING

If your students have experienced writing essays in previous years and they tend to write with honesty already . . . you may want to focus on any one of a host of qualities of good writing. For example, William Zinsser, author of *On Writing Well*, suggests that surprise is important in writing, and I have to agree. Jean Fritz, the author of many history books, seems to agree as well. She writes about the importance of surprising details: "As human beings, we thrive on astonishment. Whatever is unknown quickens us, delivers us from ourselves, impels us to investigate." Fritz includes surprising details in her books. For example, she writes that Paul Revere forgot to bring cloth to muffle his oars for his secret row across the Charles River. This little mostly-unknown detail helps the reader feel the urgency and danger of his trip. Instead of just writing that Revere was a silversmith, she lets her readers know that he did unusual jobs, such as whittling false teeth out of hippopotamus tusks. This bit of information is colorful and engaging for readers.

Fritz says, "I dote on small details . . . In researching Ben Franklin, I read in one book after another that Franklin learned ten swimming tricks. What were they?" Her inquisitive nature couldn't let that fact go unexplored. After a long search, Fritz found that one of the ten tricks involved cutting one's toenails under water! (Sutherland, p.179) Imagine that. What a detail to include in a piece about Ben Franklin!

You could use these examples to suggest to your students that they might consider putting information in their essays to surprise and engage their readers. You might say, "Writers, one of the qualities of powerful writing is that it surprises readers. It makes readers think of things they never thought about before. Essayists hope readers finish their essays and say things like, 'I never thought about it like that!' or 'I never knew that!' or 'Wow. That was full of surprising information.' But you know what? These surprises don't happen by accident. Essayists think about ways they can astound or surprise their readers. As you go through your folders full of supporting stories and supporting evidence for your topic sentences, look for places where you surprise. As you look through your folders, try to answer these questions: 'Of all these pieces, which one will draw my reader in? Which one is most astonishing?'"

You could demonstrate how to do this by going through one of your folders to find a piece of evidence that could surprise readers. You'll also want to model how to ask questions of yourself, like "Which of these is most astonishing?" as you look through your pieces. Finally, you'll want to explain the rationale for why you chose a particular piece as the one that offers a surprise to your readers.

For the Active Engagement, you have a few options, of course. You might decide to use the whole class sample essay, which in our case is the one about first-grade reading buddies. You can review the supporting evidence with your students to have them consider which pieces are most surprising. Another way to do this is to have students bring one of their folders to the meeting area and have them read through the pieces inside. Give them a sticky note to attach to the piece that contains the most surprising information.

ASSESSMENT

The minilessons in this unit of study may seem fairly clear cut, but I promise you that children will encounter an unusual number of difficulties. The difficulties arise especially because this unit invites children into logical, analytical thought, and this will push them in ways that are new for them—and perhaps new for you as well. You will definitely want to spend time outside of class looking through the files your children collect, trying to assess their understandings of this teaching.

I sometimes find that when I read children's non-narrative writing, sections of it seem to reflect breakdowns in logic. My first reaction is to push their confused, chaotic writing out of sight, saying, "This makes no sense." But, as I've written throughout this series, we need instead to scrutinize the chaotic writing, asking, "What is the source of trouble here? What can I teach that might help?" Resist the urge to ignore the entry, and instead be fascinated by it. Look at it all the more closely to determine what sort of trouble it reveals. You may find several types of problems.

The child may be repeating herself, almost as if she is saying something over and over until she finds a way to say it that works. If this is the case, she is doing good work and just needs to delete many of the problematic versions of the thought, leaving only the best draft. It will help children to know that this is exactly what people do when we talk over a complex idea—and what many writers do. Pros, however, know to cut their rejected writing after they've finally gotten their idea out. Peter Elbow has said, "Sometimes the

water needs to run for a while before it runs clear," and the same can be true for thinking and writing.

Another child may have written his idea in a reasonably clear sentence or paragraph, but he seems to think it's too short and so therefore he keeps writing more at the end of his thought, with the new material fulfilling no real function at all. In other words, the text may reveal a clear thought, followed by disjointed rambling. This child may need to learn strategies for planning and then for writing the idea in more detail in the first place. This child, at the very least, needs to see the pattern in his writing and to learn to cut the parts that don't add to his original text.

Yet another child may be trying to convey relationships between ideas, and expressing her thinking requires her to combine sentences or clauses. This level of thinking can push the child toward sentence complexity that she can't yet master. Celebrate her risk taking and the approximations in thought and sentence complexity you see in her writing just as you would celebrate a youngster's brave, inventive spellings. Teach her how to take the next step from where she is now toward where she wants to be to express herself.

Your colleagues can help you read through some of your students' work. Talk about everything you notice! Do you notice common characteristics? Are these characteristics typical of students in your grade level? Talk with your colleagues about the steps to take with each child, and steps to take with your classes in general, based on the writing you've analyzed.

IN THIS SESSION, YOU WILL TEACH CHILDREN THAT WRITERS GATHER A VARIETY OF INFORMATION TO SUPPORT THEIR CLAIMS. YOU'LL DEMONSTRATE STRATEGIES WRITERS USE FOR COLLECTING AND WRITING WITH THAT INFORMATION.

GETTING READY

- Your own essay demonstrating how observation and statistics can support a topic sentence
- Class thesis and topic sentences
- Samples of student writing where a variety of types of evidence are used to support topic sentences
- See CD-ROM for resources

GATHERING A VARIETY OF INFORMATION

When teaching narrative or poetry, *many of us feel confident teaching lessons on the qualities of good writing. We demonstrate and point to exemplar texts so that our children learn to show, not tell and to make characters talk. It is just as important to continue teaching the qualities and strategies of good writing once we're in a unit on essay writing! As Don Murray has said, "Writing may appear magic but it is our responsibility to take our students backstage to watch the pigeons being tucked up the magician's sleeve. The process of writing can be studied and understood. We can recreate most of what a student or professional writer does to produce effective writing."*

Writers don't write with words. Writers write with information. Interestingly, children are much more accustomed to relying on concrete information when they write in narratives than when they write essays. When retelling an event, children keep their eyes on the subject and their writing involves chronicling what happened. When children write about ideas, however, there's no chronology to guide the unfolding of the writing; there's no one image in the mind's eye to trace on paper. The child begins with a topic sentence: My dog is like a brother to me. The child is then apt to just pick up a pen and start holding forth on this topic, writing in circuitous, general, repetitive sentences.

This session seeks to remedy this tendency by highlighting that writers always write with specific, concrete information. Writers need to be researchers, collecting the hard data needed to build paragraphs and advance ideas: details, quotations, statistics, and observations.

This session is especially important because it acknowledges that even when children are writing structured, thesis-driven essays, it is crucial for them to live writerly lives—collecting, combining, sifting, and selecting bits of their life to become their work.

MINILESSON

Gathering a Variety of Information

CONNECTION

Tell children that artists combine a variety of materials in their writing.

"One way to make works of art powerful is to use a variety of materials so that one offsets another—in some art the variety comes from using different colors, in some it comes from textures, in some, from flavors. In essay writing, variety can come from different kinds of information. If our essays are going to be works of art, we need to make sure they have a depth, a richness that comes from variety."

Name your teaching point. In this case, teach children that essayists, like other artists, collect varied materials to assemble in their work.

"Essayists deliberately collect different kinds of information. That variety helps build your case by suggesting to the reader that evidence to support your thesis can be found in a variety of places in the world, not just in one kind of place. You will want to make sure that your files contain not only stories and lists but also observations, statistics, quotations, citations, and questions. The secret to collecting all these things is that you need to learn to see all the world as related to your topic. When you do this, you find material everywhere."

TEACHING

Illustrate all the varieties of information writers can collect around their theses by showing how you observed, interviewed, and gathered statistics on your topic.

"For example, I've been trying to collect material to go in my folders. My folder labeled 'My father taught me to love writing' is almost empty, so I really want to collect stories, quotes, and questions related to it."

"So I went to my parent's house and I said to myself, 'I'm going to try to use observation as a way to gather a new sort of information. I'll observe and record anything I see related to the idea that my dad teaches me to love writing.' Here's what I collected. Pay attention to the different kinds of information I gathered."

COACHING

It is not necessary to introduce a new metaphor in this Connection, but it is important for the children to have a visual image of this process. I try to make sure that my words make a visual image in the mind's eye.

When evaluating an essay, I sometimes ask, "Does this writer use a variety of source material?" In fact, my son is studying for the writing he'll need to produce on the SAT exam, and the test-prep books advise him to develop his idea by drawing on a variety of sources: one bit can come from personal experience, another from literature, still another from politics. This minilesson conveys to children that their essays will be stronger if they draw on a variety of sources. But it does so by turning this quality of good writing into a strategy that yields the quality.

It is tempting to bypass the process and share the products, to cut to the chase and say, "So I collected this, and this, and this," reading aloud the products. Remember that we are trying to show children how to go about doing these kinds of writing, so sharing our products alone won't suffice.

"First, Dad was at his desk. I just took a mental photograph of that scene so I could write about it later. When I wrote, I described the things I saw related to his loving to write."

> These days whenever I arrive at my father's home, I usually find him at his desk. He may be writing his memoir, an article, a speech, or architectural sketches and plans for a new sheep house or chicken coop— whatever he's writing, he's always surrounded by piles of papers and books. I get the feeling he's turned his desk into a tree fort, built with walls of books and manuscripts. He's having the time of his life writing.

"I also wanted to collect information by interviewing him, not just by observation, so I talked with him about how he thinks he has taught me to value writing, and I scrawled down his words. He said really powerful things, like, 'When I'm gone, my memoir and my articles will still be there. I'm going into the hospital for a minor operation next week, and you never know. So I'm trying to finish this writing project before I go in.' I copied down his exact words."

"I observed and interviewed, but I also wanted to see if I could collect any statistics. Dad's been duplicating his drafts, and he showed me the bill. He's done $172 of duplicating in the last two months—that statistic conveyed something, so I recorded it too."

Debrief, accentuating all the sources of information you drew upon as you gathered information on your essay topic.

"Did you notice, writers, that just during one little visit home I observed and recorded what I saw (I touched one finger to accentuate that I was making a list of resources), I interviewed to gather quotes (I touched a second finger), and third, I found a statistic that can help me make my case!"

I could have paused at this point to ask children to list across their fingers the different kinds of material I collected: images, quotes, and statistics.

Notice, once again, the use of the graphic organizer: my fingers.

Active Engagement

Ask children to collect observations, questions, and statistics to support the whole-class essay.

"Now, essay writers, let's try collecting a variety of kinds of information about an essay topic. Let's practice this with our topic, 'Working with our first-grade reading buddies is fun.'" I gestured to the list on chart paper.

> Working with our first-grade reading buddies is fun.

- One reason that working with reading buddies is fun is that you get to teach them to read.

- Another reason that working with reading buddies is fun is that you get to read really cool books.

- And finally, working with reading buddies is fun because they look up to us.

"We met with our reading buddies just yesterday, so the material we need to gather is fresh in our minds! If we were writing an essay on this, while sitting at our desks today we could mentally go back to reading buddies time, and recreate it in our mind's eye. Then we could zoom in on a moment that captures the fun of reading buddies, and describe that moment. I'm thinking, for example, of the moment when we arrived in the first grade and the kids all started saying, 'Hurrah' and greeting us. Partner 1, can you write an entry in the air in which you do an observation of that moment? Remember, it is best to observe people in the midst of actions. And remember that you won't just retell the moment, you'll angle your retelling to show that working with reading buddies is fun." They did this.

Remind the class that they could also collect other kinds of information: questions, quotations, and statistics.

"Class, you might decide that you want to collect not only *observations* but also *questions*. Partner 2, would you tell partner 1 some questions you might write? Remember, these need to relate to our topic, that reading buddies are fun."

"It is not easy to think about what statistics we could collect that relate to this thesis. But would you and your partner *see* if you could help us think of statistics we could collect to support our thesis? Partner 1, tell partner 2 some statistics you could gather."

"Now, partners, tell each other how you could gather some quotations to support our claim."

It probably would have been just as helpful for me to ask children to call one of their topic sentences to mind, and then to ask themselves, "What could I possibly observe so as to gather information to support this idea?" After they signaled with a thumbs up when they had an answer, I could move on and ask, "Who could you possibly interview so that you could collect a quote to support this idea?" Again, I'd wait for a thumbs up.

During this Active Engagement, I try to remove distracting difficulties so that the one challenge children deal with is the one that relates to today's lesson. In this instance, I first suggest children relive a particular moment, observing it in their mind's eye. I choose the moment and begin conjuring up the mental image. Having gotten them off to a running start, I can say, "Tell your partner what you'd record if you were going to include an observation in your data." I know they can do this in short order. If your children look at you blankly when you ask them to do something during the Active Engagement section of a minilesson, then you know you haven't provided a clear and supportive scaffold.

LINK

Rename the teaching point. Remind children they can use this strategy anytime, not just today.

"Writers, I hope that from this day on, you remember that writers, like many kinds of artists, gather information wherever they go. Carry your writer's notebooks with you at all times, and if you have a thought, an observation, a question, or some statistics that relate to your essay topic, jot them down. Right now, from your seat on the rug, look around the classroom and see if you can find something that relates to your topic—any little thing at all. If you don't notice something in the classroom that sparks a thought related to your topic, remember, you can look all the time, not just in school. You might see something on television at home that supports your claim, or you might hear something in the library— essayists are always on the lookout for information for their work!"

Watch, in this Link, how I circle back to the Connection, picking up terms and images from that section of the minilesson. Also notice that in a minilesson, I'm often teaching a concept and specifics. I think of this as a hand and fingers. I know specifics will be more memorable if they are integrated into a larger concept, so I usually situate details into the larger concept. In this instance, the larger concept is that writers, like artists, collect stuff. Specifically, writers collect observations, statistics, questions, and so on.

WRITING AND CONFERRING

Gathering Enough Material for Effective Essays

Within a day or two, you'll show children how to take the contents of their folders and begin the selecting, ordering, combining, and rewriting work of making an actual essay. Before you can round that bend in the unit, however, you want to be sure that all of your children have gathered enough material to be able to produce effective essays.

You may need to convene the children who simply do not have enough done, and help them make plans for how they will use today to be extra productive. Don't hesitate to make decisions for them based on what you see (or don't see) in their folders; send them off with a clear sense of direction and a lot of urgency! If children really buckle down, they can produce a lot of writing in a single day, but they often need us to add some pressure, raising their productivity a few notches. Sometimes it helps if these children all work alongside each other at a table reserved for the "we're racing to get a lot done" kids. Or, it might help to give each of these kids a "private office"—a desk, set far away from the maddening crowd. You decide.

Some children will not have an idea how they can gather information right now, in class, about their topics. Help them realize they can interview *each other*. For example, the child who is writing, "I don't want to let my grandma down," will probably think that no one in the class knows his grandma, so how could he interview a classmate? Show him that he could interview kids to learn the things *they* do to help *their* grandmothers. The writer could then cite what a friend does, using this to set off his own information. In his essay, he could perhaps end up writing something like, "Other children in Mrs. Gammet's fourth-grade class don't *expect* to help their grandmothers. For example, Jeremy says, 'My grandma does things for me, not the other way around. She fixes my clothes and helps with my schoolwork.' But it is different for me. When I visit my grandma, I try to help her. I . . . " The child could also ask someone else to interview him about his own grandma, to help him realize what he knows and what he has to say.

> **MID-WORKSHOP TEACHING POINT**   *Using Evidence from Books*   "Writers, at the beginning of the workshop today Zora and I talked about the 'scraps' she has gathered for her essay. Zora showed me a piece that she had written long ago in her notebook that she thought could be filed into one of her folders. 'Lucy' she said, 'Do you think this bit about Rob from *Tiger Rising* could support my thesis?' The example fit exactly! So Zora and I decided we should tell all of you that you can definitely use books you have read to support our ideas. Listen to how Zora did this," I said, and Zora read her entry aloud.
>
> > Sometimes bullies close themselves up and never express their feelings. They think of it as a way to protect themselves. I remember a friend who was poor and embarrassed to be poor so he put this feeling in his suitcase and shut it just like Rob did in the book, The Tiger Rising by Kate DiCamillo. Rob was a boy who kept his feelings inside like my friend did. I could see my friend and Rob both hurting, telling people to stay out of it.
>
> "If any of you are like Zora and can imagine how a book you know well could support your main idea, try writing an entry about this. Add it to your folders."

You may want to do some small-group or one-to-one conferring today to set children up for the thinking they'll soon be asked to do. In the next session, you will teach children to look through their folders, checking whether the material in them actually belongs in that folder. You may want to pre-teach this by helping children think through the concept of main idea and supporting details, (that is, of boxes and bullets.) You could give a small group of children photocopies of very clearly structured expository texts. "For each paragraph, would you underline the main idea," you could say. Tell children that if the author hasn't come right out and *said* the main idea, they can still infer the main idea, writing it in the margins. Children could then write little numbers (1, 2, 3) beside each new bit of supporting information as they study the way other writers set bits against each other in finished essays.

You could also show children that writers need to be able to look at a pile of information and sort it according to category. To do this work, writers need to keep in mind that some statements are subordinate and others are overarching. You could say to a small group of children, "Let's pretend you had these bits in your file. Would you sort these into two piles? Do all these items go into the same one file? Might one of these items be the topic sentence on the folder itself? Does everything go into one pile or another pile?" The items could be as brief and as obvious as these:

- People should take care of their silverware.

- Sharp knives help you slice through meat.

- Small spoons allow you to eat grapefruit.

- Silverware has different uses.

- Forks help you "fork in" the food.

- It helps to keep forks and knives separate.

- It's easy to let a spoon slip down the drain of the sink.

- We have a new kitchen.

Afterwards you'd want to explain why you asked children to sort through these bits of information. "The work you just did with these sentences is exactly the work that writers do as we reread and reconsider our collections. Sometimes, you'll find that the stuff you've collected doesn't go in any folder, in which case you need to set it aside. Other times you'll decide the stuff you've collected doesn't go under a big idea—but that you like the stuff you've collected more than you like the overarching idea, and so you alter the idea! All of this work teaches us not only to write well but also to think well."

SHARE

Gathering a Variety of Information

Create a chart of writing examples from students who have used different types of information. Ask students to talk over the kinds of information they've included and still could still include in their essays.

"Writers, I love the fact that you've been collecting a wonderful variety of information. Kayla's claim is that kids can help homeless people, and she's found two ways to include data. She's included figures on the number of homeless people in New York City and she's also written that last year, her school collected pennies—worth $4,400! Her statistics say a lot."

"Becca also used statistics to build her case. Here's what she wrote."

> If you've one of the people who won't back away you are not alone. 15 out of 26 people in Ms. Chiarella's 4th grade class said they have done something they don't want to do just to fit in.

> Nearly 60% of 4th grade kids in this class said they have done something they don't want to do just to fit in. Imagine all those people have done things they don't want to do and they weren't even forced to do it.

"Sasha has been conducting a survey to illustrate her claim that people shouldn't brag. She asked everyone in the class whether they thought it was okay to brag. She figured everyone would concur with her, but of those she surveyed, almost half surprised her by responding that sometimes it was okay to brag. Now she's trying to figure out how to keep that statistic from derailing her argument."

"Mike is writing about why he doesn't like having a brother. Mike wanted some statistics for his essay so he set up an experiment. He sat in his room for two and a half hours and counted how many times his brothers bothered him. He found out that his brother came into his room eight times!"

"Would each of you tell your partner about the variety of data you've collected to substantiate your claims? Use our chart of possible data and for each item on it, think, 'Have I collected *this* kind of data?' If the answer is no, talk together about how you *could* find that sort of data pertaining to your idea."

The truth is that your kids will only be able to collect a variety of evidence, as in these examples, if you give them more than a day to do this work. You'll still want to teach a minilesson in which you highlight that essayists value drawing from a variety of sources, but you need to decide whether to make this a priority and if so, you'll probably need to give children a bit more time for the research involved.

It is not necessary for an essayist to include all of this support material. However, it is helpful for children to realize that when writers want to support a topic sentence, we don't write with words alone. We write with stories, lists, statistics, and observation.

HOMEWORK *Getting Ready to Draft* Writers, we have been talking over the last few days about collecting materials for our essay. I have shown you the different kinds of data that writers can collect. Starting tomorrow, you are going to need all your materials in one place because tomorrow you'll learn how writers begin to assemble their material into essays. This means that some of you need to put on your hard hats and work overtime tonight. If you're not ready to write an essay tomorrow, then you'll need to collect more support material tonight.

Meanwhile, keep in mind that the best place to gather a variety of support information on your topic is your home. Consider interviewing a family member, or doing a small observation, or finding words from a song or a book that will help you build your case. By all means use your family members to help you—writing is usually a family affair!

Once you've collected lots of good material in each folder take some time tonight to reread mentor essays that you were given earlier in this unit, putting sticky note tags when you notice something the writer has done that you admire.

TAILORING YOUR TEACHING

If your children have worked through this unit in a previous year and you'd like to vary this minilesson . . . remember that you can add your own stories and metaphors to any session. You might vary this minilesson a bit by changing the metaphor. You could say, "Gathering information for your essay topic is much like gathering information in science class. Think about how we have used our magnifying glasses to look very closely at beetles in our tanks, counting their legs and noting the color and pattern of their shells. Many of us have also collected observations about the color and texture of the leaves in our plants, the patterns in their veins, the plants' growth, and their smells. As scientists, we've gathered and recorded the tiny details of whatever it is we're studying. We have asked questions, taken measurements, run experiments, and recorded observations. You can do all of these things as writers, too, researching the topics that will be the subjects of your essays."

If your children don't see possible ways to collect information related to their topic sentences . . . show children that researchers find valuable data everywhere. If your thesis was,"Children love to read," you could find evidence by opening up a child's desk, by noticing the circulation of a book or a library card, by interviewing a child . . . Help children be inventive and resourceful as data-gatherers.

MECHANICS

Every new unit of study provides special opportunities for work with punctuation. When children wrote narratives, for example, they needed to learn the punctuation required to show when characters were speaking, and to shift between speaking, thinking, and acting. Now that children are writing essays, they'll need to learn to add support information into a sentence. If Zora wants readers to know that Matthew was regarded as the toughest bully in her former school, she needs to be able to tuck this information into a sentence. She doesn't need to name participial phrases or predicate nominatives, but she will benefit from knowing that she can put more information into a sentence by using parentheses or commas:

> Matthew (the toughest bully in the school) had a soft heart.
> Matthew, the toughest bully in the school, had a soft heart.

Dashes can be used to accomplish a similar task. In this sentence from the foreword of Milton Meltzer's *The American Revolutionaries*, notice the way a dash allows him to insert facts into his sentence:

It took a long time to people the land. In 1650 there were only 50,000 settlers—about as many as live in Pittsfield, Massachusetts, today—huddled mostly in Massachusetts and Virginia. A hundred years later the number had grown to . . . (1993, p.2)

Becca could use a dash similarly in order to insert facts into her sentence:

> People who compromise to make yourself popular aren't alone—15 out of the 26 kids in Ms. Chiarella's class have done this—but this doesn't mean it's a wise thing to do.

Similarly, essayists often write with lists, and nothing helps a list more than a colon. Children can learn that essayists use a colon in order to make the transition from a generalization to a list of specifics. An essayist who also loves dogs might write, 'I love all kinds of dogs: flat-coated retrievers, English cockers, standard poodles.'

In all of these instances, essayists use punctuation to fill their writing with more precise, specific information.

IN THIS SESSION, YOU WILL
TEACH CHILDREN THAT WRITERS
TAKE THEIR COLLECTED FILES OF
WRITING AND TRANSFORM THEM
INTO DRAFTS BY ORGANIZING AND
PIECING THEM TOGETHER.

GETTING READY

- Your own essay with supporting evidence collected in colored and manila folders
- Copies of a story from one of your folders that doesn't support your claim, written on chart paper
- Several student essays with supporting evidence collected in colored and manila folders
- Questions to Ask of Writing Before We Draft chart
- See CD-ROM for resources

ORGANIZING FOR DRAFTING

When this country was young, barn raisings were a common occurrence. When I close my eyes I can imagine the people gathering. They bring all types of supplies: hammers and saws, lumber and nails, watermelon and pies. I can see the whole neighborhood gathered, hauling ropes, lifting first one of the barn walls into place, then another. Those barn raisings were spectacular events. People had worked for weeks preparing the walls, aligning the structures of each, gathering all the materials in place; as a result, within a single day, the smaller pieces could come together quickly, into a whole. Presto—suddenly, where once a flat field lay, now a barn stands tall, its completed form outlined against the sky.

The time has come in this unit for an "essay raising." After weeks of collecting, researching, writing, and planning the structure of the piece, after the long sessions of making sure the supports are in place, it's time to pull together the full form of the essay! Today, you will ask children to take all of their folders and all the information they've collected within each folder and make sure it does the job it was intended to do. Does each folder have the material needed to support the thesis and the topic sentence? Are all the pieces ready for the final essay? You'll offer children a small set of questions to ask of the writing in each folder, questions that can guide their thinking today and whenever they are in this phase of essay writing.

Then, in the mid-workshop teaching point and again in the next session, you'll ask children to nail together the pieces of writing into paragraphs. You'll offer them suggestions for making sensible arrangements and for organizing each little bit of information so that all the pieces fit together neatly to support the essay's claim.

MINILESSON

Organizing for Drafting

CONNECTION

Use a metaphor to infuse your students with a sense of celebration and anticipation—in short order, they'll each have written an essay.

"Once, long ago, some friends and I built a very small house—a cabin, really—on an island. I remember that it took us forever to gather the materials, to creosote the beams, to pour the cement and build the foundation, to frame out the walls, and to hammer planks onto those frames. Then one day, we tied ropes to the two upper corners of a wall that we'd built flat on the ground, and dragged on the rope until that wall stood upright. Within another hour, we'd done the same with a second wall. Almost magically, the components that'd we'd labored over in isolation rose into place and suddenly, presto! We could see that we had built ourselves a house!"

Name your teaching point. In this case, teach your children that writers have a process they use to go from folders full of entries to a draft in a day.

"I'm telling you this because today I want to teach you that after writers plan and collect for our essays (as you have done), the day comes to put everything together. Once a writer has planned and collected, then presto! The pieces of the essay can rise into place. It won't be finished—writers revise essays just like we revise any other kind of writing. But in the space of a single day, you can go from a bunch of entries in some folders to a rough draft of an essay. Today I will teach you how to do that."

TEACHING

Extend the metaphor to help explain to children how drafting happens.

"If we want to build a building, or an essay, and the day to raise it is upon us, we need to make sure we actually have the materials we need to proceed. Now is the last chance to

COACHING

It's important to recognize that any phase of this entire process can be as complex or as simple as you decide it should be. You'll see that I approach the prospect of drafting the essay in a breezy, no-nonsense fashion, conveying the impression that a writer will find it no big deal to combine his or her entries into paragraphs, paragraphs into an essay. As a writer, I also know this work can be infinitely complex. But for a child's first journey through this process, I think we need to simplify and condense the steps so that the writer can get into the swing of this kind of writing. During a second, third, or fourth cycle of essay writing, a teacher can help writers realize that nothing is as simple as it may seem.

I try to use stories from my life to teach. It gives my students a chance to get to know me better and it allows me to use a story to teach an idea.

I want to make today feel like a celebration while at the same time pushing kids' stamina. There is still more work to be done. Like our cabin, their essays will have all the necessary parts, but now they will need the trim, paint, and final details.

If you are a discerning critic of minilessons, you may notice that my teaching point was vaguer than usual. I essentially said, "Today I'll teach you how to go from folders to a draft," and yet until the Teaching component of this minilesson, I didn't zoom in and name the specific strategy I'd teach. In this minilesson, I think I'm covering so much ground that this works fairly well, but I'm aware that the teaching point was vaguer than usual, and as a result the teaching doesn't exactly align with it.

alter those plans before it's begun! We don't want to be stuck with a half-finished house—a half-finished essay! Before I write a lead saying there are three reasons why my father has been one of my most important teachers, I look over the material I've collected to make sure I have enough evidence to support all three of those reasons."

"Usually what I do is I take one folder at a time—one pile of materials—and I lay whatever I've collected out on the table and then I look over my materials. I ask a couple of questions." I pointed to chart paper on which I'd written these questions:

Questions to Ask of Writing Before We Draft
- Does each bit of material develop the idea?
- Is each bit based on different information?
- Does the material, in total, provide the right amount and right kind of support?

As I teach this I want to convey that the construction of the essay does follow a set plan. The frame needs to be just right before the materials can be added in. Double checking now that the topic sentences match the supporting evidence prevents instability in the final essay. Fixing the structure now is much, much easier than trying to revise a nearly complete draft.

When I teach students to ask themselves a series of questions, I usually make sure that I have written the questions where students can refer to and remember them after the lesson. Whenever you are preparing a set of questions you hope students remember, try to make them short and sweet. Otherwise, there's little chance they can stick in anyone's mind easily.

"After I ask each of these questions of the writing in each folder, then I decide whether these are, in fact, the topic sentences I will use, or whether I need to revise the topic sentences to match my material."

"So let me start with this folder, this idea: 'My father taught me what it means to regard a job as a hobby.' Remember that I collected a story about him taking the waffle iron into the hospital on Christmas mornings? Watch how I reread that story, asking, 'Does this really go with the idea that my dad (it will need to include that *subject)* showed me what it means to think of one's job as a hobby (it will need to show that *point*)?'" Muttering to myself, I said, "I'll reread the story I collected in this folder and when I find sections that go with my point, I'll underline them." Then I read this:

I remember on Christmas mornings after the presents had been opened, my dad always went into the kitchen and began doing the one bit of cooking that he did all year. He stirred Bisquick and eggs in a huge bowl and set off for the hospital, leaving us to finish Christmas celebrations without him. For Dad, Christmas mornings were not just a time to be with family, they were also a

<u>time to serve hot waffles to the medical residents and patients.</u> When I asked him once why he didn't send someone else with the waffles, he told me he loved being at the hospital on Christmas mornings. "It's my hobby," he said.

"So I think the answer is yes, this does support the idea that my father showed me what it is like to have one's job feel like a hobby. And I think the story is pretty persuasive. Let me continue looking through the folder."

ACTIVE ENGAGEMENT

Ask children to practice this work on another example from your folder.

"I also have another Christmas day story in my folder and I've made copies for you! It's the one from earlier in the year and it tells that my father got a cut on his head and used a bag of frozen peas as an ice pack. Would you and your partner reread this story, and ask those same three questions?" I gestured toward the list of questions on the chart and pulled in to listen as children reread and rethought this entry:

> On Christmas Day, my dad went to move a log in the fireplace and gouged his head on one of the nails from which the Christmas stocking hung. To stop the ferocious bleeding, he held a bag of frozen peas on the top of his bald head. Guests arrived for our Christmas party and he greeted them with the bag of frozen peas draped over his forehead. The guests weren't surprised to see Dad's odd ice-pack because he's always done what he pleases without much concern for fitting into social norms. It isn't important to him to dress "right." He wears his red plaid hunting cap everywhere. When I was a teenager and he wore that hunting cap to my school events, I was often embarrassed by him.

After children talked among themselves, I called on Sophie, who said, "It is a good story but I don't think it really goes in this folder 'cause it doesn't show anything about his job, it only shows about his *ways*."

Notice that during my demonstration I was thinking aloud and going through a process in front of my students. Especially when I am teaching something that has multiple steps, I want to make sure that I convey the different parts by slowing down my teaching. One technique I often use is to pause after each step.

Questions to Ask of Writing Before We Draft
- Does each bit of material develop the idea?
- Is each bit based on different information?
- Does the material, in total, provide the right amount and right kind of support?

Of course, I deliberately show children how to do this by using a text that does not support my claim!

Another time, I could certainly teach a minilesson to show children how the same bit of information could be angled differently to fit into different folders (and thus to advance different ideas).

"Oh dear," I said. "You mean I can't use this? Could it go in another one of my folders?" I reread the topic sentences:

> My father has been my most important teacher.

- My father taught me what it means to regard a job as a hobby.
- My father taught me to love writing.
- My father taught me to believe that one person can make a difference.

"Writers," I said. "This is probably going to happen to you. You'll find that you have a great entry that doesn't really fit with the essay you'd planned to write. And if that happens, you have three choices. You could tweak the story so that it does align with one of your topic sentences. You could save the story for another time—another essay or another narrative. Or you could do what I want to do right now, and that is to rewrite your topic sentence. What about if I added a new folder so now my essay shows four ways, not three, in which my father was my most important teacher? I am thinking that I could add a folder that says, 'My dad taught me that it is okay to be oneself and not worry about fitting in.' I've got other information that could go in that folder too, and I'm willing to work hard to fill the folder!"

LINK
Restate the teaching point. In this case, remind children to check and organize their materials before they draft.

"So writers, like I just demonstrated, you need to go through your files. You will find that some of the material in a file doesn't really belong in that file, and so you'll either need to tweak the story so it fits, save it for another time, or do as I've done and revise your bulleted sentence to better match the information you've composed and collected. Once you have checked your material, you'll need to organize it—line it up on the floor or make a stack on your table spot with each bit of writing resting in the order you'll put it in your essay. That's what writers do—they organize their writing into a rough draft!"

Notice how I set my students up by giving them an example that didn't fit. Sometimes highlighting what doesn't work makes the teaching point more vivid. Now we will collaborate on a solution.

This is complex work. If you feel your kids would do better with a condensed version, where you simply take away the story that doesn't fit, saving it for another day, then by all means do so!

I want children to see that although essayists do develop a plan for what we'll say and search for material that can support the ideas we plan to advance, we also know that the material we collect will often lead us to revise our original plan.

You'll have to modify this Link to describe to children the physical places they can use in the classroom to organize their writing. Can they use the hallway? The top of a bookshelf? The library? Some children will find it much easier to envision their draft if the writing is visible in a row rather than lying hidden in a stack.

WRITING AND CONFERRING

Checking Material

Lots of children will need a similar kind of help today so you'll probably want to go from table to table, convening all the children at that table to watch as you work with one child, using her as a case-in-point. For example, I drew a chair alongside Brianna, asking others at her table to pause and watch and learn.

"Okay, Brianna, what have you done so far? Have you chosen one folder, laid it out, and asked the questions?" I asked, pointing to the list. "Or were you just about to do that?"

"I was gonna," Brianna said.

> **Questions to Ask of Writing Before We Draft**
>
> - Does each bit of material develop the idea?
> - Is each bit based on different information?
> - Does the material, in total, provide the right amount and right kind of support?

> **MID-WORKSHOP TEACHING POINT** *Organizing Writing for Body Paragraphs* "Writers, can I have your eyes and your attention?" I said. "Takuma just came to me with a concern, and I bet it will be a concern for many of you. He's worried that the folder he's been working on is so full of great stuff that he can't imagine how he'll be able to hammer and nail all the contents of the folder together into a single paragraph. Would you give me a thumbs up if any of you have worried about the same thing?" Many children indicated they had.
>
> "Your worry is a wise one, and what I want to tell you is that in your final essay, a file of material will probably be turned into more than a single paragraph.
>
> *continued on next page*

"Will you get started while all of us are here to help?" I said, my eyes circling the cluster of children at the table. "Pick any entry pertaining to your folder, 'I love amusement parks because I love games.' Then ask [I gestured again toward the questions], 'Does this bit of material develop the idea?'" Gesturing to Brianna's entries, I said, "Read aloud so we can hear, okay?" Brianna read this tight list:

> When I play 'get to the top,' I get very competitive. I might try to hit the water gun out of your hand. When I play 'hit the target,' I get nervous, my palms get sweaty. When I play bumper cars, I get mean. I will bump you into a corner and keep you there.

When she finished reading, Brianna looked up at me as if to ask, "What next?" I turned to the observing group and said, "What is the question Brianna needs to ask of this entry?" The group decided that Brianna needed to ask whether this entry goes with her claim that she loves amusement parks because of the games.

Brianna said, "Yes? 'Cause it's about the games?"

I looked at the listening children, as if asking whether they concurred, and mulled over Brianna's topic sentence and her list, thinking aloud about whether I concurred. She claimed she loves amusement parks because of the games, and had certainly listed the games—but had she made her point? "Remember, Brianna, you'll answer yes if your entry is about the same subject (the games at the amusement park) *and* if it makes the same point (that the games are great, and they are the reason you love the amusement park)." Turning to all the children, I said, "Ask yourselves, does Brianna's entry talk about the *subject* of her claim? Does it match the *point* she wants to make?"

Once everyone had agreed that no, this entry didn't show that Brianna loves the amusement park because of the games, we helped Brianna decide whether to revise her entry to support her claim, or to move on to examine another bit of data. She did the latter.

continued from previous page

Your entire essay will have two or three major 'body paragraphs,' they're called, but really they make up a 'body-section.' Readers will be able to see when a new important section begins because they'll see the stem of your thesis reoccur. But within that section, there will probably be several paragraphs."

"So, Takuma, yes, as you select material to include in your essay, you can include a story that may be a page long, then a list that may be half a page. For now, just seat these beside each other."

SHARE

Teaching Our Topics

Remind students that talking through essay drafts can help writers organize their thoughts. Ask them to tell the first folder contents—the first paragraphs—of their essay to a small group.

"Writers, you'll remember that earlier this year, before we wrote our stories, we told versions of them to ourselves, to each other, to anyone who'd listen. And earlier in this unit, we taught each other about our topics. But that was before we'd lived with our topics, collecting lots of information and ideas. Now that we've moved from collecting to drafting, and each of you has not only gathered a lot of material but also thought through how you might order that material, it's time to again teach each other about our topics. And we're just going to teach each other one claim—the one folder that you've worked on. Take a few minutes right now to reread your material, wrap your brain around it, and get ready to act as a professor lecturing to a whole group of people on your topic."

After a few minutes, I stationed five children in different areas of the classroom, and set each child up to sit before a small audience. In each circle, one child—the professor—sat on a chair with other children grouped around. Then I asked the one child to teach a small class on his or her topic. When that child was done, the child selected someone to follow.

Debrief. Highlight what you hope students heard and did in their small groups.

"Writers," I said, "I just attended some lectures that were much more interesting than those I attend at the university! You are speaking with voices of authority, with clarity, and with precise, specific information—and that makes for some fabulous instruction. LaKeya's lecture went like this:" *[Fig. XIV-1]*

> Being a girl is hard because we go through a lot of changes, and have mixed/sensative feelings. I can be happy but in a moment I can be mad. I can not care how I look and then in a moment I can Look in the mirror every minute. I can feel thin and then all of a sudden my rear end is getting bigger. I can smell good one moment and the next moment my armpits stink.

Notice that again I am asking students to rehearse their writing orally. Once they practice speaking about a section in their essay, they can go back to their written work to see if they need to make any revisions.

If children aren't stepping into professional roles, listen for a minute and then say, "Can I interrupt?" and for a minute, press the rewind button on the course of study. Give the same lecture, only use your best professional tone, complete with the transition words that are part of this discourse. Then debrief, ask the child you displaced to try a new version of the lecture. The whole point of this is to help children step into the role, the voice, of being a teacher.

> Being a girl is hard because we go through a lot of changes, and have mixed/sensative feelings. I can be happy but in a moment I can be mad. I can not care how I look and then in a moment I can Look in the mirror every minute I can feel thin and then all of a sudden my rear end is getting bigger. I can smell good one moment and the next moment my armpits stink.

Fig. XIV-1 LaKeya's notebook entry

"As you taught others about your subjects, I have a hunch that some parts of your teaching felt especially vital, especially alive. Remember those sections when you go to draft your essays, because you'll add to these when you write your final draft. On the other hand, some parts of your lecture may have felt hollow or wooden or irrelevant. When you go to write your final draft, you'll want to trust your own intuitions! If some sections of your 'class' didn't work, when you go to write them, you'll want to teach them differently. But above all, remember the teaching voice you used today, because when you write an essay, you are teaching a course!"

HOMEWORK   *Telling Essays*   Earlier this year, I told you that fiction writer Robert Munsch says he tells a story a hundred times before he ever writes a draft. Today I want to teach you that essayists seize every opportunity they can to teach people about their subjects. So tonight, find two different people and teach each one of them, just as some of you just taught your classmates today. Become accustomed to talking about your information as if you were teaching a class, because writing essays has a lot in common with teaching. Then tomorrow we'll all draft our essays. Come to school tomorrow ready to write with authority, clarity, and precise information!

TAILORING YOUR TEACHING

If your students seem overwhelmed with the task of organizing the writing in their folders into a rough draft . . . you'll want to offer a couple of solutions, depending on the origins of the problem. For some students, the volume of material they've collected could be at the root of the problem. Perhaps these students have gone through their folders a few times already to make sure the entries match the idea of the topic sentence, but they are still left with lots of relevant material. You'll want to support these students as they cull through the entries yet again, this time selecting a few that 'best' support the topic sentence. You'll want to teach them to pick what they consider the very best evidence they have that supports their claim. You can also suggest that sometimes our favorite entry may not be the best evidence, so we need to reexamine our entries with essayists' eyes and minds.

Another reason your students might be overwhelmed is that they are imagining using every bit of every piece of writing they have collected. If this is the case for some of your students, remind them that as they draft they'll include only that part of their writing that is directly helpful to them in supporting their claim. The rest will be left out. For example, they may not need to include details about the setting in an anecdote they are using to support their claim. They can cross those details right out.

If your children are working through this unit for a second year and they are writing essays intended to persuade . . . then you may want to teach the particulars of persuasion. "I love my mother" is not a thesis that can be disputed, whereas the thesis "Homelessness affects all of us" is intended to persuade. One strategy you can teach children is that when writing to influence others, writers acknowledge the dissenting opinion in order to argue against it more effectively. Instead of pretending that our view is the only view, we acknowledge the other side and then make sure that our essay gives convincing reasons to support our side, or refute theirs. For more ideas on strategies writers use to persuade their readers, you could read Heather Lattimer's *Thinking Through Genre: Units of Study in Reading and Writing Workshops 4–12*.

ASSESSMENT

One beautiful spring day a few years ago, I brought my sons to visit Harvard Square in Cambridge, Massachusetts. The day glistened in sunshine, and so I bought a Frisbee and we played catch in the quad outside Harvard's library. Then I got the bright idea to rent roller skates and skate along the Charles River. I think I imagined that my sons and I would weave our way among the walkers, skating in those long, effortless gliding strokes that I'd seen others make. From the moment I strapped on the skates, it was clear to me I was in for trouble. I stood, and whomp! I was sprawled on my backside. I gingerly got to my feet and my skates took off with me riding shakily above them. We—the skates and I—rattled down the sidewalk. (I'd completely forgotten my sons, who were engrossed in their own life-and-death travails.) A cross street approached: how to stop? I careened into the people who were waiting on the curb, knocking a few of them down. Soon I was mopping blood off my knees and elbows, reexperiencing the road burns I hadn't felt since my childhood.

Whenever any of us try something new, we mess up. Until we get the hang of the new enterprise, we flail about. This is absolutely true for roller skating, but it is also true for essay writing.

When children begin to draft essays, their drafts will be full of mechanical problems. As teachers, it's easy to feel overwhelmed by all the errors we see in our children's drafts. It's important to understand that once they get the hang of this new enterprise, many of those errors will go away.

Jumping on every error will not instill confidence; however, there are a few mechanical errors you're sure to spot that do deserve speedy intervention. As I've mentioned before, you may find many drafts are mired in pronouns with unclear antecedents—as in this example from Becca.

> My sister is spoiled by my mother because she is going through the process of being adopted. She was close to her old foster mother and she was very nice.

When we read a passage and come to a pronoun (in this example, *she*), we need to be able to substitute the name of the person or thing referenced. In this passage, it is not clear just who is going through the process of being

adopted—the sister or the mother. That is, in the first sentence there is no clear antecedent for the pronoun *she*.

I recommend teaching writers to control pronouns by asking either the whole class or the children who need help with this to work together on some shared reading of a published text. I'd ask them to insert parenthetical antecedents for each of the pronouns. For example, the class could read aloud *Gorilla* by Anthony Browne, and the lead of the book would sound like this:

> Hannah loved gorillas. She (Hannah) read books about gorillas, she (Hannah) watched gorillas on television, and she (Hannah) drew pictures of gorillas. But she (Hannah) had never seen a real one (gorilla).
>
> Her (Hannah's) father didn't have time to take her (Hannah) to see one at the zoo. He (Hannah's father) didn't have time for anything.

Then children could try to read each other's drafts in a similar fashion. If one reader found that a pronoun reference wasn't clear, the writer could either substitute a name for the pronoun or add a more specific reference.

Language will be less redundant if the writer introduces a person using more than one identifying term. For example, Becca revised her draft like this:

> My sister, Star, is spoiled by my mother because Star is going through the process of being adopted. My sister was close to her old foster mother, Mrs. Luke, and Mrs. Luke was very nice.

But despite your work with pronouns, you'll probably see that children's essays are either repetitive or they sprawl all over the place. If you have a chance to show children how to eliminate redundancy in an essay, by all means point this out. But you probably won't get to all children, and it really is totally okay that their final essays are not what you would have written. After all, these children are eight, nine, ten years old! They're all roller skating for the very first time! Let them career about a bit, and hope the experience is more rewarding for them than my Harvard Square experience was for me!

BUILDING A COHESIVE DRAFT

IN THIS SESSION, YOU WILL TEACH CHILDREN THAT WRITERS CREATE COHESION WITH REPEATED PHRASES, LOGICALLY SEQUENCED INFORMATION, AND TRANSITION WORDS.

GETTING READY

- One folder from your own sample essay, entries organized into categories (extended list, tight list, quotes, and story) and written on chart paper
- List of transitional words, written on chart paper
- Second example from your essay illustrating transition words and another way to organize the material
- See CD-ROM for resources

You've taught children that essay writers combine different materials to lend more power to their claims and more artistry to their writing. In one essay, then, a writer may piece together an anecdote, a list, a statistic, an observation, a generalization—and a variety of other forms of writing as well! It's no surprise, then, that one of the challenges a writer faces when building a draft is the need to arrange these diverse materials into a single, cohesive whole. Ideas do not in themselves take a form in space or time; they do not lay themselves flat or set themselves up in three dimensions. The forms they take in words and on paper are completely up to the writer. Of course, many, many writers and essayists have taken up this challenge, and we can learn from the ways of communicating ideas that they have created.

In this session you'll teach children a couple of ways essay writers often organize their ideas and create unity in their assemblage of pieces of writing. To get started, you'll also teach them to use special transition words that indicate certain types of relationships between ideas. Also, you will explain that essayists often repeat crucial words of their thesis in each supporting paragraph so the reader hears the message again and again and knows those words are the key to understanding the essay. These repeated words become a unifying refrain that creates cohesion in the writing. All three of these suggestions, combined, should help students get off to a strong start, turning the collections of writing in their folders into whole, unified, cohesive drafts.

MINILESSON

Building a Cohesive Draft

CONNECTION

Restate the building metaphor to help students imagine their essays as materials, arranged in a structure. Tell students that today they'll learn to assemble these materials together.

"Writers, earlier I told you that to write an essay, essayists collect folders full of diverse material. Your folders are bulging with stories, lists, quotations, statistics, observations, and citations. Yesterday you began to sort through these materials, just as a builder might double-check her materials, thinking, "Is it all here? How will it look in the end?'"

"Today I want to remind you that once a builder has selected the materials she plans to use, she still needs to assemble them. Similarly, once you've selected the anecdotes, lists, statistics, or observations you'll use in a paragraph, you, too, will need to put these together."

Name the teaching point. Specifically, tell children that they'll put their materials together by selecting a system for arranging the data, by using transitional words, and by repeating key words.

"Today I'm going to teach you that writers put materials together by using a couple of techniques. First, we arrange the writing pieces in an order that we choose for a reason. And second, we use transitional words and key words from our thesis or our topic sentence like cement between bricks, holding one bit of material onto the next."

TEACHING

Demonstrate that you choose a logical way to sequence materials within a single category.

"You'll recall that I've collected lots of materials to support the broad thesis, 'My father has been my most important teacher,'" I said, gesturing to my outer folder. Turning to one of the inner folders, I said, "Let's look at this particular folder," and I read the sentence on the outside of the folder: "My father taught me that one person can make a difference."

Spreading out the folder's contents, I muttered, "I already took out the material that didn't make my case." I picked up two separate pieces of paper and in a parenthetical comment, said to the children around me, "Watch closely because this is intellectually demanding work. I actually copied these bits onto chart paper so you can watch more closely."

COACHING

You actually didn't spend much time teaching children the principles they can draw upon as they sequence their materials. You could, another time or in small groups, show children that some people organize topically, some chronologically, and others strategically, placing their strongest material at the beginning and at the end.

This information can be said quickly, but it is complicated, provocative, and important. Whenever my teaching point is especially important, I try to speak clearly and slowly to show that the words are carrying a heavy cargo of meaning. I find that if I consciously think about the significance of my words as I speak, my tone helps children to listen carefully.

Notice the way that the concrete visual materials help to accentuate the structure of my essay. The thesis is written on a colored file, and the topic sentences are written on manila files that are contained within the thesis file. Incorporating the color-coded files into my demonstration teaching serves as a way to subtly remind children of the text structures that I'm assuming they recall.

Then turning back to the work, I muttered to myself, "I have these bits, among others, in the folder. As I read through them, I'm going to think, 'What order makes sense to put these in?'" I read aloud, as if to myself, a few pieces of material from the folder that would become the paragraph supporting this sentence: "My father taught me that one person can make a difference." Children meanwhile followed along on a chart-sized version of the material.

The use of "parenthetical" comments, or asides, in the midst of a demonstration is important. This is how I keep two tracks going. On the one side, I am being a writer, working publicly. On the other side, I am being a teacher, explicitly explaining to children what the writer under scrutiny (also me) is doing. I encourage teachers to use parenthetical comments when working with small groups, too, because these comments allow us to explicitly name the transferable processes one child is learning that every child can use.

My father taught me that one person can make a difference.

A List	When patients wanted to squeeze into my father's full schedule, he always said yes. When organizations wrote to my father for support, he always said yes. And although he and my mother have nine children of their own, when a local couple died in a car accident, and someone needed to take in the their children, he said yes.
Quotes	My father often quoted Rockefeller to me: "To whom much is given, much shall be asked."
Extended List	My father got arrested for participation in a political protest. He volunteered at our church, at the local soup kitchen.
Story	My father once told me a story that made a big impression on me—it was of how he decided to be a doctor. As a teenager, he went to Camp Merryweather. One day, after lunch, the wife of the camp director read aloud from <u>The Microbe Hunters</u>, sharing stories of Marie Curie's and Louis Pasteur's research. Lying in his cot with a green army blanket over him, my father thought to himself, "That research is their job!" His father was a banker and it had never, until that moment, occurred to him that a person's job could be their hobby, their passion. The fact that my father told me his story and shared his insight has changed my life.

Demonstrate to show that you reread one bit of data, trying to figure out what exactly it is about so you can decide where it belongs.

"Hmm . . . I'm thinking that this one is about my father getting arrested when he was trying to make a difference, and this one is about him volunteering to make a difference. They aren't really about the same thing! I could make one pile for 'getting in trouble' and one for 'helping,'" I said, starting to make two piles. Pulling back and looking over the nascent organization system represented by those two piles, I muttered to myself, "But I am thinking that I won't have much in the 'getting in trouble' file." Turning to the children, I said, "Once I've decided that the pieces of information support my claim, my job is to find out what kind of order makes the most sense to say it in."

Picking up the two bits I questioned, I muttered, "Maybe I could arrange these according to the order in which they happened—chronologically!" Getting excited, I added, "I think this would work! I could start with the story of my dad telling me how he chose to be a doctor, because he told me that story when I was just a little girl. Then I could tell the parts about other children living with us because that happened when I was in grade school. Then I could tell about all the times he quoted Rockefeller because that happened even when I was older and he wanted to steer my direction. I think this will work well! This organization shows that throughout my whole life my dad has taught me how one person can make a difference."

ACTIVE ENGAGEMENT
Debrief. In this case, name again the steps you took in choosing how to line up the writing material from one of your folders.

"Now you've seen how I thought about how to order the information in one of my folders. I laid it all out, reread it, and thought about how the bits related to each other, and about the impression I want to give my reader. In the end, I decided the order for the material in that folder will be chronological. I'll have to decide on an order for each of my other folders as well, won't I? They might all be chronological, or I might figure out another way to do it. Essayists sometimes decide to put the strongest evidence for the claim first, to hook the reader in and last, to leave a strong memory. Essayists might decide to make categories with their information—maybe the first few bits of material are related to writing and the second few bits are related to reading, for example."

My actions support the words I say here. The truth is that in every minilesson, we need to use gestures and materials to accentuate our content. I am being more explicit about the use of gestures in this particular case because I know the minilesson's content is complex. I would not have dreamt of making minilessons this dense earlier in the year or in the unit, and as I talk now, I am aware that some children will need to hear this again in small groups or in another minilesson tomorrow.

I know that some people read children's "five-paragraph essays" (as some people disdainfully say) and claim that the writing is mind-deadening. I agree that the products that result from all this work are always not the most spectacular pieces of writing in the world—but I invite any critic to come backstage and watch children as they begin to grasp the complexities of composing these essays. Then I'd like those critics to tell me if they still believe this work is mind-deadening. When I am in the company of teachers and children who are struggling in their first forays through expository writing, I am watching minds challenged and growing!

Many of your students will no doubt choose chronological order for the information in their own folders, since that was your example. Finding a chronological order isn't easy in every set of materials, however—these materials are ideas, not necessarily events that happen in a fixed time. One way to make sure that every set of materials has a chronological order is to think of when the writer experienced each bit of information. In that frame of mind, there is an order to the information, set in time. It would be marked by phrases such as: I used to think; Then I learned; The next day a friend told me; Thinking about all this, I finally figured out . . . . This frame can be a helpful one to teach students, as it will always be possible (though it may not always be the best choice).

Ask students to talk with their partners about what order they will use for the information in one of their folders.

"Now, take one of your own folders and talk to your partner about the material you have and the order you might choose to present it in. Partner 1 go first, and I'll let you know when it's your turn, partner 2."

LINK
Remind students that every time they want to build a draft of an essay, they need to figure out a structure, an order, for the materials they've collected.

"Wow, guys, I've heard some wonderful ideas for ordering the information in your folders sensibly! Ho said he'll put the funny parts together in one paragraph that supports his claim, and the serious parts together in a second paragraph that supports his claim. He said he'll start the second paragraph with a sentence that goes 'In some ways, the reasons are funny, but in other ways, it is no laughing matter.' Isn't that a great idea? A lot of you had strong logical reasons for putting your materials in a certain order. Congratulations! That's a step every essay writer needs to take every time he or she writes an essay."

"Remember not to waste time copying a part into your draft that is just the same as what is in your folder—simply staple it to the page where you want it to go! You will probably also need scissors and tape so that you can piece your draft together efficiently."

Time is short, so I'm suggesting children use every moment to accomplish the job. You may decide that this Active Engagement is too messy to take place on the meeting area, in which case you could bypass it altogether.

WRITING AND CONFERRING

Recognizing Sources of Supporting Material

When you confer with children, you will certainly find that some of them have a couple of folders that are almost empty. It's tremendously gratifying to them if you help them see that they have more material than they may have realized. Suggest they read through their notebooks, looking for any entry that in any way fits with one of their topic sentences, including entries they wrote earlier in this unit. For example, at the beginning of the unit, when you taught children to consider possible stories that could support a bullet point, many children made lists that could, in fact, be pieced into their essays. You can help children see that their lists could probably be spiffed up and become part of a paragraph.

This was my earlier list:

> My father taught me what it means to regard a job as a hobby.
>
> My father confided that he couldn't wait to get back to his job after summer vacation.
>
> My father made waffles for doctors and patients at work on Christmas morning.
>
> My father realized Louis Pasteur's job was his hobby.

My list could become an entry like this:

> My dad taught me what it means to see a job as a hobby. For example, on the last day of summer vacation, my dad and I sailed together and he confided that he couldn't wait for vacation to be over so he could get back to his job. Another example occurred on most Christmas mornings. My father always went to the hospital carrying a waffle iron, ready to make waffles for the doctors and patients. I asked why he didn't send someone else and he admitted that he liked going to work. "It's my hobby," he said. Once Dad told me that when he was a kid, the wife of the camp director read a book aloud about Louis Pasteur. Dad said to me, "Listening to that read aloud, I thought, 'That research is his job.'" He explained that at the time, this was a whole new idea to him!

With this as an example, some children should be able take some of the barely developed entries in their notebooks and make them into useful material for their sparsely populated folders.

Lining Up Materials According to Importance "Writers, I want to tell you another way that essayists sometimes organize their materials. Sometimes, we look at all the material and rank it according to importance, least important bit first and most important bit last. To do that, we use transition words to introduce each part, like *first, building on that point, more important,* and *most important*."

"Can you see how that would help you line up your material into a big finale? You can try that organizational structure and those words for one of your folders if you think it could fit well with what you have to say and would help support your claim. Listen to how Takuma has used a few words to tie sections of his essay together:" *[Figs XV-1 and XV-2]*

> Not only do my grandparents play games with me but when I'm with them I feel safe and comfortable.
> I feel safe and comfortable with them when I'm lost.
> I feel safe and comfortable with them when I'm sick.
> I feel safe and comfortable with them when I wake up at the middle of the night.
> An example of when I felt safe is when I was going to a haunted house with my grandma and grandpa. I felt scared and didn't want to go.
> My grandma and grandpa said, "Just try once." So I tried to be not scared. I went in the haunted house squeezing my grandma's and grandpa's hand.
> "Don't let go of my hand," I said in a worried voice.
> "I won't," my grandparents said.
> "OK," I said. "I belive you." I squeezed even harder on my grandma and grandpa's hand.

Fig. XV-1 Takuma's essay

> "I'm scared," I said. I stuck right behind my grandma and closed my eyes. And through the haunted house I felt safe.
> It feels so good to have someone to comfort you and also make you feel safe. And this makes my grandparents precious to me.

Fig. XV-2 Takuma, page 2

SHARE

Selecting Words to Make the Organization Strong

Share with your students that once they've chosen an order for their material, writers cement it together using transition words that match the organizational plan. Tell them that writers repeat parts of their thesis and supporting sentences to help readers understand the most important parts of the essay.

"Writers, you've done a great job deciding on your organizational structures. How many of you think that you'll organize the content of this first folder into logical categories—thumbs up? How many of you think you'll organize your material in a line that has some order, perhaps chronological order—thumbs up?"

"The next thing I want to teach you is this. When you actually recopy and combine your material, we need to cement it together. One way we do this is by repeating the key words from our topic sentence or our thesis sentence often. So I will be repeating 'one person can make a difference' and, from the larger thesis, 'my most important teacher.'"

"The other way to link material together is by using the cement we call *transition words*. Transition words tell you how one thing you say relates to the other things you say in your essay. We choose transition words that go with our organizational plan. If I'm going to organize my bits by time, then I'll want to use transition words that show first one thing happened, then the next, then later something else, and so on. If I'm ordering my bits by degree of importance, I use different transitions."

Share some examples of transition words by themselves and then in the context of an essay.

"Here are some examples of transition words you could use if you choose a chronological order for your information." I read aloud the list I had prepared on chart paper.

- When I [he, she, it] was young
- This began when
- At first
- After awhile
- Later or still later
- Finally
- Recently
- Now

The children will be working with a great deal of material. Encourage them to literally staple or tape bits that they have collected so they adjoin each other, adding sticky notes or inserted sheets of paper with transition words and phrases. Then you'll need to decide whether you want their final drafts to be more correct than the children can make them when working with independence, in which case you'll need to edit these drafts. Finally, your children will make one final copy. Don't expect them to be able to write a sequence of drafts— each essay will be several pages long.

This is a trimmed-down, simple list. When children progress through this unit a second or third time, you can certainly add to the list or show them other lists. Children can help you do this by studying mentor texts and compiling other ways of using transitional words. Help them to notice that usually writers choose sets of transition words. For example, your children may notice that writers find ways to compare one example to another, using words such as similarly, along the same lines, in a similar way, *or* likewise. *Writers also use transitional words to highlight significance. They may use terms such as* notice that, it is important to note that, significantly, *or* most importantly.

"Remember I decided to organize my material about my dad chronologically. This means, I can use those words to cement my material together. But here is another way I could, on the other hand, decide to organize the same material differently. For example; I could organize my information from this folder into two categories. I could put all the materials about my father's life of service in one category, one part of my essay. Then in the next category, I could put all the materials about people who taught him how one person can make a difference. You'll hear my order, because I use transition words to tell about those two groups so my readers will know how to listen. Notice that I also repeat key words from the thesis and topic sentence to remind readers what my claim is. I'll write in the air, saying exactly what I'm going to write."

My father, my most important teacher, taught me that one person can make a difference. One way that he taught me that one person can make a difference is that he lived a life of service. For example, when I was a child, my father got arrested for participation in a political protest. Requests for donations used to flood our mailbox and I knew he always said yes. We often had other people's children living with us: three orphans for one year, a couple of international exchange students for another year. Another way that my father lives a life of service is that he volunteers. For example, he teaches Sunday school, he helps his professional organizations, he works at the soup kitchen.

Another way that my father taught me one person can make a difference is that he often told me stories about people who taught him this. For example, he often quotes Rockefeller, who says, "To whom much is given, much shall be asked." Another example is that my father once told me the story of how he decided to be a doctor. As a teenager, he went to Camp Merryweather. One day, after lunch, the wife of the camp director read aloud from *The Microbe Hunters,* sharing stories of Marie Curie's and Louis Pasteur's research. Lying in his cot with a green army blanket over him, my father thought to himself, "That research is their jobs!" His father was a banker and it had never, until that moment, occurred to my father that a person's job could be their hobby, their life project. Right then, he vowed that he wanted his job to make a difference.

This is way too long to write onto chart paper. I'd just ad lib the passage, writing-in-the-air. I probably wouldn't make it so complete.

"Did you hear the organization—in other words, did you hear the transition words?" I quickly reread the transition words to the class. "Did you hear how I echoed my thesis and supporting sentence?" I reread those parts to the class.

Ask writers to share the organizational structure and transition words from their own work with their partner. Also ask them to share where and how they've used key words from the thesis and supporting sentences.

"Writers, take this time to share with your partners the organization you chose for one of your folders. Ask your partner whether the transition words you used clearly show the reader how you are organizing the materials. You can then talk about the key words from your thesis and supporting sentences that also need to be in your paragraphs. Are they there? Where could you put them if they aren't there yet? Okay, go ahead."

HOMEWORK   *Lining Up Materials for Supporting Paragraphs*   Writers, today you've done extraordinary work. You thought through the way in which you'd sequence your material for one folder, organizing it as a paragraph, and realized which transitional words would most help you link your pieces together. You said your draft aloud in your head or to each other, then drafted one paragraph. Some of you found that your paragraph was too long to be a single paragraph so you divided it into two.

Tonight do this same work again for your next section. I know you are so excited to finish this part so we can put the essays all together! Our celebration is coming soon and we can't waste a minute!

TAILORING YOUR TEACHING

If your students seem to be getting tangled up as they organize their piles of supporting evidence . . . you may decide to devote more time to teaching students how to organize evidence chronologically (if you think that will help a majority of your writers) or how to organize according to importance (if many of your writers would benefit from more instruction on this method). For either or both of these lessons, you could use a published essay to illustrate the organizing structure you're teaching, and then for active engagement, you could have your students look through their topic sentence folders to see if any of them would be appropriate to organize either chronologically or according to importance. They can turn and tell a partner how they will organize and then go off to work to try it.

If your students have worked though this unit in a previous year and you'd like to vary this minilesson . . . you might offer students several mentor essays from published authors, from other students, or from the students in this unit to study. By analyzing the ways that other authors have arranged information, writers get ideas to try in their own writing. Here are two samples students could study in partnerships, noting their observations in their notebooks. Remember—students can learn from the mentor texts, weaknesses as well as strengths!

COLLABORATING WITH COLLEAGUES

It is important for teachers at different grade levels to meet and talk about ways in which children's work becomes more complex as they grow older and more experienced. As you try to articulate lines along which you expect children in the upper elementary grades to grow as writers, you'll also want to consider ways in which you foster children to do this increasingly complex thinking and writing.

The easiest way for a child to elaborate upon an idea is to provide one example, then another, then another. The logic is associative. For example, Ayana writes, "It is wonderful having kind friends. It is wonderful because your friends don't laugh at you if you get something wrong, your friends help you if you need help, and they never break their friendship." Then each paragraph states one claim ("It is wonderful having kind friends because your friends don't laugh if you get something wrong") and cites one example ("One day when I was in third grade . . . ") followed by another example ("Another time I was playing outside a game called 'Math Quiz' and I got an answer wrong").

> It is wonderful having kind friends. It is wonderful because your friends don't laugh at you if you get something wrong, your friends help you if you need help, and they never break their friendship. One day when I was in third grade and my friend sat next to me and my teacher asked me a math question and I got the answer wrong, everyone laughed except for my best friend. Another time I was outside playing a game called "Math Quiz" and I got an answer wrong and 2 girls laugh, but my best friend didn't laugh at me.
>
> It is wonderful having kind friends because your friends help you if you need help. One time I left my calculator at home and my friend let me use hers until I got mine. Another time I was doing my homework and I needed help with my homework and my friend helped me.

It is more challenging for children to elaborate on an idea by elucidating causes. In the preceding example, Ayana could have explored causes had she written about why kind (as opposed to unkind) friends don't laugh at each other, and why friends don't abandon each other when they need help or break friendships. Such an essay could have been interesting because of course people do sometimes have friendships with people who tend to be unkind, and those friendships probably do get strained.

When teachers scrutinize student work, asking, "What kind of thinking has this writer done?" it sometimes becomes clear that a child had nearly called on a more challenging level of thinking but settled on easier ways to elaborate. For example, although in the end Rebecca's essay about her sister is a straightforward list of all the times her sister acts in annoying ways, in one of Rebecca's earlier entries she'd explored causes for Star's behavior. *[Fig. XV-3]*

> My sister is spoiled by my mother because she is going through the process of being adopted. She was close to her old foster mother and never knew her biological mother. She cries a lot and says that she misses her foster brother, Rohny. I feel really bad for her and I would have acted just like her, however she gets me realy imotated.
> All the time before I get in bed at night Star climbs into my bed, pulls the covers over her head and waits for me to go to my bed. That also gets me extremly annoyed.
> Star can be annoying but yet, sometimes she can be cute, funny, and nice. It makes me really happy to see her happy

Fig. XV-3 Rebecca's notebook entry

My sister is spoiled by my mother because she is going through the process of being adopted. She was close to her old foster mother and never knew her biological mother. She cries a lot and says that she misses her foster brother Ronny. I feel really bad for her and I would have acted just like her however she gets me really irritated.

In this instance, if Rebecca's teacher had decided to help her explore causes and effects and make comparisons as she developed this piece, Rebecca's essay might have focused on causes for her sister's behavior instead of becoming the more simple list of times when Rebecca is irritated by her.

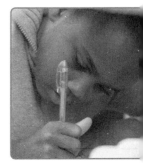

IN THIS SESSION, YOU'LL TEACH CHILDREN THE WAYS WRITERS COMMONLY OPEN AND CLOSE ESSAYS. YOU'LL HELP CHILDREN TRY THESE WAYS IN THEIR OWN ESSAYS.

GETTING READY

- List of common ways to begin an essay on chart
- List of common ways to conclude an essay on chart
- Possible introductions and conclusions for your own essay on chart
- Sample student essays with drafts of several introductions and conclusions
- See CD-ROM for resources

WRITING INTRODUCTIONS AND CONCLUSIONS

When children write stories, we hand story language over to them that can cast magical spells over their narrative accounts, turning plain-Jane recounts into stories that pull listeners close, giving them goose bumps. We do not hesitate to suggest to a child that he or she start a story with phrases like "On a dark and stormy night" or "Once, long, long ago, I . . ."

It is just as important that we also hand over language that essayists use, allowing youngsters to feel the persuasive power that special sets of words can have on listeners. In this session, I am direct. "Try these phrases on for size," I say, and hand over some of the language that I know will work for these youngsters' essays.

The results are once again magical. Try this with your own writing. Use these phrases when you address your children's parents in open-house meetings. Notice how the words work, just as the start of a story works, to cast a spell, to set the stage, to invite listeners to draw close, to lean in. Notice also how the words work on us, not just our listeners. As we say the words, essay-like language and structure flow from us more easily, evoked by tone and expectations we associate with those "expository" phrases.

I used to think each writer always needed to use brand-new words—words written for the occasion that come from the heart. But I've come to realize that for generations, people have begun stories, "Once upon a time, long, long ago" and not felt abashed to do so. Why not, in a similar way, borrow from the language of essayists and orators? I've done so in this paragraph, in fact, using borrowed phrases to frame my sentences— try doing the same! Some people begin their speeches awkwardly, hemming and hawing, but if you draw from great orators or writers, you will have words that you can rely on whenever you want to teach listeners something important.

MINILESSON

Writing Introductions and Conclusions

CONNECTION

Remind writers of the work they've done so far in this unit—the process that essayists use.

"Writers, you've done so much great work in this unit so far! Let's think again about what you've done, about how a person goes about writing essays." I held up my hand and touched my first finger, "At the start of our unit, you learned that when we want to write essays, we *first* live wide-awake lives, paying attention to things in our lives that are provocative, that make us think. We discussed a bunch of ways to gather essay entries—collecting observations and then writing off from them and from our earlier writing." I touched my second finger as I said, "Then we used thought prompts to push ourselves to extend our first thoughts."

Touching my third finger I said, "You learned that writers form a picture, an image, of the sort of thing we want to write. We do this by studying writing others have done, texts that resemble those we want to write." I held up three more fingers to go with the next three steps and said, "Then you learned to choose a seed idea, to write it as a clear and strong thesis, and to plan or frame the main sections of your essay. Next you sorted through your entries, selecting and sequencing them. And finally, you began drafting!"

Name the teaching point. In this case, writers use several phrases to help us create introductions and conclusions for our essays.

"Today I know you'll continue to cement your selected material into paragraphs, but I know you will also want to learn a bit about how essayists write introductions and closings for our essays. Specifically, I want to teach you that essay writers often use the beginning of an essay as a place to convey to readers that the ideas in the essay are important. The lead briefly places the essay into a context."

COACHING

It helps to organize and consolidate the processes and strategies that we've taught thus far so children can draw on them as they cycle through the stages of the writing process with independence, at whatever speed works for them. Although in this unit we are inching through some detailed steps in the writing process, I pause at crucial junctures to give children an aerial view of what they are experiencing. I want them to grasp the main contours of the process. The good news is they'll come to know the process better across the year because they will have chances to reexperience it.

TEACHING
Tell writers that at the beginning and end of essays, essayists often rely on some common ways to say, "This is important!"

"I think you know by now that when we want to do a new kind of writing, we often get ready for this by reading texts that resemble those we want to write. We could go on a search, collecting ways that writers usually introduce and close their essays. But this time, I'll simply tell you what I've already found from studying people's essays."

"What I've found is that often essayists want both their introduction and the closing paragraphs to say to readers, 'This essay is *really important*. Listen up!' Essayists don't usually use those exact words, however. But essayists sometimes convey that the content is important because it answers people's questions or helps with their needs or changes their mind." I revealed a chart on which I had written a few common phrases for introductions and conclusions of essays. "I might, therefore, start in one of these ways."

You'll recall that in order to teach children to write leads and endings to narratives, I invited them to pore over texts by authors they love. I invited them to find patterns in those leads and endings. As you realize by now, the truth is that I do not have a vast storehouse of exemplar essays that are simple enough for children to study and emulate. That explains why I've been the one to do this research and extrapolate these patterns, rather than sending children off to search through the essays they love, noticing how authors began and ended those essays. If you discover enough texts, you could structure a minilesson in which children extract for themselves a host of ways to start and finish an essay.

Ways to Start an Essay

- Tell a story about one person needing the information this essay will convey. What (that person) and others need to know is that . . .
- Many people (don't know, don't think, don't realize) but I've (come to know, think it's important) . . .
- Have you ever (wondered/wanted to know) . . . ? I have found . . .
- Raise a question that people ask . . . and show that this essay will answer it.

"At the end of my essay, I want to say to my readers that now that I know something, I will act differently, or other people should act differently. So I might fit what I want to say into phrases like these."

Notice that I have given my students many different phrases to choose from. You may decide to use fewer examples. I want to make sure that my students choose a phrase based on what they are trying to say to their readers. Also notice that any of these phrases could be used in an introduction or a conclusion.

Ways to End an Essay

- (My thesis) is true. Because this is true, isn't it also true that . . .
- I realize that . . .
- This makes me think . . .
- I realize that when I . . . , I feel . . .
- Other people should care about this because . . .
- This is important because . . .

These lead sentence templates can have a dramatic effect on children's essays. Just as starting with "Once upon a time" can lift the level of a story, these leads can wrap children's rather pedestrian paragraphs in an aura of drama. Be sure to emphasize that writers need to try them on for size, to revise the set phrases a bit so they fit exactly with each essay.

"So let me show you how I take these phrases and see if they might work for my essay. You'll notice that some do, some don't. They never work exactly, so I change the wording around a bit to fit what I want to say. And I often write beginnings and endings that don't use these templates. I usually list a couple of possible introductions and then choose one that will especially work for my essay."

"Here's how I might try these phrases with my essay that has the thesis 'My father's been my most important teacher.' First, I'll reread these suggestions, trying each one to see if it helps my essay get started well."

Looking at the list, I read the first item aloud. "'A story about one person needing the information this essay will convey . . .' Hmm . . . Who'll *need* to know that my father is my most important teacher? That's a big question, now that I think about it. Who *will* want to read this essay? Maybe my father? Or people who want to know him? Or parents who need to realize they could be the important teachers for their children? Let me keep that last audience in mind, and I'll try telling a story about one person who needs to know that."

> A friend of mine is expecting her first child soon, and she is already worrying about the schools that her child will attend. I tell her not to worry; what she needs to know is that she and her husband will be her child's most important teachers.

"I have to get to my thesis now," I said, so next I said:

> My father has been my most important teacher, teaching me to regard my job as a hobby, to love writing, and to believe that one person can make a difference.

"Let me go back to the list. I'll see if this next one could work: 'I used to think . . . but now I realize . . .' Let's see. I don't want to say, 'I used to think my father wasn't a good teacher' because that's not true. How about this:"

> I used to think that the teachers my children have in school would make or break them. I'd worry frantically if one of them had a teacher who wasn't superb. But I've come to realize that the teachers who matter most aren't always the official ones we have in school. In my life, my father was my most important teacher. He taught me . . .

"That one works too, doesn't it? It's totally different, but it still sets up my essay for my audience."

ACTIVE ENGAGEMENT
Ask students to try some of the introductory phrases to frame their own essays.

"Right now, would you work with your partner to see if one of these starting phrases might work for your essay? Partner 1, would you talk with partner 2 first? Does partner 1 want to use a lead that shows that this essay is the answer to someone's concerns? If so, try the first lead idea. Talk about who the reader is and how this essay could fit with the reader's questions and concerns. It might be that partner 1 wants to emphasize that this thesis is surprising, in which case both of you could talk about what the surprising aspect of it is and draw from the second batch of lead ideas."

LINK
Restate the teaching point. Remind students that writers use introductions and conclusions to help readers grasp the importance of the essay's thesis.

"So writers, I know that today many of you will be sifting through your folders, lining up the materials, taping them in or revising them as needed to finalize your supporting paragraphs, and then connecting those materials into one draft. Once you have done that (today and whenever you write an essay), write a few possible introductions and a few possible conclusions. Then choose the ones that best make your case that your thesis is important and should be listened to."

As you can see, the metaphor I mentioned in passing about "trying these on for size" is an apt one. That is exactly what this process feels like to me. You could decide to highlight this trying-on aspect at greater length.

I don't try out every single possible way to start an essay, because by now children should grasp my point—and be eager to try this themselves.

You could instead ask kids to take the third option on the chart and try it on for size, using my essay as the exercise text. "Would you and your partner help me consider whether the third suggestion on our chart might work for my essay," you could say. Instead, I ask children to try these leads out with their own essays. I know the latter is more supportive of children's work on this day; the former makes it more likely that children will learn from today's lesson in ways they can transfer to other texts and use with independence. For this class at this time, I am focused more on being sure all of them can get the job done in a timely manner and less on making sure they take these lessons home for use throughout their lives. Thus, my choice.

Whenever I link the minilesson, I try to make sure that the students understand that their work for the day is not just the work of the minilesson. Notice that I said they are drafting and trying out introductions and conclusions. If the minilesson alone is the work for the day, then this session becomes an activity instead of a workshop. Workshop teaching means that there is always something to work on.

WRITING AND CONFERRING

Turning Scraps of Paper into an Outline

You will probably find a small group of writers who are having trouble turning their materials into a draft, even when those materials are already lined up, revised, and ready to go and even though you've coached them through this process before. When I encountered this situation I handled it like this: "Writers, would all of you gather in a circle around Diego and me because I'm going to show you how Diego goes from having all these bits and pieces to having a whole rough draft of an essay."

"You'll notice that Diego has a stack of blank notebook paper and scissors and tape. Now watch." Turning to Diego, I said, "I'll coach you, telling you what I'd probably do to make an essay, and then you do it while all of us watch and learn, okay?"

"First, Diego, I'd look over your folders, your topic sentences, and the way you plan to organize the material for each one, and decide whether each folder will be one long paragraph or several different ones. If you are organizing it by saying one group first and one group second, you will probably need two paragraphs, right?" Diego had organized the information inside each folder, and showed which bits were going to be one paragraph and which the second.

"Next, I'd decide the sequence of your topic sentences. Does one somehow seem like it belongs earlier or later? If you have no other way to sequence them, put your most convincing argument last," I said, and Diego shuffled through his folders, rearranging them so his most important idea was last.

"Now take your first folder and your first sheet of notebook paper. Copy your topic sentence onto the first line of the notebook paper. It will be the start of a paragraph, so indent." Diego did this, copying "Friendship dies when there's new friends" onto the top of his paper.

MID-WORKSHOP TEACHING POINT | ***Revising Introductions*** "Writers, listen to the three different drafts Mimi has written of her introduction. You'll see she's taken ideas from our chart but switched them around so they work for her thesis, which is "School is important because you learn to work with people who are different from you, you make friends who help you feel less alone, and you learn skills that will be important for life."

"These are her first drafts of an introduction."

1. Recently I have known people to think that school is just not important and a waste of time. But I think differently. I think that school is as valuable as gold.

2. Other people have a theory that school isn't important. But lately, I couldn't disagree more. I think school is important.

3. When people talk about wishing to miss school, I just don't understand it. I think it is wrong. They should find school extremely important.

"I hope hearing what Mimi has done helps you with the work you are doing with your introduction. You can try making a list of possibilities like she did!"

"Now you need to place the bits you'll use in the order you decided. So spread the contents of this folder out in front of you, and move the bits around until they are lined up the way you've planned for them to go. I see you put numbers, right? That's a great idea." Diego did this. "Now, tell us which kind of order you have planned for this, Diego. Okay, chronological, great. So now, Diego, talk us through how this essay will go, and look at your bits as you talk to us, saying the words you will actually write. You'll be using the transition words that go with chronological essays, right? Like first and then and next? Okay, talk it through for us." *[Fig. XVI-1]*

> Friendship dies when there's new friends. When I was a friend with James when I was in first grade, but when new people came we started giving up our friendship for others. Two months past and before you knew it, he and I didn't say a word to each other and played more with others.

"Wow, you can put that down on paper just the way you told it, can't you? If you like the way you've written your entries, you can tape them in sequence onto your notebook paper with your transition words written in between. If you don't like the way you've written them, you can revise them, writing them better."

"I bet you can figure out how to keep going from here," I said, and Diego nodded and set to work with tape and scissors. Turning to the rest of the group, I said, "When you have sorted through your folders, you'll want to assemble a first draft of your essay just like Diego has done, revising as you go to make the pieces fit."

While I was working with that small group, others in the class had relied on the teaching of the minilesson to draft introductions and conclusions. *[Figs. XVI-2, XVI-3, XVI-4, XVI-5, and XVI-6]*

Sophie's introductions:

> **Times with my Great Grandmother Evelyne are special to me!**
>
> Times with her are special because, I understood her, I could tell her anything and I feel happy when I see her.
>
> Do you have a great Grandma? I do, most people don't, if you do you're really lucky. I know I'm lucky because I have one.
> Some people think that your great grandmother is just another person, but I know that's not true. Having a great grandmother is very special, this is how!

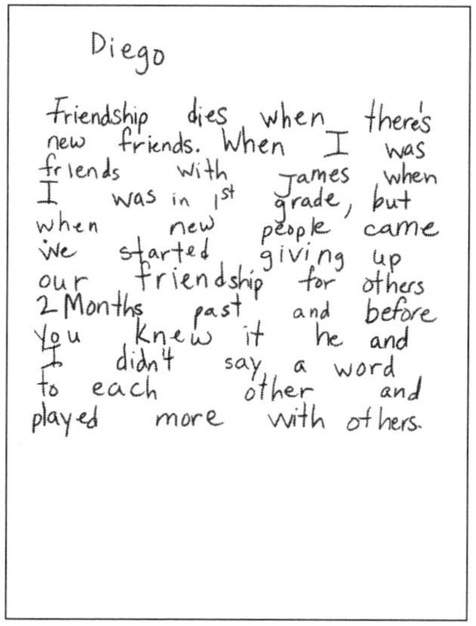

Fig. XVI-1 Diego's entry

Fig. XVI-2 Sophie's introductions

Olivia's introductions:

Sometimes I hurt peoples feelings

Sometimes I hurt people's feelings to get back at them, to fit in, and when I am having a hard time.

Do you get mad and call somebody names and hurt their feelings? I sometimes hurt peoples feelings. I hurt people's feelings to get back at them, fit in, and when I am having a hard time.

Some people think I am always nice to my younger siblings or friends, but really I get mad at my siblings almost every day and sometimes I hurt people's feelings. Sometimes I hurt people's feelings to get back at them, to fit in, and when I am having a hard time.

Some people think it is realistic that friends and siblings and some don't. But I've had experiences where I tease and hurt my friends' and siblings' feelings. Sometimes I hurt people's feelings to get back at them, fit in, and when I am having a hard time.

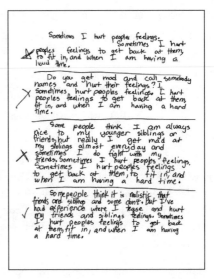

Fig. XVI-3 Olivia's introductions

Olivia's conclusions:

Endings

What I've realized now is when you are mad you say words you don't mean to say. My dad said when you hurt people's feelings you are just hurting your own feelings.

My Dad said, "When you hurt people's feelings you are just hurting your own feelings." This made me realize when I was hurting people's feelings I was really hurting my own feelings.

A few nights ago my dad told me "When you hurt people's feelings you are just hurting your own feelings. That made me realize that when I hurt people's feelings I feel hurt too. Also that I don't want to be the person who hurts people's feelings.

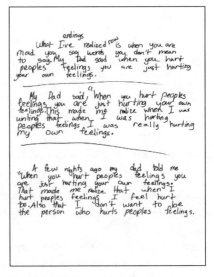

Fig. XVI-4 Olivia's conclusions

Rie's introductions:

Not everyone fears making mistakes. Many famous inventors, authors, statesman, etc. have expressed a positive view toward mistakes. For instance, Henry Kaiser said, "Problems are opportunities in work clothes."

Albert Einstein said, "In the middle of difficulty lies opportunity." Katherine Graham offered a creative view by saying, " A mistake is simply another way of doing things."

And Ralph Waldo Emerson reminded us that "Our greatest glory is not in never failing but in rising up every time we fail."

quotes

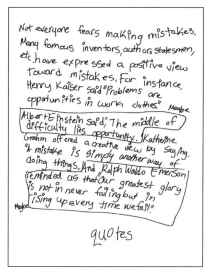

Fig. XVI-5 Rie's introductions

Rie's conclusions:

Ending

As I was writing this I realized that making a mistake wasn't a big deal.

I hope to keep on skating even if I fall. I hope that if people are laughing not to hear them.

I hope that if I make a mistake I just shrug my shoulders and I'll just laugh at myself.

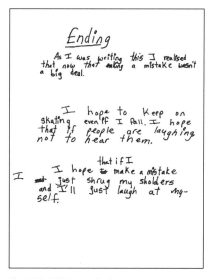

Fig. XVI-6 Rie's conclusions

SHARE

Illustrating a Thesis with a Mini-Story

Explain that essayists sometimes use a mini-story to show, not tell, their thesis.

"Writers, many of you worked on using phrases to help you convey your message in the introduction and conclusion of your essay. However, some writers do this differently. Some writers tell a little narrative, a little story to show their thesis in their introduction. It is usually a little snapshot that gives the reader a clue about the thesis for the essay. Two writers we know tried this and I wanted to share with you what they did."

Share the introductions of two students who illustrated their theses with stories.

"Here's Zoe's introduction." *[Fig. XVI-7]*

> Get down lower! That's not a side split! You're a yellow belt, you should know better!" My sensei (teacher) was yelling at me again! I was as low as I could get, practically touching the floor, yet he was still demanding perfection. He was going around barking orders. He always finds something wrong with what I am doing. <u>Karate is so demanding!</u>

"Did you notice that Zoe told a little story about karate showing us, her readers, her thesis? From her story we get the idea that karate is a lot of hard work and that much is demanded of her."

"Now listen to Yashoda's introduction."

> When I first came to the orphanage I didn't know anyone there. I was as scared as a mouse running from the cat. When I first saw them they all looked mean. I felt lonely. In a few days things started to change. Vinita and I became friends. Everyday we played together. We took turns being a leader of little kids. When we went to sleep Vinita told me stories about her life, and she slept beside me every night. <u>Vinita is such a good friend because she cares for me.</u>

In many ways, using a mini-story in the introduction, using a story to explain and support the thesis, is exactly what children did earlier in their body paragraphs. The only difference is that this mini-story illustrates the overarching topic of the essay, not just one part of the evidence. You'll have to decide if this bit of information would help your students understand this teaching point, or if it would confuse them.

> Zoe
>
> * "Get down lower! That's not a side split! You're a yellow belt! You should know better!" My sensei (teacher) was yelling at me again! I was as low as I could get practicly touching the floor, yet he still was demanding perfection. He was going around barking orders. My teacher always finds something wrong with what I'm doing. That is how karate is so demanding.

Fig. XVI-7 Zoe's introduction

Ask students to discuss how a story might illustrate the thesis of their essay.

"Can you take a moment right now and think about your thesis? Could your thesis be revealed through a snapshot story? When you are ready, turn and tell your partner a little story that could illustrate your thesis."

"Essayists, can I have your attention please? I want to compliment you on how thoughtful you were about constructing your stories to illustrate your introductions! You are thinking hard and not giving up! You can keep thinking about this in the back of your mind as we go on to other work. Sometimes the best ideas come when we think we are thinking about something else."

HOMEWORK *Reading Essay Drafts Critically* For homework tonight, I'm going to ask you to practice being a reader of essay drafts. I've made copies of the work a student in my class last year wrote. Pretend this is your essay and ask, "Is this writer's support material really aligned to her claim?" If it isn't, would you see if you could help the writer out by either revising the claim (the idea) the writer is advancing, or by revising the support material (you may need to pretend to be an expert on the topic)?

Shanice's thesis is, "I'm proud of my cat." One of her folders says, "I'm proud of my cat because she just had kittens." Tonight, read this entry and think, "Does this support Shanice's claim?" and fix it if it doesn't.

> For example one morning I woke up to a screaming noise. It was the sound of a baby kitten. I looked under my bed. My cat was giving birth. Later on I found out there was 4 baby kittens and we were giving them away. We were only keeping the mother and a brown kitten.

If your students have already worked through this unit in previous years and you'd like to teach a variation...you could teach that another technique writers use to introduce an essay is to quote a published author or a famous person. You can find many examples in this book; I often introduce a new idea by quoting another author. In the Tailor Your Teaching segment for Session XII, I wrote:

> William Zinsser, author of *On Writing Well*, suggests that surprise is important in writing, and I think he is right. Jean Fritz, the author of many history books, seems to agree. She writes about the importance of surprising details: "As human beings, we thrive on astonishment. Whatever is unknown quickens us, delivers us from ourselves, impels us to investigate."

Using the words of these two master writers helped me introduce my idea. This is something that writers do; we find other people to help us describe what we are thinking.

Another way to teach this minilesson would be to ask students to collect introductions and conclusions from published essays or from essays other students have written. Remind them how to study a mentor's writing techniques by asking, 'What has this author done that I could try?' Then invite your students to "have a go" and try the technique themselves.

COLLABORATING WITH COLLEAGUES

As you near the end of this first unit focused on expository writing, you and your colleagues may want to get together to discuss and plan how the momentum of this unit can carry you and your students toward related goals.

You might want to consider planning several days in a row to coach kids in how to write a compressed version of an essay for timed testing situations. You and your colleagues can study the past tests used in your region to determine the specifics required of essay answers. How long will children have to write, and precisely how are they expected to structure their answers? Whatever the answers to these questions, the children will undoubtedly be required to have a thesis, topic sentences and supporting paragraphs, and introductions and conclusions to their essays. With practice, children can complete an essay test using an abridged version of the writing process they've experienced in this unit, drawing on all they've learned this month, and create structured, thoughtful essays that offer opinions and provide evidence to support them. You and your colleagues can determine how best to modify the writing process to fit the demands of the tests.

Another unit extension you and your colleagues could plan together could be about listening to and/or taking notes on expository texts. Since children are fresh from creating essays and thinking about their basic components and structures, this is an opportune moment to help them listen for and read for those same structures in the nonfiction texts they encounter in life. Where is the thesis? Where are the subordinate topic sentences? What is the evidence or examples? This mental checklist can help students know which parts of what they see or hear are worth remembering or writing down. We all know that we can't take notes on everything we read, and we can't remember everything we hear. Having a structure gives us a way to make sense of the world and make thoughtful choices about the relative importance of the information we take in. It also gives us a structure on which to hang the information we take in; then, looking at the whole, we can see where the gaps are and where the information is solid. That knowledge of the essay structure gives us, as listeners or readers, a way to judge and critique texts.

CELEBRATING JOURNEYS OF THOUGHT

IN THIS SESSION, STUDENTS WILL
SHARE THE PERSONAL DISCOVERIES
THEY'VE MADE IN THIS UNIT AS THEY
CELEBRATE WITH FAMILY AND
FRIENDS. THEY WILL NOT ONLY
CELEBRATE THEIR PUBLISHED ESSAYS,
THEY WILL ALSO CELEBRATE THE
WRITING THAT LED TO THEIR ESSAYS
AND THE WAYS THIS WRITING HELPED
THEM DISCOVER IDEAS ABOUT
THEMSELVES AND THE WORLD.

GETTING READY

- Parents or other adults previously invited
- Students' writing neatly organized on tables
- Three students prepared to read during whole-class celebration
- Refreshments
- See CD-ROM for resources

During this celebration, children (and those who care for them) will celebrate not only the essays that children have written, but also the insights they've developed about themselves, their subjects, and writing itself.

Each child's work represents that child's journey of discovery, and on this occasion, these will all be proudly displayed and mined for significance.

After children participate in the rituals that will by now have become familiar, the class will disperse into corners of the room for small group sharing. Then parents, other visitors, and half the class will be invited to visit the other half the class at stations where the children will sit, with their work displayed in front of them. Visitors can browse through the child's notebook, folder, rough draft and final essay, and they'll find that throughout it, the writer will have left sticky notes saying, "Ask me." If the viewer wishes, she can point to one of those notes and say, "Can you tell me about this part?"

By this time in the year, there will be a great deal to celebrate in your class. Children will, indeed, have used writing to come to new insights about themselves. In this world of ours, where the commercialized culture of marketing and advertising spews out messages such as, "You must buy this, own this, eat this, wear this or your life will be miserable," the writing workshop conveys an entirely different message. The workshop says, "You and I can take the details of our lives and we can make something of them." The writing workshop says, "Significance and meaning aren't bought or even found, they are made, and each one of us has the capacity to take the truth of our lives and to come to new understandings, new levels of thinking about the life that we lead."

Today, we celebrate the fact that writing gives us new eyes to see and understand ourselves. We also celebrate that the youngsters in this community have grown taller as writers. Their texts are longer. Their notebooks are fuller. Their voices are stronger. Their sense of themselves and of each other as writers is more buoyant.

If we, grown-ups, can see our children's growth and help them to see it as well, they'll flourish, sprouting with new inches of power, confidence, sensitivity, zeal. So today, teaching will have a lot to do with finding a moment to look a child in the eyes, to help a child feel seen and celebrated.

CELEBRATION

Welcome visitors to the classroom. Explain how the celebration will go. In this case, again, a few children read to the entire class, and then everyone disperses to small groups for sharing.

"Welcome to this incredible occasion. Today we want to talk with you about life-journeys. When my children were young—in second and fourth grade—we took a trip to a faraway place, where we lived in a little village that was utterly different than our home town. Last summer, just before he headed off to college, my son, Miles, gathered all the photos we'd ever taken and constructed five photo albums that resurrected our life together. We were all amazed to see that there were far more photographs of that one journey than of anything else. "What if we'd never taken that journey—how much we would have lost!" I thought.

"Journeys matter. They create memories… they recreate those of us who are travelers. And the journeys that matter most may not be the ones that take us to far away places, but instead, the ones that take us to new understandings. They are journeys of thought –journeys that help us understand our own lives in a new way."

"I'm telling you this because the writers in this classroom and their teacher and I have all been on a journey together, and we have also taken a journey alone, inside our own notebooks and drafts. Today's celebration is like the class photo album, showcasing turning points from all of our journeys."

Explain that in this celebration, the readings will be in a symphony, with one person acting as conductor, using a baton to indicate the child who will read next, next, next. Voices will tumble, one against the next, with no applause or other sound in the interim.

"First, we're going to listen to three writers, as usual, reading to the entire assembly. Our reading today will be what we call a symphony. Teacher Mary Chiarella will be the conductor for these readers who will read to the whole class, then each one of those readers will be the conductor for a smaller circle of readers. One reader after another will "play his or her instrument," (you'll see what I mean) and all of us need to be as quiet as if we were at a concert. When every voice has been heard, then each circle needs to talk quietly until the others are done as well."

COACHING

One of the challenges in teaching writing is that there are many ways in which this is a cyclical curriculum. This is your third celebration, and there will be many others. So it is a challenge to find ways to keep each celebration a little bit new. There is nothing sacrosanct about the metaphor of a journey. Find your own ways to put a new spin on each Author Celebration!

The word essay means to wander, and many people define essays as trails of thought. So, it seems appropriate to celebrate, at this final moment, the new realizations children have come to about themselves as they've written throughout this unit. This celebration also gives parents a chance to notice and talk about the changes they have seen in their children as writers.

You'll notice that there is a lot of continuity between this Author Celebration and the others, and there is also some novelty. The mix is deliberate. I think people welcome a sense of continuity in the rituals of our lives. It means a lot to me that every single Christmas since I was a baby, my whole family spends Christmas Eve caroling through our neighborhood. I don't want to come up with a totally new way to spend Christmas Eves. In the same way, your children will welcome the way in which Author Celebrations are traditional events, proceeding in ways that people come to anticipate. Also, of course, there are practical advantages to Author Celebrations having a predictable structure. Parents come to understand how these events go, and then all of us can spent much less time and thought on the logistical details of the occasion (which will never be small when such a large group of people gather), and we can give more of our time and attention to the writers—to their writing and to our efforts to help them feel deeply and truly heard.

Signal for the symphony at the front of the class to begin. When they have finished help everyone move to their small groups for the rest of the symphonies.

Three writers took their places in a line of chairs, and with a pencil/baton, Mary signaled to the third child in the line. LaKeya picked up her essay and read: *[Figs. XVII-1, XVII-2, XVII-3, and XVII-4]*

We often talk about how these celebrations offer a time for offering support and affirmation for our children's writing lives. Truthfully, these celebrations can be times for support and affirmation for our teaching lives as well! Welcome these moments. We all need them in our lives.

It's Hard Being a Girl
LaKeya
It's hard being a girl. Being a girl is hard because we have mixed and sensitive feelings, we go through a lot of changes, and we worry how we look.

It's hard being a girl because we have mixed and sensitive feelings. I can be happy then in a minute I am mad. We have mood swings. For example, one time I told my sister to sing and then I told her to stop because she was making me mad. I get angry very easily. If someone hits me I will get mad and cry at the same time. One more example, I could seem very sweet but inside I hold a lot of anger from my mother's evil boyfriend. If I get what I want, I am sweet. When I am in mixed company, I am lala. Being a girl sometimes we also have surprising feelings. For example, when some one hits me I am supposed to be mad but instead I am a pool of sadness. But when I am supposed to be sad, I am happy instead. One day I will never forget is

Fig. XVII-1 LaKeya's final draft

December 16, 2003. I was getting ready to go to after school when my Uncle Duncan said we had to leave. I didn't want to leave. I felt irritated that my Uncle Duncan wanted to take me away. But when we got in front of our house, Daddy came out of his car crying. Then I wasn't irritated. I was puzzled. I stared crying because he was crying. He usually was strong about everything, Daddy sat us down and said, "Keya, Cha-cha, Grandma – our beloved grandma – is gone. She pooped the daisies. She's dead." I regretted whatever I ever said to her. I wanted to have her come back to life and see me grow up, be a writer, go to college and be there for my sweet sixteen. I would give my lungs and die then live and never see her again. That day, I had mixed feelings.

It's also hard being a girl because we go through changes. For example, our rear ends get bigger. I woke up one morning and saw that I was falling backwards. Another change is our thighs get fatter. That's hard because we get teased about them. One time at school the

Fig. XVII-2 LaKeya's final draft, page 2

class was at recess and then they were all around me. They said, "Hey fatty pants, watch you doing ham lets?" and some kids said "turkey legs." We also crave foods. One time I was not hungry but then I wanted a hamburger. We also get cramps. One time I had really really bad cramps and then I could not move. And I can smell good one moment and then the next moment my armpits stink. Another change is we act grown. One time I had a grown face on and I did not realize that. I had a grown face on and my mother said "Wipe that grown smile off your face, La'Keya!"

It's also hard being a girl because we worry how we look. I can not care how I look and then in a moment I can look in the mirror every minute. One reason is that we have to use so many face and hair products. For example, we use creams, facials, and face soaps to help our face be very radiant. One morning I just woke up and my stepfather said, "Holy Moly, your face is ashy!" I raced to

Fig. XVII-3 LaKeya's final draft, page 3

the bathroom and looked at the mirror and saw that my face was cracked all over my forehead, cheeks, and chin. By the time it was getting dark, he came home with sample moisturizers. Once he showed me that I realized I needed to put it on. It's hard because we don't care, but once we get an opinion, we worry. We also worry about how our hair looks. One time I woke up in my father's house and I saw my hair and screamed. I looked so awful. I went into the bathroom and didn't come out for half of an hour. Another example, is we are always into how we look when we were close. For example, we say this, "is this too big? This is to loose. Help me out."

Being a girl is hard. It's hard to have all these sensitive and mixed feelings, and we go through so many changes, and we worry about how you look. It's confusing and sometimes it doesn't feel good. I know this because I'm a girl.

Fig. XVII-4 LaKeya's final draft, page 4

Then William picked up his essay and read: *[Figs. XVII-5, XVII-6, XVII-7, and XVII-8]*

Love Can Build a House That Stands Forever

My mom is the best mom a kid could ever have. Believe it or not she cleans after she comes from work. She wakes up early every day and she also goes to work even when she is sick. She does all of these things because she loves the whole family.

The first way, my mom works hard for the family by cleaning after work.

One day when my mom came from work she couldn't believe it. The house was so dirty. There was dust all over the place! "What happened?!" she asked. Nobody answered. I couldn't believe it. After she came from work tired, she took the mop and broom and started cleaning. First she cleaned the kitchen. There were stains on the oven. The dishes were all dirty too. When she finished she was exhausted. I always thank her for what she does for the family.

She cleans the kitchen. She wants everything to be in order for dinner.

She cleans the bathroom. She knows I could do it but she does it anyway.

She cleans the bathroom. She knows it's nasty but she does it without complaints.

Not only does my mom work hard for the family by cleaning after work, but by waking up early every day. When I'm sleeping I can hear the creaking sound of the door of my bedroom. I could tell that she was getting my clothes. When I wake up she always has my clothes hanging from the chairs. When I put them on they fit just right and they look pretty too. If my mom wasn't beside me I wouldn't know what to do and I would be so disappointed.

She wakes up early every day to put my clothes in order. Depending on what activity I have.

She wakes up early every day to check my book bag in case I forgot a book or a sheet.

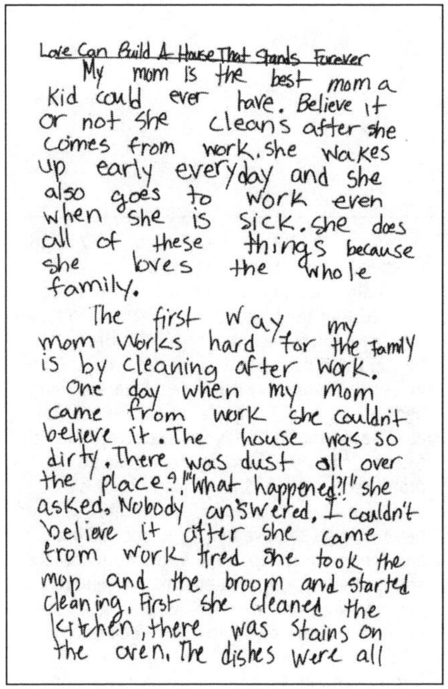
Love Can Build A House That Stands Forever
My mom is the best mom a Kid could ever have. Believe it or not She cleans after she comes from work. She wakes up early everyday and she also goes to work even when she is sick. She does all of these things because she loves the whole family.
The first way, my mom works hard for the family is by cleaning after work.
One day when my mom came from work she couldn't believe it. The house was so dirty. There was dust all over the place?! "What happened?!" she asked. Nobody answered. I couldn't believe it after she came from work tired she took the mop and the broom and started cleaning. First she cleaned the kitchen, there was stains on the oven. The dishes were all

Fig. XVII-5 William's final draft

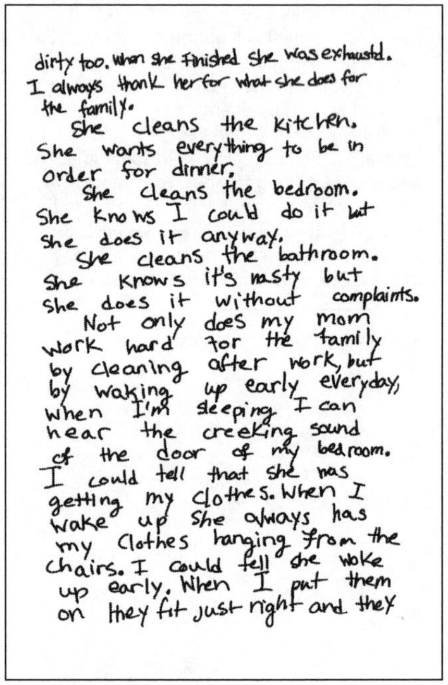
dirty too. When she finished she was exhausted. I always thank her for what she does for the family.
She cleans the kitchen. She wants everything to be in order for dinner.
She cleans the bedroom. She knows I could do it but she does it anyway.
She cleans the bathroom. She knows it's nasty but she does it without complaints.
Not only does my mom work hard for the family by cleaning after work, but by waking up early everyday, when I'm sleeping I can hear the creeking sound of the door of my bedroom. I could tell that she was getting my clothes. When I wake up she always has my clothes hanging from the chairs. I could tell she woke up early. When I put them on they fit just right and they

Fig. XVII-6 William's final draft, page 2

She wakes up early every day to see what is the temperature to see if I need a coat.

Perhaps the most important way why my mom works hard for the family is by never missing a day of work even when she is sick.

One morning my mom told me that she was sick. She sneezed. She coughed. She even wasted a pack of tissues. When she went to her job, that exact moment I felt that my mom could do anything. When she left I was worried. She left in an awful condition. When she got home she felt better.

"Hey, Mom, are you OK?" I said.

"I've never felt better" she said.

I was so relieved.

When she is sick she can still give me breakfast. She tries her best to give me something simply to eat.

When she is sick she can still put my clothes in order. She knows I put on whatever she gives me.

When she is sick she can still help me with my homework. When I'm stuck she tries her best to help me.

What I've realized is that my mom does all of this because she loves the family. She wants the family to be together and have what we need. This past week I was singing up on stage a song titled "We Will Be a Shelter For Each Other." There's a line that says "Love can build a house that stands forever." I realized that those words are how I feel about my mom. It's my mom that makes the family so strong.

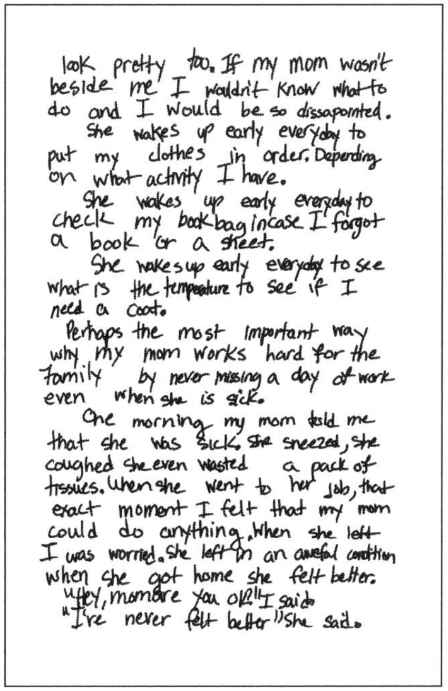

Fig. XVII-7 William's final draft, page 3

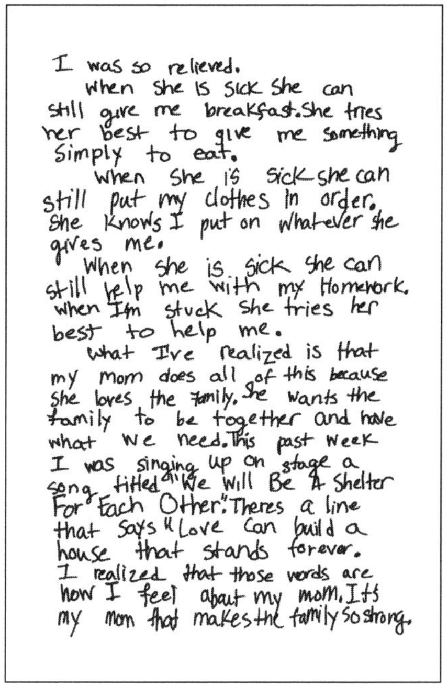

Fig. XVII-8 William's final draft, page 4

And finally, Fatmire read a portion of her
final draft: [Figs. XVII-9–XVII-13]

Love Is Missing Someone When He's Away.

Everyone has someone who is special to them.
Maybe its their best friends, their sisters or
brothers. But to me that someone is my dad
because he is so close to me My dad goes on
trips a lot. I miss my dad when he is away
because we have so much fun together He
takes care of me when I am sick and
because when I am afraid he makes me
safe.

One reason why I miss my dad is because we
had so much fun together.

During the weekend we enjoy jogging
together. We run around lakes.

Afterschool we enjoy sitting at the computer.
We play all these different kind of games.

At midnight we enjoy sitting on the sofa. We
tell stories and jokes.

But when he's not around I don't jog with
anyone, I don't sit down with anybody and I
don't stay at midnight and talk with anyone.

An example of this is when my dad went on a
trip. I was lonley sitting by myself. My sister
was doing homework and my mom was busy
doing work. I was waiting to play with some
body.

"Lena, could you play with me" I asked her.

"I can't" she said

But all of a sudden the doorbell
ring-Ring-Ring-Ring' "Hello?" I asked.

"Hello" a guy said back.

"Daddy's coming" I yelled so that
my family could hear me.

I buzzed him in. I heard footsteps.

"Daddy" I yell.

"I love you" I said to him. " Me too"
he said back.

My dad and I share good times
together, but when he is away,
I feel lonely and have no one to
play with.

Fig. XVII-9 Fatmire's final draft

Fig. XVII-10 Fatmire's final draft, page 2

Fig. XVII-11 Fatmire's final draft, page 3

Fig. XVII-12 Fatmire's final draft, page 4

Fig. XVII-13 Fatmire's final draft, page 5

After the three readers had produced their symphony, writers dispersed to smaller circles of sharing, and the original readers acted as conductors while each group produced another symphony of their own. Some of the readers read only one selected passage from their essays, leaving lots of time for a museum of sharing afterwards.

When the symphonies are finished, help children take their places in the museum display of their writing work. Coach the visitors in listening to the children.

As half the children—two of the circles—assumed their places in museum booths, with each child pulling out the stack containing the child's notebook, files, drafts and final draft, each with a few sticky-notes places here or there saying, 'Ask me' I asked the grown-up visitors to cluster around me for a moment. "Parents," I said. "Last time, you will remember that we wrote notes to the writers, giving them some feedback on their writing. Today, I am going to suggest that we don't write notes, but that we do give ourselves what the children and I call 'a self-assignment' to make a real connection with the writers. Would you try to speak to each of these writers in a way that help him or her feel as if someone has really truly listened? Every one of us knows that in life, there are not many people who really listen, and who really help us feel listened to. Let's be those people to this group of youngsters."

Then parents, along with the half the class not in stations, functioned as viewers at the museum. Drawing a chair alongside one writer, the parent would look over the child's work, dipping in to read parts of it. "Can you tell me what you did right here?" the parent would ask, gesturing to a sticky-note. At some point, I reminded parents to limit their visits to any one station to just a few minutes so they could reach several children, and then, of course, we switched so that the children who had not yet had a chance to showcase their work were able to do so. *[Figs. XVII-14, XVII-15, and XVII-16]*

My Father is My Worst Enemy

Everyone deserves a good father . Everywhere I go I see kids spending time with their fathers, but not me. My father is my worst enemy. For example, he picks his wife over me, he makes me feel like a small kid next to big foot, and he made me into a person I don't want to be.

My father is my worst enemy because he picks my stepmother over me. He lets his wife dominate him like a toy. For example, one day I was supposed to go to their house to sleep over. I was ready to go when I get a call from my father. He said " Sorry, but I can't pick you up because my wife is in the hospital." "I hope she feels better," that's what I said. Then a short while later my mom calls me and says my father was lying . My stepmother wasn't in the hospital. My stepmother just didn't want me to come. It wasn't a

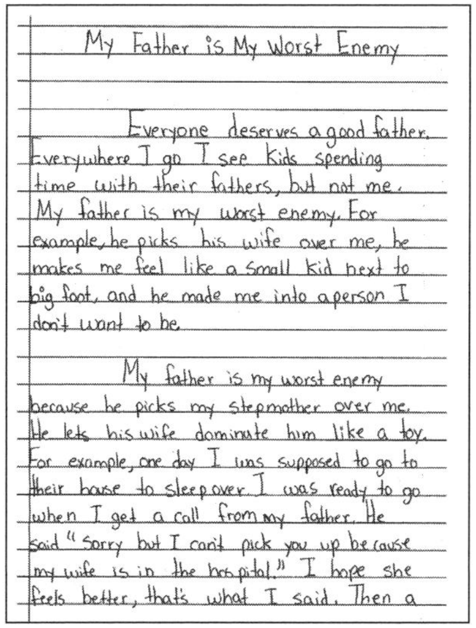

We often think about celebrations as a time for affirming children and their writing, but the truth is that these are also times for affirming ourselves and our teaching.

Fig. XVII-14 Tanya's final draft, page 1

real shock because my father has stood me up several times. I was so angry but the worst part is he couldn't tell me the truth. Another time is when I was play fighting with my step brother because he wanted me to. Then I scratched him by mistake on his neck. He told his mom that I scratched him on purpose. My stepmother came into the room and started yelling at me. My dad was right beside me and didn't even try to defend me. I got so mad I responded and said " he hit me too."

My father is my worst enemy. He makes me feel like a small kid next to big foot. I feel useless like when I was small or a younger

child. I used to wait for my father to call me. Wishing the phone would ring, for him to take me to the movies or the park. He always told me lies and excuses. I can't believe he never ran out of what to say. Every time he let me down I'd get very upset. Even though I knew he would do it again it still would always hurt.

My father is my worst enemy. He made me into a person that I don't want to be. He made me angry and mean. I remember I used to be happy, friendly, and my friends used to call me "peppy". I wish I could tell him how much he hurt me and that he made me into a person I don't wont to be. Like I used to be confident, now I'm insecure and can't make decisions on my own.

My father can be the worst father in the world but I bet there are worse. There's nothing I can do to change it, what's done is done. He will always be my dad even if I don't want him to. I guess I'll have to deal with it.

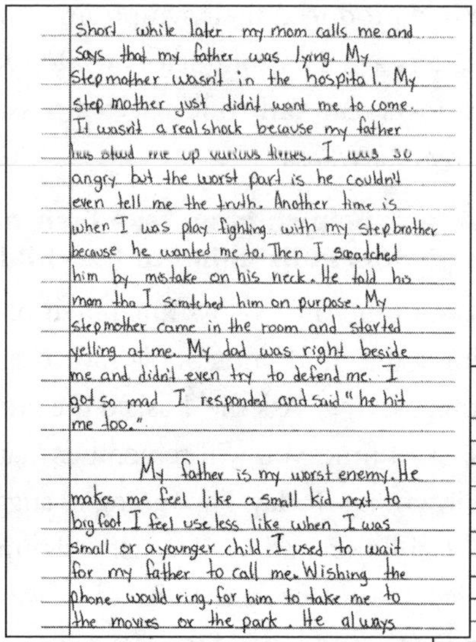

Fig. XVII-15 Tanya's final draft, page 2

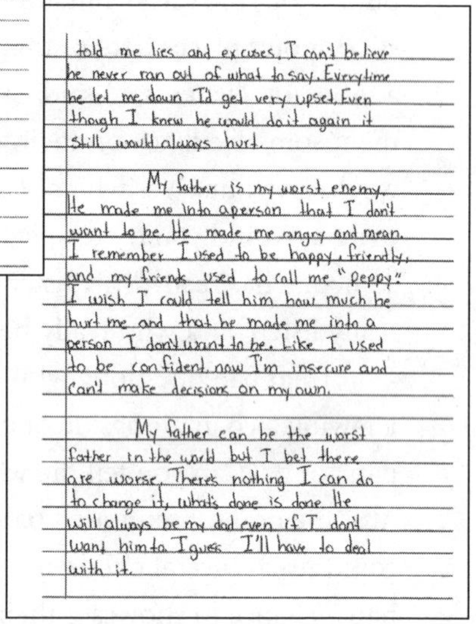

Fig. XVII-16 Tanya's final draft, page 3

At one point, Mary watched as James' father read his son's essay about how his play with his Dad has changed over the years. "When I was little, I played in the park without my dad. I played on the jungle gym while my dad sat reading a book. But now when I go to the park with my Dad, we have baseball catches together. We do funny catches and laugh together. I look back at the jungle gum and I think how things have changed."

James' father put the essay down and said to his son, "I'm proud you wrote about our relationship changing. It has gotten stronger. I think it is because you are growing up and changing—that's making the bond stronger."

Just before the celebration ended, William's mom—the mother whose love was celebrated in the opening reading about 'Love Can Build a House' whispered, "My son is becoming more compassionate. He thanks me and helps me more than he's ever done. I think writing has changed him!"

I think so too.

You'll need to circle among the groups unless you have other adults with you who can help. Folks will need just a bit of shepherding at the start of each circle of sharing. Then, once the readings have begun, you will want to model what it means to listen raptly, intensely.

LUCY CALKINS ✦ M. COLLEEN CRUZ

WRITING FICTION: BIG DREAMS, TALL AMBITIONS

This book is dedicated to Beth Neville.

FirstHand
An imprint of Heinemann
A division of Reed Elsevier Inc.
361 Hanover Street
Portsmouth, NH 03801-3912
www.heinemann.com

Offices and agents throughout the world

Copyright © 2006 by Lucy Calkins and M. Colleen Cruz

All rights reserved. No part of this book may be reproduced in any form or by any electronic or mechanical means, including information storage and retrieval systems, without permission in writing from the publisher, except by a reviewer, who may quote brief passages in a review.

Photography: Peter Cunningham

Library of Congress Cataloging-in-Publication Data

CIP data on file with the Library of Congress.
ISBN 0-325-00862-0

Printed in the United States of America on acid-free paper
10 09 08 07 06 ML 1 2 3 4 5

Excerpt from *Valentine for Ernest Mann* by Naomi Shihab Nye. Copyright © 1994
Naomi Shihab Nye. Reprinted with the permission of Naomi Shihab Nye.

Excerpt from *The Stuff of Fiction* by Gerald Brace. Copyright © 1972 by Gerald
Brace. Used by permission of McIntosh & Otis.

Excerpt from *My Name is Maria Isabel* by Alma Flor Ada. Text copyright © 1993
Alma Flor Ada. Reprinted with the permission of Atheneum Books for Young
Readers, an imprint of Simon & Schuster Children's Publishing Division.

Excerpt from *Fireflies!* by Julie Brinckloe. Copyright © 1985 Julie Brinckloe.
Reprinted with the permission of Simon & Schuster Books for Young Readers,
an imprint of Simon & Schuster Children's Publishing Division.

Excerpt from *Pippi Goes On Board* by Astrid Lindgren. Copyright © 1988 by
Astrid Lindgren. Used by permission of Puffin Books, a division of Penguin
Young Readers Group, a member of Penguin Group (USA) Inc., 345 Hudson
Street, New York, New York, NY 10014. All rights reserved.

ACKNOWLEDGEMENTS

It was a great joy to work on this book alongside co-author Colleen Cruz. Colleen has taught this unit of study many times more than I, and as the author of the young adult novel Border Crossing and other novels in-progress, she has tremendous resources to draw upon. The book was truly co-authored: we passed it from one of us to the next rather like a ball, with the receiver rereading, rewriting, and then adding on….before calling, "Your turn," and then tossing it back to the other. Sometimes, as we worked on the book or worked on the ideas behind the book in the company of teachers and children, Colleen and I would find ourselves at impasses: novelists across the world write this way, but our children seem to need something else. What a great joy it was to reach these hard parts with Colleen. She is passionate about the work, utterly dedicated to children (and especially to children who need us most), and she is also game for the hard work of thinking through challenges. We both believe the book is better off because we outgrew our own best ideas many times whole in the process of writing.

Sometimes, along the way, we tossed the ball to a third person—Katherine Bomer, and we would like to thank her. Katherine is a close friend of the Project's, a very talented writer, and a teacher who rallies kids to invest themselves with heart and soul in their work. We thank Liz Philips and the students and faculty of PS 321 for being a lab for some of the earliest thinking about ways we can best teach students to write fiction. We thank the 4th grade team at Post Road School in White Plains for their assistance in experimenting with possible modifications to minilessons. We are grateful to the upper grade teachers, staff and students at PS 94, particularly Kirsten Nordstrom, for offering valuable insights. We are also appreciative of Dr. Peter McFarlane and the PS 180 community for their generous support and their willingness to pilot this work in its early stages. We thank especially: Anisha Burke, Carolyn Montalto, Rachel Nall, Amanda Pagan and Jhimy Rodriguez. In the final days, Kathy Doyle, Shannon Rigney and Julia Mooney all contributed to this project, and we thank them.

Colleen and I, together, dedicate this book to someone who is a dear friend: Beth Neville. Beth is the architect of the Project's vast, complex network. She masterminds all of the Project's functions, interlacing the entire structure in ways unfathomable to most of us. Colleen and I are grateful to her.

A note from Colleen Cruz:

As has been the case for many people, Lucy Calkins has been a huge influence on my development as a teacher of literacy. However, almost as important to me, with the completion of this book, I can now say she has influenced my writing life too. Lucy taught me so much about what it means to streamline one's thinking in some spots and flesh it out in others. She taught me the importance of how, just as good fiction builds in an arc, so too should a unit of study. I was consistently amazed at her ability to challenge my hard-won beliefs of how fiction "should" be taught, often leading me to explore unmapped terrain. I am even more appreciative of the way she consistently (and sometimes doggedly) pushed me to challenge her own latest thinking in order for us to come to a consensus. In the end, this book is a decoupage of our work together. The seamlessness of that process is completely Lucy's doing.

WRITING FICTION: BIG DREAMS, TALL AMBITIONS

Welcome to Unit 4

WRITING FICTION: BIG DREAMS, TALL AMBITIONS

About This Unit

After students spend a month writing essays, they'll be eager to return to the land of narrative writing, especially if they are finally, at long last, able to write what students want most to write: fiction. By this time, no one will be surprised that the unit begins with learning ways to live like fiction writers, seeing ideas for stories everywhere. At the start of this unit, we let students know that fiction writers get ideas for their stories by paying attention to the moments and issues of their lives. We tell children, "When I was young, I thought fiction writers looked up into the clouds and imagined make-believe stories about castles and puppy dogs. But then I grew up and learned how real fiction writers get their ideas." We let them know that Robert McCloskey got the idea for *Make Way for Ducklings* when he was stopped in Boston traffic while a line of ducks waddled across the street in front of him.

Children collect story ideas in their writer's notebooks, learning to flesh the ideas out a bit so that they contain some of the elements of an effective story. Children learn to take the tiny details and big issues of their lives and speculate on how that could become stories. They might write entries in which they both recount a bit of their lives and then speculate (in writing) on how they could turn this into a story. A child who has recently moved could make up a story about a girl who moved, only this time she could give that girl a companion—a dog? a sister?—the writer wished she'd had. Children can reread their notebooks as well as live their lives collecting possible story ideas. In these entries, children will not actually write their stories; instead they will write plans for how their stories might go.

For a few days, children will collect entries in which they explore ideas that could possibly become fiction stories. As they do so, they will profit from trying story ideas out. A great way for them to do this is by storytelling those ideas to a partner. We teach children some storytelling techniques—for example, the beginning of their stories might sound like the beginning of a famous book or a fairy tale: "Once, not long ago, a little girl named Cissy . . . ." Elevating storytelling a bit helps each youngster bring a storyteller's voice—and an aura of literary language—to his or her own story plans.

Once children have each chosen a seed idea (which will now be called their story idea), it is important for them to develop their ideas. One way fiction writers do this is to develop their main characters, perhaps in notebook entries that never appear in the final story. A fiction writer once said, "Before you can begin writing your story, you need to know your characters so well that you know exactly how much change each one has in her pocket." When children are asked to develop ideas about their characters' traits, most children immediately list external traits, "She has red hair," and so on. We encourage children to also think of a character's internal traits. What is she afraid of? What does she want? The trick is to help children create coherent characters with characteristics that fit together in a way that seems believable. When children use broad generalizations—for example, suggesting the character is a good friend—we ask them to open these terms up, to be much more specific. What are the unique ways in which this character is a good friend? After writers gather entries developing their character, they may dramatize the character, having him perform action in a scene, a fiction writer's word for a Small Moment story.

Finally, it is important to be sure that young fiction writers think especially about a character's wants and needs. Usually a storyline emerges out of the intersection of a character's motivations and the obstacles that get in her way.

As in every unit, we remind children that what they learned once through revision and editing now needs to move forward in the writing process. Not surprisingly, then, the story mountain becomes a tool not for revision but for planning. Children use story mountains to plot their story plans and to revise these, too. We teach children, for example, that sometimes what they expect will be the prelude to their story must actually become back-story so that the actual text can focus on two or three scenes.

When children begin to draft, they rely on their story mountains as road maps. Each item (each dot) on the story mountain is usually designated its own page in a story booklet, and this, plus an emphasis on using skills developed in earlier units and on storytelling rather than summarizing, makes it more likely that children's stories will sound and feel like stories. Since the stories are long, revision needs to begin early; we help students incorporate qualities of good writing as they revise the early sections of their stories. Children incorporate all they learned during the personal narrative units of study into their texts, writing with dialogue and showing rather than summarizing their character's feelings.

We help children see that these story mountains build to a high point and that their main characters struggle harder and harder toward their goals. As they sequence their story, children learn that at the top of their mountain something happens that solves (or begins to solve) the character's problem.

Although the unit is titled Writing Fiction, it is also a unit on rehearsal and revision. Capitalizing on children's zeal for fiction, this unit encourages them to do more of both than they have done before. Although we emphasize the efficiency of revising as we write, once a draft is completed we then emphasize that writers look back on the trail of a story and consider making substantial revisions. Above all, we teach writers to consider the importance of setting in a story. Earlier, when children's dialogue threatened to swamp their story-lines, we taught them to intersperse actions with dialogue, now we highlight the need to ground the entire story (not just the introduction) in a sense of place.

Then, too, children are led to rethink the evolution of their stories. Oftentimes, they approach a fiction story planning for the character to magically receive his or her fondest dream in the form of a solution that flies in out of nowhere like Superman. With help, we show children that in fiction as in life, the solutions we find are generally those that we make, and if there are magic answers to be found, they usually have been there before our eyes all along.

The Plan for the Unit

The "bends in the road" of this unit are these:

- Children collect story ideas, imagining that everyday moments in their lives and entries they gathered previously could be fleshed out to become story ideas. They also gather story ideas by thinking about the stories they wish existed in the world. They select a story idea (as opposed to a seed idea). We channel them towards writing realistic fiction involving just a few characters, and towards stories about characters who resemble the authors, at least in age.

- Once children have selected a story idea, they continue rehearsing for the story they will eventually write. They develop their protagonist, thinking about external and also internal characteristics of that person, trying to create a coherent character. Above all children think about their character's wants and struggles. They may also develop secondary characters.

- Children plot their story on a story mountain, thinking about how to focus on just two or three scenes, narrowing the plotline based on the recognition that this will be a short story not a novel, and tucking some portions of the story into back-story. They revise their plans, taking into account more information about effective stories.

- Children draft and then revise beginnings to their stories, drawing on what they learn from studying published leads.

They write their drafts in story-booklets, with one page of the booklet for each dot on the story mountain. We remind them that front-end revisions are much more efficient than rear-end revisions.

- Children think about how they'll create rising action, making the problems get worse and worse, and continue writing their stories.

- Children revise their writing in significant ways. They reread with various lenses, including looking for "cardboard characters" and thinking about ways to ground their stories in a well-developed setting. Above all, children reconsider the resolution in their stories with encouragement to find the solution within the problem, avoiding the solution that flies in from outside the story.

- Children edit with attention especially to spelling, to making writing sound powerful, and to writing with a variety of sentence types.

IN THIS SESSION, YOU WILL TEACH
STUDENTS THAT FICTION WRITERS
GET IDEAS FOR STORIES FROM DAILY
LIFE AND FROM PAST WRITING.
YOU'LL HELP THEM GET STARTED
DOING THAT.

GETTING READY

- Anecdote you can tell to describe how fiction writers get their ideas from real life

- Entries from your own writer's notebook that you can use to demonstrate thinking about potential stories

- Several entries from your notebook copied onto chart paper, so children can practice looking for stories

- Several published stories for each child. These will be referenced in Homework. See CD-ROM for suggestions.

- See CD-ROM for resources

IMAGINING STORIES FROM ORDINARY MOMENTS

In this session, you'll teach children that writers collect ideas for realistic fictional stories by mining the details of their lives and by rereading their notebooks, spinning likely entries into story ideas.

The long-awaited day has finally arrived. At long last, you'll invite your students to begin writing fiction. This is the genre that most children especially want to write, yet it is one of the more challenging genres that they will experience and you will teach.

Children are born fiction writers. From leaning against the knees of grown-ups, listening to their stories, and absorbing the rhythms of fairy tales, picture books, and novels, they have already learned about pacing and punch lines, about the humor and tragedy of story. They have soaked up the phrasing and structures of story, from the opening invocation "Once upon a time" to the classic signals that something is going to happen—"Suddenly . . . " or "One day . . . ."

In school, children beg to write stories. Sometimes, perhaps out of fear of the runaway stories that go on and on, or out of discomfort over the retold comic book story lines, we've steered them away from this genre. How much wiser to take their energy and passion for fiction, and to channel it with crystal-clear teaching!

Although your children will probably enter this unit expecting it to be altogether different from anything they've experienced, they'll come to see that there is only a thin line between personal narrative writing and realistic fiction. But don't tell them this yet. All year long, they have practiced writing small moments, or scenes; writing with dialogue and action; and crafting tension into their stories. Now they'll join the ranks of short story writers, who know that if they conceive of and revise a plot, develop characters who interact with each other, and follow those characters through trials and tribulations, they can craft short but deeply thoughtful and realistic fictional stories.

In today's minilesson, you'll invite children into the world of fiction writers, showing one way to collect ideas for fictional stories. In the process, you'll help children fall in love with stories.

MINILESSON

Imagining Stories from Ordinary Moments

CONNECTION

Tell a true story about how, during the preceding days, you've savored the children's published work and decided that they're ready for fiction.

"Writers, I took your published essays home last night and sat on my sofa reading them, one after another. One by one, the people in my house called, 'Good night,' turning off most of the lights as they headed to bed, and I sat under a pool of light, reading and enjoying. When I finally finished reading your essays, I realized you have come such a long way as writers! You are ready to write fiction."

Name your teaching point. In this case, tell students that writers get ideas for fiction by paying attention to our lives.

"Today is an important day because we're going to begin collecting ideas for fictional stories in our writer's notebooks, and I want to teach you where writers look to find those ideas. And the most important thing I can teach you is this: We get ideas for fiction, just as we get ideas for personal narratives and essays, by paying attention to the moments and issues in our own lives!"

TEACHING

With an anecdote, tell children that you've come to realize fiction writers get their ideas from real life.

"When I was a little girl, I thought fiction writers looked up into the clouds and *imagined* make-believe stories about castles and puppy dogs."

COACHING

The challenge is to say the expected—to tell children that the texts they just published are beautiful—and yet to do so in ways that are surprising and fresh enough that youngsters don't dismiss our compliments as pap. One solution is to use compelling specifics to name what works in their writing, but we can never do this for every child within the confines of a minilesson. Another solution is to situate compliments into a scene, a narrative, as I have tried to do. I could, alternatively, have described phoning my sister to read aloud bits of their essays, or pinning excerpts from their essays onto my bulletin board. Alternatively, you could use this as an opportunity for children to tell each other about their parents' responses to the essay celebration.

Usually when we tell "I used to think . . . but now I realize" stories, we are trying to persuade kids who identify with the first way of thinking to be brought along to the new thinking.

"But when I grew up, I learned how real fiction writers truly get their ideas. Did you know that E. B. White got the idea for *Charlotte's Web* by lying on a bale of hay in his barn, watching a spider spin her web? The barn animals, the pigs, and the geese were all around, and on the rafters above them all, this little spider delicately wove her tapestry. He probably wrote an entry about that moment in his writer's notebook, and then later, sitting at his desk, he reread his notebook, remembered that moment, and thought, 'I could write a story about that!'"

"Of course, when I say that writers get ideas for writing by paying attention to our own lives, I do not mean that writers just record exactly what happened and call the text fiction. When E. B. White lay on that bale of hay and watched a spider, he did not watch her spell out the words *Some Pig*, and he did not watch her save a runt pig from the butcher."

Suggest that the imagination that matters is one that allows a writer to see story ideas in the grit of everyday life.

"Fiction writers do, however, pay attention to our lives. We cup our hands around tiny true particles of our lives, and we wait. Sometimes, while we wait, the idea for a story grows. And here is my biggest lesson of all. The imagination that *really* matters to fiction writers is this. We—like E. B. White—can find significant stories in something as ordinary as an entry we've written about a spider in the rafters of our barn. We reread an entry or remember that spider—or anything else we have seen or done—and we say, 'Wait a minute. This is giving me an idea for a story . . . Maybe I could write a story about . . . .'"

There are many similar examples. Children may want to know how Patricia MacLachlan got the idea for Cassie Binegar, *the story about a little girl who hid under the dinner table, listening to the conversations. Patricia says, "I know that child because I was that child, hiding under the tablecloth in order to watch and listen and become a writer, peering at truths from a safe place." I originally told this story as well as the E. B. White story within this minilesson; you'll find that, like me, you need to resist the impulse to tell everything you know in one minilesson.*

Notice that there are lots of ways to create cohesion or unity within a minilesson. In this one, I thread references to imagination, clouds and puppy dogs, E. B. White, and Charlotte's Web *throughout the minilesson. That, plus repetition of the teaching point, helps to make the minilesson clear to the students.*

Even though Charlotte's Web *is not realistic fiction, I use it as an example because it is a story I'm certain my children know (and I suspect your children know this story too!). If you worry that your students could get confused by the aspects of* Charlotte's Web *which don't fit into the unit's emphasis on realistic fiction, then select another book. You don't want this minilesson to seem as if it is an invitation to write unrealistic stories. You could refer instead to more realistic fiction books such as* Cassie Binegar, Fig Pudding, *or* June Bug—*or to a picture book. Be sure to refer to a story that all your students know well.*

Implicit in this minilesson is the assumption that children already have some entries to draw upon. These can be entries from much earlier in the year—they needn't have been gathered under the auspices of fiction.

Tell children what to watch for as you demonstrate rereading your notebook for bits that could be seeds for a story.

"Let me show you what I mean. I am going to reread my writer's notebook, looking for an entry that could grow into a whole story. Watch as I read; you'll notice I give each entry a little growing space, a little time to become an idea. I don't just race past entry after entry, saying, 'Nope, nope, nope' as I flick past them."

Looking at a page of my notebook, I read a bit aloud, then looked up, as if savoring what I'd written. Then I read on. This time when I looked up, I pointed at the entry excitedly. "Here's an entry about when we moved to a new town. I wrote it at the start of the year! Before we moved into that new house, I had all these ideas about how everything would look in the new place and I imagined that moving would open new worlds. I could make a whole story out of just this entry, because my hopes for the move were so high, and after we were in the new house, it echoed with awful loneliness. If I write this as a story, I think I will give my character something that helps—a friend, a pet, a cause—anything to ease her aching heart."

ACTIVE ENGAGEMENT

Set children up to practice mining entries for story ideas. Recruit children to help you find more story ideas in your own entries.

"Can you help me continue rereading my notebook and thinking of possible story ideas? On this chart paper, I copied a few more of the entries I've written. Would you and your partner reread them? Remember to reread them slowly, like writers always do when they're looking for story ideas, giving each one a chance to grow. Try to read with a writer's imagination, seeing possibilities in what at first might look pretty ordinary."

> I've been noticing that the neighbor's dog barks and runs at me whenever the boys who live there are in the front yard. When the boys aren't outside, their dog just sits on the porch and stares at me.
>
> When I was young, no one taught girls how to bat or catch the ball. I was always picked last for teams, and then the captain would put me way out in the outfield. I felt so lonely, and I knew they put me out there because if I had an important role, I would probably make the team lose. Maybe that's when I started to

Today's minilesson presents the concept that we get ideas for fiction from the moments and issues of our lives, then the minilesson channels writers to reread their notebooks, expecting to find ideas that could be developed into stories. The concepts I'm teaching in this minilesson are more complex and multifaceted than those that I conveyed at the start of the year. In this session, I am building on what children already know about writing and writer's notebooks.

Notice that although I haven't yet talked about the fact that characters struggle and change in stories, the examples I cite do already involve characters who change. That is, when I share an idea I have for a fictional story, that idea is fleshed out enough that it contains the broad contours of a story. A story always contains the three Ds: desire plus danger creates drama. My story ideas are good models, though I haven't yet talked about what those models contain.

I could have asked children to reread their own notebooks during the minilesson, looking for story ideas, but I often have children work with a case-in-point that I set up for them. There are several reasons for this. First, I can deliberately steer kids in ways that'll make it likely they'll succeed. For example, the entries I give children to work with in this minilesson contain tension, and therefore children should have success turning them into story ideas. Then, too, if I had asked children to look in their own notebooks for possible story ideas, this would probably take more than three minutes, and I want to keep my minilessons short so they don't cut into children's writing time. Also, children will be looking for story ideas in their own notebooks as the main work once they disperse from the meeting area—I don't want them to complete that work now and be at loose ends during work time. On the other hand, if the children needed extra scaffolding, I might have asked them to start finding story ideas in their own notebooks, as this could have gotten them halfway toward doing the work they'll soon do alone.

become a writer. I had a lot of time to daydream, standing way out there in the grass with nothing to do and no one to talk to.

"Turn and talk with your partner. Together, see if you could imagine growing one of these into a story." I listened in on the conversations.

Help one child demonstrate how she mined your entries for possible story ideas.

After two minutes, I convened the group. "Marissa, I'm excited by the story you imagined. You took the entry about the girl playing softball and grew it into a possible story idea. Will you share the story idea with us?"

Marissa said, "I picked the softball one because the same thing happens to me. Maybe the girl could get catching lessons and one day catch the ball and win the game!"

Joshua, Marissa's partner, chimed in: "Don't stop there. She could teach all the other girls how to catch and bat!"

"Wow! I love that your story is reversing the discrimination that led me to write the entry in the first place. That's the way that we, as writers, take the true stuff of our lives, even if it's hard or sad, and *imagine* that things could go differently."

LINK
Repeat the teaching point, celebrating that fiction writers find story ideas in the moments and issues of their lives. Send children off to do this.

"Writers, I have always known that fiction writers need imagination to write. But I used to think that most fiction writers found ideas by looking up into the clouds and imagining stories about castles or puppy dogs. What you have shown me today is that fiction writers *do* have imaginations. We look into everyday moments of our lives—into moments as ordinary as watching a spider make a web or a girl in the outfield—and we see possibilities."

"Today and for the rest of your lives, whenever you want to write fiction, reread your writer's notebook with a fiction writer's eyes. Remember to reread and then wait, and imagine. It's easy to just flick away the idea of a story about a spider, thinking, 'That's not important.' Don't do that. Have the imagination to say, 'Wait. There might be a story here.' And when you get a story idea, mark it with a sticky note, and then write a new entry based on your original entry, putting the idea it sparks onto your page."

These are the entries from my notebook, written on chart paper. You'll want to use your own. You may notice that each of my entries is very different. One is an observation; the other has more of a narrative feel. I try to be sure my examples open up possibilities for kids.

When children talk to their partners and I listen in, I get a chance to decide which child's suggestion will be especially helpful to the class. It's not an accident that Marissa has imagined a very realistic story, one which features a child who is her age and which revolves around an everyday life issue.

When we are teaching anything, we are teaching values. Be conscious of the messages that are tucked into your teaching and make sure you are empowering your children to imagine alternatives.

In the link, I generally revisit the teaching point. Here I also repeat a few tiny details from the very start of my minilesson. Writers of all sorts often find that one powerful way to end a text is to return to some of the details with which we began the text.

Because this is the first minilesson in a new unit, I want children to be inspired. I want them to believe, as I do, that there is something majestic about finding significance in the small moments of our lives and writing these as stories. I also want to spell out very concrete, doable strategies they can use today.

WRITING AND CONFERRING

Using Your Imagination to See Promise and Power in Children's Work

In today's minilesson, I have told children that writers need the imagination to look into everyday moments and see possibilities. I have urged young writers to resist flicking away the little bits of life—observations of a spider making her web—and to instead get used to saying, "Wait. There may be a story here."

Of course, this advice is even more important for *teachers* than for writers. Our students will bring us entries and story ideas. We need the imagination to look at what they bring us, and to see that these entries could become something grand. Even if we can't quite see what the writer values in his or her entry, it is important to remember that almost any topic can become a spectacular piece of writing. E. B. White, after all, wrote an essay on warts! The secret to finding something of value in all writing is to slow down, to listen to what the writer is saying, and to be moved by the details of the subject. Teachers, therefore, would be wise to be pushovers. "What a topic!" we say. "This is going to be some story! You definitely need to write the details because this is amazing stuff."

Beccah, for example, reread an entry she had written back in November, describing her observations one day during recess. She noticed the faded yellow paint lines that marked the playground boundaries, two third-grade boys who tempted nearby pigeons with cracker crumbs, the way one recess monitor clasped her hands firmly behind her whenever she walked around the playground, and the way one fifth-grade girl rolled her eyes once the girl she had been talking to turned away. At first, Beccah couldn't figure out why she was drawn to this entry; she thought she had just collected a series of random observations.

"Hi, Beccah," I said, "I noticed you keep flipping back to this page and reading this entry. There must be something rich there that you can write about."

"I don't know," she mumbled, shrugging and sighing. "I like the way I wrote these descriptions, but I don't know if there's a story idea here."

> **MID-WORKSHOP TEACHING POINT** ***Using Notebooks to Plan Possible Stories*** "Writers, can I stop you? I love the energy in this room. It feels like a fiction factory here! Marco just asked a really important question. He asked, 'How do fiction writers put ideas for stories on the page? Is it a list?' He wasn't sure which words we actually write. So I thought it might help if I shared what I wrote in my notebook when I thought about turning my entry about moving to a new place into a story." Opening my notebook, I read:
>
> > Maybe I could write a story about moving because that was a huge part of my life. I want the story to be for older kids, so I could make the main character be about 12. Yes! Cause friends really matter to kids of that age. This girl (boy?) finally finds the perfect best friend, and then she has to move to a whole different state where they call middle school "junior high," and the kids seem tough. Maybe she starts acting tough too, even before she moves away.
>
> *continued on next page*

"Hmm," I said, crouching beside her to read her entry along with her. "Well you certainly did write vivid descriptions! Your observations come to life right off the page. And remember that one way we can find ideas in stories is to think about what moves us. Something here, other than your descriptions, must have moved you enough to make you keep coming back to this entry. Maybe that's where the story idea lies."

Beccah reread her entry, twisting her lips in thought. After a few seconds, she sat straight up, pointed to a line in her entry, and announced, "Well, I thought the way that girl rolled her eyes was funny."

"I wonder why she did that?" I mused.

"I know! I thought they were friends. So maybe I could write about some girls who pretend to be friends, but really don't like each other."

"Why don't they like each other?"

I could tell Beccah had latched on to something because she began rattling off a list of possibilities: "Maybe they used to be friends, but one copied the other's homework and got her in trouble. Or maybe one of them didn't invite the other to her birthday party. Or, I know! Maybe someone else was making fun of the first one and the other one thought it was funny, so now they're not friends anymore."

"This would make a great story, Beccah. I can't wait to find out how it develops," I replied. Before I could finish that sentence, though, Beccah had already taken up her pen again. She turned to a fresh page in her notebook and started writing out her story idea.

> *continued from previous page*
>
> "Do you see how I began with some of the 'true stuff' from my entry about when I moved as a child, but then I started to imagine layers that would turn it into a juicy fiction story? And do you see how I am not actually writing *the story* in my notebook now; instead I'm thinking, planning, on the page? I even asked myself questions in the entry, questions like whether the character should be a boy or a girl."
>
> "Would you reread your notebook, take an entry you particularly like, and try to write that as story idea in a similar way? Make your entry sound as if you are thinking on the page. Write with phrases such as *I'm thinking I might* or *later I could tell about*. And write five or six sentences about that one story idea. Then, of course, skip a line, and do similar work for another story idea. You'll probably do this for about five story ideas today."

Some students, like Beccah, will become enthusiastic about the opportunity to write fiction and they'll be eager to get started. As we coach these students, it is reasonable to keep in mind some broad parameters for the stories we expect children will end up writing. Our expectation is they will write short stories, not novels. In very short stories, writers can usually handle only two main scenes. This means that if the story involves a sequence of nine major events, before the writer even sets to work, he or she will probably need to zoom in on the two or possibly three events that can then be conveyed in detail. Usually, one of these main actions (scenes) will represent a point of conflict or a turning point or a moment of change. Then, too, when writing a short story, authors usually decide to develop two (and conceivably three) characters in detail, rather than simply mentioning a whole host of people. If the child imagines a story about a girl and her parents, you may suggest that actually the story could focus on just one parent.

Keep in mind that when children write fiction, they turn first to the models that exist in their immediate, daily environment. So you might notice that their characters and plotlines resemble those they find in comic books, video games, television sitcoms and melodramas. These texts are not inherently bad, but their plotlines are difficult to write well without many years of practice.

As you listen to and read these early attempts toward story ideas, try to return to lessons from the units on personal narrative and essay writing. Remind children that over and over again, they've grown grand and beautiful ideas simply from attending to the details of their lives.

Steer children firmly toward generating ideas for realistic fiction and toward writing about subjects on which the child is an authority. Recently, a third grade teacher said to one child, "You need to know your character well, so I'd suggest you write about someone who is roughly your own age." The child said, "But I instant-message my twenty-five-year-old cousin all the time so I know all about being twenty-five." The teacher responded, "No, you know all about being nine and IM-ing someone who is twenty-five and that's different!" Celebrate also the power of making the ordinary extraordinary. Young people need to know that powerful drama exists in the details of growing up; there are stories hiding in their memories of finding a best friend, losing a beloved pet, or making a birthday gift.

Elexa

Elexa is a 11 year old girl that wants to be the head cheer leader, but her best friend Lexie also wants to, so will she do it in the cost of her friendship. She has notieed that the boy that was following her around [Max] is now following Lexie, what will happen next

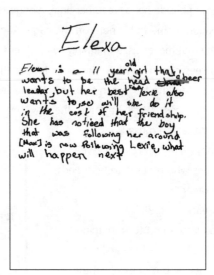

Fig. I-1 Deveonna's story idea

Story: Harrison's parents are getting divorced, his mom is dating a construction worker who only talks about jack hammers his dad is in England. In the midst of all this, Harrison is starring in a play that is the school's biggest event. Can Harrison juggle it all?

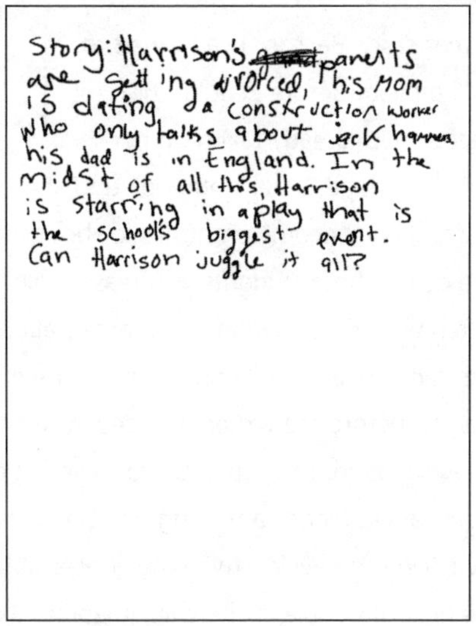

Fig. I-2 Ari's story idea

SHARE

Mining for Gold: Finding Nuggets of Stories

Offer some examples of the kinds of stories children are finding in their notebook entries. Read a story idea entry or two.

"Writers, I love seeing your notebooks filled with sticky notes that say, 'Here's a good story idea!' And I love, even more, seeing that you've each developed *old* entries into *new* story ideas by thinking on the page about what you could write about!"

"Remember Naomi Nye's poem 'Valentine for Ernest Mann,' in which she suggested that poems hide? Well, Lisa has found four places where she thinks *stories* hide. One is an entry about sitting in the park watching a bird scare another bird away from some crackers on the ground. Another is an entry about that big fight at recess a few weeks ago—remember? And this is an entry about getting Rollerblades™ for her birthday. What Lisa has already done—and what each of you needs to do—is this: Reread the story ideas you have written and star the ones that you especially like."

"Sofiya reread entries from the start of the year and several of them gave her ideas for stories she could write. She put a sticky note on an entry she wrote early in the year about the day the Nature Center woman brought a snake to our classroom. She'd been so scared to touch that snake! So she took her fear and gave it to a character. Listen to her story idea." *[Fig. I-3]*

Titles:

Elizabeth Touched a Snake!

Should I Touch the Snake or Not?

Elizabeth was a small first-grade girl. She lived with her parents. Elizabeth is afraid of snakes. The reason is because she was once bitten by a snake herself. Not even once, a few times.

Then one day her class went on a trip.

Once home, Elizabeth told her parents all about the trip. The animals, the lady, the outside lunch they had, and how Ronald got stung by a bee. She saved the best for last. When Elizabeth talked about the snake she said everything. How the snake felt, how it stared at her, its skin, everything! After she said everything about the snake, her parents asked her if she was still afraid of them. She said yes, but tame ones are okay.

Notice here that I have purposely named drastically different topics: receiving a birthday gift and seeing a fight on the playground. You will want to fill the room with a wide variety of topics that offer alternatives to themes from the latest hit movies or video games—ideas that are already in the air since they are in popular culture. We can help students find stories in places where they might never have thought to look.

> Titles:
> Elizabeth Touched a Snake!
> Should I Touch the Snake or Not?
>
> Elizabeth was a small first grade girl. She lived with her parents. Elizabeth is afraid of snakes. The reason is because she was once bitten by a snake herself. Not even once, a few times.
> Then one day her class went on a trip.
>
> Once home, Elizabeth told her parents all about the trip. The animals, the lady, the outside lunch they had, and how Ronald got stung by a bee. She saved the best for last. When Elizabeth talked about the snake she said everything. How the snake felt, how it stared at her, its skin, everything! After she said everything about the snake her parents asked her she was still afraid of them. she said yes, but tame ones are okay

Fig. I-3 Sofiya turns a personal narrative entry into a story idea.

"Sofiya also noticed that in an entry from the start of the year, she'd mentioned a stuffed animal that was especially important to her, a German shepherd named Esther. She started thinking about maybe writing a story about that stuffed animal. So she wrote an entry about Esther." *[Fig. I-4]*

> I have a lot of stuffed animals. My most, most favorite is the German shepard dog. I named her Esther, after myself. Esther is my middle and Hebrew name. When I used to play with her, I thought of Esther as a heroine. She was very brave.
>
> Whenever I look at Esther, I get courage. To me, she's a real dog. Once, when I was falling asleep, it felt like I was falling. It was the second or third time that I had that feeling. I took Esther, held her close, and fell asleep.
>
> Since the day that I had to sleep with Esther, I didn't have the falling feeling anymore. I knew the reason: Esther had given me courage.

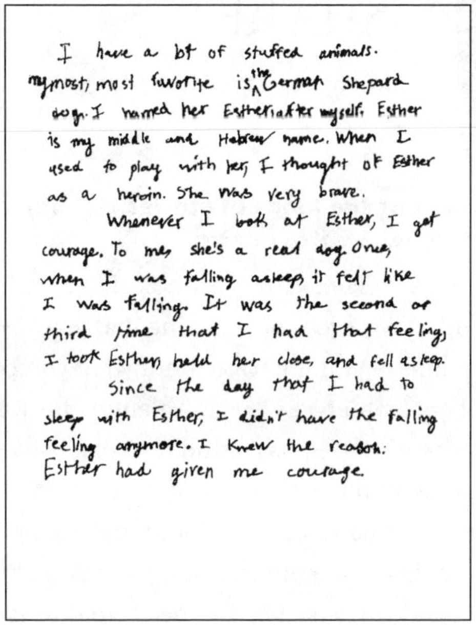
I have a lot of stuffed animals. my most, most favorite is the German Shepard dog. I named her Esther, after myself. Esther is my middle and Hebrew name. When I used to play with her, I thought of Esther as a heroin. She was very brave.
Whenever I look at Esther, I got courage. To me, she's a real dog. Once, when I was falling asleep it felt like I was falling. It was the second or third time that I had that feeling, I took Esther, held her close, and fell asleep.
Since the day that I had to sleep with Esther, I didn't have the falling feeling anymore. I knew the reason: Esther had given me courage.

Fig. I-4 Sofiya's entry

"And finally, she put sticky notes on entries about her gymnastics work because it gave her the idea she could write a story about a girl who enters a gymnastics tournament." *[Fig. I-5]*

> Every week I go to gymnastics. I go twice a week; for two hours each day. My coach's name is Mila. She's Russian and I feel extremely comfortable with her. I've been going there for four years; this is my fifth.
>
> On the days that I go to gymnastics, I do my homework extra fast. My two-hour lesson begins at six, so I have to be ready by five o'clock. I have less than two hours to do my homework, eat lunch, change, and pack.

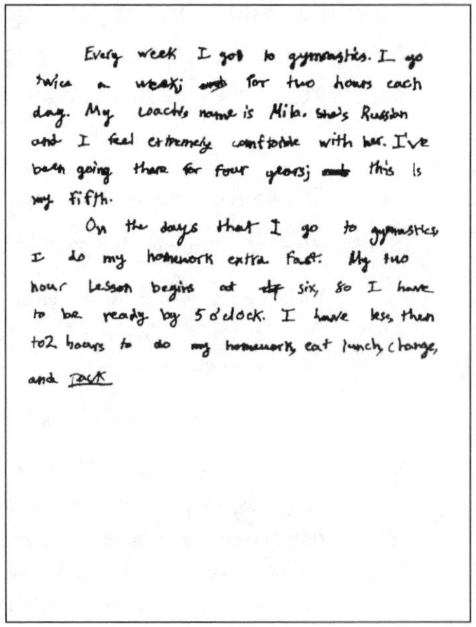
Every week I go to gymnastics. I go twice a week; for two hours each day. My coach's name is Mila. She's Russian and I feel extremely comftable with her. I've been going there for four years; this is my fifth.
On the days that I go to gymnastics, I do my homework extra fast. My two hour lesson begins at six, so I have to be ready by 5 o'clock. I have less than to2 hours to do my homework, eat lunch, change, and pack.

Fig. I-5 Sofiya's entry

Encourage children to listen to each other's story ideas with excitement and appreciation.

"So now, when Sofiya meets with her partner, she'll read this story idea (and others) aloud and she and her partner will talk together. And I hope that her partner will be appreciative and excited about Sofiya's idea—story ideas will flow more quickly in this room if the whole place is washed in a spirit of enthusiasm and appreciation. Let's all meet with our partners, then, and remember to be appreciative, responsive listeners."

Immersing Ourselves in the Sort of Text We Hope to Write You already know that when a writer wants to make a particular kind of text, we read texts that resemble the text we want to write. You are already reading fiction. My question is this: Is the book you are already reading a great model of what you'll be writing?

I ask this question because my hunch is that you may find *parts* of your novel that take your breath away, and make you think, "Ohh! If I could only write like that!" Mark those places. For example, I think there are chapters in *Because of Winn-Dixie* (a book we've not only read but practically memorized!) that resemble the fiction stories we're aiming to write. So tonight, look at the chapter-book you are in the midst of reading and notice sections of it which could be great models for your own fiction writing—and mark those sections, reread those sections, jot observations on those sections.

But mostly, you need to remember you will not be writing a novel. You won't be writing a three-hundred-page book! You will instead write a short story. So it is important for you to read short stories and picture books throughout this month. For homework tonight, would you choose one of the short stories which I've enclosed? Study it, and look at two things especially. First, let the short story help you answer the question: How do these kinds of texts tend to go? Write about that in your notebook. And second, would you think about how the story you read may have grown from the writer's life? What story idea might the writer have recorded in *her* writer's notebook? Then look at the story ideas you wrote in school today, and revise one of them in the wake of what you have just read.

TAILORING YOUR TEACHING

If you'd like to use an alternative opening to this minilesson . . . you could read aloud Marc Brown's very short picture book, *Arthur Writes a Story*. In this book the main character—Arthur—turns a bit of his life into a story. But then, Arthur feels pressured to instead write a splashy, imaginative, wild tale. In the end, he returns to the story that was grounded in his life, thereby conveying a lesson that could be an important one for your children.

If children are experiencing this lesson for a second or third year . . . after acknowledging that children already have strategies for generating ideas for stories, you may want to invite children to revisit published fiction they know well, speculating on the life work that led to those texts. Remind children that books don't come from Barnes and Noble; books instead come from writers. Say, "I wonder what this author collected in her notebook that allowed her to grow this story idea." Speculate, "I wonder whether she got this idea when she was sitting at her desk, or if it came to her when she was grocery shopping, or parking at the

---

You need to send home two short stories. See the Bibliography on the CD-ROM for suggestions.

Early in the year, you'll recall that the homework mostly asked children to live writerly lives. The homework enriched children's experiences, but it wasn't an essential part of a unit of study. By this time in the year, I expect that your children will make time for writing homework and therefore some of the homework is critical to the unit.

mall?" Then help your children think about how they can live the sort of lives that will help them generate ideas for stories. Ask them to think about how they will use their writers' notebooks differently, now that they are generating ideas for fiction. Convene the class around a discussion of homework. Now that they are writing fiction stories, maybe they want to write their own assignment ideas for homework? Use this unit as an invitation to help students author writerly lives.

If children are experiencing this lesson for a second or third year . . . be sure to acknowledge that children already have strategies for finding the stories that hide in the nooks and crannies of their lives. To talk in a new way about the process of finding story ideas in one's own life, you may want to remind children that just as a seamstress can look at a bolt of cloth and imagine it becoming a vest or a gown, a fiction writer can look at the raw material of life and think, "What kind of story might I make out of this?" Our response to such a question draws on all we know about stories. For example, because we know characters in stories have motivations that energize the story, we look at bits of life and think, "If I were to turn this into a story, who might the main character be? What might this person want? Hope for? Struggle with?"

COLLABORATING WITH COLLEAGUES

My sons and I have always loved September because it is a time for new beginnings. We make a very big deal out of the shopping trip to buy school supplies. We deliberate over a new form of datebook or a set of plastic drawers; each purchase contains all our resolve to do more, to be better, to outgrow ourselves, to reach new heights.

I hope that the start of a new unit of study contains a similar magic for you and your colleagues. Let a new unit feel like a New Year's celebration, and mark the occasion not just with an aura of celebration, but also with opportunities for reflection, looking backward as well as forward. Above all, I encourage you to take the great risk of talking about your own collaborations with each other. Have you and your colleagues found ways to support each other as you teach writing? Perhaps before embarking on this very ambitious unit of study, you could talk about the nature of your collaborations, and address issues that are sure to be there.

Roland Barth, author of *Improving Schools from Within*, points out that in every school, there are "unmentionables"—topics that are talked about in the parking lot or the bathroom or at home with one's spouse or partner, but that are not addressed in the light of day. These are the elephants in the room. Everyone knows they are there, and everyone pretends not to see them. Barth suggests that the more unmentionables one finds in a school, the more toxic that school is for those who live there. And in most schools, the greatest unmentionables of all are the relationships that exist among teachers. Talk about your relationships with each other.

What aspects of your collaboration have gone well and deserve to be built upon? What aspects of your collaboration need to be repaired?

It is easy, as teachers, to devote ourselves entirely to the challenge of helping our children learn well, but the truth is that the most important way to nurture our children's learning is to nurture our own learning. And this means talking candidly with colleagues.

I've been lucky enough to work with a leadership coach who gave me some advice regarding these "clearing the air" meetings. She suggested my colleagues and I begin such a session by agreeing upon an agenda, one that includes some time for frank conversation about what has and hasn't gone well. She suggests the time be limited—perhaps ten or twenty minutes for that conversation. Then, she advises, the conversation needs to turn toward these questions: What do we as a group want for our time together in the end? What positive steps forward can we take right now toward these goals?

As a result of this conversation, you and your colleagues may decide that reconstituting the group would be helpful. Sometimes a study group can tap into a fresh energy source by assembling a different combination of people. If you've been studying with grade-level colleagues, you might consider creating a cross-grade study group. On the other hand, you may decide the grade-level group would be more efficient if it subdivides into partnerships. Or perhaps you haven't actually been meeting, and you resolve to start doing so now.

You may want to imagine ways to give yourselves more time for more and deeper collaboration. In many schools, it is not terribly difficult for children from one grade level to have an extended playground time at the start or end of one particular day each week. For example, on Wednesday mornings, third graders might stay on the playground for an extra half-hour; if their teachers agree to come half an hour early on Wednesday, and to also meet while children are in extended recess, those two half-hours could combine to provide a nice block of time each week. Similarly, in some schools, the music teacher might be willing to convene all children at a particular grade level for an hour-long chorus period, again creating time for a study group.

Then, too, most study groups become infinitely more powerful if the group occasionally has a very long stretch of time together. Perhaps your principal would be willing to forgo the faculty meeting one month, allowing that time to be devoted to study groups? Perhaps teachers could be paid per session to convene on a Saturday? I've found that in every school, there are ways to tweak the schedule so that a group of teachers can gather together as a study group. The challenge is to be imaginative and resourceful.

The other thing I want you to remember is that the culture of a school is amenable to change—and a single teacher can make an unbelievable difference. Teachers often say to me, "In my school, everyone keeps to themselves. We don't plan together—my school isn't like that." Teachers say this as if the professional culture of a school is set in stone and as if their decisions and actions have no bearing on that culture. This is far from true!

Take it upon yourself to be an active agent. Rally yourself to have big hopes, and to make those dreams come true. The questions I suggested earlier aren't just for the other guy—they are for you!

- What do you want the learning culture in your school to be like? What are your best hopes for your school?

- What positive steps could you take today toward making those hopes into realities?

- What's getting in the way of you taking those steps and how can you address those issues?

This unit is titled *Writing Fiction: Big Dreams, Tall Ambitions* because the challenge of writing fiction can rally children's energies, tapping an unbelievable source of power. Let the unit do the same for you and your colleagues.

IMAGING STORIES WE WISH EXISTED IN THE WORLD

Today's session will help your students take the risk of writing stories that are deeply significant and personal. This can be a challenge. When we first invite children to write fictional stories, it can be as if we've opened Pandora's box. Suddenly, from all corners of the room, one finds children planning to write stories about people who win the lottery, fly into outer space, escape from kidnappers, and star on Broadway.

You'll try to bring children back to earth by emphasizing that they are writing realistic fiction and by spotlighting stories which revolve around everyday life events. But your goal is not only to encourage children to write stories about the hopes and heartbreaks of everyday life, your goal is also to show children that fiction can be a way to explore and to write about the truest and deepest parts of ourselves. Although you do not address this directly, there is no question that today's session helps children to write stories which are often more personal and more real than those they wrote during Raising the Quality of Narrative Writing unit of study. Fiction can give children a cloak of invisibility, allowing them to travel fearlessly into areas of vulnerability.

Specifically, you will teach children that fiction writers sometimes get ideas for stories by thinking about the stories we wish existed in the world. You can tuck in tips about how writers go from an image to a story idea, imbue ordinary details with significance, and live with notebooks always open, ready to record everything that catches our attention.

IN THIS SESSION, YOU'LL TELL STUDENTS THAT WHEN THEY SIT DOWN TO WRITE FICTION, THEY MIGHT GET IDEAS FOR STORIES BY IMAGINING THE BOOKS THEY WISH EXISTED IN THE WORLD. YOU CAN ALSO TEACH THEM THAT FICTION WRITERS GET IDEAS FOR STORIES BY THINKING ABOUT ISSUES IN OUR LIVES.

GETTING READY

- Example of a student who found a story idea from her own life
- Your own story idea for a book you wish existed
- Chart paper with the start of a list: How to Find Ideas for Fiction
- Your own writer's notebook or other demonstration text to use during conferring
- *The Three Billy Goats Gruff* or other fairy tale students know well
- See CD-ROM for resources

MINILESSON

Imagining Stories We Wish Existed in the World

CONNECTION

Tell a story about a child who grasped that writers often find story ideas in the details of our lives.

"During the previous share session, I heard you all telling each other story ideas that sounded like they could be written into real library books, sitting on our shelves. And this morning, as you came in, many of you told me that when you read a short story last night, the text gave you ideas for stories that *you* could write."

"At home last night, Rashann wrote a story idea that was sparked by an entry in which she'd written about just sitting on her porch, watching a squirrel crack and eat a nut. The squirrel was sitting inside a place where two branches formed a *V*; it sat right in the bottom of the *V*, all cozy and safe. Rashann watched the squirrel travel all over the tree until it found just that special, protected spot, and when she reread the story idea, she realized she could write a story about a kid watching that squirrel, a kid who doesn't have a home and is also trying to find a cozy spot, a safe spot, like the space at the bottom of a *V*. Rashann thought maybe the story would start with the girl watching that squirrel search for a nook. Inspired, the girl decides to find *herself* a similarly safe spot."

"Do you notice that Rashann's story idea began with her looking at something so tiny and ordinary? Her work reminds me of the lesson we learned yesterday when we saw that E. B. White got the idea for *Charlotte's Web* from something as ordinary as a spider, at work on her web."

Name your teaching point. In this case, teach children that writers also get ideas for fiction by thinking of books we wish existed in the world.

"Today, I want to teach you that writers collect ideas for stories not only by finding bits of life or entries that could grow into whole stories, but also by paying attention to the stories *we wish existed* in the world. Sometimes we get ideas for stories by thinking, 'How can I write a story for people like me, so we can see ourselves in books?'"

COACHING

This minilesson lays out the great work one child has done. The child's work illustrates the previous session's teaching, but describing what Rashann did also makes this one child famous to others, and this is terribly important. Many people go through life feeling invisible; by telling just this tiny story about Rashann's writing, Colleen gives Rashann a voice and shares a model of good work with the class. By likening her to E. B. White, Colleen elevates Rashann as a writer.

Over and over, you'll see that when Colleen and I tell children about a story idea, the idea is fleshed out. In this example, the story idea encompasses several scenes, and it conveys the main character's desires and struggles. Notice that the plot line in the story idea we share is not a long one. The children will write short stories not novels!

For many children, today's minilesson, about finding stories they wish they could read, involves revealing some of those injustices—revealing, perhaps, that there are too few stories of females acting powerfully in the world, or too few stories with immigrant children as main characters.

TEACHING

Point out that we each hope to find ourselves in the pages of books.

"Many times when any one of us looks through the library shelves for a book, we are looking to find ourselves in a story. I may find myself wanting a book about a kid like me who is afraid of the dark, or a book about a kid who is usually the last one picked for sports because she's not any good at them or a kid whose mother said, 'Every night before bed, you have to tip your head down and brush your hair one hundred strokes.'"

"Maybe one of you searches library shelves for a kid who lives with his grandma or a kid who likes to draw cartoon cats and dreams of having a cartoon strip in the Sunday paper. If you want to find yourself in a book on the library shelves and no book seems to tell the story that you want told, then you might decide it is important to put your truth onto the page in your own story."

Demonstrate by creating a story idea out of your longing to see books you'd like to read—in this case, books that contain people like you.

"Let me show you how I use this strategy to come up with a story idea," Colleen said. "First of all, I'm thinking about the books I want to read. For one thing, I wish there were more books about people like me who are half Mexican, kids whose fathers are Mexican and whose mothers aren't. *And* who are afraid of the dark. So in my notebook, I'll write down my story idea. I don't just write the big outline of my story—girl with Mexican dad and American mom. I want to put the stuff about a Mexican father together with true little details, like the part about being afraid of the dark and wanting a night-light. Those had been separate items on my list—the girl who is half Mexican, the girl who is afraid of the night—but in a story plan, I often combine things that were once separate. Watch."

Then Colleen wrote,

> A girl who is half Mexican lives with both her parents, but she thinks her father works too much. She wishes her father were around more because when he's home, she isn't so afraid of the dark. But his job keeps him far away so the girl usually sleeps with the light on to make her feel less alone in the night.

Notice the contribution that details make to this minilesson. The details act like pictures, and a picture is worth a thousand words. Notice, too, that when we want to speak or write with specifics, this generally means that we use more words. Children are apt to describe characters with generic terms, saying, for example, "the girl who loves soccer." How much more effective it is to use more words, as Colleen has done.

It is worth noticing that this is a unit on fiction, and the message is that we can develop ideas for fictional stories if we try to put the truth on the page. Donald Murray once helped me to write fiction by suggesting I write the Truth with a capital T, but not necessarily the exactly true story. "Change things around so that you convey the Truth of your experience," he said to me.

Naomi Nye, the poet and novelist, once said that a teacher told her when she was in school that "the things that cause you friction are the things from which you might make art." Notice that Colleen isn't shying away from the things that cause her friction.

In an earlier book in this series, I mentioned that I imagine the first few minilessons from all of the books constituting a giant course in keeping writer's notebooks. Earlier in the year, the entries your children wrote in their notebooks probably tended to be personal narratives, and most were written out in full. During the essay unit, the entries your children collected may have been observations, lists of questions or musings. During that unit, they also used the notebook as a place to draft and revise outlines boxes and bullets. Colleen and I are now hoping to let children know that writers also use notebooks as a place to mull over possible story ideas.

Debrief. Point out that you also invented a character who has desires and difficulties.

"Do you see, writers, that when writing my story idea, I didn't just say, 'I wish there were books on kids who are half Mexican'? I actually jotted a few sentences about how such a story might go. And specifically, I thought about what the character might want, and what she might struggle for. Characters in all stories have big longings."

"What I want to tell you is this: When you are collecting ideas for stories in your writer's notebook, you get ideas not only from rereading old entries, but you also get ideas for stories from thinking about books *you wish existed* in the world. Today you can use either of these ways to grow story ideas."

ACTIVE ENGAGEMENT
Set children up to try turning a wish for a certain kind of book into a story idea.

"So let's try it. Pretend that you think to yourself, 'I wish there were books about kids like me who aren't that good at sports.' Remember that to make that wish into a story idea, you need to invent some details. You can do so by asking questions of your story idea. Why isn't the kid in the story good at sports? Which sports? What has happened lately which shows these struggles?"

Ask children to turn and talk about the character traits and the struggles the character in the exemplar-story might encounter.

"Tell your partner how you could turn this into a story idea. Remember, think about the character, his or her character traits, the character's very particular struggle, about what he or she wants, and about what the character does."

In any unit of study, it is important to decide on the qualities of good writing that you want to highlight, and then you need to be sure that you refer to those qualities at many junctions in the unit. Colleen and I want children to understand story structure, and for this reason when she shows how she's devised a story idea by thinking of the books she wishes existed in the world, Colleen mentions a tip which for today is a subordinate one—the fact that her character has motivations and struggles. This will be the focus of a later minilesson.

The main point here is to help children come up with story ideas by thinking, "What stories do I wish existed in the world?" But Colleen also devotes some teaching to a subordinate tip she tucks into her main idea. She tells children that writers embellish their ideas with details. She then goes further and shows children a sequence of questions that will help them do this. These questions are carefully chosen—notice the sequence, because the questions, asked in this order, scaffold children to do some good work. First the questions channel a writer to think about the character's traits and related struggles, then the questions move writers to consider how these struggles play out in an event.

In example after example throughout this book, you'll see that story ideas contain some tension; they contain a predicament. When I was a kid and wrote fiction, my stories had magic carpets—but no tension. Hopefully, your children will sense that "a boy becomes a billionaire" is not yet the stuff out of which one makes stories.

After children talked, Colleen recruited Ramon to share. "I'd write: 'A kid comes to school at the start of fourth grade and everyone else has gotten taller. He is a shrimp, so he is no good at basketball any more. He doesn't get called on to play.'"

"I love the way you gave your character certain characteristics: He's a fourth grader who isn't as tall as the others, he used to be a great basketball player but now that height gets in the way, kids call him a shrimp. Those details really make your story start to grab me!"

LINK
Send writers off after reminding them of their growing repertoire of strategies for finding fiction ideas.

"So writers, we pretended we wished there were more stories about kids who aren't good at sports, and then imagined a character in such a book. When you are living your life as a fiction writer, you won't write about the character *I* lay out—you'll invent your own characters. As we saw yesterday, Sofiya's character may be a girl who enters a gymnastics tournament, or a child who gathers up enough courage to touch a snake. Whatever idea she pursues, Sofiya will need to think about her character's traits, and about her character's hopes and struggles. For now, you'll continue collecting story ideas. You can use any of the strategies we've learned, or others that you invent, to do this. Let's start listing these strategies in a chart," I said, gesturing to the list I had started on chart paper.

How to Find Ideas for Fiction

- Observe the world or reread entries. Mine your notebook for story ideas.
- Ask, "What books do I wish existed in the world?" Let this question lead you to invent a character with traits, struggles, actions.

"The blue table can get started . . . now the red table . . . ."

It's the second semester of the year; by now the class community is really strong. The combination of the fact that the class has lived through a lot together and that now they're writing fiction and can hide a bit under its cloak means that writing workshop will be a time when children write about huge issues in their lives. We aim to make them feel safe enough to do so.

Because you gave a hypothetical starting point, this is just an exercise. You don't expect children to write about the character from the day's minilesson, but instead to invent their own characters. There will probably be a few children, however, who decide that the story idea you have given to them could become their very own idea, and that's okay.

By now you are anticipating that in the early sessions of any unit, we'll offer children a repertoire of strategies for gathering entries that pertain to the work, and genre, of that unit.

You will find that your children are raring to go. Many of them will collect two or three ideas and they'll decide one of those ideas is perfect, and before you can say 'Jack Rabbit,' they'll have written four pages of the story. Prepare yourself for this, and galvanize yourself to deliver the news that those four pages are one draft of one possible story idea. Insist that children postpone closure, and that they continue to generate story ideas and (if they insist) story-beginnings. You will want an opportunity to teach them more before their stories are set in stone.

WRITING AND CONFERRING

Using an Exemplar Text to Respond to Predictable Problems

When you confer and lead small groups, you will probably notice that many students have long lists of undeveloped story ideas. Children won't be sure whether they are expected to write actual stories in their notebooks, or whether you are asking for lists of story ideas—and actually, you are hoping for something in between. You'll want to teach kids to stay a little longer with each idea, fleshing it out a bit. You might carry with you the first story idea you wrote in your notebook. For example, Colleen had started with this:

> Girl is afraid of the dark

Then Colleen revised her initial cryptic note to say a bit more.

> The girl is afraid of the dark. She knows she is being silly but sometimes she thinks she sees things, like monsters, in bed. She gets scared enough that she has started sleeping with the light on. Sometimes in the middle of the night, she crawls into bed with Mom. Her birthday is coming up. She wants to have a sleep over party but she is worried the other girls will make fun of her because she is afraid of the dark.

Colleen will probably want to carry both versions with her. Similarly, I could carry my story idea around with me—the idea about the girl who moved.

When conferring, it helps to carry your own exemplar text around with you so that if you decide to use the teaching method of demonstration or the "explain and show an example" method, you'll have the materials to do so. But don't let the fact that you have materials under your arm propel you into using them. As always, begin your conferences by asking, "What are you working on as a writer?" and by trying to understand what the writer has already done and is trying to do.

It will help if, before this unit begins, you and your colleagues try to predict the conferences you'll probably need to conduct early in this unit. As I mentioned earlier, you can expect that you'll often need to help children say more when they write about their story ideas. You may also:

MID-WORKSHOP TEACHING POINT

Sharing Struggles with Characters "Writers, can I have your eyes? I want to teach you one more strategy for collecting ideas for fictional stories: You can write stories in which the character wrestles with issues that are important to you. I once knew a young writer named Donald who had a big issue with 'fitting in.' In his school, cool kids all had a certain haircut. Donald wanted to be popular but he didn't have the money to go to the 'cool' barbershop. So he tried to cut his own hair, but it looked ridiculous, and kids made fun of him. He didn't just ignore that this was happening to him; Donald wrote a story about a kid who struggled with and overcame a similar issue. The kids in his story didn't have haircut troubles, but they had similar struggles."

"This was Donald's story plan":

> I'm going to write a story about a kid who tries really hard to fit in, but the more he tries, the worse it gets. Maybe he will do something bad like he steals sneakers to be like everyone else. Then he gets caught by a secret camera. Now he's in trouble with the manager, with his mom, with his principal. Maybe he gets really sick and all the people who were mad at him feel bad about it. Nah—that's dumb. Maybe he DOES something that everyone thinks is cool and makes people look at him differently. Not sure.

continued on next page

- Help students postpone closure, and to entertain the prospect of a wider range of story ideas. Some students will generate a story idea and immediately start writing that story from start to finish. Teach them that writers force ourselves to imagine more possibilities before making a commitment to one story idea. And once a child does settle on a particular story idea, the child needs to spend a lot of time rehearsing before he or she begins a draft. I think of this unit on fiction as a unit also on rehearsal and revision.

- Remind students that they know a lot about how stories generally "go," and specifically, remind them that story ideas usually originate from a character who has motivations and faces a predicament. If a child imagines a story in which an unnamed guy lives through ten daredevil activities, you'll want to explicitly teach the importance of developing a very particular character. You'll also want to show children that a character's traits and motivations lead that character to encounter struggles, and in this way a story hangs together.

- Steer children to grow story ideas from the particulars of their own lives. It is inevitable that some will want to write adult stories, and you'll want to channel them toward dramas they know from the inside.

- Anticipate that children will imagine their stories as containing a necklace-full of events. Teach them that they are writing short stories, and this generally means they'll be writing two or perhaps three Small Moment stories.

continued from previous page

"Do you see how Donald took the same issue that *he* was dealing with—trying to fit in with kids at school—and he started thinking about a story where the character wrestles in a different way with the exact same issue? Donald was incredibly brave to write about an issue that is hard in his own life." I said this because, in a subtle way, I hope to encourage children to write from the heart. "When Donald read the story idea to his class, they got really quiet; I realized that the issue wasn't important just in Donald's life, it was important to most kids in the class. It really helped them when Donald had the courage to name the issue."

"I am telling you this because I know some of you will want to think about the issues that are big in your lives or in the world. You might write an issue on the top of the page and then see if you can spin some story ideas that could possibly allow you to address the issue. We can add this strategy to our list:"

How to Find Ideas for Fiction

- Observe the world or reread entries. Mine your notebook for story ideas.

- Ask, "What books do I wish existed in the world?" Let this question lead you to invent a character with traits, struggles, actions.

- Think about an issue that is important to you and create a character who struggles with that issue.

Although it is helpful to plan for and anticipate conferences, if you find yourself giving mostly preplanned, almost canned conferences, then you probably need to listen more intently and to expect children to surprise you, to take you to new places. That is, it's helpful to expect that when you confer with children, they will stir up new ideas in you. As you draw a chair alongside a child and ask, "What are you working on as a writer?" expect that the child's response will be instructive to you.

SHARE

Storytelling

Glory in children's stories and suggest they deserve to hear each other's stories. Demonstrate storytelling by retelling a familiar tale, extrapolating pointers.

"Writers, I am so lucky because I have been able to move among you, listening in on your story ideas. So many of your stories are giving me goose bumps! You all deserve the chance I have to hear each other's stories. Right now, before you share, I'm going to give you a quick lesson in being storytellers. Then before you tell your stories to each other, we'll practice storytelling by telling just the beginning of *The Three Billy Goats Gruff*."

"After that I am going to ask some of you to tell the story of one of *your* story ideas. Are you ready for some hints on being a storyteller?"

"First, begin the story by sweeping the listeners with your eyes as if saying, 'Welcome, draw close, for I have a story to tell.'"

"Second, tell the start of the story in such a way that it sounds like a famous book or a fairy tale; start it with a phrase like, 'Once, long ago' or 'One day, a little girl . . .' or something else that sounds like a real story."

"Third, as you tell the story, be sure your mind is picturing whatever you are telling. If your mind isn't painting pictures, how will you choose the words that can help your listeners paint pictures as they hear the story?"

"I'll try storytelling first, using *The Three Billy Goats Gruff*. I'll try to follow all those tips. Then partner 1, I am going to ask *you* to storytell the same story (but in your own way) to your partner. Here goes."

> Once, long ago, there were three billy goats Gruff. They lived on one side of a stream, and everyday they would look across the stream to a lush field of grass. There was a bridge across the stream, but the three billy goats Gruff knew they were never to cross that bridge, for a mighty troll lived there.
>
> One day, however, the three goats were so hungry they decided to cross the bridge so they could eat the sweet lush grass on the far side. First the littlest goat started across the bridge. Trip, trap . . .

Colleen and I have found that in some classrooms, the children do not know The Three Billy Goats Gruff. *Obviously this reference works only if the text is familiar to kids.*

It may seem abrupt to suddenly channel students to go from generating lots of story ideas to storytelling one. We've brought storytelling into this very early session because we want the magic of literary language and the storyteller's persona and voice to help children generate and select between story ideas. But it is true that children are still generating lots of story ideas.

The hints here are ones I learned more than a decade ago when I studied with Mem Fox, author of Koala Lou. I teach these tips to children now because I think that by following these bits of advice, children will take the opportunity to storytell more seriously. I hope these tips elevate the storytelling and allow it to make a bigger contribution to children's work.

Practice telling the fairy tale you select so that you can tell it very well. As you tell the story, alter the pace of your voice, and remember the power of a pause. Appreciate crescendo—the hurrying of time and intensity. When you reach a section of the story that is especially significant, slow down, and tell these events in smaller steps. And when you reach the ending, slow your voice almost to a halt. Your timing will have terrific implications for the emotional power of the story.

Notice the literary language: The goats "knew they were never to cross that bridge for a mighty troll lived there." I'm using story language on purpose.

Set children up to retell with a partner the story you've just modeled, and then to storytell one of their own story ideas.

"Okay, partner 1, try telling the same Billy Goats Gruff story to partner 2. It doesn't matter if you remember the details of the story—you can change it as you go. But tell this story like you are a professional storyteller and this is the most amazing story in the world. Go nice and slow, create a storytelling aura."

After a few minutes I interrupted. "Writers, can I stop you? Using the same storyteller voice, will partner 1 take one of your own story ideas, any one of them, and tell your partner that story. Remember to start it in a way which signals, 'I'm telling a story!', perhaps with a phrase like, 'Once, long ago' or 'One rainy, gray day . . . .'"

HOMEWORK   *Collecting Story Ideas*   Tomorrow, writers, you are going to be choosing a story idea. This means that for homework tonight, it is really important that you do two things. First, reread a published short story you've read before, but this time, read it like a writer. Ask, "How does this story go?" Turn it inside out in your mind and notice how it's put together. Is one section of it essentially a Small Moment story? What else is there other than that? A second Small Moment story? A third? What glues these scenes (as fiction writers call the Small Moment stories) together? Write a page about what you notice when you look at the story with a writer's eyes.

And second, take some time to develop another story idea. You could use strategies we've already explored, or you could do this: story watch. Have you heard of bird watching? You know how some people tramp through meadows with binoculars around their necks, at the ready for a whir of color? "I see it," they say, after finding a scarlet tanager. Writers live in a similar way, but we're watching and listening for story ideas. Remember we learned earlier that Robert McCloskey was driving through Boston when he came to a long line of traffic. He looked ahead to see what was causing the problem and saw a line of ducks quacking across the street. Presto! The story idea for *Make Way for Ducklings* was hatched!

Tonight is your last chance to be sure you have a story idea, so in addition to reading like a writer, live like a writer.

The language of a book is different from the language of conversation. When we tell a story that begins, "Once, long ago, there were three . . . " or "There was once a little girl who . . . ," we are speaking in the cadence of story. Children need to be so immersed in story language that it is in their bones.

In Wordstruck, *Robert MacNeil writes about the importance of hearing and saying and coming to know the cadence of literary language. He writes: "Words and word patterns accumulate in layers, and as the layers thicken they govern all use and appreciation of language thenceforth. Like magic, the patterns of melody, rhythms, and quality of voice become templates . . . and the patterns laid down in our memories create expectations and hungers for fulfillment again." He goes on to say, "It was the sound of English that moved me as much as the sense, perhaps more" (p. 185).*

Teach students to carry their writers' notebooks with them on the bus or subway ride home, to sit with their notebooks open in the lunchroom and at their kitchen tables as life buzzes around them. Teach them to capture conversations, the minidramas, and the subtle nuances of character and environment for all this can be material for writing. Teach them, too, that fiction writers read newspapers and watch the news on TV, noticing ways in which the world feels unfair for some people. All this is grist for the mill.

If you'd like to give children more time to generate ideas for possible stories . . . you may want to teach them that writers live wide-awake lives, recognizing that if they look closely and listen well, they'll find ideas in the details of their lives. Cynthia Voight once saw some children sitting in a station wagon outside a mall, watching the door of the mall with a strained look on their faces—and the idea for her *Homecoming* series was born. In her memoir, *One Writer's Beginnings*, Eudora Welty wrote, "Long before I wrote stories, I listened for stories. Listening for them is something more acute than listening to them." You may want to teach children that one way to listen for stories is to visit the people in their lives, and ask them to talk about whatever they know best. Within their talk, children may find story ideas.

If you notice children want to write extravagant tales of marriages, battles, winning the lottery and so forth . . . teach them that writers usually look for stories that hide within the areas they know best. Melville traveled on a whale ship, and his story ideas reflect this! Mark Twain traveled on the Mississippi River on steamboats, and again, his novels reflect his experiences. Charlotte Brontë was a governess—and not surprisingly, her most famous character had the same career. Invite children to find stories within the terrain they know well.

If your students often find inspiration from your writing experiences . . . begin this unit by telling the story of your childhood experiences writing fiction. Your experiences might not match mine, of course. I turned the playroom into an office for myself, bought reams of paper, and began my story. Every day I added on. It became longer and longer and longer. I wasn't sure how to end it. It became so long that no one (myself included) ever read it. Now I realize that two things would have made the world of difference. I needed to take the time to plan my story before writing it. And I needed an image of what it was that I wanted to write.

COLLABORATING WITH COLLEAGUES

Just as writers begin a draft by planning, so, too, you and your colleagues will want to begin your collaboration by planning. Now that you've reconstituted your study group, spend a bit of time planning the work you'll do together this month.

You'll definitely want to be writing your own fictional stories. The idea of sitting down and writing a story is overwhelming and scary for most of us, but you'll see that this unit of study takes you along in a step-by-step fashion. Give yourselves the minilessons.

In your study group or at home in the evenings, be the student as well as the teacher, working on your own writing. You'll see that the story you write can thread its way through most of this unit. You'll want your writing to be an effective model for your children, so if you feel insecure about this, closely follow the story model we provide.

The learning that you do will be especially important in this unit because your children will probably need five weeks instead of four for this study. This means you and your colleagues will definitely need to write your own minilessons. The research you do about fiction writing, combined with your own work as a fiction writer will help immeasurably. But of course, you'll learn the most by watching what your children do as writers.

It's very important to read stories that resemble those you and your children will write. The chapter books that you read aloud can serve as models for particular techniques that fiction writers use, but there are big differences between novels and short stories. In fact, many of the problems children run into when they write fiction derive from the fact that they're modeling their writing after novels, not short stories. No one can write a strong novel in three pages!

There are lots of professional books that can inspire and inform you and your colleagues if you want to learn more about teaching children to write fiction. I recommend two books by educators: *After the End*, by Barry Lane and the fiction chapter from *Time for Meaning*, by Randy Bomer. I also recommend a number of books for adults who want to write fiction: *The Art of Fiction*, by John Gardner; *Writing Fiction*, by Janet Burroway; *The Plot Thickens*, by Noah Lukeman; and *Creating Fiction*, an anthology edited by Julie Checkoway. As you read, look for material you can include in the minilessons that you will write.

You'll also want to learn from fiction by becoming someone who watches for and listens for stories. In a staff development afternoon at a school, Don Graves gathered the teachers into the school library. Dividing them in teams of three, Graves gave each team an envelope. One team's envelope contained a note that said, "Mr. Blakely works in the furnace room. You'll find he has amazing stories about foster children. Find him and hear his stories." In another team's envelope, they found, "Mrs. Huber works in the cafeteria. Her granddaughter is a never-ending source of stories. Go and hear them!" Consider, for a moment, the people with whom you work every day. How could you hear their stories? Pull close, listen well. You'll soon find that there are stories everywhere.

IN THIS SESSION, STUDENTS LEARN
THAT, LIKE ALL WRITERS, FICTION
WRITERS NEED TO CHOOSE A SEED
IDEA (A STORY IDEA) AND THEN
BEGIN TO DEVELOP CHARACTERS BY
CREATING THEIR EXTERNAL AND
INTERNAL TRAITS.

GETTING READY

- How to Find Ideas for Fiction
  chart from preceding lesson
- Your own character and story line
  that you will use to model
  throughout the unit
- Start of a Developing My
  Character T-chart on chart paper,
  with two columns: Outside
  (external features) and Inside
  (internal features)
- Advice for Developing a
  Character chart on chart paper
- See CD-ROM for resources

DEVELOPING BELIEVABLE CHARACTERS

Today's lesson is a critical one. You'll teach children that once writers get some ideas for how a story might go, we resist the temptation to begin drafting the story and instead we rehearse for it. Often children think that the writer's job during rehearsal is to come up with a topic, a subject. But when writing fiction, we need more than just the topic, we need to create the story world, we need to know our characters. We need to know them with intensity—well enough that we can live inside their skin and see through their eyes.

Children often think that the central element of a story is plot, and they enter a fiction unit expecting that the story of a father and a son hiking will revolve around all that happens to them (perhaps they meet a grizzly bear, get caught in a rock slide, fall into a cavern, are bitten by a rattlesnake). However, the truth is that the better story will revolve not around what happens to the father and son, but rather, what happens between the father and the son, or within them.

You'll see that we suggest children begin with fairly easy work—but the level of difficulty will escalate quickly. So, although you'll begin by teaching children that fiction writers rehearse by fleshing out their characters—detailing their external features—you'll soon point out that these external features need to reflect and describe the internal features.

Throughout this work, you will teach children that fiction writers write not only drafts of a story, but also plans. Fiction writers use pen and paper to mull over possible directions, to gather and sort information, to plan. More specifically, children will learn that rehearsal is also a time for revision! By thinking through a story idea in some detail, writers progress through a whole sequence of possible ideas—even before we actually begin our first drafts.

In this session, youngsters choose their seed idea—their story idea—and begin developing that idea by developing their characters. This will involve thinking about their internal attributes—their likes, dislikes, thoughts, and feelings—as well as their external attributes, such as physical characteristics, age, and habits.

MINILESSON

Developing Believable Characters

CONNECTION

Chronicle the learning journey the class has been on in this unit to date. Emphasize that children have learned the ingredients of a good story.

"For the past few days, you've been living like fiction writers, seeing ideas for stories everywhere. You've been writing entries in which you think on the page about your story ideas. I read through your notebooks during gym yesterday and what I saw blew me away."

"Listen carefully to what I noticed because it is important. Although our minilessons have been about the strategies fiction writers often use to come up with story ideas (and the chart How to Find Ideas for Fiction, lists those ideas), you guys are so alert as learners that on your own you have gleaned a whole lot about the ingredients that go into a good story idea."

"Looking over your notebooks, I could tell that when we started this unit, you thought a good story idea might be one like this."

A girl climbs a mountain by herself and she's proud.

"And I could tell that now, many of you realize that a story idea needs to include some more specifics about the character and the story, so it might go like this."

A 9-year-old girl has had a knee injury and will never be able to bend her knee. At first she gives up on life but then something happens to change this and she decides to not give up anymore. To prove herself she sets out to climb the mountain that overlooks her house. She doesn't get to the top but she proves herself in a different way and learns something, I am not sure the specifics.

COACHING

Children are choosing their seed ideas very early in this unit because once they've chosen their story ideas, they still need to devote lots of time to rehearsal.

Colleen has a few options right now. Because today's lesson will channel children to settle on one of their story ideas, she can contextualize this session by referring to the sessions in earlier units when children chose their seed ideas, reminding them of what they already know about this phase of the writing process and then highlighting ways in which this phase will be a bit different now that they are writing fiction. Similarly, she can reference the Monitoring My Writing Process chart from previous units, reminding children that always, they begin writing by gathering ideas and then, before long they pause to make a selection. A third option is that she can summarize the previous session's work, aiming to either consolidate what students have learned so that it becomes more memorable for them or aiming to put a new slant on their prior learning. Then, too, another option is that she can simply share observations about her students' work. She decided to summarize previous learning and to do so in ways she hopes make that previous work more memorable and accessible.

The truth is that children probably have not made this much progress yet! This second version of a story idea is considerably better than those most children will be writing, but no harm is done in overstating how much they've learned.

Tell writers that today they'll select a story idea.

"Today, each of you will reread all your entries and select one seed idea to develop into a publishable story (in this unit, we'll call it your *story idea*)."

Name your teaching point. In this instance, you'll teach children that after fiction writers have chosen a story idea, they rehearse by writing — by thinking on the page — about their character.

"I am going to teach you that fiction writers don't just go from choosing a story idea to writing a draft. Instead a fiction writer *lives with* a story idea for a time. Specifically, I will teach you the thinking-on-the-page strategies that fiction writers use to live with our characters and to rehearse for our drafts."

"You will see that these strategies focus less on planning what will happen in our stories and more on bringing to life the people who will make things happen. A fiction writer once said, 'Before you can begin writing your story, you need to know your characters so well that you know exactly how much change each one has in his or her pocket.'"

TEACHING
Set the children up for your teaching by quickly summarizing your process of selecting a story idea.

"I mentioned earlier that we'll need to reread all our story ideas and select one to develop into a publishable story. Honestly, I think the truth is that usually there is one idea that chooses *us*. Usually I find that, in the end, one idea stays with me, and haunts me enough that it feels inevitable that I must write about it."

Notice that this sentence—today you will reread your entries and select (a story idea)—is not a teaching point. This is an assignment, not a lesson! Sometimes, as in this instance, we will want to tell writers to do something, and of course we can tell them so within a minilesson. But it's important to keep in mind that telling writers to do something can't substitute for teaching them a strategy or a skill.

It is often tempting to keep the teaching point vague, saying something like, "Today I'll teach you a strategy for writing good leads." Then, in the teaching component of a minilesson, we can name the strategy. However, I've found that when we force ourselves to be more explicit in the teaching point, then we are less likely to fool ourselves in the Teaching component into thinking that simply naming the strategy amounts to teaching it. Notice today's teaching point is specific and contains several sentences.

People hunger for information. Whenever possible, Colleen and I try to weave little facts, quotes, stories, and tips into our minilessons. We want children to feel as if the moments when they gather close for a minilesson are heady times. We want them to come to a minilesson expecting to learn, learn, learn. We certainly couldn't, six months into the year, pretend that children's minds could be on fire if we simply "taught" them to reread and select a seed idea—that would be old hat by now!

In a moment, Colleen will introduce a story that ends up weaving through this entire book, becoming the class' story, my story, and perhaps your story too. Ideally you'll substitute your own class' story, but the story that weaves through this book is one that can belong to many of us.

"This morning on my way to school, I realized that I had already decided to write about that girl who is afraid of the dark and wants to buy a night-light. So I put sticky notes on the pages related to that entry, and now I am going to begin developing that seed idea, that story idea."

"Notice that I don't start by thinking about what *will happen* in the story. I rein myself in, I hold myself back from doing that, and try instead to get to know my character."

When you want children to listen well to your teaching, it helps to embed your points into little vignettes such as Colleen does here when she retells the story of how she came to this realization.

Demonstrate that you develop your story idea by listing external and internal features of your main character.

"I already know she's part Mexican, so I add that to the external side of my chart. I need to give her a name that goes with the fact that she's Mexican. I'm thinking whether there's anything else about my character that could help me find a good name . . . I definitely know she's afraid of the dark." Colleen added that to the internal side of the chart. "Oh! I'll name her *Luz* 'cause that means 'light.'"

There are lots of reasons to rein children in so that they don't bolt ahead into writing a draft before they develop their characters. One reason for postponing the draft is that the work on character development will enrich the eventual draft. But another reason to ask children to work on developing their characters before they launch into a draft is that this gives us a bit more time to confer, making it more likely that children get off to as strong a start as possible.

Developing My Character

Outside (external features)	Inside (internal features)
Part Mexican	Afraid of the dark
Luz	

Shifting from the role of author to that of teacher, Colleen addressed her children directly. "Did you see that I don't just come up with any ol' random characteristics for my character? I try to put together a person in such a way that the parts of who she is fit together, they cohere, into a person who begins to come to life."

Watch the way in which Colleen weaves between demonstrating and debriefing, embedding writing tips or pointers into her debriefing. Notice, also, that although she gives a lot of pointers, her written work is lean. Within a minilesson that aims to be just ten minutes long, Colleen can't rattle on and on about her character. Everything she says here is chosen because it helps illustrate a larger principle Colleen wants to teach.

Returning to the role of author, Colleen looked at her chart and mused, "What else? I want Luz to be a bit like me—if this chart were about me, not Luz, I think that in the internal column, I'd write that I'm sensitive. I think I want Luz to be sensitive too, and sort of artistic." Colleen added this to her chart.

By explaining how she constructs her character, Colleen is sharing with children some essential fiction writing truths: characters need to be believable. They need to be real and often this means they have parts of us in them. It isn't surprising or accidental that Luz is sensitive like Colleen, or that she's part Mexican or a bit artistic. Colleen is drawing on important aspects of herself—both internal and external—because she knows that doing so will allow her to create a convincing character.

Think aloud to highlight the fact that the external and internal traits need to cohere.

Colleen reread all of what she had written. "Let's see, does being sensitive and being artistic fit with everything I know about Luz? When her father is gone, she is afraid of the dark. She's sensitive. Sensitivity often goes hand in hand with imagination and creativity. I can imagine Luz conjuring up all sorts of inventive, frightening thoughts about the dark. I can also picture her creating interesting artwork. So yes. Those go together."

Notice the way Colleen emphasizes that the traits she gives to her character need to fit together in a logical fashion. This is an emphasis we added after seeing children throw random traits together with abandon ("my character likes peach ice cream, her favorite color is purple, she walks funny," and so on). The fact that Colleen models the process of developing a coherent character does not insure that students will follow this example!

Debrief. Highlight that you first decide on the main goals for your character and let these guide what the character develops into.

Shifting again to the role of teacher, Colleen said, "Do you see that when I am creating a character, I begin with whatever I know? I knew I wanted my character to be a bit like me. You may know that you want your character to resemble someone else in your life, or that you want your character to go from being tough to being gentle. Start with whatever you know you want for your character."

"I hope you also noticed that I often pause to reread everything I have created, asking, 'Do these different things make sense within one person? Do they fit together in a believable way? Are the traits here for a reason?' I reread to test whether the character I've created thus far stands up to the test of believability."

When you debrief, you have another chance to incorporate tips into your demonstration. So be sure that when you retell what you have just demonstrated, you do so in a manner which highlights whatever it is you want children to take from your demonstration. In this minilesson, Colleen's point is a very sophisticated one. She could have made this easier for kids had she left fewer options open, perhaps suggesting that many of the children, like her, may want their main character to resemble themselves.

Alternatively, you could ask children to extrapolate their own tips for creating a character from what they saw you do, perhaps listing across their fingers the steps they saw you take that they could also take. If you do this, however, avoid trying to extract your points from them through a series of leading questions!

Show children a chart of advice for developing character and model how you might use it.

"I'm going to do one last thing that I want you to notice. I am going to look at that word *sensitive* and say exactly what it means. Lots of people can be sensitive, but what exactly does it mean for Luz? Um . . . let's see . . . I think for Luz this means she really cares about people. She is really kind."

"But as I write this, I am still keeping in mind that question, 'Does the character seem believable?' I'm worried that I just made Luz too good to be true. If she is human, she can't be all-caring, all-kind. She needs to be more complicated."

Advice for Developing a Character

- Start with whatever you've decided matters to you about your character. Is he or she like you? Like someone you know?

- Put together a character so that all the parts fit together into a coherent person.

- Reread often, asking, "Do these different things make sense within one person? Do they fit together in a believable way? Are these traits here for a reason?"

- Open up any broad, general descriptors—words like sensitive—and ask, "What exactly does this word, this trait, mean for this particular character?"

- If a character seems too good to be true, make the character more complex and more human by asking, "What is the downside of this trait? How does this characteristic help and hurt the character?"

Anne Lamot says that "Plot grows out of character. If you focus on who the people in your story are . . . something is bound to happen." Children are often tempted to skip the step of developing their characters. They may think of stories as sheer plot and want to jump right into the action. It's important to encourage them to slow down, to stay with their characters long enough to know them inside and out. Some fiction writers believe that characters begin to make their own decisions, even lead writers where they want to go. For this to happen, though, a writer needs to know her characters well.

Colleen is wise to examine what she means by "sensitive" because this will get children to think more deeply about the choices they make when naming their characters' traits. Children are often apt to throw around trite words like "mean" and "happy" without giving too much thought to what those words mean. By teaching them to think about the words they choose, we're encouraging them to be as precise as possible about who their characters are—to challenge clichés, and to get at the truth.

You could add something like, "Writers know that interesting, fleshed-out characters are at the heart of good fiction, but we often create wooden, two-dimensional characters when we're first writing. When I find myself doing this, I try to remember that the best characters are like real people; they're a mix of good and bad. Sometimes they even have contradictory traits: they're gentle yet tough, kind and cruel, self-assured but doubtful. Think about Harry in the story, "Papa's Parrot," who gets furious at his father's bird, calls it "stupid" and attacks it with peppermints. Harry is really cruel. At the same time, he sobs for his father because he understands that the parrot's words, "Where's Harry? Miss him" are just an echo of what his father has been saying. And because we relate to that mixture of anger and hurt, we forgive Harry his cruelty, sympathize with him, and grow from his complexities."

"I am going to think some more about Luz being sensitive and about her caring about people. I am thinking about why she cares for people and about how there needs to be a downside to this."

"Okay. I think Luz is really thin-skinned. Things get to her easily. Like the dark gets to her, and her father being away gets to her. People's judgments get to her too. Her feelings get hurt easily. This is why she is careful of other people. She assumes other people are thin-skinned like she is. I'll add these things to the internal side of my Developing My Character chart."

ACTIVE ENGAGEMENT
Set children up to join you in creating the main character in your story.

"So now it's your turn to try. Let's think about this character, Luz. For now, will you and your partner try to add some things to the other side of the chart—the external side? (By the way, I often develop the internal side first, and then make sure the external reflects the internal.) As you work, remember these things we've learned so far about developing characters," Colleen said, and pointed to the Advice for Developing a Character chart.

"Also, as you talk through things you might add about the external side of Luz—her hobbies, her looks, her ways of acting in the world, her friends or family, her experiences at school—remember that you are going to talk about external features that *fit with the internal ones*. So begin by rereading what we've already written, and then turn and tell your partner how the things we've already written affect your ideas about the external side of Luz." The room erupted into talk.

Intervene to lift the level of what children are saying by reminding them to use pointers from the chart.

After three minutes, Colleen interrupted. "Writers, can I have your eyes?" Then she said, "Please pause to reread the chart of Advice for Developing a Character and then use that advice to revise what you are saying about Luz's external features." Again, the room erupted into talk.

This bit of character development is sophisticated, and you may decide to postpone it for another year. But on the other hand, it is important work because we do want children to think about people, including characters in books, in complex ways. So this minilesson will be echoed in the reading curriculum. If children try to reduce characters in their novels to clichés, we say, "Most characters are not so simple." I used to point out to children that even J. R. Ewing loves his mother, but the reference doesn't mean much to the children in our classrooms today! Probably it'd be more effective to say, "Even a good guy like Harry Potter doesn't have good thoughts all the time!"

The story begins as Colleen's story but it will become a story that belongs to the entire class.

Colleen wisely steers students toward the often short-changed aspect of a character's internal nature. Young people can easily list external, physical features, and love doing it: tall, baggy clothes, dark brown hair, and so on. But we fall in love with characters not for what they look like, but for who they are— how they feel about things, their particular perspectives on the world—so the more time spent learning how to flesh out the character's interior life, the better. Still, there may be some children who begin creating their characters by elaborating on the external features. When you confer with these children, ask questions that will help them link physical and external qualities to internal states. For instance, if a character is tall for her age, ask the child how the character feels about this.

If we want a particular pointer (or a particular chart) to influence how children go about their work, we need to thread it through our conversations.

Elicit suggestions for character development from a few partnerships and add these to the list of external and internal features.

Colleen soon requested the children's attention, asking Paige to report back on what she and her partner had said. "We thought about how Luz is part Mexican so we said she has light-brown skin and then we thought she has a ponytail with long brown hair. We thought casual clothes would go with that and with her being sort of artistic. This is probably stupid but we made a sketch of some dangly earrings we thought she wore; she made them herself." Colleen added Paige and Francesca's suggestions to the chart.

Celebrate your children's imaginings about characters. It takes time for characters to unfold, for us to know them. When children find themselves thinking of tiny details about a character without quite knowing why these are so right, they're writing intuitively, creatively. They're allowing themselves to really see their characters. This is fiction writing at its best! You can help them understand the details they choose later. For now, let them enjoy the creative process.

Developing My Character: Luz

Outside (external features)	Inside (internal features)
Part Mexican	Afraid of the dark
Luz	Artistic
Light-brown skin	Cares for people
Long brown hair in ponytail	Thin-skinned
Casual clothes	
Self-made dangly earrings	

Keep in mind that just because a writer knows the color of a character's earrings and knows even why this color is special to the character, this information will probably not show up in the actual story! And bear in mind, too, that your children learn as much from the writing that does not end up in their publications as from the writing that does. You are, after all, hoping to develop great writers, not simply great writing. So nothing is wasted!

"Sketching her earrings is not in the least stupid. In fact, it is really smart to know your character well enough that you can sketch her dangly earrings. Do you know what color beads she used in the earrings? I bet you could tell me why that is her favorite color. Remember, you need to know your characters well enough to know how much change they have in their pockets!" Then Colleen added, "I'm beginning to think that Luz needs to become shared property and that this story is being co-written by all of us!"

When Colleen says, "Do you know what color beads she uses in her dangly earrings?" and suggests she's sure the children know why that color is so important to the character, she is nudging them to go further, to dig deeper—but doing so in a supportive manner. What a wonderful way to extend these children's efforts!

LINK

Rally members of the class to choose their story idea and begin charting external and internal characteristics of a character. Remind children that fiction writers do this always.

"You've got some big work to do during the writing workshop today. You'll begin by thinking whether one of your seed ideas, one of your *story* ideas, has chosen you. If nothing seems inevitable, if nothing feels like it can't be ignored, you may want to spend a bit more time collecting story ideas, going back to generating ideas. Either way, you need to end today feeling committed to one story idea. And once you have your story idea, you can begin getting to know your character."

"To think about what your character is like on the inside and the outside, you may want to use a two-column chart like the one we made together. I've got forms in the writing center. When you go to your writing spot, you can tape one of these forms into your notebook. Or you may prefer to just divide a page of your notebook into two columns. Or you can alternate paragraphs, with some paragraphs telling the internal side of your characters and others the external. You are in charge, of course."

"From this day on, I hope that whenever you write fiction, you remember that instead of launching right into a draft or focusing only on planning the plot line of a story, you always rein yourself in, taking the time to develop your character."

Listening to this, you may think, "Geez, I bet none of my kids feel as if a story idea has chosen them!" I encourage you to act as if your kids are zealously committed to their stories. Act as if they love writing. You'll surprise yourself by finding the drama becomes real life. As you've heard me say before, the literacy researcher, Jerry Harste, once said, "I see teaching as creating, in the classroom, the kind of world we believe in and then inviting our children to role play their way into becoming the readers and writers we hope they'll become." Over and over again, you'll see that in our minilessons, we speak to children as if we know they're passionately involved in their writing. We hope that our assumptions become realities.

The truth is that this minilesson channels children in a very direct way. So it helps to highlight that, within the constraints of this directive, children still have some choices.

Pause to marvel at the amount of instruction you fit into today's teaching!

WRITING AND CONFERRING

Anticipating the Help Children Will Need Developing Their Characters

As you confer with individuals or, more likely, with small groups, you'll no doubt see that many children begin by simply listing phrases to describe the character. Ariana, for example, began with the list in Figure III-1.

Don't be surprised that children are making lists—this should be what you expect. But when conferring, help these youngsters realize that their lists can be more specific and more elaborated. Pay attention to places where the child provides a bit more detail, and celebrate these. For example, with coaching, Ariana progressed from developing her character with a mere list of words toward doing this with phrases. *[Fig. III-2]*

- licks her nose with her tongue
- sometimes wears hair up half down pigtails
- puts her hair behind her ears
- she doesn't move her head when she talks
- says "well" a lot, ex—did you know that, well, the new . . .

As you confer, you will probably notice that many of the characters seem like stereotypes. This is natural. Luz, even, begins as a half-Mexican artist with dangly earrings and loose, swinging clothes. It would be tempting to teach students to think critically about the work they've done developing characters by putting their characters on trial: "Is your character a stereotype? Is your character simplistic?" I don't recommend this. For now, it is very important for youngsters to bond with their characters, and therefore we are wise to avoid treating the character or the character development work harshly. If a character seems generic, stereotypical or underdeveloped, instead of saying so, simply help the writer outgrow this surface-level character development.

For example, when a character's internal characteristics are generic, I find I can help the child open up those generic terms if I ask the right questions. If the character is "good at soccer," then I can point out that people can be good at soccer in different ways. "What is your character's *specific* way of being good at soccer?" I can even press further and ask, "What is going on inside the character that makes her so good at

---

MID-WORKSHOP TEACHING POINT   ***Building the Character's Self-View***   "Writers, I just must stop you! I've been thinking that as we work on creating the insides of our characters, we don't want to forget one really important thing. We need to think about how our characters feel about themselves. We know, as real people, that how we feel about ourselves is really important. It only makes sense that our characters would think something about themselves too. Does your character like himself, herself? Does the character think he or she is funny? If your character is strange, does she know she's strange? Is the character humble? Or does the character think she or he is the best thing since sliced bread?" *[Fig. III-1]*

Sally
- oval eyes
- a little curly
- tan skin
- jean capris
- red shoes

continued on next page

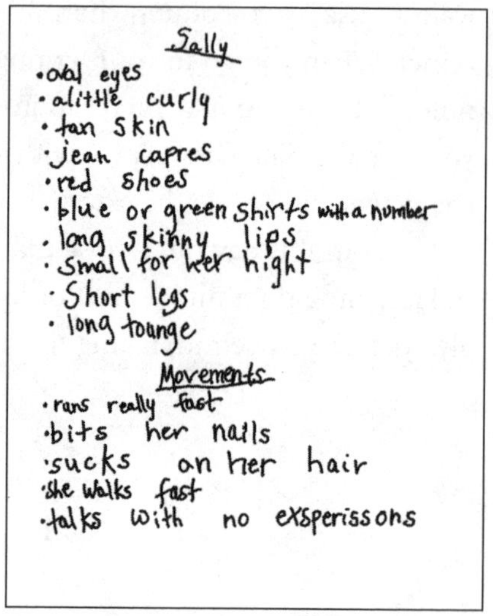

Fig. III-1 At first Ariana simply listed phrases as she developed her character.

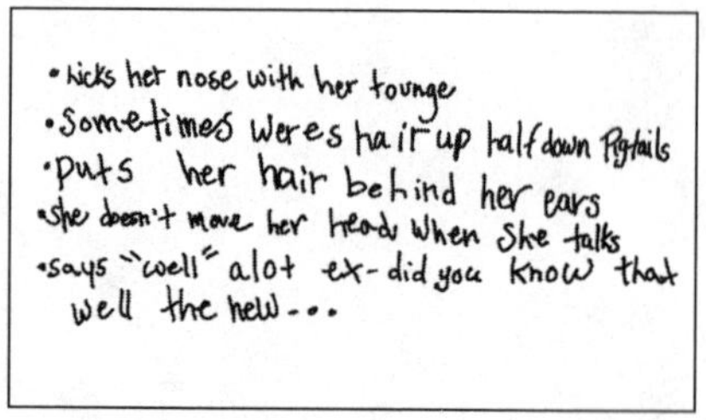

Fig. III-2 With coaching, Ariana's descriptors became more detailed.

soccer?" Once the child has answered by creating some revealing details about this one dimension of the character's life, I might ask, "How does that connect to other things the character does?" It also helps to ask, "What's the downside of this?" The character who is always pushing during the soccer game may not know when to relax. In a conference, I'll ask these questions of a child, but I will also pull back and talk about the importance of asking (as well as answering) questions such as these. That is, I will pause in a conference and say, "Will you notice, for a moment, the questions I've asked you about your character because these are questions you, as a writer, need to be able to ask yourself and each other." It helps to chart these questions. My goal, of course, is for the young writer to learn that another time, he or she can ask these same questions while writing. Children can also ask these questions of each other's characters.

If a character seems wooden, I often find the youngster has been trying to make up the character out of thin air. When this is the case, I find it helps if the child learns to lend his or her own life experience to the character. A child can do this even if the character is in many ways very different from himself. For example, a child might be writing a story about an old man who has outlived all his family members. The child doesn't know much about being old, but he can think, "When I feel lonely, what do I do?" Perhaps, when no one is home and the place echoes, the child sometimes looks through sports trophies, remembering the games. Why couldn't the old man do something similar? Perhaps the youngster finds that when the house is especially empty, he finds that he waits for phone calls, and sometimes even picks up the receiver to check that there's a dial tone so that calls can come through. Why couldn't the old man do this as well? Details grounded in real life have power.

Sometimes when I confer with a child, I find that the child feels as if he or she has hit a dead end with a character. I sometimes let the child know that problems with a character's development can be early warning signals that the story idea itself doesn't fit the writer, or that the story idea has problems that need to be addressed. As a result, then, I may encourage the writer to rethink the entire story idea.

Finally, I always keep in mind that secondary characters need to be developed too! Everything that the writer has done with the main character needs to be done with the secondary characters.

continued from previous page

- blue or green shirts with a number
- long skinny lips
- small for her height
- short legs
- long tongue

Movements
- runs really fast
- bites her nails
- sucks on her hair
- she walks fast
- talks with no expressions

"Ariana has wisely set up two columns in her notebook. One is labeled 'attitude toward self' and the other is 'attitude of others toward her.' Some of the rest of you may want to follow Ariana's example. Before we go on, look back and see if you have included what your character thinks of himself or herself." *[Fig. III-3]*

Attitude toward self
- she thinks she's dumb, grumpy, rude
- and of machas she hates her lips
- she knows all of what she thinks isn't true but she still thinks that

Attitude of others toward her
- Mrs. Jorach her teacher thinks she's great in writing
- Mr. Megrache her math teacher thinks she's good in word problems

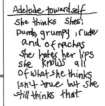

Fig. III-3 Ariana's notebook entry

SHARE

Complicating Characters

Spotlight one student who decided his character was one-sided and asked, "What's the flip side of this trait?"

"Writers, you've done some wise work today. I especially want to celebrate the wise decision Henry made when he realized that his character, Max, was too good to be true. So Henry went back to alter his early work with the character, Max. Henry had already said Max had a rich imagination. He'd already said that the character's lively imagination meant he had big, imaginative dreams, and plans and schemes, too. Henry worried, though, that Max sounded *too* perfect. He could have just added some other, less-ideal qualities, but instead he did something really smart. He thought, 'If my character has a lively imagination, this is probably bad as well as good for him.' Then Henry wrote that his character imagines everything that could go wrong, and consequently has lots of big worries and always seems nervous."

"I hope all of you learn from what Henry has done. He realized his character was too good to be true, but he didn't just jump into a list of bad as well as good things about him. Instead, Henry took one thing—that his character imagines a lot—and thought carefully about the ways this would help *and* hurt his character."

Extrapolate the larger principle. Writers develop complex characters by thinking of the bad as well as good aspects of a trait.

"Writers call characters like the one that Henry has created *complex*. With your partner today, would you look at your characters and think whether they have bad as well as good sides, and whether you've really worked through the ups and downs of your characters' personalities?"

As we listened in on partnerships, Ariana read her entries aloud and Jesse signaled with her thumb to indicate whether Ariana was showing the good side, the bad side, or a neutral side of a trait. This is what Ariana *[Fig. III-4]* read aloud.

> Seamus
> Internal Inside
> is afraid of everything
> doesn't like his father
> he likes to go on high roller coasters

You'll notice that this unit is densely packed, and that each new component of a minilesson lays out another point. There is never a time to simply share! You may decide that the sequence of these minilessons moves way too quickly, in which case you'll want to write interim minilessons. One way to do this is to take pointers that are now embedded into the Shares or the Mid-Workshop Teaching Points and use them as the teaching points in minilessons.

Although the Share session gives children one opportunity to talk about their characters, you needn't shoehorn all this thinking and talking into the writing workshop. If you want to stoke the fires of excitement that came when launching this unit, whenever you have an extra five minutes before the end of the day or before gym, assume children will be dying to talk and think about their characters and "let" them do so.

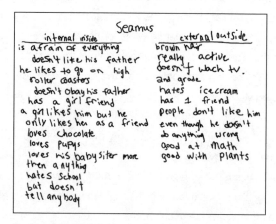

Fig. III-4 Ariana read this aloud to her partner, noticing whether she'd included negative as well as positive traits.

doesn't obey his father

has a girlfriend

a girl likes him but he only likes her as a friend

loves chocolate

loves puppies

loves his babysitter more than anything

hates school but doesn't tell anybody

External Outside

brown hair

really active

doesn't watch TV

2nd grade

hates ice cream

has 1 friend

people don't like him even though he doesn't do anything wrong

good at math

good with plants

Deveonna, meanwhile, showed Ari that she'd developed her characters by first revising her original story idea. Whereas earlier, she'd imagined that Elexa would be struggling to be chosen as a cheerleader, now Elexa struggles instead to shake off the fawning attention of Max. Beautiful, popular Elexa (the would-be cheerleader) isn't sure if geeky Max is after her or after her best friend, Lexie. This is what Deveonna wrote: *[Fig. III-5]*

> Today I was walking around the schoolyard, and I saw that Max kid, but he wasn't chasing after me, in fact he was after Lexie, and she let him catch her. Show off! She wants to be the one, so she can get the part. I wonder if I should call him over and talk and end my longest friendship over him.

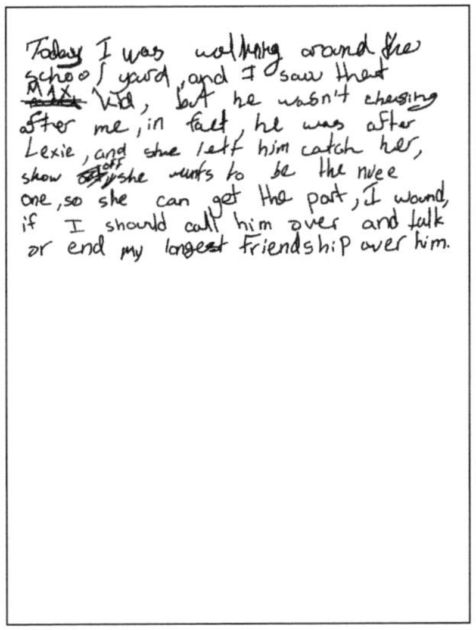
Today I was walking around the school yard, and I saw that Max kid, but he wasn't chasing after me, in fact, he was after Lexie, and she left him catch her, show off she wants to be the nwee one, so she can get the part, I wound, if I should call him over and talk or end my longest friendship over him.

Fig. III-5 Deveonna's revised story idea

HOMEWORK *Fleshing Out Secondary Characters* We've spent the last few days getting to know our main characters. We've made T-charts, compiled lists, and practiced writing scenes in order to bring our main characters to life. Yet we all know that there are other characters in our stories. Some of you remember from our reading work that we call these secondary characters. They are important characters and deserve our attention because they really help to make our stories believable. It's not enough for us to have a great main character if all the other characters in our story seem like we rushed through them.

Tonight for homework, take a look at the other characters in your story idea. Try some of the same work with a secondary character that you did with your main character. You can make an internal/external T-chart or you can explore different things about them that we have on our lists. Whichever you try, the most important thing to keep in mind is that writers know all of the characters in their story well, not just the main character.

TAILORING YOUR TEACHING This minilesson launches some important work with character development. You'll certainly want to spend another day or two helping children continue to flesh out their characters.

If your students need a more concrete way to get to the abstract idea that a character has an internal life . . . you could teach them that just as some writers brainstorm writing topics by sketching a heart and jotting on it the topics that the writer has in his or her heart— Mom, horses, rainy days—so, too, could children get to know a character by pretending that character does the same thing. Children can ask themselves, "What might the protagonist of my story put inside his or her heart?" Similarly, the child could imagine the people, places, or objects the character might write about in his or her writer's notebook.

If you notice that some students have lots of notes on their characters, yet the characters still feel like caricatures . . . it might help these children to see the world through their characters' eyes. You could teach your children that fiction writers sometimes find it productive to put a character in a situation where the character is all alone (waking up in the morning, walking home from school) and then to write what the character does, in tiny detail, interspersed with what the character notices and thinks and wonders and remembers as he or she goes about the small solitary activity. These solitary moments can be revealing, and meanwhile children practice writing scenes. For example, in Figure III-6, Ariana has done this:

In the bathroom

"Wake up, wake up," my mom calls. "Are you up yet?"

"I'm getting up." I walk in the bathroom, take my toothbrush and put it in my mouth. "This tastes like tomatoes, euh!" I brushed my teeth, got dressed and walked to school.

If you have students who are game for a challenge . . . encourage them to study how authors they admire have portrayed their characters, and to let those examples serve as mentor texts. In *Night Noises*, for example, Mem Fox describes old Lillie Laceby by saying:

Her hair was as wispy as cobwebs in ceilings. Her bones were as creaky as floorboards at midnight.

Or you could use an example from your own notebook:

Luz looked at her dresser. She knew she should maybe put on a nice blouse or something. After all, it was picture day. Instead, she pulled out her denim overalls that had the paint splatters on the knees. Her mom hated those overalls. She thought they looked like rags. Luz loved them. They were soft against her skin, and comfortable too.

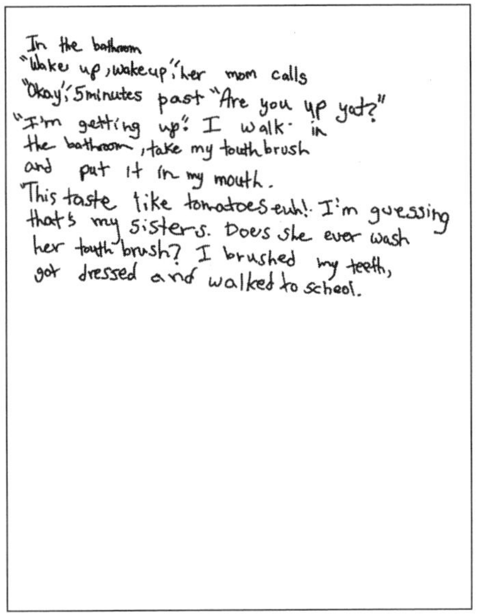

In the bathroom
"Wake up, wakeup," her mom calls
"Okay", 5minutes past "Are you up yet?"
"I'm getting up." I walk in
the bathroom, take my toothbrush
and put it in my mouth.
"This taste like tomatoes euh! I'm guessing
that's my sisters. Does she ever wash
her toothbrush? I brushed my teeth,
got dressed and walked to school.

Fig. III-6 Ariana has written a scene, bringing her character Sally to life.

ASSESSMENT

You'll definitely want to read over your children's writing at this juncture so you can plan ways to help them. Try temporarily sorting your children's work. If you create lists of children who could benefit from one kind of help or another, then you can cover a lot more ground within the writing workshop. Examine not just their work with character, but also, more fundamentally, their story ideas. Now is the time to help children revise these, so don't wait! You are apt to see that children fit into several categories.

You'll no doubt find that some children don't seem invested in their own ideas. You'll want to work with these children one on one. Perhaps ask the child to talk to you about the story idea and try listening to it really responsively, as if it is an amazing idea and deeply suited to the child. Sometimes your commitment to an idea can help the writer become committed to it as well. But if you seem to be the only one who gets excited about the idea, then name this as a problem and help the child get started on a different idea—even if this means the child is out of step with the class.

Other children may have story ideas that contain some of the most crucial elements of story, but not all of them. Gather these children together and overview the elements that all stories usually contain (or at least those your class has studied). Ask these children to look again, thinking, "Which of these is not well developed in my entry?" Then give them a chance to flesh out their story ideas so they contain all the crucial elements.

You'll almost certainly have a cluster of children who have disregarded your efforts to channel them toward writing a *focused* short story. Their story ideas might work as ideas for a novel, but are too expansive to be contained in a short story. You'll want to bring these children together into a small group. Explain the problem, point out that the short stories they're reading at home contain no more than three scenes (or small moments). Then use what you know of each child to help that child settle on a more focused story idea.

For example, if a child has a list like Marissa's in Figure III-7 or Sofiya's in Figure III-8, help that writer zoom in on just a tiny portion of her idea.

You'll probably find another cluster of children who have each developed a fragment of a story idea, but don't yet have a complete plan. For example, this child's story idea lacks tension:

> Gwen met Summer when she moved to Brooklyn with her Grandparents and started going to school. Summer and Gwen always stick together.

Perhaps they've developed a character who dreams of a goal and gets it. What's still needed in that story plan is the tension, the challenge. Perhaps this is a character with particular traits and goals, and what's missing is the plot line.

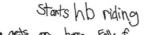

Starts hb riding
- gets on horse Falls of
- gets own horse
- Starts riding
- from Walk goes to trot
- learns to post
- from trot goes to canter
- learns how to clean house gear
- learns how to groom horse

Fig. III-7 Marissa's story idea

She won her first trophy at the age of 12

She made lots of new friends

She got on a tennis team.

She practiced a lot.

She won a lot of medals, ribbons, and awards.

Won a trophy

Fig. III-8 Sofiya's story idea

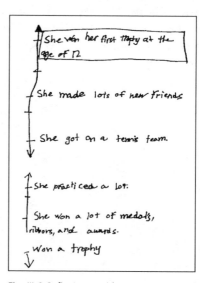

IN THIS SESSION, YOU'LL TEACH
CHILDREN THAT WRITERS CAN
DEVELOP CHARACTERS BY TELLING
ABOUT THEIR CHARACTERS'
MOTIVATIONS AND STRUGGLES, AND
ALSO BY CREATING SCENES THAT
SHOW THESE THINGS.

GETTING READY

- Chart of all the different character ideas students have developed
- Passage from a text students know well that illustrates a character's yearning
- Class story in mind that children can use for practice text
- Advice for Developing a Character chart
- Qualities of Good Personal Narrative Writing chart (from Unit 2)
- Idea for an ordinary scene with your character that you can quickly compose on chart paper
- See CD-ROM for resources

GIVING CHARACTERS STRUGGLES AND MOTIVATIONS

In today's session you will guide students into what many fiction writers consider the heart of fiction: character struggle and motivation. You will teach your students that readers will root for a character when they know what the character wants and they see the character struggle toward these goals. As Gerald Brace writes in The Stuff of Fiction, *"The first essential is the creation of believable persons who wait for something or want something or hope for something—they themselves hardly know why or what. Suspense is created by the waiting and wanting."*

We know this from our reading lives. Charlotte wants to help Wilbur, and this longing leads Charlotte to weave her web. Readers, too, want to save Wilbur. We want this so much that we flinch when Charlotte is almost discovered, and we root for a rat to bring back the much-needed newspaper clippings.

Students, like E. B. White, can rope readers in by creating characters who have desires that are intrinsic to their personalities. A shy person might dream of one day overcoming her fear of performing on stage. Encourage students to think not only about what their *characters desire, but* why *these motivations matter so, so much. This will help children create richer, more complex characters.*

In life, of course, the path is never smooth. This is true in stories, too. No one wants to read a story where the character wants something, and then promptly gets that thing. We read to find bits of ourselves in characters; and the characters we love best are often the ones whose desires and struggles mirror our own. We are more apt, then, to get lost in stories that take us on a slow journey toward overcoming a challenge or toward realizing a long-held dream rather than in the drive-through quick-and-easy stories. We want to live inside a character's shoes, facing his dragons, reaching for her gold medal. And we want to do so slowly so that we can savor the final outcome after the long buildup.

Even though students are still sorting out how they want their stories to go, this session sets them up to create the right combination of motivation and obstacles. This way, their characters can star in riveting plots.

MINILESSON

Giving Characters Struggles and Motivations

CONNECTION

Celebrate the character development work children have already done in a way that honors it.

"Writers, I feel as if a whole crowd of people came into the classroom with you this morning. You brought with you Griffen, who dreams of impressing Julie and of having a pet of his own; and Mario, who is hoping to get a chance to play jazz at his church's coffeehouse; Mrs. Randoff who has nasty teeth like an old rusty pole and who tells the black kids to get off her block; and Alex, with her horse bracelets and horse T-shirts and horse-sized hole in her life. I jotted down the sorts of details you have been inventing for your characters. Look at the list of what you have done!"

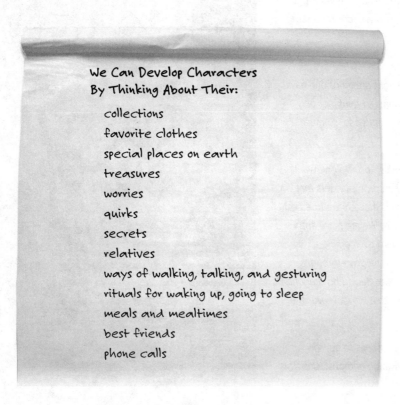

We Can Develop Characters
By Thinking About Their:

collections

favorite clothes

special places on earth

treasures

worries

quirks

secrets

relatives

ways of walking, talking, and gesturing

rituals for waking up, going to sleep

meals and mealtimes

best friends

phone calls

COACHING

Instead of beginning this minilesson by telling specific ways that I hope children have learned to flesh out their characters, I try to simply applaud their enthusiasm and show a list that records what writers have done so far. My fondest hope for the class right now is that they are absorbed in their characters, carrying these "people" with them all the time. I therefore act as if this is already happening.

Of course, I could have taught separate minilessons in which I suggest writers could think about these and other aspects of their characters, but especially by this time in the year, I try to use minilessons to teach skills and concepts that are too complicated to just mention in passing.

Name your teaching point. In this case, tell children that fiction writers must think about their characters' desires and their struggles to fulfill those desires.

"Today I want to teach you that although there are oodles of things we *can* think about as we develop our characters, there are just one or two things that we *must* think about. Specifically, I want to teach you this: Every fiction writer needs to know what his or her characters want, what they yearn for, and what gets in the way—what keeps these characters from getting what they want."

"I also want to teach you that when we know what our characters yearn for, we don't just come right out and say what this is. We *show* what our characters want by putting examples of this into little small moments, into what fiction writers call *scenes.*"

TEACHING
Show students an example of a published text in which the character wants something and encounters difficulties. Show that the author conveys this through a dramatic scene.

"I learned to do this by studying how published authors—writers like Alma Flor Ada and the authors of the short stories you've been reading—write little scenes (which could be called vignettes or Small Moment stories) that show what a character yearns for and what gets in the way for that character."

"In the book *My Name Is Maria Isabel*, remember how the teacher decided early in the story that because she had two students named Maria, she would change Maria Isabel Lopez's name to Mary. Maria Isabel, of course, doesn't feel at home in the name *Mary*. She doesn't recognize when her teacher is addressing her as Mary, and so she gets into trouble. When we read the story, we come to know that Maria Isabel *yearns* to be accepted for who she is (not Mary Lopez) and to feel that she has a role to play in the class—but the author doesn't come right out and say that Maria Isabel yearns for this. Instead Alma Flor Ada shows this by putting examples of that yearning into scenes. In the chapter titled "The First Snowfall," watch how Alma Flor Ada tells a Small Moment story (or a scene) that reveals Maria Isabel's longings and also the trouble she encounters at school."

> Once she was at school, Maria Isabel kept thinking about the snow all during math . . . Suddenly she remembered that she hadn't finished her multiplication exercises, and hurried to complete her work. Maria Isabel was so busy trying to finish the page that she didn't hear the teacher call out, in an irritated tone of voice, "Mary Lopez!" When at last she realized that the teacher was waiting for an answer from her, Maria Isabel had no idea what the question had been.

This session is very full, and of course it could have been broken into separate sessions: we need to know our characters' wants; we need to know our characters' struggles (or what gets in the way of achieving their wants); and we need to show, not tell, these details. I decided to consolidate all three of these tips into one teaching point because otherwise, I felt the children's work would be odd. I didn't think it'd be valuable for children to spend an entire writing workshop listing only characters' wants, for example. Also, I'm aware that sometimes separating items that belong together can actually make them more, not less, complicated. Notice that in an instance like this, I don't hesitate to devote a few sentences to making my teaching point as clear as possible.

Notice that I am referring to texts the whole class already knows. It would be very rare to read aloud a new text within a minilesson. There is nothing that makes My Name Is Maria Isabel uniquely suited to this minilesson—any story would work. Use one that your class knows well.

Although Colleen and I have decided that during the Teaching component of minilessons, we'll often demonstrate by showing children what we do as fiction writers and that we'll often use the Luz story, we're aware it would be monotonous if every day's teaching were built upon that story. So you'll see us vary the text we use, as I do in today's minilesson. Notice that usually there are two texts in any one minilesson. One of these is a text which threads through the Teaching component of many minilessons, and the other is a text which threads through the Active Engagement of many minilessons. In this minilesson, the teaching story is a published children's book, and the story of Luz that was once Colleen's teaching text now becomes the whole class' story, used during Active Engagement.

"Well, it looks like Mary doesn't want to take part in our Winter Pageant," the teacher said. "That's all right. You can help Tony and Jonathon greet the parents at the door and show them where they can put the food and hang up their coats."

The Winter Pageant . . . Maria Isabel couldn't think about anything else on the ride home from school . . . ."I would have loved to be a shepherd. I could have used Mama's straw basket, and it would have been so wonderful . . . "

Maria Isabel turned toward the window of the school bus so that no one would see her wiping a tear.

Debrief. Mention that writers create little scenes and then piece them together like bricks. Point out that the scenes show characters in action in ways that reveal their desires and struggles.

"Some people say that fiction is like a brick wall, and the bricks that go together to make the story are scenes, or vignettes. This scene shows what school is like for Maria Isabel. When she works so zealously on her math (after being distracted by her first snowstorm), we see her resolve to do things right. And then we see how she gets into trouble simply because she doesn't recognize—doesn't hear, really—when her teacher addresses her as Mary. We see, also, how desperately Maria Isabel wants to be part of things, and how she hides her sadness."

"When we are developing characters, then, we need to think not only about what our characters want and what gets in the way for them. We also need to think about how we can create little scenes that show all this."

ACTIVE ENGAGEMENT
Rename the longings and difficulties experienced by the character in the class' story, and then have children talk with their partners to bring these motivations and struggles to life in a scene.

"Let's try this with Luz. I'll get us started by thinking a little bit about what she wants."
I assumed the posture I usually take when demonstrating that I am thinking.

Notice that I abbreviated the text by skipping past some of the detail. Published literature (and especially novels) will be more detailed and elaborate than anything the children can write. By letting some of the detail fall away, I share a text that more closely resembles what I'm hoping children will write. You can do the same, or you can decide otherwise. There are good reasons for either alternative.

Of course, you can decide to simplify this minilesson by letting some points fall aside. You may well want to end the minilesson by simply repeating that there are many things writers can show about characters but there are just one or two things that writers must *show: a character's wants and struggles.*

Neil Simon has said, "Only recently did I discover that my plays didn't really take off until the main character wanted something and wanted it badly."

You have a choice. You can launch a class story that will function as a practice text throughout this unit, or you can invite children to coauthor the text that was, originally, your story. You'll notice Colleen and I chose the second option.

"Let's see, Luz is afraid of the dark. We've already decided she's going to have a slumber party but she doesn't want everyone to know she's scared of the dark. That's the story, but what does she really *want*? I think she wants her friends to think she is cool. She feels different because her father is Mexican, and she wants them to accept her."

"So will you guys imagine a scene that could show some of this? Let's put Luz somewhere—packing for a slumber party, climbing into her sleeping bag at the party—and she is doing *something* (see if you and your partner can come up with an idea) that shows that she is afraid of the dark but doesn't want to use her night-light when her friends come because she wants to be accepted by them. Turn and talk. See if you have any suggestions for how we could write this into a scene." The room burst into conversation.

Convene the class and ask a child or two to share a suggestion. Help the child to turn an explanation into a scene. Debrief to point out the process needed to make a scene.

After a bit, I interrupted. "Writers, can I stop you? What ideas did you have for a little scene we could write that might show all this?"

Sirah's hand shot up. "You could show the slumber party and she says, 'Good night' and turns off the light and then lies there in the dark, listening to the noises and worrying."

Ramon added, "Or you could have her lying in her own bed, a couple days before the slumber party, with the lights off, practicing sleeping in the dark. She could get scared and get up and leave the closet light on."

"Those are both exciting ideas," I said. "Ramon, help me actually write what you envision. Class, you'll notice that Ramon and I can't actually write a scene until we can picture exactly what happens in a step-by-step way, with all the tiny, tiny actions. So Ramon, let's picture the whole thing like a movie in our minds. Luz is lying in bed, trying not to be afraid of the dark. What *exactly* is she doing? More specifically, what is Luz doing or saying to herself that shows the reader that she is scared of the dark and shows the reader that she is practicing sleeping with the lights off?"

"She is just looking up. She looks where the lamp usually shines. She doesn't want to lie in the dark but she tells herself, 'I gotta practice.'"

"I can picture it: 'Luz stared through the darkness to where the light usually shone. "I've got to practice," she said to herself. She . . . ' What? What does she do next?"

"She closes her eyes so she won't see that it is dark. Then she gets out of bed and she opens the closet door and she pulls the light string on and she leaves the door open just a crack."

Notice that although this is the Active Engagement section of the minilesson (when it's the kids' turn to do the work), I review the facts and begin the work I've proposed. In this way I give the children a running start, passing the baton to them only once momentum has been well established. This makes it much more likely that children can be active and productive even within a three-minute Active Engagement section.

It is key to realize that once we decide on a character's traits or wants, we need to imbue these with life by writing them within a scene, as occurs here.

Novice fiction writers are apt to explain what's going on rather than to show it. Notice that I help Ramon take his explanation of what's going on and imagine the actions that a character might take that would convey this. I do this not because I want to teach Ramon (I could do that later in a conference) but because I know that by helping him, I can help most of the class.

You'll recall that this is the portion of the Active Engagement when the teacher calls on one member of the class to share what he or she just said or did. Usually we select carefully so that we call on children who help us make the point we hope to highlight. But sometimes we call on a child whose contribution is not exactly what we're after. Notice how, in this instance, I try to explicitly name the problem I have with Ramon's draft, and then coach him to revise it. This revision of one child's "writing in the air" is a helpful way to demonstrate complex, sophisticated writing work. Notice the way in which I coach him and scaffold his work. This is exactly the work you'll also do in conferences today.

"So let me try that," I said. "Class, pay attention to the power of Ramon's tiny, tiny details. I'll even add some more," I said, and quickly wrote this scene on chart paper:

> I stared through the darkness to where my lamp usually
> shone brightly. "I've got to practice," I said to myself. I
> turned onto my stomach and squeezed my eyes shut.
> But even through my closed eyes, I could tell that the
> comforting glow from my bedside lamp was gone.
>
> Climbing out of bed, I opened the door to my closet,
> pulled the light string on, and then closed the door
> partway, careful to leave a crack of light shining into
> the bedroom.

Notice that I accept Ramon's ideas for what could happen in this scene, but I turn his oral storytelling into text that sounds literate, or written. I act as if I'm simply restating what Ramon said. "I can see it," I say, prefacing my version of his words. The differences between Ramon's version and mine are subtle, but in this way, I'm trying to help him lift the quality of his oral storytelling to the realm of literature.

Notice that the actual writing I do in front of the class is very limited. Writing on chart paper is a slow process and minilesson time is precious!

Debrief. Reiterate that writers put their characters into situations—small scenes—that reveal their desires and their struggles.

"Ramon and I have put Luz in a situation where we can show what she wants and what she struggles with, and we have tried to write a little scene, a small moment, that shows all of this. Notice the words we chose that really brought the scene to life: 'squeezed . . . shut,' 'comforting glow,' 'crack of light.' Do you see how these words highlight Luz' struggle to overcome her fear of the dark? All of you will write lots of scenes like this for your own character today, tomorrow, and whenever you want to write fiction."

LINK
Put today's teaching point into context by reminding writers of all they now know how to do. Stress that deciding what their character wants is not an option but is essential, and add this to the chart.

"So writers, whenever you write fiction, remember there are oodles of things we *can* think about when you want to develop characters: a character's special places on earth, best friends, quirks, collections, and ways of waking up. There are oodles of things we *can* think about, but just one or two that you *must* think about: As fiction writers we must know what it is that our characters yearn for, and what gets in their way."

"We usually build the story line out of our character's motivations and struggles—so once you know what your character yearns for and struggles to have, then it's wise to create little scenes that show this. Remember how we just put Luz somewhere—in bed—and came

By this time in the year, you don't need to make a fuss over the fact that, of course, students will not write Luz stories but will instead transfer what they've learned to their own story ideas.

Notice that I pick up exact phrases I used earlier in the minilesson. There are "oodles of things you can *think about . . . and just one or two things you* must *think about." Notice, also, the parallel structure. I want this advice to be memorable.*

up with something she could be doing—practicing sleeping without a light on to get ready for the slumber party—to show what she longs for? You'll want to do this same work with your story idea, not once but many times today, and you'll want to remember to do this whenever you write fiction. The scenes you end up writing today may not end up in your stories. Writing them, like making the two-column chart, is a way to bring characters to life, and that's our greatest job right now." I added the latest point to the chart of advice.

Advice for Developing a Character

- Start with whatever you've decided matters to you about your character. Is he/she like you? Like someone you know? A person who starts out tough?

- Put together a character where all the parts fit together into a coherent person.

- Reread often, asking, "Do these different things make sense within one person? Do they fit together in a believable way? Are these traits here for a reason?"

- Open up any broad, general descriptors—words like sensitive—and ask, "What exactly does this word, this trait, mean for this particular character?"

- If a character seems too good to be true, make the character more complex and more human by asking, "What is the downside of this trait? How does this characteristic help and hurt the character?"

- Know your character's motivations (longings) and struggles.

Donald Graves has said, "Fiction is really about character. It is about showing characters wanting things, having aspirations they hope will be fulfilled, or wanting a different life from the one they are living at the moment. Of course, it isn't long before all this 'wanting' produces tough choices, and negative and positive reactions from others. Usually the main character learns something about life itself" (Inside Writing, p. 36).

Threading a single chart through a series of minilessons is a great way to keep yesterday's teaching points front and center in children's minds. It is typical for a minilesson to become the latest bullet on a chart. Be sure that your charts are sensible examples of "boxes and bullets." That is, you won't want to add a tip about editing onto a chart titled Advice for Developing a Character, nor will you want to simply create hodge-podge charts.

WRITING AND CONFERRING

Showing Characters by Writing Scenes

You may find that many of your writers could benefit from a conference like the one I had with Francesca. I pulled my chair alongside her and saw she'd written the entry shown in Figure IV-1.

> Griffen likes to act like he is 13. He likes to act really cool. Sometimes he embarrasses himself in front of Julie Colings. Griffen really loves Julie. He is always trying to impress her but this boy Mikey the Bully always takes her away.

"Francesca," I said. "You've got a great idea for your story, and you've sketched out some notes on Griffen. Your next step will be to try writing some scenes which show Griffen and Julie in action—they probably won't be scenes you actually include in your final story, but writing them will help you know these characters better. Remember in the minilesson how we remembered what Luz wants, which is for kids to think she's cool and to not realize she's afraid to sleep without a night-light. So all of us imagined a scene that might show Luz doing something around those fears and wants. Ramon started off just summarizing by saying, 'Luz is lying in her bed, practicing sleeping in the dark. She could get scared,' but then he ended up making a movie in his mind that *showed* this. He had to picture it in a step-by-step way, and he started by thinking, 'What exactly is she doing?' That scene turned out this way."

> I stared through the darkness to where my lamp usually shone brightly. "I've got to practice," I said to myself. I turned onto my stomach and squeezed my eyes shut . . .

"Francesca, you'll get to know Griffen so much better if you make him come to life in a scene in your notebook. I guess you already know he wants to impress Julie. Can you think of one particular time when Griffen acted cool, trying to impress Julie?" I waited till she nodded. "Now you need to ask yourself the same question: 'What *exactly* is Griffen doing? How does it start?'"

"He and Timmy are riding their bikes and he . . . "

"So write that!" I said, dictating, "One time Timmy and Griffen . . . "

MID-WORKSHOP TEACHING POINT *Sharing a Scene That Shows a Character's Traits* "Writers, I want to show you the important work Ariana is doing. Yesterday she wrote entries about her character. In one of them, she'd written this:"

> Sally is different in front of her friends than her mom. She tries to talk really cool. Sally hates tomatoes, but her mom keeps making stuff she has to eat with tomatoes in it. That makes her mad.

"So today, Ariana decided to try her hand at writing a scene that showed this, just like we did with Luz's fear of the night. You'll remember that to get started, we began by thinking, 'Where could Luz be? What could she be doing?' and so Ariana asked herself these same questions. She knew she wanted to show that her character, Sally, sometimes gets mad at her

continued on next page

> Griffen likes to act like he is 13 He likes to act really cool sometimes he ImBaroses hisself in front of Julie Colings. Griffen really loves Julie. He is always trying to Impress her but this Boy Mikey the Bully always takes her away

Fig. IV-1 Francesca's first draft of a scene

Francesca wrote this entry: *[Fig. IV-2]*

> One time Timmy and Griffen were riding their bikes and he went by Julie Colings. Griffen quickly stopped. "Hi Griffen," she said in a loving way. "Hi Julie," Griffen said almost falling to the floor. "Well bye," Julie said. Griffen could not say another word. Then he fell on the floor . . . .
>
> The next day Griffen saw some 13-year-olds skateboarding on a big ramp. Griffen wanted to impress Julie so he asked to try. Timmy told him that it was a bad idea but he did it. He landed flat on his face and the 13-year-olds teased him. Griffen was so embarrassed.
>
> Then Julie went over to him and pulled him up. "Are you ok?" she said. "Of course," Griffen said meekly. "Well bye," Julie said.

continued from previous page

mother for making her eat things with tomatoes, and also Sally acts differently when she's talking to her friends. Pretty soon she'd written this scene." *[Fig. IV-3]*

> I thump, thump, thump down the stairs into the kitchen.
>
> "Hurry, we are having tomato soup tonight"
>
> "Mom, I **hate** tomato soup!" I yelled
>
> "You have to."
>
> "I don't got ah" I said in a strong voice.
>
> "Go upstairs right now, young lady," she said.
>
> I thumped back up the stairs and yelled, "I hate you."
>
> That's when my mom got really mad. I picked up the phone and dialed Sarah's number.
>
> "Hello" she said.
>
> "What-up?" I said.
>
> "Nothing up, I got punished."

continued on next page

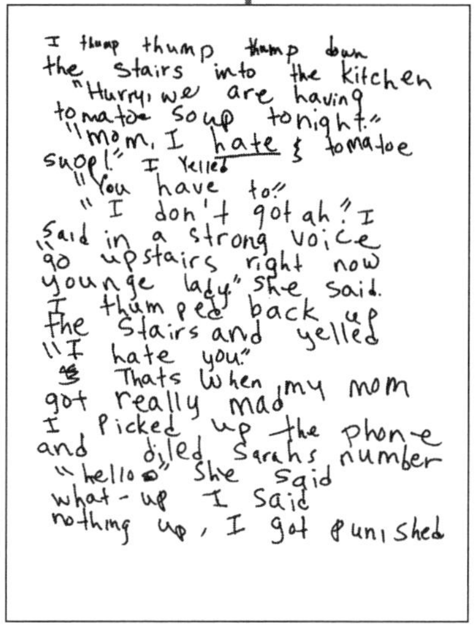
I thump thump thump down the stairs into the kitchen "Hurry, we are having tomatoe soup tonight." "mom, I hate tomatoe soup!" I yelled "You have to" "I don't got ah!" I said in a strong voice "go upstairs right now younge lady" she said. I thumped back up the stairs and yelled "I hate you." Thats when my mom got really mad I picked up the phone and diled Sarahs number "hello" she said what-up I said nothing up, I got punished

Fig. IV-3 Ariana's scene showing her character

Meanwhile, I'd moved onto Felix who'd written reams of notes about Max. "What a lot of work!" I exclaimed, and asked Felix to give me a guided tour of his entries. They seemed to have been written in a chain-of-thought style, with one detail about a character prompting the idea for a related detail. Max was at the park saying to people, "You dropped your brain," or "Your sock is untied." "He is not a bully but no bully goes near him. He wants to be a boxer. He goes to boxing lessons." The details about Max clearly conveyed complexity. Felix wrote, "Max is very scared because there's this new kid. He's as strong as a bulldozer. He might cream Max." In addition, Max is scared of clowns and horses. Felix summarized the latter fear, saying, "Because one day Max's uncle owned a farm and they were going to ride on horses and there was a mean old one. Max still has a horseshoe scar but he puts cream on to hide it." *[Fig. IV-4]*

After taking a guided tour through Felix's ten pages of entries, I asked, "What are you planning to do next as a writer?" Felix pointed out that he'd gathered entries especially about his main character, Max, and still needed to decide on his other characters and then develop them. I asked how he planned to decide on the

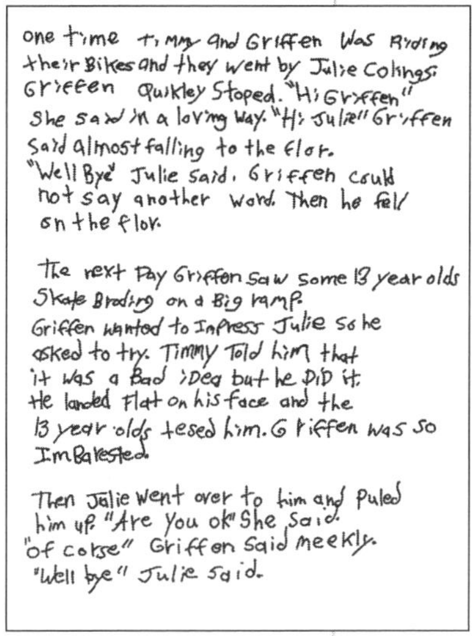
one time timmy and Griffen was Ryding their Bikes and they went by Julie Colings. Griffen Quikley Stoped. "Hi Griffen" She said in a loving way. "Hi Julie" Griffen said almost falling to the flor. "Well Bye" Julie said. Griffen could not say another word. Then he fell on the flor.

The next Day Griffen saw some 13 year olds Skate Broding on a Big ramp. Griffen wanted to Inpress Julie so he asked to try. Timmy Told him that it was a Bad iDea but he DiD it. He landed Flat on his face and the 13 year olds tesed him. Griffen was so Imbarested.

Then Julie went over to him and puled him up "Are you ok" She said "of corse" Griffen said meekly. "Well bye" Julie said.

Fig. IV-2 Francesca's 2nd draft of a scene

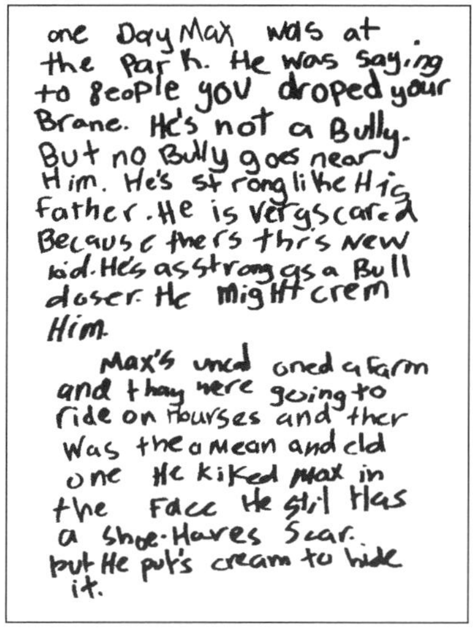
one Day Max was at the park. He was saying to People you droped your Brane. He's not a Bully. But no Bully goes near Him. He's strong like His father. He is very scared Becaus there thrs New kid. He's as strong as a Bull doser. He might crem Him.

Max's uncl oned a farm and thay were going to ride on hourses and ther was the a mean and old one He kiked Max in the Face He stil Has a shoe-Hares Scar. but He puts cream to hide it.

Fig. IV-4 Felix's entry in which he develops the character of Max.

secondary characters and he said he figured he'd need to write about Max's parents, so he might start there.

"Felix," I said. "I want to congratulate you on the fact that you've developed a really complex, interesting character. You could have just made Max into a tough boxer but you built in tension in your story idea, suggesting a new kid moves to town who could be even tougher than Max, and suggesting also that for all his cool, tough exterior, Max is still afraid of clowns and of horses. You've made him into a really human, complex, real sort of a person, and I can see why you're thinking of doing the same work for a host of other characters. You're really talented at developing characters, and I may want you to help others who struggle with this."

continued from previous page

"I love that Ariana brought her character to life, writing a Small Moment story that *showed* the kind of person she is! So when you sit with your notebook in front of you today, before you start an entry, make a choice. Will you add to your chart, listing internal and external characteristics? Will you write *about* your story idea, thinking on the paper so that your entry sounds like, 'In my story, I might show . . . '? Or will you try the new work you learned about today, and write a scene?"

Then I said, "But Felix, instead of moving on to do similar work with a host of other characters, I think you'd profit by first trying to crystallize your story. If you worked now on a secondary character, it could be someone in the park, someone he boxes with, a person at the farm . . . . I'd first zoom in a bit on the central tension of your story. I'd do that by taking some of the tensions you've created in your characters, and try to think through, 'What might end up being a turning-point moment for Max?' You could think about a time when he changes, maybe, or when he goes from being totally tough to being something else." Then I reminded Felix to zoom in on one particular moment, to envision it and to write the scene step-by-step. Before long, Felix had written these entries. *[Figs. IV-5 and IV-6]*

Should I get on that horse? No, no, no. Do it. Stop going. I won't. I will. My little brother will make fun of me. He will tell everybody in school.

I am scared of horses. What happens when it moves? Nothing. How do I stop it?

Oh no, it goes faster. Stop, stop, stop, kablam. I am not getting on a horse ever! It smells, it's ugly, everything is bad. I'd rather babysit three-year-olds. I will hate horses for the rest of my life. Why did I get on that horse?

Fig. IV-5 Felix's timeline

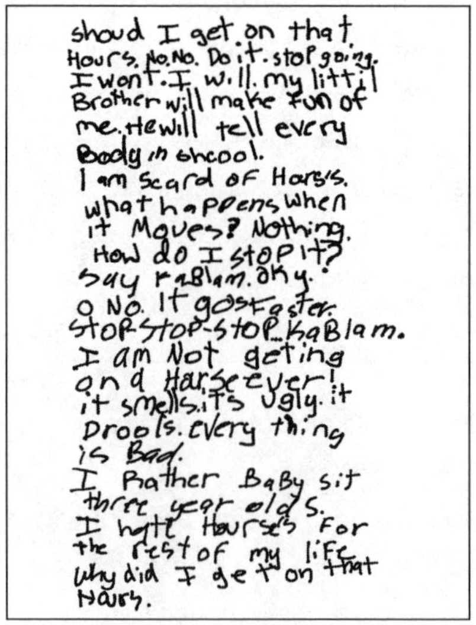

Fig. IV-6 Felix puts his character, Max, into action—riding a horse.

SHARE

Remembering What You Know About Writing Small Moment Stories

Share the work of one writer who used what he learned about writing in previous units. Explain that all writers can do likewise and invite them to begin.

"Ramon just did some important work that all of us could learn from. His story is about Marco, who knows his grandfather will leave soon for Jamaica and who wants to feel more connected to his grandfather before the old man leaves. Ramon didn't come right out and say any of this, instead he put his character—Marco—in the kitchen, cooking his grandfather some scrambled eggs as a way to do something for him. Ramon stretches out the action in the cooking scene, like all of you learned to do with your personal narratives. Marco cracks the eggs on the edge of the bowl and is afraid they'll slurp down the side of the bowl, and he's worried that the shells will go into the bowl and the breakfast will be ruined. But this is the really smart thing: When I asked Ramon how he'd thought to do this smart work, he said, 'I just wrote it like a small moment! I followed our old charts.' He keeps the charts from our narrative units on his desk as he writes."

"Based on Ramon's suggestion, I've found our chart and hung it up. Would you get with your partner now and talk about that Small Moment story chart and your efforts to write what we are calling a scene? Because really, a scene in a fiction story *is* a small moment."

"If you see qualities of good personal narrative writing that you've forgotten to try to do, I don't suggest revising your writing. Instead, I suggest you take an entry you almost like and write it all over again, an entirely new version, this time using all that we learned earlier in the year to help you write it as an effective small moment."

By this time in the year, your children will be very familiar with the term Small Moment. They will therefore have an easier time understanding what a scene is if you describe it as a small moment in a story. This is also a good way to reinforce connections between units of study and between elements of writing.

Qualities of Good Personal Narrative Writing

- Write a little seed story; don't write all about a giant watermelon topic.
- Zoom in so you tell the most important parts of the story.
- Include true, exact details from the movie you have in your mind.
- Begin with a strong lead—maybe use setting, action, dialogue, or a combination to create mood.
- Make a strong ending—maybe use action, dialogue, images, and whole-story reminders to make a lasting impression.
- Stay inside your own point of view. This will help you to write with true and exact details.

It's a good idea to remind children of strategies and charts they've used in previous units of study. Students will have better results if they understand that one unit of study often builds on another and that good writing techniques apply to many kinds of writing.

HOMEWORK   *Writing an Ordinary Scene Revealing Character*   One of my writing teachers once told me the best way to get to know your character is to write a quick scene with your character in a very ordinary situation, like taking out the garbage or going food shopping or getting dressed in the morning. Then, while writing that ordinary scene, you try to keep in mind everything you know about your character as a person: their internal qualities, their external qualities, and their troubles. Remember, I already tried this with Luz, putting her in a place she goes everyday:

> Luz looked at her dresser. She knew she should maybe put on a nice blouse or something. After all, it was picture day. Instead, she pulled out her denim overalls that had the paint splatters on the knees. Her mom hated those overalls. She thought they looked like rags. Luz loved them. They were soft against her skin, and comfortable too.

I added something about how Luz loves art, tucking in what we decided about this character:

> She could fit her extra pencils and erasers for her sketches in the back pocket.

And since I knew that Luz cares about what people think, I couldn't just have her wear her overalls. I wanted her to do something to make her mom happy, so I wrote this:

> She looked at the top drawer of her dresser and thought about what shirt she could wear. She decided to go with the purple one her grandmother gave her for her birthday. It was dressy enough for picture day, but comfortable enough to wear with overalls.

I hope you noticed that I made just a tiny scene but I incorporated a lot of what we know about Luz. We may never use this scene in our story, but it helps us get to know her even better when we begin to write a little longer about her. This is something you can do when you feel like you have a pretty good idea about your character and what she or he is like.

Tonight, continue to get to know your character. Place your character in an everyday scene to see how well you know your character internally and externally. Think about something your character probably does every day, getting dressed for school or going to the store or playing with her dog. Then place your character in that situation and see how much you come to know about your character.

It's important to have kids practice placing their characters in ordinary scenes. If we teach them only to write dramatic scenes, they'll rely on the action of the story rather than digging deeply into character. When you have students reveal their characters through ordinary, everyday moments, you're showing them that in stories, the gritty stuff is often shown with small details or actions, or with internal thought or dialogue. Mastering this is tough, but it's key to effective fiction writing. The more your students practice, the better they'll get.

This homework, like so many of them, could instead be used as the heart of a minilesson.

If your students need help creating tension in their writing . . . you might want to craft a minilesson around teaching them to show, not tell, the character's struggles. To create tension in a story, the character needs to want something. Just as important, *the reader needs to discover for himself what the character wants*! If the author comes right out and names the character's motivations, we are less apt to be caught up in them. Once we grasp the character's motivations, they become our own. In a good story, we read quickly, wanting to discover for ourselves whether the story turns out okay. We read, hoping Goldilocks gets away from the bears, that the prince will spot the girl sitting in the cinders, that Jack will make it down the beanstalk before the giant catches him.

If your students are having a difficult time with the abstract concept of motivation . . . you could develop a minilesson that teaches writers that the characters in their stories— like those in the novels they are reading in reading workshop—have troubles. You might say something like, "We all know from our reading work that characters have troubles, just like real people do. Those troubles make the story more interesting and the character more realistic. The thing is, when we think about the troubles our characters might have, we don't want those troubles to come out of nowhere. The troubles need to make sense for our characters in the same way that our characters' external qualities make sense with their internal qualities. Writers sometimes look at the internal and external qualities of a character to see if these qualities suggest hidden troubles that fit with who the character is as a person." You could say, "Watch me think about the troubles that Luz encounters," and then you could flip through the pages you'd written about her and say, "I know a lot about this character, but I don't see any troubles right away. She likes animals. She lives with her mom. She is artistic. She has brown hair. At first glance, I don't really see anything . . . But wait . . . I wrote here that she's sensitive and she cares a lot about what people think. Maybe there's some trouble there. Maybe, because her clothes are casual, someone makes fun of her and it really hurts her feelings." Then you might jot these notes on a fresh piece of chart paper:

- Somebody makes fun of her clothes
- This hurts her feelings

You could show children how you press on, asking, "What else do I know about Luz that is really important? Hmm . . . I know she's artistic. Maybe her trouble comes from making art and people not liking it. Or maybe she paints a picture for an art contest and something happens. I'm not really sure yet, but I think one of her troubles could be about art because art is something that's so much a part of her character." Here you might add another bullet to the list:

- Somebody makes fun of her clothes
- This hurts her feelings
- **Something bad happens with Luz's art**

Be sure to debrief. Do so by saying something such as, "These are realistic troubles because they come from Luz's character. They're believable. Notice how I didn't say she was disappointed she didn't make the soccer team, because soccer is not something she really cares about. Instead, I used what I knew about her and the kinds of troubles that would make sense for her to have. I just jotted a few notes so I can go back later and see which troubles make the most sense for my story when I get ready to draft."

COLLABORATING WITH COLLEAGUES

In your study group, you'll definitely want to spend time reading. Read, read, read. Read the sort of stories you want to write. Devour stories. Read them once, twice, again. Turn them inside out and notice all the decisions the author made. For example, if you and your colleagues study Peter Reynold's picture book *Ish* (which I heartily recommend), you might notice things like these:

- Within the first few sentences, readers know who is doing what. The story begins with action; it begins with an action that reveals the main character's wants. Right away, we learn that Ramon wants to draw something beautiful—a vase of flowers. Before long, we also know why Ramon struggles—his brother laughs at him.

- We aren't told what the characters want, and what they struggle over—we're *shown* this. Leon sees his kid brother's drawing, bursts out laughing, and asks, "What is that?" Ramon crumples up the drawing and throws it across the room.

- This story is composed of scenes or small moments and also of summaries. Between the vignettes there are passages such as this one:

  > [Ramon] kept trying to make his drawings look "right" but they never did. After many months and many crumpled sheets of paper, Ramon put his pencil down. "I'm done."

- The central character experiences a journey of feelings in this story. Ramon's body language alone shows that he goes from resolve to dejection before finding his way back to happiness.

- The story is held together by a central theme. The title and page one connect to the heart of the story, as does the ending.

- Some parts of the story are described in more detail—the characters' actions are detailed in smaller steps. Notice, for example, that there is more text on the pages that are at the center of the book—"the heart of the story" or "the top of the story mountain."

You and your colleagues could also study the characters in Cynthia Rylant's story, "Papa's Parrot." This is a terrific story for character study because the characters, far from being two-dimensional, are unapologetically flawed and complex. In her opening line, Rylant writes, "Though his father was fat and merely owned a candy and nut shop, Harry Tillian liked his papa." Immediately we imagine not only the rotund papa, but a boy who sees nothing wrong with disparaging his father—what he looks like, what he does—whom he also claims to (nonetheless) like. There's humor here, and sadness, too, which is on some level the point of her piece: that we're not just one way or another—good or bad—and that life, like people, can be read in various ways.

You could teach students that Rylant probably prepared for writing this story by thinking about the external and the internal features of her character. She may have made a chart of either Harry or his father. A chart on Mr. Tillian might look like this:

Developing My Character	
Outside (external features)	Inside (internal features)
Fat (blubbery stomach)	Sensitive
Candy/nut store owner	Sad
	Misses son

You could suggest to students that Rylant probably examined both the external and the internal traits of Mr. Tillian to see if they fit together. "Does the fat go with the candy and nut store owner?" she probably wondered. Then you could show children that Rylant probably thought also about whether "sensitive," "sad," and "misses son" match up.

Harry Tillian is by far a more complex character than his father, so for children who are ready for a challenge, or older, you might help them talk about how Rylant developed this character. The final scene, in which Harry both abuses his father's bird and cries for his papa, offers a great opportunity to explore the ways in which characters, like people, are often interesting mixes of seemingly contradictory traits. Harry is both soft and hard, and children might find a real connection with him imagining times when they, too, have acted one way, while feeling quite another.

When you and your colleagues think together about characters and their motivations, you'll probably notice that in most well-written stories, a character's initial desire is a smaller piece of a greater desire, one which is

initially masked from both the character and the reader. As stories unfold, we watch a character's cares as they are revealed gradually. The character initially thinks he or she wants one thing, but in fact what the character wants turns out to be different. In *Charlotte's Web*, Wilbur longs for a friend, but when he learns his life is at stake, his sole desire becomes staying alive. It is only toward the end of the book, when he discovers that Charlotte has sacrificed her own life for his, that he recognizes how much he values the gift of love and friendship. In *The Lion, the Witch, and the Wardrobe*, Lucy first wants to prove to her sister and brothers that the world she's found beyond the wardrobe really exists. Once she's accomplished this, and reentered the world, she wants to save her friend, Mr. Tumnus, and when she discovers that all of Narnia is at risk, she strives to save the entire world from the witch's clutches. By the end, Lucy accomplishes her goal and through it she finds the respect of her siblings and the power of her convictions, which is perhaps what she was after in the first place.

PLOTTING WITH A STORY MOUNTAIN

IN THIS SESSION, YOU WILL TEACH CHILDREN THAT WRITERS SKETCH OUT POSSIBLE PLOT LINES FOR STORIES, OFTEN ON STORY MOUNTAINS WHICH REPRESENT TRADITIONAL STORY STRUCTURE.

GETTING READY

- Story mountain on chart for *Peter's Chair* (used in Unit 2)
- See CD-ROM for resources

Some people imagine that writers put a pen to paper and out pours a story, or a novel, or a play, from beginning to end. In fact, that is how the writing process is often depicted in movies, giving the average person a romantic but false version of how writers work. We are fortunate to know from our own processes and through learning from countless writers over the years that the process involves as much organization as inspiration. This unit of study offers a perfect opportunity to teach children the power of rehearsal, and specifically, it gives us a chance to teach children that writers organize our ideas before we embark on a draft.

In this session, we again remind writers of a template used by countless authors to structure the plot lines of their fiction—the story mountain. As an organizing tool, the story mountain acts like a timeline or an outline. It allows the writer to step outside the details of the story to see the big picture. As children learned during the Raising the Quality of Narrative Writing *unit,* the shape of the mountain (as opposed to a timeline) can help writers visualize that in a story, characters journey uphill, against obstacles. By asking children to plan their plot against a story mountain, we steer them away from writing in a chain of equally important events. Instead of planning a story which involves just a string of episodes, children will plan a story in which a character reaches toward a goal, then meets and overcomes difficulty. Today's session goes farther and points out that just as in climbing a real mountain, the obstacles get harder to overcome as one progresses, with the most dramatic challenge occurring at the top. Often there is a sense that from the top, a character gains vision. Coming down from the mountain, the character probably feels more experienced.

This session also emphasizes that story mountains, like timelines, are tools for revision. Because children will be writing in scenes and not in summaries, they'll probably need to revise their story plans by zooming in on just two or perhaps three key moments.

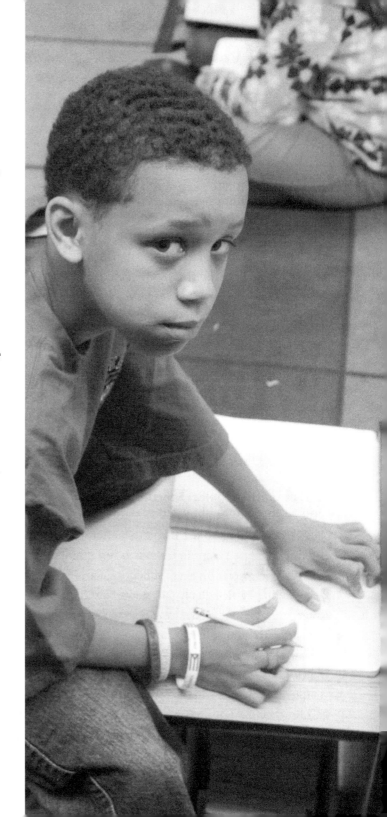

MINILESSON

Plotting with a Story Mountain

CONNECTION

Remind children that once fiction writers have brought their characters to life, we use a knowledge of the characters' wants and struggles to develop a possible plot line.

"Writers, a few days ago, I told you that fiction writers don't just go from choosing a story idea to writing a draft. Instead, fiction writers have strategies for bringing people to life, strategies like thinking about the internal and the external characteristics of the main character, the protagonist. We go through our lives thinking, 'What would my character do in this situation?' We give special attention to what a character yearns for and struggles with."

"We postpone thinking about what happens in a story, about the plot of a story, until we've done this other work. We postpone thinking about the sequence of events because eventually we take all we know about our characters—especially our understanding of what our characters yearn for and struggle with—and we use this information to create a plan for our stories."

"You'll remember that when we wrote our personal narratives earlier this year, we got ready to write by remembering what happened and plotting the sequence of events on little timelines and, later, on story mountains."

Name your teaching point. Specifically, remind children that fiction writers plan by plotting a story mountain—and specifically, by aiming to intensify the problem.

"Today I want to teach you that after we develop our characters, we draft possible story mountains. And I want to teach you something new about plotting your story, something that will help you whenever you write fiction from now on!"

"Writer Patricia Reilly Giff says that the fiction writer's job is to make every part so interesting that the reader can't wait to turn the page. She says some writers call that 'plotting,' but she calls it 'making the problem worse and worse!' Story mountains can help you do that because they remind you that you have to keep giving the characters something that makes it harder and harder to climb toward their goal. It's like each point along the mountain is just a whole new mess of trouble for your character. That's what makes readers want to keep reading, to find out how the character will solve these problems!"

"The story mountain also shows you that something is going to happen, and things are really getting tough, and then, bam, something happens right there, on the top of that

COACHING

Before now, children may have drafted scenes that put their characters into motion and revealed them as people, but those scenes will probably not comprise the start of their story. Before a fiction writer can write her lead, the writer needs to know the character, to imagine him or her in action, and to have drafted, chosen between and revised multiple plot lines for the story. Today, then, children will consider a variety of ways their stories could unroll.

We considered postponing this minilesson and this emphasis on plotting a story in order to encourage writers to spend more time putting their characters into scenes as you saw us recommending in the homework to the last session. There are lots of judgement calls to be made when designing curriculum—and you'll be in the best position to judge. So be sure you keep close tabs on your children and jettison these lessons in favor of ones you design.

Notice that I teach story mountains within the context of a bigger focus—thinking about how the story will go in general (across the pages). Only after emphasizing that the character will get himself or herself into a growing mess of trouble do I mention that this is signified by the rising slope of the story mountain. I'm trying to be sure the graphic organizer functions as a symbolic representation for the story itself.

mountain, that changes things or that solves your character's problem. After that, going along is different, easier, like your character is going down the mountain and the tough part is behind and there isn't a feeling of anticipation anymore."

TEACHING
Explain why a writer would use a story mountain to help plan a plot. Teach children that writers are not always sure of what might happen in their story when they first set out to draft a plan.

"Writers, earlier, when we were studying personal narratives, we realized that just as minilessons have a way they usually go, a pattern, so, too, do stories have a way they usually go. And we learned that usually the main character has wants, and something gets in the way of the character getting all that he or she wants. So the character encounters trouble, or a problem. And today, we learned that usually after encountering the problem, things get worse and worse, or harder and harder, or more and more complicated for a while."

"You'll remember that when we were studying personal narratives, we looked at Ezra Jack Keats' *Peter's Chair*, noticing that the story could be outlined in a story mountain that looked like this," I said, turning back to a chart the children recognized:

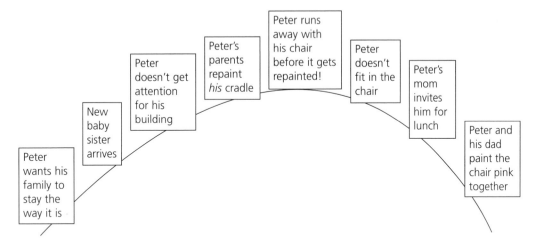

"When Ezra Jack Keats wrote this book, he probably knew he'd start it with Peter's block tower crashing down and his mother responding not by saying, 'Oh, your tower! Let me help you rebuild it' but instead by saying, 'Shush. You'll wake the baby!' And Ezra Jack Keats almost certainly knew the trouble would escalate; it would get worse and worse. But he probably didn't know, when he started to write the story, exactly what would happen. I bet he imagined one way the story might go, and another, and another."

Notice that in a single minilesson, I teach the rise and also the fall of the story arc, the story mountain. These are interrelated and need to be thought of as a broad sweeping stroke, not as discrete items. Of course, I'll need to reteach much of this!

I'm especially aware that I'm oversimplifying the resolution part of a story, setting children up to believe that in every story characters achieve all that they want which is far, far from true.

There are advantages and disadvantages to revisiting Keats' Peter's Chair. The advantage is that children not only know the book, they also know how the book can be represented as a story mountain. Therefore you can mention the book and graphic organizer in passing, and spotlight the new concept you're weaving into this session which is the idea that as one progresses through a story, trouble escalates. The disadvantage of this book is that it is not only a familiar book, it's also a story written for and about a child who is younger than your students. There are countless wonderful alternatives, if you so choose. One is Reynold's Ish, described earlier, and another is Peggy Rathman's Ruby the Copy Cat, a Scholastic book about a child who yearns to be accepted and therefore copies her idol's every move. We refer to the latter text in an upcoming session on revising one's lead. I also recommend John Steptoe's Stevie.

"Authors always know that the trouble will grow, and that characters will make choices—some of which probably won't work out. And authors know that *somehow*, in the midst of all the trouble, *somehow* there will be *something* that makes a difference. I bet Ezra Jack Keats didn't start his book realizing all the little details—he probably didn't know before he started writing that Peter would try to sit in his little chair and would find he didn't fit."

"When we plot our Luz story, I know that our character will struggle to achieve what she yearns for, our character will make choices. Some of those choices may not work out. We don't know which ones, exactly. But we do know that something will happen that makes a difference. Our character will find a way to resolve the struggle or she will change her sense of what she wants."

"And we know that just as a story mountain gets steeper and steeper, the challenges Luz faces, or the intensity of the feelings she has about them, will get stronger and stronger until finally one way or another, things will be decided. In other words, Luz will then be at the top of the story mountain."

ACTIVE ENGAGEMENT
Demonstrate planning a possible plot line based on the story idea the class has been following.

"So let's try planning our Luz story, the one that Ramon helped us start, keeping this story mountain in mind. In the draft we've already begun, we have Luz lying in bed, practicing sleeping without a light on so she can sleep in the dark at a slumber party. Then she gets up to turn on the closet light. Before fiction writers move forward to plot the whole story, it helps to rethink the start of it. Do you want to keep what we have so far as the very beginning? (This does show Luz's fears.) Or we could alter the beginning, perhaps in a way that more dramatically shows what she wants, and only then shows her fears."

"Talk with your partner and think what the first few dots on the story mountain would be. The starting scene (which will probably be the first two dots on the story mountain) must bring Luz to life, show what she yearns for, and show the trouble (which we already know will be her fear of sleeping in the dark and of being embarrassed in front of her friends). And remember, that mountain needs to get steeper, so think about how we'll then make Luz's problem get worse and worse! Turn and plan the start of our story mountain."

You'll notice that across the year, we revisit the same texts often. "Eleven" was a touchstone text for the unit, Raising the Quality of Personal Narrative Writing, *and it will resurface in* Literary Essays *and also* Memoir. *And in this instance, we bring children back to consider the story mountain Ezra Jack Keats probably made when he was planning* Peter's Chair. *It is also significant to notice that both of these texts and others that thread their way through these units are relatively simple and brief ones. When we want children to do some important new conceptual work, it's easier for them to do this when the material illustrating those new concepts is not overwhelming, complex, and gigantic.*

In this minilesson, you'll notice that the Teaching component is brief because most of the teaching is embedded in the Active Engagement. I mostly told and reviewed, and I did not show—an exception from the norm.

The story mountain is useful because it provides a concrete image for thinking about a complicated idea. When teaching students about the story mountain, I draw an actual mountain shape on a chart and model the plot points that move the character toward a moment when he or she solves a problem, confronts someone, changes, or learns something.

Many writers say that they aim to gradually raise the stakes in a story, intensifying the tension. In this instance I hope that I'm helping children imagine ways they can tweak a story plan to intensify the tension.

Annie Lamott, in Bird by Bird, *reminds us of the relationship between character development and the story mountain. "Find out what each character cares most about in the world," she writes, "because then you will have discovered what's at stake" (p. 55).*

Everyone started to talk. I moved among the partners. Marissa said, "Let's think of a different beginning, one that shows she wants friends. We could have Luz decide to hold a slumber party. Then she gets worried who'll come."

I nodded. "But try to think about that in terms of actions. What exactly might you show Luz *doing* when she decides to have a slumber party? How does the movie in your mind actually go at this starting scene?"

Marissa answered, "She realizes her birthday is just two weeks away. Then she starts writing invitations."

I nodded. "But you can't *tell* that she realizes her birthday is coming. What could she do? Imagine this as a movie. What would the character be doing that shows her realizing this?"

Marissa jumped up with excitement. "She looks at a calendar?"

Convene the class. Report on overheard ideas for how the story could begin.

"Writers, I heard some great ideas. Some of you suggested we alter the start so as to show first that Luz is hoping lots of friends come to her birthday party. Marissa thought the story could begin with Luz looking at a calendar, realizing her birthday was approaching, and beginning to address invitations. Would you be willing to have our story start like Marissa suggests?" I asked, and when children agreed, jotted an abbreviated version of Marissa and Ramon's points on the story mountain and retold those scenes from the story.

Set children up to imagine what might come next, then convene the children and add their ideas to the story mountain.

"What could come next? Remember you'd need to *show* (not summarize) her struggle and that the problems need to get worse and worse. Turn to your partner and plan."

Notice that in this Active Engagement, children are not only working on the teaching point of the day. They're also synthesizing all they know to collaboratively author a story. This is an unusual Active Engagement for this reason.

John Gardner, one of our leading novelists and the author of The Art of Fiction, *describes reading fiction by saying, "We act out, vicariously, the trials of the characters and learn from the failures and successes of particular modes of action." For fiction to do its job creating a drama in the reader's mind, it must create a vivid and continuous dream. The flow of action can't be continually interrupted by a stage manager's voice, inserting little explanatory comments. Gardner writes, "One of the chief mistakes a writer can make is to allow or force the reader's mind to be distracted, even momentarily, from the fictional dream." The writer encourages the reader to dream by presenting as many concrete details as possible. I'm trying, in this intervention, to elicit those concrete details and to remind writers that the story is carried by scenes, not summary.*

You'll see that I don't retell this conversation with Marissa in any detail to the class. I do share Marissa's idea for a lead, but I do not spotlight the way in which I coached her toward showing, not telling. In this instance, I decided it was more important to channel children's attention toward the actual plan for the Luz story. But I easily could have publicized the pointers I gave to Marissa, because they could have helped many others as well.

"The first job of a story's beginning is to start at the right time. It should not start when things are quiet, when nothing's happening, when things are much the same as they always have been. After all, the whole reason we tell the story is because something about life is new and different, something's happening that stands out—and your responsibility, as the writer, is to begin the work at that point of change" (Ebenbach, p. 60).

You'll notice that more of my pointers to you are about fiction and craft, and less about methods of teaching. This unit is a sophisticated one.

Again I listened in, and after a bit I again paraphrased what I'd heard a child suggest. Soon the story mountain contained these "dots":

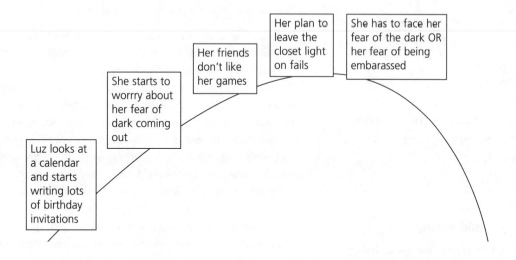

Philip Gerard, in his chapter, "An Architecture of Light: Structuring the Novel and Story Collection" suggests that stories have a "signature" that can be stated in a single sentence. The signature for Moby Dick is "Madman goes hunting for a white whale." This line defines what Gerard refers to as the "structural arc" of the story. He writes, "Think of the signature as the cable that hauls the roller-coaster cars up the long hill of suspense, round the hair pin turn of reversal, down the stomach-clenching fall". (p.152)

Most importantly, Gerard says that although writers begin with our structural arc and our characters clearly in mind, "almost everything will change." (p.153)

LINK
Remind writers that when fiction writers plot story mountains, we do so knowing the problems will get worse and worse.

"So writers, I hope you've been reminded today that the time comes when fiction writers plot possible story mountains. We are usually not sure exactly what will happen next, but we plan the start of the story against the shape of a story mountain, remembering that we can't just write any old thing next. In our Luz story, after she makes the invitations, we can't have her grandmother arrive and the family go to dinner, forgetting all about her being afraid of the dark and the slumber party! Instead, when we ask ourselves, 'What will happen next?' we already know that Luz's struggles to master her fear of the dark and to have friends will get worse and worse."

"So let's go—draft your story mountain, and do so, making the problem worse and worse, like writers always do!"

WRITING AND CONFERRING

Building Story Mountains

I drew my chair first alongside Caleb, who had taped a crude story mountain onto the far corner of his desk, and was now staring at a half-written page. "You've put your story mountain just exactly where Rachel, in "Eleven," put that red sweater," I said. "It's on the tippy top corner of your desk and if it could hang over the edge like a waterfall, I bet you'd push it there! Are you trying to get it out of sight, out of mind?"

Caleb laughed and assured me that he wasn't mad at the story *mountain*, just at the story. I glanced at the graph, noticing that instead of marking specific small-moment scenes into it, he'd labeled general trajectories he'd planned for the story. *[Fig. V-1]*

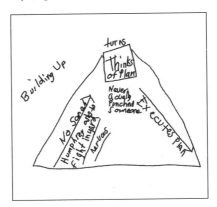

Fig. V-1 Caleb's Story Mountain

But it seemed he was preoccupied with other worries. "So what's troubling you?" I asked.

"I want to show Spencer walking to school, worrying about Humphrey, the bully. But I just keep telling what's in his brain: 'I'm worried. I'm so worried. I'm really worried.' There isn't any way to *show* his worries except if he looks up and down the block like James Bond or something," he said.

> **MID-WORKSHOP TEACHING POINT** *Finding Story Mountains in Published Stories* "I need to stop us for just a moment and tell you something really wonderful that's going on right now. I just saw Ari get up quietly from his seat and grab his folders. Then I noticed he was going back and rereading some of the realistic fiction short stories we've been reading as a class. I wasn't sure what he was doing at first, but then I talked to Ari and realized he was doing something so smart. Ari—can you tell people what you were up to?"
>
> Ari held up his notebook to show a rough story mountain. "I was getting a little confused as I tried to put my story into a story mountain. So I thought, well, if most stories have a story mountain, I'll go and see what other writers did. I went back to look at 'The Marble Champ' and I noticed that the story starts with Lupe getting her thumb all ready for the marble competition, in lots of different ways. So I decided to look for what would be the mountain peak in 'The Marble Champ' and to make a story mountain on that story. I think Lupe's last battle where she wins the championship is the very peak of that story mountain. Because after that she got everybody's cheers, and the trophy, and her family gave her that party, and then everything seems to calm down."
>
> I thanked Ari, and then said to the class, "Writers, if you can pull yourselves away from work on your own story, it'd be helpful for you to try what Ari did. Consider looking for a story you can use as a model for your own story. Plot the story mountain in the text you select as a mentor text. And remember, you need to continue thinking and writing about your characters even as you plot out possible story lines."

"Caleb," I responded. "You are doing what every fiction writer—really, what every writer—does. You've identified the writing problem that your story line poses. Some stories are hard because there are lots of characters, some are hard because time jumps backward and forward. Yours is hard (or at least the start of it is hard) because you want to show what your character is thinking and feeling, and yet he's walking all alone. So the problem you are struggling with is this: How does an author reveal a character's thoughts and still show, not tell? It is really smart for you to identify the problem!"

Then I said, "What I do when I encounter a problem is that instead of thinking about what the final solution will be, I switch my brain over and think, 'What strategies could I use to at least get me started on this?' So that means, for example, I'd probably sit here and just list optional ways to solve the problem. I'd brainstorm possible ways to go about solving it. How could you *maybe* solve it?"

Caleb generated a couple of ideas, culminating in the idea to add Sarah, Spencer's friend, into this section of the story. Soon he'd begun a new draft of the lead: *[Figs. V-2 and V-3]*

> Spencer and his friend, Sarah Mayberry were walking to school together.
>
> "I have my publishing party today," said Spencer.
>
> "What story did you write?" said Sarah.
>
> "About when I caught the foul ball hit by Jason Giambi."
>
> "GIAMBI!"
>
> "The one and only."
>
> "Uh-Oh," exclaimed Sarah, "It's Humphrey Dugball and his rats!"
>
> Humphrey was the meanest bully in the history of the earth. He crushed (or gave wedgies to) everyone in his path. Humphrey was the leader of a gang called the rats.
>
> Sarah watched as one of his rats and him pulled a kindergartner's pig tails. Then they looked at Spencer and a devilish grin formed on their faces. Spencer felt like a sheep in a wolf pack.
>
> "Well if it isn't one of Snow White's dwarves," Humphrey said. "Dopey." Humphrey burst out laughing like he had heard the funniest thing in the world. "Who's that," he exclaimed pointing at Sarah. "Is it your Girl . . . augh" by the time he got to the word 'friend' he was flat on the floor.

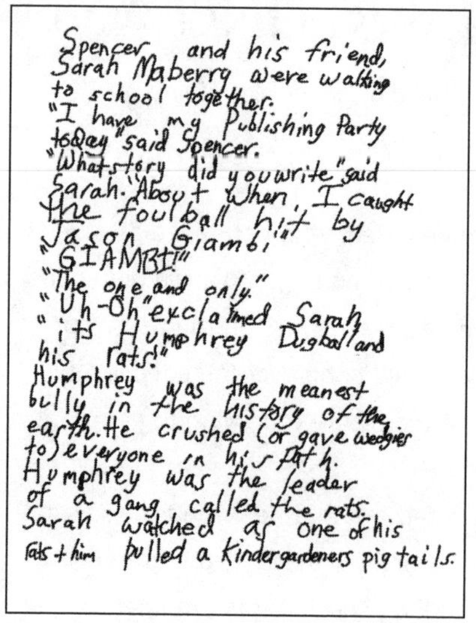
Spencer and his friend, Sarah Maberry were walking to school together.
"I have my Publishing Party today" said Spencer.
"What story did you write" said Sarah. "About when I caught the foul ball hit by Jason Giambi"
"GIAMBI!"
"The one and only."
"Uh-Oh" exclaimed Sarah "it's Humphrey Dugball and his rats!"
Humphrey was the meanest bully in the history of the earth. He crushed (or gave wedgies to) everyone in his path. Humphrey was the leader of a gang called the rats. Sarah watched as one of his rats + him pulled a Kindergardeners pig tails.

Fig. V-2 Caleb has added a second character into his lead.

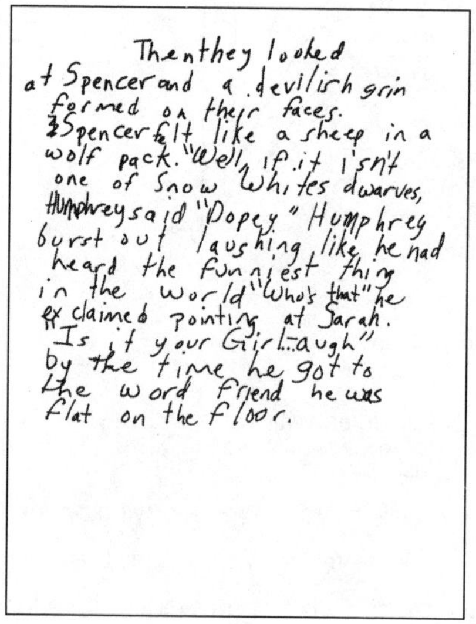
Then they looked at Spencer and a devilish grin formed on their faces. Spencer felt like a sheep in a wolf pack. "Well, if it isn't one of Snow Whites dwarves, Humphrey said "Dopey." Humphrey burst out laughing like he had heard the funniest thing in the world "Who's that" he exclaimed pointing at Sarah. "Is it your Girl...augh" by the time he got to the word friend he was flat on the floor.

Fig. V-3 Caleb's opening scene, page 2

Once Caleb had written this lead, we again conferred. I pointed out that with the arrival of Humphrey, he'd definitely created some tension, but he hadn't really had a chance to develop Spencer's character or to show what Spencer wanted before Humphrey arrived on the scene. With that in mind, Caleb decided to revise his story mountain. "Fiction writers do that a lot," I told him. "We shift back and forth between planning possible story mountains, writing a scene or two, rereading and rethinking what we've written, and revising our story mountains."

Next I gathered a group of children together for a strategy lesson. "I want to talk to all of you together," I said, "Because each of you has a great plan for a *novel*." I added, "But I want to remind you that you are writing a very short story, and before you get much farther, you need to do some rethinking. When you plot out your story mountain, the first two dots on it will probably belong to one Small Moment story, to one vignette. And then you'll probably leap ahead to a second and maybe a third moment, but by then the story will need to be complete." Then I suggested we all look together at Felix's tentative plans, using that as a case in point. Felix had already made a timeline which began with Max winning his first boxing trophy. Then Felix shows that Max practiced to win more, followed by Max having a fight with his nemesis, Mike, followed by Max's first loss, the arrival of a girlfriend . . . *[Figs. V-4, V-5, and V-6]*

"You need to go back to that question," I said. "What does Max most want? Fear? Struggle toward?" The group of children helped Felix revise his plans and sketch a story mountain, and then they each brought out their own work. Soon the children had stories which were at least somewhat focused!

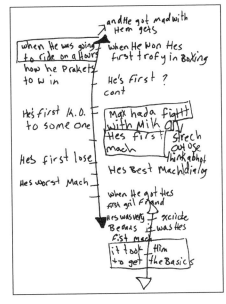

Fig. V-4 Felix's timeline

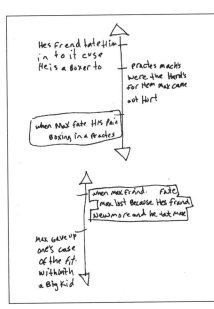

Fig. V-5 Felix's timeline, page 2

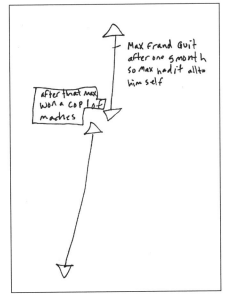

Fig. V-6 Felix's timeline, page 3

SHARE

Using Story Mountains as Tools for Revision

Share the fact that children already have strategies and tools for revision.

"Writers, I want to remind you of some work we did earlier in the year with timelines. Do you recall that we drafted timelines for our personal narrative stories and then we looked back on those timelines and asked, 'Which dot on this timeline is inconsequential to the story?' We crossed those dots out. We also asked, 'Is there one dot that's crucial?' and we often ended up rewriting that as three dots."

"We learned very early in the year that timelines are not just tools for planning, they are also tools for revision. And front-end revision is a lot more time-efficient than back-end revision."

"When we made story mountains in order to rethink our personal narratives, we again used those graphs as tools for revision. Remember how we looked between our story-beginnings, and the tops of our story mountains, and asked, 'How does the beginning relate to the real meaning of my story?' When Sophie decided her story wasn't just about going to Chuck E. Cheese's but that it was instead a story of how she and Claudia exchanged vows to be best friends, then Sophie needed to revise her lead, this time showing that en route to the restaurant, she rehearsed her proposal, feeling butterflies in her stomach."

Set partners up to share and assess story mountains with each other—and then to revise them.

"So timelines, outlines, boxes and bullets and story mountains are all tools for planning, yes, but also for revision. Would you and your partner recall what you know about stories, and look at each of your story mountains through the lenses of what you know about effective stories—then use these conversations to prompt revisions?"

HOMEWORK *Setting Yourself Up to Write Well* Writers, the work you did today in our writing workshop and the work you will do tomorrow will probably be the most important work you will do in this entire unit of study. If you can start your story well, you will set yourself up for a spectacular writing experience. So tonight, your assignment is to prepare yourself. How will you do this? You'll need to decide. Write yourself an assignment, based on your own knowledge of yourself.

Are you, like Robert Munsch, the sort of writer who benefits from telling your story to one person and then another and then another? If so, recruit your family members, your dog, your sister's teddy bear to be listeners, and consciously set yourself up with specific goals before launching into a second or third rendition. Say to yourself, "This time, I'm going to try to make my mom feel how devastated he felt," or "This time, I'm going to use my words to paint a rich picture of the place."

But you may not be the sort of writer who benefits from storytelling. Perhaps, instead, you'll want to reread texts in ways that set you up to write a lead which is saturated with mood. Read then, and also write. Write one lead, and another, and another. Fiction writers often make thirty or forty attempts at beginning a story before we settle on a lead we like, and you won't have time in school tomorrow for that amount of revision.

No matter what you decide to do in the pages of your notebook—and do fill at least a page—you'll want to carry your story with you throughout the evening. Nancy Hale, in her book on fiction, describes the slow incremental growth of a story this way:

> The story continued to rise, as stories do, in my mind as I woke up in
> the morning, each day with some new addition, as though it were a
> log of driftwood that I kept pushing down into the sea only to have
> it rise again with more seaweed, more barnacles encrusted on to it.

If you go for a walk, bring your story along. If you sit on the sofa for a bit, save some space for your story to join you. Your story will be far deeper and richer because of the life work as well as the desk work you do.

● TAILORING YOUR TEACHING

If you notice some of your students appear frustrated . . . you might find that they thought they had a great story idea until they tried to show it as a story mountain. In particular, they might be wrestling with finding a good conflict to put at the top of the mountain. If this is the case, you might want to teach your students that if a writer knows his or her character very well, he or she can imagine that character in a few common conflicts. You and your students might want to brainstorm the types of conflicts they find in the fiction they read all the time. Common conflicts can be related to:

- A misunderstanding with someone in authority (teacher, parents, etc.)
- A conflict with a family member or friend
- A loss of something or someone
- A struggle to make sense of a new situation or place
- A fight with one's own conscience
- A hardship in the natural world
- A yearning for acceptance
- A deadline

Traditional ways to describe conflicts may also help students to imagine a conflict for their characters:

- Person vs. person
- Person vs. society
- Person vs. nature
- Person vs. himself or herself

If you think your students are ready for more sophisticated work thinking about story structure . . . you could let them know that not all stories have the same story mountain structure, nor are the sides of the mountain necessarily equal. You might teach your students that some story mountains have just a short climb to the crisis, and spend the rest of the story trying to come to a resolution. Other stories have a very long climb up to the crisis, with only a short time, or no time at all, for a resolution. Some stories have a series of crises and resolutions, each worse than the last—often because the "resolutions" leading up to the main crisis weren't complete resolutions of the problem. These story mountains may look like a series of peaks. Students can spend some time in their notebooks playing with story mountains of various shapes to see how the story might change based on how and where they structure the conflict. To widen their repertoire of potential story mountain shapes, they need only look at the stories all around them.

If your students are having a hard time understanding the idea of rising and falling action . . . you might want to revisit a short story they know very well, just like Ari did in the Mid-Workshop Teaching Point. Using the text of the story as your material, work with students to create a story mountain of that familiar story.

ASSESSMENT

You'll probably want to gather your children's work and try to ascertain the nature of the stories they've set themselves up to write. When you do this, try to look not at the story mountains children will have made, but rather through them to the story the writer has in mind, and the criteria for writing effective stories that the writer has assimilated. The actual graphic organizer is relatively unimportant. It's simply a vehicle, a strategy, toward a larger goal. Your real goal will be to study children's graphs, notes and entries in order to understand their writing plans.

If you find that some children seem confused by the actual format of a story mountain, then by all means show that child he or she can plan just as well with a timeline or a storyboard. [Figs. V-7 and V-8] Nina, for example made this storyboard about taking her sick fish to the vet. Then she wrote her story "Something Fishy." [Figs. V-9 and V-10]

The core structure of a short story, in a nutshell, is that a character wants or needs something (or needs to learn something) and then encounters obstacles in reaching this goal. This continues for most of the story until something happens, or someone helps, such that the character achieves that desire. The story mountain is useful visually because everyone can relate to the difficulty of climbing straight up a mountain! But other students might relate better to different graphic representations—perhaps a timeline with stars for key moments or a blank comic strip. You'll want to encourage children to use any and all means available to organize their progression of scenes.

As you reflect on students' work at this point, look for how they are using their writers' notebooks alongside their drafts to plan and organize their writing. Notice the writers who seem to "think on the page," writing out their plans for how the story might go, and then experimenting, moving items into a different order. By all means, celebrate this!

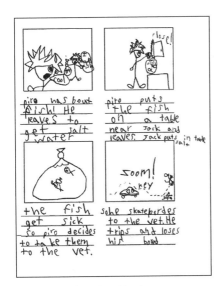

Fig. V-7 Storyboard and lead

Fig. V-8 Storyboard and lead

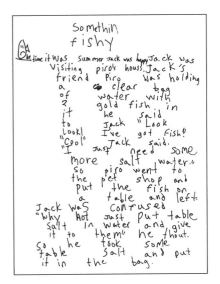

Fig. V-9 Nina's story

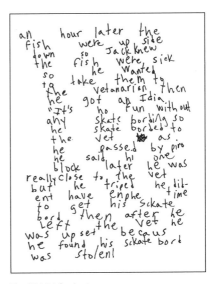

Fig. V-10 Nina's story

You will definitely, then, want to spend as much time as possible sitting alongside individuals, helping them to postpone closure on their story plans. As you teach children to brood over one idea, then another, and another, keep in mind that you are not only helping them develop a stronger story plan, you are also mentoring your students in the crucial art of revision.

You'll probably see that many of your children proceed in an all-or-nothing fashion: Either a story plan is perfect and a fait accompli or else it is terrible, and needs to be forsaken for another brand-new and totally undeveloped idea. However, it is crucial for children to learn to take a draft idea and ratchet up the level of that idea—in your assessments, try to applaud this kind of work. After all, you want to teach writers that in life, as in stories, people encounter difficulties and we persevere, eventually coming to some sort of resolution.

If you find in your assessments that children need ways to improve weak story ideas, one strategy is to teach children that a good story idea usually has the characteristics of a good mystery. When the main character encounters a problem (the mystery), the solution can't be instantly apparent and obvious to the reader; if that's the case, the story has no tension. But in the end, once the mystery has been solved, the solution can't have been utterly outlandish either. The reader should be able to look back and see that the clues were there all along.

Using these criteria, you could help children assess their own story plans, then choose one, and start drafting a lead. *[Figs. V-11 and V-12]*

> If ... I am having a friend over for dinner. My friend hates the food I am serving.
> Then... I would try to find something else in the house that they might like.
>
> If ... Two of your friends have birthday parties on the same day. You don't want to go to one person's because the other would have hurt feelings.
> Then... talk to both of the friends about how I feel, call all my other friends, tear myself apart, then decide to go to half of both.

Fig. V-11 Rena's story ideas

> If ... Two of your friends have birthday parties on the same day. You don't want to go to one person's because the other would have hurt feelings.
> Then... If both are slumber parties Bug and bug, and bug my other friend apoligizing over and over and making sure it is ok, then go to the one slumber party that I have ripped all my hair out over and decided on.

Fig. V-12 Rena's revised story idea

SHOW DON'T TELL:
PLANNING AND WRITING SCENES

Today your children will shift from planning to drafting. *You'll help them use their story mountains as guides in creating story booklets, transferring one dot from the timeline onto one page of the booklet, and then you'll help them storytell (not summarize) their plot lines. Above all, you'll help them see that show don't tell pertains to an entire draft, not just to one selected passage.*

It is easy to tell writers, "Show don't tell." But as a writer, there is never a day when I don't struggle to follow this seemingly simplistic adage. Donald Murray has referred to show don't tell as the most important quality of all dramatic writing.

In this session, you'll once again say to students, "Writers bring characters to life by setting them in motion." You'll tell children that instead of saying, "Leo was mean," a writer shows Leo kicking his cat. Instead of saying, "Sasha was upset," the writer shows Sasha tearing out of the room, calling, "See if I care!"

Your minilesson alone can't be your only vehicle for teaching children that we come to know people through actions. Watch your children, and spot one child making a generous gesture. Point out to the class that this child's actions reveal who he is as a person. "I watched Felix lend Paige his best pen, and I learned something about Felix through his actions," I recently said to the class. "I learned how generous Felix can be." Actions reveal character.

Of course, you'll also want to pause in the midst of reading aloud to talk about the character's behaviors. "He could have reacted very differently," you might say. "The fact that he did these things shows us a lot about what he's like on the inside." Then point out that in similar ways, children are using actions to bring their characters to life on their pages.

IN THIS SESSION, YOU WILL HELP CHILDREN REALIZE THAT WRITING SCENES IS, IN A SENSE, THE SAME AS WRITING SMALL MOMENT STORIES. WRITERS OFTEN BEGIN BY PUTTING THE CHARACTER INTO ACTION OR BY LAYING OUT THE CHARACTER'S EXACT WORDS, AND THEN UNFOLDING THE MOMENT STEP-BY-STEP.

GETTING READY

- A snippet of conversation between children about their writing illustrating that it's time to write
- *The Three Billy Goats Gruff* or whichever published text you've been using so far
- See CD-ROM for resources

MINILESSON

Show Don't Tell: Planning and Writing Scenes

CONNECTION

Use an overheard comment about writing to illustrate that there comes a time when writers need to move from planning to drafting.

"Writers, while you were lining up to come in this morning, I heard Emily tell Rachel that she can't figure out exactly what her character will do all along the way in her story. Emily *knows* her character wants to dance a solo in her dance recital and that every time she performs in class, she messes up—but Emily can't decide exactly *how* her character messes up."

Remind children that when the time comes to write, writers can use paper in a way that flows from the organization they've set out. In this case, tell children that writers can use a separate page for each point on their story mountain, and demonstrate by transferring dots on the class story mountain onto the early pages of a booklet.

"So I told Emily something that I want to teach you, that yes, there comes a time when writers need to stop planning, and write. Sometimes it's easier to plan once we are already writing. Often the best details are those that come out of our pens, surprising us."

"So today, I want to remind you that when we want to write a story, it helps to think carefully about the paper we'll use. In this case, I suggest we write our stories in drafting booklets that have one or two pages for the opening scenes of the story, and then several pages for the heart of the story, and a page or two for the ending scene. You may put a labeled dot from your story mountain on each page as a way to plan the contents of that page. Then we know where to start and where we're going, roughly. Writers always try to make our materials support the plans we have for writing."

"We already know that narratives are made up of scenes, or Small Moment stories. Many fiction writers get ourselves ready to write a draft of a story by gathering a booklet of paper, and thinking through plans for what we'll probably write on each page of a booklet. I usually give myself a different page, a different piece of paper, for each point on a story mountain. Two of those points usually comprise one focused, Small Moment story, so I stretch the story

COACHING

Obviously you won't tell your children about this particular overheard conversation; this was the conversation Colleen overheard, and you'll refer instead to a conversation you hear your own children saying to each other. The important thing is that you keep your ear to the ground, and that you hear evidence that your children's work on their stories is becoming the "talk of the town." Engagement matters tremendously, and it deserves your attention.

In perhaps a quarter of our minilessons, the main goal is to shepherd children toward the next steps in the writing process. In these minilessons, it is tempting to forgo a usual teaching point. Instead of saying, "Today I want to teach you that writers often . . . ," it is tempting to say, "Today, I'd like you to . . . ." When the work is complex and multifaceted, it's especially tempting to use the minilesson as a forum for giving directions and assigning work. Notice that despite the ambitious agenda she has for the day, Colleen clings tenaciously to the idea that minilessons provide opportunities to teach strategies that writers use often—meanwhile, however, she manages to lay out her particular hopes for today's work.

You'll probably use the word scene synonymously with small moment. By scene, we mean a bit of continuous drama—as in one part of a play. In your own mind, think of a scene as a Small Moment story, and keep in mind that it includes a flow of related mini-events.

across two pages of my booklet. It helps to label at the top of the paper the dot from the story mountain which will go on that page."

Looking at the first page of a chart paper booklet (on which she'd already written a dot and a sentence), Colleen said, "Marissa helped us realize we could start the story with Luz looking at a calendar, realizing her birthday is two weeks away, and sending out invitations. We realized she'd definitely be dreaming of all the friends who'd come, but she'd be nervous too."

Then Colleen said, "I copied the lead Marissa helped us write onto one page of our drafting booklet." Then she turned to page two and, drawing on the story mountain, Colleen said, "I think time will need to jump ahead until it's the day of the sleepover and Luz is getting everything ready and starting to worry about her fear of being revealed, so I put a second dot on the top of this page and wrote, 'Luz got ready for her party.' Later, after I use my story mountain to set up this whole drafting booklet, I'll come back to this page and write this dot as a Small Moment story. But for now, let me move on to thinking about what might happen later in the story."

"Writers, after you've planned out your story, you'll want to work on a lead. Before you do, I want to remind you that throughout most of your story, you'll be writing in scenes, not summaries."

You could, of course, decide against encouraging your children to write in story booklets, steering them instead toward notebook pages. We chose the booklets because they are a concrete way to encourage children to take their time, stretching out the story. But there is nothing sacred about writing in booklets.

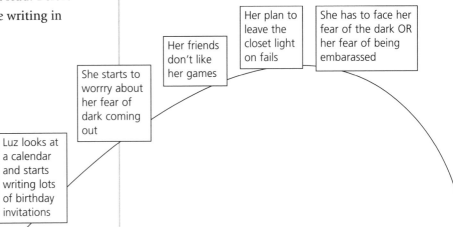

Name your teaching point. Specifically, tell children that fiction is composed of scenes, or drama, and that sometimes a line of dialogue or a small action ignites a dramatic scene.

"I want to remind you today that when we want to create a scene, we are creating drama. We sometimes use a line of dialogue—we make a character talk. Or we describe a small action—we make the character move or react physically to what is going on in the scene."

If you feel today's teaching point is not a new one, you are right. This time, Colleen has put a new spin on the now-familiar lesson of storytelling versus summarizing, but essentially this is a repackaged version of a minilesson that I've taught before. It might be interesting to contrast this version with earlier ones.

TEACHING

Illustrate the difference between summary and scene by telling a familiar tale in two contrasting ways.

"Let me remind you of the difference between writing summaries and writing scenes," Colleen said. "Listen while I tell the story of *The Three Billy Goats Gruff* in a summary way, like a stream of words rushing past."

> It's a story about three goats who are trying to cross a bridge to go eat some grass on the other side, and there's this troll who wants to eat them. So as he goes across, each goat tricks him by promising he can eat the next goat who is even bigger. The troll's greedy so he waits for the next one, but the biggest goat pushes him in the water, so they all get across safely. The end.

"Didn't you feel like that story just rushed by you? Didn't you want me to slow down and give the troll a voice, and make some sound effects, and put in some suspense to help you see and hear what is happening?"

"Now listen as I write in the air a scene from that story."

> "That's the greenest green grass I've ever seen in my life," said Third Goat. "Can we go over to that hill to eat some, pleeeeeeese?"
>
> "Yeah, we're hungry!" said Second Goat. So First Goat placed one foot gingerly onto the little wooden bridge that would carry them over the rushing river to a delightful afternoon snack. The bridge felt good and sturdy. "Nothing's stopping us! Follow me!" And First Goat stepped out onto the bridge toward the grassy hillside.
>
> "No No NO!" boomed a voice. "Who dares to cross my bridge?" Suddenly, First Goat felt the hot breath of a troll on his muzzle!

"Can you hear the difference between that stream of words, just telling, telling, telling what happened, and then the sound, when my characters talked in their character voices?"

Colleen told this story in a purposely hurried, monotone way, emphasizing the summary feeling. She does this for two reasons. First of all, it is easier to tell a story using story language and dramatic flair once the storyteller or writer has some sense for the bare bones of the story. Telling the story in summary fashion acts rather as a timeline, scaffolding the storytelling which will follow. She also summarizes the story because she wants to define what a story is by highlighting what it is not. A story is not a discussion, a summary. As Brace writes in The Stuff of Fiction, *"Fiction is not an explanation or a summary or an argument. Exposition is almost no good in fiction. Visible action and audible speech are needed. The reader must see and hear . . . the purest form of fiction is drama where everything is presented directly to the senses— the stage to be seen, the actors to be watched, and heard".*

As Colleen stretches out a moment from the story, she uses her voice purposely again, this time to give body to the words and help children really hear the difference.

There is a reason why we're appealing to the listener's sense of sound, of voice. We believe some children need to learn about story almost viscerally, from soaking it up. Mem Fox describes how she learned story; saying, "It came from the constant good fortune of hearing great literature beautifully delivered into my ear, and from there into my heart, and from my heart into my bones." Mem goes on to write, "All this makes me wonder whether we, as teachers of writers, focus too much on the mind: *have we forgotten, or did we ever know, the explosive power, the necessity of focusing also on the ear?"*

ACTIVE ENGAGEMENT

Set children up to storytell a moment from their stories to each other. Then share one child's summary, inviting the class to reimagine it as a story.

"Let's try it together. Will each of you think of a moment from your story mountain—perhaps the moment that could become the start of your story? And will you turn to your partner and take turns saying your little moment first like a summary of what's happening?"

"Okay, great! Let's listen to Caleb's summary, and see if we can help him reimagine this as a story."

> This guy named Spencer really wants to do great in school 'cause he wants to go to the same college as his big brother, but his friends think he's a geek for reading.

"Whew! That story flew by, didn't it? I want to hear what Spencer sounds like and what the other guys say to him and what books he's reading, don't you? Before you try to turn this summary into a scene, remember that during our personal narrative work, you learned that it's easiest to do this if you begin with a line of dialogue or with a small action."

Remind children that when you turned the summarized fairy tale into a real story, you started it with dialogue. In this way, help your children have success storytelling their classmate's summary.

"Remember that I began my *Three Billy Goats Gruff* scene with a line of dialogue? I said, 'That's the greenest grass I've ever seen in my life!' When a character talks first thing, it can make the scene come alive *instantly* in the reader's ears and mind."

"A second way that writers begin their scenes sometimes is with a small bit of action. Usually the story doesn't start with the main action, giving everything away in the first sentence, but with a tiny action that causes the reader to picture that movement in his or her mind's eye. So, for instance, I could have begun my Billy Goats scene by having First Goat put out his little hoof to test how steady the bridge was. So it would sound like this."

> First Goat gingerly placed one hoof onto the wooden bridge and leaned his weight into it. It seemed sturdy enough. "Let's cross to the other side and eat some of that greeny, green grass," said the First Goat.

It might be hard for children to mentally shuffle through their entries, settling on one in which they summarized a tiny moment rather than storytelling it. For this reason, we know from the start that we'll soon draw on one child's example and ask all children to help the one child reimagine a moment he's summarized, writing it as a scene.

You'll notice that this Active Engagement section involves another round of demonstration. Colleen made the decision to do this because we think children need lots of scaffolding to go from summarizing to storytelling. There are no set laws for how minilessons must progress. The most important thing is that these lessons are helpful—and our job, as teachers, is to do whatever is needed to make them so.

Ask each child to try telling the story idea as a story, not a summary.

"Okay, now let's all try to write in the air, and help Caleb turn his summary into a little scene. You can choose to make the first sentence a line of dialogue or a small action to pull your readers in right away." Colleen listened in on the children. "You've got it! I can picture so many of the scenes I heard, as if they were on movie screens in front of me! Let's hear the way Caleb rewrote his own scene."

> Spencer peeked out from behind the science portable and looked both ways. Good. No one in sight. He sat back against the wall of the portable and pulled his football jersey out of his backpack. He opened the jersey and there, hidden safe and sound, was a piece of heaven: <u>Harry Potter</u>.

Debrief by reminding writers to show their characters by putting them into action.

"Can't you see Spencer peeking out to see if any of those tough guys are around? That's the way to bring the reader right into the heart of the scene. Show us what your character is doing or saying."

LINK
Send children off to work, reminding them of the many points you've made today. And tuck in a reminder to carry these lessons with them always.

"So writers, your job today is first to transfer your story mountain onto a story booklet, and then to use that booklet as a support for storytelling your story. Try telling it so that each page or two of your booklet contains a Small Moment story. When you are ready, start working on your lead. Make sure when you start writing a scene today that the scene sounds like a story. Create a kind of word-movie with dialogue and action. Let's get to work, writers!"

In a school where I've recently been working as a staff developer, teachers have piloted the units of study described in these books, and they are accustomed to writing their own minilessons. We've been working on the Active Engagement components of their minilessons so that the teachers scaffold some aspects of these little practice-sessions, supporting and channeling children's work so they are able to have success with the one new tool or strategy the teachers will have just taught in the minilesson. In a similar fashion, you and your colleagues may want to do an inquiry into just this component of a minilesson. If you examine Active Engagements, notice the blend of support and of space we try to give children.

You can see from this Link that today's session is loaded with little lessons. Colleen could have made a different decision, choosing to end the minilesson by simply highlighting today's new point. But we wanted to help children synthesize all the particular points they've been given into an organized, multifaceted understanding for the process of writing.

Children will understand right away what you mean when you tell them you can picture their scenes being on movie screens. Their world of entertainment is largely one of moving images: television, video games, movies, etc. You can take this image further by talking about the sounds of your children's writing, the tones of voice you imagine their characters having, the ways in which they move, their facial expressions. "All this," you might say, "came from the words you chose and the way you decided to put them together!"

WRITING AND CONFERRING

Moving from Summary to Story

You'll want to make sure that every student is now drafting scenes rather than using writing as a way to think about and plan the scenes they'll soon write. Bits of story should be taking shape; they should pop off the page at you as you confer today. If students have trouble moving from entries that are *about* the story to entries that *sound like* story, you may find that it helps for you to model. Listen to the child's story, tell the child your observation about his or her work, and then say, "So I imagine it might sound like this," and rewrite the child's summary into the start of a story. Pause after just a bit to say, "Of course, I'm just making this up and *you* know how the story really goes. So now you try it. Tell it like a story." Help the child get started writing in the air.

If the child says a summary statement, quietly prompt for more specifics. You'll find that when students rehearse bits of a story out loud, with you coaching right beside them, saying things like, "What did she do? What did he say back?" students get started saying aloud beautiful stories. Jot down what the child says as a way to synthesize it and then say it back to the child. The writer will hear the difference between the first and the later version:

> I got home. I was exhausted. I went to bed.

becomes:

> I flicked on the light so that I could see my way to my bed. It looked like it was miles away from where I was standing. I closed my eyes. I wanted more than anything to be carried to my bed. Instead, I had to walk. I dropped my backpack on the floor with a thud. Then I used my feet to pry off first one shoe, then the other. The idea of bending over to untie them was just too exhausting. I trudged to the edge of my bed, step by step. "You can make it, just a few more steps," I told myself. Then I was there. I began to fall onto my bed, unable to even pull the covers back. My eyes closed as I fell. The last thought I had before I fell asleep was, "I should have taken off my jacket."

<table>
<tr><td>MID-WORKSHOP
TEACHING POINT</td><td>Revise, Revise, Revise   "Writers, can I have your attention for just a moment?" Colleen said. "The work you all are</td></tr>
</table>

doing seemed so important that I can't resist doing similar work. I could just move on to the next page, but I know that beginnings matter. So I'm going to reread page two one more time." Colleen read:

> On the day of my slumber party I put everything I would need into a corner of our family room. I propped my sleeping bag up against the corner, and my pillow on top of it. Above the pillow, I laid out my cute new pajamas. Then I added my secret night-light to the pile. I was afraid of the dark and nobody knew it.

"Hmm . . . I *could* just go on to page 3, but I like to revise as I write. This scene is about Luz getting ready for the party. I want to make it really clear that she wants people to like her, and that she's a little insecure and embarrassed about being afraid of the dark. I think I can make my character's wants and struggles a bit clearer," Colleen said. Dictating as she wrote, Colleen scrawled out this revised page:

> I checked all my stuff at least three times. I made sure my secret night-light was pushed all the way to the bottom of my pillow case where no one would see it. Then I walked over to the table and rearranged the napkins.
>
> Everything on the table was yellow. Yellow wasn't my favorite color, but a lot of the girls coming to the party wore yellow all the time, so I thought they'd like it.

continued on next page

Your conferring today will be crucial. As important as the adage "show don't tell" is to all writing, it's even more important to fiction. Fiction writer Shirley Jackson ends her *Notes for a Fiction Writer* by summarizing all that she's said in the article. She concludes, "Just remember that primarily, in the story and out of it, you are living in a world of people. Suppose you want to write a story about what you might vaguely think of as 'magic.' You will be hopelessly lost, until you turn your idea, 'magic,' into a person, someone who wants to do or make or change or act in some way. Once you have your character you will of course need another to work in opposition, a person in some sense, 'anti-magic;' when both are working at the separate intentions, dragging in other characters when needed, you are well into your story."

Help children reread their own work, noticing times when they tell the reader something that they could instead have shown. For example, Sofiya's story about a girl named Elizabeth who is afraid of snakes includes a fair number of places where she summarizes or talks about the character and the events. You and Sofiya could find those places, and work together to rewrite them. [*Fig. VI-1*]

Once there lived a little girl. Her name was Elizabeth and she lived with her mom and dad. Elizabeth was in first grade. One day her class went on a trip. The class had to sit in a circle. When the class had been there for about half an hour or so, the lady that was working with Elizabeth and her class brought out a snake. Elizabeth, who was terrified of snakes, stared wide-eyed at the snake. She heard the lady tell the class that they may touch the snake. Elizabeth got even more terrified. When the lady with the snake reached her, Elizabeth felt her hand touch the snake. Oh, how frightened she was! Poor Elizabeth thought the snake would bite her hand off, or poison her! Little Elizabeth was delighted when she didn't feel the snake harming her. The rest of Elizabeth's trip was a lot of fun. When Elizabeth got home, she told her parents all about the trip. She also exaggerated the snake part a bit, but her parents knew that.

continued from previous page

Colleen shifted back to her role as teacher. "Did you notice that I could have gone on to page 3, but instead I reread page 2, and remembered what I knew about stories and revised it. I tried to show what Luz wants and what obstacles keep her from getting what she wants."

"I hope you notice, writers, that to start drafting, I first set up a draft booklet based on our story mountain. Then I copied our lead, and wrote another page and revised that page. Fiction writers revise as we progress!"

"So writers, before you move from one page of your story booklet to another, remember to do as I just did and revise. I revised to bring out our character's wants and struggles even more, but you could revise toward any goal that seems to you to be an important one."

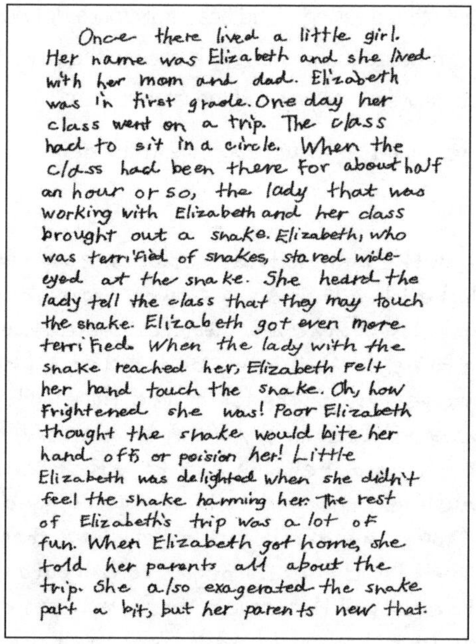
Once there lived a little girl. Her name was Elizabeth and she lived with her mom and dad. Elizabeth was in first grade. One day her class went on a trip. The class had to sit in a circle. When the class had been there for about half an hour or so, the lady that was working with Elizabeth and her class brought out a snake. Elizabeth, who was terrified of snakes, stared wide-eyed at the snake. She heard the lady tell the class that they may touch the snake. Elizabeth got even more terrified. When the lady with the snake reached her, Elizabeth felt her hand touch the snake. Oh, how frightened she was! Poor Elizabeth thought the snake would bite her hand off or poision her! Little Elizabeth was delighted when she didn't feel the snake harming her. The rest of Elizabeth's trip was a lot of fun. When Elizabeth got home, she told her parents all about the trip. She also exagerated the snake part a bit, but her parents new that.

Fig. VI-1 Sofiya's draft contained bits of summary.

In her next draft, Sofiya left off the most obvious instances of telling/summarizing, as you can see in Figure VI-2. What an important step ahead!

Elizabeth felt her hand touch the long, mean-looking snake. Its gleaming, coal-black eyes sparkled in the light as it stared at Elizabeth not even blinking. The snake kept sticking its blood-red, forked tongue out of its mouth. Elizabeth felt coil or something like scales under her fingers. Elizabeth knew that it was the snake's rough skin. She wasn't surprised that it was rough because she thought that snakes are rough and so is their skin. Elizabeth noticed the pattern on the snake's back. How she liked it! It was also the only thing she liked about the snake! Golden gleaming and sparkling diamonds on the same kind of coal black surface.

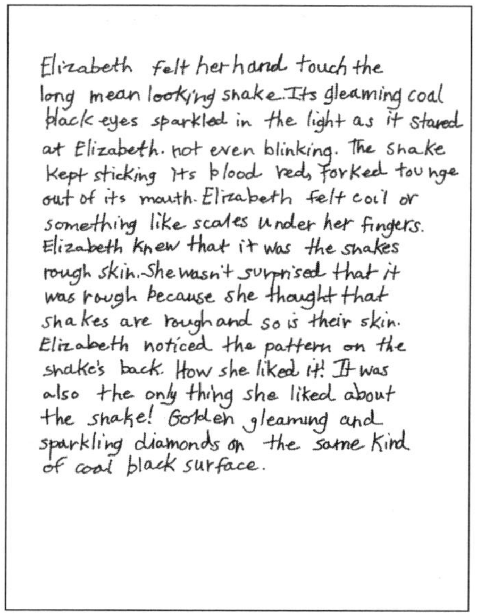

Elizabeth felt her hand touch the long mean looking snake. Its gleaming coal black eyes sparkled in the light as it stared at Elizabeth. not even blinking. The snake kept sticking its blood red, forked tounge out of its mouth. Elizabeth felt coil or something like scales under her fingers. Elizabeth knew that it was the snakes rough skin. She wasn't surprised that it was rough because she thought that snakes are rough and so is their skin. Elizabeth noticed the pattern on the snake's back. How she liked it! It was also the only thing she liked about the snake! Golden gleaming and sparkling diamonds on the same kind of coal black surface.

Fig. VI-2 Sofiya tried to rewrite so that her summaries became scenes.

SHARE

Acting Out Writing

Ask several students to direct fellow classmates in the scenes they've written to see what revisions, if any, are needed to make them "camera ready."

"Writers, I wish we had the movie cameras rolling on some of these scenes you've got going! But why don't we pretend that we *do* have movie cameras filming our scenes. Let's try acting out a couple of your scenes to see how they look and sound, to see how that helps us revise them!"

"I'm going to choose five students to be the directors of their little scenes." Colleen named them. "Will you find actors for your scenes? You have five minutes to give them the directions so they know what your characters are saying and doing, and then you all can rehearse the scene once, really fast! Then another group of kids will watch the scene you develop and see if it feels ready for filming or if the scene needs some revision. Okay, choose and rehearse fast!"

Reconvene the class. Tell a story about children resolving to do superbly well, even while knowing today's best draft will be revised.

"Ariana and Gabe and Francesca are working on a dance for the talent show. They're practicing every day after school for this whole week. Do you suppose that on Monday they grab any CD and start doing any old dance moves, saying to themselves, 'We don't need to make this good till Friday?'"

"No! Ariana and Gabe and Francesca worked really hard so that when they met on Monday, they had already chosen the song they thought would work and the moves they hoped would be perfect. As the group practiced, I hear they came up with even better dance moves—but that doesn't mean that on Monday they aimed for anything less than their best!"

"The same needs to be true for all of you as you move forward in your draft. I know you will aim to make this draft of your lead gorgeous and spectacular and significant. We've learned that writers first plan how their stories might go, sketching out possible lines of development on one story mountain after another. We try on leads, and use those leads to test out what our stories might be like if we write in one voice or another, if we start in one place, at one time, or another."

If you've never had your students practice acting out parts of stories or using their bodies and voices like this before, you may find this Share a bit chaotic. But when students are accustomed to role playing and to performing Readers Theater, like these students are, this provides a powerful way to give body and voice to the words on a page. When writers see real human beings trying to carry out the action of the scene, they realize quickly that they have important revision to do so the scene works better. (And the good news is, this comes at the end of the workshop, and you can end it early if you feel you need to!)

Capturing students' attention matters. Colleen knows that this group of students cares about the challenge of getting a dance number ready, choosing a CD, and rehearsing with friends. It strengthens her lesson about writing when she links writing to the creative endeavors that children care about most.

First Colleen makes the point that when composing a dance, children resolve to do their best from the start, despite knowing their best will turn out to be only a rough draft. Then she makes a parallel point about writing, suggesting that to do their best from the start, students must resolve to work toward all the goals they've learned so far.

HOMEWORK *Living in a Character's Shoes* Writers, tonight when you have supper, you'll be having supper not just as a child, not just as a son or daughter, but also as a fiction writer. You'll remember from earlier this year Cynthia Rylant was once asked to describe her writing process, and she said, "It is about going fishing as a writer, having relatives over for supper as a writer, walking the aisles of Woolworth's as a writer." So when you pull up a chair at the supper table, you need to think to yourself, "I wonder who my character sits with at supper?" When you plop your backpack down in its regular place in your bedroom or your kitchen, you need to pause for just a second and think about the teeny tiny rituals in your character's life. Where does your character keep his or her stuff?

Fiction writing isn't just desk work, it is life work. We carry our story ideas and especially our characters with us always, letting them grow with time and attention.

So right now, as you read this assignment, pause for a moment. Think to yourself, "Where does your character sit in order to read?" Look up at the space around you. Think to yourself, "What does your character see when he or she looks around?" And as you go about your life this evening, try to let something new about your character pop into your mind. Then remember: You could easily forget these thoughts. Tonight, when you live like a fiction writer and grow new realizations about your character, please jot those into your writer's notebooks so you are sure to hold on to them.

TAILORING YOUR TEACHING

If some of your writers need concrete reminders of the elements usually found in scenes . . . you might offer them a clear checklist of things to include. Even though your students spent a lot of time during earlier narrative units working on small moments, which are essentially scenes, some students will find the idea of scene writing in fiction a little risky. You might consider creating a chart or a handout that offers a bulleted list of things writers include in scenes.

If your students are struggling with the concept of scene versus summary . . . you might teach them that writers study texts others have written, noticing not only what the author says but also the structures in which the author writes. For example, a writer of short stories might reread a familiar short story, keeping an eye out for places where the author writes in summary and where he writes in scene. The writer might box each section and code it with notes to themselves like *sum* for *summary* and *sc* for *scene*, and then look between those sections in order to notice the differences between the two kinds of writing.

Things Writers Include in Scenes
- A beginning, middle, and end
- A setting
- Characters who want things
- Characters who feel and think
- Obstacles that get in the way of what characters want
- Action
- Dialogue (most of the time)

ASSESSMENT

You will definitely want to linger late in your classroom, with a cup of coffee (or whatever lifts your spirits) on hand. Expect that you'll be there still when the afternoon shadows become long. Give yourself the opportunity to really look closely at your children's work. Their leads, after all, represent the drafts they are angled to write. Just as leads are a sort of contract with the reader, they are also a contract between the teacher and the child. By blessing the child's lead and letting the child go forward, you are putting a seal of approval on the life work the child has taken on. So take the time to read the leads your children have written, and arrange for time tomorrow to talk with children about the problems and the promise you see in their work. You'll probably need to meet with a child or two before school, and another cluster during lunch. Investing this time will set children up for success and make the entire unit work better.

You will probably find that at least half a dozen children have begun their stories far from the main event. My friend Ralph Fletcher cautions writers, "Start when you can hear the waterfall around the next bend." Some children will need you to convene a strategy lesson and teach them this.

In order to help these children, show them that part of the story they have planned is backstory. I recently worked with Carrie whose story began with a detailed description of a girl, also named Carrie, whose best friend, Kim, was a foster child. Then Kim was adopted by an out-of-state family, and moved away, leaving Carrie feeling lonely. Then—good news! (I say this tongue in cheek) Kim's adopted family rejected her, she returned to being a foster child, and Carrie was reunited with her friend and is no longer lonely. In Carrie's original draft, the story began before the adoption, and was poised to drag on and on. I interceded to point out that the story could begin much, much later; perhaps with the lonely heroine going to the mailbox in search of a letter from her distant friend. Carrie and I studied the

start of both *Because of Winn-Dixie* and *Journey*, noticing that in both those books, before the story actually begins, a great deal has taken already place.

I also find that when I look at the leads of children's drafts, some of them raise issues about values. When you read over their leads and study their story plans, you find that sometimes the values that children weave into their stories are ones you want to question. After one afternoon assessing writing, I made an appointment to confer with three girls who were each writing a version of the same story. The story line was this: three girls go to the mall. A classmate, Kayla, is there, drinking a smoothie, carrying on about the fact that her drink contained natural ingredients. The three girls are disgusted with Kayla, and decide to retaliate. The grand climax of the story comes with the three girls inventing a way to retaliate—they fill Kayla's locker with poop and cockroaches, and when she weeps at the sight, they spray whipped cream in her face. Reading the story, the teacher and I were speechless and convinced that part of the problem was our decision to let the girls plan a story collaboratively and to include so many characters in it. The gang-mentality was shielding them from seeing the viciousness of their heroines' actions. The teacher and I decided we couldn't live with these girls investing a full month writing and role-playing such a story. So I pulled the girls together, and said, "I read your lead and I see this is a story about a gang of really vicious girls who first gang up on an undeserving victim (at the mall) and then, the gang's behavior gets much much worse and they act in really violent and hateful ways. So what do you think will happen—perhaps in the midst of that awful attack—to change your characters? How will they learn a lesson? Will one girl look Kayla in the eyes and suddenly come to her senses, or what?" In this fashion, I subtly but firmly steered the children toward work I felt would be more helpful for them.

FEELING AND DRAFTING THE HEART OF YOUR STORY

In this session, you'll set children up for something quite magical. When writing, we plan and chart, deliberate and select. But then the day comes when we do none of this. Instead, we "let it rip." We "go with the flow." We write fast and long, our eyes glued not to charts admonishing us to do one thing or another and not to mentor texts that demonstrate what's possible; but instead, to the drama that unfolds before us as we follow our characters into the thickening plot.

Frankly, it's not easy to figure out how to pass along the equation for the magic that happens when a writer finds that words and characters lead us toward meanings we didn't even know we knew! To some extent, I always approach this particular minilesson knowing my teaching will be hopelessly inadequate. But we carry on, as best we can, knowing that children can learn from their words as they appear on the page, if not from the minilesson.

In this session you will try to equip children to experience the power of what some people refer to as a "discovery draft." One way writers do this is to empathize with our characters, imagining ourselves within another's feelings, situations, and thoughts. By stepping into the character's skin, right into the story, the writer watches and listens and feels what is happening as the story unfolds—writing the story down as it happens.

Set children up to expect that as they write, their character's problems will get worse and worse, the stakes will rise. Teach them to hold their hats, expecting quite a ride! In this session, then, we'll teach children that writers draft by empathizing with our characters and letting that empathy determine the course of the story.

IN THIS SESSION, CHILDREN WILL LEARN THAT FICTION WRITERS CREATE OUR BEST DRAFTS WHEN WE EXPERIENCE THE WORLD THROUGH OUR CHARACTER'S SKIN, LETTING THE STORY UNFOLD AS IT HAPPENS TO US.

GETTING READY

- Example of a well-known text, such as *Fireflies!* in which students have probably experienced "becoming" the character
- Current lead for the class story
- Current story mountain for the class story
- Idea for a scene for the class story you can use to demonstrate writing by pretending to be the character
- See CD-ROM for resources

MINILESSON

Feeling and Drafting the Heart of Your Story

CONNECTION

Celebrate that your children have created story mountains and characters and best yet, they've begun bringing these to life on the page.

"It's a rather amazing process, isn't it? You plan, list, choose, sketch—like the old woman making that gingerbread boy. She probably thought, 'What will I use to show his eyes?' 'Will his shirt be a button-down shirt?' 'Will he wear suspenders?' But then the day comes when the gingerbread boy springs to life, calling out, 'Run, run, as fast as you can. You can't catch me, I'm the gingerbread man. I am, I am!'"

"You have each created a gingerbread child who has sprung to life. Hannah's character, Jane is standing in Central Park near the carousel, with her two friends circling her, taunting, 'Jane is scared, Jane is scared.'"

"The blood rises to Jane's face, she feels circled, caught, so she snaps back, 'At least I'm smarter than you guys!' and she huffs away. The amazing thing is that Jane's creator didn't know that Jane would snap back like that. One thing led to another, that's all; Jane was caught and she dug deep into herself and found a kernel of self-respect and shot back with, 'At least I'm smarter than you guys!'"

"This is the magical power of writing fiction. Our characters, like that gingerbread man, spring to life and suddenly we, as writers, are following them, trying as best we can to catch up."

Name your teaching point. Specifically, tell children that once writers are actually drafting, they worry less about writing and focus instead on reliving the drama.

"So today, what I want to teach you is this. Before writers actually get going on a draft, we think a lot about ways to make a draft into a really good story. But once we're actually in the midst of the story, most of us try, above all, to lose ourselves in the story. We become the characters, and writing is a bit like a drama, happening to us."

COACHING

Faulkner has said, "There are some kinds of writing that you have to do very fast, like riding a bicycle on a tightrope." Another time, he used a different analogy to convey the same message, "A writer writing is like a man building a chicken coop in a high wind. He grabs any board he can and nails it down fast." You are setting children up to draft, fast and long—and more than that, you are setting children up to produce a draft that they regard as temporary and improvable.

Once dancers and writers have produced the start of a work of art, the time comes to worry less about ratcheting up the level of their composition and to focus more on letting the dancing or writing flow.

TEACHING

Remind children that when reading, we lose ourselves in a story, becoming the character. Explain how this is true for writing as well. Give an example.

"You all know how, when we read, we feel almost like we become Gilly or Opal or Melanin Sun or the narrator in *Fireflies!* We read the words and suddenly we are that boy at the dinner table, looking out the window onto our backyard at dusk, seeing the dots of light flicker by the dark shape that is our tree house—seeing through his eyes and living in his self. We hardly need the words of the story to tell us that the boy pushes away his plate and asks, 'Can I be done?' and then rushes to get a jar for catching fireflies."

Tell children that readers can more easily walk in the shoes of a character if the writer has done this first.

"Readers can do that—we can read words on the page and suddenly be in the shoes of the character because writers first do the same. Gerald Brace, in a book called *The Stuff of Fiction*, says it this way:"

> It is not enough for a writer to tell us about a person or a place; he must give us the illusion of being the person ourselves . . . the basic failure in much writing is the failure of the writer's imagination: he is not with it . . . not trying hard enough to live from moment to moment in the very skin of his characters.

"We, as writers, need to try to do this work—live in our characters' skins as we draft their stories!"

Demonstrate to show how you go from envisioning to enacting to drafting.

"And so today, I'm going to reread the latest lead to our Luz story. At one point we'd said we wanted to start it earlier, as she writes invitations, but now we've settled on this lead, I revised it a bit since you last saw it. Today, I'm not going to be re-thinking the lead so much as writing more. To do that, I'm going to pretend to *be* Luz." Colleen reread the latest draft, written on chart paper:

> On the day of my slumber party I put everything I would need into a corner of our family room. I propped my sleeping bag up against the corner, and my pillow on top of it. Above the pillow, I laid out my cute new pajamas. Then I added my secret night-light to the pile. I was afraid of the dark and nobody knew it.

It could be a fruitful inquiry to look at all the minilessons focused on drafting in all the Unit of Study books. I believe fast-writing works to help students draft. You may not, in which case you may want to suggest that some people draft slowly and cautiously. Regardless, there is a cyclical curriculum underlying these units, and you can learn from studying it— and also from questioning it! Any one line of work is but one choice among many.

I'm reminded of tobogganing as a child. We line up the toboggan just so at the top of the hill. We anticipate its journey. We call for folks to clear the path. We give ourselves a running start. But then at some point, momentum takes over and we simply hold on tight, traveling fast. To me, drafting is a bit like tobogganing—the time for control and choice ends, and the pace quickens.

So far, Colleen has given a little lecture on the virtues of envisioning and role playing as part of the writing process. She could simply shift now to the next phase of the minilesson. Instead, she demonstrates what she's just described in the hopes that this will provide more ways to support children. You can decide whether to explicitly tell, to demonstrate, or to do as Colleen has done and combine both teaching methods.

I checked all my stuff at least three times. I made sure my secret night-light was pushed all the way to the bottom of my pillow case where no one would see it. Then I walked over to the table and rearranged the napkins. Everything on the table was yellow. Yellow wasn't my favorite color, but a lot of the girls coming to the party wore yellow all the time, so I thought they'd like it. And like me.

First Marta came in. Then Joy and Tish walked in together, helping each other carry all their sleeping stuff. I helped carry things to the corner of the room where my mom and I decided we would keep the stuff until it was time to go to sleep.

"So what are we going to do first?" Joy asked.

I looked around at all my friends. I was so excited that my party was finally happening that I almost forgot the games I had planned.

"I'm going to keep in mind that the next dot on the story mountain says, 'Her friends arrive and don't like her games and I'm going to remember that Luz wants desperately to feel popular," Colleen said, referring to the story mountain.

"But mostly I'm just going to try to *be* Luz." Colleen picked up her pen and began scrawling on her pad of paper, saying aloud the words as she wrote them. Pulling back from writing, she said to the children. "I just that second made up the idea that the games were brand-new and I pretended they were junk. I have no idea what, exactly, will happen next, so I'll reread what I just wrote and just let something come to me."

Soon she'd added (and voiced) this scene:

> "What do you wanna do?" I asked, waving with feigned carelessness to the stack of games on the table.
> They're all old," I said, hoping I'd taken the price tags and cellophane off each of them.
> "TWISTER?" Tish said, her voice incredulous. "My mom played that when she was a kid. That's such a stupid game."
> I felt the blood rise to my cheeks. "I know," I said.
> "I don't know why we even have it."

"Let your story move as naturally and as easily as possible," Shirley Jackson urges young writers. "Suppose you are writing a story about a boy and a girl meeting on a corner; your reader wants to go to that very corner and listen in; if, instead, you start your boy and girl toward the corner and then go off into a long description of the streetcar tracks and a little discussion of the background of those two characters—you will lose your reader and your story will fall apart."

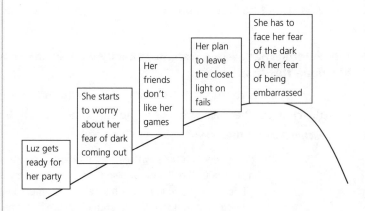

Notice that Colleen tucks little insights into her demonstration. This is important to do. Some children will hear these fleeting tips, some will probably learn only from the demonstration as a whole. The subordinate tips make the minilesson more multileveled.

ACTIVE ENGAGEMENT
Recap specific tips you hope children gleaned from the demonstration.

"Writers, do you see that when we write—when any fiction writer writes—we keep in mind the big plan for how a story will probably go, but we let the details emerge from the specific, exact actions we take. Usually, our scenes involve two characters, and one does or says something and then the next one reacts."

Set children up to extend the class story by putting themselves into the unfolding scene. Then call on one set of partners and add their work to the class story.

"To continue writing our Luz story, you need to *be* Luz, gesturing with disgust at the stack of games, pretending you agree that they're junk. You need to keep in mind that Luz desperately wants the party to go well. She's got it all planned—the games she's dismissing were her best hope for keeping everyone happy."

"Right now, pretend *you are* Luz. Picture her. The games are out on the table. The one friend has just looked in disgust at Twister. What does Luz do (remember—actions matter, not just talk). Turn and tell your partner the next bit of the story." To get them started, Colleen reiterated the last scene:

> "TWISTER?" Tish said, her voice incredulous. "My mom played that when she was a kid. That's such a stupid game."
> I felt the blood rise to my cheeks. "I know," I said. "I don't know why we even have it."

The children talked with their partners, and soon Colleen had called on one partnership and added this to the story:

> I jumped up to put the entire stack of games into the closet. The other kids, however, surrounded me, and Joy and Marta were shaking dice to see who'd go first in a game of Mousetrap.

LINK
Remind children that drafting is a form of acting on the page, and send them off.

"Writers, I want to remind you that writing is a lot like drama. Once we've written our lead, we need to reread it and become the main character. We need to stand in the character's shoes, to see through her eyes, to blush with her, and to hope with her. This way our readers will also be able to experience the story we put onto the page."

"You'll probably do as I did today, and reread your lead, then turn to page 2 of your story booklet and to the second dot on your story mountain, and act out—write out—that story."

Over and over this year, we've told children that a writer "makes a movie in the mind" and records what the writer sees. In this minilesson, Colleen brings children into this concept more deeply by inviting them to explore the close link between drama and writing.

The emphasis in this minilesson is on showing, not telling. You may determine that other qualities of good writing will help your children more. Scan students' work as they draft. The emphasis in the minilesson grew from the fact that despite all our best efforts, some students were still summarizing when they should have been writing scenes or small moments. That said, there are times when summary is the best tool a writer has at her disposal. Teach students that when we are drafting there are times when we want to show the reader everything—those are our scenes. There are also times when we might choose to summarize. Fiction writers usually summarize when they want to pass by a lot of time, when something routine happens (such as brushing teeth or putting on shoes), or when they want to quickly transition from one scene to the next by using transition phrases like the next day or that afternoon. Readers don't need to see a character pack his backpack at the end of the day, unless something compelling and unusual, like a fight, has occurred and is related to that action. In that case, we'll want to see it as a scene!

Notice that after children turn and talk, we do not hear from one child after another after another.

WRITING AND CONFERRING

Writing in Summaries and Writing in Scenes

As you confer today, you'll want to help writers make significant revisions in their story mountains and their leads. When working with children around both of these things today, help them envision what's happening. Often writers will need to go from summarizing to storytelling. If a child has written something like, "Elisabeth woke up and listened to her parents fight," you'll want to point out that this is still a summary. "Pretend you are Elisabeth," I said to Sofiya. "You are lying in your bed sleeping. Now you begin to wake up, just a bit. You hear something. What is it?" Coaching, I said, "Maybe you hear voices. Then what do you do? Sit up in bed, and listen some more? This time you make out a voice you know—whose? Can you make out any words the voice is saying?" In this way, I helped Sofiya rewrite her draft so that she storytold in a step-by-step fashion—and relived her character's experience of that morning.

As you confer with your children, remember that you are a talent scout, searching for what each child does well so that you can solicit that child to teach his or her peers. Then set children up to lead little seminars. For example, when I read Chris' work, I was blown away by his ability to convey the reciprocity and intimacy in a friendship between two best friends. And so I called a group of children together, who, like Chris, were writing relationship stories, and I asked them to study Chris' writing closely, just as we'd studied texts by other authors, and to pay special attention to Chris' talent for making a relationship seem very real. He'd written, for example:

> Jerod wasn't in Boy Scouts because it met at a church; he was Jewish and his mom didn't want him experiencing another religion. Luke understood and never brought it up.

MID-WORKSHOP TEACHING POINT — *Matching Writing with Story Mountains*

"Writers, I want to remind you that when we worked on our Luz story, we had our story mountain out beside us, and before we picked up our pens and stepped into Luz's shoes, we first checked our story mountain so we'd keep in mind the main event that we knew would happen next. Before we wrote the story of Luz bringing out the stack of games, we checked our plans. As we wrote, we kept in mind the overall game plan—one page about playing games, another page in which Luz's worries over being liked get worse and worse. Make sure you're keeping your own story mountain beside you as you write and that page 2 of your booklet is the second dot on your own story mountain." Then I added,

continued on next page

When a text provides such precise detail, readers believe the story is real. Above all, children noticed Chris' culminating metaphor:

> He and Jerod were like a chain. If it breaks, it's just two pieces of metal always looking for the other piece.

When I find a child who has done something marvelous, it is incredibly powerful if I let that child's good work become a subject for study. Once I saw Chris' beautiful metaphor capturing his character's friendship, I asked Chris if he could help revise the Luz story so that it, too, contained a beautiful metaphor. We found a possible place. The text read:

> Then, just like that, the lights were out. It was dark. Luz tried to find some light, somewhere in the living room.

With Chris' help, we rewrote this. We thought, "What else looks for something the way Luz is looking for a light? Hmm . . . she's starting to feel a bit frantic . . . ."and we wrote:

> Luz searched the dark living room like a sailor lost at sea searches for land on the horizon.

Then Chris taught a cluster of other children to do similar work on their drafts.

continued from previous page

"Remember that as you move from page one to page 2 of your story, your character's troubles escalate. They get worse and worse."

"Caleb has already started to move into the next scene in his story about Spencer, the boy who decides to face up to the big bully and meet him on the playground. Listen to the beginning of this first scene, how he sets up the problem: There is going to be a confrontation with that bully." *[Fig. VII-1]*

> I tried absent-mindedly to walk away so that the oversized tiger wouldn't prey on me. I'm as skinny as a wire and a main target for bullies.
>
> My puny frame was no match for Humphrey's bulging one. I wanted to shrink and shrink until he couldn't see me anymore.

continued on next page

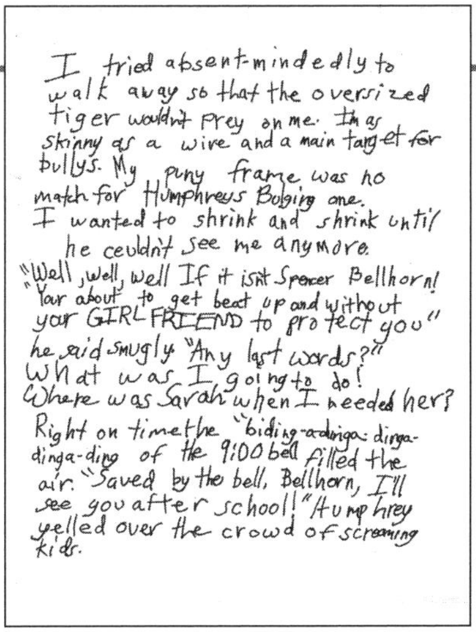
I tried absent-mindedly to walk away so that the oversized tiger wouldn't prey on me. I'm as skinny as a wire and a main target for bullys. My puny frame was no match for Humphreys Bulging one.
I wanted to shrink and shrink until he couldn't see me anymore.
"Well, well, well If it isn't Spencer Bellhorn! Your about to get beat up and without your GIRL FRIEND to protect you" he said smugly "Any last words?"
What was I going to do!
Where was Sarah when I needed her?
Right on time the "biding-a-dinga-dinga-dinga-ding of the 9:00 bell filled the air. "Saved by the bell, Bellhorn, I'll see you after school!" Humphrey yelled over the crowd of screaming kids.

Fig. VII-1 A snippet from Caleb's draft

Of course, children, too, need to be talent scouts. You can help them find talent among their classmates and among the authors whose books they admire. Becca came to me with this section of *Journey*, by Patricia MacLachlan, announcing, "Know what's amazing? It's the best description in the world and it only has two adjectives in it!"

> The first letter that wasn't a letter came in the noon mail. It lay in the middle of the kitchen table like a dropped apple, addressed to Cat and me, Mama's name in the left-hand corner.
>
> I'd watched Cat walk up the front path from the mailbox slowly, as if caught by the camera in slow motion or in a series of what Grandfather calls stills: Cat smiling; Cat looking eager; Cat, her face suddenly unfolding out of a smile. She brushed past me at the front door and opened her hand, the letter falling to the table.

I looked with her at the passage, agreed with her analysis, and pointed out to her that when I was studying with Don Murray, he gave me a list of editing tips. "Check to be sure you are writing with strong precise nouns and verbs, not relying on adjectives and adverbs to prop them up—the *young* dog is a puppy, and if the man walked *quietly*, he tiptoed."

continued from previous page

Can't you just see them? Caleb has really set this scene up, and it feels dramatic. What will happen? Will the bully hit him or not? Listen to the next scene that Caleb made." *[Fig. VII-2]*

> I couldn't pay attention in math class because I was thinking of a plan, a plan to defend myself against Humphrey. I could run away! No he would get me the next day. I could set a trap! No time.
>
> Then a thought crossed my mind. Humphrey had never actually hit someone, he had just threatened to! So why should I be afraid? A light bulb lit up in my head. I had a plan.

"Can you hear how Caleb is making a plan for how to stand up to the bully? Make sure that as you write your stories, you keep in mind where the story is going . . . but that like Caleb, you take your time getting there."

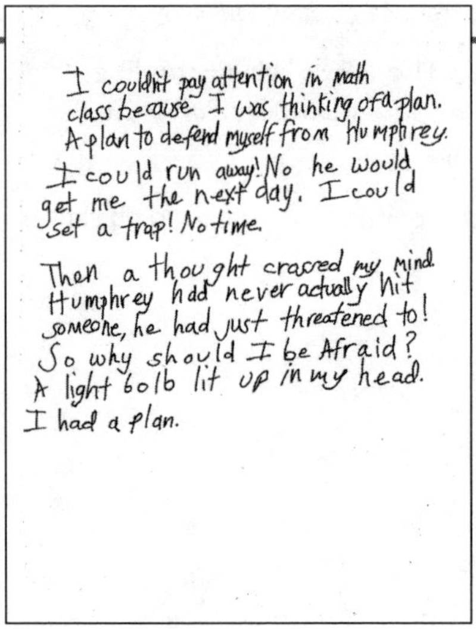

> I couldn't pay attention in math class because I was thinking of a plan. A plan to defend myself from Humphrey. I could run away! No he would get me the next day. I could set a trap! No time.
>
> Then a thought crossed my mind Humphrey had never actually hit someone, he had just threatened to! So why should I be Afraid? A light bulb lit up in my head. I had a plan.

Fig. VII-2 Caleb's draft, page 2 of his story booklet.

SHARE

Revising Leads

Tell children that you can't move fast enough to help each writer, so you'll teach them how to be writing teachers for each other. Explain that it is more efficient to revise earlier rather than waiting to revise the whole story, and tell children that they need to look at leads asking, "What story does this set up?"

"Writers, I've been racing around, conferring with lots of you. But your stories are so long and complex and interesting, that I'm not moving fast enough. And I want every single one of you to have the chance to confer with someone about your story, so that you can revise before you get a lot farther into your draft. It's much easier to write a page or two and then look at those early pages and say, 'Whoa! Let me rethink this,' rather than writing a whole ten-page draft, then rereading it and saying, 'Whoa! Let me rethink this!'"

"So right now, I want to teach every one of you how to be writing teachers for each other, and then I'm going to suggest you each meet with your partner, and try to confer in ways that help both of you rethink your lead *and your story*.

"You see, when you help each other revise your leads, you are really thinking, 'If this keeps on going and becomes a whole story, what problems might the story encounter?' I think I may have told you about the time I wanted to put a new carpet on our living room floor. But I didn't want to buy a big carpet, install it, and *then* say 'Whoa!' So I got a sweater the color of one possible carpet. I put it on the floor and I looked at it, squinting in such a way that I imagined that sweater as a whole big carpet touching the walls, and I thought, 'How would this look if it were big?' Then I put a different sweater on the middle of the floor, stepped back and squinted at it, imagining *that* sweater as a whole big carpet."

"We can reread the early pages of a story like I looked at those sweaters, thinking, 'What might this look like when it's a bigger text?' When you do this for your own writing and for each other, reread the draft and think, 'What will happen next in the story?' Talk and think about the story that this particular lead sets up."

Remind children of the common problems they're apt to see when they look at each other's and their own leads.

"Often you'll decide that your first draft starts too far from the turning point, and you'll decide the next draft needs to zoom in on an event that is closer to the main action. On the other hand, sometimes you'll decide that you've told the whole story right at the start from

I find that a unit of study on fiction quickly becomes a unit of study on revision. In part, this is true because writers are so eager for the chance to write fiction that they fill pages upon pages in short order. Then, too, there is so much involved in getting a story off to a good start that it's inevitable that children will write a less-than-ideal draft and that we'll want to ratchet up the level of that draft by helping the child make significant revisions. So ready yourself to put a lot of weight behind the importance of revision, and prepare to act utterly dumbfounded if a child announces he or she doesn't want to revise. Act as if you've never heard of such a preposterous idea! Unheard of!

As your children become more experienced as writers and as students of writing, their abilities to confer well with each other will grow in leaps and bounds. Whereas during the early portion of the year, you probably hoped that in their peer conferences, children functioned as audiences for each other (only), by now, you can expect children's conferences with each other to include assessment, planning, and suggested strategies.

beginning to end, leaving nothing for page 2 or 3. In this case, you'll need to back up and work on your story mountain again. Ask yourself, 'What episode (or Small Moment story) could occur next to show the predicament? What episode could make the predicament get worse and worse?'"

Set children up to practice conferring by asking them to consider how they'd respond to a child you describe who's written just the lead of a story. Then launch partnership work.

"Imagine, for example, that you are Rena's partner. She brings her draft to you. I'm going to read you page 1 and 2 of her story booklet and would you think to yourself, 'How will this look once she's written an entire story?' Ask yourself, 'What problems might Rena run into once this becomes a whole big story? Has she started too early in the sequence of events? Has she spilled the beans too early?'" [Fig. VII-3]

> "I got both of your invitations . . . same day . . . don't know what to do . . . can't make . . . anyone feel bad . . . ," Morgan panted after running up to Cassandra in the school yard.
>
> "Who? Wha-"
>
> "Your birthday party is on the same day as Amy's. I can't miss either, I just can't," Morgan said firmly.
>
> "Why? It's OK if you'd rather go to Amy's," says Cassandra humphily.
>
> "That's the point though, that's the point!" Morgan wailed. "Oh I just can't stand making either of you feel bad. Plus, the parties sound like so much fun, so I can't miss both, but I just can't only miss one!"
>
> Cassandra smiles and nudges me. "Hey calm down, I was only joking. Like I care if you go to Amy's . . . It's my own fault I planned it on the same day during the same hours. Plus I'll still know you're my friend."
>
> Morgan shook her head vigorously, "I can't risk offending either of you. Uh-uh, no way. I won't."

Soon the class had agreed that if they were Rena's partner, they might tell her that she'd not only conveyed the problem, she also came very close to solving it! Within just this first page, the character got herself into and out of a little scrape. So the children suggested Rena could now go back to the drawing board, quite literally, and think again about the story mountain of her story. They suggested she needed, also, to take a bit of time to allow readers

Fig. VII-3 Rena's lead

If you're accustomed to reading children's efforts to write narrative, then you'll probably have the eyes to see that Rena has made a big effort to intersperse small actions throughout the dialogue. Often children begin to do something as writers that needs to be celebrated—and extended. I think Rena needs to be more clear where the interchange is taking place, and what, exactly, her characters are doing, holding, and so forth. If Rena were clear about this, she could add actions and setting in a way which grounded the dialogue. Then she could hear your suggestions about tenses!

to identify with and care about the protagonist. "Show her in agony over the decision," they suggested. "Then make it get worse and worse." Rena agreed to return to the stage of planning and drafting her story.

With this experience as writing teachers behind them, partners convened and tried to give similarly dramatic help to each other.

HOMEWORK *Revising Story Mountains* When my sons were young, they spent much of one summer building a tree fort high in the branches of a lakeside tree. Long before they put the first logs into place, they sketched out their plans. Starting in the middle of winter, they worked on their architectural drawings. Should the fort be one story, or two? Should the second story be above and parallel to the first, or jutting out on a higher branch? What sort of stairway might link the floors?

My sons began sketching and dreaming and problem-solving in February and kept at it through the entire spring. Writers in a writing workshop don't have as much time to mull over story mountains, but it is still really important to imagine alternative ways that a story (like a tree fort) might go. John Gardner, author of *The Art of Fiction,* describes this stage of the writing process this way.

> Plotting is ordinarily no hasty process but something the writer
> broods and labors over, trying out one approach, then another,
> carrying the idea around with him, musing on it casually as he drifts
> off to sleep. (pp. 170–171)

Tonight, try a few different story mountains, and be sure that with each different sketch, you take the time to envision how that version of the story might unroll. Does it get to the heart of the action right away? Does the tension increase slowly until it is unbearable? Come to school tomorrow with a diagram of your story that feels like it's a viable plan.

If your students are rushing along in their stories and you want to give input to help their endings . . . you could say to them, "Writers, I think Patricia Reilly Giff would be proud of the heap of trouble you have all gotten your characters into! I'm out of breath just thinking of climbing your story mountains! But now we've all created some gigantic problem mountains, and we're stuck on top! How will we get our poor characters out of the situations they are in?"

Then you could tell children that realistic fiction writers work very hard on what they call the resolution. We work hard to make sure the resolution of the problems makes sense and doesn't seem to come out of the clear blue sky. It's not like a comic book, where Superman can just fly in to save the day. A good resolution feels like it fits with the rest of the story, and makes our character learn something or change in ways that feel tailored to the character.

If your students are working through this unit for the second or third year . . . you could spend some time teaching them the difference between first person, second person, and third person perspectives in writing. Second person, the "you" voice, often feels forced or too familiar. The third-person voice allows students to distance themselves from the characters and reinforces the idea that this is fiction, not personal narrative. The first person often sounds more natural, and using it can make it easier for students to integrate an internal narrative. You can teach children that writers often experiment with different perspectives before settling on one. To do this, writers would write the same scene in first, second, and then third person. Then, we choose which perspectives have the effect on the reader we prefer, and hold to that point of view. Writers could try this in partnerships.

ASSESSMENT

You'll definitely want to collect your children's work and study it. It's easy to look at student work for signs of trouble, and that will be important to do. But give yourself firm orders to first look for signs of growth. Since the start of the year, your children will have often picked up their pens and spun stories onto their pages. Look back on the earliest September entries and contrast them with the writing they did today. The fact that September's writing was personal narrative and this is fiction shouldn't detract from the comparability of these texts. What progress do you see?

I suspect you'll see that children are writing with vastly more fluency, voice, detail, and structure. If so, you'll want to point this out to the child. Bring out the first entries and contrast them with the child's latest work. "Look at the difference!" you need to say.

But you also need to point this out to yourself, because your children's growth should help you believe in the power of instruction. And the evidence that your children have already made important gains can renew your energy to teach. Be willing to look at children's writing and to see what they are almost but not quite doing.

There are a few problems that you should expect to see. These won't be new problems—chances are, they were also present during the personal narrative work. Many times, you'll see that even your most skilled writers try to carry their scenes through dialogue, not action. This was the case in the lead to Rena's story we studied in the previous share session, and you'll see the problem remains in this new effort she made to write a whole new story. [Figs. VII-4 and VII-5]

"Butthead!" Cassidy says seething.

"I didn't do anything," Carly, the sensitive one of the three is on the verge of tears.

"Did so! You kept on hurling pine cones at me when I told you to stop, and then you played keep-it-away-from-Cassidy with my favorite hat and now it's halfway downstream because

you tried to throw it across the spring to Morgan and it landed in the spring."

"I was joking," says Carly looking down. "It was funny."

Ideally, you will want to see your students weaving together action, thought, dialogue and setting to create the scenes of their stories. As you read through their work, notice which of these elements your students do and do not use.

For example, I noticed that in this section of Joey's draft, when he tried to convince his mother to give him money to buy a bicycle, he relied exclusively on dialogue:

"But Mom," Gary said. "I really want that bike."

"Sorry, but you can't afford it," Gary's mom said.

"Can't you give me the money? I'll pay you back."

"And how exactly do you think that will work?"

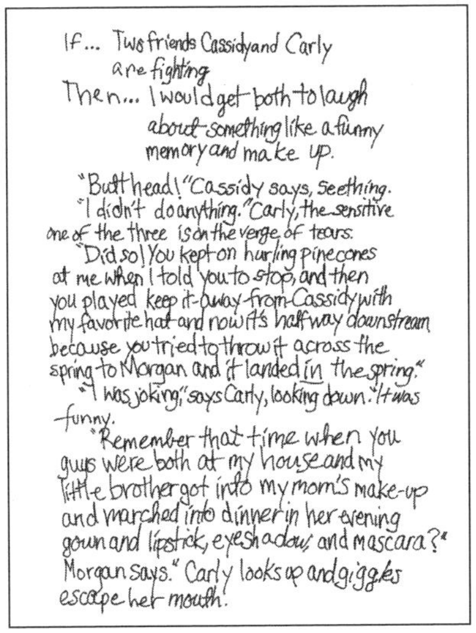

Fig. VII-4 Rena's lead

Fig. VII-5 Rena's lead, page 2

This would have been a much stronger image if Joey had added thoughts and action and setting. Revised, it might have gone something like this:

> "But Mom," Gary said, "I really want that bike. Gary sat at the kitchen table finishing his homework as his mother cooked dinner.
>
> "Sorry, but you can't afford it," Gary's mother said without looking up. Her voice was strong and final, but Gary wasn't ready to give up."
>
> "Can't you give me the money? I'll pay you back."
>
> Gary's mother stopped cooking. She turned and looked at her son. She stood with her arms folded as if she was firmly resisting his pleas. "And how exactly do you think that will work."

Children need us to give them examples of what we imagine. If we simply tell them to add actions, they don't necessarily grasp the way in which we envision setting the words into a scene. So plan on actually showing them how a bit of their text could be rewritten, and plan also on extrapolating the larger principles from this. Once we rewrote a few sentences of Joey's draft for him, we could point out that in the new version a reader could see that Gary's mother is not at all agreeable to Gary's plan, and that Gary is relentless in his pursuit to get a new bicycle.

You will probably also notice that if your students write with setting at all, they put one big blob of it at the beginning of their story and let it sit

there. The characters walk past the setting, but the setting doesn't further the main action of the story. Joey's original draft started like this:

> It was a sunny day. Gary walked through the park towards school. The ground was covered with leaves and the trees were bare. People were walking their dogs and drinking coffee. There was a chill in the air, but Gary was wearing his new fleece so he was warm.

Joey has created a sense of place at the beginning of the story, but as his story unfolds, you can see that the setting has little to do with his story line. If revised to make the setting serve his story, his beginning might instead go like:

> Gary rushed through the park toward school. It was a sunny day but Gary hardly noticed. He was too intent on hurrying. People were walking dogs and drinking coffee and chatting, but Gary's only interest was getting to the bike shop before school to catch one quick glimpse of his favorite BMX bike.

As you read through your students' writing, you'll learn what you need to know to plan your future teaching.

STUDYING PUBLISHED TEXTS TO WRITE LEADS

IN THIS SESSION, YOU'LL REMIND WRITERS OF VARIOUS STRATEGIES FOR WRITING EFFECTIVE LEADS. YOU WILL ALSO REMIND CHILDREN THAT WRITERS REREAD LITERATURE, LETTING IT TEACH TECHNIQUES FOR WRITING.

GETTING READY

- Leads of two short stories kids are familiar with
- Lead that invites further revision
- Two examples of dialogue, one empty and one revealing, written on chart paper
- See CD-ROM for resources

If you look across all the units of study that we've detailed in this series, you'll see that time and again, we ask children to draft and revise their leads. The goal in making a great lead isn't the lead itself. The goal is to imagine a work of art, and then to write a lead which points the course toward and is worthy of that larger enterprise. Opening scenes set up the drama of what will follow. We plan our leads with an eye toward all that we believe is essential for the larger experience to work.

This session, then, aims to help children remember that after drafting a lead, it's important to step back and ask, "How might this lead set up the larger text? Is that the way I want the larger text to go?" As writers revise this opening paragraph or two, they also revise the larger text.

We ask children to revise their leads because front-end revisions are vastly easier for children to embrace and more likely to lift the level of entire drafts than back-end revisions, which are much more time consuming. And by investing a minilesson (and therefore an added day) in early revision work, we slow children's progress, making it more likely that we'll be able to confer with more children at this crucial just-starting stage. Once children are deep into the first drafts of their stories, they become more and more committed to the road they've taken, and it is harder to deter them from that pathway. Soon, children won't want us to confer in ways that help them imagine other paths their story could have taken.

When we ask children to revise their leads, we aim to remind them that writers consider and reconsider not only the content of their stories, but also their craftsmanship. When a writer shifts from planning a story to writing a draft, the writer needs to think not only about what will happen in a scene (in this instance, in the opening scene), but also about how to write the scene well. Children are much more apt to write well if, just before they pick up their pens, something occurs that stirs their hearts, that raises their hopes, that fills them with a sense of momentousness. So we tell them, "Study the work of other authors"—and secretly, we say, "Put yourself under the spell of other authors. Let their magic rub off!"

In today's session you will show students how they can study the work of published writers to help them craft enticing leads for their stories.

MINILESSON

Studying Published Texts to Write Leads

CONNECTION

Celebrate that your children have begun their stories, and do so by conveying the essence of a couple of stories to the class.

"Writers, you'll see from today's schedule that the read-aloud we've scheduled for later will be a special one. Instead of me continuing to read our chapter book aloud, some of you will read aloud the leads to your stories. Something extraordinary is happening in this classroom, and we all need to be a part of it. Stories are literally coming to life in your story booklets. You need to know each other's stories!"

"You need to know that just as that gingerbread boy came to life, there are characters coming to life right in this room. You need to know that a girl named Elexa is surveying the playground, hoping against hope that the geeky boy who stalks her hasn't caught a glance of her. Elexa sees her best friend—but oh no! She is frantically gesturing that someone is close by, and with a sinking heart Elexa realizes she's been spotted."

"You need to know that Spencer is getting ready to confront his nemesis, Humphrey Dugball, the meanest bully in the history of Butts, Missouri. And you need to know that right here in this room, Jane's friend Amy has asked her yet again to sleep over, and Jane is frantically coming up with yet more excuses."

Name your teaching point. In this case, teach children that by revising their leads, they revise their entire stories, and remind them they could emulate the work of another writer.

"Today I want to teach you that just when a writer is most fired up to write, most ready to charge into page after page of writing, we force ourselves to pause. We pause, rewind, and then we listen to what we've written. And we revise it. We revise our lead because by doing so, we revise our entire story. Sometimes, we do this with help from a pro."

COACHING

Your job is to help children fall in love with their own stories and with the fiction writing workshop itself—and to then channel their energy and zeal for writing into revision. Notice that the impetus for revision is not discontent, but instead pride and commitment.

Notice that the message to children today is, "Your stories are riveting! I'm dying to learn how they turn out." It's important for children to aim toward writing riveting, absorbing stories that draw in readers.

Children can learn as much from their friend's work with a draft as they learn from your work with a demonstration text. So be sure that you help them learn vicariously by following the drama of each other's progress.

A unit of study on fiction writing is also a unit of study on rehearsal and revision. Fiction writing is such a complex enterprise that there is no way we can preteach kids all they need to know to get off to a good start. By emphasizing revision, we give ourselves opportunities to double or triple the amount of instruction we can give to our students. Meanwhile, children will experience the power and pay off of real revision.

TEACHING

Tell children that to write leads that draw readers into a story, it helps to study the leads published authors have written.

"You already know that the beginning of a piece of writing, any piece of writing, is called a *lead* because these sentences are the way an author *leads* readers into the text. A good lead functions like the Pied Piper. You remember the story of the Pied Piper, walking through town playing his flute? People would listen up, and soon all the villagers were following along wherever he led them."

"This morning, I told Francesca that I always work hard on my lead because I want it to draw readers along. But she asked the crucial question—how can a lead do that? What techniques do writers use?"

"Of course, you know how to answer that! When we writers want to learn how to do something, we study texts written by authors we admire. After we look really closely at exactly how other authors pull something off, we try the same techniques in our own writing."

Tell the class that you and one student studied the leads from familiar stories. Read one aloud, listing what the student noticed about it and then showing the resulting revisions in her own lead.

"Francesca and I decided to study leads. We first reread the lead to *Ruby, the Copy Cat*, which you'll remember is a picture book by Peggy Rathmann. The story starts like this:

> Monday was Ruby's first day in Miss Hart's class. "Class, this is Ruby," announced Miss Hart. "Ruby, you may use the empty desk behind Angela. Angela is the girl with the pretty red bow in her hair."
>
> Angela smiled at Ruby.
>
> Ruby smiled at Angela's bow and tiptoed to her seat.

"Looking at this story reminded Francesca of things she'd learned earlier: It often helps to start with the exact words one character is saying (or with a small action); and, in a short story, it's important to start close to the main event. If there's a waterfall in the story, start when you can hear the falls. The main tension in this story revolves around Ruby wanting Angela's approval, and she will try to earn this by wearing a red bow, just like Angela's . . . and by worse examples of copying too! Notice that the lead of the story hints at what will come later."

When teaching skills, we need to anticipate that we'll often revisit earlier lessons. It's a challenge to find new ways to teach a familiar concept. In this instance, I've found a new way to describe the role a lead plays in a story.

F. Paul Wilson has said: "I don't know how it is with other writers, but most of the time when I finish [reading] a story or novel, I may be pleased, I may even be impressed, but somewhere in the back of my mind I'm thinking, 'I can do that.'" The act of apprenticing oneself to a respected and more experienced practitioner is an age-old tradition.

There is nothing special about this particular story. We also use Peter's Chair, Stevie (by John Steptoe), or "Merry Christmas, My Friend," a short story from Chicken Soup for the Kid's Soul. Select any text that works!

Set children up to listen to and then talk with partners about what the one child did as she revised her lead.

"So Francesca thought about her story. She already knew that the heart of the story revolved around Griffen, the boy in her story, trying to convince his father he could take care of a pet. She remembered that often it helps to start a story with dialogue, so she decided to try a lead in which Griffen says something about getting a pet to his dad. Listen to what she wrote: *[Fig. VIII-1]*

> "Dad," Griffen said.
>
> "Can I get a pet?"
>
> "Well, a pet is a lot of responsibility," Dad said.
>
> "Please," Griffen said.
>
> "If I see that you are responsible enough you can get a pet," said Griffen's dad.
>
> The next day, Griffen told Timmy. He was amazed.
>
> "I bet we can show that we are responsible enough," Timmy said.

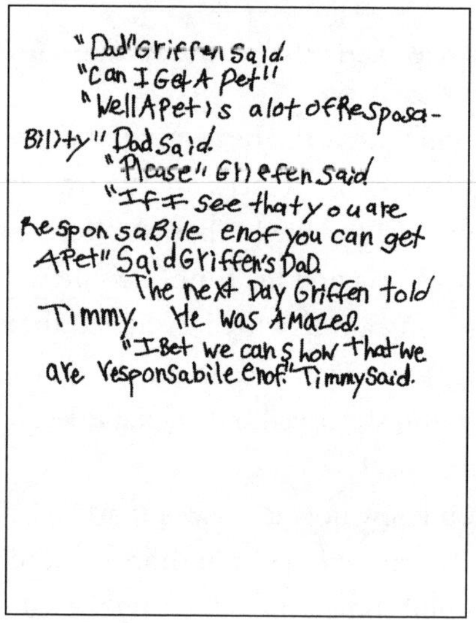
"Dad" Griffen Said
"Can I Get A pet"
"Well A pet is alot of Responsa-
Bility" Dad Said
"Please" Griffen Said
"If I see that you are
Responsabile enof you can get
A pet" Said Griffen's DaD
The next Day Griffen told
Timmy. He was Amazed
"I Bet we can show that we
are Responsabile enof" Timmy Said.

Fig. VIII-1 Francesca's lead

This is not a spectacular example of a lead. Francesca is a very capable writer, as you will have seen from following her progress throughout the year. Don't be surprised if your children's writing, like Francesca's, is not as impressive when they are writing fiction as when they wrote personal narratives. As this session unrolls, you'll point out ways to enrich this writing.

Active Engagement

Share a second lead, this time asking the class to list to a partner what they notice about it that Fransesca, and all of them, could try.

"Then Francesca and I looked at a second lead, this time from Julie Brinckloe's *Fireflies!"* We were pretty sure this story would teach us more techniques, so we read it really closely. Reread it with me now, and think, 'What has Brinckloe done that we can learn from?'"

> On a summer evening
> I looked up from dinner,
> through the open window to the backyard.
> It was growing dark.
>
> My treehouse was a black shape in the tree
> and I wouldn't go up there now.
>
> But something flickered there, a moment—
> I looked, and it was gone.
>
> It flickered again, over near the fence.
> *Fireflies*!

You've probably noticed throughout this series that I use the same texts in my minilessons over and over again. These are texts that I have read to the children, texts that they know and love, carefully selected for their teaching potential. Returning often to the same text shows students how very much we can learn through the study of one beautiful story. Keep a stash of these texts to use as demonstrations during small group and individual conferences, too. I've sometimes led workshops to show teachers how we can weave any one text into fifty very different conferences!

"Don't let your dinner get cold," said Momma.

I forked the meat and corn and potatoes into my mouth.

"Please may I go out? The fireflies—"

Momma smiled and Daddy nodded. "Go ahead," they said.

"Brinckloe's used lots of techniques here; the lead is one we could examine and talk about for hours. So let's reread it again. As you listen this time, let a section of the lead stand out for you, and then when I finish reading it, turn and point out that part to your partner. Name what Brinckloe has done that you could emulate."

I reread the lead, and reminded children of what they each needed to do in his or her own mind. After giving them a moment or two of silence, I queried, "Ready?" and when they nodded yes, I directed them to share with a partner. I listened in as the children talked.

Convene the class to talk as a group about what they noticed in the lead. Do this to lift the level of partner talk which will be continued soon.

After a moment, I said, "Who can get us started on a conversation about the techniques Brinckloe has used in her lead?"

Deveonna's hand shot up. "It has less talk."

"Hmm . . . that's interesting," I said, looking at the text. "That's a smart thing to notice. But class, do you see that if there's *less* talk, there is *more* of something else?" I asked. Then I named the larger principle. "Writers, when I try to learn from other authors, I push myself to name what a writer *has* done, not just what he or she *hasn't* done, because it's easier to emulate something positive. What *did* Brinckloe do instead of writing dialogue?"

"She takes her time showing where the story takes place; the evening is coming and the treehouse is a black shape and all?" Ramon said.

"She doesn't start with dialogue." Ari added. "First there's just the backyard, then a flicker by the fence."

"So this author first creates the setting," I confirmed, providing Ari with the words he seemed to be reaching for. "But also, even before we see the backyard, we see the narrator, sitting at the dinner table, looking outside. The backyard is growing dark . . . . It's not the author who describes the setting is it? It's the boy, the narrator, who notices the setting. And what do you make of the flicker? Why did the author write the setting in such a way that there is a flicker right from the start?" Then I said, "Let's again try to talk with partners and this time really name what Julie Brinckloe has done in this lead." I sent children to talk in pairs about this.

Convening the class, I again called on a few children.

Notice that when teaching strategies, I am careful to describe each step in sequence. I don't simply suggest that children "talk about what they can learn from this author." Instead, in order to set children up to make a reading-writing connection, I ask them to reread the text, let a part stand out for them, then point to that part and name the technique the author has used in this part that they can emulate.

This is unusual. I'm asking for a child to launch a whole-class conversation within the minilesson instead of simply retelling what I heard a child do. The teaching component of this minilesson was brief so I saved enough time for this.

The way I ratchet up what Deveonna has said is a way you too can try. I could have simply agreed that there is less talk and then asked, "What takes the place of that talk?" But whenever possible, I try to explicitly teach concepts that might apply to other situations, and so I first point out the generalizable principle—that children will learn more from looking for positive features, features that are present rather than absent.

Of course, the decision to select a story that is filled with such a sense of place and of mood, too, was not accidental. I'm hoping to expand my students' repertoire. I agree with Janet Burroway who writes, in Writing Fiction, *"Your fiction must have an atmosphere because without it, your characters will be unable to breathe. Part of the atmosphere of a scene or story is its setting, including the location, period, weather, time of day . . . " I agree, too, that we most effectively reveal setting through detail. Burroway cites this example of how a detailed movement can create the larger setting: "The bugs hung over the black water in clusters of a steady hum." I refer instead to the examples in* Fireflies!.

"I think there is action, but it is just the flicker of the firefly."

"I think some stories start with the setting, and with making a mood. That's what this lead does 'cause we know it's evening outside."

"You've noticed a lot of techniques!" I said, and listed a few on my fingers:

- Sometimes stories begin not with a big action but with a small action, and this can be an action in the setting, as when the firefly flickers on and off.
- Some stories begin by creating a mood and a place, and only afterward does the sequence of actions begin.
- Sometimes the time and the place are revealed slowly, bit by bit, as the character sees or moves into the setting.

Channel children to use what they notice an author has done in order to help one child again revise her lead.

"Let's all listen again to Francesca's first lead and think whether the techniques we've learned from Brinckloe could help Francesca as she gets ready to again revise this lead. Listen again, then tell your partner if you have suggestions for Francesca."

"Dad," Griffen said.

"Can I get a pet?"

"Well, a pet is a lot of responsibility," Dad said.

"Please," Griffen said.

"If I see that you are responsible enough you can get a pet," said Griffen's dad.

The next day, Griffen told Timmy. He was amazed.

"I bet we can show that we are responsible enough," Timmy said.

After the children talked with their partners, I called on Shariff, who said, "Francesca, I'm not sure, but I think maybe your first lead had *too* much talk. You could add in where you are, and put some setting in with it and take some talk out."

Hannah added, "Another idea is you could start the story earlier, before this when he's just sitting and dreaming about getting a pet, and have Griffen be alone, like the kid in *Fireflies!*—then he could go to his dad next. That'd show his wants more."

You could decide to create a large chart with a favorite passage from a mentor text on the left, the words children use to describe what the author has done in the center, and examples of two or three children's efforts to write similarly in the far right column. This chart could form a cohesive link, tying together several days of inquiry and apprenticeship. I recommend this sort of chart in the Authors as Mentors *book within the* K-2 Units of Study *series, and you'll see charts like this elsewhere in this book.*

I deliberately selected a student whose lead invited further revision. I wanted to make it easy for children to imagine ways they could incorporate more setting.

LINK

Restate the options your children have for today, reminding them of the step-by-step process they might take to revise their leads.

"So writers, I want to tell you a surprise—Francesca and I came to the same conclusions when we studied her lead. Francesca tried two other leads; let me read them to you." [Figs. VIII-2 and VIII-3]

First Revision

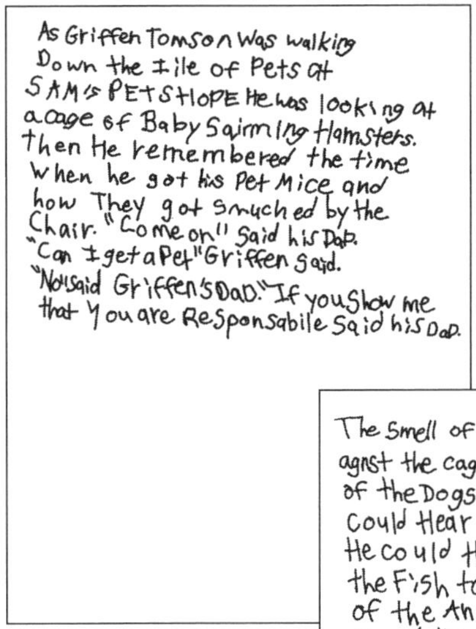

As Griffen Tomson was walking down the aisle of pets at Sam's Pet Shop, he was looking at a cage of baby squirming hamsters. Then he remembered the time he got his pet mice and how they got squashed by the chair. "Come on" said his dad. "Can I get a pet?" Griffen said. "No" said Griffen's dad. "If you show me that you are responsible," said his dad.

Later Revision

The smell in the air of the pets' fur rubbing against the cage. The smell of the dogs breath panting. Griffen could hear the hamsters squeaking as they ran. He could hear the running water in the fish tank. It felt like all of the animals were his pets. He could hear the cat's purring and he could hear the turtles walk. It smelled like dog and cat fur. He could hear the birds squawking and making loud noises. He could see the little turtles rest under their mom. He saw one little turtle all alone under its shell. He saw it go under a big rock like a cave. He wanted to take the little turtle home!

"Do you see what she learned from other authors in her own lead? Today, each one of you needs to decide what you need to do. Some of you are probably realizing that in order to write with this sort of detail, you need to rethink your story plan, figuring out how you can zoom in more on just two Small Moment stories. Some of you may decide that you need to do some revisions that are similar to those Francesca has done. Some of you will want to study published leads for yourself, learning more techniques. All of you will be drafting and revising leads, but you'll decide how to go about doing that. You're the boss of your own story!"

Of course, I could have told the children that Francesca decided to revise her lead by adding more of the setting and by working to create a mood, and then asked them to reread their leads and to consider whether Rathmann or Brinckloe's leads could help them imagine ways to improve their own leads. I would work with children's own leads if the class I was teaching was filled with resistant writers or with writers who struggled to get anything much on the page. In either case, setting the children up to decide upon and rehearse for the revisions they'd soon do could be very helpful. I didn't do this in this instance because I think it is more ideal for children to work collaboratively to revise a model, and then to disperse and initiate a review of their own leads.

Fig. VIII-2 Francesca's first revision of her lead.

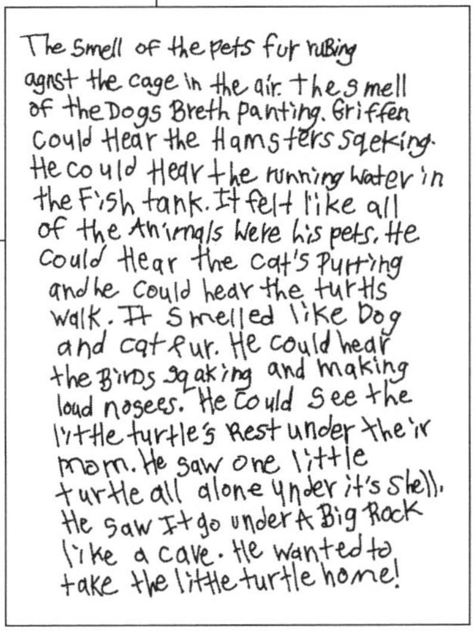

Fig. VIII-3 Francesca's second revision of her lead.

WRITING AND CONFERRING

Learning from Mentor Texts

As you move among your writers, you may want to carry a couple of short stories or picture books with you so you can refer to these often as you work with children. Keep in mind that the same text can be used to help writers with a wide array of goals. This means that your resolve to help children use mentor texts needn't control the course of a conference. Instead, you'll want to open your conferences by asking, "What are you working on as a writer?" Presumably many children will respond that they're trying to learn from Julie Brinckloe or from another author.

Don't act as if this answers your initial interest in understanding the writer's intention. Instead, press on. "And what, exactly, are you admiring about your mentor author's text?" you can ask, channeling the child to at least point to a favorite part. Appreciate that section of the text. But then quickly shift from oohing and ahhing toward helping the child think, "What has the author done in this text that worked so well?"

That's a tricky question for a child to answer. If the child makes any attempt to articulate the replicable and transferable strategies the author has used, plan on accepting and building upon whatever the child says. Act fascinated by the child's observations. "Huh! That's so interesting!" you can say. "Explain more, 'cause you are onto something!"

On the other hand, be ready to demonstrate the sort of response you hope the writer might produce in case the child says nothing. If a child says she liked the lines, "It was growing dark," "My treehouse was a black shape," and "But something flickered there, a moment . . . It flickered again, over near the fence," and if the child doesn't respond when you nudge her to articulate what Brinckloe has done that she, too, could try doing, you might help her imagine the sort of response you hope she provides. "Were you especially impressed by the way Brinckloe made us feel that *her character* was the one noticing the backyard? Was that it? You loved that we got to see the setting through the boy's eyes? Was that the aspect you especially liked?" Give the child some options. "Or were you impressed with the way Brinckloe made the setting, the place, more interesting by setting it into motion, having it be active? The backyard grows darker, doesn't it, until the tree house is just a black shape . . . and then something flickers." Then restate your question. "Were you impressed that we saw the setting through the character's eyes or that Brinckloe made the setting active, or what?" By this time, the child will probably be able to indicate which of those two options impressed her more, or she'd grasp the sort of

MID-WORKSHOP TEACHING POINT **Using Dialogue Deliberately** "Writers, can I stop you? I know by talking to many of you about your pieces and by looking over your shoulders that you are using a lot of dialogue in your stories. Give me a thumbs up if you have dialogue in your story." Most of the students gave a thumbs up.

"That's great. We know that fiction writers use dialogue all the time, so it makes sense that we're using it. I just want to give you one caution. When we use dialogue in our stories, there has to be a reason. We usually use dialogue because we're trying to show something about a character. It's important that we don't just use dialogue as filler. For example, look at this piece of dialogue." The students looked at lines I'd written on chart paper:

continued on next page

response that was expected and could contribute something of her own. Either way, ask if the writer was thinking of trying to do similar work in the next draft of his or her lead. It was this sort of conference that led Francesca to revise her lead. *[Figs. VIII-2, and VIII-3]*

Although your minilesson today was erudite and set children up for ambitious work, don't fool yourself into expecting that all your conferences will be aimed towards making good leads into great ones. Today's session gives you a final chance to check in with each student, making sure that each child has embarked on a project that is at least in the ball park that you have in mind. You are sure to find some children who, like Jasmin, have resolutely refused to follow any of your advice! Look at Jasmin's story mountain and her rough drafts of some leads: *[Figs. VIII-4, VIII-5, and VIII-6]*

Jasmin's first lead:

> "What are you doing?"
>
> "Nothin . . ." Chaos said quickly, "For now."
>
> Chaos's eyes shifted side to side. "Really?" Akyra asked, a little suspicious. I nodded. Chaos, Death, and I zoomed up the stairs. Lora and Ashley closed the door of the basement. Even though I started to hear weird noises from the basement, I kept walking. As Lora, Ashley, Akyra, Chaos, and Death walked ahead of me I turned the flashlight and laughed maniacally, "MUAHAHAHAHAH!"

Jasmin's second lead:

> I saw Death and Chaos open the door of the basement. They walked down the stairs. I tilted my head for a second, then I followed them.
>
> Chaos, Death and I were stuck in the basement . . . thanks to Death. Chaos and I looked at Death. We both yelled to Death, "NICE GOIN' IDIOT!" I thought of this situation as, DEATH'S FAULT!

continued from previous page

> "Hi" I said.
>
> "Hi," he said.
>
> "How are you?" I asked.
>
> "Fine, how are you?" he replied.

"Does everyone see how this part of dialogue doesn't do anything to help us learn more about the characters? It doesn't even move the story along. Instead, we can simply summarize what they said and write dialogue that deserves to exist, like this:

> After we exchanged greetings, I said what I had been meaning to tell him for days. "Mike," I blurted out. "I can't stand the way you pick on me all the time."
>
> "I had no idea," Mike said quietly. "Why did you wait so long to tell me? I would have stopped a long time ago."

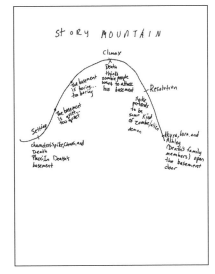

Fig. VIII-4 Jasmin's story mountain

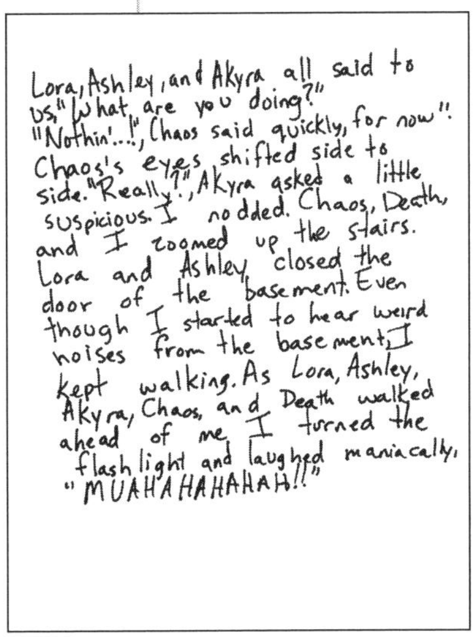

Fig. VIII-5 Although Jasmin's been directed to write realistic fiction, this is her first lead.

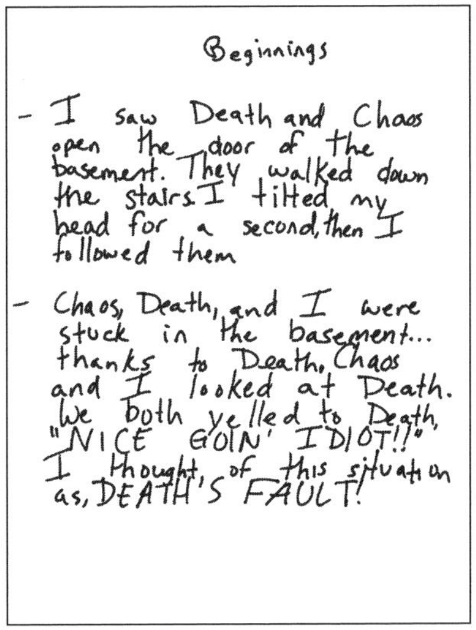

Fig. VIII-6 Jasmin's revised lead is close to the first version.

When I reminded Jasmin that we were studying *realistic* fiction, she immediately pointed out that her characters' names—Death, Chaos, and Spike were really their nicknames, and that underneath the nicknames, these are really just three normal fifth graders named Marilyn, Steven, and Lilly. "And underneath the bits about zombies and so forth, what's the simple, human story line?" I asked.

After some convoluted explanation, I finally extracted the fact that Spike-Marilyn follows the other two kids but is ambivalent about their tendency to always push boundaries and get in trouble.

"This is incredible!" I said, once I finally pushed past all the overstated drama. "Now I get it! What an incredible idea. So Marilyn wants to be friends with these kids. Do they seem to her to be powerful? What's their allure?"

Jasmin and I talked a bit more, and then I put all her drafts of the Death, Chaos, zombie story inside her folder, and pushed it to the side. I gave her a new blank sheet of paper and said, "You are definitely going to want to plan and write this story," I said. "Where will Steven and Lilly go? What sort of trouble will they get into?" Then I said, "Choose a place you know, a place you go to so that you can include realistic details, like Brinckloe did when describing the backyard."

This is the draft that Jasmin started that day: *[Fig. VIII-7]*

> Lilly, Steven, and I walked through Chinatown. "So . . . many . . . shops," I thought. Steven pointed to the fish market. "Let's go there," he said. Lilly sighed, "Ok! What about you Marilyn?"
>
> "Whatever . . ." I responded, as I shrugged. We all ran to the fish market. I could smell the seafood. It didn't really smell so bad. Lily swung the door open. Steven froze. "Look at the fishy goodness," Steven said. His eyes widened. I wasn't really amused. Lilly ran toward the fortune cookies.

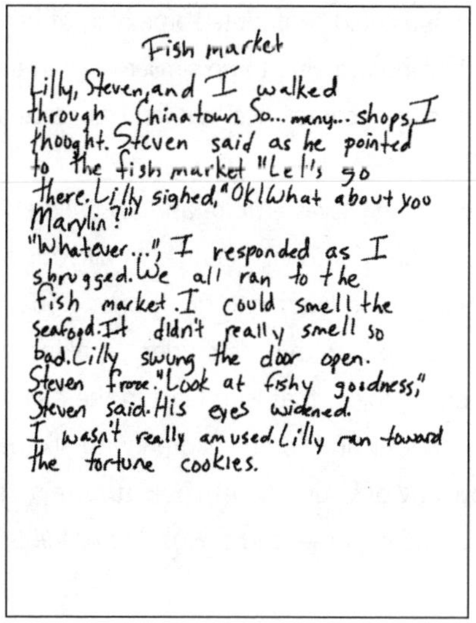

Fish market

Lilly, Steven, and I walked through Chinatown So... many... shops, I thought. Steven said as he pointed to the fish market "Let's go there. Lilly sighed, "Ok! What about you Marylin?"

"Whatever...", I responded as I shrugged. We all ran to the fish market. I could smell the seafood. It didn't really smell so bad. Lilly swung the door open. Steven froze. "Look at fishy goodness," Steven said. His eyes widened. I wasn't really amused. Lilly ran toward the fortune cookies.

Fig. VIII-7 Jasmin is now launched in a much more realistic story.

SHARE

Playing Out Leads

Remind your children that as they reconsider various leads, they are actually reconsidering various ways their entire drafts could go. Ask them to write in the air the way the next section of their story would go if they selected one lead, or another lead.

"Writers, by now many of you have written several leads, several different first scenes. I want to remind you that each of your leads will get you started telling a different story. Would you share one of your leads with your partner, then see where your lead, leads? Write in the air to help your partner imagine how that particular lead will set up your story. After that, share a second lead, and again see where it leads. Use this as a way to figure out which lead sets you up for the story you want to tell."

I listened as Valerie read first one lead to her partner, then another, pausing each time to dictate the story that would follow each lead. *[Figs. VIII-8 and VIII-9]*

Lead #1

It was a dark and gray day, kids were screaming and running inside puddles of water. All of them were screaming "Yahoo!" because school had just ended. The last day of school was sure a bad one, maybe it wasn't so bad for the other kids but it was pretty bad for Summer. She was sitting on the monkey bars wishing that school hadn't ended yet. In the back of her head she was thinking, "Oh, man, do I have to go to Catskills with Grandma & Grandpa?" Summer ran back home as fast as her feet would take her.

Lead #2

I was sitting on the school porch thinking and thinking and thinking about school. School was ending. Kids were happy. They were going home. Some of them were going away for the summer with their grandparent or their parent, others were staying home for the summer, but I was going to the Poconos with my grandparents and for me that was a disaster.

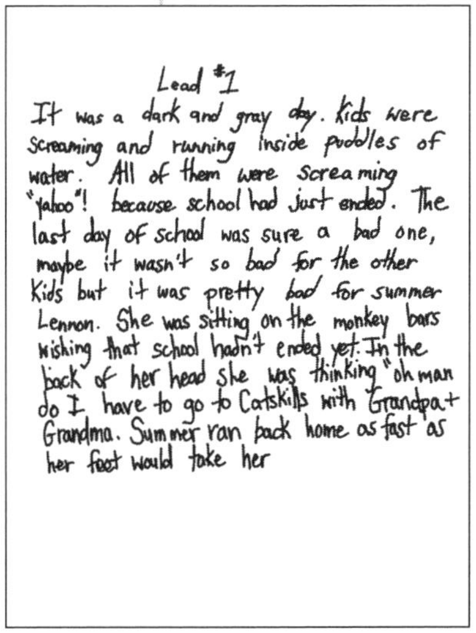

Leads set the path for the story to follow, so playing out each lead's story before choosing one is necessary work. The lead is not only a hook for the reader, it is also the rudder for the whole story.

> Lead #1
> It was a dark and gray day. kids were screaming and running inside puddles of water. All of them were screaming "yahoo"! because school had just ended. The last day of school was sure a bad one, maybe it wasn't so bad for the other kids but it was pretty bad for summer Lennon. She was sitting on the monkey bars wishing that school hadn't ended yet. In the back of her head she was thinking "oh man do I have to go to Catskills with Grandpa+ Grandma. Summer ran back home as fast as her feet would take her

> Lead #2
> I was sitting on the school porch. thinking and thinking and thinking about school. School was ending. kids were happy. They were going home. Some of them were going away for the summer with their Grandparent or their parent others were staying home for the summer but I was going to the Poconos with my Grandparents and for me it was a disaster.

Fig. VIII-8 Valerie has written this lead in third person.

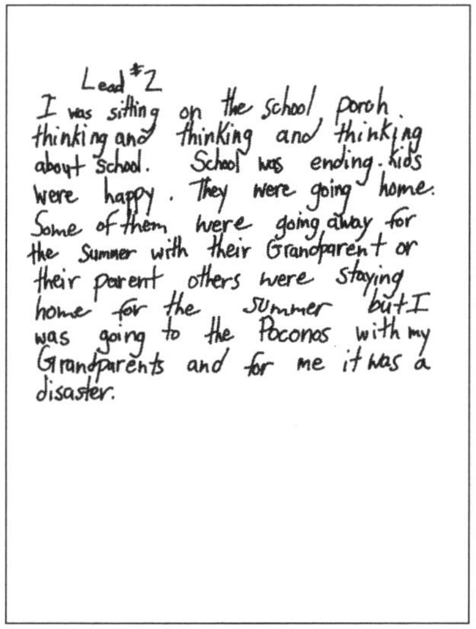

Fig. VIII-9 Valerie has written this as a first-person lead.

The girls talked over the differences, and Valerie decided she liked writing in first person, but wanted to create a mood as she'd done in the first lead. With her partner's help, she began writing a third lead which eventually looked like this: [*Fig. VIII-10*]

Lead #3

Huge lightning bolts were in the dark gray sky. Thunder was booming in my ears, rain was hitting the ground like little bits of hard rocks hitting the windows. I was standing outside and getting soaking wet. I wasn't the only one who was out in the huge storm. For some weird reason I didn't like going home, at least that's what most kids thought. Well, I thought it was a good reason. Going home to your two boring grandparents wasn't fun, especially if one of them was really fussy, grumpy and mean.

"Writers, I need to stop all of you," I said, interrupting the partner conversations. "Your leads are beautiful. Listening to them, I thought if your leads weren't handwritten, it'd be hard for me to tell which leads you wrote, and which leads had been written by professional writers! Remember, writers test out our leads as one way to help us choose and revise."

HOMEWORK ***Reading the Work of Other Authors for Inspiration*** Sometimes, when fiction writers are starting a new story, we stop and take some time to get inspired. We reread some of our favorite fiction stories and we look for some new stories we've never read before. We do that for a few reasons. We do this in order to find techniques that other authors have used that we can emulate, sure, but we do this for another even more important reason. We read other writers' work because this can change what we're feeling inside. When I reread parts of some of my favorite books—like *Because of Winn-Dixie* or *Roll of Thunder, Hear My Cry*—I get goose bumps. I get excited because those books are just so good. I want to make things that are that good, that give people goose bumps in the way Kate DiCamillo and Mildred Taylor give me goose bumps.

It might be convenient for you to take these three leads and turn them into a lesson that offers children an example of how they can try out different ways to draft and revise leads. You might also use these leads to hold a discussion with children about which leads work the best for which purposes. Children could also work together to revise these leads toward different ends, either as a class or in partnerships, and then compare and contrast their revisions.

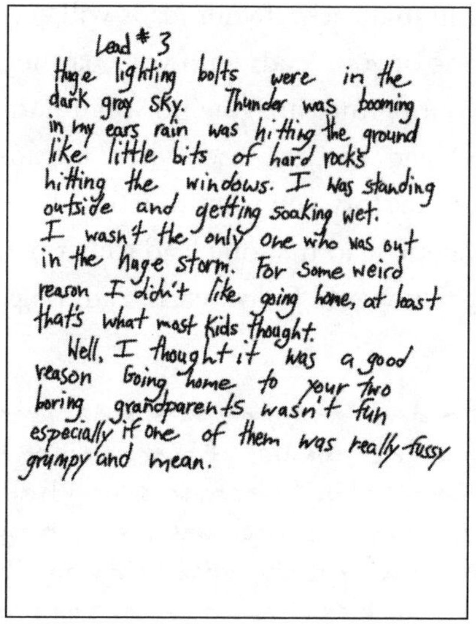
Lead # 3
Huge lighting bolts were in the dark gray sky. Thunder was booming in my ears rain was hitting the ground like little bits of hard rocks hitting the windows. I was standing outside and getting soaking wet. I wasn't the only one who was out in the huge storm. For some weird reason I didn't like going home, at least that's what most kids thought. Well, I thought it was a good reason Going home to your two boring grandparents wasn't fun especially if one of them was really fussy grumpy and mean.

Fig. VIII-10 Valerie aims to write in first person and to create a mood. She moves deeper into her story line.

Writers, give yourselves the time to be inspired by the fiction writers you know and love. Tonight pull out a book or two that you've read before and loved. Don't just limit yourself to chapter books either. Often, some of the best stories you can find are in picture books. Look through those books, and put a sticky note wherever you find a place you love. Read that part again and again. Read it aloud. Then put the book aside, and bring out the drafting booklet containing your story. Reread what you've written so far. Perhaps you'll find yourself revising!

⊙ TAILORING YOUR TEACHING

If you want to write another minilesson supporting reading-writing connections and revisions of leads . . . you could begin this way: "You know how when you go to the library or a bookstore, you read the first few lines or paragraphs of a book to see if you want to take it home? How many times do you recall passing up a book because the beginning just wasn't interesting enough? That's why it's crucial that we each write the best lead possible for our stories. Think of a lead as a hook on a fishing rod. If the bait is tasty enough, you'll catch the fish! Today I want to help you learn to write really effective leads. One way to do this is to study the leads of authors you admire. You already know that writers choose our words carefully so as to paint a picture. But writers also write for the ear, choosing words which have a rhythm. Think about the lead to Karen North's *Hot Day on Abbott Avenue*:"

> Hot day on Abbot Avenue. Too hot to even flutter a fan. Buster,
> snoozing, barely flicks flies at his ears. The cat keeps to herself under
> the house.

"The author could have just written, 'It was a very hot day on Abbott Avenue.' Instead she created a sort of rhythm out of the heat. Listen, it almost sounds like a poem. Notice the rhythm and notice also that the author, Karen North, has picked precise words that make you feel that awful heat, like 'flutter' and 'barely flicks.' Notice the repetition of words that begin with the letter 'f' (this is called alliteration): 'flutter a fan,' 'flicks flies.' This lead pulls you right into that hot, lazy day and makes you want to read on, doesn't it?" Then you'll want to reread, and to perhaps invite children to reread. You may later want to direct children also to the lead of Donald Crews' book, *Shortcut*. It's so simple:

> We looked . . .
>
> We listened . . .
>
> We decided to take
> The shortcut home.

You may want to point out that although this lead is simple, it is also suspenseful. As a reader, you're left wondering, "What are these characters looking at? What are they listening to? And what's so special about the shortcut home?" You could point out to children that Donald Crews did this intentionally; his writing style conveys that the children in the book are as apprehensive about taking the shortcut home as the reader is about what lies beyond these four short lines.

In the same minilesson, you will want to remind children that a lead should relate in some way to the heart of the story. Heat is central to the tension between the two girls in Karen North's book, *Hot Day on Abbott Avenue*, just as taking a chance—by taking a dangerous shortcut home—is central to Donald Crews' book, *Shortcut*. Leads aren't arbitrarily selected. It doesn't work just to pick an enticing opening line. The lead you write must fit in some precise way with the rest of your story, giving the reader a hint of what's to come and convincing her that she's at the start of a fascinating ride.

If students are struggling with making the leap from the story mountain to the draft . . . you can teach them how to use storyboards, just like filmmakers do. Students can take each point from their story mountains and draw a thumbnail sketch about it, then write a quick sentence or two about that scene. When they are done, the sketches will look a lot like comic-book panels. Each sketch helps students visualize what they want to happen in each scene. Often, as students sketch, they realize that some points can be consolidated or others need to be added.

MECHANICS

During the first few days of this unit, many children will have spent their time jotting lists rather than writing passages. By now, your children will have had plenty of time for writing narratives, and this means that you may want to look at their drafts with an eye toward noticing which conventions of written language have become so second nature that children are using them with automaticity even in their early drafts.

Notice, for starters, whether all your children use end punctuation and capital letters as they write, rather than seeing periods as something to scatter across the page of finished drafts. The question is not whether they use these absolutely correctly, but whether they have the instinct to punctuate as they write. If you emphasized to children earlier in the year that writers say a thought to ourselves, then write that sentence without pausing, adding a period at the end of the thought as a culminating action before pausing, then you should see that children by now show that they have the instinct to write with end punctuation.

You may notice next whether or not children use a variety of end-punctuation. If they write with periods only, then you'll definitely want to help them see the relationship between punctuation and intonation, learning that the same words can assume different meanings based on punctuation. For example, it means something very different for a child to write, "Punctuate?" or (Punctuate) rather than writing, "Punctuate!"

Notice whether children are using punctuation to show dialogue. My colleagues in the Teachers College Reading and Writing Project studied punctuation across New York City schools and found that by spring of their first year in a writing workshop, an astonishing number of children used punctuation correctly . . . and we decided that children grasped these conventions easily because they'd *first* learned to make people in their stories talk. Once stories contain lots of dialogue, it is not hard to teach children to punctuate that dialogue.

You'll want to study children's rough draft entries in order to decide on two or three tools that you believe will especially help them write more conventionally. You may decide that children need help writing in past, present and future tenses (without shifting recklessly between these). The prospect of teaching verb tenses can feel like a daunting one, but if you set children up in little role plays, you'll find they have very little trouble with tenses. If you say, "Pretend you are at a soccer game. Use your cell phone to tell a friend what's happening in the game as you watch it," you'll see that children talk in present tense. If you say, "Pretend you called your grandma and you want to tell her about an event that happened a month ago," children will talk in past tense. Once you realize that your children really do know something about tenses, then teaching them to write in consistent tenses is less scary. We can admonish them to listen to their writing, to hear whether it sounds right, and to correct it when needed.

Then, too, you may decide that there are a dozen irregular verbs that continually cause your children difficulty. Perhaps you'll want to put word pairs such as, *say, said* and *run, ran* and *think, thought* on your word wall, teaching children that these words deserve to become part of children's sight vocabulary.

IN THIS SESSION, YOU WILL REMIND WRITERS THAT AS THEY WRITE, THEY NEED TO "STAY IN SCENE," MAKING SURE THE ACTION AND DIALOGUE ARE GROUNDED IN THE SETTING.

GETTING READY

- Anecdote or metaphor you can tell to describe the disorientation caused by lack of setting
- Scene containing almost nothing but dialogue, copied onto chart paper
- Revised scene showing more story details
- Passage from the class story, on chart paper, for whole-class practice with setting
- Passage from a favorite read-aloud story that communicates setting well
- See CD-ROM for resources

ORIENTING READERS WITH SETTING

When teachers discuss predictable issues their students have had, someone invariably says, "Kids love fiction. They'll write for pages. The only problem is it's all dialogue. I can't make heads or tails of it!"

Be sure you recognize that the dialogue which swamps the pages of many drafts represents a gigantic step ahead for these children. They are no longer summarizing the main events in their stories; instead, your authors are making mental movies and recording what happens in those movies—or at least, they are recording the sound track to those movies! This is a gigantic step ahead and your children are poised to write spectacular texts. You simply need to teach them one further step!

In a spirit of "your work is halfway there," then, convene children and tell them that you can see they are making mental movies, enacting events in their minds as they write. But point out that although they can no doubt see the character walk, gesture, turn, grimace, those parts of their envisioned stories have yet to reach the page.

Once your children begin to ground their stories in precise settings, all of a sudden it is as if the stories become real. Everything becomes grounded. One character grabs her shoes, runs to the ocean's edge, then stands ankle deep in the waves. "Come in," her sister—waist deep in the waves—beckons. Before the character can join her sister, she tosses her shoes on the dry sand. One falls near the water's edge, and before the character can reach it, a wave washes over the shoe. When writers write with setting, people carry real shoes, and those shoes need to be put somewhere before the character can wade waist deep into the ocean. When we write with setting, we need to remember to put down our shoes before we go into the water.

Today, you'll teach your students that fiction writers use settings to ground our stories. We use places, like living rooms and swing sets and forests; we use the weather, like heat waves and fog and lightly falling snow; we use times, like midnight and sunrise and lazy afternoons. Our students can often orally describe the setting of a story, but those details rarely make it onto the page. Part of the bargain that writers make with readers is that the characters will take action within a very concrete, specific world. Best yet, when children learn to write with setting, they learn not only that setting allows us to anchor characters and plots. They also learn that developing setting can help them to convey tone, and hint at a character's mood, feelings, insights.

MINILESSON

Orienting Readers with Setting

CONNECTION

Tell about a time you were awakened in the dark and felt disoriented. Liken this to the disorientation some readers feel when drafts don't include enough setting.

"Last night I was sleeping, and the phone rang. When the phone woke me up, my whole room was dark and I didn't know where I was. I couldn't see anything. I couldn't tell if I was dreaming or awake. Has that ever happened to you? You wake up and for a minute, you can't remember where you are?"

"When the phone rang again, I looked at where the sound was coming from and saw a light blinking, and it dawned on me that I was in my bedroom and that I'd just been woken by the phone. My eyes got used to the dark and I saw the dresser that held the phone."

"That unanswered phone call ended up helping me. Because when I was abruptly woken in the middle of the night like that and didn't know where I was, this made me realize that sometimes readers experience our drafts as if the events in our stories happen in the dark. The sounds—the voices—come out of nowhere, and readers are disoriented and need to ask themselves, 'Wait, where am I?' and 'What's going on?' and 'Where's that sound coming from?' Readers can hear the words a character says, but it's like the words come out of nowhere."

Name the teaching point. In this instance, let children know that writers need to show the setting in a story so that readers don't feel disoriented.

"Today I want to teach you that we need to be sure that we 'turn on the lights' in our stories, to show the place and the time, so that our readers don't have that disoriented feeling, asking, 'Wait, where is this? What's going on?'"

COACHING

This little episode actually occurred the day before I wrote this minilesson. I was in a hotel which added to the sense of disorientation, but that detail seemed like a distraction. Just as writers live wide-awake lives, expecting that tiny everyday events can be grist for the writing mill, so do teachers. And of course, our teaching takes on special immediacy and intimacy when we bring the tiniest little events of our lives into minilessons. Sometimes teachers don't realize they can do this. They say to me, "But I'm not a writer. My life doesn't contain writing lessons!" So I try to show them that even a phone call in the dark can bring new life to a minilesson.

This is really a lesson on improving the quality of our students' fiction writing, and there are, of course, zillions of possible topics for this minilesson. Students' stories will inevitably be very different from the stories that mature, experienced writers produce. I selected this particular point because students' drafts frequently contain a stream of dialogue, with very little setting for orientation. Often it's as if student writing provides only the sound track for a movie. Then, too, I'm focusing on setting because this is something important that we haven't addressed very seriously yet in these units of study. I've addressed the overreliance on dialogue, of course, but before now suggested the solution lay in adding actions. Now I spotlight a second solution. The truth is that most qualities of good writing can be taught within any genre, and the decision to highlight one or another is partly arbitrary.

TEACHING

Tell children that when writing scenes, it's easy to rely only on dialogue, resulting in characters who don't seem to be anywhere in particular. Give an example of an all-talk scene in which the characters are nowhere, leaving readers struggling to feel oriented.

"Sometimes when we're writing a scene we get so caught up in our dialogue that we forget everything else. Let me give you an example. Ryan, a high school writer, wrote this." I showed a short, generic excerpt that I'd copied onto chart paper.

> I didn't know what to do. I looked at her. "Hey, are you mad at me?" I asked.
>
> "No. Are you mad at me?" she asked.
>
> I took a deep breath. "No. I don't think so," I said.
>
> "Great, then let's race," she said.

"Some things work in this scene. Characters are talking. We can tell how they're feeling. But the characters are floating. The story produces the same feeling I had when I woke up in the middle of the night and I didn't know where I was. We can't tell where the characters are, and we're not sure what they are doing."

Tell children that the child revised the scene by adding action and setting, then show the resulting next draft.

"To make sure the lights are on for our readers, we need to always include two things: action and setting. Watch how Ryan's draft became much more clear when he added action and setting."

"Ryan didn't actually know what his characters *were* doing. When he wrote the draft, his characters were just talking. So he decided to revise his draft so his characters were walking home from school. He decided it'd be a gray, rainy day. That way, one of the characters could do stuff with an umbrella and the other character could step in puddles. Ryan expected the actions would be fillers, really, to hold up the talk, but the actions ended up revealing the real story in very important way. Listen to Ryan's next draft:

> "Are you mad at me?" I asked as we walked down the sidewalk together.
>
> "No. Are you mad at me?" Zoe responded.
>
> A car whizzed passed us, kicking up water from the rain-

I deliberately chose a very brief excerpt. I know this will more than double in size when it is revised, and I want to keep my minilessons brief. Little is gained by showing large expanses of text in minilessons.

Watch the ways in which I weave threads from earlier sections of the minilesson into the later sections, creating cohesion. I believe that all writers do this, and that the aspects of a text that reoccur are central to the text's message. This is why, when I teach readers, I put more of an emphasis on helping children see intratextual connections (those that occur within a text) rather than intertextual (or text-to-text) connections.

filled gutters as it went. I thought about what Zoe was asking, and shifted the umbrella so that it protected her as well as me. With my other hand, I tugged on my back pack straps. My bag was heavy from all the homework our teacher had given us.

"No. I'm not mad," I said.

She smiled at me from beneath her yellow rain hood. "Good. Then let's race!" She took off ahead of me, splashing through every puddle on the sidewalk. The rain streamed down on her. I pulled in my umbrella, and took off after her. I caught up with her, then loped easily in her wake.

You'll recall that earlier in this series, I talked about Chris Raschka's Caldecott Honor winner, Yo! Yes? as a book that can help us teach children that their stories cannot be carried by dialogue alone. The words of that book are simple, one-word exclamations or questions. The dialogue alone isn't easy to comprehend. The book works because the author-illustrator provides pictures that describe each character, providing the gestures and body language that need to support the dialogue. Because readers can rely on the pictures as well as the dialogue, the story actually "reads" more like this: "'Yo!' called the basketball player, as he stood with a swagger, chest out and hands on his hips. Nearby, a little nerdy boy in a suit coat shrugged, hid his head, and meekly responded, 'Yes?'" With that book, it would be easy to point out to children that because their stories rely on words alone, their words need to do the work done by Raschka's drawings as well as his text. This lesson would be as appropriate now as in that previous unit. You may decide to use this book and make this point again here, even if you also used this suggestion before.

Debrief, tucking some extra tips into your description of what the student did to revise. Point out that when trying to supply the setting and actions, the writer discovered important new interactions and meanings.

"Writers, do you see how the characters are not in the dark anymore? We can really picture them. We can see what they're doing and where they are. And you know what? When Ryan wrote this, his only plan was to have the two of them walking home together. He only made it be a rainy day because he figured he could describe the rain. Then, as he wrote the scene, adding in the actions, stuff started happening between the characters that Ryan never planned for at all—it just happened on the page! It surprised Ryan that his main character decided to move the umbrella over to shield Zoe, and he was totally surprised when her 'Let's race' response left him standing behind like a fool with that open umbrella! He recovered, though, and caught up with her, but didn't need to show her that he was the faster runner. All this drama came out in the story simply because Ryan realized that he needed to get his characters out of the dark, and to rewrite the story, showing the characters as they moved and interacted in the setting."

The lessons that I tuck into my minilessons are often more advanced than the teaching point itself. I know in this instance that the writing-to-discover work that Ryan has done is beyond the reach of most of the writers in this class. He is a high-school student, and this is skilled work. But I do still want to expose all writers to the richest and deepest ideas, because who knows what will "click" for a child! And meanwhile, I am usually confident that my main teaching points are within reach and pertinent for everyone. The little subordinate tips one weaves into a minilesson are one of the ways our minilessons become multilevel, providing differentiated instruction.

ACTIVE ENGAGEMENT

Ask children to reread the Luz story from the chart paper while asking, "Will this make sense to readers?" When they encounter a passage that might be disorienting, ask them to revise it with their partner, adding setting.

"So let's try it. Let's read this section of our Luz story—I've been writing some more of it—and as we read, let's ask ourselves, 'Will this make sense to my readers? Is this clear?' If we come to a place in the story where the words seem to come out of the dark, a place where we suspect that readers might feel disoriented, you and your partner will have a chance to write in the air, sprinkling references to the setting and to small actions that characters do in that setting, into our next version."

I retrieved the draft and read a section of it aloud—a section that I knew was well-lodged into the setting and amplified with actions. I read:

> "Cake!" my mom called from the kitchen. All of us raced to the table which my mom had decorated entirely in yellow.
>
> "Everything looks so cool," Marta said as she reached for a thick slice of the yellow cake with chocolate frosting. I couldn't help grinning. I had been right to choose yellow. It was a cool color. Since I didn't really have a favorite color it didn't really matter anyway.
>
> I had barely swallowed the last bit of my cake when the other girls started to jump out of their seats to toss their party plates in the trash.
>
> "Let's go, first one there gets dibs on spots," Trish called out as she ran.

"Could you picture what was going on?" I asked. "Did you see the place?" Children gave me a thumbs up. "So let's read on," I said, and this time read the upcoming section (a part I knew was underdeveloped):

> "Here's my place," said Beccah
>
> "I'll be near," I said. "We can talk. But let's move closer to the closet."
>
> "No, this is nice."
>
> "Weellll ... "
>
> "Can we fit in," three others said.
>
> "I'll move over," I answered.

Notice that, instead of beginning the Active Engagement by saying, "Could you rewrite this scene so that . . . ," I instead ask readers to begin by rereading a fairly large passage of the Luz story using the lens of "Is this clear?" By backing up and starting with this, I not only get the chance to synthesize all the points I have made in this minilesson, I also demonstrate to writers how they might position themselves to do this work in the first place.

Notice that the whole-class text has, in this unit of study, served alternatively as the teaching text as well as the text used in the Active Engagement.

The children talked to their partners, and after a moment I intervened. "Writers, please don't simply *comment on* how you'd go about rewriting this to add setting and actions—write the new text in the air."

If you look back on the instructions I gave children, you'll see that I originally told children to write in the air to show how they'd revise this. If our words are going to mean something, we need to speak up when children ignore our instructions.

Ask one partnership to share their new version, and set up other children to act out the new version.

"Let's listen to Francesca and Jamal. While they write in the air, I'll record it. But can I have someone who will play the part of Beccah and act out what they say, and someone who'll be Luz? Are there three of you who'll be the three others who want to join?" Soon the improvisational drama was ready to begin, and the children began improvising the new story. "The first character to do something is Beccah," I said, and gestured for her to step forward on the "stage." "What exactly is she doing?" I asked Jamal and Francesca. With that, they began spinning out a story, while the actors moved about accordingly:

If you and your colleagues are looking for a way to lift the level of all these units of study, you might try to incorporate more drama into the entire series. I believe there is a very powerful connection between drama, reading, and writing. I'm convinced that these minilessons do not harvest the power of drama as much as they might.

> Beccah got her sleeping bag and found an empty spot of rug behind the sofa. She unrolled her sleeping bag. Then Beccah said, "Here's my place."
>
> I grabbed my stuff, and sat on the floor beside Beccah. "I'll be right here," I said. "We can talk." But as I said that I knew I wouldn't be able to sleep there. I couldn't see the closet where the light was on, so I knew I had to move. I tried to talk Beccah into it and said, "Let's move closer to the closet."
>
> Lying down, Beccah said, "No, this is nice."
>
> I wasn't sure. I looked over to a nice spot right beside the closet, and was about to try again to get Beccah to move closer to the closet. Then three other girls came. "Can we fit?" they asked.
>
> "I'll move over," I said, and picked up my stuff and went over to the empty place.

Ask the class to end the scene in a way that is informed by the acting.

"What could happen to end this scene?" I asked. "What might Luz watch that group of girls doing together?"

"They could all be huggin' each other and all so she feels left out?"

"Okay, but remember, we have them arranging their sleeping bags and getting ready for bed. Could they do those actions in a way that accomplishes the same thing in the story?"

These seemingly innocuous little prompts actually are fairly controlling. My question channeled the text in ways that made it much better. The children believe they've written this on their own, but meanwhile I've been directing.

Soon the class had written this ending to the scene:

> I watched as the group of girls figured out how to
> arrange their sleeping bags so they could all be close to
> each other. I heard Eliza say, "This way we can whisper
> together all night."
> I turned my back away from them, toward the closet
> where the light shone.

Debrief, highlighting the sequential steps you hope writers use with their own texts. Emphasize that revisions that begin as corrections can become entirely new creations.

"Writers," I said, "you've done some amazing revision. You reread this part of our draft and realized that readers might feel disoriented, as if the scene were taking place in the dark. So you sprinkled in a little information about the characters' exact actions in the setting, and as you did this, you—like Ryan—ended up surprising yourselves and finding that things are happening between the characters that we didn't even realize when we planned the story!

"This is what writers do. Our revisions start out as corrections and they end up as creations!"

LINK
Remind writers that today they'll shift between drafting and revising, and that to revise, they'll want to reread their draft with specific lenses.

"Writers, today you'll continue to draft and revise your stories, shifting between the two processes. And when you revise, you'll reread for all the goals that have become important to you. You'll make sure your characters feel real. You'll keep an eye on the deeper meaning of your story. You'll make sure you don't leave your readers in the dark. If there is a section of your story that seems disorienting, you can revise it like you've done today, adding more setting and actions to the scene. Please be sure that if you expect to *correct* your draft, you do so knowing that revisions that begin as corrections often take on a life of their own and become creations. Let your characters do things to and with each other that you'd never expected they'd do. Run along behind them!"

You may want to look at several minilessons and notice all the different ways in which we debrief after teaching. My hunch is that even though the debrief segments are usually brief, you'll find they are almost always sequentially organized, retelling a sequence of steps as one would in a how-to text. Although these sections where we debrief are summaries, they are also examples of how a writer can organize thoughts.

I suspect that this last line is one that deserves more attention than I give to it: Revisions start out as corrections and become creations. So true, if we let it be true!

Since the sentence—revisions that begin as corrections often take on a life of their own and become creations—will probably go over some students' heads, I may want to capture it in print and invite children to talk and think about it another time. This brings up a larger question of note-taking during minilessons. Be very careful that you don't emphasize this in a manner which slows down your minilessons!

WRITING AND CONFERRING

Weaving Together Action, Thought, and Dialogue

Beccah was busy at work adding in sentences here and there to her story. I approached her and said, "Beccah, I can see that you are busy revising your story. Can you tell me about the work you're doing?"

"Well, I realized that I don't have a lot of setting in my story, and so I'm trying to add in some setting so that my reader knows where my characters are."

"That sounds like great work, Beccah. Can you show me a place where you've done that?" I asked as I scanned Beccah's draft.

Beccah turned to the last page of her story and skimmed the page. "Right here," she said. "This is the part where Chloe and Samantha walk away from Niki and leave her standing alone. The first time I wrote it, it went like this:

> "Sorry, Niki," Chloe said.
>
> "Let's go," Samantha said, smirking at Niki. Together they turned and walked away from Niki. Niki just stood there.

"And then, I revised it by adding in setting. Now it goes like this:"

> "Sorry, Niki," Chloe said.
>
> "Let's go," Samantha said. They all stood in the hallway looking at each other. Doors were opening and closing as kids went to class.

I thought to myself, "Yes, Beccah has certainly added setting to her story. Even this little bit helps orient the reader." But I also thought about the fact that so many of my students saw revision as adding in a word or a sentence here and there. I wanted to celebrate this kind of revision but I also knew many of my students were capable of much deeper work. In this case, for example, I knew I could teach Beccah that people are affected by their environments and that adding setting to a story can be a tool for revealing what a character is feeling. This could teach Beccah about how to add in setting in a more effective way, but it could also teach her that revision is about helping oneself see more deeply into a character or situation, and that it entails more than adding a sprinkling of sentences. Beccah looked up at me and waited.

MID-WORKSHOP TEACHING POINT *Using Mentor Texts in Revision* "Writers, I want to tell you about the smart discussion Ryan and I just had. He decided to study how Julie Brinckloe lets us know where and what is going on in *Fireflies!* and so he noted all the tricks he saw her use that he could use." This is Ryan's list:

"If you aren't sure that readers will know exactly what's going on in your stories, look at your draft and ask whether you do the same things that you find in the mentor text you study. Ryan realized he hadn't done many of them. Now he knows just what his work can be. You can try the same thing he tried, now and anytime you write."

Sentences from Text	Strategy Brinckloe Uses
On a summer evening I looked up from dinner, through the open window to the backyard.	tells where narrator is/what he's doing right away
On a summer evening I looked up from dinner, through the open window to the backyard. It was growing dark. My treehouse was a black shape in the tree . . . fireflies flickered.	tells big feeling of place, weather, time, right away
• forked food into mouth • asked to go out • found a jar • polished it . . .	She tells a whole sequence of actions, of events.
First he's at kitchen table near window. Then he runs to cellar. Then he runs back upstairs. Then he returns to house . . .	Every action has a place.

"So you've let the reader know that your characters are in the hallway, and you've added in details that show what's going on around them. That works for sure," I said, and then added, "As I read this, I could see that you are ready to do even bigger revision work. What do you think?"

"Okay," There was hesitation in Beccah's voice.

I continued, "You know, Beccah, when story writers revise our writing, we are often trying to show a little more of what our characters are experiencing on the inside as well as the outside. That's what we saw Ryan do—right? He added setting but did so in a way that brought out his characters." I looked at Beccah. "When you add setting to your writing, this gives you a powerful way to reveal your characters. What happens on the outside definitely affects us on the inside, right? A rainy day might make us feel down, a stadium filled with screaming Yankee fans might make us feel excited. So, when you add setting to your writing, you need to think about how the details you add can help your reader understand what your character is experiencing on the inside."

Turning to Beccah's draft, I said, "So let's look at the part of your story where Niki is watching her best friend, Chloe, walk off with her arch-enemy, Samantha. How is Niki feeling here?"

"Well," Beccah reread the part and then said, "She's feeling all alone, and sad. She's feeling like, 'Wow, I just lost my best friend.'"

"Hmm . . . so she's standing in the hallway feeling alone. Let's think about how you might use the setting to show that Beccah feels alone."

I knew as I said this that I could always show Beccah a published text where the author does this, and there are so many—*Fireflies!*, *Owl Moon*, *Fly Away Home*. I chose, instead, to coach Beccah as she thought through her work. You'll decide how to proceed depending on how much scaffolding you believe students need.

Beccah spoke up, "Well, maybe I can show that she's feeling lonely and the halls are all empty because everyone has gone to class and she's just standing there with no one to talk to or walk to class with."

"So how might you write that? Let's turn to your draft." We both reread the part that Beccah was working on. Then, Beccah said, "Well maybe it can go like this:

> "Sorry Niki," Chloe said.
>
> "Let's go," Samantha said to Chloe. Niki watched as they walked through the blue, metal doors. She looked around, but the halls were empty. She was all alone with no one.

"Yes, Beccah, that definitely works. You are on your way! You are letting the setting reveal how Niki is feeling. Always ask yourself how your revision work is helping you dig a bit deeper into whatever you want to say—and you are definitely doing that. Nice job!"

As you confer with children, show them that it helps to shift between action and thoughts, not just record a stream of thoughts. So if I wanted to describe my worry when my son, who recently got his driver's license, returned home late, I'd write in a way which intersperses thoughts with actions. To do this, I'd create a set of tiny actions which mirrored my thoughts and feelings:

> I looked at the clock: 6:08. "Where could Miles be?" I thought. I went to the door and glanced out at the empty driveway, then at the road. Empty. "What could have kept him?" I worried. I went to the phone, picked up the receiver, and heard the dial tone. "Good. The phone's working and there have been no calls," I thought, and recalled last summer's awful phone call.

A few children in your class may well write in running commentary that sounds almost like free association, as Laurel has here *[Fig. IX-1]*:

> "Oh my god, Jessie is that you?"
>
> "Lex? Oh my god. I haven't seen you in such a long time."
>
> "I know," Jessie said. "So what's up?"
>
> "Nothing."
>
> "Like fifth grade?" Jessie asked.
>
> "It's different."
>
> "Are you still in touch with Sophie, Ali, Caitlyn, Beccah, Jamie and Alex?"
>
> "Of course. They are my best friends. So how is Hanna?" Lex asked.
>
> "Not as annoying. You know how younger sisters are from Sam. And by the way how is she?"
>
> "She is good. Just like Hanna."
>
> "How is Jenna? I almost forgot about her."
>
> "Totally great."

Free writing will end up being a wonderful skill that children can lean on, but writing always involves some coloring inside the lines (or working within the constraints) as well as some free expression. For now, these children's writing skills will come out best if they take each scene of their story, think of it as a Small Moment story, and then plot the main sequence of actions (not the thoughts) on a timeline. Some children may want to

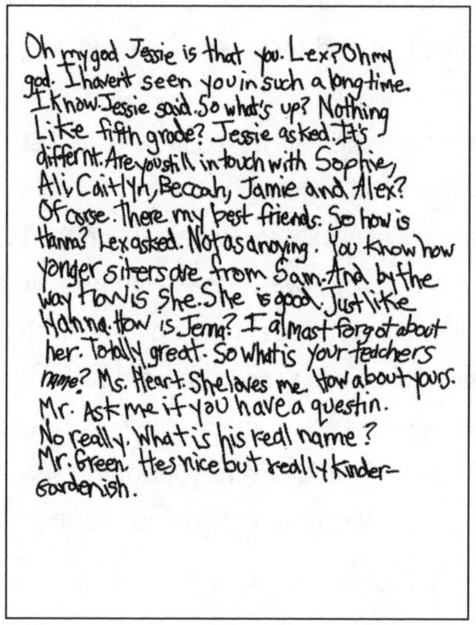
Oh my god Jessie is that you. Lex? Oh my god. I haven't seen you in such a long time. I know. Jessie said. So what's up? Nothing Like fifth grade? Jessie asked. It's differnt. Are you still in touch with Sophie, Ali, Caitlyn, Beccah, Jamie and Alex? Of corse. There my best friends. So how is Hanna? Lex asked. Not as anoying. You know how yonger siters are from Sam. And by the way how is She. She is good. Just like Hanna. How is Jenna? I almast forgot about her. Totally great. So what is your teachers name? Ms. Heart. She loves me. How about yours. Mr. Ask me if you have a questin. No really. What is his real name? Mr. Green. Hes nice but really Kinder-gardenish.

Fig. XI-1 Laurel has been free writing her story and needs to instead focus on a small moment or two.

make double timelines, with one timeline summarizing the actions, the other, the parallel thoughts or comments. Then ask children to write, alternating between dialogue, action and setting. See Laurel's second draft: *[Fig. IX-2]*

> "Let's go look at the animals first so then on the sky ride, we can retrace where we were," Jessie said. "Ok" her mom said. They were zooming along 70 mph. Hanna and her mom were singing "Ninety-nine bottles of beer on the wall. Ninety-nine bottles of beer take 1 down pass it around ninety-eight bottles of beer on the wall." When they got to sixty-six Jessie yelled "Enough! Let's play the quiet game whoever talks first loses. Ok 1, 2, 3." They stayed quiet then their mom said, "I hear that they have rides and games where you can win prizes." "And?" "We are there." They jumped out of the car and ran for the animals.

When conferring with children who struggle to pin down their free associations, I'd be apt to share my draft with them, or even to show a child how I might rewrite his or her draft. We might read a line or two and ask, "Where exactly were you? What exactly were you doing?" After the child answered, I'd say, "I asked those questions because you might want to shift between retelling your very specific actions and recording your thoughts. For example, your draft might go like this . . . " and then I'd get the child started by showing how I might start the draft, weaving between action and thought, action and dialogue. I often summarize this teaching by saying to children, "For every thought or piece of dialogue, you need to add a narrative or action." I realize this sounds like a recipe, but for students who've resisted your more generalized suggestions, this can help.

I recently pulled students who struggled with creating setting into a small-group strategy lesson. I gave each student a copy of the Luz story with a lot of white space between each paragraph. Then I modeled how to add some setting to the Beccah section, adding the sentence, "Beccah got her sleeping bag and found an empty spot behind the sofa . . . " As I modeled this, I wrote it onto my copy of the story, in the white space where it belonged.

Then I asked children to work with a partner, filling in some other setting details for the next paragraph, where the narrator speaks. I coached the partners, encouraging them to use actions and setting to help us picture what the character was doing, and where characters were.

Soon I shifted them to do similar work, adding details that allowed them to show the characters in their own pieces. I checked back with them as they continued the work after I left, prompting them. "Remember how you and Shiv worked on helping us see the room here? You wrote that 'Luz spread out her sleeping bag on the floor beside Beccah.' You said, 'Luz couldn't see the closet from where she was because the sofa was blocking her view.' Those details helped us picture this place. Are there other places in your draft where readers will be in the dark?"

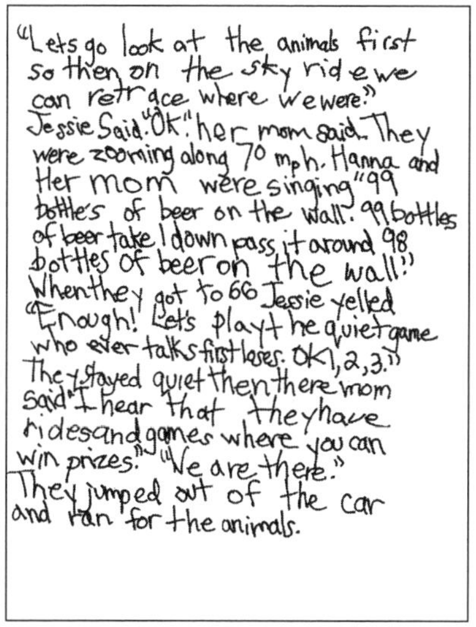
"Lets go look at the animals first so then on the sky ridewe can retrace where wewere." Jessie Said."Ok". her mom said. They were zooming along 70 mph. Hanna and Her mom were singing "99 bottle's of beer on the wall. 99 bottles of beer take 1 down pass it around 98 bottles of beer on the wall." When they got to 66 Jessie yelled "Enough! Let's play the quiet game who ever talks first loses. Ok 1, 2, 3." They stayed quiet then there mom said "I hear that theyhave ridesandgames where you can win prizes." "We are there." They jumped out of the car and ran for the animals.

Fig. IX-2 This time Laurel has situated her story into a few more concrete episodes.

When I conferred with Sofiya, she'd written this opening scene to her story about a gymnastics tournament. *[Fig. IX-3]*

> Esther could see hundreds and hundreds of seats and people trying to find good seats. Her family was going to some of the best seats. Esther had told them where the best seats were and was glad that they had listened to her.
>
> The wind was blowing from outside and she guessed that someone just walked in or out of the building. She could get a little whiff of the smell of healthy snacks cooking. Esther felt like running up to her parents—but knew that it would be better to start stretching. When she reached her stretching teammates she could taste the tension. Soon it was time for the league to begin.
>
> She sat down with her team. The judges began to introduce the teams . . .

I asked Sofiya what she had tried to do in this draft and her answer didn't surprise me. She'd tried to create a sense of place. "What really blows me away," I said, "is that even though you are only ten years old, you already realize that you can't leave the story and the character behind in order to show place. You need to have your character, have Esther, see and experience the place."

In this conference and in most of my conferences, I try to let children's work spark me to new realizations. I try not to simply admire the fact that a writer has done as instructed, but to also name what the writer has done that feels especially individual and original and new. This means, then, that conferences are one important source of new insight in my teaching.

Although I supported Sofiya's work with setting, which was her goal, this doesn't mean I didn't see some problematic aspects to her work. I noticed that Sofiya had been guided by an effort to include sensory details and was amused to see that as a result, even in the gymnasium, she had the character smelling healthy snacks (clearly Sofiya was trying to include all her senses and her repertoire of smells is a bit limited!). However, I decided that commenting on this wasn't as important as helping Sofiya understand that although she was wise to describe setting, writers need to guard against being waylaid from our main direction and message. "Your reader can't get so detoured by all the sights and sounds around the main character, that they lose hold of the main story," I said, and reminded Sofiya that her lead needs to go with her story mountain, and that she needs to remember what her story is mostly about and to highlight that in her lead. We can rephrase the question, "What's my story about?" so as to ask, "What does my character want? Struggle with?" This is a conference that is crucially important at this stage in the unit.

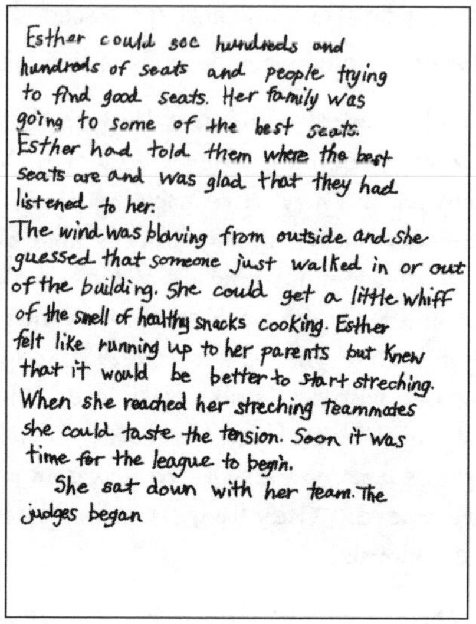
Esther could see hundreds and hundreds of seats and people trying to find good seats. Her family was going to some of the best seats. Esther had told them where the best seats are and was glad that they had listened to her.
The wind was blowing from outside and she guessed that someone just walked in or out of the building. She could get a little whiff of the smell of healthy snacks cooking. Esther felt like running up to her parents but knew that it would be better to start streching. When she reached her streching teammates she could taste the tension. Soon it was time for the league to begin.
She sat down with her team. The judges began

Fig. IX-3 Notice that Sofiya's draft shows her protagonist experiencing the setting.

Sofiya's next lead shows that, above all, this is a story about Esther wanting desperately to do well at the contest. *[Fig. IX-4]*

> Esther walked into the building—nervous from head to toe. As soon as she walked into the building—she was able to feel the tension. "Bye mom, bye dad, by Nicole. Oh yeah! There are lots of doors to the stands, but that's the door you need. Remember, Section 20, Row 5, any seats. Although the best seats are seats 14, 15, and 16. Got it?" she asked her parents. Her family nodded, said good bye themselves and left. Esther watched them leave before she left. Esther went to the changing room and took off her warm-up suit. When she came back out she looked up at the stands. People were looking for seats, she spotted her parents, they were sitting where she told them to. Esther smiled up at them. She was glad they had listened.

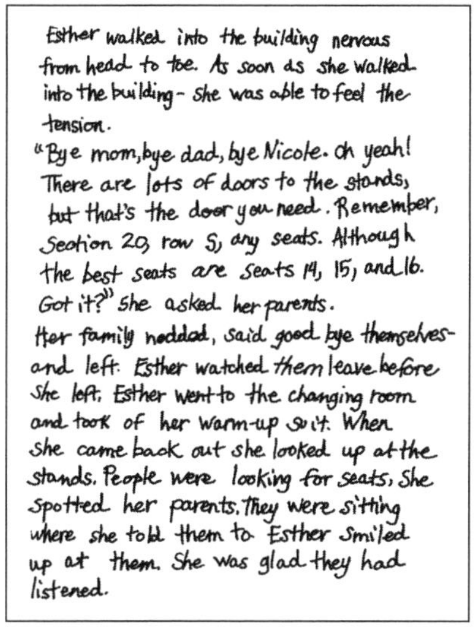

Esther walked into the building nervous from head to toe. As soon as she walked into the building- she was able to feel the tension.
"Bye mom, bye dad, bye Nicole. oh yeah! There are lots of doors to the stands, but that's the door you need. Remember, Section 20, row 5, any seats. Although the best seats are seats 14, 15, and 16. Got it?" she asked her parents.
Her family noddad, said good bye themselves- and left. Esther watched them leave before she left. Esther went to the changing room and took of her warm-up suit. When she came back out she looked up at the stands. People were looking for seats, She spotted her parents. They were sitting where she told them to. Esther smiled up at them. She was glad they had listened.

Fig. IX-4 Sofiya's next lead

As she progressed, a friend reminded her that she needs to show, not tell. This too is a piece of advice you may find yourself offering at this stage of the unit. You could use the before and after samples of Sofiya's writing to help illustrate. Here is how Sofiya tried to show instead of tell. *[Fig. IX-5]*

> Esther slowly walked into the huge gymnasium with her parents and sister, Nicole. She was nervous, slightly trembling, and her teeth were gently chattering, making a quiet clicking noise.
>
> "Bye mom, bye dad, bye Nicole. I have to run if I want to be able to stretch and practice the routines," Esther told her family as she held the door to the stands open. Her family whispered good luck and nodded.
>
> They all went through the door that Esther was holding. There, they split up. Esther's parents and Nicole excitedly went to the stands that weren't even close to being thronged, while Esther ran to the changing room.
>
> When she got there Esther took off her warm-up suit in the same speed that a cheetah runs. Then she skipped to stretch. There she warmed-up, stretched, and practiced the routines over and over again. Suddenly a loud bell rang from the judges table.

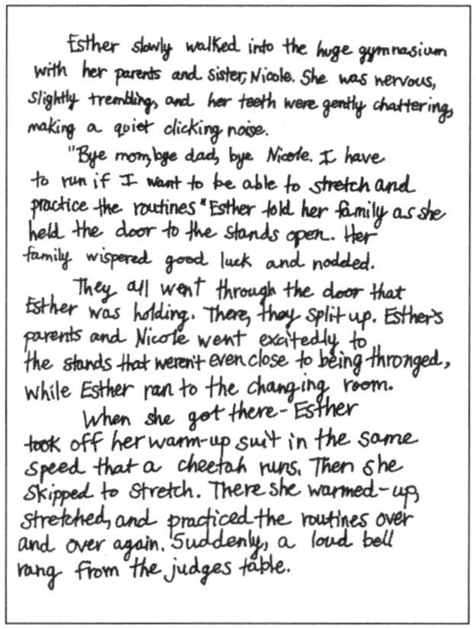

Esther slowly walked into the huge gymnasium with her parents and sister, Nicole. She was nervous, slightly trembling, and her teeth were gently chattering, making a quiet clicking noise.
"Bye mom, bye dad, bye Nicole. I have to run if I want to be able to stretch and practice the routines" Esther told her family as she held the door to the stands open. Her family wispered good luck and nodded.
They all went through the door that Esther was holding. There, they split up. Esther's parents and Nicole went excitedly to the stands that weren't even close to being thronged, while Esther ran to the changing room.
When she got there- Esther took off her warm-up suit in the same speed that a cheetah runs. Then she skipped to stretch. There she warmed-up, stretched, and practiced the routines over and over again. Suddenly, a loud bell rang from the judges table.

Fig. IX-5 Sofiya trying to show not tell

Of course, once any one child has done some significant revisions, this becomes material for a small-group strategy lesson. We could then simply pull together a small group of children, and, using the one child as an example, lead the whole group through a similar work process.

SHARE

Listening for Setting

Celebrate that children have used today's teaching point to influence their revisions and drafts.

"Today, writers, some of you have been drafting and some of you have been revising, and that is exactly how it should be in a writing workshop. And I am impressed that whether you have been drafting or revising, you have been remembering not to leave your readers in the dark. You have been sprinkling little bits of the scene and descriptions of the action into whatever happens in your story."

Ask children to share, and ask listeners to signal when they feel well-oriented to what is occurring in the story and when they feel they need more setting.

"Right now, would you find a place in your draft that you have recently written, a section of your story where you are pretty sure you've provided enough orienting information so that readers can truly make movies in their minds as they listen to your story?" I gave children a moment to find those sections. "Now would you get together with someone who is *not* your partner, someone who is a stranger to your story, and read this section aloud? And those of you who are listening, try to follow the writer's words and to dream the dream of his or her story. Show with your thumb up when you can really picture what's going on, and signal with your thumb down (as you listen) when it is harder for you to make that movie in your mind. Do this with one writer's draft, then the other writer's draft. If you have more time, look back on the drafts together and talk about revisions you might make."

Remind children they can attend to the setting of any writer's story to learn techniques for writing about setting well.

"Today you learned that writers help readers by describing what things look like in the room, the town, the place where the story is happening. The good news is that you don't need to be in a writing workshop to learn tips like this one. Whenever you read your chapter book, you can read with the eyes of a writer, thinking, 'How has this other author pulled off her story?' So right now, let's practice reading with the eyes of an insider. For now, let's look back on a section of one of our favorite read-alouds. You remember *My*

You can, of course, certainly ask students to share any part of the writing work they have been doing. You will want to angle the Share to best support whatever direction you most feel children need to take in their writing.

This share has two sections to it and of course you could select just one or the other. Always curtail your minilessons and shares if you need to do so in order to be sure that children have at least half an hour (preferably forty minutes) of actual writing time in school each day.

Name Is Maria Isabel. Listen to this bit of the story and think about what Alma Flor Ada does, in the midst of telling action and dialogue, to show the scene."

> The other kids had already taken their seats. Some were taking out their books and binders while others just seemed to be waiting for class to start. Many of them were smiling and talking to each other.
>
> Maria Isabel looked up at an enormous turkey made of construction paper on the wall behind the teacher's desk. She started to read the names that were on the tail feathers: Jonathan, Eric, Michelle, Solomon, Laurie . . .
>
> The teacher had not looked up yet. She was making notes in a large folder where Maria Isabel could see a list of names. Maria Isabel heard quiet laughter behind her. The teacher looked up only when the noise got louder.

"Okay? Thumbs up if you think you saw a technique that the author used to bring out the setting in the story."

"She told what sounds there were in the classroom," said Yasmin. "And also she described what's on the walls and what kids were doing."

"Yes! And can't you just picture that classroom in your mind's eye? Maybe it's not that different from this room we're sitting in! So from this day on, will you read whatever your chapter book is with the eyes of a writer, an insider, and notice how your author does whatever it is you are trying to do in your own story. Then use whatever the author has done to inspire you as you continue writing or rewriting your story."

Notice that we describe the techniques Alma Flor Ada has used in ways which make them accessible and replicable. It's a bit of a trick to learn to do this, but well worth learning.

HOMEWORK   ***Noticing Setting on Television***   We've done a lot of work on character and story structure in the past couple of weeks. I'm proud of all that we've done. Our stories are shaping up as we draft. But I think we need to spend a little more time thinking about the setting of a narrative.

Setting does a lot of work in a story. It can tell us something about a character's personality. If a character's bedroom is messy or it's covered in music posters, these details reveal something about the character. Setting can also tell us something about our character's mood. If the long rainy morning gives way to a bright, sunny afternoon, we might get the idea that things are getting brighter for our character. Setting also helps readers envision a story. It lets the reader really *see* what's happening and know *where* it's happening.

Tonight I'm going to ask you to do something you probably haven't ever heard me say before. I want you to spend a little time watching television. It can be a movie or a TV show, whichever your grown-ups say you can watch. I'd like you to watch a little bit with your writer's notebook in your lap. As you watch, look for the setting. Try to watch a part where the setting stays the same for a little bit. Watch, for example, a scene in a living room or in a park. While you're watching, jot a few notes about what you notice about the setting. Can you tell what the weather is? What time it is? Day or night? What colors do you see? What's high up in the setting? What's low? What does the camera show with more detail?

Once you've jotted a few notes, I'd like you to think a little bit about what parts of the setting helped you, as the viewer, understand the story more. Then make some notes on your draft, suggesting ways you can weave more setting into the draft when you come to school tomorrow.

TAILORING YOUR TEACHING

If your students have difficulty picturing the setting of their stories . . . send them back to their character development work. If you were to observe the setting of my life, you would see evidence of the kind of person I am. You would see pictures of the people I love, books strewn about the living room, dishes left unwashed far too long. My home gives clues about my personal idiosyncrasies. Anne Lamott writes that "every room is a little showcase of its occupants' values and personalities" (*Bird by Bird*, p. 74), and so it is for our fictional characters. You might tell your students, "When writers imagine the places where characters live, we must first remember what we know about our characters." Tell your students to recall their characters' interests, important relationships, and background. Then, encourage them to imagine ways to reveal these aspects of the main character through setting.

If your students develop settings that feel arbitrary . . . teach them that writers choose settings carefully to add meaning or power to our stories. You can point to many examples in books in which the setting mirrors the internal life of a character. One example is in the story "Spaghetti" by Cynthia Rylant, from *Every Living Thing*. In the beginning of the story, the main character, Gabriel, feels like a loner as he sits "on the stoop of a tall building of crumbling bricks and rotting wood" (p. 31). By the end of the story, Gabriel no longer feels lonely and the description of setting—"a room and a bed of his own in the tall building" (p. 33)—reflects the internal shift that has occurred in him.

Writers also often use the weather to create drama or interest in their stories. Some writers, like Kate DiCamillo in *Because of Winn-Dixie*, might write a scene that takes place in a violent storm to reflect the turmoil or pain that a character is experiencing. I could also imagine a writer choosing to use the weather as a foil for the character's personality, so that a scene might take place on a clear, sunny day, but no matter how warmly the sun shines, how harmoniously the birds chirp, it cannot lift a sense of gloom or sadness from the character's mood.

As adult readers and writers, we know that writers can use setting to add symbolism, metaphor, mood, and drama to our stories. Once students begin to realize what a powerful tool this is, they will make choices about setting as deliberately and carefully as they do about character and plot.

If students have worked through this unit already in previous years . . . you might teach writers that descriptions of the setting can be crafted to reflect or reveal the character's mood or situation. For example, if a character is feeling disheartened because her crush has rejected her, the school dance decorations will look different. In that case, the writer might write: "The huge overhead lights glared in her eyes, making her squint. The shiny wooden gym floor felt blinding. The bright balloons and swirling streamers all swayed with the music as if to say, 'Everyone is dancing but you!'" But, on the other hand, if the character's crush has given her some attention, the same gym will look different. In that case, the writer might write: "The overhead lights glowed like sunshine on the shiny gym floor. The balloons and streamers seemed to be winking at her and saying as they swayed, 'Come dance with us!'"

ASSESSMENT

Before long, you'll be teaching children how to write powerful endings to a story. Before you can teach this, you'll want to look at the endings your children plan to write. You'll find that many of them are planning what I call "Superman" endings. With luck, someone arrives and saves the day. Examine your students' writing to see whether the ending comes from outside the main story line. Look, also, to see if the character changes through the story. Superman endings often mean that the characters needn't experience any significant change. If a child's main character hasn't changed in some way or learned something new, you'll want to guide the child to rethink his or her ending.

Help your children learn that a story can come to a resolution without a character getting everything he or she wanted. You can draw on the mentor authors' stories to show children that often characters don't get what they want, or at least not what they start off thinking they want. For example, in *Fireflies!*, the narrator is trembling with the excitement of catching fireflies, but once he has some in his jar and sees their wings beating against the glass and their lights dim, he feels terrible. The story, which ends with the boy releasing the fireflies, is bittersweet; the narrator cries because he's losing his treasure, but smiles because he knows the fireflies will sparkle and thrive only out of captivity.

Stories can also be resolved with a change that a character can live with even if it isn't exactly what he or she wants. In *Peter's Chair*, for example, Peter is resentful of his baby sister; he doesn't like that he has to play quietly and that she's using his old furniture. But he cannot wish his sister away and by the end, Peter finds a way to live with her, filling the new role of older brother. Stories also sometimes end with a character getting something deeper (a lesson, a truth, a friend) he didn't know he was seeking. For example, in Deborah Wiles' *Freedom Summer*, the narrator thinks he wants to swim in the same pool as his friend, John Henry Waddell, but by the end he realizes what he, in fact, wants is to live in a world in which he and his friend can be treated the same way.

You'll want to be familiar with the ways in which this unit's mentor authors end their stories so you can help your students consider new ways to end their own. A child who always ends with dialogue, for example, might want to try ending her piece with internal thought or action. Encourage children to consider endings in relation to overall text structure. As with any other element of craft, endings should bring out the heart of a story and support the overall story structure.

WRITING POWERFUL ENDINGS

A few summers ago, I was glued to the gymnastics competition at the Olympics. I watched gymnast after gymnast throw her body across the floor or pommel horse or balance beam. No matter how complicated and flawless their routines were, if they did not "stick" their landings, their performances felt ruined.

It is the same way with stories. We've all had the experience of reading and getting lost in a story. We fall in love with the characters, get swept up in the plot, and then we reach the end, and bam, it's as if a door was slammed in our face. The ending is either too sudden or unbelievable or just plain unsatisfying. We all know, too, that our students often fall into these same traps when they are writing their own endings. We've all read stories about a child who toils away at a job in order to earn enough money to buy her mother something—a valentine, a charm bracelet—and then suddenly she learns she's won the lottery. We've read about the unpopular girl who is ridiculed at the start of the story and elected class president at the end of the story.

Today, our goal is to teach children that in life, solutions don't usually fly in from outer space (nor from left field). Usually no one arrives on the scene at the final moment, solving everything. Each of us, as a person and as an author, can find small solutions in the everyday truth of our all-too-human existence. No, we do not usually win the lottery. The girl who is ostracized one day doesn't usually become class president the next day. But that girl can find a place for herself, and come to realize that there's more than one way to make dreams come true.

There is no one way to write a wonderful ending. An ending may be happy, sad, funny or thoughtful. It may contain dialogue and action, or it may be a bit of setting. What all good endings have in common is they address something essential in the story. Today's session, then, aims to show children that the writers and characters, alike, can find turning points in the details of our lives.

IN THIS SESSION, YOU WILL TEACH CHILDREN THAT WRITERS OF FICTION DO THEIR BEST TO CRAFT THE ENDINGS THAT THEIR STORIES DESERVE. IN PARTICULAR, WE MAKE SURE OUR ENDINGS MESH WITH AND SERVE THE PURPOSES OF THE STORIES.

GETTING READY

- Example or anecdote to illustrate what a good ending can do for a story
- List entitled Key Questions Fiction Writers Consider in Revising Endings, prepared on chart paper
- Ending to the class story that you can use to model thinking about endings
- Display of all the read-aloud books used during the year
- Anecdote you can tell about working with titles
- See CD-ROM for resources

MINILESSON

Writing Powerful Endings

CONNECTION

Acknowledge that some children will soon draft an ending to their stories, and share author quotes which spotlight the importance of an effective ending.

"Writers, before long some of you will write your way towards the ending to your first draft. I know some of you left the mountain peak of your story mountains blank for now, and that as you've been writing, you've been rehearsing possible endings. That's smart because we all know from the television shows that end 'to be continued . . .'. that endings, like returning home from a journey, give us closure that is so important. They bring the story full circle. They are crucial. 'The opening line is a promise,' Jane Yolen has said, 'and the ending is a pay off to that promise.'"

"Rick Demarinis puts it even more strongly, 'My poetry writing teacher years ago said the ending of a poem is like a ski jump. There's the long accelerating downward glide, and then whoosh, you are thrown ballistically into space. You've been firmly fixed to earth, and now you're not.' He asks, 'Is that too much to ask of a poem or a story? Not at all,' he answers. 'That's exactly what we must ask' (*The Art and Craft of the Short Story*, p. 40).

Teach children that writers search for endings that tie up loose ends, answer questions, and bring the story's meaning home.

"Today I want to teach you that writers take our time with endings, weighing and considering, drafting and revising until we find one that fits. We know that a just-right ending will feel as if it is tailored exactly to fit our particular story. We know this ending will tie up loose ends, resolve the unresolved difficulties, and bring home the story's meaning.

TEACHING

Share something you know about how good endings go.

"When I taught very young children, I remember working with one child whose story told about a disastrous picnic but then ended with a hasty 'and we lived happily ever after.' The young writer—she was probably five—had just grown tired of her story and plopped that ending onto it. So we talked about ways she had actually appreciated the rained-out picnic after all, and I said, 'You'll definitely need to change the end of your story!'"

COACHING

Again and again throughout these books you've no doubt noticed that we make connections between the students and professional writers. Now, as we turn the final bend of the unit, when students' energy might be flagging, making those connections is more important than ever.

If your students are revisiting this minilesson for a second or third year you could instead say, "I want to share with you something one of my writing teachers told me about ending stories. She said, 'Short stories have surprising, yet inevitable endings.' That means that even though our readers may not be able to predict how the story is going to end, the ending shouldn't be unbelievable. When we finish a story we should say to ourselves, 'Yep, that's exactly how that writer needed to end that story.'"

"I came back later and she'd crossed out 'we lived happily ever after' and was instead writing a hologram of 'the end.' Each letter of 'The End' was carefully decorated with stars and stripes. 'I'm fixing up 'the end' she said cheerfully to me.'"

"We laugh, but the truth is—many of us aren't all that different from that five-year-old. We don't have a clue how to resolve our stories. We may not slap a 'they lived happily ever after' ending onto our story booklets, but in our own way, what we do is not much better. The three girls gang up on Kayla, putting cockroaches and poop in her locker and spraying whipped cream on her face. How does that story end? The principal arrives on the scene like Superman, flying in from nowhere, and brings the three mean girls to his office where they see the light of day."

"I want to teach you one bit of advice that I think can make all the difference when you draft and revise your endings. This is it: the ending is there all along, in the problem. There is never a need for another character to zoom in from outside the story to save the day!"

Offer an example that illustrates a principle of good endings.

"Let me show you what I mean. Let's go back to that story of the three girls who gang up on Kayla. It's not a sweet story, in fact it is a tragic one, but it needs an ending nevertheless. The mean girls hide around the corner in the hall, watching when Kayla pulls open her locker door. They see her step back as the turds plop out onto the floor, reeking. The mean girls laugh at the cockroaches as one drops onto Kayla's sweater. One of the girls, to top it off, approaches with a can of whipped cream in hand, ready to spray it in Kayla's face."

"What might happen?" I said. "I've discarded the idea of the principal or the therapist or the parent arriving from outer space to teach a lesson. I'm trying to find an ending—a solution—that's right here in the midst of the problem. Hmm . . . ." I paused for a long while. "I'm trying to think what could happen in that awful moment to change things."

Then I said, "Perhaps the girl with the can of whipped cream goes to spray it, brings the nozzle close to Kayla's face, and for a moment, she looks in Kayla's eyes. She sees Kayla, the person, and she sees herself, too, and drops the can onto the floor."

"Or, then again, perhaps a cockroach drops onto this girl's arm, perhaps she is terrified, perhaps Kayla reaches out to help her, and the turning point comes in that gesture."

"In order to write an ending, it'll take lots of drafts, of course. These are just early ideas, but I wanted you to see that the solution is often in the details of the problem, and that turning points often involve a word, a gesture—on the outside. Because the real turns happen on the inside."

You might point out, "We know a lot about endings from all of the work we've done in earlier units this year. The thing is, with our personal narratives, those were stories that really happened, so while we had to decide where to end the story, we didn't have to make anything up. With fiction we need to imagine our endings, which can make it a little trickier."

You might say, "It makes me think of how Fireflies! ends. We were all sort of surprised the first time we read it, but at the same time we all thought—that ending makes sense. I can't imagine it ending any other way. Of course, that ending probably didn't come to the author on the first try. She probably revised and revised until she got it just right, just like you are going to do. In fact, I'm pretty sure she thought about a few things before she wrote the perfect ending. And you guys will be doing the same thing."

Introduce a list of a few ways writers make sure endings are of good quality.

"Here are a few key questions fiction writers consider when revising their endings and imagining how they might go." I referred to the chart I had prepared:

ACTIVE ENGAGEMENT

Ask students to think about the class text in relation to one of the considerations set up in the demonstration. In this case, ask them to consider whether the class story's purposes are fulfilled in the ending.

"So writers, let's work together and see if we can imagine some possible endings to our Luz story. You'll remember that the ending will always relate to the story's real message," I said, "So we need to remember what the story is really, really about." I flipped through drafts which we'd written on chart paper.

"Hmm. So writers, it seems to me our ending needs to somehow address Luz' fears of sleeping in the dark and also of being ostracized by the girls. Would you and your partner think about two possible endings?"

The children turned to talk, and after a bit, I asked one of them to share her idea. Sofiya said, "I think Luz can be lying there in the dark getting really scared and then another girl—maybe Marta—whispers, 'Do you have a flashlight?' and it turns out *she's* afraid of the dark too."

Turning to the whole class, I said, "Sofiya had a suggestion for an ending. We need to think, 'Does it address—even resolve—Luz' fear of the dark?' 'Does it link to her desire to be popular?' 'Does it show that she's changed internally?' I'm not sure if it does the last of these but it certainly links to her fear of the dark. And there's no Superman swooping in to save everybody!"

Then Henry said, "I want Luz to get over being afraid of the dark. I want her to realize that there's nothing to be afraid of. Maybe we can have someone make a noise, and Luz and Marta realize it's a robber and they are really brave even though it's dark and they catch him."

I said, "I know Henry's not alone in thinking that in a story, a character should change—so it makes sense that Luz conquers her fears, catches the robber and so forth. But I want to remind you that we all, as people, change and grow in small ways. This is realistic fiction and realistically, Luz isn't going to get over her fears in the blink of an eye. So Henry, can I steer you towards appreciating the much, much smaller changes that human beings actually make?"

Key Questions Fiction Writers Consider in Revising Endings

- Can the reader see evidence of the main character's evolution?
- Does my ending make sense or come out of nowhere?
- Are the loose ends tied up? Have I answered the reader's key questions?
- Have I revealed everything I need to for the story's purposes?

You could also muse, "Are the loose ends tied up? Have I answered the reader's key questions? I'm not sure about that. Is Luz still afraid of the dark? I bet people might want to know that. The story isn't only about fitting in. It's also about getting over your fears. I'm going to make a note of that right here in the margin."

At first, when Henry began talking about the robber, I was worried that his idea for the story would spin into the overdramatic. Although he ended up reining in his idea, this isn't always the case. Sometimes we need to coach students if they get off track, and sometimes we simply need to celebrate that they've tried, and save the coaching for the next time—that will depend on the student and the timing. In any case, we need to decide ahead of time how to handle suggestions that are not what we'd hoped for if we're going to call on students without having heard their comment said first to a partner.

LINK

Acknowledge that you know students will be in different stages of writing today, but if they are ready, they can move into revising their endings.

"I know you are all in different places right now. Some of you may begin to write the first draft of your ending today, and for others of you it'll be tomorrow. No matter where you are in your work, when you get to the ending, remember that writers always consider whether our ending matches our story. And we look for solutions and resolutions that come from the grit, the specificity, the truth of our story. More than this, we need to remember that endings matter. Write a few different endings. Weigh which one you like best."

Here I reiterated my point from earlier in the lesson about not rushing because the students may feel tired.

Notice that I did not explicitly teach the students how to write and experiment with different endings. I assumed that the students would hold on to that strategy from our earlier work on leads and revision. If you feel that your students need that work explicitly taught, by all means do.

WRITING AND CONFERRING

Reining in Last-Minute Additions

When you confer with children in order to help them imagine possible endings, you'll find that many of them propose endings that writers refer to as Deus ex machina. The term means "god from the machine," and it refers to an ancient Greek drama in which all the conflicts of a play are miraculously solved by an actor dressed as a Greek deity who descends from the clouds to resolve everything with a timely wave of the hand. Many children will choose a quick-fix ending because they don't want their stories to go on and on or because this gives them an easy way to resolve their story's main conflict. But students' writing becomes unrealistic because the story ends abruptly or because the student has something happen that is out of left field.

I sat down next to Joey who was quickly writing furiously down the page. I waited for him to find a stopping point and then asked, "So, Joey, it looks like you've hit upon something big. Whenever I write fast and furiously, it's usually because I've had a great idea, and I want to get every word down. What have you hit upon?"

Joey looked up with a smile across his face. "I've figured out a new way to help my character with his problem, and I wanted to get it all down before I forgot."

"That's huge! You must be so relieved," I said as I picked up Joey's paper, reminding myself of his story. It began like this:

> Gary stood in front of the store window looking at the brand new BMX bike. It was candy-apple red and had shock absorbers on the front tires. He imagined himself riding this bike, doing wheelies, jumping off ramps. He imagined himself zooming down huge hills in Central Park and zooming past people. He was like a statue standing in front of this bike. How would he be able to afford it?

"So, Gary's problem is that he wants a new bike, but he can't afford it."
Joey nodded.

MID-WORKSHOP TEACHING POINT *Partnering in Revision* "When I was walking around, conferring with you, I was thrilled to see that many of you are sharing your ending ideas with a partner. I think that's a great idea. It makes me think that you know something that professional writers know—it helps to have fresh eyes look at a piece. After all, you've been looking at the same piece for a long time. It's hard to see all the things there are to see in it. Just like it's sometimes hard to see that your desk is messy because you look at it every day. It's only when someone else sits at your desk for a few minutes that you realize—oops—it's due for a cleaning!"

"Remember you need your partner to look not just at the ending itself, but also at your piece as a whole. If you haven't yet asked for a reader, do so soon."

"How have you decided to help Gary buy his bike?" I prepared to jot as Joey spoke so that I would have his words clear and straight in my mind.

Joey looked at his writing. "Well, I'm going to have an old lady who lives in Gary's building give him the money. The old lady hears Gary talking to his mom one day about the bike and how much he wants it, so this old lady decides to help Gary by giving him the money. Then, at the end, Gary goes and buys the bike."

I listened as Joey told his story, and jotted notes. "So let me make sure I have this straight." I looked down at my notes. "An old lady who lives in Gary's building is going to give Gary the money to buy his bike. Then, at the end, he goes to the store to buy the bike?"

"Yes, that's right."

"Well, I take my hat off to you Joey for working so hard to solve your character's problem. You know, it's not easy to solve a character's problem in a short story, because you don't have lots of time to do so."

"Yeah, I know. That's why I like my new ending, because Gary gets the money and can go buy the bike."

"Can you show me where this old lady comes into your story mountain?" I asked, flipping the pages of Joey's notebook to find his plans.

He quickly found his most recent story mountain and pointed to the top of the mountain. "She comes in at the middle of the story. Gary begs his mother to buy him the bike. Then, one day, this lady hears him and she tells him that she'll give him the money."

As Joey spoke, I thought to myself that there were a couple of ways that this conference could go. I could teach Joey to look at the events that had already happened in his story and then show him how he could use something that had already happened to lead to a solution. Or, I could teach Joey to introduce this new character earlier and think about how her story might unfold so that it doesn't feel as if she's come out of thin air. With those options in mind, I pressed on. "You know, Joey, having this new character in your story can add a whole new dynamic. It adds so many possibilities for how your story might unfold. So that was a very smart thing to do. But I want to give you a very important tip. Writers don't just add in characters at the last minute and have them fix all the problems that the character faces. When a solution zooms in from outside the story, this can throw a reader off and make your writing seem unrealistic. Instead, writers weave characters in from the beginning and then, sometimes those characters end up being heroes of the story." I paused so that Joey could take in what I'd said. "So let's look at your story mountain. Where might it make sense to have your neighbor come in? Remember, we want it to be somewhere close to the beginning. Introducing her in the middle is too late."

Joey looked at his story mountain and read out a point close to the beginning. "Well, here is the first time my character asks his mother for the money to buy the bike. So maybe, they can be in the hall or on the elevator and the woman is there and she hears it."

"That could totally happen. Absolutely! Now, you need to imagine a realistic reason for her to eventually give him the money. It feels unreal that she just gives him the money. What's her motivation for that?"

Joey thought. "Maybe she needs some chores done and she asks him to help her. He spends a couple of weeks doing chores for her and then he earns the money to buy the bike?"

"Yes, Joey, that's a realistic possibility. So, before you start writing, go back and revise your story mountain so that you are sure to weave your character through the whole of your story. And after this, try to be sure your solution grows out of the details of the story."

You will also find that some students, as they near the end of their stories, seem to feel insecure and therefore reach to add a little pizazz. Viktor did just that with his story about a boy who overslept for the ELA test (New York State's standardized language arts test). During the last phases of revision, he added pages and pages onto his draft. "I've been reading other people's stories and I realized my story was just not that exciting. So I decided to create more tension. So now, my character doesn't only miss the ELA test, but his father gets in a car crash," he explained. [Figs. X-1 and X-2]

I acknowledged that the car crash definitely added drama, but then continued, "You know, Viktor, a car crash is really very serious and important. In short stories, like what we've been working on, there is only room for one big event. For example, in our Luz story, we have the slumber party. We wanted to say that it was okay to be different and to be afraid of things, and the slumber party helps us show that. What important thing are you trying to say in your story?"

Viktor stopped and thought for a minute, then admitted that he was trying to talk about how stressful taking tests can be. "Maybe I should save the car crash part for another story," Viktor said, and I concurred.

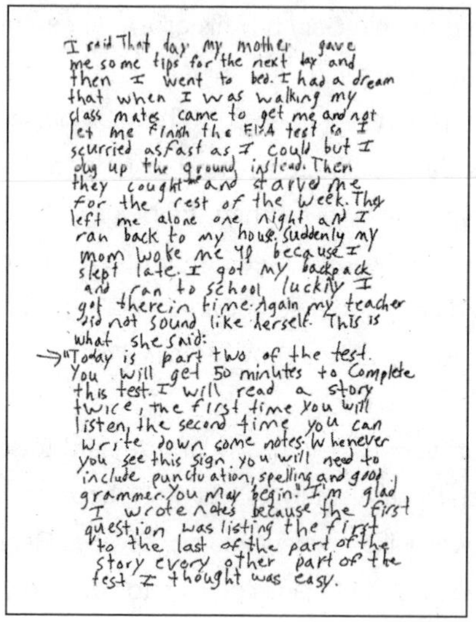

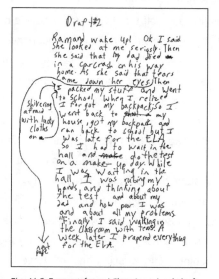

Fig. X-1 Excerpt from Viktor's original draft

Fig. X-2 Excerpt from Viktor's revised draft

SHARE
Crafting Endings

Share the story of one child's writing process that led her to write a more powerful ending.

"Writers, I want to tell you about something exciting that Deveonna realized today. Deveonna realized that she didn't need a miracle to happen at the end of her story. Let me explain. You'll remember that Deveonna's story is about a popular girl Alexa who feels as if she's been stalked by a somewhat nerdy boy, Max. In the opening scene of Deveonna's story, Alexa hides behind a tree so that Max won't find her—though of course he manages to spot her and is on her like glue. He comes close, and Alexa's friend cries, 'Run!' Later, Alexa decides she's going to confront Max and tell him she wants her privacy. She wrote": [Fig. X-3]

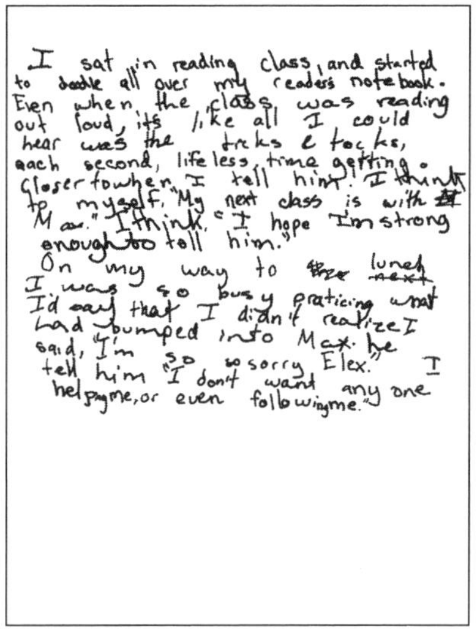

> I sat in reading class, and started to doodle all over my reader's notebook. Even when the class was reading out loud, all I could hear were the ticks and tocks of time getting closer to when I'd tell Max. I think to myself, "My next class is with Max." I think, "I hope I'm strong enough to tell him."
>
> On my way to lunch I was so busy practicing what I'd say that I didn't realize I had bumped into Max. He said, "I'm so sorry Alexa." I tell him, "I don't want any one helping me, or even following me."

"At first Deveonna wanted to write, 'He said fine, and that day after school we played chess and became best of friends.' But then she wrote in her notebook, 'I don't like that. Everything is just so peachy like an after-school special.' So she tried another ending. Will you listen to it and afterward, be prepared to list across your fingers four things that Deveonna has done in her writing that really work? This time she wrote:"[Fig. X-4]

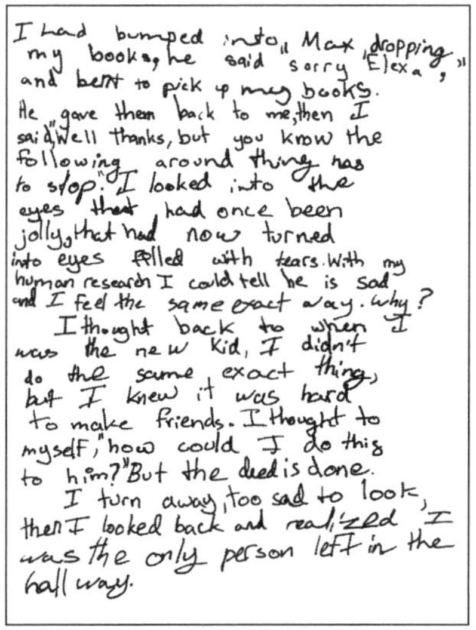

> I had bumped into Max, dropping my books. He said, "Sorry Alexa" and bent to pick up my books. He gave them back to me, then I said, "Well thanks, but you know the following around thing has to stop."
>
> I looked into the eyes that had once been jolly, that had now turned into eyes filled with tears. With my human research I could tell not only that he was sad, but I felt the exact way.

Fig. X-3 Deveonna's opening scene

Fig. X-4 Deveonna's ending

Why? I thought back to when I was the new kid. I
didn't do the exact same thing, but I knew it was
hard to make friends. I thought to myself, "How could I
do this to him?" I thought, "But the deed is done." I
turned away, too sad to look. Then I looked back and I
realized I was the only person left in the hallway.

Ask children to process what they've learned from the child's process and begin considering how to improve their own endings.

"Turn and tell your partner four things Deveonna did that really worked," I said, and the room erupted into talk. After a bit, I intervened. "If you wrote an ending today, share that ending, and talk about how it works—and how it could be better still."

HOMEWORK | *Using Mentor Texts to Explore Endings* Writers, remember that first and last impressions often matter whenever we come across something new. Just as we write strong leads to draw readers immediately into our stories, we need to write powerful endings so that readers finish our stories feeling that they've traveled with our main characters on their journeys. These endings need to be satisfying and strong, and there are a number of ways writers can do this.

Remember *Freedom Summer*? Deborah Wiles ended that story with action: "Then we walk through the front door together," and leaves us with the understanding that after the disappointment felt by John Henry and the narrator when they are not allowed to swim in the community pool anymore, the narrator is ready to stand by his friend's side through any other challenge that comes their way. Jacqueline Woodson's *The Other Side* ends with dialogue: "' Someday, somebody's going to come along and knock this old fence down,' Annie said. And I nodded. 'Yeah.' I said. 'Someday'" That final conversation between Clover and Annie lets us know how far they have come in their friendship and the hopes they share for a world in which a racial divide will be broken. *Chrysanthemum*, by Kevin Henkes, ends with internal dialogue: "Chrysanthemum did not *think* her name was absolutely perfect. She *knew* it!" This bit of thinking is the perfect way to end a story in which a character moves from fretting to feeling confident.

For homework tonight and whenever you are deciding how to end your stories, go ahead and try some of these different ways. If you've ended with dialogue, try to end the story with action. Then write another ending, this time ending it with internal dialogue. You might also look at another mentor text that ends in another way and try to use that kind of ending for your story. Then ask yourself which ending works better for your pieces. Which one best shows your character's journey in a clean, satisfying, and meaningful way?

⊙ TAILORING YOUR TEACHING

If your children need more help learning to write endings . . . you might say, "Finding the right ending for a story can be really hard! Many writers consider this the biggest challenge of writing. I've watched each of you look closely at your stories, imagining this way and that way to tie up loose ends. I know it's tempting to look toward the end of your story for hints about how to end it, but I wonder if you've thought about revisiting your story beginnings for hints about how to end it? In endings, characters find answers to questions they have on page one, or overcome a challenge they face at the start of the story. Sometimes a powerful image presented in the story's beginning reappears at its end."

You could go on and give examples. "*Fireflies!* both begins and ends with the narrator looking out a window, but, although the same fireflies dance before his eyes in both scenes, there's a clear shift in what he sees and feels when he looks at them. *Peter's Chair* begins with Peter making a building for himself and it ends with Peter helping his dad build something for Peter's sister. In both instances Peter builds, but his project at the end of the story shows that he has come to accept his baby sister and his role as older brother. At the start of "Spaghetti" Gabriel sits alone on the stoop outside, wishing for company. At the end, Rylant tells us Gabriel "no longer wanted to live outside." He takes Spaghetti, the kitten, and goes inside. Notice that Rylant uses inside and outside space to represent Gabriel's internal journey; with a kitten to care for, Gabriel gives up being an outsider, letting someone in. If you are struggling over how to end your stories, reread your beginning, and see if there is something in it worth revisiting. Remember that a beginning often holds a key to the end."

COLLABORATING WITH COLLEAGUES

By this point in the unit you have a good sense of the scope and shape of your students' pieces. This is a good time, then, to check in on the fiction writing you and your colleagues started a few sessions ago and push yourselves to try more. One of the most powerful ways writers support each other is to read each other's work and give feedback and critiques. Professional writers often call this "workshopping" a piece. It is such common practice that there are retreats for writers dedicated to sharing each other's work to get support as well as laser-sharp criticism.

Some argue that this regular practice of meeting and discussing each other's work is the single most important thing writers can do to enhance our writing skills. This offers us an audience for our writing and a reason to write on a regular basis. It allows us insights into how readers might interpret our work. And for our purposes, it allows us to experience something akin to what our students feel every day when we confer with them about their writing.

If you and your colleagues are interested in dabbling in the work of sharing and offering critiques for each other's fiction pieces, you'll want to decide several things up front:

- A private time and place to meet where there will be few interruptions. Depending on the size of your group, one workshop session might take anywhere from one to three hours.

- An agreed-upon maximum number of pages to bring so that the meetings don't go on too long.

- A plan for how the meeting will go. Will people read each other's pieces and prepare comments beforehand? Or will people bring copies of their pieces with them to the meeting and read them aloud so people can comment in person?

- Ground rules for the meeting. You might choose a facilitator who will start off the discussion. You might decide to start with compliments, then move on to suggestions. You might want everyone to share at every meeting. Or you might decide to take turns.

Once your group is up and running, you may wonder about ways to get the conversation going. What will you talk about? You needn't worry about what to discuss. You already have a wealth of knowledge at your disposal. You have the piece you are focused on, for starters. You also know a lot about good writing from your work with mentor texts, the strategies you've taught, and the qualities of good writing. If you still find yourself stymied, you can direct your focus to particular components of the text: structure, plot, character development, flow, word choice, characteristics of the genre, and so on. Of course, you can always turn your talk to the best parts of each other's writing and ways to teach students lessons that will help their writing become as powerful.

YOU WILL TEACH CHILDREN THAT WHEN REVISING, WRITERS DON'T SIMPLY REREAD, WE REREAD WITH A LENS. WRITERS VARY THEIR LENSES ACCORDING TO WHAT THE WRITER VALUES FOR HER WORK.

GETTING READY

- Latest version of the class story, on chart paper, to demonstrate revising through a lens
- Former student's draft, prepared on a transparency, for whole-class practice
- Start of a list titled Ways to Resee Our Stories on chart paper
- See CD-ROM for resources

REVISION:
REREADING WITH A LENS

In this session and the ones that follow it, you will rally children toward a serious commitment to revision. You'll pull out all stops in an effort to support revision. You'll teach revision strategies in the minilesson, confer toward revision in your conferences, and celebrate revision in your mid-workshop teaching point and your share. But above all, convey the assumption that of course children will revise.

Children generally come to us resisting revision. They often regard it as punishment for writing badly. In the series, Units of Study for Primary Writing, I introduce a unit of study on revision by telling children that when we are really proud of our work, when it is the best writing we've ever done, we revise it. Revision is a way to make our best, better. Later in that unit, I invite the youngsters to reread texts they've written, looking for whether any of them are "good enough that they deserve to be revised." My message is clear: Revision is a compliment for good writing. Lousy writing is abandoned; good writing is labored over, developed, refined, and polished.

It's important to teach and model this stance toward revision, but it is also important to equip youngsters with tools that will allow them to revise to good effect. Too many children add a clarifying phrase or insert a detail and regard that as revision!

In this session, you will teach children that revision begins as rereading, and suggest that writers can reread with any one of many lenses. This is not a new point. We can reread asking, "What is this story really about? Have I brought out that deeper story? Have I made my characters vulnerable enough to seem human?"

The larger message is that revision begins with rereading, and that writers can be deliberate and strategic, selecting a lens based on whatever we value, and rereading with that lens.

MINILESSON

Revision: Rereading with a Lens

CONNECTION

Celebrate that some of your students have finished drafts of their stories, and remind them that reaching the end allows writers to reread and revise with new perspectives.

"Hurrah! Many of you are coming to the final pages of your story booklets. And the good news is that once you reach the ending of your story, you have a chance to look over the story, and to make the whole of it fit together into a single coherent piece."

Name your teaching point. Specifically, remind children that writers revise. Writers reread, deliberately viewing their drafts through a chosen lens.

"Today, I want to remind you that even when we move heaven and earth to write our drafts really well, we will each shift from drafting to revision. And specifically, I want to teach you that revision means just what the word says—re-vision. To see again." Then Colleen leaned toward the children as if she was conveying a secret, and said, "I want to teach you that when we revise it really helps to reread with glasses." She put on a pair of glasses for effect. Then, pulling the glasses off, she said, "You don't *really* need to wear glasses to be a writer. But we do need to put on special lenses, lenses that allow us to reread our writing with one particular question or concern in mind. We sometimes call that 'reading with a lens.' We might, for example, reread looking specifically to see if our character development satisfies us, or to see if we've shown the passage of time effectively, or to study the way we've used varied sentence lengths and punctuation to create rhythm and suspense in a story."

TEACHING

Explain that, especially when writing longer texts, many writers shift often between writing and revising. Tell children that you will revise what you've written so far and ask them to notice that you start by rereading the draft through a lens.

"Let me show you what I mean when I say revision starts by rereading with a lens. Before I do, let me join you in noticing that our class story isn't finished yet—we've written three pages for our story booklet—and I want to point out that when I'm writing a long text, I usually don't wait until I'm all done before I begin to revise. I'd rather rewrite three pages than revise the whole book! Many writers do that."

COACHING

Colleen names what she hopes children learned earlier, trying to restate that teaching in a grand and inspiring way.

You will notice that here, as in most minilessons, Colleen deliberately weaves a certain amount of flexibility into the form the work of the day might take. She doesn't say, "You must look at your writing through two lenses." She says, "You might look at your writing through this lens, or this lens, or another lens that reflect something that is important to you in your writing." By doing this, she reinforces the idea that writers have to make decisions about their stories, and that the work is not the same for every writer. She entrusts these decisions to students, and they feel more invested in the process than they would if she kept a tight hold on the reins. This is one way in which we can help writers become independent.

Sometimes teachers assume that a minilesson makes literally only one teaching point, and that the one and only thing that children can learn from a minilesson is carried in that teaching point. Certainly there is one main teaching point, but there are other, subordinate points as well for those students who are ready to take them in. I worry that if our teaching isn't densely packed with interesting, helpful information, children will decide to zone out. At the same time, we have to be careful that we don't muddy our primary teaching point with the various other points we are making. Constructing a minilesson takes care.

Demonstrate rereading the draft through a lens. Explain what rereading through another lens could look like.

"So I'm going to revise the draft we've written so far. And to do so, I'm going to use a special lens—I'm going to read just a bit of it with an eye toward one issue I choose. I could choose any issue that especially mattered to me."

"Remember earlier, we said that it is really important to think, 'What am I trying to show?' and to ask, 'What is this story *really* about?' So I am going to reread our Luz story, thinking, 'Have I really brought out the idea that this isn't just a girl-has-a-sleepover story?' This is a girl-who-worries-no-one-will-like-her story, a story that revolves around Luz's worries over whether her friends will laugh that she needs a night-light."

Colleen reread the class story, underlining places that illustrated the deeper meaning. With the class' approval, she decided aloud that the class had, indeed, brought out that understory. "Did you see how I reread the draft, looking at it simply through the lens of whether I'd shown what the story is *really* about?" she asked. "As writers, we can choose any lens we want, and we usually reread and revise several times with several lenses."

Now demonstrate that you can alter the lens with which you reread your draft, thereby seeing new aspects of it.

"One revision lens that writers use is a lens that a writing friend of mine calls the 'Cardboard Character Alert.' Anne Lamott says that our stories are only as good as the characters we develop. Even if we have the most wonderful plot, we need the character to take us on the journey. We loved reading *The Great Gilly Hopkins* because Katherine Paterson created characters to take us on the journey. Writers reread to be sure that our characters, especially our main characters, look and act so real that the reader feels like the character could walk right off the pages of the book into the living room."

"Remember we talked about making sure the character had some good traits, but also some not-so-good traits? If they don't, they seem fake—they are only as real as cardboard. So when I reread our story, I'm checking that we haven't made Luz be the sweetest, most sensitive girl, the greatest artist, a straight-A student, and the perfect daughter to her parents, or else readers might go UGH! No one's like that! I find things about Luz that are not perfect—including that she is afraid of the dark. This makes her more like a flesh-and-blood person!"

"But when I put on the Cardboard Character Alert lens, I might decide we could flesh out Luz even more by giving her little traits—things only she thinks, says, and does. For instance, I might describe the way Luz eats in such a way that she'd seem unique. Maybe we

I often try to show children that when I check for whether I've done something, I sometimes find "yes," and I sometimes find "no." I do not want all my "checks" to lead to the same answer!

You'll notice that Colleen uses this form of revision to reteach a quality of writing that we emphasized very early in the unit. Early on, children thought about their characters' external and internal features, and about their characters' strengths and weaknesses. Now Colleen leads children to revisit that early work. This, again, is a rhythm you should anticipate. Plan on the fact that the qualities of good writing that you really want to highlight in a unit will need to be introduced during the first few days of the unit, and recycled later in the unit. You could, of course, harken back to this early work and even suggest that children use strategies they learned earlier to breathe life into the characters they've now settled upon.

could say she likes to eat foods that look pretty together. She is an artist after all, right? So maybe she tries to arrange food on her plate so it looks like a painting, with purple, orange, and green foods set carefully next to each other."

"So during this revision stage, a writer puts on just one lens, then another lens. We might reread asking ourselves, 'Did I show what this story is *really* about?' or 'Did I develop idiosyncratic character traits?' This rereading often prompts revisions—even before the first draft is written."

ACTIVE ENGAGEMENT
Set children up to try reading a text through the lens of a Cardboard Character Alert. Encourage them to imagine revising the draft based on what they notice when they reread it.

"Why don't we try putting on the Cardboard Character Alert lens to look at this part of a draft story by a former student? Now, really go for it! With your partner, find the places where the character feels only as real as cardboard instead of as real as your Uncle Charlie." Colleen put up a transparency with part of a draft by a former student and read it out loud to the class.

> Rex was the star quarterback of the sixth grade football team. He could kick faster and farther than anyone else on the team, and he was big too and no one could push him over. He could just catch the ball and plow through to the endline without interference. With Rex on the team, no one else ever got to play that position.
>
> "I think you should give someone else a chance to play quarterback, Rex," said his friend. (Rex had lots and lots of friends and also he was real good at school, so his teachers all liked him best too).
>
> "Okay," said Rex. Because he was really nice too.

Make sure you gather examples of student writing that will help you illustrate your teaching points. Especially keep an eye out for notebook entries and drafts in which the writer has some "typical" issue that you could teach into. For example, this piece about Rex could also be used to teach students how to add setting to their stories, how to add physical details to create a picture of their characters, or how to add a main character's internal thinking. When you find student pieces that are very flexible in this way, make copies for your colleagues. And, if you don't have any pieces from former students on hand, you can use a piece from a different classroom or a piece that you have written yourself to illustrate your teaching point.

"Do you have your Cardboard Character Alert glasses on? What do you see?" Pulling in to listen to partners, Colleen heard Caleb say, "No one is all that good at everything." He added, "I mean, who could be the star at sports *and* at schoolwork? He is too perfect."

"Yeah," Felix agreed, "and if they were, probably they wouldn't have any friends 'cuz people would hate a person who is so great. Hey! Maybe that could be Rex's big problem! He could be so super great at everything, but in his true heart, he's real lonely and just wants a good friend. So he has to change something. Break a leg or something!"

"Fantastic!" Colleen said. "You're already thinking like terrific writers and you're beginning to revise this piece of writing." Then she convened the class. "You were coming up with great ideas. Of course, it is easier to fix up someone else's stories instead of your own!"

LINK
Send children off to reread their own writing through a specially-chosen lens, and remind them to do this throughout their lives.

"Today, like professional writers, you are going to reread your writing with lenses. You might look at your own writing and ask, 'Have I brought out the real thing this story is mostly about?' You might reread asking, 'Can I make my characters seem less like cardboard cutouts?' Try other special lenses you invent to serve your purposes as well, and let your rereading lead you to revision."

"For the rest of your life, remember that writers do all we can to write great drafts, but then we return to those drafts, rereading them with different lenses in mind, expecting to revise them."

When you want to help children bring a character to life, it helps to give that character an object to hold onto. Robert Newton Peck in Fiction is Folks *writes, "Bring a thing into the scene and your audience moves an inch forward in their seats, to be close to the stage."*

WRITING AND CONFERRING

Helping Reluctant Revisers

In today's minilesson, we encouraged writers to reread drafts with a particular lens in mind. You won't be surprised when I remind you, similarly, we, as teachers, can also look over our children's work with a particular lens in mind. It is important to remember this because otherwise, we tend to believe there is something objective and universal about whatever it is we see when we look at the work being done by our writers. A researcher once pointed out, "We do not see with our eyes or hear with our ears but with our beliefs."

The good news is that we can each make ourselves aware of the lens we tend to use when viewing kids and their writing, and this allows us to make decisions. I might say, "I usually read my children's writing trying to understand the content of their pieces, but for today, I want to look mostly at the length of their writing and at whatever efforts I see them making to elaborate or to write long." There are countless lenses worth adopting for a time. Try noticing what children seem to think good writing entails. Try categorizing the scale of their revisions, or noticing what does and does not prompt them to revise.

For today, I suggest you deliberately focus your attention on one thing, however, and that is on the rereading your children do in the midst of writing. Ask children if you can watch them reread and hear what they are thinking as they reread. Your focus will surprise and please children; they'll expect you to be driving them directly toward revision. The secret truth is, most significant revision must begin as rereading, and children often don't realize this.

In any case, you will probably see that children need you to demonstrate and coach them before they understand what it can mean to read or reread with a lens. For example, you could reread, paying special attention to places where the dialogue seems especially lifelike and true. Then you can show children how you mull over what you find, thinking, "Why are these sections of dialogue so lifelike?"

Usually it is powerful to reread, searching for instances of a particular quality of writing, and then to ask, "What is it that I did here that worked so well?" By identifying and thinking about sections of a draft that work well, a writer gathers the strength and wisdom to tackle sections that work less well.

> **MID-WORKSHOP TEACHING POINT** — *Revising the Story's Sound* "Writers, you are finding so many places to flesh out your characters! The room is getting noisy with all those 'real' characters walking off the pages! Can you take off your character lenses for a moment and look at me? I want to share with you the smart revision work that Max is doing. Max has found another lens with which to view a draft. What do you call it, Max? Oh, your 'Sound Check' lens!"
>
> "Max told me he put on this lens to reread his story for how it *sounds*. That is just what professional writers do too, Max! Often they even read their stories out loud to a friend or to the mirror or into a tape recorder, just to see if they've missed words or to see if the language and the rhythm of the sentences flow and make sense. We need to read with our ears as well as our eyes!"
>
> "This lens helps us make sure our story sounds good. Consider trying Max's lens—rereading to revise the sound of your story."

SHARE

Using Lenses to Reread and Revise

Ask children to share the lenses they used to reread and then revise their work. Compile a chart for future reference.

"Writers, you've come up with so many ways writers can reread and revise our work! I think we'd better record these ideas so that we can remember them forever. These are the ways we've talked about so far:"

> ### Ways to Re-see Our Stories
>
> • Writers use a lens to reread, asking, "What am I trying to show?" and "What is this story <u>really</u> about?"
>
> • Writers use a Character Cardboard Alert lens to be sure that our characters, especially the main characters, look and act so real that the reader feels like the character could walk right off the pages of their stories.
>
> • Writers use a Sound Check lens to see if we've missed words or to see if the language and the rhythm of the sentences flow and make sense in our stories.
>
> • Writers reread our drafts, thinking, "What sections have I summarized in passing?" "What sections have I stretched out, like stories?" "Do these choices make sense?"

"Will you turn to your partner and talk about other lenses you've used to reread and think about revising your work? If you've only tried the ways on the chart, talk about ways you might try to reread and revise in the future. Then in a few minutes we'll add some more ways to the chart."

Of course, you may choose to use different questions and angles on revision than the ones we've highlighted here. The most important concept is that children do reread with a certain focus, no matter what that focus is. Rereading with a focus is a skill that will serve them for a lifetime, in both their reading and their writing.

If you notice that your students are having a hard time understanding the concept of a lens, you might want to say something like this: "Have you ever been to a movie where you got to put on those funny 3-D glasses that made everything look real, as if you could just reach out and touch it? I remember seeing a movie like that when I was a little kid. I don't remember what the movie was about at all, I just remember important things popping out in the foreground and the landscape and sky in the background. Maybe that was my first realization that what I looked at could change, depending, literally, on what pair of glasses I put on. Now I know that I can change anything if I just look at it differently. Your short story draft can be just like that movie. You can put on different eyeglasses, different lenses we might call them, and see the draft in a brand-new way in order to change it."

Rereading with a Punctuation Lens   Writers, I'm so pleased to see how you've found ways to revise your stories using different lenses, often with unpredictable and rich results. Tonight I'd like you to reread your stories using a new kind of lens. We'll call this the Punctuation lens.

I've noticed that when you read other authors' books aloud you read with beautiful intonation, making your listeners laugh uncontrollably, sit on the edge of their seats, gasp. But when you read your own stories, it sometimes sounds as if you're plodding along. I suspect part of the reason is that you're using the same kinds of punctuation over and over—a string of similarly placed commas or lots of short sentences ending with periods. You already know that writers vary our lenses when revising, making sure our characters aren't flat and predictable, rereading for rhythm and language fluidity, finding places to stretch out and places to summarize. What you may not know is that writers also reread for punctuation variation. Writers know that the kind of punctuation we choose and the way in which we use it can create mood or build tension or get readers to read with feeling.

Tonight I'd like you to reread bits of some stories you've read during this unit and notice how writers use punctuation to signal something to the reader. You might, for example, look at how Julie Brinckloe intersperses dashes with exclamation points and commas in *Fireflies!*, and what effect this creates. Or look at how Cynthia Rylant varies short simple sentences with longer ones, set off by commas. Then look at your own writing and find places where you can change the punctuation to enliven your stories, create mood or stir up emotion.

● TAILORING YOUR TEACHING

If your students tend to write extra long leads so they can give background information on their main characters . . . remind them of what they learned about leads in the *Raising the Quality of Narrative Writing* unit. You might say something like, "When you were writing personal narratives, you learned how writers don't start far, far away from the action of the story. They start their stories right at the action. Well, writers of realistic fiction do the exact same thing. They start their stories by placing the reader right in the thick of the action." If your students know the story *Because of Winn-Dixie* by Kate DiCamillo, you might show them how the author brings the reader into the thick of the action by starting with the line, "My name is India Opal Buloni, and last summer my daddy, the preacher, sent me to the store for a box of macaroni-and-cheese, some white rice, and two tomatoes and I came back with a dog." As the story progresses, Kate DiCamillo weaves in elements of the main character's history.

It is especially difficult for students to restrain themselves from giving all the background information at once if they have done a thorough job of developing a character with vivid details. Students do not want their work to go to waste, so they tend to write pages and pages of description and background, and in the process they lose their reader's attention before they ever get to the meat of the story. Help students celebrate all the work and careful attention they spent creating a rich and interesting character. Then, teach them how to artfully reveal those details to the reader. You could say, "You already know how to balance your story by weaving together details about setting, thinking, dialogue, and actions. In just the same way, you are going to weave in details about your main character. Writers don't write everything we know about our characters all at once. Instead, we need to carefully balance our stories by weaving in a bit of detail about character here and there, along with all the other kinds of details. Imagine that your story is on a stage, and you are raising the curtain ever so slowly, so the audience sees just a tiny bit at a time. Doing this creates suspense and drama in our stories."

MECHANICS

During this unit of study, children will write a very long story, and then they'll revise and edit that one draft. Most of them will make a final, clean copy of their story, but the piece will be long enough that their energy for editing at that stage will likely run dry.

Therefore, it'll probably be important for you to have children take one of the early pages in their story booklets and help them edit as well as revise that page. Then as they proceed to revise the upcoming pages, you can encourage them to draw upon conventions they incorporated into their first page. This work will be fairly individual, but meanwhile you'll also want to teach whole-class instruction around mechanics.

You'll want to study children's writing in order to decide what to teach. If you reread their pages through the lens of mechanics, noticing what they can do and what they need help doing, you may find yourself overwhelmed. The children will produce lots of text in this unit—and this means they'll also produce lots of errors!

If you stay focused, however, you can deliberately channel yourself to also notice and admire the complexity of their work. For example, both Felix and Laurel are using complex sentences, complete with subordinate clauses. They use these to show that two activities occur simultaneously:

> He was losing, but he remembered his dad telling him to pump false turn and shoot.

> "Let's go look at the animals first, so then on the sky ride we can retrace where we were," Jessie said.

It is as if the challenge to tell a dramatic, titillating story has led both writers to stretch their grammatical skills. Not surprisingly, they also make many errors.

Often, the most helpful thing that you can teach these children is that writers use paragraphs to show either when the character takes a step forward in the action, or when the camera shifts to a different but simultaneous ring in the three-ring circus that is the story. This single bit of editing will relieve the sense that the child's words are unremitting, a torrent of language.

It might also help children to study different ways in which authors convey a character's thoughts, and to realize that sometimes authors use quotes for thoughts just as they do for spoken language. It might also help enormously to remind children that when a reader encounters a pronoun—he or she or they—the reader should instantly know exactly who is being referenced. If the reader might be unclear, then it is important to use the person's name (or a synonym for it) rather than the pronoun.

If you teach one or two of these tips in an editing conference, you'll want to give writers a chance to use the advice as they edit. Then teach another tip or two, and again invite the child to edit, putting the advice into action. When you read the resulting text, it'll be important to celebrate progress and approximation, encouraging the child to continue to do this important work in upcoming pages of the story.

MAKING A SPACE FOR WRITING

In this session, you'll rally children's commitment to the project before them, that of seriously, deeply revising their writing.

When I begin work on a new writing project, my first step is not to write or even to read. Instead, my first step is to clean my office! After that, I set out all the things I will need to write or, in this instance, to revise.

When I began work on this series, for example, I put the previous series, Units of Study for Primary Writing, on the far corner of my desk. Then I gathered together the books that bring my distant teachers close to me: books by Don Murray, Annie Dillard, Bill Zinsser, John Gardner, Don Graves, and others. I pinned a few letters from readers on my bulletin board; those letters and others like them have made me care desperately about this work. On my bulletin board, I tacked a calendar of deadlines, and my brilliant editor's list of tips to remember.

Children, too, need to be encouraged to build spaces in their lives that allow them to write and to revise as well as possible, and they need to be encouraged to fill those spaces with items that can inspire and cajole and guide them as writers. By physically setting up the space in which we work, we take control of our own writing processes. As we make our writing spaces, we make ourselves. And for teachers, whose ultimate goal is to help children grow to be passionately committed, zealous writers who author richly literate lives, nothing could matter more than this.

Today, by sharing with children my own tricks of the trade, I speak to them as fellow insiders in the world of writing. And by inviting them to surround themselves with items that carry reminders of their resolutions, I encourage children to review all they have already learned, and also to renew their vows to lessons that may have slipped out of view.

IN THIS SESSION, YOU'LL TELL WRITERS ABOUT THE INTIMATE WORK SPACE YOU'VE CREATED FOR YOUR WRITING AND TEACH STUDENTS THAT THEY CAN CREATE THEIR OWN SPACES INSIDE THEIR WRITING NOTEBOOKS AND THEIR HOMES.

GETTING READY

- Anecdote you can tell about one writer's special work space
- Something special from your own writing life—a quote or object—whose significance you can share
- Charts of writing tips and strategies created during earlier units, for reference
- Copy of each child's published personal narrative from earlier in the year
- See CD-ROM for resources

MINILESSON

Making a Space for Writing

CONNECTION

Tell students that you prepare for a writing project first by cleaning your office. Explain that many writers set up work spaces, putting items nearby that remind us of our resolutions.

"Writers, I think each one of you is off to a great start, revising your fiction story. So today, I thought I'd tell you that when I turn the bend in a writing project, in addition to sketching plans for that writing, I do one other very important thing. I clean my office."

"Every writer is different, and you may decide that your needs are different from mine. But many, many writers take the time to set up spaces in which we can do our best work."

Tell the story of one writer who has set up his or her writing space in ways that convey messages about writing.

"The author Annie Dillard turned a tool shed into a study, pushing a long desk against a blank wall so that she'd have nowhere to look but at the page. She says, 'Writing a first draft requires a peculiar internal state which ordinary life does not induce'." (*The Writing Life*, p. 47)

"Annie Dillard has also pinned a photograph above her desk. It's a photo of a little Amazonian boy whose face is sticking out of river rapids. White water is pounding all around his head and his dark eyes are looking up. 'That little boy is completely alone,' Dillard says. 'He's letting the mystery of existence beat on him. He's having his childhood and I think he knows it and I think he will come out of the water strong and needing to do some good.'" (*The Writing Life*, p. 58)

Debrief. Help your students see the generalizable principles in the example of one author who organized a writing space.

"Do you see how Annie Dillard has built a place for her writing, a place that reminds her of what she wants to remember as she writes? She makes sure her place whispers a message to her—and for Annie Dillard, the message is this: Wake up. Wake up to the mystery and power of your own life. Put it on the page."

COACHING

My book Living Between the Lines *opens with a chapter titled "A Place for Writing and Reading." I do believe that when we teach writing, we are also helping children author lives in which they read and write often. This series of books doesn't spotlight the importance of a writing community and writing identity as much as I'd like—it's hard to write minilessons that could be universally applicable and yet do this work. I hope this one session inspires you to create others like it!*

This minilesson doesn't require such extensive detail about Annie Dillard's writing space. I relish detail and trust that it conveys larger principles, but you may decide to abbreviate this session—it could easily be done. Obviously, you'll want to tailor all your teaching to your children.

Although the example in this minilesson is different from that in other minilessons, you should by this point be able to see the pattern of minilessons. Over and over, we explicitly articulate a point that we hope is relevant to all children on many days. We either tell or dramatize the case in point, often tucking in little subordinate tips. Then we step back to debrief, and do so by again naming generalizable ideas and strategies. In this session, I've made a new point in the Connection section of the minilesson, which is unusual.

Name your teaching point. Specifically, teach children that writers put items and words into their writing spaces that remind us of our writing goals and hopes.

"Today as you continue drafting your story, you'll want to draw on everything you've ever learned about how to write stories well in order to make your new draft as spectacular as it can be. And specifically, I want to teach you that most writers set up spaces in which we can do our best work. We can put items and words into those spaces that remind us of all we resolve to do and be as writers."

Tell students that you like to look back on ideas learned from previous writing, bringing those lessons to bear on current writing.

"What I like to do as a writer is to look back on my writing life, and to think about all I learned before today that I resolve to remember. Remember that earlier this year, we read Sandra Cisneros' essay "Eleven," and learned that when you're eleven you're also ten, and nine, and eight, and seven, and six, and so on? Because, as she wrote, the way you grow old is kind of like an onion, or like the rings inside a tree trunk, or like wooden dolls that fit one inside the other—each year fits inside the next one. Well, I really do believe that writers also grow that way. When we're working on one piece of writing, we need to bring with us all the lessons we've learned from all the pieces of writing we've ever written. Because the way we grow as writers is like trees, with one ring inside the next, or like those little wooden dolls."

You'll see that I revisit Sandra Cisneros' essay "Eleven," making a point that is not unlike one I made earlier this year. You may wonder if I forget that I've traveled this road before. I haven't! I'm convinced that children benefit from a cyclical curriculum, and I love returning to a point made earlier, to a text that's been studied earlier, each time adding to the familiar content with more experiences, more knowledge.

TEACHING

Share the dream that each child might have a writing shed (akin to Annie Dillard's) and suggest that instead, all of them can set up their notebooks and writing spaces to convey messages about writing well.

"Wouldn't it be great if instead of putting up portable classrooms outside this school, they instead put up tool sheds, one for each of us? Then the writing workshop could be like those writing colonies I read about. We could convene for a meeting, and then each of us would head to our very own writing shed to read and write all morning. In some writing colonies, a basket lunch is left outside each writer's door so as not to disturb the writer's muse!"

"It'd be great if we could each set up a writing shed for ourselves, but in this classroom, we can only set up our writing spaces, our notebooks, our folders. Still, it is important to choose the items that we will put near us as we write, items that can carry bits of advice to us."

Notice that I repeat my teaching point here, this time in a more poetic fashion. I hope that by doing so, I increase kids' energies for this work.

Although this is playful chitchat, the underlying message is that these youngsters deserve to be taken seriously as writers. Every lesson we teach is not explicitly articulated—we also teach by our assumptions, our attitudes.

Explain that before you return to the class story or your own story, you'll first set out items that remind you of advice you want to recall. Select a quote from a book or an item from your writing life and share the significance of whatever you select.

"So before I work anymore on our class story and before I work on my own fiction stories, I'm going to choose a few items to keep near me as I write, items that carry advice for me."

"First of all, I want to keep one passage of 'Eleven' near me—the bit about how the narrator pushed one hand through one sleeve of a sweater that smelled like cottage cheese. Do you remember that passage? It told how she stood there with her arms pushed back, with the sweater itchy and all full of germs that weren't even hers."

"I know I shared that passage with you to show that a writer can describe an event in passing ('she put on the sweater') or can stretch it out, telling the story bit by bit. But for me, I love this passage also because it has a ring of truth. The details feel as if they are true details, and I want to remember the power of writing the truth, even when I'm writing fiction. So I'll tape that passage inside my notebook, and remember that advice today and always as I write."

"I think I'll also tape this calendar inside the front cover of my notebook," I said. "I want to remind myself that I can't spend too long planning for writing or I won't have enough time to revise. I think it will be helpful to me in making decisions to have the calendar saying, 'Just Get on with It.'"

Active Engagement
Help writers leaf through and revisit old charts and mentor texts, thinking, "Does any of this belong in my writing space?"

"So writers, today and tonight, would you think about ways in which you can make a space for writing both here in the classroom and at home—a space that carries messages *you* need to remember."

"Right now, I'll revisit some of the items in our classroom that *might* contain lessons for you, and as I do this, will you jot your own notes so that when I'm done, you can tell your partner whether any of these items (or others you can recall) might belong in your writing space?" I turned the pages of the chart-paper tablet back to charts from *Launching the Writing Workshop*, and read off a few items:

- Strategies for Generating Personal Narrative Writing

- Qualities of Good Personal Narrative Writing

- Monitoring My Writing Process

I deliberately selected a passage that will be familiar and memorable to children, and layered it with a somewhat new message. This is a small way to tuck another pointer about good writing into my minilesson.

I thought about whether I would also tell the class about a special stone or a rabbit's foot, just so my items would be more varied and suggest more possibilities to children for their own objects. But I couldn't come up with a brief explanation for the lessons these objects might contain. You and your colleagues might have better luck.

This lesson is reminiscent of the work in our first unit, in which we launch the writing workshop by helping students cultivate the habits of writers. Writers live with a constant, eyes-wide-open awareness, gathering ideas from the world like collecting berries in a basket. We must remind students of this often by modeling and discussing these habits. So, in addition to jotting down ideas from class writing charts during this lesson, encourage students to write or paste meaningful passages, writing advice, photographs, or other inspiring pieces into their notebooks or folders to create a rich writing space. This lesson gets to so much more than simply decorating the cover of a notebook, and it is truly the work that authors do to support their writing.

Then I turned to those from *Raising the Quality of Narrative Writing* and read off a few more:

- Lessons from Mentor Personal Narratives
- Turning Points
- When to Use Paragraphs

I continued flipping back through charts from all of our units until I reached the current one.

Ask children to talk to a partner about items they might put in their notebooks or writing spaces that can help them recall previous lessons on good writing.

After surveying these and other items, I said, "Would you turn and tell your partner if you've seen anything so far that reminds you of a message that might help you do your best writing and revision today? Because remember, writers grow like rings on a tree. When we write fiction, we still have the layers of all we've learned from earlier units of study. Which words or objects might you put into your writing space? Turn and talk."

I loved being able to come back to the passage from "Eleven" at the end of this little lesson. I think if our teaching is artful, then the teaching itself acts as a mentor text.

LINK

Put today's lesson into context by reminding writers of the many ways they can prepare themselves for writing well.

"So writers, from this day forward, remember that we can prepare ourselves for writing not only by sketching timelines, boxes and bullets, or story mountains, and not only by trying alternative leads. We can also prepare ourselves for writing by looking back over lessons we learned earlier in our writing lives and the texts that have taught us a lot. We often select passages or charts or quotations or objects to keep near us as we write, and we do this as a way of holding close the lessons we've learned."

This is sophisticated work, and it takes real self-awareness for students to identify just exactly which lessons or skills they need to keep at the forefront of their minds as they write. Think of the writing as a building. Placing the supports at random would do little to make a sound structure, and would be a wasted effort. Just as one needs architectural knowledge in order to effectively brace a building, writers need a certain amount of savvy about themselves in order to determine which words or objects will offer them the support they need.

WRITING AND CONFERRING

Learning from Our Writing Patterns

This minilesson invites each child to create an individualized work plan, one tailored to whatever particular work that child needs to do. In your conferences, you may want to help children take a larger look at themselves as narrative writers, asking, "What lessons did I learn earlier this year that really paid off for me?" and "What worked really well in my earlier stories that I'll want to remember as I revise this new story? What didn't work too well for me in my earlier stories that I could address this time, in this piece?"

To help children look back at and learn from prior work, encourage them to see the continuities between their earlier personal narrative writing and their current work with short fiction. In fact, chances are very good that a child will bring the same strengths and the same needs to both genres. Most of the problems that will show up in short fiction will also have been present in the child's personal narrative work.

The minilesson puts a spotlight on objects and texts that carry lessons—your conferences will help writers harvest insights from taking a long look at their writing over the course of the year so far. When children look across several narrative texts, you'll need to help them see commonalities. One text may be about the birth of a cousin, another about feeding a squirrel, and a third about a bully. But all three texts may be written in simple sentences, where nothing is given more emphasis than anything else nor is anything suggested, tucked in, or alluded to. In all three texts, the characters may seem indistinguishable one from the next; and all three might have strong, interesting leads. You'll want to help writers gain some ability to see patterns in how they write, patterns that show up when texts are laid alongside each other.

MID-WORKSHOP TEACHING POINT *Using Conjunctions to Communicate Complexity* "Writers, I want to interrupt you for a moment to point out ways writers use special conjunctions—connector words—to help communicate complicated situations in writing. Here's an example—have you ever tried to explain a situation and had trouble because so many things happened at the same time? Think about the word *meanwhile,* and look how Julie Brinckloe uses it in *Fireflies!* to help us feel everything that was going on, even if it all happened at once. Remember, the narrator was eating supper, *meanwhile* fireflies flickered on and off out on the lawn? Do you see how she uses the word to help her tell what's happening inside and outside the house at the same time? There are two other *meanwhiles* in this story. "The screen door banged behind me as I ran from the house. If someone *[meanwhile]* said, 'Don't slam it,' I wasn't listening." In that example, Brinckloe doesn't write *meanwhile,* but she lets us feel it there, with two things happening at the same time. Then for a third time, at the end of the story, she helps us understand that two things happen at once: The narrator lets his fireflies go and they make circles around the moon, dipping low, soaring above the boy's head. *Meanwhile,* the boy holds the empty jar in his hands. Do you see how letting two things happen at once, with a *meanwhile* or the idea of one, can be useful in your writing? It can help with complexity or add a way to make a contrast, can't it? Look over your writing quickly, and see if you can mark a place where a *meanwhile* or another conjunction could help you explain an idea or situation. Writers use conjunctions as thoughtfully as nouns, verbs, adjectives and adverbs. It's easy to think that words like *although* and *therefore* are boring, but writers know that even apparently dry words like that can contribute to our writing in powerful ways."

SHARE

Learning from Our Best Work

Share a choice that one student made about how to set up her writer's notebook in ways that support great writing. In this case, you could share the idea that our own writing can remind us to write well.

"Writers, can I have your attention please? I want to show you the smartest thing! Celena took the story she wrote earlier this year and taped it to the inside cover of her writer's notebook. She said to me, 'When I reread it, I remember all the stuff I did in that story. Then I tell myself to do it again.'"

Ask children to set up the same kind of support in their own notebooks. In this case, ask them to mark places in their own notebooks they need to continue to learn from in future writing.

"I suspect every one of us could try Celena's idea! Right now, I'm going to pass out a copy of the personal narrative you published toward the start of this year. Would each of you read your own writing to yourself and put stars at every place in your own text where you say, 'I did something that I need to remember and do again.' After a few minutes, share what you realized with your partner."

Ask children to find, note, and share with their partners great parts of the writing they've done so far in this unit.

"After you've done this, would you look over what you've written so far in this unit, and find the part that makes you most proud. It might be a place where you made an important decision, or wrote some great dialogue, or selected an exactly true word. It might be a really catchy sentence. When you find that part, but a little smiley face next to that spot."

I watched the students as they took a few minutes to look through their drafts. I coached students who needed help finding value in their work, and set some children up as talent scouts for each other.

"Now that each of you has a spot in your piece you are especially proud of, take a minute to share that part with your partner. Don't just read that bit; tell your partner why you like that spot, and talk about how you wrote it—what strategies you used. When you're done sharing, ask your partner, 'What do you think?' Partners, start with a compliment. Something you really admire about the writing. If you have a small suggestion for how the writer could perhaps make that good work even stronger, that'd be great, because after all, the time to revise is when our writing is already really strong. That way, we can make our best work even better."

This is a great way to help children see and solidify what they've learned about writing to date, but it is far from the only helpful Share possible. Nearly any words of wisdom or meaning-laden object from one child will inspire other children to find similar bits of wisdom for their writing supports. It's like stories about pets—once a child tells one pet story aloud, many other students are suddenly bursting with animal stories!

If students become inspired by this session, you may want to spend some time creating writing spaces within your classroom. You might ask children to bring in quotes, objects, and photographs that they find inspirational. If your children have cubbies or tables or cozy writing spots, you may give students some time to create writing spaces for themselves, just like yours.

There are times in a unit when the work may get a little long, and the finish line may seem far away. Often a Share can be used as a place to catch our breath and have a small celebration. Since the drafting process may be lengthy in fiction, taking some time to do just that, while in the midst of revising, may be a welcome treat.

This session might inspire some classes to spend time creating writing spaces within the classroom. Children might bring in quotes, objects, and photographs that they find inspirational. However, if you notice students spending too much time fussing with their writing spaces, gently remind them of the writing space's purpose: writing!

HOMEWORK | *Creating a Writing Space*   Writers, you won't be surprised that for homework tonight, I want you to think about the writing place (and the reading place) you've made for yourself in your house. Ask yourself, "What do I need in order to do my best work as a writer? As a reader?" Think about how you can make a place for yourself where you can do the most powerful reading and writing possible. What can you put in your reading and writing nook that will remind you of your goals?

Your special place needn't be fancy. When I was first teaching, I made a place for myself in the basement beside the furnace. I used a discarded door as a desk. That may not sound very fancy to you, but I think the first big step I ever made toward becoming a writer was creating that office for myself, down there in the basement. After that, I began a ritual of writing every evening. What big step will *you* take to further your writing? Make a sketch and write an entry about your writing space—and of course, once that place is made, press on with your story!

TAILORING YOUR TEACHING

If your students seem confused about what items to place in their notebooks to inspire their writing . . . instead of asking students to draw inspiration from a mentor text or class chart, you might suggest that students look toward their own work for powerful writing lessons as they do in the share of this session. In *The Revision Toolbox*, Georgia Heard encourages writers to reread their own writing with the purpose of finding some piece of magic. She says that as she does this, she might happen upon "the rhythm of the line that I like best, or a vivid image, or a surprising simile or metaphor" (p. 75). As students do this, they can recopy or paste that bit of their own writing into their notebooks. You might tell students to name what they did in that bit that works so well. For example, perhaps they enjoy the way they used punctuation to add meaning in a certain passage, or perhaps they used powerful language instead of ordinary words such as said, nice, and fun. Once students have named the skill they used, tell them to hold on to the idea that using punctuation to add meaning (or using powerful language, or adding dialogue, and so on) can make your story much more interesting to read. Every time they look at that bit of writing in their notebooks, they will remember to do that in their writing every single day.

When students see that they can find the qualities of spectacular writing in their own work, and not just in the work of beloved authors, they realize that they can be their own writing teachers (and, when they share these bits with their writing partners, that they can be each other's writing teachers). This rereading for their own best writing is a skill that can be added to a drafting chart and then used over and over again while gathering in the notebook, drafting, and revising.

COLLABORATING WITH COLLEAGUES

You, your colleagues, and your children can study any aspect of fiction that catches your eye. The challenges are considerable, and opportunities to learn are everywhere you look. Take, for example, the use of dialogue.

Teach children that when a character speaks, the reader needs to hear a human voice. Most writers write by ear, listening to the music of the words as we put them on the page. We choose words that fit with our characters. The phone rings, and the teenager shuffles over to pick it up. "Yeah?" he says. On the other end of the phone it's an accountant. He says, "This is Mr. Farr, with whom am I speaking?" The cadence is different, the vocabulary is different. Each character's language reflects the person, just like each child in the classroom uses language in ways which reveal that person. Each of us has a rhythm and a way of talking that's all our own. Some of us talk fast. Some of us use fancy words. Some of us say certain things all the time. And language changes based on a character's mood. A mom in a hurry sounds different than a mom sitting in a patch of sunshine and reflecting on her day.

The characters in a story need to be widely differing people. They don't walk alike, dress alike, and they surely don't talk alike. They have small individualities of speech—just as I do, and you do too. Dialogue, voice, character—they are inseparable, and worthy of study.

Once children have studied dialogue in their own drafts, they can examine books they know well. Why does Nate the Great speak in such a pompous fashion: "I, Nate the Great, am a great detective"? What makes the words spoken by Koala Lou's mother so memorable: "Koala Lou, I DO love you! I always have, and I always will!"? These jewels are precious, and writers value them.

Teach children that fiction writers use dialogue to reveal relationships more than to convey facts. We are not apt to write like this, "Ever since my friend Kay was adopted by a family from Vermont six weeks ago, I've missed her!" Instead, fiction writers find other ways to embed explanatory information into a text, reserving dialogue as a way to reveal character and relationships. For example, a fiction writer might write, "Sasha quickened her step as she neared the mailbox. Before she reached up to open the door, she whispered, 'Please, Kay, please.' But the mailbox was empty. Just to be sure, Sasha put her hand into the box, and reached all the way to the back. Nothing. No letter. No postcard. Nothing. Not today, not yesterday, not any day since that sad, awful, terrible day when Kay was adopted."

Of course, dialogue is just one of a zillion possible topics which you and your colleagues might conceivably study together. Either way, I hope that when you and your colleagues meet together in your fiction study group, you'll consider making these into potluck occasions. I love it when a group of people agree that everyone will come bearing something to share: a fruit salad, a transcript of two children in a peer conference, copies of short stories that would be perfect as exemplar texts, homemade brownies, an excerpt from a professional book. Recently I brought two items to a study group. In Patricia MacLachlan's, *Unclaimed Treasures*, two youngsters prepare for the arrival of a new baby sister, and meanwhile engage in a spirited discussion about how one goes about naming a new child (or, I infer, a character). I could imagine spinning this into a minilesson:

> "The name. What's it to be?" asked Horace at lunch.
>
> "What name?" asked Willa.
>
> "The baby," said Horace patiently. "The baby's name."
>
> Willa's father drank some water.
>
> "We have never thought about names ahead of time," he said. "We had decided that naming children was much like naming dogs or guinea pigs. You had to see them first to know."
>
> Willa's mother nodded.
>
> "Willa came first," she said, remembering. "Pushing and squalling into the world."
>
> "We almost named her Fury," said Willa's father.
>
> "You didn't!" said Willa, aghast.
>
> "No." Her father reached over to smooth her hair. "We named you after a pioneer. The writer, Willa Cather. You were, after all, our first pioneer into the world."
>
> "Nicholas we named after a horse I once knew," said Willa's mother, making them laugh. She looked at them indignantly. "I loved that horse. He was pleasant and dependable, with quirks now and then."
>
> "Such as riding too close to fences," said Willa's father, "and under low trees."
>
> "That's true, isn't it?" Willa's mother smiled at them all. "I suspect we'll think of a name when we see the baby. Her."
>
> "There's always Wanda," suggested Willa slyly.
>
> "I think," said Horace, leaning his elbows on the table, "that if I were to have a child I would name her Jane."
>
> "Jane?" Willa's mother looked at Horace.
>
> Horace nodded.
>
> "Jane," he said. "Straightforward and honest and calm."
>
> "Like you," said Willa's mother, something in her tone and look causing Willa to peer at Horace more closely.
>
> "Jane," said Horace, biting into a green Granny Smith.

I also brought an opening paragraph from Patricia MacLachlan's *Journey*:

> Mama named me Journey. Journey, as if somehow she wished her restlessness on me. But it was Mama who would be gone the year that I was eleven—before spring crashed onto our hillside with explosions of mountain laurel, before summer came with the soft slap of the screen door, breathless nights, and mildew on the books. I should have known, but I didn't . . .

I hope that you give yourself the gift of a study group of colleagues—and then, invent a host of topics to study together.

USING MENTOR TEXTS TO FLESH OUT CHARACTERS

IN THIS SESSION, YOU WILL REMIND STUDENTS THAT WRITERS STUDY MENTOR AUTHORS TO NOTICE WHAT OTHER WRITERS DO THAT REALLY WORKS. ONE THING WRITERS DO IS USE ACTIONS AND REVEALING DETAILS TO SHOW RATHER THAN TELL ABOUT OR EXPLAIN THE CHARACTER.

GETTING READY

- Excerpt from *Pippi Goes on Board* or a text important to you that shows character through actions, copied on chart paper or transparency
- Excerpt from your own writing or the class story you can use to demonstrate applying a mentor text
- Excerpt from *Fireflies!* or other familiar mentor text, copied on transparency or chart paper
- See CD-ROM for resources

Just as I hope that over time my students learn that essays, stories, and other written genres each have a "way they usually go," so, too, do I hope that you, my colleagues, will come to sense that genre-based units of study also have a familiar pattern. Early in a unit, we help students live the kind of life that writers of this genre are apt to live, collecting the sorts of entries helpful to this kind of writing. While living the life of this sort of writer, students also read texts that resemble those they aspire to write so that a bit later in the unit, they can begin to sketch or chart or outline a plan for their own first draft. Eventually, the emphasis of our teaching and our students' work shifts toward revising texts. Now students will revisit the texts they immersed themselves in earlier, only this time they'll admire and study them, asking, "What has this mentor author done that I could try?"

When I was a little girl, I often pretended to be a character from one of the novels or short stories my parents or grandparents had read out loud to me. I explored the backs of the wardrobes in my grandparents' house, hoping to find another Narnia inside them, just like in The Lion, the Witch and the Wardrobe. For a while, I acted just like Pippi Longstocking, producing a great deal more bravado than I actually felt inside, but I was trying her character on for size—yearning to live a life as full of adventure as Pippi's.

Characters are the heart and soul of fiction. Without strong characters, fiction falls apart—it becomes merely a reporting of events. Readers don't care what happens in the story unless we care about the character, and what makes us care is being able to see a flesh-and-blood character who shares thoughts and emotions similar to their own.

This final revision session, then, aims to help children flesh out their characters by make reading-writing connections. The session could invite students to consider any one of a zillion different aspects of character development in particular and well-written narratives in general, and hopefully it will serve you as a template for various other minilessons. For now, I've chosen to address an especially critical quality of character development and good writing. This session aims to help children more deeply understand the adage "show, don't tell" by applying it to character portrayal.

MINILESSON

Using Mentor Texts to Flesh Out Characters

CONNECTION

Remind children of the lessons from the previous session and connect them to today's work. In this case, remind students that revision starts with rereading through a lens.

"Writers, you have learned that revision begins with literally re-visioning, reseeing our own text, and that we do so by reading through a lens, asking particular questions. We can reread our draft asking, 'What sense will a stranger make of this?' Sometimes when we do that, we realize that our story is a lot of 'he saids' and 'she saids'—that it almost seems to float, without being grounded in the specific world of the story."

Remind students that they can go to texts they love to figure out what the authors have done and then apply that to their own writing.

"Today I want to be sure you realize that there is a place that we, as writers, can go to get new glasses—new lenses—with which to view our drafts. And this is the place: We can go to stories that resemble the ones we hope to write. We can let specific parts (or aspects) of a story matter to us. We can feel the lump in our throat, or see ourselves pull in close at a favorite part, or sense ourselves getting hooked by the story. Then we can ask, 'What did this author do that seems to work so well?' And we can reread our own draft, asking, 'Are there places in my draft where I could use that same technique?' And then, reseeing can lead us to rewriting."

TEACHING

Explain that all writers read, first to be open to the power of the story, and later to learn how writing is made. Demonstrate this with a text that is important to you.

"Most writers—writers like Walter Dean Myers and Eve Bunting and Eloise Greenfield—don't have a daily schedule with time in each day set aside for instruction in writing. But authors know that they can make their own writing workshop, and to do so they read. 'I learned how to write from writers,' Cynthia Rylant says. 'I didn't know any personally, but I read.'"

"If we want to learn from another writer, we first need to open ourselves to that author's story. Then, once we let a story get through to us, we stop and say, 'Why am I crying?' or 'Why is my heart ready to burst?' and we ask, 'What has the author done that makes this part of the story so powerful for me?'"

COACHING

Notice that this is the third time in this unit of study when I've emphasized the importance of studying texts written by other authors in order to develop our own repertoire of techniques. If I hope this unit will truly lead children to learn to rely on mentor texts, I need to do a lot more than merely mentioning the value of mentor texts!

"I've been rereading *Pippi Goes on Board,* a book that was incredibly important to me as a child; I've been remembering that Pippi was a hero to me. She had such bravado, such strength. Now, rereading this book, I find myself gasping at the power of even seemingly ordinary sections. For example, last night I read about how Pippi walked to town. That was it. Nothing great happened in the story. But for some reason, this section of the story really got to me. So I reread it, asking, 'What has Astrid Lindgren done in her story that makes it so powerful?' Listen to it and see what *you* think."

> A few minutes later they were marching down the road to town—Tommy, Annika, and Pippi with Mr. Nilsson on her shoulder. The sun was shining so gloriously, the sky was so blue, and the children were so happy! And in the gutter along the roadside the water flowed merrily by. It was a very deep gutter with a great deal of water in it.
>
> "I love gutters," said Pippi and, without giving much thought to the matter, stepped into the water. It reached way over her knees, and as she skipped along briskly it splattered Tommy and Annika.
>
> "I'm making believe I'm a boat," she said, plowing through the water. Just as she spoke she stumbled and went down under.
>
> "Or, to be more exact, a submarine," she continued calmly when she got her nose in the air again.
>
> "Oh, Pippi, you're absolutely soaked," said Annika anxiously.
>
> "And what's wrong with that?" asked Pippi. "Is there a law that children should always be dry? I've heard it said that cold showers are very good for the health."

"I realized that Astrid Lindgren didn't just *say* what Pippi did—that Pippi walked down the street en route to town. She *showed* Pippi doing this, and did so in a way that put a Pippi-like imprint on the experience. Pippi didn't walk to town in the same way that you and I might. She walked in her own uniquely adventurous way."

Demonstrate applying the technique you've noted from the mentor text to your own writing. Debrief.

"So class, after I notice something that an author I admire has done, I think to myself, 'Are there places in my draft where I could use the same technique?' So let me reread our Luz story and see if I can not only tell what Luz does, but show how she does that thing—and in so doing, convey what she's like as a person."

Notice that we do not approach a text looking for examples of literary devices. We read with receptivity, letting ourselves be blown away by the story. Only later, after weeping, gasping, laughing, do we pause to think, "What did the author do to create such an effect?"

*Jane Burroway reminds us, "Your fiction can only be as successful as the characters who move it and move within it . . . we must find them interesting, we must find them believable, and we must care about what happens to them." (*Writing Fiction, *p. 100)*

Lots of people grow up believing that they don't have what it takes to be a writer. "Writers," they think, "have very special talents." In a writing workshop, we try to help children realize that in fact, the skills and talents writers draw upon are available to all of us. In this minilesson, I essentially say that we can learn how to be great from the books around us. I intend this to be a powerful, lifelong lesson. In this way, I try to lure all the children into believing that becoming a great writer is possible for them.

I quickly reread the story and circled a section that described Luz trying to fall asleep at the slumber party. "I think I could write this in more detail, and this time really show Luz's fears—and show her, too," I said. I wrote:

> I pulled my sleeping bag as high as it would go without covering my nose. I heard a strange noise by the window and imagined big hairy beasts slamming though the front door, grabbing us up in our sleeping bags and carrying us away. I squeezed my eyes shut, so tightly I could see stars. "Don't think about those things," I said to myself.

"Do you see how I used some actions by Luz to show more about what she's like? That's what Astrid did with her character Pippi, and so that's what I tried to do."

ACTIVE ENGAGEMENT

Ask children to use the text you offer as a mentor text, studying an excerpt for what they might try. Ask them to discuss with their partner ways to apply what they discover to the class story.

"Now let's try to do this whole process together. We've talked about how you love this section of *Fireflies!* when the narrator traipses off to bed, his jar of fireflies in hand. Tell your partner what Brinckloe has done here that works so well that you could, conceivably, try doing in your writing."

> Daddy called from the hallway,
>
> "See you later, alligator."
>
> "After a while, crocodile," I called back.
>
> "I caught hundreds of fireflies—"

I listened as children talked to teach other, and then convened the class.

Henry said, "The author uses the real words that kids say, so the story sounds true."

"So let's look back at this section of our Luz story, and could you and your partner think together about whether *Fireflies!* gives you ideas for how you could revise our story:

> The doorbell rang. "Welcome, come in," Luz said. Soon the room was filled with girls.

Before long, this section had been revised:

> The doorbell rang. "Hey!" Luz said jumping aside in a gesture that said, "Come in!" Then Luz added, "Pizzas comin', lots of them."

My apprenticeship in this instance is very open-ended, and you may decide to be much more explicit about the way in which a writer can emulate another text. For example, you may decide to teach children to copy sentences they love from the mentor text, to name what specifically they love about a particular sentence and then to emulate that quality.

If you feel it's likely your students can't yet follow this process easily, you might lengthen the active engagement section of this minilesson to include charting together the steps writers need to take to learn from mentor authors. The chart would end up something like this:

Studying Mentor Texts for Our Own Writing
- *Select a part of the story that works for you.*
- *Name specifically what the author did on the page.*
- *Suppose why the author did this particular thing.*
- *Look at your own writing and find places where it would help the text to try something similar.*
- *Try it!*

Remind the children of all their options for revision today and anytime they revise. Remind them they can always turn to mentor texts to discover ways to revise.

"So writers, you already know that for the next few days, you'll shift between writing scenes of your story and revising scenes. If you want to revise, you can definitely reread with the lens of 'Does my story make sense?' You may notice, as we discussed yesterday, that some scenes seem to float—in which case, be sure to detail who is talking, where the person is, and what the person does. And you may decide to find another lens for revisioning your draft. You can learn ways to resee your draft if you find a text you admire, notice a section of the text that seems to work especially well, and then ask yourself, 'What did this author do that I could try?'"

WRITING AND CONFERRING

Helping Struggling Readers

When you confer today, you'll probably check in with your struggling writers first to be sure that each one has a mentor text in hand that he or she can read. You may feel tempted to leave the child with a text that the student "knows by heart" but the truth is that you're asking children to reread and examine the wording an author has used, and this is challenging enough when we can read the text.

Mel Levine says: "Writing is the largest orchestra a kid's mind has to conduct" (*The Myth of Laziness*, p. 7). There are enough things for a struggling student to contend with when writing—reading should not be one of them.

Once you've made sure that each of your strugglers has a mentor text he or she can read, you'll want to coach the child to notice something admirable in the mentor text. Help the child do so by taking any paragraph at all, and then thinking, "What do I like in this passage?" It doesn't help to scan the whole text, over and over, looking for a noteworthy feature. Zooming in early on makes it more likely the child will notice craftsmanship. Help the child to talk about what the author has done. Then show the child that he or she could take that same technique and apply it to his or her own writing. You'll probably want to demonstrate this, saying, "I could imagine your story might go like this . . . " You may want to give two or three examples of the way the child could use that one technique in a variety of ways.

Of course, you'll also want to confer with your stronger writers. Resist the urge to only go to the students who need us the most and leave the more sophisticated writers alone, rationalizing that they know about writing. The truth is, even professional writers rely on the advice and suggestions of their editors to help them develop their work. It is crucial that we offer our strong writers opportunities to develop their skills as individuals.

We can offset the concern that we'll have nothing to teach our skilled writers by taking time to plan some possible teaching points.

MID-WORKSHOP TEACHING POINT | ***Naming an Author's Techniques*** "Writers, today we reminded ourselves that we can take courses from any writer, living or dead, as long as we are willing to really study what that author has done. We studied the way the father and son in *Fireflies*! said good night to each other—'See you later, alligator. After a while, crocodile.' But we didn't say, 'We liked the way Brinckloe's characters said good night to each other' and we didn't have Luz turn off the light and say to her friends, 'See you later, alligator.' Instead, we named our observations, saying, 'The author uses words that people actually say to make the story sound true.'"

"But some of you have been telling me that you didn't really get how to do this. Let me try to help you. First I explain to myself what an author has done. Let's use Brinckloe's description of the dying fireflies in the jar."

> And the light grew dimmer, green, like moonlight under water.

"Then I try to talk about what I notice she actually did. (I don't say how it worked: 'I can picture it.') I say what she has done."

continued on next page

Colleen pulled up a seat next to Hannah, curious to know how Hannah was doing with her character who was only five years old—the same age as Hannah's little brother.

Hannah explained that she had changed the character to a little girl, "Angelina," so her story would be fiction. "Now I won't be tempted to copy my little brother," she said.

"Hannah, it's brave of you to choose a character who is five years old, and I'm glad you are drawing on what you know from your brother. And that you are taking the risk of writing about a character who is a bit different from you. Good writers are risk-takers—but then, you knew that right?"

Hannah nodded, clearly pleased by her teacher's support.

"I want to let you in on something. Lots of fiction writers say that every character in a story contains a bit of the writer. Even though I'm not like Luz, because I'm grown-up and I'm not having slumber parties anymore, I still know what it's like to want to fit in with other people. And I also know what it's like to be afraid. I can take those parts of myself and let them help me as I work on my character so that she becomes even more believable—more real—because she has bits of me inside her. Do you think there's a way you can do some of that work?"

Hannah's whole face lit up, "Well yeah. I'm already thinking of my brother to get ideas of what a five-year-old does and thinks. And my brother is kind of a part of me. But I can also think about what *I* was like when I was five. Like, I loved art and sometimes I would get in trouble for getting into things I shouldn't have gotten into, and I could never figure out what the big deal was. I could make Angelina a little like that too." Hannah started to jot some things down right away.

---

continued from previous page

"She wrote one sentence that has three parts to it. The first part tells what the light did (it grew dimmer), then the next phrase describes it (green), and the final phrase compares it to something else (like moonlight under water)."

"Then, I try to figure out why she wrote like that. I think Brinckloe probably wanted to tell what happened, then to show how it happened. Now, having spelled out what the author did, I can try it in my own draft. So right now, reread a mentor text that matters to you, and follow these same steps. For me, I'd tell what something did, then I'd describe it, then I'd compare it to something else. Do this with your own text now, with your partner's help."

SHARE

Highlighting Revision

Share examples of actions revealing emotions. Remind writers they can do this in their own writing.

"Writers, this morning, as I was waiting for you to line up in the yard, I took a few minutes to watch the kindergartners lining up. I noticed they line up differently than you. First of all, most of them weren't talking. Yet I could still sort of tell how they were feeling. One little girl fell on the ground, then started rubbing her knee. At first she didn't cry, but then all of a sudden her lip started to tremble and a big fat tear rolled down her cheek. I could tell she was kind of surprised that her knee hurt. Then I noticed a little boy who was clutching a teddy bear to his chest. He couldn't stand still. He kept smiling and hopping up and down. I could tell he was really excited. I didn't need to hear their words to guess how they were feeling. Just by watching their actions and gestures, I could tell their feelings."

"I'm telling you this because it is really important, when you write, to use actions to show your character's feelings. Let me share with you some smart work I saw Leo do today. He studied *Fireflies!* and he noticed this section of it:"

> I tried to swallow,
> but something in my throat would not go down.
> I shut my eyes tight and put the pillow over my head.
> They were my fireflies.

"He decided that Brinckloe used actions to show feelings: the character tried to swallow, he put a pillow over his head. So, Leo made a little tiny scene at the start of his own story, and had his character do an action that showed her feeling of loneliness. You can do this too! Listen:" [Fig. XIII-1]

> Alicia was a nobody. She had no friends and always sat in the corner. She was always seen walking home from school alone. None of the kids in her fourth grade class cared if she was there or not.
>
> Each night Alicia thought about friends. She dreamed about them too. One night Alicia looked out the window and saw a beautiful starry sky. She had been thinking about Tatiana, Alicia's dream friend. Alicia looked up and saw a star shoot across the night sky.
>
> Alicia made a wish, "I wish I had a friend."

> Alicia was a nobody. She had no friends and always sat in the corner. She was always seen walking home from school alone. None of the kids in her fourth grade class cared if she was there or not.
>
> Each night Alicia thought about friends. She dreamed about them too. One night Alicia looked out the window and saw a beautiful starry sky. She had been thinking about Tatiana, Alicia's dream friend. Alicia looked up and saw a star shoot across the night sky.
>
> Alicia made a wish, "I wish I had a friend."

Fig. XIII-1 Leo's notebook entry

⊙ HOMEWORK   *Naming Our Stories*   "Writers, have you ever named someone? A brother or sister? A pet? It is an amazing responsibility. Tonight, it is time for you to consider names for your story. List ten titles, considering the significance of each. Your title, like *Charlotte's Web*, might have a double meaning. *Charlotte's Web* is a book about a spider who weaves a web, but we know that webs are also seen as things that are very craftily made—like the way that Charlotte craftily saves Wilbur's life. And *Because of Winn-Dixie* has one of the main character's names in it, but it also tells us something about the book. Things happen to Opal because Winn-Dixie is in her life.

Tonight, I want you to spend some time thinking about your favorite titles for books, then try to figure out why you think the authors chose them. After you've done that, don't just slap the first title that comes to mind on your story. Jot down a list of titles, then choose the one that you think really connects to some big ideas you have in your story, one that will really catch a reader's interest.

⊙ TAILORING YOUR TEACHING

If your students characters simply aren't fleshed out much yet . . . you might try simply letting them have more time to focus on their characters. You might start a minilesson with the purposes of allowing students more time to focus on their characters something like this: "The other day, I told you about a story—*Pippi Longstocking*—that really mattered to me when I was a child. And the reason the story mattered was that the character Pippi mattered. You and I can listen to the news and hear about all sorts of bad things happening to people, and we don't usually find ourselves reduced to tears. But in the stories we really love, when bad things happen to the character, we find ourselves totally devastated—almost as if these things were happening to us. When we know a lot about a person or character, even if we've never met him or her, they matter to us. Have you let your readers know enough about your characters so that the reader can really care about them? Writers do that. Today, would you reread your story, and find ways to let your character shine through even more? If your character walks down the street, ask yourself, 'How can she—or he—so this in a way that shows who she is as a person?' Then try some revisions."

Naming characters is no small project for some writers! Colleen once wrote a list seventy-five titles long to find the perfect name for her own book. You might find, as Colleen did, that students will still need input from other writers to help narrow down the options and commit to a final title.

COLLABORATING WITH COLLEAGUES

As you and your colleagues help children find ways to create memorable characters, you might want to consider some of the less obvious or direct ways in which this can be done. For example, you might think about how writers reveal things through characters' observations of other characters, or of places or things.

You'll notice that many of the stories you've read with your students include animals, and that the animals often have profound effects on the characters. In "Spaghetti," for example, the kitten Gabriel finds brings Gabriel out of his isolation and loneliness. Gabriel feels an immediate connection with the kitten. His observations of it tell us a great deal about who Gabriel is and how his experiences have shaped him.

When Gabriel sees the kitten, he notices its "skinny stick-legs, wobbling to and fro." Gabriel doesn't see an infected animal, or think the kitten is pathetic or ugly or something to avoid. He sees an animal that is small, weak, and underfed. We know that Gabriel lives in a run-down building and that he doesn't have much to eat himself (recall that he thinks about his "butter sandwich"), so we can surmise he is poor. It's not surprising, then, that he would notice the kitten's thin legs and its wobbly state. Gabriel is someone who notices other creatures' needs and can empathize. It's telling, too, that Gabriel thinks the kitten smells like noodles—a pleasant, comforting smell. Later Rylant writes that "Gabriel was amazed. He had never imagined he would be lucky enough one day to find a kitten." Gabriel can't imagine his good fortune. How could he have been so lucky? Someone who has had more in life than Gabriel might not consider this kitten such an extraordinary find. Gabriel's amazement reveals

how much he wants to be needed, to have something to love, to find a friend. Gabriel isn't used to having much of anything at all.

As we see the kitten through Gabriel's eyes, we learn volumes about Gabriel himself. We see not only how Gabriel's life and experiences have shaped him, but also what he longs for and how he comes out of his shell. It would be interesting to have students think about how they would describe a kitten they saw in the middle of the road. They also might think about how Cynthia Rylant might have added to Gabriel's observations of the kitten–how the kitten might have triggered memories that would reveal details about Gabriel's backstory, or his dreams. Have kids imagine things authors can show about characters through their observations.

To help children understand how description reveals character, you might find it useful to have them do exercises in which they observe a place or an object through different eyes. For example, one teacher I know tells her students to imagine a barn and then to describe the barn as if they're one person (someone from the city) and then as if they're someone else (a person seeking shelter) and then someone altogether different. She says to children, "Look at the barn. Imagine you're an angry farmer. What do you see? What do you notice?" You could also try an exercise that focuses on objects. Picture the same people who were looking at the barn now holding something in their hands instead. What are they holding and how does this object reflect who they are? Or what thoughts do they have about the object? How do the objects bring these characters to life? You'll want children to imagine all sorts of ways they might reveal their characters without directly describing them.

EDITING WITH VARIOUS LENSES

In this session, as in other editing sessions, you will remind your children of all the editing skills you have already taught including paragraphing, use of end punctuation and capital letters, use of quotation marks, use of tenses, use of high frequency words, use of common irregular verbs and so forth. Now you will add onto that list, with the new skills joining the others on a cumulative editing chart that remains posted in your classroom year-round. As the list grows, so do your children's abilities to effectively and independently edit their work.

Fiction stories pose special editing challenges. The stories tend to be long, which means that editing and recopying will take more than a day. The children will be chomping at the bit to share these stories, and the fact that their author celebration can't occur until they've edited and recopied will frustrate some of them. For you, the trick will be to show children that just as you earlier taught them revision is a way to honor their best efforts, so, too, editing is also a way to celebrate a text.

The second major challenge that children usually face when editing these stories is that the excitement of writing fiction will have inspired them to use more sophisticated vocabulary than they might normally use, and their stories will be chock full of invented spellings. Fixing every misspelled word can feel like an impossible task. You will need to remind students of all the resources they already have in their "spelling toolboxes" as well as teaching them some strategies they can use to figure out correct spellings on their own. You might have already taught your class some of these strategies in your Word Study curriculum. If this is the case, all the better!

In this session, you will teach students how to edit their work by rereading with great care and thinking about everything they know about grammar and punctuation. You will ask them to think especially carefully about spelling, and you will teach them how to use the wealth of strategies and resources available to them.

IN THIS SESSION, YOU WILL EXPLAIN THAT JUST AS FICTION WRITERS REVISE WITH "LENSES," THEY EDIT WITH THEM AS WELL, REREADING THEIR WRITING SEVERAL TIMES FOR SEVERAL REASONS, MAKING EDITS AS THEY GO.

GETTING READY
- Passage from the class story you can use to demonstrate rethinking word choice
- See CD-ROM for resources

MINILESSON

Editing with Various Lenses

CONNECTION

Remind children that editing involves bringing all that the writer knows and is able to do to the draft. Tell students they will be rereading carefully, and relying on class editing lists, on resources such as dictionaries, and on each other as they seek to correct and clean up their drafts.

"You've all worked hard and should be so proud of yourselves. I know you are as excited as I am to share your stories with the rest of our community. But, before we do that, there is important work ahead. We still need to edit these stories so that not only the ideas and craft of the stories, but also the spelling, punctuation, and grammar of them will all reflect the best that you can do."

"Remember, as you prepare to edit your stories, that a writer calls to mind everything that he or she knows about spelling, punctuation, and grammar—you can recall those tools and mentally lay them out for yourself even before you reread, rather like a carpenter lays out the necessary tools as a way to prepare for his work. Keep these tools in mind as you re-read your story. While you reread, be especially on the lookout for misspelled words because I know that many of you pushed yourselves to reach for the precisely right word as you wrote and that this led you to write with words you haven't tackled before. You were inventive spellers in this unit of study and that's been great to see—but you will want to be sure you spell conventionally before you bring your stories to the world."

"Remember that when we want to fix up our spelling, we rely not only on the strategies we have for effective spelling but also on resources that are outside ourselves in order to be sure our spellings are accurate. In specific, we rely on distant teachers—the authors of written materials—and on nearby teachers—the writers in our community—to help us go beyond what we can do on our own."

COACHING

As you teach this minilesson, you will want to have the cumulative chart of all that the class has learned thus far in the year close by you as you teach. That chart will contain skills you have taught during word study time as well as the writing workshop, and of course it will be a very different chart for third graders than for fifth graders, and for more inexperienced writers than for children who have grown up in a writing workshop.

Name your teaching point, Specifically, tell children that when rereading their drafts, if they find misspelled words they should circle these, and then try them again. Teach them strategies for progressing from a spelling that is invented to a spelling that is conventional.

"Today I am going to teach you, (actually, I will be reminding rather than teaching you), that before or after you edit your draft for other concerns—paragraphing, punctuation and so forth—you will want to read your draft, checking on your spellings. Usually this means eyeing each word and thinking, 'Does this look right?' It also means rereading the letters in each word to double-check that those letters actually do spell the word you have in mind. When a writer is uncertain whether a word is correctly spelled, we generally mark that word (in this class, circle it) and then we try spelling the word again and again, drawing on all we know and on all the help we can locate to assist us with those spellings. I will show you how to go through this progression of work."

TEACHING

Referring to the good work one child has just done, emphasize that writers reread a draft many times, checking for first one sort of editing concern, then for another. Include in your summary of the work one child has already done an overview of how you hope children go about checking for punctuation and tense and consistency.

"Deveonna finished drafting and revising her story yesterday and without my saying anything to her at all, she began editing it. She did something really smart that I want to remind all of you to do. She reread her draft, looking first for one 'kind of thing,' and then she reread it, looking for another 'kind of thing.' Each writer will proceed in a different sequence, but none of us can simply reread our draft once, fixing everything we want to fix! We all need to do as Deveonna did, and reread it multiple times."

"Deveonna read her draft first for punctuation and capital letters. She read it aloud to herself, adding in any periods that she'd missed. Like the rest of you, she didn't have a lot of trouble with end punctuation—she mostly adds periods when she drafts. But because Deveonna had tried to write this story in a way which built up tension and created suspense, she'd written with some sentences that required pretty complicated punctuation, so in this draft, she included ellipses, parentheses, and lots of sentences that used commas in complicated ways. If Deveonna *had* noticed that she hadn't used a variety of punctuation, she might have regarded that as a clue that she could use editing as a time to

It would have been very easy to simply say, "Today I will teach you how to edit your draft." The reason that this teaching point is long and clunky is that I try to do more than name the subject of the minilesson. I try to actually tell children the answer to the question—in this case, I try to tell them how to edit their drafts—so that this section of the minilesson crystallizes the most important message of the session.

When the children write fiction, we teach them that after they come up with a gigantic sequence of events, they need to decide which of those events will be backstory. Which will happen before the opening scene actually plays out? So in Because of Winn-Dixie, *for example, while Opal shops for tomatoes at the local grocery store, the reader learns that she has already suffered the loss of her mother, and she has already moved to this new Florida town. Similarly, when teaching a minilesson, we need to think of the entire sequence of work that we want to support and then we, too, can decide which part of that sequence of work will have happened off stage, and which part of it will be emphasized because it actually unfolds on stage in the minilesson. In this minilesson, I summarize what Deveonna has already done, hoping as I do so to lightly support children in doing similar work. The "story" actually begins with me demonstrating how Deveonna does the one thing I want to highlight now, which is checking for tenses and misspellings.*

really listen to her sentences, combining some or tweaking others so they built up the drama of the story."

"After Deveonna checked for punctuation and capital letters, she decided to reread using a different lens. This time, she paid attention to her tenses. And again, she found that especially in the sections of her story where she really reached to write beautifully and well, she'd sometimes written in ways that shifted between past tense and present tense. Deveonna thought to herself, "I better be clear. Am I writing about something that is happening now, or about something that happened a while ago, like last year?" She decided she wanted the story to be in past tense, so watch and join me as I show you how she doubled-checked for tense consistency. Let's look at this section of her story. It tells that the protagonist, Elexa, hides behind a tree with her best friend, Lexi, hoping to hide from her stalker."*[Fig. XIV-1]*

> When I reach her, she puts her hand on her face, and shakes her head, then points behind me. I turn, and there was the most unwanted person ever... "Sir Stocker Max." On the inside, I could have made my head exploaded. I hide behind Lexie, as if I were a baby and she was mom that has to protect me.

"Deveonna reread the first sentence. 'This sounds like it is happening now: "When I reach her, she puts..."that is now. If I want this to be past tense, I better change it.'"

> When I reached her, Lexi put her hand on her face, and shakes her head....

"Hmm...that sounds wrong. Did I just switch back out of past tense? Let me look...I did. I can fix that."

> When I reached her, Lexi put her hand on my face and shook her head, then pointed behind me... "Sir Stocker Max."

Describe and then demonstrate how the child reread, checking spellings. Highlight the fact that the writer tried the word in question several times, seeking outside resources after she'd drawn on her own resources.

"After rereading first for punctuation, then for tenses (checking that the action was either consistently in the past or consistently in the present tense), Deveonna paid special attention to spelling. She inched her way through the text, checking each and every word. When she came across a misspelled word that she knew, that was easy! She simply corrected it right then and there."

It is crucial for you to notice that I don't go through this student's entire draft. Why do so? I can make my point much more succinctly by focusing on just a tiny chunk of the text. Notice this is not the lead of the story: the lead didn't pose as many editing issues as did this excerpt. Notice also that in the summary of how Deveonna dealt with tenses, I taught briskly and incompletely. I can't go back and teach an entire hour-long session in which I define tenses, go through the fact that action words can be called verbs, show children that verbs change in past and present and future tenses and so forth. In order to write, children need to orchestrate a vast number of skills and strategies. There is absolutely no way to teach any one of those in enormous detail at one time in a minilesson. In order to maintain the full orchestration that comprises writing, we often teach incompletely, over-simplifying. Even if we decided to teach a subject fully and completely, children can only learn one or two increments at a time, so I think it is wise to resign oneself to the fact that we will revisit all that we teach over and over, month after month and certainly year after year, and each time our teaching can become a bit more complex.

> While I ran to her, I shouted, Hey Lexie, over here, its me Elexa. She waved to me a kind of wave that meant stay back, but I didn't! When I reached her, she had put her hand on her face, and shook her head, then pointed behind me. I turned and there was the most unwanted person ever... stalker Max. On the inside I felt like I was going to explode. I thought back to the last person that was followed by him... they had to move to Queens! I hid behind Lexie, as if I were a baby, and she was the mother that had to protect me.

Fig. XIV-1 Deveonna edits her tenses in the midst of her draft.

"But, since Deveonna is the kind of writer who pushes herself to use sophisticated language in her work, she also found words that she was not sure how to spell. For example, in this paragraph, she used some very specific, colorful words—'explode' and 'protect'—and she wasn't sure how to spell those. This is what she did, watch." I said and then circled those words. Then, I showed that Deveonna pulled out a sticky note tag and put one beside each of the troublesome words. Before having a second "go", with *protet*, I showed that Deveonna reread her first try at the word, thinking aloud to herself, "Is *part* of this right?" She copied the first syllable as she'd written it. Then I showed her saying the word again, hearing the sound she'd deleted (the *c* sound) and adding that into her new version of the word. "Does this look right now?" Deveonna asked herself, and when she thought yes, she copied the new spelling into her draft.

"After going through a similar sequence with the word, "explode," Deveonna was still not able to correct her misspelled version: *exploaded*. At that point, Deveonna asked herself whether she might be able to find that word written somewhere close at hand: perhaps on a chart in the classroom, a word list, in a story in her writing folder, or a reference book such as an atlas. Deveonna decided that she would be better off in this case asking her writing partner, who she knew was a strong speller, to help her fix up her spelling. With the help of her partner, she picked the version of the word that looked correct and made the change in her story."

Debrief, highlighting the replicable process one child demonstrated that you hope others follow.

"Did you see that first Deveonna reread for punctuation, then for keeping the action in her story consistently in the past tense or in the present tense. Then she reread for spelling and marked words that looked wrong, trying them again on the side. In order to try them again, she examined her initial spelling to ask, 'Is part of this right?' and copied that part. Then she tried the puzzling part first by listening again to be sure she'd represented all the sounds, then by thinking if there were class resurces that could easily help her, and finally by recruiting her partner to help. This is the sort of work each of you will want to do today and whenever you edit your writing."

Of course, this minilesson must be revised so that it teaches your kids whatever is most essential for them to know. It may be that if you teach third graders who struggle with spellings, you may decide to emphasize simply the fact that writers say words really slowly and try to listen to be sure they have recorded each of the major sounds they hear when articulating the word. A version of this could also teach that writers don't simply sound out the missing sections, they ask, "Do I know of other words which include that sound?" That is, you could tuck lessons in using what you know in order to spell what you do not know how to spell.

You may decide to ask your children to pull out their drafts and reread the first paragraph to check for punctuation, perhaps talking with each other about what they notice. Then they can reread for tenses, and again they could (or could not) talk about what they notice. You'd need to decide how to work your time so this process doesn't extend the length of the minilesson. Sometimes when teachers ask children to get started on the work of the day while they are still sitting in the meeting area, the teachers decides to bypass the link and to simply gesture to one child, then another, to move to his or her seat, continuing the work in that place.

ACTIVE ENGAGEMENT

Set students up to follow the model you have given them, editing the next paragraph of the child's story.

"Now, you're going to assume the role of editor. With your partner, could you read the next section of Deveonna's story?" I said, passing out copies of just the next paragraph. Read it once, checking for and fixing punctuation. Then read it again, checking for and fixing tenses, then put on your 'check-for-spelling' lenses. If you find a misspelled word that you can't fix immediately, have a go on the side of the page, spelling the word several possible ways. Remember that you can use resources outside yourselves, such as other writers in our community."

> He comes even closer. Lexie whispers "oh, no." then I shout "RUN!" That's when we heard the bell, "dinnnnggg." We tried to run as fast as we can, but being so populur we don't run a lot but we try. We rush for the door, trying to slip into class without being noticed by a hall monitor or a teacher.

"Writers, as I talked to some of you about your editing work on this section, I heard many of you say that you had found places where you could fix punctuation and grammar, such as changing the verbs to past tense and capitalizing the *t* in *then*. Many of you are also thinking especially hard about spelling."

LINK

Recall what you have taught and send children off to edit their own work.

"Writers, as you edit your fiction stories or any other piece of writing, remember that all of us, as writers, take editing very seriously. We generally reread our writing once, twice, three times, and often we make a decision, saying, 'This time I will read with this lens,' or 'This time I will rereads with that lens.' I have emphasized rereading for punctuation, tenses and spelling, but you may know that you need to reread and think about characters, or about being sure your draft makes sense. You are in charge of your own writing, and the real goal is to make sure that every word, every dot, is the best that it can be."

I hope you notice Deveonna's understanding of the ways being popular constrains the behavior of her protagonist. Elexa and Lexie are popular. "We tried to run as fast as we could, but being popular, we don't run a lot . . . ." You will need to decide when you want to open up some of the social issues that these stories will bring to light. I don't suggest you use this minilesson as a time to embark on a big discussion of Deveonna's understanding of what popular kids need to do in order to maintain their status. But you may well want to make an aside at some point, saying something like, "How sad that this character lives in a community of kids where kids feel that being liked by other kids is such a fragile thing that by merely running, a person jeopardizes her social status!"

> He came closer! Lexie whispered "OH, NO," then I shouted, "RUN!" We tryed to run as fast as we could, but we knew that wasn't fast. We rush for the door, trying to slip into class without being noticed by a teacher or just a hall monster.

Fig. XIV-2 Deveonna edited her story based on input from her peers.

WRITING AND CONFERRING

Making Editing Choices

"Writers, I gathered this group because I think that as you reread your story, you will find that you are not using a variety of punctuation marks. If almost every sentence of yours ends with a period and if you do not use parentheses, ellipses, colons or semi-colons, these are signs that your sentences plod along a bit. This is also a sign that there is one, fairly easy thing you can do to make your writing a whole lot better! Right now, I can show you how you can become writers who use a variety of punctuation marks, and the important thing about this is that writers who use a variety of punctuation marks are also writers with a more elastic sense for how sentences and paragraphs of print can create mood, tone, rhythm, and feelings."

"So take just a minute, and make a list of the punctuation you have already used in your story. See if I'm right when I said that I think that you've used mostly two or three forms of punctuation." The children did this, and concurred. "This means your writing can get better really easily. Writing with only a few kinds of punctuation is a bit like writing with half the alphabet!"

"Try revising your sentences—not toward the goal of using more punctuation because I don't think any writer on earth has ever sat down with the goal of writing with three semi-colons and an ellipsis! But try revising your sentence so that when people read your sentences, they'll be swept along in the feelings you want them to experience." Then, to demonstrate what I mean by this sort of sentence, I deliberately used one, gesturing with my hand at the places in my very long, oral sentence where the commas might go. "Try writing with a more elastic sense for how sentences can go, so that some of your sentences are long ones, with parts that pile up, one on top of the next, phrase after phrase, as you hear in this sentence of mine."

> MID-WORKSHOP TEACHING POINT **Editing with Attentiveness** ""Writers, can I stop you? I really, really need your attention. All eyes up here, all minds up here."
>
> I waited an extra-long time. "Writers, right now, I have your attention. You are listening keenly, attentively, with your minds turned onto high. What I want to tell you is this: this is the sort of keen attentiveness you need to bring to the job of editing. I know this will sound unbelievable to you, but I have actually seen some people leaning back in their chairs, editing like this", I said, and role played a lackadaisical, sloppy editor. The word editing should bring to mind a person who is sitting up, pencils sharpened, with extra-keen eyesight, eager to catch each and every little item."
>
> "In order to edit well, then, you need to have checklists at your side to remind you of details that deserve your attention. But you need your own personalized checklist for the ways of acting that can help you shift from playing the part of writer to playing the part of editor. Usually people use a special pen to edit. Usually people sit at a desk to edit. Often people read aloud (either actually, or in our minds) in order to edit. This can force us to really see and register each and every word. You need to devise your own personalized checklist for what you need to do in order to remake yourself from being the passionate writer who writes with great fervor toward being the meticulous, attentive editor who doesn't let anything go by, unchecked."

At this point my voice abruptly switched so I could demonstrate the opposite kind of sentences. "Try the opposite. Try making curt, brief points. Say what you mean. Be blunt. But then, turn a corner in your thinking, and suddenly let your sentences be large rambling ones once again, with ideas that link together, building off each other, expanding on earlier bits."

"Just to practice writing with sentences that convey your mood, would you right now imagine that you are running, running, through the school. Partner 2 [I reappointed people into these roles] say a long, rambling sentence to your partner, showing what you pass by as you run, how your body is feeling as you get more tired. Start, 'I ran out the door' . . . (keep going)."

"Now, just to practice writing in abrupt sentences, partner 1, would you be the principal who catches the runner. Tell the runner to stop. Order the runner to do one thing. Then order the runner to do another thing. Show your anger. But do so in very short, abrupt sentences. Partner 1, start by saying, "Stop . . . ."

After the writers did that, I said, "Right now would you look at your draft of a story and see if there is one place where the sentences should push readers to read faster and faster, in a piling up, expansive, warm (or frantic) kind of way. Mark that section with a marginal note: long sentences with commas and parenthesis. Then read your draft over and see if there is one place where the sentence structure should signal that this section is abrupt. Brief. Cold. Mark that section with a marginal note: Short sentences. Perhaps ellipses. Perhaps colons before a list."

"Once you have marked sections of your draft where you could revise your sentence structure, would you go back and write in the air with your partner, each of you taking a turn writing an oral version of each person's draft. Then see if you can get a small sheet of paper, rewrite the section on it, and tape it right on top of the original draft. Make sure the flap can lift up so I can later admire this important editing work."

"If you'd like a mentor test, use a copy of this draft of Ari's. In her editing she's made use of every conceivable punctuation mark—to strong effect! Listen to this:" *[Fig. XIV-3]*

> The next day, I was ready. Of course it was 5:07; the family had just sat down to dinner. I looked at them, both of them, squarely in the eyes. My palms sweat; my hand bounced; my pulse kicked into turbo drive.
>
> "Dear," my mom started, looking guiltily at me.
>
> "Yeah?" I said, looking up from the takeout Chinese food. "We . . . have to tell you something," said Dad, exchanging glances with Mom. I propped my head on my hand.

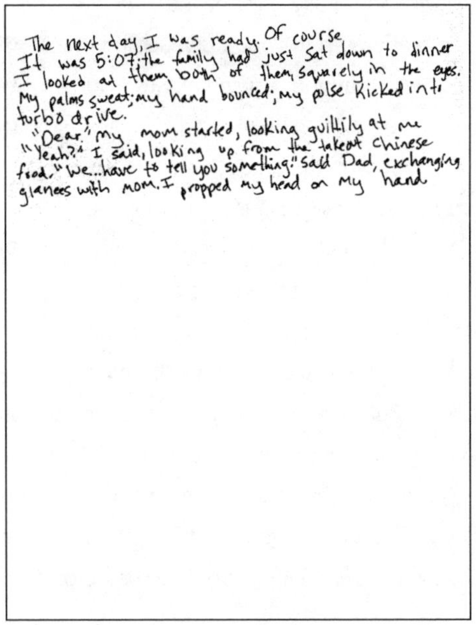
The next day, I was ready. Of course It was 5:07; the family had just sat down to dinner I looked at them, both of them, squarely in the eyes. My palms sweat; my hand bounced; my pulse Kicked into turbo drive.
"Dear," my mom started, looking guiltily at me "Yeah?" I said, looking up from the takeout chinese food. "We...have to tell you something," said Dad, exchanging glances with Mom. I propped my head on my hand.

Fig. XIV-3 Ari uses a variety of punctuation to strong effect.

SHARE

Working with a Partner

Ask children to share their work with a partner, asking for particular editing feedback, as writers do.

"We writers know that even after we've done our most careful editing, there can still be some mistakes in our stories. Sometimes we miss mistakes because we ourselves don't know exactly how to spell or punctuate properly and sometimes we miss mistakes because we just get so used to reading our own writing that we have a hard time seeing our errors. Every piece of writing needs fresh eyes. Remember that your writing partners can provide those fresh eyes for your story. In addition to helping you with accurate spelling, your partners can help you effectively edit your story for sense, punctuation, and grammar. So, let your partner provide you with a fresh pair of eyes. Partner 2, will you reread and edit partner 1's writing? As you do this, remember that the writer is the ultimate decision maker, and if someone else writes on our drafts, they do so lightly and respectfully, in pencil not pen!"

HOMEWORK   *Creating an "About the Author" Paragraph*   Since we're almost done with our stories, I realized that we can start thinking a little about how we want our pieces to be published. I know one thing many published stories have is an "About the Author" paragraph. It's the place readers can learn more information about the writer. There's usually a picture of the writer and a few facts about the writer's life—where she lives, whom she lives with, any hobbies she has. That sort of thing.

Tonight, I'd like you to work on your "About the Author." Find a picture of yourself. Maybe a grown-up will let you have one. Or, better yet, you can draw one. Then write a small paragraph about you, including the things you think your readers will want to know. If you're not sure what to include, read a few examples and see what those authors say and how they say it. One thing you're going to notice right away is that almost all of the "About the Authors" are written in third person.

If your children get caught up in the story every time they read and have a hard time reading with an eye toward editing . . . you might decide to teach them that writers at the editing stage of their writing process often go through their daily life thinking hard about grammatical structure choices, word choices, punctuation choices and paragraph choices. You might ask children to try living their daily life thinking about editing, and collecting ways they might make their own work stronger.

One way to help children learn about editing from their daily life is to direct them to replay a conversation they've had or heard that embodies the tone they are trying to create in their writing, in a particular place. Where were (and how long were) the pauses in that conversation? How could we recreate those kind of pauses in punctuation? What particular kinds of words did the speakers use? How could we find that kind of word to fit with our topics to help give us that same feel? How could we help create the tenor and urgency of that conversation with our own written words?

Of course, this same kind of thinking could be applied to any bit of text that holds the right tone, not just an overheard conversation. Does the marketing copy of a catalog hold just the right slick, overbearing tone your character uses to convince her mother to buy her an over priced tea set? Does the lead paragraph of the day's news story have just the right flat, unemotional tone the character in your story uses to tell her friend she doesn't care about her any more? What is it about each of these kinds of texts we encounter throughout the day that we can use for our own writing? Children might write in the margins of their drafts the tones they are aiming for, think of some common texts that might carry these tones, and then study them, seeing what from those texts could be imported into their own work to help create the same tone, then trying it.

COLLABORATING WITH COLLEAGUES

While the children are working on editing their stories, you and your colleagues will, no doubt, be busily preparing for your upcoming units of study. I hope that you have allowed yourselves time enough to teach a unit of study on poetry and another one or two on topics of your own choosing. You will want to reread the chapter I wrote on "Creating Your Own Units of Study" in *A Guide to the Writing Workshop*.

If your upcoming unit of study is on poetry, which I suspect will be your decision, I suggest you start by talking together about some of the over-arching decisions you need to make. First of all, you will want to decide whether you will put a different spin on poetry in third grade, in fourth grade, and in fifth grade. That's what I'd recommend. The children will absolutely benefit from having opportunities to revisit a genre year after year, but you will want them to feel as if there are lots of ways in which each year's unit of study opens new horizons.

You may decide, for example, that in third grade your unit of study on poetry will emphasize revision and reading-writing connections. Then in fourth grade, the unit could incorporate revision and reading-writing connections, but perhaps this time, children will especially attend to the contribution literary devices can make to a poem. And finally, in fifth grade, perhaps the unit will spotlight the importance of metaphoric thinking, with children learning that even their use of white space, can, in a sense, be regarded as metaphoric. Of course, the list I just made is fairly arbitrary (though I did try to build in rising complexity.) You and your colleagues will want to think about poetry across the years.

Then, too, you will want to think about the fact that I haven't written a book in which I share the minilessons we give to children when we teach

poetry. This was a deliberate choice. I know that you and your colleagues will need to develop lots of units of study in order to support your children's learning journey across all the years of upper-elementary school, and it makes lots of sense for you to do this first with poetry because there are so many wonderful resources available to help you. If your children didn't study during the K-2 grades with teachers who were relying on the primary set of Units of Study books, then they will never have had the chance to experience the poetry unit that Stephanie Parsons and I laid out for them. That book was the final one in our series, and the most sophisticated. As I wrote it, I was pretty clear that I could rely on that book to guide my teaching of college students as well as first graders, so I know it can be a resource to you.

Then, too, there are all the wonderful books that Georgia Heard has written. Georgia was one of the very first members of the Teachers College Reading and Writing Project's initial team, and she has continued to work closely with the Project ever since. So you will find that her ideas are closely aligned with ours. She's written lots of books that are spectacular—don't miss the chance to teach with either *For the Good of the Earth and the Sun* or *Awakening the Heart* at your side.

Although I definitely hope you give yourselves shoulders on which to stand, I also hope that you regard this gap in our Units of Study as an invitation for you and your colleagues to invent lots and lots of your own ideas. By now, you know that the way to do that is to bring a couple of poetry books and set them in the middle of your table, and bring, also, some sharpened pencils.

GETTING READY

- Children need to have been assigned roles for leading the day
- Small group of children need to have prepared a choral reading of a poem
- Bound (stapled or otherwise) anthologies of the students' short stories, including "about the author" paragraphs for each child
- Gift box or bag to hold all the anthologies
- Class of peers needs to join the celebration
- Sheets for reader feedback for each author, headed "Critics Agree"
- Refreshments
- Decorations—streamers, balloons, or just a few carnations in a cup—to create a festive atmosphere
- See CD-ROM for resources

PUBLISHING ANTHOLOGIES:

A CELEBRATION

When a novelist or short-story writer's book is released, *it is common practice to have a book party. First the author reads a bit of the book, and then copies of the book are available. The author autographs copies of the book. Friends and fans attend the party, and sometimes reporters come too.*

Today you'll want to give your young authors a taste of what it feels like to be a famous author at a book party. The guests this time will be other children, rather than parents. The stories to be shared are longer than children's other published texts have been, and it will probably be important for the writer to have a chance to read whole stories. This means that instead of convening the entire group to hear a few shared texts before dispersing people into small reading circles, you may want to start the small circles from the start—and you may have more of these circles, each containing fewer readers, to keep the pace up.

Writers always long to hear a response to our writing. One writer said that writing can feel like dropping rose petals into a well and waiting to hear the splash. So today, be sure that each child has a page titled "Critics agree . . . " (as in advertisements for novels which feature acclaim for the text) and be sure you create time for children to write on each other's "Critics agree . . . " pages.

Finally, remember that although children want responses from each other, probably you will be the reader who matters most to them. How will you let each and every child know that you have thought carefully about his work? I urge you, if you possibly can, to select a book that you believe in some way matches each writer in your class, and inscribe a message inside the front cover. If you can't afford books— give each child a poem!

> "Dear Author Claudia, When I read this book, Baylor's I'm in Charge of Celebrations, I thought of you because you have the gift of seeing and celebrating the small miracles that are everywhere in our lives. Cherish this talent of yours, because it makes you an extraordinary writer . . . and friend." or "Dear Lakeya, I've chosen . . ."

CELEBRATION

CELEBRATION

Create a drum roll leading to the event by recruiting the class to help make class anthologies of short stories and by inviting children to help ready the classroom for a book party.

Before the appointed time arrives, you will want the room to be dressed up for the festivities. Earlier, in Collaborating with Colleagues, I described the way in which children could work together to create carefully planned anthologies of stories, and to practice reading aloud and prepare for signing autographs. On the day of the event, children can help you roll butcher paper over the tables to keep soda and crumbs from spilling everywhere, and they can decorate that paper to turn it into festive tablecloths. They can also put a carnation in a paper cup at the center of each table and drape a roll of crepe paper wherever they think best.

Ask children to perform different roles in today's celebration. Two can greet visitors at the door, four can escort visitors to their assigned small circle, one can explain how the

COACHING

This celebration will have a different feel than the other events. Those celebrations probably felt to the kids as if they were engineered by you, and given in their honor. This occasion will feel to the kids as if it is by and for kids. They'll probably enjoy it all the more (you may enjoy it less!), but in any case, this allows for the occasion to feel new, not like a replica of all the other author celebrations in your classroom.

Mirror Magic By Hannah

Angelina felt as though the devil started controlling the neighborhood children and made them not want to play with her during this beautiful weather. She felt as though a gate separated her from happiness and led her to misery. She felt as though she was captured in a paper bag that led her to boredom, nothing going on in her mind except for terribly horrid thoughts about the children playing outside without her – thoughts that are too horrible to tell you. So guess what she did? She dreamt her day away.

The dream wasn't that nice either but it wasn't as bad as her thoughts. She dreamt of one day sprouting out of her small five-year old self and blooming way up into the fluffy white clouds that tickled her nose. Then she stepped on all the children who didn't welcome her into their games. If they ran away she would reach out her longs arms and grab them, shaking them up and down, throwing them up into the air and catching them just before they hit the hard sidewalk.

Her dream ended when she heard her mother call from the kitchen to brush her hair. Angelina tossed and turned, moaned and groaned and finally rolled off her comfortable couch. Her knotted golden hair lay spread out on the white carpet. She felt as tired as a baby cuddled up in their mother's arms in the middle of the night, and she felt as heavy as an elephant sinking in sixty feet of deep water. So she pushed and pulled herself to roll over again and again towards the wooden stairs to get to the bathroom.

Yawning heavily, she pulled herself up the stairs. At the top she lay down and rested, practically falling asleep again until she felt a wet

Fig. XV-1 Hannah's final story

---

glob drop onto her face, which could only mean an Emimay alert! Emimay was Angelina's pet lab. She was as brown as a chocolate bar, and as friendly as when your best friend in the whole world smiles and waves at you.

Angelina quickly wiped the glob from her face away with her palm, and now with some energy she shooed Emimay off and walked into the bathroom. Her bathroom had tiled walls that were turquoise with white stripes and her bathtub had little paws to hold it up that always made her laugh when she was younger.

Angelina looked at herself in the mirror for a few seconds. She not only saw herself but the reflection of the kids that were playing outside. That was enough for her, she practically bounced off the walls. She jumped up and down again and again and then ran to the sink and banged her head on the white porcelain.

"What are you doing up there?" screamed her mother, who was confused and worried about Angelina. She lifted her face from the sink. Her head was a little red but otherwise no harm was done. "Nothing mother" she said, "I'm fine." Then she looked down to see if the sink was okay and to her surprise instead of the white porcelain, she saw something that looked like whipped cream! She dipped her finger into the soft cream and put that finger into her mouth. In that second her face turned pea green and she spit it out of her mouth onto the mirror. She looked as the slimy white cream that had trickled down and thought that it tasted like something she had eaten before when she was younger, not knowing what it was.

"That's it!" she cried out loudly. "It tastes like my father's shaving cream, he must have left it out!" Her face looked even greener as she

Fig. XV-2 Hannah's final story, page 2

---

remembered. Staring at the cream intently, she realized the it looked like an eyeball and made another eyeball next to it.

Her grandmother was visiting and she had put all of her make-up neatly around the sink. Angelina dipped her finger into one of her tanning creams that had bumpy lumps in it and she flung it at the mirror to make a messy nose. Now she needed a mouth. She used a red make-up pencil to trace her mouth onto the mirror. This delighted Angelina so that she also traced her eyebrows with the pencil even though they weren't red. The make-up that really caught her eye was a glittering gold body spray bottle that was the exact color of her gold shimmering hair. She gripped the bottle nice and tight and sprayed all around the eyes, nose and mouth. Now all she needed was to color in the eyeballs. She found a bluish bottle that glistened on the shaving cream. The best part of it was that it smelled like blueberries.

There staring back at Angelina was her masterpiece of all masterpieces that enchanted her heart. It had changed her boring day into a fabulous day. "Angelina" she heard her mother call. "Dinnertime, hurry, the landlord will be coming soon." Angelina glanced one last time at the picture in the mirror before she needed to go down to dinner and then gleefully skipped down the stairs.

She smiled throughout dinner eating all her veggies and slowly savoring her dessert. But her smile turned around when the doorbell rang and the landlord walked in. He hated them. He thought they were slobs and didn't like their sense of humor. Angelina and her family didn't care for him either.

His tie was purple, resting on his green shirt. His thick eyebrows were neatly combed but Angelina couldn't be 100% sure because the hair on

Fig. XV-3 Hannah's final story, page 3

---

his head was resting down on them, just about covering his green as grass eyes. He had a habit of fiddling his fat fingers, which bothered Angelina.

"So how's my baby doing?" he said as he patted a table to his left. "Fine" said Angelina's father, Tony. "Was I talking to you?" questioned the landlord as Tony turned around and grumbled under his breath. That basically kept happening between the two as they walked throughout the first floor.

Walking up to the second floor, Angelina felt as bored as she had in the morning but then she remembered her masterpiece in the bathroom. They were all heading in that direction when she stopped and decided to wait in case she was going to be in trouble. She heard her mother gasp and the landlord exclaim, "wonderful!" Her dad never liked anything the landlord liked, so as he was about to say "ugh" instead he said, "It *is* wonderful." They looked at each other, slapped each other's backs with a loud "thud" and chuckled, as they walked down the steps to have dessert together.

Angelina sat down at the table looking at her half eaten dessert of cherry pie and whipped cream listening to her father and the landlord chatter away gleefully.

"I guess my artwork brings people together", she said proudly. Then she frowned and said "Now I need to make something for my mother and the neighbors." She quickly gulped down her dessert and took out some paper, glue, string and a few markers.

Angelina's day had definitely changed.

Fig. XV-4 Hannah's final story, page 4

---

sharing will proceed, and several can be sitting in the small groups to welcome the visitors to those groups.

When the actual appointed time arrived, Colleen and I assumed our posts, and the children assumed theirs. Two were at the door, ready to say, "Welcome to our fiction celebration." Others escorted the visitors to the appropriate group, based on preplanned rosters for each group. Still other authors sat in the small groups, holding their stories, ready to welcome the newcomers to the small group.

Welcome the guests. Mark the occasion, and unveil the anthologies.

"Writers," Colleen said, waiting for the room to grow silent and for an aura of significance to grow. "Today we will have a book party which exactly resembles the book parties that are held for many writers across the world." Then she said, "In this class, we mark many of our biggest occasions by the sharing of a poem," and on cue, four children stood, gathered, and did a choral reading of a poem they'd chosen.

"Now's the big moment," Colleen said, and I brought a large box to her, setting it on the table. The children craned their necks to see what was happening. Colleen stood and bit by bit, unwrapped the beautiful paper from the box. Finally, she opened the box, peered in, and then back up as if to say, "Wow. You won't believe it." Reaching ever so gingerly into the box, she produced a stack of published anthologies—one for each writer and one for each visitor.

The books are delivered to each sharing circle, and one child after another read his or her story aloud. Afterward the class had a party, and during this time, children signed each others Critics agree sheets.

After the readings are complete, celebrate! During this time, children write responses on critics claim sheets.

You'll want to decide how to make the party a happy one for children. Do you want it to be the prelude to a special outdoor play time? Do you want the class to take a field trip after the party to the local library, which may have agreed to showcase the children's writing in a giant display case? Do you want to gather the class for some reflection about how the unit went for them and what they learned?

You can open the box in a manner which creates rising action—all the components of a story are components of an occasion as well!

If you decide to give your writers the gift of a story or a poem, at the end of the day, as children leave to go home, you'll want to give these out. Be sure that you also send a copy of the child's publication home with an accompanying letter to parents, asking them to give the writer very specific, detailed responses.

Superficial

Niki and Chloe walked into school. Kids were slamming lockers and papers were thrown everywhere. Suddenly, there was a smell so great it could make the flowers pop up. The smell traveled through the halls, past the lockers and over the garbage that was everywhere. It was fruity passion Herbal Essence. Niki looked. Soft blonde hair was swaying in the distance. There was only one thing it could be . . . Samantha Stillman.

Niki pulled on Chloe's arm. "C'mon, Chloe." They moved behind the lockers.

"What?" Chloe asked, still looking down the hall at Samantha.

"I don't want her to see me. She's probably going to make fun of my clothes again." Niki lifted her backpack shaking with fear. "I hate her!" Niki glared.

"She's not that—" Chloe stopped herself mid-sentence and looked at Niki.

"Don't tell me you were going to say that she's not that bad. She's terrible!" Niki wanted to scream out, but she didn't want anyone to see her behind the lockers.

"Hey!" a voice said. Niki's heart beat out of her chest. She looked up to see Samantha Stillman standing in front of her.

Niki opened her eyes wide and looked straight up at Samantha. "What do you want?" she asked shaking. It seemed like the walls were closing in on her. She wanted to walk behind the lockers, turn and run the other way, but she didn't.

"I just wanted to see your new, I mean, your clothes from the back of the closet," Samantha said laughing. Niki stared at her hard. Chloe looked at the floor. "C'mon, Chloe. We have class," Niki said. But Chloe just stood there. Niki wanted pull Chloe away and run down the hall. But she did nothing.

"I have a question for you, Chloe," Samantha said gritting her teeth at Niki. "Why are you friends with her?" Samantha motioned with her chin in Niki's direction.

"Because," Chloe said proudly. Niki gave her a nudge. Samantha stared. Chloe's face turned red. "She, um, well, I don't know. I mean—" Niki wanted to crawl away.

"I mean, like she has the worst taste in clothes, right?" Samantha said cutting Chloe off.

"Yes. I mean no. I mean I don't know!" Chloe whined. Niki turned away. She didn't get it. She and Chloe had made a pact—Best Friends Forever.

"Sorry, Niki," Chloe whispered.

"Chloe," Niki said, turning around and wiping the tears from her face. But it was too late.

"Let's go," Samantha said. They all stood in the hallway looking at each other. Doors were opening and closing as kids went to class. Samantha pulled Chloe by the shirt and together they followed the rush of other kids.

The doors shut behind them as they walked off to class. Niki stood alone and wondered if it was worth being class president. I should have known after beating her last year in the election. If you mess with Samantha Stillman, she'll mess with you.

Niki started to walk to class, not sure which way to turn now that she was all alone.

Fig. XV-5 Beccah's final story

Fig. XV-6 Beccah's final story, page 2

Jane's First Sleep Over

One spring, sunny day Jane and Abby's families all went for a picnic in Central Park. They played baseball, tag, duck-duck-goose, and other fun games. Abby's brother Jack and Jane's brother Rob thought the baseball game was the most fun because they both scored runs. Jane's sister Anna and Abby's sister Robin thought the picnic was fun and they should plan another one again soon. The parents—Mary, Chris, Mel, and Kevin—thought it was a great idea to have another picnic in Central Park because it was big and there were great places to play.

Later in the day when the sun was setting over the carrousel and they were about to leave Abby asked, "Hey Jane, do you want to sleep over at my house tonight?" Jane's face froze for a second she didn't say anything; then Jane said, "I can't sleep over."

"Why not?" questioned Abby. Before Jane was able to say anything Abby added, "You aren't scared, are you?"

"No way, of course not," said Jane. "I just can't."

All of a sudden Robin and Anna started to chant, "Jane is scared. Jane is scared."

"At least I'm smarter than you guys!" Jane said as she huffed off. But Jane thought about how Robin and Anna were right about her being scared. She felt like a baby which made her feel bad inside. Why couldn't she sleep over at Abby's house? She'd played there a million times but she'd never slept anywhere but at her own house with her parents right across the hall.

Coincidentally, two weeks later, Jane and Abby's families had tickets to "Typo" at the New Victory Theater. After the show, Abby asked again, "Jane do you want to sleep over at my house?"

"Why don't you sleep over at my house?" said Jane.

"But I always sleep over at your house and you never sleep over at my house. I think Robin and Anna are right when they say you're scared to," said Abby.

"Well I'm not . . . it's just . . . I don't want to," said Jane.

"You don't want to! That hurts my feelings! Anyway, I think you're scared and you're lying to me. Maybe if you tried to sleep over at my house you might like it," said Abby.

"Fine," said Jane. "I'll do it just to show you I can. See you Friday night after school."

When Jane walked away she thought "I hope I won't embarrass myself and start crying like a baby for my Mom and Dad or worse wake up in the middle of the night and want to go home. Yikes! I can't believe I just said 'Yes'," thought Jane. "But I have to because Abby looked so excited and I did say I would."

Friday came along quickly and Jane was pretty nervous and excited at the same time to sleep over at Abby's house. At first the girls were having a blast. Jane and Abby watched their favorite movie "Elf" and said the lines they knew by heart. They played Candy Land and watched the Disney Channel. They painted each other's nails and put on make-up. They ordered Chinese food and ate until their stomachs ached. Abby's Mom came in the room and told the

Fig. XV-7 Hannah's final story

Fig. XV-8 Hannah's final story, page 2

girls it was time for bed. As Jane got into the bed next to Abby she started thinking about her mom and dad. She got quiet and her eyes filled with tears. Abby noticed and said, "Let's play one more game in the dark with a flashlight so my parents won't see the light on." The girls played game after game of War until Jane and Abby fell asleep.

Jane woke up the next morning when she heard Abby in the bathroom brushing her teeth. As she laid in bed she smiled thinking about all the fun she had and how proud she was that she made it through the night without her parents. She couldn't wait to tell her family how much fun she had and how she wanted to to do it again soon.

Spencer Bellhorn is not a Wimp by Caleb

Fifteen minutes had past and I was tired of watching the charcoal-black squirrel run up and down the big oak tree that shaded Kolben St. from the bright morning sun.

Where was Sarah? Had she forgotten? No, Kolben St. had been our meeting spot for the past three years. She's probably sick, I reassured myself. "Yeah," I mumbled, "sick." and set off to school.

"How's it going?" yelled Mr. Crabapple from his porch.

"Great!" I lied.

Then Mr. C smiled a smile I wish I could smile. But I couldn't. I could only manage a frail grin; like the one you see from a sick grandmother. I bit my lip until I couldn't feel it anymore. My eyes twitched side to side like a nervous squirrel. I closed my eyes and repetitively muttered, "Sarah's with me, Sarah's with me, Sarah's with me." trying to convince myself she really was . I walked past every house like in it was a man with a knife.

That day elm trees leading to the playground of the Mario Gabinetto School seemed bigger, but then again, so did everything.

"Auggghhh!" screamed a voice as something

Fig. XV-10 Caleb's final story

collided with my chest. Then all I felt was the hard playground concrete against my cheek.

"Sorry." I apologized as I stood up and brushed myself off.

Watch where you're goin'!" growled a voice that I thought I had heard before. All at once I realized I what I had bumped into.It was Humphrey Dugbill, the meanest bully in the history of Butts, Missouri.

I absent-mindedly tried to walk away so that the oversized predator wouldn't prey on me. My puny frame is no match for his bulgingm one. I wanted to shrink and shrink till he couldn't see me anymore. Well, well, well if it isn't Spencer Bellhorn! About to get beat up and without your girlfriend to protect you!" he emphasized the word girl a lot.

"Any last words?"he asked smugly. What was I going to do? Where was Sarah when I needed her?

Right on time the 'Bading-A Dinga-Ding" of the 9:00 bell filled the air. "Saved by the bell, Bellhorn I'll see you after school!" Humphrey yelled over the crowd of screaming kids.

I couldn't pay attention to Mr. Jimenz in math class because I was thinking of a plan, a plan to defend myself against Humphrey. Could I run away like all the other kids had done? No, I would have to stick

Fig. XV-11 Caleb's final story, page 2

Fig. XV-9 Hannah's final story, page 3

up to him. Then I a thought crossed my mind. Humphrey had never actually punched someone, he had just threatened to! So why should I be afraid? It was a risk, But also, it was the only way.

I stood in the playground of the Mario Gabinetto School to await my fate. If my plan worked, I would never need Sarah to defend me again. If it didn't, I would.

"Spencer?!!" growled a voice behind me, "I thought you would run away like all the other wimps. Oh well, all the better for me!" I didn't have to turn around to know who it was.

"Whatever, Humphrey." I said calmly. Kids of all shapes and sizes gathered to watch. I could hear a "Yeah Humphrey" chant starting in the crowd.

Humphrey braced himself. With his fist up and the grimace on his face he looked like a heavy weight boxer. I didn't pose like him. I just stood there, arms folded, and a grin on my face. He picked up his fist and pointed his elbow towards the clouds behind him.

Sarah's definitely not my girlfriend!!!!!!!

This is gonna work!" I thought and grinned.

His fist shot forward. The grin faded from my face. I felt like Roger Clemens had thrown a fastball at

Fig. XV-12 Caleb's final story, page 3

my face. My head hit the ground. I lowered my hand to my upper-lip. I lifted it back up. I saw red.

Humphrey and the other kids smirked. Their smirk turned into a giggle and they started to walk away like I wasn't really there. I needed help, couldn't they see that. They just left me, in the dirt, like I wasn't there.

I wanted to cry, I really did.

Then I remembered Humphrey's words; 'I thought you would run away like all the other wimps' I didn't run away! I wasn't a wimp. Even though I was standing there with a bloody nose, I felt like I had won. It was then that I realized that everyone at one point in his or her lives needs to be protected. Even the mighty Roger Clemens has bodyguards, and he isn't a wimp, I'm not a wimp.

Spencer Bellhorn is not a wimp.

Fig. XV-13 Caleb's final story, page 4

LUCY CALKINS ✦ MEDEA McEVOY

LITERARY ESSAYS: WRITING ABOUT READING

This book is dedicated to Carmen Farina and Laura Kotch.

FirstHand
An imprint of Heinemann
A division of Reed Elsevier Inc.
361 Hanover Street
Portsmouth, NH 03801-3912
www.heinemann.com

Offices and agents throughout the world

Copyright © 2006 by Lucy Calkins and Medea McEvoy

All rights reserved. No part of this book may be reproduced in any form or by any electronic or mechanical means, including information storage and retrieval systems, without permission in writing from the publisher, except by a reviewer, who may quote brief passages in a review.

Photography: Peter Cunningham

Library of Congress Cataloging-in-Publication Data

CIP data on file with the Library of Congress.
ISBN 0-325-00865-5

Printed in the United States of America on acid-free paper
10   09   08   07   06   ML   1   2   3   4   5

Excerpt from "Spaghetti" Reprinted with the permission of Atheneum Books for Young Readers, an imprint of Simon & Schuster Children's Publishing Division from *Every Living Thing* by Cynthia Rylant. Text copyright © 1985 Cynthia Rylant.

Excerpt from "The Marble Champ" from *Baseball in April and Other Stories*, copyright © 1990 by Gary Soto, reprinted by permission of Harcourt, Inc.

Excerpt from *Fly Away Home* by Eve Bunting. Text copyright © 1991 by Eve Bunting. Reprinted by permission of Clarion Books/Houghton Mifflin Company. All rights reserved.

Eudora Welty book review of *Charlotte's Web:* Reprinted by the permission of Russell & Volkening as agents for Eudora Welty, copyright (c) 1952 by Eudora Welty, renewed in 1980 by Eudora Welty.

Excerpt from "Eleven" from *Woman Hollering Creek.* Copyright © 1991 by Sandra Cisneros. Published by Vintage Books, a division of Random House, Inc., and originally in hardcover by Random House, Inc. Reprinted by permission of Susan Bergholz Literary Services, New York. All rights reserved.

"Turn! Turn! Turn! (To Everything There Is a Season)", Words from the Book of Ecclesiastes. Adaptation and Music by Pete Seeger. TRO-© Copyright 1962 (Renewed) Melody Trails, Inc., New York, NY. Used by permission.

ACKNOWLEDGEMENTS

This book is dedicated to Carmen Farina and Laura Kotch, the Deputy Chancellor for Instruction and the Director of Instruction for the New York City Department of Education. Because of these two people and their commitment to ensuring that every child receives the richest and most rigorous education possible, thousands and thousands of New York City children are growing up as avid readers and writers. We thank them for their resolve, their untiring efforts, and their friendship.

The contributing author of this book, Medea McEvoy, is Director of Literacy for the New York City schools and works with Laura Kotch and Carmen Farina to support literacy instruction citywide. Before assuming this role, Medea was a fifth grade teacher at PS 6, and her classroom was a laboratory for learning par excellence. This unit of study stands on the shoulders of work in the teaching of reading that many of us at the Project developed together, that Medea pioneered in her classroom. Medea also helped me pilot this specific unit in Kathy Doyle's wonderful classroom, and the two of them joined me for a writing retreat in order to turn our teaching into a text. Medea has been a willing contributor, helping out with Tailoring Your Teachings and with other portions of the book as well, and she has provided all the artwork. Above all, she has been a thought companion in the adventure of learning to teach not only writing but also reading.

This book could not have been written were it not for the invaluable support of Kathy Doyle, a fifth grade teacher at the Smith School in Tenafly, New Jersey. Whereas many of these books draw upon the teaching that has been done in hundreds of classrooms over a decade, this book relies very specifically on the work that Kathy, Medea and I did with Kathy's wonderful group of fifth graders. Kathy's willingness to open her classroom to Medea and I, her sense of adventure and of appreciation, and her vast knowledge of books and of her children, made all the difference.

Julia Mooney and Grace Enriquez, two Project colleagues, helped elaborate on sections of the text. Kathleen Tolan, the Deputy Director for Reading, read the entire draft and contributed dozens of ideas as well as many pages of text. Many of the ideas that fill these pages reflect the Project's thinking about teaching reading, and Donna Santman, Randy Bomer, Ginny Lockwood, Kathy Collins, Maggie Moon, Emily Smith, Katherine Bomer, Daria Rigney, Mary Ehrenworth and Amanda Hartman (along with many others) have all contributed to those ideas. My ideas on teaching reading benefit from the work done by other researchers. I am especially grateful to Ellin Keene, Kylene Beers, and Dick Allington.

Production of this book was especially complicated, and I am indebted to both Jean Lawler at Heinemann and to Tasha Kalista, whose considerable talents for composition and organization helped editor Kate Montgomery and I bring out the infrastructure in the book.

Literary Essays: Writing about Reading

Welcome to Unit 5

WELCOME TO THE UNIT

LITERARY ESSAYS: WRITING ABOUT READING

In personal essays, many children will have written about lessons they learned from people they know and interact with. But writing also helps us learn from the characters in the books we read. Just as writing allows us to pause in our hurried lives and really notice and experience and reflect on things that have happened to us, so, too, writing allows us to pause in our hurried reading and really pay attention to the characters in our books.

In order for children to write about reading in this way, they need to be reading! Children who are learning to write literary essays while they are still very young—in grades three, four, and five—will profit from writing these essays about short texts they've read, reread, and discussed. In this unit, I invite children to read and study small packets of short texts that merit close study. A teacher might thread one short story through many minilessons, showing children how she reads, thinks, and writes about that one story and then suggesting that children try similar techniques with a story from their packet. The stories in a child's packet need to be ones the child can read. Therefore, children may not all have the same collection. I encourage teachers to provide stories that are rich, complex, and well-crafted enough to reward close study.

On each of the first few days of the unit, I demonstrate a lens that readers can bring to a text, reminding children that all of these lenses accumulate so they have a repertoire of possibilities to choose from whenever they read. I teach children that just as essayists pay attention to our lives, expecting to grow ideas from this wide-awake attentiveness, so, too, literary essayists pay attention . . . but this time, the attention is directed to texts. Each child chooses a story that especially speaks to her and then collects entries about that story. The process of choosing a seed idea in this unit has two stages. First, a child chooses a story. Then, the child lives with that one story and gathers entries about it. Eventually, the child rereads those entries to chose a seed idea.

I remind children of their work in the personal essay unit, when they observed their lives and then pushed their thinking in their notebooks by writing, "The thought I have about this is . . . " or "This makes me realize that . . . ." In this unit, children can pause as they read to observe what is happening in the text and then develop an idea using the same conversational prompts. I teach children that their thoughts can be extended by using phrases such as "another example of this is," "furthermore," "this connects with," "on the other hand," "but you might ask," "this is true because," and "I am realizing." If we hope children will write literary essays in which they articulate the lessons they believe a character learns in a story or name the theme or idea a text teaches, then it is important to provide children with strategies for generating these sorts of ideas.

After children have collected reading responses in their writer's notebooks for at least a week, I remind them that they already know how to reread a notebook in order to find a seed idea. In the essay unit, students found seed ideas, and they'll need to do something similar now. I encourage students to search for a portion of an entry that tells the heart of the story in one or two sentences. I ask them to look for a seed idea that is central to the story and provocative.

I also help children generate possible seed ideas. Some children find it helpful to write inside this general structure: This is a story about [identify the character] who [has this trait]/[wants/cares about such-and-so] but then [what happens to change things?] and s/he ends up [how?]. In other words, I encourage some students to try writing a sentence or two in which they lay out what the character was like at the start of the story, what happened to change things, and how this was resolved at the end: "*Because of Winn-Dixie* is the story of a lonely girl, Opal, who befriends a stray dog, Winn-Dixie. The dog helps Opal make friends with lots of people." "'Spaghetti' is the story of a lonely boy, Gabriel, who learns from a tiny stray kitten to open himself to love." We also encourage children to think of a story as containing an external as well as an internal storyline, and to write an essay which highlights the internal (and therefore, sometimes the overlooked) story.

It is important to help each child revise her seed idea so that it is a clear thesis, making sure it is a claim or an idea, not a fact or a question. I help children imagine how they can support the thesis in a few paragraphs. Usually for children in grades three through five, the first support paragraph will show how the child's claim was true at the start of the story, and the next support paragraph(s) will show that it was true later in the story as well. It may be that the first support paragraph shows how the claim was true for one reason, the next, for a second reason.

Once children have planned their "boxes and bullets" for a literary essay, they will need to collect the information and insights they need to build a case. We encourage each child to make a file for each topic sentence (and each support paragraph). For example, if the child's claim is "Cynthia Rylant's story 'Spaghetti' is the story of a lonely boy who learns from a tiny stray kitten to open himself to love," the child might title one file "Gabriel is a lonely boy," and another "Gabriel learns from a tiny stray kitten to open himself to love."

I also teach writers how to cite references from a text and how to "unpack" the ways these references address the relevant big idea. Before this unit is over, we teach children that writers of literary essays use the vocabulary of their trade, incorporating literary terms such as *narrator*, *point of view*, *scenes*, and the like. We may also teach students to write introductory paragraphs that include a tiny summary of the story and closing paragraphs that link back to the thesis and that link the story's message to the writer's own life, or to another story, or to literature as a whole.

The Plan for the Unit

The "bends in the road" for this unit *Literary Essays* are as follows:

- Children read from a packet of short stories (and other texts) and write entries responding to their reading. I teach them a repertoire of ways in which literary essayists might write about texts that they are studying including teaching them they might observe the text closely and then push themselves to have thoughts about what they notice. I suggest that readers know it pays off to give special attention to characters, writing about their traits, motivations, struggles, changes and lessons. It is also helpful to think, "What is this text really about?" Part way through this phase of collecting entries, children narrow in on one text from the packet that particularly speaks to them and collect entries just about that text. Classroom time is spent not only writing but also talking about these texts.

- Children reread their entries and select an idea that they'd like to bring forth in a literary essay. With help, they craft this into a thesis statement. In most of their thesis statements, the child will either state her idea of what the text is *really* about, or the child will write about how a character changes or learns across the story. In either case, the child generally sets him or herself up to support the thesis with topic sentences like this: "Early in the book . . . and late in the book . . . ."

- Children set up a system for collecting support material for each of their topic sentences. This system replicates the system of folders children used when writing personal essays. Once again, each of the child's internal topic sentences is written on a file, and as the child collects support materials, these are filed in the appropriate file. All the files are in one folder labeled with the child's thesis statement.

- Children reread the text under study as literary essayists do, finding mini-stories which support their claims. We remind children that it is important to angle these stories to make the point and to unpack them, showing how the story makes the point.

- Children collect lists, quotations and other materials to support their claims, as literary essayists do.

- Eventually, children take one file at a time, sort through its contents, decide on particularly compelling support material and sequence this material. They staple it together, rewriting only some of it, to make a rough draft.

- Children create cohesion among the bits that comprise their drafts by using transition words and repeating key words from their thesis and topic sentences. They may or may not revise the draft. They edit and recopy it for publication.

WRITING INSIDE THE STORY

IN THIS SESSION, YOU'LL TEACH CHILDREN THAT GOOD READERS FLESH OUT STORIES BY ENVISIONING THEM AND LIVING VICARIOUSLY THROUGH THE CHARACTERS. YOU'LL TEACH CHILDREN TO TRY THIS FIRST ON PAPER, IN PREPARATION FOR TRYING IT MENTALLY.

GETTING READY

- Anecdote you can tell to illustrate that writers live intensely
- Enlarged copy of "Spaghetti," by Cynthia Rylant (or other touchstone text), prepared on chart paper for use throughout the unit
- List of tips for writing about reading—Write Inside the Story to Help You Read Well—prepared on chart paper
- A packet of four or five short, accessible texts for each child, marked in places where child could pause to envision
- See CD-ROM for resources

Because you have already taught many units of study, you enter this unit with an expectation for how a unit of study will probably go. You can count on the fact that Session I will invite writers into the big work of the unit while also equipping them with a particular strategy for generating the new kind of writing. You can also count on the fact that the first few minilessons will give students a repertoire of strategies for generating this new kind of writing, and for lifting the level of writing.

But this unit is a bit different from all the others. To write well about reading, children not only need to learn more about writing, they also need to learn more about reading. These sessions, then, must support reading well in addition to writing well. Specifically, this first session is intended to help children to read actively—and to write about the literature they are reading.

When children write essays about texts, they need to first experience the text, dreaming the world of the story, walking in the shoes of the characters. Only after reading the story with empathy and imagination will the reader who wants to write analytically *shift to reread with a critic's eyes,* looking closely at the text and constructing a logical argument about what he or she sees. In this session, then, children will talk and write about stories not as commentators or expository thinkers, but instead as active, participating readers. This session invites children to draw from their lives, to fill in the gaps in a story, as readers do. If I read a story in which a small girl pulls on the door to her school, I see the girl, leaning back to slowly pull the mighty wooden door open—and it is the door from my own elementary school. Readers co-construct texts as we read, using both the words in texts and images from our lives.

In this session, you will invite children to fill in the details as they read. You'll teach children that when the character walks outside early one morning just after a long rainy night, good readers are apt to see the character step over the wet grass and pass the worms that writhe on the pathway. The purpose of today's writing is to help children read with engagement, writing inside the text as preparation for the writing they will do about the text.

MINILESSON

Writing Inside the Story

CONNECTION

Use a metaphor or anecdote to remind children that writers first live intensely and only then write about their experiences.

"As we learned earlier in the year, the great writer Annie Dillard has a photograph above her writing desk of a little boy standing firm in the river rapids, only his head above water. Annie posts that picture beside her writing desk because, she says, 'That little boy is completely alive. He's letting the mystery of existence beat on him. He's having his childhood and he knows it.' Annie uses that picture to remind herself that writers need to live intensely wide-awake lives, and then we write about those lives."

Tell children that, in the same way, we first read intensely and only then write about that experience.

"In this unit of study we will be writing about our reading. Reading is one way to wake up to the intensity and meaning and truth of our own lives. The famous essayist Donald Hall has said, 'Great literature, if we read it well, opens us up to the world and makes us more sensitive to it, as if we acquired eyes that could see through things and ears that could hear smaller sounds.' Before we can write a literary essay, we first need to climb inside a story, just as that little boy climbed inside the whitewater. We need to let the experience of the story pound down on us. Then and only then will we decide what we want to say about the story."

Name your teaching point. Specifically, tell children that to write a literary essay, they first need to live in the world of a story. Writing inside the story can help them do that.

"Specifically, what I want to teach you today is that when we want to make something of our reading, we first need to read as deeply as possible. We first need to experience the story as intensely as possible. And writing can help us do that."

TEACHING

Demonstrate close, empathetic reading. Show especially that as you read, you infer and envision, filling in details.

"When I want to read a story well, I don't read like this," I said, turning pages quickly and disinterestedly. "I don't just skim the story, then push it aside to stare up into the heavens trying to come up with something to write about the story."

COACHING

I know that this introduction has a high beauty quotient and may be a bit low on practical nuts-and-bolts information. I'm aware that when I preach a little sermon like this, some kids won't actually take in all of what I am saying. That's okay by me. I think they still glean that I'm trying to start the unit by talking about really important issues.

With this session, I am trying to reclaim writing about reading as a beautiful, glorious thing. I'm trying to make writing about reading feel personal—even intimate—and intense. For many children, writing about reading is a dreaded enterprise. Often children are asked to do this simply as a way to prove they read the text. Often no one reads the writing children do about reading, and nothing happens to that writing. It's not read, shared, revised, discussed—and consequently, it feels wooden and lifeless. This unit attempts to reclaim writing about reading.

Sometimes when young people are asked to write a literary essay, the assignment turns reading itself into a search for a main idea and supportive detail. This lesson aims to convey that when we read a story, we need to bring a narrative frame of mind (not an expository one) to our reading. This lesson channels children toward empathizing, envisioning, anticipating, and experiencing vicariously—all actions that writers take when writing narratives and that readers take when reading narratives.

"Instead I read closely, trying to stand inside the character's shoes. Let me show you what I mean by reading just the start of 'Spaghetti,' a short story many of you know by Cynthia Rylant." I began to read aloud as if I were doing so privately, to myself:

> It was evening and people sat outside, talking quietly among themselves. On the stoop of a tall building of crumbling bricks and rotting wood sat a boy. His name was Gabriel and he wished for some company.
>
> Gabriel was thinking about things. He remembered being the only boy in class with the right answer that day, and he remembered the butter sandwich he had had for lunch. (1998)

I paused after reading this aloud and looked up, as if musing about the story. "I'm picturing Gabriel sitting on the stoop of his building. He remembers being in the school lunchroom; in my mind, he sat at a corner of a table, by himself, at lunch. I can see him pulling out a sandwich; it's not much of a sandwich, it just has butter on it." Then I paused, thought some more, and said to myself, "What else do I see?" I glanced back at the text, then again looked up and thought aloud. "I think Gabriel ate his sandwich, taking tiny bites, a little at a time, because he wanted to make it last. Now, sitting on the stoop, he is hungry. He probably wishes he'd kept some of the sandwich, that it was in his pocket still."

Setting aside the role of reader and resuming the role of teacher, I leaned close to the children and spoke directly to them. "Do you see how I read just a tiny bit and then I pause to get a picture in my mind?"

Debrief. Emphasize that as you read, you see the story in your mind.

Continuing to process my reading aloud, I said, "Do you see that when I want a story to be important to me, I don't just rush through it? It's almost as if I live inside the story. When I read, I act the story out in my mind as if it is a play and I'm the main character. You'll remember that the novelist, John Gardner, once described reading this way: 'It creates for us a kind of dream, a rich and vivid play in the mind. We read a few words at the beginning of a book or the particular story and suddenly we find ourselves seeing not words on a page but a train moving through Russia, an old Italian crying, or a farmhouse battered by rain. We read on—dream on—worrying about the choices the characters have to make, listening in panic for some sound behind the fictional door.' (1991) In our case, we read remembering butter sandwiches and feeling the hollow hunger as if it's not just Gabriel's but also our own."

In this unit of study, minilessons often require the teacher to shift between reading aloud and thinking aloud. It's easy for these two to become indistinguishable, something that creates confusion for the observing children. So from the first, find a way to signal when you shift from reading aloud to thinking aloud. When you are thinking about the text rather than reading it, lower the book and look up toward the sky: Don't hesitate to be a bit overly dramatic in ways that convey, "Now I'm not reading. I am, instead, musing over what I've just read."

You may squirm uncomfortably over the fact that as a reader, I am filling in details that are not there in the story, but I am totally convinced that all good readers do this. We read, "She stepped out into the whirling snow," and some of us see blinding snow, driven by winds. Some of us see a scattering of flakes, each one distinct, dancing daintily toward the ground. As we read on, the upcoming words in the text alter the images we create. But an active reader doesn't wait till all the information has been amassed before creating mental pictures. The talking I've just done (and the talking and writing I will soon ask children to do) embodies the mental activities that I hope good readers do as they read. I want children to experience a text deeply and fully. Later, I will also want children to hold the text at arm's length and to think about the messages in it, rereading in ways that lead them to use sections of the text to defend ideas. At that point, I will ask them to bring an expository frame even to narrative texts, generating ideas (and entries and essays) that are shaped like expository texts. But for now, I don't want to hurry children toward thinking and writing entries that feel like little expository essays about their reading.

The Gardner quote is one of my favorite descriptions of reading. I want children to become so absorbed in a text that they see not words on the page, but a train moving through Russia. Because I want to support envisionment, during read-aloud time as well as during these minilessons, I'll sometimes pause in the middle of a read-aloud, look up with a faraway expression, and say, "I can picture it. I'm seeing . . . ."

ACTIVE ENGAGEMENT
Set children up to practice envisioning as they read by explaining their mental pictures to a partner.

"Let me read on. As I read, try to be in the story. See Gabriel, hear him—try to sense through Gabriel's eyes, ears, skin. When I come to a good place to stop, I'll pause so we can each see the story in our minds and say what we are sensing, what we are envisioning, to our partners." I read this aloud:

> Gabriel was thinking that he would like to live outside all the time.
> He imagined himself carrying a pack of food and a few tools and a
> heavy cloth to erect a hasty tent. Gabriel saw himself sleeping among
> coyotes. But next he saw himself sleeping beneath the glittering
> lights of a movie theater, near the bus stop. (1998)

"Turn to your partner and say, 'I see . . . ,' then say what you see."

After this tiny interval for talk, I resumed reading, repeating the previous section of the text just a bit and then reading on:

> Gabriel was a boy who thought about things so seriously, so fully,
> that on this evening he nearly missed hearing a cry from the street.
> The cry was so weak and faraway in his mind that, for him, it could
> have been the slow lifting of a stubborn window. It could have been
> the creak of an old man's legs. It could have been the wind.

"Turn to your partner and say, 'I see . . .' or 'I hear . . . !'" After a moment, while children were still talking, I resumed reading. As usual, I reread a bit of the story, knowing that some of the children would miss the start of my read-aloud because they were still finishing their partner conversations and repositioning themselves to listen.

> Gabriel picked himself up from the stoop and began to walk carefully
> along the edge of the street, peering into the gloom and the dusk.

"Turn and envision," I said.

Sometimes instead of demonstrating how I envision as I read, I set children up to do this. Pausing while reading aloud, I say, "Let me reread that . . . ." I might invite children to turn and talk for a moment with a partner. "What city block are you picturing?" I might ask, then add, "Turn and talk." If children aren't sure how to supply the details in those mental pictures, help them understand that readers bring the city blocks from our own lives into stories we read. Sometimes as we continue to read, the text causes us to revise those pictures, and this revision is a crucial part of reading.

As you listen in, you may see a child sort of shrug to a partner and then repeat exactly what you just read aloud, saying, "I see him sleeping by the movie theater?" Don't despair, and definitely don't reveal your disappointment! For now, you want to help all children begin this new work. So nod generously, and add on. "I see that too! The movie theater I'm picturing is huge. It has eight shows all showing at once; it has great crowds of people lined up. This is a city! The people sort of circle around the lump on the sidewalk that is Gabriel, wrapped in a blanket, trying to sleep. He realizes as he lies there, sleeping alone isn't all that fun!" Be sure to ask, "What do you see? Is your theater huge, or small, or what?"

The children don't yet have much to go on in their effort to fill in the gaps in this story. If you were leaving gaps like this halfway through a novel instead of a short story, the children could use the whole first half of the story to supply missing details. Because the story I was reading aloud—"Spaghetti"—is brief and sparse, I kept the gaps that children were asked to fill very small. Alternatively, you may decide to do this work with a chapter from your read-aloud novel! If you ask children to supply too much detail without providing enough text to guide the detail selection, your request can lead children away from the story as it is written.

Show children that instead of saying what they envision and sense for the character while reading, they can write inside the story, and this can help them read more deeply.

As the children again voiced what they were picturing, I recorded the last phrase I'd just read on chart paper. Then I said, "Partner 1, keep making a movie in your mind, only this time, *write* rather than saying aloud whatever you are envisioning. Partner 2, do the same in your notebook. Do that now while I do the same thing on this chart paper." I reread the line from "Spaghetti" I'd copied onto chart paper, then paused thoughtfully to model envisioning. Then I wrote what I envisioned on chart paper:

> "Gabriel picked himself up from the stoop and began to walk carefully along the edge of the street, peering into the gloom and the dusk." He peered behind a trash can, piled high with garbage. "Was the sound coming from there?" he wondered. But only a rat skittered out from the shadows. Walking down the street, Gabriel listened hard, hoping to hear the tiny cry again. He looked again into an alley, this time seeing stuff (a bike, a bucket of purple flowers).

"Writers, do you see that instead of *talking* to convey what I saw and heard in this bit of the story, I wrote—and you did this as well. We each copied a sentence from the text and then we each added into the story, almost as if we were the author of the story. In this case, I filled in what Gabriel probably thought and noticed. Most of us wrote just a small step that the author left out, to help us really feel that moment right after what was described in the story." At this point, I turned a page of my chart paper tablet to reveal this chart.

Write Inside the Story to Help You Read Well

- Read trying to experience the story.
- Choose a part that matters.
- Step into the story. As you envision, fill in details.
- Write a bit to help you go into the story. Write a few lines that could belong in it. Resume reading.
- Pause to write again when it feels right.

In the Active Engagement sections of minilessons, it is important for us to provide children with assisted practice doing what we have just demonstrated. In this instance, I know the Active Engagement stands a chance of being confusing, so I take extra steps to set children up and get them started, making it is as likely as possible that they'll be able to do this work successfully—and in short order.

I write publicly on chart paper while the children write alongside me so my demonstration provides extra support for those who don't quite grasp what I've asked them to do. Because this is a three-minute activity and I won't have a chance to get around to every kid, a few children will probably spend this interlude watching me model rather than actually getting started on their own work, and that's okay. The fact that I am writing alongside the others, then, makes the lesson more multilevel.

Be sure you give children only a very brief amount of time to fill in the gaps of the story or they'll veer far from the story as it's written!

I could decide to say, "Partners, would you show each other what you wrote, and talk about whether you did all these steps? This was your very first time doing this so I know some of you will see that you haven't been clear about what this work entails. That's okay—just talk about it!" But, in this case, time is short, and I know some children are confused enough that I'd rather clarify by sharing an example or two.

When I show children a chart like this, I don't necessarily read it aloud. I'm just showing them that this chart exists, and children can use it if they want this scaffold. For some children, the chart is unnecessary. Let this chart be a resource rather than a lesson!

Point out that the mental movies readers create are grounded in the texts themselves. Ask children to point to the textual details that informed their mental movies.

"I heard amazing descriptions of what you are picturing and sensing through Gabriel. Of course, we didn't all picture the same things, which is as it should be."

"When Gabriel walked down that street, searching for the source of that thin cry, Max filled in that Gabriel saw a large brown dog, curled up asleep in the alley. On the other hand, I filled in that he saw a bike and a bucket of purple flowers. The movies we make in our minds won't be exactly the same. When John Gardner said that readers create—we imagine— a kind of dream, a play in the mind (when he said we listen for some sound behind the imagined door, for that thin cry to come again from the shadows along Gabriel's street), remember that we *invent* this imagined story, this dream, out of both our lives and the text."

"Both Max and I remembered, however, that the author has told us that Gabriel sat on the stoop outside a tall building of 'crumbling bricks and rotting wood' and sees himself 'sleeping beneath the glittering lights of a movie theater, near the bus stop.' We'd be misreading the story if we had Gabriel search for the source of the cry by looking in posh doorways of boutique restaurants, stopping for an éclair and a frozen frappe."

"Would you go back to your partner and point to the lines from the story that provided a rationale for the bits you created to fill in the gaps of 'Spaghetti'? For example, if you added the line, 'He peered behind a trash can, piled high with garbage,' tell your partner the grounds for this image. If your picture wasn't grounded in the text, say aloud a new way to fill out the text."

LINK
Rally children to the big work of this unit and to the goal of wide-awake, attentive reading. Explain that for the next few days, they need to read deeply the texts from the packet.

"Writers, today we embark on a new unit of study. Earlier this year, you wrote about experiences and people that have left their mark on you. Today, I hope you've learned that the first step in writing a literary essay is to be the kind of reader who lets *stories* leave a mark on us. We need to read a few sentences on a page, and all of a sudden see a train rushing through Russia; we need to read sentences and all of a sudden see a small boy, peering into the alley. And today you learned that one way to help you step into the story is to write from inside it. You learned that you can write in ways that help you feel a story. Doing this writing will help you see more, hear more, think more, feel more as you read."

"I've put a small packet of stories on each of your desks; for the next few weeks, we'll read and reread, think, talk, and write about these stories, and about 'Spaghetti,' too.

I added this extension to the Active Engagement because I found that some children thought my invitation to fill in the gaps in the story gave them license to imagine any old thing. I hadn't meant to suggest this. However, I did expect children to add specific details that are not actually in the text, as in the example from my demonstration of the bike and the bucket of flowers. I am convinced that all good readers embellish, add on to, infer. However, good readers make sure that the text guides this process appropriately.

The qualities of good writing are also the qualities of good teaching. I could have made this same point without referring to the frozen frappe or the éclair, but I try to make general points with revealing specifics.

Sometimes we intervene during the active engagement to lift the level of children's work. This extension of the Active Engagement could easily have been a separate minilesson, but I'm trying to devote only a little bit of this unit to this deep reading.

You'll want to give each child a packet of four or five short texts. Be sure there are several texts in the packet that are easy enough for your struggling readers. We've had great success, for example, with "Alone" from Frog and Toad Are Friends by Arnold Lobel. That story works because it is beautifully written—as are the other texts we recommend. Include texts your class has reread often and come to love. On the CD-ROM, I've included a list of possible texts. If you use picture books, we usually give children typed copies of the texts (with permission from the publishers) so children can write on them (while reading the beautiful versions).

Today, choose whatever story catches your eye, and then read and write. Writers sometimes do this kind of thinking from inside a text before we write from outside a text—before we write *about* it."

"When you read today, you won't want to read like this," I said, flipping through pages and looking away. "Instead, read slowly, as if your job is to climb inside the words of this text and *live* the text. You'll see I've marked places to pause in each text, and when you come to one of those places, copy the underlined bit from the text and then keep writing, adding what the character was probably seeing, thinking, remembering. Just write a tiny bit, then return to the text to read some more. Go intensely through one short text, and maybe another, today. You will be doing something *on the page* that good readers do *in our minds' eyes* whenever we read really well."

During the Link in most minilessons, we generally say to children, "The strategy I've taught you today should help you from this day forward, whenever you . . . ." However, I am aware that the strategy I've taught children today is not one they will actually use "from this day forward." Instead, I've asked children to do something in writing that I hope they end up doing in their minds' eyes as they read. We earn kids' trust by acknowledging that what we ask them to do from time to time may not be a strategy readers or writers use often—and by explaining why we nevertheless believe it matters.

WRITING AND CONFERRING

Supporting Deep Reading

At the start of any new unit, you'll hustle among children, helping them begin the new work you've laid out. Children will need quite a lot of help getting started with the work of today's minilesson. You have asked them to engage in something that requires a different orientation than their usual writing workshop work. You have asked them to read—and the reading you hope they do probably differs from their usual reading as well as their usual writing work. Specifically, you have asked children to read much more intensely than usual, inching through a text with frequent shifts between reading and writing.

So at the start of today's workshop, I suggest you survey the room and notice right away the children who are flying through a text. Notice also those who are writing at a distance from the texts rather than from deep inside them; the children who concern you will be evaluating or commenting on texts rather than writing as if they were the authors, filling in gaps. These two groups will each need a quick intervention to bring them on course.

If the entire class needs guidance, rely on a mid-workshop teaching point; otherwise, I suggest using table conferences. When I taught this unit recently, I spent this first workshop time going to one table after another. At each table, I did similar work. Gathering the attention of all the children, I said, "Will you watch me work with . . . ." Then I worked with one child to get that one youngster doing what I hoped all the children would do. Specifically, I asked that child, "Where are you in reading the story?" Once the child showed me the spot, I said, "Let's read it together," and I scanned the surrounding group of children, saying, "She's reading . . . " (and I named the text). The watching children often pulled out their copy of that text so they could follow along. "Watch." Then the one child and I read silently for less than a minute. Then I paused and said to the one child, "I'm picturing this, aren't you?" In a voice that was loud enough for all the listeners to hear, I described what I was picturing. Then we read on.

> **MID-WORKSHOP TEACHING POINT** *Writing Inside the Text* "Writers, can I have your eyes and your attention please? Some of you are writing about the story; to use writing to read deeply, it helps to try writing inside the story. Let me share something very smart that Judah did. First I'm going to read the bit of text she read—it's from 'Boar Out There' by Cynthia Rylant—and then I'll read how she recorded what she envisioned. You'll remember that the story starts by saying everyone knew there was a wild boar beyond the rail fence in the woods. Then the story zooms in on one moment:
>
> > Jenny would hook her chin over the top rail of the fence, twirl a long green blade of grass in her teeth and whisper, "Boar out there."
>
> "First Judah wrote *about* the character, about Jenny in 'Boar Out There.' Here's how she did it at first":
>
> > Jenny cares about animals. She seems lonely—sitting, looking at the boar.
>
> "But then Judah said to herself, 'No, that doesn't help me really feel from inside the story. I want to get more in it.' So this time Judah wrote about the moment when Jenny was in the woods, sensing the boar is close.
>
> *continued on next page*

In one such conference, I asked Carmen to show me where she was reading in "The Marble Champ" by Gary Soto. She pointed to a section where the protagonist, Lupe, poured her brother's marbles onto the bed and picked five marbles. I read the section of the familiar text aloud to myself (knowing the observing children were listening in). It said, "She smoothed her bedspread and practiced shooting, softly at first." (2000) I pointed to that passage and said to Carmen what I was picturing: "She reached for the can full of marbles. Then she poured the whole canfull onto the bed. As she did this, the marbles clattered against the tin can. She picked out five marbles, one at a time, then scooped up the rest and returned them to the can. Then she lined up the five marbles on the bedspread." Then I paused to name what I'd just done for Carmen and for the others who were listening. "Do you see how I used what I know from my life—like the clatter of the marbles against that tin can—*and* what I learned from the story—the text told me Lupe's brother's marbles were in a can—to get me deeper into the story? Let's read on," I said, and after a minute, I again paused and said, "I can see it, can't you?" Then I whispered to Carmen, "Take it from there. What do you see?"

Carmen was speechless, so I looked at the children who were watching, as if to signal, "You should be able to do this. Could any of you do it?" No one leapt in, so I went back and reread the text in a way that allowed Carmen to regain momentum. This time, I started Carmen off. She stumbled through a tiny bit of envisionment and I resumed where she left off, adding on a bit more. I then turned our focus back to the text. "Let's read to the mark on the page and again, you tell me what you are imagining." This time, once Carmen began to tell me what she envisioned, I said, "Write that down!" As Carmen recorded two sentences, I debriefed with the observing children. Carmen looked up in the middle of this and I gestured as if to say, "Perfect," and then said, "Read on," returning her focus to the text. Then I asked the watching group of children to get started doing similar work with whatever text each of them chose.

In these ways, you'll provide the help that some children will need. You'll probably recognize that there is reciprocity between this work—teaching children to make movies in their minds as they read—and previous work you've helped children do as writers of short fiction and personal narratives.

continued from previous page

Judah wrote": *[Fig. I-1]*

> Jenny is slowly walking. The leaves crumble beneath her feet. She looks around, nervously she tries to be quiet, so she doesn't startle the boar.
>
> She starts to feel all closed in. She looks up to the sky to try and feel out of the woods.
>
> She eats a leaf and relaxes a little She leans against a tree, looks around, adn freezes. She stops breathing.
>
> He ran through the trees toward her. Her heart starts beating fast.

"Do you see how Judah wrote that part from inside the story? We can really see Jenny looking around and we can hear the leaves crumbling beneath her feet! That's what you need to do in your work too! Remember you, too, can use your eyes, your ears, your skin to experience the story you've chosen to read."

"Would you go back to the writing you've done so far? Read it over to see if you are writing in a way that helps you get deeper into the story."

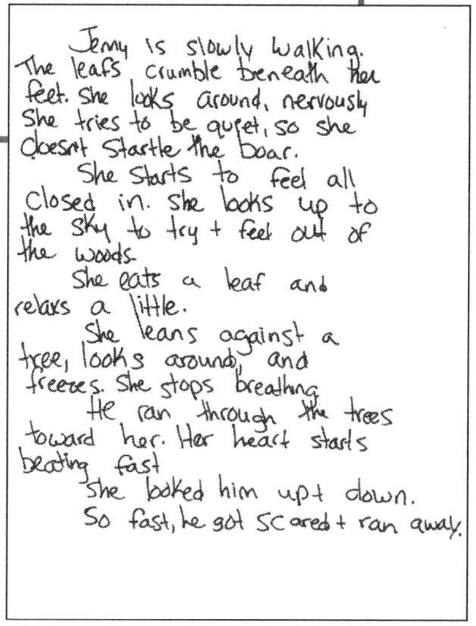
Jenny is slowly walking.
The leafs crumble beneath her feet. She looks around, nervously she tries to be quiet, so she doesn't startle the boar.
She starts to feel all closed in. She looks up to the sky to try + feel out of the woods.
She eats a leaf and relaxs a little.
She leans against a tree, looks around, and freezes. She stops breathing
He ran through the trees toward her. Her heart starts beating fast
She looked him up + down.
So fast, he got scared + ran away.

Fig. I-1 Judah continues envisioning the story

Max, for example, read "Slower than the Rest," another Rylant story, (1988) this time about a turtle. Max copied a line of the text onto his page (see italics) and then added on to it:

> "Both his little sisters squealed when the animal stuck its ugly head out to look at them, and they thought its claws horrifying."
>
> I see a dark turtle in the trunk of a big tree, scared and standing still, slowly sticking out its head. Leo would put Charlie down and he would sniff at the air for a moment, then take off as if no one had ever told him how slow he was supposed to be.

Then Max resumed reading, and soon paused again to copy a line from the text and add what he saw: *[Fig. I-2]*

> "Leo settled Charlie in a cardboard box, threw in some lettuce and radishes, and declared himself a happy boy."
>
> I see a small box with two holes for handles, just big enough for the turtle to sit in. He is in a kitchen, eating radishes.

A few youngsters may still find this difficult. With those children you'll need to decide upon your level of commitment to the work you laid out today. How invested are you in having every child grasp what it means to use writing as a medium in which they dream the dream of the story? Some of you will decide that it is crucial to be sure your children are reading with a level of alertness, empathy, and investment, but not crucial that they do this sort of writing today. Others of you will decide to linger with this session, and the extensions that follow can help you do this.

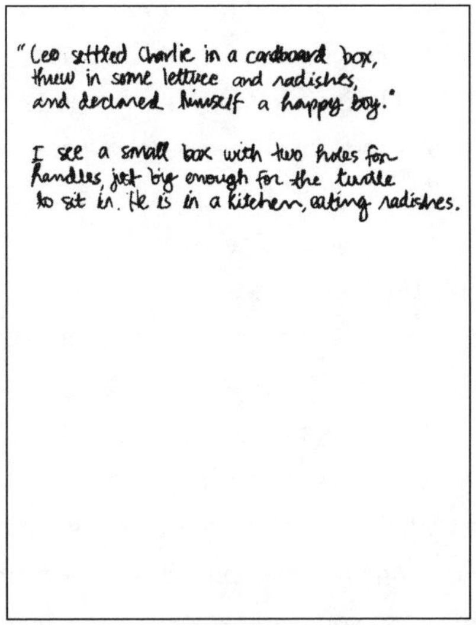
"Leo settled Charlie in a cardboard box, threw in some lettuce and radishes, and declared himself a happy boy."

I see a small box with two holes for handles, just big enough for the turtle to sit in. He is in a kitchen, eating radishes.

Fig. I-2 Max copies a line from Rylant's text and then writes about what he envisions.

SHARE

Reading Empathetically

Ask children to share their writing with their partners, discussing how this writing changed their reading.

"Right now, would you share with your partner what you wrote? Would you also talk with your partner about how this work helped you experience your story more deeply? And here is an important question: How could you do this sort of reading even if you don't have a pen in hand?"

I listened as Ali read aloud entries she'd written inside "The Marble Champ." In the story, after Lupe, the protagonist, realizes her marble-shooting thumb is weaker than the neck of a newborn chick, the text says, "She looked out the window. The rain was letting up but the ground was too muddy to play." (2000) Ali had copied that line and then filled in the details of what Lupe did next: *[Fig. I-3]*

> She looked out the window. The rain was letting up. She gripped the brown silk bag of marbles in one hand and a piece of chalk in the other hand. She got up and walked to the door to the outside. She took a deep breath and walked back to the marbles on the bed.

Later, Ali extended another section of the text: "To strengthen her shooting, she decided to do 20 pushups on her fingertips, five at a time." (2000) In her notebook, Ali wrote:

> Lupe got into the push up position. 1, 2, 3, 4, and 5. She fell down. But decided to push herself 10, 15, 20. "Yes!" she screamed.

Ali told her partner that writing these extra bits made her realize how hard it was to practice all the time, and she could feel how much each little pushup hurt.

Explain that empathy for real people works in much the same way as empathy for characters.

"Wow, I can hear that you all have really been reading deeply! The writing in support of reading that you have been doing today should definitely help you read empathetically, seeing through the character's eyes. Have you ever tried this kind of envisioning in your lives?"

You will definitely want to know well the stories you've given to your children to read. This will allow you to model, and also to quickly grasp what they've done.

> She looked out the window. The rain was letting up. She gripped the brown silk bag of marbles in one hand and a piece of chalk in the other hand. She got up and walked to the door to the outside. She took a deep breath and walked back to the marbles on the bed.
>
> . . . .
>
> Lupe got into the push up position. 1,2,3,4,5. She fell down. But decided to push herself 10,15,20. "Yes!" she screamed.

Fig. I-3 Ali envisions and writes off from "The Marble Champ"

"Have you ever tried to really imagine the senses of another person, perhaps a girl being bullied or a boy who is new to a school? This kind of careful attention to the world through someone else's eyes can help us learn how to have friends and be a good citizen in the world. From reading, we can learn empathy."

[HOMEWORK] *Reading, Writing, and Living with Empathy* The great writer, Joyce Carol Oates, has said, "Reading is the sole means by which we slip, involuntarily, often helplessly, into another's skin, another's voice, another's soul." Anna Quindlen agrees: "It is like the rubbing of two sticks together to make a fire . . . this making symbols into words, into sentences, into sentiments and scenes and a world imagined in the mind's eye." During reading time tonight and always, be sure to let the words on the page create a movie in your mind.

All year long, you've learned that *writers* make movies in our minds and then capture those movies in print. Tonight, be the *reader*. Take in the letters, words, and sentences, and let them be like the film of a mental movie. Read the print, learn that it is winter in the story, and let yourself shiver with the cold.

You can read or reread one of the short texts we'll be studying in the writing workshop—"Eleven," "The Marble Champ," "Boar Out There," "The Birthday Box"—or you can read your novel. But after you read a bit, put down the page and write what you see in that mental movie. Then resume reading. Shift between reading and writing, reading and writing. Here's an example of the kind of writing you can do: [Fig. I-4]

I look into the tent, seeing Ma laying in a tent of pain begging for water. Smelling like roasted meat. The burns from the kerosene were so severe it made Ma's skin black. I feel so bad for burning Ma. People say it was my fault but Dad says not.

I knew I would never play again. My hands were also burned in the accident. Everybody thought I was no good and they were better than me because I was motherless. The kerosene ruined my dream of being a pianist.

I turned from Ma and the tent of pain and go to Ma's piano and wipe the dust off with a quick swipe of my tender

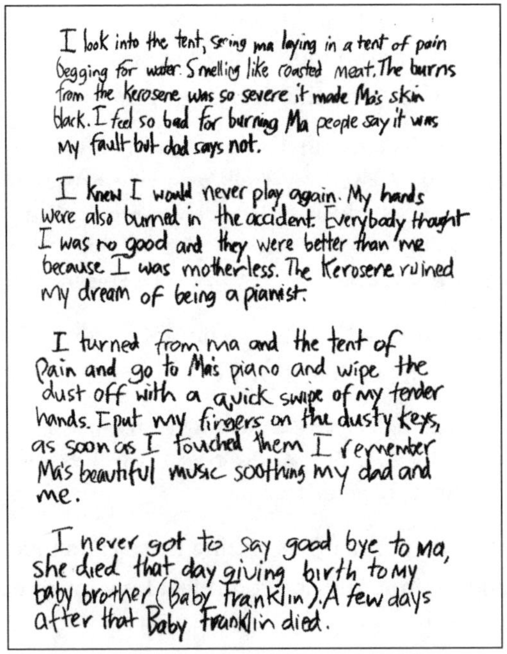

You may wonder about my use of "big words" such as empathetically. I make a point of weaving what I suspect will be unfamiliar vocabulary into my teaching. I do not usually stop to provide a definition, but I do try to surround the difficult term with an explanation of its meaning. That is, I try to enable children to use contextual knowledge to grasp the meaning of the term. This is how most human beings learn the thousands and thousands of new words we learn each year. I recognize that you will alter these minilessons so they work for your kids, and this may include altering the level of vocabulary.

I look into the tent, seeing ma laying in a tent of pain begging for water. Smelling like roasted meat. The burns from the kerosene was so severe it made Ma's skin black. I feel so bad for burning Ma people say it was my fault but dad says not.

I knew I would never play again. My hands were also burned in the accident. Everybody thought I was no good and they were better than me because I was motherless. The kerosene ruined my dream of being a pianist.

I turned from ma and the tent of Pain and go to Ma's piano and wipe the dust off with a quick swipe of my tender hands. I put my fingers on the dusty keys, as soon as I touched them I remember Ma's beautiful music soothing my dad and me.

I never got to say good bye to Ma, she died that day giving birth to my baby brother (Baby Franklin). A few days after that Baby Franklin died.

Fig. I-4 David's notebook entry in response to *Out of the Dust* by Karen Hesse

hands. I put my fingers on the dusty keys, as soon as I
touched them I remember Ma's beautiful music soothing
my dad and me.

I never got to say good bye to Ma, she died that day
giving birth to my baby brother (Baby Franklin). A few days
after that Baby Franklin died.

TAILORING YOUR TEACHING

If your children need more work to help them read deeply . . . you may decide to set
children up to turn and talk inside the story during your read-aloud sessions. For example, if
you are reading aloud *Because of Winn-Dixie* and you have just read that Opal brought a
stray dog, Winn-Dixie, home to her father, the Preacher, you might read, "The Preacher
looked at Winn-Dixie. He looked at his ribs and his matted-up fur and the places where he
was bald." And then you might say, "Partner 1, you are the father. You are looking at that
dog. What are you thinking? Tell partner 2." After a bit, you could intervene, "Partner 2, you
are Opal. Talk back to your father . . ." Once children have done this work orally in the
context of the read-aloud, it will be far easier for them to do similar work in response to the
short stories you are asking them to read as part of the writing workshop.

**If children need more time envisioning the story and writing from the character's point
of view in order to read more deeply** . . . you could lead a minilesson helping them rely on
close reading when they envision. You might start off by saying, "Yesterday you put
yourselves into 'Spaghetti' and wrote your mental movie of moments from those stories.
You used what you knew about the characters to imagine what they might have seen, heard,
and felt. Today I want to remind you that readers need to rely on the clues in a text to help
us picture the world in which the story takes place. You and I have talked about how every
story has a setting, and we talked about the importance of discerning that setting . . . but I
want to go a step farther and tell you that readers need to not only be able to name the
setting, we need to create it around us as we read. If it is a damp, gray day in the book, we
read and feel a chill. When I read, the setting unfolds like a movie in my mind."

To demonstrate you could read a bit aloud from "Spaghetti" and say something such
as, "Watch how I create the setting out of the clues I'm given. I see Gabriel slowly getting up
from the stairs of his building. He walks carefully along the edge of the street next to the
sidewalk. It is not easy to see because it is a gray, gloomy day—since Gabriel is peering into
the dusk, I know it is late in the day. Gabriel heard the cry and quickened his pace."

Then you'll want to debrief, pointing out what you did. "Writers, did you notice how I went back to where Gabriel was—sitting on the stoop—and I imagined the place where he was, then I followed him down the street, picturing exactly when and how he walked, on the edge of the sidewalk. Did you notice also that I made sure I paid attention to the word 'dusk' because it was a clue in the text, letting me know it was not morning or afternoon? I was walking in Gabriel's shoes, so when he heard the cry, I knew he would start walking faster and so would I. I was so into the story that I felt as if I (like Gabriel) wanted to discover who or what was making that sound."

During the active engagement, you might read a bit further in "Spaghetti" and ask children to make movies in their minds of the text and then turn and tell their partners what they see. Don't worry that you are revisiting "Spaghetti" over and over—rereading is crucial! You might end this minilesson by saying something like, "When we make a little movie in our minds as we read and specifically, when we create the world of the story, this helps us understand what the character is feeling and thinking because we have similar thoughts and feelings." As you send children off, remind them to play the movie in their minds . . . writing down what they see, think, feel . . . so they can connect with the characters and places in their story.

If your children worked through this unit during a previous year and they are ready for the minilesson to be a bit more challenging . . . you'll want your touchstone text to be more complex than "Spaghetti." I recommend that you and your colleagues choose a short story or a picture book and work with it together, using the repertoire of strategies conveyed in these minilessons to help you talk and write about the text you select. As you do this work, you'll find yourself deepening the lessons in this book, and inventing new ones. A group of teachers in a school I know well decided to work with Eve Bunting's picture book, *Fly Away Home*. Julia Mooney, one of the teachers at that school, read bits of the text and then envisioned the world of the story. Below you'll see the portion of the text that preceded her envisioning, and then what she wrote in her reading log:

> *Fly Away Home* (an excerpt)
>
> My dad and I live in an airport. That's because we don't have a home and the airport is better than the streets. We are careful not to get caught.
>
> Mr. Slocum and Mr. Vail were caught last night.
>
> "Ten green bottles on the wall," they sang. They were as loud as two moose bellowing.
>
> Dad says they broke the first rule of living here. Don't get noticed.

Dad and I try not to get noticed. We stay among the crowds. We
change airlines.

Julia wrote (although when teaching this, she might say this aloud):

> I'm picturing Andrew and his dad walking slowly through an
> airport with fluorescent lighting and people rushing all
> around them. They're trying not to get caught so they act
> like everyone else, pretending to be going on a trip or
> returning from one. Sometimes they wait in front of the
> conveyor belt, looking for bags that aren't actually coming.
> Other times they browse in the airport shops, reading
> magazines and admiring souvenirs.
>
> I see Andrew looking a little sad as he thinks about Mr.
> Slocum and Mr. Vail. Andrew feels bad for them, for their
> being caught. He's relieved that he and his dad are so
> good at keeping a low profile. But part of him is envious of
> Mr. Slocum and Mr. Vail. Part of him longs to be noticed, too.

Julia continued to read from *Fly Away Home*.

> Everything in the airport is on the move—passengers, pilots, flight
> attendants, cleaners with their brooms. Jets roar in close to the windows.

Julia wrote:

> Everything and everyone whirs past dad and me.
> Sometimes I wonder what all that rushing is about—where
> people are going and what they'll do when they get there.
> I wonder what it would feel like to have something to do,
> somewhere to be. Other times I don't even notice.

You and your colleagues can do similar work, and then mine this work for minilessons
you could teach. For example, in one minilesson, you could point out that you (like Julia)
brought your own ideas to the text.

If some of your children are envisioning the text by repeating the exact words of the text
. . . you might want to explain that making a movie in your mind as you read includes more
than simply repeating the story. I might say, "When I read, I am using *all* of my senses to
help me make the movie."

In a minilesson or a strategy lesson, I might say, "I'm going to reread the part of 'Spaghetti' we looked at yesterday and help you get a picture of Gabriel. Close your eyes and listen to the text. Do what I say, and this will help you get a clear picture." Then I'd reread an excerpt:

> It was evening . . .

After pausing, I'd say quietly, "See the sky . . . add the colors to your picture in your mind." Then I'd pause and continue reading:

> It was evening, and people sat outside, talking quietly
> among themselves.

"Add the people to your picture. Where are they sitting? What are they sitting on?" I'd pause. Then, "See their faces. What expressions are on their faces?"

Then I'd read on:

> On a stoop of a tall building of crumbling bricks and rotting wood
> sat a boy. His name was Gabriel and he wished for some company.

"See Gabriel. What's he wearing?" (Pause.) "What does he look like?" (Pause.) "Look closely at his face. How is he sitting? (Pause.) Right now, be Gabriel and show me what he looks like as he sits on the steps in front of his building. Sit like Gabriel's sitting."

Then I say, "Let's all look at Sabrina acting like Gabriel. Let's write in the air by putting words to what we see her doing. Turn to your partner and write in the air."

By this time, I'd want to debrief. "Writers," I might say. "Did you notice how I read a tiny bit and we worked on getting a picture in our minds by using our senses as we read? As you read today, pause and write what you are picturing."

COLLABORATING WITH COLLEAGUES

You and your colleagues can invent other ways to help children read deeply by identifying with characters. Notice what your students are doing pertaining to characters, for example, and think about how you can nudge them toward deeper work. If you want your children to identify with characters, to walk in their shoes, then it should concern you if you hear many children in your class dismissing and judging the protagonists in their books, saying things like, "*Why'd* he do that? I would *never* act like that." In these instances, you may want children to take their own questions more seriously, pausing to really consider why the character *did* do something. You might help children to ask themselves, "What is it about the character that makes him do this?" Usually in a well-written story, a character's actions are motivated. This means that although a child may not have done the same things, hopefully the child will be able to read what the character has done and say, "I can understand where this character was coming from."

Alternatively, you and your colleagues may decide to show children that writing about reading can be an opportunity for envisioning. Instead of asking partners to talk, you could have them write: "I can see it, can't you? Stop and jot what you see in your mind." Following are entries that two third graders wrote during a pause in the middle of a read-aloud from Gary Paulsen's book *The Monument*. [Figs. I-5 and I-6]

Entry 1, Writing in response to *The Monument*:

> Light, light, light is everything. All you need is a dry room and light. While he talked on about light and a dry room and how much light really is, very strange thing happened. Python walked over to him and put his jaw against the leg. Then he bent down and stroked Python's silky fur but Python did not mind at all. This was the first time he had let anybody touch him....

Entry 2, Writing in response to *The Monument*:

> "Look at the light coming down from the old wall! See how it comes down, gold and across your face! Oh god, see the light? It comes down like a blessing, like a kiss from the gods. I've got to get it. Don't move. Stay there." He sketched fast with his head bent over and sweat coming down his head. I still think, "What is he sketching?"

An extension of this would be to suggest that during independent reading, children put sticky notes on places in their independent reading books where they make movies in their minds. Then after reading silently for a half hour or so, children could meet with partners to share their notes and their mental movies.

Another day you could convey the thin line between envisioning and predicting, again doing this first in the read-aloud. As you read aloud, pause at key moments to speculate over what the character will probably do next. The character reaches into his wallet and finds no money there; the good reader is one step ahead, expecting the character to turn the wallet upside down and shake it. The reader expects the character to progress to checking his pockets, trying to recall the last time he saw that ten-dollar bill. In this way you can demonstrate that reading is an intricate weave of envisionment, prediction, and revision.

light, light light is everything. All you need is a dry room and light. While he talked on about light and a dry room and how much light really is, a very strange thing happened. Python walked over to him and put his jaw against the leg. Then he bent down and stroked Python's silky fur but Python did not mind at all. This was the first time he had let anybody touch him ...

Fig. I-5 Amelia envisions and writes in response to Paulsen's *The Monument*.

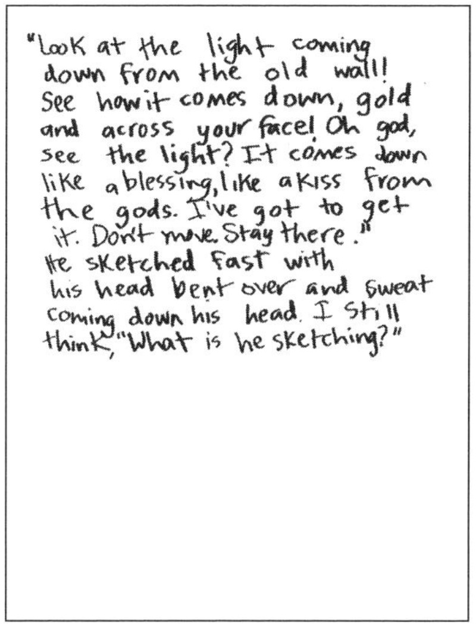

"Look at the light coming down from the old wall! See how it comes down, gold and across your face! Oh god, see the light? It comes down like a blessing, like a kiss from the gods. I've got to get it. Don't move. Stay there." He sketched fast with his head bent over and sweat coming down his head. I still think, "What is he sketching?"

Fig. I-6 Annie envisions, seeing through the artist, Mick's, eyes.

Later, you and your colleagues may want to talk together about ways in which this session can affect teaching and learning throughout the day.

For example, during your *reading* workshop, you could invite children to walk in the shoes of the main character in a story. You'd probably begin by demonstrating this in your read-aloud. Before you read aloud, read the text silently and note places where you find yourself picturing a character, a scene. The first two or three of those places can become places where you demonstrate for children.

In class, convene the children and read aloud. Pause at the first place you've marked and say something like, "I can just see this. She's . . . ." After saying aloud what you envision, read on. Your initial picture may be altered by incoming information, which is fine. Just say "Oops!" and make a quick alteration. Within a few minutes, you'll read a section in the text where you want children to do as you've done. Pause in the reading to say, "I can see it, can't you? See it in your mind." You might repeat a phrase or two. Then say, "Partner 1, tell partner 2 what you see." After a minute, interject by reading on. Don't stop and talk as a class. Read on, dream on!

IN THIS SESSION, YOU'LL REMIND
CHILDREN THAT WRITERS READ WITH
AN ATTENTIVENESS TO DETAIL THAT
CAN SPARK LARGER IDEAS. YOU'LL
SHOW AGAIN HOW WRITERS CAN
USE CONVERSATIONAL PROMPTS TO
EXTEND THEIR THINKING AND THEIR
WRITING ABOUT A TEXT.

GETTING READY

- "Spaghetti," by Cynthia Rylant, or other touchstone text, copied onto chart paper
- Idea for an entry you can use to demonstrate writing about a detail from the touchstone text, then having a larger thought about it
- Start of a chart, Strategies for Writing in Response to Reading
- Story you can tell about a child who initially had trouble making observations, then found lots to notice
- See CD-ROM for resources

GATHERING WRITING ABOUT THE STORY BY CLOSE READING

I recently watched a child come to the end of his novel, snap it shut, and sling it onto the bookshelf. "I'm done," he said. "I've read sixteen books. I've got to put another star by my name." Before Derrick raced off I asked what he thought of the book. "Umm . . . ," Derrick said. He hastened to reassure me. "I read it, I promise," he said. "I just don't remember it."

Too many children are growing up believing that comprehension is an optional "bonus" to reading. I hasten to tell them that if they have neither a memory of the text nor new ideas as a result of their reading, then they haven't really read the book at all. "Reading," I tell them, "is thinking, guided by print. Reading is response. Reading is your mind at work." We teach children that readers envision, synthesize, question, categorize, connect, and so forth, and then we give them tools for externalizing this brain work—we ask them to write what we hope they will later think. They may use notebook entries or sticky notes or graphic organizers or sketches: In all these cases, readers use tools to make invisible thoughts visible, to render fleeting thoughts lasting.

This session invites children to shift from the writing that helps the reader enter the story toward writing to develop ideas about stories. In the personal essay unit, writers learned that essayists observe the world, then push themselves to have thoughts about what they see. In this session, however, you'll invite your children to "observe" the texts and the worlds these texts represent, then push themselves to have thoughts about what they "see."

You'll teach children that literary essayists notice details to spark big ideas. Often, children either focus on the details of the text or make sweeping generalizations. As a result, their "thinking" amounts to little more than recapitulating the text or writing empty generalities. In this session, you'll tell children that when we read (or live) with a wide-awake attention to details, we are in the best position to grow big, compelling ideas.

MINILESSON

Gathering Writing About the Story by Close Reading

CONNECTION

Contextualize today's teaching by reminding children of strategies they used earlier in the year to generate writing for their personal essays. Tell them they'll follow a similar process to write literary essays.

"Yesterday, when we began our new unit, you learned one strategy for writing in response to reading. The writing we did yesterday helped us get lost in stories, seeing through the character's eyes and feeling all the character feels."

"Today, we will start writing to help us generate ideas about the texts we are studying. Remember back to when we wrote our personal essays? Remember how we generated writing for those projects? What you already know about writing personal essays can help you write literary essays. Writers grow like those little nested Russian dolls, carrying our past experiences as writers inside us as we move forward. In that unit, we learned that writers get big ideas by paying close attention to the details of our lives, to details like cicada bugs shedding their skin. Then we push ourselves to have thoughts about what we see and experience."

COACHING

Not surprisingly, I begin this unit by teaching a repertoire of strategies for generating the new kind of writing that children are studying.

In Session I, children brought a narrative frame of mind to their writing about reading. They wrote within the frame of the author's story. Today, the writing I'm teaching is more similar to the traditional expository writing one might expect in a unit designed to help children write literary essays.

You will see that the strategies children learn in this unit parallel those they learned in the previous personal essay unit. This time, their essays will be about texts rather than about their lives. Our most powerful teaching gathers up all the instruction that has preceded it, using that instruction and taking it just a little bit farther.

Remind children that when writing big ideas about a text, just as they do when writing big ideas about their lives, they must begin by paying close attention.

"Similarly, I want to teach you that when essayists want to grow big ideas about texts, we don't stare up into the heavens and wait for Big Ideas to descend on us. Instead we pay close attention to the details of what we see and hear and notice inside the story."

"If we can live wide-awake lives as readers, paying attention to the little details—to the cicada bugs—of texts, and letting those details lead us to develop fresh, provocative ideas, then we'll be well on our way toward writing powerful literary essays."

The reason I suggest students look closely at the text to grow new insights is that I'm convinced writers are more apt to develop fresh ideas when we begin by attending to detail, rather than generalizing and then supplying details to illustrate those generalizations.

Name your teaching point. Specifically, tell children that to write well about reading, essayists need to be alert to details.

"Today I hope you'll learn that to write well about reading, you need to be wide-awake readers. Some people say they read themselves to sleep, but because you and I are writers, we read ourselves awake! We use writing to help us become especially wide-awake as we read, noticing little details that others would probably pass by."

TEACHING

Demonstrate by rereading the touchstone text. Highlight the fact that you pause to attend closely to what's in the text, saying or writing what you notice.

"I want you to notice how I read 'Spaghetti,' paying attention to little details that some might pass by."

"Watch me as I read, trying to pay close attention to the details of what I see in the text. Notice that I see little details, and then push myself to have a thought about what I see."

> It was evening, and people sat outside, talking quietly among themselves. On the stoop of a tall building of crumbling bricks and rotting wood sat a boy. His name was Gabriel, and he wished for some company. (1998)

"Okay, I could read on. Nothing stands out to me. But I am going to force myself to pause, and to notice details that I could just zoom past. I've learned that there is always something to see, if we have the eyes to see it, so let me look more closely."

I looked at the text, and then I looked up, dramatizing that I had shifted from reading aloud to voicing what was on my mind: "I see that people are sitting outside in the evening, talking among themselves. They are sitting close to each other, talking quietly." Then I said to the observing children, "Now watch," and I shifted into thinking aloud about the text: "The thought I have about this is that Gabriel seems to be sitting far away from others. I wonder, Does he purposely sit far away? Or do his neighbors choose to sit away from him?"

I have come to believe that the sequence of our instruction in writing is incredibly important, because once skills have become automatic, learners can use those skills effortlessly to tackle new and more complex mental operations. This session assumes children have already learned to write entries in which they observe, then shift into reflecting on what they observe. The session also assumes that children already know how to work with conversational prompts, using these to extend their first thoughts. They are already accustomed to letting phrases such as I think or This makes me realize that lead them to write new ideas. All of this was taught during the personal essay unit and in reading workshop.

When I say that I hope readers notice that I pay attention to the little details in texts, I'm choosing those words carefully because I want children to transfer strategies they learned in the personal essay unit, where I also used that phrase, to this new unit. For this reason, I try to preserve my vocabulary from one unit to the next.

Notice that I role-play the fact that I'm tempted to read on, to say, "There's nothing noteworthy here." Over and over you'll see me role-play the very thing I hope children will not do, correcting myself in ways that I hope will also help them. I use role playing as a way to dramatize what not to do, as well as what to do.

When I first wrote this entry about "Spaghetti," I bypassed the actual words I see and The thought I have about this is, but when I revised I added them. It is important that our demonstrations match what we say. This means that during a demonstration, I don't try to dazzle children with my prowess. Instead, I illustrate what I have just explicitly taught in a manner that provides a model. For now I'm asking children to structure their responses to stories so they take in (or see) details in the text, then to think and write the thoughts they have about whatever they see. Therefore, I do likewise.

Shifting out of the role of reader into the role of teacher, I leaned close toward the children and said, "You already know how to shift between *recording* what you see into your notebook, on the one hand, and on the other hand, *thinking about what you see*. It is important to do this even when you're not sure that you *do* have a thought! Something magical often happens when you write or say, 'The thought I have about this is . . .' or 'I realize that . . .' or 'To add on . . .' Brand-new thoughts sometimes spill out."

"Now I'm going to record what I am thinking and push my brain to have more thoughts about this, like we did when we wrote essays before. Watch." I picked up a marker pen, scrawled on chart paper what I'd already thought aloud, and then said "Umm . . . ," pausing for a moment before adding on:

> I <u>see</u> that people are sitting outside in the evening, talking among themselves. They are sitting close to each other, talking quietly.
>
> <u>The thought I have about this is</u> that Gabriel seems to be sitting far away from others. I wonder, Does he purposely sit far away? Or do his neighbors choose to sit away from him?
>
> <u>To add on</u>, the lead shows a friendly place, full of people who know each other. I think Gabriel feels especially alone because everyone else has friends. Loneliness is hardest when you are alone in a group. <u>This reminds me of</u> riding the school bus, as a kid; everyone else sat with a best friend, I sat alone.

Resume reading, again pausing to notice aloud what's in the text and again writing in response to what you see.

I resumed reading:

> Gabriel was thinking about things. He remembered being the only boy in class with the right answer that day, and he remembered the butter sandwich he had had for lunch. Gabriel was thinking he would like to live outside all the time. He imagined himself carrying a pack of food and a few tools and a heavy cloth to erect a hasty tent. Gabriel saw himself sleeping among the coyotes. But next he saw himself sleeping beneath the glittering lights of a movie theater, near the bus stop.
>
> Gabriel was a boy who thought about things so seriously, so fully, that on this evening he nearly missed hearing a cry from the street. (1998)

This unit begins by asking children to spend a week or two writing about reading in their notebooks. One reason I do this is to teach children that writing is a vehicle not only for communicating but also for growing ideas. You will see, then, that I encourage children to write about ideas that are not yet fully formed in their minds, to let ideas come out of the tips of their pencils, fresh and surprising.

The most important word that I've said might be the umm. It's crucial for us to show children that ideas don't come to any of us right away. We wait for them to nibble, like a fisherman waits for the fish to bite. So often children expect ideas to be right there, fully articulated, in their minds, and they don't understand the experience of fishing for, waiting for, an idea to nibble.

Keep your writing as brief as possible. Minilessons become cumbersome and we overwhelm children if we allow ourselves to read or write too extensively. Students don't need dazzling and extensive demonstrations to grasp the teaching point.

You'll notice that when I name what I see in the text, I focus on the main thing. I don't advise skirting past the main drama of the story to point out a tiny quirk that catches your eye. Instead, read aloud just a paragraph and write (and think aloud) in a way that shows children that you noticed what most readers in your class probably noticed.

This time I said, "The story tells that Gabriel was thinking about things so intently that he almost didn't hear the cat," and as I spoke, I underlined the line that conveyed this.

I underline the lines from the story that ground what I say and think because I want this physical way to remind children that our ideas are grounded in a close reading of the story. Often children glance at a text and then spin out ideas that are only tangentially related to the text. Ideally, I will have made an enlarged, laminated copy of the entire text to use throughout this unit, but if not, I can simply copy the first portion of it onto chart paper. I could also just underline or use a sticky note to mark my own personal copy of the story, demonstrating how I do this without actually showing the text on which I write.

"But the story doesn't come right out and say *why* he doesn't hear things around him. I think readers are supposed to figure out why Gabriel doesn't hear the cat's cry. It's the same in my life—recently my mother has been acting cranky. She doesn't come right out and tell me that her back hurts her, but I can draw on everything I know and fill in that part of the story. In the same way, we all need to fill in when we read. Although the story doesn't come right out and say why Gabriel is lost in his thoughts, we, as readers, can fill that in."

You'll of course teach children during the reading workshop that bits of a story can be windows to a character. Children need to learn that when they notice what a character does, for example, they might also reflect on how the character could have acted differently. What do the character's actions reveal about the person? Children can attend not only to what a character does, but how he or she acts, because this too is a window to the character's traits.

Explain that you underline or mark with a sticky note what you see, and then write what you think.

"So now I'll try writing an entry to think about what I noticed in that section of 'Spaghetti,'" I said, and I wrote:

> My idea is that Gabriel is alone so often that he has built a wall around himself. He doesn't even listen for people to talk with him. He doesn't expect anyone on the stoop will speak to him. He has tuned everyone out, and he is lost in his thoughts, oblivious. That's why he almost doesn't hear the cat's cry.

I decided to write this particular insight because I want children to notice really important aspects of a story. A character's changes are almost always worth consideration. It is no accident, then, that I'm thinking about how the protagonist, Gabriel, changes across the text. Specifically, I see Gabriel changing from the well-defended, stalwart (but lonely) child at the start of the text to a child who eventually lets a kitten through his wall of defenses. I decided to highlight the "before" version of this change in Gabriel now because doing so will pay off for me later when I want to contrast the "before" with the "after." I am setting myself up for later minilessons.

Debrief. Remind writers that when using this strategy to generate writing about texts, you note details in the text, then write your thoughts about those details.

"Writers, do you see that after I read a bit, I look back at the story, noticing details? If I own the book, I underline the details—otherwise I leave a sticky note to mark what I notice. Then I pick up my pen, and push myself to write. I could write what I actually saw in the text—in the personal essay unit, we usually recorded what we saw in life—but when writing literary essays, I usually just *point at* what I saw in the text and then write the thoughts I have about whatever I've noticed. I write, 'I think . . .' or 'My idea is . . .'. As I write those words, I'm often not sure quite what I will end up thinking, but ideas come to my pen."

ACTIVE ENGAGEMENT

Set children up to read and scrutinize the upcoming passage in the touchstone text, then to share their thoughts by writing in the air.

"If I hadn't been writing about 'Spaghetti,' I would have zoomed right past the fact that other people were chatting in a friendly fashion on the stoop while Gabriel sat there alone. Writers see more, notice more; we live more wide-awake lives. So let's try writing to see more and think more. Partner 1, will you read aloud a bit more of 'Spaghetti,' and then pause. At that pause, partner 2, try to really pay attention to the text. Point at and reread details that matter. You *could* just glance at the text and say some generalization like 'Gabriel's outside,' but good readers look more closely, expecting that the details will be worth noticing. Then, partner 2, write in the air, saying what you see when you really look closely at the details of the text."

"After a tiny bit, partner 1, remind your partner to say something like, 'And the idea I have about this is . . .' or 'I'm realizing . . .' or 'I think . . .'. Okay? Partner 1, start by reading a paragraph aloud." I listened to a few of the partnerships.

Celebrate. Perhaps tell the story of a child who underlined what he noticed in the text and then composed ideas.

After a few minutes, I called for attention: "Writers, eyes on me please." Once I had everyone's attention, I said, "I want to share with you what Tony just said and did. He first listened to Marie read aloud this bit of the story":

> Gabriel was a boy who thought about things so seriously, so fully,
> that on this evening he nearly missed hearing a cry from the street.
> The cry was so weak and faraway in his mind that, for him, it could
> have been the slow lifting of a stubborn window. (1998)

Many of the subordinate points that I tuck into this minilesson come from previous units in the writing workshop, or, for this unit, from previous units in the reading workshop. Just as we want children to hold a whole text in their heads, not just the chapter they have just read, we also want to them to hold all of our past teaching in their heads. Tucking lessons from previous teaching into our new minilessons, as subordinate points, is one way to do that.

The lilt with which you say, "And the idea I have about this . . ." is important. You hope that partner 1 tucks this into partner 2's sentence in a way that puts words into partner 2's thoughts, words that shift this child from observing to mulling over, growing meaning around those observations.

"Then Tony pointed to the section that said that Gabriel nearly missed the cry, it seemed so weak and faraway. He also went back and pointed to a line from earlier in the text in which Gabriel thought that he'd like to live outside, and saw himself sleeping in a homemade tent surrounded by coyotes. Tony said, 'I notice Gabriel is sort of alone. He sleeps with the coyotes and he doesn't hear stuff around him.'"

"When Marie wisely nudged Tony by saying, 'The thought I have about this is . . . ,' Tony added, 'I think Gabriel is brave. He isn't afraid to sleep outside.' Then he said something really smart: 'He's sort of tough. To add on, it's like he has gotten hardened and toughened so he almost doesn't hear the weak cry.'"

LINK
Reveal a chart showing the two strategies you've now taught for generating writing in response to reading. Invite children to draw on both strategies today and always.

"Today, writers, you learned a second strategy for writing as you read. You now have two strategies you can use anytime, for the rest of your life, when you write about reading":

> ### Strategies for Writing in Response to Reading
> - Find a significant moment from the story. Copy the start of it into your notebook; envision it; fill in details, sounds, actions, thoughts, feelings.
> - Be a wide-awake reader. Notice and underline details others might pass by. Then write a thought about what you notice.

"For today, you will again read as well as write during our writing workshop, drawing on all the stories in your packet. You will probably want to reread the stories you read yesterday. You'll probably shift back and forth: reading, jotting, reading, jotting. And from this day on, remember that if you want to write about your reading, you can use either of these strategies—or others you invent."

You won't report on Tony's thinking, of course, but about what a child in your own class says. As you listen to partners talk, find or help a child to say an idea about Gabriel (or the character in whatever text you read) that you believe is worth revisiting. Record the child's exact words on chart paper. You'll see that I return to what Tony has said in tomorrow's small-group work, when I teach children that as we read further in a story, we revise our first draft ideas of it.

You'll notice that I'm not making the chart in front of children, as I would have done earlier in the year. By now, the minilessons already verge on being too long, and children grasp the relationship between what we say and demonstrate and what is recorded on the chart. Notice, however, that a new item is recorded each day, even if this happens offstage.

When I talk to children about a strategy, I am less apt to make global comments about the strategy and more apt to articulate the steps that comprise the strategy. Notice the chart captures those small steps.

As Vladimir Nabokov advises readers, "There is nothing wrong about the moonshine of generalization after the sunny trifles of the book have been lovingly collected. If one begins a reading by making generalizations, one begins at the wrong end and travels away from the book before one has started to understand it." This is the message of today's session.

WRITING AND CONFERRING

Celebrating Successes, Anticipating Struggles

Expect that children will encounter challenges in this unit, and welcome these challenges as opportunities to teach. That is, if you find yourself saying, "This is hard for my kids," don't assume hard is bad. At this point in the year, your children are probably game to do a bit of ambitious work. They'll learn all the more because the work stretches them. But of course, it will be important to find triumphs to celebrate. Assign yourself the job of reading student writing, looking for bits to celebrate.

Point out places where a child has written powerfully. Let children know when one of them has come up with an insight that stops you in your tracks and makes you go, "Wow." For example, perhaps you will decide to simply circulate the room, making little check marks beside instances in which a child's writing is more insightful than usual. "Bravo!" you can whisper. "That's such a fresh, original idea!" In this way, you can let a child know when he or she has used a powerful word or image or insight. Sari wrote that Zachary, a child in a divorce story, feels *hopeless*. Sari's teacher pointed to the term and said, "That is such a powerful word! You've said something really strong here." Sari was so fueled by her teacher's recognition of what she had done that she ended up rereading her entire entry, erasing some of her other words and substituting more powerful synonyms. Sari's teacher could have taken this a step further and taught the whole class the importance of selecting precise terms. One could say a character is friendly, but is the character outgoing? Empathetic? Loyal? Supportive? Gregarious? Steadfast? Precision in word choice matters, because each word has a different nuance.

Watch as a child uses a conversational prompt to extend his or her thinking, and help the child really comprehend the power of the transitional phrase he has just written. If you watch as a child writes, "Jenny lies in bed thinking about the boar, loose in the woods. I *realize* . . . ," point to the phrase *I realize* and say, "Wow! I can't wait to read what new thought comes to you, what the idea is that you realize. It is so

---

MID-WORKSHOP TEACHING POINT *Noticing Language* "Writers, can I have your eyes and your attention? You learned today that to write about texts, essayists read with wide-awake attention, noticing the details in texts and then growing ideas about those details. And as I worked with you today, I found that many of you especially noticed what your characters do or want. This is wise, especially if you then push yourself to have a thought about this. Remember earlier we noticed that Tony, for example, wrote, 'Gabriel wants to sleep with the coyotes.' Then he pushed himself to have a thought and wrote, 'I think Gabriel is brave. He isn't afraid.'"

"Another really important way you can grow an idea about a text is to notice how the author has written the story—the words she has chosen. Max noticed in 'Spaghetti' that Cynthia Rylant used the word *so* before the word *seriously* (and again before *fully*): 'Gabriel was a boy who thought about things so seriously, so fully.' Max was struck by the repetition of the word, deciding it might be important that instead of writing that Gabriel thought about things 'seriously and fully,' she wrote, '*so* seriously and *so* fully.' He wrote down his observation on the author's craft and began to grow a thought about it. Max wrote, 'I think Cynthia Rylant wanted us to realize something important about Gabriel … he's a very, very serious, thoughtful boy.' I was impressed that Max got all that from the repetition of the word *so*. Keep in mind that you can always get ideas from studying the language an author has chosen—even a tiny word like *so*!"

exciting to see brand-new ideas emerge!" In that way, you can help the child understand the meaning of a phrase that he could otherwise use in a rote fashion. React similarly if a child writes, "The important thing about this is . . . ." Tell the child you can't wait to see what it is she selects as the most important thing, and act as if that choice is a weighty one!

When I praise the strong aspects of what a child has done, I try to be very specific and to name what works in a way that can provide guidance for another day when the child is writing about another topic. For example, Ali wrote this about "The Marble Champ":

> I see that Lupe is laying on her bed and she is flicking marbles, eyes droopy. I think she is so into this she is like a magnet getting pulled into this game. I think she is determined to win and play as if it is her destiny.

I pointed out to her and to others that Ali had used a strategy that could help all of us as readers. "I absolutely love the way you brought your own ideas to this," I said to Ali. "The text does not come right out and tell you that Lupe worked so long that her eyes were droopy, but you figured this out, you brought that detail to the text. Wise move. And it is even smarter that you deduced that Lupe has a magnetic relationship to marbles; she's drawn to them as if with a magnetic force. That is a really smart theory, grounded in the text *but made up in your mind!* Brilliant."

With this support to goad her on, Ali continued working with zeal. Not surprisingly, she continued to shift between writing what she saw and writing the significance she attached to what she saw and thought. You'll notice in these few pages from her writer's notebook (*Figs. II-1 and II-2; emphasis is my own*) that Ali is writing a hybrid sort of entry, one that merges some writing to envision the gaps of a story with thoughts about what she envisions in those gaps:

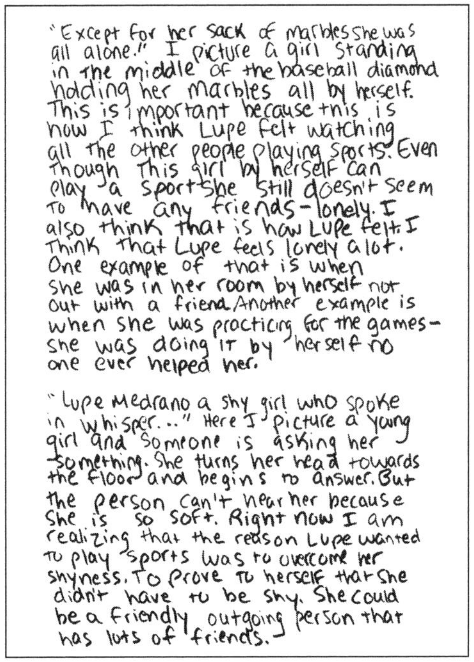

> "Except for her sack of marbles, she was all alone." I picture a girl standing in the middle of the baseball diamond holding her marbles all by herself. <u>This is important because</u> this is how I think Lupe felt watching all the other people playing sports. Even though this girl by herself can play a sport she still doesn't seem to have any friends—lonely. <u>I also think</u> that is how Lupe felt. I think that Lupe feels lonely a lot. <u>One example</u> of that is when she was in her room by herself not out with a friend. <u>Another example</u> is when she was practicing for the games—she was doing it by herself no one ever helped her.
>
> "Lupe Medrano a shy girl who spoke in whisper . . ." <u>Here I picture</u> a young girl and someone is asking her something. She turns her head towards the floor and begins to answer. But

Fig. II-1 Ali shifts between envisioning, looking closely at the text, and reflecting.

the person can't hear her because she is so soft. Right now <u>I am realizing</u> that the reason Lupe wanted to play sports was to overcome her shyness. To prove to herself that she didn't have to be shy. She could be a friendly outgoing person that has lots of friends.

<u>I find it interesting</u> that Lupe does all the really great things and wins awards, yet she is really shy. Usually when I think of a person like Lupe I would think that she would be outgoing and not shy. <u>I wonder</u> if she thinks if she played sports she would become more outgoing and not shy. I think that does happen. When she wins her first game against Rachel and she asks her to join them. I think that when she began playing marbles, she began having confidence. <u>I think</u> it was when she became more like other people, kids, girls. I think that she kind of wanted to be able to compare herself to other kids. Because she could do all of these things you have to be very talented to do.

This kind of writing is very fertile ground for essay writing about literature—there is plenty to celebrate here. Ali will have rich material to draw from as she begins her literary essay.

You can enter today's teaching ready not only to notice and fuss about children's successes, but also to scaffold children to use the new strategies you have taught. You can predict that a surprisingly large number of children will have difficulties coming up with thoughts about books. These children are apt to restate facts rather than invent their own new thoughts. So they'll write, "I think Gabriel wants company" or "I think Gabriel goes looking for what is making the sound." Neither of those is a new idea—both are stated outright in the text. To help children understand the difference, I sometimes tell them that their ideas won't be *right there* on the page of the story. If I can point to the section of the text that comes right out and says what the child has stated, then the child is retelling the story, not growing an idea. I also sometimes tell children that ideas are often debatable.

If children are recording facts about the story rather than writing ideas, I find it helps to teach them that ideas hide inside facts. For example, it's a fact that Gabriel thought about a *butter* sandwich. To grow a thought, I need to linger with that for a fraction of a minute, asking myself, "And what do I think about that?" Sometimes a child's first instinct is to think by asking a question, which I believe often reflects timidity. The child might think, "Why a butter sandwich, not peanut butter and jelly?" Nudge the child to speculate on an answer. "Maybe Gabriel remembers his butter sandwich because he's poor and it's basically just bread."

If children struggle to generate ideas about texts, you may want to teach them the kinds of topics that many readers find fruitful. For example, you could share any combination of these topics,

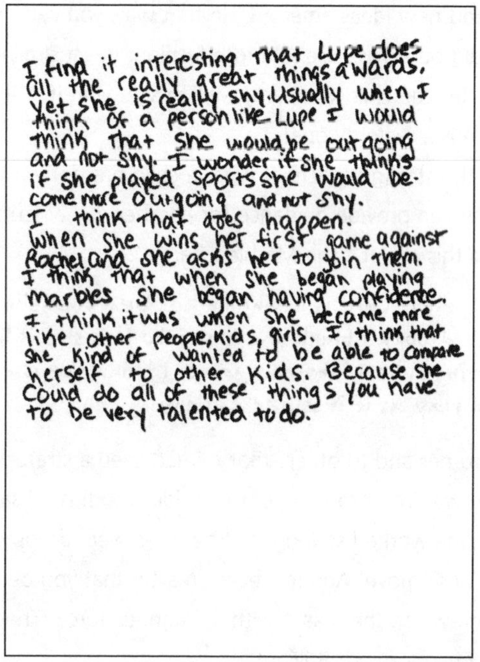

I find it interesting that Lupe does all the really great things & awards. yet she is really shy. Usually when I think of a person like Lupe I would think that she would be outgoing and not shy. I wonder if she thinks if she played sports she would become more outgoing and not shy. I think that does happen. When she wins her first game against Rachel and she asks her to join them. I think that when she began playing marbles she began having confidence. I think it was when she became more like other people, kids, girls. I think that she kind of wanted to be able to compare herself to other kids. Because she could do all of these things you have to be very talented to do.

Fig. II-2 Ali's response to "The Marble Champ" page 2

remembering that usually we are more thoughtful when we think extensively about one topic rather than race from one to the next.

Characters: What kind of person is this? What does this character want? Struggle with? What do these characters get from and give to each other? What is the nature of the relationships in this story?

Connections to other works of literature: How does the meaning in this text fit with the meaning in another related text?

Craft: Why might the author have made the decisions he or she made? Why did the author title the text this way? Start this way? Use this emphasis? Choose this setting? End this way?

Significance: What does the text teach us? What is the text *really* trying to say?

Genre: What kind of text is this? How does the text seem like, or unlike, other texts of this genre?

But the most important thing you can do to help children develop their thoughts about texts is to devote more time to helping them have grand conversations about texts. I write about this elsewhere in this book and in *The Art of Teaching Reading*.

SHARE

Developing the Eyes to See What Others Overlook

Tell the story of a child who looked at a text and couldn't find much of interest in it. Use a metaphor or anecdote to explain how one can learn to see with new eyes.

"I want to tell you about Raffi. When I came to him, he was reading the short story 'The Marble Champ.' He looked up at me and shrugged, like this, and said, 'There's not that much to see in here.'"

"But I said, 'Raffi, remember when you dipped your cup into the pond, then looked at your water? You said, "I didn't get any bugs or anything," and you almost threw your water back? But instead, you looked more closely, then studied the water through a magnifying lens, and you found your water was swarming with creatures!'" Shifting away from reenacting my conversation with Raffi, I looked out at the class, and said, "So Raffi looked again at Soto's story, and this time, he saw a whole lot and wrote all this." I held up his notebook to illustrate that he'd filled more than a page with observations.

"Writers, if some of you read a story and then think, 'What's there to see?' remember Raffi. And remember that Cynthia Rylant once said that a writer walks the aisles of Woolworth's and has relatives over to supper and goes fishing *as a writer*. Raffi and I realized that we can add to Cynthia Rylant's list. Writers walk the aisles of Woolworth's and have relatives over for supper and go fishing and *read books* as writers. Like writers the world over, we see more, hear more, notice more, and most of all, we *think more* because we are reading like writers."

Ask children to look again at a text, this time with a partner, and see it with new eyes.

"Would you get with your partner, put a story you've both read between you—it may be 'Spaghetti' if that's the only story you have both read so far—and this time, try to *really see* what's there! Point out intriguing things you notice and talk about what you see. Especially talk about what you think about what you see. Grow ideas together!"

I find that when I want to teach a lesson, it often helps to do so through an anecdote. Notice that my stories of children are written in a manner that illustrates the tips I share about how to write stories. When I tuck an anecdote into a minilesson, I try to recall qualities of effective stories. For example, I generally make characters speak. In this instance, for example, I didn't really recall Raffi's exact words, so I supplied the words I suspected he probably said. Like a good Small Moment story, the episode starts close to the heart of the problem. After I tell the story, I unpack it, or debrief, just as I ask children to do after they cite an anecdote from literature in a literary essay.

I find that it can be tricky to talk a lot about the mental work that readers do because that work is invisible. Often, then, I'll describe a more concrete kind of work, then I'll say, "Isn't reading similar?" I did this in the anecdote about Raffi looking at pond water.

HOMEWORK *Reading with Passionate Attentiveness* A friend of mine, Bess, lost her mother to cancer last spring. Her mother was dearer to her than you can possibly imagine, and the loss was devastating. Bess wondered how she'd face life—summer days at the beach, her thirtieth birthday, the first autumn colors—without sharing all this with her mother. Bess' thirtieth birthday came, and with it, a giant feeling of loneliness. Bess walked to the mailbox that day, remembering the previous birthday and her mother's presence. In the mailbox, there were the usual magazines and letters. And there was a package. Turning it over, Bess' heart stopped. The front of the package had her mother's handwriting. In place of a return address, there was a heart. How could this be?

Once inside the kitchen, Bess sat down with the package. She held it and for a moment, imagined the impossible. Finally, she loosened the tape, letting the paper fall open. And there, before her, was a letter from her mother and a scrapbook. "Bess," the letter began. "You can't imagine how much I wanted to be with you today. Knowing it wasn't in the stars, I made this gift for you, wrote this letter, and asked Dr. Marcus to be sure you received it."

Imagine the miracle of that letter—those words, coming to Bess like a letter in a bottle, one that had traveled across the sea of time. The books you and I read are all, like Bess' message, miracles. Consider how extraordinary it is that Patricia MacLachlan sat at her desk in Amherst, Massachusetts, remembering her son in Africa, her childhood on the prairie, and wrote *Baby*. Now, years later, in an utterly different place, you and I can pick up the book, read her words, and dream the dream of that story.

Mortimer Adler, a reading researcher, once said, "There is only one situation I can think of in which men and women make an effort to read better than they usually do. When they are in love and reading a love letter, they read for all they are worth. They read every word three ways; they read between the lines and in the margins . . . they even take the punctuation into account. Then, if never before or after, they read."

Tonight, would you read one of the stories we've chosen to study? Read it as if that story came as a message in a bottle, thrown across the seas of time. Read it as if it were a gift from someone you love who is now gone. Read it as if this were a love letter. And write about whatever you notice, whatever it makes you think and feel and wonder and remember. Write this in a long entry.

If your children have already experienced this unit in a previous year and if, therefore, you've decided to ratchet up the complexity of the lesson . . . you'll want to do the work you're asking children to do, and to pay attention to what skills you find yourself needing to use. Julia Mooney and her colleagues worked with Bunting's picture book, *Fly Away Home*. In a minilesson, Julia pointed out that she first observes the text and then pushes herself to have a thought about it. She read aloud this section of the book:

> "Delta, TWA, Northwest, we love them all," Dad says. He and I wear blue jeans and blue T-shirts and blue jackets. We each have a blue zippered bag with a change of blue clothes. Not to be noticed is to look like nobody at all.

Then, thinking aloud, she said:

> I <u>see</u> that Andrew and his dad dress alike, all in blue, and that they carry matching blue bags. <u>The thought I have about this is</u> that they are trying to blend in by not standing out. I wonder if the author picked the color blue to show that Andrew and his dad are sad—that they're blue. <u>To add on to this</u>, the blue clothes and bag seem like a mirror of how Andrew feels: "like nobody at all." <u>This is giving me the idea</u> that the blue clothes are a symbol of this feeling. I think Andrew is blue because he feels unimportant, almost invisible. This reminds me of how I felt when I moved to this country at age six. I didn't speak English yet so I couldn't talk to anyone except my parents. I felt like I was invisible.

Then she returned to reading:

> Once we saw a woman pushing a metal cart full of stuff. She wore a long, dirty coat and she lay down across a row of seats in front of the Continental Gate 6. The cart, the dirty coat, the lying down were all noticeable. Security moved her out real fast.

This time when Julia paused to think aloud, she said:

> Here the story says that Andrew observes a homeless woman being removed by security because of the things that make her noticeable (that distinguish her as homeless): the cart, the dirty coat, the lying down.
>
> This is just one of the many observations Andrew makes about being noticeable as a homeless person.

Debriefing, Julia pointed out to the children, "Do you see how I come up with ideas that the author doesn't come right out and say? The story doesn't come right out and say *why* Andrew collects ways homeless people are noticeable. Readers are supposed to figure out why he does this all the time. It's the same in life. I have a friend who sometimes doesn't return phone calls. She doesn't have to tell me this is because she's feeling sad over her husband's recent death. I can take what I know about her and her life and fill that part of the story in."

Then Julia said, "So now I'll try to write an entry to think about what I noticed in this section of the text."

> My idea is that Andrew is a boy who understands the dangers of being noticed when you're homeless. He's found ways <u>not</u> to be noticed (or caught) out of the need to survive. This is why he makes so many observations about those homeless people who stand out.

> Another thing I notice in *Fly Away Home* is how many times and ways Andrew says the he and his dad are careful not to get noticed, that it's dangerous to be noticed, what makes you noticed and what doesn't. There are mentions of being noticed on many of the pages in this story.

COLLABORATING WITH COLLEAGUES

In this unit, as in every unit, your teaching will be exponentially enriched if you and your colleagues give these lessons to yourselves, doing the same reading and writing that you ask children to do, while maintaining a researcher's awareness. This unit is an especially rich and provocative one, full of nooks and crannies that have not yet been explored. I hope you are especially eager as you teach this unit, ready to add your own ideas, gleaned from your own research.

One fruitful source of insight will be this. Take ten minutes in a staff meeting to read one of the texts your children are reading and then record the thinking you do as you read the text. I call this mirror writing because the goal is to look at the marginalia you wrote as a way to make visible the invisible work you did as a reader.

With a colleague, look at your writing. Ask first, "What was I trying to do as I wrote about my reading?" You may see that you are still acting as if you are in a classroom, reading to write so as to convince a teacher that you did do the assigned reading! If your writing about reading seems wooden, if it feels as if it simply records facts to prove that you read, then read a bit more, and in your notes try to really capture your fleeting thoughts.

Look at writing that conveys your thoughts and notice that this writing, when done well, does not resemble finished literary essays. The goal is not full sentences, or ideas that are spelled out and carefully supported with evidence. The characteristics of effective writing to learn are very different from those of finished expository essays.

Try looking at the writing you do as you read as a reflection of your *reading,* not your writing. Which qualities of good reading do you practice a lot? Do you predict? Envision? Ask questions? See ways in which one section of a text is linked to another section of the text? Consider what the author's message might be? Question why the author wrote the text as he or she did, and how these decisions relate to the author's message?

If you contrast your own writing about reading with that of your colleagues, you'll probably learn a few very interesting things. First, you'll probably notice that each one of you has one or two things you tend to do as you read, and you do those things often. One of you may respond personally to texts, another may notice the author's craftsmanship, yet a third may judge and talk-back-to the character. You will probably find that the lens you use a lot is one you already model for children. If you find that you often predict as you read, you'll probably see that your children are doing this as well. It helps to deliberately decide that you can take on a new lens for reading and thinking, borrowing one of your colleague's ways of seeing a text.

Of course, you'd want to process this work together with your colleagues by naming what it is you all have done together. You may decide that the repertoire of ways you have to read is limited, that you usually lean on one or two qualities of good reading, and you may decide to expand your repertoire by reading with a lens which is not your usual. When you expand your repertoire by deliberately borrowing a lens that your colleague uses, you'll want to let your students know that you are doing this so they can emulate you and expand theirs as well. It is very powerful to give ourselves and our children new lenses for seeing a text. If a reader rarely pauses to think, "What is this author's view of the world? Do I agree? Disagree?" then learning to read critically will lift the level of that person's reading and thinking.

If you are really serious about teaching children that writing can be a tool for thinking, you'll need to invest more time and attention in this instruction. You may invite children to look over past writing about reading that they've done, coding that writing so that it is divided into two piles—one for the writing that represents powerful thinking, the other for the writing that represents recording a rather obvious thought. Help children understand that the latter form of writing won't help their reading or their writing! Then you and your class could launch an inquiry into the characteristics of writing when it is meant as a tool for thought. My hunch is, your community will find that this writing:

- Is often written in incomplete notes full of abbreviations, diagrams, lists

- Raises and then entertains (or lingers with) questions

- Looks chaotic and all-over-the-place

- Can be unclear and confusing. Thoughts don't come to us in a succinct fashion.

- Is dense. That is, it has a high number of what I refer to as TPWs (thoughts per word).

You can teach children to watch themselves as they write about reading, keeping in mind the purpose of this kind of writing. If the purpose is to grow ideas and the writer is merely repeating the facts of a text or recording the obvious, help writers know they can stop mid-sentence, so as to shift to writing in ways that contain ideas. You or your children can reread the writing about reading and make a check alongside entries that are insightful—remember, the entry may be a sentence in length! Now you may want children to reread any writing they've done all year in response to reading, giving themselves pats on the back when that writing was a tool for thought. Encourage your children not to be writers who fill up pages and pages with words which, in the end, say very little.

GATHERING WRITING BY STUDYING CHARACTERS

IN THIS SESSION, YOU WILL TEACH CHILDREN THAT EXPERTS KNOW THAT CERTAIN FEATURES OF THEIR SUBJECT—FOR LITERARY ESSAYISTS, CHARACTERS—MERIT SPECIAL ATTENTION. THEREFORE, ESSAYISTS READ AND WRITE ABOUT DETAILS OF CHARACTER TO GROW SIGNIFICANT TOPICS.

GETTING READY

- "The Marble Champ," by Gary Soto, and "Spaghetti," by Cynthia Rylant (or other touchstone texts)
- Thinking About Characters chart, prepared on chart paper
- Strategies for Writing in Response to Reading chart, updated with tips from previous session
- See CD-ROM for resources

My son began his college application essay like this:

When I enter the class of 2009, I will bring my experiences of trekking through the mountains of Viet Nam and my memories of a 227-day stint in a lifeboat, accompanied by a Bengal tiger. When I attend freshman classes, my role will bear the imprint of my tortuous hours standing above the town square, a scarlet letter emblazoned on my chest. Reading has given me the water I swim in, the heroes I emulate, and the imagination to believe that I can make the world a better place.

I often say that as an educator, I want to give all children what I want for my own sons. I can think of few gifts that have mattered more to my sons than the gift of Nathaniel Hawthorne's Hester Prynne, Katherine Patterson's Gilly Hopkins, A. A. Milne's Eeyore, Brian Jacques' mouse, Martin, and all the other characters who have enriched their lives. In this world that we live in today, it's not easy finding heroes in the newspapers. But our children can find heroes in the books they read, and better still, they can become these characters, standing for a time in their shoes.

I want all children to empathize with and think deeply about characters—just as I want them to think deeply about one another. Helping children write well about literature, then, involves helping them to care about characters, and to understand what makes characters tick. This session encourages readers to think about characters' traits, motivations, struggles, and changes. These terms are easy to list, but they are potent. They hold unbelievable potential for revealing insight.

This session continues where the last one leaves off—teaching children another way to find and develop interesting, original, true ideas about texts. Those who analyze and write about texts know to pay close attention to characters.

MINILESSON

Gathering Writing by Studying Characters

CONNECTION

Remind children of the strategies for generating writing about reading that they've already learned.

"Over the past two days, you've learned a few strategies for thinking and writing in response to reading. You've learned that you can pause as you read, make a movie in your mind of what's going on, and fill in gaps in the text, thinking and writing about what the main character is seeing, hearing, and feeling."

"You also learned you can use writing to grow ideas about texts. Just as during the personal essay unit, you observed on the playground, in the cafeteria, and at your family's dinner table, you now observe in the text that you are reading. Then, after noticing details others might pass by, you write an entry in which you ponder over what you've seen. You might start by writing, 'The thought I have about this is . . . .'"

Name your teaching point. Specifically, tell children that skilled readers pay attention to characters.

"Today, I want to teach you that skilled readers of fiction pay special attention to the characters in a story to unlock secrets the text holds for the reader."

TEACHING

Remind children that experts on any subject know the features of that subject that merit attention. Illustrate with subjects you know well.

"I've been reading a best-selling book, *Blink*. Malcolm Gladwell, the author of this book, suggests that experts on a subject can gather a small amount of data and from it deduce important and surprisingly accurate insights about a larger subject. For example, an expert can listen and observe an hour of a conversation between a married couple and can predict with 95% accuracy whether the couple will still be married fifteen years later" (2005, p. 21).

"Of course, the secret is that the person who makes those observations is an expert, and therefore he or she knows which aspects of the interactions between married people are especially noteworthy."

"I've noticed something similar when I watch the Westminster Dog Show on television. I love to put myself in the judge's place, eyeing the Welsh corgis, cairn terriers, and wire-

COACHING

Early on in a minilesson, I know that I need to heighten children's interest, grab their attention. Sometimes I try to do this in my Connections, making those segments rich and elaborate; other times (as in this instance) I recruit children's interest in the Teaching component of the minilesson, allowing me to settle for a more commonplace Connection.

Draw from whatever you are reading, doing, learning to make your point clear to children. If I'd been reading about glaciers, I'm sure I could have used that as a metaphor to make my point!

haired dachshunds. But inevitably, I am still checking out the dog's coat, ears, and shape when suddenly the judge signals, 'Walk him.' Then, before I've had a chance to really take in all that new data, the judge moves on to the next dog! Expert dog watchers, like expert marriage analysts, make judgments in the blink of an eye!"

"*Blink* reveals the secrets. Malcolm Gladwell, the author, says that a good part of the secret lies in the fact that experts on a subject know which features merit our attention. The same is true for good readers. Good readers know that when reading fiction, it pays to think about characters, in general, and specifically, it pays to think about a character's traits, motivations, struggles, and changes."

Tell students that expert readers know it pays off to attend to specific aspects of a story. Discuss these and demonstrate how you read, attending to these aspects—in this case, character.

"It's easier to say this than to do it, because authors don't come right out and say, 'Lupe's character traits are . . . , she yearns for . . . , but the hard part for her is . . .' Instead, readers read, paying close attention to details (as I mentioned in the preceding session). We know that the details of a story will reveal a character's traits, motivations, struggles, and changes."

"When I mention Lupe, I'm referencing one of the stories that will be central to this unit, 'The Marble Champ.' Right now, I'm going to look back at that story and think about Lupe. Watch how my observations and thoughts about Lupe are guided by my sense of what matters to expert readers of fiction. I notice, for example, that the story says that Lupe's thumb was swollen from practicing marbles. That detail wouldn't be here if it weren't important. I need to think about what this suggests about Lupe, about her traits, motivations, struggles, and changes. Hmm . . . I think it shows that she is really persistent. She doesn't give up, even when her thumb is sore."

"Do you see that the story often gives us concrete details, and then we need to fill in what these details probably suggest about the character? We read on, looking either for confirmation or for those initial ideas to be revised."

"The truth is, all of you do this all the time. Yesterday you had a new substitute teacher. I just bet that when you came in yesterday morning and saw you had a new substitute teacher, you looked for signs that would suggest what sort of person he would be. You probably watched Mr. Harrison closely, knowing that his actions could give you clues. That's exactly what it is like for me when I meet a new character in a story. I watch that character, thinking to myself, 'Oh! Now I get it! He's *that* kind of a person.'"

By now you must realize that I'm a fan of dogs. But dogs may be the last thing on your list of loves! I'm sure that a connoisseur of yarn knows what features of yarn merit attention. Bring your loves into your teaching, and the passion you feel for your subject will come into your teaching as well!

This list of what stories reveal about character is a weighty one, so I say each term slowly, giving time for each term to sink in.

You'll notice that although "Spaghetti" is the text that weaves through most of my minilessons, I deliberately reference other texts as well. I think a steady drumbeat of references to "Spaghetti" could be dull—but for some classes of children, that'd be preferable. You'll need to decide. In any case, I try to refer to stories that children already know, because children can more easily focus on the particular point I'm hoping to make if the text itself is not new to them.

Watch how I extract particular pointers from my demonstration. It's not enough to simply say, "Watch me," and then hope the children will be enthralled by simply watching

"Of course, every detail in the story won't be of equal interest to me. If I go for a walk in the woods to think about trees, I don't pay attention to the dirt granules on the trail, but I *do* notice the shapes of leaves. When I want to learn from stories, I know that I'll probably learn something significant from paying attention to the pressures that a character feels, the struggles that he or she experiences, the choices the character makes and how they play out. When you and I read, we can see moments of courage and strength in the lives of characters and learn from those moments, just as we can learn from people and events in our own lives."

ACTIVE ENGAGEMENT

Set children up to try the work you've demonstrated and discussed. In this instance, ask children to look for a character's motivations, traits, and so on.

"We've talked a lot about the ideas we developed about Gabriel at the *beginning* of 'Spaghetti.' We noticed that Gabriel separates himself from other people, and we decided that he is a tough, brave, lonely boy who has learned to build a wall around himself. But Gabriel changes, doesn't he, as the story continues? Listen to another part of the story, later on, and notice what you learn about Gabriel's traits and motivations at this point. Remember to be a wide-awake reader, paying close attention to the details of the text."

> Gabriel was amazed. He had never imagined he would be lucky enough one day to find a kitten. He walked into the street and lifted the kitten into his hands.
>
> Gabriel sat on the sidewalk with the kitten next to his cheek and thought. The kitten smelled of pasta noodles, and he wondered if it belonged to a friendly Italian man somewhere in the city. Gabriel called the kitten Spaghetti. (1998)

"Turn and tell your partner the ideas you have about Gabriel's character—his traits and motivations—at this later point in the story."

LINK

Remind children that expert readers know which features of a story are usually worth studying. In this case, remind them that readers generally find meaning in studying a character's traits, motivations, relationships, struggles, and changes.

"So readers, today, and whenever you want to grow ideas about stories, it helps to remember that expert readers know the features of stories that are worth our attention. Among other things, expert readers pay attention to the main character's traits, motivations,

Although there are advantages to using demonstration as a teaching method, this can be a slow way to convey information. By tucking bits of information into demonstration minilessons, we keep these minilessons jam packed with helpful tips and also make them more multilevel. Some children scarf up everything we mention, while others tend to hear only the main teaching point.

Notice that I don't suggest children pull out copies of one of the stories they've been reading during the workshop and think about the character in that story. Had my children needed lots of support, I would have chosen that option. Instead, I imagine they'll do this during the workshop itself. I don't usually want the work of the workshop to be launched (and I certainly don't want it to be compressed) during the Active Engagement section of a minilesson, leaving students little new to try once I say, "Off you go." However, when working with high-need groups of children, I do want to launch the day's work during the minilessons, and therefore I'd adjust my teaching accordingly.

relationships, struggles, and changes. We read, asking and writing in response to questions like these." I pointed to the list I had prepared on chart paper.

This unit has a heavy cargo of content. In your classroom, you'll no doubt teach a reading as well as a writing workshop, and the reading workshop can carry some of this content. The list of questions shown here is very full. You'll probably decide that some of these questions are just right for third graders and others are best saved for later grades, or for a second cycle through this unit.

Thinking About Characters

- What kind of person is this character?
- What does this character long for? Fear?
- What is the character struggling against? What gets in the character's way?
- What relationships does the character have and how do these relationships play a significant role in the story?
- How does the character change over the course of the story?
- Does the character learn lessons or come to realizations?

"Today, continue reading and rereading your file of short texts and jotting entries containing your thoughts. Remember, you can draw on any strategy to help you think well about these texts." I pointed to the updated chart on the wall:

Strategies for Writing in Response to Reading

- Find a significant moment from the story. Copy the start of it into your notebook; envision it; fill in details, sounds, actions, thoughts, feelings.
- Be a wide-awake reader. Notice and underline details others might pass by. Then write a thought about what you notice.
- Think about an author's language choices, even in small words like so.
- Pay special attention to aspects of texts that are noteworthy, including a character's actions, motivations, struggles, and changes.

WRITING AND CONFERRING

Revising Initial Theories

You may decide to convene a small group of children to give them supported practice drafting and revising their ideas as they read. With one group, I said, "Once you form an idea about a character, it is important to read on, expecting you'll probably revise that idea. Let me show you what I mean. Remember yesterday, when Tony (who was a member of this small group) read 'Spaghetti,' he had this idea." I gestured to where I'd written Tony's idea on chart paper:

> I notice Gabriel is sort of alone. He sleeps with the coyotes and he doesn't hear stuff around him. The thought I have about this is I think Gabriel is brave. He isn't afraid to sleep outside. He's sort of tough. To add on, it's like he has gotten hardened and toughened so he almost doesn't hear the weak cry.

I decided to return to Tony's idea because I knew that if children kept track of Gabriel's toughness, it would pay off for them. Some of my decisions are calculated ones! I knew that in this story, the little scrawny kitten pierces Gabriel's armor of toughness. In most stories, the protagonist undergoes a change, and in this small group I subtly set kids up to watch for the very part of Gabriel that I knew would undergo a change.

I passed out copies of "Spaghetti" and continued, "I'm going to read on in the story while you follow along in your copy. Let's all keep Tony's idea in mind as we read. That's what readers do. We form an idea, then carry it along with us as we read further. When I pause as I read, would you underline sections of the story that add on to or clarify or challenge Tony's claim that Gabriel wants to be alone and that he is tough? Read with me, thinking, 'Does what I see and hear confirm the idea that Gabriel is tough? Could the story be saying something more complicated than that? Could Gabriel be changing?'"

I read more of the story, and paused a bit after the passage that said Gabriel's "ears tingled" as he walked the street, searching for the source of the cry. The children underlined and then talked about this section with partners; some of them proposed that he followed the cry because he was looking for someone or something, which suggested that at least deep down, he didn't want to be alone. Then Gabriel finds the tiny gray kitten, and I read:

MID-WORKSHOP TEACHING POINT   *Revising Theories About Characters*   "Writers, can I have your eyes and your attention? Many of you have been paying attention to characters, noticing their actions and speculating on what those actions reveal about the characters as people. I want to remind you that the ideas you develop about characters start as rough drafts. Once we have drafted an idea about a character, scrawling our idea on the page, we can hold that idea in our hands and say to ourselves, 'I'm going to continue to read, and see if upcoming sections of the text push me to *add on to* this idea or to *revise* it.' Often when we read more, we learn that our first idea was only partly warranted, and so we discard half of it. Often our ideas change in the light of new information. Our ideas need to undergo constant revision as we read more of the story, and also as we reread and rethink the story."

continued on next page

> Gabriel was amazed. He had never imagined he would be lucky
> enough one day to find a kitten. He walked into the street and lifted
> the kitten into his hands.

To me, this section of the text is very revealing: Gabriel could never have imagined he'd be lucky enough to one day find a scrawny, stray kitten! I'm not suggesting that this section will resonate for every reader, but it is really important to bring the things that speak to us into our teaching. You may want to highlight an entirely different section of this story.

"What are you thinking now about Gabriel's toughness?" I asked. I again gave children a few seconds to underline relevant sections of the text as a way to prepare for conversation. Then they talked.

Raffi said, "I think this shows that Gabriel isn't tough. He feels like the luckiest boy in the world to have found a kitten. That means he doesn't have a wall around him, or how come he feels so lucky?"

"So do the rest of you agree?" I asked. Then, upping the ante, I pushed on, gesturing to Tony's entry. "When Tony suggested at the start of the story that Gabriel was tough, that he almost wanted to be alone and had built a wall around himself—do you think that the evidence *wasn't* really there to support that claim? Or what do you think is going on? Could Gabriel be changing?" Then I added, "Right now, each of you, reread the story and try to figure out your position on this. Do you think Tony will need to revise his initial thought, or do you agree with Raffi's conclusion that Gabriel has let a kitten into his heart—or what? Underline sections of the text that help you think about this." After a minute or two of silence, I said, "Tell your partner your thinking."

Frankly, I was hoping to bring out the fact that Tony's idea and Raffi's idea could both be true. At first Gabriel had a wall around his emotions; now the cat is getting through that wall.

Soon Tony spoke. "I still say Gabriel *was* tough because he wanted to live outside, all by himself, with just the tent and the wolves, and he doesn't even hear people 'round him and almost doesn't hear the kitten. But I think Raffi's right, too, at the end. The kitten got through his wall. The kitten changed him."

Wanting to extrapolate the lessons that pertain to other days and other texts, I said, "This is the work that readers who write do all the time. We read, we notice things in texts, we push ourselves to grow tentative ideas and we talk about those ideas, and then we read on, knowing our first ideas will be revised. Sometimes we can make our ideas more specific. Sometimes we cross them out. And sometimes, we can

---

continued from previous page

"Let me show you what I mean. You already know that after I read that Gabriel sat on the stoop of a tall building of crumbling bricks and rotting wood, I theorized that Gabriel is poor. I wrote that down in my writer's notebook," I said, and pointed to chart paper where I'd copied the entry. "After I wrote my idea, I put it beside me as I continued to read, knowing new data would confirm or challenge this initial idea." I picked up "Spaghetti" and resumed reading:

> Gabriel was thinking about things. He remembered being the only boy in class with
> the right answer that day . . .

"'Does this relate in any way to my idea that Gabriel is poor? No.' I continued to read:

> . . . and he remembered the butter sandwich he had had for lunch.

"Again I ask myself, 'Does *this* relate to my idea that Gabriel is poor?' I'm not exactly sure of the answer. Gabriel could conceivably just *like* butter sandwiches, but I am pretty sure that Rylant wouldn't add that detail (or describe the crumbling bricks and the rotting wood) if she hadn't wanted to suggest that Gabriel is poor, and didn't have anything else to put in his sandwich. Probably the detail about the butter sandwiches supports my theory that Gabriel is poor."

follow a story and see that the events in characters' lives lead them to change over time. Characters make decisions, they confront their problems, they resolve tensions—and they change."

"You'll probably want to crystallize ideas *you* have fashioned about a particular story and then reread that story with that idea beside you, seeing if further rereading helps you revise that initial idea. You can, if you want, use the left-hand side of your writer's notebook to rethink what you've written on the right-hand side. [I opened a notebook and gestured to the blank left side of an open page.] Or just write additional thoughts that address earlier ones."

"I hope you noticed that because I've written my idea about 'Spaghetti,' I can keep it beside me as I read, and check it as I keep reading. If the upcoming text challenges my idea, I'll need to decide whether my initial idea was wrong, or if the character is changing. Either way, I'll write my thoughts. As you continue reading, expect that your story may lead you to revise your initial ideas. If your ideas turn out to be partly right or partly wrong, fix them. If your ideas suggest the characters in the story are changing, note that. As you read on, your ideas can become more specific or more precise."

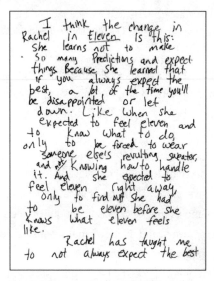

Fig. III-1 Max writes about the change he sees in "Eleven".

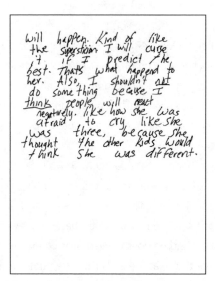

Fig. III-2 Max's entry page 2

SHARE
Writing to Know Characters

Tell children that when we read fiction, we live with a character and see the world through that character's eyes.

"A friend of mine, Ralph Fletcher, once said, 'If you want to get to know a person, don't go out to dinner with that person—instead have a flat tire together, get caught in a rainstorm together.' When we read, we're caught in rainstorms—or in whatever happens in the story—with the characters we meet on the pages. By living through the storms of life together, we form relationships with characters in books—and we learn not only *about* them, but also *from* them."

"So readers, remember that to develop ideas about characters, it helps to first live with that character through the storms of life. If you want to grow ideas about Rachel in 'Eleven,' then you first need to be Rachel. Imagine that *your* teacher has told you, 'Put that sweater on,' and *you* are looking at it, knowing it's not yours. As you read, you should be practically cringing at that sweater that's hanging over the corner of *your* desk. When you are climbing inside a story and experience the story within the skin of a character, you should find that the character's reactions make sense to you."

"Another time, you could read differently, asking, 'Do I agree with this character?' and 'Would I see the world as this character does?' But during some of your journeys through a text, try to take on the character's point of view and empathize. If you read with this amount of empathy, perhaps writing to envision or perhaps just envisioning as you read, *then* you'll be able to come to smart, new insights about the character—about people in life! And *that's* your goal!"

Ask children to reflect with a partner about what they've written about literature so far, checking whether they've empathized with a character.

"Right now, would you share what you've written with your partner, checking to see if you have stood in the shoes of a character? If not, that's okay, but sometime, try reading with empathy, as Judah and Max both did in reflections on 'Boar Out There,' a story from your packet. Judah actually empathized with the wild boar. She wrote": [*Fig. III-3*]

> My big idea is: you need to think of everyone in the
> situation's feelings. I think this might be the moral of

When I was at college, I had a poster on my wall that said, "Love does not come from gazing into each other's eyes, but from gazing together in the same direction." When we read, we and the character gaze together in the same direction. We encounter storms, predicaments, heartaches together—and because we live through life side by side, we bond with characters.

Notice that this Share essentially reminds readers of the first minilesson in this unit. You'll often want your teaching to hark back to earlier instruction; the larger lesson here is that readers and writers share a repertoire of strategies.

> my big idea is: You need to think of everyone in the situation's feelings I think this might be the moral of the story... I felt sorry for the boar because nobody paid him any mind other than Jenny. I would be hurt if someone treated me that way.

Fig. III-3 Judah's notebook entry

the story . . . I felt sorry for the boar because nobody paid him any mind other than Jenny. I would be hurt if someone treated me that way.

"Max, like Judah, read 'Boar Out There' with a wide-open heart, and he let himself feel for both Jenny and the boar—which is good reading and good living!" *[Fig. III-4]*

I think that Jenny is lonely. Maybe she goes out to find the boar to either befriend him or to show everyone she is brave. Which she is. She is brave to go find the boar. The boar is also brave because he stays there with Jenny without attacking. But he is not all brave because he gets scared when he sees or knows that someone is after him. Also Jenny knows that there is more inside the boar than most people think. Even a wild boar can have a true kind heart inside. People pre-judge him, but Jenny knows not to.

"Share your entries with your partner, especially entries in which you (like Judah and Max) have empathized with your characters."

Remind children that their talk about texts will be clearer if they refer to characters by name and try to use precise language.

"Writers, can I stop you? I can see that many of you are excited about ideas that you are growing, but when I try to learn about your ideas, I'm having a hard time understanding you. I want to give you a few tips on how to be clear:"

- "When you speak of a character, use his or her name. If you say, 'This kid, he . . .' and then say, 'Then he . . . ,' I am often unclear what person your pronouns are referencing."
- "Try to avoid talk that sounds like this: 'Well, you know, he likes all that stuff, you know.' Assume your listeners *don't* know what you are getting at. Say outright what you mean!"

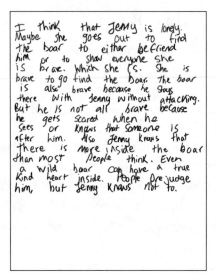

Fig. III-4 Max's notebook entry

Notice that whenever we send children off to do some work, we listen and watch to be sure they are on the right track. If we see indications that they need further channeling, we intervene, as in this example.

When children try to describe characters, some of them will reach for sweeping, generic terms, describing characters as "nice" or "friendly" or "happy." When the opportunity arises, either in conferences or in discussions about books, encourage precise language. Show children that words differ by nuance. Help children brainstorm webs of related but different words. Is a character proud? Haughty? Arrogant? Imperious? Outspoken? Condescending? Each term connotes a different quality. You'll want to teach children that writers search for the precise term. Some words have positive or negative connotations. For example, "outspoken" and "verbose" differ in that one term is more positive than the other.

It is very important to ask children to focus their efforts on one text. Although this work is lodged in a homework assignment, it is not expendable.

HOMEWORK *Studying How a Mentor Author Portrays a Character* In a few days, you will each reread your notebook to select a seed idea that you can develop into a literary essay about one of the stories you've been reading. Tonight, select a story from your packet that speaks to you. This will be the text you write and think and talk about during writing workshop for the next few days. Tonight, spend some time thinking about the protagonist, the main character, in the story you've chosen.

It is often helpful to study the ways in which people who write book reviews and literary essays capture the essence of a character. The famous author, Eudora Welty, wrote a review of a book you know, *Charlotte's Web*. In her review, Welty describes the pig, Wilbur, this way:

> Wilbur is of sweet nature—he is a spring pig—affectionate, responsive to the moods of weather and the song of the crickets, has long eyelashes, is hopeful, partially willing to try anything, brave, subject to faints from bashfulness, is loyal to friends, enjoys a good appetite and a soft bed, and is a little likely to be overwhelmed by the sudden chance for complete freedom. (*New York Times*, October 19, 1952)

There are dozens of lessons to be learned from this. Tonight, jot a list of lessons you can learn from what Eudora Welty has done. For example, on my list, I'll record that I notice that when Welty wants to convey what a character is like, she lifts tiny, emblematic details about the character's actions from the story, condensing these to create a collage that represents the character in all his or her idiosyncrasies. But you'll make your own list of observations.

After you've thought about what Eudora Welty has done to describe Wilbur in her book review, write an entry in which you use similar techniques to describe the protagonist in the story you have selected.

TAILORING YOUR TEACHING There is no question but that children will need more time and help learning to pay attention to what characters do—to their actions, their dialogue, their choices—and they'll need help regarding what's written about a character as windows to the person. You may want to read *The Art of Teaching Reading*, paying special attention to chapters twelve, fifteen, and eighteen.

If your students are ready for further study of character . . . you may want to teach them to ask whether a particular character represents an archetype. For example, in *Cinderella*, the stepmother definitely fits the archetype of the mean stepmother. Cinderella also fits into a kind-of-character that one meets often in stories. Children will enjoy thinking about possible archetypes. Fairy tales are full of these. In many fairy tales, one character fits the stereotype of the youngest son, the one whom everyone underestimates, who rises to the challenge in the end. Many stories contain a scheming, wily fox-like character who outsmarts the others (and in the end, is outsmarted)!

When readers recognize that a character fits into an archetype, this helps the reader anticipate the role the character may play in the book. Of course, you may want to teach children that there can be a thin line between archetypes and stereotypes. Wise readers sometimes resist an author's way of conveying characters. Such a reader may say, "I question why the author needed to write one more story about the handsome boy who gets the lovely girl," or "I resist the idea that the father has a job and the mother in this book bakes cookies and drives her children from place to place."

If your students are ready for further study of character . . . you may want to teach them that narrators often merit special attention. The narrator's voice may not necessarily be one which the wise reader trusts as a universally true perspective. For example, in John Steptoe's picture book, *Stevie*, the eight-year-old narrator calls young Stevie a crybaby, but the reader is meant to bear in mind that this is the older child's jealousy speaking and as such, says as much about the narrator as it says about Stevie.

If your students are ready for further study of character . . . you may want to teach them that there is a saying: "When you go over the bumps, what's inside spills out," telling them that this is true for characters in books as well. When a character struggles, what's inside spills out . . . and for this reason, experienced readers pay special attention to what a character does in the face of difficulties. Often when characters struggle, they end up finding strengths inside themselves that they never knew existed, and this is one force which accounts for the way a character changes.

If you'd like to help students eventually form sound thesis statements about characters . . . you might help steer them toward opinions about characters even now. In the end, when children write literary essays, they'll each need to develop a thesis statement (or a claim about the text). You'll steer children toward choosing a thesis which relates to the whole story, not just to one small part of it. Many of your children are apt to write a thesis such as this: "With persistence and hard work, Lupe learns that she can succeed in sports as well as in academics." You can prepare children for writing thesis statements about characters by teaching them to pay attention to the difficulties their protagonist faces, and the resources she relies on to meet those difficulties. Don't mention the upcoming search for a thesis statement yet, but teach children strategies writers use to grow entries about characters that will yield the ideas that can eventually be central to an essay.

ASSESSMENT

As you move among your children, assessing their work to help plan your one-to-one, small-, and whole-group instruction, remember that you've asked children to use writing to grow new ideas. The measuring stick a writer uses to assess writing differs based on the goals the writer brings to a piece of writing. You may, for example, show children that when they write to grow ideas, they'll reread their writing in a special way. They won't ask, "Is this a well-organized text?" or "Is my writing correctly punctuated?" Instead, they might ask, "Have I written ideas that seem true and interesting?"

When I pulled my chair alongside Adam, he'd already written this entry. Read it closely, as I did, and see if you can follow his logic (and lack thereof): [Figs III-5, III-6, and III-7]

> "Because the way you grow old is kind of like an onion or like the rings inside a tree or like my wooden dolls that fit one inside another, each year inside the next one. That's how being eleven is."—quotation from "Eleven"
>
> I think that Rachel feels that being eleven is a big turning point for her where she feels like she is supposed to be very mature, because in the next part she says, "Today I wish I was one hundred and two" so she feels the older she is, the smarter you are.
>
> I think Rachel isn't enjoying being a kid as much as she should be, because she is wishing she is older than she really is. That is basically stereotyping that kids aren't ever as smart as grown-ups. This leads me to the idea that Rachel is a push-over to all her friends because her friends think they've smarter than her. I think this because Rachel calls the two girls stupid.

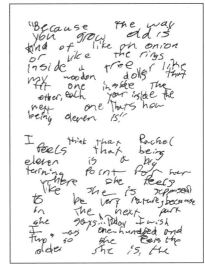

Fig. III-5 Adam's notebook entry

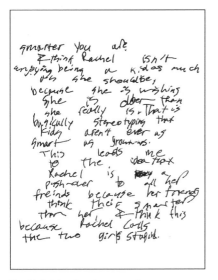

Fig. III-6 Adam's entry page 2

Using Rachel as a mentor, I have learned to respect adults but also respect my friends and my self. I also learned that it is okay to cry when you feel like it. It taught me to not care what other people think about you and only what you think matters. Rachel also taught me that sometimes you have to be tough and strong while other times you just have to cry and that is alright because you can be tough and still cry.

I told Adam that the writing he'd done was meant to grow ideas, and that he'd done half the work: He'd written a thoughtful entry, using thought prompts to develop ideas. But he still needed to

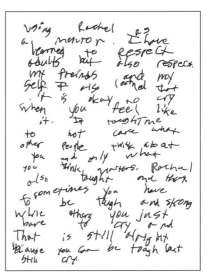

Fig. III-7 Adam's entry page 3

harvest the thoughts that he valued from his own entry. I told him that to harvest our own best ideas, we reread our musings, stopping at the end of each chunk, each bit of thinking. At the end of each bit, it is helpful to paraphrase what we just said, and think, "Is this *really* true?" As we do this, we keep in mind that often we find we've written ideas that are close to true but not *exactly* true. Giving our own ideas the truth test is one way to clarify what we really think.

I showed Adam what I meant by rereading a chunk of his text and then scrutinizing, with him, what his text said:

> I think that Rachel feels that being eleven is a big turning point for her where she feels like she is supposed to be very mature, because in the next part she says, "Today I wish I was one hundred and two" so she feels the older she is, the smarter you are.

Then I said, "So this first part says that Rachel thinks that growing older is a big deal because she believes that grown-ups are smarter than kids. You'll need to weigh whether you really believe that the evidence shows Rachel believes this." (I jotted a note reminding Adam to double-check on this claim.) "For now, let's read on."

"Let's find the next chunk of your text." I gestured for Adam to reread the next part of his entry:

> I think Rachel isn't enjoying being a kid as much as she should be, because she is wishing she is older than she really is. That is basically stereotyping that kids aren't ever as smart as grown-ups. This leads me to the idea that Rachel is a push-over to all her friends because her friends think they're smarter than her. I think this because Rachel calls the two girls stupid.

Adam said, "This says Rachel's friends think they are smarter than she is."

I intervened, "Adam, it does say that Rachel's friends think they are smarter than she is—but you need to read your own writing more slowly and carefully, because your evidence only says Rachel calls them stupid!" Then I said, "It's so wise to reread your writing and realize there are places in your entry where your ideas aren't clear or aren't warranted by the text. You do say Rachel's friends think they are smarter than she is, but as evidence you point out that *Rachel* calls her friends stupid! You never back up the idea that Rachel's friends think they are smarter than she is. When you reread your writing, you need to pause and think, 'What did I just say? Is it what I want to say? Do my different points go together?' There *may* be some connection between Rachel calling her classmates stupid and your earlier claim that she believes grown-ups are smarter than kids, but you'll need to figure that out."

Then I said, "When you reread your own entries, you'll often see that your ideas are at first a bit confusing and contradictory. That's how people grow new ideas—because they often *are* tangled at first. It can be really helpful to box out places where you've expressed an idea in a confusing fashion and rewrite that idea, this time aiming to really capture exactly what you think. Often the places where your entries are confusing are the places where really smart ideas are hiding under the surface."

"After I go, there are two things you can do—and these are things you can do *whenever* you write about reading. First, continue reading your entry, giving each chunk of it the truth test. And second, revisit sections where you have made claims you need to check or written ideas that seem confusing. Try to rewrite those sections, seeing if you can name exactly what you really do think."

In this fashion, assessment will feed into your conferences.

ELABORATING ON WRITTEN IDEAS USING CONVERSATIONAL PROMPTS

IN THIS SESSION, YOU WILL TEACH CHILDREN ONE WAY WRITERS ELABORATE ON THEIR IDEAS—IN THIS CASE, IDEAS ABOUT CHARACTER. YOU'LL GUIDE CHILDREN THROUGH A DISCUSSION THAT HAS THE SAME FEATURES AS A WRITTEN ANALYSIS OF A TEXT, REMINDING CHILDREN THAT THE CONVERSATIONAL PROMPTS THEY KNOW ARE ALSO USEFUL AS WRITING PROMPTS.

GETTING READY

- Pushing Our Thinking chart from personal essay unit
- Sample of student work from personal essay unit showing use of conversational prompts from the Pushing Our Thinking chart
- Prompts for Pushing Our Thinking About Reading chart, prepared as a handout
- Transcript of teachers' book talk that uses conversational prompts
- "Spaghetti," by Cynthia Rylant, and "The Marble Champ," by Gary Soto (or other touchstone texts)
- Student notebook entry that shows observations about the text and responses to those observations, prepared as handout for homework
- See CD-ROM for resources

When we write a narrative, the sequence of events is usually determined by chronology. We can record events in the order in which they happen, making it very easy for us to say more. We recall the first thing that happened, then the next, then the next thing, and as long as we are taking small steps through the sequence of events, we don't quickly run out of things to say.

When we write expository texts, however, and especially when the expository text conveys our ideas, it is no easy matter to say more. To say more, to elaborate, the writer needs not only to recall what happened, but also to think more. This requires that the writer have not only stuff to say but also a plan, a structure, that determines the sequence of what he or she will say. Many students have enormous trouble with elaboration when writing expository texts, and as a result, their writing ends up with "a muddle in the middle." We worked through this challenge first in the personal essay unit, and of course, will work through it again in the current unit.

Your job today will be to lure your students into learning how to elaborate upon their first thoughts—in this lesson, their first ideas about character. You'll help children to do this in writing by first encouraging them to elaborate in conversation. If children can talk well about a text they have read, making and defending and elaborating upon their ideas, then it is not difficult to teach them to write well about the text. But the first goal is not a small one! In this unit, you need to value talking well in addition to writing well about texts.

Schools often treat talk as if it's to be avoided. If a principal says to a teacher, "I passed your classroom and your children were talking," the teacher doesn't generally regard this as positive feedback. If we describe a child as "a real talker," we don't usually intend this as a compliment. Yet in our own adult lives, we recognize that talking is a way to grow. If we need help working through an issue, we meet with someone to "talk things through." If we want to imagine possible ways to teach, we're apt to "talk over our options" or "talk out a plan."

Today you'll encourage children to tap the power of talk as a tool for thinking. Moreover, you'll help children realize that the features of a probing, generative discussion are also the features of probing, generative writing.

MINILESSON

Elaborating on Written Ideas Using Conversational Prompts

CONNECTION

Remind children that when writing personal essays, conversational prompts can serve as thought prompts, helping them extend their first ideas.

"You'll remember that when we were writing essays, we found that at first, we wrote only very briefly about our ideas. We'd write our idea—say, 'soccer teaches sportsmanship'—and then we weren't sure what else to say, so our entries were often short. But we came to realize that we could rely on the conversational prompts we use in book talks to help us talk back to our own ideas as they emerge on the page. Remember?" I refer to the "Pushing Our Thinking" chart.

"I won't forget, for example, when Ellie wrote this entry during the personal essay unit; she used our conversational prompts to help her get more good ideas."

> I hate it when I am doing something important and then I get interrupted.
>
> <u>For example</u>, when I'm reading a book and my mom calls, "Ellie, it's time to go to sleep" but I really want to finish the book because that's what I am into. <u>I realize that</u> this happens a lot to me, like when I'm watching TV or having fun with my friends. <u>What surprises me</u> is I always have a lot of time and no one interrupts me when I am doing things I don't like, like homework or practicing my oboe or other things.

Name the teaching point. In this case, tell children that they can use the same—and some new—thought prompts to extend their thinking about reading.

"Today I want to teach you that when we write about our reading—and specifically, about a character—we can use the same prompts we use in conversation and in our other essay writing to help us grow ideas. I will also teach you a few new prompts that readers often use to help us talk and think more about our reading."

COACHING

Notice the way that one minilesson stands on the shoulders of an earlier one, and in this way brings children toward more sophisticated work. We strive to do this as much as we can.

Pushing Our Thinking

For example . . .

Another example is . . .

To add on . . .

This makes me realize . . .

This is important because . . .

This is giving me the idea that . . .

The reason for this is . . .

Another reason is . . .

This connects with . . .

On the other hand . . .

Usually in a teaching point I lay out more precisely what I will teach, but in this instance, I couldn't tuck the Prompts for Pushing Our Thinking About Reading *chart into a teaching point.*

TEACHING

Dramatize a discussion between you and a few colleagues about a text that is familiar to your class. Set children up to notice that you incorporated "thought prompts" into your conversation.

"Yesterday at lunch, the other teachers and I decided to read and talk about a story that you know: 'Spaghetti.' We transcribed a bit of our book talk so you could see how we used 'thought prompts' to help us grow ideas. We realized afterward that there are a few thought prompts we use specifically when we talk about reading, and so I've made a big list for each of you." I handed out this list.

Prompts for Pushing Our Thinking About Reading

For example . . .

Another example is . . .

To add on . . .

This makes me realize . . .

This is important because . . .

This is giving me the idea that . . .

The reason for this is . . .

Another reason is . . .

This connects with . . .

On the other hand . . .

I partly agree but . . . because . . .

Could it also be that . . .

Might the reason for this be . . .

This is similar to . . .

This is different from . . .

I think this is important because . . .

I noticed that section, too . . . and I think this connects to the whole story because . . .

I see (the item you are discussing), and then a similar thing happens (in this place); I think this is repeated because . . .

There is one thing in the story that doesn't "fit" for me and it's . . .

This might be present because . . .

In the beginning . . . then later . . . finally . . .

In the beginning . . . in the middle . . . at the end . . .

Many people think . . . but I think . . .

I used to think . . . but now I'm realizing . . .

Notice that there is a general progression in these prompts towards increasing sophistication. It is easier to add another example, and it is more complex to compare and contract them. Usually a reader first uses one of the earlier promptss adn the moves up the level of abstract thinking towards one of the later responses.

This list is too long to actually use with your class. Cull from it, saving some of these suggestions for another year.

"Instead of just reading you the transcript of our book talk, I'm going to help you imagine it by asking four of you—you and you and you and you—to come up and take a role, helping me reenact how that book talk went."

We organized this simulation of a book talk among teachers, giving each child the role of one teacher. I gave away my role as well. "We'll reenact a little bit of the teachers' book talk. I want the rest of you to notice (and underline) the thought prompts that the other teachers and I used in our conversation about 'Spaghetti.' You'll see that these prompts helped us extend and revise our first ideas."

"As you listen, would you also notice the number of times we go back to the text, reading specific bits of it to illustrate our points? You'll see that we don't just talk and think generally, in the abstract, about the text; we instead attach our ideas to specific parts of the text. After you listen to a bit of the book talk, I am going to give you and your partner a chance to take our places and continue the conversation."

Ms. Errico: I think Gabriel chooses to be alone. <u>For example</u>, when Gabriel is outside on the stoop, there are many neighbors sitting around talking, but he chooses not to join their conversation.

Mr. Nineteman: I agree. <u>Another example</u> of Gabriel choosing to be alone is in the second paragraph:

> Gabriel was thinking he would like to live outside all the time. He imagined himself carrying a pack of food and a few tools and a heavy cloth to erect a hasty tent. Gabriel saw himself sleeping among the coyotes. (1998)

Ms. Boland: <u>I used to think Gabriel was lonely, but now I am realizing that</u> maybe Gabriel chooses to not be with *people*. But maybe he likes being with animals. In the example Mr. Nineteman just gave, Gabriel imagines that he will be sleeping among coyotes. <u>I think this is important because</u> later, when Gabriel finds Spaghetti, he starts to feel less lonely. He likes getting company from animals.

Ms. Errico: So, are you saying that Gabriel feels more comfortable with animals?

Ms. Boland: Yes, some people are that way. They can communicate with animals better than with people. <u>So in the beginning</u>, Gabriel wants to sleep with coyotes and <u>then at the end</u>, with a cat.

Ms. Errico: <u>There's one thing that doesn't fit for me:</u> coyotes. If the author was saying Gabriel liked being with animals, why wouldn't she pick a more warm-fuzzy animal? 'Cause I think of coyotes as being in the distance, howling, and to me they are all about loneliness.

Sometimes we refer to this as fishbowling. *It is great to find new ways to demonstrate because novelty ignites interest. The sheer fact that this is a new configuration will draw kids' attention. You or your colleagues may want to take on the topic, Developing New Methods for Teaching Within Our Minilessons. You can certainly use fishbowling a lot more often, with people reading or talking in front of the class.*

Notice that here and nearly always, before we ask children to observe something instructional, we highlight what it is we hope they notice and set them up for the work they will soon be doing in response to what they see.

Notice that we tend to begin with the conversational prompts that come earlier in the list. It is easier to say and think in associative ways (Another example of this is . . .) than in analytical ways (I am realizing . . . I think this is important . . .).

Of course, instead of bringing in a conversation among teachers, I could have simply demonstrated how I go from reading and having a thought to developing that thought, and do so using conversational prompts and repeated references to the text. For example, I could have reread the opening paragraph of "Spaghetti" and then paused, pointing out (in an aside), "Sometimes I almost force myself to pause, to pause and to look and to think." Musing to myself, I would reread one line of it aloud, " . . . he remembered the butter sandwich he had had for lunch," and then say, "Gabriel's sandwich contained just butter. It wasn't a ham sandwich, it wasn't roast beef. It was just a butter sandwich."

Debrief. Tell children that when they use thought prompts to talk or write about an idea, the idea deepens.

"Readers, I hope you saw that we used this list of prompts to push our thinking about reading, to help us talk longer and deeper about our first ideas. We also referred to and read particular passages in the midst of our discussion. When we do these things, we end up growing thoughts that surprise even ourselves! The conversations we had let us extend and revise our first ideas, and made them more powerful, more specific, more true."

ACTIVE ENGAGEMENT
Set children up to carry on the book talk with their partners, using thought prompts to refer specifically to the story. Then have them continue this work in writing.

"So that's a fragment of our book talk. Instead of analyzing it, pretend you are part of the conversation and continue it—only you'll be talking just with your partner. Continue to use the thought prompts and refer specifically to the story, just as we were doing." I listened in on one set of partners:

Jessica: <u>This is giving me the idea that</u> being alone is different than being lonely. Being alone is just being by yourself. It's not lonely, it's just doing something without anyone there.

Alex: <u>To add on</u>, sometimes being alone is fun. <u>For example</u>, when you're part of a big family. Then it's kind of nice to be alone for a change.

Jessica: Yeah, yeah, I agree.

Alex: <u>This makes me realize that</u> sometimes people think they want to be alone but then they really don't. <u>For example</u>, <u>in the beginning</u> Gabriel kept to himself and got used to being without people. He didn't try to make friends. But in the middle, when he heard the kitten crying, he was curious and then when he found the kitten he really wanted to be around it. <u>At the end</u>, he made the kitten his friend.

"Can I stop you?" I asked, and waited until I had everyone's attention. "Remember that these conversational prompts also work for writing! Once you've written one idea, you can extend it using one of these prompts."

Then I would look up at the class, cueing them to notice what I would do next. <u>"The thought I have about this is</u> that Gabriel's sandwich is only butter because his family can't afford fancy sandwiches. <u>To add on,</u> even though Gabriel's sandwich isn't much, it hit the spot. He still remembers it, hours later. He probably ate that butter sandwich in tiny little bites, wanting it to last as long as possible, and then he probably used his finger to scoop up the crumbs and ate those too. <u>This connects to</u> times when I was a kid; I remember looking longingly at the pink marshmallow snowballs that Susan Downer had in her lunch box, wanting to heave my bruised pear into the trash. When kids open our lunch boxes, the stuff we find there feels like a letter from home. Gabriel is lonely, I'm not sure if he has a mom or a dad who packs his lunch."

Children may ask you whether they should speak and write about characters from books in the past or present tense. They will wonder whether it is better to say, "Gabriel was lonely" or "Gabriel is lonely." Generally, when writing about character traits, readers use the present tense. In the story "Spaghetti," Gabriel is a lonely boy.

LINK

Remind children of the teaching point. In this case, remind them that they can always use conversational prompts to extend their thinking when they talk or write.

"So readers, today and always, when you say your first thoughts about a story or put them onto the page, it is important to push yourselves to revise those first thoughts. One way to do this is to use thought prompts to nudge yourself to say (and think) more. Keep the thought prompts with you during the writing workshop this month, and whenever you write or talk about texts you've read, use these to extend and revise your first thoughts. Soon you'll use them just from habit. It's more fun and interesting to talk and write in ways that dig deep, so I'm pretty sure you'll end up using these prompts as you talk on the phone at night. You'll invent other thought prompts too."

WRITING AND CONFERRING

Elaborating on Theories About Characters

When you and your colleagues plan for today's (and every day's) teaching, be sure you plan for the conferences and small-group work as well as for your minilesson. Today, you can expect that some children will list rather than describe their ideas about a character, and many of them, like Sophia, will merely name one character trait after another. *[Fig. IV-1]*

Peter's Chair

My character is Peter
He is very jealous
He loves his baby sister
He likes toys
He tries to help the baby

Eleven

My character is Rachel
She feels weird (not eleven)
She feels bad when she wore the sweater
She hates her teacher

You'll probably want to carry a short text with you and to be prepared to demonstrate thinking hard about how to find words that precisely describe a character's trait. Sophia, in the example here, has said that Rachel, the main character in "Eleven," feels "weird." Then Sophia clarifies this by saying that Rachel "doesn't feel eleven." What *does* she feel? Encourage children to speak in whole sentences, and to be explicit. Once children have made their claims—about, say, a character's traits— you'll want to show them that writers then choose ways to elaborate. It often works for children to provide examples of this trait while using transitional phrases such as *In the beginning of the story; then in the middle; finally, at the end of the story; for example; and another example of this is . . . .*

MID-WORKSHOP TEACHING POINT **Developing Powerful Thoughts** "Writers, can I have your eyes and your attention? Right now, if you haven't done so already, reread what you've written. Find a thought that seems powerful, and make a box around it. After you find one, look for another or help someone near you recognize power on his or her page." I circulated, helping children find powerful thoughts. "Sometimes, writers, the way you've written a thought is *almost* powerful, but not quite. You can rewrite your thought to make it more powerful."

"Once you've boxed off a powerful idea, use your thought prompts to elaborate on it. If you are having trouble using the conversational prompts to grow your ideas on paper, then remember you can also talk about your ideas. I sometimes take my ideas to a friend, and say, 'Will you listen to my thoughts about this?' and we talk about my idea. The other person listens, saying, 'Can you explain that more to me?' or 'Why do you think the text does this?' Writing and talking should fire you up so that you're able to put more ideas and insights onto the page. Then you can go back and write some more."

Peter's Chair
my character is Peter
He is very Jealous
He loves his baby sister
He likes toys.
He tries to help the baby

Eleven
my character is Rachel
She feels weird (not eleven)
She feels bad when she wore the sweater
She hates her teacher.

Fig. IV-1 Sophia's entry merely lists character traits

In the following notebook entry, Ali makes a claim about Lupe. In the entry, Ali seems to brainstorm a host of possible terms that could possibly be apt ones for Lupe. *[Fig. IV-2]*

> I think Lupe had, before, put herself down. But now, she will try to prove herself wrong. This is important because she was insecure. She thought badly of herself. She thought she was only a brainy person. But she was good at things. It doesn't matter if you can't do it, it matters what's on the inside. Even though she wasn't good, she was nice and good on the inside. "She tried again and again." This shows that she doesn't give up. She works and works at a goal. She won't disappoint herself. This takes a lot of self-confidence and courage. She tries to believe in herself.

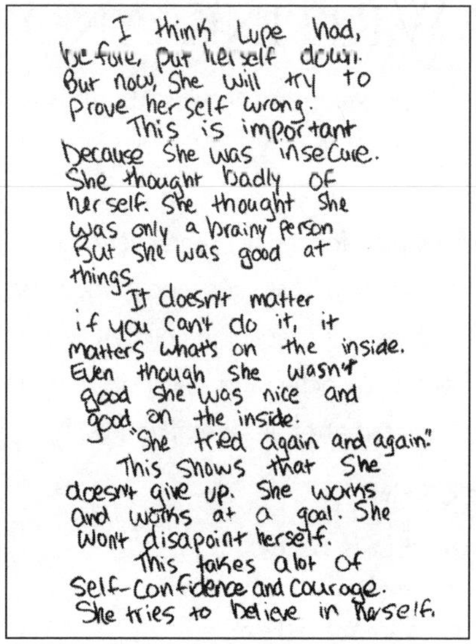
I think Lupe had, before, put herself down. But now, She will try to prove herself wrong.
This is important because She was insecure. She thought badly of herself. She thought She was only a brainy person But She was good at things.
It doesn't matter if you can't do it, it matters whats on the inside. Even though she wasn't good She was nice and good on the inside.
"She tried again and again."
This Shows that She doesn't give up. She works and works at a goal. She won't disapoint herself.
This takes alot of Self-Confidence and Courage. She tries to believe in herself.

Fig. IV-2 Ali reaches for the words to capture Lupe.

When I conferred with Ali, I showed her that characters can't always be shoehorned into a single description, so her effort to locate the one precisely right term could actually be doomed from the start. I suggested that Ali might have more success if she tried for sentences that capture Lupe. For example, Ali might say, "Lupe was full of contradictions. Although she had rows of trophies and awards that showed her academic prowess, her inabilities at athletics made her insecure."

Angelina begins her entry by summing up Clover, a character in Jacqueline Woodson's *The Other Side*, in a single term. Clover, Angelina suggests, is courageous. Although this is a short entry, Angelina not only advances her idea, she also tries to convince others of it. She cites a particular passage from the text to support her point and returns to her claim at the end of this entry. But what I find most impressive is that at the end of her entry, Angelina comes to a rather remarkable insight: Clover is a courageous person because she dares to bend the rules. Writing, for Angelina, has been a tool for thought. *[Fig. IV-3]*

> **The Other Side**
>
> Clover is a very, very courageous person. Because in the book, I could tell that she is courageous since she would dare to bend rules. Clover was not supposed to go over the fence that separates the town of whites and blacks. But she instead sits on the fence with a white girl named Annie. "My momma never said anything about sitting on the fence," said Clover. She knew better than to sit on the fence or even go near it. This is why to me Clover is a courageous person. Because she dares to bend rules that were actually laws in her time.

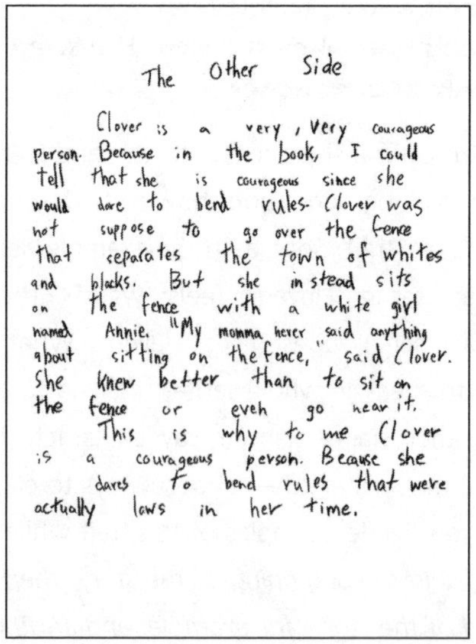
The Other Side
Clover is a very, very courageous person. Because in the book, I could tell that she is courageous since she would dare to bend rules. Clover was not suppose to go over the fence that separates the town of whites and blacks. But she instead sits on the fence with a white girl named Annie. "My momma never said anything about sitting on the fence," said Clover. She knew better than to sit on the fence or even go near it.
This is why to me Clover is a courageous person. Because she dares to bend rules that were actually laws in her time.

Fig. IV-3 Angelina advocates for her claim, then grows a further idea!

After I saw Angelina's work, I stopped the class and said, "Eyes on me." I waited until I had their attention. "Class, I want to show you the smart work Angelina just did. In her entry, she doesn't ramble from one idea to another idea to another. Instead, Angelina puts forth one idea, one claim, and then she takes the time to develop that idea. This is really smart. When writing ideas about characters or texts, it is helpful to focus, to zoom in. Only this time, you'll zoom in on a single idea you want to advance, and then you'll develop that idea across the text as Angelina has done. But best of all, as she says more about her idea, she actually *thinks* more—and comes to a better idea! Listen," I said, and read Angelina's entry.

SHARE

Discussing Texts Aloud to Prepare for Discussing Them in Writing

Invite children into a book talk. Coach them to brainstorm ideas and select one that is especially provocative and important to the story as a starting point for discussion. Explain that essayists proceed in the same fashion.

"Readers, can you gather for today's share?" I said, and waited until they'd convened in the meeting area. "You have been talking a lot with your partners—I am dying to hear some of your ideas! Today, let's let our share be a bit longer than usual so we can have a whole-class book talk about 'The Marble Champ.'"

"This story talk is going to help you with your literary essays. Over these weeks as you work toward a literary essay, you'll first brainstorm ideas as we've been doing, Then you'll select one that will make a great essay and you'll develop that one idea. For now, we'll do a miniature version of the same process. We'll brainstorm ideas and select one that will lead to a great discussion (instead of a great essay). The ways we make a great discussion and the ways we make a great essay are often very similar."

"We need to start by laying out a bunch of thoughts about the story. First, look back at the story and your writing about it, and think of a provocative or interesting claim, an idea, about the story we could use to get us started talking; we'll list several of them." I gave them a moment to think. "So what ideas do you have about this story?"

As children spoke, I listed the ideas on chart paper quickly:

> Lupe shouldn't be so competitive.
>
> Lupe learns that with hard work you can accomplish anything.
>
> Lupe really, really wants to be good at some sport and so she doesn't give up. She's got a good attitude so that changes her from being a poor marble player into a champion.
>
> Lupe's father encourages her.

"Let's think about which of these ideas might spark an especially great talk. That's what writers of literary essays do. We know we'll be writing about an idea, and we want to choose an idea that'll be worth pursuing. It's the same for people who want to have a good book

Notice that I let children know that the share will be a bit longer than usual. I want children to develop an inner sense of timing so they come to expect the time frames within which we work. So today, when we won't stay within those time frames, I'm explicit about this change.

In other units, I've found other ways to give children an aerial view of the terrain they're traveling. If we want children to internalize the rhythms of the writing process and to feel as if they control it, it helps to let them see the path they'll take.

The work children do in class discussions, small-group talks, and partnerships on the set of texts the class is analyzing provides invaluable support, because the class will have opened up many of these texts. Each child will be able to approach his or her writing with lots of ideas about the text.

talk. We need to choose an idea that'll pay off. To do this we choose an idea that feels close to the heart of the story, and one that is grounded in the whole text. We also want an idea that is interesting: I choose an idea that gets me excited to think more about it. Would you join me in looking over our list of possible ideas, asking yourself, 'Which of these ideas might start a really provocative story talk, one that will get to the best and most important parts of the story?'"

"Which idea do you think is provocative enough to initiate a great talk, and is also central to the whole text?" We discussed this for a minute, chose one, and then talked together as a class about that idea. I reminded kids to use thought prompts when they talk back to each other's ideas.

Debrief. Retell the sequence of work the class just did, and tell readers they'll follow a similar sequence of work when they set out to write literary essays.

After the talk about the text continued for ten minutes, I intervened. "Readers, I am hoping that every one of you noticed that we began this talk by generating a bunch of possible ideas; then we asked, 'Which one of these is central to the story? Which is provocative?' Then we selected an idea that we expected would generate a great book talk. When you write about reading, you need to view your possible ideas with the same lens, asking, 'If I write about this idea, will it generate some interesting writing? Will my writing address something that is central to the story?'"

The work that I describe here could easily happen almost every day in reading workshop or in response to your read-aloud. Try it. Read, then ask children to talk in pairs to get their ideas flowing. Then elicit a bunch of ideas. Then ask the class to select one idea, using the criteria I've just described. Once an idea has been agreed upon, I find it helps to give children a moment to either jot thoughts about that idea or to talk with a partner. Then you can convene a whole-class talk in response to the idea. Encourage children to use the thought prompts to grow and talk back to the idea, and to gather new ideas.

You will see that when children talk with each other, they often say, "I agree with that." Ask children to restate the exact part of the idea they agree with. This gives them practice talking about ideas and allows them to listen for and work together to find the words that carry ideas. It also helps children feel comfortable disagreeing a bit, as debate sparks great conversation. Give them words for such discussion, such as on the other hand, could it be that . . . or I partly agree but in one way, I think differently because . . .

⊙ HOMEWORK   *Bringing More of the Text to Reading Response* Writers, I wonder if any of you have ever taken a photograph and decided one portion of that photograph was really important. If a photographer looks at a picture and decides that the tree in the upper-right-hand corner is important, he can zoom in on just that one tree. In the same way, literary essayists look over all that they have written about a text and ask, "Is one portion of this writing especially provocative and central to the text?" We did this in our share today. We generated lots of ideas about "The Marble Champ" and then we chose one idea, and spent a while talking about just that one idea. When we write about texts, we often reread all we've written and box a line or a passage that feels to us to have potential. Then we copy that onto the top of a fresh sheet of paper, and assign ourselves the job of expanding our first idea.

There are many ways to expand ideas. Of course we use thought prompts, and I know you each have a list of them that you've taped into your notebook. But another thing writers do is we reread the text, looking much more closely at it, listening much more closely to it. If we look really closely, if we listen really carefully, we can generally find more places that help us think in new ways about our original idea. Logan Perrsal Smith has said, "What I like in a good author is not what he says, but what he whispers" (Burke, p. 89). Literary essayists learn to listen for ways in which a text whispers.

So tonight, before you write just anything, select an idea that is worth expanding about the short text you selected as the focus for your work this month. Try to stay with that idea for a little while—write lots and lots about it. Reread the text and find more sections that connect with your idea, then write about them. Give examples of your idea. Use thought prompts to nudge yourself to say more. Then, I challenge you to also ask, "What part of the story *doesn't* fit with this idea?" You may find that all of this leads you to revise your original idea, and that'd be incredibly exciting.

I'm sending home an entry that Judah wrote, which I think can serve as an example of the sort of writing and thinking you can aim toward doing tonight: *[Fig IV-4]*

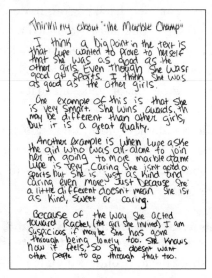

Fig. IV-4 Judah's entry

Thinking about "The Marble Champ"

I think a big part in the text is that Lupe wanted to prove to herself that she was as good as the other girls. Even though she wasn't good at sports, I think she was as good as the other girls. One example of this is that she is very smart. She wins awards.

Another example is when Lupe asked the girl who was all alone to join her in going to more marble games. Lupe is very caring. She isn't good at sports but she is just as kind and caring, even more. Just because she's a little different doesn't mean she isn't as kind, sweet, or caring. Because of the way she acted toward Rachel, (the girl she invited) I am suspicious if maybe she has gone through being lonely too. She knows how it feels, so she doesn't want other people to go through that too.

This part doesn't "fit" for me: I can't tell if Lupe has or doesn't have self-confidence. She does for going to play marbles and being so brave and courageous. She doesn't for having to prove to herself that she was as good as the other girls. I think she does and doesn't

> have self-confidence. No matter if she does or doesn't,
> she is caring and sweet and kind on the inside. That's
> what matters the most.

You'll notice that Judah's entry is shaped a bit like an essay, and some of you will probably find that the same thing sometimes happens to your writing when you make a point of staying with and elaborating upon an idea before jumping to the next one.

TAILORING YOUR TEACHING

If you are teaching a class of children who are revisiting this unit for the second year . . . you will probably want to remind them of the important lessons they've already learned about the way conversational prompts can help talkers and writers grow our own ideas. But you'll also want to teach them other strategies that can help accomplish this purpose. Here are a few:

- Teach children to monitor what they say and write, asking, "Will this contribution take the thinking further?" Some children—some adults, too—act as if it's not a problem if one person after another says the same thing in a conversation, and similarly, some children seem to not feel that there's any problem with repeating oneself over and over in a piece of writing. Coach children to be able to listen to a group conversation, notice when the talk recycles over the same terrain for long enough, and say, "So we have established that . . . Can we move on to a further point?" Children can also learn how to find further points. Sometimes, it works to think, "If this *is* true, then what are the implications for . . . ?" Then again, sometimes it works to stand back and imagine that an idea which feels resolved and finished could be regarded as tentative. "Could it be otherwise?" one can ask.

- Teach children that if they find themselves saying (writing) what everyone else is apt to think, it can help to ask, "What ideas might I have about this that are uniquely mine?"

- Teach children that one way to take a conversation deeper is to ask questions. It can help to generate several questions, then to look back on them and select one which stands a chance of yielding productive thought. It's important to build on the question, just as one builds on an idea. Let the question snowball. Then, once it is a question that fires up the child's mind, it is wise to entertain the question rather than to simply answer it. Nothing closes an inquiry down faster than a hasty answer.

MECHANICS

You and your colleagues will want to look at children's entries through a variety of lenses. When you do this, use a lens that allows you to notice the demands this unit places on their syntax.

When children talk and write about contemporary (or at least familiar) objects or events, they can rely on what some refer to as the register of social English. This is the sort of English we use during everyday interactions. If children are instead speaking about times and places that are distant and unfamiliar (especially if they are speaking about language itself), then they must use what some call academic English. This is the register that children must use when writing literary essays.

The linguistic demands on children who attempt to write literary essays are high. This is especially true for English language learners. Sometimes this struggle is evident because children write their thoughts only in a very brief, bare-bones fashion. Other times, a child's struggle with syntax results in the child restating the same thing over and over. Still other times, the child may write in garbled prose: "The influence shown by the character on his interactions with others shows the relationships and the tensions and the feelings that are important to all." If a teacher presses for more clarity and explicitness, the child's language can become even more tangled. Usually, the tangled prose represents a child's efforts to sound impersonal, objective, and scholarly, relying on passive tense and strings of noun phrases. Be forgiving; it's impressive that the child is trying to take on a new role and a new way of using language. All of us need support when we take the great risk of outgrowing ourselves!

Still, it is crucial to let children know that getting an idea across to the reader is more important than a scholarly tone. If a child says or writes something you sense is important, but you can't discern the message because of the convoluted syntax, tell her! Don't think for a moment that you do the child a favor by neglecting to mention that the message is confusing to you. You might say, "I'm trying to follow what you are saying but I don't understand." If the child tries to explain by making unwarranted assumptions, such as saying "you know" when in fact you don't know, then let the child know you are not exactly sure what she means. "I don't know what you are getting at," you could say, "but I want to understand. Can you try again to explain it and let me see if I can follow you?"

As in the personal essay unit, you'll probably find that children struggle with pronoun references. It may be helpful to remind them that readers must always know the person to whom a pronoun refers. Children make dramatic progress toward this goal when they learn and use characters' names—often they make vague references to "this guy" and "that other guy" because they neither learn the character's name nor look back at the text as they talk, think, and write about it. Children need to become accustomed to rereading their own work and detecting places where a reader won't be sure which character is being referenced. Ask children to exchange their notebooks and to observe their partners' efforts to comprehend their entries. You may suggest that partners read each other's writing aloud quietly, adding (in oral parentheses) the proper name referenced by each pronoun. If the reader is unclear of the antecedent, the writer then needs to use the proper name or a more precise reference. By the way, you can ask children to do this without teaching complex, long lessons on parts of speech—simply list pronouns (he, she, me, etc.) and tell your children that readers need to know who is signified by each of these words. To help children specify pronoun references, teach them to include modifying clauses (again, without using that term) in their writing so that when they introduce a character, they give themselves more than one way to reference that character. If a child writes, "Gabriel, the protagonist in this story, is a lonely boy," then she can later refer to Gabriel not only by his name but also as "the protagonist" or "the lonely boy."

Of course, there are many reasons to use modifying clauses apart from having additional ways to refer to a character. Descriptive clauses also enable the writer to tuck tiny bits of information about a character immediately after mentioning what the character has done or said. The added information often allows readers to picture not only what is being done, but also how that action occurs. Watch meanings become more specific as sentences become more complex:

> Gabriel picked up the kitten.
>
> Gabriel, the main character in this story, picked up the kitten.
>
> Gabriel, bursting with pleasure, picked up the kitten.
>
> Gabriel, bursting with pleasure, picked up the kitten, putting it close to his cheek.

Or

> Gabriel ate his sandwich.
>
> Gabriel, ravenously hungry, ate his sandwich.
>
> Gabriel, sitting alone on the stoop, ate his sandwich, savoring the thin layer of mayonnaise between two slices of Wonder bread.

You can use examples such as these in conferences or in a minilesson to help children learn how to use subordinate phrases to make their writing more clear and nuanced.

DEVELOPING PROVOCATIVE IDEAS:

"WHAT IS THIS STORY *REALLY* ABOUT?"

This session stands on the shoulders of Session III, *in which you taught children that expertise in any field involves knowing what does and does not merit attention, and that skilled readers know it pays to think about character. You will now teach them that skilled readers also know it pays to read with an interpretive lens, thinking, "What's this story really about?"*

The lesson for today links also to your earlier instruction on narrative writing. Many times this year, you've called children's attention to the fact that when writing both personal narratives and short fiction, it is important to ask, "What's this story really about?" You helped children understand that a story about riding the Ferris wheel could really be a story about how, when one grows older, childish thrills aren't the same, or about how the author conquered fears. In those earlier units, children learned that deciding what their story was really about influenced their choice of a lead and an ending as well as which sections of the story deserved to be stretched out and which could be less elaborated upon. Children learned that all details aren't equally important to a story, and that once a writer has decided what her story is really about, the writer can add the details that support her meaning.

Now the tables have turned. Now you will help children read someone else's narrative, asking the same question: "What is this text really about?" You'll help children examine the way in which the text has been crafted, recognizing that the meaning in a story is often conveyed by the craftsmanship. You'll teach children that just as they worked hard to write leads that were linked to the heart of their stories, now they'll examine the lead that another author has written, thinking, "Why might the author have chosen this particular way to start this story?" Similarly, readers can consider why some parts of a story are told in detail, have been stretched out, asking, "Why might this author have decided that this particular moment of the story was such an important one?" Implicit in these questions is the understanding that as authors we make deliberate choices as to how we will write, and those choices reflect what it is we want to say.

IN THIS SESSION, YOU WILL TEACH CHILDREN THAT LITERARY ESSAYISTS ASK, "WHAT'S THIS STORY REALLY ABOUT?" AND THEN ANALYZE THE WAYS THE AUTHOR DELIBERATELY CRAFTS THE STORY TO CONVEY THIS MEANING.

GETTING READY

- List of provocative questions— Interpretation: What Is This Story *Really* About?—prepared on chart paper
- Passage from "Spaghetti," by Cynthia Rylant (or other touchstone text), copied onto chart paper
- Strategies for Writing in Response to Reading chart, updated with bullet points from today's lesson
- See CD-ROM for resources

MINILESSON

Developing Provocative Ideas: "What Is This Story *Really* About?"

CONNECTION

Rally your children's commitment to thinking deeply about texts by suggesting that as we read, we can learn life lessons from characters just as we do from people in our lives.

"Writers, earlier this year you wrote essays conveying lessons you've learned in your lives. In those essays you mostly wrote about people who have helped you learn things about the world and about yourselves. In this unit, you'll again write about life lessons, but these will mostly be lessons you learn from characters in books."

"There is a psychologist who says kids grow strong based on the number of people they have in their lives from whom they can learn. Her theory is that kids are lucky if they have a grandparent, a coach, a preacher or rabbi, an older cousin, a big sister or brother, a camp counselor, a friend—people who can act as mentors."

"I agree that learning relationships make kids (also grown-ups) strong, but I don't agree that we need to just sit around and *hope* that we luck out and get people in our lives who can teach us. The good news is that when we read, each of us can give ourselves our own learning relationships. When we read, we can let people into our lives and our hearts and we can learn from them. Just as we learn from our moms, our grandparents, and even our pets, we can bring characters into our lives and learn from them."

"You already know how to write personal essays in which you hold tight to what you learn from your life relationships. I want to propose that we work for the next couple of weeks to become the kind of people who can learn from the characters in stories. Are you game for that?" The kids indicated they were.

"In another day or two, you will each reread your writer's notebooks, searching for an idea that can become the seed idea for your literary essay. You'll want to find an idea that not only matters to you, but that is also central to the story."

Name the teaching point. In this case, teach readers that important ideas about stories often reside in the question, "What's this story *really* about?"

"Specifically, today, I want to teach you that many readers find important ideas in stories when we reread, asking, 'What is this story *really* about?' We may ask more specific questions, such as, 'What is the character learning in this story? Is this a lesson that pertains also to my life?'"

COACHING

When I teach minilessons, my goal is not simply to follow the architecture of good minilessons. I'm also hoping that my minilessons illustrate the qualities of good teaching. To me, this means that my minilessons need to be memorable. I use a variety of techniques to achieve this, but few are as effective as the use of metaphor.

When I describe literary essays in this way, saying that children will be learning life lessons from the characters in stories, I am angling children toward writing interpretive essays. By channeling them to look for messages in stories, I'm directing them toward the work that high school educators refer to as literary interpretation. For the past few years, I've felt as if I have been attending high school along with my sons, trying to learn from their teachers' instruction. One thing I've learned is that the standard secondary school essay assignment asks students to identify a theme in a work of literature and show the ways in which the author used literary devices to support that theme. I've also learned that when they assign writing tasks, secondary school teachers rarely teach students what they need to know to be successful. This unit of study is my attempt to give kids the foundational skills they will need to fare well under the regimen of secondary school English classrooms!

I don't summarize the sorts of questions I hope readers ask; instead I literally put words in their mouths. This is true across the entire series. I'm hoping to put words not only in my students' mouths, but also in their minds.

TEACHING

Remind children that earlier in the year, they learned that once they, as writers, asked, "What is my story really about?" their choice of lead, details, places to elaborate, and so forth all reflected their answer.

"Earlier this year, we learned that a writer could angle a story about riding on the Ferris wheel so it is really about how that writer looks for occasions to be alone. Alternatively, written another way, it could become the story of how he wants to cling to the joys of childhood. Then again, it could highlight his relationship with his father. We learned that writers need to ask, 'What is my story *really* about?' and the answer then influences our lead, our points of emphasis, the thoughts the character reveals, which actions are told in detail versus which are quickly summarized, and many other aspects of the story."

"There is a reciprocal truth. When we read stories *others* have written, we can ask, 'What is the significance this author wanted to highlight?' We can notice the craft decisions an author made and think, 'How does the author's decision to title the story like this, to start it at this point or to elaborate on this section, convey a meaning that resonates in us, long after we've completed the story?'"

Show children that readers have a repertoire of questions to ask to develop interpretive ideas about a text.

"What I am suggesting is that readers don't just finish reading a text, close the book, look up in the air, and think, 'What was that story really about?' Instead, we study the way a text was written, and we develop a tentative idea about a story's central meaning. For example, when we want to know what a story is really about, we often use these subordinate questions as stepping stones." I gestured to the chart I had prepared.

Teaching your students to entertain provocative, significant questions of a text is worthwhile work because in real life, there are no questions at the ends of chapters. Skilled readers need to be able to generate as well as to muse over questions.

This list is long—choose just a few of these questions to teach during any one year.

> **Interpretation:**
> **What Is This Story Really About?**
>
> What single section—or which two related sections—best capture(s) the story's meaning?
>
> Is there one object or one moment from the story that symbolizes the whole message of this story? How does this object or moment convey the overall meaning?
>
> What does the character learn in this story? Is this a life lesson that readers are also meant to learn?
>
> What life lesson can I draw from this story? How does this story teach me a lesson that can help me live my life differently?
>
> How might all the elements of this story contribute to the message of the story? How does the title contribute? The beginning? The setting? The way the character changes? The form? The end?

ACTIVE ENGAGEMENT

Demonstrate reading with interpretation, asking questions about a well-known text. Have children make silent observations of the moves you make with this story, noticing these are moves they could also make with the stories they're studying.

"So watch me as I start to bring these questions to 'Spaghetti,' and then I'll ask you to name what I've done, and to step in where I leave off and continue doing this work."

"I'm going to reread the list of questions and choose one that'll get me started. Um . . . I think I'll ask, 'What did the character—Gabriel—learn?' Let me look back at the story with that in mind." I turned to the text that was written on chart paper, then reread and mused aloud as I did so. "I better tell the before and the after," I muttered to myself. "At the start of the story, Gabriel wears a tough shell that keeps him from feeling how lonely he really is. But in the story, he learns—" Abruptly, I paused.

Reenact what you've just done, asking children to list with their partners the steps you took to apply an interpretive question to the text.

Shifting out of the role of being a reader, I leaned toward the children and said, "Let me stop. I'm going to rewind and replay what I just did. As I do this, would you list across your fingers particular moves that I make with this story that you could later make with your own story." Quickly, I reread the questions from the interpretation chart (gesturing with an upraised finger to show this was the first step I took) and then I chose one question—What did the character learn? (When I chose the question, I gestured that this was my second step.) Next I looked over the story with the question in mind, thinking about what specifically I needed to find to answer the question. I realized that I needed to notice the before and after in order to illustrate how a character changes. This, then, was the third thing I did, and I gestured to a third finger to indicate I'd made another move that the children, too, could take with their texts. Then I asked the children to list with their partners the steps I had taken. After a few minutes, I convened the class' attention. I could have reiterated what they said, but instead moved on to make my larger point.

Sometimes we, as teachers, listen to children talk about texts and we despair. "They're always jumping away from the text," we say. "They veer off to their own lives so often," we complain. If we're not happy with what children do, then we need to teach them what we'd like them to do. This session teaches children how to generate questions that keep them close to the central issues of a text.

I often pause very early on to process what I'm doing. There's not much reason to postpone this move.

Instead of asking children to name what I did, I could have asked them to look at another text, asking, "What's this really about?" I might have encouraged students to notice unusual craft moves the author made and think, "How might this bit of craftsmanship support the meaning the author was trying to convey?" For example, children are apt to say that Gwendolyn Brooks' poem 'We Real Cool' is really about the futility and pain that teenagers experience when they try to be cool. It is productive, then, to look at Brooks' odd use of white space. One can speculate why her lines end with a jagged edge, as in this example: "We real cool. We . . . ." I did not look at craft moves at this point, however, because I know this is something I will invite children to do later.

LINK

Remind children of the strategies they can draw upon when writing about reading.

"So writers, from this day on when you want to write about texts, remember that you have lots of options." I showed the chart that I had updated with the latest strategies.

"I can't wait to see the choices you make today as you continue to use writing to help you think in deep, smart ways about the text you've selected."

Strategies for Writing in Response to Reading

Find a significant moment from the story. Copy the start of it into your notebook; envision it; fill in details, sounds, actions, thoughts, feelings.

Be a wide-awake reader. Notice and underline details others might pass by. Then write a thought about what you notice.

Think about an author's language choices, even in small words like so.

Pay special attention to aspects of texts that are noteworthy, including a character's actions, motivations, struggles, changes.

We ask, "What is this story really about?" More specifically, we look at:

- the section(s) that best capture the whole story's meaning
- what the character learns in the story
- how all elements of the story contribute to the story's message

---

As you help children interpret texts, it is important to remember there are different schools of thought in the world of literary criticism. Some people argue that by close reading, a student can detect the author's message. Others, and I count myself among them, believe that texts do not carry a single message. Texts aren't fortune cookies that can be cracked open to reveal a single moral. I believe that by close and responsive reading, readers co-construct meanings. I'm convinced that readers will not (and should not) all arrive at the same meaning for a text, because reading involves integrating all that we know from the text and all we know from our own prior reading and prior experiences. Although I do not believe there is any single message encoded into a story, I am not uncomfortable suggesting that children read closely, trying to ascertain what an author has tried to convey. With older children, I reword this, asking them to attend to what the text says, because often the author is not accessible. But with upper elementary children, I try to help them reach toward an understanding of what the author might be saying; in doing so, I avoid channeling them toward a single consensus about "the author's meaning," because this can close down conversation and thoughtfulness.

Whichever school of thought you represent, it is important that children learn to read closely and to bring their own constructive minds to the job of asking, "What's this story really about?"

WRITING AND CONFERRING

Choosing a Tone

When I drew my chair alongside children, I found that the questions about the themes of the texts seemed to have nudged some children, including Emily, to believe they should give definitive responses and assume the authoritative stance of a literary expert. Many of these children seemed to feign confidence in their entries but at the same time seemed insecure over their conclusions. In one entry and then another, Emily had taken a stab at crystallizing the message of "Eleven." *[Fig. V-1]*

> In the story "Eleven" by Sandra Cisneros, Rachel is a girl who has confidence on her birthday, but when is singled out it causes her to lose confidence.
>
> Rachel does not act old as eleven should. Rachel is stuck in her childish ways. Rachel is older but old habits of her being young aren't completely hidden.
>
> Rachel has no power in the story "Eleven." Sylvia and Mrs. Price are the ones with power. Without the power, Rachel had to take more responsibility.

I began my conference by asking Emily how her writing was going. She said, "It's hard because I am not sure what to say." She expected that next she'd try to write about a different story. When I asked if she'd write differently or in a similar way, she wasn't sure what the question meant, but seemed to suggest she'd again try to pinpoint the text's "real meaning."

I nodded, feeling like I'd grasped enough information to be able to help, and then made a double-decker compliment. "Emily, I love the fact that after you asked a giant question like, 'What is this story really about?' you didn't just point to what's right there in the story as the response. You didn't say: 'It's about a girl whose teacher makes her wear someone else's red sweater.' Instead you read between the lines and talked about meanings that are *suggested* but not *stated*. That's brave work because you are adding your own ideas to the text—and as a result, you've said things that are really interesting!"

"For example, I think it is fascinating that you think Rachel is stuck in her childish ways. I'm also so interested that you think she has no power, and that Sylvia and the teacher have all the power. We could

MID-WORKSHOP TEACHING POINT   *Entertaining, Rather Than Answering, Questions*   "Writers, can I have your eyes and your attention? The questions that I posed today are big and difficult questions. They are meant to make a person think; they are meant to be puzzling. So in this instance, you probably won't ask yourself one of these questions and then just pop out with an answer. Instead, you will take one of the questions and then muse about possible responses. If you come to a quick answer, you may want to force yourself to say, 'So that's one idea. How else could I respond to this question?'"

"The writing you do when you are musing over something difficult (and when you don't want to become clear too quickly) has a different quality to it than the writing you do once you are sure of your ideas."

continued on next page

> In the story 'Eleven' by Sandra Cisneros, Rachel is a girl who has confidence on her birthday, but when is singled out it causes her to lose confidence.
>
> Rachel does not act old as eleven should. Rachel is stuck in her childish ways. Rachel is older but old habits of her being younger arent completely hidden.
>
> Rachel has no power in the story 'Eleven' Sylvia and Mrs. Price are the ones with power. Without the power Rachel had to take more responsibility.

Fig.V-1 Emily assumes an authoritative tone in her entry about "Eleven."

definitely gather the class together and have a grand conversation over your ideas. They are provocative; they stir up thoughts! So congratulations for doing that."

Then I shifted. "I have one thing I'd like to teach you, if that's okay." Emily nodded, and I pressed on. "What I realize is that when we talk or write about our big ideas about texts, we need to make several choices. We need to choose not just the strategy we'll use to generate our ideas. (You decided to think about 'What's the story really about?' and to think about the character, too.) We also need to choose what role we want to play as we talk and write about the text."

"You have a choice when you write about a text. You can talk and write as if you are a professor, teaching others the smart theory that you've settled upon. If you decide to play this role, you'd probably talk a bit like an announcer, using a strong, declarative voice." (I illustrated the tone by altering my own voice to match what I was describing.) "You'd talk like this":

> In the story, such and such happens. This is evident from . . . Clearly, . . . It is important to notice . . . Furthermore . . . In conclusion . . . .

"On the other hand, you could decide to talk and write about the text as if you are an explorer, a wanderer. In that case, your voice would be tentative and exploratory. For example, if I were writing about 'Spaghetti' in that voice I might write":

> Spaghetti is a story about a boy who learns to love. He learns this from a cat. Some people might say it's not really love he felt. He just held the cat and his heart opened. Or was it already open? Would he have picked up the cat and put it by his cheek if he was so hardened? I don't think so. He maybe learns love from his own life, not just from the cat, but I'm not sure.

"Do you hear how I used a wondering, thinking voice?"

"I'm saying this to you, Emily, because the ideas you've recorded are really smart, but you seem to be struggling, and therefore you want to hop to the next text. I'm thinking that you may have been pushing yourself not only to take on Big Questions, but *also* to write in a professor voice, and perhaps you've pushed yourself to do so before you were ready for that voice. You have a choice as a writer about literature. You can write or talk in a professor voice or you can write or talk in a tentative, exploratory voice."

continued from previous page

Listen to Max's writing about 'Eleven' and notice its musing, explorative, unsure quality." *[Fig. V-2]*

> At the beginning of the story, I thought that she was kind of immature, but a kid. Because of the way she talks about the sweater and they all yell "not mine."
>
> Then I thought she was kind of sensitive, or she gets a little more upset at things or people then she should. Like when Sylvia just said "I think its' Rachel's" and she got all upset and called her stupid.
>
> Then I thought she was the sort of person who held in her anger without expressing it. I think this because of all her closing her eyes shut tight and big.
>
> I have been thinking that Rachel's expectations are too high. That's because she expected to feel eleven when she woke up on her birthday. Also, when she expected the kids in her class not to know about the different ages. Now I am thinking, and maybe, it is not that she expects things to happen a certain way. Maybe she thinks these things because that is the way someone taught her to think. Maybe she is just naïve. I think that she thinks that everything will go as she thinks it will. This makes me think that maybe she has to think for herself sometimes. And maybe what happened in the class will teach her to make her own decisions. Or, to work it out and see.

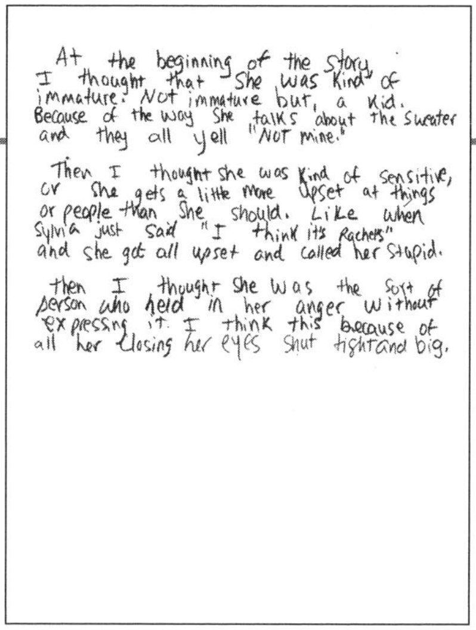
At the beginning of the story, I thought that She was Kind of immature. Not immature but, a Kid. Because of the way She talks about the Sweater and they all yell "NOT mine."

Then I thought she was Kind of sensitive, or She gets a little more upset at things or people than She should. Like when Sylvia just said "I think it's Rachel's" and she got all upset and called her Stupid.

then I thought She was the Sort of person who held in her anger without expressing it. I think this because of all her closing her eyes shut tight and big.

Fig.V-2 Max's entry reflects his exploration of "Eleven."

Later I came back to Emily and she had written this: *[Figs. V-3 and V-4]*

> Rachel wants to grow up and she's still young. Maybe she's not very nice because she called Sylvia stupid or maybe that's the reason she said it was Rachel's. Why does Mrs. Price believe Sylvia? It's interesting how she says "because she's older and the teacher, she's right and I'm not." That could be another reason why she doesn't want to be eleven and younger than Mrs. Price. She doesn't want the sweater. Rachel tries to cheer herself up. If she doesn't feel eleven why would she be one hundred two, even older.
>
> This is true because if she was one hundred two then she would be older than Mrs. Price and be right. This is important because if she was older she would have been right and she wouldn't have to wear the sweater, or cry. This connects to fairness because it's not fair she's only eleven.

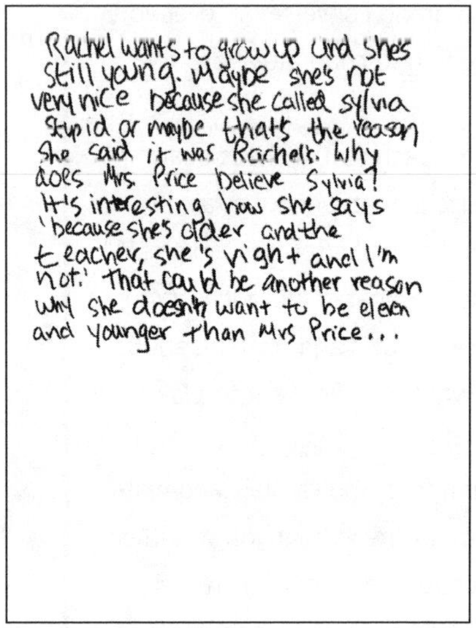

Rachel wants to grow up and she's
still young. Maybe she's not
very nice because she called sylvia
stupid or maybe that's the reason
she said it was Rachels. Why
does Mrs. Price believe Sylvia?
It's interesting how she says
'because she's older and the
teacher, she's right and I'm
not.' That could be another reason
why she doesn't want to be eleven
and younger than Mrs Price...

Fig. V-3 Emily tries to write in the voice of an explorer.

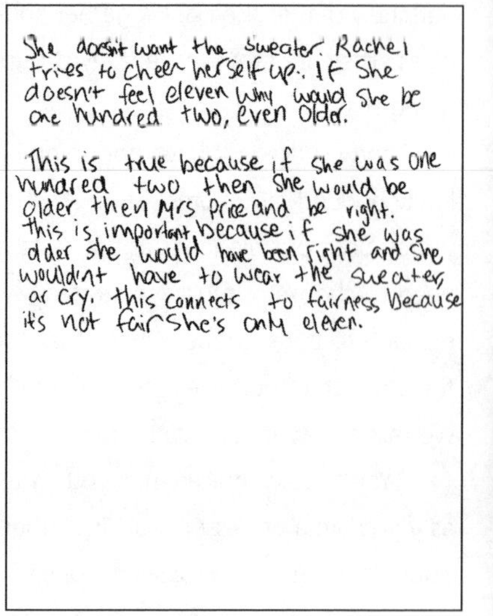

She doesn't want the sweater. Rachel
tries to cheer herself up. If She
doesn't feel eleven why would she be
one hundred two, even Older.

This is true because if she was one
hundred two then she would be
older then Mrs Price and be right.
this is important because if she was
older she would have been right and she
wouldn't have to wear the sweater,
or cry. this connects to fairness because
it's not fair she's only eleven.

Fig. V-4 Emily page 2

Other children showed that they needed very different instruction. When I pulled my chair alongside Adam, I found that in his effort to pinpoint the main idea of the story and then "write long" about it, he ended up writing about a host of very tangentially related subjects. Within the space of a brief entry, he crystallized what he regarded as the main idea of "Eleven" and then related it to Iraq, Osama bin Laden, to school bullies, and to Jenny from "Boar Out There." *[Fig. V-5]*

> I think that this is a social issue and if it isn't a social issue then it connects to each social issue. If we all thought of everyone's feelings, this world would be twice as nice. Almost half of the reason we are in Iraq is because we don't think about their feelings or even thoughts.
>
> If Osama bin Laden cared about what we think or what the families who lost someone would think he may not have done this. Everyone is mean from school bullies to evil dictators. They don't think of others' thoughts like Jenny does.

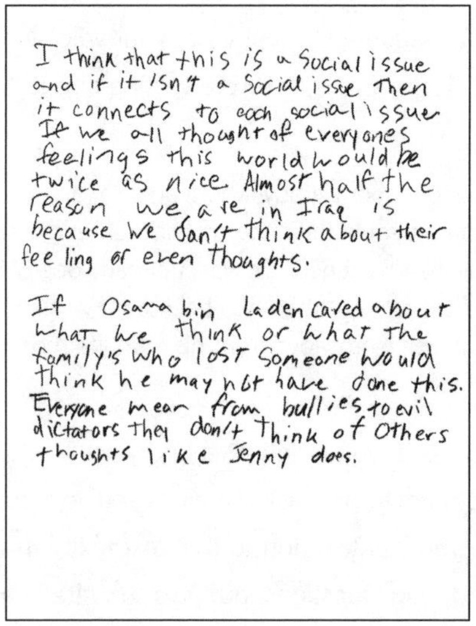

I think that this is a Social issue
and if it isn't a Social issue Then
it connects to each social issue
If we all thought of everyones
feelings this world would be
twice as nice. Almost half the
reason we are in Iraq is
because we don't think about their
fee ling or even thoughts.

If Osama bin Laden cared about
what we think or what the
family's who lost Someone would
think he may not have done this.
Everyone mean from bullies to evil
dictators they don't think of Others
thoughts like Jenny does.

Fig. V-5 Adam's writing could profit from focus!

It was not hard for me to point out to Adam that the lessons he learned during the personal essay unit of writing still pertain to his entries. "When you write, keep in mind that each time you shift from one idea or one topic to another, you need to indent and start a new paragraph. And you don't want paragraphs that are one or two sentences long! When you see yourself writing in two-sentence paragraphs, ask, 'Am I jumping too quickly from one topic to another? Should I spend a bit longer elaborating on whichever idea I put forward?' The answer will probably be yes."

As you move among children, conferring with them, you'll probably see that today's session led many children to talk about their ideas about texts. Often they'll try to name an idea with just a single word. It's not enough to say that "Spaghetti" is about loneliness. Try saying to kids, "Can you use more words to say that idea?" This can help readers phrase ideas as propositions or claims, rather than as topics.

You'll find that many times young readers develop an overall interpretation of the text, and then they want to paint the entire text with that one idea. So if a child thinks the story is about loneliness, he decides that everyone in the story is depressed because of loneliness—and overlooks all evidence to the contrary. You may want to teach readers that if a story addresses an idea, the characters in the story will probably take different stands on that idea, and some may well alter their relationship to the idea over the course of the story. For example, in Jacqueline Woodson's *The Other Side*, the narrator longs to be friends with a girl "from the other side" while both her mother and her friend, Sandra, hold people who live on the opposite side of the fence at a distance. They are cautious about keeping the worlds—and the people who inhabit them—separate. But by the end of the story, when the narrator has eased the tension by befriending the girl from the other side, sitting with her on the fence that serves as a barrier, both her mother and her friend soften to the possibility of a time when the two worlds can come together.

"I hope you are realizing that there are some times in life when we answer a question crisply and clearly. There are other times when we take a question and we 'entertain' it. Have you ever entertained a guest in your home? You know how you say, 'Have a seat, stay awhile'? You may ask, 'Can I get you something to eat?' You try to make the guest feel at home. In a similar way, when we *entertain a question*, we try to be sure that question lingers, that it stays a while. We make the question feel at home; we chat back and forth with it."

"For a second, let's practice responding to questions in two very different ways. Here's a question for you *to answer* (to your partner): What happens most days during writing workshop? (Before you answer, get your mind clear. You want to answer in a crisp, clear, direct style.) Here's a question for you *to entertain*: What is one moment from this year that best encapsulates the writing workshop for you? (Before you answer, think through different possibilities, and different lenses you could use to approach the question. Remember, this time you don't want to *answer* the question, you want to entertain it, to linger with it and grow thoughtful insights.) To entertain this question, you'll use phrases such as *it might be . . .* , *it could be that . . .* , *on the other hand . . .* , and *one way to think of this is . . . .*"

"Writers, get back to your work. Try, as you proceed, to *entertain* rather than to answer questions."

SHARE

Finding and Developing Provocative Ideas

Invite children into a book talk. Coach them to brainstorm ideas and to select one that is especially provocative and important to the story as a starting place for discussion.

"I am dying to hear some of your ideas! Let's have a whole-class story talk about 'Spaghetti.' Would one of you who has written about this story share an entry in which you've advanced an idea (made a claim) about the story." A few children indicated they could start a conversation.

Speaking to just these children, I said, "Before you read your entry or say your thought, would each of you share your entry or your thought with the group of kids sitting near you? Then would that group talk together about whether the idea feels provocative enough to initiate a great talk, and whether it is also central to the whole text?"

Ask children to select one entry as the discussion-starter, and let the discussion begin. At times, invite children to write to grow their ideas from the conversation.

After children talked in these informal small groups, I asked for a group to nominate a child's entry as starting material for a class conversation.

Adam read aloud this entry:

> Gabriel is brave, but not very smart. The reason he can be brave is because no one told him how dangerous picking up a stray cat is. We never heard about a guardian or anything. So I think there was something sad that made Gabriel brave. The cat is like Gabriel.

"Would you talk in partners about Adam's entry, just to get your thoughts going?" I said. After they talked for a few minutes, I said, "Keep 'talking' over Adam's idea, but now *jot* your next thoughts instead of saying them. That is, each of you write down your thoughts. Then exchange notebooks, and reread your partner's idea and jot a further thought into your partner's notebook. You'll be passing notebooks back and forth among yourselves."

After another few minutes, I asked, "Jill, would you get us started in a conversation?"

"I am thinking about the difference between tough and brave. Tough means brave to some people."

I nodded, repeated what she'd said, and asked everyone to think about it and be ready to talk about it. "You can be tough on the inside or on the outside," Tyler said first.

The work that I describe here could easily happen almost every day in response to your read-aloud. Try it. Read, then ask children to jot their thoughts, then to talk in pairs or small groups to sift through their ideas and find some that are worth pursuing, and then begin to pursue them. Then elicit either a small bunch of ideas (which you'd then narrow) or just one idea. Invite children to help assess whether the idea is provocative enough to generate a good discussion and is central to the text—and then hold a whole-class talk in which everyone uses the thought prompts to grow related ideas.

You'll notice that in the next unit of study, one child—Ali—uses this question to frame a memoir in which she explores the bravery she believed she showed in the face of her father's illness. You'll notice that children—people, actually—do not always invent big ideas. They take a big idea that is floating in the world around us, and apply it to a near situation and voila! Insight!

Max added, "I don't think he's tough here, but he is brave. He needs courage to be himself, to be the only one with the right answer, and to live so alone."

"This connects to what Tyler and I were talking about. There's a tough, mean kind of bravery and there's a caring kind of bravery. We think Gabriel is the second kind of brave. We think he cares about the kitten because he's lonely. He needs the kitten. The kitten has a personality for him," Judah responded.

Emily chimed in, "Gabriel being lonely reminds me of Journey and Bloom. Journey was lonely—'and then the cat came,' Patricia MacLachlan said. Bloom helped cure Journey's loneliness. Bloom also helped connect Journey to the rest of his family. I wonder if Spaghetti will do that for Gabriel."

"To go back to what Judah said, I agree there are lots of types of bravery. A fireman, for example, going into a fire—that's pure bravery," Harrison said.

As the children talked, many of them jotted notes. Here are Adam's jottings during this conversation:

> What does it mean to be tough?
>
> Tough is a thought, brave is what you do.
>
> Gabriel thinks of the NOW, not the "what can happen."

After the conversation, I asked each person to again jot his or her thoughts about the text. "Take a minute and think back over the many ways you talked about Gabriel and his bravery. Look at something you wrote earlier, take that sentence, and write off of it using one of the ideas we grew in this conversation."

Set children up in partnerships to develop ideas about the texts they have selected just as they have just done as a class.

After the children did this for a bit, I intervened to say, "These are unbelievably powerful ideas that you are growing today! All of these ideas, however, are about 'Spaghetti.' Many of you may find that your mind is especially on fire about 'Eleven' or 'The Marble Champ' or 'Boar Out There' or 'The Birthday Box.' Right now, would you each reread your entries on the text that especially interests you and box out an idea that feels provocative and central enough to that story that you'd like to develop it." I let the children do this for a moment or two. Then I said, "I've regrouped you into partnerships based on the story you are focusing on especially. I'm going to read off some partnerships, and when I finish reading my list, would you meet at the desk of the partner's name I read first (that will be partner 1 in these new groupings), bringing your writer's notebook and your story with you." I then read the list, and let the class regroup.

You'll notice that this is really more like the Active Engagement portion of a minilesson than like a share. Sometimes more practice with a new way of learning helps children more after the workshop time than making public some of the work they've done, which is more usual for a share.

"All eyes on me. Partners, I suggest that you discuss one partner's idea only, and talk about it just as we talked about Jill's idea. After you and your partner have agreed on a claim that you want to discuss, take a minute to look back at your chosen short text so that you get yourself ready to talk more about the one idea you select. Mark sections of the text that relate to that idea. Afterwards, try to talk as long as you can about that one idea. You may find other sections of the text that relate to that idea, in which case, talk about them, too."

"You may decide the original idea can be revised so it is more specific and more true. You may find exceptions to the idea. You may talk about whether the idea is true in your own lives or in the lives of characters in other books. Your job will be to talk as long as you can about one person's idea, always referring to the text as often as you can."

HOMEWORK *Finding Elusive Meaning in Texts* For homework tonight, reread the text you have been studying and this time, pay attention to a part of the text where nothing much happens. Ask yourself, "Why is this section of the text here?" Don't settle for "Who knows?" as the answer. There must be a reason—so speculate. Ask, "Could it be . . ." and then say, "On the other hand . . ." Entertain the question!

As you do this, you may find that you come up with several central ideas. Good readers generate lots and lots of ideas about a text's larger meaning.

TAILORING YOUR TEACHING

If children need more practice learning how to use interpretive questions to lead them to interpret . . . you might want to first ask one child to do this, and then use that one child's work as a demonstration text. For example, a fifth grader, Jose, used these questions to reflect on "Boar Out There." He felt that the section which best captured the story's meaning was the one where Jenny sees the boar and cries because he's been hurt. She isn't afraid anymore. It's important to notice that this one section of the text pertains to both the start of the text—to the fearful rumors associated with the boar—and to the turning point in the text, when Jenny develops sympathy for the boar. When reflecting on what object from the story symbolized the message of the story, Jose wrote this:

> The boar's torn ears are the object that symbolizes the whole message of the story. The ears represent the hurt part of the boar, and maybe of all of us. They are also what allow Jenny to sympathize with the boar.

The question which really nudged Jose to do some important work, however, was this one, "How do all the elements in the story contribute to the message?" This question. . . especially following the others . . . scaffolded Jose to make a journey of thought. He wrote this:

All the elements of this story are about imagining something that isn't really true. Jenny thinks the boar is this really wild, scary beast but in fact he's hurt and scared. So the message is that we shouldn't make assumptions about people. The title, "Boar Out There" shows that the boar isn't a part of Jenny's world; he's "out there," which is why she imagines him to be something he's not.

The beginning of the story shows this, too: "Everyone in Glen Morgan knew there was a wild boar in the woods over by the Miller farm." Right away Cynthia Rylant shows that all the people in the town, not just Jenny, know there's a wild boar. Cynthia goes on to describe the boar that everyone knows exists, but then she says, "No one in Glen Morgan had ever gone past the old back Dodge and beyond, as far as she knew," so we know that what these people think about the boar has nothing to do with the way things actually are.

The setting shows that fear is big in the story. The rail fence that separates the boar from the town is "splintery," the trees are "awful," the leaves are "damp" and "dark" and the air of the woods presses "deep into" Jenny's skin. This isn't a warm friendly place. It's an uncomfortable, heavy, dark place.

Jenny changes from a scared girl to a caring girl. She cries when she sees that the boar is hurt and from then on she doesn't fear him anymore, she just feels bad for him.

The end of this story shows that it's possible to think new things about people or animals. Jenny realizes that the boar has as little to fear about the people of Glen Morgan (the "bluejays and little girls") as the people have to fear about the boar.

From this story I can learn to not judge people too quickly, before getting to know them and I can learn to be more sympathetic to people who are strangers. I hope I'll keep this in mind as I meet new people.

COLLABORATING WITH COLLEAGUES

Today's session opened up the topic of teaching children to interpret texts. For those of you who teach fifth or sixth grades, this should be an especially important topic, because it is a huge priority in secondary school English courses. I remember when I was in high school, my teacher asked me, "What does the light at the end of the dock mean?" I remember thinking, "It means a lamp, a lantern, at the end of the pier"—but of course I knew from my teacher's penetrating gaze that he wanted a deeper answer. I ventured forth. "Does it mean heaven?" I bravely queried.

"Any other ideas?" my teacher asked, scanning the room. When no one else put forth a hypothesis, my teacher proceeded to explain the deeper meaning of the text. How well I remember sitting at my desk thinking, "How did he get *that* out of *this*?" I learned from that day and others like it that I didn't have what it takes to read literature well—and decided against majoring in English, as I'd always planned.

Too many children come to feel that because they don't see the meanings that the teacher sees in a text, this means their ideas about texts are somehow "wrong." I once sat in on a class discussion where the teacher asked her class to describe the relationship between Frog and Toad in Arnold Lobel's Frog and Toad series.

A child suggested they were adventurous friends—a reasonable thought—but the teacher had a particular answer in mind that she wanted her children to produce. "No," she said. "It begins with *d*."

"Damp?" I thought, wracking my brains for the correct answer (and I was an adult at the time!).

To help the children out, the teacher asked a leading question. "Are Frog and Toad the same, or are they . . . ?"

A child produced the requisite word. They are different. That is a perfectly reasonable (if not very surprising) conclusion about Frog and Toad, but it is not reasonable for us to work so hard to elicit our ideas from children that we silence them.

With your colleagues, talk and think about the role of leading questions in your teaching. Teachers are taught, of course, to ask leading questions. We are taught to elicit information and ideas from children. Basal textbooks tell teachers the questions to ask and the answers to expect.

But I believe this sort of teaching silences children. I often tell my graduate students that as a rule of thumb, it is best to aim never to ask a question for which we know the answer. This means that instead of saying, "Are Frog and Toad good friends?" the teacher might ask, "What aspect of their friendship especially interests you?" I hope, then, that today's session invites you to rethink the role of leading questions, and to entertain the notion that it is not important for children to see the same big meanings in a story that you have seen.

What *does* matter is that children grow up to be the kinds of readers who pause in the midst of reading to ask, "What is this really about?" To support children in doing this, be sure that when you read aloud chapter books, you sometimes demonstrate the way in which you pause to think about a book's message. Show children, for example, that when you pause to think about *Because of Winn-Dixie*, you think first that it is the story of a girl, Opal, who goes to the grocery store and ends up adopting a stray dog. To earn money for the dog, she gets a job, and in the process, meets lots of people. But then show children that you entertain other ways to think about the book.

If readers ask questions such as, "What do the characters want? What choices do they make? Why does this matter?" we read more deeply. Perhaps you might think, "In this book, Opal adopts a stray dog and this matters because she is lonely. The dog helps her make a relationship with her father, she and her father get to talking. The dog also helps her make relationships with people at the pet store, and with a recluse." Or you might think, "This story starts by introducing a girl who is not only an only child. She's also a child who is isolated. In the end, she and her dog are part of a network of relationships."

SESSION VI

DEVELOPING PROVOCATIVE IDEAS:

"How Does This Story Intersect with My Life?"

In this session, you will teach children some ways that literary essayists draw on their life experience to understand and develop ideas about texts.

Getting Ready

- Story you can tell of an instance when reading changed a person's life (perhaps your own)

- Example of an important issue from your own life

- "Spaghetti," by Cynthia Rylant (or other touchstone text)

- Idea for a shared life issue children can discuss in relation to a text

- See CD-ROM for resources

My family and I gather every Sunday at 10 p.m. to watch Grey's Anatomy, a show chronicling the drama experienced by a cluster of surgical interns and the attending surgeons. We all watch the same show at the same time, but when it's over and we share our responses, we invariably find that the story has meant something very different for each of us. I'm a sucker for Meredith: I love her resolute efforts to hold herself together, even when her insides are coming out. My husband admires George, who rarely asks to be in the limelight, but in his quiet way does countless small acts of generosity. Each of my sons has his own favorite character and his reasons for championing that person. Each of us constructs our own meaning of the story. We each construct meaning out of all that we are and long to be. I suspect that a person who knows John and me well would suggest that my affinity for Meredith, and John's for George, mirrors our own life stories. But that's not surprising—after all, we bring ourselves to the books we read, and to the shows we watch!

We read, in part, to know that we are not alone. Who among us has not looked up from the pages of a book and thought, "That's it! That's exactly what I've been feeling." Just as we take exquisite comfort in having a friend who understands us— even the parts of us we don't understand—so, too, do we find solace in opening a book and finding ourselves there on the page.

In this session, you'll provide children with one strategy for making personal connections to a book. You'll suggest that when we approach a book aware of our own issues and struggles, and expect the story to speak to us in a deep and profound manner, the chances are great that it will do just that.

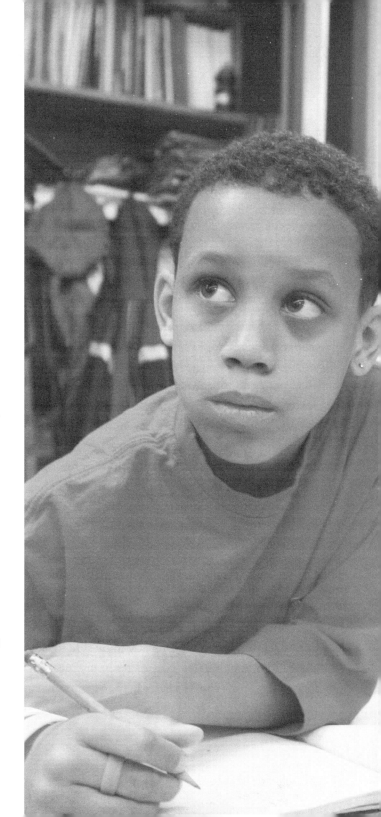

MINILESSON

Developing Provocative Ideas: "How Does This Story Intersect with My Life?"

CONNECTION

Tell your children a story of when reading changed a person's life or your own life. Suggest that by writing about reading, we make it more likely that books will "get through to us."

"I remember last year, one of my students—Ramon—was reading about the author Walter Dean Myers. Ramon brought me a passage in which Myers said, 'The book that changed my life was . . . .' Ramon said to me, 'I don't get this. How could a *book* change someone's life?'"

"I hope that in this unit of study, you come to understand that texts can, indeed, change our lives. And I hope you learn that we write about our reading so that it will be more likely that texts get through to us and make a difference."

"Books have definitely changed my life. When I was your age, I read a book about people who lived in an Israeli kibbutz—they were willing to risk their lives to build their promised land, and I was envious of their sense of mission. I remember thinking, 'I wish I were Jewish!' I suspect that I am a teacher today because books taught me that some people don't just have jobs, they have missions—and I wanted a sense of *mission* in my life as well."

"Sometimes I see kids read a book and when they reach the last page, they just throw the book to the side and say, 'I'm done!' They don't seem to understand that we read to be affected by what we experience on the page."

Name your teaching point. In this case, teach children that we write so that stories we read will be more apt to matter to us. Give writers a strategy for connecting personally to the texts they are studying.

"Today I want to teach you that when readers write, we can make it more likely that stories get through to us. One way to be sure that stories speak to us and to the issues in our lives is to think, 'What are the issues in my life?' Then we can read or reread a text, thinking specifically, 'How can this story help me with my issue?'"

COACHING

In this unit of study, I am trying to rally children not only for a particular kind of writing but also for a love of reading. My connections, then, have more work to do than usual. Over and over again, I plead with children for their attention, their dedication.

Shirley Brice Heath has said that one of the most important gifts we can give our students is allowing them to form bonded relationships with richly literate adults. To that end, we need to wear our love of reading and writing on our sleeves. Minilessons provide opportunities not only for teaching but also for preaching.

Notice that my teaching points are often several sentences long. In the first sentence, I name the general goal of the minilesson and in the second or third sentence, I spell out the specific strategy I will teach students so they can reach the goal.

TEACHING

Show children that they can become aware of the issues in their lives by rereading their notebooks, looking for the topics and themes that reoccur.

"Writers, some people can just say, 'Hmm . . . what are the issues in my life?' and those issues pop into their heads. Other writers need to go on a search for those issues. We can find them if we look back through our writer's notebooks, glancing at the personal narrative and personal essay entries we've written, thinking, 'What's this *really* about? Is that a big topic, a big concern in my life?'"

"I did that work at home already, and I'm aware that in my life, one of my big issues is that I am bracing myself to deal with a feeling of emptiness. My son Miles will be going off to college very soon, and there will be a gaping hole in my heart when he is gone."

Demonstrate to children that once a person is aware of an issue, he or she can reread literature, looking at it through the lens of that concern, asking, "How can this story help me deal with my life issues?"

"So watch me think (and write) about 'Spaghetti,' letting this story help me with my issue."

"How can Rylant's story help me deal with the hole that will be in my life when Miles goes? Let's see . . . at the start of 'Spaghetti,' I get the feeling that Gabriel has a hole in his life too; I'm just going to reread the story again and think about what Gabriel does with that hole in his heart." I did this, and said, in a musing tone, "I think Gabriel had steeled himself to not feel the hole in his heart . . . but as a result, he hardly heard or felt *anything*. I hope that when I need to deal with Miles' departure, I don't wall myself up like Gabriel started to do." As I spoke, I jotted some of this in an entry on chart paper. I continued musing and jotting, "I'm thinking about the fact that Gabriel got himself a kitten, and found a way to fasten his love onto something. This reminds me of how I've always wanted to adopt a little girl from China. I'm tempted to race to China right now! But actually, I've got people at home already waiting for me, and some of them have been as neglected as that kitten."

Debrief. Replay the sequence of work you've done, giving added tips.

"Readers, do you see how I reread my notebook and came upon an issue that was important to me—the hole that will be in my heart when my son leaves for college? Then I reread the story, asking, 'Does this story speak to my issue?' and I wrote about it. I could have looked at 'Spaghetti' and just said, 'No, this isn't about my issue. I'm not poor or homeless. My issue involves my son going to college and Gabriel's not going to college.' But I think when you look to the root of any issue, often that issue is universal. Sometimes, of course, one particular text won't speak to an issue, but I recommend you don't give up too quickly."

I'm telling the truth when I let children know this is a big issue in my life. Obviously, you'll need to think about your own issues, and to speak the truth of your life. Your children will be much more apt to open their hearts to the stories you are studying together if you do so. I may not initially be moved by "Spaghetti," but if I read this story while thinking also about Miles' upcoming departure, suddenly it all means more to me.

When writing in front of children, you have choices. You can write on chart paper, a white board, an overhead transparency, or in your own notebook (in the latter case, your children won't see your script but you can voice what you write as you go, and/or you can write silently and then reread later). I find that even if I decide to simply write in my own notebook, this has some visual power, and of course writing in my notebook is vastly faster than the other formats because I can use shorthand.

Of course, if need be, you can always think of another issue in your life and see if the text can help with that second issue.

ACTIVE ENGAGEMENT
Ask children to pretend they have a shared life issue and to view the class text through the lens of that problem.

"So let's pretend you've already read over your notebook and found that one of the issues that is huge in your life is the pressure that so many of us feel to fit with the in crowd and to be popular. So now you think, 'How does Rylant's story help me deal with the issue of feeling pressured to fit in and be popular?' I'll give you a minute to think about that."

After some silence, I said, "You could think, 'Rylant's story isn't about a kid and his friends—it doesn't really speak to the issue of peer pressure.' But if you give things a chance, I bet you and your partner can find that Gabriel struggles (in his own way) with some of the same pressures to fit in that many people feel, and he's made some choices that might teach you. Would you turn and talk with your partner about how Gabriel and this story could perhaps help you, or someone else who is struggling with feeling that the only way to be popular is to remake yourself to fit in with everyone else."

LINK
Review optional ways writers can generate entries about the texts they are studying.

"So writers, by this time in the year, you have become skilled at making decisions about the work you need to do. Today you may decide to continue to entertain big questions such as, 'What is this story really about?' You may read, trying to be the kind of reader upon whom nothing is lost. That is, you may read closely, noticing details others would pass by, and then write an entry in which you linger over a description of one thing you see in the story. Afterwards, skip a line and write, 'The thought I have about that is . . .' If you want to reread your notebook, grasp onto a life issue, and then think, 'How can this story help me with an issue in my life?' that'd be especially great. The important thing is that you read, reread, reread, and do all this as a wide-awake writer. Let your mind be on fire, and write what you think."

Over and over you'll see me making decisions for children so that during the active engagement section of a minilesson, they are set up to accomplish what I've named and demonstrated. Notice that if I set up the active engagement well, children usually waste no time on peripheral or lead-in activities.

You can be sure that I've already thought this through, and I'm pretty convinced this will be in reach for these kids. If I'd felt it was important to be even more supportive, I might have asked them to keep that question in mind while rereading the story, and I would then have selected a particularly relevant part to read aloud, pausing at the most pertinent sections.

Whenever possible, I want to end a minilesson by reminding children of the array of options available to them so they learn to be the job captains of their own writing. In this Link, I list options, but for variety or for engagement's sake, I could instead ask children to list across their fingers three different ways they could write about reading.

WRITING AND CONFERRING

Making Personal Connections to a Text

"Adam," I said, "You look very serious."

Adam answered, "I can't find anything in my notebook like in 'Eleven.'" He shook his head, discouraged. "I haven't had a birthday. I haven't had a mean teacher like Mrs. Price. I've never been forced to wear someone else's clothes—or not that I can remember."

"To make personal connections with a story," I said. "I usually *start with my own life*. Remember I suggested you reread your writer's notebook and ask, 'What issues do I talk about a lot?' Let's try that together."

"I looked through my notebook but there isn't anything in my life about turning eleven or anything."

"Let's just take an entry," I answered. "For example, this one." I pointed to an entry Adam had written about his brother pounding his arm as they rode in the car to his grandparents' house. "So what's the issue here for you?"

"Oooh! I get it. Jon—he's kind of mistreating me like the teacher is mistreating Rachel."

"You are so smart! You see, when we read, we *do* bring our own lives to texts, but it helps to start by reading your notebook or thinking about a specific issue in your life. Then (and only then) look at the story and think, 'How might this story help me with my life issue?' You'll find this works often."

Adam nodded and began to write:

> Whenever we ride in a car with my parents, Jon and I sit together in the back. Sometimes he hits me hard on the shoulder. I tell him it hurts, but he says, "I'm just trying to toughen you up." When Mrs. Price tells Rachel to put on the red sweater that isn't hers, she is mistreating Rachel the way my brother mistreats me when he punches me.

Interrupting the class I said, "Can you give me a thumbs up if you are finding it a bit hard to make significant personal connections with your text?" Half a dozen kids indicated yes, so I rounded up a small group, and we huddled together. "I just had a conference with Adam, who was struggling to find important ways to bring his life

MID-WORKSHOP TEACHING POINT *Celebrating* "Writers, can I have your eyes and your attention? I need to tell you that the work you are doing today is blowing me away. I am amazed by the reflective thinking and writing you are doing today! You are combing through your writer's notebooks in search of entries that feel meaningful to you and rereading, asking yourself 'Why does this entry matter to me? What does this reveal about me?' Emily, for example, found an entry in her notebook about how she likes to dress up in grown-up clothes, and now she has realized that there are times in her life when she, like Rachel in 'Eleven,' feels both old and young at the same time! And Dominic found just a sentence in one entry that reminded him of a time when he forced himself to act in brave, tough ways (even though he felt something very different). For him, 'Boar Out There' is a story of a character who has done this same thing. But for Harrison, our animal lover, 'Boar Out There' is instead a story about the fact that animals that act mean are often really just hurt."

"You are pushing past your initial thoughts, and making connections between your life and the text you are reading. This is the work that great readers and writers do and this enables texts to change our lives. When we read a text together each one of us brings along our life experiences . . . it is the lens we read through. When I read 'Spaghetti,' I bring the hollow feeling of Miles leaving for college. Oona may bring the lens of loneliness based on her personal essay about being an only child. Zach, after getting a puppy for his birthday, may read through the lens knowing that animals make great company."

to the text he is studying. He did some great work, and I thought maybe you'd be willing to try some similar work—am I right?" The children indicated they were game.

"Take just a second and open your notebook to almost any page—but choose a place where you wrote about something important to you. Reread that page. If it reveals an issue in your life, name that issue. For example, my entry was about my son packing for college, and my issue is that I'm bracing myself for this giant hole I am going to have in my life. Adam's entry was about his brother pounding on his arm, and his issue is that Jon sometimes mistreats him. Usually if you've written about a subject that is important to you, you'll find an issue or a hard part right there. Take just a second to reread your entry and find the issue that is lurking there." After a moment the children looked up, signaling they were done. "It is easier than you think to find issues within your own writing notebook," I said. "The trick is to not spend too much time flipping the pages—settle on one page, and trust that there is definitely an issue on that one page." Then I said, "Zach, tell us the issue you've realized is there in your life," and I motioned to all the children that they should watch what I did to help Zach take the next step.

Zach replied, "Leaving for camp."

I wasn't totally convinced this qualified as an issue, but I tweaked what he'd said a bit so that it would suffice. "That's such an important time, isn't it? Are you saying you have lots of feelings when you are leaving for camp?" I asked.

Then I glanced at all the children. "Once you know an issue that is important in your life, you can pause in the midst of your reading and think, 'How does this text speak to (or help me with) my issue?' So Zach, in what ways does 'Eleven' speak to the deep issues that are wrapped around your leaving for camp?"

"Because sometimes when I go to camp, I feel like crying like a kid, and Rachel feels like that?" Zach said, his voice tentative.

I nodded. "That's huge, Zach. You know the feeling of being both eleven and three years old, and you know that when you feel like crying, you feel as if you are three." Then I asked, "Does Rachel's struggle to deal with that sweater and with the feelings the episode caused in her help you learn ways you could deal with your feelings?"

"'Cause she should have talked; she should have said something," Zach said.

"You need to write that down. It is really important." To the others, I said, "Do you all see what Zach did here with his entry?" As I spoke, I jotted a list of what Zach had done. "First he reread an entry from his notebook and found an issue in his life. Then he asked, 'How does this text speak to the issue in my life?' and he took his first answer deeper. Finally, he asked, 'How might this text help me think more about or realize some new things pertaining to this issue in my own life?' That's how you can let stories matter in your lives! Can you all do this now? Follow these steps," I said, sliding the list I'd made into the center of the table. "I'm going to go work with some other children but I'll be back in five minutes to see how you've done. Stay right here and do this work beside each other, okay? I can't wait to see what you do!"

SHARE

Helping Friends Connect Personally with Texts

Share the story of a child who struggled to make a personal connection to the text and then did, with the help of someone else's eyes.

"I want to share something with you that Max did this morning. When I conferred with him, he shook his head and whispered to me, 'I can't . . . I can't do this!'"

"Max," I said, "What's the matter?"

"'There's nothing here that matches my life. I can't see the stuff I noticed in "Eleven" in my life! I tried, but really, my life is not like hers.'"

"I asked Max to show me what he'd tried to write today and he pointed to this entry," I said and read it aloud to the class: [Fig. VI-1]

> I think that people don't understand Rachel. They don't
> understand her being eleven, ten, nine, eight, seven, six,
> five, four, three, two, and one. I see this in the text
> where it says, "I don't know why but I'm feeling sick
> inside, like the part of me that's three wants to come
> out of my eyes, only I squeeze them shut tight . . . and
> try to remember today I'm eleven . . . " This tells you
> that she is afraid to be three, because other people
> don't know she is also three. She may be too afraid to
> be herself because the other people don't know the
> real her. And they are also probably three, and can cry
> like they are three, but are too afraid to. Because it's
> different. And Rachel is different. But she as well as
> her classmates are afraid to be different.

After I read that, I said to Max, "Sometimes, when we write about a text, issues from our lives leak through into what we notice and think. Sometimes, we're not aware that our lives have affected what we notice in a text until someone else points out possible connections to us."

Then I said to Max, "Do you remember an entry you wrote about how you love to bake—remember we had a huge class discussion about the fact that you don't always share things because you (like many others) get uneasy over what people think? And do you remember the entry you shared with the class about not liking sports and being different in

Fig. VI-1 Max's notebook entry

You may be surprised that I'm willing to talk in this honest way about one writer's struggles. The truth is, writing workshops become intimate places and we do talk about struggles as well as successes. Also, Max is an especially capable writer, so I'm more apt to spotlight his struggles than those of another student. Of course, in an instance such as this, I'll check with the child before using his story as the centerpiece in a lesson!

that way from a lot of kids? Well—look again at what you wrote about Rachel. You said she 'may be too afraid to be herself because the other people don't know the real her.' And you wrote, 'Rachel is different. But she, as well as her classmates, is afraid to be different.'"

"Max's eyes got big behind his glasses and a smile spread across his face when I said that. He knew his issues in his personal life had already leaked into his response to 'Eleven.' *His* life had leaked into his thinking about Rachel."

Point out the ways the one child's struggles and solutions could apply to everyone's. Ask children to work with their partners to explore potential personal connections to the texts in their writing.

Looking around at the class, I said, "Max didn't realize at first that his life issues had leaked into his thinking and writing about Rachel. I bet the same thing has happened in your writing today. I know Ali, for example, has paid a lot of attention to the relationships Lupe had in 'The Marble Champ.' Ali, I'm wondering if you realize you may be noticing Lupe's relationship with her father especially because *your* relationship with your dad has been on your mind a lot lately?"

Then I said to all the children, "My guess is that your lives have been leaking into what you see in texts and that, like Ali and Max, you may not even realize it. Partner 1, tell partner 2 what you have noticed especially in your short text, and share a few entries you have written about the text. Partner 2, listen carefully and give your partner feedback if you see that some of your partner's life issues may have been leaking into your partner's thinking about the text. Then switch so that you both get this sort of help. Think hard—be smart and try to *make* the writing connect to your partner's life."

🌐 HOMEWORK   *Learning from Characters* Writers, tonight as you read, instead of focusing on how an overall text speaks to you, instead think about a single quality of a character you admire—one you'd like to have yourself, or one you have deep inside you but haven't yet found a way to express. You might, for example, notice that someone in your book finds ways to deal with her anger without shouting or losing control. If you're someone who does get heated when angry, you might think about how you could let this character in, learning from her, maybe even finding ways to change yourself. You might find that it isn't always the main character who affects you. Often secondary characters, in their quiet and sometimes quirky ways, touch us more immediately or more deeply. Once you've

This may seem to you like a lucky coincidence that Max noticed in "Eleven" what he also deals with in his own life. You may be surprised at how often you notice this "coincidence" of a match between a response to literature and the readers's response to his or her life. Even if at first there appears to be no connection at all, ask children to assume the connection must be there and free write about it until they surprise themselves by finding it really is there. We all share the human experience, and there is always a way to empathize with other people or characters, even those with very different lives.

identified a character who speaks to you in some way, spend some time jotting down your thoughts about the quality you admire in this character, the ways in which he or she demonstrates the quality. What it is about the quality you identify with, long for, or are trying to bring out in yourself? You might use prompts like, "The quality I admire is . . . ", "This quality makes me feel . . . ", "I notice in my own life that . . . "

TAILORING YOUR TEACHING

If children are making personal connections that veer very far from the text . . . then you'll want to help them deepen this response. Often, a child reads a text, sees a word or passage in the text that reminds the child of her own experience, and suddenly it is as if the text no longer exists. All the child can think about is her own experiences. Reading, then, becomes an orgy of self-expression. Be sure, with these children, that you help them to shuttle back and forth between the text, their lives, and the text. That is, if a child pauses in reading to say, "The same thing happens to me," it is helpful to ask, "So how was this character's experience the same as yours? How was it different? What can you learn from this?" Then too, some children regard personal response as a conversation stopper. You'll hear these children make comments such as, "Well, that is just my own idea," or "There is no one right way to read this." Be sure these children know that responding personally to a text needs to be the beginning, not the end, of conversation.

If your children are having trouble getting started making personal connections with the text . . . you might try teaching them a different way to go about it than the way presented in this session. Robert Bleich, author of *Readings and Feelings*, suggests a different set of steps to try that can help readers recognize ways in which their own lives and experiences affect what they see in a text. A reader can read a text, and then search for and mark what he believes is the most important sentence, image, or word in the text, the bit that represents what the text is really about for him. If a number of different readers do this work with the same text, it will immediately become apparent that different aspects of a text stand out to different readers. It is helpful, then, for a reader to ask himself, "Why was it this, out of everything else, that stood out for me especially in this text?" "What is there about my own life that can help me understand my experience of this text?"

COLLABORATING WITH COLLEAGUES

I've previously shared with you the wise advice the poet Lucille Clifton gave me and my colleagues when she visited us almost fifteen years ago. "Nurture your imaginations of what's possible," she said. "We cannot create what we cannot imagine."

That advice has been important to me as I help school districts imagine and plan for large-scale reform in the teaching of writing. It's also advice that helps me when I coach teachers in developing units of study. And I think we need to remember this advice when we work with writers.

Children need an image of the sort of thing we hope they will write in a unit of study, so you and your colleagues will need to find or to write exemplar essays. Before you can proceed, you need to clarify for yourself what it is *you* hope your children will write.

Over the year in my community of practice, we've taught toward a variety of templates for literary essays, and no one template is more right than another. You may choose any one of these templates as the one you want to teach toward, or you may invent yet another, or you may spread the array of options before your children and let them know they can sculpt their essays in any of these ways.

The first template described below is the one we taught with the children in this class. The accompanying pieces of student writing are available on the CD-Rom.

I. A claim, with several parallel supporting ideas drawn from the text

- Introductory paragraph which generally begins with a broad statement about literature or life and often (but not always) includes the author, genre, and text summary, which ends by stating a claim about the story. This claim, the thesis statement, overviews two or three subordinate ideas.

- One subordinate idea is restated at the start of body paragraph #1 and that idea is supported with evidence from the text

- A second subordinate idea is restated at the start of body paragraph #2 and supported with evidence from the text

- A third subordinate idea may or may not be restated in body paragraph #3—if it is, then it is also supported with evidence from the text

- In the last paragraph, the claim is reiterated. The writer may make a personal connection, or put a new spin on the writer's initial claim.

Literary Essay on "Eleven" by Sandra Cisneros written by Jill

In my life, not everything ends up like a fairytale. I like to read books where characters are like me. They don't live fairytale lives. We have the same kinds of problems. Many people read Sandra Cisneros's essay "Eleven" and think it's

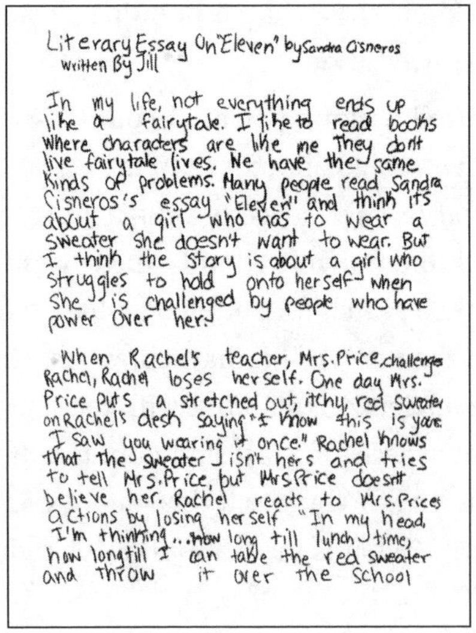

Literary Essay On "Eleven" by Sandra Cisneros written By Jill

In my life, not everything ends up like a fairytale. I like to read books where characters are like me. They don't live fairytale lives. We have the same kinds of problems. Many people read Sandra Cisneros's essay "Eleven" and think its about a girl who has to wear a sweater she doesn't want to wear. But I think the story is about a girl who struggles to hold onto herself when she is challenged by people who have power over her.

When Rachel's teacher, Mrs. Price, challenges Rachel, Rachel loses herself. One day Mrs. Price puts a stretched out, itchy, red sweater on Rachel's desk saying "I know this is yours I saw you wearing it once." Rachel knows that the sweater isnt hers and tries to tell Mrs. Price, but Mrs. Price doesn't believe her. Rachel reacts to Mrs. Price's actions by losing herself "In my head, I'm thinking...how long till lunch time, how long till I can take the red sweater and throw it over the School

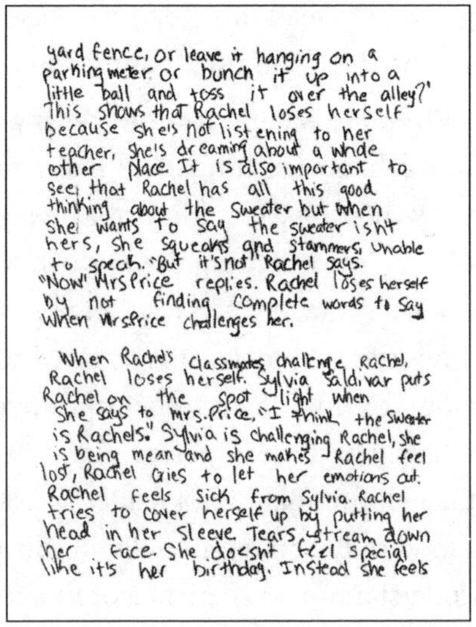

yard fence, or leave it hanging on a parking meter or bunch it up into a little ball and toss it over the alley?" This shows that Rachel loses herself because she's not listening to her teacher, she's dreaming about a whole other place. It is also important to see that Rachel has all this good thinking about the sweater but when she wants to say the sweater isn't hers, she squeaks and stammers, unable to speech. "But it's not" Rachel says. "Now!" Mrs. Price replies. Rachel loses herself by not finding complete words to say when Mrs. Price challenges her.

When Rachel's classmates challenge Rachel, Rachel loses herself. Sylvia Saldivar puts Rachel on the spot light when she says to Mrs. Price, "I think the sweater is Rachel's." Sylvia is challenging Rachel, she is being mean and she makes Rachel feel lost, Rachel cries to let her emotions out. Rachel feels sick from Sylvia. Rachel tries to cover herself up by putting her head in her sleeve. Tears stream down her face. She doesn't feel special like it's her birthday. Instead she feels

Fig. VI-2 Jill page 1

Fig. VI-3 Jill page 2

about a girl who has to wear a sweater she doesn't want to wear. But I think the story is about a girl who struggles to hold onto herself when she is challenged by people who have power over her.

When Rachel's teacher, Mrs. Price, challenges Rachel, Rachel loses herself. One day Mrs. Price puts a stretched out, itchy, red sweater on Rachel's desk saying, "I know this is yours. I saw you wearing it once!!" Rachel knows that the sweater isn't hers and tries to tell Mrs. Price, but Mrs. Price doesn't believe her. Rachel reacts to Mrs. Price's actions by losing herself. "In my head, I'm thinking . . . how long till lunch time, how long till I can take the red sweater and throw it over the school yard fence, or leave it hanging on a parking meter, or bunch it up into a little ball and toss it over the alley?" This shows that Rachel loses herself because she's not listening to her teacher, she's dreaming about a whole other place. It is also important to see that Rachel has all this good thinking about the sweater but when she wants to say the sweater isn't hers, she squeaks and stammers, unable to speak. "But it's not," Rachel says. "Now," Mrs. Price replies. Rachel loses herself by not finding complete words to say when Mrs. Price challenges her.

When Rachel's classmates challenge Rachel, Rachel loses herself. Sylvia Saldivar puts Rachel on the spot light when she says to Mrs. Price, "I think the sweater is Rachel's." Sylvia is challenging Rachel, she is being mean and she makes Rachel feel lost. Rachel cries to let her emotions out. Rachel feels sick from Sylvia. Rachel tries to cover herself up by putting her head in her sleeve. Tears stream down her face. She doesn't feel special like it's her birthday. Instead she feels lost in Sylvia's challenge.

In "Eleven," Rachel is overpowered by both Mrs. Price and Sylvia Saldivar and this causes her to lose herself. I used to think that when people turn eleven they feel strong and have confidence but I have learned that when you're eleven, you're also 10, 9, 8, 7, 6, 5, 4, 3, 2, and 1.

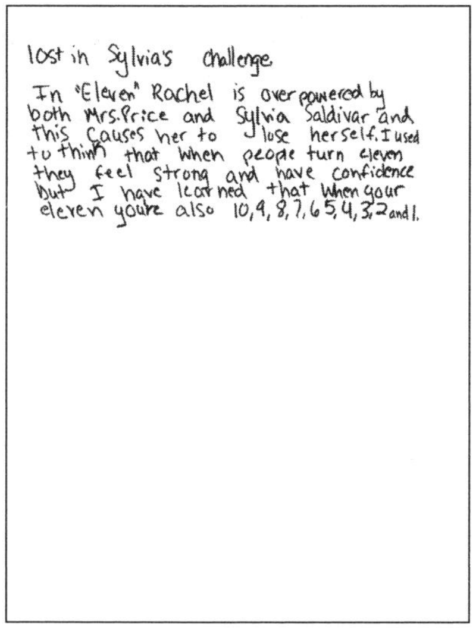

II. A journey of thought: one claim leads to another

- The introductory paragraph may or may not be a summary, but it mentions the title and author and makes a claim.

- The claim is supported, perhaps with subordinate ideas but certainly with examples or instances from the text.

- A secondary claim, one that pushes off from the first or turns a corner from the first, is made.

- The secondary claim is also supported.

- The writer finds a way to end the essay.

Two Sides of Esther
by Miles

The story begins in 1941 in the Polish town of Vilna. Esther Hautzig, the ten-year-old heroine of Esther Hautzig's fictional memoir The Endless Steppe, lives an idyllic life. Esther lives together with her extended family in a mansion encircling an amazing garden. Her father is a successful engineer. She has a summer cottage on the bank of River Wilja. During the

lost in Sylvia's challenge.
In "Eleven" Rachel is overpowered by both Mrs. Price and Sylvia Saldivar and this causes her to lose herself. I used to think that when people turn eleven they feel strong and have confidence but I have learned that when your eleven youre also 10, 9, 8, 7, 6, 5, 4, 3, 2, and 1.

Fig. VI-4 Jill page 3

school year her days are full of lessons—piano lessons, dancing class, and trips to the library. Her problems were small ones, she fought with the librarian for grown-ups' books and she fought with her mother for silk underwear that the other girls wore, instead of her white cotton ones that her mother made her wear.

She was happy, carefree, trusting and optimistic. In the early pages of the book you start seeing how optimistic and trusting she really is. Even when her world starts to collapse she still acts as if her life is perfect. Because she is Jewish and this is taking place during World War II the Russians confiscate her father's job and her family's property, but they do not evict her—yet. It was amazing to me that instead of being panicked and depressed she continues to live blissfully on, playing in the garden with her cousin and happily skipping down the street to school. Things get worse and she continues to believe that her life will improve.

When the Russians come to evict her she assumes she can take all her precious belongings as if they were headed to a hotel. When she is on her way to Siberia she is optimistic in thinking of Asia as a land full of men with long beards and turbans and the air heavy with spices.

You could say that Esther is optimistic and trusting. But you could also say she is blind and that she was deluding herself. Two on one coin. Maybes she deludes herself and acts like she does not see how bad things are because of the family custom to share one's joys and hide one's sorrow. Maybe she hides them so well that she hides them from herself.

III. A claim, with support from the text and from the writer's life

- The introductory paragraph usually includes the author, genre, and a summary of the text, and a hook to draw the reader in.

- The author makes a claim or thesis about the story, usually at the end of the introductory paragraph.

- The writer offers a comment about why the text matters to him or her.

- The writer provides one example or instance from the text that supports the claim.

- The writer gives another example or instance from the text that supports the claim.

- A final story, usually contained within a concluding paragraph, shows how the claim pertains to the writer's own life.

Who says you're supposed to be a certain age on your birthday? Eleven, by Sandra Cisneros, is an admirable story. Many people don't know that whatever age you are, you're also all of the ages you've ever been. Those ages are inside of you. In Eleven, it's Rachel's 11th birthday. She can't pull out her other ages and tell her teacher, Mrs. Price, that a certain hideous sweater does not belong to her. I think that a lot of people don't know how to get the other ages out of themselves. Some people don't even know that these ages are there. Mrs. Price thinks she's the best because she has only one age—the oldest one in the class. Also, Rachel doesn't know that she can bring out her younger ages. I'll be 11 in a week and now I know it's okay to be all my ages if I have to.

In Eleven, Mrs. Price thinks she's the best because she's the oldest in the class. She thinks she's always right because she's older and wiser. "Of course [this sweater] is yours," Mrs. Price says when Rachel tries to say that the sweater isn't hers. Just because she thinks that the ugly sweater is Rachel's, she won't let anyone tell her otherwise. Also, Mrs. Price does a good job of getting people to think she's always right. During the sweater situation, Rachel thinks, "Because [Mrs. Price] is older and the teacher, she's right and I'm not." Mrs. Price doesn't know that she's not only the oldest in the class, she's also the same age as everyone else in the class. She doesn't know that she has every age she's ever been inside of her. Therefore, she's not always right, and she's not the best. She's the same as everyone else.

Also in Eleven, Rachel doesn't think she's allowed to bring out her other ages. She knows that she's not only 11, she's also 10, 9, 8, 7, 6, 5, 4, 3, 2, and 1, but she doesn't think she can use those ages. She thinks she always has to "act her age", as people say. Rachel is embarrassed to bawl like she's 3 again, or to have a tantrum like she's 5 again, or to use any of her other ages to let Mrs. Price know that the sweater belongs to someone else. She holds all of the ages in, even though they're practically bursting out of her.

Rachel has just turned 11, and she feels like she has to "act her age." But her age won't let her do anything about the big heap of red, itchy material that is hanging like a waterfall over the edge of her desk. That's when 10, 9, 8, 7, 6, 5, 4, 3, 2, and 1, come out and she starts crying. All because she can't let herself let her other ages out.

Eleven teaches us that age isn't just a number. Age is what you are. Many people think that everyone is only one age. If this is true, and if age is what you are, then you'd only be one thing, like a one-way street, or a house with nothing inside. This is impossible. A person is like an encyclopedia. There are so many pages, so many chapters, so much information in a person! Mrs. Price doesn't know this. She's missing a page—no, a chapter.

Rachel knows that she is not only 11, she is also 10, 9, 8, 7, 6, 5, 4, 3, 2, and 1, but she is holding these ages in. She learns that you can't hold in something that is a part of you. She can be all her ages at once.

Fig. VI-5 Final draft linking "Eleven" to the writer's life, page 1

Fig. VI-6 Final draft, page 2

Fig. VI-7 Final draft, page 3

Fig. VI-8 Final draft, page 4

SESSION VI: DEVELOPING PROVOCATIVE IDEAS: "HOW DOES THIS STORY INTERSECT WITH MY LIFE?" 93

IV. A universal claim, with support from several texts

- The introductory paragraph makes a claim about literature or life.
- Several subsequent paragraphs each suggest that a different text elucidates this theme/claim.
- An ending paragraph relates back to and resembles the opening paragraph.

If you think about it, people are capturing beautiful things constantly. They do so with memory, and creativity, but before that, they use sight, smell, sound, taste and touch. But only with wisdom can you realize what you've captured.

In "Morning Assignment," a little girl and a woman capture buttons and ribbons for royalty. Do you think the average eye could have captured that? Or would the eye just see fabric?

In "Window" and the excerpt from "Music," the poet captures something fairly simple. Notes. Light. But when music and brightness are caught by the wise ones, they turn into complex pieces of art.

In the piece from "Living," a salamander is caught with the hand. Using the mind, paper, and a pen, the creature was transformed into the magnificent dragon of the imagination.

Only when a wise one captures something simple can the philosophy be released. Everything has majesty. Everything has one love.

GETTING READY

- "Spaghetti," by Cynthia Rylant
- Your own sample seed ideas from "Spaghetti" you can use to demonstrate choosing and testing possible thesis statements
- Start of a chart: Questions Essayists Ask of a Thesis Statement
- Manila file folders
- Sample of student work where ideas are boxed and bulleted
- Sample thesis statements that illustrate using a template—juxtaposing the internal and external story lines
- See CD-ROM for resources

FINDING AND TESTING A THESIS STATEMENT

I remember well the analytical papers I was asked to write when I was a young girl. I bought myself several packets of index cards, took the bus into the city of Buffalo, made my way to the library, and spent days recording my data about my assigned author. When children in today's world are asked to write academic papers, the challenge has far less to do with collecting data—that they can do with one click—and far more to do with synthesizing it.

After this watershed session, children will no longer write assorted ideas about the text they've chosen. Instead, they will invest themselves in shaping, organizing, drafting, and revising entries that elaborate on their claim.

As you approach this session, you and your children bring all that you know from previous cycles through the writing process and specifically from Session VI of Narrative, Session VI of Essays, and Session V of Fiction. You may want to reread those minilessons so that you can help children remember them. Earlier, you reminded children that writers grow like nesting wooden dolls, one inside the other. "When we are in our second unit of study," you said, "we are also in our first, drawing on all we already know as writers." Of course, now you could say, "When we are in our fifth unit of study, we are also in our first, second, third, and fourth units of study."

Hopefully, children will bring to this session an understanding of the relationship between the seed idea (the claim, the thesis) and the subordinate ideas they will develop in their essays. Today, we hope each child not only searches for and selects the best possible thesis statement, but also imagines the categories of support that idea needs and revises that thesis accordingly. That is, you hope children shift between crafting a thesis and imagining the ways they would support that thesis.

In this unit you're asking children to make a claim (that is, to write a thesis) about a short text. The claim needs to be interesting to the writer and defensible with evidence from the text.

MINILESSON

Finding and Testing a Thesis Statement

CONNECTION

Celebrate the writing and thinking your writers have generated thus far in the unit. Remind children of earlier work they did with thesis statements and supporting ideas.

"Writers, your notebooks are brimming with ideas about the short text you've chosen to study. You've each got reams of ideas about 'Eleven,' 'The Marble Champ,' 'Boar Out There,' 'The Birthday Box,' or 'Spaghetti.' Today I want to remind you that in the end, you need to decide on *one idea* for your essay. It's never easy to focus on just one idea. Fred Fox, a famous speechwriter for President Dwight Eisenhower, once said, 'You ought to be able to put your bottom-line message on the inside of a matchbook.' He was talking about a speech, but he could have been talking about a literary essay or a short story or a memoir or any text at all."

"A few months ago, you looked over all that you'd written and selected a seed idea for your personal essay. You rewrote it as a thesis statement and then framed your essay using boxes and bullets. Writers do similar work in writing literary essays. We find a main idea that is really important to us—writers call it a claim, or a thesis."

Name your teaching point. In this instance, remind children to reread their notebooks, collecting materials that could become a thesis. Teach them to collect an excess of possible seed ideas.

"Today I want to teach you that when we are writing literary essays, as when we write personal essays, we find our seed ideas (our thesis statements) by, first, rereading all our related entries and thinking, 'What is the main idea I really want to say?' We often star lines in our notebooks or copy material from our notebooks onto a special page, one we title 'possible seed ideas.' Then writers usually spend time—at least half an hour—drafting and revising a thesis statement and supporting ideas (boxes and bullets) until we settle on something that feels right."

TEACHING

Demonstrate your own process of rereading your entries and starring possible seed ideas.

"So let's pretend it's time for me to write a thesis statement for a literary essay about 'Spaghetti.'" Sitting in the front of the children, I opened up my notebook and skimmed it for a moment, circling a few bits.

Showing children the page on which I'd just worked, I said, "As you can see, I first reread my entries and then I circled or starred sentences that express ideas that especially

COACHING

For a moment, consider the ways in which your children's ideas on focus have developed across the year. Earlier in the year, your children believed that focusing mainly involved narrowing in on a smaller subject. More specifically, a focused story was one that involved less time. By now, the locus of focus has shifted. A writer could be writing about a very big topic and still write a very focused text. Writers focus by asking, "What is the meaning I am trying to convey?" and by having an answer that one could write on the inside of a matchbook!

Visual cues and props can make a big difference in our minilessons, and I haven't emphasized them enough. In this instance, for example, I held one of the working folders we'd used from the earlier essay unit so that as I mentioned boxes and bullets, the object—in this case the folder—nudged children to recall the entire process they experienced in that unit.

This teaching point contains mostly reminders, but when the point of my minilesson is to remind children of something they already know, I try to add a new layer of complexity.

It may seem odd to you to sit in front of the class and reread your notebook silently. Don't make the decision to instead read your notebook aloud! This minilesson already contains as much detail as it can hold. Don't convince yourself that children need to hear all your entries and your entire thinking process. And the truth is that it's rather impressive to actually watch someone reading silently at the front of the room! Do this for twenty seconds—it's an important demonstration.

matter to me. I'm looking in my notebook for *ideas*, not for facts. An idea refers to something that occurred to me, something not actually stated in the text. I've circled a couple of sentences from my entries in which I express an idea about 'Spaghetti.'" I copied two of these onto chart paper, saying, "Here are two possible seed ideas":

> Possible Seed Ideas
> Gabriel is a lonely boy who has steeled himself to accept being lonely.
> Gabriel has a hole in his life.

Demonstrate testing your possible thesis statements with questions and revising them based on the answers.

"After I've chosen a few seed ideas, I look these over, think these over, and revise them. I first reread each idea and ask, 'How does this idea relate to the whole story—both the first and the second half?' Often this question leads me to revise my seed idea so that it becomes an umbrella idea—one that stretches over both the beginning and the end of the text."

"Watch how I go about letting this question lead me to revise my seed idea," I said, and pointed to my first possible seed idea:

> Gabriel is a lonely boy who has steeled himself to accept being lonely.

"I'm thinking that this relates to only the start of 'Spaghetti.' Let me try to revise the idea so that it relates also to the ending. Umm . . ."

> Spaghetti is the story of a lonely boy who has steeled himself to accept being lonely but then lets a cat into his life.

"That's awkward," I said, and tried again:

> Spaghetti is the story of a lonely boy who lets a cat into his life and isn't lonely anymore.

Turning back to the children, I said, "That thesis fits the beginning and the end of the story now, doesn't it? So one way I rethink my thesis is to ask, 'Does this relate to both the first and the second halves of the text?'"

"A second way that I rethink my seed idea is to ask, 'How would I support this?' I think about what I might write for my categories, my supporting ideas. Very often, I support a thesis in a literary essay by showing how the thesis is true *at the start of the text*, then *at the end of the text*. But I might alternatively support a thesis by showing how it is true *for one character*, then *for another character*, or *for one reason*, then *for another reason*."

You'll notice that I return often to "Spaghetti." This unit is complex enough that I do not aim for variety in the texts I use. This one short text threads through many minilessons because the children have enough shared knowledge of the text and our work with it that I do not need to do a lot of reminding and summarizing; instead I can spotlight each new point I want to make.

There are a number of reasons each thesis needs to pertain to the entire text. First of all, when children are writing thesis statements about very short texts, if the thesis pertains to only one portion of the text, it will be almost impossible for the child to garner enough support for the claim. The texts are too sparse! Then, too, I am steering children toward writing interpretive essays, and this means I am hoping they consider lessons they can learn or messages they can carry from the text. An effective interpretation of a story requires that the reader take into account the most important features of the complete text, including the first and the second halves of the text, certainly, and including a great many smaller features as well.

Pay especially close attention to this instruction, because helping children write effective thesis statements and supporting ideas is far more complicated than you might imagine. This session and the one that follows it were far and away the most difficult to write in the entire series. Hopefully the teaching seems simple and clear now—but the trail of thought leading to this point has been quite complicated and challenging!

> **Questions Essayists Ask of a Thesis Statement**
> - Does this relate to both the 1st and 2nd halves of the text?
> - How would I support this?
>   - At start of story, then at end of story
>   - One character, then another
>   - One reason, then another

"Let me think whether I could support the idea 'Gabriel had a hole in his life.' I could write one paragraph that shows how Gabriel had a hole in his life at the start of 'Spaghetti' and another paragraph showing that this is also true at the end of the story." As I spoke, I made notes:

> Gabriel, the protagonist of "Spaghetti" had a hole . . .
> - in the first half of the story
> - in the second half of the story

"But let me just think whether I have the evidence I need to prove my point!" I glanced at "Spaghetti." "The start of the story *does* provide enough details about Gabriel's loneliness, so yes, I could probably write that at the start of the story Gabriel had a hole in his life. But I'm not at all sure I could get enough evidence to make that case for the end of the story! So I have some options. I could change this seed idea so it *is* something I could support with references to both of the beginning and end of the text. Or I could try to find other ways of supporting the idea. For example, I could try to develop the idea by thinking instead of different *reasons*." I wrote this example on chart paper:

> Gabriel, the protagonist of "Spaghetti," has a hole in his life. He has this hole because:
> - reason 1
> - reason 2

In front of the class, I silently mulled over possibilities for a moment, shaking my head to show that no, nothing was coming to mind. Turning to the class, I said, "If I can't figure out a way to support my thesis, this pushes me to revise it!"

This is a great deal of important material to convey simply through talk, so at this point, I revealed a page of chart paper on which I'd written both the questions I ask of possible thesis statements and those I ask of subordinate questions. Notice that I don't take the time to write these in front of the class.

I could, alternatively, have shown children how I ask these questions of the thesis statement I'd already been developing. That thesis will not prove to be a very workable one, however, and for now I wanted to show that these questions prompt revisions.

Again, don't convince yourself that the children need a more detailed account of your thinking here. If anything, they may need less detail—you may decide to leave off all reference to the fact that a writer can try out other ways to support a thesis.

ACTIVE ENGAGEMENT

Set children up to work in partners, testing out another possible thesis. Remind them to ask whether the thesis pertains to the whole text and whether it can be supported with references to the text.

"Let's try another one of these possible thesis statements," I said, and gestured toward the first seed idea.

'Spaghetti' is the story of a lonely boy who lets a cat into his life and isn't lonely anymore."

"Right now, working with your partner, would you test out this thesis? Be sure to test it by asking the questions on the chart." I pointed to the chart.

By now you should realize that if your class brims with struggling or resistant writers, and moving kids through the process of writing anything at all is a big problem, you may need to tweak the active engagements throughout the series so that students are working with their own writing while sitting in the meeting area. In this instance, you would need to first give children time to reread their entries, selecting and revising their seed ideas; then you could nudge them to test out their chosen seed ideas while sitting together in the meeting area. This is not ideal, but it does allow you to shepherd kids along.

> **Questions Essayists Ask of a Thesis Statement**
> - Does this relate to both the 1st and 2nd halves of the text?
> - How would I support this?
>   - At start of story, then at end of story
>   - One character, then another
>   - One reason, then another

I listened in as children did this work in pairs, and then asked for their attention. "So many of you found ways to make this thesis statement really work! I can't wait for us all to label folders, one for each supporting paragraph, and to begin collecting evidence in each folder!" I pointed to the place where the materials lay waiting.

I did not elaborate on the materials because for now, children are just at the very start of this work, rereading their notebooks to find seed ideas. I know I will need to work in small groups, reiterating ways to test a possible thesis statement. I have indicated where the materials are for making folders so that if some children progress quickly, they won't create a logjam.

LINK

Recap that writers reread entries looking for possible thesis statements, then revise their theses by asking questions of them.

"So writers, today and whenever you write a thesis statement for a literary essay, look over the entries you've collected about the text, and ponder your thoughts about it. Box or star or list the ideas you've written about the text, ideas out of which you will shape your boxes and bullets, your thesis statements and supporting sentences. And then remember that writers ask questions to test out their possible seed ideas." I pointed again to the list of questions.

Notice that prior to this point in the minilesson, I've emphasized the final actions children will take at the end of the upcoming workshop. This Link allows me to bring children's attention back to the work they need to do right away.

WRITING AND CONFERRING

Anticipating Predictable Problems

For students to write a great literary essay, it is essential that they start with a strong, clear thesis statement. The thesis is like a car engine—without one that works, a car, or an essay, cannot move forward. You'll need to confer often today and tomorrow!

Encourage your children to make multiple drafts of their boxes and bullets—their thesis statements and supporting ideas—and to regard these as one organic unit. Children often encounter difficulties imagining the paragraphs they could write to support their theses, which should prompt them to revise their theses. Judah, for example, boxed these ideas in her notebook:

> Lupe wanted to prove herself that she was as good as the other girls.

> Lupe was insecure. She had put herself down.

> Even though she wasn't good, she was nice and good on the inside. She tried again and again. This showed that she doesn't give up.

> Lupe is very caring. She is good on the inside. She doesn't need to be on the outside.

> I used to think Lupe was a goody-goody two-shoes. She got all of those awards and seemed so perfect. I realized she isn't perfect. She has to work and practice like everyone.

Then Judah consolidated her efforts, settling for this more modest possible thesis statement:

> Lupe works hard to overcome her difficulties.

I helped her add the expected trimmings to this:

> Lupe, the protagonist in Gary Soto's short story, "The Marble Champ," works hard to overcome her difficulties.

MID-WORKSHOP TEACHING POINT *Using a Template to Create a Thesis* "Writers, can I have your eyes and your attention? Many of you have lots of possible thesis statements—you are well on your way. If you are struggling, though, I want to give you a bit of advice to use today or whenever you are stumped in trying to write a literary essay. Usually, you can arrive at a pretty solid thesis if you think about the story mountain for the story you've read, and think not only about the external but also about the internal story line. The internal story line shows what happens on the inside of the main character from the beginning, through the turning point, to the end of the story. These two story lines can give you a pattern, a template, for constructing a thesis statement."

continued on next page

Fig. VII-1 Judah's boxed ideas

Then Judah began to imagine how her bullet points might go. She considered whether she wanted to provide *examples* to establish (to prove) that Lupe works hard. Did she want to write about the *kinds of work* Lupe does? To write about the *reasons* Lupe works so hard to become a marble champ? Did she want the fact that Lupe works hard to be one factor and to cite another factor that helps Lupe overcome her difficulties?

The truth is that these ideas are not all equal in sophistication. The simplest way to elaborate upon the claim that Lupe works hard would be to provide two examples of the fact that she does this. If Judah simply provided examples for her point, this would not require her to be analytical. In contrast, to elaborate upon *the kinds* of hard work, or the *reasons for* her work, Judah *would* need to be analytical. This was Judah's next draft of her thesis:

> In the short story, "The Marble Champ," by Gary Soto, Lupe learns to overcome her difficulties by working hard and by believing in herself.

This thesis set up the topic sentences that Judah then developed: Lupe overcomes her difficulties through hard work; Lupe also overcomes her difficulties by believing in herself. Notice that in each of her subordinate points, Judah repeats the stem (as I call it) of her thesis.

Some children will need help finding possible thesis statements in their notebooks. Help them reread their notebooks respectfully, looking for possible thesis statements and paying attention to ideas that resurface often as well as patterns that reoccur across entries. It can sometimes be very productive to take two ideas that may not at first seem connected, and to write in an effort to connect those ideas. Teach children that, from time to time, it helps to ask, "How might these two different ideas go together?"

You'll find that once children have developed an idea that is rooted in one section of the text, they often want to comb that one idea through the entire text and will do so even if there is no supporting evidence. Help children understand that applying an idea to an entire text does not mean painting the whole text in one monolithic color. The statement that Gabriel is lonely can apply to the whole text without the reader suggesting he is lonely in every paragraph of the story! Perhaps his loneliness evolves? Is resolved?

As you work with children individually and in small groups, you will find that some of them tend to write about small stuff. These children's pages will be full of specific, concrete, detailed references, and they will not have grown many ideas. Other children will be just the opposite. They will tend to write expansive, abstract ideas without much detail or grounding. A rule of thumb is that if children start small, they profit

"Then usually you can write a strong thesis if you say, '*Some* people think this is a story about (and you summarize the external sequence of events), but *I* think this is a story about (and you summarize the internal sequence of events).' Just for practice, let's try that for 'Spaghetti.' I could write a thesis that goes like this":

> Some people think that Cynthia Rylant's short story "Spaghetti" is about a homeless boy who adopts a stray cat, but I think this is really a story about a lonely boy who learns to love again.

"Of course, writers change the words around a bit. So I could say it differently":

> When I first read Cynthia Rylant's story "Spaghetti," I thought it was a story about a boy who adopts a stray cat but now I realize it is really a story about a lonely boy who learns to love again.

"Or I might write":

> A first read of Cynthia Rylant's story "Spaghetti" suggests that it is a story about a boy who adopts a stray cat; a careful reread, however, shows that it is really a story about a boy who learns to love.

continued on next page

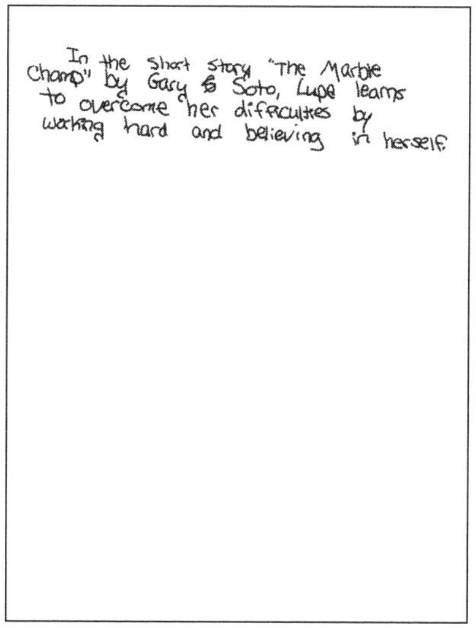

> In the short story "The Marble Champ" by Gary S Soto, Lupe learns to overcome her difficulties by working hard and believing in herself.

Fig. VII-2 Judah's draft thesis statement

from instruction that helps them shift toward big, abstract, general ideas. That is, if a child starts by writing, "The character's Australian shepherd went for a walk and didn't return," he will profit from being nudged to shift toward writing, "Things are always leaving this character." On the other hand, if a child tends to start by writing big, abstract ideas, such as, "This story is about loss and dealing with loss," she will profit from being encouraged to write that the character's Australian shepherd went for a walk and didn't return.

You will also want to help children realize that most of their ideas have parts, and it helps to articulate the parts of an idea. Eventually, writers will probably develop one part fairly completely before progressing to the next part.

Often children's ideas seem obvious to them, and therefore they don't feel compelled to defend their ideas. Help those children to realize that others may see an idea differently, and they need to address that different view.

Another common pitfall is that when writing about their thesis statements, students do not state their ideas as clearly as possible. Children need to try writing their ideas in four or five ways, until they can read them to a partner and the partner understands them. Their statements need to be simple and clear, and pop out to the reader.

For example, at first Max wrote his thesis statement this way: "Rachel is a girl who acts, wants to be or feels different ages on her birthday." While at first glance that seems clear, Max is waffling. Then, too, when I talked with him and learned what really fired him up as a reader of this text, it was clear to me that his rough draft thesis lacked the part of the statement that tells the reader his real thesis—the *why* of it. Finding the whole of the thesis takes time and thought. The final draft of a thesis is not apt to be in the notes the students have written already—instead, students need to explore, write, and talk more to push their thinking. In Max's case, he needed to figure out which of his three statements about Rachel he really wanted to advance. Then he needed to figure out *why* he thought she did that. Or, *what happens inside of her* because of this.

After some talking and writing and conferring, Max changed his thesis statement to: "Rachel is a girl who wakes up on her eleventh birthday expecting to feel older on her birthday, but ends up feeling disappointed by the way the day goes." This thesis statement more clearly shows the reader what he is going to prove as he continues the essay.

continued from previous page

"Listen, for example, to Jill's lead. You'll see that her content is very different, but she follows the same template for a thesis statement":

> Many people read Sandra Cisneros's essay, "Eleven," and think it is a story of a girl was has to wear a sweater she doesn't want to wear. But I think it is about a girl who struggles to hold onto herself when she is challenged by people who have power over her.

"So if today or another day, you find yourself struggling to write a strong thesis statement, you can usually move past this impasse if you think of your story's internal story mountain. Then write, 'Some people think this is a story about (and retell the external story mountain), but I think this is a story about (and retell the internal story mountain).'"

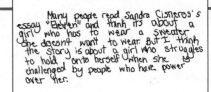

Fig. VII-3 Jill's lead with thesis statement

SHARE

Interpreting Texts

Tell students that when writers decide what to write, they think about the story—the events and the place they happen—as well as its deeper meaning—what the story is really about.

"My favorite writer, Annie Dillard, wrote a memoir called *An American Childhood.* She said that when she was writing it, she thought, 'What shall I put in?' She decided what it was she really wanted to say. 'It's about the passion of childhood. It's about waking up.' That's the internal part. But Annie had to use something concrete to show that deep message. So she decided to use the landscape of her childhood as the external part and then angle the text to show her waking up over and over again: noticing things, loving the rocks, the tiny creatures, the adventures she has. Every story has that same dynamic: the plot and the deeper meaning. As readers, we need to consider both of them as we think and write about texts."

"So readers, as you work on framing your thesis statements and planning your boxes and bullets, remember to pause and think about the internal and external story mountains in the texts. Annie Dillard isn't really writing about the rocks and the butterflies she saw, she's really writing about how it felt to grow into an awareness of herself and the world. In the same way, Cynthia Rylant and Gary Soto and Sandra Cisneros are not really writing just about finding a kitten, learning to shoot marbles, or a red sweater that didn't belong to Rachel. They are writing about deeper, more powerful ideas."

Ask children to work with a partner to read their thesis statements and notice whether they have included both the external and internal story mountains for their stories.

"Right now, would you share your thesis statement with your partner? Look at what you have said to see if you have included the internal and external story mountains in your statements. When you look at what you have written, does it include what the story seems to be about (the plot or external story)? Does it also include what the story is *really about* (the internal story, the character's change, or the deeper meaning)? If not, don't worry. See if you can help each other revise the thesis statement. Ask each other that very important question: 'What is this story *really* about?' Another way to think about that is to ask, 'What is the significance the author wants to highlight?' Or, 'What does the character learn in this

This session guides students to consider the internal and external story lines in the texts under study. Some students will need to hear more about this before they can successfully incorporate the strategy into their writing. This session focuses on choosing and crafting a seed idea, but it also expects that children will be able to consider what the story is really about— the internal aspect of the story. If your children need help doing this, you'll need to either teach this in strategy lessons and one-to-one conferences or develop additional minilessons.

I could have reminded writers that they already learned about Annie Dillard's writing shed and the photograph she has there of a boy standing deep in rapids, a picture with a deeper message about feeling all of life intensely.

Notice that this lesson reminds students of what you have just taught as well as important things they have worked on as readers all year.

Listen in on students' conversations. Take note of the students who are still struggling to name and/or phrase the internal story. You might intervene now, as in the example following. Or you can convene them for a group conference later.

story?' Once you answer one of those questions out loud, think about whether the answer can in some way fit into your thesis statement. Let's add this new question to our chart":

Questions Essayists Ask of a Thesis Statement
- Does this relate to both the beginning and end of the text?
- How would I support this?
  - At start of story, then at end of story
  - One character, then another
  - One reason, then another
- **Does the thesis address what the story is really about, the internal as well as the external story?**

"Janica, can I stop you? I heard you telling Peter that you are not sure what the story 'The Marble Champ' is really about, because you think it could be about lots of things. That's such a good point. But let me teach you something that good readers do: They realize there are lots of possibilities for what a story is really about—but they choose one, because it seems the most important or powerful to them. So out of all your possibilities for 'The Marble Champ,' which one do you think is most important?"

HOMEWORK *Crafting Theses Quickly Using a Template* In class today, we spent lots of time crafting and revising our thesis statements and our plans for essays. In many situations, however, you'll want to write a thesis really quickly. So tonight, would you practice writing thesis statements quickly? Try this:

Think of a fairy tale you know well. For now, let's take "Little Red Riding Hood." Quickly think, "What's the external plot line of the story?" Remember that it helps to think of the main character, what he or she wants, what gets in the way, how this is resolved. Quickly plot the external story line. For example, for "Little Red Riding Hood," you might sketch this story mountain:

Story Mountain for Little Red Riding Hood

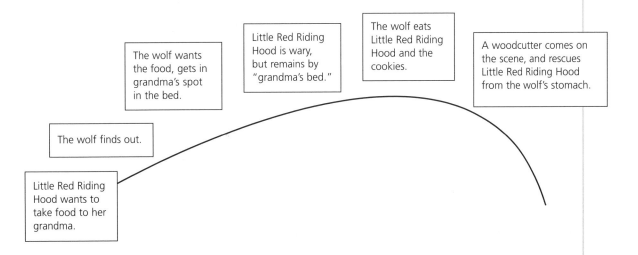

Now think, "What might this story really be about?" or "What life lessons does the character learn?" You are now thinking about the internal story. For "Little Red Riding Hood," you might write this:

> Little Red Riding Hood is naïve and trusting, unaware and unsuspicious. She therefore gets into trouble, and almost dies.

> The story is really a reminder that evil lurks along our pathways, and we need to be less naïve, more suspicious.

Now use the template I gave you earlier for one way a thesis statement could go—contrasting the external and internal story mountains—and draft one possible thesis. For "Little Red Riding Hood," for example, my thesis might be:

> Some people think "Little Red Riding Hood" is the story of a girl, dressed in a red hood, who wants to give cookies to her grandma but instead is eaten by a wolf. I think, however, this is also a story of a girl who goes into the woods of life utterly trusting and naïve, and learns that she needs to be more suspicious.

Tonight try using this template to produce an instant thesis about the story you have in mind: "Some people think (the fairy tale you've chosen) is a story about (the external story line), but I think it is also a story about (the internal story line)."

TAILORING YOUR TEACHING

If your students are voicing shallow, wooden responses to texts . . . you could teach them that when they form a thesis, the important question isn't "What is the author saying?" but "What idea does this text support?" In our own education, many of us were taught to write literary essays as though there was only one possible thesis to argue. We were taught to ask, "What is the author trying to say?" or "What is the author's message?" These kinds of questions erect barriers for us, limiting our thinking and making us doubt insights we glean from reading. Students need to believe that readers can come away from texts with different understandings, so long as sufficient evidence in the text exists to support them. Imagine how productive and provocative their writing will be if they have the chance to share and argue those understandings, rather than timidly putting forth guesses as to the author's one and only True Meaning.

If your students are having a hard time figuring out if a seed idea would make a good thesis . . . you could teach them to study the work of literary critics. Literary critics usually focus on a few key ideas in stories when they write their reviews: how a character's journey progresses, how a plot and setting mirror a real-world social issue, how a story compares or contrasts with previous works by the same author. Students who have a hard time figuring out if a seed idea would make a good thesis can lean on literary critics as mentors for writing about reading and ask themselves questions like, "Does this seed idea deal with a character's journey? Does it deal with a social issue that's reflected throughout the text? Is this seed idea similar to (or different from) something the author has written about in another text?" As we teach these growing writers about literature, we need to give them lenses that help them recognize the kinds of seed idea that will carry them through an entire essay.

ASSESSMENT

When I wanted to put down new carpet in my living room, I wasn't sure whether I wanted pink, blue, or green. I didn't have carpet swatches so I found a few shirts and sweaters that matched the optional colors. I first laid the grayish blue sweater onto the floor, then stepped back and squinted, trying to see only the sweater, and to imagine it stretching out between the wallpapered walls. "If this little patch of color were room-sized, how would it look?" I asked. Then I tried this with a spring-green T-shirt.

Today, you'll want to reread each of your student's efforts to frame out thesis statements and bullet points in a similar way, trying to imagine what the work will "look like" when it's expanded into an essay. It's usually more helpful to intercede now, setting the child up for success, rather than to let the writer go forward with a plan that is flawed from the start.

For students to be able to write a great essay, it is essential that they start with a strong, clear thesis statement. Students will feel easily discouraged and find it hard to proceed unless they have an idea that is central to the story and that matters to them.

Let me show you how I read and assess drafts of thesis statements.

When I first read Harrison's thesis, it sounded very professional. I know, however, that it's easy to be conned by a thesis statement that sounds overly polished, so I resisted the temptation to give his thesis only a cursory glance and a stamp of approval. Instead I deliberately and carefully looked it over, almost as if I were expecting to find problems. After all, the work is being written by nine-year-olds, writing their first thesis statements about a literary text—chances are great their efforts will require revision. This was Harrison's draft of a thesis statement:

> In the short story "The Marble Champ" by Gary Soto, a girl named Lupe through practice, devotion, and persistence, has to overcome not being an athlete and not being a good athlete. This is all new for Lupe because she is very academic.

Right away, I reduced this to its simplest form, just so I could see the plan Harrison had laid out for himself. I may or may not teach him to do this in the end, but to think through the work entailed in supporting the thesis, it definitely helps me to consider whether a clarified version of the thesis could be easily defended.

> In the short story "The Marble Champ" by Gary [Soto] Soto, a girl named Lupe, through practice, devotion + persistance, has to overcome not being a good athlete. This is all new for Lupe because she is very academic.

Fig. VII-4 Harrison's draft thesis statement

> Through practice, devotion, and persistence, Lupe overcomes not being an athlete and not being a good one. This is hard because she is academic.

I thought to myself, "What will Harrison need to prove?" To support his claim, Harrison would need to support many claims.

Through practice, Lupe overcomes not being an athlete.

Through practice, Lupe also overcomes not being a *good* athlete.

This (practicing and overcoming not being an athlete/ a good athlete) is hard because Lupe is academic.

Through devotion Lupe overcomes not being an athlete.

Through devotion she overcomes not being a good athlete.

This, also, is hard because Lupe is academic.

Through persistence, Lupe overcomes not being an athlete.

Through persistence she overcomes not being a good athlete.

This, also, is hard because Lupe is academic.

Looking at this, I realized that this configuration of claims was so complicated that it would be very difficult to defend. Also, of course, it would be tricky to defend the idea that the difficulties Lupe faces over not being athletic derive from the fact that she is academic. Why would being academic make it especially hard for her to deal with the fact that she's not an athlete? Because these issues popped up, I encouraged Emily to consolidate and clarify her thesis. I also suggested that once she did this, she'd want to be really sure she could prove her points. In the end, she wrote this:

In Gary Soto's short story, "The Marble Champ," an academically talented girl named Lupe through persistence and practice becomes also an athletic success.

Now I weighed what Emily would need to prove, and the answer was much more reasonable.

Lupe is an academically talented girl.

Through persistence, Lupe becomes an athletic success.

Through practicing, Lupe becomes an athletic success.

I wondered, still, if the two main claims would be significantly different from each another, but at least the plan seemed workable.

I'm accustomed to eyeing categories, asking, "Are these significantly distinct, one from the next?" When I ask this, I'm trying to predict whether, when the writer goes to elaborate on each bullet point (each topic sentence), he or she will find that the same content belongs in several categories. I also am accustomed to asking, "Is this claim warranted in the text?" The two questions sometimes overlap. For example, although one could conceive of practice and persistence being distinctly different, in this text I suspect the lines between them will blur.

Often we must decide whether to tell children the issues that we see with a thesis or let them encounter these problems along the way. In this instance, I decided it was likely that Emily would see for herself that her two bullets overlap once she began gathering and sorting evidence. Even if she collapsed these two categories into one, she would still have a viable thesis, so I let the categories stand.

IN THIS SESSION, YOU'LL TEACH STUDENTS THAT WRITERS PLAN THEIR ESSAYS, MAKING SURE THEY CAN DELIVER THE EVIDENCE FROM THE TEXT THAT THEIR THESIS PROMISES. YOU'LL DEMONSTRATE SOME WAYS ESSAYISTS REVISE THESES AND SUPPORTING PARAGRAPHS.

GETTING READY

- Child's draft and revised thesis statements that illustrate the process of analysis and revision
- "Spaghetti," by Cynthia Rylant
- Class thesis statement for "Spaghetti," written on chart paper
- Questions Essayists Ask of a Thesis Statement, updated with latest bullet points
- List prepared as a handout: Tips and Tools for Writing a Thesis and Topic Sentences for a Literary Essay
- See CD-ROM for resources

FRAMING ESSAYS

Once I decide to write a nonfiction text to address a particular theme or topic, one of my earliest steps is drafting and revising a succession of outlines. My outlines aren't complete with Roman numerals and capital and lowercase letters, but they do divide the terrain into subordinate categories, and then divide those subordinate categories into subsections. Just as I can look at a timeline of a narrative and mull over whether I want to eliminate some dots or clump other dots together, I can also look at a rough draft of an outline, imagine the text it represents, and weigh whether that is the text I want to write. I anticipate the problems that I will encounter writing the text I've outlined. I revise my outline countless times, and love doing so. It's much more efficient to revise an outline than to revise an entire book!

For children, it is equally important that they draft and revise outlines before they begin to write their essays. A child's energy for revision is far from endless, and the texts children write for this unit will be longer than most that they've written. It's not likely that they'll be game for writing a succession of entirely new drafts.

Today's session will hark back to Session VIII of *Breathing Life into Essays*. In this session, you'll help children draft, reflect on, and revise possible outlines for their now-literary essays. You'll coach the whole group through the sequence of work involved in imagining the boxes and bullets that can provide the framework for their essays. But most of your teaching will occur as you help individuals and small groups of children see and resolve difficulties that are inherent in the essays they've outlined. Eventually children will be able to draw on prior experiences writing essays (and especially literary essays) to anticipate problems, but for now they'll be fairly dependent on you to help them foresee difficulties.

To help children critique their rough-draft boxes and bullets, you'll need to hone your own abilities to read these very closely and critically. This is not a time to skim!

MINILESSON

Framing Essays

CONNECTION

Tell children that you stayed up late reading their boxes and bullets. Acknowledge that even though the texts are short, reading a pile of thesis statements is nevertheless demanding.

"Writers, I took your thesis statements home last night and stayed up very, very late reading them. I put them beside me while I ate dinner, and read them as I ate. I told my family they'd need to clean up from dinner—that I had a ton of reading to do. All evening I read your thesis statements, and I was still reading them as, one by one, the people in my family went to bed. Finally, when it was very, very late, my husband asked, 'What have you been reading anyhow?' I showed him the stack of pages—one for each of you—on which you'd written your thesis statements and bullets."

"'Okay,'" he said, eyeing the stack. "'And what else have you been reading?'"

"'Just this,'" I said.

"'And it's taken you *all these hours*?'" he asked. "'How is that possible?'"

"How could I explain the kind of reading that you and I have been doing? How could I tell him that we read our thesis statements and imagine the implications that each word has for our essays? How could I explain that a thesis isn't just regular writing—that it's almost a blueprint for a building, a contract for a business relationship? It lays out terms, makes promises. How could I convey to John how important it is for us to read our thesis statements and understand what we are setting ourselves up to do?"

Name your teaching point. In this case, tell children that it is far easier to revise a thesis statement and topic sentences than to revise whole essays.

"Today I want to teach you that writers need, at this juncture, not only to read with critical, cautious eyes. We also need to be tilted forward, expecting to revise. It's much more efficient to do the front-end work of revising a thesis rather than the rear-end work of repairing a problematic essay."

COACHING

This is not a usual Connection. I'm not naming the work the children have been doing or the lessons I've tried to teach.

William Zinsser, author of On Writing Well, *suggests that one of the most important qualities of good writing is surprise. If we can surprise our readers (and our listeners), we earn their attention. In this minilesson I deliberately go a little bit off track, telling an anecdote that I know will surprise children, and I do this because I want their attention.*

Notice these terms. A thesis is a blueprint for a building. A contract for a business relationship. Say these words so that children hear them. You are saying, "Writing matters."

Notice the parallel structure here. "It's easier to do the front-end work of revising a thesis rather than the rear-end work of . . . ." I'm trying to use rhetorical devices to make my teaching memorable.

Teaching

Tell children about one child who scrutinized her thesis statement, imagining implications and potential problems.

"Oona drafted a thesis statement yesterday, then began the hard work of rereading what she'd written. She's got what some people refer to as 'lawyer's eyes.' When I wanted to buy a new house, I had a lawyer read the contract, the deal. Lawyers are trained to have eagle eyes. They can spot potential problems. My lawyer read my contract and pointed out all the risks I was undertaking, all the trouble I could get myself into. And yesterday, I saw that Oona was able to do that for her own thesis! She read what she'd written": *[Figs. VIII-1 and VIII-2]*

> In "Boar Out There," by Cynthia Rylant, Jenny is a girl who believes that the wild boar in the woods is fearless and is hurt. She feels sorry for him and goes to look for him. When she finds him, she realizes that he has fears after all. The boar runs through the woods ignoring the sharp thorns and briars. The boar cries at the moon.

"And then she said, 'To support my thesis, I'm going to need to show that'":

Jenny believed that the wild boar was fearless.

Jenny believed the boar was hurt.

Jenny felt sorry for the boar.

Jenny wants to find the boar.

When she finds him, she realizes he isn't fearless.

"'That's a lot to show!' Oona realized. Then she looked at her planned bullet points and decided to revise her draft of the thesis statement. She cleaned it up, so now it read":

> Jenny is a girl who believes that the wild boar in the woods is fearless, but after finding the boar she comes to realize that he is not.

"Then she thought, 'What would my paragraphs be?' and tried planning her bullets. Then she used her lawyer's eyes to spot problems with that plan. She wisely questioned whether she could write a whole paragraph about Jenny finding the boar in the woods, so she tried a new outline":

- In the beginning Jenny believes the boar is fearless (runs through the thorns and briars).

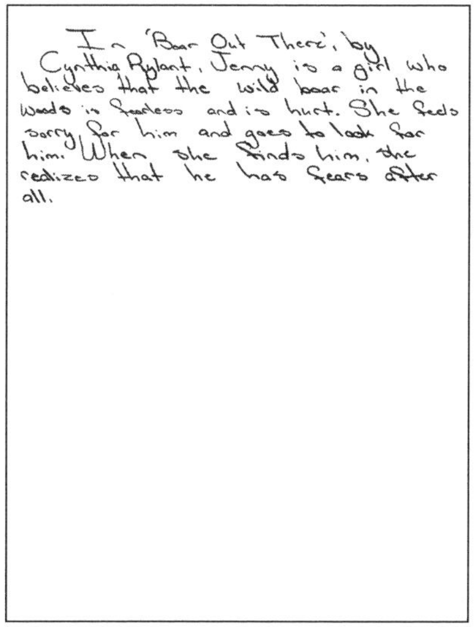
In 'Boar Out There', by Cynthia Rylant, Jenny is a girl who believes that the wild boar in the woods is fearless and is hurt. She feels sorry for him and goes to look for him. When she finds him, she realizes that he has fears after all.

Fig. VIII-1 Oona's draft of a thesis statement

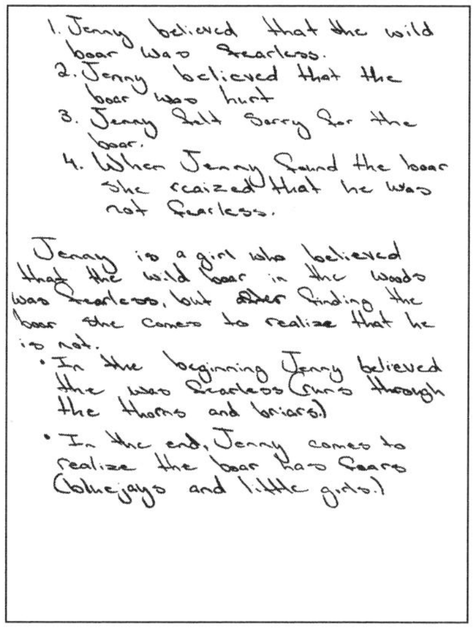
1. Jenny believed that the wild boar was fearless.
2. Jenny believed that the boar was hurt
3. Jenny felt sorry for the boar.
4. When Jenny found the boar she realized that he was not fearless.

Jenny is a girl who believed that the wild boar in the woods was fearless, but after finding the boar she comes to realize that he is not.
- In the beginning Jenny believed the was fearless (runs through the thorns and briars)
- In the end, Jenny comes to realize the boar has fears (bluejays and little girls)

Fig. VIII-2 Oona realizes her first thesis is too complex and writes a simpler one

- In the end, Jenny comes to realize the boar has fears (bluejays and little girls).

"Do you see how Oona first read her essay plan with a lawyer's eyes, trying to understand what she'd set herself up for and to make sure she could do it? Then she wrote the plan for a literary essay imagining what she might put in each paragraph, just to test out whether her thesis would work."

ACTIVE ENGAGEMENT

Using the latest thesis from the class story, set children up to read with a lawyer's eyes.

"Let's try this with the thesis statement we worked on yesterday for our 'Spaghetti' essay," I said, and flipped the chart paper to reveal this draft of a thesis statement:

> Some people think that Cynthia Rylant's short story "Spaghetti" is a story about a homeless boy who adopts a stray cat, but I think this is really a story about a lonely boy who lets a stray cat into his life and learns to love again.

- At the start of the story, Gabriel is lonely
- Then Gabriel lets a stray cat into his life and learns to love again.

"Would you and your partner read this over with a lawyer's eyes, searching for potential problems? Remember to ask questions such as these:"

"Remember to read each word very carefully, and to check whether this is precisely what we want to say." The children worked with each other for a few minutes.

Convene the class. Coach them to see potential problems with the planned boxes and bullets based on content that classmates propose.

Soon I convened the class, and gestured first to one partnership, then another.

"We couldn't figure out if the first paragraph has gotta support the first part of the thesis when we wrote that some people think this is a story of a homeless boy who adopts a stray cat," James said.

I nodded, "Good question, James. I don't think there is a right or wrong answer to that—this first sentence could be considered part of your thesis and therefore needs to be supported, but it could also be the lead-in to your thesis, a place for background facts, in which case you can assume your readers will trust you. Did you want to devote your first paragraph to that point, James?"

"Not really, 'cause it'd be dull."

I deliberately use a thesis statement that I know resembles the statements many children have written. This way, the class work will scaffold their work. I intentionally write this in a way that I know is somewhat problematic. Can you spot the problem? Practice reading with a lawyer's eyes!

Questions Essayists Ask of a Thesis Statement
- Does this relate to both the beginning and end of the text?
- How would I support this?
  - At start of story, then at end of story
  - One character, then another
  - One reason, then another
- Does the thesis address what the story is really about, the internal as well as the external story?
- Can I deliver with my planned categories what I promise in my thesis?

"I think you're okay with not defending it, then," I said. "But that was really close and careful reading! What did others decide?"

"We figured how to show he's lonely at the beginning," Ali said. "We can tell that 'cause he's sitting on the stoop alone. Other people are talking but he doesn't join. Plus he daydreams that he's away by himself like living outside on the street."

I coached her to write in the air, dictating what she might claim in that paragraph and what her supporting information might be. She said aloud, with intonation that suggested she was dictating boxes and bullets:

1. At the start of the story, Gabriel is lonely.
   - Even though Gabriel was sitting on the stoop surrounded by other people who were talking to each other he was not included or did not join in.
   - He daydreamed about being other places:
     - Living outside
     - Sleeping under the movie theater lights
2. At the end of the story, Gabriel learns to love again.

"What do the rest of you think of Ali and Emily's plan?" I asked. "Read their plan for the first support paragraph with a lawyer's eyes!" Soon the class agreed that the second point (that Gabriel daydreamed about other places) didn't necessarily relate to the claim that he was lonely, and the class reworded this (Gabriel had become so used to being alone that he imagined sleeping outside alone).

The class turned to the big idea and at first had no trouble with it. I then told them I could imagine arguing that the second topic sentence was not defensible. They read it again, this time realizing that the story doesn't *actually* show that Gabriel learned to love again. They revised this bullet point to read, "Gabriel isn't lonely anymore."

LINK
Remind writers that they'll soon make files for each of their bullet points, but caution them that it's efficient to first critique and revise their planned boxes and bullets.

"Writers, I know it's tempting to get started making files for each of your bullet points, and you'll no doubt do that today. But I hope that first you'll remember that it's much more efficient to do the front-end work of revising a thesis than the rear-end work of repairing a problematic thesis. So take the time right now to read your thesis and supporting statements with a lawyer's eyes, spotting potential problems. Have the courage to revise your plans many times before you go forward."

One of the many advantages of asking children to first talk with partners is that, before I call on a child, I already know what he or she will say. I can deliberately call on children who will bring up what I regard as the big, main questions.

It's possible to write one paragraph that relays the plot line of the story and then another that reveals the deeper story, but in "Spaghetti," the text is so simple that there is not a huge difference between the external and the internal story. For this reason, I don't especially recommend that children write one paragraph on the external and another on the internal story.

I deliberately jot Ali's proposed content because I already know from hearing her share it in her partnership that it is somewhat problematic (as well as being impressive). I plan to seize this opportunity to give children practice reading with a lawyer's eyes.

This session relies upon you to teach youngsters how to read closely and critically. Notice these examples of careful reading. It would have been very easy to let the claim that Gabriel "learns to love again" slide right past us. Frankly, you'll need to decide how rigorous you want to be. If I am teaching third graders who are new to this work, I might not bat an eye at the notion that Gabriel learns to love again. But with more sophisticated students, I want to teach them to triple check whether their claims are accountable to the text. But keep in mind: You'll be able to teach children to scrutinize their claims and imagine how they could be different only if you become accustomed to doing so yourself.

I like talking about the fact that revision requires courage. I actually believe that most qualities and strategies of effective writing rely on personal character: honesty, empathy, accountability, tenacity, high standards, optimism, confidence, a willingness to be vulnerable. Of course, I think qualities of good teaching are not very different!

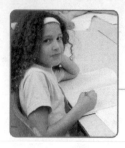

Writing and Conferring

Revising Essay Plans

I pulled my chair alongside Max and watched as he reread what he'd written: *[Figs. VIII-3 and VIII-4]*

In the story "Eleven" by Sandra Cisneros, Rachel is a girl who wakes up on her eleventh birthday expecting a lot, but ends up getting disappointed by the way the day went.

She expects to feel eleven.

- "When you wake up on your 11th birthday you expect to feel 11 but you don't."
- "You don't feel eleven, not right away. It takes days, weeks even, sometimes even months till you say 11 when they ask."

She expected the other kids not to understand all the ages she has.

- "I feel sick inside like the part of me that's 3, but I shut my eyes down tight . . . and remember I'm eleven."
- "Rachel you put that sweater on and no more nonsense!"

She expected everything to go perfect because it's her birthday.

- "Mama is making a cake for tonight and Dad will come home and everyone will sing happy birthday, happy birthday to you"
- She does not think she will get in trouble while fooling around with the sweater because it's her birthday.

Max set to work, looking first at "Eleven" and then at his outline, adding yet more references to the text under each of his topic sentences.

"Can I stop you?" I said to Max. "What are you working on?"

"I'm making my boxes and bullets, like you said," Max responded. "I'm on my second page."

"Max," I answered, "I love the way you are not just reading *your plans* closely, you are also reading the

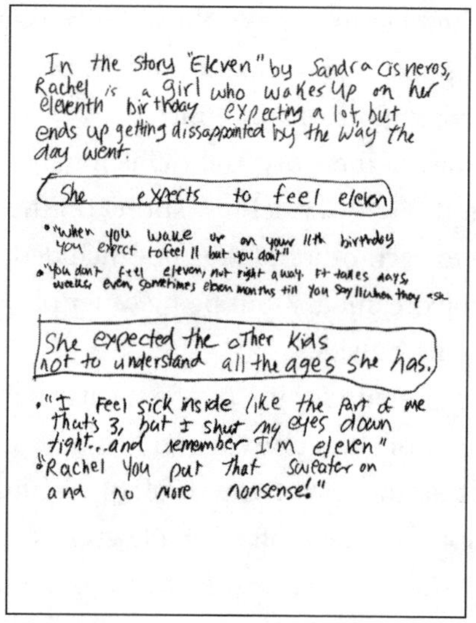
In the story "Eleven" by Sandra Cisneros, Rachel is a girl who wakes up on her eleventh birthday expecting a lot but ends up getting dissappointed by the way the day went.

She expects to feel eleven

• "when you wake up on your 11th birthday you expect to feel 11 but you don't"
• "You don't feel eleven, not right away. It takes days, weeks even, sometimes eleven months till you say 11 when they ask.

She expected the other kids not to understand all the ages she has.

• "I feel sick inside like the part of me that's 3, but I shut my eyes down tight...and remember I'm eleven"
• "Rachel you put that sweater on and no more nonsense!"

Fig. VIII-3 Max, page 1

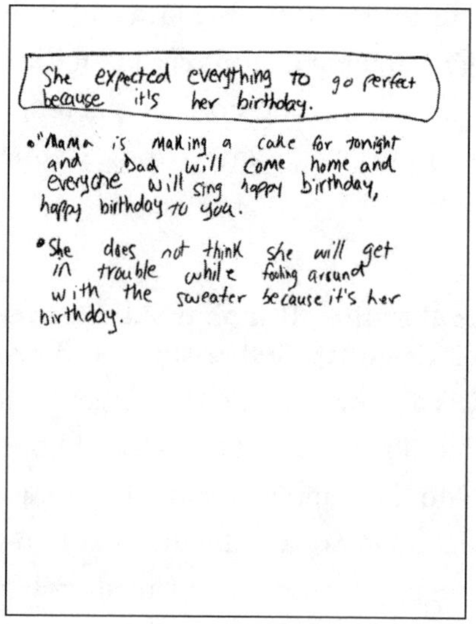
She expected everything to go perfect because it's her birthday.

• "Mama is making a cake for tonight and Dad will come home and everyone will sing happy birthday, happy birthday to you.
• She does not think she will get in trouble while fooling around with the sweater because it's her birthday.

Fig. VIII-4 Max's work, page 2

short text closely. I love seeing you look back and forth between the text, your outline, the text, your outline. And I think it is really smart that you are looking for the textual evidence for each point."

Then I shifted my voice, saying, "But can I teach you one thing?" I waited for Max to nod, then said, "Writers really profit from being able to give ourselves self-assignments. And especially early on in our writing process, instead of doing one thing on and on and on, it helps to do one job for a bit, then to pull back and think, 'How's this working?' Instead of continuing on and on, you'd be wise to reread this with a lawyer's eyes, like I suggested today, thinking, 'What will I need to prove if this is my thesis?' and imagining possible problems."

Max looked stunned, "But I have the evidence," he said.

"Actually, I think a lawyer would tell you that your boxes (your topic sentences) don't match your thesis," I said. I did not point out that certainly his second box— "She expected the other kids not to understand all the ages she has"—didn't fit with his thesis. Instead I said, "You are smart enough and hard working enough to see

> **MID-WORKSHOP TEACHING POINT** *Using Partners to Help Scrutinize Essay Plans* "Writers, can I have your eyes and your attention? I want to remind you that when I wanted to buy a house, I hired a lawyer and asked that lawyer to read my contract with eagle eyes, helping me imagine potential problems. You may need to recruit another pair of eyes to help you scrutinize your plans. I've set up extra conference areas around the edges of the room. If you think your boxes and bullets are okay, would you recruit someone other than your partner to read your planned thesis and supporting statements, to hear your intentions, and to help you see potential problems? And those of you who are recruited as lawyers, be sure you cosign the writer's plans. Your signature acts as a promise. Your signature says, 'You can go forward with this and not encounter problems.'"

this if you give yourself the job of really scrutinizing what you promise in your thesis, and really looking at the match between your thesis and your topic sentences," I said. "You also need to make sure the evidence you are gathering *really*, truly matches the point you are making."

Then I said, "Max, you've got a talent for getting a ton of work done, and for keeping on and on and on in a job. Those are very special talents. But you need to be not just the worker who grinds out a lot of sheer work. You also need to be the lawyer who is critical, thoughtful, and makes cautious decisions. To become the lawyer as well as the worker, you need to be willing to believe that a plan that feels great to you—one you want to get started with—could conceivably have problems. So right now, switch from being a builder to being a lawyer, from writing to reading, from going forward to looking backwards."

The next day, I returned to find that Max had made a few important revisions. He had altered his plan. This time, I congratulated Max and suggested he simplify, imagining that his essay might have only two or perhaps three body paragraphs.

> In the story "Eleven" by Sandra Cisneros, Rachel is a girl who wakes up on her eleventh birthday expecting a lot, but ends up getting disappointed by the way the day went.

She expects to feel eleven.

- "When you wake up on your 11th birthday you expect to feel 11 but you don't."

- "You don't feel eleven, not right away. It takes days, weeks even, sometimes even months till you say 11 when they ask. And you don't feel smart eleven, not until you're almost 12, that's the way it is."

She expected everything to go perfect because it's her birthday.

- "Mama is making a cake for tonight and Dad will come home and everyone will sing happy birthday, happy birthday to you."

- She does not think she will get in trouble while fooling around with the sweater because it's her birthday.

- She expects someone to come and take the sweater so she does not have to keep it.

She learns that Eleventh Birthdays can be disappointing and not bringing what you expect.

- You wake up expecting to feel eleven but you don't.

- You don't feel eleven. Not right away. It takes days . . . weeks . . . even months to say eleven when they ask you.

- You don't feel smart eleven. Not until you're almost twelve.

- And maybe one day when your all grown up you will need to cry like you're 3. And that is fine. That's what I tell mama when she's sad and needs to cry. Maybe she is feeling three.

She understands that you can still feel a different age, even if you're older.

- Someday you may say something stupid and that's one part of you that's still ten. And that's okay.

- Or maybe sometimes you are scared and need to sit on your mama's lap, and that is the part of you that still is five.

SHARE

Writing Thesis Statements on Demand

Compliment children on crafting and scrutinizing their essay plans.

"Writers, lawyers, can I have your attention? You've done some powerful work today. Most of you will end today with a viable thesis and with a plan for your topic sentences, and that will mark an enormously important step forward. We have been working for more than a week, and as a result of all this work, we'll each have a plan—one we can write in three or four lines—that is solid and trustworthy."

Ask children to join you in charting the tips and tools for planning an essay.

"It's pretty amazing, isn't it, to think that we've been writing and reading and revising and thinking and planning for more than a week—and we end up with about fifty words! But of course, the truth is that we've not only written a strong thesis, we've also each developed a whole backpack full of tips and tools for writing a thesis statement and for planning our supporting paragraphs. Before we go forward, let's gather some of the tips and tools we've learned. This time, would you talk not just with your partner but with another set of partners as well, and see how many helpful tips and tools you can recall."

Soon I solicited their input and compiled this chart:

Tips and Tools for Writing a Thesis and Topic Sentences for a Literary Essay

- First gather lots of ideas about the text you've read. Be sure you read closely, really noticing stuff and then write, "The idea I have about this is . . . ." Use thought prompts to write long. Reread, looking for ideas that are true and interesting. Box them and write more about them. Then reread again, looking for ideas that are true and interesting.

- Pay attention to characters and their traits, wants, struggles, changes, and lessons. Think about the whole story as a story of a character who wants something, struggles, and then changes or learns a lesson.

- Think about the issues in your life and ask, "How does this story go with my issue?" This can help you find something to say that really matters to you.

The chart you make in your class will be slightly different from this one. You can certainly use this one as the handout for children to keep in their notebooks or folders, but it is still important to allow children the process of creating this list together.

Tips and Tools for Writing a Thesis and Topic Sentences for a Literary Essay (continued)

- Ask, "What's this story <u>really</u> about?" Look how the author wrote it, and think, "Why did the author do this?" Expect the author to make craft decisions that highlight the meaning the author hopes to convey.

- Reread all your ideas and find things that seem interesting and true and important. Compile these.

- Draft a possible thesis statement, then test it out. Ask, "Does this go with the whole story?" and "Can I support this?"

- Maybe write, "Some people think this is a story about . . . but I think it is <u>really</u> about . . . ." Consider whether your thesis addresses the internal as well as the external story line of the text under study.

- Write your thesis and plan your paragraphs. Your paragraphs might be organized to show how your thesis is true at the beginning and the end of the story, or in one way and another way, for one reason or another reason.

- Reread your thesis with a lawyer's eyes. Look at what you have promised to prove and make sure you can do that. Check every word. Be sure your subordinate claims match your thesis. Rewrite over and over.

This list might be too wordy or too lengthy to be helpful, depending on your children's developmental stage. Alter it as you see fit!

"We've spent many days writing a thesis and planning an essay, but I'm pretty sure that you've also learned that you can do this really quickly if you need to do so. Let's try it."

Ask children to go through the whole process again in a condensed, faster version, using a text they all know well.

"Pretend you are writing a thesis about Gary Paulsen's book *The Monument*, which we read earlier this year. Let's imagine you want your thesis to address a deep message in the book. Work with a partner, and see if you can come up with a thesis in exactly five minutes. Remember, if you are stuck you might think about the external and internal story lines and use the template, 'Some people think such and such is the story of . . . but I think it is really the story of . . . .' Remember, too, you might think about what two or

This quick drill is something you can ask children to try throughout these units at nearly any stage of the writing process. Not only is it a way for children to consolidate and review what they know about the writing process of a given genre, it also helps prepare them for the writing on demand that they will invariably be asked to do.

three things the main character learns or ways the main character changes. Are you ready? Go!"

Soon I'd written some of the children's best ideas on chart paper:

> Some people think this is a story about a girl who is adopted and goes to live in a dull Kansas town, but I think this is a story about a girl who learns to be an artist.

> In The Monument, a girl named Rocky learns to see the world as an artist and to not be so tough.

> In Paulsen's story, The Monument, an artist teaches with examples and with advice.

"So remember, it may be that you'll be asked to write literary essays quickly on tests— look how well you are set up to do that, already! The process you'll use when you write essays on demand is the same as the one you already know."

● HOMEWORK *Providing Thinking About Texts by Making Connections* Writers, this morning I asked many of you to tell me all about the new ideas you came up with at home about "Spaghetti," and many of you looked at me like I'd just asked the stupidest question. You said, "I didn't even take the story home!" But you did. I know I gave it to every one of you. I read it to you! Once we've read (or heard a text read to us), that text is ours. We carry it with us. And we not only carry the text with us, we continue reading it—even if it's not there! We continue reading it because reading is mulling, thinking, questioning, and envisioning. I have a quote over my bed, the words of a great poet, and it says, "The poet is working," meaning that poets work on poems even in their sleep! But I *could* also have a quote over my bed that says, "The reader is reading." Readers, you need to carry texts with you all day long, all night long, mulling over them, finding new significance in them. To help you do that, notice intriguing bits of stories and life around you—collect anything fresh you can get your hands on, and use it to help you think about the text you are working on! The material you collect might not exactly make sense with the text you are reading at first, but if you work at it, you can often make extraordinary connections that will eventually help make your points in fresh and intriguing ways! Tonight collect some interesting tidbits, some great quotations, and try to make them apply to the reading you are doing now. See what you can come up with!

If your students are writing theses that are complex and confusing . . . you might highlight the importance of simplicity and elegance in thinking. In order to write a strong thesis statement, one that is both thoughtful and clear, a writer needs to take a complex idea and make it simple. You may, therefore, want to teach a minilesson on the importance of simplifying. It may help to tell a story about the genius, Albert Einstein. He insisted always on using hand soap for shaving, despite the discomfort. When asked why, Einstein replied, "Two soaps? That is too complicated!" This, from a man who created theories of relativity and so forth! Many people believe that Einstein's genius came from a willingness to be dissatisfied with anything which wasn't simple, elegant, and clear.

If students need help in planning the categories that support their theses . . . we can remind them to draw on the strategies they learned while writing personal essays. Some theses are more easily supported by discussing them in terms of *parts* or *kinds*. Here, we can show how this essay will explore the kinds of risks the main character faces in the story:

> Despite the risks and dangers that challenge her on the long, perilous journey to the duchess' palace, Irene continues on and shows her love and devotion to her mother in *Brave Irene*, by William Steig.
>
> - Despite the strong, biting wind, Irene continues on to the palace.
>
> - Despite twisting her ankle in a hole, Irene continues on to the palace.
>
> - Even despite the approaching darkness, Irene continues on to the palace.

Students need to understand that we are not teaching a set of disconnected lessons for writing, but that we are arming them with a cache of strategies to fuel their writing throughout life.

COLLABORATING WITH COLLEAGUES

You and your colleagues will probably want to spend some time together looking over your children's thesis statements and supporting claims. Help each other to sort the children's work into two piles: on track, and in need of help. In this way, you can triage your problems and guard against children doing a great deal more work if their entire plan is totally flawed.

As you reread children's plans, consider whether there are ways to help children simplify and consolidate what they have written. For example, this is Judah's plan for her essay: [Fig. VIII-5]

> In the short story "The Marble Champ" by Gary Soto, a girl named Lupe does good in everything she tries. But, she is not good at sports. To overcome this problem, she practices every day and believes in herself to become good at marbles.

> In the beginning Lupe wins a lot of academic awards, but she is not good at sports.

- Ex. of what she won
- Explanation about Lupe not good at sports

> Lupe decides to play marbles. She practices and believes in herself to become good.

- Lupe likes the idea of marbles
- She starts practicing right away.
- She really believes in herself and she practiced three good hours.

> In the end Lupe has overcome not being good at marbles. She won the championship.

- She won! Practicing paid off.
- Self belief—kept going, never gave up.
- Her awards—she worked at goal, finally overcame it.

Fig. VIII-5 Judah's plan for her essay.

With a bit of help, Judah consolidated her thesis statement. She first rewrote it this way:

> In Gary Soto's short story, "The Marble Champ," Lupe changes from being good only at academics to being good also at sports. By practicing everyday and believing in herself she becomes a marble champ.

Her final draft of her thesis statement and supportive claims is as follows: *[Fig. VIII-6]*

In literature, characters face challenges and learn to survive. In the short story, "The Marble Champ" by Gary Soto, Lupe learns to overcome her difficulties by working hard and believing in herself.

- Lupe overcomes her difficulties through hard work.
- Lupe overcame her difficulties, not only by hard work, but also because she believed in herself.

Fig. VIII-6 Judah's revised thesis and topic sentences

Paulina's draft looked like this: *[Fig. VIII-7]*

This essay shows how Rachel—the girl in Cisnero's "eleven" the story—feels about growing up and being eleven. Sometimes growing up feels slow—like when the teacher makes Rachel wear the sweater, or right after your birthday—and sometimes it feels fast—like when Rachel stops being excited about her birthday cake or like when you act younger than you are.

- Sometimes growing up can feel really slow. When you want to be older than you are, growing up feels slow.
- However, growing up can also feel fast.

Growing up is hardly ever right on schedule ... or maybe it is—just not a schedule you agree with. Sometimes growing up is behind schedule and sometimes it's ahead.

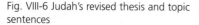

Fig. VIII-7 Paulina's boxes and bullets

IN THIS SESSION, YOU'LL
DEMONSTRATE WAYS THAT
ESSAYISTS COLLECT AND ANGLE
MINISTORIES AS EVIDENCE TO
SUPPORT THEIR CLAIMS.

GETTING READY

- First portion of "Spaghetti," by Cynthia Rylant, on transparency, chart paper, or as handouts
- Timeline of "Spaghetti" that you can quickly summarize
- Specific ministry from "Spaghetti" you can retell to support a thesis
- See CD-ROM for resources

USING STORIES AS EVIDENCE

Throughout the year, your children *will have written about tiny moments in ways that convey the biggest meanings of their lives. My stories about searching for a place to sit at the basketball game, and about hoping that by receiving a part in the school play I'd also receive a place in the popular group, both conveyed my yearning to find my place in the world. Stories can be powerful vehicles for conveying Big Truths.*

Earlier in the year, your children collected stories to support the main ideas in their personal essays. Now you'll invite them to collect stories that support the ideas they've chosen to advance in their literary essays.

You may need to reteach lessons from the personal essay and narrative units, reminding children to bring what they know about writing effective stories to this unit. Above all, children will need reminders about the differences between summarizing and storytelling. Although there are appropriate times to summarize a bit of the short text to make a particular point, today you will emphasize the value of storytelling bits of the text, and of angling their rendition of the text to illustrate an idea. Today, then, you'll help children recall how to write short chronological stories, and you'll teach them to angle these stories to convey big ideas. This may sound easy, but it's actually very complex and challenging work.

Interestingly enough, in our minilessons, we as teachers are constantly required to do just what we're teaching children to do. That is, we are frequently called upon to retell a story, angling it to make one point or another. We therefore have a repertoire of strategies to bring out our angle (or our interpretation) of an event. For example, we may highlight the point we want to make by mentioning counterexamples, saying something like, "Donald Crews didn't write about his whole summer down south; instead he wrote about just one episode on the train tracks." This is a technique children can learn as well. We also angle our stories by starting with an overarching statement that orients listeners: "Listen to what I do," we say, "and notice especially . . . ." Children, too, can learn to preface their stories with comments that establish their angles.

MINILESSON

Using Stories as Evidence

CONNECTION

Remind children that in the personal essay unit, they collected and filed evidence that supported each of their topic sentences. Ask children to do the same when writing literary essays.

"Writers, you'll remember that after you wrote your thesis statements and planned your supporting statements during the personal essay unit, you each became a researcher, collecting the evidence that would allow you to make your case."

"So it won't surprise you when I suggest that you need to do similar work now. In fact, you can look back on our charts from the personal essay unit, and remind yourself of materials you can collect to support your thesis. Many of you, I'm sure, will decide to collect Small Moment stories that support your claim, your thesis."

Name your teaching point. Specifically, tell children that when writers want to tell stories in the service of an idea, they tell these stories with an angle.

"Today I want to remind you that when you are telling a story in the service of an idea, you need to angle that story to highlight the idea you want to convey."

TEACHING

Demonstrate that before a literary essayist can tell a story to illustrate a topic sentence, the writer must reread the text and identify bits that could make the point.

"I first need to reread 'Spaghetti,' looking for small moments that could illustrate my first point—that at the start of the story Gabriel is lonely." I used an overhead projector to enlarge the text, and skimmed the first half of it, writing stars in the margins whenever I found a potential story.

"I could tell a tiny story about Gabriel sitting alone on the stoop," I said. "Or alternatively, I could tell a tiny story about how he didn't hear the meow at first, then did, and wondered if someone was calling for him."

Ask children to watch as you tell one portion of the text as a story. Highlight the steps you take.

Then I said to the children, "Watch how I write the first story, and then you'll have a chance to use similar techniques to write the second story."

COACHING

It'd be great to display the chart you and your class made during the personal essay unit, and to point toward it at this point. Teaching must be cumulative, and it's very powerful when one day's teaching harkens back to lessons learned earlier in the year. After all, as Sandra Cisneros has reminded us, people grow like trees, with one ring of growth added upon earlier ones. When we are eleven, we are also ten, nine, eight . . . .

I let children know when the teaching point contains a reminder of something they learned earlier. Obviously there will be times when we teach children to use a strategy they learned earlier, and there is no reason to pretend differently. Ideally, we will add a new layer of complexity, as I try to do in this instance.

If you don't have access to an overhead projector, then you'll want to use either a chart-sized version of the first portion of "Spaghetti" or individual copies for each child. You'll notice that I don't refer to the overhead projector often. I think that on the whole, chart paper is a more effective way to provide enlarged print during a minilesson. Chart paper has a concreteness, and of course it lingers after the minilesson is over.

The first is more challenging than the second because it doesn't already follow a plot sequence. For this reason, I'm doing the first example myself and giving the children the second example.

"First I'm going to reread the text and just get the timeline of what happened straight. But I need to remember that I won't be simply telling the story of what happened; I'll be telling the story of what happened that shows Gabriel was lonely."

"I'm going to retell what happened in order. Some of these things might have happened all at once, but I'll put them on a timeline. I'm going to fill in some of the details that the author didn't exactly say but did suggest." Then, touching one finger after the next, I listed these events:

First Gabriel was sitting on the stoop alone.

Other people around him were chatting with each other but he didn't hear them.

He remembered his sandwich and wished he still had it.

He remembered being alone in school too when he was the only one who knew the answer and the kids were mad at him.

Then he imagined that he'd like to sleep outside alone.

Then he heard something.

"Now I'll tell it as a story, remembering to start at the beginning and remembering, every line or two, to say something about how this story shows Gabriel being lonely."

> One evening Gabriel sat on the stoop outside—

"No," I said, "I should tuck in something about him being lonely so people know from the start that this story shows his loneliness."

> One evening Gabriel, a homeless boy, sat alone on the stoop outside the shelter where he lived. Other people sat on far corners of the stoop, but they were all talking with each other.

"I better mention the alone parts again."

> Gabriel sat alone. He remembered his lunch sandwich and wished he still had it.

"I want to make the sandwich relate to the fact that he is lonely. Umm . . . ."

> He felt extra lonely because he was hungry.

When children retell portions of a novel to make a point, the text itself is long enough that it's not challenging to cull a sequence of events. When writing about a very short text such as "Eleven," however, the entire text is so abbreviated that writers must really zoom in on microevents to extract a sequenced story. But a sequence is necessary to create a story.

We always make decisions over whether something is worth recording. In this instance, I do not plan to revisit this timeline or ask children to work with it, so I don't think it needs to be written on chart paper. If you decide otherwise, I'd record only a word to signify each new dot on the timeline.

When retelling a sequence of events to make a particular point, children are apt to abbreviate the start of the event, instead starting the story at the climax because it is usually the section that most pertains to the idea the child wants to advance. I try to remind children that even ministries must have a beginning, a middle, and an end.

"Writers, do you see that I first extracted the timeline of activities, retelling the sequence of events across my fingers and making sure to tell the events that illustrate that Gabriel is lonely? Then I storytold, but after every line or two, I thought, 'How do I highlight the "Gabriel is lonely" theme?'"

I advise you and your children to literally return to the key words—in this case, to the word lonely—after every sentence or two. Many of us are taught to avoid repeating a word—don't take that instruction too seriously. Repetition can be an important source of cohesion.

ACTIVE ENGAGEMENT

Describe the way you've created a file system in anticipation of data collection. Tell children you plan to collect a few tiny stories to support each topic sentence.

"Like most of you, I've already made files, so I'll have a place for the material that I will gather to support each of my bullets. I have one file that says, 'At the start of the story, Gabriel is lonely,' and another file labeled, 'Then Gabriel lets a stray cat into his life and isn't lonely anymore.' Today, I'll want to collect at least one or two tiny stories for each of my files."

Although my real point will be to show children ways writers angle stories to illustrate a particular idea, I have minor points that I'm also hoping to make. One concerns productivity. I find some children call it a day's work after they've retold one tiny snippet of a short text, and I'm modeling a very different expectation for productivity.

Reiterate the steps you hope students take: finding an episode, extracting a sequence of events, recalling the main idea, telling the story. Help one partner start doing this.

"So remember that after finding a little bit of the text that could illustrate my point, my topic sentence, I reread it and extracted a timeline. I retold the sequence of events across my fingers. Remember how I kept threading my big idea in and out of the story."

"Would you try that with the second small moment we've marked? We've already located the episode. Remember, this is the episode when Gabriel is sitting on the stoop and there is a meow, but Gabriel almost misses hearing it because he is lost in his own thoughts. When he does hear the small cry, at first he wonders if someone is calling him, and goes looking, looking."

If you feel your children would profit from extra support during Active Engagement, you could retell two-thirds of a story only and then ask them first to retell the story you've just told, and then to continue, adding on the rest of the story. This, of course, would provide them with much more scaffolding than the request to proceed in a similar way, retelling an entirely new small story.

To get them started, I said, "Partner 1, extract the sequence of events, telling them across your fingers. Start at the beginning—'Gabriel sat alone on the stoop imagining sleeping outside all alone . . .'" I paused, then added, "Keep going," and gave them a moment to do this.

Notice that when referencing the small moment, I provide children with subtle help seeing this as a sequence of microevents all pertaining to the main idea.

Record the sequence of events that many are articulating on chart paper. Remind children that the goal is to storytell, angling the events to make a point. Launch partners into doing this.

As partners talked, I recorded the sequence of events they mentioned on chart paper. "Writers, most of you retold a sequence that goes like this," I said, and showed this timeline:

You'll notice that I helped children get started retelling the sequence of events. By telling the first dot on the timeline, I made it considerably easier for them to be successful with this activity. My role is often to function as training wheels so that children get a felt sense for what the strategy I've taught feels like.

Gabriel sat alone on the stoop, imagining sleeping outside alone.

There was a meow.

Gabriel almost didn't hear it because he was lost in his thoughts.

Meow again

"Is someone calling me?"

Looked

Heard again

Excited, looked more

"Now, partner 2, would you storytell this to partner 1? Remember, after every dot or two, you'll want to highlight ways this story shows that Gabriel was lonely and longing for company."

Demonstrate, recruiting children to help you angle the story toward the point.

Children did this, and I coached those that I overheard to bring out the loneliness theme. "Writers, can I stop you?" I said after a bit. "I'm going to storytell and I'll pause after every dot or two. Will you help me highlight the theme of loneliness?"

> One day Gabriel sat on the stoop outside his building, imagining sleeping outside.

I gestured to Emily. "Emily, I'm going to repeat my story. Then will you write in the air what you might add next to bring out the message about Gabriel being lonely?" I said, and repeated my lead.

> One day Gabriel sat on the stoop outside his building, imagining sleeping outside.

Emily added:

> He sat all alone. He imagined sleeping alone with just coyotes and on the grate outside the movie theater, all alone too.

I continued:

> There was a meow.

Again, notice that I find a way to intercede with additional support. Of course, not all the children will have arrived at this timeline of events. By recording this on a chart, I offer children a leg up as they approach the second portion of this work.

Because I know that children will need help fully understanding what it means to angle a story to make a point, I add this extension.

I deliberately call on Emily to work with me here because I know she's fairly adept at this, and I want her to provide yet another demonstration.

I gestured for Emily to add her part, and she said:

> Gabriel didn't hear it. He was off in his dreams.

I gestured for her to say even more.

> He wasn't expecting anyone to call or anything. He was just used to being alone.

I added:

> There was another meow.

Emily added:

> Gabriel thought someone was calling him.

I gestured for her to say more, and to stay with the lonely theme.

> He was glad someone was calling. He was so lonely that he couldn't believe someone was calling him.

You'll notice that I don't complete this; earlier, too, we began but didn't finish a demonstration. After a bit, I think the point has been made and that children won't benefit from prolonging the demonstration.

LINK
Remind writers that essayists collect ministories to advance their point. Remind students that literary essayists can collect several stories for each topic sentence within a single day.

"So writers, you already know that when you are writing an essay, you need to collect material to support each of your topic sentences, and you already know that essayists often collect stories to make a point. Today you've seen how writers of literary essays reread, finding portions of the text that can be told as stories, and then how we angle those tiny stories to make the point we want to make."

"Today, I know each of you will collect several stories. You may collect a story for each file, or several stories in one file. The challenge will be to angle those stories to highlight the idea you are advancing, as Emily just helped me to do."

Just before sending them off to work, I remind children of the productivity goals for today.

WRITING AND CONFERRING

Collecting and Angling Stories to Support Ideas

You'll probably want to conduct table conferences today. That is, you will probably not need to invest lots of time in research. You can count on the fact that children will profit from help, and you can anticipate the sort of help they'll need.

For starters, children will need help seeing the microstories they can extract from these short texts. For example, if a child wants to make the point that Rachel is silenced by Mrs. Price, she is apt to see only one possible story that might illustrate this, and that story encompasses the whole text of "Eleven." (Mrs. Price says she's seen Rachel wearing the sweater, Mrs. Price doesn't listen to Rachel's protests and moves on to math, Mrs. Price makes Rachel put on the sweater, Mrs. Price acts as if it is no big deal when the sweater turns out not to be Rachel's.)

You'll need to show children that they can also regard "Eleven" as containing several different episodes, each of which shows Mrs. Price's disregard for Rachel. For example, one of these episodes happens early:

- Mrs. Price asks whose sweater it is and Rachel thinks, "Not mine."

- Mrs. Price listens to Sylvia and not Rachel, believing Sylvia when she says that the sweater is Rachel's.

- When Rachel sputters "Not mine," Mrs. Price ignores her and acts as if she knows better than Rachel.

- When Rachel tries to protest, Mrs. Price turns to math as if the sweater question is now resolved.

- Rachel is about to cry but Mrs. Price doesn't notice.

Then, too, children will need help retelling a sequence of actions as a story. Many will be apt to cut to the chase, summarizing rather than storytelling the event. For example, a child might write:

> When Rachel tried to tell Mrs. Price the sweater wasn't hers, Mrs. Price ignored Rachel.

MID-WORKSHOP TEACHING POINT — **Finding Ministories to Illustrate Topic Sentences** "Writers, can I have your eyes and your attention? Writers, you all are doing a superb job at finding tiny ministries inside your short texts and then telling these to advance the ideas you've chosen. Ali, for example, wanted to tell a story to show that Lupe had never been good at sports. She reread the start of 'The Marble Champ'—listen to it and think about whether you could find a ministry here":

> Lupe Medrano, a shy girl who spoke in whispers, was the school's spelling bee champion, winner of the reading contest at the public library three summers in a row, blue ribbon awardee in the science fair, the top student at her piano recital, and the playground grand champion in chess. She was a straight-A student and—not counting kindergarten, when she had been stung by a wasp—never missed one day of elementary school. She had received a small trophy for this honor and had been congratulated by the mayor.
>
> But, though Lupe had a razor-sharp mind, she could not make her body, no matter how much she tried, run as fast as the other girls'. She begged her body to move faster, but could never beat anyone in the fifty-yard dash.

continued on next page

You will want to let this writer know that he has just summarized rather than storytold. Although essayists *do* sometimes summarize pertinent bits of a text to defend a point, a wise writer recognizes the difference between a summary and a story, and can produce either one.

Above all, children will need help angling their storytelling so that every line or two references the point they want to make. You could teach children these tips:

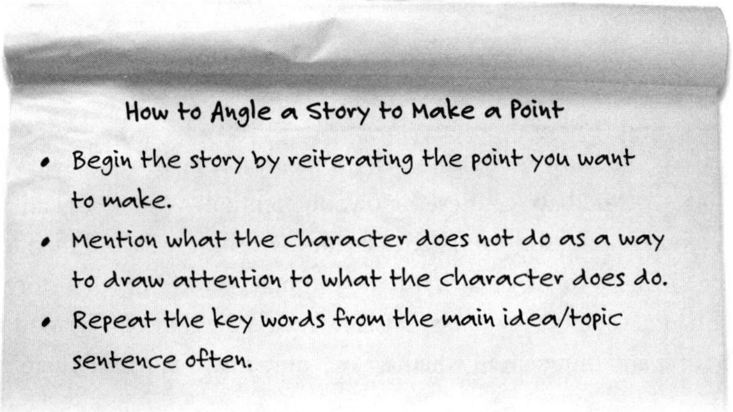
How to Angle a Story to Make a Point
• Begin the story by reiterating the point you want to make.
• Mention what the character does not do as a way to draw attention to what the character does do.
• Repeat the key words from the main idea/topic sentence often.

As you conduct table conferences, don't hesitate to ask every child to stop what he or she is doing and watch you work with one child. For example, I asked children to watch while I worked with Harrison, who had decided to retell the story of Lupe's dinner conversation so as to support the idea that Lupe overcame her difficulties through the support of her family. The excerpt from "The Marble Champ" that Harrison wanted to storytell goes like this:

> That night, over dinner, Mrs. Medano said, "Honey, you should see Lupe's thumb."
>
> "Huh?" Mr. Medrano said, wiping his mouth and looking at his daughter.
>
> "Show your father."
>
> "Do I have to?" an embarrassed Lupe asked.
>
> "Go on, show your father."
>
> Reluctantly, Lupe raised her hand and flexed her thumb. You could see the muscle.
>
> The father put down his fork and asked, "What happened?"
>
> "Dad, I've been working out. I've been squeezing an eraser."
>
> "Why?"

continued from previous page

"Listen to the story Ali wrote": *[Fig. IX-1]*

At the start of "The Marble Champ," Lupe had never been good at sports. She lay on her bed wishing she could play a sport. There was never a sport she could play. She stared up at her awards shelf. She looked at awards—for spelling, reading, science, piano, chess, and for going to school every day of the year. Not one of her awards was for a sport. "I wish I could win at a sport," she thought.

continued on next page

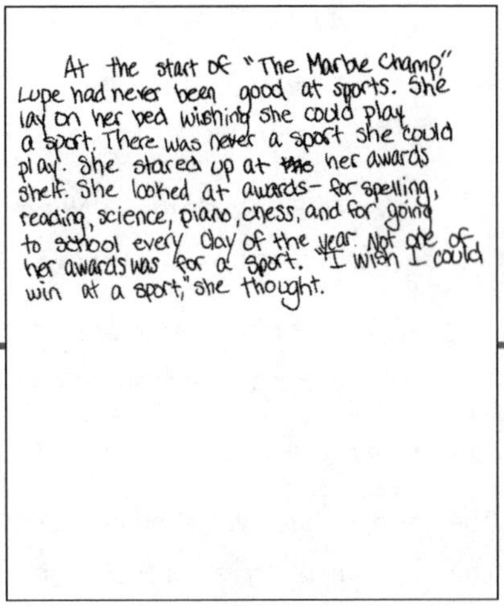
At the start of "The Marble Champ," Lupe had never been good at sports. She lay on her bed wishing she could play a sport. There was never a sport she could play. She stared up at her awards shelf. She looked at awards- for spelling, reading, science, piano, chess, and for going to school every day of the year. Not one of her awards was for a sport. "I wish I could win at a sport," she thought.

Fig. IX-1 Ali's ministory

"I'm going to enter the marbles championship."

Her father looked at her mother and then back at his daughter. "When is it, honey?"

"This Saturday. Can you come?"

The father had been planning to play racquetball with a friend Saturday, but he said he would be there. He knew his daughter thought she was no good at sports and he wanted to encourage her. He even rigged some lights in the backyard so she could practice after dark. (Soto, p.116)

Harrison had initially written:

> For example, one dinner Lupe asks her father to come to the marble competition. "When is it?" her father asks. She said, "This Saturday." The date wasn't good for him but he decided to come anyway.

I said, "Harrison, when I reread my stories to check whether I've angled them to support my claim, I do this: I underline the parts of my rough-draft story that directly show my main idea. Right now, could you underline the parts of your microstory that show that Lupe overcame her difficulties through the support of her family?"

Harrison began doing this. Partway through, he paused and said, "I get it. I stretched out the wrong point 'cause my details about Saturday are ones that don't really show the big idea. I need to add on to the part about the dad switching his plans to support her." In the end, this is what Harrison wrote: [Fig. IX-1]

> Lupe overcomes her difficulties through the support of her family. For example, one dinner, Lupe asks her father to come to the marble competition. Her father drops his fork and drops into deep thought. He had finally planned to spend that very day playing racquet ball, his favorite activity. But he looked into Lupe's eyes, thought about how important it was that she was risking entering a sports competition, and announced he would be there. Lupe grinned.

I debriefed for the observing children. "Do you see that Harrison reread his draft and realized he'd stretched out and provided details for an aspect of the story that didn't make his point? So he redid it. Notice in the next version, he ends by talking about how this episode shows his claim, his idea."

"Harrison added into his version of these events the notion that Lupe's father thought about the racquetball game he'd planned and then thought about the risks his daughter was taking before he made his decision."

continued from previous page

"Ali has done just what essayists often do, finding a ministory that illustrates the idea she wants to advance. And I want to point out something special Ali has done that can help the rest of us. As you did, she paraphrased sections of the text that go with her big idea. But she did something else—she added her own insights and her own envisionment. Listen again to the excerpt from 'The Marble Champ' and then to Ali's ministory, and you'll see that Ali inferred, she added bits to her story that *aren't in the text itself.*" Then I read both aloud.

"Ali's reading between the lines in this instance, seeing what's not quite written in the actual words and showing how that supports her ideas too. Today, if you find yourself copying or paraphrasing bits of the actual text that go with your idea, that's fine. But try to do as Ali has also done and sometimes collect evidence that is suggested but not explicitly stated in the texts."

SHARE

Celebrating the Use of Ministories and Other Bits of Wonderful Writing

Remind writers of the teaching point. Celebrate an aspect of their writing that is going particularly well, and ask them to reread their writing with their partner, talking about both ministories.

"Writers, earlier today I taught you that literary essayists search for sections of a text that can make our point, and then we storytell those sections, starting at the beginning of the story and angling the story. But today, *you've* shown me other things writers do that are so, so important. Your stories are incredibly powerful because they act like the smells of salt air and sea roses, which for me always conjure up the presence of the ocean. You include tiny, emblematic details in your ministories that evoke the entire story in your literary essay. I'm not sure what makes some details have such magical power—but there is no mistaking these details when I see them in your folders."

"Would you and your partner each reread one of the stories you wrote today and notice ways it is angled to highlight the point you want to make. And would you notice, also, specific details you've used that have magical powers?"

HOMEWORK *Studying a Literary Essay* During the next two weeks, you'll be working toward writing a literary essay. It helps, I think, to be able to imagine the sort of text you're hoping to make. For homework, then, I'd like you to study Jill's essay on "Eleven." I've made a copy for each of you. *[Figs. IX-2, IX-3, and IX-4]*

Literary Essay on "Eleven" by Sandra Cisneros written by Jill

In my life, not everything ends up like a fairytale. I like to read books where characters are like me. They don't live fairytale lives. We have the same kinds of problems. Many people read Sandra Cisneros's essay "Eleven" and think it's about a girl who has to wear a sweater she doesn't want to wear. But I think the story is about a girl who struggles to hold onto herself when she is challenged by people who have power over her.

Literary Essay On "Eleven" by Sandra Cisneros
written By Jill

In my life, not everything ends up
like a fairytale. I like to read books
where characters are like me. They don't
live fairytale lives. We have the same
kinds of problems. Many people read Sandra
Cisneros's essay "Eleven" and think its
about a girl who has to wear a
sweater she doesn't want to wear. But
I think the story is about a girl who
struggles to hold onto herself when
she is challenged by people who have
power over her.

When Rachel's teacher, Mrs. Price challenges
Rachel, Rachel loses herself. One day Mrs.
Price puts a stretched out, itchy, red sweater
on Rachel's desk saying "I know this is yours
I saw you wearing it once." Rachel knows
that the sweater isn't hers and tries
to tell Mrs. Price, but Mrs. Price doesn't
believe her. Rachel reacts to Mrs. Prices
actions by losing herself. "In my head,
I'm thinking...how long till lunch time,
how long till I can take the red sweater
and throw it over the School

Fig. IX-2 Jill's literary essay page 1

When Rachel's teacher, Mrs. Price, challenges Rachel, Rachel loses herself. One day Mrs. Price puts a stretched out, itchy, red sweater on Rachel's desk saying, "I know this is yours. I saw you wearing it once!!" Rachel knows that the sweater isn't hers and tries to tell Mrs. Price, but Mrs. Price doesn't believe her. Rachel reacts to Mrs. Price's actions by losing herself. "In my head, I'm thinking ... how long till lunch time, how long till I can take the red sweater and throw it over the school yard fence, or leave it hanging on a parking meter, or bunch it up into a little ball and toss it over the alley?" This shows that Rachel loses herself because she's not listening to her teacher, she's dreaming about a whole other place. It is also important to see that Rachel has all this good thinking about the sweater but when she wants to say the sweater isn't hers, she squeaks and stammers, unable to speak. "But it's not," Rachel says. "Now," Mrs. Price replies. Rachel loses herself by not finding complete words to say when Mrs. Price challenges her.

When Rachel's classmates challenge Rachel, Rachel loses herself. Sylvia Saldivar puts Rachel on the spot light when she says to Mrs. Price, "I think the sweater is Rachel's." Sylvia is challenging Rachel, she is being mean and she makes Rachel feel lost. Rachel cries to let her emotions out. Rachel feels sick from Sylvia. Rachel tries to cover herself up by putting her head in her sleeve. Tears stream down her face. She doesn't feel special like it's her birthday. Instead she feels lost in Sylvia's challenge.

In "Eleven" Rachel is overpowered by both Mrs. Price and Sylvia Saldivar and this causes her to lose herself. I used to think that when people turn eleven they feel strong and have confidence but I have learned that when your eleven you've also 10, 9, 8, 7, 6, 5, 4, 3, 2, and 1.

Would you circle Jill's thesis statement and her topic sentences? Notice where they are in her essay, and notice the way in which they channel everything she writes.

Would you also notice (and star) her use of a story to illustrate one of her topic sentences? Notice and star ways Jill angles her story so that it develops her topic sentence. Finally, notice that after Jill tells a story from the text, she writes a sentence discussing how the story addresses her topic sentence. This sentence begins, "This shows that . . . ."

Finally, would you look again at the ministories you wrote today and revise them, using what you learn from Jill's essay to help you? Be sure that, like Jill, you include a sentence that discusses how your ministory addresses your topic sentence. Your sentence, like Jill's, can begin, "This shows that . . ." and it needs to refer back to the topic sentence.

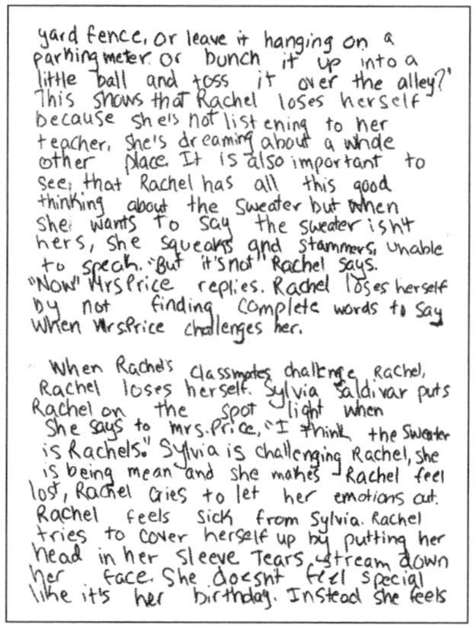

yard fence, or leave it hanging on a parking meter or bunch it up into a little ball and toss it over the alley?" This shows that Rachel loses herself because she's not listening to her teacher, she's dreaming about a whole other place. It is also important to see that Rachel has all this good thinking about the sweater but when she wants to say the sweater isn't hers, she squeaks and stammers, unable to speak. "But it's not," Rachel says. "Now!" Mrs Price replies. Rachel loses herself by not finding complete words to say when Mrs Price challenges her.

When Rachel's classmates challenge Rachel, Rachel loses herself. Sylvia Saldivar puts Rachel on the spot light when she says to mrs. Price, "I think the sweater is Rachels." Sylvia is challenging Rachel, she is being mean and she makes Rachel feel lost, Rachel cries to let her emotions out. Rachel feels sick from Sylvia. Rachel tries to cover herself up by putting her head in her sleeve. Tears stream down her face. She doesnt feel special like it's her birthday. Instead she feels

Fig. IX-3 Jill's literary essay page 2

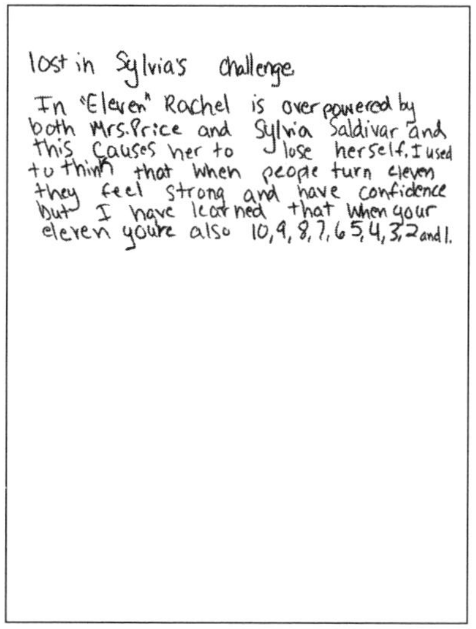

lost in Sylvia's challenge.

In "Eleven" Rachel is overpowered by both Mrs. Price and Sylvia Saldivar and this causes her to lose herself. I used to think that when people turn eleven they feel strong and have confidence but I have learned that when your eleven you're also 10, 9, 8, 7, 6, 5, 4, 3, 2 and 1.

Fig. IX-4 Jill's literary essay page 3

TAILORING YOUR TEACHING

If your class of children studied this unit during a previous year and you want to add complexity . . . you might teach a variation of this lesson to more clearly illustrate that the way we angle our story—the point we want to make—alters the story. You could, for example, point out that if you wanted to say that Jenny, the protagonist in "Boar Out There," was curious towards the boar, you'd retell the story one way. If, alternatively, you wanted to suggest she's sympathetic towards the boar, you'd tell it differently. In such a lesson, you could first timeline a section of the story:

- The people of Glen Morgan knew about the boar.
- Jenny whispered to the boar sometimes.
- Jenny imagined the boar as fierce.
- Jenny went looking for the boar.
- Jenny heard the boar.
- Jenny saw the boar.
- The boar left.
- Jenny felt a new understanding for the boar.

Then you could demonstrate a retelling that shows Jenny is curious about the boar:

- Jenny whispered to the boar sometimes. Leaning over the fence that separated its world from hers, she imagined that it could talk back and wondered what it would say.
- Jenny imagined the boar as fierce. She could see his large angry eyes as he charged through the woods, spearing everything in his path with the golden horn on his head.
- Jenny went looking for the boar. As she walked quietly through the woods, Jenny felt afraid. She thought of how the boar could come charging at any moment, and wondered if it would even spear a little girl.
- Jenny heard the boar. She heard loud, stomping feet that could have been the feet of a giant. Jenny was terrified as the sound grew louder and louder, and the branches on the trees starting swaying back and forth. She was scared but didn't move. She wanted to see what the boar looked like.

Finally, you could demonstrate how the retelling would be different (and the same) if Jenny instead felt sympathetic towards the boar. You could, for example, simply retell the rest of the story to show this:

- Jenny saw the boar. He was large and ugly, but also sad looking. His ears were bloody and torn and he shivered, silent. Jenny felt sorry for him right away. He seemed so fragile even in his large frame that she started crying.

- The boar left. It went charging past Jenny as quickly as it had arrived. The boar looked scared. Its eyes were very large and gleaming. Jenny wished she could put her arms around the boar and convince it she didn't mean it any harm.

- Jenny felt a new understanding for the boar. Now, whenever Jenny leaned on the fence, she felt both sad and happy when she thought about the boar. She was glad he wasn't the mean beast she'd imagined, but felt sad that she could never be his friend. He was still wild and didn't understand that she would never hurt him.

COLLABORATING WITH COLLEAGUES

You'll probably find that before you can help your children with this minilesson, you need to spend some time with your colleagues developing your own skills at this work. I suggest you reread minilessons from earlier in this series, searching for instances when I have angled a story to make a particular point. Notice exactly what I do to accomplish this goal. For example, in the personal narrative unit, in Session VI, I model how I can tell the same story about the classroom window getting stuck to show two different things. First, I show children how to angle this story so that it's about how broken items in the classroom make it impossible to get through a single lesson. This is how I begin that version:

> Yesterday, our teacher read aloud. It was so hot that sweat was rolling down our faces, so our teacher stopped and went over to open the window. She pushed. Nothing happened. Flakes of paint rained down.

Notice that I include details to show how the window is stuck shut: the teacher pushing and nothing happening, flakes of paint raining down. The emphasis in this story is on the window being beyond repair. Next, I tell the same story, but this time I angle it to be about how the class works together, as a community, to overcome problems:

> Yesterday our teacher read aloud. She looked out and saw that we had sweat rolling down our cheeks. So she knew she had to help us. She went over and tried to open the window. It was stuck. Soon Ori had jumped up.

Here, the emphasis is on how members of the class—the teacher, Ori, and presumably, as the story continues, others—help each other solve problems. Many of the details from the earlier version have been dropped from this new story.

Once you've studied how we have angled stories in minilessons, you'll develop your own list of tips for doing this. My list is given here, but use your own. Next, tell an angled story by working together (orally if it is easier) on a

joint text. For example, if you and your colleagues have been pulling your hair out over the pressures wrought by standardized testing, then you could retell a shared moment showing how this is true. You could retell the story of a recent faculty meeting that prioritized standardized tests, using these tips:

- Name what did not happen, but could have happened, in a way that highlights the aspect of this event that you want to highlight.

- Mention the specific actions that further your point and bypass others that don't do this.

- Bring out the internal story—your thoughts, observations, remarks, worries—in a way that allows you to elaborate on the aspect of the story you want told.

- Frame the story with explicit comments that make your point.

Your story might begin like this:

> Last Monday we gathered as usual for our after-school faculty meeting. But this time when we gathered, no one was smiling and jovial. Ms. X (the principal) especially didn't smile. She looked as if she were gritting her teeth in anxiety. We sat in our usual places but this time, instead of a gorgeous children's book as a place setter, we each had a stack of bubble paper and copies of printout tests. "Let's skip the usual amenities," Mrs. X said, bypassing all the rituals that made us a community. I glanced at my grade-level colleague and we rolled our eyes. This faculty meeting would contain no small-group collaboration, no collegiality, no problem solving—it would contain none of what sustains us. School systems need to realize that tests only wreak havoc on morale, dissipate energy, and jettison all that works well in schools.

USING SUMMARIES AS EVIDENCE

The Inuit are rumored to have dozens of different words for snow—one for falling snow, one for the last grey patches that remain long after most of winter has melted away, and words for all the kinds of snow in between. Because many Inuit work closely with snow, it makes sense that they have specialized terms for it. Children will need specialized terms for their essay writing as well. When children first learn to write about literature, they will probably talk often about the need to cite evidence (or examples) from the text. The goal will be to "give evidence." Most third, fourth, and fifth graders will not know that, just as the Inuit might call on a specific set of words and phrases to refer to snow, literary essayists draw on a set of terms to help state claims and make cases. Literary essayists have a vocabulary to help us incorporate evidence from a text into an essay. Starting in this session, we'll introduce children to some of this specialized vocabulary.

The majority of this session, however, will be devoted to helping children learn how to summarize bits of a text as evidence to support their theses and claims. In the preceding session, children learned that they can find bits of a text that illustrate the idea they are advancing, and then retell those bits as microstories. Today you'll help children learn that as literary essayists, they have a palette of optional ways to refer to the text under study. They will sometimes choose to tell a story to make a point, but other times, they'll summarize (paraphrase) or quote a section of the text to provide evidence.

IN THIS SESSION, YOU'LL EXPLAIN SUMMARIES AND OFFER AN EXAMPLE, THEN DEMONSTRATE HOW ESSAYISTS USE SUMMARIES TO HELP THEM SUPPORT THEIR POINTS. YOU'LL OUTLINE THE STEPS CHILDREN CAN TAKE TO CREATE SUMMARIES FOR THEIR ESSAYS.

GETTING READY

- Example of a paragraph that summarizes a book, transcribed onto chart paper

- Passages from "Spaghetti," by Cynthia Rylant, transcribed onto chart paper and as a handout

- Example of a paragraph that summarizes an episode from "Spaghetti" as supporting evidence for an idea

- Transitional Phrases to Link Evidence in Essays chart

See CD-ROM for resources

MINILESSON

Using Summaries as Evidence

CONNECTION

Point out to children a place in their lives where they encounter summaries. Tell them that essayists use summaries just as they use stories to support their claims.

"Have you ever asked a little kid—say a five- or six- or seven-year-old kid—'What was the television show about?' and then had the kid take this huge breath of air and start off, telling one thing and then the next, the next, on and on and on? After a bit, you interject and say, 'So how did it end?' because you're trying to nudge the child to finish the retelling. Well, today I want to tell you that what you wanted the kid to give you—what you expected when you asked the question, 'What was the show about?'—was a summary. You hoped for a brief, encapsulated synthesis of the plot. You hoped for something resembling the blurb on the back cover of a book."

"I want to talk to you about summaries, today, because all year long I've nudged you to storytell, not to summarize. Today, I want to take that all back and teach you that essayists sometimes decide to storytell and sometimes decide to summarize—and we need to be skilled at doing both."

"Essayists make choices. When we want to cite evidence (or give an example),we can decide to *storytell* the detailed, step-by-step timeline of what happened first, next, next—or we can quickly *summarize* just the main highlights. These are closely related but distinctly different ways to bring bits of a text into our literary essays."

Name the teaching point. Specifically, tell children that writers use summaries to support their claims.

"Today I will teach you that literary essayists often summarize bits of a text. When we summarize a story, we convey a miniature version of a text. We mostly use our own words, but we also often borrow a few specific words from the story—words that capture the feel of the story's language."

TEACHING

Explain the elements of a summary and offer an example.

"A few years ago, hundreds of New York City teachers created a list of books that we hoped our city's mayor would put in every classroom across the city. The mayor did put

COACHING

You'll recall that earlier in this series I stressed that writers show, not tell, and then later I recapitulated, pointing out that although that is an adage of good writing, it is nevertheless true that writers actually show and tell. Now I'm going to—in a similar fashion—retrieve summarizing from the "reject" pile, and teach the craft and purpose of a summary.

those books in classrooms, and the teachers produced the series *Field Guides to the Classroom Library* that gave teachers and children just a glimpse of each book's contents. What these teachers and I wrote were summaries, and I want to share one with you. It's a summary of a book you know well: Karen Hesse's *Come On, Rain*."

"I want you to notice that this summary, like most summaries, tells the main features of the story. Usually that will mean that a summary captures the main character, conveying his or her traits and motivations. The summary will capture the story's setting, too, and the main sequence of events, especially those that involve a struggle and a resolution. I also want you to notice that often a story summary will use a few words from the text in a way that captures the tone and color of the text. Listen, then, for the elements of story, the story language. In a minute, I'm going to ask you to try to create an even more miniature version of this summary."

Turning the pad of chart paper, I read this summary:

> This jewel of a book uses poetic language to tell the story of a little girl, Tessie, who lives in the sweltering hot city. From her apartment balcony, Tessie stares past chimneys and roof tops to see, way off in the distance, a bunch of grey clouds bulging under a purple sky. Tessie whispers, "Come on, Rain!" Soon Tessie and her friends are in bathing suits, waiting for the rain, which finally comes after great longing. "The first drops plop down big, making dust dance all around us," Tessie says, and soon the Mamas have thrown off their shoes and stockings and joined the girls in a glorious dance through puddles. After the joyful rain celebration, Tessie and her mom head home "fresh as dew."

"Do you see how just that short little bit of text about *Come On, Rain* captures the important parts of the whole story? That's what a summary needs to do."

Demonstrate summarizing a short episode from a known text.

"Let's pretend we have claimed that Gabriel, in 'Spaghetti,' is determined, and let's pretend we decide that instead of storytelling the moment when he searches for and finally finds the cat as an example of him being determined, we will *summarize* that episode."

"Okay, we have to summarize that bit of the story that proves that Gabriel is determined. The first thing we need to do is reread the story, marking off the section that describes Gabriel finding the cat—with determination. The sections don't always come right next to each other in the story." With my pen, I highlighted the section of "Spaghetti" in which Gabriel almost missed hearing the cry. I also marked the sections of the text

There are lots of sources you can turn to in order to illustrate the components of book summaries. The American Library Association Web site, http://www.ala.org, contains lots of book lists, many with summaries.

In this minilesson, I demonstrate how I go about summarizing bits of a text. I'm scooting right past a potential lesson, showing children how I go from wanting to show that Gabriel is determined to locating the sections of the text that demonstrate that quality. I'm aware, however, that many children, when looking for evidence of a character trait, would skim through the text looking for explicit mention of that trait (here, determination). When that word isn't mentioned, these children would decide the text doesn't show the trait! This instruction, in this instance, will need to be reserved for small groups.

where Gabriel picked himself up and walked down the street. As I did this, I pointed out that there were sections of the story I wasn't marking.

"What I do next is I think back over what I have read and try to restate it in just a sentence or two, in a way that covers the highlights of it. I want to remember to mention the character, what he wants and does. I might repeat just a very few specific words or phrases from the story that help me summarize it and make my point. For example, the story said that the cry was so small it *could have been the wind* but Gabriel still picked himself up. I think it is important that a cry as quiet as the wind got him to get up from that stoop! It also says that he didn't just look in the alleys, he *peered* into them. *He peered!* Here's my summary":

> In one section of the story, Gabriel heard a cry as weak as the wind. He was determined, so he picked himself up and started walking in the direction of the cry. He didn't just glance around to find the source of the cry, instead, he peered, determined to see what was making the noise. He didn't see anything but he knew something was there.

Debrief. Point out the steps of summarizing that you took and you expect they will take as they try this strategy for creating evidence for their essays.

"To recap, here's what I do when I want to summarize an episode to use it as evidence to prove an idea":

- I read and find the exact section of a story that supports my point (that Gabriel was determined).
- I reread the section and think about how I could tell it in my own words, more briefly, conveying the main elements of story.
- I notice and underline the key words in the text.
- I retell the section, trying both to get my point across (that Gabriel's determined) and to recap a bit of the story for people who haven't read it. Although I mostly use my own words, I also incorporate a few key terms and weave in the main idea I want to advance.

ACTIVE ENGAGEMENT

Get children started summarizing another section of the touchstone text. Set them up to do this by recalling the components of a story summary.

"So let's pretend we are writing that Gabriel is a soft-hearted person and we want to summarize (not storytell) what happened when Gabriel saw the cat and decided to take him in. On your copies of the text, would you and your partner mark the sections of 'Spaghetti' that show he is soft-hearted? These will be the sections that, for now, you want to summarize."

It is important to stress that a literary essayist often lifts key words from a text, bringing those words into the essay itself. Children may worry about plagiarism, and it is true that a writer doesn't borrow more than four or five consecutive words without using quotation marks, but this doesn't mean there's a problem with lifting a sprinkling of key words.

In this instance, I am teaching a few complex ideas at once. For example, it is complex enough to simply teach children to summarize—and I am teaching them to summarize in an angled fashion to make a specific point. You may decide to teach summary at another time—perhaps during reading—so that this minilesson isn't too ambitious. If you are teaching children to summarize a story, it can help to teach them that a summary usually answers the who, where, when, why, and how questions. Alternatively, it can help to teach them that a summary is generally structured like a tiny story, containing a character who has traits and motivations, and who goes through a struggle and changes in the process.

You may decide that during this Active Engagement, you'd like to switch to another text altogether. You could ask children to think of a part of the story that they could cite as evidence for a claim you state, and to summarize that part of the story. Alternatively, you could ask them to try this with a fairy tale.

"Reread the section and think how it conveys elements of story—a character who wants something, does this and then this, and perhaps changes. Now will you circle any exact words that either help your case or that capture the flavor of the excerpt?" I waited a few minutes while the children worked in pairs. Then I said, "Thumbs up if you've done this." Most of the children indicated they were done. "Okay, writers, now would you write in the air a summary of this section, weaving in the idea that he was soft-hearted. Start by saying: 'Gabriel is soft-hearted. In one section of the story, Gabriel . . . .'"

Present the thinking of the group for comment. Demonstrate that after we write a summary, we have the opportunity to revise it.

As I listened, children summarized. I then convened the class, and retold (and improved upon) one child's summary. "I heard many of you summarize like this," I said:

> Gabriel is a soft-hearted boy. In one section of the story, Gabriel saw
> a scrawny kitten. Gabriel held the kitten next to his cheek. It smelled
> of pasta so he named it that, and it purred.

"After we write a summary, we often reread it to see what we could delete. You could, of course, do this," and I deleted some phrases before their eyes, resulting in this summary:

> Gabriel, a soft-hearted boy, picked up a scrawny kitten that smelled
> of pasta and held it against his cheek.

LINK
Remind children of the repertoire of options before them.

"Writers, artists make masterpieces by drawing on a palette of colors, and today when you collect more evidence for your files, you'll draw on a palette of choices. You may write ministories to illustrate your topic sentences, filing each one in your folder for all the writing that goes with that topic sentence. On the other hand, you may take some time to reread one of the stories you have already written and decide to angle that story to bring out the idea you want to advance. Or you may decide that instead of storytelling to make your point, you'll summarize bits of the text. Whenever you write literary essays, you'll want to remember that as a writer, you have options. You need to provide evidence from the text to support your claims, but you can do so by telling stories or by summarizing portions of the text, among other options."

You could say, "Let's try this with 'The Three Little Pigs' . Let's say your claim is that the three pigs work hard to be safe from the wolf. Can you summarize the part of the story that illustrates this claim? I've got copies of the fairy tale if you need it."

The work you are asking children to do is very complex. Expect rough approximations. It would help if you find summaries elsewhere and point them out to the class.

Your children may not know the term 'palette'. When this is the case, tuck a synonym into your sentence and use gestures and drama to help convey your meaning. But don't detour around unfamiliar words!

WRITING AND CONFERRING

Summarizing to Support a Claim

To help Tyler, Rebecca, and John understand how to summarize in ways that develop a claim, I convened them into a small group. "Let's practice together first by differentiating between how a writer storytells and summarizes. Let's take something—anything—you guys did together. Say . . . what you did in art class this morning. (For now, we'll pretend you aren't making a special point about art.)"

"If you want to storytell the events of this morning's art class, first recall what you did. (I gave them a few seconds to do this.) Now go back to the start of art class when Mrs. Pressley walked into our room. Can you recall her entering, dragging that cart behind her? Make a movie in your mind of it." I gave them a moment to do this. "Okay, Rebecca, storytell art class, starting with, 'I heard a bump on our door and looked up to see Mrs. Pressley pushing through the door, dragging the art cart.' What did she say or do?"

Rebecca continued, "She said we were going to make God's eyes today and asked if we ever made them. Then she showed us some God's eyes. She said, 'Aren't they beautiful?' Then she passed out two sticks to each of us."

Taking over because I wanted the story to be especially drawn out and step-by-step, I added, "Then she passed out a pattern, didn't she? Then she passed out the yarn. Then she showed us how to attach the yarn to the stick. Then she showed us how to turn the yarn to get our God's eyes started. Then she showed us how to change yarns. She called it magic."

As Rebecca and I storytold, I scrawled the main events that we repeated onto the pages. Turning to the group, I said, "Now let's try to summarize this," and I gestured toward the list. "Before we do, would you think about where there are places in this version that Rebecca and I detailed in a step-by-step, drawn-out way that could instead be described in a phrase. Like instead of saying, 'I went on the swings, the seesaw, the slide,' I could say, 'I played on the playground equipment.'"

Children agreed that the summary could say that the teacher passed out the supplies (not listing each item) and gave directions (instead of listing each instruction). Then the youngsters worked with partners to jot down a summary. Most went something like this:

MID-WORKSHOP
TEACHING POINT ***Linking a Sequence of Summaries*** "Writers, can I have your eyes and your attention? Earlier today I taught you *how* writers summarize episodes from a story, but I didn't teach you *why* we do this. Usually we decide to summarize episodes because no single example is powerful enough to make our point, and therefore we gather a few examples, chaining them together. So, for example, if I wanted to convey that Gabriel is lonely, I might decide that it would be hard to write really well about Gabriel sitting alone on the stoop; I might instead decide to summarize a few different examples that showed his loneliness."

"Max, for example, has a folder titled, 'Rachel realizes when you are 11, you are also 10, 9, 8 . . . .' He decided to summarize a time when Rachel feels younger than she is. So he wrote this":

> In the story, Rachel sits at her desk staring at the nasty red sweater Mrs. Price made her keep. She was disgusted with it and wanted to cry like she was three.

continued on next page

Today in art, Mrs. Pressley told us we'd make God's eyes and showed us examples. Then she passed out the supplies and gave us directions.

"Now let's try something trickier," I said. "You just summarized *everything* that happened in art. You could, instead, summarize those things that support a claim that you have about art class. Then you would need to pick and choose what to say. Let's imagine you wanted to say, 'It is hard for Mrs. Pressley to teach art from a cart,' and you wanted to explain that lots of time is taken up just giving out stuff. How might you summarize that part of art class in a sentence or two that makes your point?"

The children looked back on the storytold version. I called on John, reminding him to start by saying his claim. He said:

It is hard for Mrs. Pressley to have art on the cart. Today in art she had to pass out about five things so we could make God's eyes.

"Let's say we want to make the point that having art supplies on a cart is hard by writing a couple of summaries in a row," I said. "What *else* happened in art that shows it is hard to have it on a cart?"

Then children recalled the way art class had ended, and soon had written a chain of two summaries to make their point:

It is hard for Mrs. Pressley to have art on the cart. Today in art she had to pass out about five things so we could make God's eyes. At the end of art, we weren't done and we couldn't leave them in the room, so we had to mark which God's eyes was ours, and that is hard because you can't write on yarn. She couldn't fit them all on the cart so some of us carried them to her closet.

"So now," I said, "could you turn to your writing, think about what you'll do next, and get started while I watch."

"My hunch is that if you've collected one summary, you'll probably find that there is another episode in the story you could also summarize, to help you make the same point. If so, you'll want to use a transitional phrase such as Max used when he said, 'There are other sections of the story where Rachel . . .' and 'For example . . .' and 'Another example is when . . . .' Or like Diana did when she said, 'At the beginning of the story, Jenny . . .' and 'Later . . . .' I've written several transitions on chart paper—you can use these to help you now and whenever you write essays! Essayists have special words they use to help them, and little by little we'll learn lots of those words in this unit."

continued from previous page
"Then Max wrote":

There are other sections of the story where Rachel understands that when you are eleven, you are also all the ages inside. For example, she says "When you are scared and need to sit on your Mama's lap, that is the part of you that is still five." And another example is, "When you say something stupid, that is the part of you that is still three."

"So Max has strung together three examples, one of which is a summary, all of which prove his point."

"Diana has a folder on 'Boar Out There' titled, 'Jenny imagines that the boar is ferocious and special.' Diana compiled a list of instances in the story when Jenny thinks about the boar in ways that support this claim. Then she summarized each of those two parts. She wrote this":

At the beginning of the story, Jenny imagines the boar as a wild and ferocious beast. For example, early on, she leans against the fence and whispers to the boar, and pictures that he is fierce. Jenny also imagines the boar as magical, with a golden horn.

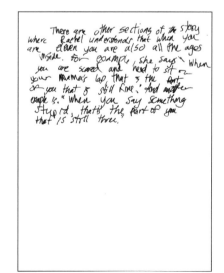

Fig. X-1 Max's examples

SHARE

Studying Collections of Entries

Ask children to study and talk over their work with their partners, paying careful attention to the parts of the essays they've worked on to date.

"Writers, last night for homework you studied Jill's essay, and looked especially closely at the way in which she used stories to support her topic sentences. It seems to me that we need to also study *your* work, because so many of you have found wise ways to use both stories and summaries to support your claims. Would you share your stories and summaries with your partner? Just as you noticed Jill's thesis statement and her topic sentences, would you notice each other's thesis statements and topic sentences? Notice your stories, too, and your summaries. Talk in detail about the ways in which you've angled these to support your topic sentences. If you've neglected to write a sentence after your story or summary that refers back to the topic sentence, help each other to do so." The children shared, and I listened in.

HOMEWORK *Using Quotations as Evidence* Jill did something in the exemplar piece we have been studying that some, but not all, of you have done. She included a quoted section from her story in her essay. Read Jill's essay again and notice that she has used a quotation that is a complete sentence—it doesn't rely on Jill's words to prop it up. It stands alone even though it has ellipses showing that a section of the sentence has been left out.

Jill could have *instead* written with a partial quote, lifting just a phrase from "Eleven" as I do here: "Rachel was unhappy putting on a sweater that wasn't hers. She thought it was disgusting to put on a sweater that was 'full of germs' that weren't even hers." That phrase, *full of germs*, isn't a full sentence, it is just a few words that support your claim. Essayists use both kinds of quotations.

Find a few different sections from the text you have been studying that you could quote to support your claim. Copy those sections onto separate pages to file in the folders you've made for each supporting section. Bring them to school tomorrow and file them in your folders.

If your students are not seeing a difference between storytelling and summarizing . . .
you might design a minilesson to help them see the difference. It might go something like this: "Writers, I am blown away by the stories and summaries that you are telling to support your ideas. And most of you are telling these in ways that highlight the meaning you are trying to show!"

"One thing I've learned about writing about reading is that our readers don't always notice what we want them to notice. Yesterday when I was reading an essay in the *New York Times* about Lance Armstrong, I read quickly and when my friend and I were talking about it, I realized I'd completely missed the part where the writer said Lance Armstrong is a hero of our country!"

"When you write your literary essays, you need to keep in mind that your readers might be in a hurry and do the same thing. They might fly right past whatever you have said. The way you can help prevent that is to unpack your stories or your summaries and stretch them out a bit."

"For example, earlier we summarized part of 'Spaghetti' like this:"

> In one section of the story, Gabriel heard a cry as weak as the wind. Still, he got himself up and started walking in the direction of the cry. He didn't just glance around, he peered and when he saw the cat waiting, he was amazed. (That's the summary.)

"Now, watch what I add on to the end of that story as I unpack it so that my readers really get my point:"

> This episode is important because Gabriel might have just looked up and returned to his daydreaming. But instead he went forward, into the gray street. Most people wouldn't have done that—they'd have chickened out or ignored the cry. Gabriel did not. This proves he was determined to find out what the cry was.

Teaching writers to summarize has implications across the curriculum, and it will be important for you to show children how they can summarize in math, social studies, and science as well as in literary essays. Although all year long you will have taught children to write with details, summaries are a place where generalizations can be helpful. Show children that they can describe the step-by-step sequence that occurred in a specific battle at the start of the Revolutionary War—say, at the Battle of Bunker Hill or the Battle of Lexington—or they can, alternatively, say something general that acts like the overview on the back of the DVD box, conveying the main idea of those early battles.

COLLABORATING WITH COLLEAGUES

In today's minilesson, you taught children that when they want to support an idea by citing evidence from the text, they can summarize or storytell to make a point. In a study group with colleagues, you will probably want to consider ways to use the reading workshop and read-aloud time to help children develop the requisite skills.

For example, it's not necessarily easy to read a text and find specific instances that support a specific idea. In today's minilesson, I suggested that I could show that Gabriel is determined by showing that he persisted in tracking down the source of the sound he heard. It's important to bear in mind that it's no easy matter for a child to recognize that Gabriel's tenacious search for the source of the noise shows determination. Many children would survey the details of this vignette, see that Gabriel is not described as determined, and decide this episode can't be used to support the claim that Gabriel is determined.

Some children, then, will find it very challenging to locate sections of the text that support a claim they've made. You and your colleagues can consider

Examples of Increasingly Advanced Textual References

1. Gabriel is determined. An example is when he finds the cat.

2. Gabriel is determined. We see this when he looks and looks for the cat.

3. Gabriel is determined. When he hears a cry, he gets up to look for what is making the sound. He peers into the alley. He finds the cat.

4. Gabriel is determined. When he hears a cry, he doesn't just glance around for the source of it. He actually gets up and walks down the street, looking for the source. He doesn't just glance in the alleys— he peers into them. When he hears the noise a second time, he walks faster and searches more. Other people might just glance around, looking for the source of the noise, but Gabriel's determination makes him look until he spots the tiny kitten.

ways to teach the requisite skills during your read-aloud. For instance, you might pause in the midst of reading and ask yourself, aloud, "So what kind of person does this character seem to be?" You could proceed to demonstrate developing a theory, generating a variety of words that could possibly suffice, and then read on, saying, "Let's see if the upcoming text supports or challenges that theory."

Of course, as you read on, chances are good that nothing in the text will exactly match the words you've used to characterize the character, so you can show children the process of weighing whether or not an event in the story can function as evidence for the theory the class is advancing.

Similarly, you may want to suggest that children record on sticky notes the ideas they form as they read their independent books. When children are midway into a book, they can reread all their notes, thinking, "So what is one big idea that feels important to this whole story?" Again you could suggest that children read on, expecting the upcoming text to either support or challenge their theories. They may, in fact, want to create "theory charts," accumulating page numbers that support, extend, revise, or dispute their theories.

In these ways, then, you and your colleagues can invent ways to be sure that the work you are doing in the writing workshop pertains also to the reading workshop. If you want to go a step farther and use summarizing in the context of a reading workshop, you could show children how to transform a theory chart into a summary.

You and your colleagues will want to work together to develop wise responses to the summaries your children produce. It can help to spend time talking about what it might look like for children to progress from beginning-level summaries to more intermediate-level summaries, and from intermediate to advanced summaries. Then you'll need to imagine specific ways in which a child's efforts could become more skilled.

You can create such a ladder of difficulty by collecting examples from your children's work and thinking, "Is this a more mature version? How so?" In this way, you can slot children's work into a ladder of development . . . and design teaching that helps children progress along a pathway you've imagined.

USING LISTS AS EVIDENCE

When this nation was young, rhetoric was part of each school's core curriculum. Children grew up with as firm a foundation in oration as in multiplication. In school, they learned to articulate their ideas loudly and clearly, using their voices to gather and command attention, and to rally listeners to action.

Essay writing was inexorably linked to public speaking. Children delivered their essays at speaking contests, and learned to write in ways that would appeal to the ear. Perhaps for this reason, parallelism is a crucial part of many essays—and many speeches. Think of the greatest, most memorable speeches you can, and you'll probably find yourself remembering lines that were repeated: "Ask not what your country can do for you, ask what you can do for your country" and "I have a dream."

Today's work with lists invites children to use the parallelism of the list structure to bring rhetorical power to their writing. This session also invites children to write with attentiveness to sound as well as to meaning.

IN THIS SESSION, YOU'LL REMIND CHILDREN OF WORK THEY DID DURING THE PERSONAL ESSAY UNIT IN USING LISTS TO SUPPORT THEIR CLAIMS. YOU'LL AGAIN ENCOURAGE THEM TO WRITE "TIGHT LISTS" IN WHICH THEY WRITE WITH PARALLELISM.

GETTING READY

- Examples of well-known repeating phrases from familiar children's texts
- "Spaghetti," by Cynthia Rylant, and "The Marble Champ," by Gary Soto
- Example of a thesis used as the repeating chorus for a list
- Example of one student's thesis and supporting ideas, written on chart paper, from which the whole class can develop a list using parallel structure to support a claim
- Types of Evidence to Support Claims, listed on chart paper
- See CD-ROM for resources

MINILESSON

Using Lists as Evidence

CONNECTION

Celebrate children's powerful read-aloud voices. Point out that the repetitive phrases in the books children are reading act as signals for how to read in powerful ways.

"The other day I listened while you read aloud books to your first-grade reading buddies. Every one of you read aloud really well. Your voices were rhythmic and flowing, and you used your voices to hold parts of the books together. I've been thinking about the read-aloud voices you use when you work with first graders, and it occurs to me that you don't use equally powerful voices when you read your own writing aloud. Part of the secret may be that many of the books you read to your reading buddies contain lists, held together with repetitive phrases, and those repetitive phrases help you read aloud in powerful ways."

"'When I'm five...' one book says, listing over and over what the young narrator will do when she is five years old. 'When I was young in the mountains...' is the refrain in Cynthia Rylant's list of memories from when she was young, growing up in the mountains of Appalachia. We all know the famous words of 'The Little Engine That Could': 'I think I can, I think I can.' When texts contain lists, held together by phrases or repeating lines, it's almost as if the texts become a song containing a chorus."

Name your teaching point. Specifically, remind children that their writing should appeal not only to the eye but also to the ear. Lists, held together by repeating phrases or lines, can hold an essay together.

"I'm telling you this because as writers, you need to remember that you are writing not only for readers' eyes but also for their *ears*. And readers' ears welcome lists and repetition. Lists, held together by repeating lines, can hold an essay together, just as repeating verses can hold a song together."

TEACHING

Demonstrate that literary essayists often use a claim, a thesis, as the repeating chorus for a list. Then show students that any important simple sentence can be used to create and extend a list.

"Often when writing literary essays, you'll find yourself making a claim. That claim might be your thesis or one of your bullet points (these become topic sentences), or it could just be a claim that you make in the middle of a paragraph. Either way, once you've made a

COACHING

Initially, I'd also written an example from my family, but I try to delete any example that doesn't contribute something new. This is the deleted example:

"In my family, my brothers and sisters seem to know all the verses to every Christmas carol. Meanwhile, I often stumble along through those verses. But when the chorus comes, I'm always happy. The repetition of those lines allows me to join in heartily to sing 'Oh! Jingle bells, jingle bells, jingle all the way...' or 'Oh-oh, Star of wonder, Star of night, Star with royal beauty bright. Westward leading still proceeding, guide us to thy perfect light.'"

This session introduces a skill which has turned out to be more challenging for youngsters than I ever anticipated. You'll invent your own adaptations.

claim, stated an idea, you can often use that claim as the basis for a list. For example, let's take the claim, 'Gabriel is lonely.' Once I have a claim, I think to myself, 'How could I extend this claim by adding some detail?' I'd probably think, 'I could list *times* when he's lonely, *places* where he's lonely, or *reasons* why he's lonely!' Then I could take one of these and try it. I'll think about times when Gabriel is lonely. As I write my list, I lift specific terms and details from the text itself. The list, then, is less original than it might seem."

"You should notice that I develop a claim into a list in the same ways that I develop a thesis. Earlier we learned that after we have made a claim (My father's been an important teacher), we can think of reasons (because he taught me to write, to fail, and to be my own person). Alternatively, we can think of times—instances—or of parts; the work I do here is reminiscent of that."

"For example, we could instead have said, 'Gabriel is lonely because he lives alone, Gabriel is lonely because he's isolated by his classmates, Gabriel is lonely because he distances himself even from the people who are around him.'"

> Gabriel is lonely when he eats his butter sandwich at school.
>
> Gabriel is lonely when he sits on the stoop outside his building.
>
> Gabriel is lonely when he walks the dark street, peering into alleys.

"I can create a list by starting with almost any claim, any sentence that conveys one of my ideas and feels important. I just need to think, 'Can I repeat part of this sentence in a way that creates echo lines?' For example, I could write":

> Gabriel doesn't mind that the kitten smells like pasta.

"Then I could try extending this. When I go to do this, I have no idea what I will say, but I just repeat the phrase I've chosen and squeeze my brain to see if I can come up with something":

> Gabriel doesn't mind that the kitten smells like pasta.
>
> Gabriel doesn't mind that kitten's legs are wobbly.
>
> Gabriel doesn't mind that the kitten meows pitifully.

Much of education includes learning to apply what one already knows to new situations. When children learned to plan an essay considering whether they could support their claim with reasons, times, or places, they can apply this to lots of different situations.

ACTIVE ENGAGEMENT
Enlist children to work in pairs, helping a classmate write a list, with support from you.

"Let's help Harrison write a list. His thesis is this":

> Lupe overcomes her athletic difficulties through hard
> work and family support.

"Remember yesterday, we heard Harrison's story of the father at dinner time, agreeing to come to Lupe's game? Well, today Harrison wants to list other ways in which Lupe's family supports her. Harrison has already reread the story and looked for and starred sentences that show what Lupe's family did to support her." I read aloud from chart paper:

> So Lupe . . . listened to her brother, who gave her tips on
> how to shoot: get low, aim with one eye, and place one
> knuckle on the ground.

> (The father) even hung some lights in the backyard so
> she could practice after dark.

> (The mother) asked why her thumb was swollen.

"So writers, can you help Harrison turn these into a list? Your items won't necessarily progress in this order, and you needn't include all of this data, or use these exact words. Work with a partner to decide first on the repeating stem, then plug in the details. Turn and talk."

The children immediately began talking. Many of them simply lined up these excerpts, using the exact words of the text.

Intervene to lift the level of the children's work. In this instance, remind them that for the most part, their lists will contain their words, not the words of the text they are referencing.

"Writers, can I stop you? The author, Gary Soto, may have used beautiful words, but your essay can't just repeat his story. You will need to *replace* many of his words with your words! That's hard to do, I know, because it feels almost arrogant. It's easy to think, 'His words work so well; why get rid of them?' But remember, *you* have an angle on this that you want to bring out—you are trying to highlight how helpful Lupe's family has been—so that's one reason to use your own words. Go back and work some more."

Notice that during an active engagement, we do everything possible to set children up for success with the strategy we've taught. Typically, we do half the task, leaving the children with only the part of the task that is most pertinent to that lesson. In this instance, Harrison and I fed the children the data to draw upon in making their lists, and got them started with an initial claim that they could build upon with success. The examples we've provided could be channeled into a list of people who support Lupe, of times when the family supports her, or of places or ways in which the family supports her.

You will want to watch for times when children's work during the Active Engagement is not exactly what you want. You can intervene, coaching the class as a whole with more specific pointers, and let them have a second go at whatever you are hoping they practice.

After children had worked for a bit longer, I said, "Let's listen to the lists a couple of you suggest for Harrison." Soon we'd heard (and I'd charted) these lists:

- Lupe's brother gave her tips on shooting well, Lupe's father gave her lights for practicing in the dark, Lupe's mother gave her attention.

- Lupe's family gave her tips, materials, and interest.

- Her family did all they could. Her brother told her tips, her father rigged some night lights, her mother tried not to doubt her too much.

- Lupe's family supported her with tips on shooting low and with one eye, with lights for practicing late at night, and with observations of her thumb.

LINK
Remind children of the options they have when collecting material to support their topic sentences.

"Writers, today, and whenever you write literary essays, you'll draw on lots of different options as you collect material to gather in your files. Some of you may draft and revise *stories* to support your topic sentences, rewriting those stories so they are angled to make your point. Some of you will *summarize* a bunch of small sections that illustrate your point. And some of you will try your hand at writing *lists*, using parallel structure. You'll want to write several items for each folder today."

Types of Evidence to Support Claims
- Stories
- Summaries
- Lists

Try creating a list yourself before you read the children's ideas, because you want to be able to say to a child in a conference, "Might you want your list to go something like this?" and then get them started with the first two items in a list.

When you cite options, those choices should be on a chart, and you'll want to gesture toward the chart as you speak. Make it likely that children rely on it as a resource.

WRITING AND CONFERRING

Arguing on the Page

As you confer, be sure that you are helping children draw from their entire repertoire of ways to collect evidence. You'll want to begin every conference by asking the writer what he or she is working on. Richard looked up from Cynthia Rylant's story "Slower than the Rest" to say, "I am proving that Charlie matches the turtle 'cause they are both slow. I'm not sure if it is a summary or a story because it is a little of both." He showed me what he had written:

> Leo said that "It wasn't fair for the slow ones." This shows that Leo hates being slow. He thinks that it isn't fair for the slow ones. Leo talked about how there are great things about Charlie. He was really saying that even slow kids have things that they are good at. Charlie represented Leo and all of the other slow kids in Leo's class.

I asked Richard what he thought of what he'd written, and he said it was good but he had more stuff to say and hadn't figured out how to put it—whether it was a list or a summary or whatever.

"Richard," I responded, "you have just taught me something that I need to tell the kids. Because when I tell you about the different kinds of things you can collect in your files, I definitely do *not* want you to be so worried about whether you are writing this kind of thing or that kind of thing that you focus on the rules for how to write rather than on what you really want to say! I am so glad that your mind is fired up about this story. That is like you: You always are someone who pushes yourself to have smart ideas on any and every topic. That is a great gift of yours. Different people have different talents, and your talent is that you have so, so much to say. Never forget that."

Then, shifting from the compliment section of the conference to the teaching part, I said, "And I need you to know that another way to fill up your files is to talk on the page, saying whatever it is you'd say if you were arguing your point and wanted to be sure people understood your claim." To get him started and to test whether my advice would work, I said, "Can you and I just talk together a bit about this story— writers sometimes do that, we find a friend who is interested and we talk over what we are going to write. So tell me more about Charlie the turtle, representing Leo the boy, and them both feeling trapped. Is this story saying it is really awful to be slow?"

"Yes and no. 'Cause when Leo said that Charlie (that's the turtle) was sluggish, he said, 'It wasn't fair for

---

MID-WORKSHOP TEACHING POINT   ***Arguing and Collecting Like Essayists***   "Writers, can I have your eyes and your attention please? I want to remind you of something that the writer Philip Lopate said in his preface to a book entitled *Best Essays of 1999*. Lopate read thousands of essays in order to select the very best for his anthology, and from all that reading, he learned that very few things can be said about all essays. Essays are different, one from another. Some contain long narratives; some take inventory (like a shopkeeper takes inventory of merchandise). But Lopate does say that *all* essays are both arguments and collections."

"I want to suggest that all of you in this class are natural at doing both things. You argued very convincingly for an extra-long recess yesterday, in fact. And you are born

continued on next page

> Leo said that "It wasn't fair for the slow ones." This shows that Leo hates being slow. He thinks that it isn't fair for the slow ones. Leo talked about how there are great things about Charlie. He was really saying that even slow kids have things that they are good at. Charlie represented Leo and all of the other slow kids in Leo's class.

Fig. XI-1 Richard's notebook entries

the slow ones,' but he also talked about the good things for Charlie. 'Cause Charlie was a phenomenal turtle and he helped Leo win an award."

"So why do you think Rylant put a turtle in here," I asked, "and not a frog?"

"Because turtles are slow like Leo and she wanted Charlie to be like the slow kids."

"You mean, she wanted to use Charlie as a metaphor for the slow kids, so as to teach a lesson about slow kids not being only slow?" I replied, tucking some literary language into my retelling of what Richard had just said. Then I added, "You definitely need to write this." I pushed paper in front of Richard. Before he resumed work, I said, "You could start one entry, on one of these pieces of paper, by saying, 'You might ask, "Why did Rylant decide to make Leo a turtle?"' because essayists do that; we take other people's questions and put them right into our essays." This is what Richard gathered: [Fig. XI-2]

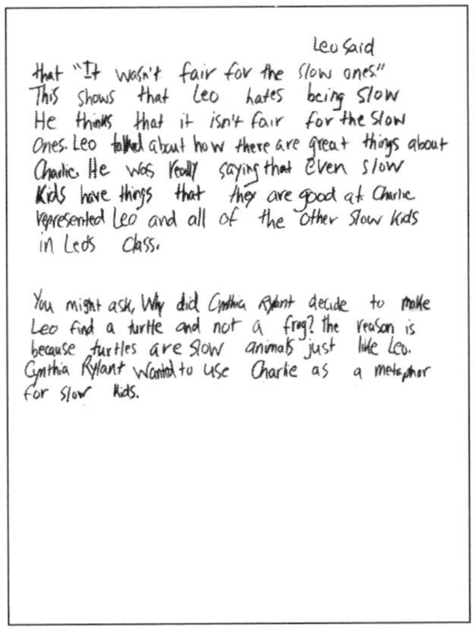

> Leo said that "It wasn't fair for the slow ones." This shows that Leo hates being slow. He thinks it isn't fair for the slow ones. Leo talked about how there are great things about Charlie. He was really saying that even slow kids have things they are good at. Charlie represented Leo and all of the other slow kids in Leo's class.
>
> You might ask, "Why did Cynthia Rylant decide to make Leo find a turtle and not a frog?" The reason is because turtles are slow animals just like Leo. Cynthia Rylant wanted to use Charlie as a metaphor for slow kids.

Later, when I saw Richard's work, I turned what he'd done into a brief Mid-Workshop Teaching Point, reminding Richard and all the other kids of a few things. First, sometimes they will simply have ideas pertaining to one of their claims, and it is a great thing to fill their folders with those ideas, not worrying whether those ideas are written as a list, a summary, a story, or whatever. And if a child wants to realize that he or she has lots of ideas, it can help to talk to someone about the story. Then, too, if people in those discussions ask us questions about our ideas, we can record the questions, and our answers to them. Often these make very strong additions to an essay.

continued from previous page

collectors—as is clear from the pins and badges on your backpacks, the songs on your iPods. Because you are already good collectors, could you look over your files and think, 'What else could I collect that might help me make my case?' Because as essayists, we especially collect evidence and ideas that will help us make our cases, win our arguments."

"In the end, an essayist is like a trial lawyer. You will go before a jury (yours will be a jury of readers) and you will argue for your claim. Adam will argue that Mrs. Price took her fury out on Rachel who, in turn, passed it on to others. Jill will argue that 'Eleven' is about a girl who struggles to hold on to herself. Many of you will make claims about other stories. Either way, each of you will each make an argument, and hope to be convincing. Like Perry Mason, you will present evidence to support your claim—and to do that, you need to collect! You need to decide what to collect, too; I have given you some ideas but in the end, you need to collect whatever ideas, facts, information, or observations can allow you to make your case. Right now, would you talk with your partner about the collecting you plan to do, and make yourself a planning box?"

Fig. XI-2 Richard's notebook entries

SHARE

Reading Lists Aloud

Gather children on the rug with their list work from today. Ask them to take a list they've written and practice reading it really well to themselves and to a partner.

"Writers often read their work aloud, so we can hear the words we've written, to hear how they sound—and lists especially are meant to be read aloud. So let's do this share like a symphony. Each of you, and your lists, will be a part of the music we create. So take a second and find, in your files, a list you wrote today that you really like."

"First, you need to practice reading your list aloud *really* well. You won't want to read it like this." I read the first part of my list very quickly, running the words together as if they were one word: "'Gabriel is lonely when he sits on the stoop outside his building. Gabriel is lonely when he eats his butter sandwich at school.' Instead I will want to read my list as if the words are worth a million dollars." (This time I read my list slowly and rhythmically— giving each word weight.)

"Practice reading one of your lists to yourself in your head before we begin," I said, and gave them a minute to do so. "Now would you work with your partner? Give each other help and advice, so each person's words sound as wonderful as they can be."

After a few minutes, remind children how the symphony works, and elicit their contributions.

"I'll be the conductor. When I gesture to you with my baton, read your list aloud in your best voice. Do this even if it is practically the same as a list we heard previously. Remember, in a musical symphony, the composer uses a repetition of phrases to make the symphony sound beautiful and resonate for the listener!"

I gestured to one child, then another, not in a round-robin fashion and not including every child. For example, I gestured to Judah and she read, "Lupe believes in herself to try and win those academic awards. Lupe believes in herself to work and try to become good. Lupe believes in herself to go to the game and win." Finally, I closed the reading by saying, "The music of words, Room 203."

Not only is this Share lovely and exciting for students, it also helps them develop a felt sense for parallelism in structuring language. Developing this felt sense makes teaching parallelism later much easier. Often, powerful language and powerful structures are easier to feel than to explain.

You may find that one child's lists resemble another's. This is not surprising considering they are working with the same short texts.

Saying Essays Aloud You've all heard the expression "Practice makes perfect." It's no secret that when you want to get good at something—anything—you need to practice. In the story "The Marble Champ," Lupe, a girl who's never been good at *any* kind of sport, proves that hours of practice can help her overcome the odds. She outshines even the expert marble players at the marbles championship. Lupe doesn't just *decide* to enter the competition and win, though. She spends hours each day for weeks and weeks exercising the precise muscle—her thumb muscle—to perfect the skill of shooting marbles.

It's impossible to master something all at once. Mastery takes time and practice, and practice involves steps. Singers sometimes warm up by singing some scales. Basketball players warm up by shooting some hoops. And writers sometimes warm up by talking in the voice, the persona, we want to assume. Sometimes before I write a minilesson or a letter to your parents, I practice by saying the words aloud to myself. When you wrote personal narratives, you practiced by storytelling to each other, trying to give each other goose bumps, but now that you will be writing a literary essay, you need to practice by using your professor voice.

Tonight, put a fresh sheet of paper in front of you, write your thesis, and write your first topic sentence. Then use your professor voice to fast-write a little lecture on that topic. Do the same for your second topic sentence. As you do this, pretend you are actually giving a little course on your topics. Bring your papers to school. They will be first drafts of your essays!

TAILORING YOUR TEACHING

If you find your children are stuck on old ideas or that the content of their writing isn't as complex as it could be . . . you might suggest that these children spend some time writing simply to think harder about their topics. Sometimes children are so caught up with the structure of essay writing that they don't spend enough time developing their thinking. Freewriting is a great way to get new ideas flowing, to ask questions and entertain answers, and to push thoughts forward. Specifically, children might ask themselves, "Do I believe what I've written?" "What have I not considered in all that I've said?" "Is the opposite of what I'm saying also true?"

If children are quoting whole paragraphs of text from the stories to support their claims . . . you may decide to teach them ways to use only exact, meaningful quotes to support their arguments. When children are first learning to quote, they may be tempted to replace their own writing with large portions of the texts they're writing about. Explain that using quotes often involves going back to the text and taking just bits of it to support, not replace, your argument. For example, a child arguing that Lupe's father in "The Marble Champ" is a supportive, proud father wouldn't cite Soto's entire paragraph on this, but would instead pick parts of it that highlight the thesis. Often this involves a bit of summarizing, interspersed with portions of quotes. Here is an example:

> Lupe's father is incredibly supportive and proud of his daughter. He sacrifices his Saturday racquetball game because "he knew his daughter thought she was no good at sports and he wanted to encourage her." He even goes out of his way to help Lupe practice at night, rigging lights in her backyard. It's clear that Lupe's father is not only supportive but also proud of his daughter because Gary Soto writes that Lupe's father is "entranced by the sight of his daughter easily beating her brother."

For an active engagement, children could take paragraphs such as the above and, in partners, talk about the use of quotation marks and summary to support a claim or topic sentence.

MECHANICS

If you collect your children's folders and pore through them, you'll see that this unit has posed new challenges to your children's command of conventions. You may decide to design minilessons and strategy lessons to address these challenges.

This is probably one of the first times your children will have been asked to craft literary essays. Just as kindergartners and first graders write with incomplete, approximate spellings when writing is new for them, your children will in a similar fashion write with an incomplete and approximate command of the conventions that accompany this form of academic writing. If you decide to address the most common problems that crop up in this unit, the following are some you'll want to highlight.

Past Versus Present Tenses   Your children will not know whether to write about a short story in present tense (because Gabriel, in the story, is still there on the page, holding his cat) or in past tense (because it was yesterday that the child read about Gabriel, and the child's life has moved on, and because the author wrote this book long ago). Some children may write in whichever tense the text is written.

When your children are in secondary school, they'll be taught that when retelling what they found in the pages of a story, they should generally use present tense. This is not usually the tense in which the story is written (stories are more often told in past tense). For this reason and others, your children will quite frequently shift between present and past tense as Max does in this summary:

> In the story, Rachel sits at her desk, staring at the red sweater Mrs. Price made her keep. She was disgusted with it, and wanted to cry like she is three . . . she then realizes that she was not just eleven . . .

Max will need to correct his summary to put it in the present tense:

> Rachel sits at her desk, staring at the red sweater Mrs. Price made her keep. She is disgusted with it, and wants to cry like she is three . . . she then realizes that she is not just eleven . . .

Transitions   Transitions can be tricky, but they are essential to the flow of writing, so make it a priority to help children understand them. Transitions are connections between two thoughts on a page. A transition can be a word, a sentence, or several sentences.

> One example of this is her saying Mrs. Price is older.

> And one more place is when she blabbed and stuttered to Mrs. Price when she wanted to say something.

> It is interesting how she says "because she's older and the teacher, she's right . . . "

> Other parts of the text where I see that Rachel thinks being eleven can be a let down are "You don't feel eleven . . . "

Pronoun-Verb Agreement   Pronoun-verb agreement becomes more complicated when the pronouns are indefinite. You may want to teach your most advanced students that words such as *anybody, anyone, nobody, no one,* and *neither* are all singular. It is correct to say, "Neither of his friends *is* going." When subjects are separated by *or* (as in Paul *or* Jerry) the verb must be singular (is going).

> Gabriel *is* a lonely boy who *wants* company.

> Gabriel and his cat *want* a home, but Gabriel *sits* on the stoop.

IN THIS SESSION, YOU WILL TEACH
CHILDREN THAT WRITERS STUDY THE
CHOICES AUTHORS MAKE IN THEIR
TEXTS IN ORDER TO FIND EVIDENCE
TO SUPPORT THEIR CLAIMS. YOU
WILL SUPPORT CHILDREN IN
LEARNING TO DO THIS.

GETTING READY

- "Things," by Eloise Greenfield
- Your own thesis and supporting folders related to "Things"
- Recording of a talk or lecture, demonstrating a "professor's voice"
- See CD-ROM for resources

USING DESCRIPTIONS OF AUTHOR'S CRAFTSMANSHIP AS EVIDENCE

Literary essays, historical essays, and personal essays all resemble each other. In each one, the writer articulates a claim and several subordinate ideas. To support their ideas, writers draw on anecdotes, quotations, lists of examples, and so forth.

One of the few features that set literary essays apart from other essays is this: Literary essayists pay attention to the author's craftsmanship and to the literary devices an author has used. That is, the writer of a literary essay notices not only what a text says, but also how the text creates emphasis and meaning.

In this session, you'll teach young essayists that they are wise to notice not only the content but also the craftsmanship of the text under study. The session could introduce a whole series of minilessons (teachers of middle school students may decide to stretch this one session into several). For most elementary school classrooms, however, it's enough to expose children to the notion that they will want to notice how an author uses literary devices to convey the deeper meanings in a text.

MINILESSON

Using Descriptions of Author's Craftsmanship as Evidence

CONNECTION

Celebrate that students have collected a variety of evidence in a variety of ways and have learned ways to connect it to their claims.

"Yesterday we talked about essays being collections. You all are natural-born collectors, so it is no great surprise to me that you have collected dozens of entries in your files. And the great thing is that just as you all collect a variety of songs on your iPods, and just as Harrison collects a variety of hats and Diana collects a variety of horse statues, most of you have collected a variety of evidence to support your ideas. Give me a thumbs up if you've collected ministories. If you've collected summaries? Quotes? Lists? I am glad you've collected such a rich variety of materials, because your essays, like quilts, will be more interesting if they are constructed from variety. But I am glad not only that you have learned to gather a variety of evidence to support your ideas, but also that you know strategies for collecting evidence in general. For example, you know to restate your ideas often, threading them in and out through your information. You know to angle your information so as to highlight the point you want to make. I'm starting to worry about whether I'll ever win another argument in this class, because you are definitely learning to be convincing!"

"In another day or two, we're going to piece together the evidence and construct our essays."

Name your teaching point. In this case, tell children that writers of literary essays pay attention to an author's craftsmanship techniques, trusting that authors use these techniques on purpose, hoping to highlight deeper meanings.

"Before we do this, I want to teach you that good readers pay attention not only to character development, to the author's message, and to ways in which texts speak to the issues of our own lives. Good readers also pay attention to literary devices. Good readers know that an author deliberately crafts a story—or any text—in ways that highlight the deeper meanings of that text."

COACHING

During the lead of a minilesson, we have a chance to help children recall what we've taught them. The way in which we recall previous instruction matters because we can make students feel as if prior lessons contained armloads of hard-to-remember, discombobulated instructions and directions—or we can make them feel as if our teaching had turned the light on in a new space, illuminating the way. By suggesting that children already love to make collections and that this is what an essayist does, I hope to help children feel at home with these strategies.

TEACHING

Show children that authors use literary devices to highlight what they want to say. Share your own thesis and folders related to a short and familiar text. Demonstrate rereading to study craftsmanship.

"I want to show you how I pay attention to what people refer to as literary devices, looking to see ways in which these literary devices support the message conveyed in a text. To show you this, I'm going to work with a poem you know well, 'Things,' by Eloise Greenfield ." (1978)

"I've already written and thought about this poem, and I've come up with a tentative idea, a tentative thesis: '"Things," by Eloise Greenfield, is a celebration of poetry.'"

"Things" celebrates poetry by showing that it is joyful, it reaches everyone, and it lasts forever.

"I've already made folders for each of my bullet points, and collected some evidence in my folders. Now I want to specifically look to see if the writerly devices Eloise Greenfield has used, the craft moves she's made, match the idea I have about her text."

"In my mind, I have a list of literary devices that authors sometimes use: language decisions (these include sound effects, dialect, incorporating words from another language, alliteration, and repetition) and comparisons (known as metaphors and similes)."

"Watch while I think about the language decisions Greenfield has made."

> "Things"
>
> Went to the corner
>
> Walked in the store
>
> Bought me some candy
>
> Ain't got it no more
>
> Ain't got it no more

"I notice that the narrator says things like 'ain't' and speaks in half-sentences, as when she writes 'went to the corner.' Before I read on, I'm going to think whether this language decision goes with one of my topic sentences," I said, as I scanned my folders and then the poem. Taking hold of one of my folders, I said, "The language decision to use casual talk *does* support the idea that poetry is for everyone. So I'll write an entry about this. Watch."

Of course, the way in which I went about forming my thesis involved reading the poem carefully and letting its literary devices work their magic on me. So it is not surprising that when I look back to see why the poem created the effect it did, I find that Greenfield used particular techniques. Perhaps in an ideal world, this minilesson might have come before the lesson on developing a thesis statement so that the sequence of instruction first conveyed the idea that readers attend closely to the choices authors make, and grow ideas about the text from this close, analytic reading.

There is nothing subtle or complex about my ideas. I think that when I'm demonstrating, it's helpful to choose examples that are extraordinarily clear.

Picking up a marker pen, I wrote on chart paper:

> The way that Eloise Greenfield wrote "Things" shows
> that she wants to convey that poetry is for everyone.
> She doesn't use fancy, elitist language. For example, she
> says "Ain't got it no more" instead of "I'm not still in
> possession of the candy."

To the children, I said in an aside, "Notice that to describe the craft decisions Eloise did make, I mention other choices she did not make."

"So let me think about another literary device: comparison or metaphor. Hmm . . . I better read on":

Went to the beach

Played on the shore

Built me a sandhouse

Ain't got it no more

Ain't got it no more

Went to the kitchen

Lay down on the floor

Made me a poem

Still got it.

Still got it.

"She doesn't *exactly* compare things, but . . . hmm . . . she *does* line up three things—building a sand castle, buying candy, and writing a poem! So it's sort of like she compares them. In a way, she's saying writing a poem is like eating candy or making sand castles. And that's comparison! That's metaphor! And it goes with my idea that she makes poetry seem joyful. So now, I could write an entry on that."

"I've still got to think whether there is craftsmanship that supports the idea that this poem is a celebration of poetry—and I bet the evidence is here!"

I use a very brief and familiar poem because the concept I am teaching is a complex one, and I think couching it in this well-known poem makes the lesson itself more accessible.

ACTIVE ENGAGEMENT

Set children up to work with partners, looking for other literary devices the author you have been examining used. Help children see how the author's use of a literary device supports one of your ideas about the text.

"Why don't you try it? Take repetition, for example. See if you find instances of it, and then ask, 'Did Eloise Greenfield use this literary device in a way that supports the idea that poems are lasting, joyful, and for everyone?' If you find evidence that Greenfield's use of repetition supports this view of the poem's message, then tell your partner what you'd write about this." The children did this.

"I heard many of you say that it's probably important that she repeats 'Ain't got it no more, ain't got it no more' and the contrasting line 'still got it.' And you felt this *does* go with the idea that 'Things' is a celebration of poetry. Smart work."

LINK

Send children off, reminding them that they now have yet another way to collect evidence supporting their idea.

"Usually I'd tell you that you have lots of optional ways to collect evidence to support your ideas, but tomorrow we're going to move on to actually write our essays, so it's important that you spend today doing one of two things. First, if you have a folder that is somewhat empty, try to gather some material for that folder, or check whether the idea is really arguable. You may want to eliminate it. And second, you will definitely want to pay attention to literary devices."

There is absolutely no question that Eloise Greenfield's use of repetition helps to convey her messages, so I definitely have set children up for success in this Active Engagement. As usual, I use the trickier examples in my demonstration, leaving for students the work that is bound to work for them.

The work you teach today is important enough to the genre of literary essays that you'll probably want to insist children look at ways in which an author's craft supplies the text's meaning. This work definitely merits more than a day—extend the work if you can!

WRITING AND CONFERRING

Supporting the Study of Craftsmanship

You won't be able to spin among your children fast enough to reach them all today, and most of them would profit from some scaffolding and encouragement. Therefore, I suggest you convene small groups of children who are studying the same text. Each child will have his or her own unique angle, of course, but they can help each other apply the new lens to their text.

Once you convene a group, you may want to teach them that instead of scanning the text, hoping a craft move or literary device will pop out, saying "Here I am! Look at me," it can help to almost arbitrarily take a passage and think, "I'm *sure* there are literary devices and craft decisions within this paragraph. Let me read very, very closely to find them, and see whether they support my claim."

"Let's pretend that your claim for an essay on 'Eleven' is that Cisneros is actually writing about how and why she became a writer. Your claim is that Cisneros has written an essay that celebrates the importance of writing."

"Zoom in on any paragraph. Let's take the top of page two":

> Not mine, not mine, not mine, but Mrs. Price is already turning to page thirty-two, and math problem number four.

Show children that you squeeze your mind and try to come up with something to say about the way Cisneros has crafted this sentence. Let the children see that you at first feel speechless. "Umm . . . well . . . it's long!" Let the children see that you are tempted to brush your first thought aside but resist. "The sentence is not just long, it also has lots of parts. 'Not mine, not mine, not mine' is what Rachel is thinking. But there isn't a period at the end of it. Instead the sentence keeps going, almost as if it is a run-on sentence, and at the end of it Mrs. Price is ignoring Rachel, turning to page thirty-two."

MID-WORKSHOP TEACHING POINT

Using Descriptions of Authors' Craftsmanship as Evidence

"Writers, can I have your eyes and your attention? Writers, I'm seeing amazing insights. It's as if your minds are on fire. Listen to what you've discovered!"

"Max says that because Cisneros wants to emphasize that when you are one age, you are also all the ages you've ever been, she stretched all those other ages out into a long repeating list, saying, 'When you are eleven, you're also ten, and nine, and eight, and seven, and six, and five, and four, and three, and two, and one.' She could have just said, 'You are all the other ages,' but instead she stretched out what she means by being other ages."

"The way Max thought about what Cisneros *did do*—by considering choices she *rejected*, alternatives she opted against—is really smart. I suspect others of you will borrow that strategy."

"Ali wrote that Gary Soto uses lists in the beginning of the story to convey the point that Lupe has been a winner. For example, she's 'the school's spelling bee champion, winner of the reading contest three summers in a row, blue ribbon awardee in the science fair, the top student at a piano recital and the playground

continued on next page

"I'm realizing that Cisneros sometimes uses long, run-on sentences, and in this instance, she does so in a way that shows that Rachel's voice gets lost in her teacher's actions."

You'll want to show children that you shift between very close reading of the text and consideration of your claim. "Now how might this connect to the idea that this is an essay about writing? Hmm . . . Maybe Cisneros' sentence structure reinforces the idea that Rachel feels voiceless? Rachel's thoughts get lost in this long sentence that ends up being all about the teacher's actions and decisions. Perhaps 'Eleven' is not just the story of Rachel but also of Sandra Cisneros and how she struggles to find and claim her own voice. Perhaps the story culminates in the fact that Cisneros gets the last word in. She—that's Cisneros but also Rachel—perhaps *does* find her voice because look—she's writing this essay! She's gotten the last word in, even if at the time Mrs. Price rolled right over her."

You'll need to demonstrate this in an efficient manner so that the conference is not a soliloquy. Shift soon to a second passage, and suggest that children assume there's a craft move in that paragraph that relates to each child's different thesis. (Of course, this may prove incorrect, but that is unlikely.) Then support children in identifying that move.

---

continued from previous page

grand chess champion.' Soto wants readers to notice that although Lupe has excelled in many areas in her life, she has not been good in sports."

"Judah wrote: 'I notice the way that Gary Soto uses lists in the beginning of the story really carries through the point that Lupe was no good in sports. For example, "she could not catch a pop-up or figure out in which direction to kick the soccer ball." This is a place where Gary Soto uses a list to show some things that Lupe tried but never succeeded in.'"

"Both Ali and Judah noticed that Soto uses lists to emphasize his point that Lupe was good at many things but not at sports. I know that many of you will be noticing when authors use lists to prove a point."

"Harrison noticed that Soto also uses repetition, like 'Tried again and again' and 'Practice, practice, practice, squeeze, squeeze, squeeze,' to show the character's determination."

"So writers, if at first you don't notice literary devices that support your idea, look again, more closely. Look at what the author did and didn't do, as Max demonstrated. Pay attention even to something as clear as repetition, as Harrison did. And notice more craft moves that merit attention so we can add them to our list, just as we added Ali and Judah's observations about using lists for emphasis."

SHARE

Taking a Teaching Tone

Tell children that essayists sometimes write in the voice of a teacher, a professor. Set children up to talk in groups about how a teaching voice differs from a storytelling voice.

"Tomorrow you'll begin drafting your literary essays. You'll recall that before we wrote stories, I told you that the author Robert Munsch tells his stories at least a hundred times aloud before he writes them. We all did a bit of storytelling in our narrative units, and I think that helped us write in the voice of a storyteller."

"When we write essays, we need to write in the voice of a teacher, a professor. I know you tried this last night. Before we try it again, I want to teach you a bit about how to write and talk in a professor's voice. I tape-recorded a professor who was on television last night, giving a little lecture on bird migration. I want you to listen for just a second to her teaching voice, the explaining voice she uses. Jot down phrases you notice, phrases that go with the role. For example, she says, 'Notice . . . .' Imagine how she stands, too, and imagine her relationship with her readers, her audience. Jot notes on what you notice. After I play a bit of the tape, I'm going to ask you to talk in groups of four—two partnerships can clump together—about ways in which this woman's teaching voice seems different from a storytelling voice."

Share some of the children's observations with the class and then have children teach each other their ideas.

We did this, and I listened to what children said. Convening the class, I said, "Many of you pointed out that the teacher seems to be trying to be clear. You said that even though you couldn't see the written version of her words, you still sensed that she was speaking in paragraphs because she talked on one clear topic, then the next. You said that you could almost imagine her holding up fingers to say, 'My first point is . . . ,' 'My next point is . . . .' You said that she came right out and spoke to her listeners, saying, 'It is important to notice . . .' and 'You may ask why . . . the reason is . . . .'"

"Now I'd like you to take a few minutes of silent time to get ready, and then I'm going to set you up to act as professors, teaching each other your ideas."

"Follow your essay plan. You can lay materials out in front of you to help you remember what you want to say, but don't read your entries. Instead, say aloud what you might write—and then say more. Add on. Elaborate."

Obviously, as these units of study unroll and you come to know your particular class of children better and better, you'll use your own experience with previous units to inform your work in this unit. If it has been incredibly helpful to set children up to say what they'll eventually write, you may have brought this share activity into an earlier session. If your class was chaotic last time you tried this, you'll anticipate the potential problems and tweak my words so they channel your children in productive ways.

Notice that in this Share, I ask children to engage in table conversations involving two partnerships. You may decide to invite these larger conversations often.

Considering Purpose in Crafting In today's session, you learned that it is important to notice not only what an author has written about, but also how that author has written, noting ways that the author's craft supports his or her message. This minilesson could launch another whole bend in the road of our unit. But time is short. Let's extend today's lesson at least for tonight, however. One way to do this is to reread the text under study and to notice what the author *did* do by noticing what he or she did *not* do!

When you and I write our own stories, we make choices about what to expand and what to skip past. We look over our own writing and think, "What is the heart of the story?" and then we stretch out that part. The authors of these texts that you are reading have made similar choices. They write with a lot of detail about some things, and bypass others altogether. So one way to learn what matters to an author is to think, "What has this author written about with extensive detail? What has the author skimmed past? And how might this support the author's real message?"

For example, we can look at Rylant's story, "Spaghetti," and we can ask, "What's missing here? What has she seemed to pass right by?"

I notice, for example, that Rylant doesn't say why Gabriel is lonely, or why he is sitting by himself. I think we are supposed to get the idea that he is homeless and to infer that this means he doesn't have any friends. So I think Rylant is trying to sort of push poverty and loneliness together, blurring the line between them, making them into one overlapping category.

Once I have developed and written this thought, I need to decide which folder can best hold this thought, and then I'll file it just as I have filed other bits I have collected. If I want to hold on to the thought and it doesn't fit under any category, I will make myself a file titled "Other."

Tonight, will you reread the story you have been studying, and notice what your author has developed and what the author has skimmed past? Notice the details that are missing. Does one character not have a name? Is there a feeling in the story that is never really explained? Once you have noticed what's missing in the story, ask yourself, "How does the author's decision reflect the message of this story?" Write your thoughts, one on a page, and file those thoughts.

If you decide that your children are ready for a challenge . . . you might extend this session. As part of this, you could help them know that specialists in an area usually know and use specialized vocabulary. A chemist refers to valence and isotopes. A person who studies literature, too, has a tool chest of terminology and many of these terms are words we can use to describe authors, ways-with-words. You might begin by reviewing terms that children know but may not always incorporate in their essays. They should identify the text's genre by name, refer to the speaker as the 'narrator' and describe parts of a text using terms such as 'stanza' for poetry, 'climax' or 'resolution' for story.

Children probably know terms such as metaphor, but may not know and use terms such as alliteration, image, assonance or hyperbole. In a single minilesson, you wouldn't want to dump fifteen terms on top of your kids, but you could definitely stress that they can convey that they are experts by using the specialized terminology of this field.

If you decide to extend this minilesson another day . . . you could teach children that when trying to surmise why an author made a decision to write in a particular way, they'll be conjecturing. That is, many children will notice that an author has done something, and not feel confident that they can discern *why* the author wrote as he or she did.

Children need to be encouraged to guess. Teach them that no-one *knows* the answer. The difference between a person who is a very skilled literary essayist and a person who just sits there saying, "I don't know *why* Soto did that," is not that the first has more facts, more knowledge. The difference is that the skilled literary essayist is willing to surmise, to speculate, to conjecture, to hypothesize. That is, this is a person who is willing to think, 'Could it be that he does this because . . . ?"

Of course, once we make a tentative guess as to why an author could have decided to write in a particular way, we think this through. One way to do this is to ask ourselves, "How *might* he have written this? What different effect would he have created had he written it in that manner?" Then, too, we can say, "Is there any other evidence to suggest this might be why the author did this?"

Teach children that reading and thinking about literature is not altogether different than being a crime solver. We see what looks as if it could, possibly, be a clue and we speculate . . ."Could it be?" Then we look for more clues, hoping to see a pattern.

COLLABORATING WITH COLLEAGUES

It's essential that you and your colleagues take time to study the ways that craftsmanship can convey meaning in a text. You might choose several stories to read together to examine the variety of ways in which writers use craft to reveal meaning. You might, for example, look at "Spaghetti," and notice how Cynthia Rylant uses soulful, plaintive sounds—"the slow lifting of a stubborn window ... the creak of an old man's legs ... the wind"—to describe how Gabriel envisions the kitten's cry. Some people feel that implicit in these imagined sounds is the loneliness and longing Gabriel hears in the kitten, and feels himself. Rylant also uses repetition here: "It could have been ... it could have been ... it could have been ... But it was not." Does this not show how vivid an imagination Gabriel has, how he spends so much time in his own mind that he can imagine not one, not two, but three sounds he might be hearing?

You could next study "Eleven" by Sandra Cisneros. You might study the author's use of comparisons. About growing older and turning eleven, Rachel says, "Because the way you grow old is kind of like an onion or like the rings inside a tree trunk or like my little wooden dolls that fit one inside the other, each year inside the next one. That's how being eleven years old is." What do you make of the fact that the comparisons Cisneros has Rachel make are to physical things in her world that she can touch and see? They are also all layered things—circles and shapes that fit together—why might Cisneros have chosen those things? In another simile, Cisneros has Rachel compare the sweater to something from her world of childhood, calling the sleeves "all stretched out like you could use it for a jump rope." Why that image? What specific purposes do you suppose it serves?

There are many more literary devices you might notice in these or other stories: metaphor, alliteration, consonance, hyperbole, analogy, to name just a few. Why might the author have chosen to use these devices right where she does? What purpose does it serve? Bring the thoughts you and your colleagues come up with about these texts back to your students and share the thinking that led you to them.

Sometimes, studying literary devices can lead essayists to further evidence to support their claims. If the reasons we think authors have chosen specific comparisons and images don't fit with our claims about the story as essayists, what then? Sometimes, close reading of the story, of the crafting an author has done, may lead essayists to revise their thesis statements. If this happens to you or your colleagues as you study a text in depth, be sure to bring that story to your young essayists!

GETTING READY

- Enlarged copy of first two paragraphs of Jill's essay from in Session IX
- Copies of Jill's essay for each child
- See CD-ROM for resources

PUTTING IT ALL TOGETHER:
CONSTRUCTING LITERARY ESSAYS

When I was younger, a singing group named The Byrds sang a song—"Turn! Turn! Turn! (To Everything There Is a Season)"—and the refrain went like this:

> To everything—turn, turn, turn
>
> There is a season—turn, turn, turn
>
> And a time for every purpose under heaven

Those words mean a lot to those of us who are writers because in writing, as in farming, there is a rhythm to our work. The farmer plants, waters, weeds, and harvests, and the writer plans, gathers, outlines, drafts, revises, and edits. This ancient rhythm is in our bones; we remember it like a river remembers its seasonal rise and fall.

I hope the rhythm of writing is in your students' bones now as well. I hope that your students remember it, and can sense that the time has come to turn, turn, turn.

Today you'll help your children perform that miracle of miracles. They'll begin with a pile of folders and that will turn, turn, first, into a writer's version of solitaire. Throughout the room, your children will sort through their material, deciding what to keep and what to discard. Then they'll turn, turn again. With scissors and tape, they'll place one entry next to another, constructing an essay. They have a feel for how to do this by now—it's in their bones.

Also today, you will remind writers about that special kind of reading that writers do. You will teach them, first, to read the work of another author, one who has written something similar to the essay they'll be writing. You will teach them to look over this other writer's work, thinking, "How has she constructed this text? What has she done with her text that I, too, can do with mine?"

Also, you will teach your students to critically reread the notes and entries they've accumulated, scrutinizing their own drafts of stories, lists, and reflections in order to say "yes" and "no" to each bit of their material. You will teach them to read with imagination, too—with the imagination that allows them to envision ways in which one piece of thinking can be linked to another, and another, creating a path of thought. There is a tall agenda for today!

MINILESSON

Putting It All Together: Constructing Literary Essays

CONNECTION

Celebrate that children are ready to construct their literary essays.

"Writers, yesterday, you and your partner spent time talking about the material you have collected. You pretended you were literature professors, teaching each other about your theories. You took on the voice of teachers, of professors; you gave little talks to each other about your theories. That was your dress rehearsal: Today's the day!"

"You no doubt can already feel that this will be the day to draft your literary essay. And you no doubt can recall this day from our earlier unit of study on the personal essay. I bet you recall how, in the space of a day, you went from having scraps of paper to having a draft of an essay. It was like magic. Presto! That same magic will happen today."

"I do not need to teach you that you will open up the file you want to write first, lay out the contents, and sift through all of the stuff you have collected, thinking, 'What should I throw out?' and 'What should I keep?' I do not need to teach you that you'll tape one bit of data alongside another."

Name your teaching point. Specifically, tell children that before constructing their raw material into essays, it's useful to read other writers' work, examining what works well.

"Today I want to teach you that writers take raw materials and piece them together to form a coherent essay and that writers especially need to be strong, smart readers. One kind of reading that writers do just before we make a draft is this: We read the work of other writers, asking, 'What has she done that I, too, could do?'"

COACHING

It is a bit harder to rally children to step into the role of being literary essayists. They know fiction writers or poets, and aspire to create texts like they create. Still, it's important to try to help children know that they are not just producing a text, they are also becoming the kind of person who makes this sort of text.

I am hoping that by listing all that I do not need to teach children, referencing appropriate visuals for each stage that I mention, I manage to remind children of those very things! That is, while saying, 'I do not need to teach you this,' and 'I do not need to teach you that,' I allow myself to quickly review both. In art—and teaching must be an art—selection is crucial. Although I mention in passing what I hope children already know, I highlight the one new goal for today—and it is contained in my teaching point.

You could look back across the series and locate half a dozen other similar teaching points. One challenge in teaching writing is that the strategies we talk about are more easily said than done, and therefore our teaching will often revisit what we taught earlier. If we simply repeated the same minilessons six times, students might well tune us out, so we're always working to find ways to make old ideas feel new enough to be noteworthy.

TEACHING

Demonstrate that before writing a draft of an essay, it helps to look at an example and box the parts, noticing how it is put together. Use one child's draft to model this.

"When I was your age, my sister and I loved jigsaw puzzles—the more pieces the better. Every Christmas we would ask for a harder, more intricate puzzle than the year before. After unwrapping our newest challenge, we would clear off the round table in the corner of the living room and start to discuss our plan. First, we'd dump out all the pieces and turn them right side up. Second, we'd separate out all the 'edge pieces.' Third, we'd each pick a side that would be our responsibility. Fourth, we'd study the picture on the cover of the box and build the frame."

"Once we had accomplished those steps, we would still spend hours sorting the remaining pieces into piles. We often consulted the picture on the cover of the box to see where the pieces might go best, and then we would slowly piece together the puzzle. Sometimes we were determined that certain pieces went together and we would push and push until they lay flat and looked liked they belonged. Each night after dinner, my father would come and survey our progress. He would compliment each of us on the work we had accomplished, but he also always seemed to notice the one or two spots where my sister and I had forced pieces together that didn't fit smoothly. He'd ask, 'How do these two pieces fit together?'"

"When your audience reads your work, they will be piecing together your essay and asking themselves, 'How does this part fit with the part I just read?' They will be thinking about your thesis statement and combining it with one bit of evidence, like two puzzle pieces, and then with another bit of evidence, like more pieces of a puzzle. So you need to be smart about how you piece your bits together."

"Specifically, before you begin to piece together your essay, it is helpful to look at another author's essay and to examine how it is constructed. Let me show you how I go about doing this. I'm going to study the first section of Jill's essay—remember, you worked with this essay earlier in this unit. I want to study Jill's first body paragraph, because today you'll each write a body paragraph or two. So let's study the ways Jill pieced together that paragraph." I used an overhead projector to enlarge Jill's opening paragraph and her first body paragraph, and read it aloud. *[Figs. XIII-1 and XIII-2]*

> In my life, not everything ends up like a fairy tale. I like
> to read books where characters are like me. They
> don't live fairy tale lives. We have the same kinds of
> problems. Many people read Sandra Cisneros's essay
> "Eleven" and think it's about a girl who has to wear a

Over the sequence of units, I've used a variety of metaphors to depict this process. I've likened the writer's work to the work of a builder, a quilt maker, and now a person who constructs jigsaw puzzles.

sweater she doesn't want to wear. But I think the story is about a girl who struggles to hold onto herself when she is challenged by people who have power over her.

When Rachel's teacher, Mrs. Price, challenges Rachel, Rachel loses herself. One day, Mrs. Price puts a stretched out, itchy, red sweater on Rachel's desk saying, "I know this is yours. I saw you wearing it once!! Rachel knows that the sweater isn't hers and tries to tell Mrs. Price, but Mrs. Price doesn't believe her. Rachel reacts to Mrs. Price's actions by losing herself. "In my head, I'm thinking ... how long till lunch time, how long till I can take the red sweater and throw it over the school yard fence, or leave it hanging on a parking meter, or bunch it up into a little ball and toss it over the alley?" This shows that Rachel loses herself because she's not listening to her teacher, she's dreaming about a whole other place. It is also important to see that Rachel has all this good thinking about the sweater but when she wants to say the sweater isn't hers, she squeaks and stammers, unable to speak. "But it's not," Rachel says. "Now," Mrs. Price replies. Rachel loses herself by not finding complete words to say when Mrs. Price challenges her.

"Okay, I'll first box Jill's thesis:"

> I think "Eleven" is about a girl who struggles to hold onto herself when she is challenged by people who have power over her.

"I'm noticing that Jill begins her first body paragraph with her topic sentence, the one she had probably written on the outside of her folder, her first bullet point." I said, circling that section of the essay as I read it aloud again,

- When Rachel's teacher, Mrs. Price, challenges Rachel, Rachel loses herself.

"Then Jill tells the story of how Rachel loses herself (how she struggles to hold onto herself) by not being able to speak up and tell her teacher that the sweater isn't hers. Jill thinks that when Rachel tunes out of class, sitting in the room dreaming of ways she might get rid of the sweater, this shows that Rachel is losing touch with herself." I circled those several sentences where Jill summarized that part of the text. "Let me see how Jill connected

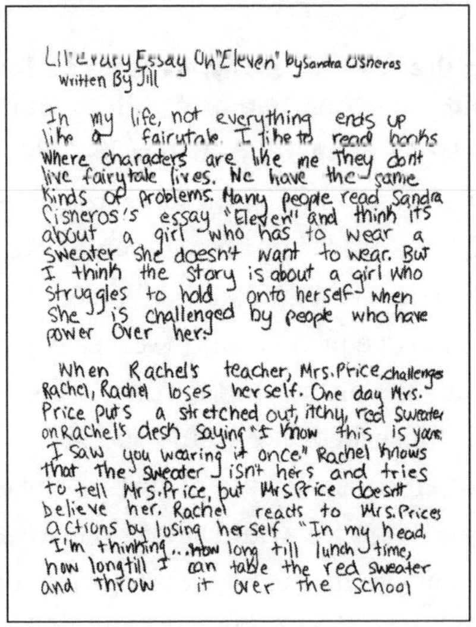

Fig. XIII-1 Jill's final literary essay, page 1

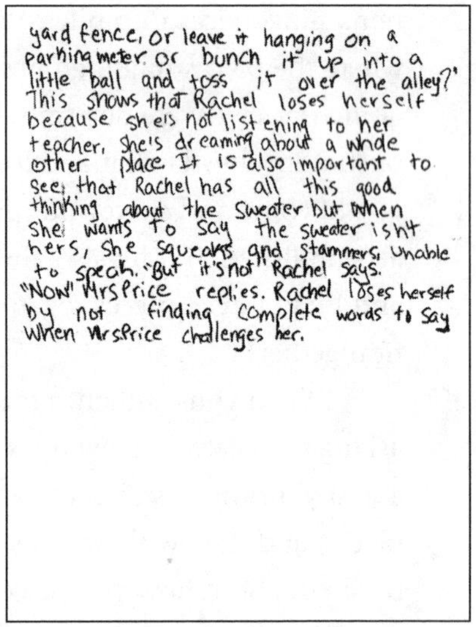

Fig. XIII-2 Jill's final literary essay, page 2

Of course, literary essayists often structure essays differently than this one. For example, essayists often entertain points of view other than their own, writing, "Some might argue differently . . . " and then providing a counter-argument. Then, too, essayists often compare and contrast the one text to other texts, or to life. The actual components you teach aren't especially crucial, and I encourage you to make your own decisions, taking into account the standards in your region.

her topic sentence to this example, this story that illustrates her point—oh! After her topic sentence, Jill just jumped right into this story with only the connector words 'One day' to signal she is telling a story." I underlined the words 'One day.'

I continued to reread:

> This shows that Rachel loses herself because she's not
> listening to her teacher, she's dreaming about a whole
> other place.

"I'm noticing that Jill has 'unpacked' how this example refers back to her topic sentence. Do you see how she does that? She explains how the little story about Rachel dreaming of ways to get rid of the sweater relates to her topic sentence, doesn't she?"

Then I reread the next bit of text:

> It is also important to see that Rachel has all this good
> thinking about the sweater but when she wants to say
> the sweater isn't hers, she squeaks and stammers,
> unable to speak. "But it's not," Rachel says. "'Now,' Mrs.
> Price replies.'

I pointed to the chunk of text, rereading it several times to myself. "What point is Jill making here, I wonder? What kind of evidence is this? Oh! Now I see! Jill is pointing out that Rachel's actions highlight the fact that Rachel loses herself. Rachel had lots of thoughts but when she went to talk, Cisneros made it so Rachel couldn't get words out, she only stammered. How does Jill connect that bit of evidence to her paragraph? Ah-ha, she uses the transition 'It is also important.' I'll underline that so we remember she used a connector for that bit of evidence too."

"Does Jill explain that bit of evidence too?" I read on:

> Rachel loses herself by not finding complete words to
> say when Mrs. Price challenges her.

"That's Jill explaining her evidence again, isn't it? Yes, she is saying exactly why that part of the story supports her point, just like she did the first time she had evidence."

ACTIVE ENGAGEMENT
Ask children to work in partners to study and label what the author has done to construct her second paragraph.

"Now it is your turn. Would you sit with your partner and study Jill's second paragraph? Do as I did, noticing each sentence and thinking, 'What is this? Is it a story? A list? A discussion of the writer's craft moves?' Would you pay special attention, as I did, to

This may be more detailed than your children can handle. If so, select the items you want to showcase. Alternatively, you can analyze just the start of this paragraph before sending children off to do the same for the start of the next paragraph, continuing with both paragraphs in the Mid-Workshop Teaching Point.

You always have the option of using this brief interval as a time for children to help each other get started doing whatever you've just taught them to do. So you could say, "Let's get started on our own essays right away," and then ask children to lay out the materials from one of partner 1's files, and begin to think about which material needs to be eliminated because it doesn't align with the claim, is repetitive, and so forth.

how Jill makes her transitions from one bit of data to another, and to the times when she unpacks the data she has just shared? Mark up the text of Jill's essay that I have given you and label what it is that Jill has done. Notice what Jill has done that you could also do when you build your body paragraphs." *[Fig. XIII-3]*

> When Rachel's classmates challenge Rachel, Rachel loses herself. Sylvia Saldivar puts Rachel on the spot like when she says to Mrs. Price, "I think the sweater is Rachel's." Sylvia is challenging Rachel, she is being mean and she makes Rachel feel lost. Rachel cries to let her emotions out. Rachel feels sick from Sylvia. Rachel tries to cover herself up by putting her head in her sleeve. Tears stream down her face. She doesn't feel special like it's her birthday. Instead, she feels lost in Sylvia's challenge.

Children may notice that in the sentence, "Sylvia is challenging Rachel, she is being mean . . . " Jill has listed all the bad things Sylvia does to Rachel. The reader feels as if there is a giant pile of evidence because Jill writes this as a list. Then again, Jill writes another list, this time cumulating all the ways in which Rachel acts distressed in response to what Sylvia has done. The paragraph ends with a sentence which returns to the thesis.

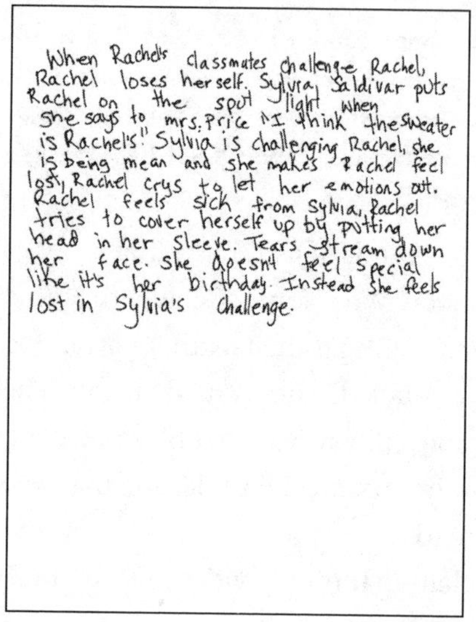
When Rachel's classmates challenge Rachel, Rachel loses herself. Sylvia Saldivar puts Rachel on the spot light when she says to mrs. Price "I think the sweater is Rachel's." Sylvia is challenging Rachel, she is being mean and she makes Rachel feel lost, Rachel crys to let her emotions out. Rachel feels sick from Sylvia, Rachel tries to cover herself up by putting her head in her sleeve. Tears stream down her face. She doesnt feel special like it's her birthday. Instead she feels lost in Sylvia's challenge.

Fig. XIII-3 Jill's body paragraph

I gave children a couple of minutes to do this. "You've done some really good thinking and decision-making."

LINK

Set students up to review the contents of their folders, deciding what to include and how to sequence the information within each of their paragraphs. Ask them to decide which bits need to be revised.

"So writers, today you will want to reread Jill's essay, thinking again about what she has done that you could also try. I have given you a copy of it. And from this day forward, always remember that when you go to write something, it helps to study—to analyze—similar texts that other authors have written."

"After you study Jill's essay, you will be doing the work that you know how to do. You'll take one of your folders, and you'll spread the contents out before you. Then you'll reread each bit that you have collected, deciding, 'It this really powerful evidence? Is this something to include?' Keep in mind the overall shape you intend to follow in your essay. You'll need to decide how to sequence the information within your paragraph. Finally, you'll need to decide whether all that is required is some tape—or whether bits of information need to be revised before they can be put into your essay. Off you go!"

WRITING AND CONFERRING

Making Parts into a Cohesive Whole

As you confer with young writers today, you can predict that you'll need to show them how to write sentences that link their bits together into a cohesive whole. For example, when I pulled my chair alongside Harrison, he had spread before him the contents of a folder titled, "Lupe overcame difficulties through hard work." He had two micro-stories in his pile. One read:

> Lupe lay in front of her shelf full of academic trophies and medals. She wished there was at least one trophy that showed that she could do sports – but there were none. She decided that she would work hard, day and night, to win a marble tournament.

Another story began:

> Lupe came home from school and immediately tossed down her backpack and got out her marbles . . .

Harrison's first job was to decide on the sequence of his stories, and he decided these would follow the order I just described. His next job, then, was to link his topic sentence with the start of his first story. If he simply stapled these alongside each other, they'd read:

> Lupe overcame difficulties through hard work.
> Lupe lay in front of her shelf full of trophies.

I told Harrison, "You need to set readers up for the story by coming right out and explicitly telling us that this story pertains to Lupe overcoming difficulties through hard work. Then I said, "I could imagine it might go like this," and I wrote-in-the-air to give Harrison a sense for sure of his options. "Lupe decided to work hard and become a marble champ one day when she lay . . ." or "Lupe didn't just become a marble champ by luck or talent. She worked hard to become a marble champ. This hard work began one day when . . ."

Harrison needed less help building a bridge between the one story and the next. I simply reminded him that generally writers use transition words such as these:

MID-WORKSHOP TEACHING POINT   *Piecing Together Evidence*   "Writers, once you've selected a few pieces of evidence that you believe should be brought together in one of your body paragraphs, you'll want to use a stapler or transparent tape to literally piece together a rough draft of your essay. Use a sheet of notebook paper as your foundation, and leave space between the assembled bits so that you can write transitional sentences that link your various pieces together. We'll learn more about how to write those transitions tomorrow, but have a go at them if you can, and in any case, leave space for them."

"As you construct your essay, keep in mind that you are arguing for your claim. You may be claiming that Cisneros believes that growing up is hard. If that's your belief, then you need to think, 'How can I really drive my point home?' Sometimes, you'll realize that the material you've collected doesn't really speak as forcefully as you'd like, and so sometimes you'll decide to put one of your notes on the corner of your desk, and you'll pick up your pen and say exactly what you meant to say all along. Don't hesitate to do this. None of the early reading and thinking and writing and collecting will be wasted, because all of that good work has brought you to the place where you are now."

- Another example
- Not only did she . . . but she also . . .
- Later
- Furthermore

I told him, "I just take one, try it out to see how it sounds and fits, then take another."

I also find that children need lots of encouragement letting go of materials. If they've collected four stories, three quotes and a few lists, they want to stick all of those together to make a gigantic paragraph. Over and over I find myself reminding children that they can't revisit the same material three times in a single paragraph, first, and furthermore, that in general less is more. "Choose the most compelling, best-written material," I say. "Decide which evidence will be especially convincing."

Then, too, when conferring with children today it's important to think about the help they'll need editing their essays so that the instruction we give in the ensuing days can be as targeted as possible.

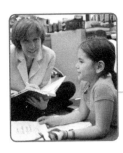

SHARE

Rereading as a Means to Revise

Advise writers to stop and to revise as they construct their essays.

"Writers, it's been exciting to see you sort through your materials, and begin constructing your essays. Look at what a change Adam made today!"

Adam's thesis began like this: *[Fig. XIII-4]*

> Some people might think "Eleven" is about a girl whose teacher yells at her to put on an ugly red sweater. Really it is about how Rachel has to cope with her teacher who won't listen to her.

He then revised it in this way: *[Fig. XIII-5]*

> In literature, authors write a lot about one character being upset and taking it out on another person. Sandra Cisneros' essay, "Eleven," is about a girl named Rachel who is mistreated by her teacher and in return mistreats her classmates.

- Rachel is mistreated by her teacher.
- In return for Mrs. Price mistreating Rachel, Rachel then goes on to mistreat her classmates.

"He realized his evidence was supporting a different thesis from the one he' d written. You could either continue sorting, selecting, and assembling until you've constructed all your body paragraphs, or you can pause midway to look over your work and revise it. I tend to suggest pausing earlier, rather than later, because I think if we not only construct but also revise one paragraph before proceeding on, we can avoid making the same mistakes twice. Today, let's use our share session as a time to read what we've assembled with critical eyes so that we leave school with a plan for revision work we need to do at home tonight."

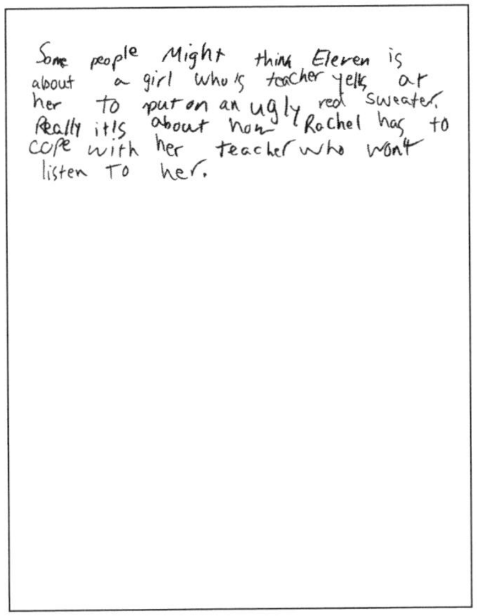
Some people Might think Eleven is about a girl who's teacher yells at her to put on an ugly red sweater. Really it's about how Rachel has to cope with her teacher who won't listen to her.

Fig. XIII-4 Adam's first thesis

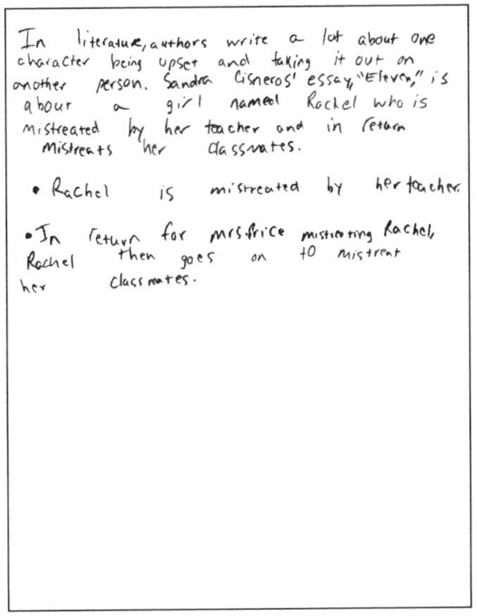
In literature, authors write a lot about one character being upset and taking it out on another person. Sandra Cisneros' essay, "Eleven," is about a girl named Rachel who is mistreated by her teacher and in return mistreats her classmates.

• Rachel is mistreated by her teacher.

• In return for mrs. Price mistreating Rachel, Rachel then goes on to mistreat her classmates.

Fig. XIII-5 Adam's revised thesis

Advise children of some predictable problems writers encounter when constructing essays. Ask children to help each other reread and revise.

"Would you and your partner look at first one person's writing and then the next person's writing. Reread the section that you assembled today and as you read, would you check for a couple of the predictable difficulties that essayists often get ourselves into, and see if you've encountered any of this trouble."

"First of all, sometimes we find that we have collected so much evidence that each paragraph in our essay could be three pages long! Harrison, for example, has at least two pages of evidence showing that Lupe overcame her difficulties through hard work. If you're in Harrison's predicament, you can be very selective, choosing only the most compelling evidence."

"Meanwhile, however, keep in mind that you can write several paragraphs to support one of your ideas. So Harrison's thesis is that Lupe overcomes her difficulties through hard work and support from her family. If we wanted to do so, Harrison could show that Lupe received support from her family early on, and then again later—and these could be divided into two paragraphs. Or Harrison could tell in one paragraph about the support she received from her father, and in another paragraph, about the support she received from her brother. So in the end, you may have two or three paragraphs supporting each of your topic sentences."

"Then too, it is important to reread a rough draft essay checking for clarity. A stranger should be able to read the essay and understand it. Sometimes, for example, a reader will be unclear over the pronouns. 'Who is he?' the reader might wonder. Every writer needs to be able to shift from writing to reading, and to reread our work looking for places which will be confusing, and those places need to be revised for clarity."

"So writers, take some time to reread your own and each other's work, checking to be sure you've selected the most compelling and pertinent evidence, written in shapely paragraphs, and that you've been clear."

⊙ HOMEWORK *Revising for Strength and Clarity* Writers, tonight you have an opportunity to revise the draft that you assembled in school today. Revise it first for power. You are writing an essay that aims to be persuasive. You'll be most convincing if every portion of your argument is fresh, new, and compelling. So read over the bits of evidence you've collected, and decide whether some sections of it seem redundant or unnecessary. Do what any skilled writer would do—and cross those out. Then look at the evidence which is compelling and convincing enough to remain in your essay and think, "How can I make this even stronger? Even more convincing?" Finally, double check your draft for clarity. If you can rope someone from home in to listening, read your draft aloud. Notice where you stumble as you read, or when your words no longer feel like they are reaching your listener. Revise these places, aiming to be precise, clear and convincing!

TAILORING YOUR TEACHING

If your children need more time to construct and revise their body paragraphs . . . which is very likely, you might teach them that they, as writers, need to do their very best work before passing the draft on to you for final corrections.

Don Murray, author of *A Writer Teaches Writing*, once told me the story of a senior editor at a publishing company who sent his people out to do some writing. "Bring your articles in on Friday," he barked.

Friday came, and the writers brought drafts to the great editor. He collected them in a folder, then tucked them in his briefcase, saying, "Come in on Monday morning and we'll discuss these."

Monday came, and the writers assembled. Pulling the folder of drafts from his briefcase, the editor waved them in front of his team, asking, "Was this your best?"

The writers shifted uneasily from one foot to another, looked at their feet, shrugged. One said, "I tried but . . . " Another said, "Mine started strong but . . . "

Brushing aside their excuses, the editor said: "Take your drafts. Make them your best. Bring them back tomorrow at 3:00 p.m."

The next day came and again the great man collected them. Hours later, he again convened the team and again asked sharply: "Was this your best?" And again, their excuses were met with a wave of dismissal. "Take these then, and this time do your best."

That Friday, he again collected the papers, and this time, after he collected them, he turned to his team. Holding the stash of drafts he said, "Now for the third time, I ask you—'Is-this-your-best?'"

The people looked him in the eye and said, "Yes."

"Good," the editor said. "Now I'll read them."

In the same way, your children need to do their very best before they bring their drafts to you for help. Use this story to remind them that it is the writer's job, not the editor's job, to make the text the very best that the writer can possibly make it. Then the editor can make the best, better.

If your children need help constructing a coherent text out of the bits and pieces they've collected . . . then you'll probably want to spend another day helping them to grasp the big picture of how literary essays go. You might decide to do this by teaching children how writers go about writing "instant essays," a lesson your children will probably need to learn anyhow as part of test prep.

You might alter the normal schedule of the day, keeping children with you in the meeting area for a collaborative work session. Give them each a copy of a text—and teach them that after reading a text, a literary essayist thinks, "What interesting idea do I have about this text? Is it one that pertains to the whole text?" Writers can try asking some of the questions we generated earlier, or can simply read the text and think, "The thought I have about this is . . . "

Say the text was "Papa Who Wakes Up Tired in The Dark" from Cisneros' *House on Mango Street*. Show children that you come up with a claim: "Although this text focuses on one moment, it uses that moment to show the whole of the narrator's life." Then push yourself to say how the text does this, or the reasons why it does this: "It does this by portraying the narrator's father and by revealing many of her family traditions."

In a similar manner, show children how a writer drafts a very quick literary essay. Let the children do the work of finding a story—or example—to build each topic sentence. Show them that often writers link two stories with some connections. Encourage children to quote a section and then unpack that quotation.

You'll only need to do a single paragraph together as a class, but this work should remind children of the overall task they're doing as they assemble their pieces into a draft. Remind them, too, that when writers decide to write a new draft of a chunk of material rather than merely stapling things together, this is cause for great celebration.

MECHANICS

You'll need to decide when and how you want to help children turn their rough drafts into final pieces. It is likely that you'll need to build another day or two into your unit of study, and that you'll read students' work in progress outside of the writing workshop, correcting some aspects of it, leaving other work to be done during and after editing conferences.

Most of the editing help children will require for this unit will not be unique to the unit. That is, they'll still be working on spelling, punctuation, logic, clarity, and the rest. But there will be a few issues that are unique to the genre, and I want to help you with these.

First, as I mentioned earlier in this session, you'll find that children want to include everything but the kitchen sink in their essays. If they collected four examples to illustrate that Jenny, in "Boar Out There" has created a mythical idea of the boar, they'll want to include every example. You may find it helpful to suggest an ideal length for your children's literary essays so they have more motivation to select.

If you have a chance to do so, you'll find that children's essays benefit enormously from tightening, from consolidating. I doubt if you could easily convey the art of this in a minilesson, but you could certainly gather a small group of children together and show them that a three-page-long typed essay can become two and a half pages without actually losing any content at all. One way to consolidate texts involves eliminating redundancy using lists.

Harrison, for example, had written:

> Lupe overcomes her difficulties by squeezing an eraser 100 times. She overcomes her difficulties by doing "finger ups" for finger strength. She also overcomes her difficulty by practicing after dark even when she could be tired.

He took out redundancy, so now his draft read:

> Lupe overcomes her difficulties by squeezing an eraser 100 times, by doing "finger ups" for finger strength and by practicing marbles even after dark.

You'll also find that children need lots of help with citations. This is a time to review the conventions around quotations marks, but also you'll want to teach children how to pick and choose the most pertinent sections of a citation, using ellipses in place of the irrelevant material. For example, Judah wanted to show that Lupe changes from the start to the end of the story. She found sections of the story that suggested that at first, Lupe wasn't strong. She was "a shy girl who spoke in whispers" and her thumb "was weaker than the neck of a newborn chick." In the sentence I just wrote, notice that following Judah's lead, I excerpted only the tiny sections of "The Marble Champ" which made the point Judah wanted to make, and notice also that I needed to write some words that set up the excerpts. Judah must do similar work.

Let me explain more clearly. A child may want to show that Lupe encountered frustration when she first tried to play marbles. The child might identify this sentence from the text as relevant:

> She tried again and again. Her aim became more accurate, but the power from her thumb made the marble move only an inch or two.

If the child's topic sentence was: "Lupe battles frustration," the child can't simply attach the citation to the topic sentence, or the resulting text would be confusing:

> Lupe battles frustration. "She tried again and again. Her aim became ..."

In your editing conferences, then, you'll need to teach children that writers tuck explanatory information into our sentences. This, of course, asks children to not only recognize places where more information is needed but also to have the linguistic dexterity to tuck subordinate clauses into texts:

> Lupe battles with frustration. One day, after pouring marbles onto her brother's bed, she set to work trying to flick one marble at another. "She tried again and again. Her aim..."

As you meet with children in one-to-one and small group conferences, remember that your children will probably be brand new at the complex work of inserting text references into an essay. They need not master this! Teach those who seem ready the gist of this work, and be ready to do as any editor might do and to insert a phrase, add a sentence into a draft. The final texts need to make sense, and when working with this brand new and challenging aspect, you'll find that some children need your help in order to make their texts comprehensible.

PACKAGING AND POLISHING YOUR LITERARY ESSAYS

IN THIS SESSION, YOU'LL PASS ALONG SOME TRICKS OF THE TRADE WHICH WILL ALLOW CHILDREN TO TAKE THEIR ROUGHLY CONSTRUCTED ESSAYS AND MAKE THEM LOOK MORE PROFESSIONAL. SPECIFICALLY, YOU'LL SHOW THEM WAYS TO WRITE INTRODUCTORY AND ENDING PARAGRAPHS, TO IMPORT SOME SPECIALIZED LINGO, AND TO HANDLE CITATIONS WITH MORE FINESSE.

GETTING READY

- Examples of leads written for secondary school essays
- Example of one child's process for writing and revising a lead, using an essay children have studied
- See CD-ROM for resources

Just as stories often rely on traditional beginnings, so, too, literary essayists can draw on the traditions of their field. When high school and college students are taught to write essays on Hamlet and Beloved, teachers tell them to begin their essay with a few sentences which situate this essay within its larger context. Interestingly enough, this is exactly what I do in minilesson—in fact, in this very paragraph! My writing is shaped like a funnel. First I talk abut texts in general, then narrow in to talk about the lessons older children are taught about literary essays. If you keep reading, you'll see that I continue funneling you, my reader, in toward the specific point I plan to make today. Specifically, today I try to teach children to write opening sentences which gesture toward situating their essays within larger contexts.

I also show children that once they've written an introductory passage, it's easy to write a corresponding closing passage, suggesting that it's 'no-big-deal' to write these components of a literary essay.

Finally, I invite children to spend any extra moments polishing their essays. They'll especially learn more about making citations and about using the specialized jargon of literary scholars.

MINILESSON

Packaging and Polishing Your Literary Essays

CONNECTION

Orient children by telling them that once they've constructed rough body paragraphs, they need to package and polish their essays. One way to do that is to write an introductory paragraph.

"Today, some of you will finish selecting and combining the bits that will make the mosaic of your first, second, and perhaps third body paragraphs. Once literary essayists have written, selected, and roughly combined the evidence to support our claims, then it is time to think about packaging and polishing our essays. One way we can do this is to write introductory paragraphs that prepare readers for our thesis statements (the thesis traditionally ends the first paragraph of a literary essay, setting readers up for what will follow)."

Remind children that they already have a repertoire of ways to start a narrative.

"You already know that narrative writers have a host of ways to begin stories. Sometimes narrative writers and storytellers begin by showing the character in action: 'I grabbed my sneakers and ran barefoot across the beach.' And sometimes narrative writers begin instead with dialogue': "Race you to the water," I said, and, grabbing my shoes, ran barefoot across the beach.' Some begin with classic story openings: 'Once upon a time' or 'Once, long ago' or 'One day, not long ago.'"

"Earlier this year, you also learned templates that writers of personal essays sometimes find helpful. You learned that essayists sometimes find it helpful to begin an essay by showing their journey of thought, saying something to the effect of, 'I used to think . . . but now I realize . . .' or 'I once believed . . . but recently I've come to think that . . .'."

Name your teaching point. Specifically, stress that literary essayists often write leads that contain broad statements about literature, life, stories, or about the essay topic. The introductory paragraph aims to put the essay into context.

"Today what I want to teach you is this. Literary essayists are usually taught to begin an essay by putting this particular essay and/or this particular text into context. We write a generalization about literature or stories or life—one that acts as the broad end of a funnel, channeling readers so they are ready for the specific point we set forth in our thesis."

COACHING

Chances are very good that children will need another day of composing their essays before they are ready for you to help them with their introductory paragraphs. Don't teach this lesson if few are ready for it, or your instruction will fall on deaf ears. Instead, use the extensions or your own sense of what your children need to provide another minilesson to help them go from folders to drafts.

Refer to the panoramic view at the start of some movies, and to the way the camera later zooms in on a single character, making his or her way through that larger context, to help writers sense the function that lead paragraphs often play in literary essays. Share examples of leads written for secondary school literary essays.

"You know how some movies begin by panning the whole landscape and then the camera seems to zoom in on some specific place—perhaps a winding country road—and eventually, we see an old man cycling down that road. In a similar fashion, literary essays often begin by panning the whole landscape and then the camera zooms in. But in a literary essay, the landscape is not a hilly countryside and the camera doesn't zoom in on a single road. Instead, when a literary essay begins with a wide view, it often means the essay says something general about how literature tends to go, or about stories, or about life. Of course, the writer says something that provides the big-picture context for this particular essay, this particular journey down a road of thought."

"You will learn a lot more about this when you are in middle school, high school, and college. Let me read to you three leads that my sons wrote for their high school essays. Remember, these were written by high schoolers, so they will be complicated, but see if you can sense how they begin broadly, talking about big topics, and then funnel down to the particular theory that the essay will develop."

- The desire for love and for money has motivated much of human history. Western literature is filled with novels which address the conflicting feelings a woman and her family feel when the woman must decide between marrying a man she loves and marrying a man who can provide for her financially. Many of the characters in Jane Austin's novel, *Pride and Prejudice*, personify one view or another of the advantages and limitations of marrying for love rather than for money.

- Some researchers suggest there are stages to accepting death or great loss. These stages include denial, anger, and finally acceptance. Characters in Chris Crutcher's book, *The Crazy Horse Electric Game* go through these stages as they deal with a great loss in their lives.

- I am a lacrosse player. When decisions must be made in the heat of a game, our coach has always told us that the worse thing to do is to stall. It is always better to make a decision, however bad it may be, rather than to freeze in indecision. When I first heard this advice, I was skeptical. Now, after reading Shakespeare's *Hamlet* and Heller's *Catch-22*, I understand the wisdom of my coach's advice. A bad decision is always better than no decision at all because every decision leads to some amount of progress, even if the progress comes, as in *Hamlet* and *Catch-22*, from mistakes made and lessons learned.

Here is another example, one I chose not to read aloud but which also makes the point: The headlines of recent newspapers spotlight our nation's desperate search for justice. Did our president knowingly deceive us about Iraq's weapons of mass destruction in order to take us into war? Was the office of the vice president involved in criminal deception to the grand jury? Questions about right and wrong are basic to what it means to be human. In the tragic play Hamlet, *Shakespeare explores this fundamental aspect of life. The play suggests that, in a world filled with corruption and betrayal, it is difficult to live as a just man because our information is inevitably fragmented and because a person who walks this path is doomed to loneliness, unsure of whom to trust and therefore alienated from the world.*

Tell the story of how one child went about writing the lead to a literary essay that the children have already studied. Highlight the steps taken, including asking, "What is my essay really about?" and brainstorming a variety of choices.

"When Jill worked on her essay, she had already written her thesis:"

> Many people read Sandra Cisneros's essay 'Eleven' and think it's about a girl who has to wear a sweater she doesn't want to wear. But I think the story is about a girl who struggles to hold on to herself when she is challenged by people who have power over her.

"So she began with the idea that 'Eleven' tells the story of a girl who struggles to hold on to herself. Jill asked herself, 'What is the broader context—the larger landscape of kinds of texts—that this belongs in?' To answer that question, Jill needed to think about what she wanted to highlight in her essay. She could have said her literary essay about 'Eleven' was really about voice, or about girls, or school, or about people who struggle over power differentials. And depending on which of these she chose, she might have put her essay into a different landscape. Jill decided that she wanted to highlight—to pop out—just the idea that Rachel *struggles*. Jill gathered a cluster of friends and together, they brainstormed a bunch of possible lead sentences that each talk about the big picture of characters and their struggles. They suggested these were possible leads:"

> • Whenever I watch a movie, I know there will come a part when the music changes and I need to worry about the character. That part is sure to come because in the movies, as in all stories, characters struggle.
>
> • My life is full of problems. Everywhere I turn, it seems that there are problems. When I read stories, I realize I am not alone. Characters in books, too, struggle with problems.
>
> • In school I learn from lessons that teachers teach but when I read stories, I learn from problems that characters encounter. When I see how people in books face their problems, I become better at facing my own problems.

"In the end, Jill wrote this as her lead:"

> In my life, not everything ends up like a fairy tale. I like to read books where characters are like me. They don't live fairy tale lives. We have the same kinds of problems.

To write a lead to a literary essay, it helps to be able to look at some thing—any item, really—and think of it as one instance of a larger category or class of items. In a small group, you may have to give some children practice at shifting between specifics and generalizations. Earlier I mentioned that you could teach children to realize that a fork is one instance of the more general category of a piece of silverware (or a tool for eating). A cat is one instance of the more general category of family pets or the feline category of animals or of companions. A rug could be thought of as a floor covering, a decoration, or a way to warm one's house. Help children see how in each of those instances, the thinker is shifting between a specific—a cat, a fork, a rug—and a generalization. Similarly, if one's thesis claims that "With determination and hard work, Lupe overcame her problem and became a marble champion," the author needs to think, "What is this an instance of?" The author might generate a list of possibilities, such as:

> • *In life, all of us face problems. The ways in which we respond to these problems reveal a great deal about our inner character.*
>
> • *Stories usually contain a character who yearns for something, and struggles to achieve his or her motivations.*

ACTIVE ENGAGEMENT

Ask children to join you in thinking of the lead for the class literary essay by first thinking of the essay's larger landscape. Ask them to work with partners to generate lists of possible leads.

"Let's try writing introductory paragraphs by thinking about the lead to our essay on 'Spaghetti.' Remember, we first need to think about the general topic that our essay addresses, and we have some choices. The thesis is 'Gabriel is a lonely boy who learns from a cat that he doesn't need to be lonely anymore.' So we could say this is an essay about cats as companions (though I doubt that is really the main thing the essay addresses). Could you talk with your partner and generate a few other possibilities for the general topics? If you don't think this essay advocates cats as companions, then what general category would you file it under?"

The children talked, and soon I called on a few for suggestions.

"The essay could fit under the category of essays about animals that make a difference."

"The essay could fit under the category of characters who learn from surprising teachers."

"The essay could fit under the category of characters who change their attitudes."

"The essay could fit under the category of characters who feel as if they are misfits and find a way to belong."

"To write a lead for this 'Spaghetti' essay, we first need to decide which of these will provide the larger landscape for our essay, and that is up to us. Which do you choose?" I asked, and soon the class had decided that the essay would fit under the broad category of characters who learn a lot from animals. Once that choice was made, children worked with partners to brainstorm options, generating a list of several possible leads. In no time, the first paragraph was completed.

> Pet lovers know that animals are not just cute and companionable. They can change a person's life. In Cynthia Rylant's story "Spaghetti," Gabriel, a lonely boy, adopts a stray cat and learns that he doesn't need to be lonely anymore.

LINK

Remind writers that they now have a process they can go through to write a lead paragraph for a literary essay. Summarize the steps of the process.

"So writers, when you have combined your material into a rough draft, you will want to begin packaging and polishing your essay. One way to package your essay is to work on an introductory paragraph. When doing so, begin by asking, 'What general themes might this essay address?' and come up with some options, as we did. Then, once you have decided on the landscape in which you want to set your essay, try different ways to draft a lead, and then choose one from those options. This is good work for you to do today, and whenever, in your life, you need to write a literary essay."

As practice for teaching literary essays, you and your colleagues may want to try imagining how you could turn these other options into possible lead sentences. When I coach children to do this, I sometimes bring out a pretend violin, puff my chest up, wave my arms, all in an effort to convey the sweeping, grand tune that many writers assume when writing a lead. Let's take, 'characters who learn from surprising teachers' as a case in point. For a lead, I might start:

> Throughout my life, I've had the opportunity to learn from many remarkable teachers. Few, however, have taught me as much as my scruffy little English cocker, Tucker. In Rylant's short story . . .

or

> Great teachers come in many shapes and sizes . . .

or

> Life is full of lessons, and oftentimes teachers come from surprising places.

or

> We attend school in order to learn from teachers, but many of us find that our most important teachers are those we stumble upon when we least expect to find them.

You'll need to decide on the actual logistics involved in helping children go from rough to final drafts. Can you ask children to use word processors and type their drafts at home, allowing you the opportunity to reread and edit them? If many of your children don't have access at home to computers, they'll need to write a rough draft at home, and in school, and then you'll still need to take their drafts home, edit them, and give children time to make final drafts. The scheduling of all this must be in your hands.

WRITING AND CONFERRING

Unpacking Evidence

I pulled my chair alongside Tyler, who had laid six or seven slips of paper out across his desk and now sat, immobilized in front of the intricate design. "What's up?" I asked.

"I got my first sentence," Tyler said, "and my evidence. But I don't know how to combine it so it goes."

"What's giving you trouble?" I asked.

"My big idea is that 'Eleven' isn't really a story. And I'm on the first reason—because it doesn't have a problem and a solution," Tyler said, then pointed to the lines he'd cited as proof:

> Mrs. Price says, "That is enough nonsense. Put the sweater on."
>
> "But"
> "Now"

Could also say:

> When Mrs. Price said, "Of course it's yours. I remember you wearing it," Rachel couldn't say anything. Her power was taken away from her.

"So why do you think it is hard to combine these?" I asked, but Tyler didn't have an answer.

"Tyler," I said. "Do you remember that when I taught you to collect mini-stories that illustrated your big idea, I told you that after you tell the story about one time, then you need to unpack the story, showing how it relates to your big idea? You need to say something such as, 'This shows that . . .' and 'This is important because . . .' Well, I'm realizing that I should have taught you that in fact writers 'unpack' almost any evidence that we include in an essay. And I think the reason you are struggling to combine your claim and your evidence is that you haven't really unpacked your evidence yet." Then I added, "What I mean by 'unpacking' the evidence is that you need to be able to take a quotation from the text (like those you have copied) and you need to talk about how that quotation serves as evidence for your point." Then I urged Tyler to take hold of one of his notes. "Hold this," I said, and talk to me about how this bit of evidence goes with the point that you are trying to make."

MID-WORKSHOP TEACHING POINT   *Revising for Clarity and Cohesion*   "Writers, can I have your eyes and your attention? Earlier today I pointed out that after you have assembled a rough draft of your essay, you will want to begin packaging and polishing it. I gave you some pointers for how to write a lead paragraph, and later I will do the same for a closing paragraph. But meanwhile, it is also very important that you read over your draft and work on creating something called cohesion. Cohesion means stickiness, but I don't mean you need to pour glop on your essay to make it sticky! Let me explain what I do mean."

"Earlier, I read you leads to literary essays that my sons wrote when they were teenagers. The really odd thing about grades 7 through 12 is that practically the only genre my sons wrote in was literary essays! So I tried to learn everything I could about that genre from their teachers, because it is not a kind of writing I see a lot in the world."

"I won't forget the day I was walking down the school corridor with the chairman of Ridgefield High's very fine English department, and she said to me, 'The students really struggle with essays. And we are all clear about what the hardest thing is for them.' She continued walking and my mind raced through all the possibilities: Was the hard part

continued on next page

Tyler read aloud his evidence:

> Mrs. Price says, "That is enough nonsense. Put the sweater on."
>
> "But"
>
> "Now"

"This shows she's really mean and gets mad?" he said, his intonation suggesting this was more of a question than an answer.

"Tyler," I intervened. "Remember, your point is, 'Eleven is not really a story,' and one reason for this has to do with Mrs. Price saying,'That is enough nonsense.' How does that show that this isn't really a story?'

"Cause she keeps on getting mad at Rachel, she never stops," Tyler said.

"So Tyler, that is important. The way you'd write this, then, might be like this," I said, and started to write in the air:

> "Eleven" is not shaped like a story because stories usually have problems and solutions, and in this text, there are problems but those problems don't have solutions. From the start of the text to the ending of it, Mrs. Price doesn't listen to Rachel. That problem never goes away, it is never solved. Even towards the end of the story, when Rachel protests, she only gets to say, "But" before Mrs. Price . . ."

Then I said, "So Tyler, when you go to glue bits of evidence together, remember that you need to unpack the evidence. You need to talk about how that particular bit of evidence goes with the main point you are trying to make."

The next child I approached was Judah, who had already written a draft and was rereading it. She'd written this:

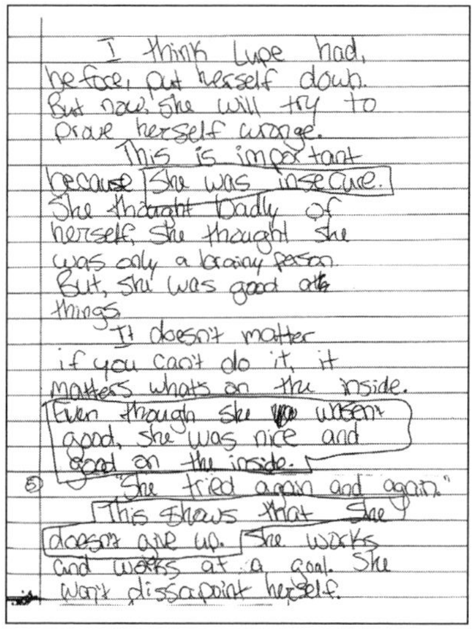

> I think Lupe had before, put herself down. But now, she will try to prove herself wrong.
>
> This is important because she was insecure. She thought badly of herself, she thought she was only a brainy person. But, she was good at things.
>
> It doesn't matter if you can't do it, it matters what's on the inside. Even though she wasn't good, she was nice and good on the inside.

developing insights about texts? Writing with correct control of conventions? Studding their essays with ideas? Then the department chair finished her sentence.' Yep, the hardest thing for all of them is writing transitions'.

"At that point in the conversation, we arrived at wherever she was going—I don't recall now where it was. But I do recall that she abruptly left me at that point. And I stood there in the hall, trying to get my brain around what she had just said. 'The hardest thing of all is writing *transitions*?' I thought. I wondered how that could possibly be, and frankly, I still wonder. But meanwhile, I want to be sure you understand transitions—because transitions are indeed one important way in which you can make sure that all the parts of your essays stick together."

"Strong essayists don't just use tape to combine our bits and pieces together to make an essay. We also use words. Sometimes the words function as bridges between one bit and the next one. In these instances, writers often use phrases that act as glue: *for example, another example, furthermore*. But writers also create cohesion with repetition. If I want to show that Gabriel is lonely, when I describe him sitting on the stoop, I will come right out

continued on next page

Fig. XIV-1 Judah's draft

She tried again and again. This shows that she doesn't give up. She works and works at a goal. She won't disappoint herself.

"So what are you working on?" I asked Judah.

"I got a draft started. I'm putting everything together and writing what I think about her," Judah said. "It is coming really good because I have most of a page already."

"How do you feel about what you've written?" I asked.

"Good because she is really good, she just doesn't know it," Judah answered.

"Judah," I pressed. "When I asked how you thought about your draft, I was really wondering how you think of this as a literary essay. Your answer was focused more on how you feel about Lupe. What do you think of this as a draft of a literary essay?"

"Good?" she asked, unconvinced.

"You don't sound too sure," I responded, "and that is okay. Because this is the first literary essay that you've written, so you are just figuring out now what makes a really good essay. There are a couple of things that matter a lot in a literary essay. Why don't I remind you of some of the criteria, and then you look over your draft and think, 'Do I have that already, or is that something I want to work on?' Okay?" Judah nodded.

"An essay always involves a claim. The writer needs to come out and say an idea, and readers should believe the idea matters to the writer," I said. "Do you think you have done that?"

Judah nodded. Then I pressed on, "And an essay needs to back those claims up with evidence that is convincing. Essayists often write with big ideas and then specific examples. Do you think you've done that?"

Judah reread her draft, her eyes scanning back and forth across the page. "I think I left that out," she said. "I have it but it is in my folders." I nodded, agreeing with her, and pointed out that sometimes in life when we are really persuaded of something, we assume others will buy into our ideas. But we always need to remember to be as persuasive as possible.

---

continued from previous page

and say that he is *alone*. I could describe his fantasy of sleeping out with the coyotes without using the term *alone*, but I will use that exact term—I will say, 'Gabriel imagined himself sleeping *alone* under the stars, surrounded only by wolves '(or even, by the *lonely* cry of wolves). I will do this because I know that repetition can act as a cohesive tie, as word glue. And when I have been giving a sequence of examples, I will sometimes remind readers that the upcoming example is just one more in a whole chain of examples. I might say, 'Not only does Gabriel sit alone on the front stoop of his building and think of sleeping alone among the coyotes, he also wanders alone down the street.'"

"I suspect that one reason high school students still have trouble with transitions is that it is not easy to teach how to use words to tie an essay together. But I can tell you that it helps to reread your essay, trying to make it sound like it's connected. Sometimes as I read aloud, my voice tells me places where I can add cohesive ties. Then, too, I think it helps to read over your essay and pay special attention to the breaks in your text, and see if you can use words as tape to help with those breaks. Write in a word or a phrase, but reread the whole draft to see if your addition actually sounds right and works. And definitely, get your partner or someone who has not yet seen your draft to read it over with you, pointing out little places where the pieces of your text—like pieces of a puzzle—don't yet fit smoothly."

SHARE

Writing Conclusions

Tell students that literary essayists craft their conclusions with care. List some choices writers have for their conclusions.

"Something terrible happened to me last night. I was watching a television show–an enthralling one. I kept wondering how it would all come together at the end . . . and it never did. Suddenly, the words came onto the screen "'To be continued . . .'"

"Has that ever happened to you? It's an awful feeling, isn't it, to be left in the lurch?"

"So I want to take a few minutes to remind you that your essays need endings. You'll probably want to try three or four endings(just like you often try three or four leads)."

"Remember that we learned that literary essayists begin their essays with a generalization about literature or life in order to set up the broader context for stating a particular thesis about text? Well, the conclusions you write are just as important as the beginnings for similar reasons. Literary essayists conclude their essays by reconnecting to that broader context, leaving readers with something to think about, to linger over—to carry around in their minds and perhaps to revisit later on, in discussion with others."

"The conclusions you write matter especially because they are the last impression that your readers will be left with. The conclusion puts forth the final thoughts you want to emphasize about the text you have read. Remember that you have choices. For example, Judah returned to her thesis, emphasizing why the claims and evidence she used support that thesis. Adam linked the essay to himself, sharing the lesson he learned from reading the text. Both students, of course, made sure their conclusions still related to that broader context they introduced at the beginning of their essays."

"Constructing your essay is like constructing a building. All your hard work will be for naught if you have only a strong foundation and sturdy floors, but no roof! So, tonight, you will need to reread what you have drafted today and then make a strong final statement about your journey of thought."

HOMEWORK *Using the Language of Literary Scholars*   Writers, we looked at some of the leads that high school students used for their literary essays. I know you aren't in high school yet, but I'd like to teach you one trick that can make your essays look as if you are in high school! This is the trick: Your essay will look much more professional if you use the tools of your trade.

This is true for any endeavor. My niece and nephew raise and breed chickens. They are eight years old—they are twins—but they want to be taken seriously by other poultry breeders so they can purchase good birds from them, and sell their birds for a good price. As a result, when Abigail and Hugh write and speak to adult poultry breeders, they use the words of their trade. They say things like this: "This bird has strong coloring on the undercoat, and its vent is clean and pink." Or they'll say to a breeder, "We are looking for a good showmanship bird, one with smooth legs and a good head." They answer inquiries by saying, "We have a hatch in February for the Rhode Island Reds and in April for the Call Ducks."

If you want your literary essays to be taken seriously, you need to use the words of your trade. The main character, as you will recall, is the *protagonist*. The text is written in the voice of the narrator. The start of the story is its *lead*. You might describe a story by speaking of its *setting*, *plot*, *theme*, or *tone*. Tonight, read over your draft and see if you've used the words available to you, and make sure that you have included the vital information in your essay—the title, genre, and author's name of the text you are examining.

TAILORING YOUR TEACHING

If your students are having a hard time writing introductory paragraphs . . . you might enlist the whole class's help to create one for a story children know well. Take a simple, childhood tale like *Cinderella* or *Jack and the Beanstalk* and prompt children to think of large, familiar themes. Tell children that the themes of fairy tales are repeated throughout literature. *Cinderella*, for example, which explores the notion of good triumphing over evil, and, more precisely, someone with little power triumphing over someone with significantly more, is mirrored in *The Lion, the Witch, and the Wardrobe, Peter Pan, Skinny Bones, Pinky and Rex and the Bully, Dancing in the Wings, The Meanest Thing to Say*. Children might also notice that the character Cinderella is similar to other literary characters they know well—Harry Potter, for instance, also adopted by reluctant family members, or Ella Enchanted, a modern –day Cinderella. Children might start to see additional themes, for example, an abused family member, forced to do housework wearing rags, rises above her situation with the help of a fairy godmother, and goes, literally, from rags to riches. Once you have come up with themes, guide children to pick one and formulate a thesis statement. Then see if together, they can move from this larger, more universal (or general) idea to say something specific about the book itself and its characters. Children might have an easier time doing this work for their own essays if they first do it for a story they've known since they were little.

If you have children who need help laying out their materials and deciding what to include . . . tell them that selection is a very important part of the art of essay writing. Just as a painter doesn't take all his or colors and put it on a canvas, but instead chooses a particular shade of orange and another of pink to draw a sunset, so too essayists realize the importance of selecting the material that will be the most powerful for their essays. You might ask your students to consider a time they went to an art museum and saw an exhibit in which only one piece of art was spotlighted in a large display area—a large painting or a single vase.

If you notice your children have a tendency to be redundant in their essays . . . caution them against using the same excerpt to support several arguments. the same excerpt from the texts they're writing about to support several arguments, while others make the same point with three or four examples. Tell children that after they put their pieces together, to some extent, the challenge is to reread their essays with critical eyes, eliminating redundancy. Encourage children to think about what does and doesn't hold their attention. For example, if a character faced the same challenge over and over, or fought the same battle with the same enemy in every book in a series, they, as readers, would grow frustrated and bored. Remind children that just as they are hungry for new thoughts, ideas, storylines, so too are their readers wanting to be challenged by new ideas in each paragraph of an essay. Once you've made your point, move on to the next. The last thing you want is for your readers to be eyeing the clock. And sometimes, less is more.

COLLABORATING WITH COLLEAGUES

In this unit of study, you will have helped your children develop many of the muscles that they'll need in order to write literary essays in middle school and also on standardized assessments. Before this unit can really pay off in those contexts, however, children need to be able to use most of what you taught quickly, writing a literary essay over the span of an hour or two, not a week or two!

With your colleagues, then, it will be important to think about ways in which you can transplant bits of this unit into other parts of the day, and ways in which you can help children do more of this work internally.

For example, look over the sessions that were geared toward helping children read thoughtfully, gathering entries that could, in the end, become seed ideas for an essay. The work that you invited children to do within the writing workshop is really work that thoughtful readers do on the run as we read, or in moments of reflection after we put a text down in order to mull it over and to talk it over. Could you imagine suggesting that children read their independent books with sticky notes at the side, marking places in the text where the character changes or acts out of character or learns a big lesson? Could you imagine suggesting that children always read with our own life issues like an open book before us aware that oftentimes we can find help with our own lives in the books we read? These early sessions in this unit can surely nurture a culture of thoughtfulness around children's independent reading, their shared reading, and around whole-class read alouds.

Then, too, you'll want to find opportunities for children to consolidate what they really want to say about a text into a claim that they believe is

thoughtful, provocative and central to the text. After you read a chapter of your read-aloud book to the class, why not pause and say, "What claim would you like to put forth? Talk with your partner and see if you could get us started in a conversation by putting a claim, an opinion, in the middle of our community."

Children could become accustomed to weighing whether a claim feels central to the text and grounded in the text and then they could learn to talk-long about that claim. Talking long about an idea is a lot like writing-long about the idea.

In the whole group conversation, you can coach children to do all that they learned in this unit of study. After a child cites an excerpt from the text, for example, you could ask, "Can you unpack that citation? How does it link back to the big idea under discussion today?"

Of course, children could do similar work around their independent books. If they read, jotting ideas on sticky notes, children could then have time after half an hour of quiet reading to look over their sticky notes "and prepare for a partner conversation." Meanwhile, you could teach children that the way to prepare for a partner conversation is not unlike the way they prepare for writing a literary essay or preparing for a whole–class talk. Readers scan their roles, review their thoughts, thinking, "What big idea do I want to put forth?" "How might I support this idea?" That is, they turn sticky notes into what the kids come to speak of as "boxes and bullets." Of course, those boxes and bullets take on new life when they are challenged, added to, rewritten through spirited conversation.

LITERARY ESSAYS:
A CELEBRATION

IN THIS CELEBRATION, YOU AND YOUR COMMUNITY OF WRITERS WILL CELEBRATE THE LITERARY ESSAYS THAT YOU CHILDREN HAVE COMPLETED.

GETTING READY

- Children need to have created anthologies from their essays.
- See CD-ROM for resources

In the real world, there is a whole group of people who spend their lives thinking about the real message behind a beloved story, noticing the ways in which an author's craftsmanship supports the author's message. The people who do this are literary scholars, and they spend a good part of their lives writing essays about texts. For example, hundreds of literary scholars have written about the deeper meanings in Mark Twain's Huckleberry Finn. These literary essays are then circulated among the "club" of people who devote their lives to literary scholarship. This means, that when these people talk and think about texts, they have all the advantages of being in book-club conversations with people who, like them, have pored over these texts . . . only they are not in the same room, let alone the same state, as those people. What this means is that actually, what literary scholars do when they write about texts is they write in response to what others have said. A literary scholar might begin her essay on, say, Huckleberry Finn, by writing, "So and so has argued that although some may think Huckleberry Finn is a story about . . . it is really a story about . . . I want to partly agree and partly disagree with So and So's claim . . .

It is fitting, then, that your children celebrate their literary essays by circulating them among other literary scholars. The children in your class will already know each other's texts and interpretations of texts (because in fact, their ideas will have been co-authored through extensive conversations), so it will be important for your children's ideas to be circulated among a classroom full of readers who have read the texts under consideration, and have become invested in thinking about those texts, but whose ideas are still just emerging. More specifically, the children in your class who have written about "Boar Out There" will collate their texts into an anthology of literary essays on this story, and this group of children will go to another classroom, listen in to a book talk about this story, and after a few minutes, offer their essays that extend or at least 'go-with' that child's reading of the story. "Read this," the author will say, "and mark it up. Get ready to cite it in your book talk." When the children in the book talk resume reading, they'll be asked to bring the views of the essay-authors into the conversation, actually reading bits of the essays. All the members of the book club will be expected to talk-back to the views of the absent (though really, the eavesdropping) essayists using the same conversational prompts as they use to talk back to each other's ideas.

CELEBRATION

Before the actual celebration day, convene small-groups of children whose literary essays addressed a particular text. Coach them towards compiling an anthology of related literary essays—rereading and sorting each others' essays according to an organizational structure they design.

"Writers, tomorrow we will publish our literary essays, and we will do so following the tradition of literary scholars. Across the world, there are people whose job in life is to do what you have been doing. They are professionals at writing literary essays, and we're going to publish just like they do."

"The pros at this work don't read their literary essays aloud at public readings or hold book parties, as short story writers and poets do. Instead, these professional authors publish their essays in anthologies of literary essays. For example, I have here in my hand a book of essays about Mary Twain's famous novel, *The Adventures of Huckleberry Finn*. This book has a name on the spine, and this is the name of the person who edited the anthology of essays."

"In our classroom, you will not only author articles, you will also co-edit the anthology that brings together all the articles written about a particular text."

"So in a few minutes, we're going to gather in small groups of co-editors. The four of you who wrote about Rylant's 'Boar Out There' will form one group, those who wrote about 'Eleven' will form another group, and so on."

"But before you can decide on the sequence of your articles and write a forward to your anthology, I need to tell you about your audience."

"Literary essayists write for other people who study literature. The average Joe on the street won't pick up this anthology of articles about Huck Finn, but people who are deep into a book club conversation about this novel will absolutely want to know what other smart readers think. So your essays need to go to other people who are deeply involved in thinking about 'Eleven' and 'The Marble Champ' and 'Spaghetti.' Those people are the children in Mrs. Rosenblum's class. They've been reading these same short texts, but they haven't spent as much time thinking about them as you guys have. Tomorrow, we will go to their classroom when they are in book club conversation. Those of you who've read 'The Marble Champ,' will listen to those kids talking about that text . . . and then you'll give them your anthology, let them read your ideas, and you'll listen as they use those ideas in their

COACHING

In this session, you and your community of writers will celebrate the literary essays that you children have completed. In considering the best way to publish children's final writing projects, it is always helpful to think about the real-world ways in which this particular kind-of-writing reaches readers. For example, if children had written songs, publication might involve bringing out the xylophones and putting the lyrics to music, performing the music in a celebration and sending visitors home with cassette recordings. If children had written editorials arguing for causes they believe in passionately, then publication should involve mailing those editorials to local newspapers. For this unit, then, you need to mull over the real-world ways in which literary essays reach readers. And that is a tricky question because mostly, literary essays are a school genre, and they are read only by a teacher, usually a middle school, high school or college teacher. If you and I think a bit harder and longer about the genre of literary essay, however, I think we can find the answer to the question, "What are the real-world ways in which literary essays reach readers?" and we'll find, also, a marvelous way for children to publish their literary essays.

In this instance, we are not envisioning that the buddy-class is a younger group of children because a lot of responsibility will fall on the shoulders of the children who will read the literary essays and incorporate them into their book talks. You may decide that this class needs to have the literary essays for a day or two, and to talk in partnership with the authors of these essays before they incorporate them into their book talks.

continued book club. In that way, you'll see how it really works in the real world of writing literary essays!"

"So gather in your editorial circles."

On the day of the celebration, sit children from your room who have written about a particular text in a ring around the children from another class who've recently read that text. Launch book talks, with your children listening. After a few minutes, each of your children will give copies of his or her essay to two children.

Once the two classes of children had come together, and everyone had taken their appropriate places, I convened attention. "Literary scholars. In science, when we study biology, we try to do as field biologists do, peering closely at drops of water and carefully recording what we see. Today, we will try to do as literary scholars do. Mrs. Rosenblum's class, you began studying some short texts yesterday, and I know you are just about to talk about those texts. We've studied the same texts, working for several weeks with them. We're going to listen in on your book-club conversations about these texts, hoping that there are ways that our ideas, written in our essays, might talk-back-to your ideas. So right now, will Mrs. Rosenblum's book clubs get started?"

As the children talked, their teacher and Medea and I circulated, pointing out to the ring of listeners ways in which their ideas added onto or challenged the ideas the readers were discussing.

After a very short while, I asked for children's attention. "Mrs. Rosenblum's readers? We've been listening to your ideas about these texts—'The Marble Champ,' 'Boar Out There' and so forth—and we have ideas we'd like to bring into the conversation. One way for that to happen is for you to move your chairs apart, and make space for us to literally squeeze into the circle. But among literary scholars, there is another very important way for people to bring ideas to a book talk. We write literary essays! Then we put those essays out into the world, often making anthologies of them or magazines of them. So right now, the

Readers, please be sure to actually read the literary essays included in this book, noticing the way in which all the lessons of this book set children up to write this way. Spot Harrison's effort to write micro-stories which are angled to support his claim. Note how he tries to 'unpack' his evidence, showing how it relates to his claim. Enjoy his efforts at an ending!

Literature often tells the story of underdogs who rise up in the end. The Mighty Ducks is the story of a rag-tag hockey team that ends up winning the state championship. Cinderella tells the story of the rejected youngest sister who ends up marrying the prince. "The Marble Champ," by Gary Soto, is also an underdog story. It tells not only about Lupe winning the marble championship, it also tells that she overcomes her athletic difficulties through hard work and family support.

Lupe overcomes her difficulties through the support of her family. For example, one dinner, Lupe asks her father to come to the marble competition. Her father drops his fork and drops into deep thought. He had finally planned to spend that very day playing racket ball, his favorite activity. But he looked into Lupe's eyes, thought about how important it was that she was risking

Fig. XV-1 Harrison's final draft

entering a sports competition, and announced he would be there. Lupe grinned. There are other ways in which Lupe's family showed their support. Her parents let her practice marbles even after dark, her brother gave tips on how to shoot marbles, and her whole family was there to encourage her when she was worried. Gary Soto shows how important family support was to Lupe. His story contains a full page description of the family dinner. This section was not important to the plot of the story but it needs to be in the story because it shows how supportive Lupe's family was to her.

Lupe also overcame her difficulties through hard work. Lupe' decision to work hard and succeed in sports was made when she lay in front of her shelf full of academic trophies and medals. She wished there was at least one trophy that showed

Fig. XV-2 Harrison's final draft, page 2

that she could do sports – but there were none. She decided that she would work hard, day and night, to win a marble tournament. A bit later, she came home from school and immediately tossed down her backpack and got out her marbles. Let me point out Lupe usually came home from school and did her homework - that is why she had a shelf full of academic trophies. She put on a determined face, and started to flick her marbles. At five o'clock, she hadn't started homework. It's six o'clock, she had flicked 500 times, and she hadn't started her homework. At seven o'clock, she'll die if she goes on any longer. Final score—marbles: three hours; homework: zero hours.

Lupe overcomes her difficulties by squeezing an eraser 100 times for thumb strength, by doing "fingerups" for finger strength, and by practicing after dark even

Fig. XV-3 Harrison's final draft, page 3

when she could be tired to improve her overall marble game.

Gary Soto shows Lupe's hard work through repetition. For example, he says unnecessary lines like "Tried again and again," and "Practice, practice, practice, squeeze, squeeze, squeeze." These lines support my idea that Lupe is working hard,

I enjoy underdog stories because they make me have a feeling of strange success inside. I have experienced being an underdog, in soccer. But in the end, like Lupe, my soccer team succeeded. The hidden lessons I learned from this story taught me that even if you don't think about it, there is a part inside of you that says your parents are there; just remember who held you when you learned how to swim.

Fig. XV-4 Harrison's final draft, page 4

writers who have been working with me want to give you their literary essays, and we're going to watch as you read them, and as you mark up points that you think you could bring into your book club. So readers—you'll each get an essay, maybe two. And my class, just watch as people read your essays!"

After a few minutes, I said, "Would each literary essayists talk with someone who read your essay? Make sure they see the points that might be relevant in the essay to the book club conversation."

Restart the book talks. Only this time, encourage the readers to weave the views found in the literary essays into their book club conversations. Remind your writers that they can nudge readers to reference their essays, whispering in to them.

"Readers, could you return to your book clubs. Only this time, make a point of bringing not only your own ideas to the conversation, but also the ideas you read about in an essay. And essayists, if you hear times when you think your ideas could be brought into a conversation, whisper a hint to the reader. Nudge them to cite your essay!"

"The talks here are amazing—and that is what happens when a group of readers can stand on the shoulders of so much thinking. That's the power of writing essays about reading."

As essayists talked, I circulated, encouraging children to use phrases such as, "As one literary critic suggested . . . " or, "In an essay on this text, so and so suggests that . . . " Encourage children also to use conversational prompts—"I agree because . . . " '"This is giving me the idea that . . . " to raise the level of the conversation.

Literary Essay to "Eleven" By Maxwell
Some people think that growing up is fun, or exciting, having birthday parties and blowing out candles. But smart kids know that growing up is not all fun. Your old clothes don't fit anymore, and you can't play the same games, and you need to worry about new things, like money or work. In the story, "Eleven," by Sandra Cisneros, Rachel comes to an understanding of what being eleven really feels like.

Rachel comes to understand that when you are eleven, you are also ten, nine, eight, seven, six, five, four, three, two, and one. In the story, Rachel sits at her desk, staring at the nasty red sweater Mrs. Price made her keep. She was disgusted with it, and wanted to cry like she was three. She tried not to let her three come out though. Why did she want to cry over a sweater? She thought she was eleven, old enough not to cry over something silly like a sweater. She then

Fig. XV-5 Max's final draft

---

realizes that she was not just eleven, but ten, nine, eight, seven, six, five, four, three, two, and one. There are other sections of the story where Rachel understands that when you are eleven, you're also all the ages inside. For example, she says "when you are scared and need to sit on your Mama's lap, that is the part of you that is still five." And "When you say something stupid, that is the part of you that is still ten." Another section of the story where Rachel sees that she has all the ages is "When you are sad and need to cry, that is the part of you that is still three." And one more place is when she blabbed and stuttered to Mrs. Price when she wanted to say something. That was the part of her that was still four. Her understanding that when you are eleven you are also all the ages inside is important because the way Sandra Cisneros stretches out "10, 9, 8, 7, 6, 5, 4, 3, 2, and 1" instead of just saying "all the other ages"—she really wants to show that that is

Fig. XV-6 Max's final draft, page 2

---

the most important part.
Something else that Rachel comes to understand is that turning eleven can be a let down I see this in the text here: Rachel expected to feel eleven on her birthday as soon as she woke up. But she did not. She opened her eyes and everything was just like yesterday but it was today. She went to school and expected to feel like a big eleven-year-old, cut instead has a terrible day. Mrs. Price forces her to wear a nasty, disgusting sweater. She cries in front of the whole class like she was three. At the end of the day, she just wanted it to be gone and forgotten. Other parts in the text where I see that Rachel understands being eleven can be a let down are "You don't feel eleven. Not right away. It takes a few days, weeks even, sometimes even months until you say eleven when they as you." And "You are not smart eleven. Not until you are almost twelve." And when she realizes that she does not know

Fig. XV-7 Max's final draft, page 3

---

what to do when Mrs. Prices forces her to wear the sweater. She does not have enough ages yet. I can really tell that Rachel does not feel eleven because Rachel says "I'm eleven" or a variation on that a lot, and that shows that she really has to remind herself, because that is not the way she feels. Also, Sandra Cisneros made a list of examples at the end of the story of things that are far away like "I wish I was 102 or anything but eleven" and "far away like a runaway balloon" or like "a teeny tiny little o in the sky." This really shows how much Rachel wants the day to be over with. Because she did not have a happy birthday. She had a let down birthday.
Literature can help you understand things better. For example, I have come, through Rachel's thoughts and experiences, to a conclusion that growing up is not all birthday parties and blowing out candles. And I have learned that I should appreciate being young, while I am.

Fig. XV-8 Max's final draft, page 4

ELEVEN

By Adam

In literature, authors write a lot about one character being upset and taking it out on another person. Sandra Cisneros' essay, "Eleven," is about a girl named Rachel who is mistreated by her teacher and in return mistreats her classmates.

Rachel is mistreated by her teacher. Mrs. Price finds an ugly, old sweater in the coat room and forces Rachel to put it on. Rachel says "That's not . . . mine." But Mrs. Prices moves on to the next math problem without understanding Rachel, saying "of course it's yours." Mrs. Price says, "I remember you wearing it once." This is mistreatment because Mrs. Price isn't respecting Rachel. Mrs. Price doesn't care about what Rachel has to say. Later, right before the bell rings, Mrs. Price pretends as if everything's ok, ignoring the real pain Rachel is feeling.

In return for Mrs. Price mistreating Rachel, Rachel then goes on to mistreat her classmates. Rachel thinks of her classmates in a derogatory way. An example of this is when Rachel commented, "Maybe because I am skinny, maybe because she doesn't like me, that stupid Sylvia Saldivar says" . . . I think it belongs to Rachel!" Then later on, Rachel comments " . . . But the worst part about it is right before the bell that stupid Phyllis Lopez who is even dumber than Sylvia Saldivar says she remembers the sweater is hers." In both these examples, Rachel is calling her classmates dumb and stupid. She's doing this in her mind, but her feelings probably effect her actions too. Sandra Cisneros also shows Rachel mistreating her classmates when Rachel describes the sweater as smelling like "cottage cheese" and " . . . all itchy and full of germs that aren't even mine." This shows that Rachel is disgusted with wearing her classmate's clothes. The sweater, it turns out, belongs to Phyllis and she must feel awful, seeing Rachel cry over the fact that Rachel needs to wear her sweater.

This story teaches me that when someone mistreats a person, that person needs to protest so that they don't pass on their fury to other people. When someone gets mad at me, I sometimes don't protest and instead pass it on to someone else. Sandra Cisneros in "Eleven" teaches me to speak up.

Fig. XV-9 Adam's final draft

Fig. XV-10 Adam's final draft, page 2

Fig. XV-11 Adam's final draft, page 3

THE MARBLE CHAMP

By Judah

In literature, characters face challenges and learn to survive. In the short story "The Marble Champ" by Gary Soto, Lupe learns to overcome her difficulties by working hard and believing in herself.

Lupe overcomes her difficulties through hard work. Soon after Lupe decided to become skilled at marbles, she came home from school and decided to waste no time before playing marbles. But this wasn't just play. This was serious work. Lupe had never been good at sports. So this time she was determined to become good at marbles. She picked five marbles that she thought were her best. Lupe didn't practice on any old table; she smoothed her bedspread to make it into a good surface for her marbles. She really thought about what to do to get good at this sport. She shot softly at first to get her aim accurate. The marbles rolled and clicked against one another. Lupe was disappointed, but didn't give up. She decided her thumb was weak and decided to strengthen it. Lupe worked to get her thumb strong by spending three hours flicking at marbles. She worked to get her wrists strong by doing twenty pushups on her fingertips, and she worked to get her thumb even stronger by squeezing an eraser one hundred times. Gary Soto uses a lot of repetition to emphasize that Lupe worked hard to become good. For example, he wrote, "she tried again and again," and "Practice, practice, practice. Squeeze, squeeze, squeeze."Lupe overcame her difficulties, not only by hard work, but also because she believed in

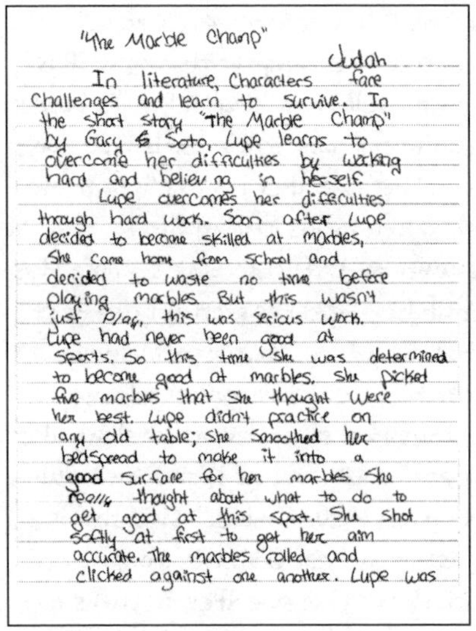

Fig. XV-12 Judah's final draft

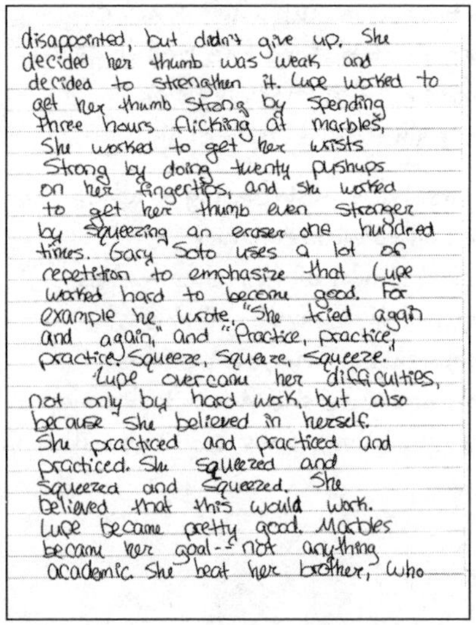

Fig. XV-13 Judah's final draft, page 2

herself. She practiced and practiced and practiced. She squeezed and squeezed and squeezed. She believed that this would work. Lupe became pretty good. Marbles became her goal—not anything academic. She beat her brother, who played marbles. And, she beat a neighbor friend who, not only played marbles, was a champ. She believed in herself to play against them and she might win. The friend said, "She can beat the other girls for sure, I think." This didn't stop Lupe. It didn't even make her nervous! She kept going and still believed in herself. Lupe believed in herself to try and win the academic awards. Lupe believed in herself to work and try to become good. Lupe believed in herself to go to the games and try to win.

In the beginning, Gary Soto writes, "Lupe Medrano, a shy girl who spoke in whispers . . ." It is important to notice that Gary Soto is writing about a character who is complicated. He writes that she is shy. But she sits and looks at all of her awards. Then, as the story goes on, Lupe changes to a girl who believes in herself. In the beginning, Lupe was shy. Then, in the end, she shook hands with people who watched her, even a dog! At first, her thumb was "weaker than the neck of a newborn chicken." Then, after she exercised it, it was swollen because of the muscle. Her thumb was so strong, that when she shot, she shattered a marble. Gary Soto writes to make us think that Lupe is determined to become good at marbles.

played marbles. And, she beat a neighbor friend who, not only played marbles, was a champ. She believed in herself to play against them and she might win. The friend said, "She can beat the other girls for sure, I think." This didn't stop Lupe. It didn't even make her nervous! She kept going and still believed in herself. Lupe believed in herself to try and win the academic awards. Lupe believed in herself to work and try to becom good. Lupe believed in herself to go to the games and try to win. In the beginning, Gary Soto writes, "Lupe Medrano, a shy girl who spoke in whispers..." It is important to notice that Gary Soto is writing about a character who is complicated. He

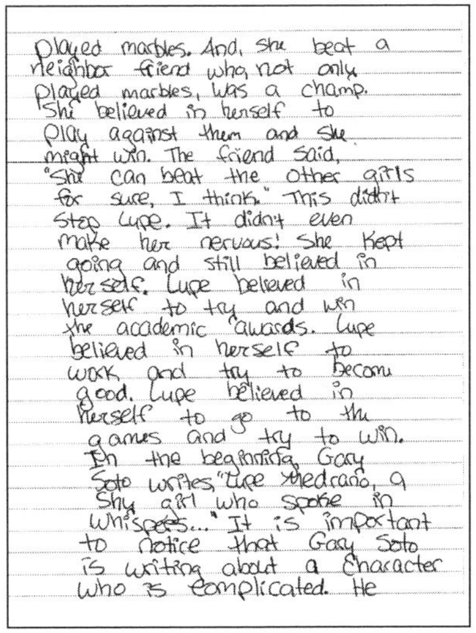

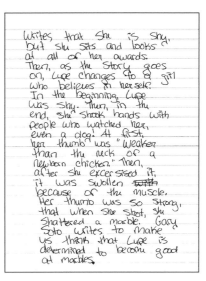

Fig. XV-14 Judah's final draft, page 3

writes that she is shy, but she sits and looks at all of her awards. Then, as the story goes on, Lupe changes to a girl who believes in herself. In the beginning, Lupe was shy. Then, in the end, she shook hands with people who watched her, even a dog! At first, her thumb was "weaker than the neck of a newborn chicken." Then, after she excersised it, it was swollen ~~with~~ because of the muscle. Her thumb was so strong, that when she shot, she shattered a marble. Gary Soto writes to make us think that Lupe is determined to becom good at marbles.

Fig. XV-15 Judah's final draft, page 4

A Literary Essay on "The Marble Champ"

By Ali

When I read I am often drawn to stories that are about people my own age who have problems that I might have, because than I can really feel how the character is feeling. In the short story "The Marble Champ" by Gary Soto a girl named Lupe has never been good at sports, but through determined effort she will do something she has never done before—win a sport.

At the start of the story Lupe had never been good at sports. She could not catch a high pop, kick a soccer ball, or shoot a basketball. One afternoon, Lupe lay on her bed staring up at the shelves that held her awards. Her awards were for spelling, reading, science, piano, chess and for never missing a day of school. Not one of her awards was for a sport. "I wish I could win something, anything, even marbles."

Gary Soto uses lists in the beginning of the story to convey the point that Lupe has been a winner. For example "…the school's spelling bee champion, winner of the reading contest three summers in a row, blue ribbon awardee in the science fair, the top student at her piano recital, and the playground grand champion in chess." Soto wants readers to notice that although Lupe has excelled in many areas in her life she has not been good in sports.

Through determined effort Lupe will win in a sport. One night after dinner, Lupe and her dad went outside. It was dark, but with a couple of twists the porch light went on. The light shone down on the circle Lupe had drawn earlier in the dirt. Lupe set the marbles inside the circle and she dropped down to her knee, she released her thumb. Even through she completely missed the marble she did not stop. She was determined to perfect her shot. She practiced again and again and again. It started to become a regular movement in her thumb. It was getting late and she continued to work her way around the circle. Dropping, aiming, releasing. Lupe prepared for the championship by squeezing an eraser 100 times, by shooting marbles for three hours, and by pushing up and down on her finger tips 20 times.

Gary Soto uses repetition to illustrate determined effort as an important part of Lupe's character. For example "Squeeze, squeeze, squeeze … practice, practice, practice." Repeating these words show how Lupe's determination to work hard in order to succeed.

From this story I have learned that determined effort can have surprising results. Lupe had motivation to succeed, but I don't think she was expecting to win her first game. I think she had prepared herself as best she could and she was going to try her hardest. What I realize is that having determined effort to always do your best is important, because it can help make your wishes come true.

Fig. XV-16 Ali's final draft

Fig. XV-17 Ali's final draft page 2

Fig. XV-18 Ali's final draft page 3

LUCY CALKINS ✦ MARY CHIARELLA

MEMOIR: THE ART OF WRITING WELL

This book is dedicated to Kathy Doyle.

FirstHand
An imprint of Heinemann
A division of Reed Elsevier Inc.
361 Hanover Street
Portsmouth, NH 03801-3912
www.heinemann.com

Offices and agents throughout the world

Copyright © 2006 by Lucy Calkins and Mary Chiarella

All rights reserved. No part of this book may be reproduced in any form or by any electronic or mechanical means, including information storage and retrieval systems, without permission in writing from the publisher, except by a reviewer, who may quote brief passages in a review.

Photography: Peter Cunningham

Library of Congress Cataloging-in-Publication Data

CIP data on file with the Library of Congress.
ISBN 0-325-00867-1

Printed in the United States of America on acid-free paper
10   09   08   07   06   ML   1   2   3   4   5

Excerpt from *What You Know First* by Patricia MacLachlan. Text copyright © 1995 by Patricia MacLachlan. Used by permission of HarperCollins Publishers.

Excerpt from "The Writer" from *New and Collected Poems*, by Richard Wilbur. Copyright © 1988 by Richard Wilbur, reprinted by permission of Harcourt, Inc.

Excerpt from *Journey*, by Patricia MacLachlan. Text Copyright © 1993 by Patricia MacLachlan. Used by permission of Yearling, a division of Random House.

Excerpt from "Laughter" from *The House on Mango Street*. Copyright © 1984 by Sandra Cisneros. Published by Vintage Books, a division of Random House, Inc., and in hardcover by Alfred A. Knopf in 1994. Reprinted by permission of Susan Bergholz Literary Services, New York. All rights reserved.

Excerpt from *Mama Sewing*, by Eloise Greenfield. Text Copyright © 1992 by Eloise Greenfield. Used by permission of HarperCollins.

ACKNOWLEDGEMENTS

This, the final book in the series, is dedicated to Kathy Doyle who has opened her classroom to me for almost two decades. Most of the teaching described in this book took place in Kathy Doyle's fifth grade classroom at Smith School, and Kathy was very much a partner in all of this. Kathy's teaching is remarkable. She cares deeply about her children and is absolutely dedicated to giving them the richest, deepest literacy education one can imagine. Kathy has studied the teaching of reading and writing for decades, and every year, approaches her teaching as a grand learning adventure. She never fails to outgrow her own best thinking, and in doing so, has given the Teachers College Reading and Writing Project a lab site par excellence.

This book also relies on the brilliant teaching of Mary Chiarella, the book's co-author. When the ideas behind the book were developed, Mary was a staff developer at the Teachers College Reading and Writing Project. She was able to sneak away from that work on occasion to join me in Kathy Doyle's classroom, and I think the time alongside the children who star in this book—Adam, Ali, Jill, Harrison, Justin, Tyler, Emily, Judah and the others—finally tipped the balance. This year, Mary has once again been a classroom teacher and I have once again had the chance to learn from her extraordinary teaching. After the first draft of the book was written, Mary launched the unit with her children, and some of those children have joined Kathy's children in a few of the minilessons. More of them are featured in the wise Tailoring your Teaching's that Mary wrote; these will help readers live off this unit for many years. Meanwhile, Mary's students and her ideas about teaching have enriched every book in the series, and she and her children are featured on the DVD collection that will accompany these books.

The ideas benefit from conversations with Katherine Bomer, author of *Writing a Life*, a spectacular book on memoir which needs to be studied alongside this one. This book is filled, also, with an emphasis on teaching towards independence, and our thinking on that topic is enriched by the resourceful work of Colleen Cruz, co-author of our *Fiction* unit and of her own book for teachers *Independent Writing*.

Finally, this book, like all the books in the series, is only possible because of wise, wonderful school leaders who have allowed us to work in ways that make dreams come true. Earlier I mentioned school leaders in New York City but now, just before I write the final page of the final book and send them all, winging their way into the world, I want to also thank the school leaders from across the nation who have created long-distant-partnerships with Teachers College Reading and Writing Project and have led extraordinary curriculum work in their regions. I specifically want to thank the teachers in Harford, California, and their leader, Becky Pressley; the teachers in San Ramon, California, and their leader, Robert Alpert; the teachers in Pinellas County, Florida, and their leaders, Cathy Torres and Leesa Peerson; the teachers in Chappequa, New York, and their leader, Lyn McKay; the teachers and principals in Washington, DC and their leader, Sheila Ford; the teachers in Lakota, Ohio, and their leader, Cecilia Schnidt; and the teachers in Union County, North Carolina and their leader Trudy Griffin. These people, plus hundreds of others, have helped me to learn from rough drafts of the ideas that fill the pages of these books, and I am grateful for their enormous energy and their dedication.

A word from Mary Chiarella:

No one has shaped my teaching more than Lucy Calkins. From Lucy, I've learned to see the potential in a child's ideas and to listen closely so that I might celebrate them. I've learned what it means to teach explicitly without losing sight of the art and inspiration required of writing teachers. I've learned to find my voice as a teacher of writing and to have the courage to share my practice with others. I thank Lucy, not only for her influence on my work as a classroom teacher, but also for including me in this project—another opportunity to find my voice.

MEMOIR: THE ART OF WRITING WELL

Welcome to the Unit

WELCOME TO THE UNIT

MEMOIR: THE ART OF WRITING WELL

About This Unit

This final unit aims to teach children that they can compose not only pieces of writing but also lives in which writing matters. Children will write memoir, and in doing so, they will draw not only on everything they have learned all year, but also on all the writing strategies they can create for themselves and each other. The unit invites children to join in creating methods of writing with power and depth.

At the start of the unit, we invite children to search for Life Topics. We suggest that Life Topics can be found by rereading our notebooks, reconsidering our lives, and living, wide-awake to the topics that feel intensely alive and close to the heart. We know children will begin by writing about gigantic Life Topics: ambivalence over growing older, worries over weight, an appreciation for Grandmother. And we know, too, that we will need to remind children of the saying, "The bigger the topic, the smaller we write."

We will also tell children, "This time, you need to compose a writing life for yourself. You can draw on any strategy you have learned this year, or invent new strategies. Your job is to decide what to do in order to write texts that capture all you want to say." This unit, then, recognizes that the scaffolds we have provided for children all year can also become limiting, and the unit encourages children to push off from scaffolds that limit, to make resourceful use of scaffolds that help, and to do all of this in the service of their own important writing projects. As children invent this last and biggest writing project of the year, we know they will also be inventing their own identities as writers, preparing themselves to go forth with independence, into the rest of their lives.

We help children learn that in order to put themselves on the page with honesty and intensity, they need to write within a community of trust. And so now, as children 'round the final bend of the year, we again teach them what it means to really listen to each other and to themselves.

When writers really listen to themselves and each other, an entry or a topic can grow in significance. In some classes, children in this unit of study refer to their seed idea as a *blob* idea, imagining a glowing, living, amorphous form. Children learn that the process of choosing a seed idea is a more flexible one than they'd at first learned, for as they live with a Life Topic, their sense of what it is they really want to say changes. We encourage writers to use writing as a way to develop their own ideas and associations around a Life Topic, writing-to-learn in their writers' notebooks.

In this unit, the emphasis is not so much on strategies for *generating* writing but on strategies for *writing with depth*. For example, we teach children that writers sometimes find it helpful to write about a single topic from several perspectives. Usually our ideas about a topic are complicated, so once we've written about one set of ideas on a topic, we can come back and revisit the topic, writing an entry that begins, "On the other hand . . . " In the end, some of our best writing will result from efforts to get our mental and emotional arms around the full breadth of a topic. Then, too, we teach children the wisdom of Eudora Welty's advice, "Write what you don't know about what you know." How powerful it is to take the topics we know best and ask, "What are the mysteries, for me, of this topic?"

Children will read literature in this unit first because great literature can serve, as Kafka writes, "as an ice-axe to break the frozen sea within us." Literature calls us from our hiding places, helping us to bring ourselves to the page. The importance of this can't be over-emphasized. Of any quality of good writing, the one which matters the most may be that elusive quality writers refer to as *voice*. We write with voice when we allow the imprint of our personalities to come through in our texts. But children also read literature in order to study the craftsmanship of other writers. Because children have responsibility for imagining a way to structure their memoir, they will read the memoir that other authors have written with a special attentiveness to structure. That is, in this unit we do not say, "This is how your writing will be structured." Instead, we teach children that writers often begin with an emerging content, and then combine and create structures (drawing from our internalized repertoire of structures) that will allow us to say whatever it is we want to say. We teach children to read published memoir from an aerial perspective, noticing the component sections and asking, "How did this writer construct this text? What can I learn from the way the writer put component sections together to make this text?"

Although writers can make calculated decisions to organize a text in one way or another, the actual process of writing is more passion-hot than critic-cold. Milton Meltzer, the great non-fiction writer for children, has said, "In the writer who cares, there is a pressure of feelings which emerges in the rhythm of sentences, in the choice of details, in the color of the language." When children draft, we hope their intense commitment to their meaning gives their writing this sort of pressure of feelings.

Some children will write their narratives as a story, some will write a collection of short texts, some will write essays that are more journeys-of-thought rather than traditional thesis-driven essays. Mostly, children discover that the structures they've learned to use throughout the year are not as inflexible as they once thought, and they create texts which are hybrids, containing perhaps one long narrative section set off against a thesis-driven expository paragraph.

As children create structures that will support their content, they learn about revision in a whole new way. They come to understand that writing is a process of growing meaning, and that writers use strategies as needed, as we reach to create meanings that feel deeply significant and personal.

The Plan for the Unit

The "bends in the road" of this unit, then, are as follows:

- Children draw on every strategy they have ever learned in order to find their Life Topics. They're reminded "The bigger the topic, the smaller we write."
- Children learn that writers do not always, on one given day, reread our entries and select a seed idea. Sometimes the process of coming to know what we really want to say is one that involves more of an evolution, with a writer narrowing in towards what some call a *blob* not a *seed* idea. Writers write-to-learn in order to explore the significance of their emerging focus.
- Children learn that as writers progress toward a clearer idea of what we want to say, we draw upon strategies that can help us write and think with depth. These include writing about a topic from several different perspectives, and identifying the mysteries that lie at the heart of a subject.
- Children learn that writers find it often helps to read texts that resemble the text we want to write. It is important to look at these texts, asking, "What component sections does this contain?" and "Why might the author have structured

the text in this manner?" and "What can I learn about structuring my memoir from studying how other authors have structured theirs?"

- Children draft, doing their best to write with honesty and power and intimacy. Children reflect on what they have written, asking, among other things, "What is it I want to show about myself? About my life? How can I bring this meaning out in my draft?"

- Children revise and edit to bring forth significance, to explore different possible ways to structure a text, and to make their writing more powerful and more graceful.

UNCOVERING LIFE TOPICS

IN THIS SESSION, YOU WILL TEACH CHILDREN THAT WRITERS USUALLY HAVE SEVERAL THEMES THAT SURFACE IN OUR WRITING AGAIN AND AGAIN. YOU'LL INVITE CHILDREN TO UNCOVER THESE TOPICS FOR THEMSELVES BY REREADING THEIR NOTEBOOKS LOOKING FOR CONNECTIONS AND ASKING, "WHAT'S THIS REALLY ABOUT?"

GETTING READY

- Notebook for each child
- Your own, filled writer's notebook
- Prominently displayed basket containing exemplar memoirs of various kinds (this might include *Been to Yesterdays, When I Was Your Age: Original Stories About Growing Up, What You Know First, The Relatives Came*)
- See CD-ROM for resources

It will not be long now until the final day of school arrives. You can picture the final moments. The children will drag wastepaper baskets to their desks; they'll go through each piece of work, thinking, "What do I throw away? What do I hold onto?" You'll disassemble your sections of the room, too, asking your own version of that question. Then, suddenly, the buses will arrive and before you are ready for it, the room will be almost empty. Just a few children will remain, waiting for the final bus. You'll chat about the summer, the year ahead, and promise to write each other. Then you'll hear the call—Bus 29 has arrived—and those final few children will shoulder their backpacks and head out the door. One will linger in the doorway. "Bye," he'll say. "Have a good summer."

"Bye," you'll answer, and as the door closes behind his departing figure, you'll whisper, "Have a good life." And in the quiet of that classroom, before the faculty lunch, you'll savor the memories of your year, and wonder if your time with these children left a mark.

Philosophers tell us that human beings are shaped by our awareness of our own mortality. I do not know if this is true—although as I age, I begin to believe it—but I do know that a consciousness of loss threads through my life as a parent and as a teacher.

As surely as day follows night, my sons grow up. First one and then the next climbs into the yellow school bus and heads off to kindergarten and to a life that is separate from me. They come home speaking phrases from a different world, caring about sneakers that light up when you walk and plastic action figures with gigantic guns.

Now my oldest is heading off for college. I watch him pack and pray that our time together has been intense enough that he will carry much of it with him. Then, in the blink of an eye, Miles has shouldered his backpack, and is standing in the doorframe. "Bye," he says.

As parents and as teachers, we watch our children grow up and leave the nest. And a consciousness that they will leave us does thread through all of our parenting, all of our teaching. For me, this unit of study is about preparing for those final moments when our kids shoulder their backpacks and head out the door. I want this year and this unit to be intense enough that it leaves a lasting mark.

MINILESSON

Uncovering Life Topics

CONNECTION

Show writers that you've thought hard about this final unit, deciding to aim toward helping each child learn to compose a writing life for himself.

"Writers, many of you have been asking, 'What will we study in our final unit?' I didn't answer you partly because I, too, have been mulling over that question. 'What unit could be *big* enough, could be *worthy* enough, to culminate our year together?'"

"You have learned this year to compose personal narratives and essays, short stories and poems. As important as this learning has been, I think it is equally important that you learn to compose lives in which writing matters. Before this unit is over, before this year is over, I want to be sure that each and every one of you has learned to compose a writing life for yourself."

"In this final unit, then, I will not say to you, 'We are all going to work on this particular structure of writing,' nor will I teach you to follow along in a step-by-step process toward making a particular piece of writing. You see, six weeks from now, you won't be in this writing workshop. You'll be at home, or at summer camp, or with your grandparents . . . and you will need to know that wherever you are, even when there is no teacher in sight, you can tackle writing projects that feel big and important to you. And you will need to know that your drafts of writing can teach you to write."

Tell children that they'll create a memoir using their own process and choosing their own genre. Remind children to draw on their repertoires of strategies for gathering entries and finding Life Topics.

"In this final unit, then, each one of us will find a Life Topic for ourselves, and we will write *something*—an anthology of poems, an essay, a true story, a picture book—that allows us to put our lives onto the page. We will each write a memoir, but I won't say to you, 'This is how memoirs tend to go,' because a writer can write memoir as an anthology of poems," I said, holding up Lee Bennett Hopkins' collection of poems—titled *Been to Yesterdays*, "or as a narrative," I said, holding up James Howe's memoir, "Everything Will Be Okay" "or as a picture book," I said, holding up MacLachlan's *What You Know First* and Rylant's *The Relatives Came*.

COACHING

I've sat for a long while before this first day of our final unit of study. I am brim full of hopes for this unit; I want it to be gigantically important. I want it to be deep and vast and pure. I want it to matter so much that the unit, and the year-long writing curriculum, leaves a mark on children long after the year is over. At the start of this minilesson, I am trying to create a drumroll around the unit, the same drumroll, the same sense of heightened anticipation that you and I feel over the prospects of this unit. We hope this session helps children approach the now-familiar work of collecting writing ideas with a renewed sense of agency and of zeal.

At the start of this unit, as of every unit, we need to try to give children a big picture of the unit. It is easier to assemble a jig-saw puzzle if one has seen the picture on the cover of the box. Similarly, I am convinced that children will feel more in control and more active in a unit of study if they feel as if they have a handle on the goals for a unit. As you can see, this unit—like most units—aims towards several related goals. I am trying to emphasize not only the kind-of-writing that I hope children will do, but also the spirit which I hope they will bring to this unit.

These texts will all go into a basket of memoir texts. Over the next few days, you and your children will add other texts to this basket. Be sure that it is prominently displayed and that you bear in mind that throughout the writing workshop, it is always wise for children to take time from writing in order to immerse themselves in reading the sort-of-text they hope to write.

"In this unit, you will each decide on what you want to say and you will each choose (or create) the form [and I held up the collection of memoir, representing an array of optional structures] to say it in." I put the texts I'd referenced into a basket entitled "Exemplar Memoir."

"You already know that to get started, you will need to find a way to collect entries that are worthy of this final project. You can draw on your entire repertoire of strategies for collecting entries."

Name your teaching point. Specifically, teach children that most writers have only a few Life Topics that we revisit often, and that writers reread what we've written in order to name those Life Topics.

"Today I want to teach you that when writers look for Life Topics, we often reread our writer's notebooks, looking for subjects that thread their way through much of what we have written."

TEACHING
Tell children that a writer once told you that most of us have a few topics we revisit repeatedly, and explain that this has been true for your writing

"Don Murray, who as you will recall is one of my writing teachers, once came to work with my colleagues and me on our writing. We all gathered around him, and Murray began. 'As writers,' he said, 'most of us have just three topics that we continually revisit. Even when we think we are writing about new topics, we are really, deep down, revisiting one of those three topics.' Then Murray said, 'List your three Life Topics.'"

"I was flabbergasted. I thought about all the writing that I do in my life . . . . How could he suggest that I really only write about *three* subjects? I quickly peeked back into the entries in my writer's notebook. To my astonishment, one after another after another was either about my father, about my sons, or about the teaching of writing."

"Since then, I have found that other great writers agree that most of us, as writers, have a few great Life Topics that we continually revisit. F. Scott Fitzgerald, for example, says this: 'Mostly we writers repeat ourselves—that's the truth. We have two or three great moving experiences in our lives—experiences so great and moving that it doesn't seem at the time that anyone has been caught up and pounded and dazzled and astonished and beaten and broken and rescued and illuminated and humbled in just that way ever before.' And as writers, he suggests, we continually mine those experiences."

It is rare for us to bring brand new texts into a writing workshop. If children know other memoirs rather than these, I will draw from the texts they know in describing some of the ways to structure a memoir. It will be much more powerful if the texts that I reference in passing are ones that children have already heard read aloud.

Over and over again you will see that minilessons themselves demonstrate many of the principles that we try to teach young writers. Notice that I tell a micro-story, then lay two quotes alongside it, unpacking the quotes so as to relate them to my main point.

The word author *connects to the word* authority. *It makes sense that all of us write best on topics in which we are authorities.*

"I've been thinking, for example, about Patricia MacLachlan, the author of so many books that we love. I recently heard her speak and she said that she always keeps a bag of prairie dirt near her as she writes, because it reminds her of her childhood home. And she said that she believes that every book she ever writes is really about a child's longing for home."

"When I heard her say that, I was puzzled. I thought to myself, '*Journey* is not about a boy's journey toward home—it is the story of a boy who lives with his grandfather and tries to reconstruct his life in the absence of his mother.' But as I started to think about it, I realized that really *Journey* is all about that boy coming to feel that he's at home when he is with his sister and his grandparents. Then I thought about *What You Know First*, and again my first thought was that this is not about a child's longing for home. I thought, 'It is about moving.' But then I remembered the ending:"

> What you know first stays with you, my Papa says. But just in case
> I forget I will take a twig of the cottonwood tree. I will take a little
> bag of prairie dirt. I cannot take the sky.

Explain that when writers want to find Life Topics, we reread our writing looking for the few topics or patterns that underlie our entries.

"So today, and whenever you want to find your Life Topics, you may decide to reread your own writer's notebook, looking for the themes that underlie many of your entries. Watch how I do this, and notice that often my entries address one topic on the surface, but deep down, they address another, more universal, topic."

I opened my notebook to entries I'd gathered at the start of the year, and began skimming. "This entry tells about the time I went to the basketball game. But it is really a story about wanting to fit in with the kids, and also about my father who embarrassed me that evening." Then I paused, and looked up at the children. "Do you see that when I first read this, I commented that the entry is about attending a basketball game . . . but then I looked a bit more deeply at it, thinking, 'What life issues does the entry address?' When I did that, I recognized that it is really about my longing to fit in, and about my mixed feelings toward my father. No, let me be more specific. The entry shows that my relationship with my father is all mixed up with feelings of judgment—with him judging me, and me judging him." Then, shifting from my role as a writer to my role as a teacher, I said, "I'm going to read more and see if there are any patterns across many of my entries."

I do not usually give quite so many examples—Murray, Fitzgerald, MacLachlan. I'm trying to rally children's enthusiasm for this new unit, and I know that the particular strategy I am teaching today is not one which requires a great deal of demonstration.

Patti told me that she got the idea for that ending from a fourth grader. Patti had told the girl that she was having a hard time writing because she'd recently moved, and she felt disconnected from her new house; she missed the old house, with its snakes in the basement and mice everywhere. She told the girl that she always carried a bag of prairie dirt with her, to remind her of her childhood home. Patti then said, "Maybe I should take this bag of prairie dirt and toss it into my new yard. The two places could mix together that way!" "No!" cried a boy who was listening in. "Maybe the prairie dirt will blow away!" And then the little girl said, "I think you should put that prairie dirt in a glass bowl in your window so that when you write you can see it all the time. So you can always see what you knew first." That gave Patti the idea for her book, What You Know First. I tuck stories like this into my memory-bank because I know there will be a minilesson or a conference when I need just this story to make my point.

You will see that the role of demonstration is very small in this minilesson. I do not think kids need to spend a lot of time today watching me reread entries. So, I opt for only a small bit of demonstration and a larger bit of time rallying children for the important work on this unit. Still, during the demonstration, I am active and strategic enough that kids can see me doing work that they can emulate. For example, I show them that I push past an easy, surface-level answer to "What is this entry really about?" I show them that I find more than one answer to that question, pushing myself to be more specific and true. A demonstration can't be effective unless we enact replicable activities.

ACTIVE ENGAGEMENT
Ask children to reread their first few entries looking for underlying Life Topics and to write an entry about what they find.

"Writers, would you open up your notebooks to the entries you wrote at the very start of this year. Reread them, and as you do so, think to yourself, 'If it is true that as writers, most of us have just a handful of Life Topics that we visit over and over, what might be my Life Topics?' Read just an entry or two, and remember to read thinking not only of the surface-level meaning, but also of the underlying theme. I've given you each some sticky notes. You can jot your observations and thoughts on those notes, right in the margins of your entries."

LINK
Remind children that in this unit, each child will be expected to compose her own writing process. Remind children that today they will invent ways to find their Life Topics.

"So writers, today we begin our final unit of study. In this unit of study, your job will be to compose a writing life for yourself. To do this, you need to make choices. Those choices start today, as you leave this rug and head for your writing spot. Your job will be to begin thinking about the topics that matter so much to you that you may want to write about them in your final memoir. You'll be collecting entries and living toward your draft for a long while. You can draw on any strategy you've learned this year," I said, gesturing to charts gathered across the year, "or you can invent new strategies. Among other strategies, you may want to reread previous entries, asking yourself that question that Murray asked my colleagues and me: 'What do I write about again and again, sometimes without even realizing it?' 'What are my Life Topics?'"

"I can't wait to admire the choices you make and the work you do today."

This unit requires that children dig deep into themselves in order to grow insights about their own lives. You will find that fairly often, instead of asking children to turn and talk during the active engagements, I ask them to stop and jot. I know that tiny interludes of reflection and writing can provide a forum for some powerful new thinking and that the work children need to do in this unit and often as they write does not necessarily become stronger and deeper by being discussed.

Now that it is near the end of the year, you will see that I am more apt to have children stop and jot during the Active Engagement section of minilessons. Prior to now, I worried that jotting would be slow and cumbersome for them, but there comes a time when I think the children's writing abilities should be strong enough for quick-writes to begin to play more and more of a role in instruction. In your classroom, you may decide that it is still too cumbersome for children to write during a minilesson . . . or you may have been doing this (in lieu of turn-and-talks) for a while.

I want children to feel that this unit is a more rigorous, demanding one than any that preceded it, and so I overstate the amount of independence they'll be given. I act as if this unit will be altogether different, and I hope that more and more of the children do become increasingly deliberate, strategic, purposeful, and active as writers. But the truth is, we will still shepherd the class along, and as always, we will allow children varying amounts of independence depending on children's abilities to make good use of it.

WRITING AND CONFERRING

Supporting Reflection

You and your colleagues will want to anticipate the sort of work your students will be apt to produce today, and to rehearse for how you will respond to that work. Because I've taught this unit of study so many times and have watched other teachers teach it as well, I can almost promise you that the work your children do today will be disappointing. Gone will be all the detail and fluency you've come to expect in their writing; instead, children will produce lists of clichés. This, for example, is what Jill wrote: *[Fig. I-1]*

Things I love/are important
Similarities/differences
Everyday thinking   Relationships
Childhood memories   Home
Grandmother   Change
Seeing the world in different ways
Excitement   Times
Leisure time   Anxiety
Obsession   Thinking
Feelings

Many children write as Jill does here, listing generalizations. You won't be surprised to learn, therefore, that I was tempted to skip this minilesson. But I decided, in the end, that even though the writing that most children produce today will be far from their best, it is still important for them to spend time rereading their notebooks and thinking about the Life Topics that thread through their entries. I realized, also, that if I did the work that this session asks children to do, the list of Life Topics that I would produce would probably seem as commonplace and clichéd to you as Jill's list seemed to me. But in fact, for me, every word on my list would brim with poignancy:

My Life Topics
Miles and Evan
Dad
Nostalgia for the creek, the farm ... for some aspects of my childhood
Teaching writing

> **MID-WORKSHOP TEACHING POINT**   *Searching for Patterns*   "Writers, can I have your eyes and your attention? When you reread your entries and look for the Life Topics that thread through them, remember that sometimes those Life Topics will be hidden. Maybe on first glance, an entry will seem to be about shopping with your mom, but if you look closer, you will see that there is a hidden theme underneath that entry, and it may well be a theme that underlies other entries as well."
>
> "One way to see those themes, themes that sometimes seem to be hiding, is to look across a bunch of your entries and to think, 'What are the topics that I address over and over?'"
>
> "When Judah first read these entries, they seemed to have nothing in common. But she reread them, and said, 'These do sort of connect!'" *[Fig. I-2]*
>
> My home is a place that I am loved at. Everyone can be their self.

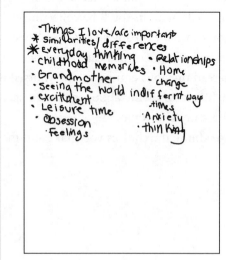

Fig. I-1 Jill's list of Life Topics

I think it is helpful for children to approach the writing workshop brimming with an awareness of their own precious lives. I've come to believe, therefore, that it can be very powerful for a child to pause in the midst of her writing life, to reread all that she has written and to think, "What are the Life Topics (the writing territories) that I revisit often?"

In our conferences today, the job will *not* be to help children improve the quality of their lists. The goal for today will not involve helping writers *write* well but will instead involve helping them *reflect* well. Our first job will be to affirm the importance of each child's Life Topics.

As you confer today, remember this. There are only a few times in the lives of each of us when we feel truly heard. It can be an extraordinarily powerful thing to have someone listen and say, "What you're onto is really huge." When someone listens like that, really taking in the significance of what we only gesture towards, suddenly our eyes well with tears, and we find ourselves saying more than we knew we had to say. A goal for this unit will be to help children write with honesty, intensity, and openness; it is, therefore, important that we, as teachers, begin the unit with an enormous spirit of receptivity and empathy.

I will not forget the day Maya read me an entry that began, "My brother can be mean sometimes." The entry told about the day Maya's friend came over to play. The two girls raced up to Maya's bedroom, planning to play bride with Maya's dolls. They'd chosen the flower girls and the ushers. All of a sudden, they opened the bedroom door, and there, in front of them, they found all Maya's dolls and teddy bears hanging helplessly from nooses. Hearing this entry, I gasped in utter horror. How awful, how devastating!

Of course, I could have responded differently. Those were dolls and teddy bears hanging from nooses, not pets or children. The event was not *really* one of life's worst tragedies. But in the life of this one child, that moment brims with pathos. I have come to believe that I cannot teach writing well if I cannot walk in the shoes of the writer, trusting that Maya's life experiences are as intense to her as my experiences are to me.

As teachers of writing, in general, and especially as teachers of memoir, we need to be people who gasp and wince and weep and cheer in response to the heartbreak and the happiness that children bring into the writing workshop. Ultimately, a child will only be able to write well about his own life if that child can re-experience it. We need to listen deeply and to be profoundly moved by children's life-themes so that children can do the same. The most important work we can do today, then, will be to listen, to acknowledge the gigantic significance of children's Life Topics.

continued from previous page

> We trust each other. We care about each other.
>
> My home is a security blanket. I am away from rude, mean, bad people. I am inside my turtle shell and the big animals can't get me.
>
> My fears are outside. My bad times are outside. The protection of my soul is left on the doorstep.
>
> At my home, I am my siblings' second Mom. I read to them, give them baths, fix their hair, and most importantly, love them.
>
> My home holds everything that makes me. My home is me.

"Another of Judah's notebook entries":

> Whenever I am with my Mom, I miss my dad. Whenever I am with my dad, I miss my mom. It's like life can never be perfect. It's not that I don't love one or the other, it's just that I miss the one I'm not with. I have always, my whole life, been missing someone.

"'I'm realizing,' Judah said, 'that both the entries are about my sense of home, and the second one shows that even when I am home, I'm a little bit homesick for the one that isn't there.' "

"If you find yourself just flipping past your entries, saying, 'This is about shopping with Mom,' 'This is about going out for pizza,' 'This is about buying a new goldfish' . . . slow down, and look for the Life Topics that may be underneath these entries, and may be connecting them. One way to see those topics is to do as Judah has done, looking across many entries to see the subjects that reoccur."

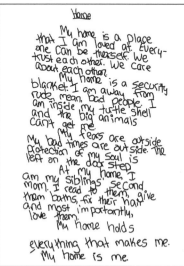

Fig. I-2 Judah's notebook entry

SHARE

Recording Self-Assignments

Celebrate the choices children have made. Ask them to record their self-assignments beside their entries.

"Writers, can I stop you? I've been really pleased to see that you made choices today, and you began selecting strategies that will work for you. Would you once again record your self-assignment beside your entry? That is, during this whole unit, before you pick up your pen to write an entry, jot down the strategy you will be using or the goal you are aiming toward! For example, before you, Tyler, reread your writer's notebook and thought and wrote about the topics that threaded through your entries, you could have written: 'Reread notebook, look for Life Topics.' Then before you took one of those Life Topics and began writing a two-page entry about just it—about messiness—you could have written in a self-assignment box: 'Write long about Life Topic messiness!' And Tyler, that was a wise self-assignment because usually when we write long, we find ourselves generating ideas we never knew we had."

"Some of you have used strategies from earlier this year, and again, it would be great to record those. Right now, would you look back on the work you did today, and write belated self-assignment boxes at the top of today's work?"

The work you have asked children to do today is not especially ambitious work. Remember that during the first day of a unit, it is important to be sure that every writer feels he can be successful with this new work. Today's session sets the stage for those to follow, and as you will see, the pace of work will quickly pick up.

My example spotlights a child who has not only listed Life Topics but has also chosen one and written a long entry about it. I know some children will have stayed in the safe harbor of lists, and I'm deliberately showcasing the value of writing long.

Notice I suggest each child will write more than one self-assignment box. I do expect that most of the children will have done one thing for a while, then switched and done something else. Often a writer will first list or brainstorm, and then the writer will select and expand.

Ask children to share their work with a partner, noticing especially the strategies each chose to use today.

"Will you share the work you did today with your partner, and take note especially of the strategies that each of you chose to use? Remember that in this unit of study, you will work hard to compose writing lives that really work for you. Talk about whether the strategies you used today seemed to you to be helpful, and if they did not seem helpful, talk about what you can learn from today's work."

Although I speak as if many children have been drawing strategies from across the year, the truth is that I am fully aware that most of them did not, in fact, do this. Listing big topics one finds in one's notebook is an easy, comforting enough activity that many children will have devoted most of the workshop to just that. I'm hoping, however, that this share session helps remind children that they are expected to be drawing from the full repertoire of strategies they have learned across the year. Tomorrow's teaching will make a giant step towards ensuring that kids actually do this.

Uncovering Heart-Opening Images Writers, today in class you reread your notebook looking for Life Topics. Tonight, I want to invite you to do something similar. This time, would you reread your notebook, from beginning to end, but instead of looking for Life Topics, would you look for *images* that matter to you. The writer, Camus, once said, "A man's work is nothing but this slow trek to rediscover, through the detours of art, those two or three great and simple images in whose presence his heart first opened." When you reread your notebook, looking for images—for pictures, objects, scenes, places— that matter, my suggestion is this: don't think too much. Don't try to go through a logical process of weighing one image versus another. Just reread your notebook looking, as Camus said, "for those great and simple images in whose presence your heart opens."

Sandra Cisneros found little wooden Russian dolls, one inside another, as one of her images. One of my heart-opening images is that stump that stood alongside the playground at my elementary school. That stump became our chariot, our castle, our underground railroad station. Whereas many children played on a plastic and metal playground, I always spent recess at the stump. I am not sure why that stump stands out in my memories, but I have a hunch that it is one of those images that Camus meant.

See if you can find an image or two that feels at the heart of who you are as a person. Write or draw one of those images, and then write about the power this image has for you. As you do this, you may want an example. Listen to Nicole's entry, in which she uses the image of washing clothes with her grandma to symbolize their relationship: *[Fig. I-3]*

> When I was 5, I would dash upstairs after school to help my grandmother put the wrinkled, stained clothes in the washer. I remember bouncing up and down, watching the sideways hurricane go 'round and 'round.
>
> Sometimes my grandma would sit in a chair and bounce at the exact same time as me.
>
> I also loved heaving the damp clothes out and loading them heavily into the dryer, where the clothes became a tornado.
>
> When we were finished, I would love to hold the warm clothes because they felt like a warm sunny day when my grandma and me washed all the stains and wrinkles out of the clothes.

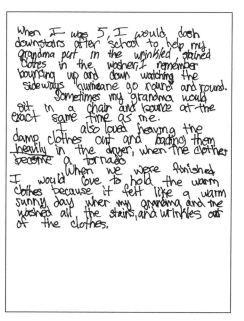

Fig. I-3 Nicole's entry

If your students have identified some key entries, but need support thinking about the Life Topics under them . . . you might decide to teach students to ask themselves a question to provoke thinking as they reread. Some questions that might help do this are:

- What surprises me about this entry, or about the pattern of entries I find in my notebook?

- What specific line or entry or images evokes a strong feeling in me? What is that feeling? How does that feeling—or the text that evoked it—fit into the whole of my life?

- What isn't said in an entry? What isn't included in this notebook? What parts of me have I omitted? Why aren't they here?

If you find that your students are skimming across the pages of their notebooks, instead of reading each page carefully . . . show them how you read a page of your notebook underlining and highlighting parts of an entry as you go. Show them that Life Topics may be hidden inside of bigger entries and for this reason it is worth slowing down and sifting through each entry. One way to make sure students reread slowly is to put speed bumps in their paths. Simply showing them how you stop at the end of a paragraph or page and say to yourself, "I'm not moving on until I dig up an idea or a topic here," will give them the image of how to read slowly and sift.

You might also give them some lenses for rereading so that they know what they're looking for as they revisit what they've written. For example, they might look for a line in an entry where they seemed to change in some way. They might look for sentences that hold strong feelings. They might even do something as simple as underline the names of people who continue to show up across their notebooks. Our goal is to show them that slowing down will pay off and that they're certain to find inspiration *for* their writing *from* their writing, if they just take the time to reread.

COLLABORATING WITH COLLEAGUES

Today you told children that in this unit, you would not teach them one particular way memoir to structure their memoir. Instead, you suggested that they'd create a structure which matched their message. Although you will not be teaching children one specific blueprint for writing a memoir, you still need to be as knowledgeable as possible about the genre, and specifically, you need to imagine various shapes for your children's memoirs.

It is important, then, for you and your colleagues to embark on a course of study of memoir. There are lots of wonderful resources you can draw upon. My chapter on memoir in *The Art of Teaching Writing* could be a place to start. Bill Zinsser has edited an anthology of articles on memoir, *Inventing the Truth*, and the book includes chapters by Toni Morrison, Annie Dillard, and Russell Baker. My close friend and colleague, Katherine Bomer, has written a powerful, gorgeous book on the topic entitled *Writing a Life*.

You may be wondering about the difference between personal narrative and memoir. The two genres overlap. A personal narrative recounts an episode in one's life; a memoir may or may not recount an episode, but a memoir must reveal the person. The purpose of a memoir is to say, "This is me. This is my life." So, a memoirist might write about a day at the zoo with one's dad, but the purpose of the story is to use this day, this episode, to reveal something enduring about the writer.

You may also wonder about the differences between autobiography and memoir, and again, these genres overlap. An autobiography is an attempt to account for an entire life, whereas a memoir is a slice of life, an angle on life. The memoirist does not attempt to tell the whole story, but instead tries to tell one view of it. Annie Dillard's memoir is the story of her coming awake to her own life. James Howe's memoir is the story of his learning to differentiate himself from his brothers, and learning that being a man need not mean being tough.

Of course, different writers define memoir differently, but there is a consensus that memoirs are retrospective. That is, in a memoir an author looks backwards in time. In a memoir, then, there is almost always a *now* and a *then*. There is a sense that the text is being written by someone older and wiser who is looking backwards in order to make sense of prior experience. Memoir involves not just memories, not just a re-experiencing of one's experiences. It also involves bringing meaning to memories, it involves a writer trying to find the truth and the significance of his own experiences.

Memoir come in a variety of structures, which is why I do not teach the genre early in the year when I still want children to learn to write inside the constraints of one structure or another (narrative or essay). Before you can help your children understand the scope and breadth of this genre, it will be important for you to immerse yourself in the genre. Read a wide variety of memoir and sort it into different categories, including categories that are organized by structure.

You will find that some memoirs are structured as lists. For example, there is an excerpt from Paul Auster's *Invention of Solitude* that my colleagues and I often share with children (see Session VI), and it is structured as a list of memories, held together by the refrain, "He remembers . . . ." Rylant's *When I Was Young in the Mountains* is also structured as a series of snapshots. Each snapshot in this book is very short. In some memoirs, these are longer, but the structure is what my colleagues and I refer to as "pearls on a string." The string represents the common theme, and the pearls may be snapshots, vignettes, Small Moment narratives, or scenes.

Other memoirs are structured as stories or narratives. *Angela's Ashes* by Frank McCourt, for example, is one of many narrative memoirs that you may have read. James Howe's poignant text, "Everything Will Be Okay" is a far briefer narrative; it is one of eight memoirs in a wonderful collection entitled *When I Was Your Age: Original Stories About Growing Up* (edited by Amy Ehrlich).

Then, too, some memoirs are structured in sections, with a section of exposition and a section of narrative. If you consider "Eleven" to be a memoir (which is open to debate, although I think it is), then this text can illustrate the fact that some memoirs are written in sections, with a section of exposition standing alongside a focused story angled to illustrate the point of the exposition. "All-Ball," Mary Pope Osborne's short memoir from the *When I Was Your Age* anthology, also fits into this category.

As you and your colleagues immerse yourselves in these and other examples of memoir, you will want to decide upon a few that represent the diversity of the genre and read these aloud to your children so that they, too, can learn through immersion. Depending on the age of your students and on whether you wish to align reading workshop with writing workshop, you may ask students to plunge into their own deep study of memoir by reading independently—a list of suggested texts is on the CD-ROM.

WRITING SMALL ABOUT BIG TOPICS

All of us remember the scenes from *a devastated New Orleans after Hurricane Katrina. I remember the faces of people left behind to cope with the floods; an old woman, clinging to a rooftop as the water rose around her. I remember Ivory, who had been a garbage collector and now sat on a cot in the Convention Center, listing on a little sheet of paper all he'd left behind. Somehow Ivory found solace in simply writing the words of what he had lost: my radio, my picture of Agnes, the rocking chair. For many of us, the particular details captured in those New Orleans photographs conveyed gigantic truths about America today. In the faces of those people who were left behind, who had no way to leave the city, big ideas became poignantly real to us: the gap between rich and poor became real, the unfairness of it all became real. When I think about the impact that those specific images and stories from New Orleans have had on me and on so many others, I am reminded that Big Truths are carried through specific images and stories.*

Over and over throughout this year, you and I have helped children learn that when we write, we use tiny particulars to convey big ideas. In Units of Study for Primary Writing, *even children as young as kindergarteners learned that writers don't write with "big watermelon ideas" but instead with "little tiny seed stories." They learned that writers focus, writing not about "I love my grandma," but instead about "The morning when my grandma braided my hair."*

Now, years later, you and I will continue to remind children that writers write with tiny details. But as children become older and their understanding of good writing matures, concepts that were once hard-and-fast must now become more flexible, and ideas that were once one-dimensional must now become more complex. By now, it is important for children to learn that in fact writers do write about big (watermelon) ideas . . . but that we use tiny (seed-like) stories to represent those ideas. A writer might tell the story of her grandma braiding her hair and do so in order to convey a truth that is too big for ordinary words—the fact that yes, indeed, she loves her grandmother very much.

IN THIS SESSION, YOU WILL TEACH CHILDREN THAT WRITERS OFTEN WRITE ABOUT SIGNIFICANT TOPICS AND BIG IDEAS BY WRITING FOCUSED STORIES TO ILLUSTRATE THEM. YOU'LL TEACH CHILDREN WAYS TO TAKE THE WRITING STRATEGIES THEY'VE LEARNED TO DATE AND APPLY THEM TO THIS TASK.

GETTING READY

- Exemplar piece of writing that uses a small moment to convey a larger Life Topic
- Memoir that demonstrate writing small about big topics (these might include "My Grandmother's Hair," "Eleven," "Papa Who Wakes Up Tired in the Dark," "Alone," "Statue," "Eating the World," "Last Kiss," "Everything Will Be Okay," *Hey World! Here I Am!*, poems from *Been to Yesterdays*
- Copies of the list of conversational prompts from the *Breathing Life into Essays* unit
- See CD-ROM for resources

MINILESSON

Writing Small About Big Topics

CONNECTION

Celebrate that children have reread their notebooks, finding Life Topics that feel huge and significant.

"Yesterday many of you read over your writer's notebooks; you ran your hands over entries about falling off your scooter and buying a sweater that matches your mother's and standing in a hospital room beside your sick grandmother and getting your puppy from the dog pound. Like you, I also reread my writer's notebook yesterday; it was powerful, turning through the pages, turning past all those parts of my life. Although there were many topics that threaded through my entries, when I put my notebook down, there were just a couple of big Life Topics that welled up in me and felt huge. Can you give me a thumbs-up if the same thing happened to you, if you come from yesterday with a few big topics welling up inside of you?" Many children signaled that yes, they, too, were entering this second day of the writer's workshop conscious of gigantically important Life Topics.

"Before we go any farther, let's try a symphony. I'll be the conductor, and when I motion my baton toward you, just say—in a single word or phrase—one of the Life Topics that you are carrying with you today! Say your Life Topic in a crystal clear voice, like it's priceless."

We did this, with voices chiming in, saying aloud words that bristled with power:

"My brother leaving for college."

"Going to summer camp."

"When I couldn't read and felt bad."

"My grandmother."

"My divorced parents and how I am always missing one or the other."

"Moving to America."

I left a ring of silence after the symphony ended. Then, speaking very quietly, I said, "These are so important. They *are* Life Topics."

Remind children that earlier they learned that writers do not write about big watermelon topics but instead about small seed stories. Invite children to wrestle with the fact that their Life Topics resemble watermelon topics.

"But you know what? These could also be called 'watermelon topics.' The term doesn't do these topics justice, of course, but do you agree that these topics—'My grandmother',

COACHING

When you compose your own units of study, you will find that one day's minilesson often leads almost inevitably to the next day's minilesson. Yesterday's teaching definitely set the stage for today's minilesson. Although you will, of course, tweak these sessions so that they work for you, I suspect that you'll find it non-negotiable that the message in today's minilesson follows yesterday's work.

You'll remember that children have participated in similar symphonies earlier in the year. Cherish these activities that become rituals, and use them across the entire day. Teach children to do these with eloquence. If a child interrupts to chat over the ups and downs of his or her Life Topic, for example, I'd point out that there is a time and a place for everything. For now, you are asking children to sing out their topic, almost as if one child was the bass viola, another the cello, in a symphony.

If you notice this Connection is unusual because it includes voices, you are right. Now that children know that the start of a minilesson is mostly a time to listen and learn, inviting them to speak no longer means you run the risk of turning minilessons into rambling discussions.

'Going to Summer Camp,' 'Being a child of divorce'—resemble those watermelon topics that you learned, earlier this year, to avoid?"

"Remember that in September, we learned that writers don't write about big watermelon ideas, but that instead write little seed stories? Kids in the younger grades practice telling the difference. Their teachers might say a topic such as, 'I love my grandmother'—and the little kids use gestures to show whether 'I love my grandmother' is a big watermelon idea," I showed the gesture, using outstretched hands to measure an imaginary watermelon, "or a teeny tiny seed story." I again gestured, showing that such an idea could fit between pinched fingers. "So why are we looking for these topics now? Before we go any farther, I think we need to wrestle with the question of whether or not it is true that writers don't write about big topics."

Name your teaching point. Specifically, tell children that the bigger the topic, the smaller one will need to write.

"This is what I want to teach you today. A poet named Richard Price said it well. He said, 'The bigger the meaning, the smaller you write.'"

TEACHING
Suggest that writers need to write with topics that are both big . . . and small. Share a text in which the writer has used tiny details to convey a Life Topic.

"Earlier, when I told you that writers do not write with big watermelon ideas but with little tiny seed stories, I was oversimplifying the truth. Because the truth is that sometimes writers *start with* a gigantic Life Topic that wells up inside of us and feels huge. And on the other hand, sometimes writers *start with* the teeny tiniest glimpse of life, with a little sliver of experience (as we did earlier this year). But either way, in the end, good literature needs both big meanings and tiny details."

"Earlier this year, you started with tiny moments and asked, 'What is this story really about?' and revised to find the big meanings in those tiny moments. Now many of you have begun this unit of study instead with big meanings, and that is okay too . . . as long as you remember, 'The bigger the meaning, the smaller you write.'"

"My brother, Geoff, is the sports columnist for *The Commercial Appeal*, Memphis' newspaper. Usually he writes about sports topics: Mike Tyson coming to town, Shani Davis' gold medal. But a few years ago, Geoff decided that for his January 1 column, he would break stride and write instead about the importance of pausing to remember what we value most. Geoff had a big meaning he wanted to convey, but he didn't begin his article by sermonizing. Instead, his article went something like this":

Piaget has said that growth involves disequilibrium, and more specifically, both assimilating and accommodating. As children learn more, some of their new learning will lead them to revise previous learning. When a child learns to read, a teacher will teach that child to point under each word as she reads it. At another point, the same teacher will tell a child to stop pointing under each word. Similarly, the teacher of writing might first suggest that writers do not write "all-about" pieces, choosing instead to focus, but that generalization cannot stand for too long, for in fact it is not completely true.

One of the challenges of teaching writing is that there are not a vast array of concepts to guide us. The list of qualities of good writing is not an endless list! The challenge is not to name these qualities, but to actually use them in one's writing. The lesson I am trying to teach today is not a new one, but I do believe that writers need reminders often to renew our commitment to this concept. My challenge, therefore, is to find a way to make this familiar idea feel exciting and important.

I suspect that different writers find it easier to proceed differently. Some start with a big idea, others start with specifics. Eudora Welty, for example, says, "What discoveries I've made in the course of writing all begin with the particular, never the general."

The games I remember most from my childhood aren't Little League or hoops. Instead the game I remember most was penny pitching. This was usually played in hospital waiting rooms. I grew up with leukemia and spent a lot of time in hospital waiting rooms. To pass the time, my mother would take off her shoe, push it onto the middle of the rug, and we'd take turns pitching pennies into her shoe.

Now when people ask me what it was like, growing up with leukemia, I do not tell them about the scabs around my mouth or the IV lines. Instead I tell them that what I remember most is the thrill of the perfect arc and the soft thud as the penny landed squarely in my Mum's shoe.

I am writing this column not because this has anything to do with Memphis or sports, but because I do not want another year to go by without saying "thanks." My mother took a potentially scary time and made it sweet.

And isn't that the lesson of September 11? Whatever it is we have been meaning to do—we need to do it, and do it now. Write that letter. Go for that job. Make that phone call. Not because at any moment, a plane might come out of the heavens and reduce our world to smithereens, but because we are still here on this fragile spinning earth, and never has that seemed so precious.

I'm paraphrasing this column because I no longer own a copy of it—and because I've learned it by heart, too. It is one of my very favorite pieces of writing. I believe that by this time in the school year, kids will benefit enormously from studying the author's craft in a text such as this. But for now, I am using this text to give children a felt sense for the sort of writing I hope they'll produce during this unit of study.

Watch the way in which this article shifts between close up writing and wide-angle lens writing. Notice the odd combination of details that Geoff welds together. There are lots of lessons to be learned from this column. Geoff is a columnist; his picture is always there beside his column. Columnists are expected to put their personal imprint onto their articles, and Geoff has done that.

"You see that Geoff has written about a huge Life Topic . . . and he's embedded that Life Topic into a tiny small moment story."

ACTIVE ENGAGEMENT
Invite children to think of and to collect examples of texts where the writer has used tiny details to convey a big Life Topic.

"It was fun for me to make this minilesson. In order to make it, I needed to think of a time when someone wrote about a big Life Topic, and wrote small. It doesn't seem fair for me to have all the fun. Right now, could you take a second and look through one of the memoirs we've gathered in our memoir basket. Some of these texts will be very familiar to you. Would you and your partner read a text over—just read the first part of it for now—and see if the author wrote about a big Life Topic, and yet wrote small."

Soon children, in pairs, were looking at "My Grandmother's Hair" by Cynthia Rylant, "Eleven" or "Papa Who Wakes Up Tired in the Dark" by Sandra Cisneros, "Alone" by Jacqueline Woodson, "Statue," "Eating the World," or "Last Kiss" by Ralph Fletcher, "Regrets" by Richard Margolis, and "Everything Will Be Okay" by James Howe and talking together about the way in which the author of each of these texts writes both big and small.

Remember that independence is a goal in this unit of study. Throughout the unit, you will see that I try to hand over control to children, and to help children learn not only how to write a particular kind of text, but also how to go-about-learning-how-to-write.

Don't give children a great deal of time for this because children can quickly grasp the notion that many memoirs contain tiny detail and convey big ideas. This is not the time for deep study— you'll invite children to revisit these and other texts soon.

After a bit, I said, "Writers, I have an idea. If any of you know of other memoirs that we could study, would you be willing to bring them in and put them into this basket?" I gestured toward the basket that held the memoirs the children were poring over. "If you need me to make copies of a particular part of a book, just stick the book in here with directions on a sticky note. That way, we'll all be able to study texts that resemble those we will be writing."

LINK
Send children off to write with generalizations and particulars. Tell them ways they can use strategies they've learned across the year to generate writing that is both gigantic and tiny.

"So today, if you have been writing *small*, ask yourself, 'What's the Life Topic here?' And if you have been writing about a Life Topic, pause to think, 'What *small* seed stories are contained inside this?'"

"Remember, writers, that so far this year, we have learned a handful of strategies for generating writing. Some of those strategies help us generate Small Moment stories, and some help us generate big ideas . . . but by now, you have learned that writers can begin with either one of these—big ideas or small moments—as long as we write our way toward the other!"

"Today and throughout this unit, you will want to draw from strategies that are already in your backpack of strategies for generating writing. You have already learned that writers sometimes write about first times, last times, turning points, or moments when we learned something. Now, you may decide to write about first times pertaining to your Life Topic— for example, Adam's Life Topic may be his brother going off to college. So he may write about the first time his brother left for college, or about the last time his family was all together. Whatever your Life Topic may be, you could write about a turning point pertaining to that topic, or a time you felt a strong feeling pertaining to that topic, or about ideas you have pertaining to that topic."

"You may want to look back on previous writing, and write new insights and thoughts that you have, but this time, you won't look back on any old previous writing—you will look back on the entries pertaining to whatever Life Topics are emerging for you."

"Remember that you will each use a writing process that works for you. Keep an eye on your writing, making sure that you choose strategies that work for you, and that you record those strategies in self-assignment boxes. If you get started on an entry and your writing feels ho-hum and perfunctory, don't continue it. The goal, today and always, is to find your own way to write with power."

One of the reasons that it helps to preplan many of the minilessons in a unit of study is that this way, we can use one minilesson to lay the foundation for future minilessons as we are doing here.

Read this Link with care. Usually the Link is my least favorite part of a minilesson but this is an exception. I think this one is particularly helpful.

Don't underestimate the importance of making passing references to strategies kids have learned earlier in the year. Because they have lived with these strategies, just a word or two can bring them to mind. So, whereas usually we do not teach by merely mentioning something, in this instance, I do.

I refer to Adam's Life Topic and I act as if each child has a Life Topic so as to convey my meaning to children more concretely. But, in fact, I definitely do not expect that children will have made a lasting commitment yet to any one Life Topic. As I confer with children today, I will need to make sure they understand that yes, they can for a time take on one particular Life Topic and write a variety of focused entries pertaining to that one watermelon idea . . . but on the other hand, they still need to move between one watermelon idea and another.

In many minilessons, I have used the Link as a time to remind children to draw on their cumulative repertoire of strategies, and of course I am doing this here as well. But in this unit, you will see that I shift my emphasis a bit from encouraging children to use one strategy or another toward encouraging children to be purposeful and deliberate as they proceed. In the end, a strategy is not a strategy unless it gets the writer somewhere. If a strategy is "something the teacher wants me to do so I do it," then it is only an assignment, an exercise, and it serves no writing purpose. In this unit, then, you will find that I continually remind children to keep their eyes on their writing goals, and to do whatever it takes, use whatever strategies or processes are helpful, to make progress towards their goals.

WRITING AND CONFERRING

Settling Down to Write Well

Yesterday, your focus was not on helping children write well but instead, on helping them to list important Life Topics. Today, you will definitely want to help many of your children recall what they learned earlier in the year about writing powerful narratives. It is important that children quickly resume writing well. Magical writing is contagious, and today you will want to do everything possible to set children up to write magically well. Your hope is that within today's workshop, many of your children will write poignant, detailed, true small moments about events that are charged with emotional significance for them—events related to the Life Topics they are choosing. If this happens, the unit will be off to a strong start, and the children who are well-launched will be able to sustain themselves and help you bring the others along. By now you know how to do the conferring necessary to scaffold your children in these early days of the unit. Reread the conferring sections of *Launching* and *Personal Narrative* to remind yourself!

Today when you confer, you will either help children who are writing with big ideas ground these in focused narratives, or you'll help children who write with focused narratives mine these for big ideas.

When you approach a child, expect that the child will be writing on a topic of great importance, even if the part of the topic that's on the page doesn't yet reveal that importance. Remember that often a draft of writing is like an iceberg: beneath the bit that shows, there's a tremendous part that doesn't show. Confirm the significance of the child's topic (even if you are doing so on faith only). Say, "I can tell you are onto something that's big for you," and act as if it is absolutely clear to you that this topic has depths that merit exploration.

If the child has written about ideas, you'll probably want to remark on this, using your observation to help the child develop her identity as a writer. "What I notice is that today, when given a choice over how to proceed, you've begun by writing about ideas. Many kids will choose to first capture little moments, and then later they'll need to reach for the ideas that fit with those moments. But you are special because as a writer, you seem to be especially at home writing about ideas." You'll want to be more specific, too. For example, when I read Rie's idea-based entry, I congratulated her on writing with honesty and precision about ideas. To highlight what she *did* do, I juxtaposed it with the commonplace. "You didn't write in general about ideas. You reached for exactly true, specific words to convey your feelings." This was Rie's entry: *[Fig. II-1]*

MID-WORKSHOP TEACHING POINT ***Growing Provocative Ideas*** "Writers, can I have your eyes and your attention? It is a great joy to see the enormous variety of strategies you are drawing upon to generate writing. How many of you have chosen a potential Life Topic, and are using strategies to help you write small moment stories related to it? That's great. You will probably want to try out a sequence of Life Topics. You can begin, of course by writing either small moment stories or entries in which you grow big ideas. Remember that just as you each have a repertoire of strategies for writing about small moments, you also have strategies for writing about big ideas."

"For starts, you learned yesterday that you can reread your entries, looking for the hidden themes that underlie several entries. But that is not the only strategy you have for writing about big ideas! Earlier this year, remember that you learned that you can take anything—an entry, an observation, a mental picture—and write, 'The thought I have about this is . . .' and then write long, trying to let new ideas come out of your pencil point as you write."

continued on next page

Rie

I sometimes have a hard time being myself. I try to be like other people. It sometimes feels like everybody else does everything right, and I just mess up everything. So I'm always looking to see what other people do. All I want is to be like other people, and this makes me feel really bad. When I think about this, I realize that I should be happy to be myself rather than being like someone else.

Fig. II-1 Rie's entry

I sometimes have a hard time being myself. I try to be like other people. It sometimes feels like everybody else does everything right, and I just mess up everything. So, I'm always looking to see what other people do. All I want is to be like other people, and this makes me feel really bad. When I think about this, I realize that I should be happy to be myself rather than being like someone else.

After supporting what Rie had done, I told her that her challenge would be to shift between writing ideas and writing stories. For Rie and others like her, it helps to have a repertoire of questions these writers can use to help them make this shift. For example, a writer might ask, "How can I show this idea by telling the story of one time in my life?" If a writer is most at home in the land of idea-based essay-like entries, this writer may need to be reminded that in order to capture a story on the page, it helps to make a movie in one's mind, to go to the start of the episode and record it, to write step-by-step, not rushing over details. This is the small moment Rie wrote about the idea addressed in the entry cited earlier: *[Figs. II-2 and II-3]*

"Up, up, down. Up, up, down . . ." my ballet teacher shouted out to the class. Oh, I wish this was over, I thought.

"Rie!" Her voice called over the music right to me. "Your knee is not straight!" I looked down at my knee. This is all I can do. I don't have a skinny American knee.

She came over to me and pushed my knee down like she was making dough flat. Why do you have to do this to me? I screamed out in my head. I looked at the girl next to me. Her knee was back and flat. Oh, if she is like that, why can't I be like that? As I stood there, my mother's voice came into my head. She said, "Be yourself, Rie. You're not Kathy or Paula or Helen . . ."

Meanwhile, if a child is writing focused narratives, you'll want to proceed similarly. First name what you see the child doing in ways that help the child develop a sense of himself as a writer. Then compliment more specifically, being sure you also convey your absolute trust that the small moments contain big meanings. Then teach the child to shift between writing focused narratives and exploring these narratives, mining them for insights.

continued from previous page

"You will want to grow big ideas about whatever 'precious particle' emerges as important to you. You'll write about your ideas in order to figure out what you think, believe, hope for, and fear. What do you want to say about this topic, this entry? What are the really important, provocative ideas you might want to convey? You may want to choose a Life Topic, and then take an entry or an observation or a mental picture or a fact or a quotation or anything pertaining to that Life Topic, and write long about it, starting by saying, 'The thought I have about this is . . . .' So Adam, who has chosen the Life Topic of his brother leaving for college, could mentally look-over his brother's packed bedroom (even if he hasn't yet packed) and write an entry that describes what he sees, and then says, 'The important thing about this is . . . .'"

"Then, too, I hope you remember that the list of conversational prompts we used earlier in the year is yours for life. (I've got a new copy of that list for each of you, which I will pass out in a second.) Whenever you want to push your mind to have a new thought, it can help to assign yourself the job of writing long, using phrases such as, 'The surprising thing for me is . . .' or 'I wonder . . . .'"

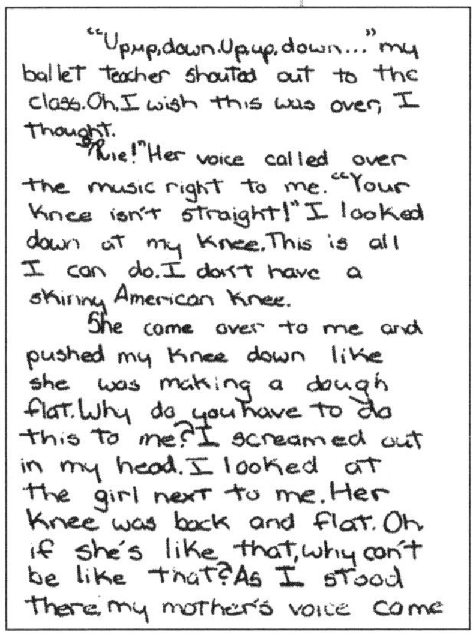

"Up,up,down.Up,up,down..." my ballet teacher shouted out to the class.Oh,I wish this was over,I thought.
"Rie!"Her voice called over the music right to me."Your knee isn't straight!"I looked down at my knee.This is all I can do.I don't have a skinny American knee.
She came over to me and pushed my knee down like she was making a dough flat.Why do you have to do this to me?I screamed out in my head.I looked at the girl next to me.Her knee was back and flat.Oh if she's like that,why can't I be like that?As I stood there,my mother's voice come

Fig. II-2 Rie writes with honesty and precision

into my head.She said, "Be yourself,Rie.You're not Kathy or Paula or Helene..."

Fig. II-3 Rie, page 2

SHARE

Believing in the Writing

Use a poem, anecdote, or metaphor to celebrate the writing intensity in the room.

"Writers, this is wonderful. The intensity in this room reminds me of a poem by Richard Wilbur. The start of the poem goes like this:

> The Writer
>
> In her room at the prow of the house
> Where light breaks, and the windows are tossed with linden,
> My daughter is writing a story.
>
> I pause in the stairwell, hearing
> From her shut door a commotion of typewriter keys
> Like a chain hauled over a gunwale.
>
> Young as she is, the stuff
> Of her life is a great cargo, and some of it heavy:
> I wish her lucky passage.
>
> But now it is she who pauses,
> As if to reject my thought and its easy figure.
> A stillness greatens, in which
>
> The whole house seems to be thinking.

"Today, I found myself pausing, taking in the ferociousness with which so many of you were writing. I thought to myself, 'Young as you are, the stuff of your life is great cargo, and some of it heavy.' And there were many times today when a stillness greatened in this classroom."

Point out a problem you are noticing, suggest a reason and propose a solution. In this case, tell children you think the desire to write about something important may be luring them into giving up on potential topics too early.

"There is no question but that all of you are writing about gigantically important topics. But writers, what I have noticed is that for some of you, the effort to write really well about a gigantic topic has made you a bit insecure. It's as if you are a kid looking for treasure. You know it is somewhere, so you run about with a shovel, digging just a little here and then just a little there. You never get to really digging deep because you are frantically worrying that first this place and then that place won't, in the end, hold any treasure."

I've only read the first half of the poem aloud. The rest of it goes like this:

> And then she is at it again with a bunched clamor
> Of strokes, and again is silent.
>
> I remember the dazed starling
> Which was trapped in that very room, two years ago;
> How we stole in, lifted a sash
>
> And retreated, not to affright it;
> And how for a helpless hour, through the crack of the door,
> We watched the sleek, wild, dark
>
> And iridescent creature
> Batter against the brilliance, drop like a glove
> To the hard floor, or the desk-top,
>
> And wait then, humped and bloody,
> For the wits to try it again; and how our spirits
> Rose when, suddenly sure,
>
> It lifted off from a chair-back,
> Beating a smooth course for the right window
> And clearing the sill of the world.
>
> It is always a matter, my darling,
> Of life or death, as I had forgotten. I wish
> What I wished you before, but harder.

I wish I'd woven more poems through these series. What an intense way to communicate! If I could write these books over, I'd weave much more poetry into the minilessons. Ah, hindsight!

Remind children that they, too, can look to see what's happening in their writing, figuring out the problems and making solutions.

"Of course, I am sure that many of you *don't* have this frantic feeling of racing here and there, frantic to find the right spot for digging deep. But my bigger point is that you need to be in charge of your own writing process. So you (not I) need to step back and think, 'Is my writing process working for me?' And you need to think, 'If it isn't quite working, why isn't it? What can I do about it?'"

"Before we go any farther in this unit, then, will you look over the writing you have done so far, and think, 'Have I found a process that is working for me?' Think quietly about this, and in a moment I will ask you to share what you are realizing with your partner."

The children worked alone first, then talked with each other. I listened in on Judah, who said to her partner, "I think I AM racing around and not really writing long about anything. I tell a story in about two paragraphs and then I jump to something else." To illustrate, she read this entry aloud to Katherine: [Fig. II-4]

> Many memories that I have about my mom and I carry questions. Every day when I was little, I would stand on the back of the toilet and put on my makeup for day care, as my mom put on her make up for work. She would put something on, then I would take it and put it on in my own way. I would put mascara on my eyebrows, a lot and very thick! She would try to give me advice, but I stuck to my opinions.
>
> Will she be there for me my whole life? Will we keep in touch so she can give me advice on life? One thing I don't understand is that sometimes when my mom gives me advice sometimes I don't like it.

Point out that from now on, children can analyze what's working and what's not working in their writing and revise their processes accordingly.

"My first suggestion is to do this periodically: Stop and think about the work you are doing. Is the writing yielding powerful thoughts? If not, change what you are doing! My other suggestion is that as writers, you need to trust. Trust that the truths of your life are hidden there in your writing—any one of those moments might carry a great cargo!"

When you plan your own minilessons, I suggest you aim to teach ambitious minilessons that convey content that the kids will feel is substantial, and that you anticipate difficulties your children will encounter as they try to apply your suggestions. Plan to teach in ways that will scaffold, coach, and assist them with these difficulties . . . but keep in mind that children will surprise you, finding some things easy, and finding other things surprisingly difficult.

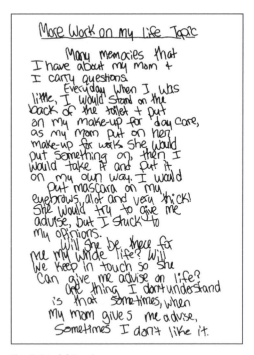

Fig. II-4 Judah's entry

HOMEWORK *Exploring a Topic from Another Side* In our writing workshop, all of us have become skilled at looking at an entry and thinking, "What do I really want to say?" or asking, "What's my big idea about this?" and then using details to support the one idea we decide to advance. *However,* most of the time in life, we do not have just one big idea or one big feeling about a subject. Usually our ideas and feelings are more complicated than that. Many of the things that I love are also things that trouble me. In *Hey World! Here I Am!* many of the notebook entries that Jean Little has included are about the friendship between Kate and Emily. Jean shows different sides to Kate and Emily's friendship. In "Maybe a Fight," Jean Little shows that friendships aren't always peachy:

> "Emily Blair," I said, struggling with my conflicting emotions, "are you trying to pick a fight with me?"
>
> "I wasn't, but I will if that's what you're after," she growled.

But in the very next notebook entry, "Not Enough Emilys", Kate writes as if Emily is the only person in the world who really understands her.

> There are not enough Emilys in the world.
>
> What I mean is . . . Emily is the kind of person
>
> Everybody needs to have sometimes.

Relationships aren't just one way. Maria's notebook is filled with entries about her annoying little brother. Here's an entry she wrote about how annoying he is.

> The apartment was so quiet without my brother. I sat on the sofa and flipped through every channel over and over again. Nobody complained or stood in the way so that I couldn't see. If my brother was here he would try to wrestle with me instead of letting me relax. The only problem is that I don't have anybody to talk to. My grandmother is in the kitchen talking with her friends.

But right in the middle of telling how annoying he is, Maria starts to write about how she misses him when he's away. Maria's entry, like Jean Little's writing, includes a whole new perspective about her brother. Maria uses tiny details to show that her brother is good company.

Tonight, will you take an entry about a Life Topic that matters to you, an entry in which you write with details and also show a big idea? Perhaps it's an entry about loving your family's homeland in Missouri, or about grieving over your big brother's upcoming departure. Write another entry, this time, write in a way that is the opposite of what you wrote earlier! Writing from opposite sides of an idea will help you think about your ideas with more depth.

TAILORING YOUR TEACHING

If your students are writing stories in their notebooks, but still need help angling them so that they reveal more . . . you might show children that the same story can be told in a variety of ways so as to convey a variety of meanings. You may want to tell about a person you know who often retells stories, each time shaping the story to make a different point. In the minilesson, you'd want to show how the person in your life can retell a single story differently based on the point that person wants to make. For example, Mary could tell children that one of her grandmother's favorite stories is the story of how she skipped a grade when she was seven. Sometimes she wants everyone to know that the day she was "moved up" was one of the proudest days of her life. On those days, she angles her story so that it goes something like this:

> Sister Corona walked over to my desk and picked up my math test. Her eyes scanned the page. A smile grew across her face. "Catherine Zinzi," she said, "you're too smart for second grade." I put my hand over my mouth and muffled the laughter that seemed to bubble through every inch of my body. "You know all of your math. Your writing is beautiful and you read well, too. I'm putting you in the third grade." I sat up very tall in my chair. All eyes were on me.

Mary's grandmother makes sure to include the details of Sister Corona's smile and to quote the exact words Sister Corona used to announce to everyone that my grandmother was "too smart for second grade." She includes the details of sitting up straight in her chair.

But her grandmother holds other very deep feelings about her life that she sometimes reveals through this same event. She holds feelings of shame and embarrassment that came from being poor—that came from being the kid in the class who was the recipient of other children's hand-me-downs. When she wants her family to see this part of her, she angles the story something like this:

> Sister Corona walked over to my desk and picked up my math test. I tried to cover the frayed rags tied to the end of each of my braids. "Catherine Zinzi," Sister Corona said. "Please stand." All eyes were on Sister Corona. All eyes were on me. Out of the corner of my eye, I could see one of the older students whispering behind her hand. I pulled the hem of my skirt down trying to cover my boots, but my skirt wasn't long enough to cover the ruffed-up, hand-me-down boots.

Like all writers and storytellers, Mary's grandmother knows that the details she includes in her story will angle it to reveal what she wants her listeners to know. For the Active Engagement part of the minilesson, you could ask children to think about a recent event the class experienced together, and to consider different ideas they might want to advance about that event. In pairs, children could write-in-the-air one way and then another way to tell that one story, and could be reminded that as writers, they always must choose what parts of stories to highlight.

MECHANICS

While children reread their notebooks and rethink their lives, searching for what it is they want to say in this final unit of the year, you and I need to take time to do our own reflecting. We, like the kids, need to think, "What is it I really want to say?" and "What matters so much to me that I'm going to put it front-and-center during this final unit of study?" Good teaching and good writing have a lot in common.

We need to approach this unit (and any unit) with overarching goals for the month, and also with goals for each line-of-growth. It is important, then, to think about our children's developing skills with punctuation, spelling, syntax, vocabulary, and grammar, and to clarify our goals for this important dimension of their writing development.

Clearly, one goal is for children to incorporate their skills and knowledge of mechanics in all they write. That is, if it takes a child just a few seconds of attentiveness in order for that child to spell *although* correctly or to punctuate dialogue correctly, then we'll want to nudge that child to take those few seconds, realizing they're on the brink of forming a new habit, one that will be useful to the child.

Another goal is for children to learn that there is a time and a place for everything, and in the early stages of writing—as a child collects entries or scrawls rough drafts—the child's primary focus needs to be on content and meaning and not on correctness. By this time in the year, all our children should be fearless writers, and they should be willing to incorporate words they don't quite know into a draft, spelling them as best they can without delaying themselves to obsess over correctness.

A third goal is for each child to have a personal agenda, a set of goals for himself. One child should know that he tends to write with unclear pronoun references and needs to keep that in mind; another should aim to spell the class set of high-frequency words correctly and to use the words she knows to help with words she does not know how to spell.

Finally, it is important for children to feel that they are on a shared journey, learning exciting new things . . . and they need to have this sense of anticipation in every aspect of their writing development. So now is a good time for you and me to think about what the exciting new work might be in the area of mechanics.

My suggestion is that we take this unit as a time to remind children of the importance of writing with *voice*. Many published writers agree that there are few qualities of good writing that matter more than this hard-to-define quality. I write with voice when the imprint of my personality comes through in my words. If you, my reader, can sit wherever you are—perhaps you are at your desk in your classroom on the fourth floor of a gigantic school in the heart of Los Angeles, or perhaps you are in the middle seat of a plane flying from Miami to Puerto Rico—and if you can pick up this page, read the little black letters that march across it, and feel as if I'm there with you, telling you something that matters to me, then I write with voice.

I bet you are wondering how voice relates to mechanics. The one seems almost spiritual, the other, mundane and workaday. But remember how magic always happens. The wizard doesn't make his magic potion by adding a handful of pearls into the finest apricot wine. He mixes the most basic, earthy of ingredients—three hairs from a rabbit's ear, the top of one yellow acorn, goat's milk. In writing, too, powerful effects come not from fancy phrases but from mixing the most basic of ingredients—words and commas, white spaces and parentheses. Writers know this and so we take time, fooling around with our print. Remember the writer who said, "I spent yesterday morning adding a comma into my story. I've worked really hard today and finally, I've made a decision: I took the comma out."

In order to help your children approach this unit caring about the way their words sound, you may want to encourage children to reread their writer's notebooks looking not only for places where they've written about important topics, but looking also for places where their writing feels alive. Tell them about the magical quality of voice, and ask them to look for places where they think that they, as a human being, shine through their words. Judah needs to read her writing looking for places where she says, "Ah, yes. This is Judah," and where she says, "Here I am" and "This sounds just like me." The topic in those sections may not be important, the writing may not fit the writer's internalized checklist of qualities of good writing, but if Judah sees herself (hears herself) in these parts of her writing, then she needs to take note. Just as we study published authors, asking, "What did he do here that I could emulate?" we need to study our own writing, asking, "What have I done here that I could emulate?"

You can help your children write with voice also by asking them to reread their own writing aloud (with internal voices). It is not an accident that writers name the magical quality I've been describing using the term *voice*. Lines of little black marks will only come to life if readers can run our eyes across those letters and turn syllables and sentences into the voice of a storyteller, a preacher, a counselor, a teacher, a companion.

We can help children write with voice also if we give them opportunities to hear us read aloud the texts that other authors have written. We will definitely want to read aloud whichever texts we use as touchstones in this unit of study. If, for example, you decide to study "The Bike," a beautiful excerpt from Gary Soto's *A Summer Life*, after you've read it aloud once or twice for other purposes, you'll probably want to give children a copy of parts of the text, and to ask them to follow as you read, noticing how Gary Soto put the sound of his voice onto the page. How does he use punctuation and words to create emphasis, to channel us, his readers, to read in such a manner that we tuck in a quick reference here, and slow

down there? Try reading some of these passages (describing Gary as he rode his first bike) aloud, and ask yourself, "How does he want me to read this?"

> When I squinted, I could see past the end of the block. My hair flicked like black fire, and I thought I was pretty cool riding up and down the block, age five, in my brother's hand-me-down shirt.
>
> Going up and down the block was one thing, but taking the first curve, out of sight of Mom and the house, was another. I was scared of riding on Sarah Street. Mom said hungry dogs lived on that street, and red anger lived in their eyes. Their throats were hard with extra bones from biting kids on bikes, she said.
>
> But I took the corner anyway. I didn't believe Mom. Once she had said that pointing at rainbows caused freckles, and after a rain had moved in and drenched the streets, after the sparrows flitted across the lawn, a rainbow washed over the junkyard and reached the dark barrels of Coleman pickle. (19-20)

Ask children, too, to read a passage like this aloud, and to do so more than once. Help them to read it so that they feel the way that a comma reins in their voice. Help them feel in their bones the power of those short sentences: "But I took the corner anyway." Help them see that Gary Soto could not have turned that corner without indenting, without leaving the white space that a new paragraph provides. Help them feel that the way that meaning and punctuation and white space all combine to channel the voice of a reader.

If you invite children into such a study of the prose, of the nuts and bolts of prose, you will be imbuing written language with significance. Your attentiveness and respect for the tools of writing well will make the world of difference.

IN THIS SESSION, YOU WILL TEACH CHILDREN THAT WRITERS OF MEMOIR DIVE DEEP INTO THEIR TOPICS. YOU WILL SHARE SOME STRATEGIES FOR WRITING WITH GREATER DEPTH THAN EVER BEFORE AND WILL INVITE CHILDREN TO JOIN YOU IN CREATING MORE STRATEGIES TO ACHIEVE THIS.

GETTING READY
- Example of writing that asks and explores important questions about a Life Topic
- Strategies for Writing with Depth chart
- See CD-ROM for resources

EXPECTING DEPTH FROM OUR WRITING

Last night my son pointed out to me that studying for his math mid-term will not be difficult because the course has been cumulative. Each new unit has built on the material he learned in earlier units, thus keeping all that earlier learning alive. My hunch is that all good education is cumulative—that in a well-taught history course, for example, as students study the Great Depression, they learn about ways that financial, social disaster compares and contrasts with the depression of 1832, and they learn also how seeds for the Great Depression were sown earlier in the Roaring Twenties.

A year-long curriculum to support children's growth as writers should be cumulative. Children should constantly revisit skills and strategies they learned earlier in the year in order to use them in the service of more complex, multifaceted operations. Today's session aims to help children revisit the earlier sessions in which they learned strategies for generating writing, this time rallying children to a more ambitious goal than that of simply generating any writing. Today, you support children in generating writing that is thoughtful, writing that dives deep.

Of course, there's no easy sequence of steps that you can lay out for young writers, assuring them that if they compliantly follow this prescribed route, they'll arrive at a "Eureka!" moment. It will never be the case that compliance produces depth of thought!

For this reason, in this session you summon children to join into an inquiry, an investigation. "Which strategies do lead to deeper, more insightful writing?" you ask. You know there will be answers, and that your teaching and their inventions will combine to create a list of suggested strategies, but more than this, you know that writers will profit from approaching writing with an intention to go deep. Your hope is that this session (and this unit) will help children approach a page, wanting not just to fill the page but wanting to discover new insights, to surprise themselves by saying something they never knew they knew.

When young writers worked in an author study of Angela Johnson (in the Authors as Mentors unit of our Units of Study for Primary Writing series), one very young child decided that Angela Johnson had taught her, above all, that on every page of her writing, she needed to do something beautiful. This intention, alone, changed everything about that child's writing. In this session, your hope is that children come from it resolving that in every entry they will write something that is deep and true and important. You hope, too, that children approach their writing with a spirit not of compliance but of adventure, willing to climb every mountain until they find their dream.

MINILESSON

Expecting Depth from Our Writing

CONNECTION

Tell children they are ready to graduate from focusing on strategies for generating writing to focusing on strategies for writing with depth.

"You all have become skilled at generating writing—writing about small moments, and writing about big ideas. So I think the time has come for us to think less about generating *writing*, and more about generating *writing that is powerful*. And frankly, I am not altogether sure what the strategies are that I use—or other writers use—to generate writing that is powerful!"

"Have you ever watched a duck swimming across the surface of a lake? It swims along very peacefully for a while, and then suddenly the duck tips its head down and dives deep underwater? Writers are like ducks, in a way. We often swim along the surface of a subject for awhile, and then all of a sudden, we make a deep dive."

"Over the next few weeks, I hope that together, we figure out a bunch of strategies that we can use to help us take deep dives as writers."

Name your teaching point. Specifically, teach children to write what they *don't know* about what they *know.*

"Eudora Welty, a famous memoirist, taught me one strategy that she uses in order to write with depth. She once gave me this advice (actually she wrote it in a book, but when I read the book it was as if she was speaking directly to me). She said this: 'Write what you *don't know* about what you *know*.'"

TEACHING

Share an example of a child who has taken a Life Topic he or she knows well, generated questions about that Life Topic, and used writing to entertain those questions.

"Welty is suggesting that we take a topic we know well and ask, 'What *don't* I know about what I know?' Ask, 'Where's the mystery in this topic?' For example, I could take the topic of my father, and I could ask, 'Where is the mystery pertaining to my father?' One thing that is mysterious to me is this: 'Why do I write so often about my father when it is my mother who is the truly influential person in my life?'"

"Once you have found a possible Life Topic (or even just an entry that you somehow like) you may want to borrow Eudora Welty's strategy. Ask yourself (as I asked myself), 'What don't I know about what I know?' Ask, 'Where's the mystery here?'"

COACHING

I am deliberately beginning this minilesson by requesting children's help in an inquiry that will thread through much of this unit. The question I pose here is, "What strategies can writers use to write with depth?" For now, I will share one tentative answer, but I also want to set the stage for kids to be collaborators in this inquiry.

I know this might seem like a silly image to you. Find a better one! My family has a cabin alongside an Adirondack lake, and so for me, this image holds great romance. It carries with it all that I feel when I am in that summer place. But I know it probably won't hold as much power for many of my readers, and so you will want to find your own way to communicate that writers go deep.

When we taught children to write narratives, we urged them to write with the exact words that a character spoke rather than paraphrasing the character. Similarly, you'll notice that I rarely paraphrase within minilessons. Instead of saying, "Ask yourself what the mystery is in your topic," I say, "Ask yourself, 'Where's the mystery in this topic?'" I believe that it is helpful to give kids the exact words I use to think about my writing. This doesn't mean that you need to incorporate those exact words into your teaching or that children need to incorporate those exact words into their thinking about writing, but that option is available and the choice is yours and your children's.

"I'm remembering a young girl that I taught years and years ago. She'd written an entry about how, by mistake, she shaved one eyebrow off. She didn't know what to do so she went to her sister. To help, her sister shaved off the other eyebrow! Alongside the entry describing this, that girl wrote a marginal question. She wrote, 'Why do I always do weird things like this? Am I the only one in my family who does weird things like this? When my mom was little, did she used to do weird things?' She was essentially looking back on her writing and identifying the mystery."

"Adam, too, took the risk of asking hard questions about his Life Topic (which for now, anyhow, is the fact that his brother, Jon, will soon be leaving for college). Adam wrote this": *[Fig. III-1]*

> My brother. What does he think I think of him? Would he rather spend time with me or his friends? What does he think about me? Do his friends know a lot about me? Do I want them to?

"But this is the important thing. After listing these questions, Adam thought and wrote about them. He entertained those questions. (You'll remember us learning to do this during our last unit of study.) Listen": *[Fig. III-2]*

> I hope that he will still have time for me and not only his friends. I think that my brother is going to do something special with his life. We do this thing called hugs. I think it is because he doesn't want to give a real hug so he can maintain his big brother personality. I think he is almost helping me through life. He is almost like a young dad to me. He is almost like a jester sometimes. We share a lot of things but we both have our own personal lives.

"Did you hear how Adam entertained those questions? He thought and wrote more and more about them, didn't he?"

Active Engagement

Invite your students to join you in reading one child's writing in order to ascertain the strategies that writer has used to write with depth.,

"Writers, I'm hoping that you'll join me in a study of the strategies that we, as writers, can use to write with more depth just like the ducks diving deep below the surface. Listen to Max's entries, and as you listen, think about what Max has done to get himself thinking and writing more deeply. In a moment, you'll have a chance to talk about what you notice."

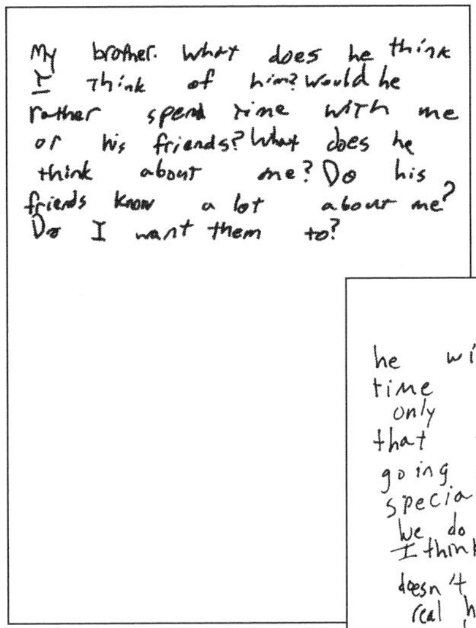

My brother. What does he think I think of him? Would he rather spend time with me or his friends? What does he think about me? Do his friends know a lot about me? Do I want them to?

Fig. III-1 Adam asks questions of his Life Topic

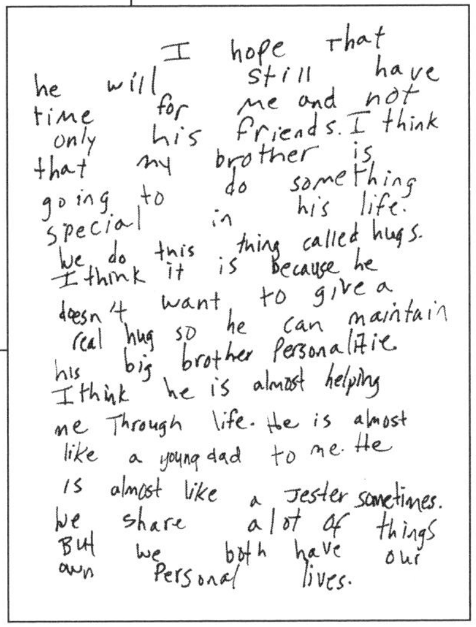

I hope that he will still have time for me and not only his friends. I think that my brother is going to do something special in his life. We do this thing called hugs. I think it is because he doesn't want to give a real hug so he can maintain his big brother Personalitie. I think he is almost helping me through life. He is almost like a young dad to me. He is almost like a Jester sometimes. We share a lot of things But we both have our own Personal lives.

Fig. III-2 Adam entertains his questions

One of the interesting things for you to notice in a minilesson is that you will find yourself doing all the things you suggest kids do when they write essays. If you look back over the last few minutes of this minilesson, you will notice that after talking about an idea for just a few sentences (and during that time I quote Eudora Welty), I then shifted into telling a small story, which illustrated the thought I laid out. The story ends with a sentence that unpacks how this story connects to the idea I'd laid out. Then there is a second example, with just a single word (too) acting as a transition. Again, after this example, I unpack it, this time using the phrase, "But this is the important thing . . . ." After citing this example, I unpack it, then I pose a second idea, one that builds on the first. If this were, in fact, an essay, and I developed this second idea, then the essay would be structured not as a traditional single-thesis essay but as a journey of thought essay, with one claim leading to a second, higher-level one.

I read Max's entry with gestures and intonation which highlighted the ways Max "dove for depth": [Fig. III-3]

> Whenever I used to read the entry I wrote about getting injured on the boardwalk, I thought it was about safety.

As I read, I cupped my left hand as if holding that small moment.

> Now I realize it's also about pressure.

I brought my right hand towards the small moment I held, trying to show that this was another possible angle on that same small moment.

> My sister pressured me into wearing shoes. I didn't have to listen, but I was pressured.

As I continued reading, I showed with my right hand that Max had suggested a second angle on that same small moment. My intonation suggested that the word "now" signaled yet a third, alternate angle Max would take toward the same small moment.

> Now I think and realize that I may get pressured even more than that.

I dropped the small-moment I had been holding in one cupped hand and moved my arms wide apart, implying that now Max is thinking beyond this one focused topic to a big Life Topic.

> For example, if my friends are gossiping about someone, sometimes I feel pressured to join them. Sometimes I have to step on the brakes and stop and think about what I am doing and stop before I get pressured into doing something.

Ask children to tell partners the strategies they observed the writer using in order to write with depth.

Children turned and talked with their partners, and then one or two of them spoke, as did I, suggesting that Max thought deeply because he revisited his subject, thinking one thought about it, then thinking another thought about it, then another. I told children that this is one way that writers make deep dives. "Let's listen to another entry that Max has written and see if this time, like last time, he thinks and rethinks his subject," I said. This time when I read, I used my intonation and hand gestures to

As a minilesson progresses, you have has several opportunities to restate the teaching point of the minilesson, each time angling it one way or another. For example, at this moment in the minilesson, I could have said, "Writers, you've learned that it is important to ask, 'Where is the mystery in my topic?'" Alternatively, I could have said, "Writers, I hope you have learned that it is important to ask yourselves questions as you write, questions that help you think not only about the topic but about why the topic matters to you."

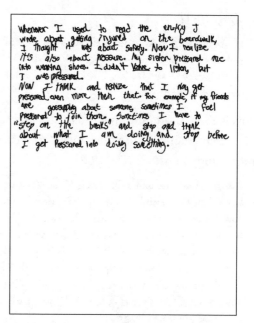

Fig. III-3 Max "dives for depth"

highlight the fact that in the entry, Max described standing beside his grandmother's bed in the hospital, reliving a whole chain of thoughts, questions, associations . . . revisiting his subject repeatedly. *[Fig. III-4]*

> If Grandma is so strong, how is it that she looks in need for the first time in a while in the hospital? She has never made me cry before. And as a matter of fact, I've never seen her in bed before. And her hair feels so soft and warm. She can't stay awake while she speaks with us, and she looks so bad, it makes me so sad. She always knew how to keep strong, and supported us to do that. But she isn't speaking now and I have trouble keeping strong. Those drafted movies always make you think that when you are in a hospital bed with tubes going into your body, you are going to die.
>
> Those were the thoughts going through my head. I found it my duty to stay beside her, making her strong, as she does for me. But I had a problem. She had never really explained how to keep yourself strong. I never thought it was important because when would I need to do so? I was just a happy little kid with a good life.

"Do you feel how powerful this writing is? Do you see how Max keeps diving deeper into his own thinking? So writers, I hope that from this, you are learning strategies for posing and pursuing questions as you write. Remember that your goal is not just to *write* well, but to *think* well too."

Link

Remind children that their goal is to generate *thoughtful* writing. Encourage them to draw from their full repertoire of strategies for doing this.

"Writers, I can teach you strategies for generating narrative or essay writing, but in this unit of study, our goal is not just to generate writing, it is to generate thoughtful writing. Our goal is to write like ducks, who may swim along the surface of a subject for a time but who then dive deep. And frankly, I don't know the strategies that you in particular can use that will make your writing deep. My hunch is that above all, you need to approach the page yearning for and reaching for depth. My hunch is that you need to write with a spirit of adventure, and to be willing to risk going off the beaten path."

Instead of asking children to turn and talk about ways that Max dove deep in his writing, I could have asked children to write about what they noticed. Either way, I need to invite them to do likewise. The cycle of noticing what another writer has done and then giving ourselves the task of doing likewise allows any writer to write in ways that are getting progressively deeper and smarter. Either way, my goal is to help writers to aim towards depth, and to help them understand that honesty, surprise, questions, and approaching topics through new tangents can all help to create provocative thoughts.

Fig. III-4 Max tries a variety of perspectives

"Today and always, take charge of your writing. Do whatever you need to do so that your writing leads you to surprise, to discovery, to significance. I've made a chart of what we've said thus far in the unit, and in case this helps, I'll have it on the easel. Off you go."

Don't feel as if you have to read this to your class!

This entire chart could be retitled Strategies for Revising with Depth. Consider each bullet and you'll see that actually, each of these techniques invites students to revise. When a writer revisits two or three Life Topics over and over, the writer is revising his or her understanding of the topic. When a writer looks between several seemingly separate entries in order to build a bridge uniting those entries, this, too, is revision.

Strategies for Writing with Depth

- Many writers have a few Life Topics that we return to often, mining these topics for new insights, stories, images, ideas. We ask, "What do I write about again and again?" "What might my Life Topics be?"

- Sometimes writers look at seemingly unconnected entries and ask, "How might these connect with each other?" Oftentimes, there are underlying issues or truths beneath the seemingly separate bits.

- Sometimes a writer finds he or she has one or two great images—places or objects or scenes—within which the writer's heart opens. We search for those images.

- Writers remember, "The bigger you write, the smaller you write." Writers shuttle between writing big insights and writing with minute details.

- After a writer has written about a subject by advancing one idea or claim on that subject, the writer may deliberately try to write about the same subject, advancing the exactly opposite idea: I love to write, I hate to write. Oftentimes, two contrasting ideas can be simultaneously true.

- Writers take topics and territories we know well and think, as Eudora Welty has suggested, "What don't I know about what I know?" and "Where's the mystery here?"

- Writers write to explore new ideas and do so by asking and entertaining hard questions, and by visiting a subject, repeatedly, from different perspectives.

WRITING AND CONFERRING

Supporting Thoughtfulness in Writing

As you confer with your children, you will help them use writing as a vehicle for learning more about their Life Topics. In preparation for this, you may want to make yourself a little chart, with children's names along the top and a list of strategies/qualities that pertain to writing-to-learn down the left-hand margin. Then when you confer with children, the list you've generated can remind you of things to compliment and things to teach.

If I were to make such a list, I'd probably decide to list qualities of thoughtful, deep writing. I would start with *honesty*, and this would be one important thing to watch for, to compliment, and to teach toward. I think it is all too easy to write with glib clichés, and that when I hold myself accountable for writing the exact truth, my writing is much more apt to take me to surprising places. More specifically, I'd look for evidence that a writer understands that the process of writing involves a writer working toward the goal of putting the truth into words. I'd celebrate any evidence I saw that a writer tried one way to say something, felt dissatisfied, and then tried another way to say that message. I think Adam was doing this in the entry I cited earlier in this session in which he wrote about his brother. When Adam wrote, "I think he is almost helping me through life. He is almost like a young dad to me. He is almost like a jester sometimes," it seems to me Adam is reaching for the precise words and metaphor to capture the role his brother plays in his life. I'd support that and teach toward that.

I'd look for *length*, too. Peter Elbow, the great writing researcher, once said, "Writing is like water. You need to let it flow for a while before it runs clear." There are lots of ways for writers to write longer—the most important is for them to shift between generalizations and examples generous with detail. Children can also use the conversational prompts they learned earlier in the year. "Remember how, earlier this year, we

> MID-WORKSHOP
> TEACHING POINT
>
> **Inventing Strategies for Writing with Depth** "Writers, can I have your eyes and your attention? Would you reread what you've written today and see if you made a deep dive? If you can find a place in your writing where you suddenly took a deep dive (even a little one), look at what you did as a writer. Did you ask questions of your subject, as Eudora Welty suggests? Did you invent another strategy?" After a few minutes during which time children reread the work they'd done that day, I said, "Share the place where you took a deep dive with your partner! Read the surface writing you'd been doing, and then read the deep dive. And writers, if either you or your partner took a deep dive, would you ask yourselves this question: What, specifically, did you do to get yourself to go deep?"
>
> After a bit I intervened to say, "Earlier today we saw that both Eudora Welty and Adam asked questions in order to make deep dives into their subjects; they both explored the aspects of their subjects that were mysterious to them. Remember that Adam asked, 'Would my brother rather spend time with me or his friends? What does he think of me?' Those were risky, probing questions, and they channeled Adam towards deeper thinking. Would you give me a thumbs-up if today, you used questions for diving deeper?"
>
> *continued on next page*

learned to use conversational prompts to grow important ideas? This is probably a time to use those thought prompts, or to use any other means you have available, to grow insights about your Life Topics," I might say.

Within writing of length, I'd look to see if the writer seemed to be making choices, deliberately assigning himself or herself particular strategies and topics in the interest of writing with power. Sometimes it almost seems to me that a child's goal is simply to fill the page, and I'd want to be sure that children's writing looked as if the writer had other goals: to learn, to be surprised, to capture the truth on the page, to convey something significant. I might teach specific strategies for making choices. For example, I might encourage children to shift between writing about their Life Topics and rereading what they have written, boxing out the most important line and then expanding upon that one line.

But most importantly, I would want to encourage children to be writers with *purpose*, writing toward the goal of learning more about themselves. "Remember," I might say, "you are in charge of your own writing process. You need to think about how you can gather entries that will help you to write about the issues and moments of your life. Many of you have made lists of Life Topics and that is important. What will you do next? Don't wait for me to tell you what to do because you are the author of your writing life."

continued from previous page

"I need your help to think about yet other strategies we can use to make our writing dive deep. I've never taught kids to do this before so I could use your help. My hunch is that if we work together, we can invent our very own repertoire of strategies. We could share those strategies with each other, like Adam has already done with us, and we could all try the strategies out to figure out how to use them in powerful ways. Are you game for this? It will require that we do some inventing together . . . ."

The children all signaled that yes, they were game to work together to invent strategies for writing with depth. To get themselves started, they talked among themselves about ideas they had for doing this and shared ways they'd already found that helped them write with depth. "Writers, I'd love to have a grand conversation about the ideas you've developed for writing with depth," I said. "But why don't you show me rather than tell me those strategies. In the remaining time we have, try to write in a way that feels deep or significant or honest, and later we'll study and learn from what you do, as we learned from Adam's and Max's work."

SHARE

Entertaining, Rather Than Answering, Questions

Offer one student's writing up for study. Ask children to find, with a partner, something in the writing they could all try to do as well.

"I've made copies of an entry that one of your classmates has written. I thought that we'd try to look together at an entry, asking, 'What exactly has this writer done that the rest of us could perhaps do as well?' Read over Emily's entry, and then make marginal notes as you think about the question, 'What has Emily done that you and the rest of us could try as well?'" [Figs. III-5 and III-6]

> I am still a child and still have childhood memories but when is it over? Maybe it's never over, it is just you believe it's over. On Adam's poetry notebook it says you don't stop playing because you are old—you are old because you stop playing. So maybe if we always believe in this, no one is old. Just because the world says, "You are 90 and that's old" doesn't mean it is true. So like Naomi Shihab Nye says, "Reinvent things." Ninety-year-old people may not be old anymore. You will always have a piece of child-ness in you.
>
> When I was seven, my mom called me a little cub. Because I was a baby. When I was a baby I would lie on my mom's stomach and listen to the beat of her heart and fall asleep. And even now I do the same and I say, "Little cub." She says when I'm a hundred I will still be her little cub. Even now I am scared of thunder, scared of monsters in my closet. It feels like I am little always. My sister is the big sister so I always feel small. But even my sister is a little baby. There are times in my life where I feel stuck small. But there are many times when I feel big and want to stay a kid forever.

Collect observations from the class and add some to the class chart.

Children talked with their partners about their observations, and then I asked a few children to say aloud what they'd noticed.

Jonah pointed out that in Emily's entry, as in the entry that Max wrote and the class studied earlier, Emily thinks about a topic in one way, then in another way, then in yet another way. But Emily gets those varied ways of thinking by linking specific things to the

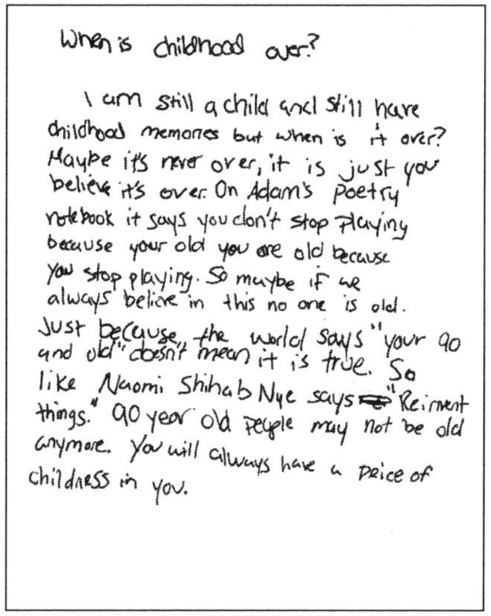

When is childhood over?

I am still a child and still have childhood memories but when is it over? Maybe it's never over, it is just you believe it's over. On Adam's poetry notebook it says you don't stop playing because your old you are old because you stop playing. So maybe if we always believe in this no one is old. Just because, the world says "your 90 and old" doesn't mean it is true. So like Naomi Shihab Nye says ← "Reinvent things." 90 year old people may not be old anymore. You will always have a piece of childness in you.

Fig. III-5 Emily explores her Life Topic

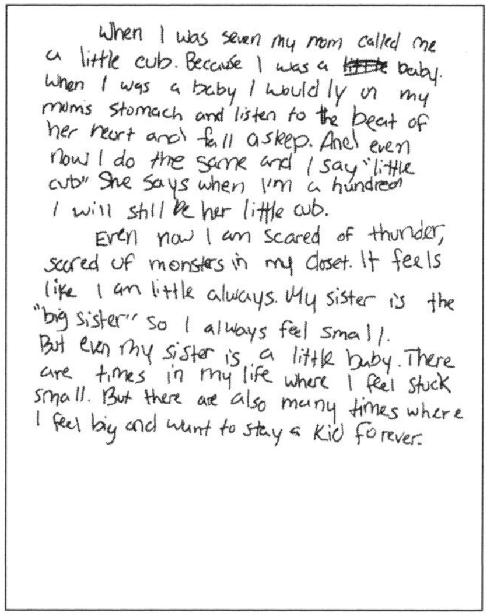

When I was seven my mom called me a little cub. Because I was a ~~little~~ baby. When I was a baby I would ly on my moms stomach and listen to the beat of her heart and fall asleep. And even now I do the same and I say "little cub." She says when I'm a hundred I will still be her little cub.

Even now I am scared of thunder, scared of monsters in my closet. It feels like I am little always. My sister is the "big sister" so I always feel small. But even my sister is a little baby. There are times in my life where I feel stuck small. But there are also many times where I feel big and want to stay a kid forever.

Fig. III-6 Emily's entry, page 2

question. She builds bridges from her idea to a quote from a poet, from her idea to an idea from a classmate, and from her idea to an anecdote from her life. "You can all do this same sort of work," I said to the class, and added this strategy for writing with depth to the chart:

Strategies for Writing with Depth

- Many writers have a few Life Topics that we return to often, mining these topics for new insights, stories, images, ideas. We ask, "What do I write about again and again?" "What might my Life Topics be?"

- Sometimes writers look at seemingly unconnected entries and ask, "How might these connect with each other?" Oftentimes, there are underlying issues or truths beneath the seemingly separate bits.

- Sometimes a writer finds he or she has one or two great images—places or objects or scenes—within which the writer's heart opens. We search for those images.

- Writers remember, "The bigger the idea, the smaller you write." Writers shuttle between writing big insights and writing with minute details.

- After a writer has written about a subject by advancing one idea or claim on that subject, the writer may deliberately try to write about the same subject, advancing the exactly opposite idea: I love to write, I hate to write. Oftentimes, two contrasting ideas can be simultaneously true.

- Writers take topics and territories we know well and think, as Eudora Welty has suggested, "What don't I know about what I know?" and "Where's the mystery here?"

- Writers write to explore new ideas and do so by asking and entertaining hard questions, and by visiting a subject, repeatedly, from different perspectives.

- Sometimes a writer thinks about a topic or a question by linking that one starting subject to one thing, another, another (to a quote, a statistic, a memory, a classmate's idea).

HOMEWORK ***Thinking About Topics from Different Perspectives*** Writers, when you were younger and less experienced as writers, you probably thought that the content of writing depended upon the subject. But you're older and more sophisticated as writers now, and so you've probably come to realize that as a writer, you can take a topic and then choose the way you write that topic. We've talked a lot about the fact that a writer needs to decide whether the story about a ride on the Ferris wheel is a story about a child overcoming fear of heights or a story about a child not wanting to outgrow childish pleasures, for example. As a writer, you need to decide what it is you want to show in a story and then highlight that meaning.

In memoir, the understanding that a story can be told in different ways to highlight different meanings is very important. We can take an incident, for example, and write what how we used to think the incident involved. Then we could write about how something happened to change the way we regard that initial incident—perhaps time passed, or perhaps we came to a new realization, or perhaps someone made a passing comment that changed our thoughts—but one way or another, we can write that we came to question the way we once regarded that initial incident. Then we could write about it from a very different perspective. For example, maybe you and your friend had an argument and at the time, you felt angry. You could recreate the argument from that perspective. Now, looking back, you can recall the entire sequence of events and from your more distant perspective, you can understand your friend, sympathize with that person, and regret your own role. You could write the story of the argument twice, each time from a different perspective.

To do this, you will probably want to start by rereading your notebook, looking for an entry that pertains to one of your Life Topics. The entry will probably capture one way of thinking about an event or a topic. You may need to recall a time when your perspective on that topic or that incident changed so that you can write from another perspective. You might start your first entry by saying, "At the time, I was mad . . . " and then write another entry by saying, "At the time, I was mad. But now, looking back, I realize . . . "

Here's an example of James' entries about making origami ornaments with his mom when he was little. He's not sure how he wants to use this story yet so he's writing it in different ways: *[Figs. III-7* and *III-8]*

My mom folded another piece of paper. I leaned in and watched every fold she made.

"What are you trying to make?" I asked.

"A boat," said my mom. "Finished!" I got the boat from the table. I pretended it was sailing up my arm.

"Can you teach me how to make one?" I asked.

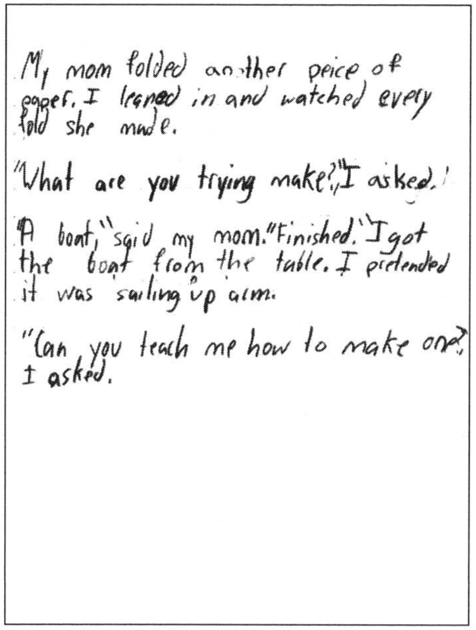
My mom folded another peice of paper. I leaned in and watched every fold she made.

"What are you trying make?," I asked.

"A boat," said my mom. "Finished." I got the boat from the table. I pretended it was sailing up arm.

"Can you teach me how to make one?" I asked.

Fig. III-7 James looks at origami as magic.

My mom folded another piece of paper. I looked out the window. Origami wasn't fun.

"Hey, James, look what I made," said my mom.

"A boat. Who cares", I thought. "Try to make something else," I said. Only girls like to do origami, I thought as I looked out the window again. Why do I have to do this? Why can't I play outside with my dad instead?

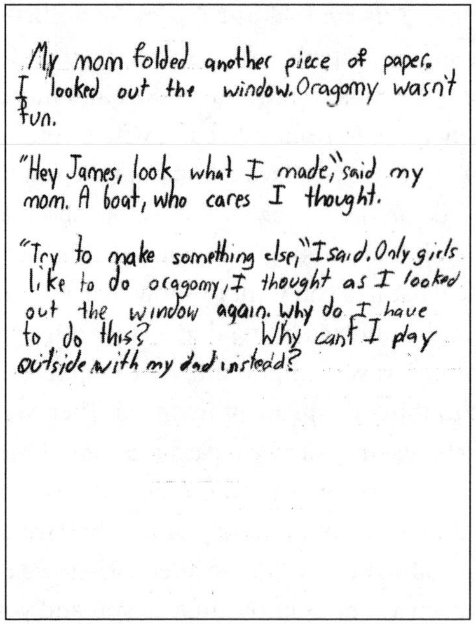
My mom folded another piece of paper. I looked out the window. Oragomy wasn't fun.

"Hey James, look what I made," said my mom. A boat, who cares I thought.

"Try to make something else," I said. Only girls like to do ocagomy, I thought as I looked out the window again. Why do I have to do this? Why cant I play outside with my dad instedd?

Fig. III-8 James looks at origami as dull.

TAILORING YOUR TEACHING

If your students are writing about their Life Topics, but seem to be letting go of much of what they know about writing well . . . you might teach students to apply what they've learned so far this year about writing with focus, detail, and structure by demonstrating how you read from your list of Life Topics and then go through your list of strategies for writing well. In a minilesson or small group you might say, "I'm going to look at my current list of Life Topics. I'm going choose one and then I'm going to recall what I know about writing well as I write." For example, if my Life Topics are:

- Fun activities
- Embarrassing mistakes
- Hurtful words

I might demonstrate by saying to the children, "As I look at this list, I immediately recall that writers often narrow our topics, we don't write all about a topic, but rather we take a small piece of a topic so that we can focus our writing. 'Fun activities' is too broad! I need to focus that topic. One way writers focus a topic is by thinking, 'What do I want to say about this?'" I could proceed, saying something like, "The word 'fun' always makes me think of my friend Amanda. Now I need to ask myself, 'What do I want to say about this?' Well, for sure I want to say that I can always be myself around Amanda, because she never judges me. That's why I have so much fun with her."

Then I might say to children, "So you see how I use what I know about writing to get myself started. Now watch how I continue to use what I've learned all year. The next questions I'll ask myself are key: 'How will I write this? What structure will I use? Will I write it as a small moment entry or an essay entry?' If I write it as a small moment, I need to think about a particular time that shows how Amanda and I have fun together—and it needs to pertain also to the idea that Amanda doesn't judge me. I'll need to remember specific details that show this. If I write it as a essay entry, I'll need to begin with this idea, 'I can always be myself around Amanda,' and then I'll need to support this idea with evidence. So, writers, did you notice how I looked at my list, chose a topic, and applied what I've learned about writing well? I applied what I know about writing with focus, detail, and structure?"

If your students are asking questions to delve deeper into their writing, but the questions don't seem to be leading them anywhere . . . show students that questions can be more or less powerful. For example, Tyler reread his entry about his grandmother and realized his questions were not ones he could answer without further research and may not yield depth anyhow. In one entry, he'd written these questions: *[Fig.III-9]*

> In my grandmother's childhood, did she have a good relationship with her Mom or her grandmother? When I am at my grandmother's apartment and she isn't at work I wonder what does she do all day? Does she go outside and do stuff in New York City? Does she go to our house and help my Mom? Does she go shopping with my Mom or my cousins? In my grandmother's home does she read? What are my grandmother's hobbies? What does she enjoy doing when she isn't busy?

These questions will probably not take him very deep. Writers will benefit more from questions which promote deeper thinking. Because this is a memoir unit, writers will benefit most from questions that pertain not only to the subject but also to the writer. Tyler, for example, realized he could ask:

- Why is my grandmother so important to me?
- What is the unique role my grandmother plays in my life?
- Why does my grandmother mean so much more to me than she seems to mean to my siblings?
- Have I always cherished my grandmother as much as I do now or has this changed over time?
- What do I want to say to my grandmother that I haven't yet said?
- How does my grandmother fit into the whole of who I am as a person?

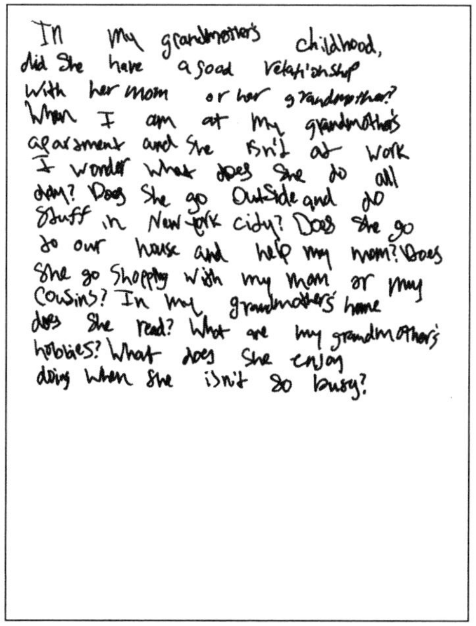
In my grandmother's childhood, did She have a good relationship with her mom or her grandmother? When I am at my grandmother's apartment and She isn't at work I wonder what does She do all day? Does She go Outside and do Stuff in New York city? Does She go to our house and help my mom? Does She go Shopping with my mom or my Cousins? In my grandmother's home does She read? What are my grandmother's hobbies? What does She enjoy doing when She isn't so busy?

Fig. III-9 Tyler asks questions.

ASSESSMENT

You'll need to spend some time looking over the work your children have done so far in this unit so that you can chart your course for the next few days. It is likely that children will need you to spend a day or two reminding them of all that they have learned earlier in the year about writing focused narratives.

As you look over their writing, divide the notebooks into several piles. Make a pile for children who are intending to write focused narratives in the service of Life Topics, but who seem to be summarizing rather than storytelling. Don't be discouraged if you find that a fair proportion of your class is doing this. The units on personal narrative writing taught children to write tiny, tiny focused narratives, and this new unit is, after all, asking children to write about big Life Topics . . . only to do so by writing tiny focused narratives. That is, this new unit is asking children to shift between big ideas and focused narratives, and so it should not surprise you if some children have been pulled farther into writing in generalizations than they have before. But yes, you may need to take a detour away from the minilessons I suggest so as to first reteach your children how to write focused narratives when they want to do so.

You could couch this teaching in a bigger principle. For example, you could teach children that whenever a writer decides to tackle a particular kind of writing, she must pause for a moment, thinking, "What do I already know about how to achieve this challenge?" That is, once a child has taken on a particular writing task, the child needs to take the time to access what she already knows about how to do that task. For example, if the child is writing a focused narrative in her notebook, then she needs to recall what she knows about how to do this well. Having said this, you can then remind children that in this case, it can help to make and revise a timeline or a story mountain, it can help to think about what the story is really about and to start it in a way that links to the real meaning of the story, it can help to start with dialogue or with a small action, and so forth.

While dividing the notebooks into piles, make a pile also for children who do not seem to be making self-assignments. That is, you will see that some notebooks seem to brim with random accounts of events from the last few weeks, conveying the impression that the child is writing on autopilot. Despite your efforts to lure children to dig deep, to explore Life Topics, some children will yet approach memoir writing as if it is business as usual. For example, James' new section of his notebook contained many entries like this one in which he recorded recent events. He wrote: *[Fig. III-10]*

We walked into Avery Fisher Hall. People were all around and the lights were on. Me and my grandfather took our seats. We were so close that we could see all the musicians.

The lights went out and the music started to play. I don't know what the name of the music was, but it was really beautiful. I could have listened to the music play all night.

> We walked into Avery Fisher Hall. People were all around and the lights on. Me and my grandfather took our seats. We were so close that we could see all the musicians.
>
> The lights went out and the music started to play. I don't know what the name of the music was, but it was really beautiful. I could have listened to the music play all night.

Fig. III-10 James' writing "as usual".

Later, when I asked James how this entry helped him to think about his Life Topics, he said, "Well, it doesn't really, but it was really fun to go to the concert, and I thought it would be a good story." If you have several children like James, who haven't yet understood that this unit asks something more of them, you'll want to convene this group and talk to them about the differences between personal narrative writing and memoir writing. When writing memoir, a writer is called upon to ask, "Who am I? What is it I want to say about the whole of my life?"

You may also create a pile of notebooks representing students who are filling their notebooks with listlike entries about their Life Topics. Here's an example from Stella's notebook: [Fig. III-11]

> I love my uncle a lot. We have so much fun whenever I go to visit him. I also love him because he is about my age and we have a lot in common.
>
> I love my uncle because we like to do the same things. We can spend all day together and never get bored.
>
> This is why I love my uncle.

When you see lists of topics, each summed up in a phrase, your initial reaction may be to want to steer the child away from mere listing. Be careful that the child doesn't end up feeling as if you reject the items on his or her list! Remember that each of those items is probably gigantically important to the child who has written it. Respond with trust and appreciation. "These are so, so huge, aren't they? They give me goose bumps." Read the child's list as if you were reading names from the Vietnam Memorial Wall. Each word will capture a person, a place, a time in the child's life, and as such it will brim with significance. Then (and only then), take this energy and the feelings of significance that will well up in the child's chest, and rechannel them toward entries that are long and specific. They may be small moment entries (which will be easier than essay-like stories) in which case, help the child use the advice you gave in the Link section of Session II's minilesson.

Fig. III-11 Stella's list entry

READING LITERATURE TO INSPIRE WRITING

Adrian Peetom, a Canadian literacy leader, *once told me, "If I could say just one thing to teachers of writing, I would tell them this. Trust the books. Trust the books and get out of their way." It is true that the authors who write the books we love can become co-teachers, helping us teach children to write. Authors teach not only by demonstrating craftsmanship but also by inspiring children to dig deep into their hearts and souls. In this session, you will let children know that we can read to be moved. We read in order to feel something stirring within us—to feel awake to our own feelings and lives.*

I'm thinking of Andrew, a fifth grader. During fourth grade he'd written an entry about his camp. In the piece, he told only a superficial, comic story. Then, in fifth grade, Andrew's teacher Kathy Doyle created a trusting community where it was okay for Andrew and the others in his class to reveal themselves. Kathy did this especially by using literature as an ice ax, as Kafka has said it can be, to break the frozen sea within us.

From the safety of this new community, Andrew looked back at the piece he'd written the preceding year. "The truth is, camp was nothing like this in the story," he said. "When I wrote it, in fourth grade, there was a school-Andrew and a home-Andrew. Back then, I acted completely different in school than I really am." Andrew again wrote about his camp and this time, he wrote about how, on the last day of camp, he'd struggled to keep from weeping when he paused to say goodbye to the goats and to the gravel driveway. His memoir ends:

> We took pictures until finally Soren joked, "Now it looks like we're all peeling onions!" Driving away, we stopped to say goodbye to the goats who had been with us the whole time. We drove up the gravel driveway, still crying. I thought the magic was gone. At the end of the gravel driveway, just before the paved road began, we stopped to pick flowers and to wave one last goodbye to the goats and to the gravel driveway.
>
> In the car, I knew one thing. I could never truly explain what happened at camp. I couldn't explain the magic. I'd try to explain, to tell my parents what it had been like, how we'd felt, but I would never really explain and secretly, I didn't mind. These were my friends, these were my memories.

Today, you will help children to bring the truth of their lives into your own classroom, into their own writing—in this case by using literature to evoke depth.

IN THIS SESSION, YOU WILL TEACH CHILDREN ANOTHER STRATEGY WRITERS USE TO WRITE WITH DEPTH—READING LITERATURE AND LETTING ITS POWER HELP US WRITE ABOUT OUR OWN TOPICS.

GETTING READY

- Evocative published piece (this might be the chapter "Alone" from Jacqueline Woodson's *Notebooks of Melanin Sun*)
- Passage from a book children know well, one which is either a memoir or which has a memoir like quality (this might be *Journey*)
- Example of writing that models the strategies the above author uses
- Example of writing after reading a published text
- Strategies for Writing with Depth chart
- See CD-ROM for resources

MINILESSON

Reading Literature to Inspire Writing

CONNECTION

Celebrate that writers have begun finding ways to think about and reveal the mysteries and depth of their writing.

"Yesterday, we talked about ways to make our writing more powerful. We talked about how to write what we *don't* know about what we *do* know—how to ask the questions that get at the significance and mystery of our Life Topics. We noticed that many writers write about a subject in one way, then another way, then yet a third way, working to reach a more honest, more thoughtful relationship to the subject."

Name your teaching point. Specifically, tell children that a strategy writers use to dive deeper in writing is to write in the wake of reading great stories.

"Writers, today I want to teach you that when a writer wants to take a deep dive in her writing, one strategy that we use is to read (or listen) to literature and then write. We let the story wash over us, and then in the silence afterwards, we write what we need to write. We don't write about the text; we write in the direction the text has pushed us."

TEACHING

Tell children that reading can be a way for us to get in touch with our deepest thoughts and feelings. Show an example of a text you read and wrote off from.

"A great writer once said, 'If you can't cry, how can you read?' and I believe those words are true ones. I would go farther and say, 'If you can't cry, how can you *write*?' because writers, like readers, really do need to work with open hearts. Now I know that in minilessons, I often say to you, 'Watch me as I . . .' But I can't really imagine saying to you, 'Watch me as I read this story and bawl my eyes out . . .' (and of course, readers and writers don't literally need to *weep* in order to read and then write well!) But I do want to show you that reading can be an ice ax to break the frozen sea within us."

"What I often do, as a writer, is that I take a text that I know will be evocative for me. It is often a text I already know. Then I simply read the text, taking in the words and the images. Then, when the text is done, in that little ring of silence after the words of the text are no longer there, I write. I don't write *about* the text, and I don't write more of the text,

COACHING

There is a trim, candid, personal feel to this connection which I like. Many of the deepest messages we say to each other are simple ones: "I love you." "Goodbye." "Help." When I really want to feel as if my minilesson allows me to make an I-Thou connection with children, I often talk simply and briefly.

I often refer to this as writing "off from" literature.

You have two choices. You can demonstrate this, or you can show an example. If you decide to demonstrate, then you will actually do the work in front of the class. That is, you'll actually read a text and then pick up a marker pen and free write on the white board as the children watch. You'll probably want to choose to read a poem if you are going to demonstrate because time will be an issue. If you do this, be sure you write fast, without worrying about your wording, without censoring yourself. You will see that in this instance I decide not to demonstrate but instead to show the writing I did at a different time.

I write *off from* the text. So for example, I recently reread my favorite chapter from Jacqueline Woodson's *Notebooks of Melanin Sun*, titled "Alone." Let me read just a little bit of it to you, and then I'll read what I wrote off from this:

> Alone
>
> Some days I wear alone like a coat, like a hood draping from my head that first warm day of Spring, like socks bunching up inside my sneakers. Like that.
>
> Alone is how I walk some days, with my hands shoved deep in my pockets, with my head down, walking against the day, into it then out again.
>
> Alone is the taste in my mouth some mornings, like morning breath, like hunger. It's lumpy oatmeal for breakfast when Mama doesn't have time to cook and I still don't know how much oatmeal and water and milk will make it all right . . . .

Debrief, pointing out that you didn't write about the text, or even about the subject in the text. Highlight the fact that you free wrote.

"This is what I wrote, and you'll notice that I didn't write *about* Woodson's text, or even about the same topic. I just let the words of her writing roll over me and I wrote whatever was in my mind. I wrote practically without thinking, all in a rush, very quickly":

> Some days I feel as if stress has seeped into every nook and cranny of our classrooms. It's there, on teachers' faces, when we try to nudge more and more into the day, when we read the practice tests with a sinking feeling, when we glance up at the clock, the calendar, and realize time is passing.
>
> Stress is what we feel as we approach the meeting area: what did I forget? What must I cover? Will my students understand the heart of today's lesson?
>
> Stress presses in to our minds and bodies, making our hearts beat quickly, our skin get damp, our heads pound. Stress clings to us like a great, dark shadow that won't leave our side.

I love this text. I love the images of everyday ordinary things and routines that characterize the feeling "alone" so precisely. I love that I get a pit in my stomach —the same one kids get though it's been years since I felt alone in these ways.

ACTIVE ENGAGEMENT
Set children up to try this. Read a text aloud and ask them to free write in the wake of that text.

"Let's try. I will read aloud a passage from our read-aloud book—this is a passage that I know you heard earlier. I will read it aloud, and then in the silence after I finish reading, would you pick up your pen and write *off from* the story I read. Don't write *about* the story, write *off -from* it." Then, opening Patti MacLachlan's novel, *Journey*, to pages 11–13, I said, "This is a passage that I think holds the heart of the book—and it speaks right to my heart. I hope it speaks to yours as well." Before I read, I reminded children that Grandma brings a bowl of soup and a photo album to her grandson, Journey, and together they look through the pictures until they come to one of the whole family:

> In the picture the girl who was my mama sat behind a table, her face in her hands, looking far off in the distance. All around her were people laughing, talking. Lancie, Mama's sister, made a face at the camera. Uncle Minor, his hair all sunbleached, was caught by the camera taking a handful of cookies. In the background a dog leaped into the air to grab a ball, his ears floating out as if uplifted and held there by the wind. But my mother looked silent and unhearing.
>
> "It's a nice picture," I said. "Except for Mama. It must have been the camera," I said after a moment.
>
> Grandma sighed and took my hand.
>
> "No, it wasn't the camera, Journey. It was your mama. Your mama always wished to be somewhere else." "Well, now she is," I said.
>
> After a while Grandma got up and left the room. I sat there for a long time, staring at Mama's picture, as if I could will her to turn and talk to the person next to her . . . The expression on Mama's face was one I knew. One I remembered.
>
> Somewhere else. I am very little, five or six, and in overalls and new yellow rubber boots. I follow Mama across the meadow. It has rained and everything is washed and shiny, the sky clear. As I walk my feet make squishing sounds, and when I try to catch up with Mama I fall into the brook. I am not afraid, but when I look up Mama has walked away. Arms pick me up, someone else's arms. Someone else takes off my boots and pours out the water. My grandfather. I am angry. It's not my grandfather I want. It is Mama. But Mama is far ahead, and she doesn't look back. She is somewhere else.

Be careful to give children all the directions for the entire activity before you begin to read so that once you finish reading, you will not need to reiterate directions. You will not want instructional words to break the spell of the story, to separate the text from their writing off from that text.

Journey is a demanding book. It's the Teachers College Reading and Writing Project, it has been one of our most important touchstone texts. Many of us look forward to the day when we begin reading it aloud, and know that the classes will be transformed by this book. I encourage you to read it with care and consider it as a potential touchstone. Consider Paulsen's The Monument, *too. Like* Journey, *that book has a great deal to teach writers.*

The silence after I finished reading was palpable; children looked up at me, as if to ask, "Tell us again what you want us to do now?" but I didn't meet their eyes, and instead picked up my pen, looked intently at the page, and began writing intently, scrawling words onto my own page.

Share the writing of one child for whom this strategy seems to have worked well.

When I eventually pulled in close to see what Adam had written off of the *Journey* excerpt, it seemed to me that the resulting entry felt very different than most of Adam's writing. "Class, listen to the entry that Adam has written. I think you'll agree with me that some of MacLachlan's power as a writer has rubbed off on Adam, and that's what can happen when you try this strategy:"*[Fig. IV-1]*

> Somewhere else, I am crying. I am maybe 3 or 4. I am laying in bed with my covers pulled up.
>
> My Dad in the doorway, trying to calm me down. There was a feeling something was missing. There was a pit in my stomach. My throat was itchy.
>
> I started to calm down. Thoughts and memories of my brother ran through my mind. "He will be back soon." That's what my Dad had said to me.
>
> "Not soon enough," is all I could think. It was my brother who told me he would tell me about his whole summer when he gets back. That was all I could think of. It was all I could look forward to. Spending time with Jon.
>
> When my brother leaves, I get an emptiness. There is a special relationship between brothers that in our case can't be broke.

"Do you feel it? Do you feel the power in Adam's writing? He took the direction from *Journey* and pushed himself toward his Life Topic, didn't he?"

LINK
Send children off to write, reminding them of their options and alerting them to the short texts on their tables in case they want to continue to read and write off from literature.

"Writers, it is time to write. You'll have forty-five precious moments today, in school, to write. Time is the most precious resource you'll ever have—so use these forty-five minutes to do some important work."

"Some of you will probably reread an entry you've already written, and you'll think, 'Where's the mystery here?' and you'll dig down underneath that first entry, asking hard

I deliberately do not look up and scan the room, as if giving children the eagle eye. There is something unbelievably powerful about simply writing in front of others, losing oneself in the page, and I know that my demonstration will be more powerful if I model absolute absorption. There are times, of course, when I am not able to sit at the front of the room and truly engage in my own writing. Sometimes, to tell you the truth, what I am writing is: "Geez, I hope they are doing this. I am dying to look up but I am going to force myself to keep writing instead. I haven't even thought about what to say but oh well. They don't need to know that . . . ."

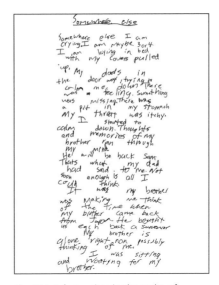

Fig. IV-1 Adam writes in the wake of literature.

In the tiniest of ways, we can convey an urgency to write, to work, to do important work. Notice ways in which you send children off to work. What a difference it makes when instead of saying, "I don't want any excuses today. You all need to write at least . . . ." we say, "You'll have forty-five precious moments to write . . . ."

Strategies for Writing with Depth

- Many writers have a few Life Topics that we return to often, mining these topics for new insights, stories, images, ideas. We ask, "What do I write about again and again?" "What might my Life Topics be?"
- Sometimes writers look at seemingly unconnected entries and ask, "How might these connect with each other?" Oftentimes, there are underlying issues or truths beneath the seemingly separate bits.
- Sometimes a writer finds he or she has one or two great images—places or objects or scenes—within which the writer's heart opens. We search for those images.
- Writers remember, "The bigger the idea, the smaller you write." Writers shuttle between writing big insights and writing with minute details.
- After a writer has written about a subject by advancing one idea or claim on that subject, the writer may deliberately try to write about the same subject, advancing the exactly opposite idea: I love to write, I hate to write. Oftentimes, two contrasting ideas can be simultaneously true.
- Writers take topics and territories we know well and think, as Eudora Welty has suggested, "What don't I know about what I know?" and "Where's the mystery here?"
- Writers write to explore new ideas and do so by asking and entertaining hard questions, and by visiting a subject, repeatedly, from different perspectives.
- Sometimes a writer thinks about a topic or a question by linking that one starting subject to one thing, another, another (to a quote, a statistic, a memory, a classmate's idea).
- Sometimes writers read powerful literature, and then in the wake of that reading, we write. We do so hoping some of the magic rubs off on us.

questions. Some of you will probably decide that you want to write some more entries, and perhaps some more compelling ideas about something that's been on your heart and mind lately. You may take some time to list thoughts you have about a Life Topic. You may take one of those thoughts, and write long about it. You may feel as if there is still a frozen sea within you, and you may decide to use reading as an ice ax to help you break that frozen sea. You may simply want to reread 'Eleven' one more time, writing off from it again. You may want to select a different text to read and to write-off-from, and if you wish to do that, I've left a small folder of texts that I think are especially powerful in a folder on the center of your table."

"Right now, will you do some rereading and decide what your first self-assignment will be? Fill in your self-assignment box, and once you have done that, you can just get started."

WRITING AND CONFERRING

Writing Guided by Literature

As I conferred with Tyler, I glanced at others at the table, noticing that several of them were reading short texts and writing off from them. Adam, for example, selected Ralph Fletcher's "Last Kiss" from the file of short texts. In this memoir, Ralph contrasts his mother and his father—their goodnight kisses, and their roles in his life—and ends by saying, "If nothing else, my childhood had symmetry . . . ." After reading this, Adam wrote an entry. Later, when I pulled close to see what Adam had been working on, I saw that the entry contained three different attempts to write off from Fletcher's text. He explained to me that he read the text, then wrote off from it. Then he reread the text, and again wrote off from it, and the same for the third time. [Figs. IV-2 and IV-3]

1. If it had nothing else, my relationship with my brother had conflict. He would wake up early, me late. He would go to bed late, me early. He would play defense, him a lefty, him liking the flat backyard; I would play offense, me a righty, me liking the woods behind the backyard.

2. If my brother had anything in our relationship, it was power. If I was in the den first, he still got the remote. If I wanted to go outside with my friends, he got to go outside with his friends.

3. This conflict seemed to happen rarely. It grew from little fights before bed. It was Jon who picked on me. At bedtime, he would come to my bed and turn the lights on or ask me questions and watch me sleep, talking.

MID-WORKSHOP
TEACHING POINT

Combining and Layering Strategies "Writers, can I stop you? I want to celebrate how so many of you have found *yourselves* in those texts you are reading. When Ali reread 'Eleven,' she found in it not only a teacher who uses power over her students, but also herself—a girl who uses her power to tell her father (who as we all know has been sick and absorbed by being sick) that she wants him to come back to being a father who cares again about her spelling tests and her soccer goals. When Max read 'Eleven,' he found in it not only a girl who turns eleven and is also ten, nine, eight, seven, six, five, four, three, two, and one . . . but also, Max found himself—a boy who is moving on to middle school and is still holding tight to a childhood tree fort."

"Before you go on, I want to remind you that you can combine strategies that work for you. I've been learning about this from talking to Max. For example, after Max reread 'Eleven'

continued on next page

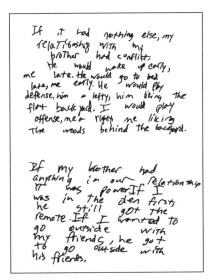

Fig. IV-2 Adam writes "off from" Fletcher's "Last Kiss".

Fig. IV-3 Adam writes "off from" Fletcher's "Last Kiss".

After Adam wrote several entries in response to "Last Kiss," he decided to write off from another text and this time selected a very familiar one: "Eleven." *[Figs. IV-4 and IV-5]*

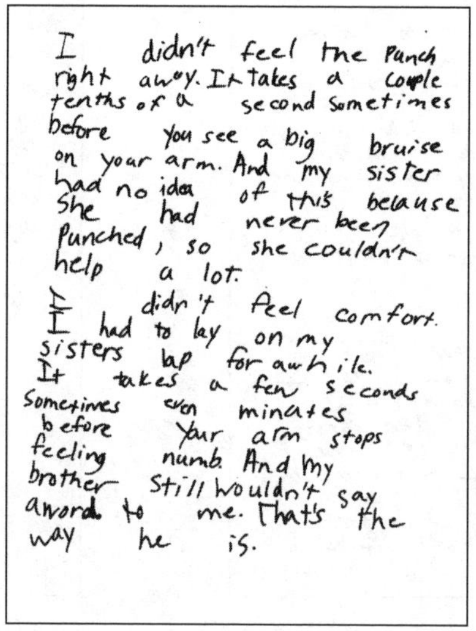

> I didn't feel the punch right away. It takes a couple of tenths of a second sometimes before you see a big bruise on your arm. And my sister had no idea of this because she had never been punched, so she couldn't help a lot.
>
> I didn't feel comfort. I had lay on my sister's lap for a while. It takes a few seconds sometimes, even minutes, before your arm stops feeling numb. And my brother still wouldn't say a word to me. That's the way he is. I didn't feel comfortable with him. Not right away. It takes minutes and sometimes even hours before my brother and I talk. I really try to keep away from him after I get a punch. That's how it is.

You may wonder about the fact that Adam borrows phrases from "Last Kiss" and "Eleven," using another author's words to prime his pump, to get his ideas going. I noticed this, of course, but kept in mind that Adam is not writing for publication here. He's writing in the privacy of his writer's notebook, fully intending that his purpose is to generate seed ideas. By leaning on other authors Adam is giving himself a scaffold that is allowing him to write much more powerfully than he's ever written . . . and as long as this dependency is temporary, I'm all for it.

At the start of the year, Adam had been one of the students in Kathy Doyle's classroom who wrote flat, safe entries. Many of his September entries resembled this one: *[Fig. IV-7]*

> First, we all climb into the car to go to Degrentore's, a pizza parlor. When we got there we went into the bathroom to wash our hands. When we finished washing our hands, we all picked out a bottle of soda. Then we sat down at a

and wrote off from it about loving his old house, he then asked, 'What's the mystery here?' and this is what he wrote": *[Fig. IV-6]*

> The mysterious thing about my old house is that I don't know what about it made me love it so much. Maybe the clubhouse. I remember on cool autumn nights, we would go up there with a single candle, telling ghost stories. And though they all had silly or funny endings, I loved them.

"Max has been doing something else we can all learn from as well. He shifts often from writing one way to writing another way. So, after asking himself, 'What's the mystery here?' and exploring that for half a page, he left a bit of white space, and then he thought a different way, wrote a different way. This time, he zoomed in on a small moment related to his topic. After he wrote about a small moment, he switched again: he posed some hard questions to himself about that

continued on next page

I didn't feel the punch right away. It takes a couple tenths of a second sometimes before you see a big bruise on your arm. And my sister had no idea of this because she had never been punched, so she couldn't help a lot.
I didn't feel comfort. I had to lay on my sisters lap for awhile. It takes a few seconds sometimes even minutes before your arm stops feeling numb. And my brother still wouldn't say a word to me. That's the way he is.

Fig. IV-4 Adam writes "off from" Cisneros' "Eleven".

I didn't feel comfortable with him. Not right away. It takes minutes and sometimes even hours before my brother and I talk. I really try to keep away from him after I get a punch. That's how it is.

Fig. IV-5 Adam's "flat" entry from September.

The mystyrious thing about my old house is I don't know what about it made me love it so much. Maybe the club house. I remember on cool autumn nights we would go up there with a single candle, telling ghost stories. And though they all had silly or funny endings I loved them.

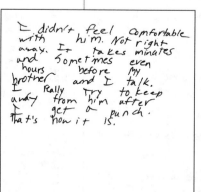

Fig. IV-6 Max answering "What's the mystery here?"

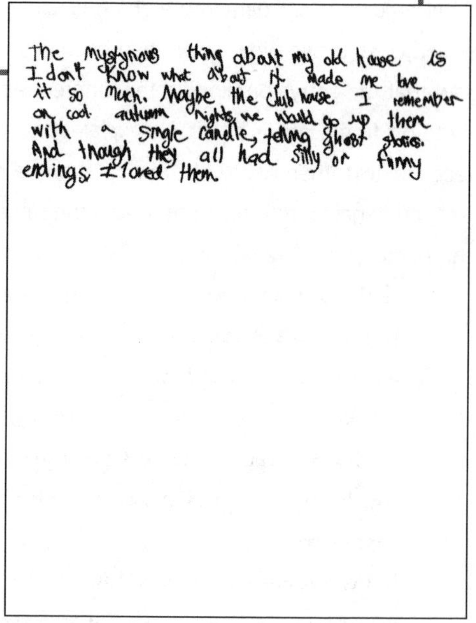

table and talked. It was my friend who used to live in Tenafly's birthday so he had a lot of us over to his house. When we got to the pizza parlor we were all hungry. We each ate about two pieces of pizza. All of us left. Then we filed back into the cars and we drove to an ice cream parlor . . . .

Adam and I together contrasted the writing he did at the start of the year with the writing he was doing now, and tried to name the differences. They were substantial. "I'm writing what I think and feel," Adam said. "It's like I have turned inside out now."

Dr. Spock advises parents, "Catch your child in the act of doing good," and that advice is important for teachers of writing too. The invitation to write in response to literature led Adam (and others, too) to write with a new level of honesty and of detail, so I made a great fuss over what Adam had done, trying to help him redefine himself based on this new work he'd produced. "So from now on," I said, "You need to remember that you have become the kind of person who writes really true, deep entries."

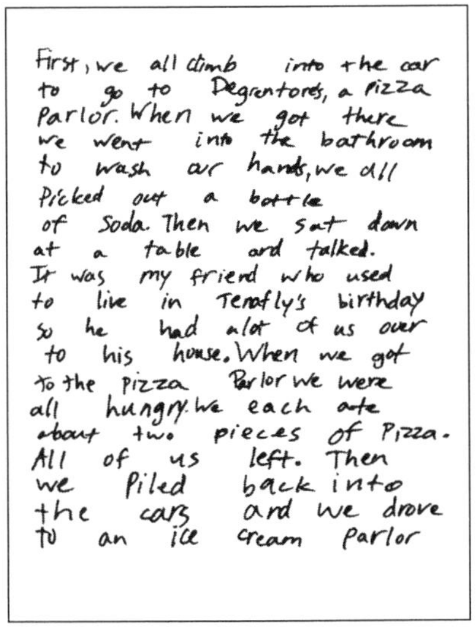

Adam and I wondered, together, over what had led to the change in him, and Adam suggested that writing about a topic that was so, so important to him had made a big difference. We agreed then, that from this day on, Adam would make a point of taking an extra few minutes to gauge his own level of commitment to a topic. "Don't keep writing entries when you aren't really that involved in them," I said. "Instead, pull back and say, 'Wait, this isn't working,' and then get yourself off to a new start."

---

continued from previous page

moment. He's layering one kind of writing and thinking right on top of another and another. Listen:" [Fig. IV-8]

> I stood at the bottom of the tree that was much taller than me. I felt almost unworthy. The green leaves fluffed out at the top. Alex and her friend Emi were climbing up so I started. I felt like a monkey, holding the small branches in my grip, with the bigger branches under my feet. That's when it hit me:

> I climbed down the majestic tree and ran inside. Not a minute later I came back outside with my Georgie Porgy book. Holding the picture book in my teeth, I once more climbed the tree and sat on a branch towards the top.

> I started to read. I thought I was so cool. A kindergartener who could read in a tree, with two second grade girls doing their homework.

> I thought that these moments were the moments that really made me want to hold on to that clubhouse/swing set/tree. My new backyard is really big. There is about 3/4 an acre of woods. I love to be there but it is a different happiness than my old backyard. This backyard is clubhouseless.

"Let yourself be inspired by Max's writing—try combining and layering strategies and see where it can take you in your own writing!"

Fig. IV-7 Adam's "flat" entry from September

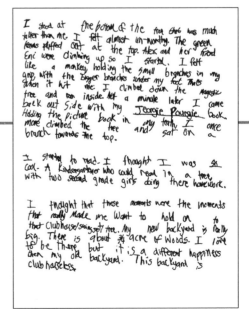

Fig. IV-8 Max combines and layers strategies

SHARE

Reflecting and Making Resolutions

Ask children to reflect on what the writing process has been like for them thus far in the unit and then share that thinking with a partner. Ask them also to plan for their future writing with a partner.

"We've shared our writing a lot so far in this unit, but I think it is important to also talk about what it feels like to write. Think and jot for a moment about the writing work you've been doing. What are you learning as a writer? What's been new for you lately? What's been important for you? Just jot some thoughts and in a moment, I'm going to give you a chance to talk about this."

After a few minutes of silent writing, I divided the clump of children sitting on the carpet into five clusters (one at each corner, and one in the middle) and children shared their thoughts. "Writers, you have been looking backwards and thinking about what has and has not worked for you," I said. "Could you shift now and think forwards to the work you want to do tonight and tomorrow and the day after? What new resolutions do you have?"

HOMEWORK *Collecting Memories* Writers, before long you will be choosing a seed idea to develop into a finished memoir. Before that time comes, you want to be sure to have gathered lots of poignant, intense, powerful entries in your notebook. Tonight, would you gather a couple of pages of entries? I suggest you write a glimmer of a memory that has flashed across your thoughts, like the fireflies that Julie Brinkloe describes in her picture book. Expect the memory of your early days to come to you when you are in the midst of something else. The writer Katherine Bomer has said this: "Memories come to people most often while they are doing something else; washing the dishes, driving to work, listening to music, walking the dog. Memory comes in split-second images, it hides in the cracks of daily activity, and to capture it, sometimes we have to sneak up behind, pretend we are doing something else, like scrubbing the bathtub, and memories will come" (*Writing a Life*, p. 90).

Once a memory occurs to you, try to hold onto the intensity of it: the colors, the feel of the air, the sounds. And write to make that memory searing and real on the page. Here's an example: [Fig. IV-9]

So often my message to children is "Write fast and long." I want them to get into the habit of putting their thoughts on paper and writing with stamina. Today is one of those rare moments when I instead ask children to slow down and reflect about their writing. What I'm telling children is that it's as important for them to think about their process of writing as it is for them to think about what to write. My hope is that their thoughts will spur new understanding of themselves as writers and that this will bring about, above all, more precise, true writing.

OLIVIA

I took a sip of my hot choclate and turned the page of my book. It was snowing outside and I was nice and cozy inside, reading.

"Perfect," I said. My mom walked in and wiped her hands on her jeans.

"Well, laundry's done," she said looking out the window. She didn't look at the blue jay or the dog running across the field, She looked at my brother and sister playing in the snow.

"Olivia, why don't you go play with them?" she said.

I looked down at my book and back at my brother and sister struggling to get the head on the snowman.

"Sure," I said putting down my book and finishing up my hot chocolate.

"Tell them I'll be out there to help them in a minute," I said heading to go get my stuff.

Fig. IV-9 Olivia's memory

I took a sip of hot chocolate and turned the page of my book. It was snowing outside and I was nice and cozy inside reading.

"Perfect," I said. My mom walked in and wiped her hands on her jeans.

"Well the laundry's all done," she said looking out the window. She didn't look at the blue jay or at the dog running across the field. She looked at my brother and sister playing in the snow.

"Olivia, why don't you go and play with them?" she said.

I looked down at my book and then back at my brother and sister struggling to get the head on their snowman. My sister turned and looked at me and smiled. She motioned for me come out. "Sure," I mouthed back at her as I put my book down and took a last gulp of my hot chocolate. "I'll be right there!" And I headed off to get my snow gear.

TAILORING YOUR TEACHING

If your students are finding great success writing in the wake of literature, or if they are undertaking this unit for a second or third year . . . you might decide to teach them to study the literature they have written off from in order to try to learn what craft moves the author has made to make the texts so powerful.

Some teachers may find it helpful to use charts to nudge students to channel their thinking in particular ways (other teachers find that charts box in and curtail students' thinking and writing—you decide!).

If your students are trying to write ideas about their Life Topics, but could use support . . . you might teach them that writers borrow other writers' thought processes to help us delve deeper. G. H. Mead has said, "Just as the sparrow picks up the note of the canary. So too we pick up the dialects of those about us." You can teach your students that when they listen to or read a piece of literature, they can look for the trail that a writer took in order to come to an idea. For example, in the column I cited earlier, my brother Geoff began: "The games I remember most from my childhood aren't Little League or hoops. Instead, the game that I remember most was penny pitching."

"Not Enough Emilys"—Jean Little

What are you thinking as you read this text?	What part of the text makes you think this?	What craft moves has the author used to make you think and feel in these ways?
The world would be a better place if people had friendship and understanding in their lives.	There are not enough Emilys in the world. . . . maybe the world needs—not only better laws but more Emilys.	The writer used similar language in the beginning and ending.
Everybody has the right to be understood and accepted by others.	Everybody should . . . Everybody should . . . Everybody should . . . But mostly, everybody should . . .	The writer used a list with a twist to make her idea stand out.
Kate felt frustrated—like everyone was pulling her down. So she went to Emily's where she knew she'd be happy.	Oh, it's understandable. I didn't yell at them or anything. They were making perfect sense. But who needs to make sense every minute? . . . Emily is usually with me. But what if she wasn't?	The writer used the character's inner voice to show us her perspective on the whole of the text.
Emily and Kate are lucky to have each other because they're so sensitive to each other's ideas and feelings.	"Not by my thermometer it isn't," he **grunted**. Emily **laughed** at me, just sat on her bed and laughed. "Hey, lets have a picnic . . ."	The writer used contrasting images. The adults were stern. Emily was playful.

Geoff began by thinking about what the reader might say to the question he asked himself, "What games do I remember most from my childhood?" Then, once he'd decided what the reader might reply, he writes in a way that tells the reader he is different: *The games I remember most from childhood aren't Little League or hoops.* Then, he distinguishes himself: *Instead, the game that I remember most was penny pitching.*

Gabriel, a fourth grader, deliberately followed Geoff's lead with one of his Life Topics—Living in Rome for the Past Seven Years—and was able to move from writing about the Pantheon and the Roman Forum to a more intimate memory. *[Fig.IV-10]*

> What I remember most about Sunday afternoons in
> Rome is not visiting the Pantheon or the Roman Forum.
> What I remember most is walking along the Tiber holding
> my dad's hand, eating gelato.

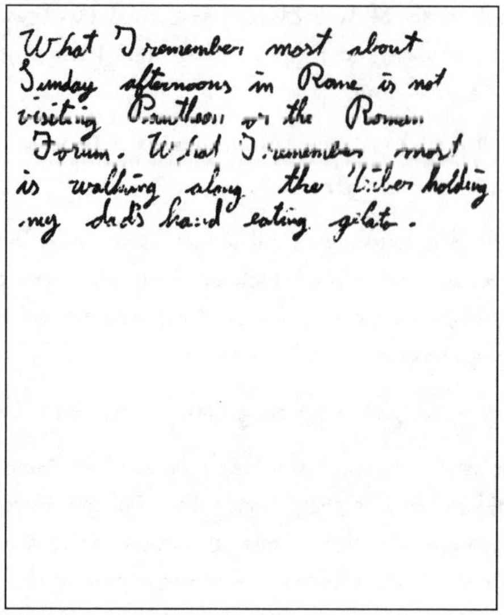
What I remember most about Sunday afternoons in Rome is not visiting Pantheon or the Roman Forum. What I remember most is walking along the Tiber holding my dad's hand eating gilato.

Fig. IV-10 Gabriel's entry

COLLABORATING WITH COLLEAGUES

When I was a child, all the neighboring kids often gathered at dusk to play giant games of kick the can. How I recall that final cry, when the game was over and it was time to reveal our hiding places: "All-y, all-y in free!" we'd hear. "Come out, come out, wherever you are."

Great literature can call all of us from our hiding places. When we talk in the wake of a great story, it is as if those stories have called out, "All-y, all-y in free." For us too, as teachers, stories can be an ice ax to break the frozen sea within us, within our faculty rooms. Too many of us, as teachers, understand what Andrew meant when he said, "In fourth grade, there was a home-Andrew and a school-Andrew," because we, also, keep our real selves away from the classroom . . . and, oftentimes, from the faculty room as well! The problem is that good teaching and good writing, both, rely on an elusive quality that many people refer to as "voice." We write with voice and teach with voice when we allow the imprint of our personalities to come through in our work. We write and teach with voice when we take that awful risk of putting ourselves on the line.

There are many, many teachers who have stopped me in the hallway or spoken to me at a conference, saying, "Lucy, our work on the teaching of writing has helped my kids but what I really want to thank you for is the fact that it has changed relationships at my school." These teachers tell me that even just fifteen minutes of writing alongside each other has made a difference. This is most likely to happen if the writing is preceded by reading. Try it. Suggest that you and your colleagues write off from literature so you have examples of writing to share with the kids. Then ask one person from your group to read aloud. Follow Rylant's advice:

> Read to them. Read them *The Ox Cart Man*, *The Animal Farm*, and *The Birds and the Beasts and the Third Thing*. Read them with the same feeling in your throat as when you first see the ocean after driving hours and hours to get there. Close the final page of the book with the same reverence you feel when you kiss your sleeping child at night. Be quiet. Don't talk the experience to death. Shut up and let those kids feel and think. Teach your children to be moved and you will be preparing them to move others."

You and your colleagues will want to find texts that might be especially evocative ones. In the Teachers College Reading and Writing Project community, we've had great success reading aloud this excerpt from Paul Auster's *Invention of Solitude*:

> He remembers that he gave himself a new name, John, because all cowboys were named John, and that each time his mother addressed him by his real name he would refuse to answer her. He remembers running out of the house and lying in the middle of the road with his eyes shut, waiting for a car to run him over. He remembers that his Grandfather gave him a large photograph of Gabby Hayes and that it sat in a place of honor on the top of his bureau. He remembers thinking the world was flat. He remembers learning how to tie his shoes. He remembers that his father's clothes were kept in the closet in his room and that it was the noise of the hangers clicking together in the morning that would wake him up.

We've had great success inviting people to write in response to "Alone" by Jacqueline Woodson. This is part of it:

Alone

Some days I wear alone like a coat, like a hood draping from my head that first warm day of Spring, like socks bunching up inside my sneakers. Like that.

Alone is how I walk some days, with my hands shoved deep in my pockets, with my head down, walking against the day, into it then out again.

Alone is the taste in my mouth some mornings, like morning breath, like hunger. It's lumpy oatmeal for breakfast when Mama doesn't have time to cook and I still don't know how much oatmeal and water and milk will make it all right . . . .

For example, here is a student's response to "Alone." Rie is responding to the subject of the text: *[Fig IV-11]*

I need to be alone sometimes. If I'm not alone when I'm in a bad mood, I can do something really mean for no reason. Maybe I'm just having a bad day and I can't handle it or I can't control myself, and I begin to get wild. Nobody understands that. It's better for me to be alone when I'm feeling bad.

Fig. IV-11 Rie's response to "Alone"

IN THIS SESSION, YOU WILL REMIND CHILDREN OF THE WAYS THEY HAVE FOCUSED IN ON A SEED IDEA IN PREVIOUS UNITS. YOU WILL TEACH THEM THAT WRITERS USE ALL THESE WAYS AND MORE TO DEVELOP WRITING, AND THAT EACH WRITER NEEDS TO INVENT AND ADAPT A UNIQUE PROCESS TO REACH EACH WRITING GOAL.

GETTING READY

- List of what a child does to come up with a seed idea
- List of what you do to come up with a seed idea
- Examples of children's reflections about their seed (or blob) ideas
- See CD-ROM for resources

CHOOSING AND DEVELOPING A SEED IDEA

Chances are good that your children know enough of the rhythms of writing that they will have begun the process of selecting a seed idea well before today. In this session, you will teach children that different writers approach writing in different ways. The differences reflect different writing tasks, and they also reflect differences in personal style.

Early in the year, we taught children that writers of personal narratives look for a focused, true stories as seed ideas. Later, we taught children that writers of personal essays look for key sentences turning these into thesis statements. Sometimes, however, a writer may begin with a compelling metaphor, a longing to accomplish a particular purpose, an assigned topic, an excerpt that we want to extend . . . or with a still amorphous (but very much alive) Life Topic. We need to let our children know that writers do lots of different things, as called for by the demands of the task.

Then, too, today you will show children that although writers do make some choices, narrowing in on whatever it is we will write, there is not often a single day, a single moment, when a writer chooses a seed idea. Instead, a writer writes toward an emerging sense of what it is we mean to say. We may start by saying we are not writing about something. We may have a general intent, saying something like, "I'm going to write a memoir that explores my homesickness for the old house, maybe for the old tree or the tree fort or for both of those." Then, as we work, we zoom in with increasing decisiveness.

In this session, you will help writers choose and develop, re-choose and re-develop a seed idea. You will help children postpone closure, letting their emerging sense of direction and their image of what it is they will write grow within them. Earlier in the year, children had fewer strategies for planning a piece of writing and less knowledge of what does and does not pay off when writing. Their rehearsal, then, was short. By now, you will want children to draw on all they know in order to rehearse for their writing because revising as you begin your writing is vastly more efficient than revising as you end it!

MINILESSON

Choosing and Developing a Seed Idea

CONNECTION

Celebrate the fact that your children already anticipate that they'll soon shift from collecting entries to selecting a seed idea.

"Writers, I bet I don't even need to tell most of you that the time has come for you to shift from collecting entries to selecting your seed idea. Can you give me a thumbs-up if you *already knew* that it'd be time, soon, to look back and ask, 'So what am I going to select as my seed idea?'"

The children all indicated that yes, indeed, they had already anticipated this shift. "What you are showing me is so important. You are making me think that when you go to work on a story or a poem or an article for the paper this summer . . . you'll know, without me being there, that after collecting some ideas for writing, you need to look back and think, 'Out of all the possibilities, what stands out for me?' You might not realize it but this is a HUGE lesson, one you need to remember for the rest of your life. Writing will always be more powerful if you take some time to generate different possibilities, to mull over them and to select one choice among many options."

"This is true even when you get older and need to take writing tests where the test gives you an assigned topic. My son has been taking a course to learn to write instant essays inside the SAT exams (those are tests kids take to get into colleges). Last week, the test-prep expert said to my son, 'Even if you have only half an hour to write your entire essay (and remember it has to be almost two pages, so that's not much time), you still need to take a few minutes before you write anything and you need to think, 'What are the different possible ways I could focus my essay?' And you still need to imagine one way the essay could go, then imagine another way the essay could go, and *make a choice*."

"So far this year, I taught you that writers of narratives reread our entries and select one focused moment as the seed idea for a narrative. And I taught you that writers of essays reread our entries and select a sentence or two as the seed idea (the thesis) for our essays."

COACHING

You will see throughout this unit that I am hoping to use this one last cycle through the writing process to crystallize in children's minds the fact that they now have a repertoire of strategies for proceeding through the writing process and do not need to rely on my help every step along the way. You'll also see that I describe the "steps" of the writing process in ways that depict them as increasingly flexible. I know full well that when working on their own independent writing projects, it is highly unlikely that children will collect entries for a week, for example, before selecting a seed idea. So this time, as I articulate what it is that I hope children carry with them as they go forth into the world, I'll make the process sound especially transferable to their future, independent work.

Obviously the paragraph about test writing is expendable—you could leave it out of your minilesson if you so choose. I do want children to understand that even if they are writing under time constraints, it is still efficient to go through a version of the process they've experienced throughout this year's writing workshop. You may decide your writers already know that or that your writers need other points more than this one, at the moment.

Name your teaching point. Specifically, tell students that writers rely on lots of different possible ways to generate a seed idea.

"But today I want to teach you that writers need lots of ways to accomplish almost any job. Writers have lots of strategies for choosing a seed idea, and we know that sometimes the process of focusing our writing, choosing a seed idea, happens over the course of many days."

TEACHING
Remind students that the goal of the unit will be to write a memoir. Suggest that some writers prefer to zoom in on a seed idea, or focus, early; others prefer simply to establish a general direction and focus more gradually.

"You already know your goal in this unit of study will be to make something—a true story, an essay, an anthology of poems, a feature article—that conveys an important message about the whole of your life. You will be writing a memoir. Like so many memoirists, you will spend time choosing (or creating) the form, the structure, that will best carry your message. But before you can think about that, you need to figure out the heart of this particular writing project."

"Let me be clear that although some of you will be able to reread your entries today and find a focused narrative or a compelling idea that can become your seed idea, others of you probably won't be ready to narrow yourself down to one, clearly focused seed idea. Writers are different. Some writers find it works best to zoom in very early on the writing process, and others delay in order to let our subjects develop a bit. But no matter what, you will want to make *some* choices. If you don't leave today's workshop with a seed idea yet, you will at least have your mind on a glowing, amorphous, very powerful blob of an idea!"

Interview an adult who will demonstrate strategies that writers use to generate and select between possible directions for an upcoming writing project. From this interview, select and highlight certain strategies that writers can use often.

"So how do writers select our blob idea? What I'm going to do right now is to interview a writer and teacher we know well, Mary Chiarella. Let's be researchers, keeping track of the strategies Mary has used to decide on her 'blob idea.'"

Mary said, "I started by reading all of the entries I had collected. I read each one slowly.

When I originally wrote this, my teaching point also included this sentence: "The most important thing for you as a writer is to hold tight to your goal, and to try a variety of strategies for reaching that goal." I took this sentence out because I think it is important to say less, to pare down. You'll probably take the teaching points I've written and pare them down even more, doing so with your particular kids in mind. It is always hard to say less, but choosing what not to say is as important as choosing what to say.

Mary and I first taught this unit of study, as it now stands, in collaboration with Kathy Doyle, a fifth grade teacher from Tenafly, New Jersey, who has been a major figure in all of my books for decades. Kathy and her children had been doing some community-building work that involved passing a brilliant pink rubbery, elastic "blob" from one child to another, using that blob to signal "it's your turn to speak your heart." When I described seed ideas in a more amorphous and organic manner than Kathy and I had been describing them in previous units, the children supplied the term "blob idea," and for this class, the metaphor worked magic on their understanding of how focus in writing can evolve.

In our community of practice, terms are born out of the specifics of one classroom or another, and oftentimes those terms have staying power. Across many classrooms, now, children in this unit of study refer to their seed idea as their blob idea. This isn't necessary, however, and in fact the term blob idea really means just a more sophisticated notion of a seed idea.

Across these books, you will have seen me use a variety of methods to teach children. It is important to teach in various ways. Sometimes we demonstrate by writing publicly, sometimes we share an example that we or an author or a child has written. Sometimes, too, children role-play or re-enact in front of the class. And today, I have recruited a colleague, coauthor Mary Chiarella, to play the role of writer while I join children in learning from what she has done.

Frankly, as I read, I realized in some of my entries I kept saying one thing over and over again. Like this one here":

> My father gives me confidence to believe that I can do whatever I want to do. <u>He acts all confused when I feel overwhelmed by something. He bunches his face up really tight and says sternly, "What's the big deal?"</u> When I feel like I can't do something my dad gives me the confidence to push myself. My dad gives me that extra push. Without him, I'd be insecure. He makes me feel like I can do whatever I want.

"I wanted to push aside this entry, and others I didn't love, because they weren't the best, but I forced myself to pay attention to what they were saying. I realized, for example, that in the entry I just read, it was important to me when I said my dad bunches his face up and speaks sternly. My dad's not the kind of guy who gets all mushy. He has his own way, and it is a tough way."

Mary went on, "I continued to read, asking, 'How do these entries connect?' And then I asked, 'Do any of my other entries connect to the idea about my dad that is bubbling below the surface?'"

"An entry about my nephew connected. I described my dad with two-year-old Antonio. Dad had to bend his knees so he was low enough to reach Antonio's hand, and Antonio waddled on tiptoes. One part of the entry went like this":

> They turned the corner and made their way onto the sand. I watched as my father picked up my two-year-old nephew and carried him into the water. They looked into each other's faces and laughed.

Debrief by listing what you saw the writer doing to select her seed idea.

At this point, I interrupted Mary's account of her writing process and said to the children, "So let me think about what Mary has done that all of us could do as well. Hmm . . ." Then I said, jotting notes as I spoke, "It seems to me that in order to find her 'blob' idea, Mary did these things." I listed:

- Read entries and marked the ones that lit sparks, trying not to disregard any
- Marked small parts that stood out
- Reread marked entries, looking for connections and patterns

As students reread their notebooks, you may notice that they have the tendency to skim over their writing quickly. Sometimes they don't realize that each entry holds jewels that can be unearthed and used to inspire new, richer writing. In addition to demonstrating particular strategies for rereading, you'll probably want to show students to stop and think as they're rereading an entry. This will help them see things they might otherwise miss.

To help your students reread with intention and value the outcome of looking back in order to move ideas forward, you'll want to give them specific lenses for rereading that will help them see what they're looking for. A powerful lens to teach them is to look for connections across entries that might not, at first glance, feel connected. This will require children to look closely and to think about the larger ideas that an entry holds. Once they do so, they will likely begin to see connections. That is the strategy Mary is demonstrating here.

This is, of course, a typical move that you make after a demonstration. Listing the steps in the process that you've just revealed to your students will help them have a structure to follow when going off to reread and think about their own writing.

ACTIVE ENGAGEMENT
Ask children to think about what the writer has done that they might also do.

"Let's continue to listen to Mary's process of finding a seed idea, and this time, will you join me as researcher, thinking, 'What has she done that we could also do?'"

Mary continued, "Then I found an entry about a time when I was little and supposed to stand on a ramp and act like a little Miss America, but I was totally scared. My father helped me out. I wrote this":

> "Dad!" I screamed. "Dad!" Tears started streaming down my face as I sat on the floor, lost. Bolts of fabric lined the walls. I knew I was supposed to walk down the stage pretending to be Little Miss America, but instead I was crying and shivering.
>
> "There you are." My father reached out his hand and picked me up off the floor. We walked out to the end of the runway. "Right there," he said, setting me on the runway. "Beautiful," he said. I smiled my best Miss America smile.

"I kept on reading entries and sorted them into categories with sticky notes. I put yellow sticky notes on entries about My Relationship with My Dad and green ones on entries about Fitting In. Some of my entries about Fitting In also pertained to entries about my dad, so I put two sticky notes on those! After I finished, I thought about which category of entries felt most powerful and I chose My Relationship with My Father as the general territory to explore. Then I realized that in several of my entries, my dad was lifting a child up in his arms. This image seemed important."

Then Mary said, "Now, I have been reading all the entries that relate to My Relationship with My Dad and I am getting myself ready to write. I have been thinking about what they say that is deep and true and surprising to me. I tried to form them into one blob—one seed idea. This is what I wrote":

> When I was little, I thought my dad was very strict and that was all. I thought that he was the person who reminded us to turn off the lights, the person who told us we were talking too loudly in the car, or the person who wouldn't let us watch I Dream of Jeannie. But as I got older, I realized that he was also the person who taught me how to swim and ride a bike, the person who dragged me and my siblings up our steep street on a saucer sled in winter and the person who planned our summer vacations.

By writing about this, I've come to realize that I'm able to do so many things because of my dad. I don't mean just that I can swim and ride a bike because of my Dad. I mean things like believing in myself and believing that anything is possible for myself.

Mary finished her explanation of her process, "So, that is how I got my seed idea!"

Ask partners to tell each other what they observed the writer doing in order to select her seed idea.

"Writers, Mary has just demonstrated a whole sequence of steps that she went through in order to write her blob idea. Would you and your partner reconstruct these steps?" The children turned and talked.

"So writers," I concluded. "What you are noticing is that your teacher did all these things when she wanted to decide upon her blob idea. She":

- Read entries and marked the ones that lit sparks, trying not to disregard any
- Marked small parts that stood out
- Reread marked entries, looking for connections and patterns
- Categorized most powerful writing into several possible Life Topics
- Chose one Life Topic and reread the entries on that topic
- Wrote an entry, combining various images and ideas related to this blob idea

LINK

Encourage students to draw on the various strategies they have learned to select a seed idea. Highlight that what works for one child, or one piece of writing, may not work for another. Celebrate their independence.

"These are all things that you and I, as writers, can also try. But the most important thing that Mary did, and that writers do, is figure out what would work for this writing project. She tried to find entries that held powerful ideas. She simply underlined an image that she wanted to highlight. Do you see that she figured out her own ways to help her get to her goal?"

"Writers, what works for one writer—or for one piece of writing—may not work for another. Try different approaches each time you sit down to write and make lists of what you do to choose your seed idea. You've gotten so good at drawing on the strategies we've learned this year that I have no doubt that you'll be able to use them independently and in ways that are effective. I can't wait to see what you come up with!"

WRITING AND CONFERRING

Finding Potent Topics

One of the reasons to ask children to postpone closure on their seed idea is that this way, you'll have time to confer with more children, checking to be sure they've settled on an idea that will yield for them. These conferences are challenging because of course we can't listen to a phrase-long description of a seed idea and be in any position to judge whether that idea will yield insight and powerful writing for that specific writer. Instead, we need to read the child's entries, observe the interaction between writer and topic, and think, "Does this topic/seed idea seem to bring out the best in this writer?"

When I conferred with Jill, she told me that she was having no trouble determining her seed idea. "I'm going to write about my Mom because I really, really, love her," she said. Jill's comment made me a bit uneasy because as a writer, I know that sometimes it is hard to write about happy, happy times without sounding Hallmark-card clichéd. A writer (I can't recall who) once said, "I don't write about my marriage because I have a happy one," and there is wisdom in this. When I looked at Jill's entry about her seed idea, my uneasiness grew: [Fig. V-1]

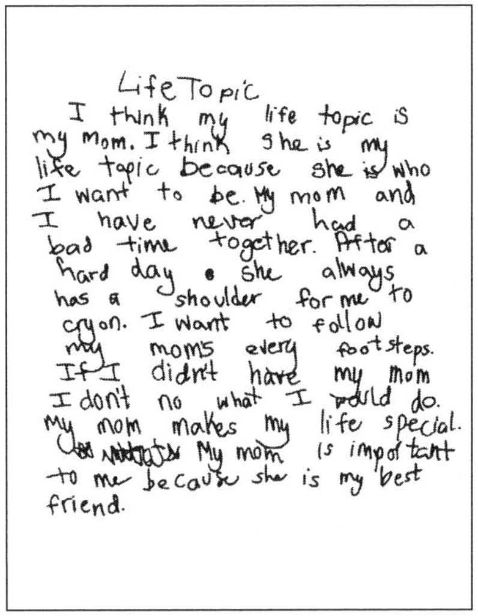

Life Topic

I think my Life Topic is my mom. I think she is my Life Topic because she is who I want to be. My mom and I have never had a bad time together. After a hard day, she always has a shoulder for me to cry on. I want to follow my mom's every footstep. If I didn't have my mom, I don't know what I would do. My mom makes my life special. My mom is important because she is my best friend.

Reading this, it seemed to me that although Jill might be very committed to a rhapsody about her mother, I suspected that if Jill—who is, after all, a budding adolescent—reached

MID-WORKSHOP TEACHING POINT *Writing Seed Ideas* "Writers, can I have your eyes and your attention? Some of you are beginning to define your blob, and I'm glad to see that you are using lots of words to write your current best-draft idea for your blob. For example, Max has written this about his blob idea:" [Fig. V-2]

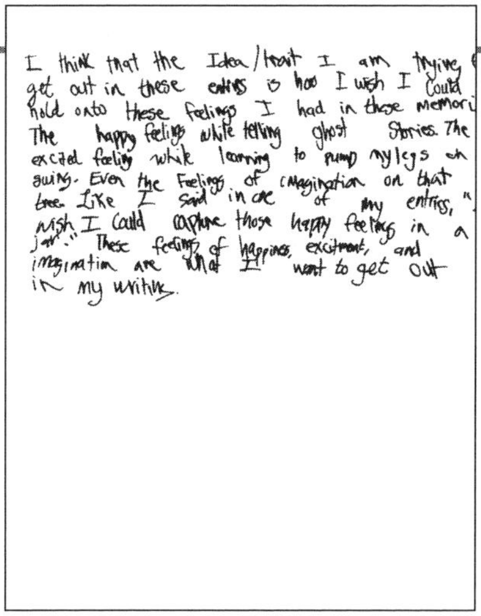

I think that the idea/trait I am trying to get out in these entries is how I wish I could hold onto these feelings I had in these memories. The happy feelings while telling ghost stories. The excited feeling while learning to pump my legs on a swing. Even the feelings of imagination on that tree. Like I said in one of my entries, "I wish I could capture those happy feelings in a jar." These feelings of happiness, excitement, and imagination are what I want to get out in my writing.

continued on next page

Fig. V-1 Jill's early seed idea

Fig. V-2 Max's best-draft idea

toward honest, deep writing, her writing work would require her to take on a less one-dimensional, all-is-bliss stance on her mother. I wasn't sure she wanted to go there, or that it was my role (or her teacher, Kathy Doyle's role) to nudge her toward that. I needed to spend more time looking at Jill's writing about this topic.

So, I asked Jill if she had any more entries that she'd written about her and her mom. She showed me an entry about how they went pumpkin picking together. It was a love-fest; every other line of Jill's entry restated Jill's appreciation for her mother. Reading it, I couldn't help but admire both the way Jill had learned to angle a story to make a point about her relationship with her mother. Still, I was worried. *[Fig. V-3]*

> Pumpkin picking seemed like the coolest thing when I was little. But what was even cooler was that my mom was with me. Since I was little my mom was my best friend. We were on a field trip to the pumpkin patch. Lucky for me, my Mom was chosen to come help. I think we picked the heaviest pumpkin possible. But it wasn't the pumpkin that made me love the trip so much, it was that I was with my mom. When we came back from pumpkin picking, everyone was saying they had a good time because they picked a big pumpkin. I said that too, but the real reason I had a good time was because I was with my Mom.

Jill also told me she'd begun writing an entry about shopping with her mother, because that was an activity they loved to do together. Continuing my research, I asked, "Jill, remember how earlier I suggested that writers ask deep, probing questions about our topics and use those questions as a way to dive deep into our writing?" She nodded.

"I'm wondering, have you asked that sort of question about your relationship with your mom, and allowed those questions to take you deeper?" Jill indicated that no, she'd just gathered more examples of loving-her-mom moments.

continued from previous page

"Emily, on the other hand, has written this": *[Fig. V-4]*

> Life Topic/Blob
>
> A Life Topic is childhood. I wonder when will my childhood end. Sometimes I want to be older and grow up quick and sometimes I want to stay a little baby. It is something I am. It is a part of me, my life.

"Max and Emily are not alone in trying to put down on the page what it is they really want to say. One of my favorite memoirists, a writer named Annie Dillard, did the same thing. This is her 'blob' idea":

continued on next page

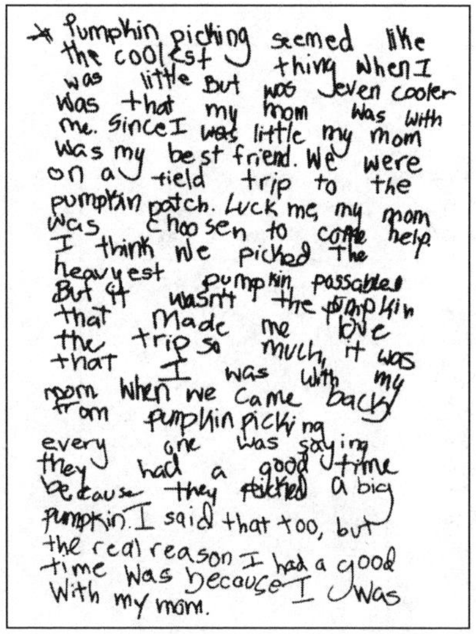
Pumpkin picking seemed like the coolest thing when I was little But was even cooler Was that my mom was with me. Since I was little my mom was my best friend. We were on a field trip to the pumpkin patch. Luck me, my mom was choosen to come help. I think we picked the heavyest pumpkin passable But it wasn't the pumpkin that made me love the trip so much, it was that I was with my mom When we came back from pumpkin picking every one was saying they had a good time because they picked a big pumpkin. I said that too, but the real reason I had a good time was because I was with my mom.

Fig. V-3 Jill's first seed idea

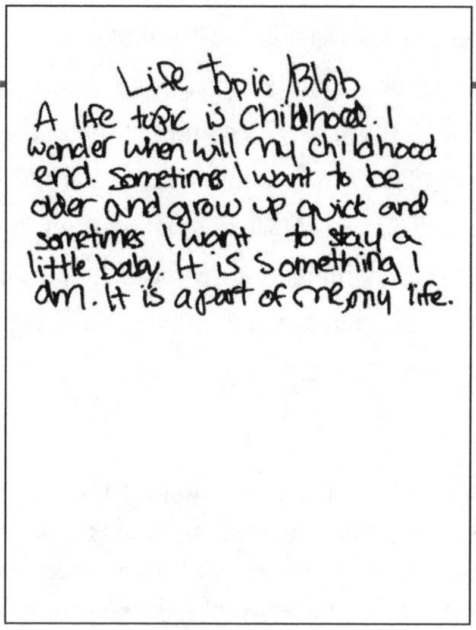
Life Topic Blob

A life topic is Childhood. I wonder when will my childhood end. Sometimes I want to be older and grow up quick and sometimes I want to stay a little baby. It is something I am. It is a part of me my life.

Fig. V-4 Emily's Life Topic

Often I think it helps children to understand where our questions are coming from, so I tried to explain. "The reason I'm asking this, Jill, is this: You know how the books we read usually have a poignant mix of intense feelings, with characters who want things and who struggle? The way you are writing about you and your Mom makes me know this is a huge and happy part of your life, and I totally understand why you'd want to write entries that celebrate your closeness with your mom. You may want to turn these entries into a letter to her, maybe into a Valentine or a Mother's Day card. You could turn these into a memoir, too, but I think that if these entries are going to become a memoir, you'll want to find some trouble within this topic, some issues lurking there, some mix-of-feelings."

"My suggestion to you as a writer, then, is to ask those questions that can help you dig deeper: 'Where's the mystery in this topic about loving my mom?' 'Is it really totally true that all my feelings about this topic are blissful, happy, wonderful feelings?' If you think of this as a story, Jill, are there any struggles in this story?"

Then I said, "You might also, Jill, consider whether there are other topics that are important ones for you—topics that contain a mix of feelings, or contain some hard parts," and I shared with her the quote from the writer who said, "I don't write about my marriage because I have a happy one." Jill set to work immediately. By the end of that day's workshop, she'd written this entry: [Fig. V-5]

My Weight

My weight makes me mad because I am constantly thinking about it. I don't see anything good about not weighing enough. I get angry when I think about this because its something I drive myself crazy about. It sounds like something good to be skinny, but for me it's my nightmare.

I have trouble with my weight. Weighing 67 pounds at age 11 is not enough. I have to push myself to eat more. I have to worry about it. This issue is on my mind all the time. It's something I have trouble talking about it. It's something I'm not proud of. It's like a nightmare to me.

By the time I had circled back to Jill for a follow-up conference, she'd written a storm of intense entries about her struggle over feeling too thin, and then she had put those entries aside and returned to the story

> *continued from previous page*
>
> I thought, "What shall I put in?" Well, what is it about? <u>An American Childhood</u> is about the passion of childhood. It's about a child's vigor, and originality, and eagerness, and mastery, and joy. It's about waking up. A child wakes up over and over again, and notices that she's living. She dreams along, loving the exuberant life of the senses, in love with beauty and power, oblivious of herself—and then suddenly, bingo, she wakes up and feels herself alive. She notices her own awareness.
>
> "Before today is over, take some time to record your current best-draft idea for your blob idea!"

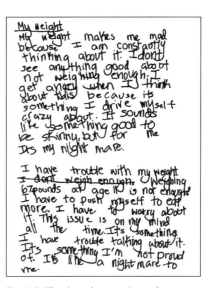

Fig. V-5 Jill writes about an issue that concerns her deeply of pumpkin picking with her Mom. "I thought about all my options and I think that pumpkin picking day was really important to me because I really remember it and it could make a great story," Jill said, and showed me a beautiful lead she'd written for that story.

As you can imagine, I was not sure how to respond. We tell children they are in charge of their writing and that the choice of topics is their own. Jill had made a choice.

I felt as if I was ready to take a parachute jump from a plane. I took a big breath, and went for it. I don't recall what I said exactly, but it went something like this. "Jill, I want you to know right from the start that the decision about your topic will be (and has to be) yours. But let me tell you what I'm thinking. It is safe for you to write about how you love your mom, and about how, one day when you were three or four years old, you and she went pumpkin picking. And I know you could get a good piece out of that because you write well enough that you could write a good piece about anything. But I think you can ask more from this writing project. I think this memoir unit can show you that writing can be a way for you to work out your issues and fears and concerns and struggles—because Jill, every one of us has hard stuff that we deal with in our lives. And at least for now, you are writing and living inside an incredible community. If there is ever going to be a time and a place for you to write about your issues, your struggles, the real times of your life, it will be right now in this classroom in the company of friends."

I pressed on. "Next year, you will be in middle school. You won't have Kathy Doyle as your teacher, and you and your friends won't gather on the carpet and pass the blob between you and try to talk truthfully and carefully with each other. So I want to suggest that right now, this is a time and a place in your life for you to write about the most important stuff in your life—stuff that isn't perfect, stuff that's on your mind." I didn't stop. "I thought it was amazing and brave of you to write about your weight. I can tell from your writing that this is on your mind."

"But I know, Jill, that you need to be the one to make the decision. You may decide to at least try writing about your weight . . . maybe write a small moment entry pertaining to feeling too thin. That is, you may stick one toe into that topic and test the waters. Or you might go back to listing possible topics. I am going to leave the decision up to you because after all, this is your very last unit in your year, and you need and deserve the chance to work on something that feels right to you."

End of sermon.

Jill decided to write about her weight. And, in the end, she was very glad to have made that choice. Phew. Sometimes we, as teachers, take risks. They don't always turn out as happily as this one did . . . but we have to take risks anyhow.

SHARE

Reflecting on Seed Ideas

Share an observation with students about the work they've been doing. Share a strategy to make the work stronger. In this case, point out that writing evolves more quickly if the writer asks and responds to probing questions.

"Writers, I want to talk to you about a concern I have. Some of you are filling your notebooks with new stories pertaining to your Life Topics, and losing sight of the fact that you are on a journey to specific, deeper ideas about these broader topics. You may be collecting story after story about how you have a good relationship with your uncle, but you aren't necessarily naming or realizing, even, how your idea is changing—and so your idea isn't becoming more specific and deeper. I want to encourage you to take a reflective stance by answering questions such as":

- What are the reasons I keep writing about this?
- I've written what's obvious about this, what else can I write?
- What do I want to show about myself?
- What does this say about me?

When I help my graduate students at Teachers College write their own units of study, I emphasize to them that a certain amount of our teaching will introduce children to brand-new ideas, and a certain amount of our teaching will respond to the difficulties that kids encounter when they try to use those ideas. This is an example of a bit of teaching that aims to respond to the problems that kids encounter as they set out to do some of the work we've laid out. Because my colleagues and I have helped hundreds of teachers teach various versions of this unit of study, we can already anticipate a certain amount of the difficulties that kids will encounter. You'll see lots of other problems arise in your class, however, and you need to realize that it is not bad news when problems arise. Instead, this simply shows you where you can be helpful. So when you see that lots of your kids are getting mired in one problem or another, say to yourself, "Great! Now I know where I can be helpful."

Share the work of a writer who used the strategy. In this case, share the work of a writer who asked herself questions about her evolving seed idea.

"For example, one of Olivia's Life Topics is swimming. She has collected tons of entries about swim practice and winning races and losing races. When I asked her where she feels this writing is going, she said, 'I'm not sure. But I'm going to keep writing 'til I see something.' But Olivia and I talked some more, and she realized she won't see something deeper unless she pushes herself to go back, slow down, and think. So, guess what? She did this with an entry she'd written about winning a race. She was so happy because her cousin was there and, more than winning a trophy, she felt proud that her cousin got to see her win. After rereading the entry, Olivia wrote this entry, and I want you to notice that she has taken a reflective stance in this entry. This is something I hope all of you do."

Knowing the larger meaning behind your writing is no easy feat, so it's no surprise children often write about an event or episode without exploring its possible significance. Spotlighting one child's process of reflection is a way to encourage children to push themselves to reach for the truth of their writing.

> The reason I keep writing about swimming is because
> it's the thing that I have in common with my cousin
> and I want to be just like her. I keep writing about how
> happy I am each time I win, but what I haven't written
> about is how each time I win I feel a little bit closer
> to my role model.

Ask students to try to review their writing, asking "Am I reaching toward new depth?".

"Usually I ask you to share your writing with your partner, but right now, will you review your writing by yourself and think about whether you might be writing entry after entry without really thinking about how your idea could become more specific and more significant. Try, right now, to put onto the page your current best thinking about your topic."

HOMEWORK *Composing a Writing Life* There is a saying, "Today is the first day of the rest of your life." Today can become a turning point in your life as a writer. Today you made a commitment to a Life Topic, to a new writing project. You are leaving school, carrying with you new resolve.

Remember, your job in this final unit of study is not only to make a piece of writing. Your job is also to make a writing life for yourself. Tonight, you will definitely want to think about building a writing place for yourself. How will you build a house for your thoughts?

Some of you have told me that you go into the quiet of your rooms to write with no disturbance—to block out the world. Others of you have said that you like to take your writer's notebooks with you wherever you go. If you want to create a writing life for yourself, it seems that you'll need to imagine both of these possibilities as you walk through the world. The writer James Cross Giblin has written about his writing space: "It's a quiet room with windows on two sides and views of New York skyscrapers, but it's close enough to the street so that I don't feel disconnected" (*Speaking of Journals* 1999). Writers need quiet and focus to write, but we also need the world around us to seep into the words we choose to put on the page.

Writers, I want to say one final thing. After you've found a place to work quietly, a source of inspiration, words to live by, routines that help you to be productive . . . then you will want to do the one most important thing in a writer's life. You will want to write.

TAILORING YOUR TEACHING

If your students could use more time learning ways to let writing lead to discovery . . . you might start a minilesson or small-group lesson something like this, "Writers, when you go on a trip, you want to see as much as possible—you want to discover new things, right? If you stayed close to home and walked around the block over and over again, that wouldn't really get you anywhere, would it? That wouldn't be much of a trip. You'd see the same buildings and the same people that you see every day. In order to see new things, you need to move forward a bit, away from what's familiar to you. That's what you need to do in your writing. If you want to discover what's new about your Life Topics, you need to venture away from what's familiar to you to what feels new—to what looks a bit different. One way writers do this is by taking a new route. They look at their topics from another perspective—from the inside out. They write about what's going on in their minds and in their hearts instead of what's easily seen by the human eye."

"The other day when I was conferring with William, he realized that he was writing the same idea over and over again in his notebook." *[Figs. V-6 and V-7]*

Entry 1:

> My mom does everything for me. She cooks, she cleans, she helps me with my homework. When I think about this I realize that it's because she loves me. She would do anything for me. Even when she's tired or doesn't feel well, she still takes care of me.

Entry 2:

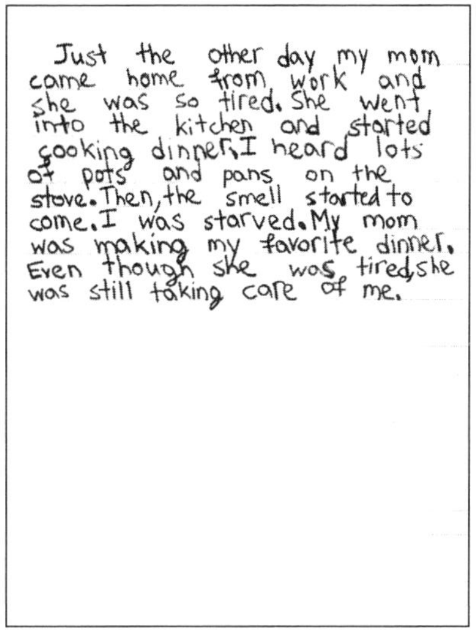

> Just the other day my mom came home from work and she was so tired. She went into the kitchen and started cooking dinner. I heard lots of pots and pans on the stove. Then, the smells started to come. I was starved. My mom was making my favorite dinner. Even though she was tired, she was still taking care of me.

"William said, 'These entries feel exactly the same. I'm not seeing anything new. I feel stuck in this place.' So, William did a really smart thing. He reread his entries and wrote about them from a new angle. Instead of writing about what his mother does for him, he wrote about how his interactions with his mom affect him on the inside. William wrote this entry:" *[Fig. V-8]*

> The other day my mom came home from work and she was so tired. I looked at her and I could see that her

My mom does everything for me. She cooks, she cleans, she helps me with my homework. When I think about this I realize that it's because she loves me. She will do anything for me. Even when she's tired or doesn't feel well, she still takes care of me.

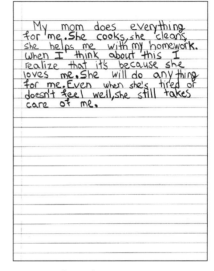

Fig. V-6 William's first entry

Just the other day my mom came home from work and she was so tired. She went into the kitchen and started cooking dinner. I heard lots of pots and pans on the stove. Then, the smell started to come. I was starved. My mom was making my favorite dinner. Even though she was tired, she was still taking care of me.

Fig. V-7 William realizes his entries were repetitive

eyes were tired. I went over and gave her a kiss and a hug. Her eyes started to look less tired.

She went in the kitchen and starting filling pots with different things. A delicious smell started coming out of the kitchen. I stood by the doorway to watch. I was amazed that after working all day, my mother was able to come home and work more with a big smile on her face.

"By recalling the interaction between him and his mom and by thinking about how he was affected on the inside by his mom's goodness, William was able to write an entry that felt different from the first. It's leading him in a new direction. It's leading him to see something he hadn't seen before. Right now, look through your notebooks for a place where you think you could try what William tried . . . . "

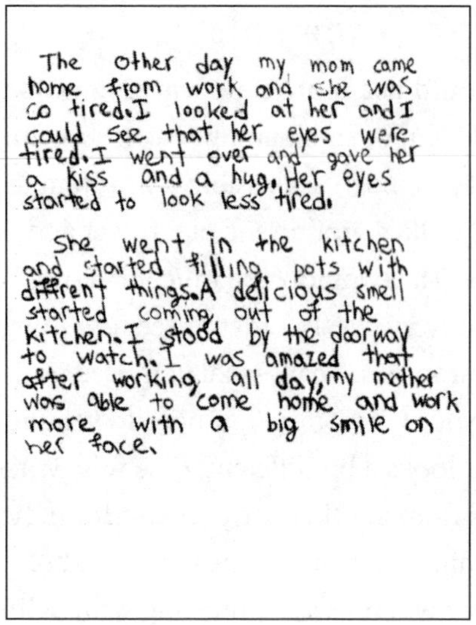

Fig. V-8 William's final entry

ASSESSMENT

I suspect you'll find, as I did, that it is very important for you to spend time reading through all that your children have written since the start of this unit. This will not be a small endeavor, because they will have produced a tremendous volume of writing. Whereas when children wrote personal narrative entries, each entry was a stand-alone text, now most of their entries will explore different aspects of the Life Topic the child has chosen. This means that an entry Max wrote a week ago is utterly connected to an entry he wrote today. Staying abreast of all that your children are writing will be an enormous enterprise!

As you read through your children's writing, be aware that your reading will probably be more powerful if you assign yourself a lens through which to look. For example, you may decide to look closely at the work of two writers who seem to you to be struggling with this unit, and also at the work of two writers who seem to you to be soaring in this unit. Your task might be to think about what it is that the more successful writers are doing that could, perhaps, be taught to the two who are struggling (and to others). "What are the really essential differences between those who are soaring and those who are struggling?" you'll ask.

As you read through your children's work, you will want to find places where their writing takes your breath away. Children profit from specific examples, and, of course, it is transformational when a teacher says to the class, "I want all of you to study the important work that so and so did" . . . and that child is a classmate! It is especially important that you find instances where a struggling writer has done something that you hope everyone will learn from. Look especially hard to find treasures in the pages of your more novice writers.

As I do this work, time after time I find that the novice writers who are struggling (and not all do) are those who spend most of their time writing about generalities. The call to write Big Important ideas has derailed them from writing detailed, chronological narratives, which was something they could do with success. These children have trouble with the open-ended nature of the unit, and are trying so hard to write something Big and Significant that they write in clichéd generalizations, one after another.

IN THIS SESSION, YOU WILL TEACH CHILDREN THAT WRITERS STUDY PUBLISHED TEXTS TO GET IDEAS FOR WAYS TO STRUCTURE THEIR OWN TEXTS. YOU WILL DEMONSTRATE READING A TEXT AND STUDYING ITS STRUCTURE TO HELP STUDENTS LEARN HOW TO DO THIS.

GETTING READY

- *Invention of Solitude* by Paul Auster (or another memoir that shows a describable structure)
- Ways to Structure a Memoir chart
- See CD-ROM for resources

STUDYING MEMOIR STRUCTURES

This year, you have taught your children that texts can be structured as narratives, and they know that narratives are organized chronologically, with a main character proceeding through a sequence of events. You have also taught your children that texts can advance ideas, and they know that these texts usually set forth a claim and then support that claim with several subordinate ideas.

Before your children fly the coop, you will want to let them in on the fact that actually, writers organize our texts in lots of different ways. We may write a traditionally structured narrative or a traditional thesis-driven essay, but we may also structure our text according to a vast range of different templates. Just as painters paint with a palette of colors and can choose the color that allows them to convey their meaning, so, too, writers write with a palette of optional structures and can choose the structure that allows us to convey our meaning.

In today's session, you will invite children to read texts taking special note of the ways in which the writers have structured those texts. This session serves two main purposes. In this session, you'll introduce children to a way of reading—reading to find and study ways to structure a text. In this session you will also introduce children to several templates, several potential structures for the texts they will write within this unit.

MINILESSON

Studying Memoir Structures

CONNECTION

Remind children of the ways they have learned to structure texts.

"Writers, this year you have learned that writers sometimes structure our texts as narratives—and you know how narratives tend to go. You have learned that writers sometimes structure our texts as essays—and you have learned ways that essays tend to go."

Name your teaching point. Specifically, teach writers that they can learn a variety of ways to structure a memoir by studying the structures in published memoirs.

"Today I want to let you in on a secret. Writers structure our texts in lots of different ways. And one way we learn to structure our texts is by reading texts other authors have written and by studying the structures they have used or made."

TEACHING

Tell children that finding patterns in writing is much like seeing patterns in the land from an airplane, since you need to take in more than what's right in front of you to discern the patterns.

"Have any of you ever looked out the window of a plane to see that the world below looks like patchwork? It's funny because when you fly far above the world, you'd think that would mean that you see less . . . but the truth is that when I've looked at the world from the window of an airplane, even though I see less detail, I also see more. I see patterns. I see component sections. I see the way different component sections fit together. I may see that a city or a swatch of farmland is organized into a grid. I may see that the plots of land are smaller alongside the river; that as distance increases from the river, the plots of land are larger."

Demonstrate this with an excerpt from a memoir that has been organized like a list.

"I'm telling you this because when a writer wants to study the ways other authors structure their texts, we read texts as if we are flying above them, looking down at them. Let me show you what I mean. Let's look again at the excerpt we listened to earlier from Paul Auster's memoir. Remember, when I reread this bit of memoir, I'm going to look at it as if I'm flying above it. This time I won't be reading in order to pay attention to the specific images Auster has created. Instead, I'll look at the component chunks, at the dimensions of those chunks, and at how these chunks connect to each other. I will, of course, read the text

COACHING

Your Connection and Teaching Point need not be fancy or elaborate. The first draft of any minilesson you write may well be as short and to the point as this one, and as you revise the minilesson, there may not be a need to elaborate on this early part. By now, kids know that if they listen, they'll be rewarded by learning something to help them with their writing—we hope that often that will be hook enough!

In the Units of Study for Primary Writing *series, in the unit on writing poetry, I wrote a minilesson to help young children consider ways in which the structure of a poem often supports its meaning. This is one of my favorite minilessons. You may want to borrow from that minilesson now. In that minilesson, I asked children to use only two words—"up" and "stop"—to write a poem about how they go up the stairs, and to use the same two words to write a poem about how their grandfather goes up the stairs. Children wrote poems that reflected their ascent, which went something like this: "Up/ up/ up/ stop." On the other hand, poems representing the grandfather's ascent went more like this, "Up/ stop, stop, stop. Up/ stop, stop, stop." Notice how the patterns convey the meaning of both a brisk young person's movement and an older person's more labored progress.*

and think a bit about how the specifics of it fit with the structure. Okay, let me look at this," I said and began to shift between scanning and quietly rereading the text:

> He remembers that he gave himself a new name, John, because all cowboys were named John, and that each time his mother addressed him by his real name he would refuse to answer her. He remembers running out of the house and lying in the middle of the road with his eyes shut, waiting for a car to run him over. He remembers that his Grandfather gave him a large photograph of Gabby Hayes and that it sat in a place of honor on the top of his bureau. He remembers thinking the world was flat. He remembers learning how to tie his shoes. He remembers that his father's clothes were kept in the closet in his room and that it was the noise of the hangers clicking together in the morning that would wake him up.

Point out the structure of the text. In this case, the memoir excerpt is a list, with each part linked to it by a repeated line.

"I am noticing this part of the memoir is organized sort of like a list. Every two or three lines, Auster shifts to another memory, and the sequence of these memories seems to be random. But Auster links the different memories together with the repeating refrain of 'He remembers . . . .'" Then I said, "I wonder if all the phrases describing memories are the same length, and if each phrase about a memory has a similar structure? Let me look back, and read on, and see."

"So I have my answer. Some of the memories are more elaborate than others. Some are described in two sentences, some in just one. Let me compare some of the longer memories to see if they, at least, have the same structure," I said, and pointed to one and then another, reading each aloud:

> He remembers that his father's clothes were kept in the closet in his room and that it was the noise of the hangers clicking together in the morning that would wake him up . . . .

> He remembers that his grandfather gave him a large photograph of Gabby Hayes and that it sat in a place of honor on the top of his bureau . . . .

"These two parts of the list, even though they are both long, are not patterned alike in any way I can see," I said.

By now you should not be surprised to see that I use a familiar text rather than a brand-new text. I don't ever say to a class of children, "Listen to this new text and as you listen, pay attention to the structure of the text." I think all of us should read a text first to hear it for what it is in its entirety, letting the text work its magic on us. Then we can reread it with a specific lens, looking for any one particular thing.

When I read a text, looking at its structure, I look for component parts. Paragraphs can help me do this. Some kinds of words also signal the microstructures in a text. Some signal words suggest the text is organized chronologically (the word next) and some suggest the text is organized to highlight contrasting information (words like yet). Still other signal words suggest the text reveals a cause-and-effect relationship (therefore). Often, I need to read the whole excerpt to notice when the author has shifted from writing in one microstructure into writing in a second microstructure. Is the text composed of a list of items? Does the text contain one small story after another? Is it a single, extended narrative? Is it comprised of questions and then answers? Is it a claim followed by one reason after another?

I decided to use this text and talk about this structure for several reasons. First, it is a structure that I want to invite children to adopt. Second, it is a simple structure so I can make my point quickly and move on.

When you teach this unit, you may want to borrow some of the texts that children write that are included in this book, using those texts as well as published ones as examples of different ways to structure memoir.

ACTIVE ENGAGEMENT

Set children up to read a text to notice its structure and jot down their observations of it. Give them a text that includes both sections of exposition and sections containing narratives.

"Let's try reading texts that other authors have written as if we're in an airplane, looking down at the lay of the land—at the map of their structure, okay? I've copied a memoir you know onto chart paper. Please read it quickly, in almost a skimming-like way, and then make a map of the two or three major chunks you see in this text. Then look at each of the chunks and ask, 'What kind of text is this section?' Jot your observations about the text's structure in your notebooks," I said, and turned the page of the chart tablet to reveal this excerpt from *The House on Mango Street*:

> Laughter
>
> Nenny and I don't look like sisters . . . not right away. Not the way you can tell with Rachel and Lucy who have the same fat Popsicle lips like everyone else in their familiy. But me and Nenny, we are more alike than you would know. Our laughter, for example. Not the shy ice cream bells giggle of Rachel and Lucy's family, but all of a sudden and surprising like a pile of dishes breaking. And other things I can't explain.
>
> One day we were passing a house that looked, in my mind, like the houses I had seen in Mexico. I don't know why. There was nothing about the house that looked exactly like the houses I remembered. I'm not even sure why I thought it, but it seemed to feel right.
>
> Look at that house, I said. It looks like Mexico.
>
> Rachel and Lucy look at me like I'm crazy, but before they can let out a laugh, Nenny says: Yes, that's Mexico all right. That's what I was thinking exactly.

Explain how the text is a combination of an essay and a narrative. Chart some ways to structure a memoir.

After children had a chance to turn and talk, I called on them to explain their observations. After a bit we came to the conclusion that this text begins as an essay and ends as a narrative. "It's a combo," one child said. At this point, I began a chart.

If I worried that children would have difficulty with this. I could have scaffolded their work by boxing the text into chunks myself and simply asking children to think about what kind of text is in each of the chunks. There is not only one right way to talk about the structure of this text. However, I chose it because to me it seems to have a section of exposition followed by a vignette (or focused story). I expect that children will think of this as a mix of two structures they know well. That is, I expect them to say this text starts with an essay and ends with a narrative. I'd be willing to let those terms stand in a classroom as descriptions of this memoir, although technically it is probably more accurate to say that the entire text is an essay, and that it is comprised of a section of exposition followed by a vignette.

Ways to Structure a Memoir

- Write in a list-like structure that resembles beads on a string. The beads can be Small Moment stories linked by theme (example: times when a writer was shy) or the scenes could be linked by a common element (example: scenes from my childhood alongside the creek). The component parts can be as brief as a sentence or two, or as long as a page or two.

- A hybrid text in which the writer writes some exposition and sets a related story or two alongside this.

LINK

Remind children that they are the authors of their writing lives, that they have options in the work they do of structuring, planning, and writing memoir.

"Today, writers, you need to remember that each one of you is the author of your writing life, and you need to decide what the work is that you need to be doing. Some of you may want to spend some time thinking about alternate ways to structure a short memoir; you'll see that I have left a folder of short memoirs on each of your tables. You can tape a memoir into your notebook, and write right onto it—boxing out the component sections, labeling what you think the author is doing."

"You will, of course, want to spend some time thinking about how you might end up structuring your memoir and . . . (this is the important part) thinking about ways in which your tentative writing plan might tell you how to spend your time. For example, if you are thinking that your blob idea seems perfectly suited to a memoir that involves a collection of tiny scenes, then you may want to begin collecting those scenes in your notebook. If, on the other hand, you are thinking that your entire memoir might be one long story, then you may begin sketching out a possible story mountain."

"On the other hand, many of you are not yet ready to be thinking about how your text might go because you need to spend time thinking and writing deeply about your blob idea. You will want to gather a lot of entries related to your blob idea, and then later you'll be in a position to look over what you have collected and to think, 'So what shall I make out of this?'"

"Before you leave the rug, would you reread the entries you've been writing and write yourself an assignment box, committing yourself to start with a particular line of work today? But remember, as Max showed us yesterday, that when you are on the trail of important meanings, sometimes you'll want to shift between doing one thing and doing another."

I encourage you to include "Alone" by Jacqueline Woodson, "Eleven" by Sandra Cisneros, and "Not Enough Emilys" from Hey World, Here I Am *by Jean Little.*

You may decide this unit grants children too many options, and you may therefore rein your children in a bit. Even if you decide to do so, I'd recommend you give children choices when possible because part of the power of this unit derives from the invitation you give the children to research what works for them.

You will also need to decide whether you think writers should be taking notes during your minilessons or not. The answer to this probably depends on their age, but different teachers will of course make different decisions.

I am aware that in this series of books, I have not been steadfast in my commitment to students using the planning boxes (sometimes we refer to these as "self-assignment boxes.") You will need to decide whether you want your students to use these, and if so, whether you expect them to write a self-assignment/planning box at the start of each day or at the start of each new bit of work the writer tackles. In most cases, I'd prefer the latter, but this is your decision.

WRITING AND CONFERRING

As you confer with children today, you'll be listening to the writer's tentative ideas for a focus, hearing the work plan the writer has made for herself, and learning, also, whether the writer has any notion of the sort of text she will probably end up writing. For example, when I pulled alongside Ali, she briefly showed me an entry she'd written about her blob idea. I scanned the entry: [Fig. VI-1]

> My blob is not following directions, being free. But to be free you have to be brave, trust in yourself. You have to be your own person and be unique to be truly free. Being brave and being unique has helped me at steps in my life. This is important to me because being brave and different has in a way saved a part of me. Sometimes being brave hurts.

I had some internal reactions to Ali's write-up of her seed idea—it seemed too vague to me and I was tempted to encourage her to remember that writers need to write both big and small. When a writer starts with something small such as a detailed vignette, the writer needs next to reach towards big ideas. On the other hand, when a writers starts with big ideas (as was the case with Ali,) the writer's next job will probably be to reach towards details.

But of course I didn't want to simply read a half-page write-up and leap into providing Ali with a prescription. First I needed to hear if she'd written or thought anything else, and I needed to know her own assessments of her work and her own plans for her next steps. As it turned out, Ali had, in fact, read a short memoir and listed a few options for herself. In each option, she used the term "thinking" to refer to expository sections of a text. These were the options she'd imagined she could write. [Fig. VI-2]

> Forms I could use:
> • Small moment with thinking
> • Thinking/small moment/thinking
> • small moment, small moment, thinking.

MID-WORKSHOP TEACHING POINT *Examining a Published Memoir* "Writers, can I stop you? Earlier today we looked at two texts from an aerial view, noticing how they were structured, and we began a chart of possible ways to structure memoir. Tyler and Michael continued to research this, while the rest of us were writing, and they are going to suggest that we add another structure to our list."

Tyler stood alongside me. "We looked at 'Statue,' a chapter in Ralph Fletcher's book, *Marshfield Dreams*, and it is really one story—it is just one small moment." I asked Tyler to say more, to tell the story, so he explained that the story tells about how, on Saturday mornings when Ralph was little, as soon as he saw his parents coming home, he'd run to a special place on the lawn and freeze like a statue. They always pretended to believe he was a statue and they'd buy him for one hundred dollars and bring him home. Then the dad would say, 'He looks almost alive,' and at that point, young Ralph would come alive."

continued on next page

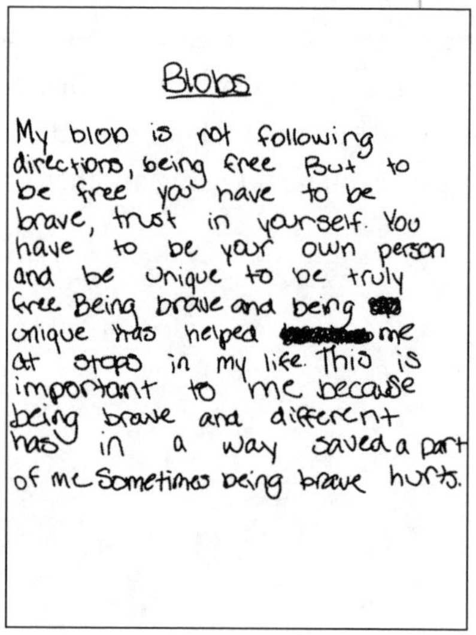

Blobs

My blob is not following directions, being free. But to be free you have to be brave, trust in yourself. You have to be your own person and be unique to be truly free. Being brave and being unique has helped me at steps in my life. This is important to me because being brave and different has in a way saved a part of me. Sometimes being brave hurts.

Fig. VI-1 Ali's synthesis of her seed idea

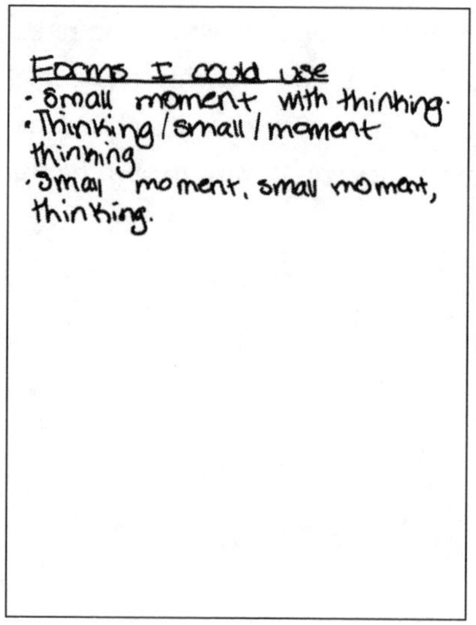

Forms I could use
- Small moment with thinking.
- Thinking/small/moment thinking
- Small moment, small moment, thinking.

Fig. VI-2 Ali's list of structures she might use

That list didn't necessarily amount to much, but making the list seemed to have helped Ali. Without any input from me, she'd realized that her final memoir would probably contain a narrative or two—which was exactly what I hankered to teach her!—and she'd also realized that therefore she needed to begin collecting more memories pertaining to her topic. She'd made herself a to-do list, and started to work on the first item: *[Fig. VI-3]*

What I need to do as a writer

- Think back on more memories about my topic
- Talk to people about it
- Revise some things I already wrote
- Think about more memories of my blob. Maybe put in some thinking. 1½ pages.

A time when I was being brave was when my dad got into a car accident. I sat wrapped in a blanket on the couch, crying and praying. Before my mom left to go help my Dad she whispered, "Be brave." So I sat there, sobbing quiet sobs, trying not to scare my brother and his friend. I was being really brave. But I was being brave with my tears.

When my dad had to have surgery on his back, he lied in bed and never got up. He listened to the TV and to me talk about my day. My dad told me himself that he was afraid. But he was brave by lying on his back.

Ali told me that her plan was to continue collecting more small-moment narratives, each capturing a time when she had been brave.

By this point in the conference, it was very easy for me to know what I could compliment and how I could teach Ali. I first gushed over the deliberate, plan-ful progression of work that Ali had accomplished and at the way in which she shifted between thinking about what her next steps should be as a writer, then carrying out one of those steps, then thinking again about her next steps.

"So class," I said, "Here is a question that I have for you. Do you think that 'Statue' *is* a memoir *and* a snippet of personal narrative . . . or do you think it is only a personal narrative?" Then I went on to explain, "We know it is a personal narrative because it retells a chronological incident, in sequence, and readers can almost experience that incident. It is only a memoir if it is a window to the person, if the story is written not just to tell about one time but also to reveal Ralph, and his childhood, his family, his life."

"Let me read just a bit of this aloud to you and will you all listen and think, 'Is this simply a story of One Event . . . or is it a window into a life, a family? Is it a memoir?'" I read just a bit of the text aloud:

continued on next page

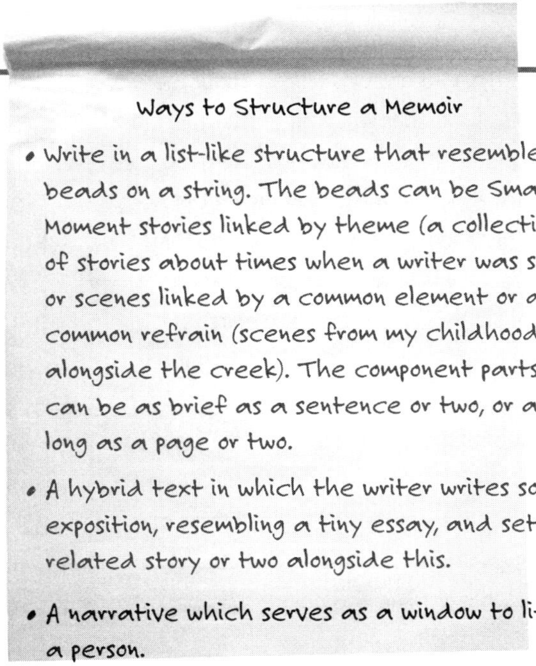

What I need to do as a
writer
· Think back on more memories
about my topic.
· Talk to people about it.
· Revise some things I already
wrote.

Think about more memories
on my blob. Maybe put in
some thinking 1½ pages

A time when I was being
brave was when my dad
got into a car accident I
sat wrapped ~~on a~~ the
~~~~ in a blanket on the
couch. Crying and praying Before
my mom ~~left~~ to go help
my dad one whispered, "Be
Brave." So I sat there, sobbing
quiet sobs, trying not to scare
my brother and his friend. I
was being really brave. But
I was being brave with
my tears.

Fig. VI-3 Ali's plans for her writing and the first part of her entry

Ways to Structure a Memoir

- Write in a list-like structure that resembles beads on a string. The beads can be Small Moment stories linked by theme (a collection of stories about times when a writer was shy) or scenes linked by a common element or a common refrain (scenes from my childhood alongside the creek). The component parts can be as brief as a sentence or two, or as long as a page or two.

- A hybrid text in which the writer writes some exposition, resembling a tiny essay, and sets a related story or two alongside this.

- A narrative which serves as a window to life, a person.

"But Ali," I said. "Very often our strengths are our weaknesses. And although I am really pleased with the way in which you are shifting between being the job captain who gives yourself a job to do, and then starting and accomplishing that job, then returning to your job captain role to think again about the work you should do, I feel as if your day is a mosaic of so many little activities that you aren't giving yourself the time to really lose yourself in any one activity," I said. "It seems like you are spending five minutes writing a narrative, then spending three minutes reflecting on the narrative, then spending another five minutes on a different narrative . . . "

I went on to tell Ali that a writer once said, "It is Spring in my book. I look up and am surprised to see it is snowing." That author was talking about the feeling he gets as a reader when he is utterly lost in a text . . . but I think that good writers, like good readers, get totally lost in a text. We dream the dream of a story and it is as if we are reliving that story. And for a very long time, we don't hear anything that is going on around us; we are totally absorbed in reliving a moment and capturing it on the page.

In conclusion, I told Ali that she had done a great job taking charge of her own writing life, but I suggested that she assign herself bigger blocks of time, expecting that much of the time she'd get utterly lost in whatever she was doing.

---

continued from previous page

"A statue of a little boy!" Dad exclaimed. "It's beautiful. It's absolutely perfect! Amazing!"

Mom knelt to touch my nose. I could feel the eyes of my whole family studying me closely. Jimmy laughed. The baby just started.

"A little boy carved in stone!" Mom exclaimed. "You think we could buy it?"

"Hey, look!" Dad said. "There's a price tag right here on the sleeve!"

I remained absolutely still, barely breathing while Dad examined the invisible tag.

"How much?" Mom asked impatiently. "How much is it?"

"It's a lot—one hundred dollars!" Dad told her. "But who cares? It's worth every penny! I'd pay five hundred dollars for a statue like this! I'd pay a thousand!"

I tried hard not to smile.

"Which is it? A personal narrative? Or a personal narrative that is also a memoir? And why? Turn and talk."

For a few moments the children talked about all the ways in which this text revealed Ralph as a young child—his imagination, his delight in being appreciated—and the ways in which it revealed above all the abundant appreciation and the rich, playful imagination that saturated relationships in Ralph's family. Everyone agreed this was memoir. "Writers, we will definitely add this structure—story—onto our chart. Will each of you, as you continue to work, think not only about various ways in which you may end up structuring whatever you write . . . but will you think also about ways in which *your* writing is a memoir. How does *your* writing reveal you?"

SHARE

Examining Your Entries for Structure

Remind children that earlier they read memoirs noting the structure of those texts. Ask children to read one of their own memoir entries, looking again at structure. Ask them to box out component parts and share those with a partner.

"Writers, so far today we have looked at several published memoirs, noticing the structure of each one. We've seen that some are structured like lists, like beads on a necklace. Some are structured as hybrid texts, in which the writer writes some exposition (like a tiny essay) and sets that alongside a narrative. And we have seen that some memoirs are structured as stories."

"Now that you know how to look at a text from an aerial view, noticing the component parts of the text and the pattern in which it has been written, take time to read your own entries, noticing how you are structuring those entries. Right now, would you look back at one of the entries you've written during this unit that particularly pleases you? And would you read it as if you are on an airplane, looking down at it. Read it closely, too, thinking about when your writing changes from talking in one way, to talking in another way . . . or from talking about one subject, to talking about a different subject. Box out the different component parts, and make marginal notes about how you've structured the text."

I gave children time to do this, and then asked partner 1 to share his text with partner 2. "As you talk over the structure you find in your text," I said, "you may see ways in which you wish you'd written differently. That will be important work—because as you know, re-vision begins with seeing again, and this is one way to see again, and to imagine new possibilities for our own writing."

While the children worked with their partners, I joined in on Tyler's conversation with Michael. Tyler had written this entry about his grandmother's apartment: [Figs. VI-4 and VI-5]

> My grandmother's apartment is always a place I know that I will be able to have fun. When I walk in, I see the tiles on the floor, the pictures of my family on the wooden counter. The kitchen has really big spinning chairs that me and my brother used to play with.
>
> My brother and I had so much wonderful memories here. Like when the time we bought those really hard Legos to build. We

You and your colleagues will definitely want to practice reading texts for their architecture. Gather a bunch of student texts and try doing this kind of reading together. You will need to read the piece carefully, especially when you are looking for a nascent structure that the writer has not yet finished or brought forward. Accustom yourselves to reading in such a manner that you see structures that are almost but not quite evident. Notice how I do this work with Tyler's text, below, and with Judah's text in Collaborating with Colleagues. Try using these as models.

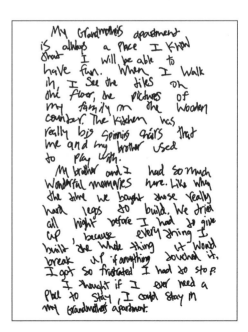

Fig. VI-4 Tyler's notebook entry

tried all night before I had to give up, because everything I built the whole thing it would break up if anything touched it. I got so frustrated I had to stop.

I thought if I ever need a place to stay, I could stay in my grandmother's apartment.

I remember the time when me and my brother played a little soccer game and we were having a really fun time. My grandmother said, "You guys are allowed to play but just don't break anything."

"We won't," my brother and I said. So we started playing and I am goalie. My brother shot and I blocked and it hit one of the pictures and it fell and broke. Me and my brother tried to fix it but we couldn't so we told my Grandmother and she wasn't screaming at us, she just fixed it. Then we put the soccer ball away.

When we get to the apartment after a day in the city we play Monopoly for a long time. My grandmother and I have such a good time playing Monopoly. My grandmother never wins! I think I saw her win once.

Tyler and I read this together. I pointed out to him that writers sometimes give readers signals that make readers expect that the piece will be structured in certain ways. It is important that writers keep track of the signals we give to readers and make sure we keep to our promises.

My grandmother's apartment is always a place I know that I will be able to have fun. When I walk in . . .

"Tyler," I said. "Your first sentence seems almost to be a thesis statement, setting us up to expect that your piece will develop the claim that in your grandmother's apartment, you expect to have fun. When you go from saying the apartment is fun to saying, 'When I walk in . . . ,' you made me expect you'd describe what you see and how each of those things makes you anticipate the fun you will soon have. You sort of, almost, follow through on that first promise. I showed Tyler that he could reorganize his piece a bit and add topic sentences so as to bring out a structure that was almost but not quite evident in his first draft. His next draft could read like this:

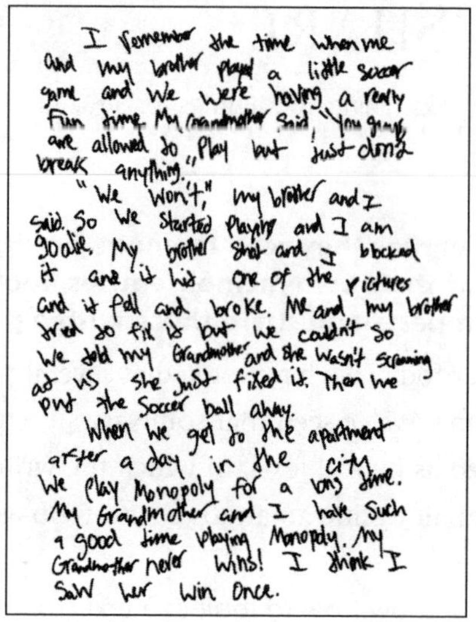
I remember the time when me and my brother played a little soccer game and We were having a really fun time. My Grandmother said, "You guys are allowed to play but just don't break anything."

"We won't," my brother and I said. So We started playing and I am goalie. My brother shot and I blocked it and it hit one of the pictures and it fell and broke. Me and my brother tried to fix it but we couldn't so We told my Grandmother and she wasn't screaming at us she just fixed it. Then we put the Soccer ball away.

When we get to the apartment after a day in the city We play Monopoly for a long time. My Grandmother and I have such a good time playing Monopoly. My Grandmother never wins! I think I saw her win once.

Fig. VI-5 Tyler's entry, page 2

My grandmother's apartment is always a place that I know I'll have fun in. When I walked in I saw the big spinning chairs that me and my brother used to play with.

I noticed a crate of Legos. Those Legos brought back memories of the time when my brother and I bought really hard Legos to build. We tried all night before I had to give up, because everything I built the whole thing it would break up if anything touched it. I got so frustrated I had to stop.

Then I noticed a soccer ball in the back of a closet. That soccer ball brought back memories of time when me and my brother played a little soccer game and we were having a really fun time. My grandmother said, "You guys are allowed to play but just don't break anything."

Then I saw the Monopoly game. That Monopoly game brought back memories of when we got to the apartment after a day in the city and we played Monopoly for a long time. My grandmother and I have such a good time playing Monopoly. My grandmother never wins! I think I saw her win once.

HOMEWORK | **_Researching for Memoirs_** Writers, I know that you realize that the people who write articles in *US News, Time, People,* and *Sports Illustrated* all spend time researching those articles before they write them. And when you write reports for social studies, you spend time researching those reports so that you have lots of specific information to weave into your writing. But I am not sure that you realize that almost all writers of almost every genre regard research as an important part of writing.

Research is not just something you do for a report on penicillin or Switzerland, writers research even when we are writing about our families, our feelings for a nook in our home. We research because we know that whatever we write, our writing will be stronger if it is filled with specific, factual details. Many students have the misconception that writers write with flowery, lush language that they pull from the sky. Actually, good writing is always built with precise, factual information.

So tonight, think of your writer's notebook as a reporter's notepad or a researcher's data collection. Live attentively, trying to collect precise information related to your idea. Collect the telling quote, the relevant newspaper article, the descriptive detail. If you are writing about your teenage sister, capture the expression she uses a lot. Go into her closet and count how many pairs of shoes she owns. Record the way she answers the phone. If you are writing about your early days as a reader, go back and reread the books from long ago. Interview your mother to learn her memories of your early forays into reading. You'll probably collect lots—heaps, really—of data. That'll be a rich brew!

TAILORING YOUR TEACHING

If your students have worked through this unit in previous years . . . you might want to talk in new ways about shaping texts. You may want to teach students to think of shapes and objects and how they function, then show students that their stories could follow those functions and forms. For example, some authors structure their memoirs to follow a camera's telescopic capabilities; that is, the memoir can begin with a wide-angle frame—a reflection or exposition about a theme—and then zoom in to focus on small moments that illustrate and provide more intricate detail about that larger perspective. Some students may decide to write two Small Moment narratives which contrast with oneanother. Perhaps one could show Sunday mornings before the divorce that changed everything, and the other could show Sunday mornings since that fateful day. Children could think of the two moments as mirror images. You might encourage them to think about how a mirror returns an opposite image. They can then structure their memoirs so that the two narratives oppose each other, connected by a reflective piece between them. In this sense, we remind students that writers are artists, and like all artists, they can find inspiration and create beauty from the everyday.

If your students are writing tight, beautiful small moments, but they are not necessarily revealing anything about themselves . . . you might say in a minilesson or a small group, "Writers, you are writing tight, beautiful narratives. I can see that you recall all you've learned from our other narrative units. How wonderful that you are carrying all that you know about writing well with you as you proceed through this study!"

You may decide to read them a personal narrative from the second unit of study and show how it could have been revised to become a memoir. You might take a subject that was typical for many of them, for example, learning to ride a bike or going swimming in the ocean. Then, you could show children that by angling these stories or adding some explicit reflection, those narratives could be turned into memoir.

"Today, I'm going to teach you that when writers write memoir, we don't just recall an event from our lives, but rather we decide what we want to show about ourselves and we use our stories to show this." You could then take a narrative and demonstrate how to take the same event and make it into a memoir.

ASSESSMENT

You will be a lucky person, indeed, if you have the chance to gather armloads of writer's notebooks and to meet with a small group of like-minded colleagues who are working with their children in similar ways. Be careful of and cherish these times that you have together because ultimately, the education you can provide to students has everything to do with the learning environment you can create among yourselves. Seymour Sarason, author of *The Culture of Schools and the Problem of Change,* has said (and I believe), "The notion that teachers can create conditions that are alive and stimulating for children when those same conditions do not exist for us has no warrant in the history of mankind."

When you gather together around your children's notebooks, remember that you can choose the lens with which you want to view this work, and I recommend you do so. For example, I think it would be useful to say, "Why don't we look at the trajectory of writing that one or two sort-of-representative kids have done across this unit. Let's each just read the whole of their work quietly for ten minutes, and then talk about the bigger ideas and issues that this brings to mind."

If you do this, you'll probably want to follow some guidelines for how this leads you into a discussion. I find it helpful to first gather people's thoughts without really delving deep into any one topic of conversation, and then, after developing a list of optional topics for further discussion, to select one of these at a time to talk about.

When my colleagues and I did this, these were some of the thoughts that emerged for us:

- Some children wrote gorgeous bits and seemed not to realize the power of that writing. They kept writing more and more new stuff, and not looking back on what they'd already written. We decided we need to talk to children about the importance of reading their own writing with a discriminating eye, separating out the good from the less good. How does one give children the ability to judge? We decided to try reading over some children's work starring sections that we thought were particularly powerful, then asking children to look at and talk about our assessments. Our hope was that it could help them know the bits of writing which we felt were powerful.

- Some children still seemed to be like kids in a toy store. These children seemed to race from one delectable subtopic to another, then to another. Were they overwhelmed by their options? We decided that some children needed more structure; we decided we'd tell those children that they needed to write focused narratives (although the writer could decide whether to write some exposition before or after the narrative).

Of course, there are other lenses you can choose. Try looking over a student's entry and thinking about the different component sections of the writing. For example, look at the architecture of Judah's entry: *[Figs. VI-5 and VI-6]*

> My mom and I have a unique relationship that is very different than other mother-daughter relationships. But not only is that different, we have Missouri in us. That is very different than other people who live in New Jersey.
>
> When we first moved to New Jersey, I was in first grade. This is what happened one day:
>
> "Here is it," my mom said cheerfully. She bent down in front of me and squeezed my hands, "You don't need to worry, you will love it here."
>
> "Okay, Momma," I said, looking at the ground.
>
> "Are you excited?" she asked.
>
> "Yes, Ma'am," I said, as the bell rang and a group of kids walked by. "I love you."
>
> "I love you too," she smiled, but it was a nervous smile. I walked through the giant metal doors.
>
> Some girls came up to me. "Hi. Are you new?" they asked. "What's your name?"
>
> I was overloaded with many questions. I tried to answer them quickly. Then one person asked, "Why did you say, 'Yes, Ma'am?'"

> "Ummm," I mumbled. My face got red. I was embarrassed. I weaved my fingers together. "That is manners," I said, unsure of every move.
>
> In school we are reading a book about foreign cultures. The people who live in these countries live such different lives than we do. This book reminds me of my Mom and I. Our relationship is so different than other mother-daughter relationships. We have Missouri in us. Missouri is foreign to people who live in New Jersey.

Judah makes a claim at the start of her entry, suggesting, "My mom and I both have Missouri in us." Then she tells a story and by the end of it, the story has illustrated her point. Judah again takes a step backward, restating her new strengthened claims. Some children feel that the entry is shaped like a capital I.

Fig. VI-5 Judah's notebook entry   Fig. VI-6 Judah's entry, page 2

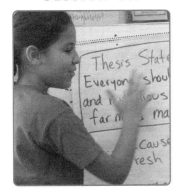

IN THIS SESSION, YOU WILL TEACH CHILDREN WAYS TO CONFER WITH THEMSELVES. YOU WILL TEACH CHILDREN A FEW QUESTIONS TO ASK THEMSELVES IN ORDER TO ASSESS THEMSELVES, PLAN THEIR GOALS, AND CHOOSE THEIR PATHS TO THOSE GOALS.

GETTING READY

- Questions Writing Teachers Ask chart
- "Alone" by Jacqueline Woodson (or another mentor text your children echo in their own writing)
- Example of a child's writing that echoes a mentor author's text
- See CD-ROM for resources

BEING OUR OWN TEACHERS

There is a time, midway into most units of study, when each writer is apt to be working on something different. This is a time for minilessons that essentially rally children to carry on. That is, it can't be that every day in our minilesson we describe a new hoop for children to jump through, a new strategy to try, because it is important that each child has the time to determine the goals that she needs to pursue, and then to work according to those plans, choosing the strategies she needs to achieve those goals.

This session, then, essentially says to children: "Keep going!" There are a variety of ways to convey this message. You could, for example, decide that this should be a minilesson that spotlights the role that writing friends can play in a writer's life, inviting children to confer well with each other. On the other hand, you could decide that the session should remind children that writers turn to authors and mentor texts when we have goals for ourselves as writers. You could return to the notion that writers build places that are conducive to writing and fill these places with objects and texts that remind us of what we know as writers.

As it is, this particular session encourages children to step up to the role of being their own first teachers. You will name for children what it is that you do when you confer with them, and remind them that each writer needs to confer with himself. Tucked into the session, there will be reminders of all that children already know, and encouragement for each child to review options and to make plans for his or her own writing life.

MINILESSON

Being Our Own Teachers

CONNECTION

Tell children that your one-to-one conferences have been slow and ask if they'd be willing to take over your job, becoming teachers for themselves.

"Writers, I wanted to share with you a problem that I have been having and ask for your help. I'm finding that in this unit of study, it is hard to keep my conferences short and efficient. You've written a whole lot of entries, all of which pertain to this writing project, so even just reading what you've written takes time. And you've put so much thought into your plans and concerns that it also takes a lot of time to hear and understand those plans and concerns. I love conferring with you . . . but I am not getting to as many of you as I'd like."

"Here is my request: Would it be okay if I taught you how to confer with yourself? I'll still confer as much as I can, but if you can each confer with yourself, then you won't be waiting for me. This would not only help with my problem; it would also mean that when you write this summer—when you are at home or at camp or at your grandparents and decide to tackle a writing project—you'll know how to be not only the writer, but also the writing teacher."

Name your teaching point. Specifically, teach children that good writing teachers listen and reread before generating new goals and plans.

"Specifically, what I want to teach you is this: When a writer can't go to a writing teacher, we can become our own writing teacher. But before we can suggest next steps for ourselves, we need to spend time listening. A good writing teacher looks backwards in order to look forward."

TEACHING

Confer with one child in front of the class, first asking children to note what you do and to consider ways to confer with themselves in similar ways.

"Writers, how about if I confer with Ali right up here, in front of you, and meanwhile you and your partner keep shared notes on what you see me doing? (Maybe two of you could work together to take public notes up here on the chart paper while the rest of you take notes in one partner's notebook? You can both write onto one page.) After I confer with Ali I'll ask you to look back on what I did in this conference, and think, 'Is this something I could do for myself?'"

COACHING

During this unit, I hope to elevate each child's self-concept—and to solidify each one's independence and commitment to writing. Lecturing children on the virtues of believing in themselves as writers won't work well, however, so it is important to draw on other ways to teach these important lessons. I ask for children to function as teacher-replacements in part because I know that by talking to them in these collegial ways, I can invite them to see themselves as more powerful and more in-control.

It is true that conferences each take more time in this unit. They are more intimate, too.

I almost said, "And a good writing teacher generates several options before deciding upon one," which is another important thing that good writing teachers often do. But, then as I reread the entire minilesson, I realized that in fact, I do not demonstrate that good writing teachers generate several options! I always double-check to make sure there is alignment between my teaching point and what I, in fact, demonstrate.

Notice that I set children up to share a single piece of paper. I'm trying to put a new spin on note-taking, one which imbues it with some new energy and which meanwhile helps children learn through collaboration. You may decide you need to introduce the idea of shared note-taking before asking children to work in this way within a minilesson. Do this if your kids tend to get freaked when you ask them to do something new and give them incomplete directions.

Start your conference by researching what the writer has aimed to do and has already done.

"So, Ali, how's your writing going? I haven't talked to you since we had that conference about you needing to give yourself bigger stretches of time on each bit of work that you do. Did you try that?"

"Yeah, I wrote a few different small moments, but this time I wrote them longer. Like here," she said, gesturing to a two-page-long narrative entry. "I wrote about when I didn't want to ride the roller coaster with my dad. I stretched each bit of it out," she said.

"Can you show me what you mean by stretching it out?" I asked. "Show me a stretched-out part."

Ali pointed at this section of the entry: *[Fig. VII-1]*

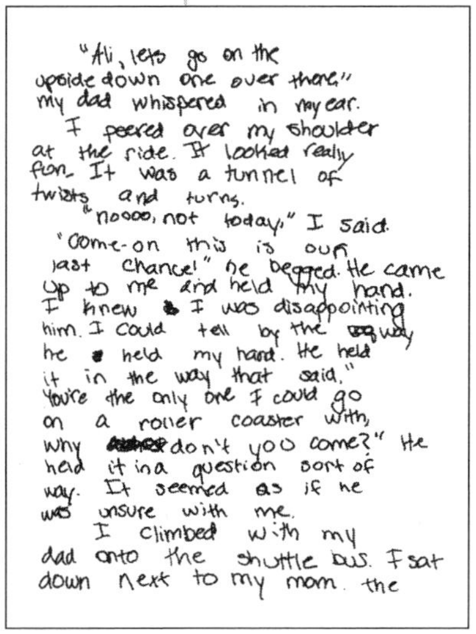

> "Ali, let's go on the upside down one over there," my dad whispered in my ear.
>
> I peered over my shoulder at the ride. It looked really fun. It was a tunnel of twists and turns. "Noooo, not today," I said.
>
> "Come on, this is our last chance," he begged. He came up and held my hand. I knew I was disappointing him. I could tell by the way he held my hand. He held it in the way that said, 'You're the only one I could go on a roller coaster with, why don't you come?" He held it in a question sort of way. It seemed as if he was unsure with me.

After skimming this, and being flabbergasted by the power of her details, I wondered about the context for writing this particular small moment and therefore asked, "Ali, you said you had written several different small moments. Were they all small moments about a particular big idea, or small moments about you and your dad, or what?"

"They were small moments about times when I felt brave or didn't feel brave," Ali responded. "I wrote about the roller coaster because after that time, I regretted not being brave enough to go on it with my dad." Then she said, "I also read 'Eleven' and after that I wrote some 'thought patches' to go with the small moments." *[Fig. VII-2]*

> When you're brave, it doesn't always end up in the right way. You're kind of in a bottomless pit. Or maybe sometimes when you are brave, it makes you want to smile and be proud of yourself. Maybe, one day, when you aren't brave, you will feel bad, feel like you let someone important in your life down.

You will notice that I began this conference with the traditional opening question, but then went on to ask more specific questions based on my knowledge of Ali and her writing. Journalists have a rule of thumb: In order to learn information, it helps to give information. The more you know, the more you can learn. Therefore, if we have a hunch about what children have been working on, we should put that hunch forward in our conferences, thereby nudging children to elaborate upon that and to tell us things we don't already know.

In a conference I will often act as if I am not sure what a writer means when he uses one of the terms that is common in the classroom—I do this because of course the term can mean something very different to a child than it means to me! This is why I say, "Can you show me what you mean by stretching it out?"

"Ali, lets go on the upside down one over there," my dad whispered in my ear.
I peered over my shoulder at the ride. It looked really fun. It was a tunnel of twists and turns.
"Noooo, not today," I said.
"Come-on this is our last chance!" he begged. He came up to me and held my hand. I knew I was disappointing him. I could tell by the way he held my hand. He held it in the way that said, "You're the only one I could go on a roller coaster with, why don't you come?" He held it in a question sort of way. It seemed as if he was unsure with me.
I climbed with my dad onto the shuttle bus. I sat down next to my mom. the

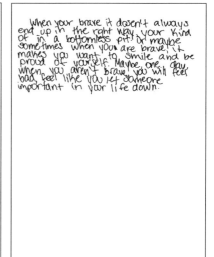

Fig. VII-1 Excerpt in which Ali stretches a small moment

When your brave it dosen't always end up in the right way. your kind of in a bottomless pit. Or maybe sometimes when you are brave, it makes you want to smile and be proud of yourself. Maybe, one day, when you aren't brave you will feel bad feel like you let someone important in your life down.

Fig. VII-2 Ali's "thought patch" to follow one of her focused narratives

Nodding, I said, "So is that where you are as a writer? You've stretched out a few moments, including one about riding the roller coaster, and written some expository text which elaborates on those moments? Do you have plans for what you MIGHT do next?"

Ali nodded, and showed me a diagram she'd made which resembled a capital *I* with boxes for each section—one for the first section of a piece, and then a subordinate box for an illustrative story, then a final box parallel to the first. I looked over the diagram and said, "So does this mean you are preparing to draft? You are thinking of writing a draft that has three sections—an expository section like what you wrote in response to 'Eleven' about braveness, then a small moment in which you describe not riding on the roller coaster, and then another very tiny expository section in which you sum up your feelings about that moment?"

She nodded, and I turned to the observing students and said, "So now my research is done. Watch what I do next."

Shift from researching the writer to giving a compliment and teaching

"Ali, I think I grasp the status of your writing," I said, "and I want to let you know that the way in which you wrote about holding your father's hand was drop-dead gorgeous. I absolutely loved that you could take something as simple as walking across a carnival with your dad and use that very ordinary time to reveal so much about your relationship with him. You are right that you stretched the small moment out . . . but more than that, you studded it with jewels! For the rest of your life, Ali, you always want to remember that this is something you can do. It is one of your best writing talents."

"Can I also make a suggestion?" She nodded. "I worry that you are rushing towards completing your piece. I want to tell you what a writer, Virginia Woolf, once said. She said this: 'Wait.'"

Then I said, "I think you've found an enormously important Life Topic, Ali. But you will want to explore for a while so that you really understand what you want to say about bravery, and so that you select a moment where that message really shines through. You may want to write about bravery in terms of the roller coaster ride that you didn't go on . . . but I think it is premature to make that decision. Try writing about some other small moments where you were called upon to be brave." Then I said, "And Ali, when you write about other small moments . . . remember to write about them in ways that show yourself, like you did when you wrote about you and your father walking across the tarmac towards that roller coaster ride."

You may notice that I noticed that Ali's work was stellar but chose not to say so. I could have oohed and ahhed appreciatively, but for the most part during the research component of a conference, I withhold all my various and assorted thoughts. In a minute, I will think through all the possible compliments I could make and choose the one that I think will be especially apt.

It is always important to learn about a writer's self-assessments and plans. I try to remember to ask about both in a conference.

I try to go on and on and on when I am complimenting a writer, and to be as personal and specific as I can be. I'm totally convinced that kids (and the rest of us) can learn as much from having someone identify what we have done well and extrapolate out the replicable aspects of what we have done as we can learn from having someone critique our work.

More precisely, Virginia Woolf wrote, "As for my next book, I am going to hold myself from writing it until I have it impending in me: grown heavy in my mind like a ripe pear, gravid, asking to be cut or it will fall."

I often debrief at the end of the teaching component, but in this minilesson the Active Engagement is nothing more than an opportunity to debrief, so I instead shift directly into that.

ACTIVE ENGAGEMENT
Set children up to debrief, to name what they saw you do that they could also do in a conference with themselves. Listen in on what they say, and use it to compile a list of questions writing teachers ask.

"Writers, would you turn and talk with your partner about what you saw me doing with Ali. Talk also about whether it makes sense to think about conferring in similar ways with yourself." The children talked, and as they did so, I compiled notes of what they were saying. After a few minutes, I reconvened the group. "So let's make a chart of what you saw me doing or asking." Soon we'd created a chart.

LINK
Suggest that writers take time to reflect on what they have done and to give themselves assignments. Encourage writers to notice what has worked well in their writing so as to do more of that.

"Writers, many of you have been taking about thirty seconds at the start of each writing workshop to decide on the work you are going to do each day and to write your self-assignments. But I hope that today has helped you to realize that it is important for you to take a little bit more time to function as a writing teacher for yourself, making sure that you are on the best possible course. Try asking yourself some of the questions that I ask in conferences: 'What was the last thing you decided to do, and how did it turn out? What else, other than that work, have you been doing, and how has that worked out?'" I pointed to the chart as I read these questions.

"As you ask these questions, remember that you need to notice what you have done well. Noticing what you've done well is very important. Sometimes we stumble almost accidentally onto doing some really good work, and if we don't stop and notice what we've done and dedicate ourselves to doing more of that . . . then it becomes just a one-time-lucky accident, instead of a new discovery that happens again and again. Think also about the course of action you have chosen, and allow yourself to reconsider that choice, to imagine there might be another route to travel."

There were, in fact, some other things that weren't visible but that were part of the conference. These included my thinking, "What has really worked for this writer that she will want to do more often?" and "What hasn't seemed to work?" and "What course-of-work does the writer seem to be on? Can I imagine another course which might work even better for the writer? Why might that other course work even better?"

Questions Writing Teachers Ask
- What was the last thing you decided to do, to work towards? How did it turn out?
- Why did you do this exactly? What else could you have done to reach the same goal?
- What else, other than that work, have you been doing and how has that worked out?
- Do you have specific plans for what you might do next?

Of course, advice for writers is really advice for teachers, advice for people. I've sometimes used a leadership coach to help me become a better leader, and my coach has taught me to reflect in just those ways on my role as a leader.

WRITING AND CONFERRING

Writing in the Wake of Reading

Because children, by this time in the year, are able to carry on without constant teacher-input, working with some independence, you will probably find that you rely on one-to-one conferring more than small group strategy lessons. Still, you will probably find that sometimes several of your children need help with one thing or another. If you cluster these children together into small groups, you can economize your time, saving as much of it as possible for more extended conferences.

Recently, I found that a few children, for example, had taken so enthusiastically to the idea of writing off from a short text that their drafts echoed the cadence of texts written by other authors. For example, it didn't take me but a second before realizing that Emily's text harkened back to Jacqueline Woodson's "Alone." Listen to the two, one after the other:

"Alone"

By Jacqueline Woodson

Some days I wear alone like a coat, like a hood draping from my head that first warm day of Spring, like socks bunching up inside my sneakers. Like that.

Alone is how I walk some days, with my hands shoved deep in my pockets, with my head down, walking against the day, into it then out again.

Alone is the taste in my mouth some mornings, like morning breath, like hunger. It's lumpy oatmeal for breakfast when Mama doesn't have time to cook and I still don't know how much oatmeal and water and milk will make it all right . . . .

> **MID-WORKSHOP TEACHING POINT** *Revising Seed Ideas* "Writers, can I have your eyes and your attention? Earlier this year we talked about the fact that one day, somewhere in the midst of the process of working on a piece of writing, a writer chooses his seed idea. But I am hoping that by now you realize that really, for many of us, the process of choosing what it is we will say in a piece and deciding which material will help us to say our message can take several days, sometimes even weeks."
>
> "You saw that Ali began her conference with me feeling pretty sure of exactly what she planned to say in her writing. She had resolved to write about bravery in her life, then to retell one time with her Dad when she wasn't brave and regretted it afterwards, and then sum up her writing with another few sentences about bravery in general. You saw me suggest to Ali that she postpone establishing closure. The story about the roller coaster *might* be the best moment for conveying her content, but it might *not* be the best moment."
>
> *continued on next page*

"Childhood"

By Emily

Somedays I wear childhood like a jacket, a backpack draped from my back the first day of school, like shoes that are too small, like that. Childhood is how I pretend to be old, my posture straight as a pencil, talking about behavior, and acting serious, trying to get onto a roller coaster too old for me. Childhood is trying to get onto the roller coaster too old for me. Pretending to drink coffee, when it's really hot chocolate.

Childhood is believing my sisters' lies. "There's a secret door in the attic and a skeleton in there," she said. "If your belly-button is an out-y, you're an alien." And believing I came from the baby-bird that dropped me off in a basket on the front porch.

Some days childhood creeps over my shoulder and makes me do stupid things like saying "like" too much. "Like, um, like I was swimming and like, I like almost like drowned."

Today childhood is the dirty shirt, squished with the other dirty clothes in my laundry basket. Today childhood is the quiet room, and tiny mothball in my laundry, small as it can be.

continued from previous page

"Ali's not the only one who has found that she wants to rethink her blob, imagining possibilities she hadn't necessarily considered. Max, for example, has written an entry about the magnolia tree in his backyard. But instead of just narrowing in on that one story right away, he is writing about related subjects—about his nostalgia for his old tree fort, about his feelings about his new backyard. And he has rewritten his synopsis of his seed idea several times. This is what he recently wrote".

> This entry changes my blob by making my thinking wider. When I wrote my first small moment, my thinking was thin. When I thought about these new subjects inside my topic, it made me think about my blob more.

"Many of you will want to do the same sort of work that Max and Ali have been doing. You can do this work by re-articulating your seed idea or by gathering more entries that pertain to your seed idea. These entries may become part of your eventual draft, or they may just give you more options to choose from when you go to write your final draft."

After gathering a group of children who, like Emily, had written off from short texts, I congratulated them. It is great when a writer can stand on the shoulders of a text like "Alone," or "Eleven," or "Papa who Wakes Up Tired in the Dark." But I told these children that just as a rocket relies on a booster rocket to give it lift off for a time but then, once it has broken into space, lets that starter rocket drift away, so, too, they need to let the original text float away . . . and then decide how to take their own writing farther. "In the end, you'll probably take what you've written with the help of another author, and you'll keep just a part of it. Because you probably won't want your final memoir to be such that when someone reads it they say, 'Isn't that written by Sandra Cisneros?'" With that advice, I suggested the children work in partners to imagine how they could write off from their own pieces.

SHARE

Conferring with Each Other

Share with writers that we can deliberately choose to care deeply about our subjects.

"Writers, the great writing teacher, Don Murray, has given some advice that I think is important for us to hear, today and every day. He says this, 'If I am going to make you care about my subject matter, I need to care deeply about it first. I have to find in what I write some echoing cord of my own being: my fears, hopes, language, appetites and ambitions.' Right now, would you reread the work you are doing with your seed idea—your blob idea? In a minute I am going to ask you to consider whether you care about your subject, but before I ask that question, I want to tell you that *you can make the decision* to care about a subject. Caring is not something that is imprinted into our DNA. It is a choice we make. Often when I pick up my pen to write, I am not immediately enthralled with my topic. But I try to follow Murray's advice and 'find some echoing cord of my own being' in a topic . . . even if that topic is not, at first glance, my very favorite thing in the world."

Ask children to write about their commitment to their subject. Then, invite them to share their thinking with the children at their table, helping each other become invested in the writing.

"So right now, will you think about this: Are you able to find some echoing cord inside of you that allows you to bring yourself to this topic? For a moment, would you write about that echoing chord, and then I'll give you a chance to talk."

After a few moments, I intervened. "Writers, instead of sharing with just your partner, would you share this time with the other children who sit at your table. Talk to your table about whether you are finding a way to really care about your blob idea. Would you make sure that the writer who speaks first is someone whose response is, 'yes,' and would you make sure also, that you help each other become invested in your writing. Because a writer can do all the technical revisions in the world, but if you are writing a memoir and your writing doesn't really affect you, then you won't be doing your best writing!"

I hope that you see that often during this unit of study, I am returning to messages that I conveyed earlier in the year, messages which oversimplified the complexities of writing well. Now is a good time to confide in students that actually, the strategies they learned are more conditional than they were initially led to believe. For example, we don't always start out caring deeply about our topic. Then, too, most qualities of good writing are not absolute—although it is true that writers have a saying, "Show, not tell," it is also true that writers show and tell, and sometimes, writers tell, not show! I rather like this way of teaching something with heart and soul, then returning to that lesson later to add nuance and conditions. You may decide, however, to be more nuanced and conditional from the start.

You will see that in this Share session, I don't ask children to talk only to their partners, I instead suggest they have table conversations. My colleagues and I just came up with this idea when thinking about how we might help teachers rally as much energy for reading and writing as possible. We think that interspersing "table-shares" might bring new energy to the writing workshop. We can also imagine that sometimes those table-shares might uncover a shared problem that the class is facing and the next day, the share session might be a whole-class problem-solving session. In any case, we came up with this idea yesterday, and so I am popping it into this session before the books go off to print!

The reason I am telling you this is that, of course, all of these ideas simply represent my current best-draft of thinking, and every idea that is written on any of these pages is now, because it is written, an improveable draft. Just as my colleagues and I are rethinking possible structures for share sessions, you will do the same!

HOMEWORK *Picking Subjects You Care About* Writers, I talked with you about the importance of caring about your subject. You know Don Murray's advice is: "If I am going to make you care about my subject matter, I need to care deeply about it first. I have to find in what I write some echoing cord of my own being: my fears, hopes, language, appetites and ambitions."

Yet there are times when I've seen you all leaf half-heartedly through your writer's notebook and your drafts, dismissing one page after another of it, "Don't care, don't care, don't care . . ." My message is this: you can decide to care about your own writing. Tonight I want you to practice deciding that your pieces of writing are unbelievably important to you. Good writers have some processes for revving ourselves up so that we *do* care about our piece of writing. Try whichever of these ideas you think might help you:

- Reread your writing and find the line in it, the word in it, the paragraph in it that at least sort of matters to you. Copy that part over and reread it, this time telling yourself that this is really huge, that now that you think about it, this actually does matter. Psych yourself up like an athlete before a big competition. After you have decided that this bit does matter, write off from it. Make it bigger. A great deal of power in writing comes from finding the strong parts of our writing and making those parts bigger.

- When you and I go about doing the details of our lives—say, washing dishes—we always have a choice. We can do that action as if it is monotonous, or we can try to be awake to whatever we are doing. Reread your writing and notice when you described yourself doing something, anything, in a half-awake fashion. Tape a new sheet of paper over the part of your draft, and plan to re-experience whatever it was you wrote about. Were you shampooing your dog? If so, do that action—not really, but in your mind's eye—but this time, be awake to whatever you are doing.

- Reread your writing and find a place where you wrote with whatever words came first, using the one-size-fits-all words that anyone could have used. Try rewriting that part of your text, this time holding yourself to the goal of being exactly, precisely honest. You will find you tap a new source of power when you reach for honesty.

TAILORING YOUR TEACHING

If your students are writing furiously, but rarely reread with the eyes of an editor . . . you might set up regular times throughout the workshop where they stop and reread so that they begin to internalize their editing knowledge. Before each minilesson begins, you might say to your students, "Writers, before we begin, I'd like you to reread what you wrote yesterday and last night as an editor. Have your pencil in your hand poised to circle misspelled words, add in punctuation, and fix capital letters. Underline anything that doesn't seem to make sense, and be sure to figure out how to rewrite it so that it does."

Alternatively, you can use the mid-workshop teaching point as a time to remind children to edit their writing. You might stop your class and remind them of something that you've taught. Perhaps you say something like, "Writers, can I stop you? Make sure that as you're writing, you separate your draft into paragraphs. If you haven't been doing this, please take a moment, reread, and mark where you meant to start a new paragraph. Then, from now on, be certain to think about where to begin new paragraphs as you write."

Then too, when students gather for the share, you may want to set them up to first reread their writing as editors. Constant reminders will help students develop the habit of editing their writing as they cycle through the writing process.

If your students aren't noticing when parts of their writing detract from their meaning . . .
you might teach them to reread their writing deciding whether or not all the thoughts they've included add to their message. You might show them how to place boxes around paragraphs and then jot quick notes in the margin explaining what thought they were trying to convey. Then, they can reread the paragraph closely, asking themselves: "Does each part here support my meaning or is there a part that takes my writing off the track?"

You might begin a minilesson or small group by saying, "Writers, it's important for us to make sure that each line in our writing leads readers towards our meaning. We want to be sure that we are not sending our readers mixed messages by including details that show a different feeling or idea than the one that we want to convey."

"I know that sometimes we remember the details of something that happened and we include each one. However, each true detail might not fit with our true meaning. The other day, Dakhari was working on the beginning to his memoir. It began where he is walking out of the hospital room after visiting his uncle who was very ill. He said that he was trying to show that he was feeling very worried. When he sat down in a chair to wait for his mom, he started to play with his pocket video-game. When Dakhari reread this, he realized that the detail about his pocket video-game pulled his writing away from the tragic feeling he wanted to convey. So, Dakhari decided that he was going to take this detail out." Students might then try rereading their memoir, looking for off-track lines.

ASSESSMENT

One of the big questions that you will need to think about as you teach is this: In your classroom, what differences do you expect to see when children are collecting entries in their writer's notebooks compared to when children are writing and revising drafts? There is no right or/ wrong answer to this question. Many knowledgeable teachers and writers believe that the notebook should be utterly different—that this is the place for writers to write quickly, with abandon, with a focus only on telling the truth and capturing life onto the page. On the other hand, many knowledgeable writers and teachers believe that if children get the impression that they can fill their notebooks with any ol' thing, they won't aim for the precisely right word, the detail that brings something to life, and as a result, their writing will be lifeless.

The answer, obviously, rests in a skilled teacher making informed assessments. You absolutely want children to take risks in their writing notebooks and to be able to write fast and long sometimes, without worrying about the conventions that are not within their easy grasp. On the other hand, you want the risks to be taken in the service of writing well, which means that it is important for children to approach the writer's notebook with high aspirations.

If you want to raise the level of your students' writing in the notebook without making the notebook feel a bit like a grammar exercise book, you may suggest occasionally that children take a few minutes to work in their writer's notebooks, playing with the way in which they craft their sentences. You could, for example, tell children that writers sometimes take a sentence that matters to us, and put it on the top of a page. Then we try to rewrite that single sentence, so that we capture that bit of life more precisely. This is what Max has done in these pages of his notebook: *[Fig. VII-3]*

Original: **I came back out the side screen door with my Georgie Porgie book.**

First revision: **I felt the dull sides of my book as I walked out. It was the book with the most pictures I saw, which was good considering I was just six.**

Second revision: **I skipped outside with a thin book of rhymes. It was easy for a beginner, because the rhyming helped me read.**

Original: **I once more climbed the tree, and sat on a branch towards the top.**

First revision: **Feeling the tough bark in my palms, I looked lower down at Emi and Alex, who had started to do their homework. I sat down on a branch so I could see them, suddenly turning into a pirate lookout.**

Second revision: **I hoisted myself up, onto my favorite branch, and took a seat for reading. Feeling the tough bark in my palms, I looked down below at Em, and Alex who had started to do their homework. I hoisted myself up onto my favorite branch and took a seat for reading. When suddenly, I imagined, I transformed the tree into a pirate lookout, looking down below at the two eight-year-old girls.**

Fig. VII-3 Max tries rephrasing each in multiple ways

The next line from his draft which Max set out to improve was this:

> I jumped down the sunny side of the tree, and ran inside the side door.

This time, Max decided to improve his writing by learning from a Mentor line from a text he loved. He selected this line from *Journey*, which was the read-aloud book at that time in his classroom:

> The cat stared at me, its face like a pansy, and then, without claws, it lifted a paw and hit the window screen.

This is Max's revised line:

> I watched the grass, hoping it would catch my fall when I hopped off the tree. Then, without even trying to open the screen, it swung open and I sprinted in.

Max's language and syntax became richer as he tweaked and spliced his sentences, inserted subordinate clauses, and substituted one word for another. But I believe Max's understanding of a writer's notebook also became richer, and he and his classmates learned that caring about the conventions of written language needn't feel like coloring within the lines.

I jumped down the sunny side of the tree, and ran inside the side door.

I watched the grass, hoping it would catch my fall when I hopped off the tree. Then, without even trying to open the screen, it swung open and I sprinted in.

Fig. VII-4 Max's revised line

GETTING READY

- Example of a draft by a child who has overcome writing struggles
- See CD-ROM for resources

FINDING INSPIRATION BEFORE DRAFTING

I have devoted my entire adult life to an effort to make writing easier for children. For decades now, I have moved heaven and earth in an effort to help children realize they have something to say and the words with which to say it. Every word of every book in this series has been written in the hope that somehow, we can help children feel ready and able to put themselves on the line.

Yet the truth is that writing a first draft is one of the hardest things I do. I am terrified of the blank page. After all these years as a writer, I still approach the page with trepidation. I never fail to feel inadequate to the challenge. Will I . . . can I . . . deliver? I hold the pen over the page, poised, and feel as if I'm poised to parachute from a plane, to dive from a high diving board. My heart is in my throat.

Sometimes the truth is complicated. Sometimes we human beings want two conflicting goals. This is one of those times.

I do want children to write with ease and confidence. I want every child to know that he or she has something to say. But yes, I also want children to be overwhelmed by the awesome challenge of the blank page. I want each child to pick up his or her pen, and to feel for a moment as if he or she is on the verge of a high dive.

When children are accustomed to writing and writing a lot, as they will be in your classroom, then I think there is a place for increasing the drumroll leading up to a first draft. And that is the goal of this session.

Then, too, there are important lessons to teach at this critical moment. You will want to remind children that their writing will be stronger and more vivid if they write about a subject that they care very much about, and if they fill themselves with those feelings before they approach the page. You'll want to remind children that many writers find it helps to read beautiful writing just before we write and to do so in the hopes that some of that good stuff rubs off on us. You will want to remind children that even if they are writing a text that has lots of different components, they can't write all those components at once. They need to decide what subject comes first and what kind-of-writing they will be doing first, to conjure up what they know about that one kind of writing, and to write that one component to the best of their ability. Then, onward.

MINILESSON

Finding Inspiration Before Drafting

CONNECTION

Remind children that because they are the authors of their own writing lives, they'll decide when they are ready to write a first draft.

"I told you earlier that this time, you will be authoring your own writing life. So I am not going to tell you, 'Today is the day to start writing your draft.' That day may be today, tomorrow, the day after . . . you'll need to decide. When you do begin to write your first draft, you already have a tool chest of strategies and advice to rely on. I have just one final piece of advice."

Name your teaching point. Specifically, encourage children to find ways to inspire themselves before they embark on a first draft.

"Before you begin your first draft, the one written on white paper outside your notebook, be sure you think hard about how you can inspire yourself to do your best work. Writing well requires talent and knowledge and skill, yes . . . but also magic."

TEACHING

Tell a story about a published writer who has found ways to lift the level of her first draft writing. Specifically, teach children that the writer needs to feel an emotion towards a subject before the writer can make readers feel that emotion.

"I want to tell you about a great writer and writing teacher,. Bill Zinsser. Zinsser, who has written lots of books on writing well (including one titled *On Writing Well*) ends his most recent book, *Writing About Your Life*, with a chapter on playing the piano. In this chapter, a musician named Mitchell gives Bill this advice: 'If you feel a certain emotion while you're playing the piano, your listeners will feel it too.' Mitchell elaborated by telling about a time when he was expected to provide the music for a wedding and was given a piano that played like a factory reject. 'I learned it does no good to complain. You think, "This damn piano," and you get mad at it and when you get angry you play angry, and you can't project who you really are because you have been transformed into an angry person.' About this, Zinsser said, 'Much of what Dwight Mitchell taught me about playing the piano has nothing to do with music. It has to do with conduct and character.' The lesson, of course, relates also to writing."

"When the day comes for you to write your first draft, you will want to find a place inside yourself from which you can write better than you ever thought you could write. And to do this, it helps for you to think, 'How can I inspire myself to do my best work?'"

COACHING

Milton Meltzer, the great nonfiction writer, has said, "In the writer who cares, there is a pressure of feelings which emerges in the rhythm of the sentences, in the choice of details, in the color of the language." I believe that all of this is present also in the voice of the teacher who cares. We can imbue our teaching with the urgency that comes from caring enormously about our message, and in so doing, demonstrate for kids the importance of commitment.

You may be wondering whether some children will have already written what they regard as a first draft. The answer is yes. This session can help them imagine writing a whole new version of that first draft!

It shouldn't surprise you that when I want to give advice to students, I follow Zinsser's model and convey not only the advice but also the context, the story. I know that the advice will be more memorable if it is wrapped in a story.

When my colleagues and I meet in think tanks, I have a habit of taking notes which ramble across pages. Then, sometimes, I pause to "draw a line," as we call it. That is, I literally draw a horizontal line to close one topic of conversation and to signal that the next bit of talking and thinking will be fresh and new. I am hoping in this minilesson to show children that they won't want to slide between drafting entries and writing a first draft. Instead, they'll want to "draw a line" between the two stages of writing, and to do this in hopes that their draft is imbued with extra significance, extra magic.

Set children up to use the boxes-and-bullet format to take notes as you talk about strategies writers can use to raise the level of first draft writing.

"Let me share with you some of the ways in which I try to raise the level of my writing so that my first drafts feel like they are of a higher order than my everyday entries. As I do this, will you take notes? Would one of you be willing to take notes up here on chart paper? Will someone be willing to take notes on the chalkboard? And the rest of you, take notes in your writer's notebook. Your notes will probably need to be shaped in boxes and bullets."

Backing up to reiterate my topic, I said, "There are many things I do to raise the level of my writing so that my first drafts are more special than my everyday writing." I looked at the charts and notes that were emerging under children's hands to be sure that note-takers had recognized that this was probably an overarching main idea and recorded it as such. "First of all, before I write, I reread wonderful writing. I often reread writing which resembles the sort of text I want to write—in this unit, perhaps I'd read 'Alone' or 'Eleven' or 'Everything Will Be All Right.' I don't necessarily read the whole text—I am not reading for any one particular purpose. I just want that feeling of awe, grandeur, and intensity to well up inside of me."

"Also, I reread bits that I have written that I love. Often these are passages I've written pertaining to my seed idea, but sometimes I read one of my earlier publications. Whatever I choose to read, I read that text as if every word is sheer gold. I don't read in a cranky mood, looking for errors. Instead, I pretend the text is magical, and I read it to convince myself that I can write really gorgeous stuff."

"Then, just before I start, I map out a plan. After I sketch a plan, I usually say to myself, 'I'm going to write just the first component, the first bit, of this draft.' I try to think, 'So what *kind of writing* will I be doing? Will this be a narrative?' If so, I recall what I know about writing effective narratives. 'Or will this first section be expository? If so, will I start with a claim? With a question and an answer?'"

"I do all that I have described briefly, for perhaps ten minutes. And then finally, I pick up my pen, and write a lead. If I like it, I keep going. If I'm not sure that I like it, I pause and try again, hoping to get a solid foundation, a good start, for the upcoming draft. But soon I am writing, writing, writing, fast and furious, until I get to the end of one component, one section, then I pause, then I make plans for the upcoming section."

ACTIVE ENGAGEMENT
Set children up to use their notes as a prop to help them recall and re-create your little lecture. Then ask them to talk with a partner about your talk, adding their ideas to yours.

"In a minute I will ask you to share your notes with each other. Before you do this, listen carefully for how we use notes to remember what a person said. When you and your

---

Notice that several times throughout this minilesson, I coach children towards taking notes. When children are younger and less mature and less fluent as writers, I am not convinced that they can listen and jot at the same time. But somewhere towards the end of elementary school, this usually changes. Of course, the work children do in the personal essay and literary essay units, thinking about main ideas and support information, provides them with skills that they can draw upon when taking notes. You'll notice that as I talk in the upcoming section, I deliberately structure my message so that children will have an easier time capturing my message in boxes and bullets.

I think it is helpful to talk in paragraphs. Notice that in order to support children's note-taking, my little speech has an especially clean structure.

This section of advice is particularly important because I find that when children set out to write a text that incorporates sections of narrative writing, sections of exposition and so forth, they often create a muddle. You will notice that later in this minilesson, I suggest that children write their drafts in component sections, working first to write whatever the starting component will be—perhaps a list, perhaps a small story, perhaps a stretched-out narrative. Only then do I suggest the children plan the next component, and again, I hope their plan includes not only their content but also the micro structure.

partner meet, read just a little bit of both notes—merging the notes that the two of you wrote about that one first item—and then together, reconstruct that part of my message. Then read the next bit of your notes—yours and your partner's—and again, talk in such a way that you re-create what I said, remembering more than either of you wrote down. Continue in that way to use your notes as a scaffold, a prop, to help you remind yourself of what I said."

"Then after you have done that, would you and your partner go back and look over what I said, this time talking not about my information but about your own ideas. Talk and think together, asking 'What does she do to prepare for writing a first draft that I will also want to do?' and ask also, 'Can I think of other ways to set myself up to write my first draft really well?'"

LINK
Use the story of one child to caution writers against clinging too tightly to the one best entry they've written thus far. Encourage writers to risk embarking on a draft that doesn't rely upon a previous entry.

"As you will recall, you are the author of your own writing life. You will need to decide what the work is that you need to do today. Your writer's notebook will tell you what you need to do, if you listen to it!"

"You'll remember that yesterday, Ali and I looked back over all that she'd collected. We knew she had an important Life Topic—her struggle to be brave—but I cautioned her against deciding prematurely to settle upon the Small Moment story about the roller coaster ride. Ali came to me this morning and said that she realizes now that she'd been clutching onto that roller coaster episode simply because she'd managed to write it well. Yesterday and last night, she listed a whole bunch of small moments, and she realized that with her father getting into an accident, and her family struggling over his injuries, she's had lots of chances to be brave. There's a lesson for all of us in this. First of all, just because you have some good writing in your notebook . . . this doesn't necessarily mean that your one bit of good writing should be at the heart of your draft! If you have written well once, you can do it again."

"Then, too, your choice of content *does* matter. Ali wrote well about that roller coaster ride . . . but I suspect, if she wants to write about her struggle to be brave, she'll be able to write even better about a moment that is closer to her heart. Remember the advice that the musician named Mitchell gave to Bill Zinsser. This advice is important enough to Bill Zinsser that he ends his book with it: If you feel a certain emotion while you're playing the piano, your listeners will feel it too."

I adore this section of this minilesson. Over the past ten years, as my sons have traveled through secondary school, I've learned that students are expected to know how to do all sorts of things that they are rarely taught to do. My son's sixth grade social studies teacher, for example, announced during the first week of sixth grade that her students were to outline the textbook. But no one taught my son how to do that. No one showed Evan (and all the other kids) that expository texts are written in such a manner that they articulate a big idea, then support it, then shift to a second idea. Sometimes the big ideas are all related under an umbrella topic. Furthermore, no one showed my son how to read outlines, using them to conjure up the content of a written text or a spoken lecture. I'm hoping to right the wrongs my son experienced by teaching one rather traditional way of note-taking.

Read this carefully because the subordinate points that I mention are meant to be tucked so that the main message shines through.

How I identify with Ali! When we've written something that we like, we're tempted to hold tight to it whether or not the text really serves our larger purposes. How important it is to learn to trust ourselves.

If we can recruit children to take the great risk of truly inventing themselves in writing that is enormously important to them, we'll accomplish something very important.

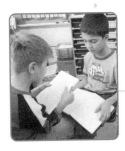

WRITING AND CONFERRING

Choosing the Right Story and Blending External and Internal Story Lines

By the time I reached Tyler, he had already rewritten his entry about his grandmother so that it was now a first draft. He'd progressed past his earlier plan to write about two fun aspects of his grandmother's apartment, and had now decided to zoom in on one fun time they'd had together. It was immediately clear to me that Tyler had made an effort to write his draft as a compelling story, one imbued with feeling: *[Figs. VIII-1 and VIII-2]*

Tyler's entry: One time I was going to my grandmother's house and I was so excited. I got there with my mother and we were wondering what we could do. So we took our jackets off and started talking to Grandmother. In New York City there is always something you could do. So we decided to go to the lunch place. When it was time for lunch we went to Dr. Jeckle and Mr. Hyde. This restaurant was scary and that is why I liked it. It was funny/scary and had good food.

Tyler's first draft: I could feel the excitement taking over my body. I am going to be able to go to Dr Jeckle and Mr. Hyde. I was bouncing around. Somehow the air felt as fresh as it could be even if it is in New York City. Everything felt different. It is as if this is so important. I am about to turn the corner to see the restaurant but I had to tie my shoe. I was so angry that this was holding me up. It felt like I was tying my shoe for one week. Inside it was destroying me every second it took and every minute. Finally the ten-second shoe tying was over and we turned the corner. It felt like I got punched in the face at a boxing match and got knocked out.

Still, reading this first draft made me uneasy, as if I'd perhaps steered Tyler astray because although the level of his writing had risen significantly between his entry and his draft, the draft didn't seem to be a memoir. And frankly, I worried that Tyler's efforts to "write a good story" had lured him away from writing a story that conveyed emotional truth. His exaggerations made me not trust his text. This wasn't the first time that I'd seen a child make an effort to tell an event with excitement and end up distorting the emotional truth of it. Looking up from reading what Tyler showed me, I was careful to avoid making any suggestions or pronouncements based on the drafts alone. "So what are you thinking?" I asked.

"I think the draft is better because I was filled with feelings—I was hungry when I wrote it!—and I *showed* my excitement to get to the restaurant. I didn't *say*, like, 'I was excited to go out to lunch;' instead, I *showed* it by the part about tying my shoe and 'Arrrrrg! I want to stop doing this and get to the restaurant!'"

MID-WORKSHOP TEACHING POINT ***Truth-telling*** "Writers, can I have your eyes and your attention? Writers, can we gather for a moment? I know that is unusual but what I have to say is so important that I need all of you to pull close," I said, and waited till everyone had taken a seat on the carpet. The room bristled with some tension because I'd just broken stride, and the children clearly wondered what was powerful enough to alter the normal routine.

Jill sat beside me at the front of the meeting area. "Writers, I need to talk to you about Jill," I said. "The other day, when I conferred with Jill, she was thinking about writing about her golden relationship with her mother, telling in specific about pumpkin picking with her mother. Jill had some good writing on that topic, and it is something she feels strongly about."

"But in her notebook, Jill also had some entries about a problem that haunts her like a nightmare, a problem that is so difficult that she doesn't like to talk much about it. Jill

continued on next page

One time I was going
to my Grandmother's house and
I was so exited. I got there
with my brother and we were
wandering what we could do. So
we took our jackets off and
Started talking to Grand mother.
In Newyork City there is allways
something you could do. So we
decided to go to the lunch place.
When it was time for
lunch we went to Dr. Jakle and
Mr. Hyde. This restaurant was scary and
that is why I liked it. It was
funny/scary and had good food.

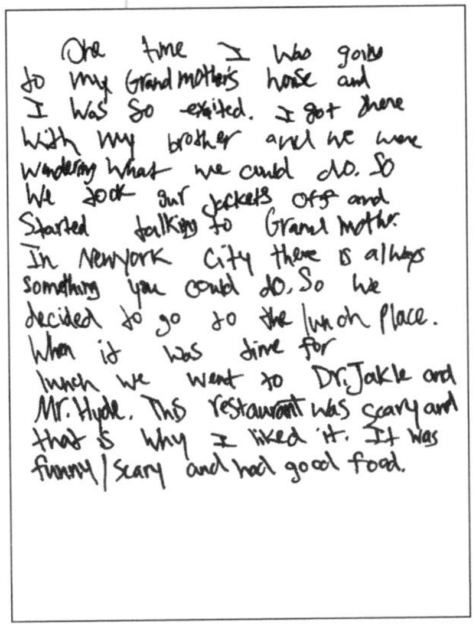

Fig. VIII-1 Tyler's entry

I could feel the excitement taking
over my body. I am going to be
able to go to Dr. Jackle and
Mr. Hyde I was bouncing around.
Somehow the air felt as fresh
as it could be even if it
was in New York City.
Everything felt different. It is as
if this is so important.
I am about to turn the corner
to see the restaurant but I
had to tie my shoe. I was so
angry that this was holding me
up. It felt like I was tying my
shoe for one week. Inside it was
destroying me every second it took
and every minute. finally the ten second
shoe tying was over and we turned
the corner. It felt like I
got punched in the face at a
boxing match and got knocked out.

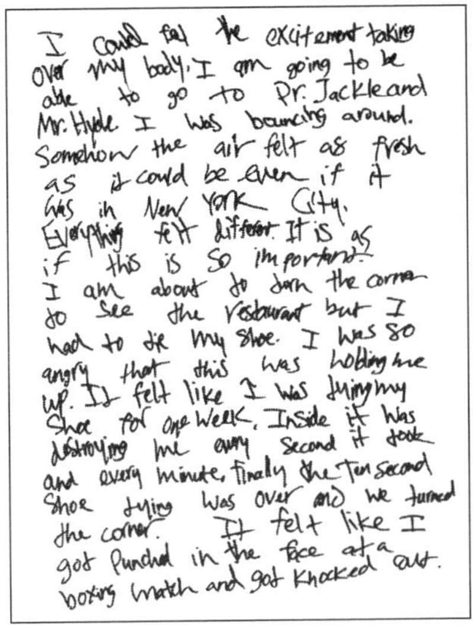

Fig. VIII-2 Tyler's first draft

"Did that shoe-tying bit really happen?" I asked.

"Wellll . . . " Tyler said. "It is one of those true but not True parts. I don't really know if it DID happen or not, because it was a year ago, but I WAS happy to be going out for lunch 'cause it is a cool place."

"What are you thinking you should do next?" I asked. "Is this going to be part of a larger memoir? Are you thinking of stretching this out, or of laying other events alongside it, or what?"

"I gotta put some other things with me and my grandma because this isn't really that much about us; it is mostly about the lunch place," Tyler answered.

Seizing on this statement as an indication that Tyler had some reservations about this excerpt as his memoir, I confirmed the importance of the hard work he'd done and even more, of the evaluation he'd almost (but not quite) made of the entry. "I love that you didn't just copy your entry and call it a draft but instead, you deliberately worked to remember all that you know about a story, writing the draft with a problem and a solution, and angling it to convey a feeling," I said. "But Tyler, what I love best is that even after all that good work, you have the courage to look back on what you have done and to say, 'I'm not sure this really shows what I want to show, which is my relationship with my grandmother.' That is incredibly smart, and I definitely agree that although this is a well-written story that shows how hungry you were, it probably is not going to be the heart of a memoir about you and your grandmother." Then, in an effort to be sure Tyler didn't veer off course again, I said, "Can I help you get started on another moment, one which will show what you want to show?"

When I asked Tyler if he had an idea of another event—one that might show the relationship even more—he said he was thinking about writing how his grandmother went on a roller coaster ride with him.

Recalling the harrowing trip I'd once had on a roller coaster and wanting to rally Tyler's energy for the idea he'd proposed, I said, "Oh my gosh, Tyler. Your grandmother went on one of those rides?" Then I added, "I went on a roller coaster a few years ago and it was brutal. My head was practically jerked off my neck. And when the cart paused on top, before plummeting down . . . it was harrowing! I can't imagine your grandmother did that!"

"She didn't want to—she yelled her head off," Tyler agreed. Then he confided, "I think she did it just for me."

"No wonder you want to tell this story! It is so revealing of your grandmother, isn't it! It is so touching that she would do *even that* for you! It is so smart of you to realize that your story about having lunch at a restaurant

continued from previous page

and I got to talking, and I suggested that this year, you guys are such a close community, that maybe Jill could take the gigantic leap of faith and write about the problem that haunts her." Then I said, "Can you talk to the kids about this, Jill?"

As Jill started to talk, children shifted in their seats and one or two whispered to each other. Sitting beside her, I signaled for her to wait. "Wait 'til their eyes are on you, 'til you have their full attention." After the room grew quiet, Jill began to talk. "I realized that pumpkin picking with my Mom wasn't really on my mind or anything so I'm writing about my weight."

"Class, earlier we talked about bravery, and how there are lots of kinds of bravery. Ali, you are writing your essay on that, aren't you? I think that Jill has just shown us one kind of bravery, don't you? Jill has a draft . . . and is willing to share it with us. So let's listen. As you listen, will you jot down things that you notice Jill doing which makes her draft a powerful one?"

Jill glanced up just once, and then began to read:

> Some days I want to crawl in a hole and hide, hide under a blanket like when I was five and didn't have to worry about my weight, when I could still jump into my bed thinking about jump-ropes and hula-hoops and not having to think about the weight monster coming out from under my bed.
>
> I walked into my parents' bathroom. My eyes skimmed the room and spotted the scale. Gray and yellow. I dreaded going on it. What will it say? I thought. 67 pounds was the minimum, I thought. Should I? Should I not? Should I? Should I not? I didn't want to disappoint myself but I thought maybe I would surprise myself and gain more pounds. I put one foot on the scale. I lifted the other foot slowly off the floor and placed it on the scale next to the other foot. 63 pounds. What! was all I could think. I shouldn't have gotten on the scale. I knew I was going to disappoint myself. I ran from the room, crying.

continued on next page

doesn't show you and your grandmother's relationship but that this moment definitely *does* show that relationship!" Shifting, I said, "Can you tell me how the whole thing happened? What happened first?"

"We were standing in line, watching the ride and the people were screaming. Then we got on."

"Tyler," I said. "Tell it in smaller steps. And Tyler, you want to tell what you saw and did—the external story—*and* what you felt and thought, too, the internal story." To get him started, I said, "So stand up and show me what you were doing exactly as you stood in line, watching the people."

Tyler acted to show that his eyes followed the roller coaster as it traveled along the rails.

Prompting him, I provided words for his actions. "I stood in line . . . " Then I said, "That's the external action, what were you thinking, feeling?"

"I was amazed at the roller coaster," he said. When I prompted him to shift next to again telling what he did or saw next (returning to the external story line), he said, "My eyes were following the roller coaster like, like, it was the strongest magnet in the world!"

"That's beautiful," I assured Tyler. "Write it!" and I dictated the words he'd said while he recorded them. Soon Tyler had written this: [Fig. VIII-3]

> I stood in line to get on the roller coaster next to my grandmother amazed at the roller coaster. My eyes follow it as it was the strongest magnet in the world, and every second it got closer, closer, closer. And nothing can stop me from getting on it. And before I know it, the roller coaster zoomed right next to me as it almost knocks me off my feet. Impatiently I wait to get on. I jump up and down like a kangaroo. My grandmother has a scared face. I see people get off, "That was awesome," they say.

"Tyler," I said. "Do you see how, at the start of this, you shift between the external story line, telling what you did or saw, and then the internal story line, telling what that made you feel or think?" I reread the draft, underlining the external and letting the internal stand.

> <u>I stood in line to get on the roller coaster</u> next to my grandmother amazed at the roller coaster. <u>My eyes follow it</u> as if it was the strongest magnet in the world, and every second it got closer, closer, closer. And nothing can stop me from getting on it. And before I know it, <u>the roller coaster zoomed right next to me as it almost knocks me off my feet.</u> I am so excited <u>I jump up and down like a kangaroo.</u>

"The draft has a pattern that really works," I said, as if this had been his invention. "It goes like this, 1) I do or see something, something happens in the external world. Then 2) I respond by thinking or feeling. Then 3) I do or see something, something happens in the external world, and it continues."

continued from previous page

Throughout the class, hands shot up. Justin spoke first. "I think you are brave to write about that because it is so personal. And I don't think you should worry about being thin because your age is a time for changes and it will probably change because I grew like, four inches in a year!" he said.

Max added, "When you wrote that you hide under your blanket like when you were five, it sounded like Sandra Cisneros in 'Eleven' talking about all her different ages." Others followed.

After a few minutes I brought the class back to the central point. "Let's take Jill as a mentor. All of us have the courage to tackle the real topics that are on our minds. The truth is, we will end up writing in powerful ways when we select a subject that has some angst, some struggle involved in it. So if any of you are writing All-Is-Perfect entries, you may want to think, 'Where's the struggle in this subject?' and 'Is this the truth of what has been on my mind lately?' A writer—I forgot who it was—once said, 'I don't write about my marriage because I have a happy one.' Tackle the hard stuff and your writing often becomes more powerful."

"Tyler," I said. "This is going to be a drop-dead amazing piece, I can just tell. It is amazing how a little story about you and your grandmother riding the roller coaster can really and truly be a window onto your relationship. As you write today and whenever you write stories, remember that you have a skill for shifting between the external story, and the internal story. Would you work on this now and maybe at lunch time—because you are onto some important work—and bring it to me at the start of tomorrow's workshop so that we can use it in the minilesson to teach all the other kids?"

On most days, this would certainly be the end of an already lengthy conference. However, today I made the decision to not end the conference just yet. I instead took Tyler a little farther in hopes that I could use his draft as an example in tomorrow's minilesson—and meanwhile assure myself that he was well on his way towards writing a piece that would work for him. Pressing on, I said, "That is really a brilliant way to write a story, Tyler. But the pattern seems to be disrupted when you get to this part about your grandmother. When you say, 'My grandmother has a scared face,' I am unclear. You were in line, your eyes totally on the ride, oblivious of your grandmother. So when the text says, 'My grandmother has a scared face,' is this what you, the kid in the line for the roller coaster, saw?"

Tyler nodded, "Yeah, because suddenly I looked over and hey! She looked scared and she was clutching her pocketbook and all."

"That's a huge part of the story, isn't it? If this is about your relationship with your grandmother, I think it is really smart that you decided to first show that you were oblivious of her, wrapped up in the roller coaster. Are you suggesting that then something happens to pull you out of your reverie and suddenly you remember that she is there? Will you have her do something or say something that all of a sudden makes you look at her?" Tyler nodded. "After you show yourself looking at her—the external story line—will you shift and show the internal story line [I motioned to the underlined sections of his draft] so that you keep up the pattern of external, then internal, then external . . . ?"

To get Tyler started, I redirected him back to the last lines he'd written and suggested he cross out "My grandmother has a scared face," substituting instead whatever it is that she does to call his attention away from the ride and to her.

> And before I know it, the roller coaster zoomed right next to me as it almost knocks me off my feet. Impatiently I wait to get on. I jump up and down like a kangaroo. My grandmother has a scared face. I see people get off, "That was awesome," they say.

"I can't remember what she did,"-- Tyler said.

"Make it up," I coached, "That's what writers do. Imagine you are in line, you've been watching the roller coaster, your eyes glued to it. Then what happens next?"

"I look over and she is reading the sign? 'Cause it said 'The Intimidator.'"

"Great. And Tyler, as you write, make sure things happen (in your external story and then, in reaction, in your internal story,) between you and your Grandmother because that is what the story is really about.

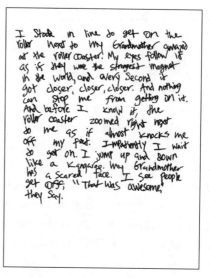

Fig. VIII-3 Tyler includes internal and external story lines.

SHARE

Writing Less

Tell the story of one writer who collected an excess of entries and drafts and then paused to ask, "What do I really want to say?" and used that question to lead him to start an entirely new draft.

"Writers, I want to talk with you again about courage. That seems to be the subject of the day! I want to tell you about another writer who showed great courage today, and that is Adam."

"Adam, as you know, has been writing about his relationship with his brother. Before I conferred with him today, he'd collected about ten long entries about moments he has spent with his brother. For example, he had written an entry which began like this":

> My brother and I go to restaurants. We always play a game named napkin. Whoever sits down first says, "Napkin." If you are the first one to say this you get one point . . .

"And one that began":

> "Why isn't Jon coming?" I asked as my sister, mom and dad pile into my dad's car.
>
> "Jon's with his friends," replied my mom. We drove down into Englewood. We all sat together, talking and laughing. After our meal we were talking about colleges. It came up that we would be together next year at the same time except without Jon. "Next year at the same time we'll be together without Jon," I said. Then I thought, "Oh, no, I shouldn't have said that." Everyone one of us went quiet.

"And he'd written an entry about Jon teaching him to be a goalie, and about Jon writing to him when he was at camp, and about rough housing with Jon in the car, and on and on the list goes. When I asked Adam his plans, he said he thought he'd recopy the entries, and find a refrain that could hook them together. Instead of saying 'Alone is . . .' he'd say something like, 'My brother is . . .'"

"But as we talked, Adam said something really important. He said, 'I don't know if these *really* show what I feel.' I asked him to say more, and he talked about how he's feeling like his childhood with Jon will soon be over. Then Adam did something really brave. He put all those entries aside and went over to the computer and sat with a blank screen in front of him. 'I'm going to try writing just one really long story about the day when he

You will see that this share session encourages children to be willing to begin a draft without hanging onto an entry they liked. This is an important message for me because I often find that to comfort myself when I'm approaching a new piece of writing, I try to bring along something I have already written or said, using that as the starter-dough for the new piece. But as a result, I end up rehashing something I've written before instead of being willing to take the great risk of saying something new. This quote by Murray hangs alongside my desk as a personal reminder: "Emptiness is the starting point of writing and I have to remind myself of that. After all, I don't want to write what I have written before, and write it in the same way. I have to remember that in despair, in terror, in hopelessness, I have come to the beginning of my writing. Now I can find a new country to explore."

In this unit, you'll see the way in which one day's conference becomes the next day's mid-workshop teaching point or minilesson. I think of conferences as the power chip that energizes all of our teaching.

It is very hard, when writing, to let go of texts we've written. When you see a writer put one draft aside and embark on a new draft, celebrate. When you see a writer cross out an entire page, celebrate.

leaves,' Adam said. 'I'll pretend it already did happen, and stretch it out and put all my feelings in.' Then he added, 'If it doesn't work, I will go back to my other entries.'"

Ask children to respond to the writer's work, offering an opinion.

"Listen to this draft, and then let's tell Adam whether his decision was a good one": [Fig. VIII-4]

> "Noooo, please can't I go?" I plead.
>
> My sister and I are going to be staying at my aunt's house. Without Jon. Last time we did this my sister had gone off to college. This time was different. This time I would be crying instead of her.
>
> It was already happening. My eyes stung. I tried to blink back tears, but they were inevitable. Tears started pouring over my eyes. I looked up and saw tears in my brother's eyes. I ran to my brother, he hugged me. I was surprised at this. I didn't want to let go.
>
> I knew he was moving on. My childhood with my brother would end this very moment. It won't be the same when he comes back, because all the spaces and gaps that would be left when he was gone. Like our talks about soccer games, our talks about school and most importantly our talks about each other. These are all ways we would bond. It will only be a matter of time before he has graduated college and gets married and has kids.

"The draft continues, but let me stop," I said. "What do you think? Talk to Adam." For the next few minutes, one child after another talked to Adam about the great emotional power in this piece, and about the power of his stretched moment.

Celebrate the support writers have offered one another and ask students to share further thoughtful suggestions about the draft presented.

"Writers," I said. "When you have done as Adam and as Jill have done and taken the risk of writing with heart and soul about a topic that really matters to you, it will be really important that people help you feel like you have made a good decision; you guys have just done that. Thank you. But it is also important that people give your writing the respectful attention it deserves, and this means helping you to make it even better. Adam and Jill and many of the rest of you have written brave, strong first drafts . . . but these are *first drafts*. And they deserve smart, honest responses. So would you listen again to just the start of Adam's draft, and this time give Adam and his writing the honor of your thoughtful suggestions." I handed out copies of his draft, saying, "Mark up the text and get ready to give him some feedback."

You'll notice that I describe what Adam has done as if all the decisions were his alone. Adam laid out all the entries he'd written, then Adam questioned whether the entries really conveyed his feelings, then Adam set the entries aside . . . .The truth is that Adam did not round all these corners on his own. I was at his elbow, asking, suggesting, nudging. But typically, when I want to retell what one writer has done so that others can learn from it, I find that I want to relate the blow-by-blow story of how the writer progressed from one state of affairs to another. I want to tell the story so as to suggest that others in the class might follow the one child's example and do likewise. So it makes sense that I factor out the role I played, and allow the writer to be the one star of the show.

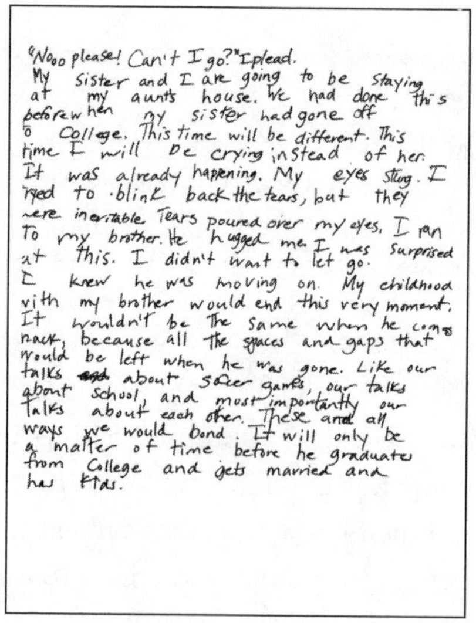

Fig. VIII-4 Adam's first draft

Children read quietly for a few minutes, and then I gestured for one and then another to speak to Adam. "It was really sad," Judah said, "but I was actually a little confused. Where were you?"

Adam launched into a long and convoluted explanation of how, when Jon and Adam's sister left for college she left not from home but from the aunt's house so that will probably hold true when Jon leaves as well. I intervened to point out that writers can take poetic license; just because Jon actually will leave from college in this unusual fashion does not mean that Adam needs to tell the story that way. "It might be simpler and more straightforward, Adam," I said, "to tell the story of Jon packing up and driving away from your home. You may even leave out your sister entirely." This led the class into a bit of a talk about the difference between literal honesty and emotional honesty. Sometimes writers write what is "True with a capital *T*, but not true with a small *t*." Children also suggested to Adam that his piece might become too full of explanations. "Keep the story going longer," the children suggested.

Ask partners to offer each other the same kind of supportive, thoughtful feedback they've just offered the writer in the spotlight.

Once the class had given Adam this thoughtful feedback, I suggested partners get together and decide which of them needed help most urgently, and then confer in a similar way, giving that person help.

As often as possible, I want to celebrate good work by revising it. In Units of Study for Primary Writing, *we launch a unit of study on revision by asking children whether the work they have just published is their best writing ever. When the children chorus, "Yessssss!" then teacher Pat Bleichman and I say, "Because what writers do when we really, really like what we have written, when it is the best writing we have ever done, is this: we revise it!" Another time in that unit of study, we ask children to look back on writing they've finished to see if any of that writing is good enough that it deserves to be revised. In this share session, I try to make a similar point.*

When children have gathered in the large group and they are giving one writer feedback on her writing, be sure the child directs his remarks to the writer, not to you. You may need to intervene and say, "Your eyes should be on Adam."

⊙ HOMEWORK *Conferring with Yourself to Make a Writing Plan* Writers, in school today and recently, you've been learning how to confer with yourself, just as I confer with you. You've learned to ask questions:

Questions Writing Teachers Ask

- What was the last thing you decided to do, to work towards? How did it turn out?
- Why did you do this exactly? What else could you have done to reach the same goal?
- What else, other than that work, have you been doing and how has that worked out?
- Do you have specific plans for what you might do next?

Tonight, have a conference with yourself the way every writer in this whole world does. Tonight, though, ask yourself also, "Am I being a brave writer? Am I writing the truth?" There are lots of ways to be brave and lots of ways to answer these questions.

So, tonight, read over your own work, entertain questions, consider your options for what to do next, think about which options might pay off especially . . . and then create a plan for your work for tonight, and henceforth. Write a planning box that reflects your decisions and plans. And then begin the work that you lay out for yourself.

TAILORING YOUR TEACHING

If children are not getting a lot of writing accomplished and you suspect they are worrying about writing texts which are weighty enough . . . perhaps you will decide to emphasize the fact that writing often gets better, through sheer hard work. If students are taking too long to draft, perhaps this is because they feel so pressured to write about their lives in a profound way that they are frozen. You may need to downplay the inspirational aspect of writing and emphasize the virtues of persistence and hard work. Writing about our lives in ways that help us discover ways we have grown is not always an easy task—especially if we are just learning how to reflect on our experiences in that way. Productivity matters. Writing a lot matters. You might remind students of Thomas Edison's quotation: "Genius is 1% inspiration, 99% perspiration." If we just keep writing, we may surprise ourselves and turn that perspiration into inspiration after all.

Another way to loosen writers a bit from the pressures of writing with significance is to ask them to talk with their partners about the sources of inspiration they draw upon. We can never underestimate the social nature of learning. Writing is never a solitary activity, streaming from only the mind to the pen in a direct flow of ideas. "Writers," you might say "I've noticed that throughout this unit, you've been doing a fabulous job writing and thinking independently about your memoirs. But writing isn't always an isolated thing. The classic adventure novelist Robert Louis Stevenson once said, 'Keep your fears to yourself, but share your inspiration with others.' Right now, would you push all your worries about this piece aside and share your inspiration, your hopes for your memoir, with your partner? Partners, would you listen for and think about ways your partner could turn those hopes into a draft?"

If you suspect that this genre is a very ambitious one for your students . . . you may want to remind children that writers sometimes find it helps to draft different parts of their writing on separate sheets of paper. Perhaps, for example, one child will use a different sheet of paper for each of three Small Moment stories (or scenes) that she decides to write, and then other sheets of paper for two passages in which the writer reflects on the scenes. Once they have a few parts written, then students can physically move the sections around so that they have a better vision of how they want their drafts to flow.

COLLABORATING WITH COLLEAGUES

My hunch is that there have been several times throughout this book when you have read student work and thought, "That's pretty good!" Then you turn the page and find that I have nudged the student to revise the exact text which you admired earlier. This may have made you uneasy. "Wasn't it good enough the way it was?" you may have asked. "When is a piece of writing good enough?" you may wonder.

The truth is that I am an unabashed enthusiast for revision. I remember once, I was scheduled to speak to a large auditorium of teachers, and just before I began my speech, a messenger entered the room carrying the very first copy of my book, *The Art of Teaching Reading*. A teacher saw me holding—stroking—the brand new book and murmured, "Imagine, you wrote *all those words*!"

I looked at her and said, "You don't know the half of it." When we redid our kitchen, the contractor brought one of those industrial trailers into our yard and parked it beside the house, filling it with debris. When I wrote that book—or any book since—I think I filled five industrial trailers with discarded drafts!

I *love* to revise. I put myself on the page; the best that I can. I put all of me there—my experiences, my priorities, my knowledge, and my ignorance and biases too—and then I reread and see myself. And then—glory be!—I get to fix myself up, to make myself into the kind of person I want to be. I revise to make myself (and my ideas) more clear, more generous, more informed, more helpful.

In life, I don't get a chance to recall my first draft efforts: I say something, I do something, and my words and actions are out there in the

world, creating waves of reactions. I can't call those actions and words back in order to make them wiser, better. But when I write, I get a chance to pull myself up by my bootstraps. When any one of us has done our very best, and can then stand on the shoulders of our best work in order to produce work that is better yet, this is a great treat.

So yes, you will see that I purposefully act on the assumption that children will welcome revision as I do. You will see that I regard good work as an invitation to revise. And yes, I do believe that our writing, like our lives, can be made better, better, better. And so I assume that children will want to revise their writing until the whistle blows and time is up.

Please don't interpret this as meaning that I want children to slog away at endless revisions, letting their energy for writing wane. I'm totally and absolutely convinced that revision can feel like an honor, a compliment, and that we can make revision feel this way when we take care of the culture we create in our classrooms and our own attitudes towards writing and revision.

So I encourage you to wear a love not only for writing but also for revision on your sleeve. Let children see that you can't imagine that they wouldn't love the chance to revise. Study ways in which you can help children care enough about writing, and about their specific text, so that they, too, feel personally invested in those drafts.

And if the day comes when you really do believe that by encouraging a child to revise his writing, you will make that child value writing less, then by all means, back off. Invite the child to start a second piece on the same seed idea. And the truth is, you'll be luring the child into revision through the back door!

IN THIS SESSION, YOU WILL TEACH CHILDREN THAT AS EACH POINT ON THE EXTERNAL TIMELINE OF A STORY AFFECTS THE CENTRAL CHARACTER (IN A MEMOIR, YOU) ON THE INSIDE, THIS CREATES THE INTERNAL TIMELINE OF A STORY. TODAY YOU'LL TEACH CHILDREN WAYS THAT WRITERS CRAFT STORIES THAT INCLUDE INTERNAL JOURNEYS.

GETTING READY

- "Mama Sewing," from *Childtimes* by Eloise Greenfield
- Chart of Internal and External Timelines for "Mama Sewing," see below
- Copies for each student of a student's writing containing internal and external story lines (Perhaps Tyler's)
- See CD-ROM for resources

THE INTERNAL AND EXTERNAL JOURNEY OF A STORY

The most important lessons that you will teach your students are not ones that are simply taught, then checked off from your list—"Done!" Instead, the most important lessons are the ones that your children revisit over and over, in a cycle of continuous study, with your teaching and your children's understandings becoming more complex and sophisticated over time.

It should not surprise you, then, that this session revisits lessons you have taught often. From the start of the year, you have emphasized to children that when a writer writes a story, a narrative, the writer needs to ask, "What is my story really about?" Although your children are writing memoir in this unit, not personal narratives, most memoirs contain stories. In memoir, it is essential that the stories carry larger meanings. So you will want to remind children that based on the writer's answer to the question, "What is my writing really about?" the writer will tell the story differently. You have already taught children that if the writer is writing about riding a Ferris wheel and the point is that the writer still cherishes childhood pleasures, then the writer may describe how she stood in the ticket line, surrounded by a sea of little children, none higher than her waist, and realized that old as she is (ten!) she still appreciates childhood pleasures. On the other hand, if the Ferris wheel story is about the writer appreciating the chance to look out over the entire fairgrounds, the writer will probably bring out the internal thinking which occurs when the Ferris wheel approaches the top of its spin.

Today, you take these lessons another step and suggest that writers actually approach a story anticipating that across the story, the main character (who in this instance is the author) will go through an internal journey of feelings that parallels (and is in response to) the story's external journey of actions. This means that if the writer wants her memoir to convey that she still appreciates childhood pleasures, she can do better than putting that one unchanging feeling throughout her entire draft, beginning, middle, and end. Instead, she might in the draft reveal an internal journey, one that shows a conflict and a resolution. Today, then, children will consider how an internal journey might fit into their writing.

MINILESSON

The Internal and External Journey of a Story

CONNECTION

Reiterate all the options your children have as memoirists, and then tell them they have no option when writing a memoir but to reveal themselves through it.

"Writers, for the past few weeks, we've been studying options that are before you as writers. I've told you that you have options for how you will structure your memoir; that your memoir can be one story, a necklace of related ministories, an essay, or even a collection of poems. Then, too, you know that you have options about your subject. Your memoir can shine a spotlight on your relationship with your father, on the tree-fort in your backyard, on your homesickness for Missouri, on your childhood struggles to learn to read. You have lots and lots of choices as a writer of memoir."

"But as a memoir writer, you have no choice but to reveal yourself. The point of writing a memoir is to make a statement about yourself—about the kind of person you are. So yes, Max can write about the tree-fort that used to be in his backyard, but *really* his memoir needs to be about a boy who is nostalgic for that tree house. And Adam can write about his brother Jon, leaving for college, but *really* the memoir needs to be about Adam, the younger brother, who is left behind when Jon heads off to college. And Ali can write about her father's bravery as he lies in bed, recovering from an awful injury, but really Ali is writing about the girl who stands beside her father's bed. And Tyler can write about a grandmother who is so loving that she even rides that roller coaster ride—but really, this needs to also be a memoir about what a grandmother's generosity means to her grandson."

"So keep in mind that when you are working on a story within your memoir, this can't just be the story of *an event*, this needs to be the story of *you as a person*. I am pleased that many of you are writing not only the external story of what happened to you, but also the *internal* story of what you thought and wondered and remembered and worried."

Name your teaching point. In this case, tell children that the internal, as well as the external, story line needs to evolve over time, and that as points on the external story line affect us, the internal story line is created.

"Today I want to teach you that both the external events *and* the internal feelings of a story need to evolve across a timeline, a story mountain. When we write a story, we know there will be a sequence of actions—that one thing will happen, then another thing will

COACHING

You should be able to hear the drumroll in my language. "You have choices about one thing, you have choices about another thing, but you have no choice but to . . . "

Whenever you can name what your students are doing in ways that are beautiful, you'll lift the level of their work and their self-concepts. It is important to do this. Notice that when I want to speak beautifully, I use techniques that we teach children—in this instance, parallelism. My list is parallel, and detailed.

Connections are meant as a time to consolidate what children have already learned, and as a time to convey the "why" of a minilesson. You may want to look back at Connections across this series, and notice commonalities and differences. As children become more experienced, the connections should consolidate larger armfuls of material and should be more nuanced.

happen, and another. But we are not always aware that when writing a story, there needs to be a parallel sequence of *re-actions*, of feelings and thoughts and dreams and fears that the main character (in a memoir, that will be you) experiences."

"The external and the internal story line, of course, need to be utterly connected. With each external event, the narrator or the main character sees and thinks and feels a bit differently on the inside. Something happens and we realize something we hadn't realized before. Something else happens, and we feel something we hadn't felt before."

"Today, therefore, I hope you come to understand that as each point on the external timeline of a story affects the central character (which, in a memoir, is us) on the inside, this creates the internal timeline of a story."

TEACHING
Reiterate the teaching point in different words, emphasizing that writers approach the narrative section of a memoir thinking, "What feeling do I want to show in the beginning? Which one in the middle? Which in the end?"

"I want to remind you that when you plan the sections of your memoir that contain a narrative, you need to plan for how you will show the journey of feelings that you experience as you moved through time. So you can't just ask, "What feeling do I want this story to show?" and then put that one feeling into all the parts of your entire draft. Instead, you need to think, "What feeling or thought do I want to show *at the start* of my story? How does that feeling change *in the middle* of my story? What does that feeling become *at the end* of my story?"

Illustrate your point by reading aloud a short text and showing children the external and internal story lines in it.

"In 'Mama Sewing,' Eloise Greenfield has very clearly organized the *external* story line of her story. In a similar way, all of you write with very clear external story lines."

"But what I noticed last night when I was reading 'Mama Sewing,' trying to learn from this mentor text, is that in this memoir, each event in the external story line affects Eloise—and the effects that the events create are a big part of the memoir. More than this, I noticed that the way Eloise is affected—the way she feels as a result of various happenings—creates the *internal* timeline of this memoir."

"In 'Mama Sewing' by Eloise Greenfield, the text is a story that jumps over long spans of time. Eloise Greenfield writes in this way to show that her ways of understanding her mother have changed over time."

"Listen as I read 'Mama Sewing,' and let's think, 'What is the first external event?' and

I say this as if of course we are aware that a story contains an external and internal story line, each of which evolves, and that the two are bound together into actions and reactions, but the truth is that I didn't comprehend this myself 'til I worked to help Tyler bring out the external and the internal journey across his roller coaster story. I'm a lot older than the kids and this lesson just dawned on me a year ago! So it's not as obvious as I make it sound.

You will notice that in a sense this session has a double teaching point. Don't worry about condensing everything you want to say into a single sentence. Worry instead about clarity and explicitness.

Sometimes people decide that it is important to simplify the teaching point by consolidating it into a single sentence. I advocate for clarity over brevity and believe there is often a trade-off between the two.

Notice that as these units of study unroll, children revisit the same concepts of good writing over and over, each time dealing with them with increasing sophistication. So at first children asked, "Where is the heart of my story?" Remember the author of that "Al is Dead" story decided the heart of the story was the moment of finding the fish, Al, dead in the trash can? The young writer expanded that section of the narrative, and did so towards no conscious, deliberate purpose. Next children learned to ask, "What is my story really about?" and to comb their answer through the whole text. They worked to be sure their lead and end addressed the peak of their story mountains. Now I'm teaching children that their internal as well as their external story unrolls in a progression—the internal story evolves as much as the external one.

then let's think also, 'What internal response to that external event does the story convey?'"
I read this aloud:

Mama Sewing

I don't know why Mama ever sewed for me. She sewed for other people, made beautiful suits and dresses and got paid for doing it. But I don't know why she ever sewed for me. I was so mean.

It was all right in the days when she had to make my dresses a little longer in the front than in the back to make up for the way I stood, with my legs pushed back and my stomach stuck out. I was little then, and I trusted Mama. But when I got older, I worried.

Mama would turn the dress on the wrong side and slide it over my head, being careful not to let the pins stick me. She'd kneel on the floor with her pin cushion fitting the dress on me, and I'd look down at the dress, at that lopsided, raw-edged, half-basted, half-pinned *thing*—and know that it was never going to look like anything. So, I'd pout while Mama frowned and sighed and kept on pinning.

Sometimes she would sew all night, and in the morning I'd have a perfectly beautiful dress, just right for the school program or the party. I'd put it on, and I'd be so ashamed of the way I acted. I'd be too ashamed to say I was sorry.

But Mama knew.

"Do you see, writers, that Eloise Greenfield's memoir tells one thing that happened on a story line of happenings, and then tells the internal response," I said, turning the chart paper tablet to reveal the chart I'd made of the external and internal story line in this memoir. Gesturing to the chart to illustrate my remarks, I said, "Then the memoir tells the next thing that happened on the external storyline . . . Each event affects Eloise in some way. The way she is affected—the way she feels as a result of various happenings—creates the internal timeline."

Timelines in "Mama Sewing"

External Timeline	Internal Timeline
Mama sewed for me when I was little . . .	. . . my response was that this made me happy.
Mama sewed for me when I was older . . .	. . . my response was that this made me irritable.
Then Mama made me a beautiful dress for the school dance . . .	. . . my response was that I was ashamed of my earlier behavior towards her.

This excerpt comes from Childtimes, *a memoir written by Eloise Greenfield and her mother. Like* House on Mango Street *by Cisneros and* Marshfield Dreams *by Fletcher, this memoir is an anthology of short passages, making it a wonderful text for children to study.*

This chart made the organization of the text very obvious to the students, highlighting how each point on the external timeline of the story affects what happens inside the character, therefore creating an internal timeline.

This text is organized chronologically. It is not a small moment because it takes place over the course of years. It does, however, very explicitly illustrate the connection between external actions and internal feelings. If most of your students are writing across shorter periods of time, you may choose to use a small moment from another text.

Highlight the fact that the external events move the story forward. The character's responses to those events constitute the internal story line, conveying the impact the events have on the person or on the relationships.

"When you lay these timelines side by side, you can see how Eloise has changed her way of understanding her mother as a result of this series of events from her life. At the start of the story, Eloise appreciates her mother's sewing. But as the story line unfolds, Eloise goes through a journey of feeling. When Eloise is a teenager, she has no patience for her mother or for her mother's sewing. Her feelings have evolved. Then, one day, Eloise wakes up and finds a beautiful dress that her mother had worked on all night to sew, and now, Eloise becomes ashamed of the way she has treated her mother."

"In this memoir, and in many memoirs, the internal story is important because this helps us see what the character realizes about himself or herself and about the character's relationships. Pay attention to what I just said. It is crucial."

ACTIVE ENGAGEMENT
Tell students about a child who deliberately shifted between the external and the internal story and whose internal story line follows a clear sequence. Ask children to mark a copy of the child's text to track the journey of feelings it shows.

"So writers, when you plan the sections of your memoir that contain a narrative, remember to plan for your internal journey of feelings. Tyler has been writing a beautiful memoir about a time when he and his grandmother went on a roller coaster ride together."

"I'm going to ask Tyler to read the start of his draft aloud. You each have a copy of it. As you listen, notice the way Tyler records the *external* event (sometimes in just half of a sentence) and then his *internal* response to that event. Then he records the next *external* event, and his next *internal* response to that event. As you listen, keep in mind the evolving *internal* story line. How does Tyler feel at the beginning? After a bit? Later? Soon you'll have a chance to talk about Tyler's journey of feelings."

Tyler read the beginning of his draft aloud: [*Figs. IX-1* and *IX-2*]

> I stand in the line, my eyes drawn to the roller coaster as if it were the strongest magnet in the world. I follow the cart as it swoops and swirls. It jets along the tracks over my head. "I can't wait," I think.
>
> I count how many people are ahead of me in line. Nothing is going to stop me from getting on the ride!
>
> "The intimidator," my grandmother reads from the sign. I look at

You could also point out that Eloise's journey of thought is both circular (at the start she trusts her mother's sewing, in the middle she is irritated by it, and at the end she is again trustful) and linear: As she ages, Eloise not only appreciates her mother's gesture of love, she feels shame for having ever scorned it.

I try to keep my minilessons short and clear so kids can grasp their meaning without feeling overwhelmed. Nonetheless, there are times—like now—when I stop to say, "Listen up!" highlighting one part of my lesson so that kids know it's something especially important.

I've deliberately chosen to spotlight Tyler's piece because the external story of a roller coaster ride is so dramatic and action-filled that the internal story might easily have been lost. Yet Tyler has managed to write an equally powerful internal story, and I want kids to learn from this.

Tyler's writing now becomes a mentor text for the entire class. Not only Tyler but also other kids who regard themselves as similar to him benefit from this. As I wrote earlier, during my work with Tyler and his roller coaster story, I first came to the ah-ha that a writer can't simply ask, "What am I trying to show in this story?" and then identify a single feeling ("I worried about my grandmother"), combing that one feeling throughout the text. It was my work with Tyler which actually illuminated for me the fact that there needs to be an internal as well as an external progression. So, longer conferences can help not only the child but also us, as teachers!

her and see that she is clutching her pocketbook in her hands and brushing the dust off her vest. I start to worry.

The roller coaster cranks to a stop near us. And the people get off. As they flood past us, I hear someone say, "That was awesome." And, "Let's do that again." Out of the corner of my eyes I see my grandmother sigh with a scared face. I worry more.

We step into the cart. "Grandma, you don't have to go on. It's a pretty big ride," I say, wanting to get her off the ride. I hear a click click as the handle bar locks against our stomachs. I feel like my grandma is trapped in her worst fear. "This is our last chance. Do you want to get off?"

"So did you see Tyler's feelings evolve? What was the main feeling at the start of the story?" The children chorused that at the start of the story, Tyler felt excitement. "If excitement was the main feeling at the start, then what was the next main feeling?" I asked, and in the ensuing conversation, I talked up the fact that Tyler was really smart to not show himself worrying about his grandmother from the start but to instead let this come out over the sequence of events.

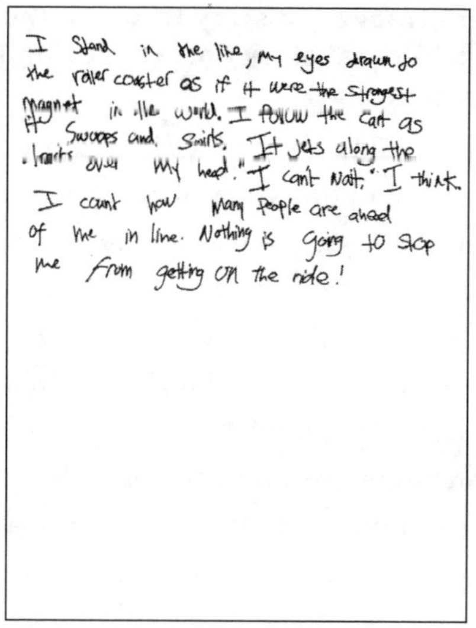

Fig. IX-1 Tyler's entry

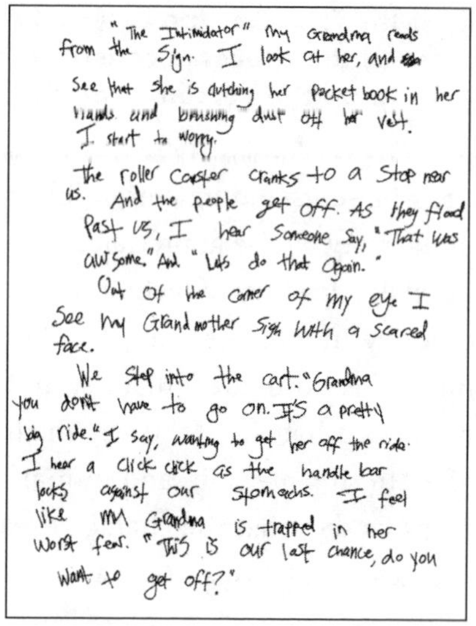

Fig. IX-2 Tyler's entry, page 2

Tyler's memoir is rich with so many elements of good writing: alliteration, simile, dialogue, sounds, detail, observations, external and internal story, and a clear change in the narrator. You could have kids point out these elements of good writing, highlighting the fact that writers draw on all they know about writing even when their focus is on just one aspect of writing—in this case, internal and external story.

If a child writes a story, "I got a puppy from the dog pound and I was happy," the child may need to add the external as well as the internal beginning to that story, so that the story can contain a progression of feelings. Perhaps in the new draft, the story begins, "I entered the dog pound, full of worry and anticipation." Then it ends "I found Rufus and I was happy."

One way to think about the components of minilessons is to think that the Connection of a minilesson is a time for the "why" of what we are teaching, the Teaching is a time for the "how" of what we are teaching, and the Link is a time for the "when." This is our opportunity to remind students what the circumstances will be which will lead them to use the strategy or to apply the knowledge learned in the minilesson.

LINK

Remind writers that when they work on the narrative sections of their memoir, they need to plan for a journey of feelings, and to remember that the external storyline is intertwined with the internal one.

"So writers, as you work on the drafts of your memoir, many of you will spend some time working to write a story—the story may be your entire memoir, or the story may be part of your memoir. Either way, remember that when we write a story, there is a sequence of events that moves the story forward through time. And with each event, the main character will begin to see and think and feel differently. Each point on the external timeline of a story will affect the character—in this case, us—on the inside and, as a result, the internal story line will be created."

WRITING AND CONFERRING

Writing About Internal Changes

I pulled my chair alongside Ali who was rereading the draft of the narrative section of her memoir. "I tried to divide it into tiny chapters based on my feelings," she said, "But it was mostly one feeling 'cause Dad wasn't able to do anything but lie there." Then Ali pointed to a section of her draft (see below) and said, "I added more feelings here so I have a journey of feelings."

Ali was writing about the feelings she experienced during her father's long convalescence after major back surgery. She had produced dozens of drafts of both the Small Moment story when she went into the room where her father lay, wanting desperately to feel that he cared about the little events of her school-life, and she'd also written many reflective rumination which encircled this narrative. Most of the reflective writing explored an issue that first surfaced during the literary essay unit when children talked about Gabriel, the protagonist in "Spagetti," as tough and brave.

This was the draft Ali had before her: [Fig. IX-3]

> My father stared at the ceiling. It was like there were strings coming out of his eyes that were attached to the ceiling and the strings wouldn't let his eyes move. I sat on the side of the bed. "Today at school . . ." I said. "When will you be better?" He kicked his leg. "And I ate pizza, ice cream and strawberries for lunch. I played with Jill. I had a good day as always."
>
> I missed him but I let him be. He was in pain. I was surprised he didn't cry. But maybe he did.
>
> After some time I got up and left his bedroom. I stood outside the door and looked at him for a long time expecting him to talk to me. If I stood there long enough he would get up and run around and play ball with me. But he never did. I went downstairs to watch TV. His silence stayed with me. His silence was one I felt and one day I would feel again.

MID-WORKSHOP TEACHING POINT *Writing with Specific Actions* "Writers, can I have your eyes and your attention? I've been reading the revisions that you're making to your memoirs, and I can see that your writing is becoming much more powerful as you concentrate on telling your internal stories. Many of you are adding in lots of internal thinking. I want to remind you of something. You can also convey the internal story by using very specific actions that show how you were feeling! The internal story isn't just *telling* your feelings, you can also *show* them. That can be tricky because we have been talking about the external story as where the actions happen and

continued on next page

My father stared at at the ceiling. It was like there were strings coming out of his eyes that were attached to the ceiling and the strings wouldn't let his eyes move. I sat on the side of the bed. "Today at school . . ." I said "When will you be better? He kicked his leg. And I ate pizza, ice cream, strawberries for lunch. I played with Jill. I had a good day as always.
I missed him but I let him be he was in paid I was surprised he didn't cry. But maybe he did
After some time I got up and left his bedroom. I stood outside the door and looked at him for a long time expecting him to talk to be me. If I stood there long enough he would get up and ron around and play ball with me. But he never did. I went down stairs to watch tv. His silence stayed with me. His silence was one I felt and one day I would feel again.

Fig. IX-3 Ali interspersed the internal story into her sequence of events.

"Can you tell me about the journey of feelings that you are trying to show," I said, and heard from Ali that she hoped her draft first showed hopefulness as she tried to interest her Dad in the details of her life, then showed loneliness and sadness as she responded to his disinterest, then showed that she tried to feel better by leaving to watch TV but found that the sadness lingered.

"So what are you planning to do next?" I asked, and learned that Ali had decided that she needed to stretch out each feeling more, and she also wanted to build up one more feeling. To do this, she'd written a number beside the phrase at the start of her final paragraph in which she had written: "After some time I got up and left his bedroom. I stood at the door and looked at him for a long time expecting him to talk to me." On another page, Ali was trying to write more about what she felt as she stood outside the door of her father's room, waiting, willing him to react to her and to get over his injury. When I arrived, she had been in the midst of writing this insert: *[Fig. IX-4]*

> After some time I got up and left his side. I stood outside the door and looked at him for some time. Waiting. Expecting him to talk to me. Expecting him to push his pain behind him. If I stood there long enough he would get up and run and play ball with me and we wouldn't have to wait. Wait. That was my least favorite word. I went downstairs.

"Ali," I said. "You are doing really important work, aren't you? It gives me goose bumps. And I absolutely love the way you are thinking about the chapters of your feelings, and trying to show how your feelings evolved across the sequence of this piece—from hopefulness, to loneliness, to whatever it is you are showing yourself feeling when you stood outside the door (perhaps anger). I also love the way you are planning your work, giving yourself assignments."

Then, shifting, I said, "Can I give you just one tip?" Ali nodded. "You may want to watch the ratio of external actions and internal feelings because as you stretch out the sections in which you write what you are feeling, you may find yourself writing one sentence of actions—I stood beside my dad's bed—and then a huge paragraph of feelings and thoughts. What you can do to solve this is to invent small actions you could have done at the time. For example, you could say:

> I stood beside Dad's bed. I thought . . . I felt . . . I reached out and touched Dad's hand, running my finger over his bumpy veins. I remembered . . . A breath of wind rippled through the curtains. For a moment I glanced outside. I wondered . . .

continued from previous page

the internal story as more introspective. But you can use actions to convey feelings. For example, Rie is trying to show that she feels embarrassed and out of place in dance class. She shows this to her reader at the very beginning when she walks into the dance studio, pulls out her ballet shoes, and then quickly shoves them back into her bag because she doesn't want anyone else to see them. This tiny action is a window into Rie's feelings. So as you revise, remember you can convey the internal story with external actions too."

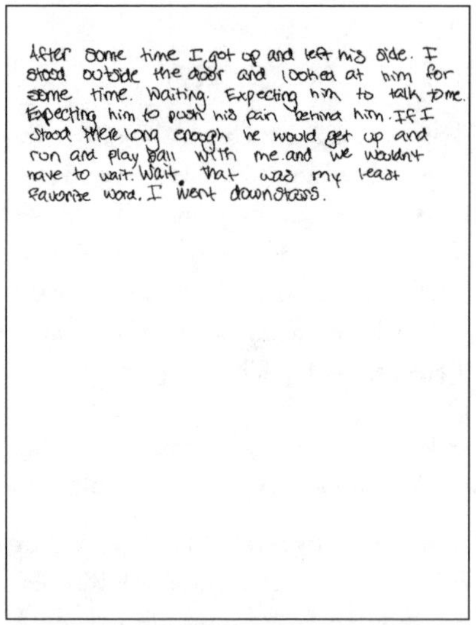
After some time I got up and left his side. I stood outside the door and looked at him for some time. Waiting. Expecting him to talk to me. Expecting him to push his pain behind him. If I stood there long enough he would get up and run and play ball with me and we wouldn't have to wait. Wait. that was my least favorite word. I went downstairs.

Fig. IX-4 Ali zoomed into one moment of her narrative, stretching that one moment out.

"Do you see how that version intersperses actions in between the thoughts and feelings?" Then I said, "Let's try it. Start with when you walked into his room. Slow down and tell tiny, tiny actions so you keep up the balance of an action, then a feeling or a thought, then an action . . . " Then I said, "Start, 'I pushed the door open. I didn't go in, not yet. I thought . . .'"

Ali picked up where I'd left off. Soon she'd gotten a strong start on another draft: *[Fig. IX-5]*

> I pushed the door open. I didn't go in yet, not yet. I thought of what I was going to say. I knew I was going to say what I had said for the last two weeks: "When will you be better?" I wasn't just putting off what I was going to say. I was preparing myself. I didn't want to run away like my brother.
>
> I walked in about two feet, then I started to turn around. I stopped mid-turn. "No, Ali, stay," I said inside my heart. I jumped on to the bed and crawled over to his side. "When will you be better?"

"You got it!" I said. "And after this, remember to yes, think about the journey of your feelings as you've done here. And also to remember to braid your writing so that you weave the external story to the internal story."

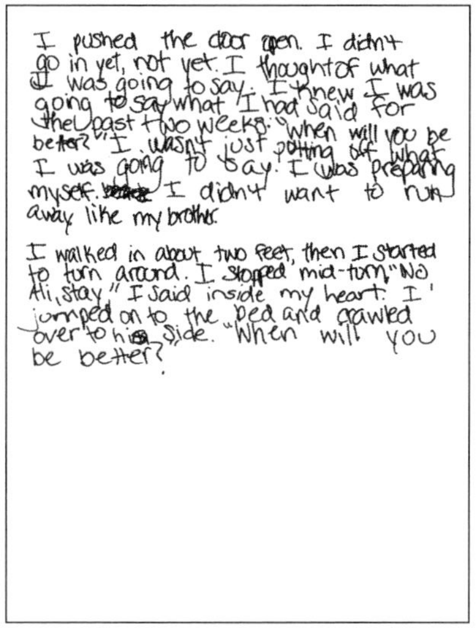
I pushed the door open. I didn't go in yet, not yet. I thought of what I was going to say. I knew I was going to say what I had said for the past two weeks: "When will you be better?" I wasn't just putting off what I was going to say. I was preparing myself. I didn't want to run away like my brother.

I walked in about two feet, then I started to turn around. I stopped mid-turn. "No, Ali, stay," I said inside my heart. I jumped on to the bed and crawled over to his side. "When will you be better?"

Fig. IX-5 Ali brings out more story actions, using them to support her introspection

SHARE

Putting Feelings onto the Page

Contrast the way in which novice writers describe feelings—usually summarizing the generic feeling in a single word—with the way that skilled writers capture feelings. Share examples of the latter.

"Writers, in this session we have talked a lot about the importance of writing not only what was happening *to* you, but also, what was happening *in* you. I want to remind you that it is not easy to put feelings onto the page. What novice writers sometimes do is they try to find a single word that will sum up a feeling, and they write, 'I felt sad,' or 'I felt lonely,' or 'I was worried.' But writers like you, who study the qualities of powerful writing, know that usually when we want to convey a feeling, we need to do so by writing sentences or paragraphs that capture the feeling. And you know that a writer takes seriously the challenge of helping people know the specific way in which the writer experienced that particular feeling."

"Once I worked with a fourth grader, Gerthruder, who wrote about getting up late in the night, and feeling afraid as she made her way down the hall towards the bathroom. Listen to how she captured her particular experience that night of being afraid":

> It was terrifying getting closer to the bathroom and feeling like my heart was running ahead to the light switch.

"And once a boy named Birger wanted to describe what it felt like just after he learned that his cat had been run over by a car. He described himself walking out towards the scene of the accident, and he captured his feeling by writing":

> It was hard, smelling the fresh Spring air, and thinking that a part of me had just died.

Ask children to share with their partner instances in which they captured their feelings in print, or to help each other do this if they haven't yet had a chance to do it.

"Right now, would you and your partner look over your drafts and find places where you've tried to put a feeling you had onto the page. See if you found a way to capture the precise, the particular experience you—and only you—felt. And if you haven't yet done this, help each other. Turn and talk."

You will no doubt notice that I am not explicit about whether share sessions are delivered with the children sitting in their workspaces and the teacher standing in the midst of them, or whether teachers convene the writers into the meeting area for the share session. This is really a matter of personal preference . . . or of time. Of course there is something special about having whole-class meetings bookend most of your writing workshops. On the other hand, the one thing that none of us have enough of is time, and one way to economize on time is for the share session to be delivered with kids sitting in their workspaces. If you do this, then you will need to have children sitting close to their writing partners, and you will also want to work with children to remind them that you do want their eyes to be on you. I am convinced that children are much more apt to listen well to us if they are watching as well as listening.

I knew Birger twenty years ago. He is out of college now, and recently tracked me down and wrote to me. After all these years, I still remember his sentence. One message, then, is that I find myself totally blown away by writing which is startlingly true. But another message is this. As teachers, save the writing you love. Be collectors. Twenty years from now, you'll still be using the bits and pieces that you've stored away.

Notice my language in the bold writing. "Ask children to share . . . and to help each other if they haven't yet "had a chance to do it." The language we use conveys so many of our assumptions about literacy and learning and children. I do want children to know that I regard it as a privilege to "muck about in sentences," as Annie Dillard puts it.

Ask children to read a particular section of their writing in a "symphony" fashion. In this case, ask them to choose sections where they've captured a feeling in words.

After a few minutes, I organized a symphony. When I gestured to one writer, then another and another, each writer read aloud a section of his or her text in which the writer had tried to capture a feeling. This was what Ali read: *[Fig. IX-6]*

> I climbed into my father's bed, and leaned over to his ear so that he would hear me. "When will you be better?" I asked. No reply. This was the same answer I had gotten for two weeks. I felt awkward, even more than how I feel in a room full of people I don't know. But I was with one of the people I know best. I stared at my father. He tilted his head towards me, his face pale, his eyes telling me "soon." "Soon" wasn't good enough.

"Writers, when you write about feelings, remember that sometimes, there is no one word that can capture the particular way that loneliness or hunger or nostalgia feels when you are the one wearing that feeling."

Of course there are lots of published texts that I could have referenced in this Share, but the one that comes most to my mind is the chapter Jacqueline Woods wrote titled "Alone." The advantage of this chapter is that children will have been studying it already in this unit.

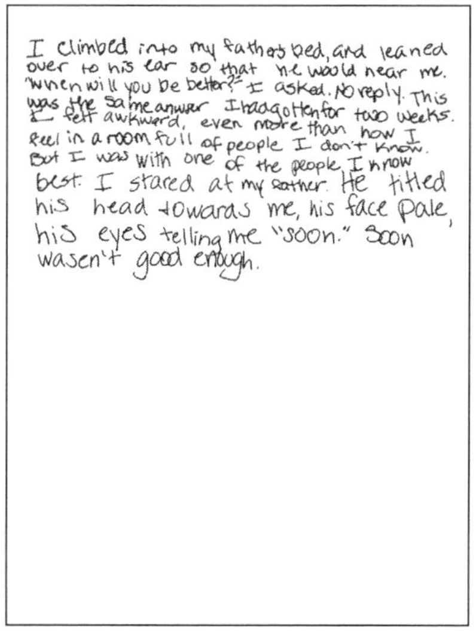
I climbed into my fathers bed, and leaned over to his ear so that he would near me. "When will you be better?" I asked. No reply. This was the same answer I had gotten for two weeks. I felt awkward, even more than how I feel in a room full of people I don't know. But I was with one of the people I know best. I stared at my father. He titled his head towards me, his face pale, his eyes telling me "soon." Soon wasen't good enough.

Fig. IX-6 Ali uses many words and sentences, too, in order to capture her precise feeling.

HOMEWORK ***Unpacking Tiny Moments*** Life whizzes along so quickly that each moment often blurs into the next. At the end of the day we might recognize that something big has happened to us, and that perhaps we're different in some way, but it's sometimes hard to unearth the particulars inside of each moment. The writer Natalie Goldberg says, "Writers live twice. They go about their lives, as fast as anyone . . . . But there's another part of them that they train towards. The part that lives everything a second time." That's what we do as writers. We train ourselves to slow down the crucial moments in our lives. We can do this by imagining an itsy-bitsy dot of time as an inner-journey—something that changed us in some way. Listen to Gary Soto's beautiful description of his inner journey, bike riding down the street and around the bend. ("The Bike," *A Summer Life*)

> My first bike got me nowhere, though the shadow I cast as I pedaled raced along my side. The leaves of the bird-filled trees stirred in a warm breeze and scuttled out of the way . . . . Going down the block was one thing, but taking the first curve, out of sight of Mom and the

house was another. I was scared of riding on Sarah Street. Mom said hungry dogs lived on that street and red anger lived in their eyes. Their throats were hard with extra bones from biting kids on bikes, she said.

But I took the corner anyway . . . . After a few circle eights I returned to our street. There ain't no dogs, I told myself.

We stand back from an event, remember, and ask ourselves: How did this moment change me? How am I different because of it? And then we write, slowing down time and showing how change occurred inside of us in this tiny bit of time.

Today, would you find a place in a book where the writer takes a single moment of time and slows it down, stretching that moment out. See if you can find an excerpt from literature in which one action—packing up a suitcase, feeding the dog, entering the front foyer of a house, approaching and entering a friend's home—is told as a sequence of small actions and of feelings.

Then write about an action in your life in this same way; take any tiny bit of your life tonight, and stretch it out, showing the internal journey that accompanies the external one. If it works to do so, take a part of your memoir and write it like this.

TAILORING YOUR TEACHING

If your students seem to need further support understanding external and internal timelines . . . you might show them more examples. You might show them how the same event has the potential to affect people differently and therefore will create different internal stories. As we experience an event, the details we choose to include—what we're thinking, how we're acting, what we're saying, what we're noticing—will be different. These details are what will make our writing personal and give us our own point of view.

So, for example, a first-year teacher could tell the story of a fire drill to show that she worries about her students misbehaving. A child could tell the same story in a way that shows he's relieved to get out of math class (and the discovery that he hadn't done his homework). Another child could tell the fire drill story from her perspective of having once been trapped in a fire. Each story reveals not only the events, but also one person's response to those events.

Students could fill in the rest of the chart with their partners, seeing how the external story might be the same for each, but that the internal story reveals the narrator specifically. Children would then need to go back to their own writing and add in internal stories that reveal themselves in all their specificity.

Event	Response to the Event
The fire alarm rang.	**Teacher:** (Face got hot anticipating the embarrassment) I felt sick. I hope my class behaves. **Student 1:** Yippee, saved by the bell. **Student 2:** Paralyzed by fear.
We filed out of the classroom and down the stairs.	**Teacher:** Calling out: Get over to the side. **Student 1:** Looked at his watch. Math will be over by the time we get up stairs. **Student 2:** Feet moved quickly. Head down. Focused.
The side doors were locked.	**Teacher:** Looking at other classes. Looking at mine. Are they acting the same? **Student 1:** Another delay. Another deep sigh of relief. **Student 2:** Grabbed the holy medal in his pocket. Closed his eyes. Prayed.
We waited while the principal opened the door.	
We stood on the sidewalk until it was safe to go back inside.	

ASSESSMENT

Although for a few days the minilessons will focus on helping children write and rewrite the narrative sections of their memoir well, you will meanwhile want to keep an eye on your children's larger plans for their drafts. As children work with either the narrative or the expository components of their drafts, their plans for their memoir will evolve and change. For example, if a child ends up telling a story that is very challenging for the child to write—and if that story seems to be central to what the child wants to say—you may decide to help this child realize that the one story could in fact become the memoir. This is what happened with Tyler, who initially intended to collect a sequence of small moments pertaining to his grandmother, but, in the end, decided to tell only the single story of his grandmother riding the roller coaster. On the other hand, if a child writes the expository section of a text with special power, you may decide to show the child how he or she could take what initially was meant to be one section of a text and then let that become the entire text.

For example, Max initially intended to follow this plan for his memoir:

Non-Narrative

I use my imagination a lot unintentionally

It makes me have more fun using my imagination

Using my imagination takes me to new ideas and new actions/things

Small Moment:

Beginning: I look at tree and see Alex, Em

Next: I start to climb the tree imagining I'm a monkey

After: run inside and come out with book

Idea: I will be a lookout in the tree while reading/My imaginatioin brought me something new

Non-Narrative Thinking:

I think my imagination gives me newer and better ideas

Max's next self-assignment said: "Write, using form."

This is what he wrote: [Fig. IX-7]

I realize I used to use my imagination a lot, unintentionally. It always made everything more fun. In a new way, it took me to new thoughts even actions.

I glance up at the tree. I felt almost unworthy to her big, poofy crown of leaves. Alex and Emi push their feet onto her limpy arms, and pull themselves up to her thicker shoulders. I start to climb after them. I am a lot faster though because I turned into a monkey. I bruised my knee when I got the idea . . .

Hoping the grass would catch my fall, I flew off the tree onto the patch of dandelions. I glided into the side door not long before I came out again, holding it. I felt the dull sides as I walked back. It held the most pictures of the books I saw in my bedroom, which was good considering I was only six.

I felt the tough bark in my hands as I looked down at the two eight year olds who had already started their homework. I am a pirate lookout . . .

Max, however, decided that the expository section of his draft lacked life, and so he returned to "Eleven," studying what Cisneros had done in this section of her text, and compiling a list of attributes. His list went like this: [Fig. IX-8]

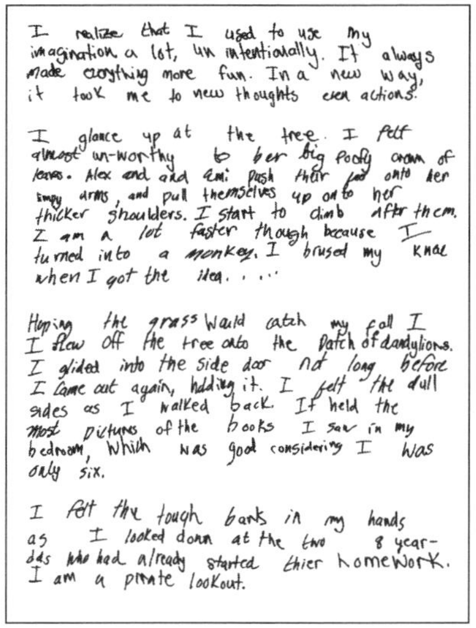

Fig. IX-7 Max's plan for his memoir

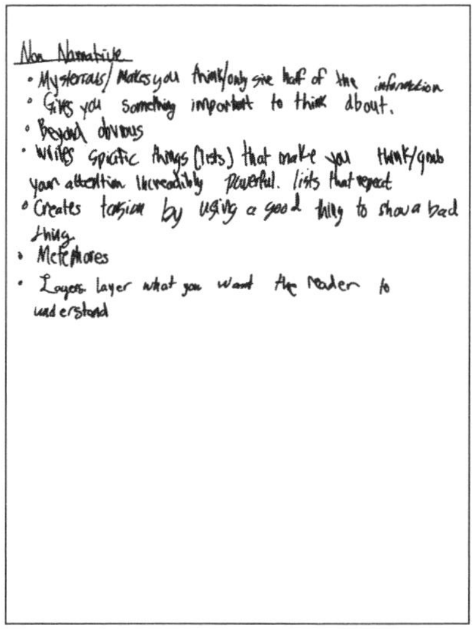

Fig. IX-8 Max's plan page 2

Non-Narrative

Mysterious/makes you think/only gives half of the information

Gives you something important to think about

Beyond Obvious

Writes specific things (lists) that make you think/grab your attention. Incredibly powerful. Lists that repeat.

Creates tension by using a good thing to show a bad thing

Metaphors

Layers. Layer what you want the reader to understand

Max's next self-assignment was this: "Choose a part of 'Eleven' and try to write like it. One NN [non-narrative] paragraph with lists etc. Write about missing ch [childhood] and m.t. [my tree]."

This is what he wrote: *[Fig. IX-9]*

> What construction workers and handymen and gardeners don't have a single clue about is this: When you build a clubhouse or a swing set in some kid's backyard, or when you plant a big, branch-filled, perfect-for-climbing magnolia tree in some kid's front yard, they are gonna love it. And what makes those guys sooo ignorant is you can't bust it down! Even if that kid does not live there anymore!
>
> I think about how much I miss them. Well, my tree is still there even if I'm not. And hey! I have something a construction worker or any of those guys can't bust down, something you can't tear up in photos. Something you can't stain with grape juice and never wear again.
>
> I've got memories!!

> You can't take away my memories. Not in a million years. And when I am old and gray and can't remember my last name, I will still have these memories.
>
> Wanna know why? Because it is sort of like when you are blind. You can hear and feel better than when you could see.
>
> Since I don't have my clubhouse or my tree, I can't make new memories with them. And they aren't there to see, hear, feel, etc. but they are still there in my heart and soul, and memories!

Once Max finished this quick-write, he reread it and knew that it was more powerful than the narrative he'd been toiling over for so long—the one retelling his tree-climbing book-reading effort. And so he did something that many writers find hard to do. He let go of a draft he'd worked on for a long while, and began instead to see this new entry as the foundation for his memoir. As Don Murray writes,

"The writer must be open to these changes, for writing is a continual process of discovery. He is doing something, building something, creating something, and it will change under his hands. This is part of the terror and the excitement of writing." (*A Writer Teaches Writing*)

Fig. IX-9 Max's self assignment

IN THIS SESSION, YOU WILL TEACH CHILDREN THAT WRITERS CAN REVEAL CHARACTERS (OURSELVES) NOT ONLY BY BRINGING FORTH INTERNAL THOUGHTS, BUT ALSO BY SPOTLIGHTING SIGNIFICANT DETAILS.

GETTING READY

- Example of writing that includes details that are distracting rather than emblematic (or use Diana's)
- Example of writing that includes emblematic details (or use Miles')
- See CD-ROM for resources

CHOOSING EMBLEMATIC DETAILS

If you think of the people you love, and allow yourself to just sit for a moment, holding the image of those people in your mind, you will probably find yourself savoring particular details. I find myself tenderly taken by Evan's teenage spread in our bathroom. His tidy line of cologne, hair spray, zit medicine, and mouthwash says so much to me about the drama of being sixteen years old. When I think of my son, details such as these act like Aladdin's magic lamp; I hold one of these details in my mind, and lo and behold, the detail conjures up the person, as real as life. Tiny details make our writing intimate.

Of course, to be truly powerful, the details need act as Aladdin's lamp not only for the writer, who knows the people, the places, represented in the details. Those details also must have magical conjuring power for readers.

In this session, then, you will help writers realize that every detail counts. In previous sessions, you have emphasized that a memoir always reveals a person, the author, and you will have helped children think about ways in which they can develop their internal story line so as to convey a journey of thought and emotion. In this session, you will remind children that writers bring ourselves to the page not only when we write our thoughts and feelings—"I remembered . . . " and "I worried . . . "—but also when we select details that reveal who we are and what the world in which we live is like for us.

You will teach students that writers do not include a detail—say, the color of their kitchen counter—simply because the detail happens to be true. The details that find a way into a brief memoir must be those that are emblematic. We, as writers, choose which details to include and which to exclude by thinking, "How does this detail help create a portrait of me and of my life?"

MINILESSON

Choosing Emblematic Details

CONNECTION

Celebrate the way in which children have created a progression of feelings across the narrative sections of their memoir.

"Writers, you've worked really hard to be sure that when you work on the narrative sections of your memoir, you write not only the *external* but also the *internal* story line. And many of you, like Tyler and Eloise Greenfield, think about how your internal story line will evolve across your story. Adam, I know, is rethinking whether he wants the whole entire scene with his brother packing up for college to just have one feeling—sadness—or whether he might go through a progression of feelings as the events unfold . . . even if that progression is just sad, sadder, then saddest of all . . . This is smart work."

"Today I want to talk with you about the way you describe the events in your memoir because, as I think you realize, every single part of your memoir reveals who you are."

Tell about a writer who included details simply because they were true, explaining that writers learn to choose details with care, selecting ones which are emblematic.

"I spoke with one writer recently, Diana, who'd written, 'I walked up to my brown front door, and went in. I left my bookbag by the door and walked through the kitchen.'"

"So I said, 'Diana, why did you decide to say that you walked to your *brown* front door?'"

"Diana looked at me like I was nuts. 'Because it is brown,' she answered, exasperated by my question. I could tell from her voice that she wanted to add, 'Duh . . . .'"

"But," I persisted. "I totally understand, Diana, that your front door *is* brown. But I still need to ask, 'Why did you put that in your memoir?'"

"I'm telling you this story about Diana because writers don't add details into our drafts simply because they are true. It is no doubt *true* that Diana's door is brown. And that it includes a doorknob. And hinges. And maybe there is a slot for the mail. Maybe there's a plant on the doorstep. Lots of details will be true details . . . but writers don't include details just because they are true. We include them because they are important to a text. And in a memoir, usually this means the details say something about the kind of person we are, the kind of life we lead."

COACHING

Whenever possible, I like to make a list of writers that includes a published author and a child or two. I'm hoping this feels like a compliment to kids!

This point harkens back to our Raising the Quality of Narrative Writing *unit of study, when I reminded children that the details they should include in a narrative are those that are true to that moment in time, from the narrator's vantage point. A child who is running across the lawn and into the front door of her house is not apt to make a mental note that the front door is brown, unless it was painted that day. This detail, therefore, is jarring in the mental movie a writer hopes to create for the reader. Although I could make this point, in this minilesson, I am highlighting a different aspect of it.*

Notice that I make my point with specifics. Qualities of good writing and of good teaching are similar!

Name your teaching point. In this case, teach children that every detail a writer adds into a short text is chosen because it furthers the writer's message.

"Today I want to teach you that as you work to reveal yourself through your memoir, you need to remember that you can show yourself not only by bringing out your internal thoughts, but also by spotlighting details that reveal whatever it is you want to say about yourself."

TEACHING

Tell children that you have realized that the details that are shown in televised mysteries always end up being significant to the solution. Similarly, details included in a memoir always need be revealing, emblematic ones which convey bigger meanings.

"In my family, we watch that television show, *Monk*. At the start of this mystery show, some extraneous detail always happens—a cat runs across the living room, a neighbor makes a cake and brings it by—and I have learned (finally) that those details are never included in the story by accident. They always turn out to be part of the solution to the mystery! That's how mysteries go . . . and frankly, that's how well-written texts go."

Share ways in which the writer you described earlier could have rewritten her writing so as to include revealing details.

"When Diana and I thought some more about the sentence she'd written—'I walked up to my brown front door, and went in the house'—we realized that if she *did* want to write about walking up to her house and going into it, she could have done so in ways that revealed what her family is like, what her life is like. She realized, for example, that she could have said, 'I walked up to the front door, past the discarded bikes and hula hoops, left over from our last day of summer, our last day of play.' Or she could have said, 'I raced off the bus and started to tear across the lawn towards the house. Then I glanced up and saw a figure behind the living room curtain. "Is Dad home?" I thought, moving quickly from the carefully manicured lawn onto the cement path.' That is, she could have chosen details that create a portrait of her family."

ACTIVE ENGAGEMENT

Share an example of a writer who used detail to paint a family or a life. Ask children to point to (and to talk with partners about) places in the text where the author used emblematic details.

"My son Miles recently wrote a memoir about visiting his grandparents—my parents—at my childhood home. I've made copies for you. I'm going to read an early section of Miles' memoir aloud. Would you follow along, and as you do, notice and mark places where Miles reveals something about the sort of person he is, and the sort of family he

As much as possible I show children that elements of writing are all around them—even on television! If children understand that stories are crafted similarly—be they picture books, television mysteries, Harry Potter books, or memoir—they'll have a better time grasping how to master the craft of any kind of writing.

Notice that in this teaching component, I am not demonstrating how a writer might go about doing the work, instead I am simply showing children the difference between problematic and good writing. You may decide your children need you to share specific strategies for accomplishing the goal you detail here. That is, you may decide that you need to demonstrate how Diana can go about producing the more effective version.

There is no question in my mind but that the examples I've provided are beyond the reach of most elementary school children. I'm hoping, however, to give children a felt sense for writing with effective details. You may notice that the details are generally longer than a word or a phrase. I think children at first believe they can add details by inserting a word here or there in a draft, as in Diana's inclusion of the color "brown." Actually, effective details often require a paragraph, not a word! You may also notice that the details in Diana's improved draft are woven into the sentence that also contains action. Sometimes children divide their writing into parts. One sentence tells one thing the character did. A separate section tells where or how the character did something. I recommend interweaving the two, and make sure my examples do that.

belongs to? Then you'll have a chance to talk with your partner about craft moves that Miles made which you could also make in your own writing." I began to read: *[Fig. X-1]*

A Family Portrait

As we approached my grandparents' sprawling farmhouse last Christmas, my brother and I went silent. In single file, suitcase in hand, we marched down the ramshackle brick path. The storm door slammed shut as we entered the mud room, then trooped up the short flight of stairs, past the boxes of apples, home-laid eggs, the dog food, and into the kitchen. Catalogs were strewn across the tables, Christmas cards dangled from the walls. Dogs lay curled under tables and chairs, and cousins of all shapes and sizes— thirty-four in all—perched on every surface. In the corner, Virginia's parrot squawked, "Hello Charlie, Hello Charlie" as he swung chaotically in his cage.

Virginia, the matriarch of the family, furtively scanned the room. In a conspiring tone, she asked, "Did you hear what happened . . . "

Pausing at this point, I said, "Would you turn and point out to your partner particular places where Miles used details which revealed something about him or his family?" Children talked in partnerships.

I know you will probably not want to share my son's writing with your children. You'll choose other texts that work within your lessons. But I do want you to see that I bring all the things that I love into my teaching, and I hope you feel invited to do the same. At the very end of my friend Georgia Heard's book, Awakening the Heart, *she cites Michael Fox, who once wrote, "The Celtic people insisted that only the poets could be teachers. Why? I think it is because knowledge that is not passed through the heart is dangerous." I don't think that either Georgia or Michael Fox meant that literally we all need to be poets in order to be great teachers, but I do think it is true that we need to weave love and intensity into our teaching, and one of the best ways I know to do this is to bring my sons and my parents and my husband and my friends and yes, even my favorite television shows into my teaching. Do the same!*

A FAMILY PORTRAIT
By Miles

As we approached my grandparent's sprawling farmhouse, my brother and I went silent. In single file, suitcase in hand, we marched down the ramshackle brick path. The storm door slammed shut as we entered the mud room, and then trooped up the short flight of stairs, past the boxes of apples, home-laid eggs, the dog food, and into the kitchen. Catalogs were strewn across the tables, Christmas cards dangled from the walls, dogs lay curled under the tables and chairs, and cousins of all shapes and sizes— thirty four in all—perched on every surface. In the corner, Virginia's parrot squawked "Hello Charlie, Hello Charlie" as he swung chaotically in his cage.

Virginia furtively scanned the room. In a conspiring tone, she asked, "Did you hear what happened to Bobbie?"

We had all heard the news. Nevertheless, the room grew silent.

"He wrote a lousy essay and got wait-listed at Harvard."

We shook our heads in collective pity. No one spoke. It was as if church bells had rung and the clan was grieving. Bradley had blown it.

It wasn't long before we gathered in the living room. A large fire roared in the fieldstone fireplace. The Christmas tree leaned precariously from its corner; only a book, wedged under its L.L.Bean stand, kept the tree from toppling. I found a place on the floor and leaned against the hard edge of the fireplace. Knee socks, masquerading as Christmas stockings, dangled over my head. Talk filled the room as the aunts and uncles, cousins and dogs each found a patch of floor…

Fig. X-1 One page of Miles' memoir containing emblematic details

Ask children to imagine that they were writing a narrative about entering their home, and ask them to tell this narrative to each other, weaving in revealing details.

Rather than eliciting from children a list of what they'd noticed, I decided to challenge them to follow Miles' model. "Right now, would you think about your own home, your own entrance way. Remember the first things you see and do when you arrive home? And would partner 2 turn and tell partner 1 the story of a time when you arrived home and walked into your place. Use details not because they are true, but because they will reveal whatever it is you want to show about yourself, your family, your home."

Link
Remind writers of options they have for proceeding. They may need to reflect on what their memoir aims to show. They may decide to rewrite their draft so as to include more revealing details. They may tuck today's pointers into the recesses of their mind to call upon later, during revision.

"Writers, can I stop you? Mystery writers include details that will later turn out to help solve the case . . . and memoirists include details that help to make the text we write into a statement about ourselves."

"You can decide what the implications of this minilesson are for you. Some of you may decide that you need to think a bit more about how your text is a window onto yourself. You may need to pause and write an entry or have a conference in which you think, 'What is it I want to show about myself?' and 'What do I want my reader to know about me and my family?' Others of you may have begun a draft and may decide that before you get any farther, you want to rewrite the start of your text so that you are more careful to choose details that reveal yourselves. Others of you will keep this advice in mind as you write, or when you get ready to rewrite. Before you head off to work, will you talk for a moment with your partner about how you will use the advice from today's minilesson? Then when you feel clear about what you are going to do, you can get yourself started."

"But today, I want to remind you that as you write and revise, you need to remember that it's not just the internal thinking that reveals you. *Every detail* in your memoir reveals you . . . creates you . . . on the page. Writers know this and therefore we choose our details carefully, thinking, 'What does this detail show about the kind of person I am, the kind of life I live?'"

One of the significant things to notice about Miles' description of the family manse is that even though the paragraph is part of a story, not part of an essay, Miles is still advancing one idea and providing supportive details. I doubt if he thought of that as he wrote it—I suspect, instead, that he made a movie in his mind and replayed that movie, selecting the particularly apt images. Still, every detail Miles selects adds to a single impression of ramshackle chaos! I hope the impression brims with life, too, because after all this is my son's impression of the scene when my family convenes and I'm partial to it!

You'll notice, of course, that these minilessons brim with personal details of the show I watch, of my son's description of our family home. When Mary teaches, she relies on the details from her life, and when you learn from these minilessons, you will of course alter them so they reflect your own life, and your children's writing, too.

By comparing memoirists with mystery writers, I'm hoping children will put on imaginary detective hats and delve into the details of themselves and their lives.

As you know by now, I often give children a number of choices so they can select the plan of action that will be most useful to them in their own writing process. I believe this allows children to step up to the role of job captain, thinking meaningfully about what precise step will best help their writing.

WRITING AND CONFERRING

Managing Conferring

You will probably find that your conferring is inefficient in this unit, but incredibly important. Conferences in this unit are often saturated with the poignancy and intimacy that can come when children's subjects are so very important to them, when children's work is especially self-propelled, and when we have such a wonderful shared history to draw upon.

My suggestion is to try to give yourself extra time for these conferences. Can you sneak some moments before school, after school, or during lunch for conferences? Are you game for having children e-mail their writing to you so you can write back to them? It won't be long now before you no longer have these kids under your wing, so these opportunities to confer are precious.

If you can't give yourself extra time to confer, you may want to give your children extra writing partners. Above all, encourage children to truly confer with each other. Help them to reflect on what you do in your conferences and to work in similar ways with each other. By this time in the year, children can ask each other, "What are you working on as a writer?" and "Can you show me where you have done that?" They can ask each other, "What are you planning to do next?" "How will you go about doing that?" "Is there anything else you are thinking of doing with the piece?" and "What help are you needing?" Those questions can launch wonderful exchanges between children.

I also encourage you to invite parents or community members into your classroom to join you in conferring. Just be sure that you take some time to teach people what you know about conferring. If you don't have time to teach conferring, then ask visitors to function as readers for children, letting children know what they felt as they read the child's piece. It is valuable for a child to simply hear a reader's chronicle of what she thought, felt, experienced, wondered as the person read the text.

MID-WORKSHOP TEACHING POINT *Inventing Details* "Writers, can I stop you? I wanted to talk with you a little about something that Justin just said to me. As many of you know, Justin is writing a story about a time in second grade when he froze with fright when he was asked to read aloud in front of the class. He said to me, 'Lucy, I'm stuck. I want to write with details but I don't have a good memory.' Then he added, 'I can remember how I felt, which is embarrassed, but I can't remember what book I was reading or what Mrs. Buckley said or hardly any details!'"

"I wanted to thank Justin for asking that question because it is a question that I'm sure you are asking. What I want to tell you is this, Justin. (The rest of you should listen, too.) What you do is this: you make up the details. The secret is that you invent the details which reveal the truth of your life."

"When Miles continued his essay about that Christmas morning at my family's house, he described the family going into the living room to gather for a Bible

continued on next page

Meanwhile, you will probably not talk with, confer with, every child as much as you'd like. If you find that you aren't able to have a prolonged, deep conference with a child, you can still assign yourself the job of reading even just a bit of the child's work so that you can talk back to what the child has done. If you have no time to confer, you can still catch a moment to say to the child, "Last night, I told my husband about the way you described those knee socks, masquerading as Christmas stockings! What a telling detail. You have a real knack for telling the truth." Consider, for a moment, times when your principal has passed you in the hallway, or spoken to you on the run in the staff room, saying even just the tiniest compliment. Those comments may be said in passing, but for those of us who are teaching our hearts out day after day, wondering if anyone at all notices or cares about what we are doing, even just a sentence said in passing can make an enormous difference. So remember that with power comes responsibility. Isn't that the lesson of *The Little Prince*?

---

continued from previous page

reading. He said that he sat underneath knee socks, masquerading as Christmas stockings, near the Christmas tree, propped up with a book. I am sure that when Miles went to write about that particular Christmas Eve, he did not recall whether or not he sat near the fireplace, under the Christmas stockings, and I'm sure he isn't certain whether on that particular Christmas Eve, people had in fact hung knee socks rather than the more traditional Christmas stockings. Miles supplied those details from all the Christmases he has ever spent with my family, and he selected the details which captured what he wanted to show about my family."

"So Justin you can make yourself stand in front of the classroom to read aloud or you can sit yourself on a rocking chair. You can decide what book—and what page of the book—you will read. The details may not be true with a small *t*, but they will be True with a capital *T*."

SHARE

Unpacking Tiny Events

Celebrate that children are writing with an awareness that events always have both an external and an internal timeline.

"Writers, I am totally blown away by the way in which you are writing with details and the way in which you are writing about the external and the internal journey-through-time in your memoir. What I saw a few of you doing today that I want to remember to do in my own writing is this. You are describing the tiniest actions with an awareness that any one of these tiny, tiny actions can involve a whole sequence of events and responses to those events."

Teach children that even an event as tiny as a single hug can be stretched out so that it contains a sequence of external events, and a journey of changing feelings.

"I learned this especially from Adam who has been writing about saying goodbye to his brother during those last moments before Jon heads off to college. Adam wrote first about the major events. He wrote that they packed the car, they hugged, Jon got in the car and drove away. But then Adam realized that he could take any one of those actions and write about the steps involved in it."

"He's been working on writing a whole mini-story about one hug. You need to remember that Adam's brother has not really yet left for college at all, and that Adam is writing about how he imagines the goodbye will go. So now, as Adam works to write the story of this one hug, he has been creating that hug in his mind. He's been asking himself, 'Knowing Jon, how will the hug probably start? Then what will happen? Then what?' And of course, he is writing the external story and the internal story. Adam, will you read your latest draft?"

Adam read this: *[Fig. X-2]*

> Our eyes met when he turned around. Sadness seemed to flow straight into me just like the mournful sound of Jon's bassoon when he practices. I ran to my brother, he embraced me in his tight hug. I pulled him closer.
>
> It was already happening, my eyes stung. I tried to blink back the tears, but they were inevitable. Tears started

By telling children I want to try what they have done in their writing in my own writing, I am telling them that they are not just absorbing my lessons, they are also creating their own. I hope to help children feel ownership of their writing decisions.

Remember—Adam is is writing about saying goodbye to Jon . . . but none of this has happened yet!

Adam has done two remarkable things; he's written especially small about a large topic, and he's written about something close to his heart that hasn't yet happened . . . as if it has! I hope that all children will challenge themselves to do equally difficult work. This sort of writing involves knowing your subject so well—and caring about it so deeply—that it rings true even when still only imagined.

pouring out of my eyes. I remembered when I was taken by the ambulance corps and Jon being there to help. I remember how I was with him there. Much safer, much calmer and much less scared. It reminded me of the letter I got from him when I was in camp, the laughs I got from it and the warmth of him being my older brother and the one who can kid around but also has a duty to set a good example. I looked up and saw tears in my brother's eyes. All those feelings came together.

I was surprised.

Ask children to share with their partners places in their own writing where they could learn from the example you just spotlighted.

"I know many of you have already been doing this work, and some of you were just about to do it. Would you share places in your draft where you've done something close to this, or talk with each other about how you could learn from Adam's work?"

The children talked in partners. After a bit I said, "So remember, as a writer you can always take a tiny action (and it can be an action you recall happening or one that could have happened). And you can write the whole tiny timeline of that action."

HOMEWORK *Using Details to Reflect Point of View* Writers, early this year you learned that details are important to writing, and today you learned a lot more about how writers go about writing details that will be powerful ones. Tonight, take a moment and write what it is you are trying to show about yourself and the way you see the world. Of course, as we're learning, you probably want to show that you are feeling and thinking one thing early in the piece and something else at another time. Record in the margins what it is you want to show about your point of view on the world at each point in your story. Then go through your draft and find some places where you could write with more precise details. As you do this, remember that the details you notice will say as much about you as they say about the world before your eyes. If I am feeling generous, I might describe the antics at my bird feeder this way:

① Action for Jon exp.

Our eyes met. when he turned around Sadness seemed to flow straight into me just like the sorrowful sound of Jon's bassoon when he practices. I ran to my brother, he embraced me in his tight hug. I pulled him closer.

It was already happening, my eyes stung, I tried to blink back the tears, but they were inevitable. Tears started pouring out of my eyes. I remembered when I was taken by the ambulance corps and Jon being there to help. I remember how I was with him there. Much safer, much calmer and much less scared. It reminded me of the letter I got from him when I was in camp, the laughs I got from it and the warmth of him being my older brother and the one who can kid around but also has a duty to set a good example. I looked up and saw tears in my brother's eyes. All those feelings came together.

I was surprised.

Fig. X-2 Adam's draft

I watched as two sparrows landed on the birdfeeder, and immediately began pecking at the seed. "Poor birds, they look hungry," I thought, and reminded myself to buy more birdseed at the grocery store. Then a large black crow settled beside the two smaller birds and they spun away. "I should hang up another feeder so there is space for everyone," I thought.

If I am feeling cranky, I could see the same antics through very different eyes:

Two sparrows landed on the birdfeeder and immediately began pecking at the seed. "Golly these guys are so dependent on my hand-outs," I thought. "Can't they get any food for themselves at all?" Then a black crow approached and they spun away. "Scardey cats," I thought. "What's their problem?" All afternoon I continued to watch the neurotic social life that took place outside my window.

So tonight, make sure the details reveal whatever it is about yourself that you want to reveal. Notice that I didn't add details by inserting a word or two into my draft. You'll find that in a similar way, writing with details usually requires that we write with paragraphs.

TAILORING YOUR TEACHING

If your children have regarded this unit as a time to write life stories rather than as a time to grow ideas about their own lives . . . you may decide to teach a single minilesson or a sequence of minilessons in which you help writers write-to-learn in their writer's notebooks. As part of this, you could teach children that many writers believe that in order to write well, we need to write badly. Actually, it is probably more accurate to say that in order to write well, a writer needs to be willing to write badly. You may want to teach children a strategy that Peter Elbow made famous in his book, *Writing with Power*, in which he teaches children to free write. The goal of free writing is to keep writing, fast and strong, letting one thought lead to another without you worrying whether the writing is good or not good. Later, after generating reams of writing, a writer looks back to say, "Did anything I say seem especially important? Vital? True?" Then the writer can box that line, that image, and copy the boxed section to the top of a clean sheet of paper and again write fast and strong off of that bit of powerful writing.

There are other ways to teach children to write to learn. Certainly, you could help them understand that sometimes the goal is not good writing but instead good thinking, and that writers can take that word—thinking—and open it up. If Justin was to write about—think about—the time when he was younger and he became frozen with fright when he tried to read aloud in front of the class, he could say to himself, "What do good thinkers do?" and then do those things:

- He could ask questions.
- He could entertain those questions.
- He could connect this moment with another moment and write how they were similar and different.
- He could list other similar moments, and then write about how all of those moments connect to each other.
- He could try to see that one moment, long ago, in an opposite way, writing not only about his embarrassment but also about his pride.

If your children are thoroughly enjoying (or struggling with) writing with detail . . . you might want to teach them that writing with details begins with living with details. You may want to say to them, "Annie Lamott, author of *Bird by Bird*, gave me a minilesson last night. Has that ever happened to you? Sometimes I read books about writing and I say to myself, 'This, right here, is a minilesson. My own private minilesson.' Annie Lamott said this to me":

> I honestly think that to be a writer you have to learn to be reverent. If not, why are you writing? Why are you here? Let's think of reverence as awe, as presence in and openness to the world. The alternative is that we stultify, we shut down. Think of the times when you've read poetry or prose that is presented in such a way that it gives you a fleeting sense of being startled by beauty or insight, by a glimpse into someone's soul. All of a sudden, everything seems to fit together or at least for a moment to have meaning. This is our goal as writers, I think; to help others have this sense of—please forgive me—wonder, of seeing things anew, things that can catch us off guard, that break in on our small, bordered worlds. When this happens, everything feels more spacious. Try walking around with a child who's going, "Wow, wow! Look at that dirty dog! Look at that burned-down house! Look at that red sky!" And the child points and you look, and you see, and you start going, "Wow! Look at that scary dark looking cloud!" I think this is how we are supposed to be in the world—present and in awe.

"Talk with your partner about what this means to you!"

ASSESSMENT

Reading your children's writing requires a special kind of imagination. It will be as if you are reading through postcards from a journey. You'll see one entry or draft, written at one point along the writer's journey, and you will try to use that bit of writing to help you conjure up all that was in the writer's mind and the writer's environment at that time. What minilesson might you have given on the day the child wrote this text? Did you or someone else confer with the writer near to the time when she wrote the entry? You will read through the entry and try to extract from it some sense for what the writer was trying to do during this day's work. You can also speculate over the images of good writing that guided the child, and the sources for inspiration the child drew upon. As much as possible, it helps if you can create a rich, layered, accurate portrait of each child as a writer, and a sense for the journey that each child is taking. This, of course, is a tall order! We never have enough time. You will, therefore, need to decide how much of your time you are willing to invest into a close study of your children and their growth as writers.

What I can tell you is that, frankly, there is very little that you could do that could enrich your teaching more than closely studying your children and their journey as writers. When I was new to the teaching of writing, I spent two years sitting alongside four writers, studying and documenting their every move. When one of those four writers picked up his pen to delete a sentence, I was usually able to figure out what had prompted the child to make that cross out, and when the child replaced the one sentence with another, I could discern the probable sources of influence over that decision. Of course, since then I have never had the luxury of sitting alongside a tiny collection of writers and tracing their day-by-day evolution. But I do approach kids' work believing that if I study it closely, I can understand each child's evolution as a writer. I think this commitment to understanding and the trust that if I read closely and imaginatively enough, I can re-create the child's learning journey, has helped me immeasurably as a teacher of writing. I also think it is incredibly helpful to a child to know that we are taking lessons from her. Children become accustomed to articulating what they are doing and why they are doing it, and this makes them more metacognitive, more planful, and more strategic and purposeful as writers.

Just to give you a glimpse into one child's mind at work during the second half of this unit of study, let me share with you some of the planning boxes and reflections and goals one writer kept during the final two weeks of this study. Ali's work is within range of what many children can do if they've grown up in a school that values their writing development. *[Fig. X-3]*

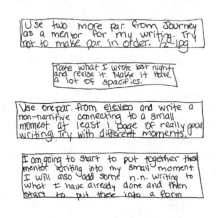

Fig. X-3 Ali's planning boxes

You may want to notice your own responses to Ali's work. Oftentimes, when confronted with examples of children whose work is especially strong, we try to distance ourselves from that work. "Oh, she's definitely gifted," we say to ourselves, and the message we convey to others, perhaps, and to ourselves is, "Don't blame me for the fact that my kids aren't doing work at this level!" I am sorry that in too many schools, assessment is equated with blame, and blame, like Dr. Seuss' red splotch in *The Cat Comes Back*, lurks, just waiting to be affixed to the next person. Wouldn't it be wonderful if we could all enjoy examples of good work without battling with feeling defensive?

When a young person wants to become an artist, the young person travels to museums and sits in front of a masterpiece, studying the technique and working to emulate it. The apprentice doesn't have the need to dismiss da Vinci, saying, "He's definitely gifted," as if that means no one has anything to learn from this master!

And the truth is that Ali is gifted. She has been gifted with a teacher, Kathy Doyle, who has given this child, and all the others in the classroom, the opportunity to learn and reach and grow and reflect in ways that are frankly dazzling. I never fail to gasp when I am in the presence of a truly great teacher. Part of what impresses me so much is the sheer quality of work that children do when they have the opportunity to live and learn in such a teacher's classroom. In our profession, there are teachers who have been working at their craft for decades, and are really good at it. Kathy is one such teacher, and there are thousands of others. We can look at their children's work with appreciation, and say to ourselves, "If I learn the art of teaching writing really, really well, my children will do likewise." So let's draw a chair alongside the masters.

WRITING ABOUT IDEAS

IN THIS SESSION, YOU WILL TEACH CHILDREN THAT WHEN WRITERS WRITE ABOUT IDEAS, JUST AS WHEN WE WRITE ABOUT EVENTS, IT IS IMPORTANT TO FIND OR CREATE A STRUCTURE THAT ALLOWS US TO SAY WHAT WE WANT TO SAY.

GETTING READY

- Example of writing that contains both exposition and narration (or Ali's writing)
- Example of writing that is organized in a boxes and bullets structure
- Example of writing that is organized by following a progression of thought
- See CD-ROM for resources

Education is a cyclical process. Children learn to do something in a fairly simple, concrete, rudimentary fashion, and then they cycle back and relearn to do it, this time learning more sophisticated ways of working. In this session, children revisit the topic of writing-about-ideas. Earlier, we told children that writers have premade templates into which we can pour our thoughts. Now we will tell children that writers think about what they want to say, and then step back to decide if there are parts to that message, or if there is a sequence to the message, imagining the shape it could take based on the shape it already has.

It is complex to teach children that when writing on a concrete topic—a tiger—it is important to sort information so that facts about the tiger's habitat go on one page, and facts about the tiger's enemies go on another page. In this session, you will teach children that even when our topic is less concrete, we still need to think about how to organize it. Even when our topic is writing our thoughts about one of our mini-stories, writers profit from looking over those thoughts, asking, "Can these be divided into a couple of groups?" Writers ask ourselves, "Are some of these thoughts about one thing? Are some about another thing?" Then writers decide where each category of thoughts might go, in the draft.

This session invites children to think about their thinking. It does so by telling a rather long story about one child—Ali—who wrote the story of visiting her invalid father in bed and feeling a chaos of conflicting feelings. As Ali writes this memoir, she sorts through her feelings and decides not only what she felt but also what she wants to bring forth in this memoir. Ali writes countless drafts, each offering a different interpretation of her bedside journey-of-feelings. The thinking and writing work she does is very sophisticated, and it will be too complex for some students. You'll obviously tell a story of a child's work which seems to you to be within the zone of proximal development for your writers, keeping in mind that it is okay for our teaching to give kids (and ourselves) horizons to reach for. The lyrics from South Pacific are wise: "If you don't have a dream, how are you going to have a dream come true?" This session can help you and some of your kids reach towards big dreams for the conceptual work they can do as they draft and revise the expository sections of their memoir.

MINILESSON

Writing About Ideas

CONNECTION

Celebrate the wonderful memories that fill the classroom, but remind children that the goal is not only to remember but also to think.

"Writers, our work in this unit has been saturated with memories. I think every one of us has found that as we write about something that happened once upon a time, long, long ago, we are flooded with lots of memories. These memories are precious because they remind you that now when you are nine or ten, you are also the you that was once six or seven. Just like we carry skills and strategies from earlier in the year with us as we grow older, we also carry the selves we used to be with us, the memories. I am still the earnest girl who grew up alongside a creek, fighting for a place to belong in a family of nine kids. And each of you is still the child you were, five years ago."

"And the good thing is that you have been writing not only to remember, but also to think. By writing, you have given yourselves the chance to think about your lives and about yourselves."

"And I think you've learned that in order to grow ideas through writing, writers say to ourselves, 'Right now, I am not writing for an audience. I am writing in my notebook and my goal is not good writing but good thinking.' Many of you have lots and lots of entries—some good, some less good—in which you explore the idea you want to convey in your draft."

Name the teaching point. In this case, tell children that in order to write reflective paragraphs, writers generate a lot of material and then reread it asking "What am I saying?" and "How will I structure this?"

"Today I want to teach you how writers go about crafting the sections of our writing which aren't stories. I have emphasized all year that writers show, not tell, but of course the truth is that writers show and tell. Today I want to help you think about how you go from a pile of rich, chaotic, idea-based writing to a draft."

"Specifically, what I want to teach you is that just like whole pieces of writing often have a structure—with narrative writing often organized chronologically by time, and essay-writing often organized into big ideas, then supportive details—so, too, a single paragraph or a single chunk of a text often will also have a structure. After writers generate what

COACHING

I might have used "Eleven" to demonstrate how we carry our earlier selves with us throughout life. When we teach children to write memoir, it is essential that we encourage them to put all of who they are, from birth to now, into their pieces. Memoir writing is about discovering and revealing something essential about oneself, and this sort of discovery happens not over a few weeks or years, but over a lifetime.

By this time in the year, children's understanding of the writing process will have changed dramatically. Whereas in September, revision meant deleting a dot from a timeline or extending one sentence of a draft into a paragraph, by now there will be no real separation between rehearsal, drafting, and revision. The entire process will feel like exploration.

amounts to a pile (you could say, a hodge-podge) of ideas, the writer rereads all of these and figures out how she will structure the chunk of text. And there are ways that texts often go that sometimes can help a writer structure her paragraph."

TEACHING
Use an example of one child's work in order to show the steps a writer can take in order to generate and shape expository sections of a text.

"Often during this part of my minilesson, I write in front of you or tell you about a famous writer and his or her work. Today I want to tell you about a writer who is famous in our community and that is Ali, and I want to tell you about the steps that Ali has gone through in order to write what she is calling a patch of expository writing (or a patch of thought) that will go before and after the narrative sections of her draft."

"As you recall, Ali's work on this memoir began with her writing a focused story about one day when she walked into the room where her father was lying in his hospital bed, and tried to tell him about her spelling test only to find him looking blankly back at her. Standing there, at her father's bedside, Ali felt a lot of different feelings as she struggled with the fact that because of his injury, her father wasn't there for her."

"Ali knew from the start that she is trying to write not just the story of one time, but to write a piece which conveys who she is as a person. Early on, after writing this narrative, she tried using the prompt, 'And the thought I have about this is . . .' to grow some ideas about this. She inserted thoughts she generated into her story: [Fig. XI-1]

1. The most important thing I learned was that silence is very powerful. Because silence can say a lot without saying anything.

2. Feeling a small braveness inside yourself is a very strong feeling. Because it makes you think.

3. Wait. That was my least favorite word. But I couldn't help myself. Hadn't I waited long enough?

"Then later, when Ali wanted to develop the thinking section of her writing, she took each of these and wrote longer about it. In the end, she combined the ideas about waiting and about silence, writing entries about them. And she wrote entries about how this incident related to bravery."

Part of our job in this unit is to reinforce for children that writing, like thinking, doesn't always go one way. It's essential that children understand that there are times when writers tell, and times when they show. Likewise, they must now learn how to combine what they know about narrative structure and essay structure to understand how to structure their ideas into powerful memoir.

Notice how I refer to Ali as a "famous writer." If you make celebrities out of the children in your class, they will begin to view themselves and each other as people with talent, with voice, and with words that matter.

Notice how again I bring in teaching from an earlier unit, highlighting how Ali has drawn on the prompts chart to grow ideas about her writing. It may not be exactly true that Ali did all of these things, but I am telling the story of her writing so as to set children up for the work that I believe will pay off for them to do in the future. So I take some license.

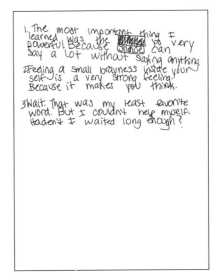

Fig. XI-1 Ali writes the thoughts she had during the event she retells.

As you chronicle what one child did in order to write the expository sections of her essay, pause to debrief, highlighting the points you want children to abstract from this example.

"I could show you all of those entries but there are dozens of them. And the first thing I want you to know is that, in the end, Ali didn't jam all the ideas she had about various subjects into one paragraph. Instead, she made a choice. She said to herself, "How could I categorize my thoughts?" and she decided she had two main topics—one about the agony of waiting for her father to get better, the other about bravery. And she decided that one of these ideas was going to be the framing idea for her essay, and the other would be just tucked into her story. She could have chosen either one of these as her framing idea, but she chose bravery. Later, when you read the story of her walking in and standing by her father's bedside, you will see that in three or four places, she has a whole tiny paragraph in which she tucks her thought-patches about waiting into the midst of her story."

Show that after the child generated some ideas off of her narrative writing, she took those ideas and expanded on them. Name the strategies the writer used, but be sure to emphasize that the writer generated lots of material, then selected from that excess.

"But let's look at what she did with bravery."

"She wrote a lot of stuff, writing freely, and much of this writing stood on the shoulders of Jacqueline Woodson and Sandra Cisneros' writing. You'll hear that Ali borrowed some of the song of 'Alone' and of 'Eleven' to get herself going, talking about bravery. Listen": *[Fig. XI-2]*

> I think my dad was being brave but in a very little way. He wasn't talking to me. I thought this was brave of him because it taught me to think for myself. I didn't realize he was being brave until now. Because all I thought was just (he was) in a lot of pain.

"Then there was this version": *[Fig. XI-3]*

> Some days I wake up to bravery like a chicken cawing at the sun, like slurping down fresh squeezed orange juice. Like that.
>
> Brave is how I go to sleep some days, listening to the crickets outside my window, hugging my bear real tight.

"And this version": *[Fig. XI-4]*

> When you're being brave really brave like Superman, you don't always know it. Not right that very second.

One of the things that you may notice is that the writing process that children have experienced—gathering entries, selecting a seed idea, developing that seed idea, and so forth—repeats itself in the microcosm of a writer's work on components of a text. For example, Ali has essentially experienced the entire writing process in order to write a bit of reflective writing at the start and finish of her memoir.

Throughout the year, I emphasize the importance of choice. I encourage children to push themselves to make wise choices about their writing, choices that get to the heart of what and how they want to write.

I think my dad was being brave but in a very little way. He wasent talking to me. I thought this was brave of him because it taught me to think for myself. I didn't realize he was being brave until now. Because all I thought was that he was just in a lot of pain.

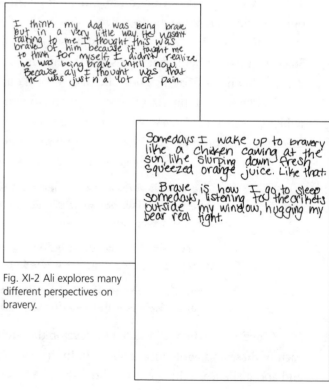

Fig. XI-2 Ali explores many different perspectives on bravery.

Somedays I wake up to bravery like a chiken cawing at the sun, like slurping down fresh squeezed orange juice. Like that.

Brave is how I go to sleep somedays, listening to the crikets outside my window, hugging my bear real tight.

Fig. XI-3 Borrowing from the syntax of "Alone" Ali continues to explore bravery.

Sometimes it takes a few minutes to realize, a few thoughts. A few gazes before you know, "hey, I was just being really brave by standing up to my fears." It could be that you won't know your braveness until the next time that you are the least bit brave. That is just the way the system of braveness works.

"So when Ali wanted to go from entries to a draft, and to write something about braveness, she needed to decide two main things: what did she want to say, and how would her writing be structured. To make this decision, she did what writers the world over do. She reread, thinking, 'What is the true idea I want to get across?' She looked to see how many different things she was already saying about bravery. This was smart—she knew it was not enough to say, 'I am writing on bravery.' She needed to think, 'What specific ideas am I claiming?'"

"And smarter yet, she realized that she had said a bunch of different things, and that she actually didn't agree with everything she said! She realized that when she wrote that her father was brave—that really was not the truth of how she felt. She felt angry at him. And Ali came to the gigantic realization that she was the one who had been brave. So now she had her idea, which was, 'Standing beside my father's bed, I was brave.'"

"Then Ali had almost a conversation with herself. She said, 'Of course, I wasn't brave in a Superman way . . . .' So pretty soon Ali had an even more specific idea she wanted to get across to her readers: 'When my father was an invalid for so long, I acted in brave ways. This wasn't a Superman-kind-of-bravery, and in fact I didn't even realize until recently that I was being brave!'"

Teach children that when writing about ideas, it helps to make a plan for how your writing will go. Expository writing is usually either organized by boxes and bullets or it is a journey-of-thought.

"Now I want to teach you one last thing, and it is really important. When you write about ideas, as when you write about events, it can help to plot out a plan for how your writing will go. And when writing about ideas, usually you organize your writing in one of two ways. Either the writing is organized by boxes and bullets—with a main idea, which is developed with details or with supporting ideas and then details. Or else the writing is a journey-of-thought. And if it is a journey-of-thought, you usually write about the first idea and then the next, related idea and then the next idea that builds on the first two . . . with your writing following a structure that is not chronological, but instead a logical progression of thought."

Fig. XI-4 Continuing to explore bravery, Ali writes ideas that she ends up holding onto.

It is not an accident that I highlight that Ali's decisions about structure and content were really decisions about the message she wanted to convey.

ACTIVE ENGAGEMENT

Set children up to examine one student's draft, looking for the structure in it.

"You already know how to write expository writing which is organized with a big idea, followed by supportive ideas and/or details. But let me show you how a writer can write in a sort of trail of thought. I'm going to pass out copies of Ali's latest drafts of her first and her final paragraphs (these will bookend her story). Would you and your partner read this, and imagine the trail of ideas that Ali might have laid out before she wrote each of these paragraphs": *[Figs. XI-5 and Fig. XI-6]*

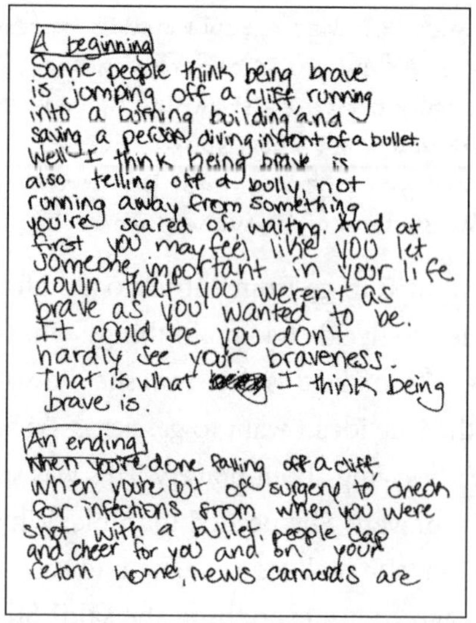

A beginning:

Some people think being brave is jumping off a cliff, running into a burning building and saving a person, diving in front of a bullet. Well, I think being brave is also telling off a bully, not running away from something you're scared of, waiting. And at first you may feel like you let someone important in your life down, that you weren't as brave as you wanted to be. It could be you don't hardly see your braveness. That is what I think being brave is.

An ending:

When you're done falling off a cliff, when you're out of surgery to check for infections from when you were shot with a bullet, people clap and cheer for you and on your return home, news cameras are waiting to interview you. Those people's signs of bravery are on the outside. But when you walk away from a bully that you left behind wide-eyed, or when you stand close to the thing you were once scared of, those peoples' signs of bravery is the feeling of proudness, the feeling of people clapping that is on the inside of you. My sign was little sparkled, like a fairy sparking her golden dust over me.

Review the steps this student took to structure her writing and timeline her thoughts, steps that you also hope other writers might take.

After children worked together for a bit, I intervened. "Writers, I hope you have learned a lot of things from what Ali did. Let's go back and talk about all you've figured out that she probably did":

"First, Ali wrote a story and knew she needed her writing to say something important about herself and her life so she reread her narrative, and used the thought prompt, 'This

Fig. XI-5 Drafts of Ali's openings and closings

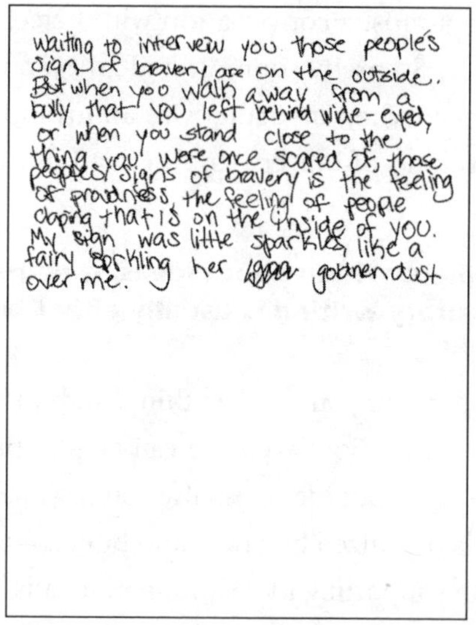

Fig. XI-6 Ali's drafts, page 2

makes me think . . . .' Or 'This makes me realize . . .' to write a few tiny bits of ideas, bits that could get inserted into the draft."

"Then Ali free wrote lots of entries about each of these ideas, using some mentor texts to prime her pump and help her write long and well."

"Then Ali reread these and realized that really, they could get sorted into two main topics: waiting and bravery. She decided that her thoughts on one of those topics could get inserted into key spots in her narrative. She could have decided to insert all her thinking into her narrative—I think Tyler and John and others of you will be doing that. But she decided she wanted to have an introductory and a closing bit of writing in which she wrote about her ideas, with the story inserted in the middle."

"Then Ali reread what she'd written about bravery and realized she didn't agree with all she said. She figured out one claim she wanted to make. Then she talked back to it, and figured out another idea or two."

"Then Ali thought of what she might say about bravery, thinking what she might say first (which would be something sort of obvious that everyone agreed with) and then what she wanted to say next (which would be building off that idea), and next. Then she wrote a paragraph in which she said one thing, then the next, then the next!"

"Of course, some of you will tuck everything that I taught you today into your tool kit to use later and for now continue doing other work. You are in charge of your writing, and I know that right now, some of you have other work that demands to be done. That's as it should be."

WRITING AND CONFERRING

Flaborating with Lists

William continued to write as I read the first paragraph of his memoir. He began with exposition, and I could see that he tried to make it organized and concise. His beginning went like this:

> Some people think that oldest children don't need attention. But I'm an oldest child, and I miss my mom's attention.

"Can I stop you, William?" He finished making a note on his draft, and looked up at me. "I was reading the beginning of your memoir, and I noticed that you've begun by setting it up with exposition. Tell me a bit about how you decided to begin this way."

William took a moment to reread his beginning and then said, "Well, this is my idea. It's what I'm trying to show about myself through my memoir. So I decided to say it at the very beginning."

"That makes a lot of sense, William. We've read lots of memoirs, and we've seen that many writers begin this way." I paused before making my next point. "I also can see that you tried to make it direct and to the point. That's important, because we don't want our ideas to get swamped by too many words."

"Yeah," William said, "I know that so I tried to make it short. It was much longer, but it was too confusing. I couldn't even understand what I was saying." We both laughed.

"That's so true, William. Longer writing does not always make better writing. But as I read your writing, while I applaud the revision work you've done here, I also wonder if what you've written is too brief. I think that there's a way to say more and still keep your idea focused. When writers say more, they are often able to make their ideas clearer and sometimes even a bit deeper. Are you game for some tips?"

William picked up his pencil ready to write. "Sure," he said.

"One way that writers say more about their ideas without losing their focus is by using a list of brief examples. This list helps the writer elaborate without losing focus. And, with each example, the idea can become clearer and deeper." William was listening and waiting for more. "Let's look at the first line of your exposition. 'Some people think that oldest children don't need attention.' I'm going to try to imagine a brief list that to elaborate on this idea." It was going to take me a moment to imagine how this might go. I didn't want to confuse William by creating a list that veered off in a direction other than the one he was taking, nor did I want to make the list redundant.

MID-WORKSHOP TEACHING POINT   *Studying Mentor Texts*   "Writers, can I have your eyes and your attention? If you are writing about your thinking and you feel like your writing is not as strong as you'd like it to be, remember that one thing writers do when we want to lift the level of our writing is this. We study what other writers have done. We think, 'What do I like that this writer has done?' and 'How could I use a similar technique in my writing?' We have lots of models that you can learn from in this class. You can learn from the lead and ending that Ali wrote which we studied earlier today. Or you can learn from the opening section of 'Eleven.'"

"Remember, one way to study a writer's craft is to reread the text, and to simply notice parts that make you go, 'Wow.' So, for example, I could reread the place

continued on next page

"I'm going to start by thinking about the idea and then make the list. So let's see," I referred to William's draft. "'Some people think that oldest children don't need attention.' Maybe my list goes like this":

> They think that being the oldest means that you want to be independent and mature. They think that being the oldest means that you want to shine all your attention on younger kids who might need more guidance.

"Did you see how I took your idea and used a very brief list to say a bit more about it? Saying just a couple of sentences more actually seems to make it more focused." I looked at William who was smiling and nodding his head. "Are you ready to try this with the second line of your exposition?"

"Okay," William said. He read the line out loud, "'But I'm an oldest child, and I miss my mom's attention.'" He thought for a couple of moments, rereading his idea out loud. Then he said, "Maybe it could go like this":

> I miss the way she used to run the bathtub for me and make sure the water was just right. I miss the way she used to sing to me until I fell asleep each night.

"Wow! Let's see what that sounds like all together." We laid out William's draft and together pieced the work we had done together, helping each other remember what had been said.

> Some people think that oldest children don't need attention. They think that being the oldest means that you want to be independent and mature. They think that being the oldest means that you want to shine all your attention on younger kids who might need more guidance. But I'm an oldest child, and I miss my mom's attention. I miss the way she used to run the bathtub for me and make sure the water was just right. I miss the way she used to sing to me until I fell asleep each night.

"That seems to really work, William. You've said more without swamping your idea, and those extra thoughts elaborate on your idea in a way that feels clearer and deeper, don't you think?"

"Yeah, I'm going to get that down!" As I walked away from William, I could see him rewriting the work of our conference.

---

continued from previous page

Sandra Cisneros says, 'Because the way you grow old is kind of like an onion or like the rings inside a tree trunk or like my little wooden dolls that fit one inside the other, each year inside the next one. That's how being eleven years old is,' and I could say, 'Wow.' And then I could try to name exactly what it is that she did that I could try also. So, for example, I think that Cisneros decided to use images of real-life things that show the relationship to time she's describing. After naming this technique, then I could look at my own writing and I could say, 'So where might I try the technique Cisneros just used? Where could I use an object to describe a relationship?' and I could revise with her technique in mind."

SHARE

Writing Our Ideas About Our Stories

Share the way one child writes a narrative about her life then writes reflectively about that narrative. Highlight what the child did that is replicable. In this case, the child wrote from one perspective, then from another.

"Writers, I want you to listen really carefully to the work Claudia has been doing. Claudia, as you know, has been writing about the day she visited the nurse's office in her school and had to tell the nurse that she doesn't have a dad." Claudia took a seat in a chair at the front of the meeting area and said, "Well, I had my story part written. This is it": [Figs. XI-7 and XI-8]

> I sat in the bean bag chair in the nurse's office feeling all queasy and sick and about to throw up. My head started turning and everything started to blur. The nurse came over and touched my forehead with her hand. She shook her head and took a deep breath. "Is your mom at home?" she asked.
>
> "No she's at work," I said weakly.
>
> "What about your dad?" she asked. I just sat there unable to answer. What about my dad? I closed my eyes and touched my forehead with my own hand. My seashell bracelet scratched my skin and I immediately remembered that day on the beach with my dad when we collected shells in our blue-striped bucket.
>
> "Hey dad, I found one and it's a beauty," I said as I held the shell up for him to see. I ran to him. He kissed my forehead and took my hand.
>
> "I don't have a dad," I said to the nurse. I sunk down lower into the bean bag chair and fought hard to keep from crying.

"Today Claudia began to really work hard on writing her *ideas* about this narrative. Just like explorers explore a new land, writers explore our topics. Watching Claudia work, it reminded me of a person holding a piece of sea glass in her hand, turning it this way and that way. Claudia was sort of holding her memory of that visit to the nurse's office in her hand, thinking about it one way and then another way."

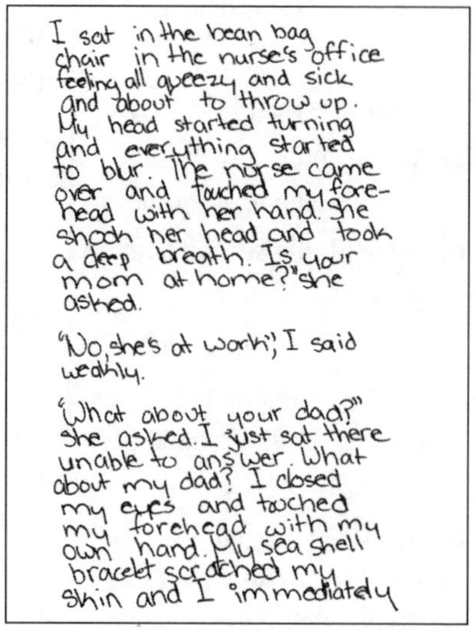

I sat in the bean bag chair in the nurse's office feeling all queezy and sick and about to throw up. My head started turning and everything started to blur. The nurse came over and touched my forehead with her hand. She shook her head and took a deep breath. Is your mom at home?"she asked.

"No, she's at work," I said weakly.

"What about your dad?" she asked. I just sat there unable to answer. What about my dad? I closed my eyes and touched my forehead with my own hand. My sea shell bracelet scratched my shin and I immediately

Fig. IX-7 Claudia's story

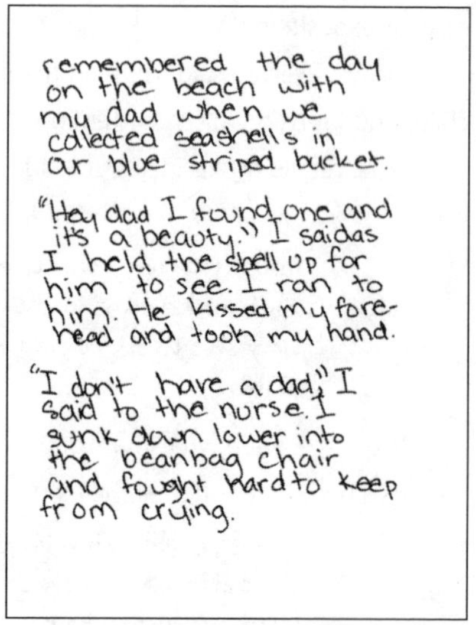

remembered the day on the beach with my dad when we collected seashells in our blue striped bucket.

"Hey dad I found one and its a beauty." I said as I held the shell up for him to see. I ran to him. He kissed my forehead and took my hand.

"I don't have a dad," I said to the nurse. I sunk down lower into the beanbag chair and fought hard to keep from crying.

Fig. IX-8 Claudia's story, page 2

You will notice that oftentimes, I either share children's work, or I have them share it but then I extrapolate the points I want to make rather than trying to elicit these from the child. I can imagine that you might want children to assume a teaching role for their classmates more often. Just keep in mind that the point of the share session cannot be to make the one child in the spotlight feel proud of herself. Granted, that will happen. But if twenty-eight children have stopped their work in order to listen, the intervention must be helpful to those kids who are listening.

Extrapolate from the one case-in-point whatever it is you hope your students learn from the example.

"After she wrote, 'The thought I have about this is . . .' and wrote about the entry one way, she purposely tried to think about it in a whole different way. Then afterwards she reread everything she'd written, and now it was almost as if she were fishing for something she felt was really good: a good line, a good idea, a good image. She liked most of this entry, but then decided to reread it, and look for the best part of it. She decided to look for the surprising part, the part that wouldn't be obvious to most people. So this is what she chose":

> The thought I have about this is . . . there are so many times in my life when I need my dad and he's not there. Like in this story, I needed him because I was sick. I try to remember things about him when I'm feeling bad, but that sometimes just makes me feel worse.
>
> Sometimes people ask me what it's like to live in a new country and what's hardest about living here. They always think that learning a new language or eating different foods is what's hard, but none of that is hard for me. What is hard is that I had to leave my dad and I haven't seen him in three years.

"After she reread this, Claudia said, 'Well, my story shows that I needed my father but he wasn't there. That's kind of obvious. But I don't really say anything about how leaving Poland was hard, because I had to leave my dad, and I haven't seen him in three years.'"

"I told Claudia that she is really smart to identify which of her ideas is especially interesting, and I pointed out to her that she could, if she wanted to do so, start right in with her observations about how people think the hard part of moving is learning a new language, and they don't realize that the hardest thing can be that sometimes you need to leave people you love at home. To help Claudia get started I said, 'I could imagine, for example, that you might begin your essay by saying, "When people hear that I moved from Poland to the United States, they always ask me: 'Was it hard to learn a new language? Was it hard to get used to a different way of eating?' But none of that was hard for me. What was hard for me . . . "' And then you could continue."

"Claudia added onto that oral version of her draft, saying . . . 'What was hardest for me is that now I don't have my dad when I need him!' Then she said, 'That's it! That's it exactly!'"

It isn't an accident that I use an ocean image to talk about Claudia. I want her to know that her powerful memory has carried over to who she is today, that I can imagine her on that beach with her dad holding a seashell, or a piece of sea glass in her hand. This is the beauty of memoir writing.

It's always much easier to write generally about emotions than to name the reasons behind them or to write about them with exact detail. Claudia's discovery of the link between missing her dad and leaving Poland is at the heart of her experience. With this discovery, her more general longing for her father grows in precision and power. And her piece becomes much more interesting and poignant.

When I nudge kids to consider a new way of structuring their writing, I'm hoping they'll see that sometimes a simple shift in angle can bring their writing to life. By suggesting that Claudia begin with the expected reasons a person might struggle when leaving a native country, I'm giving her a way to make her own, personal reason stand out.

Ask all the writers to look at the expository parts of their own writing, and to consider if the structure is right for that section of their text.

Then I said, "Writers, can you look at the thinking part of your writing, or at entries when you explore your thoughts on your blob. And can you do as Claudia and Ali have done and think, 'What am I really trying to say?' Ask yourself, 'Is there a way that I can divide my ideas into a couple of categories? Are all of these categories necessary right in this part of the text? Should I be saying one thing? And even if I am saying one thing, what might come first in my writing? Next?'"

HOMEWORK *Studying Published Memoir* Writers, you've spent a lot of time all year studying the work of published authors and it's always paid off, hasn't it? When we look to see what another author has done, it allows us to imagine possibilities for ourselves. Right now, many of you are still deciding if you want to have exposition in your memoir and, if so, where will it go. But before you can decide, you need to do some research. You need to study the work of other writers to see what you can learn and to see if you can apply this learning to your own writing. So, for example, when I read the beginning of "Not Enough Emilys":

> There are not enough Emilys in the world.
>
> What I mean is . . . Emily is the kind of person
>
> everybody needs to have sometimes.
>
> and suppose I didn't?

I try to understand the moves that Jean Little made, and I name them for myself: Well, she starts with an idea, then she says another line about it and then she asks a question to set up her story. Now I can try this out with my writing!

So tonight writers, I'd like for you to choose your two mentor texts that have exposition, and, in the margin near a particularly powerful part, jot down the structure the author followed. Then, when you want to write your own ideas in a clear, concise, compelling style, you'll be able to refer to your notes. Maybe you can use one of the structures you've found and described.

If your students are having difficulty writing exposition, but their stories are angled to reveal something about themselves . . . you might teach them to embed reflection into their narrative writing. Students can learn, for example, that when they write a personal narrative, they can give themselves, the narrator, internal thoughts that in fact, they may only have grown through the process of writing.

For example, William wrote a memoir to show that ever since his sister was born, he's felt as if he is invisible to his mother. Instead of constructing exposition to explain this idea to his reader, William chose to write a story which illustrated this, and then he tucked some lines into the end of his narrative which addressed his feeling straight on. In the narrative, William is sitting and watching his mother feed his sister and he's trying to tell his mother about his day, but she pays no attention to him. He wrote: "My lips were moving and words were definitely coming out of my mouth, but it was as if someone had pressed the mute button. My mother didn't seem to hear a word I said." Teach all your children that they, too, can bring forth their internal timelines with stories rather than exposition.

If some of your students are writing memoirs which contain chunks of straight exposition and you find their ideas are difficult to follow . . . you might teach students that they can look back at ideas which they developed through stream-of-consciousness writing and think, "How will I sequence these thoughts so readers can follow them?"

Some children, like Ali, will move from more general ideas to more specific and personal ideas. If you see that some children have sequenced their writing in this fashion, point out what they have done. On the other hand, some children's expository sections will be sequenced in the opposite way, with the child progressing from a specific example to a general point, as Sandra Cisneros did in "Laughter." Help children realize that they can plan a way to sequence their writing.

COLLABORATING WITH COLLEAGUES

In any unit of study, it is extremely helpful if you and your colleagues study the types of texts your kids will be writing. For this unit, you could look at any of the memoirs you've selected for your class to read—"Eleven," "Papa Who Wakes Up Tired in the Dark," or a selection from *When I Was Your Age: Original Stories About Growing Up*, or from another memoir you find. You might want to select just two to read closely, in which case I recommend that one of the texts be one which contains sections that read like focused narratives as well as at least one section which reads like a miniature essay. Probably the other text which you study should be one in which the big idea is conveyed mostly through the narrative. The structures that memoir authors use must allow them to reveal the discoveries they've made about themselves and their lives.

You and your colleagues might begin by looking at a selection from *The House on Mango Street* by Cisneros. You will definitely want to own this book—and to look closely at "Papa Who Wakes Up Tired in the Dark." You will probably notice right away its circular structure; that is, it begins with a brief narrative, then it shifts to an extended section of exposition and reflection, and then returns to narrative. The way in which the author relives a moment in time and then steps back from that moment to reflect on it suggests that this author makes sense of life by pausing to reflect.

You might see that this piece begins with dialogue, setting, and action, which are all elements that children studied when they learned to write narratives. The narrative, however, is told through the eyes of the narrator, and it conveys as much about the narrator as it does about the events themselves. When the narrator describes her father, sitting on her bed to tell her about the death of his own father, she says that he "crumples like a coat." This detail reveals the narrator's sensitivity and her attention to her papa's feelings.

The narrator is revealed all the more when she says that this is the first time she has seen her "brave Papa" cry. It is important to notice that when we write memoir, we may write about a single moment, but that moment is always emblematic of a whole life. Here, when the narrator says she has never before seen her brave Papa cry, the narrator is allowing this one moment to reveal the whole of her life.

In the next paragraph, the narrator pulls away from that moment by revealing her larger knowledge of her family's cultural traditions around death. She progresses gradually from talking about the events that are happening right before her eyes to talking about her father and his role in the family to then talking about the roles her extended family (her aunts and uncles) will play and about the customs of her culture.

Because of all of this, the narrator is able to consider her role as oldest child, and then to think about what it would mean to lose her own father. Then and only then can she determine what to do in this moment, with her grieving father. "I hold and hold and hold him." By returning to narrative by describing this small, yet large, gesture, Cisneros completes the circle, revealing what that initial moment has shown her.

You and your colleagues will also want to look closely at James Howe's beautiful piece, "Everything Will Be Okay." Notice that Howe starts by writing a vignette from his childhood, and in the end, this memory serves like a stone, thrown in a lake. The ripples go out as Howe reflects on this moment and relates it to others. In the end, he makes and reveals larger discoveries about what it means to be a man. This memoir shows Howe's realization that he must decide for himself "what kind of boy I am, what kind of man I will become."

Howe's memoir begins with a detailed observation of a physical discovery: "The kitten is a scrawny thing, with burrs and bits of wood caught in its hair, where it still has hair, and pus coming out of its eyes and nose." Howe speaks to the kitten with a child's naiveté: "Everything will be okay," he tells it, though the animal is clearly sick. Howe's portrait of himself shows that at the start of the story, he is someone who just goes along with things: " . . . sometimes you just play with the kids on your same street, even if they're mean, sometimes even to you," he writes. Later he writes about a dog, "He called the new one Bucky and said that Bucky could be mine . . . I feed Bucky some days and play with him . . . He is my father's dog, really."

As you study this memoir, you will notice that the chronological narrative in interrupted by flashbacks. For example, in a reflective flashback of a family dinner, James Howe remembers how he pushed away some venison from a deer his father and brothers killed, a deer whose eyes have "life in them, still."

Howe does not interrupt the story in order to share reflections. But he does convey his interpretations of events as well as the events themselves. Young James Howe comes to realize that his brother, whom he so reveres, has a cruel side to him. The good memories of times spent with Paul are also tainted with memories of Paul's insensitivities: "He's the brother who tells me how to be a man. He is also the brother who plays tricks on me and sometimes the tricks are cruel."

These two memoirs are well worth your close study. And once you have examined them closely, you will find that they can be resources, helping you to teach almost anything.

IN THIS SESSION, YOU WILL TEACH STUDENTS WAYS THAT WRITERS REREAD OUR WRITING INTENTLY, IN ORDER TO LEARN FROM IT HOW WE NEED TO REVISE.

GETTING READY

- Writing sample on transparency to be used to demonstrate different kinds of reading
- Overhead projector
- See CD-ROM for resources

LETTING OUR PAGES LEAD OUR REVISION

Just as there is a story line to a narrative, there is also a story line to a unit of study, and in specific, to this unit of study on writing memoir. At the start of this unit, you probably hoped that writers' eyes were on their lives; your teaching helped writers put those lives on the page. Early in the unit, your conferences and minilessons helped writers reminisce, re-experience, and write freely. But by now, you will want your writers to focus less on the content of their writing and more on their craft. You will want writers to be less consumed with the question, "What shall I tell about myself?" and more consumed with the question, "How can I write this so the text works?"

The writer needs to read her own writing first as an open-hearted, receptive reader, ready to be touched and moved by her own words and to sense the potential they hold. Such a reader notes her own response to the text, asking, "Where does the meaning pop off the page with freshness and energy? Where is the meaning crystal clear and startlingly significant?" Such a reader knows that a great deal of a writer's craft involves finding what works and building upon this.

The writer also needs to read her own words as a stranger might, no longer filling in all that the writer knows but hasn't yet said, and as a busy person might, ready to set the page down if ever the pace sags and the meaning becomes mired. The writer, too, needs to read her own words ready to pull back in askance and say, "What? This makes no sense." Such a writer cannot give the draft just a cursory glance. Instead, this writer reads each word, each sentence, and asks, "Where is this vague? Where does this say two contradictory things?" This writer-turned-reader needs to read precisely and exactingly and yes, ruthlessly. But this kind of reading is also full of loving attentiveness.

Of course, writing is a cyclical and recursive process. The questions that writers ask as we read our own writing take us right back to the beginning, and even though the unit of study is in its final moments, the writer is back to generating writing—and to thinking, "What do I want to say?" But the writing we generate during these final moments stands on the shoulders of all the earlier writing and is often deeper and more true than any before it.

MINILESSON

Letting Our Pages Lead Our Revision

CONNECTION

Find a way to compliment the students on their involvement in their writing work. Be inventive!

"A friend of mine told me a story the other day. Her daughter, Rachel, is a high school student, taking a class in Developmental Psychology and working with children. The teacher of this class decided she wanted the high school students to realize that having a child is a big responsibility—something best left to adulthood—so she purchased a baby doll that is programmed to cry, to need to be burped, to fuss . . . to need constant attention. Last weekend, Rachel's homework assignment was to care for that baby all weekend and to keep a log of her responses. She did it: getting up five times in the night, carrying the baby with her everywhere. But she came out of the weekend saying just the opposite of what the teacher wanted her to say. 'It felt great to have a child!' she said. 'I didn't mind at all giving the baby all that attention. I can hardly wait until I can have my own child!' That wasn't the lesson the high school teacher meant to teach, but it was an important lesson for Rachel nonetheless. She learned that she has a greater capacity to care, to be invested (even in a doll!) than she'd imagined possible."

"I'm thinking of contacting that high school teacher and suggesting that she doesn't need to send a doll home in order to teach kids what it feels like to be *so* involved, *so* invested, that they don't mind the time and work required. She could, instead, invite her students to do what you have done—write memoir!"

Let children know that writers the world over find ourselves surprisingly invested in our emerging writing.

"Annie Dillard, a famous memoirist, said—not in these exact words—'There's a notion that writers are really self-disciplined. We grit our teeth and go to our desks to work on our writing.' Then she said, 'This is a deep misunderstanding of what impels the writer. What impels the writer is a deep love for and respect for language, for literary forms, for books. It's a privilege to muck about in sentences all morning . . . . You don't do it from willpower . . . .'"

"She explains: 'If you have a little baby crying in the middle of the night, and if you depend only on willpower to get you out of bed to feed the baby, that baby will starve. You don't do it out of willpower, you do it out of love . . . . You go to the baby out of love for that particular baby. That's the same way you go to your desk'" (1987, p. 75–76).

COACHING

I know, I know. This is an odd story to tell kids. Call it an attention grabber! Minilessons can get to feel rather similar, one to the next, so sometimes we go a bit "out there" for the sake of being interesting. You'll see that my real goal at the start of this minilesson is to wax sentimentally over the kids' amazing dedication to this work. I find I can't be mushy for long so I'm using this little tidbit of news as my way in. Watch how I get from this odd (but true) story to my point . . . and realize you can find ways to tuck almost anything you find interesting into a minilesson!

I love these words of wisdom from Annie Dillard, and I am utterly convinced that Dillard is not talking only about writing but also about teaching. The amount of time and care that we invest in our work is boundless. We don't do it out of willpower. Contrary to what the federal government seems to think, we don't pour ourselves into our teaching because tests hold us accountable. No, we are invested in teaching because we care about the kids in our care, and about the mission to bring up a new generation that will safeguard this fragile world of ours.

"I'm blown away by your investment in your writing, and I can tell you are not going to your notebooks out of willpower but out of love. I am glad that you are willing to work hard on these writing projects."

Name your teaching point. In this instance, tell children that near the end of a writing project, writers shift into becoming readers of our own work, reading with enough careful attentiveness that our pages teach us how to write.

"Today I want to teach you that the hard work you do as a writer needs to change as you work through the writing process. Pretty soon, you'll want to spend a good deal of your writing time *reading*, not writing. And today I want to teach you that there is a special sort of reading writers do when we read our own writing. We do not skim over it as if we've seen the draft a hundred times. Instead, we examine the draft in all its particulars. If we read what our draft actually says (and if we read also for what it *could* say) then our page will teach us how to write."

"'Who will teach me to write?' a reader wanted to know. 'The page,' Annie Dillard answered . . . . The page that you cover so slowly with your crabbed thread of your gut . . . that page will teach you to write'" (*The Writing Life*).

TEACHING

Tell children that when you near the end of a writing project, you often shift into being a succession of different sorts of readers of your writing.

"Once I can see the end of a writing project, I sometimes feel tired and am tempted to call it a day. I have learned, however, that this is a time instead for me to shift from being a *writer* to being a *reader*. I usually take my writing and go sit in a different place. I bring a different color of pen with me. (I think I'm trying to dress up, almost, as if I am no longer the writer of this piece.)"

"I deliberately decide what sort of reader I'm going to be, and then I read my writing as that reader. Usually, I first read as a big-hearted, responsive, involved listener. I expect to be blown away by parts of the writing, and to see incredible, amazing meaning in it . . . sometimes meaning which isn't yet on the page. I usually look up from that first experience of the text and say to myself, 'This particular section is just so huge and important. You have no choice but to develop it!' Sometimes I find just tiny places in a draft where it is clear there is more, just under the surface of the story; more that deserves to be heard and said. So I mark those sections. 'Slow down,' I might jot in the margins, or 'Say more.'"

You'll see that as this minilesson evolves, I mention a few specific ways that writers read our rough draft writing. Normally, I would bring all these specific strategies into my teaching point so that I'd be articulating not only the goal but also the strategy. I couldn't find a way to tuck the information into this teaching point without bogging it down.

Recall that very often, during the Teaching component of a minilesson, I tell a story of one specific time when I've done whatever it is I am teaching. If I'd threaded a particular piece of my own writing throughout this unit (such as the Luz story in the Fiction *unit of study), I could now show children how I reread that evolving piece of writing. You'll notice, however, that for the first unit yet this year, I haven't used my own writing. In this unit, the children's work was so compelling to me that I wanted to spotlight it.*

You will have noticed how often this "reading with a deliberately chosen lens" enters into our teaching of writing. The ability to do this is, of course, equally essential for readers. Reading through a lens is as important to us as teachers as it is to our children. I always find that when teaching reading and writing, I grow as a teacher, and as a reader and a writer. It is intriguing to teach a subject where good work is not all that different whether one is six or sixty!

Show your children how a student in the class went about rereading his draft as one kind of reader, then as another kind of reader. Role-play being the child, reading in one way, then thinking aloud and annotating the writing.

"Adam reread his draft," I said, enlarging half a page of his draft by means of the overhead projector. "He reread this, trying to be a really responsive reader, one who wanted to hear more. Watch how he reread it. I'll role-play Adam," I said, and read this aloud:

> "Nooo, pleeese can't I go," I pleaded. My mom just ignores me. I knew she would but I was desperate.
>
> My brother walked outside where my mom and I were standing. Our eyes met. Sadness seemed to flow straight into me just like the sound of Jon's bassoon when he practices. I ran to my brother. He embraced me in his tight hug. I pulled him closer.
>
> It was already happening. My eyes stung.

Then, talking as if I were Adam and looking still at the draft, I said, "Those last minutes can be really important and sad." Then I looked at the page and said, "This is a great scene to show. But I should slow it down and show more. I gotta show the packing more. I gotta think of what specific things Jon could have packed that might say something about our relationship. And I should slow down the hug even more, too, and show what I felt at the start of it and in the middle." Then, continuing to role-play Adam, I read on:

> I am in camp, running up a hill. The scene of my brother pulls me forward. The sun is shining but shadows are keeping me cool. As I run my feet push the rocks aside, as I run faster my feet start to slip. When I look up my brother is on the top of the hill. He opens his arms. I am happy and a smile spreads across my face. Tears almost pour out but I control myself.
>
> I tried to blink back tears but they were inevitable. Tears started pouring out over my eyes. I looked up and saw tears in my brother's eyes. I was surprised at this.

Role-playing Adam, I jotted another note in the margins of the draft. "It's great to put what I was remembering into that moment, but I should think about more memories, more times Jon and I had had, and remember them and put them in too."

There will be lots of times when the material you have with you to use in a minilesson is an artifact of another person's writing. In this instance, I have Adam's annotated draft; in another instance, I will have a writer's published text. Either way, I always have the choice of teaching through demonstration or teaching through explaining and showing an example. In this instance, I teach through demonstration, playing the role of writer, reenacting what he did as he progressed through the process. Of course, I am not certain of the exact thoughts in Adam's head as he reread and annotated his draft, but I fill in the gaps with what I imagine Adam was probably doing and thinking.

Shift into role-playing and show that the same child then shifted into being another kind of reader, approaching the same draft differently. Again shift between reading aloud, thinking aloud, and making marginal annotations.

Now shifting out of the role, I leaned towards the children and said, "Then Adam reread, thinking less about that time in his life and more about the words he'd written. This time, he read every sentence and tried to translate that sentence into a mental movie so that he could be sure that the words conveyed just exactly what he wants to show happening."

Then I said, "Adam did this, and realized there were places where his sequence of action wasn't clear. Watch how he did this rereading," and I began slowly reading each bit aloud, registering what it said in my mind, then reading the next bit:

> "Nooo, pleeese can't I go," I pleaded. My mom just ignores me. I knew she would but I was desperate.

"I'm not sure what exactly is happening here. The action isn't clear. It is hard to start the mental movie because what, exactly, is going on?" I read the next sentence or two aloud. "So let me read on, still pretending to be Adam," I said:

> My brother walked outside where my mom and I were standing. Our eyes met.

As Adam I said, "This is clearer, but I didn't say we were packing up the car, or any of that. (And then class, Adam continued rereading his work that way.)"

Tell children that writers also read in different ways, summarizing a few. Then show the child's earlier draft and revised draft, asking them to talk with partners about the revisions they notice.

"Adam, like most writers, also read the writing in other ways—to make sure it rang true, that it felt absolutely emotionally honest (because sometimes to make a good story we hype something up in a way that is not exactly precisely honest). And he read his draft like he was in an airplane, flying over, looking at the structure and thinking, 'How else could this have gone?'"

"Adam left these marks on his first draft, and then rewrote it. I'm going to read Adam's next draft of this section, and then would you and your partner talk about what you notice Adam has done differently as a result of his reading?" *[Fig. XII-1]*

> "Nooo, Pleeese can't I go," I pleaded. My mom just ignores me. I knew she would but I was desperate.

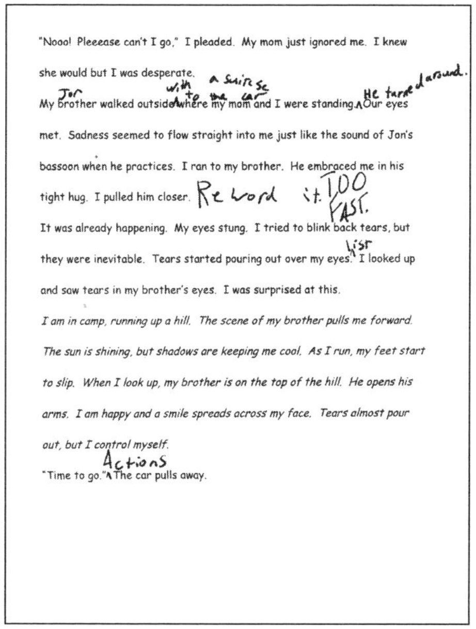

Fig. XII-1 Adam's draft

My brother (Jon) walked outside (with a suitcase to the car) where my mom and I were standing. (Action. He turned around.) Our eyes met. Sadness seemed to flow straight into me just like the sound of Jon's bassoon when he practices. I ran to my brother. He embraced me in his tight hug. I pulled him closer. (reword it. Too fast.)

It was already happening. My eyes stung. I tried to blink back tears but they were inevitable. Tears started pouring out over my eyes. (list ex) I looked up and saw tears in my brother's eyes. I was surprised at this.

I am in camp, running up a hill. The scene of my brother pulls me forward. The sun is shining but shadows are keeping me cool. As I run my feet push the rocks aside, as I run faster my feet start to slip. When I look up my brother is on the top of the hill. He opens his arms. I am happy and a smile spreads across my face. Tears almost pour out but I control myself.

"Time to go." ACTIONS. Car pull away.

"This was Adam's next version": [Fig. XII-2]

My brother came outside with one last suitcase in his hand. He crammed it into the back of my mom's car with all the others. Then Jon slammed the back of my mom's car shut.

Our eyes met when he turned around. Sadness flew straight into me as clear as the mournful sound of Jon's bassoon. My brother hugged me. I pulled him closer. "I'm going to miss you badly," he said. "I will too," I managed to squeak out. My voice was hoarse. It was already happening; my eyes brimmed, I tried to blink back tears, they wouldn't stop. Tears started pouring from my eyes. It reminded me of when I was playing basketball and I fell, pain throbbed through my arm. Jon came and took me to the hospital. With Jon there, I'd felt safer, calmer, less scared. It reminded me of when I was in camp and I hadn't gotten a letter for days, and loneliness was starting to haunt me. Jon's letter came and filled me with laughs and warmth and a feel that it was good to have a big brother. I looked up and saw one tear roll down my brother's cheek. He brushed it away but I remembered it.

This bit of Active Engagement is tucked here, in the teaching component of the minilesson, because it is not a proper Active Engagement. The children are talking about Adam's revisions—and these revisions are somewhat tangential to the point of the minilesson. The children are certainly not practicing doing the strategy that I've taught in this minilesson, as one would expect them to do (and as they do do!) during an Active Engagement.

My brother came outside with one last suitcase in his hand. He crammed it into the back of my mom's car with all the others. Then Jon slammed the back of my mom's car shut.

Our eyes met when he turned around. Sadness flew straight into me as clear as the mournful sound of Jon's bassoon. My brother hugged me. I pulled him closer. "I'm going to miss you badly," he said.

"I will, too," I managed to squeak out. My voice was hoarse. It was already happening; my eyes brimmed, I tried to blink back tears, but they wouldn't stop. Tears started pouring from my eyes. It reminded me of when I was playing basketball and I fell, pain throbbed through my arm. Jon and took me to the hospital. With Jon there, I'd felt safer, calmer less scared. It reminded me of when I was in camp and I hadn't gotten a letter in days, and loneliness was starting to haunt me. Jon's letter came and filled me with laughs and warmth and a feeling that it was good to have a big brother. I looked up and saw one tear roll down my brother's cheek. He brushed it away, but I remembered it.

Fig. XII-2 Adam's next version

"Turn and talk," I said. "What revision do you notice that Adam has done as a result of his careful reading?"

ACTIVE ENGAGEMENT

Ask children to read the first section of their own draft as an especially responsive reader, noticing when the draft's potential deserves to be developed.

"Right now, would you bring out your most recent draft?" I waited for them to do this. "Would you read just the first section of this draft, reading it as a big-hearted, responsive, involved listener. Be blown away by parts of the writing. Find a bit of it which you can point to and say, 'This is just so important. There's more here!' Then jot in the margins, something like, 'Say more' or 'List more examples' or 'Tell with tinier details.'"

Ask children to read the first narrative section of the same draft differently, this time trying to translate the words into a mental movie. Are the actions explicit and clear?

After the children read and annotated for a few minutes, I said, "I know you could work a lot longer on this, but you can go back to that. For now let me ask you to shift and be a different kind of reader. This time, read a passage which is a narrative and read it as a stranger might. You don't know more than is on the page. Try to make a movie in your mind from the words, translating each sentence into the next bit of the mental movie so that you can be sure the words are conveying exactly, precisely what is happening. When you aren't exactly, precisely clear, mark your draft so that you can rework it."

LINK

Remind writers that when they see the end in sight and their energy flags, this is a time for fresh resolve.

"Dag Hammarskjöld, the famous Secretary General of the United Nations, once said, 'When the morning freshness has been replaced by the weariness of midday, when the leg muscles quiver under the strain, the climb seems endless, and suddenly, nothing will go quite as you wish—it is then that you must not hesitate.'"

Ask children to dig into their reserves of energy, to believe their writing can become even better, and to shift from writer to reader.

"This is a good time for you to dig into your reserves of energy and to find new energy for writing. Remember that writers go to our writing desks not because of self-discipline, but because of love for the particular bit of writing. Trust that your piece can become so, so much better—as we saw with Adam's writing—if you allow yourself to shift from writer to reader, and to let the page teach you how you can write even better than you've written so far!"

"Push it," Annie Dillard suggests. "Examine all things intensely and relentlessly. Probe and search each object of a piece of art . . . do not course over it, as if it were understood, but instead follow it down until you see in the majesty of its own specifics and strength."

WRITING AND CONFERRING

Drawing on All We Know to Draft and Revise

While Emily reread her draft, trying to see a section with enormous potential, I sat beside her and did the same thing. The draft had originally been an entry in which Emily wrote off from Woodson's collection of images in "Alone." In a similar fashion, Emily had accumulated images about her topic, growing up. The draft began with this list of images and thoughts about growing up, written by this young girl at the brink of adolescence:

> Whenever I wonder about my childhood, the first thing I think about is when is it over? You don't stop skipping down the street because you're old; you're old because you stop skipping down the street. I'm not exactly old and I'm not exactly young.
>
> Childhood is me. No one ever talked about when it's over. When I play the game of life, I like to think how I'd end up in twenty-three years. A successful business woman or a cashier at MacDonald's, living with three children happily, or still living in my parent's house.
>
> The trampoline sits alone during the winter but in the spring, I'm all over it. I go on it a lot. When I did, Mama was right there with me. Jumping and laughing. Having fun. My mom is a grown-up and still jumps around like me.
>
> When I try to act old trying so I can go on a roller coaster too old for me, I start dancing like a five year old. "La-la, la la, la, la, la . . ." I sing while I dance.
>
> "Stop, Em', everybody's watching," my embarrassed sister says. I ignore her.
>
> One, two, one, two, I say to the beat of my step. And I notice I'm not acting very old.

MID-WORKSHOP TEACHING POINT *Sticking with the Writing Process* "Writers, can I stop you? Freeze where you are exactly. Writers, I know that many of you are wanting help from your teacher and from me and also from each other, but I need to tell you this room is feeling more like a farmer's market on a busy weekend than a writing workshop. Just for a second look around at the room. Notice what each person seems to be in the midst of doing. Notice how few of you were actually in the midst of writing! Writing well takes attentiveness. It takes putting one's butt on the chair and staying there. It takes getting to hard parts and pushing past them, instead of using the hard parts as an invitation to wander around hoping someone is going to deliver a magic solution. So writers, sit back down. Reread your writing. If you have a problem, decide that you can invent a solution to that problem, as well."

At some point in the entry, Emily stopped gathering associated images reflecting her relationship with growing up, and instead wrote one longer narrative about a time when her sister put makeup on her and dressed her in her mother's fur coat. This section of Emily's entry would end up becoming an exquisite memoir, but of course I did not know this at the time: *[Figs. XII-3 and XII-4]*

After my sister graduated elementary school, something changed. The shine in her eye was gone, her smile wasn't as bright. She wasn't the sister who dressed me up in grown-up clothes. "Come on my bed," Jenn said, patting the bed next to her. "Now stay still," she took a suitcase that looked heavy. My eyes watched the suitcase, wondering what was in there. She opened it and told me to close my eyes. "Don't move," she whispered while putting something on my eyes. It felt cold. "Okay open," then she put pink powder on my nose.

"That tickles," I said giggling.

Then she puts goop on my lips.

"Ptth," I spit the yuck off. And wiped the remaining off with my sleeve. But she puts more on again. This time I don't budge.

"Voila. Done." But I'm guessing she wasn't because she turned me around and messed with my hair. "Come here." She went around the house taking clothes. "Wear this and this."

I looked at what she was holding. A furry coat was my mom's. I listened to her orders and when I came out of the bathroom door, Click. She takes a picture I'll remember my whole life.

What I like to do, being a child, are very weird things. Reading the instructions on a shampoo bottle, reading nutrition facts, and spinning on my mom's "merry-go-round chair," the twirly chair.

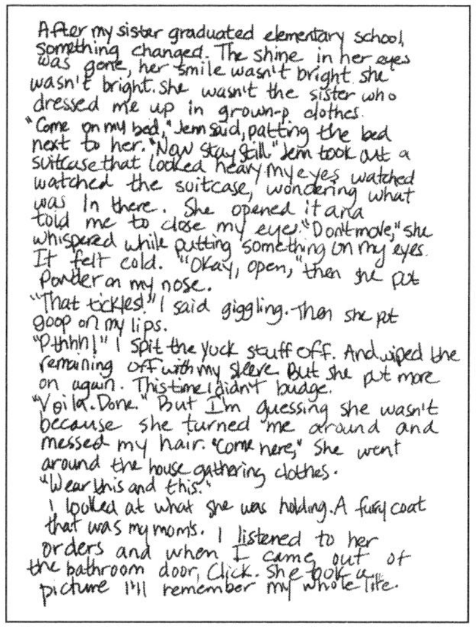

After my sister graduated elementary school, something changed. The shine in her eyes was gone, her smile wasn't bright she wasn't bright. She wasn't the sister who dressed me up in grown-p clothes.
"Come on my bed," Jenn said, patting the bed next to her. "Now stay still." Jenn took out a suitcase that looked heavy. My eyes watched watched the suitcase, wondering what was In there. She opened it and told me to close my eyes. "Don't move," she whispered while putting something on my eyes. It felt cold. "Okay, open," then she put powder on my nose.
"That tickles!" I said giggling. Then she put goop on my lips.
"Pthhh!" I spit the yuck stuff off. And wiped the remaining off with my sleeve. But she put more on again. This time I didn't budge.
"Voila. Done." But I'm guessing she wasn't because she turned me around and messed my hair. "Come here," She went around the house gathering clothes.
"Wear this and this."
I looked at what she was holding. A fury coat that was my mom's. I listened to her orders and when I came out of the bathroom door, Click. She took a picture I'll remember my whole life.

Fig. XII-3 Emily's entry

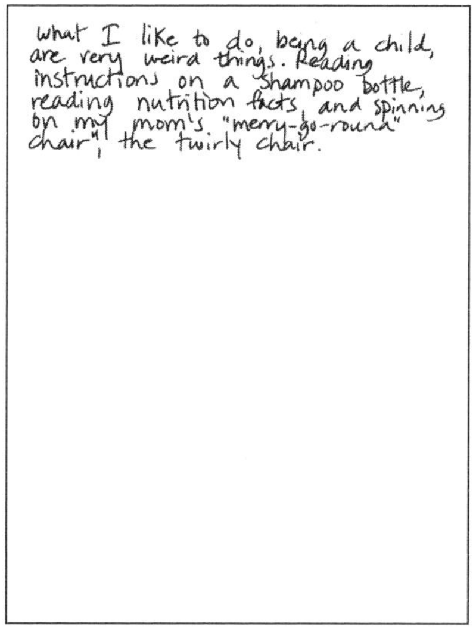

What I like to do, being a child, are very weird things. Reading instructions on a shampoo bottle, reading nutrition facts, and spinning on my mom's "merry-go-round chair", the twirly chair.

Fig. XII-4 Emily's entry, page 2

As soon as Emily finished reading the end of the draft, she pointed to the final half of it, and said, "I think this is the best part." I agreed with her, and for a moment we looked at the way in which Adam, like Emily, had begun trying to write all-about his Life Topic, his brother, by creating an anthology of vignettes. Emily saw, too, that Adam had more recently decided to focus on just the story of Jon's departure, and that he was trying to embed much of what he wanted to say into that narrative.

"Maybe I could try a new draft and just write about that final section where my sister dresses me up," Emily suggested. I nodded, and added, "And try writing it as if the story of your sister dressing you up will be your whole entire memoir. It might turn out to just be part of the memoir, but try taking it so seriously that it could be the whole memoir."

When I returned, Emily had written this new draft: [Figs. XII-5 and XII-6]

Before my sister went to middle school, after she graduated elementary school, and when her shine in her eye was still there, matching her bright smile, she used to play with me. Once she called me to her room.

"Come on my bed," Jenn said, patting the bed next to her. "Now stay still," she took out a suitcase that looked heavy. My eyes watched the suitcase, wondering what was in there. She opened it and told me to close my eyes. "Don't move," she whispered while putting something on my eyes. It felt cold. "Okay, open," then she put pink powder on my cheeks and nose. "That tickles," I say, giggling. Then she put goop on my lips. "Pthh!" I spit the yuck stuff off. And wiped the remaining off with my sleeve. But she puts more on again.

"Voila. Done." But I'm guessing she wasn't because she turned me around and messed with my hair.

"Come here," she went around the house gathering clothes. "Wear this and this." I looked at what she was holding. A furry coat, my mom's furry coat. I go into the bathroom and put it on. I'm finally old. I've always wanted to be. I look in the mirror. I look like one of the actresses with big fur coats, curly hair, walking down the red carpet in the old days. I scrunch up my hair. "Omigod!" I say to myself trying to be like my sister. I point to the tub. "Omigod it is so blue," I walk over to the toilet. "Omigod, that's gross!" I walk over to the mirror. "Omi—" I stop. Something is wrong. This isn't me! I'm not the thirteen-year-old I'm trying to be. Is this me? Is this who I really am? I stare at the girl who isn't me. I am a child. I won't grow up.

Fig. XII-5 Emily's new draft

Fig. XII-6 Emily's new draft, page 2

Emily wasn't pleased with one section of this, the lead which described her sister, so she worked on it and before long, it read:

> After my sister graduated elementary school, something changed. The shine in her eye was gone, her smile wasn't as bright. She wasn't the sister who dressed me up in grown-up clothes. "Come on my bed," Jenn said, patting the bed next to her. "Now stay still," she took a suitcase that looked heavy. My eyes watched the suitcase, wondering what was in there. She opened it and told me to close my eyes. "Don't move," she whispered while putting something on my eyes. It felt cold. "Okay open," then she put pink powder on my nose.
>
> "That tickles," I said giggling.

"Emily," I said, "I absolutely love the fact that you are the kind of writer who rereads your own writing and finds parts that aren't the best you can do, and then you make them better. You are going about this like a professional." Then I nudged her to ask, "What other sections of my draft could take work?" She wasn't sure, so I taught her that often writers look for sections of our writing that we like a lot (not just those we don't like), and we think, "How can I build this up even more?" With that impetus, she set out to add details onto and to expand the section showing her sister rounding up things for her to wear.

At this point, I made notes to myself of a variety of things I could eventually teach Emily, though I would not do it now. First, I was quite clear that I'd want to tell Emily—and others, for she was not alone in this— that she needs to remember that when we write memoir, we are writing about ourselves. So in the end, I would say, Emily will need to focus less on her sister, more on herself. Then, too, I'd want to teach Emily ways to expand particular scenes to reveal more about *herself* and her life. Then, too, I'd want to teach her ways to think about the internal timeline of her pieces, as Tyler did with his roller coaster story.

In the end, Emily decided to show that at the start of the episode, she was happy to be dressing herself up to look older. She stretched out the dressing up part of her piece, adding actions, dialogue, and images that show us how special she felt, at first, wearing makeup and her mom's fur coat. Emily also decided to show that her response changed. She described a turning point of looking in the mirror and seeing how wrong grown-up looks on her. Emily writes: "I stare at the girl who isn't me. I am a child. I won't grow up." And we readers understand that the longing for and imagination about being grown up is just that. She isn't ready and she doesn't recognize herself as a grown-up. But this work is still just a glint in her eye for now.

SHARE

Looking for, and Revising for, Structure

Tell children that writers read our own drafts noting the component sections, asking, "How is this draft almost-but-not-quite structured?" Then we make revisions to bring forth and complete the nascent structures.

"Writers, earlier in this unit, we read published memoirs as if we were flying above them, trying to see their overall layout. We noticed that some memoirs are a single story, usually made of several closely linked scenes held together by a story arc. We noticed that some memoirs are shaped like a necklace of beads, a series of sections of writing strung together with something repeated over and over—perhaps an image or a vignette. And some memoirs contain exposition and one or two narratives. Then, too, some memoirs are essays that advance a thesis, and contain a few supporting paragraphs."

"Today I want to remind you that writers do not merely plan the structure of our writing, we also reread our writing to pay attention to our structure. Sometimes we see that our writing is almost, but not quite, structured in a specific way, and we revise to bring out the shape that is just under the surface of a text. Right now, would you reread your writing and ask yourself, 'What structure is sort of, but not quite, evident in my writing? How could I clean up my writing so that this structure shines through more clearly?' Would you think about this quietly, and in a moment I will ask you to share what you have discovered with your partner."

Remind children that writers often decide to study texts that are structured like the texts the writer hopes to write. Encourage children to select a text to study.

"When you are pretty sure of how you will be structuring your final piece, could you select a short text from the folders I'm putting at the middle of each table? Select a short text that you already know and that you like a lot. Select a text that is structured similarly to the way you want your writing to be structured. Then read it over to see if it can be helpful for you for your writing."

I think that resonance in what we say is a quality of good teaching and good writing. There is a satisfying feeling when a text, or a lesson, returns to something which was taught earlier.

We often ask children to study memoir texts at the start of a unit. Now, as children round the final bend, they can return to these texts, this time viewing them with new eyes.

HOMEWORK *Seeking Trouble* Writers, today we talked about becoming readers of your own writing, and it is important to do that. I want to let you know a secret to keep in mind as you reread: You can't ignore trouble. A writing teacher, Peter Elbow, once said this:

> The mark of a person who can make progress in thinking—who can sit down at 8:30 with one set of ideas and stand up at 11 with better ideas—is a willingness to listen, to notice those inconvenient little details, those annoying loose ends, instead of impatiently sweeping them under the rug.

So tonight, reread your entire draft again. And try to be the sort of person who doesn't sweep the loose ends, the annoying knots and tangles, under the rug. Deal with those parts of your writing that give you trouble.

TAILORING YOUR TEACHING

If your students are writing about one deep feeling or change after the next . . . you might teach them to identify the one most important place in their writing where their feelings changed and then teach them to elaborate on that part.

When you read your students' writing, you might see that they are moving quickly from one extreme emotion to the next in a way that feels unrealistic. If you find this, you might want to start a minilesson by saying, "Writers, so many of you are writing about very complex emotions. That's wonderful because memoir is about uncovering what's sometimes hidden deeply inside of us. But when you make your feelings change in your writing, the reader needs to know why! To make sure our readers understand the changes, writers find the spot in their writing where their feelings change from one to the next and then they elaborate on that moment. We often sit with our feeling and try to capture our thinking, writing down each internal shift that takes place on the page."

If your students are trying to write with a complexity of emotion . . . they may benefit from learning to add flashbacks to their writing so that they can let the reader in on their experiences. Relationships are complex and sometimes it is difficult to get this complexity on the page in a single story. Using a flashback is a way to help readers understand past experiences that might explain why a writer is responding as he is to what's happening now. When teaching students to write flashbacks, you might teach them to think about what they want to show about themselves and then find an event from their pasts that will reveal what's inside of them more fully.

If your students are rereading their writing, but seem to be reading past places that are in obvious need of editing . . . encourage them to have editing conversations with their partners. It sometimes happens that students become so familiar with their writing that it's as if they have it memorized. To them it makes perfect sense and feels absolutely correct. Pointing out that this is not the case has only limited benefits. A partnership where the students are discussing the editing decisions that a writer made, however, can help both students learn to analyze writing in a way that can lead to more accurate and thoughtful editing choices. When students have editing conversations, one student is not simply correcting the other's draft, rather, students are asking each other about choices they've made. The goal is to have students elaborate on their editing choices so that they might become more aware of how to effectively compose their ideas for an audience. Some questions that students might use in an editing conversation are:

- Would you explain to me what this sentence means?
- Will you tell me why you've chosen to put this punctuation mark here?
- Why have you chosen to make this sentence this length?
- How could this sentence (or paragraph) be reshaped, or edited to convey your meaning even more strongly?

COLLABORATING WITH COLLEAGUES

Finding Metaphors in the Moments

The upcoming session focuses on metaphor. To prepare for it, you will want to study your children's writing to see the metaphors that are almost there that you can help children bring forth. You will become more skilled at this if you spend a bit of time revisiting the memoirs you have been studying in order to see the role that metaphor plays in those texts. As you reread these, bear in mind that we want to help children recognize ways in which authors capture large feelings with small, sometimes ordinary images. It isn't as important for children to write elaborate metaphors as it is for them to understand how to pinpoint their own big ideas, feelings, and meanings with symbols.

When reading for metaphor, you might want to first consider smaller, more concrete metaphors within a text. In "Eleven," for example, you will notice that the red sweater is much more than just a stretched-out, ugly garment that the narrator knows isn't hers. It's the focal point of the burden of being a young girl who feels powerless in the face of authority. When Rachel is unable to convince her teacher that the sweater isn't hers, its repugnance grows and grows, just as her years (in her mind) shrink. The sweater becomes repository of the feeling of having all your younger years well up in you. It has become a symbol. Rachel, who has lost her voice, pushes the sweater away, and with it tries to push away the frustrations of being "ten, nine, eight, seven, six, five, four, three, two, and one."

If you consider "Eleven" in its entirety, you might also notice that it can read as a metaphor for growing up. Rachel, who has turned eleven the day of the sweater incident, imagines she should feel her new age right away but doesn't. What she is grappling with is the knowledge that growing up is a gradual process, and a new age doesn't erase who you were each prior year of your life. She says, wisely, " . . . the way you grow old is kind of like an onion or like the rings inside a tree trunk or like my little wooden dolls that fit one inside the other, each year inside the next one." Rachel names

growing up with images she can understand, physical things with layers—the circles of an onion, the rings of a tree trunk, her nesting dolls—and so creates her own metaphor for age and experience. By the end of "Eleven" Rachel has learned something else about age; she's learned that having many years, and a position of authority, as does her teacher, doesn't mean being right or all-knowing.

"Eleven" is rich with simile and metaphor and there's much more you and your colleagues will notice beyond what I've described. This text is a good model for children because they will no doubt be able to identify with Rachel, whose feelings are too big to voice. Rachel's way of naming those feelings using images she understands—"sleeves all stretched out like . . . a jump rope," "animal noises," "a runaway balloon," etc., may resonate with children, who will see that the tangible pieces of their lives can be powerful symbols for large ideas. In writing their own memoir, your students are trying to put on paper large emotions and ideas that reveal something essential about who they are, and they may be better able to do this if they understand how to write, and think, with metaphor.

Sometimes I think that we, as teachers, are brought up to think of metaphor as something like a trinket. We say the piece of paper is "as white as snow" and think we've created a metaphor. I hope that this session helps you reconsider and see that the entire texts that children—and you and I—have been writing are metaphor. Most of my favorite bits of minilessons are metaphor, and you may want to leaf through the pages of these books to see the many times when a minilesson begins with a metaphor. Or read wonderful literature, and find times when the entire piece is a metaphor. I think "Grandma's Hair" is a metaphor, for example, as is James Howe's "Everything Will Be All Right." Below, I've cited the final story at the end of my *The Art of Teaching Reading*. This is a metaphor, too, and I think this story helps me remember that really, making metaphor is what writers do. We live our lives and then turn back on our tracks thinking, "Wait, what was that really all about?" We think, "What can I learn from that?" and devise answers. Here is the ending of *The Art of Teaching Reading*:

> Twenty-five years ago, when I founded Teachers College Reading and Writing Project, a fellow named Jim was our fiscal manager. Jim seemed to adopt the Project as his family. After hours, he'd busy himself about the office, listening to classical music and doing nice things for people. He'd lay out a new blotter on my desk, wash out all our coffeecups, take a coat to the tailor's for mending.
>
> After many years of service, Jim began to get sick. He grew thin before our eyes. No one knew what was the matter. He said he was being tested for parasites. Eventually he developed red blotches on his arms, hands, and neck, and it became clear that he had AIDS; he was the first person I knew to have the disease. Before long, Jim left on disability.
>
> Often after our Thursday meetings at Teachers College, someone would head off to the distant parts of Brooklyn to visit him, to help him with grocery shopping or to clean his apartment. My son Evan was an infant then, and because we lived an hour in the opposite direction, I couldn't often make it on these visits. Feeling inadequate, I'd watch as people left for Brooklyn, and say, simply, "Give Jim my best."
>
> A year later Jim entered Columbia Presbyterian Hospital, and I stopped in to visit him. It was heartbreaking to see how much he'd changed. He was so thin, his head like a skull, but still with blue blue eyes. He held my hand and looked at me with such intensity that I was embarrassed. Looking for a conversation topic, I scanned his barren hospital room. "Jim, you don't have a radio," I said. "Remember how you always listened to classical music? Can't you have a radio here?"

> "Oh, I could have one," he said. "Mine got lost along the way."
>
> Glad to finally have found something, however small, I could do to help, I said, "Jim, I'll get you a radio."
>
> "Oh, Lucy, that'd be great," he said. "Beethoven would be good right about now."

> I left soon after that, hurrying back to the college. My plan was to get the radio the next day. I just had to write a grant first, and grade my student papers and answer some phone calls. A week later a colleague came back from a visit with Jim. "He told me about the radio," she said.
>
> "I'm going to get to it right away," I answered, making a mental note to get the radio as soon as I'd plowed through the pile on my desk. There just were some things I had to cover, and finish, and get through, and check on first. Then my own appendix ruptured, and I was in the hospital with tubes in my nose. The phone rang. "Jim died."

> I held the receiver in my hand. All I could think was, "He never got the radio."
>
> Now I drive past Columbia Presbyterian Hospital every day on my way to work, and every day, I see that hospital and I vow, "May I never again be the kind of person who forgets the radio." I end with the story of Jim because in the teaching of reading, there are always so many details to plow through, to cover and finish and check, that it's only too easy to forget the radio. In the end, my wish for all of us is this: Let's hold tight to what matters most.
>
> Let's hold on for dear life.

Hold on to what matters most . . . and high on that list is the human ability to bring significance to our lives.

METAPHORS AND MEANINGS

Jerome Bruner, the great developmental psychologist, has asked should we not celebrate the day the child begins using combinational grammar? Isn't that the day, he asks, that marks a child's "entry into the human race"? At first, the toddler uses single words to represent things. But, one day, the child will come home from a walk and out of the clear blue sky, say, "Doggy bye-bye." A two-word sentence! And then, Bruner says, this new language work will lay down new mental tracks—suddenly the child makes himself understood in terms of things and actions. Bring out the trumpets and the confetti! As writers grow, they make many breakthroughs in language that, like the one Bruner celebrates, lift the level of that child's thinking.

When we teach writing, we are teaching thinking. We are helping children lay down new mental tracks. Upper elementary children come to us already speaking in sentences. But there are still unbelievably important language lessons to learn, and these lessons can give children whole new layers of understanding and experience. One of the truly gigantic lessons that we can teach during a memoir unit of study is the power of metaphor.

I remember learning about figurative language. I concentrated on the fact that similes used like or as; metaphors didn't. Now, as an adult writer, and especially as a teacher, I know that metaphor is so much more than this. Metaphor is grasping big ideas and feelings . . . the meanings that sometimes feel hard to explain. My brother Geoff wants to thank our mother for the whole of his life, and he knows that it won't work to say, "I am thankful for the Whole Works. It's all been great." So he finds one shining moment—the times, when he was a little boy with leukemia, when Mum would help to pass those long hours in the hospital by taking off her shoe, pushing it into the middle of the room, and taking turns with her son, pitching a penny into that shoe. Years later, when my brother writes the story of the penny pitching, Geoff isn't thinking about like or as; instead, he is thinking, "How can I take the gigantic feelings of gratitude that well inside me and somehow put them onto the page?"

Your children, too, will be holding gigantic feelings, feelings too pure and too impassioned for ordinary words. It is time for teaching your children the power of metaphor. If they really learn what metaphor can be, then bring out the trumpets, the confetti, because glory be! They'll be laying down new mental tracks—They'll be thinking in entirely new ways.

IN THIS SESSION, YOU WILL TEACH CHILDREN THAT WRITERS TAKE A TINY DETAIL FROM OUR LIVES— OFTEN SOMETHING THAT COULD BE VERY ORDINARY—AND WE LET THAT ONE DETAIL REPRESENT THE WHOLE BIG MESSAGE OF WRITING.

GETTING READY

- Story of a child's process of using metaphor in his writing with examples (or use Justin's writing below)
- Examples of powerful metaphors in writing
- See CD-ROM for resources

MINILESSON

Metaphors and Meanings

CONNECTION

Tell children a story that leads you to talk about the times when you—or any writer—wanted to capture something in print that felt too big for words.

"One of my favorite movies is *The Sound of Music*. At the start of the movie, Maria is apprenticing to become a nun, and runs into difficulties because when she is supposed to be in prayer sessions, she instead heads into the hills, where she breaks into song, singing 'The hills are alive, with the sound of music . . . .' In this particular monastery, traipsing through the mountain meadows isn't nun-like behavior: she isn't solemn enough. At one point, the nuns gather and, trying to find the words to describe the way that Maria can't be contained in the confines of the abbey, they sing, 'How do you hold a moonbeam in your hand?'"

"When I write, I often have the same trouble. The meanings that I want to convey sometimes well up inside me, and the more important those meanings are, the harder it is to find the words for them. They are like moonbeams—I feel them, but I don't know how to pin them down. I sit beside the page and think of big, elusive meanings, and the question I ask is, essentially, 'How do you hold a moonbeam in your hand?'"

"How does Adam find the words to capture what his house felt like after his dad and his brother had driven off? How will Judah find the words to capture the feelings that well up in her for home, Missouri?"

Name your teaching point. Specifically, teach children that sometimes writers cup our hands around a detail from our lives, letting that one detail symbolize our message.

"What I want to teach you today is that writers often take a tiny detail from our lives—often something that could be very ordinary—and we let that one detail represent the whole big message of our story or our memoir."

COACHING

If you think of it, right here in this minilesson, I am using a metaphor to teach children about writing. I quote those nuns at the start of The Sound of Music, *talking about Maria, asking, "How do you hold a moonbeam in your hand?" but I am also reaching for the words to talk about the challenge every writer faces when we try to capture something fleeting, multi layered, nuanced, and alive in little black letters that march across the page. In the last session, I began the minilesson by telling about the high school child who was given an assignment to carry a baby-doll with her throughout the weekend . . . and somehow, even that became a metaphor for writing!*

TEACHING

Remind children of a story they've learned about an author who has a big content she wanted to convey in her story, and did so by embedding that big meaning into an object, a metaphor.

"You'll remember that when we started this unit of study, when we were beginning to think about Life Topics, I told you that Patti MacLachlan once told me that every book she writes is in some way about a child's longing for home. One day, just after she'd moved into a new home, when she was having a lot of trouble writing, Patti visited a school and told the children there that she thought she was having a hard time writing because she felt disconnected from her new house; she missed the old house, with its snakes in the basement and mice everywhere. She told the children that she always carried a bag of prairie dirt with her to remind her of her childhood home. Patti then said, 'Maybe I should take this bag of prairie dirt and toss it into my new yard. The two places could mix together that way!' 'No!' cried a boy who was listening in. 'Maybe the prairie dirt will blow away!' And then the little girl said, 'I think you should put that prairie dirt in a glass bowl in your window so that when you write, you can see it all the time. So you can always remember what you knew first.'"

"When Patti MacLachlan went to write a memoir, she had big feelings welling up inside of her, just as you all do now, feelings that sometimes feel too pure and deep for words. But she remembered that little girl who'd suggested she put her prairie dirt in a glass bowl in her window so that when she wrote, she could look at the bowl and remember what she knew first. Patti borrowed just a part of that memory, giving her memoir the title *What You Know First*."

"And the final page of the memoir, you'll remember, tells about a girl bracing herself for leaving her home on the prairie. She considers staying, letting the family go on without her":

> Mama says the baby would miss me
> If I stay
> My Mama says how will he know about the way the
> Cottonwood leaves rattle when it's dry,
> If I don't tell him.
> And how will he know Uncle Bly's songs,
> If I don't sing them.
> What you know first stays with you, my Papa says.
> But just in case I forget
> I will take a twig of the cottonwood tree
> I will take a little bag of prairie dirt
> I cannot take the sky

Sometimes when our goal is to teach artistry, when we want to convey a quality of good writing that is very special, it helps a lot to refer to published writing. There are lots of advantages. First, you and I can't hold a candle to Patricia MacLachlan's abilities, so leaning on her brings extraordinary power into our minilesson. But also, if MacLachlan serves as the writer in the minilesson, then we are freed up to model learning from the writer, which after all is what we hope our children will be able to do.

Debrief, explaining that the author, in the example above, created a metaphor to say something too big for words. Perhaps share a second example of a time when a writer used a very concrete image in order to convey something bigger than words.

"Patti MacLachlan has done something that writers do often. She has found one very specific object, and one line of dialogue, too, and used those two things to represent the huge longings for home that well up in her. I do this often in my own writing. For example, in a book I called *The Art of Teaching Writing*, I wanted to find a way to tell about the fact that writers can take all the littlest details of our lives and make them matter. So I wrote this":

> In her book, *Roxaboxen,* Alice McLerran tell about how, as a little girl, she and her friends invented a kingdom. Roxaboxen,as the kingdom was called, started out as a scraggly desert hill with nothing but cacti, sand, and some broken-down boxes. Then Marian dug up a rusty tin box. Everyone gathered around and declared it treasure. And it was. Inside the box there were smooth black stones. After that, there were treasure hunting days, and a town grew, with streets lined with white stones, and a jail, and a cemetery. The kingdom of Roxaboxen began with Marian holding a rusty tin box in her hand and declaring it a treasure. That is why I write.
>
> I write to hold what I find in my hands and to declare it a treasure. I'm not very good at doing this. When I sit down at my desk, I'm like my students. "Nothing happens in my life," I say. I feel empty-handed. I want to get up and rush around, looking for something Big and Significant to put on the page.
>
> And yet, as a writer, I have come to know that significance cannot be found, it must be grown. (p. 7)

Active Engagement

Tell children that in the act of writing narratives that represent something big about their lives, the children are each making metaphor. Suggest that children bring out the metaphoric aspects of their writing more, and ask them to help one child do so.

"When you write memoir, in a sense, each one of you is creating a metaphor for your life. You are taking particular bits of your life and saying, 'Look closely at this bit of life, because this one bit of my life sort of stands for who I am as a person.' Or you are saying, 'Listen to this story of my father and me, because this story stands for my relationship with my dad.'"

"Every one of you is already writing a metaphor of your life, but some of you will want to bring that metaphor out a little more explicitly. Let me tell you about and read you

You could, of course, decide to use one of these examples or the other and not both. I think I decided to include the second example because in a sense, this is a metaphor about metaphor!

Justin's memoir. Then let's see if we can help Justin bring out the metaphor which is right beneath the surface, ready to be highlighted."

"Listen to the story, and let's all of us think, 'How might this story represent something huge about Justin and his life?' Something huge just like that story about penny-pitching represented something huge about what my mother has done for my brother? It won't be easy to think of this, so listen really hard," I said. Then I paraphrased part of his memoir, and read other sections of it aloud.

"Justin opens his memoir by telling the story of a time in second grade when another classmate, a struggling student, read aloud. Justin has written about this one turning point moment. His story starts, 'Hearing him read was the funniest thing in the world to me,' and then he continues, telling about how after Daniel stuttered his way through the text, other boys sat around at snack time, impersonating Daniel. 'I . . . want . . . ttto . . .' After snack, the children reconvened and this time a girl named Natalie read aloud beautifully. Justin wrote, 'I felt as if I was in the ocean and all the waves were rocking me to sleep.' But soon it was Justin's turn to read, and suddenly he was gripped by fear. He wrote":

> "Justin, your turn," Mrs. S. said. I stepped up and walked to the brown chair. I sat down. Chills scattered through my bones as I cradled the book in my hands like a feather floating down the water. My stomach was tossed around. I opened my mouth . . . nothing came out. I tried again as if every word on page 106, chapter 8 would come stumbling out. Still nothing.
>
> I tried one last time. Only a squeak came out. I wish all my troubles disappeared like a popped bubble. They started laughing, then, "Stop! You can't laugh at someone if they did not laugh at you!" I could not believe it. Thanks Danny.
>
> He stood up for me after he had no reason. The teacher lost her temper and ended reading short. I got up and walked over to my locker.

"Justin," I said. "What do you want to say about you and Danny? What do you want your readers to know at the end of this story?"

Justin thought and then said, "That we started to be friends?"

I selected Justin's draft because he is not a child who finds writing easy, and yet he has done a very significant piece of work. I suspected that he'd benefit a lot from children's help because with their input, he could take his draft to a whole new level. Meanwhile, it is great for Justin to have the entire class learning to do something very advanced and challenging by standing on his shoulders.

Oftentimes you won't need to read the whole of a piece of writing aloud in your minilessons, so become accustomed to interspersing paraphrase with reading aloud.

Notice the way Justin reaches for the precise words that capture what fear felt like for him. Notice, too, that this boy, on the cusp of adolescence, trusts his classmates enough to write this beautiful piece.

I nodded, and said, "So class, would you think about it. What might Justin have himself do, or have Danny do, as the ending action of this story? What could one of them do or say that would show that they became friends? Turn and talk."

Soon children were making suggestions to each other. I gathered a list from what I overheard. "I heard some of you suggest that Justin could pull some food out of his locker and offer it to Danny, or that he could look at something Danny owns—his coat, maybe, and say, 'Nice.' Or that Justin could say, 'You want to come over later?' Those are all good ideas. And each of you, in a similar fashion, may find that you can bring objects or actions into your story that carry the deeper meanings you want to convey. You can do this with memoir—and you can do this anytime that you want to write a really significant text."

Before the day was over, Justin had added an ending to his memoir: *[Fig. XIII-1]*

> I shut my locker and walked down the hall with Danny talking.
>
> "So friend, what's new?"

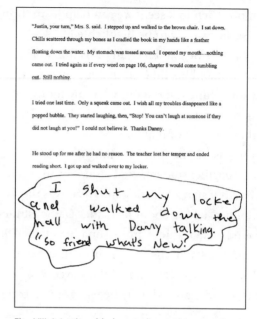

Fig. XIII-1 Justin added an ending to his memoir.

WRITING AND CONFERRING

Letting the Metaphor Emerge

Takuma sat at his table writing, rereading, and then erasing frantically. I approached him, sat down and asked, "Takuma, how can I help you with your writing today?"

He cleaned the eraser bits from the page with the back of his hand and said, "I've been trying to find a way to end my memoir, and after today's minilesson I thought that ending with a metaphor would really help me. But I can't seem to find one that really fits."

I wondered how Takuma was trying to find a metaphor. Was he rereading his writing to see the possibilities that already existed? Or was he trying to create a new metaphor that fit with what he'd already written? So, I pressed, "Takuma, tell me. How are you searching to find this metaphor? Let me into your brain. What's your thinking?"

Takuma immediately began, "Well, I was trying to think of a metaphor that fits my relationship with my dad. I'm writing about how he always helps me and makes me feel safe when I'm scared. So, I was thinking that my dad is like a security blanket, but that didn't really work. Then, I was thinking that I could say that my dad's a nightlight, but that sounded weird too."

I understood why Takuma was having difficulty. He was trying to think of a metaphor that was not emerging from his memoir. How smart he was to be able to see that this was making his writing inauthentic. "Takuma," I said. I wanted to find the words to repeat what he'd said in a way that might more specifically name the trouble he was having. "I understand why you're feeling frustrated. You are trying to find a metaphor for your relationship with your dad, but when you reread your writing to see if it fits, you discover that it feels out of place. Is that right?" Takuma nodded.

"You really understand something that is so important about writing well, Takuma. You understand that writing needs to have unity. That means that the parts must all fit together as a whole. Writing with metaphor should help to create unity across your writing, not make it feel like it's in separate pieces. One way to make this happen, Takuma, is to try to let a metaphor emerge from the writing that already exists. You don't need to hunt around outside of your writing, rather you should let your writing show you the possibilities."

> **MID-WORKSHOP TEACHING POINT** *Using Refrains* "Writers, can I stop you? As I walk the room reading your drafts and conferring with you, I can see how you've focused so intently on crafting powerful lines as you compose—lines that hold meaning that is enormous to your writing. Writers often search their writing for lines such as these looking for ways to highlight them, because highlighting a particularly strong line can also highlight a particularly strong idea. One way to make a powerful line stand out is by repeating it here and there across a piece of writing."
>
> "In 'Eleven,' Sandra Cisneros, repeats the line, 'Mama is making a cake for me for tonight, and when Papa comes home everybody will sing Happy birthday, happy birthday to you.' Each time I read that line I get goose bumps, because I understand that
>
> *continued on next page*

I decided that I would use Takuma's writing to teach him how metaphor can create unity in his writing. I wanted to help him see that, if he thought through the writing he had already done, he would be able to see that a metaphor already existed. They nearly always do, in our writing, when we look hard enough! His job would be to recognize it and make it stand out. "Tell me how your memoir goes, Takuma."

"Well, I'm writing a story to show how my dad makes me feel safe. Just knowing he's there makes me feel like everything's okay, even when I'm scared. So, I wrote this story to show this idea. It's about this time when I was on the beach with my dad, and we had built a tunnel deep in the sand. I started to go through the tunnel, but as soon as my dad let go of me, I panicked because everything was dark. Then, he lifted me out of the tunnel, and I was no longer scared." I listened as Takuma retold his story. I wanted him to hold the whole of it in his mind so that he might imagine both how his ending could go, and how a metaphor might tie his ideas together.

continued from previous page

there is an enormous idea behind it. One idea that Sandra might be trying to show through this line is that birthdays are supposed to be wonderful occasions that celebrate the beauty of growing up."

"Sandra repeats this line across her writing somewhere near the beginning and then again towards the ending. Sandra wants us to pay attention to this idea across the entire piece, so she repeats it to help us say, 'Yes, yes, I see what you're trying to say!' So, right now, writers, can you take a moment to reread your writing for lines that could be highlighted. When you find one, think about where else you might try writing it so that it helps your ideas really stand out."

I pointed out to Takuma that he already had the beginnings of metaphor in his writing. "When you are very frightened, Takuma, there is darkness all around you, right? Well, that's a metaphor. You are trying to show something about how you are feeling by using an image—in this case the image is darkness. Hold that in your mind, Takuma, and think for a moment. At the end, you want to show that you come out of the tunnel and you are no longer scared. How can you show this feeling with an image that fits with the image of darkness and feeling frightened?"

I had put a good bit of scaffolding into place because I wanted to reflect to Takuma the tracks of his thinking and allow him to follow them right into his ending. Takuma began, "When I come out of the tunnel, I'm on the beach and it's no longer dark and scary. The beach is filled with sunlight. I'm looking up at my dad and up at the bright sky."

"Takuma, that metaphor is perfect for your ending! You've taken the image of darkness that you used earlier and changed it to an image of brightness. This shows how you are affected by your father's absence and presence. You retold your writing and were able to find a metaphor for your ending that fit with a metaphor that you used earlier. If you remember this each time you write with metaphor, you will not run across the trouble of your writing feeling disjointed. Rather, it will help to give your writing unity!"

SHARE

Finding an Object to Act As a Metaphor

Tell of one child who wanted to find a significant ending and therefore searched for an object that could stand for something big. Highlight that writers can make actions happen on the page that didn't happen in real life.

"Adam needed to find an ending for his story, and decided that maybe he could find a way to use part of his writing as a metaphor. So today he reread his draft looking for some very specific details that he used early in the story, that he could revisit in a way that made those items or those actions represent the huge big feeling that he had, the feeling that is hard to put into words."

"Adam realized that he'd made references to the mournful sound of Jon's bassoon. But there was another object that represented his brother, too, and it wasn't in the early sections of the memoir—yet. So Adam did something very smart: he added that object—his brother's hat—into an early section of the draft. Now when Jon goes to climb into the car, he puts his Penn cap on backwards, like always."

"Listen to the ending Adam has written for his piece":

> Jon rolled his window down and motioned me over. I walked up to the car, not sure what to say or do. He gave me a little punch, this time I didn't mind. "I'll miss you," he said.
>
> "Yeah, me too," I said. He handed me his hat.
>
> The car pulled down the driveway. I knew my childhood with my brother was ending this very moment. My brother opened the sunroof and waved his hand. I waved back even though he probably couldn't see me. The car made a left and climbed the hill til it was out of sight. I walked to the end of the driveway to see if I could get one last glimpse of the car. I knew Jon was moving on. It will only be a matter of time before he has graduated from college, gets married and has kids.
>
> I stood there for a moment, then slowly made my way back up the driveway. I remembered I was holding Jon's Penn hat, and put it on backwards just as he always did. I walked to his room and sat down on his bed. I squeezed his pillow and looked for any sign that Jon was once there. I picked up Jon's bassoon and put each piece

This is a beautiful example of a child finding a metaphor within the details of a life story. You can help one of your students find a metaphor too, and use your own students' work as an example. The writer must first think, "What should the message be at the end of the piece?" So, if this is a story about a grandparent dying, for example, perhaps the writer wants to say at the end of the piece that she remembers that person still. Once the writer knows what she wants to say at the end of the story, then the writer has to think, "What action could the character do that would convey that?" The writer can brainstorm possibilities. The narrator who remembers a lost grandparent could place a photograph beside his bed, add a photo into his wallet, whisper a message to the missing person at a key moment, imagine an upcoming event and know that the grandparent won't—yet will—be there. Try helping a child imagine possibilities; kids will need your help to imagine the possibilities in doing this.

together the way Jon had taught me. I went over to the chair Jon always sat in when he played, and I played the deep mournful sound I had heard coming from his room so many times.

Extrapolate from the example lessons that every child can learn, reminding them of the step-by-step process a writer can go through to create a metaphor. Set children up to help each other.

"So writers, many of you may want to learn from what Adam and Justin have done. If you want to use a metaphor at the end of your piece, think about what message you want to convey at the end of your piece. Do you want to say you are filled with hope for tomorrow? Then look across your lawn and see the sun rising, its rays turning the world golden. Do you want to say you'd ended one chapter in your life? Then say that you said goodbye, turned to walk away but then paused and came back. Taking hold of the door, you closed it securely. Touching the door, you whispered a second 'bye' and turned your back. You—every one of you—can make metaphor! Turn and help each other."

HOMEWORK   *Describing Our Writing Processes*   Our unit of study will soon end, and so, too, will our year-long journey through the writing workshop. Before the year is over, would you take some time to think about what you have learned about the writing process? I will be sending home a chart which we used earlier in the year to track our progress through the writing process. Would you look at the chart tonight and remember how, earlier this year, I taught you that writers first live like writers, collecting lots of entries. Then we choose one entry to become our seed idea. Then we make a timeline or some other plan for our writing, and read other texts like those we want to write. Then after we plan, we write, rewrite, and edit. By now, you have come to realize that the writing process is more complicated than that. Every day for the last week, you've been shifting between writing, rewriting, planning, and writing some more. So tonight, I want you to think about how you might describe your own writing process, now.

When you think about this, ask yourself whether there is a beginning, a middle, and an end to the story line of your work with a piece of writing. Is it the case that earlier in your work with a particular text, your focus is not on the piece of writing but on the piece of life we're trying to capture? Early in your work with a piece, are you making movies in your mind, remembering and envisioning and re-experiencing? Is there a time when your focus shifts? How are your strategies of writing different at the start and towards the end of a process of writing? Write about what you have now learned about your own process of writing.

If your students feel like they're finished revising . . . you might add new fuel to their work by having them meet with a partner to discuss the revision decisions they've made. Students might prepare for their partnership talk by rereading their drafts and marking the crafting techniques they've used in their writing. When they meet with their partners, they can each discuss the work they've done and name how each technique somehow improved the quality of their writing. Then, they can lean on each other to make further revision plans. They might ask questions such as: What work has my partner tried that I might try? Or: What have we learned that I've yet to apply to my writing? You might emphasize that writers try to re-imagine their writing and sometimes the revision work they do pays off and sometimes it doesn't. What's important to remember when revising, however, is that stretching one's way of thinking will often lead to new discoveries.

If your students sprinkle figurative language on their writing, but it doesn't reinforce their ideas . . . you could teach them to identify the places where they might have used similes, metaphors or another form of figurative language, and have them ask themselves: How does this writing help to show my idea? It is common for students to enjoy writing with figurative language. Once they are exposed to it through their reading or writing lives, it tends to show up everywhere. You may find, however, that they are more focused on the language and less focused on how this crafting technique will help develop their ideas.

If this is the case, you might teach a small group lesson or mini lesson that begins, "Yesterday, Marlin and I were reading his memoir. There's a scene where he's sitting with his mom at the vet's office waiting to find out if his dog has survived surgery. He does such a great job helping us understand the depths of his sadness and worry. But when the nurse comes into the waiting room to tell him the news, he writes, 'I jumped from my chair like a Jack-in-the-Box.' As Marlin was reading this, he said, 'Wait! That sounds really happy, but I was actually still really worried.' Wasn't that so smart for Marlin to catch that? He was using a simile, which was a cool thing to try, but he realized that it was not at all showing his idea. So, he decided to take it out unless he could find one that actually fit what he was trying to show."

You might have a text that has a simile or metaphor or another form of figurative language that seems to be taking the idea of the writing off track, and have students identify how the line interferes with what the author is trying to say. Students might also benefit from studying an author's use of figurative language to identify how these crafting techniques are used to bring meaning to the surface. This will benefit their reading comprehension as well as their writing work.

MECHANICS

In the upcoming session, you will remind your children that writers edit not only to make our work conventional and correct, but also to make our work powerful. We edit by ear, listening to the rhythm of our language, hoping to create a powerful effect for readers.

Before the year ends, you need to make an important statement to your children—and such a statement needs to be made regarding the power and the pleasure of editing.

So before you go into tomorrow, spend just a little time thinking about ways you can help children understand that writers take great pleasure in making decisions about how we will use even the littlest marks on a page—a period, a comma, a parenthesis.

You may want to linger after school with a few picture books. Try one by Patricia Polacco or Tomie De Paola or Cynthia Rylant. Those authors all use luscious punctuation. Take Hesse's *Come On, Rain* or Rylant's *Night in the Country*, perhaps. Once you know the stories, open to any page, and study the punctuation that the author has used. In your mind, think to yourself, "Why did Rylant write with these dashes? With these short sentences and periods? With this exclamation point?"

It is easiest to answer these questions if you think, "How would this have been different had she punctuated this sentence differently?" Try rewriting a sentence, and then reading it according to the new road signs, new punctuation that you provide. You will quickly become aware of the effect of the author's decision.

Pico Iyer says, "Punctuation then is a matter of care. Care for words, yes, but also, and the more important, for what words imply. Only a lover notices the small things: the way the afternoon light catches the nape of the neck, or how a strand of hair slips out from behind an ear, or the way a finger curls around a cup. And no one scans a letter so closely as a lover, searching for its small print, straining to hear its nuances, its gasps, its sights and hesitations, poring over the secret messages that lie in every cadence. No iron can pierce the heart with such force as a period put at just the right place . . . Punctuation, in fact, is a labor of love." (1996)

IN THIS SESSION, YOU WILL TEACH
CHILDREN TO LISTEN TO OUR
WRITING CAREFULLY, THEN TO
CHOOSE WORDS, STRUCTURES,
AND PUNCTUATION THAT HELP US
TO CONVEY THE CONTENT, MOOD,
TONE, AND FEELINGS OF THE PIECE.

GETTING READY

- Two samples of writing to edit for sound
- See CD-ROM for resources

EDITING TO MATCH SOUND TO MEANING

In this session, we'll teach students *that editing involves, among other things, listening to the sound of writing and refining our text so that it sounds right. Too often, when our students think about editing, they think only about getting each period, comma, and capital letter into place. They check their spelling and their paragraphs, but they do not check their rhythm or tone. Their eagerness to correct errors is important, but before the year is over, it is also important to be sure that students understand that editing entails more than correcting.*

When writers edit our writing, we read it out loud to hear the sound of each word, to hear the rhythm of our sentences. Truman Capote writes, "To me, the greatest pleasure of writing is the inner music the words make." The sound of our words is powerful. It's an important part of what communicates our ideas to others. Writers choose words to communicate the mood, the tone, the feelings that we want to convey.

We can help children think about the power of punctuation if we ask them to consider how a passage might sound differently (and mean differently) if the punctuation were different. "Why do you suppose this author made such a long sentence, with all these commas," we can ask, "instead of writing several shorter sentences?"

In this session you will help students learn that in order to edit their writing, writers pay attention to the sound of each word, reading the draft aloud over and over. You'll teach children to reconsider their word choice and sentence constructions as well as their punctuation decisions. They will begin an inquiry, studying the editing moves that published writers make in order to learn techniques which they too can use to strengthen their writing.

MINILESSON

Editing to Match Sound to Meaning

CONNECTION

Acknowledge that children already know writers edit so as to correct errors.

"Writers, you know that it is important to edit in order to check for misspellings and to indent our paragraphs. You know that in order to be taken seriously as a writer, it is important to scrutinize our drafts, reading our writing over and over so that we can find and mend places where our ideas tumble onto each other or places where our thoughts hang awkwardly in mid-air."

Name your teaching point. Specifically, tell children that writers edit for sound, rereading our writing aloud and refining words, sentences, and punctuation so that the texts sounds right.

"But today what I want to emphasize is that when we, as writers, edit our writing, we read it out loud to hear the sound of each word, to hear the rhythm of our sentences. Truman Capote wrote, 'To me, the greatest pleasure of writing is the inner music the words make.' The sound of our words is powerful. Writers communicate with readers by choosing words that convey not only the content but also the mood, the tone, and the feelings that we want to convey."

Tell children that it helps to closely examine passages—and punctuation—in published texts.

"In order to learn how to write for one's ear, it helps to look at texts that other authors have written. Remember when we read the scene from *Journey* that describes Journey's grandmother bringing soup and a photo album to Journey's room?"

"You all felt like you could see right into Journey's heart and see how hurt he was. When we looked closely at this scene later, you all commented on Patricia MacLachlan's ways with words. You commented on the lengths of her sentences, on her word choice, on the different kinds of punctuation that she used. You noticed how she used list-like sentences and short, abrupt sentences and long sentences that seemed like they would never end. We discussed how the sound of Patricia's words were forceful and direct and created clear, elaborate images that helped us understand Journey's feelings on a very deep level."

COACHING

By reminding children of what they already know, we re-emphasize the importance of these foundations. Notice that when I try to bring life to a subject, I pay attention to my action words. Here, I have described run-on sentences by saying ideas tumble upon each other and thoughts hang in mid-air.

Early in the year, most of our teaching was channeled towards lifting the level of the content in children's writing. By now, more and more of our focus can be on the craftsmanship. It is very important for writers to think about the tone, rhythm, and pace of our prose.

Again, this minilesson revisits a text that children already know and care about. It would be odd to pull out a brand-new text and read only to study its punctuation. This lens makes more sense if we are examining a text we know well to see how the author created the meaning on the page.

TEACHING

Show students how reading writing aloud can help them to edit for sound. Demonstrate using your own writing or the writing of a colleague.

"Let's look again at a draft of the memoir that your teacher Mary Chiarella has been writing. Mary will read it aloud and as she does, will you really listen to its sound? Mary will pause from time to time to tell us the images, feelings, and ideas that she wants to convey, and together, we'll help her see if the sound of her writing communicates this. Listen to Mary's draft, and then we'll talk about what we notice."

Mary read this:

> I stood on the platform. I watched the swimmers speed across the water. I looked down at my dad. I reached to him. I let his hands carry me into the water. "Don't let go!" I cried out. I clung to my dad's neck with both hands.

Turning to the children, I said to them, "Did you hear that Mary starts many of her sentences in a similar fashion?" When many of them had not noticed this, I suggested Mary reread, and this time they concurred.

Interrupting, Mary said, "You are right that I do this! That is so interesting."

Highlight that writers decide how to punctuate once the writer knows what she wants to communicate.

Then I added, "The important thing for Mary to decide, class, is whether she wants those parts of her draft to sound the same. That depends on what she is trying to say, doesn't it? What do you want to convey in this piece?" I asked Mary.

She replied, "I want my reader to understand that there's lots of movement going on around me and that the pool can be overwhelming for me," Mary said. "But meanwhile, I'm so focused on my dad that I'm able to go into the pool, even though I feel afraid." Then, looking at her draft, Mary added, "Oh! I know! I need to rewrite this bit about swimming to show that more things were happening. Instead of writing, 'I watched the swimmers speed back and forth across the water,' maybe I should stuff more things into a sentence so the sentence sounds fuller and crazier, like the pool." For a second Mary closed her eyes, imagining the scene, and then she said, "What if it went something like this?"

> Swimmers sped into and out of the water making quiet splashes with each stroke and creating short, rough waves.

"Writers," I said. "Did you see that when Mary first read her writing, her words and sentences lacked variety? Then, she edited this one part of her draft—and did so by first, deciding

My goal is to help the students begin to hear the rhythm that their words and sentences create. I want them to see that if they vary their words and reconstruct their sentences, they can give their writing a new sound and, as a result, create clearer images. Mary has deliberately chosen to share sections of her draft that will bring out the point of the minilesson.

Remember that Mary made the decision earlier to focus her memoir on her relationship with her father, and that she specifically noticed that in many of her entries, her father's hands were holding up a child.

to write a long sentence and then, by thinking hard about what she wanted to communicate. The sound of her writing has changed and she has also made her image clearer, hasn't she? Let's begin collecting ways to make the sound of our writing align with the ideas we want to convey!"

ACTIVE ENGAGEMENT

Set the students up to listen to a shared text and then to edit it, making the sound match the meaning.

"Let's listen to a scene from Sirah's memoir. She wants to show how scared she was when she thought that her little sister was in danger. Keep the meaning she wants to convey in the back of your mind as you listen to the rhythm of her words, thinking, 'Does the sound of Sirah's writing match the content of it?'" I read aloud this passage, reading from the chart paper version of it: *[Fig. XIV-1]*

> The doors of the train shut. I saw my sister concealed behind them. She was alone. I didn't know what to do. I just stood there. I watched the train pull away.

Partners talked among themselves, and I listened in. Justin said to his partner, Jill, "I like how it sounded when it said, 'I didn't know what to do. I just stood there." Pressed to elaborate, he said, "The words go with what happened. I can picture not knowing what to do and just standing there."

Jill wasn't convinced that Sirah's piece did justice to the moment. "Wouldn't it have more excitement," she said, "like this":

> Slam! The train doors shut behind me as I stepped from the train onto the platform. My sister wasn't next to me where she had been a moment ago! When I turned to find her, the subway started with her in it. All I could see was ...

Sirah completed the sentence, saying, "All I could see was her tiny face looking out the the closed train door."

LINK

Remind writers that today and every day, they can edit their writing to make sure the writing sounds in a way that communicates our ideas as best it can.

"So writers, as you make editing decisions today, and on other days throughout your life, remember it's not enough to make sure each word and sentence looks right. It's not enough to say, 'Oh, I've used capital letters and I've made sure to use punctuation.' We also need to make sure our writing sounds the way we want it to. We need to make sure the sound communicates our ideas."

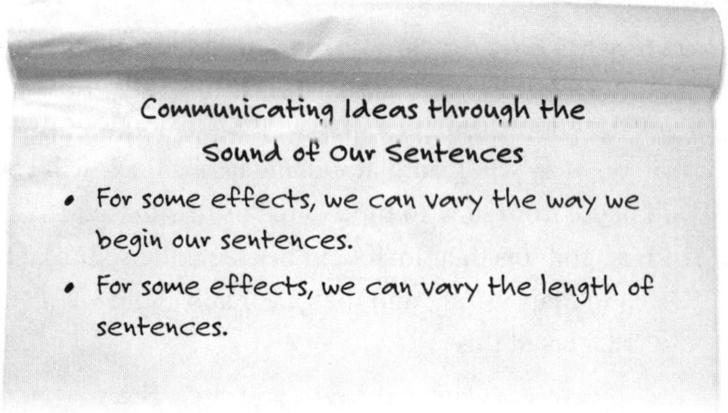

Communicating Ideas through the Sound of Our Sentences

- For some effects, we can vary the way we begin our sentences.
- For some effects, we can vary the length of sentences.

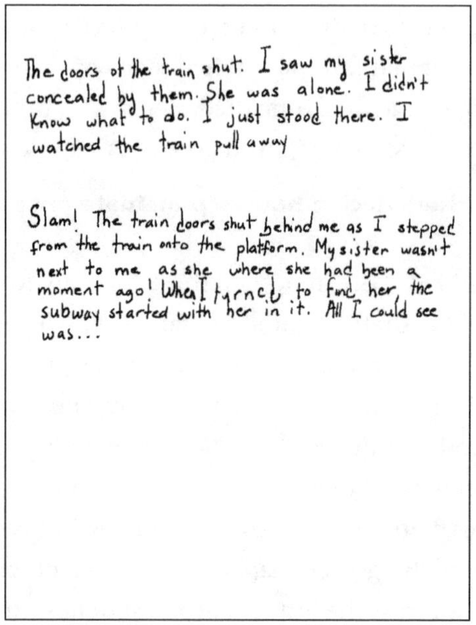

The doors of the train shut. I saw my sister concealed by them. She was alone. I didn't know what to do. I just stood there. I watched the train pull away

Slam! The train doors shut behind me as I stepped from the train onto the platform. My sister wasn't next to me as she where she had been a moment ago! When I turned to find her, the subway started with her in it. All I could see was...

Fig. XIV-1 Sirah's passage

WRITING AND CONFERRING

Using Sentence Structure to Vary the Sound

William was reading his writing aloud to himself. Every now and then he stopped and wrote a note down on his draft. I walked over to listen as he read, and this is what I heard:

> I walked into the bathroom. I turned on the water. I poured bubble bath into the tub. I tested the water with my toe.

I could see that William was trying to write this moment bit by bit, but }I noticed that he read right past these lines and didn't seem to pay attention to how this paragraph sounded. So, I asked him, "William, can I act as your writing partner? Will you reread this part of your writing to me so that together we can listen to its sound?"

William picked up his draft and read the first paragraph aloud. He stopped, looked and waited for me to comment. "I like the way you've slowed down this part by using a series of small actions." I paused and let William take in the compliment. "But as you read it aloud, I noticed that each sentence seemed to have the same beat." I showed him what I meant by reading the paragraph aloud and hitting my thigh with my hand so that he could hear the rhythm of my words.

"Oh, I get what you mean. Yeah, I can hear that. Each sentence sounds so much the same." William looked down at his paper and reread that part. He nodded his head and looked up.

"You know, William, what you've said is really true. Each sentence sounds so much the same. Did you mean to do that?"

"Well, I did mean to slow down each action, but I didn't want each sentence to sound the same."

"Yes, if your words all sound similar your meaning can get lost. It's hard to make any one thought stand out. I'm going to remind you of something that you know about writing narrative that will improve the rhythm of your writing. Are you up for it?"

"Yes." William nodded his head and gave me his full attention.

I could have taught William a way to combine sentences like these, using commas to set off each action. That would improve his writing now and in the future. But I decided that William also needed to stretch himself by using something other than a series of actions to tell his story; he needed to use all that he's learned about narrative this year to lift up his ideas and improve the craft of his writing.

MID-WORKSHOP TEACHING POINT — *Using Punctuation to Create Sound* "Writers, can I have your eyes and your attention? As I walk around the room, I can hear your memoirs. I can see you editing them and listening to them again to hear how your changes sound. Many of you are reading your writing to your partners asking them to listen and give you feedback. That's a great idea because sometimes we have a hard time hearing the sound of our own words because we've heard them so many times."

"You're working on varying your word choice and sentence lengths as well as rewording your sentences to add variety to your writing. But there's another choice that writers make that affects the sound, and therefore the meaning, of their writing. That's our punctuation choices. Remember when we read *Night in the Country* by Cynthia Rylant and many of you were talking about how still and quiet her writing sounded? There are two lines in particular that go":

continued on next page

"When narrative writers craft their writing, they vary the kinds of details they use. They might use some small actions, but in-between, they use details about the time or about the place or about the thoughts they're having—all to help the meaning of the story come forward. Let's look again at your paragraph and try this." William and I read the paragraph silently. Then I read aloud the first line and said, "So let's see how I might add some details about the time and place and the thoughts you might have had after the first action." I read the sentence aloud. "You're getting ready to run a bath for yourself so that you can relax, right? That's what you are trying to convey?" William nodded. "How about if we add details like this?":

> I walked into the bathroom. The tiles were cold under my feet, but the shag bathmat warmed me up. All my favorite bubble baths lined the rim of the bath tub, leaving me too many choices.

"What do you think?"

"That makes it different! It gives more information about what's going on."

"Okay then, William. Try the next line." I pointed to the page. "Remember, you want to add in details other than actions."

William read the line over several times and then said, "Maybe I could write":

> I turned on the water. Steam started to fill the bathroom and fog up the mirror. It was toasty and the temperature was perfect for taking a bath.

"That makes me feel relaxed even reading it! Let's try to put all of that together":

> I walked into the bathroom. The tiles were cold under my feet, but the shag bathmat warmed me up. All my favorite bubble baths lined the rim of the bath tub, leaving me too many choices. I turned on the water. Steam started to fill the bathroom and fog up the mirror. It was toasty and the temperature was perfect for taking a bath.

"Wow! Now, the sentences no longer sound the same, and these new details make this scene feel how you intended it to feel! Remember, William, when you are reading your writing aloud to see how it sounds, listen for sentences that sound too similar to each other. Then, ask yourself: Where can I add in a new and different kind of detail that helps convey my meaning? Do you know what your work can be right now?"

"Yes, I'm going to try that some more in this paragraph and then I'm going to see if I've done that in any other places."

continued from previous page

> And, if you lie very still, you may hear an apple fall from the tree in the back yard.
>
> Listen: Pump!

"That last line is what really brings out the tone and mood. She uses a colon after 'Listen' to set up the sound that the apple makes as it falls. Then, she adds an exclamation point after 'Pump' to make that single sound—one that would normally be so quiet—ring out."

"You can play with punctuation as you write so that you can bring out the tone of your writing. Right now, take a minute to reread your writing to see how the punctuation choices that you've made help to bring out the tone in your writing. If you don't find that they do, find a spot that you might rewrite. From now on, remember that using punctuation is another way you can make your writing sound the way you intend!"

SHARE

Editing for Simplicity

Remind writers of the importance of writing with clarity. Ask them to find new partners and together read their writing to be sure every bit rings with clarity.

"All year, we have stressed the importance of writing with clarity. You know that adding in lots of lush language can sometimes throw dust in the eyes of our readers—keeping them from seeing clearly the worlds which we've created. One of the greatest rules of editing is this: Simplify. As E.B. White and his writing partner, Strunk, wrote in a book about writing, 'A sentence should contain no unnecessary words, a paragraph no unnecessary sentences for the same reason that a drawing should have no unnecessary lines and a machine no unnecessary parts.'"

"So today, would you meet with someone other than your partner who can help you edit. Put one person's writing between the two of you, and read it through, inch by inch, asking whether each sentence creates a clearer image and moves the idea along."

HOMEWORK   *Using the Sound of Language to Convey Meaning*   Today's workshop focused new attention on the sound of our writing and how word and sentence and punctuation choices affect that sound. Being able to listen closely is a tremendously important part of being a writer. The way our writing sounds on the page helps us to convey meaning. Tonight, I'd like you to read your writing aloud and think about how your writing sounds. Ask yourself: Does my word choice (and sentence structure and punctuation) convey what I'm trying to say? Underline places where your writing has a strong sound—lonely or confused or elated. Then, ask yourself: Is this the feeling that I want my reader to have?

If your students seem to be writing with an inconsistent use of mechanics . . . you might choose to teach them to find mentor sentences in their own writing. You've taught them to notice the technique of other writers, and this has certainly helped them improve the quality of their craft. So often we read our students' writing and see a sentence that is glistening. This may be because of its structure or the use of punctuation or the choices they've made for word placement. You might point out to them that when writers do something beautiful and brilliant, we set new expectations for ourselves. Now our writing needs to be lifted to new heights.

After identifying wonderfully crafted sentences, you might have the students specifically name what they've done with a partner. Then, they can look across their writing and name other places where they might do the same work. You might decide to make a bulletin board of "Mentor Sentence, from the Work of Class 5-314". Students might begin conducting conferences using their expertise to teach each other and to create a sense of celebration around these carefully crafted pieces of writing.

If your students struggle with spelling words conventionally . . . teach them to live their lives as students of spellings. You've taught them that writers live wide-awake lives and pay attention to the sights and sounds in their environments. Well, good spellers live a similar life. They listen to words and study their spellings, develop curiosities and theories and in the process develop the experiences needed to accurately spell words in their writing.

You might teach them that good spellers sometimes make up rhymes (or learn rhymes that already exist) to remember rules. You might also teach them to notice patterns in words and show them how knowing the spelling of one word will open the door to the correct spelling of many more words. It's also important, of course, to teach students how to use dictionaries quickly and efficiently and to value this tool as a place where they can come and savor words.

MECHANICS

One lens that you might use when assessing your students' writing is the lens of punctuation choice. You might be relieved to find that your students have a sense of where to end their thoughts and that they are writing clearly, but do they possess the knowledge of how to express their ideas with more complexity? As students try to write about more complicated ideas, something they are called on to do in this unit, they often benefit from learning a variety of punctuation marks that will give them the power to say what's in their hearts and on their minds with greater sophistication.

Learning how to use a semicolon, for example, might help your students understand how they can take their ideas and develop them in a single sentence. When teaching students about the functions of semicolons, you're not simply teaching them the rules of how to use it, you're also teaching them the ways semicolons challenge them to think very precisely about what they will say. Would a semicolon make my meaning more clear, more intense?

In the sentence below from *Journey*, Patricia MacLachlan uses semicolons instead of commas, and elaborates on each character, painting a picture for her reader. This is the sentence where she describes the photographs that Grandfather has taken since Mama left.

Patricia could have written:

> Grandfather has taken photographs of Mary Louise, our least trustworthy cow, my grandmother reading a book and of himself.

Instead she wrote:

> He has, in the weeks Mama left, taken many photographs— one of our least trustworthy cow, Mary Louise, standing up to her hocks in meadow muck; one of my grandmother in the pantry; reading a book while bees, drawn to her currant wine, surround her head in a small halo; and many of himself taken with the self-timer device he's not yet figured out.

Patricia has gone beyond simply making a short list of the people that Grandfather has photographed. Instead, her use of semicolons has created a list-like description of each character mentioned in this sentence. The semicolon has added power to the words that she's used.

You'll decide which punctuation choices you feel your students will benefit from learning. Teaching them to understand the function of a wide variety of punctuation marks, however, has the potential to help students think more and say more about their ideas.

IN THIS SESSION, CHILDREN WILL READ ALOUD THEIR MEMOIR TO THEIR FRIENDS AND FAMILY. LISTENERS WILL SAY A FEW LINES OF A CHORUS BETWEEN READINGS.

GETTING READY

- Introduction to the celebration, or the introduction below
- Pre-assigned readers for the whole group, and for the small groups
- Few lines of a chorus for the audience to say after each reading
- See CD-ROM for resources

AN AUTHOR'S FINAL CELEBRATION:
PLACING OUR WRITING IN THE COMPANY OF OTHERS

You will approach this celebration with poignant feelings. You will be sad because another year is over, and these children are about to walk right out of your life. You'll look at them, each so quirky and so intense and so very much himself, herself. The sadness will be there too because, as we watch the kids, each shouldering a back-pack for that one last time and walking away, we see that there is too much letting go in life. Every year, it seems, we have to let go of even more. Perhaps your son, like mine, will be going off to college, or to kindergarten.

But of course, there will be new beginnings around the bend. Author celebrations—especially this final one—help us not only look backward but also forward. We celebrate in order to name, plan, resolve, re-make ourselves.

You and your children will need to talk together about how this final celebration should go. My advice is this: Don't make the event so complicated that you lose sight of the people. Kathy Doyle and Mary Chiarella both held very simple celebrations to culminate this unit, this year. In both, the children and their teacher decided to return to rituals that were by now imbued with great significance for their classroom communities.

In this celebration, family members gather. That alone can be momentous. The Art of Teaching Writing was released for publication just before a large conference at Teachers College. I knew my colleagues had planned a small get-together at the end of the day to toast the book's arrival. I keynoted that conference, as was typical for me. Only this time, as I started speaking, I caught the sight of a white-haired man in the back of the auditorium. I continued speaking and as I did, it dawned on me that I was looking at my father. Then beside him, I saw Mum. "How could they be here? They live in Buffalo," I thought as I continued, somehow, giving my keynote. As I spoke about writing, I watched each of my words reaching my mum, my dad, and it was as if each word meant something more because it was said in their presence. My talk about writing became also a talk about growing up and families and childhood and values . . . it was as if I'd written this keynote just for them, as if I'd waited all my life to say these things to them. They sat there, listening to my talk and through my talk, to me. It is eighteen years later, but I still have a lump in my throat as I recall what it meant that were there for me that day. Your children will be reading texts that say, "This is my life." It will be intense for them to read these aloud in the presence of their families.

CELEBRATION

Welcome everyone and set the tone for the ceremony with an introduction or a story.

"We gather here together for one final celebration. When I was a child, I went to Camp Aloha. Each summer would end with all of us campers gathering on the shores of Lake Wannabee. Just as the sun was setting, we'd convene, as all of us are convening now, only at Camp Aloha, each one of us held a handmade wooden boat—it was just a block of wood, really, with a hole drilled in the center so the boat could hold a candle. Standing on the shores of Lake Wannabee, for that final ritual, we'd light the candles on our boats and sing, "This little light of mine, I'm gonna let it shine, let it shine, let it shine, all the time." Then as we sang, one camper, and another, would approach the lake, crouch down by the water's edge, and cast our boat off. Then we'd step back into the group and, linking arms, we'd watch the little flames of light bob across the lake, into the dark corners, and we'd sing. "This little light of mine, I'm gonna let it shine. Hide it under a bushel? No. I'm gonna let it shine. Don't you try to blow it out! I'm gonna let it shine, let it shine, let it shine, all the time."

"I say this to you now because in a sense, each of the children here is holding his or her own little flame of light, and today, these children will send their light into the world. Their ideas, their stories, their voices."

And our message to these children of ours is, "This little light of yours, you've got to let it shine, let it shine, let it shine, all the time."

Explain the way the ceremony will go. In this case, explain that a few children will share with the whole group, then the group will divide and the rest of the children will share with one of the two smaller groups. Suggest the audience join in a chorus after each child reads.

"We'll begin, as we are accustomed to doing, with a few writers sharing their memoir with all of us, and then we'll disperse into just two groups. These are larger groups than usual, but I know on this occasion that you'll want the chance to hear more, and I know all of the youngsters here are eager for the larger audience."

"After a child reads, let's all look at that child and tell her, tell him, 'This little light of yours, you've got to let it shine, let it shine, let it shine, all the time.' We'll say those words in unison, and try to say them in a way that sends this writer off into the world, launching the writer to go forth differently because of this day, this year, this community.

COACHING

For this final celebration, family members do gather. Mary Chiarella and Kathy Doyle both scheduled their celebrations so that working parents, grandparents and siblings could come. Adam's big brother Jon was there to hear Adam's story of his sadness at his brother's leaving home. Tyler's brave grandmother was there to hear the story of how she'd cared so much to even ride that roller coaster with her grandson. Ali's parents were there—her father, well again, and so very present for his daughter, and her mom too. For these children, the Author Celebration was held on the evening proceeding graduation, and it became part of that larger rite of passage.

Saying Good-bye
By Adam

My brother came outside with one last suitcase in his hand. He crammed it into the back of my mom's car with all the others. Then Jon slammed the back of my mom's car shut. Through the tinted glass I could see the soccer ball that we would shoot into our goal on hot summer evenings. Our eyes met when he turned around. Sadness flew straight into me as clear as the mournful sound of Jon's bassoon. My brother hugged me. I pulled him closer. "I'm going to miss you badly," he said.

"I will, too," I managed to squeak out, my voice hoarse. It was already happening: my eyes brimmed. I tried to blink back tears, but they wouldn't stop. Tears started pouring out over my eyes. It reminded me of when I was playing basketball and I fell. Pain throbbed through my arm. Jon came to take me to the hospital. With Jon there, I felt safer, calmer, less scared. It reminded me of when I was in camp and I hadn't gotten a letter for days, and loneliness was starting to haunt me. Jon's letter came and filled me with

Fig. XV-1 Adam's final draft

laughs and warmth and a feel that it was good to have a big brother.

I looked up and saw one tear roll down my brother's cheek. He brushed it way, but I remembered it.

My dad appeared from the house, carrying an old picture of my brother close to his chest like it was a billion dollars. My brother's face was fat and round in the picture. Hair was starting to grow in on the top of his head as if it were a flower, sprouting. I looked up at my dad and he was wiping his eyes with the back of his hand. My dad sat down on the hood of the car and studied the picture like a textbook. He couldn't stop looking at it.

"It's time to go," said my dad "Say your good-byes now." Wearing his Penn hat backwards, Jon walked over to the passenger seat of the car, climbed in and closed the door. He rolled the window down and motioned me over. I walked up to the car, not sure what to say or do. He gave me a little punch. This time I didn't mind. "I'll miss you," he said.

"Yeah, me too," I said. As I walked away, he handed me his hat.

Fig. XV-2 Adam's final draft page 2

The car pulled down the driveway. I knew my childhood with my brother was ending this very moment. My brother opened the sunroof and waved his hand. I waved back even though he probably couldn't see me. The car made a left and climbed the hill till it was out of sight. I walked to the end of the driveway, to see if I could get a last glimpse of the car.

I knew Jon was moving on. It will only be a matter of time before he has graduated college, and gets married and has kids.

I stood there for a minute, then slowly made my way back up the driveway. I remembered I was holding Jon's Penn hat and I put it on backwards, just as he always did. I walked into his room and sat on his bed. I squeezed his pillow and looked for any sign that Jon was once there.

I picked up Jon's bassoon and put each piece together, the way Jon taught me. I went over to the chair Jon always sat on when he played, and I played the deep mournful sound I had heard coming from his room so many times.

Fig. XV-3 Adam's final draft page 3

Writing by Emily

Before my sister went to middle school, when the shine in her eyes was still there, matching her bright smile, she used to play with me. We used to play merry-go-round-chair on my mom's spinning chair, but all that changed when she went to middle school.

One afternoon she called me to her room. "Come on my bed," Jen said, patting the spot beside her. "Now stay still." She took out a suitcase from under her bed and put it beside us. She opened it and told me to close my eyes. "Don't move," she whispered while putting powder on my eyes. She spread it around and around with a brush. It felt cold. "Okay open," she said. She moved back to get a far view of me.

Then she dabbed pink powder on my cheeks and nose. Her brush swept up and down. "That tickles!" I said, giggling. Soon Jen was putting goop on my lips. She spread it around with a lip-gloss wand. "Pthhhh!" I spit the yucky stuff off, and wiped the remaining goo. Jen put an extra dab of blush on my cheeks and finished.

"Voilá. Done." But then she changed her mind and started putting curlers in my hair. "While we wait, come here," she said. I followed her around the house as she gathered clothes. "Wear this and this." I looked at what she was holding; my mom's furry shawl.

Fig. XV-4 Emily's final draft

I went into the bathroom and wrapped it on. I stared at myself in the mirror. I took the curlers off and fluffed my hair. I looked great! I was finally old; I'd always wanted to be. I looked like one of those old Hollywood actresses with big fur coats and curly hair, walking down the red carpet. I scrunched my hair. "Omigod!" I said to myself trying to be like my sister. I pointed to the tub. "Omigod! It's so round!" I walked over to the toilet "Omigod! That's so gross!"

To the mirror, I said, Omi-" I stopped. Something was wrong. "This isn't me!" I thought, "I'm not the thirteen year old I am trying to be." I splashed water on my face, scrubbing the teenager away. I combed water through my hair and the curls unraveled.

Being a child means jumping on the bed, having laughing contests, making funny faces. I don't want to loose that. When guests come over and look at my baby pictures, or if they haven't seen me in a long time, they say, "Awwww, you've grown so much!"

I have grown taller, but inside I'm still the little girl who plays with Barbies, and the one who's still afraid of lightning. I am the little girl who needs my mom right by my side me. I don't want to grow up! Not yet.

But I did look pretty good in that shawl.

Fig. XV-5 Emily's final draft page 2

My Grandmother
By Tyler

Have you ever made someone go on something you hated? Did you ever say, you don't have to go on? Or let's not do this! Well, that is the part of you that is eleven years old. Or when you say, please can you go on? That is the part of you that is four. And when you don't let her get off, that is the part of you that is two. Well, this happened to me once.

I stood at the line to get on the roller coaster, next to my grandmother. I was amazed at the roller coaster. My eyes followed it as if it were the strongest magnet in the world, and every second I got closer, closer and closer. The sun beat down on my grandmother and me. Nothing could stop me from getting on. And before I knew it, the roller coaster zoomed right next to me as it almost knocked it off my feet. Impatiently I waited to get on. I jumped up and down like a kangaroo. My hands shook from side to side, not wanting to wait any longer.

I saw five people get off and I heard, "That was awesome, let's do that again." That only got me wanting to go on even more. I heard the cranking of the roller coaster as it went up and up. And then it stopped for a half a second and dropped like a cannon ball getting shot out of a cannon. I heard a scream as the roller coaster hovered over my head. But in a theme park with a lot of roller coasters, you shouldn't be so surprised

Fig. XV-6 Tyler's final draft

when you hear screams from a roller coaster.

Then it swooped up to the left, then another drop and another scream. Out of the corner of my eye, I spied my grandma sighing with a scared face. The ride tracks made a sharp left and the people were tugged to the left, then up. I heard nothing else, noticed nothing else. There was only the roller coaster. A drop, and a thunder scream, then it tugged to the right and suddenly stopped! And then they got off. I saw the big sign that read THE INTIMIDATOR. I waited impatiently, wanting to block everyone off from moving and just cut the whole line. I could not pay attention to anyone or anything else.

Suddenly I noticed my grandma was acting strange. She stared wide-eyed, like it was some kind of monster. She shouldn't be going on this ride, I said to myself, feeling sick inside.

"Grandma, if you don't want to go on you don't have to. It is a pretty big ride."

"Tyler, I want to do this. If I don't go on this is roller coaster, I will be afraid of roller coasters for the rest of my life," she announced to me.

"This is our last chance; do you want to get off?" I said to her.

"No, Tyler. I want to stay." She said this, but anybody could know that she was lying.

We stepped into the roller coaster and sat down. As we

Fig. XV-7 Tyler's final draft page 2

sat, we pulled the handle bar against our stomachs. I heard a click, click as it locked. And I realized my grandma was trapped into her worst fear. Like when you have the scariest nightmare and you just can't wake up and it feels like forever.

We were cranked up like a huge fish. We moved up and up and up and her hand tightened, harder and harder on mine. At the top we stopped and, just before we began to fly down, I heard a scream so loud it felt like my ears drums had exploded. I pulled my hand away from her and tried to close my ears as hard as I could.

As I covered my ears I said to myself, why would I make my grandma go on a scary roller coaster? Who else can I blame but myself? I knew she would scream like a crazy person from the beginning to the end. She wouldn't do it for anybody but me. I turned my head and saw her face. She was still screaming and so scared.

As we got off the ride, she said, "I am sorry for ruining your ride, Tyler. I kind of overdid it on the screaming."

"You made it better by going on with me. And if you didn't go on I would forget it after a while. That was a ride I will never forget," I said, my ears still hurting.

"That is the last ride in my life. I will never go on that again — or any other ride," Grandma panted.

"Until tomorrow. Then we will go on a bigger ride," I replied with a smile.

Fig. XV-8 Tyler's final draft page 3

When You Stay
By Ali

Some people think being brave is jumping off a cliff, running into a burning building and saving a person, diving in front of a bullet. Well, I think being brave is also telling off a bully, not running away from something you're scared of, waiting. And at first you may feel like you let someone important in your life down, that you weren't as brave as you wanted to be. It could be you don't hardly see your braveness. That is what I think being brave is.

I stood in the dark hallway in front of my parents' bedroom door, which led to the bed where my dad was lying. I pushed open the door. It swung all the way back to the wall and made a little clicking sound when it hit. I saw my dad, a pile of pillows and blankets all around him. I didn't go in, not yet. *I am going to go in there and act normal, as if nothing is wrong. I will tell him about my almost goal and my 95% in spelling. This time he will say, "Good!" to me.*

I walked in, then started to turn around. I stopped mid-turn. "No, Ali, stay," I told myself. I took a deep breath. I began to walk toward the bed again.

Fig. XV-9 Ali's final draft

I crawled up onto the bed, being very quiet, trying not to wake him if he was asleep. He wasn't.

"Today at soccer I was running down the field. I wound up for a big shot, kicked it . . . ! It stopped about two feet from the goal. We can work on my shooting together," I said.

No reply.

Does he not care? Is he in too much pain? That was it, that was the whole reason he was in bed. Too much pain! The pain had not only taken over my dad's life, it had taken over mine.

I stared at him with tough eyes. I wanted him to know that I was upset with him. He had caused me a lot of pain. He didn't get to see my almost-goal and he didn't get to help me study for my spelling test.

He looked back at me with sad puppy eyes. He was sorry.

I don't know if I wanted to forgive him. Giving me a little twitch of his eye, a little brush of his hand against the blanket. That wasn't normal for him. It amazed me. He was such a full guy. His movements were always full, not half.

I had to forgive him, though. He needed me and I needed him. I stayed, waiting for him. I sat next to

Fig. XV-10 Ali's final draft page 2

him, holding his hand, watching the clock tick by. 3:33 . . . 3:34 . . . 3:35 . . .

I gently let go of his hand and placed it by his side. I got up and walked back to the doorway. I stood leaning against the wall, looking at him. I stood there, waiting. Expecting him to talk to me, expecting him to push his pain behind him. If I stood there long enough, he would come, get up, and practice my shot with me.

No, he couldn't. I knew that. So I guess I was just going to have to wait awhile. So I stayed.

When you're done falling off a cliff, when you're out of surgery to check for infections from when you were shot with a bullet, people clap and cheer for you and on your return home, news cameras are waiting to interview you. Those people's signs of bravery are on the outside. But when you walk away from a bully that you left behind wide-eyed, or when you stand close to the thing you were once scared of, those people's signs of bravery are the feeling of proudness, the feeling of people clapping that is on the inside of you. My sing was little sparkled, like a fairy sparking her golden dust over me.

Fig. XV-11 Ali's final draft page 3